MARKETING: THE CORE
Eighth Edition

Roger A. Kerin
Southern Methodist University

Steven W. Hartley
University of Denver

MARKETING: THE CORE, EIGHTH EDITION

Published by McGraw-Hill Education, 2 Penn Plaza, New York, NY 10121. Copyright © 2020 by McGraw-Hill Education. All rights reserved. Printed in the United States of America. Previous editions © 2018, 2016, and 2013. No part of this publication may be reproduced or distributed in any form or by any means, or stored in a database or retrieval system, without the prior written consent of McGraw-Hill Education, including, but not limited to, in any network or other electronic storage or transmission, or broadcast for distance learning.

Some ancillaries, including electronic and print components, may not be available to customers outside the United States.

This book is printed on acid-free paper.

1 2 3 4 5 6 7 8 9 LWI 21 20 19

ISBN 978-1-260-71145-5 (bound edition)
MHID 1-260-71145-5 (bound edition)
ISBN 978-1-260-08886-1 (loose-leaf edition)
MHID 1-260-08886-3 (loose-leaf edition)

Executive Brand Manager: *Meredith Fossel*
Senior Product Developer: *Kelly I. Pekelder*
Senior Marketing Manager: *Nicole Young*
Lead Content Project Manager: *Christine Vaughan*
Senior Content Project Manager: *Danielle Clement*
Senior Buyer: *Susan K. Culbertson*
Senior Designer: *Matt Diamond*
Lead Content Licensing Specialist: *Carrie Burger*
Cover Image: *©@by Feldman_1/Getty Images*
Compositor: *Aptara®, Inc.*

All credits appearing on page or at the end of the book are considered to be an extension of the copyright page.

Library of Congress Cataloging-in-Publication Data

Names: Kerin, Roger A., author. | Hartley, Steven William, author.
Title: Marketing : the core / Roger A. Kerin, Southern Methodist University, Steven W. Hartley,
   University of Denver.
Description: Eighth edition. | New York, NY : McGraw-Hill Education, [2020] |
   Audience: 18+
Identifiers: LCCN 2018048487| ISBN 9781260088861 (alk. paper) |
   ISBN 1260088863 (alk. paper)
Subjects: LCSH: Marketing.
Classification: LCC HF5415 .K452 2020 | DDC 658.8—dc23 LC record available at
   https://lccn.loc.gov/2018048487

The Internet addresses listed in the text were accurate at the time of publication. The inclusion of a website does not indicate an endorsement by the authors or McGraw-Hill Education, and McGraw-Hill Education does not guarantee the accuracy of the information presented at these sites.

mheducation.com/highered

WELCOME FROM THE AUTHORS!

Is technology an integral part of your life? Are you innovative and entrepreneurial? Do you consider purpose-driven work important? Have you ever thought you could change the world? If the answer to any of these questions is yes, your decision to study marketing is a perfect match! In addition, if you are curious about robots in the marketplace, virtual reality and augmented reality in advertising, wearable technology, YouTube channel brand advocates, shopping on Pinterest, or the gamification of almost everything, you will be excited by the insights you will learn during your studies. And we are excited to have the opportunity to help you along the way with our textbook about this exciting field!

We know from our experiences in the classroom that students choose to study marketing for many reasons. For marketing majors this course is the first of many on the way to a marketing degree. For students from other business majors this may be a required course in a business "core." For many other students, marketing is an elective chosen because of a personal interest in the marketplace. Regardless of your reasons for taking this course, it is our pleasure to help you explore the many new trends, concepts, practices, challenges, and opportunities that are part of marketing today. We encourage you to use your own past experiences and future interests to create a personalized journey of exploration and study.

The dynamic nature of the marketing discipline necessitates equally dynamic learning resources. As a result, we have focused our time and energy on ensuring that our textbook provides the most current, insightful, and comprehensive coverage of the marketplace today. The dramatic changes in student learning styles—from traditional observational styles to contemporary collaborative styles—are also reflected in our efforts as we have included many features to match these interests. Our approach to presenting the complexities of marketing and facilitating the changes in learning is based on three important dimensions:

- **Engagement.** As professors we have benefited from interactions with many exceptional students, managers, and instructors. Their insights have contributed to our approach to teaching and, subsequently, to our efforts as textbook authors. One of the essential elements of our approach is a commitment to active learning through engaging, integrated, and timely materials. In-class activities, an interactive blog, marketing plan exercises, and in-text links to online ads and web pages are just a few examples of the components of our engagement model.

- **Leadership.** Our approach is also based on a commitment to taking a leadership role in the development and presentation of new ideas, principles, theories, and practices in marketing. This is more important now than ever before, as the pace of change in our discipline accelerates and influences almost every aspect of traditional marketing. We are certain that exposure to leading-edge material related to topics such as social media, data analytics, and marketing metrics can help students become leaders in their jobs and careers.

- **Innovation.** New educational technologies and innovative teaching tools have magnified the engagement and leadership aspects of our approach. *Connect*, *LearnSmart*, and *SmartBook*, for example, provide a digital and interactive platform that embraces the "anytime and anywhere" style of today's students. In addition, we have provided new videos and increased the visual impact of the text and PowerPoint materials to facilitate multimedia approaches to learning.

Through the previous 7 U.S. editions—and 19 international editions in 11 languages—we have been gratified by the enthusiastic feedback we have received from students and instructors. We are very excited to have this opportunity to share our passion for this exciting discipline with you today. Welcome to the 8th edition of *Marketing: The Core!*

Roger A. Kerin
Steven W. Hartley

PREFACE

Marketing: The Core utilizes a unique, innovative, and effective pedagogical approach developed by the authors through the integration of their combined classroom, college, and university experiences. The elements of this approach have been the foundation for each edition of *Marketing: The Core* and serve as the core of the text and its supplements as they evolve and adapt to changes in student learning styles, the growth of the marketing discipline, and the development of new instructional technologies. The distinctive features of the approach are illustrated below:

Marketing: The Core 8/e *Pedagogical Approach*

Rigorous Framework
A pedagogy based on the use of learning objectives, learning reviews, learning objectives reviews, and supportive student supplements.

High-Engagement Style
Easy-to-read, high-involvement, interactive writing style that engages students through active learning techniques.

Personalized Marketing
A vivid and accurate description of businesses, marketing professionals, and entrepreneurs—through cases, exercises, and testimonials—that allows students to personalize marketing and identify possible career interests.

Traditional and Contemporary Coverage
Comprehensive and integrated coverage of traditional and contemporary marketing concepts.

Integrated Technology
The use of powerful technical resources and learning solutions, such as Connect, LearnSmart, SmartBook, the Kerin & Hartley Blog (www.kerinmarketing.com), and in-text video links.

Marketing Decision Making
The use of extended examples, cases, and videos involving people making marketing decisions.

The goal of the 8th edition of *Marketing: The Core* is to create an exceptional experience for today's students and instructors of marketing. The development of *Marketing: The Core* was based on a rigorous process of assessment, and the outcome of the process is a text and package of learning tools that are based on *engagement, leadership,* and *innovation* in marketing education.

ENGAGEMENT

The members of this author team have benefited from extraordinary experiences as instructors, researchers, and consultants, as well as the feedback of users of previous editions of *Marketing: The Core*—now more than one million students! The authors believe that success in marketing education in the future will require the highest levels of engagement. They ensure engagement by facilitating interaction between students and four learning partners—the instructor, other students, businesses, and the publisher. Some examples of the high-engagement elements of *Marketing: The Core* include:

In-Class Activities and Digital In-Class Activities. The in-class activities, located in the Instructor's Manual, are designed to engage students in discussions with the instructor and among themselves. They involve surveys, online resources, out-of-class assignments, and personal observations. Each activity illustrates a concept from the textbook and can be done individually or as a team. Examples include: Designing a Candy Bar, Marketing Yourself, Pepsi vs. Coke Taste Test, and What Makes a Memorable TV Commercial? In addition, digital in-class activities have been added to selected chapters. These activities, located in the Instructor Resources, focus on the use of web resources and the marketing data they can provide students.

Interactive Web Page and Blog (www.kerinmarketing.com). Students can access recent articles about marketing and post comments for other students. The site also provides access to a *Marketing: The Core* Twitter feed!

Building Your Marketing Plan. The Building Your Marketing Plan guides at the end of each chapter are based on the format of the Marketing Plan presented in Appendix A. On the basis of self-study or as part of a course assignment, students can use the activities to organize interactions with businesses to build a marketing plan. Students and employers often suggest that a well-written plan in a student's portfolio is an asset in today's competitive job market.

LEADERSHIP

The popularity of *Marketing: The Core* in the United States and around the globe is the result, in part, of the leadership role of the authors in developing and presenting new marketing content and pedagogies. For example, *Marketing: The Core* was the first text to integrate ethics, technology, and interactive marketing. It was also the first text to develop custom-made videos to help illustrate marketing principles and practices and bring them to life for students as they read the text. The authors have also been leaders in developing new learning tools, such as a three-step learning process that includes learning objectives, learning reviews, and learning objectives reviews and new testing materials that are based on Bloom's learning taxonomy. Other elements that show how *Marketing: The Core* is a leader in the discipline include:

Chapter 17: Using Social Media and Mobile Marketing to Connect with Consumers. *Marketing: The Core* features a dedicated chapter for social media and mobile marketing. This new environment is rapidly changing and constantly growing. The authors cover the building blocks of social media and mobile marketing and provide thorough, relevant content and examples. The authors discuss major social media platforms like Twitter, Facebook, LinkedIn, and YouTube. They explain how managers and companies can use those outlets for marketing purposes. Chapter 17 also includes a section titled Social Media Marketing Programs and Customer Engagement that addresses criteria for selecting social media, how social media can produce sales, and methods of measuring a company's success with social media and mobile marketing. This chapter is one of many ways *Marketing: The Core* is on the cutting edge of the field.

Applying Marketing Metrics. The *Applying Marketing Metrics* feature in the text delivers two of the newest elements of the business and marketing environment today—performance metrics and dashboards to visualize them. Some of the metrics included in the text are: category development index (CDI), brand development index (BDI), load factor (a capacity management metric), price premium, sales per square foot, same-store sales growth, promotion-to-sales ratio, and cost per thousand (CPM) impressions. The feature is designed to allow readers to learn, practice, and apply marketing metrics.

Color-Coded Graphs and Tables. The use of color in the graphs and tables enhances their readability and adds a visual level of learning to the textbook for readers. In addition, these color highlights increase student comprehension by linking the text discussion to colored elements in the graphs and tables.

New Video Cases. Each chapter ends with a case that is supported by a video to illustrate the issues in the chapter. New cases such as IBM, Toyota, Justin's, and Body Glove, and recent cases such as GoPro and Coppertone provide current and relevant examples that are familiar to students.

INNOVATION

In today's fast-paced and demanding educational environment, innovation is essential to effective learning. To maintain *Marketing: The Core*'s leadership position in the marketplace, the author team consistently creates innovative pedagogical tools that match contemporary students' learning styles and interests. The authors keep their fingers on the pulse of technology to bring real innovation to their text and package. Innovations such as in-text links, a Twitter feed, hyperlinked PowerPoint slides, and an online blog augment the McGraw-Hill Education online innovations such as Connect, LearnSmart, and SmartBook.

In-Text Links. You can see Internet links in magazine ads; on television programming; as part of catalogs, in-store displays, and product packaging; and throughout *Marketing: The Core*! These links bring the text to life with ads and videos about products and companies that are discussed in the text. These videos also keep the text even more current. While each link in the text has a caption, the links are updated to reflect new campaigns and market changes. In addition, the links allow readers to stream the video cases at the end of each chapter. You can simply click on the links in the digital book or use your smartphone or computer to follow the links.

Twitter Feed and Online Blog. Visit www.kerinmarketing.com to participate in *Marketing: The Core*'s online blog discussion and to see Twitter feed updates. You can also subscribe to the Twitter feed to receive the Marketing Question of the Day and respond with the #QotD hashtag.

Connect, LearnSmart, and SmartBook Integration. These McGraw-Hill Education products provide a comprehensive package of online resources to enable students to learn faster, study more efficiently, and increase knowledge retention. The products represent the gold standard in online, interactive, and adaptive learning tools and have received accolades from industry experts for their Library and Study Center elements, filtering and reporting functions, and immediate student feedback capabilities. In addition, the authors have developed book-specific interactive assignments, including (a) auto-graded applications based on the marketing plan exercises, and (b) activities based on the Applying Marketing Metrics boxes and marketing metrics presented in the text.

Innovative Test Bank. Containing more than 5,000 multiple-choice and essay questions, the *Marketing: The Core* Test Bank reflects more than two decades of innovations. The Test Bank also includes "visual test questions" in each chapter to reward students who made an effort to understand key graphs, tables, and images in the chapter.

> Students—study more efficiently, retain more and achieve better outcomes. Instructors—focus on what you love—teaching.

SUCCESSFUL SEMESTERS INCLUDE CONNECT

FOR INSTRUCTORS

You're in the driver's seat.

Want to build your own course? No problem. Prefer to use our turnkey, prebuilt course? Easy. Want to make changes throughout the semester? Sure. And you'll save time with Connect's auto-grading too.

65%
Less Time Grading

They'll thank you for it.

Adaptive study resources like SmartBook® help your students be better prepared in less time. You can transform your class time from dull definitions to dynamic debates. Hear from your peers about the benefits of Connect at **www.mheducation.com/highered/connect**

Make it simple, make it affordable.

Connect makes it easy with seamless integration using any of the major Learning Management Systems—Blackboard®, Canvas, and D2L, among others—to let you organize your course in one convenient location. Give your students access to digital materials at a discount with our inclusive access program. Ask your McGraw-Hill representative for more information.

©Hill Street Studios/Tobin Rogers/Blend Images LLC

Solutions for your challenges.

A product isn't a solution. Real solutions are affordable, reliable, and come with training and ongoing support when you need it and how you want it. Our Customer Experience Group can also help you troubleshoot tech problems—although Connect's 99% uptime means you might not need to call them. See for yourself at **status.mheducation.com**

FOR STUDENTS

Effective, efficient studying.

Connect helps you be more productive with your study time and get better grades using tools like SmartBook, which highlights key concepts and creates a personalized study plan. Connect sets you up for success, so you walk into class with confidence and walk out with better grades.

©Shutterstock/wavebreakmedia

> " I really liked this app—it made it easy to study when you don't have your textbook in front of you. "
>
> —Jordan Cunningham,
> Eastern Washington University

Study anytime, anywhere.

Download the free ReadAnywhere app and access your online eBook when it's convenient, even if you're offline. And since the app automatically syncs with your eBook in Connect, all of your notes are available every time you open it. Find out more at **www.mheducation.com/readanywhere**

No surprises.

The Connect Calendar and Reports tools keep you on track with the work you need to get done and your assignment scores. Life gets busy; Connect tools help you keep learning through it all.

Learning for everyone.

McGraw-Hill works directly with Accessibility Services Departments and faculty to meet the learning needs of all students. Please contact your Accessibility Services office and ask them to email accessibility@mheducation.com, or visit **www.mheducation.com/about/accessibility.html** for more information.

Asset Alignment with Bloom's Taxonomy

Principles of Marketing

We Take Students Higher

As a learning science company we create content that supports higher order thinking skills. Interactive learning tools within *McGraw-Hill Connect* are tagged accordingly, so you can filter, search, assign, and receive reports on your students' level of learning. The result—increased pedagogical insights and learning process efficiency that facilitate a stronger connection between the course material and the student.

The chart below shows a few of the key assignable marketing assets with *McGraw-Hill Connect* aligned with Bloom's Taxonomy. Take your students higher by assigning a variety of applications, moving them from simple memorization to concept application.

artBook

- Adaptively aids students to study more efficiently by highlighting where in the chapter to focus, asking review questions and pointing them to resources until they understand.

eit! Videos

- Short, contemporary videos provide engaging, animated introductions to key course concepts. Available at the chapter level. Perfect for launching lectures and assigning pre- or post-lecture.

deo Cases & Case Analyses

- Mini-cases and scenarios of real-world firms accompanied by questions that help students analyze and apply marketing theory and other core concepts.

arketing Analytics

- These newest auto-graded, data analytics activities challenge students to make decisions using metrics commonly seen across Marketing professions. The goal of this activity is to give students practice analyzing and using marketing data to make decisions.

arketing Plan Prep

- These exercises use guided activities and examples to help students understand and differentiate the various elements of a marketing plan.

ni Simulation

- Marketing Mini Sims help students apply and understand the interconnections of elements in the marketing mix by having them take on the role of Marketing Manager for a backpack manufacturing company.
- Mini Sims can be assigned by topic or in its entirety.

NEW AND REVISED CONTENT

Chapter 1: Update of Chobani's Success Story, New Showstopper Analysis, and New Material on Ritz-Carlton and Patagonia. Chobani's continued success at creating customer value is discussed and updated. The company's guiding mission, "Better food for more people," new products such as Drink Chobani, Chobani Flip, Smooth Yogurt, and Chobani Savor, and advertising campaigns such as "Love This Life" are presented. Discussion of Elon Musk and his success with entrepreneurial endeavors such as Zip2, PayPal, SpaceX, and Tesla has been added to the Marketing and Your Career section. New-product examples such as smart glasses and the YoYo car subscription service have been added to the discussion of potential "showstoppers" for new-product launches. Discussion of the Ritz-Carlton's use of relationship marketing concepts and Patagonia's Common Threads Initiative have also been added.

Chapter 2: New IBM Video Case, Updated Chapter Opening Example, Addition of a New Example of Social Entrepreneurship, and New Discussion of Uber's Changing Business Definition. The Chapter 2 opening example discusses Ben & Jerry's mission to make fantastic, sustainable, world-changing ice cream. Free Cone Day has been added to the discussion of creative marketing strategies used by the company to help accomplish its mission. The social entrepreneur venture NexGenVest has been added to the *30 Under 30 Forbes Social Entrepreneurs* discussion in the Making Responsible Decisions box. In addition, the discussion of business definitions and business models now describes how Uber has changed its definition from a cab service, to a ride-sharing service, to a delivery service. The application of the Boston Consulting Group business portfolio model to Apple's product line has been updated to include changes related to the Apple Watch, the iPhone, and the iPad/iPad mini tablet devices. The end-of-chapter video case is completely new, and features the recent IBM campaign and strategy: "Let's Put Smart to Work."

Chapter 3: New Toyota Video Case, Update of New Trends in Marketing, New Discussion on Generation Z, and New Discussion of Gender-Neutral Marketing Actions. The discussion of new trends, such as the growing popularity of brand advocates, the increasing application of virtual reality and augmented reality, and the surging scrutiny regarding the collection and use of consumer data, has been updated. Generation Z, the post-millennial generation, has been added to the discussion of generational cohorts. The Making Responsible Decisions box includes new examples such as P&G's recyclable shampoo bottles, Unilever's "brands with purpose," and Apple's "greenest building on the planet." New gender-neutral marketing actions have been added to the Culture section. A discussion of new trends in technology, such as the growth of automation (e.g., autonomous cars, drones, and robots), digital assistants (e.g., Amazon's Alexa), and wearable technology, has also been added. In addition, the chapter ends with a completely new video case about Toyota, its transition to a "mobility" company, and its marketing activities related to the hydrogen fuel-cell vehicle, the Mirai.

Chapter 4: New Section on Consumer Touchpoints and Consumer Journey Maps, and New Figure to Illustrate a Consumer Journey Map. A new section describes consumer touchpoints, the product, service, or brand points of contact with a consumer, and consumer journey maps, the visual representation of all touchpoints where a consumer comes into contact with a company's products, services, or brands. The new Figure 4–4 illustrates consumer touchpoints and a consumer journey map for electronic devices sold by Apple in stores. The Marketing Matters box has been updated to reflect the latest procedures for BzzAgents.

Chapter 5: New Examples Including Lockheed Martin and BMW, and Updated Marketing Matters Box Regarding eBay Business Supply. The description of government markets has been updated to include the Orion Multi-Purpose Crew Vehicle being developed by Lockheed Martin. In addition, the Buyer–Seller Relationship section now includes GT Advanced

Technology's $578 million contract with Apple to produce iPhone camera lenses and screens as an example of a long-term agreement. BMW's purchase of a Cloud-based data management system from IBM has been added as an example of a new buy. In addition, the Marketing Matters box has been updated to reflect eBay's trading platform, eBay Business Supply, which generates $4 billion in sales annually.

Chapter 6: Updated Chapter Opening Example Regarding Amazon in India, and Addition of UK Withdrawal from the EU. The chapter opening example is completely updated to describe the opportunities and challenges Amazon faces as it invests billions of dollars in India. The Economic Integration among Countries section has been revised to reflect increasing economic protectionism, including the withdrawal of the United Kingdom from the European Union, and discussions regarding possible changes in the North American Free Trade Agreement. In addition, Listerine has been added as a new example of product adaptation in the Product and Promotion Strategies section.

Chapter 7: Updated Chapter Opening Example, New Primary and Secondary Data Coverage, and New Discussion of Artificial Intelligence. The chapter opening example has been updated to reflect the use of marketing research in movies such as *Atomic Blonde, Edge of Tomorrow,* and *War Dogs*. An update of the Secondary Data section reflects the upcoming 2020 Census. The Primary Data section has been updated to include new Nielsen program ranking data, an example of Gillette's use of observational data, a discussion of the growing use of neuromarketing technologies, and a description of McDonald's use of test markets in developing its delivery service. In addition, artificial intelligence is discussed as part of the Intelligent Marketing Enterprise Platform presented in Figure 7–5.

Chapter 8: Update of Zappos's Use of Behavioral Segmentation, New Segmentation Examples, and New Patronage Example Data. The chapter opening example has been updated to describe how Zappos uses behavioral segmentation to deliver "happiness" to its customers. The Multiple Products and Multiple Market Segments section includes a new discussion of Ford's shift in strategy to reduce its product line and provide higher quality at lower prices. In addition, in the Patronage of Fast-Food Restaurants section, the patronage and user/nonuser data have been updated; also, the Future Strategies for Your Wendy's Restaurant section has been updated.

Chapter 9: New Discussion of the Apple-Enabled iCar and New Marketing Matters Box Coverage of Feature Fatigue. The chapter opening example has been updated to include a discussion of Apple's next innovation—the Apple-enabled iCar. The concept of feature bloat and fatigue is now introduced and illustrated in the Marketing Matters box. Keurig Kold and the HP Tablet are introduced as examples in the Marketing Reasons for New-Product Failures section. An example of the success of Aaron Krause's Scrub Daddy, originally pitched on *Shark Tank,* has been added to the section on inventors as a source of innovation.

Chapter 10: New Justin's Video Case, New Material on Gatorade's "Smart Cap," New Co-Branding and Brand Dilution Coverage, and New Examples. The Chapter 10 discussion of Gatorade in the chapter opener now includes material on the microchip-fitted "smart cap" and the digital sweat patch for athletes and fitness buffs. In addition, new discussions of co-branding and brand dilution have been added to the Multiproduct Branding Strategy section. New examples include Olay Skin Care Advisor, the NFL and NBA, and P&G's acquisition of Gillette. The chapter ends with a new video case titled Justin's: Managing a Successful Product with Passion, which describes the inspiring story of entrepreneur Justin Gold, and the application of product management concepts to the Justin's brand of organic nut butters.

Chapter 11: Updated Chapter Opening Example about VIZIO, and Discussion of Apple iPhone X, 8,

and 8-Plus Pricing. The updated chapter opening example describes VIZIO's approach to pricing the 50 million HDTVs it has sold since its founding. Microsoft's approach to pricing its Xbox One X videogame console is now included in the Skimming Pricing section. In addition, examples of penetration pricing, odd-even pricing, standard markup pricing, and cost-plus pricing have been updated to reflect the current marketplace.

Chapter 12: New Chapter Opening Example about Multichannel Marketing at Eddie Bauer, Updated Marketing Matters Box about IBM's Watson, and Updated Making Responsible Decisions Box. A new chapter opening example describes Eddie Bauer's "brick, click, and flip" multichannel marketing strategy. The Marketing Matters box has been updated to reflect IBM's use of artificial intelligence to manage its supply chain. In addition, the discussion of recycling e-waste in the Making Responsible Decisions box has been updated.

Chapter 13: Updated Chapter Opening Example about Smart Stores, Updated Making Responsible Decisions Box, and New Discussion about YouTube Programming, Robocalls, and EDLP 2.0. Chapter 13 opens with a description of the potential impact of smart stores on the customer journey. The Internet of Things, biometric scanners, virtual reality, 3D modeling tools, and wearable technology are discussed. The Making Responsible Decisions box now includes information about California's "zero-waste" laws. New information, such as banks' attempts to change ATMs into smart self-service devices, has been added to the Self-Service section. In addition, YouTube's live programming, the FTC's discussion regarding robocalls, and Walmart's development of EDLP 2.0 are discussed.

Chapter 14: Expanded Discussion about Personalization; New Section Titled How Consumers Shop and Buy Online, including Coverage of Social Commerce; Broadened Implementing Multichannel Marketing Section; and New Figure Illustrating a Multichannel Consumer Journey Map. The Interactivity, Individuality, and Customer Relationships in Marketspace section has an expanded discussion about the differences between collaborative filtering and personalization and includes Sunglass Hut as an example of a company using personalization techniques. The use of chatbots has been added to the Communication section. A new section titled How Consumers Shop and Buy Online has been added and covers *social commerce*—the use of social networks for browsing and buying. In addition, the Implementing Multichannel Marketing section has been rewritten with new coverage of cross-channel consumer behavior, mutually reinforcing channels, and monitoring and measuring channel performance. New Figure 14–5 illustrates a multichannel marketing consumer journey map. This chapter was previously located later in the sequence of chapters and has been moved to follow coverage of marketing channels and supply chains (now Chapter 12) and retailing and wholesaling (now Chapter 13).

Chapter 15: Updated Chapter Opening Example, New Advertisements, New Example of an IMC Program for a Movie, and New Discussion of the Media Agency of the Year. The chapter opening example has been completely updated to reflect Taco Bell's recent IMC activities. The company's Love & Tacos Contest; new restaurant in Las Vegas; Happily Ever After sweepstakes; superbowl ads; collaborations with Sony, the NBA, and Airbnb; and social media tactics such as Taco Tales and Clip Show posts are all discussed. New advertisements include examples from The North Face, Sony, and Humira. The IMC program used to promote the movie *Star Wars: The Last Jedi* has been added to the Scheduling the Promotion section. In addition, the work of *Advertising Age*'s Media Agency of the Year, PHD Media, is discussed.

Chapter 16: Updated Chapter Opening Example about Virtual Reality and Augmented Reality in Advertising, New Advertisements and Sales Promotion Examples, and New Discussion of the Advertising Agency of the Year. The growing impact of virtual reality (VR) and augmented reality (AR) on advertising is discussed in the chapter opening example. New examples of VR and AR campaigns include McDonald's Happy Goggles and Lowe's Holoroom. Coverage includes new advertising examples from

Mercedes-Benz, Progressive, Duracell, Milk Life, Amazon, AG, and Sonos and new sales promotion examples from Nabisco and Ben & Jerry's. The Identifying the Target Audience section now includes Mountain Dew and Lululemon campaigns as examples, and the Message Content section includes a discussion of the increasing use of gender—neutral advertising. The chapter also includes new discussion of *Advertising Age*'s Agency of the Year—Anomaly. In addition, the results of a recent Association of National Advertisers survey about the most common forms of compensation for ad agencies are discussed.

enough retweets to win free chicken nuggets for a year. The Marketing Matters box has been updated to describe how vloggers are becoming the online version of traditional celebrities and the Pepsi MAX "Friend Finder" YouTube video is included as an example of Pepsi's use of social media. The revised section titled Social Media Marketing Programs and Customer Engagement introduces new key terms and definitions for social media marketing programs and customer engagement. The chapter ends with a new video case about Body Glove and the role social media play in the company's marketing plan.

Chapter 17: New Body Glove Video Case, New Discussion on Internet-Connected Cars, New Section on Influencer Marketing, New Material on Live Streaming at Facebook, and Updated Marketing Matters Box on Vloggers. Chapter 17 opens with a discussion of the new level of mobile marketing enabled by Internet-connected cars. The discussion addresses three channels that can reach cars—social media, e-mail, and messaging apps. In addition, a new section titled Emergence of Influencer Marketing addresses the growth of social media influencers such as Kendall Jenner who has close to 100 million Instagram followers. New discussions about Facebook's privacy protection, its new dating feature, and Facebook Live have been added to the section on Mobile Marketing at Facebook. The overview of Twitter now includes an example of teenager Carter Wilkerson obtaining

Chapter 18: New Material on Upselling and Cross-Selling, Updated Marketing Matters Box, and New Discussion of Customer Relationship Marketing Systems and Technology, including Sales Force Automation, Marketing Automation, and Customer Service and Support Automation. The Consultative Selling section now includes discussion of upselling and cross-selling. The Marketing Matters box has been updated to include the most recent emotional intelligence test and the current link. In addition, the discussion of CRM systems and technology includes new material on the consolidation of customer and sales information, how *marketing automation* emphasizes sophisticated analytical techniques to track the behavior of anyone showing an interest in a product or service, and how *customer service and support automation* provides services such as "live chat."

INSTRUCTOR RESOURCES

Test Bank
We offer almost 5,000 test questions categorized by topic, learning objectives, and level of learning.

Instructor's Manual
The IM includes lecture notes, video case teaching notes, and In-Class Activities.

Video Cases
A unique series of 18 marketing video cases includes new videos featuring IBM, Toyota, Justin's, and Body Glove.

In-Class Activities
Chapter-specific in-class activities for today's students who learn from active, participative experiences.

PowerPoint Slides
Media-enhanced and hyperlinked slides enable engaging and interesting classroom discussions.

Digital In-Class Activities
Digital In-Class Activities focus on the use of web resources and the marketing data they can provide students.

Marketing: The Core 8/e *Instructor Resources*

Connect, LearnSmart, and SmartBook
The unique content platform delivering powerful technical resources and adaptive learning solutions. Includes new Marketing Analytics Exercises.

Blog
www.kerinmarketing.com
A blog written specifically for use in the classroom! Throughout each term we post new examples of marketing campaigns, along with a classroom discussion and participation guide.

Practice Marketing (Simulation)
Practice Marketing is a 3D, online, multiplayer game that enables students to gain practical experiences in an interactive environment.

Practice Marketing
Practice Marketing is a 3D, online, single or multiplayer game that helps students apply the four Ps by taking on the role of marketing manager for a backpack company. By playing the game individually and/or in teams, students come to understand how their decisions and elements of the marketing mix affect one another. Practice Marketing is easy to use, fully mobile, and provides an interactive alternative to marketing plan projects. Log in to mhpractice.com with your Connect credentials to access a demo, or contact your local McGraw-Hill representative for more details.

Marketing Mini Sims—Now Assignable within Connect!
Marketing Mini Sims are building-block sims based on our full Practice Marketing simulation that require students to take on the role of a marketing decision maker for a backpack manufacturing company. Each of the 9 Mini Sims focuses on one aspect of the marketing mix and serves to both reinforce the understanding of key concepts as well as allow students to make business decisions.

   To view a demonstration video and/or see a list of available simulations, please visit the McGraw-Hill Marketing Discipline Landing page at http://bit.ly/MHEmarketing.

Acknowledgments

To ensure continuous improvement of our textbook and supplements we have utilized an extensive review and development process for each of our past editions. Building on that history, the *Marketing: The Core,* 8th edition development process included several phases of evaluation and a variety of stakeholder audiences (e.g., students, instructors, etc.).

Reviewers who were vital in the changes that were made to the 8th and previous editions and its supplements include:

A. Diane Barlar
Abe Qastin
Abhay Shah
Abhi Biswas
Abhik Roy
Adrienne Hinds
Ahmed Maamoun
Al Holden
Alan Bush
Alexander Edsel
Alicia Revely
Allan Palmer
Allen Smith
Amy Frank
Anand Kumar
Andrei Strijnev
Andrew Dartt
Andrew Thacker
Andy Aylesworth
Angela Stanton
Anil Pandya
Ann Kuzma
Ann Little
Ann Lucht
Ann Veeck
Annette George
Anthony Koh
Anthony R. Fruzzetti
Aysen Bakir
Barbara Evans
Barbara Ribbens
Barnett Greenberg
Barry Bunn
Bashar Gammoh
Beibei Dong
Ben Oumlil
Beth Deinert
Bill Curtis
Bill Murphy
Bill Peterson
Blaise Waguespack Jr.
Bob Dahlstrom
Bob Dwyer
Bob E. Smiley
Bob McMillen
Bob Newberry
Brent Cunningham
Brian Kinard
Brian Murray
Bronis J. Verhage
Bruce Brown
Bruce Chadbourne
Bruce Ramsey
Bruce Robertson
Bryan Hayes
Carl Obermiller
Carmen Powers
Carmina Cavazos
Carol Bienstock
Carol M. Motley
Carolyn Massiah
Casey Donoho
Catherine Campbell
Cathie Rich-Duval
Cathleen H. Behan
Cathleen Hohner
Cecil Leonard
Cesar Maloles
Charla Mathwick
Charles Bodkin
Charles Ford
Charles Schewe
Cheryl Stansfield
Chiranjeev Kohli
Chris Anicich
Chris Ratcliffe
Christie Amato
Christine Lai
Christopher Blocker
Christopher Kondo
Christopher Ziemnowicz
Chuck Pickett
Cindy Leverenz
Clare Comm
Clark Compton
Clay Rasmussen
Clint Tankersley
Clyde Rupert
Connie Bateman
Corinne Asher
Craig Stacey
Cristanna Cook
Cydney Johnson
Dan Darrow
Dan Goebel
Dan Sherrel
Dan Toy
Daniel Butler
Daniel Rajaratnam
Darrell Goudge
Dave Olson
David Erickson
David Gerth
David J. Burns
David Jamison
David Kuhlmeier
David Smith
David Terry Paul
Deana Ray
Deb Jansky
Debbie Coleman
Debra Laverie
Deepa Pillai
Dennis Pappas
Dennis Rosen
Diana Joy Colarusso
Diane Dowdell
Diane T. McCrohan
Don Weinrauch
Donald Chang

Donald F. Mulvihill
Donald Fuller
Donald G. Norris
Donald Hoffer
Donald Larson
Donald R. Jackson
Donald V. Harper
Donna Wertalik
Doris M. Shaw
Dotty Harpool
Douglas Kornemann
Duncan G. LaBay
Eberhard Scheuling
Ed Gonsalves
Ed Laube
Ed McLaughlin
Eddie V. Easley
Edna Ragins
Edwin Nelson
Elaine Notarantonio
Eldon L. Little
Elena Martinez
Elizabeth R. Flynn
Ellen Benowitz
Eric Ecklund
Eric Newman
Eric Shaw
Erin Baca Blaugrund
Erin Cavusgil
Erin Wilkinson
Ernan Haruvy
Eugene Flynn
Farrokh Moshiri
Fekri Meziou
Frances Depaul
Francis DeFea
Francisco Coronel
Frank A. Chiaverini
Fred Honerkamp
Fred Hurvitz
Fred Morgan
Fred Trawick
Frederick J. Beier
Gail M. Zank
Gary Carson
Gary F. McKinnon
Gary Law
Gary Poorman
Gary Tucker
George Kelley
George Miaoulis

George Young
Gerald O. Cavallo
Gerard Athaide
Gerald Waddle
Glen Brodowsky
Glen Gelderloos
Godwin Ariguzo
Gonca Soysal
Gordon Mosley
Greg Kitzmiller
Guy Lochiatto
Harlan Wallingford
Harold Lucius
Harold S. Sekiguchi
Havva Jale Meric
Heidi Rottier
Heikki Rinne
Helen Koons
Herbert A. Miller
Herbert Katzenstein
Howard Combs
Hsin-Min Tong
Hugh Daubek
Imran Khan
Irene Dickey
Irene Lange
Ismet Anitsal
J. Ford Laumer
Jacqueline Karen
Jacqueline Williams
James A. Henley Jr.
James A. Muncy
James C. Johnson
James Cross
James Garry Smith
James Gaubert
James Ginther
James Gould
James H. Barnes
James H. Donnelly
James L. Grimm
James Lollar
James Marco
James McAlexander
James Meszaros
James Munch
James Olver
James P. Rakowski
James V. Spiers
James Wilkins
James Zemanek

Jane Cromartie
Jane Lang
Jane McKay-Nesbitt
Janet Ciccarelli
Janet Murray
Janice Karlen
Janice Taylor
Janice Williams
Jarrett Hudnal
Jason Little
Jay Lambe
Jean Murray
Jean Romeo
Jeanne Munger
Jeff Blodgett
Jeff Finley
Jeffrey W. von Freymann
Jefrey R. Woodall
Jennie Mitchell
Jennifer Nelson
Jerry Peerbolte
Jerry W. Wilson
Jianfeng Jiang
Jim McHugh
Jo Ann McManamy
Joan Williams
Joanne Orabone
Jobie Devinney-Walsh
Joe Cronin
Joe Kim
Joe M. Garza
Joe Puzi
Joe Ricks
Joe Stasio
John Benavidez
John Brandon
John C. Keyt
John Coppett
John Cox
John Finlayson
John Fitzpatrick
John Gaskins
John H. Cunningham
John Kuzma
John Penrose
John Striebich
Jonathan Hibbard
Joseph Belonax
Joseph Defilippe
Joseph Myslivec
Joseph Wisenblit

- Juan (Gloria) Meng
- Judy Bulin
- Judy Foxman
- Judy Wagner
- Julie Haworth
- Julie Sneath
- Jun Ma
- June E. Parr
- Karen Becker-Olsen
- Karen Berger
- Karen Flaherty
- Karen Gore
- Karen LeMasters
- Kasia Firlej
- Katalin Eibel-Spanyi
- Kathleen Krentler
- Kathleen Stuenkel
- Kathleen Williamson
- Kathryn Schifferle
- Kathy Meyer
- Katie Kemp
- Kay Chomic
- Kaylene Williams
- Keith B. Murray
- Keith Jones
- Keith Murray
- Kellie Emrich
- Ken Crocker
- Ken Fairweather
- Ken Herbst
- Ken Murdock
- Ken Shaw
- Kenneth Goodenday
- Kenneth Jameson
- Kenneth Maricle
- Kerri Acheson
- Kevin Feldt
- Kevin W. Bittle
- Kim Montney
- Kim Richmond
- Kim Sebastiano
- Kim Wong
- Kimberly D. Smith
- Kimberly Grantham
- Kin Thompson
- Kirti Celly
- Koren Borges
- Kristen Regine
- Kristine Hovsepian
- Kristy McManus
- Kumar Sarangee
- Kunal Sethi
- Lan Wu
- Larry Borgen
- Larry Carter
- Larry Feick
- Larry Goldstein
- Larry Marks
- Larry Rottmeyer
- Laura Dwyer
- Lauren Wright
- Lawrence Duke
- Lawrence Marks
- Lee Meadow
- Leon Zurawicki
- Leonard Lindenmuth
- Leslie A. Goldgehn
- Leta Beard
- Linda Anglin
- Linda M. Delene
- Linda Morable
- Linda Munilla
- Linda N. LaMarca
- Linda Rochford
- Lindell Phillip Chew
- Lisa M. Sciulli
- Lisa Siegal
- Lisa Simon
- Lisa Troy
- Lisa Zingaro
- Lori Feldman
- Lowell E. Crow
- Lynn Harris
- Lynn Loudenback
- Marc Goldberg
- Maria McConnell
- Maria Randazzo-Nardin
- Maria Sanella
- Marilyn Lavin
- Mark Collins
- Mark Weber
- Mark Young
- Martin Bressler
- Martin Decatur
- Martin St. John
- Marton L. Macchiete
- Martyn Kingston
- Marva Hunt
- Mary Ann McGrath
- Mary Beth DeConinck
- Mary Conran
- Mary Joyce
- Mary Schramm
- Mary Tripp
- Matt Meuter
- Max White
- Mayukh Dass
- Melissa Clark
- Melissa Moore
- Michael Callow
- Michael Drafke
- Michael Fowler
- Michael Mayo
- Michael Peters
- Michael Pontikos
- Michael R. Luthy
- Michael Swenson
- Michelle Kunz
- Michelle Wetherbee
- Mike Hagan
- Mike Hyman
- Mike Luckett
- Milton Pressley
- Miriam B. Stamps
- Nadia J. Abgrab
- Nancy Bloom
- Nancy Boykin
- Nancy Grassilli
- Nanda Kumar
- Nathan Himelstein
- Neel Das
- Nikolai Ostapenko
- Norman Smothers
- Notis Pagiavlas
- Ottilia Voegtli
- Pamela Grimm
- Pamela Hulen
- Parimal Bhagat
- Pat Spirou
- Patricia Baconride
- Patricia Bernson
- Patricia Manninen
- Paul Dion
- Paul Dowling
- Paul Jackson
- Paul Londrigan
- Paul Myer
- Peter J. McClure
- Philip Kearney
- Philip Parron
- Philip Shum
- Phyllis Fein
- Phyllis McGinnis

Poh-Lin Yeoh
Pola B. Gupta
Priscilla G. Aaltonen
Priscilla LaBarbera
Priyali Rajagopal
Rae Caloura
Rajesh Iyer
Rajiv Kashyap
Ram Kesaran
Randall E. Wade
Randy Stuart
Ravi Shanmugam
Raymond Marzilli
Reid Claxton
Renee Foster
Renee Pfeifer-Luckett
Rex Moody
Rhonda Mack
Rhonda Taylor
Richard C. Leventhal
Richard D. Parker
Richard Hansen
Richard Hargrove
Richard J. Lutz
Richard Lapidus
Richard M. Hill
Richard Penn
Rick Sweeney
Rita Dynan
Robert C. Harris
Robert Jones
Robert Lawson
Robert Luke
Robert Morris
Robert S. Welsh
Robert Swerdlow
Robert W. Ruekert
Robert Williams
Robert Witherspoon
Roberta Schultz
Roger McIntyre
Roger W. Egerton
Ron Dougherty
Ron Hasty
Ron Larson
Ron Weston
Ronald A. Feinberg
Ronald Michaels
Rosemary Ramsey
Roy Adler
Roy Klages

Ruth Ann Smith
Ruth Rosales
Ruth Taylor
S. Choi Chan
S. Tamer Cavusgil
Sally Sledge
Samuel E. McNeely
Sanal Mazvancheryl
Sandipan Sen
Sandra Robertson
Sandra Smith
Sandra Young
Sang Choe
Sanjay S. Mehta
Santhi Harvey
Scott Cragin
Scott Swan
Scott Thorne
Shabnam Zanjani
Sheila Wexler
Sherry Cook
Siva Balasubramanian
Soon Hong Min
Srdan Zdravkovic
Stacia Gray
Stan Garfunkel
Stan Scott
Starr F. Schlobohm
Stephen Calcich
Stephen Garrott
Stephen Pirog
Stephen W. Miller
Steve Hertzenberg
Steve Taylor
Steven Engel
Steven Moff
Sudhir Karunakaran
Sue Lewis
Sue McGorry
Sue Umashankar
Suman Basuroy
Sundaram Dorai
Sunder Narayanan
Susan Godar
Susan Peterson
Susan Sieloff
Susan Stanix
Susie Pryor
Suzanne Murray
Sylvia Keyes
Tamara Masters

Teri Root
Terrance Kevin McNamara
Terry Kroeten
Theodore Mitchell
Theresa Flaherty
Thom J. Belich
Thomas Brashear
Thomas L. Trittipo
Thomas M. Bertsch
Thomas Passero
Tim Aurand
Tim Landry
Timothy Donahue
Timothy Reisenwitz
Tina L. Williams
Tino DeMarco
Tom Castle
Tom Deckelman
Tom Marshall
Tom Rossi
Tom Stevenson
Tom Thompson
Tracy Fulce
Vahwere Kavota
Van R. Wood
Vicki Rostedt
Victoria Miller
Vincent P. Taiani
Vladimir Pashkevich
Vonda Powell
Walter Kendall
Wendy Achey
Wendy Wood
Wesley Johnston
William B. Dodds
William Brown
William D. Ash
William Foxx
William G. Browne
William G. Mitchell
William J. Carner
William Motz
William Pertula
William R. Wynd
William Rodgers
William S. Piper
Wilton Lelund
Yi He
Yue Pan
Yunchuan Liu

Thanks are due to many people, including current and past students, marketing educators around the globe, university staff, business journal and periodical authors, company representatives, and marketing professionals of every kind. Their assistance has been essential in our efforts to continue to provide the most comprehensive, up-to-date, and integrated teaching and learning package available. We have been fortunate to have so many people be part of our team! In particular, however, we continue to benefit from the insights and guidance of our long-time friend, colleague, and coauthor, William Rudelius. His contributions to the textbook are truly timeless.

Nancy Harrower of Concordia University, St. Paul, led our efforts on the Instructor's Manual, the PowerPoint slides, the In-Class Activities, and the new Digital In-Class Activities. In addition, she provides the content for our blog (kerinmarketing.com). Tia Quinlan-Wilder of the University of Denver was responsible for the Test Bank and Quizzes and the LearnSmart component of our interactive learning package. Erin Steffes of Towson University was responsible for the Connect application exercises and the new Marketing Analytics exercises. All of these professors are exceptional educators and we are very fortunate that they are part of our team. Michael Vessey, our long-time collaborator who recently passed away, also provided assistance in the preparation of materials that are still in use.

Thanks are also due to many other colleagues who contributed to the text, cases, and supplements. They include: Richard Lutz of the University of Florida; Linda Rochford of the University of Minnesota—Duluth; Kevin Upton of the University of Minnesota—Twin Cities; Nancy Nentl of Metropolitan State University; Leslie Kendrick of Johns Hopkins University; Lau Geok Theng of the National University of Singapore; and Leigh McAlister of the University of Texas at Austin. Rick Armstrong of Armstrong Photography, Dan Hundley and George Heck of Token Media, Nick Kaufman and Michelle Morgan of NKP Media, Bruce McLean of World Class Communication Technologies, Paul Fagan of Fagan Productions, Martin Walter of White Room Digital, Scott Bolin of Bolin Marketing, and Andrew Schones of Pure Imagination produced the videos.

Many businesspeople also provided substantial assistance by making available information that appears in the text, videos, and supplements—much of it for the first time in college materials. Thanks are due to Ann Rubin, Teresa Yoo, and Kathleen Cremmins of IBM; Jana Hartline, Rommel Momen, Joanie Swearingen, and Amy Ulloa of Toyota; Justin Gold and Mike Guanella of Justin's; Lisa Selk of CytoSport; Jeff Ettinger of Hormel; Russ Lesser, Billy Meistrell, Nick Meistrell, and Jenna Meistrell of Body Glove; Peter Maule of Marquee Brands; Daniel Jasper, Jill Renslow, and Sarah Schmidt of Mall of America; Mike Pohl of ACES Flight Simulation; Chris Klein, Jaime Cardenas, Casey Leppanen, Heather Peace, and Lori Nevares of LA Galaxy; Ian Wolfman and Jana Boone of meplusyou; David Ford and Don Rylander of Ford Consulting Group; Mark Rehborg of Tony's Pizza; Vivian Callaway, Sandy Proctor, and Anna Stoesz of General Mills; David Windorski, Tom Barnidge, and Erica Schiebel of 3M; Nicholas Skally, Jeremy Stonier, and Joe Olivas of Prince Sports; Brian Niccol of Pizza Hut; Tom Cassady of JCPenney, Inc.; Charles Besio of the Sewell Automotive Group, Inc.; Lindsey Smith of GE Healthcare; Beverly Roberts of the U.S. Census Bureau; Sheryl Adkins-Green of Mary Kay, Inc.; Mattison Crowe of Seven Cycles, Inc.; Alisa Allen, Kirk Hodgdon, Patrick Hodgdon, and Nick Naumann of Altus Marketing and Business Development; and Nelson Ng from Dundas Data Visualization, Inc.

Those who provided the resources for use in the *Marketing: The Core,* 8th edition textbook, Instructor's Manual, and/or PowerPoint presentations include: Todd Walker and Jean Golden of Million Dollar Idea; Karen Cohick of Susan G. Komen for the Cure; Liz Stewart of Ben & Jerry's; John Formella and Patricia Lipari of Kodak; Erica Schiebel of 3M; Joe Diliberti of *Consumer Reports*; Patricia Breman of Strategic Business Insights (VALS); Brian Nielsen of the Nielsen Company; David Walonick of StatPac; Mark Rehborg of Schwan's Consumer Brands (Tony's Pizza); Jennifer Olson of Experian Simmons;

Kitty Munger and Mary Wykoff of Wendy's; Mark Heller of RetailSails; Nicky Hutcheon of ZenithOptimedia; Amy Thompson and Jennifer Allison of Dell, Inc.; Adriana Carlton of Walmart and Rick Hill of Bernstein-Rein Advertising (Walmart); Janine Bolin of Saks, Inc.; Dr. Yory Wurmser of the Data and Marketing Association; and Elizabeth Clendenin of Unilever (Caress).

We also want to thank the following people who generously provided assistance with our *Marketing: The Core,* 8th edition In-Class Activities (ICAs) and associated PowerPoint presentations: Mitch Forster and Carla Silveira of Ghirardelli Chocolate Company; Karolyn Warfel and Betsy Boyer of Woodstream Corp. (Victor Pest); Leonard Fuld of Fuld & Co.; Maggie Jantzen of Starbucks Coffee Company; Michelle Green and Victoria Glazier of the U.S. Census Bureau; Lisa Castaldo of Pepsi; Muffie Taggert of General Mills; Robert M. McMath, formerly of NewProductWorks; Greg Rodriguez; Jeremy Tucker, Julia Wells, and Lisa Cone of Frito-Lay (Doritos); Susan Carroll and Bob Robinson of Apple, Inc.; Willard Oberton of Fastenal Company; Scott Wosniak and Jennifer Arnold of Toro; Kim Eskro of Fallon Worldwide (Gold'n Plump); Robin Grayson of TBWA/Chiat/Day (Apple); Katie Kramer of Valassis Communications, Inc. (Nutella/Advil); Triestina Greco of Nutella/Ferrero; Tim Stauber of Wyeth Consumer Healthcare (Advil); and Yvonne Pendleton and Lucille Storms of Mary Kay.

Staff support from the Southern Methodist University and the University of Denver was essential. We gratefully acknowledge the help of Jeanne Milazzo and Gabriela Barcenas for their many contributions.

Checking countless details related to layout, graphics, and photos, and managing last-minute text changes is essential for a sound and accurate textbook. This also involves coordinating activities of authors, designers, editors, compositors, and production specialists. Christine Vaughan, our lead content project manager, of McGraw-Hill Education's production staff provided the necessary oversight and attention to detail while retaining an extraordinary level of professionalism, often under tight deadlines. We are very fortunate that Christine was part of our team. Thank you again!

Finally, we acknowledge the professional efforts of the McGraw-Hill Education staff. Completion of our book and its many supplements required the attention and commitment of many editorial, production, marketing, and research personnel. Our McGraw-Hill team included Susan Gouijnstook, Meredith Fossel, Nicole Young, Kelly Pekelder, Danielle Clement, Susan Culbertson, Matt Diamond, Carrie Burger, and many others. In addition, we relied on David Tietz for constant attention regarding the photo elements of the text, and Claire Hunter for management of the details of the online authoring system. Handling the countless details of our text, supplement, and support technologies has become an incredibly complex challenge. We thank all these people for their efforts!

    Roger A. Kerin
    Steven W. Hartley

BRIEF CONTENTS

Part 1 — Initiating the Marketing Process

1. Creating Customer Relationships and Value through Marketing 2
2. Developing Successful Organizational and Marketing Strategies 26
   - Appendix A Building an Effective Marketing Plan 56
3. Understanding the Marketing Environment, Ethical Behavior, and Social Responsibility 72

Part 2 — Understanding Buyers and Markets

4. Understanding Consumer Behavior 98
5. Understanding Organizations as Customers 128
6. Understanding and Reaching Global Consumers and Markets 148

Part 3 — Targeting Marketing Opportunities

7. Marketing Research: From Customer Insights to Actions 178
8. Market Segmentation, Targeting, and Positioning 210

Part 4 — Satisfying Marketing Opportunities

9. Developing New Products and Services 236
10. Managing Successful Products, Services, and Brands 266
11. Pricing Products and Services 298
12. Managing Marketing Channels and Supply Chains 324
13. Retailing and Wholesaling 350
14. Implementing Interactive and Multichannel Marketing 378
15. Integrated Marketing Communications and Direct Marketing 402
16. Advertising, Sales Promotion, and Public Relations 428
17. Using Social Media and Mobile Marketing to Connect with Consumers 460
18. Personal Selling and Sales Management 488
    - Appendix B Planning a Career in Marketing 516

Glossary 531

Name Index 539

Company/Product Index 549

Subject Index 558

DETAILED CONTENTS

Part 1 — Initiating the Marketing Process

©Diane Bondareff/Invision for Chobani/AP Images

1 CREATING CUSTOMER RELATIONSHIPS AND VALUE THROUGH MARKETING   2

Creating Customer Value: The Chobani Way!   2
    Creating an Exceptional Product   2
    Connecting with Customers   2
    Chobani Today   3
    Chobani, Marketing, and You   4
What Is Marketing?   4
    Marketing and Your Career   4
    Marketing: Delivering Value to Customers   5
    The Diverse Elements Influencing Marketing Actions   5
    What Is Needed for Marketing to Occur   6
How Marketing Discovers and Satisfies Consumer Needs   7
    Discovering Consumer Needs   7
    The Challenge: Meeting Consumer Needs with New Products   8
    Satisfying Consumer Needs   10
The Marketing Program: How Customer Relationships Are Built   11
    Relationship Marketing: Easy to Understand, Hard to Do   11
    The Marketing Program and Market Segments   12
    3M's Strategy and Marketing Program to Help Students Study   13
How Marketing Became So Important   15
    Evolution of the Market Orientation   15
    Focusing on Customer Relationship Management   15
    Ethics and Social Responsibility in Marketing: Balancing the Interests of Different Groups   16
    The Breadth and Depth of Marketing   17

Learning Objectives Review   18
Learning Review Answers   19
Focusing on Key Terms   19
Applying Marketing Knowledge   20
Building Your Marketing Plan   20

Video Case 1: Chobani®: Making Greek Yogurt a Household Name   20

Chapter Notes   24

©McGraw-Hill Education/Evelyn Nicole Kirksey, Photographer

2 DEVELOPING SUCCESSFUL ORGANIZATIONAL AND MARKETING STRATEGIES   26

Ben and Jerry Are on a Mission: To Make Fantastic, Sustainable, World-Changing Ice Cream   26
Today's Organizations   28
    Kinds of Organizations   28

> Making Responsible Decisions: New Types of Organizations Help Entrepreneurs Focus on Passion and Purpose 29

    What Is Strategy? 30
    The Structure of Today's Organizations 30
Strategy in Visionary Organizations 31
    Organizational Foundation: Why Does It Exist? 31
    Organizational Direction: What Will It Do? 32
    Organizational Strategies: How Will It Do It? 34
    Tracking Strategic Performance with Marketing Analytics 34
Setting Strategic Directions 36
    A Look Around: Where Are We Now? 36

> Applying Marketing Metrics: How Well Is Ben & Jerry's Doing? 36

    Growth Strategies: Where Do We Want to Go? 37
The Strategic Marketing Process 41
    Principles Underlying the Strategic Marketing Process 41
    The Planning Phase of the Strategic Marketing Process 42
    The Implementation Phase of the Strategic Marketing Process 44
    The Evaluation Phase of the Strategic Marketing Process 46

Learning Objectives Review 48
Learning Review Answers 49
Focusing on Key Terms 50
Applying Marketing Knowledge 50
Building Your Marketing Plan 50

Video Case 2: IBM: Putting Smart Strategy to Work 50

Chapter Notes 53
Appendix A   Building an Effective Marketing Plan 56

3 UNDERSTANDING THE MARKETING ENVIRONMENT, ETHICAL BEHAVIOR, AND SOCIAL RESPONSIBILITY 72

Fortune's Businessperson of the Year: "I'm in This to Build Something Cool!" 72
    Facebook in the Future 73
Environmental Scanning 74
    An Environmental Scan of Today's Marketplace 74
Social Forces 74
    Demographics 74
    Culture 76

> Making Responsible Decisions: Balancing Profits and Purpose—Millennial Style 76

©David Paul Morris/Bloomberg via Getty Images

Economic Forces 77
    Macroeconomic Conditions 77
    Consumer Income 78
Technological Forces 79
    Technology of Tomorrow 79
    Technology's Impact on Customer Value 80
    Technology Enables Data Analytics 80
Competitive Forces 81
    Alternative Forms of Competition 81
    Small Businesses as Competitors 81
Regulatory Forces 82
    Protecting Competition 82
    Protecting Producers and Consumers 82
    Control through Self-Regulation 83
Understanding Ethical Marketing Behavior 84
    Societal Culture and Norms 84
    Business Culture and Industry Practices 85
    Corporate Culture and Expectations 85
    Your Personal Moral Philosophy and Ethical Behavior 86

> **Making Responsible Decisions: Corporate Conscience in the Cola War** 86

Understanding Social Responsibility for Sustainable Marketing 87
    Three Concepts of Social Responsibility 87
    Sustainable Development: Doing Well by Doing Good 89

> **Marketing Matters: Will Consumers Switch Brands for a Cause? Yes, If . . .** 89

Learning Objectives Review 90
Learning Review Answers 90
Focusing on Key Terms 91
Applying Marketing Knowledge 91
Building Your Marketing Plan 92

Video Case 3: Toyota: Where the Future Is Available Today 92

Chapter Notes 95

Part 2 — Understanding Buyers and Markets

©Whisson/Jordan/Corbis/Getty Images

4 UNDERSTANDING CONSUMER BEHAVIOR 98

Enlightened Carmakers Know What Custom(h)ers and Influenc(h)ers Value 98
Consumer Purchase Decision Process and Experience 100
    Problem Recognition: Perceiving a Need 100
    Information Search: Seeking Value 100
    Alternative Evaluation: Assessing Value 101
    Purchase Decision: Buying Value 102

    Postpurchase Behavior: Realizing Value   102
    Consumer Involvement Affects Problem Solving   103

> **Marketing Matters: How Much Is a Satisfied Customer Worth?**   103

    Situational Influences That Affect Purchase Decisions   105
    Putting the Purchase Decision Process into Practice: Consumer Touchpoints and Consumer Journey Maps   105
Psychological Influences on Consumer Behavior   107
    Consumer Motivation and Personality   107
    Consumer Perception   109
    Consumer Learning   110

> **Making Responsible Decisions: The Ethics of Subliminal Messages**   110

    Consumer Values, Beliefs, and Attitudes   111
    Consumer Lifestyle   112
Sociocultural Influences on Consumer Behavior   113
    Personal Influence   113

> **Marketing Matters: BzzAgent—The Buzz Experience**   115

    Reference Group Influence   116
    Family Influence   116
    Culture and Subculture Influences   118

Learning Objectives Review   121
Learning Review Answers   121
Focusing on Key Terms   122
Applying Marketing Knowledge   122
Building Your Marketing Plan   122

Video Case 4: Coppertone: Creating the Leading Sun Care Brand by Understanding Consumers   123

Chapter Notes   125

5   UNDERSTANDING ORGANIZATIONS AS CUSTOMERS   128

Organizational Buying Is Marketing, Too! Purchasing Publication Paper for JCPenney   128
Business-to-Business Marketing and Organizational Buyers   130
    Organizational Buyers   130
    Organizational Markets   130
    Measuring Organizational Markets   131
Characteristics of Organizational Buying   132
    Demand Characteristics   132
    Size of the Order or Purchase   132
    Number of Potential Buyers   133
    Organizational Buying Objectives   133
    Organizational Buying Criteria   133
    Buyer–Seller Relationships and Supply Partnerships   134

Courtesy of JCPenney

> Marketing Matters: At Milsco Manufacturing, "Our Marketing Philosophy Is Designed to Develop Partnerships" and Deliver a Great Ride for Customers' Seats 135

The Organizational Buying Function and Process and the Buying Center 136
    The Buying Function in Organizations 136

> Making Responsible Decisions: Sustainable Procurement for Sustainable Growth at Starbucks 136

    Stages in the Organizational Buying Process 137
    The Buying Center: A Cross-Functional Group 137
Online Buying in Business-to-Business Marketing 140
    Prominence of Online Buying in Organizational Markets 140
    E-Marketplaces: Virtual Organizational Markets 140
    Online Auctions in Organizational Markets 141

> Marketing Matters: eBay Means Business for Business-to-Business Marketing Entrepreneurs, Too! 141

Learning Objectives Review 142
Learning Review Answers 143
Focusing on Key Terms 143
Applying Marketing Knowledge 143
Building Your Marketing Plan 144

Video Case 5: Trek: Building Better Bikes through Organizational Buying 144

Chapter Notes 147

6 UNDERSTANDING AND REACHING GLOBAL CONSUMERS AND MARKETS 148

Photo: ©Andrey Arkusha/ Shutterstock, Logo: ©Editorial/ Alamy Stock Photo

Transforming the Way India Sells and Transforming the Way India Buys: Amazon India Builds a Multibillion-Dollar Operation from the Ground up to the Cloud 148
    Amazon's Awesome Opportunity in India 148
    Amazon's Awesome Challenges in India 148
    Failure Is Not an Option 149
Dynamics of World Trade 150
    Global Perspective on World Trade 150
    United States' Perspective on World Trade 151
Marketing in a Dynamic Global Economy 152
    Economic Protectionism by Individual Countries 152

> Making Responsible Decisions: Global Ethics and Global Economics—The Case of Protectionism 153

Economic Integration among Countries 154
    Global Competition among Global Companies for Global Consumers 155
    The Presence of a Networked Global Marketspace 158

Marketing Matters: The Global Teenager—A Market of Voracious Consumers 158

    Prevalence of Economic Espionage 159
A Global Environmental Scan 160
    Cultural Diversity 160
    Economic Considerations 163
    Political-Regulatory Climate 165
Comparing Global Market-Entry Strategies 166
    Exporting 166
    Licensing 167

Marketing Matters: Creative Cosmetics and Creative Export Marketing in Japan 167

    Joint Venture 168
    Direct Investment 168
Crafting a Worldwide Marketing Program 169
    Product and Promotion Strategies 169
    Distribution Strategy 171
    Pricing Strategy 171

Learning Objectives Review 172
Learning Review Answers 173
Focusing on Key Terms 173
Applying Marketing Knowledge 173
Building Your Marketing Plan 173

Video Case 6: Mary Kay, Inc.: Building a Brand in India 174

Chapter Notes 176

Part 3 — Targeting Marketing Opportunities

7 MARKETING RESEARCH: FROM CUSTOMER INSIGHTS TO ACTIONS 178

Hollywood Loves Marketing Research! 178
    A Film Industry Secret 178
The Role of Marketing Research 180
    What Is Marketing Research? 180
    The Challenges in Doing Good Marketing Research 181
    Five-Step Marketing Research Approach 181
Step 1: Define the Problem 181
    Set the Research Objectives 182
    Identify Possible Marketing Actions 182
Step 2: Develop the Research Plan 182
    Specify Constraints 182
    Identify Data Needed for Marketing Actions 183
    Determine How to Collect Data 183
Step 3: Collect Relevant Information 184
    Secondary Data: Internal 184

©Moviestore Collection Ltd./Alamy Stock Photo

Secondary Data: External   185
Advantages and Disadvantages of Secondary Data   185
Primary Data: Watching People   186

Marketing Matters: Online Databases and Internet Resources Useful to Marketers   186

Primary Data: Asking People   188
Primary Data: Other Sources   192

Applying Marketing Metrics: Are the Carmex Social Media Programs Working Well?   194

Advantages and Disadvantages of Primary Data   195
Step 4: Develop Findings   195

Making Responsible Decisions: No More Personal Secrets: The Downside of Data Mining and Predictive Modeling   197

Present the Findings   198
Step 5: Take Marketing Actions   199
Make Action Recommendations   199
Implement the Action Recommendations   200
Evaluate the Results   200
Sales Forecasting Techniques   200
Judgments of the Decision Maker   201
Surveys of Knowledgeable Groups   201
Statistical Methods   201

Learning Objectives Review   202
Learning Review Answers   203
Focusing on Key Terms   204
Applying Marketing Knowledge   204
Building Your Marketing Plan   204

Video Case 7: Carmex® (A): Leveraging Facebook for Marketing Research   205

Chapter Notes   208

8   **MARKET SEGMENTATION, TARGETING, AND POSITIONING**   210

Segmentation Rules in the Kingdom of Happiness!   210
Zappos's Secret to Success   210
Delivering WOW Customer Service   210
Why Segment Markets?   212
What Market Segmentation Means   212
When and How to Segment Markets   213
Steps in Segmenting and Targeting Markets   216
Step 1: Group Potential Buyers into Segments   216
Step 2: Group Products to Be Sold into Categories   220
Step 3: Develop a Market-Product Grid and Estimate the Size of Markets   222

©Brad Swonetz/Redux

Step 4: Select Target Markets 223
Step 5: Take Marketing Actions to Reach Target Markets 224
Market-Product Synergies: A Balancing Act 226

Marketing Matters: Apple's Segmentation Strategy—Camp Runamok No Longer 227

Positioning the Product 228
Two Approaches to Product Positioning 228
Writing a Positioning Statement 228
Product Positioning Using Perceptual Maps 228
A Perceptual Map to Reposition Chocolate Milk for Adults 229

Learning Objectives Review 230
Learning Review Answers 230
Focusing on Key Terms 231
Applying Marketing Knowledge 231
Building Your Marketing Plan 231

Video Case 8: Prince Sports, Inc.: Tennis Racquets for Every Segment 232

Chapter Notes 234

Part 4 Satisfying Marketing Opportunities

9 DEVELOPING NEW PRODUCTS AND SERVICES 236

Apple: The World-Class New-Product Machine 236
Apple's New-Product Development Successes 236
Apple's New-Product Development Stumbles 237
The Next Chapter in Apple's Story: An Apple-Enabled iCar? 238

What Are Products and Services? 238
A Look at Goods, Services, and Ideas 238
Classifying Products 239
Classifying Services 239
The Uniqueness of Services 241
Assessing and Improving Service Quality 242
Product Classes, Forms, Items, Lines, and Mixes 242

New Products and Why They Succeed or Fail 244
What Is a New Product? 244

Marketing Matters: Too Much of a Good Thing: Feature Bloat and Feature Fatigue in New-Product Development 245

Why Products and Services Succeed or Fail 246
How Applying Marketing Metrics Can Monitor New-Product Performance 249

©John Ziomek/Courier- Post via USA TODAY NETWORK

> Applying Marketing Metrics: Which States Are Underperforming? 249

The New-Product Development Process 250
    Stage 1: New-Product Strategy Development 250
    Stage 2: Idea Generation 251
    Stage 3: Screening and Evaluation 253

> Marketing Matters: Was the Google Glass Half Full or Half Empty? 254

    Stage 4: Business Analysis 255
    Stage 5: Development 255
    Stage 6: Market Testing 256
    Stage 7: Commercialization 257

Learning Objectives Review 258
Learning Review Answers 259
Focusing on Key Terms 260
Applying Marketing Knowledge 260
Building Your Marketing Plan 260

Video Case 9: GoPro: Making All of Us Heroes with Exciting New Products 261

Chapter Notes 264

10 MANAGING SUCCESSFUL PRODUCTS, SERVICES, AND BRANDS 266

©J. Meric/Getty Images

Gatorade: Bringing Science to Sweat for More Than 50 Years 266
    Creating the Gatorade Brand 266
    Building the Gatorade Brand 267
Charting the Product Life Cycle 268
    Introduction Stage 268
    Growth Stage 270
    Maturity Stage 271
    Decline Stage 271
    Three Aspects of the Product Life Cycle 272

> Marketing Matters: Will E-mail Spell Extinction for Fax Machines? 272

Managing the Product Life Cycle 276
    Role of a Product Manager 276
    Modifying the Product 276
    Modifying the Market 277

> Applying Marketing Metrics: Knowing Your CDI and BDI 277

    Repositioning the Product 278

> Making Responsible Decisions: Consumer Economics of Downsizing—Get Less, Pay More 279

Branding and Brand Management 280
    Brand Personality and Brand Equity 280
    Picking a Good Brand Name 282
    Branding Strategies 283
Packaging and Labeling Products 286
    Creating Customer Value and Competitive Advantage through Packaging and Labeling 286

> Marketing Matters: Creating Customer Value through Packaging—Pez Heads Dispense More Than Candy 287

    Packaging and Labeling Challenges and Responses 288
The Marketing of Services 289
    Product (Service) 289
    Price 289
    Place (Distribution) 290
    Promotion 290
    People 290
    Physical Environment 290
    Process 291

Learning Objectives Review 291
Learning Review Answers 292
Focusing on Key Terms 293
Applying Marketing Knowledge 293
Building Your Marketing Plan 293

Video Case 10: Justin's: Managing a Successful Product with Passion 293

Chapter Notes 296

11 PRICING PRODUCTS AND SERVICES 298

Vizio, Inc.—Building a Smart TV Brand at a Great Value 298
Nature and Importance of Price 300
    What Is a Price? 300
    Price as an Indicator of Value 301
    Price in the Marketing Mix 302

> Marketing Matters: Does Spirit Airlines Engage in Value Pricing? For Some Yes, for Others No 302

Common Pricing Approaches 303
    Demand-Oriented Pricing Approaches 303
    Cost-Oriented Pricing Approaches 304

> Marketing Matters: Energizer's Lesson in Price Perception—Value Lies in the Eye of the Beholder 305

    Profit-Oriented Pricing Approaches 306

©CTK/Alamy Stock Photo

Competition-Oriented Pricing Approaches 307

> Applying Marketing Metrics: Are Red Bull Prices Above, At, or Below the Market? 308

Estimating Demand and Revenue 309
    Estimating Demand 309
    Price Elasticity of Demand 311
    Fundamentals of Estimating Revenue 311
Determining Cost, Volume, and Profit Relationships 312
    The Importance of Controlling Costs 312
    Break-Even Analysis 312
Pricing Objectives and Constraints 314
    Identifying Pricing Objectives 314
    Identifying Pricing Constraints 315
Setting a Final Price 316
    Step 1: Select an Approximate Price Level 316
    Step 2: Set the List or Quoted Price 317
    Step 3: Make Special Adjustments to the List or Quoted Price 317

> Making Responsible Decisions: The Ethics and Economics of Surge Pricing 318

Learning Objectives Review 319
Learning Review Answers 320
Focusing on Key Terms 320
Applying Marketing Knowledge 320
Building Your Marketing Plan 321

Video Case 11: Carmex (B): Setting the Price of the Number One Lip Balm 321

Chapter Notes 323

12 MANAGING MARKETING CHANNELS AND SUPPLY CHAINS 324

Eddie Bauer: The "Brick, Click, and Flip" Pick for the Active Outdoor Enthusiast 324
    Eddie Bauer's Multichannel Marketing Strategy 324
    Supply Chain Dynamics at Eddie Bauer 325
Nature and Importance of Marketing Channels 326
    What Is a Marketing Channel of Distribution? 326
    How Customer Value Is Created by Intermediaries 326
Marketing Channel Structure and Organization 328
    Marketing Channels for Consumer Products and Services 328
    Marketing Channels for Business Products and Services 329
    Internet Marketing Channels 330
    Direct and Multichannel Marketing 330
    Dual Distribution and Strategic Channel Alliances 331
    Vertical Marketing Systems 332

©Bonnie Kamin/PhotoEdit, Inc.

> Marketing Matters: Nestlé and General Mills—Cereal Partners Worldwide   332

Marketing Channel Choice and Management   334
    Factors Affecting Channel Choice and Management   334

> Applying Marketing Metrics: Channel Sales and Profit at Charlesburg Furniture   336

    Managing Channel Relationships: Conflict and Cooperation   337

Logistics and Supply Chain Management   338
    Supply Chains versus Marketing Channels   339
    Sourcing, Assembling, and Delivering a New Car: The Automotive Supply Chain   339
    Supply Chain Management and Marketing Strategy   340

> Marketing Matters: IBM's Watson Supply Chain—Delivering a Total Solution for Its Customers   341

Two Concepts of Logistics Management in a Supply Chain   342
    Total Logistics Cost Concept   342
    Customer Service Concept   342

Closing the Loop: Reverse Logistics   343

> Making Responsible Decisions: Reverse Logistics and Green Marketing Go Together at Hewlett-Packard: Recycling e-Waste   344

Learning Objectives Review   345
Learning Review Answers   345
Focusing on Key Terms   346
Applying Marketing Knowledge   346
Building Your Marketing Plan   346

Video Case 12: Amazon: Delivering the Earth's Biggest Selection!   347

Chapter Notes   349

13 RETAILING AND WHOLESALING   350

Smart Stores Are Changing the Customer Journey!   350
The Value of Retailing   352
    Consumer Utilities Offered by Retailing   352
    The Global Economic Impact of Retailing   353
Classifying Retail Outlets   353
    Form of Ownership   354

> Making Responsible Decisions: How Green Is Your Retailer? The Rankings Are Out!   354

    Level of Service   356
    Type of Merchandise Line   356
Nonstore Retailing   357

©Jiraroj Praditcharoenkul/Alamy Stock Photo

　　　　Automatic Vending　358
　　　　Direct Mail and Catalogs　358
　　　　Television Home Shopping　359
　　　　Online Retailing　359
　　　　Telemarketing　360
　　　　Direct Selling　361
Retailing Strategy　361

> Applying Marketing Metrics: Why Apple Stores May Be the Best in the United States!　365

The Changing Nature of Retailing　366
　　　The Wheel of Retailing　366
　　　The Retail Life Cycle　367
　　　Data Analytics　368
Wholesaling　368
　　　Merchant Wholesalers　369
　　　Agents and Brokers　369
　　　Manufacturers' Branches and Offices　370

Learning Objectives Review　370
Learning Review Answers　371
Focusing on Key Terms　371
Applying Marketing Knowledge　372
Building Your Marketing Plan　372

Video Case 13: Mall of America®: America's Biggest Mall Knows the Secret to Successful Retailing!　372

Chapter Notes　375

14　IMPLEMENTING INTERACTIVE AND MULTICHANNEL MARKETING　378

Courtesy of Seven Cycles, Inc.

Seven Cycles Delivers Just One Bike. Yours.　378
Creating Customer Value, Relationships, and Experiences in Marketspace　380
　　　Marketing Challenges in Two Environments　380
　　　Creating Customer Value in Marketspace　380
　　　Interactivity, Individuality, and Customer Relationships in Marketspace　382
　　　Creating a Compelling Online Customer Experience　383
Online Consumer Behavior and Marketing
　Opportunities and Practices　386
　　　Who Is the Online Consumer?　386

> Applying Marketing Metrics: Sizing Up Site Stickiness at Sewell Automotive Companies　386

　　　What Consumers Buy Online　387
　　　Why Consumers Shop and Buy Online　387
　　　When and Where Consumers Shop and Buy Online　391
　　　How Consumers Shop and Buy Online　392

Making Responsible Decisions: Who Is Responsible
for Internet Privacy and Security?   392

Cross-Channel Consumers and Multichannel Marketing   393
    Who Is the Cross-Channel Consumer?   393
    Implementing Multichannel Marketing   393

Learning Objectives Review   395
Learning Review Answers   396
Focusing on Key Terms   396
Applying Marketing Knowledge   397
Building Your Marketing Plan   397

*Video Case 14: Pizza Hut and imc²: Becoming
a Multichannel Marketer   397*

Chapter Notes   401

15 INTEGRATED MARKETING COMMUNICATIONS AND DIRECT MARKETING   402

Sometimes Taco Bell Leads to Wedding Bells!   402
The Communication Process   404
    Encoding and Decoding Messages   405
    Feedback   405
    Noise   406
The Promotional Elements   406
    Advertising   406
    Personal Selling   407
    Public Relations   408
    Sales Promotion   409
    Direct Marketing   409
Integrated Marketing Communications—Developing
the Promotional Mix   410
    The Target Audience   410
    The Product Life Cycle   410

©Walt Disney Studios Motion Pictures/Photofest

Marketing Matters: Hey Marketers, College Students Are
Digital and Mobile!   411

    Channel Strategies   412
Developing an Integrated Marketing Communications Program   413
    Identifying the Target Audience   413
    Specifying Promotion Objectives   414
    Setting the Promotion Budget   414
    Selecting the Right Promotional Tools   415

Applying Marketing Metrics: How Much Should You
Spend on IMC?   415

    Designing the Promotion   416
    Scheduling the Promotion   416
Executing and Assessing the Promotion Program   417

Direct Marketing 418
    The Growth of Direct Marketing 418
    The Value of Direct Marketing 419
    Technological, Global, and Ethical Issues in Direct Marketing 419

> Making Responsible Decisions: What Is the Future of Your Privacy? 420

Learning Objectives Review 421
Learning Review Answers 421
Focusing on Key Terms 422
Applying Marketing Knowledge 422
Building Your Marketing Plan 423

Video Case 15: Taco Bell: Using IMC to Help Customers Live Más! 423

Chapter Notes 425

16 ADVERTISING, SALES PROMOTION, AND PUBLIC RELATIONS 428

©Ray Tang/REX/Shutterstock

Fantasy Is Becoming Reality for Advertisers! 428
Types of Advertisements 430
    Product Advertisements 430
    Institutional Advertisements 431
Developing the Advertising Program 432
    Identifying the Target Audience 432
    Specifying Advertising Objectives 432
    Setting the Advertising Budget 432
    Designing the Advertisement 433
    Selecting the Right Media 435

> Applying Marketing Metrics: What Is the Best Way to Reach 1,000 Customers? 436

    Different Media Alternatives 437
    Scheduling the Advertising 441

> Making Responsible Decisions: Who Is Responsible for Preventing Click Fraud? 441

Executing the Advertising Program 442
    Pretesting the Advertising 442
    Carrying Out the Advertising Program 443
Assessing the Advertising Program 443
    Posttesting the Advertising 443
    Making Needed Changes 444
Sales Promotion 444
    Consumer-Oriented Sales Promotions 444
    Trade-Oriented Sales Promotions 448
Public Relations 449

Learning Objectives Review 450
Learning review Answers 451
Focusing on Key Terms 452
Applying Marketing Knowledge 452
Building Your Marketing Plan 452

Video Case 16: Google, Inc.: The Right Ads at the Right Time 453

Chapter Notes 455

17 USING SOCIAL MEDIA AND MOBILE MARKETING TO CONNECT WITH CONSUMERS 460

Mobile Moments Will Soon Include a Nice Ride! 460
Understanding Social Media 462
    What Are Social Media? 462
    Why and How Social Media Transformed Marketing Communications 463
A Look at Four Important Social Media 465
    Comparing Four Social Media 465
    Facebook 465
    Twitter 467
    LinkedIn 468
    YouTube 469
Social Media Marketing Programs and Customer Engagement 471
    Selecting Social Media 471

Marketing Matters: Vloggers Are the New Power Players, Worldwide! 471

    Selecting Social Media Content 472
    Measuring the Results of Social Media Marketing Programs 473
    Carmex Goes Viral with Luck and a LeBron James Bear Hug 475
The Future: Convergence and Mobility 477
    The Convergence of Real and Digital Worlds 477
    Mobile Marketing: Tightening Links to Marketing Actions 478

Learning Objectives Review 480
Learning Review Answers 480
Focusing on Key Terms 481
Applying Marketing Knowledge 481
Building Your Marketing Plan 482

Video Case 17: Body Glove: Helping Consumers Do What They Love! 482

Chapter Notes 485

Background: ©Pozdeyev Vitaly/Shutterstock; Icons: ©Hilch/Shutterstock

©Hillsman Stuart Jackson

18 PERSONAL SELLING AND SALES MANAGEMENT 488

Meet Today's Sales Professional 488
Scope and Significance of Personal Selling
and Sales Management 490
    Nature of Personal Selling and Sales Management 490
    Selling Happens Almost Everywhere 490
    Personal Selling in Marketing and Entrepreneurship 491
    Creating Customer Solutions and Value through Salespeople:
    Relationship and Partnership Selling 491
The Many Forms of Personal Selling 492
    Order-Taking Salespeople 492

> **Marketing Matters: Science and Selling: Is Customer Value Creation in Your Genes?** 492

    Order-Getting Salespeople 493
    Customer Sales Support Personnel 493
The Personal Selling Process: Building Customer Relationships 495

> **Marketing Matters: Creating and Sustaining Customer Value through Cross-Functional Team Selling** 495

    Prospecting: Identifying and Qualifying Prospective Customers 496
    Preapproach: Preparing for the Sales Call 497
    Approach: Making the First Impression 498
    Presentation: Tailoring a Solution for a Customer's Needs 498

> **Marketing Matters: Imagine This...Putting the Customer into Customer Solutions!** 500

    Close: Asking for the Customer's Order or Business 501
    Follow-up: Solidifying the Customer Relationship 501
The Sales Management Process 502
    Sales Plan Formulation: Setting Direction 502

> **Making Responsible Decisions: The Ethics of Asking Customers about Competitors** 503

    Sales Plan Implementation: Putting the Plan into Action 504

> **Marketing Matters: What Is Your Emotional Intelligence? You Might Be Surprised.** 505

    Salesforce Evaluation: Measuring Results 506
    Customer Relationship Management Systems and Technology 507

> **Applying Marketing Metrics: Tracking Salesperson Performance at Moore Chemical & Sanitation Supply, Inc.** 508

Learning Objectives Review 510
Learning Review Answers 510
Focusing on Key Terms 511
Applying Marketing Knowledge 511
Building Your Marketing Plan 512

Video Case 18: Xerox: Building Customer Relationships through Personal Selling 512

Chapter Notes 514
Appendix B Planning a Career in Marketing 516

Glossary *531*
Name Index *539*
Company/Product Index *549*
Subject Index *558*

MARKETING: THE CORE

1

LEARNING OBJECTIVES

After reading this chapter you should be able to:

LO 1-1 Define marketing and identify the diverse factors that influence marketing actions.

LO 1-2 Explain how marketing discovers and satisfies consumer needs.

LO 1-3 Distinguish between marketing mix factors and environmental forces.

LO 1-4 Explain how organizations build strong customer relationships and customer value through marketing.

LO 1-5 Describe the characteristics of a market orientation.

Creating Customer Relationships and Value through Marketing

Creating Customer Value: The Chobani Way!

Are you a health-conscious consumer? Are you determined to find food products that are a good value for you? Then you may have noticed Chobani yogurt while you were shopping!

If you purchased Chobani and enjoyed the product, it was the result of an extraordinary marketing success story. Just a few years ago the U.S. yogurt market was dominated by Dannon and Yoplait. Then Hamdi Ulukaya created Chobani with less sugar and more protein to better match the changing tastes of American consumers. Today Chobani has more than $1.5 billion in annual sales and was recently recognized as one of the most innovative companies in the world "for stirring it up in the grocery store."[1]

What is the secret to Chobani's success? Read on to hear the rest of the story!

Creating an Exceptional Product

The Chobani website proclaims that its guiding mission is "better food for more people." The process starts with milk from local sources and then uses a straining procedure that makes the yogurt extra thick and gives it twice as much protein. Finally, only real fruit and natural sweeteners are added. The recipe is the result of a commitment to a high-quality product. "I was very picky. It took us 18 months to get the recipe right. I knew I had only one shot, and it had to be perfect," says Ulukaya. To produce the yogurt, Ulukaya purchased a closed dairy in a small town in New York using a Small Business Administration loan. He remodeled the facility using sustainability as a theme to reflect a focus on environment and community.[2]

Connecting with Customers

Chobani had little money for traditional advertising, so it relied on positive word of mouth, with one happy customer telling another about the new style of yogurt. In addition, Chobani used social media such as Twitter and Facebook to connect with consumers and a mobile yogurt food truck

Source: Chobani, LLC

Source: Chobani, LLC

Source: Chobani, LLC

called the CHOmobile to hand out free samples to encourage consumers to try Chobani's Greek Yogurt for the first time. One of Chobani's biggest breakthroughs in gaining public awareness was its sponsorship of the U.S. Olympic and Paralympic Teams.

Chobani also pushed for distribution in major grocery chains, rather than smaller niche stores, and encouraged placement of the product in the main dairy cases of the stores, not the specialty or health food sections. Ulukaya was convinced that Americans would really like Greek yogurt if they tried it and that they would try it if they heard about it and could find it easily in their grocery store.[3]

Video 1-1
Chobani Fruit Symphony Ad
kerin.tv/cr8e/v1-1

Chobani Today

Chobani continues to monitor changing consumer tastes and offers new products to accommodate them. For example, the company recently introduced a yogurt drink called Drink Chobani, a package with a second compartment of crunchy toppings to add to the yogurt called Chobani Flip, a less tart product called Smooth Yogurt, and a squeezable package called Chobani Savor. The products are designed for new and existing consumers and for new eating occasions.

Located in New York City, Chobani SoHo is the brand's first-of-its-kind retail concept, serving yogurt creations with innovative toppings.
©Diane Bondareff/Invision for Chobani/AP Images

One way Chobani stays in touch with consumer interests is through its yogurt cafés in New York's SoHo and Tribeca neighborhoods. New ideas are continually tested on the menu and the feedback has been so useful that Chobani plans to open similar outlets in Los Angeles, San Francisco, Chicago, and other U.S. cities. Chobani also recently announced a plan to open the Chobani Food Incubator, which is designed to invest in and cultivate ideas from emerging food entrepreneurs.

Today, Chobani boasts a 40 percent market share of the Greek yogurt segment, which makes up almost half of the $8 billion yogurt market. Chobani advertising, such as the "Believe in Food," "No Bad Stuff," and "Love This Life" campaigns, are featured on the Chobani YouTube channel. The company's success has even led to a Super Bowl ad featuring a 1,400-pound bear in search of a healthy snack![4]

Chobani, Marketing, and You

Will Hamdi Ulukaya and his Chobani Greek Yogurt continue this fantastic success story—especially with the recent appearance of competing Greek yogurts from Yoplait, Dannon, Annie's, Noosa, and Fage? For Ulukaya, one key factor will be how well Chobani understands and uses marketing—the subject of this book.

WHAT IS MARKETING?

Are you a marketing expert? If so, what would you pay for this cutting-edge TV?
©Kobby Dagan/VWPics via AP Images

The good news is that you are already a marketing expert! You perform many marketing activities and make marketing-related decisions every day. For example, would you sell more LG Signature 77-inch 4K OLED TVs at $24,999 or $7,999? You answered $7,999, right? So your experience in shopping gives you some expertise in marketing. As a consumer, you've been involved in thousands of marketing decisions, mostly on the buying and not the selling side.

The bad news is that good marketing isn't always easy. That's why every year thousands of new products fail in the marketplace and then quietly slide into oblivion.

Marketing and Your Career

Marketing affects all individuals, all organizations, all industries, and all countries. This book seeks to teach you marketing concepts, often by having you actually "do marketing"—by putting you in the shoes of a marketing manager facing actual marketing decisions. The book also shows marketing's many applications and how it affects our lives. This knowledge should make you a better consumer and enable you to be a more informed citizen, and it may even help you in your career planning.

Perhaps your future will involve doing sales and marketing for a large organization. Working for a well-known company—Apple, Ford, Facebook, or General Mills—can be personally satisfying and financially rewarding, and you may gain special respect from your friends.

Start-ups and small businesses also offer marketing careers. Small businesses are the source of the majority of new U.S. jobs. So you might become your own boss by being an entrepreneur and starting your own business.

The chief executive officer of Tesla and SpaceX began building businesses shortly after graduating from college.
©Reuters/Alamy Stock Photo

Shortly after leaving Stanford, Elon Musk, for example, started and sold a web software company called Zip2. With the proceeds from that business he started another business which merged with another and became PayPal. When PayPal was purchased by eBay, Musk founded another venture called SpaceX, which develops and manufactures space launch vehicles and currently launches satellites and delivers cargo to the International Space Station. Since those initial business start-ups, Musk has also started the electric car company Tesla and a solar power company called SolarCity. In addition, he has started a design competition for a high-speed transportation system called Hyperloop, a not-for-profit artificial intelligence company called OpenAI, and a neurotechnology company called Neuralink. Perhaps your interest in marketing will lead to new business successes like Musk's![5]

Marketing: Delivering Value to Customers

 Define marketing and identify the diverse factors that influence marketing actions.

The American Marketing Association represents individuals and organizations involved in the development and practice of marketing worldwide. It defines **marketing** as the activity, set of institutions, and processes for creating, communicating, delivering, and exchanging offerings that have value for customers, clients, partners, and society at large.[6] This definition shows that marketing is far more than simply advertising or personal selling. It stresses the need to deliver genuine value in the offerings of goods, services, and ideas marketed to customers. Also, notice that an organization's marketing activities should also create value for its partners and for society.

To serve both buyers and sellers, marketing seeks (1) to discover the needs and wants of prospective customers and (2) to satisfy them. These prospective customers include both individuals, buying for themselves and their households, and organizations, buying for their own use (such as manufacturers) or for resale (such as wholesalers and retailers). The key to achieving these two objectives is the idea of **exchange**, which is the trade of things of value between a buyer and a seller so that each is better off after the trade.[7]

marketing
The activity, set of institutions, and processes for creating, communicating, delivering, and exchanging offerings that have value for customers, clients, partners, and society at large.

exchange
The trade of things of value between buyer and seller so that each is better off after the trade.

The Diverse Elements Influencing Marketing Actions

Although an organization's marketing activity focuses on assessing and satisfying consumer needs, countless other people, groups, and forces interact to shape the nature of its actions (see Figure 1–1). Foremost is the organization itself, whose mission and objectives determine what business it is in and what goals it seeks. Within the organization, management is responsible for establishing these goals. The marketing department works closely with a network of other departments and employees to help provide the customer-satisfying products required for the organization to survive and prosper.

Figure 1–1 also shows the key people, groups, and forces outside the organization that influence its marketing activities. The marketing department is responsible for facilitating relationships, partnerships, and alliances with the organization's customers, its shareholders (or often representatives of nonprofit organizations), its suppliers, and other organizations. Environmental forces involving social, economic, technological, competitive, and regulatory considerations also shape an organization's marketing actions. Finally, an organization's marketing decisions are affected by and, in turn, often have an important impact on society as a whole.

The organization must strike a balance among the sometimes differing interests of these groups. For example, it is not possible to simultaneously provide the lowest-priced and highest-quality products to customers and pay the highest prices to suppliers, the highest wages to employees, and the maximum dividends to shareholders.

FIGURE 1–1

A marketing department relates to many people, organizations, and forces. Note that the marketing department both *shapes* and *is shaped by* its relationship with these internal and external groups.

Marketing doesn't happen in a vacuum. The text describes the four factors needed to buy a product from Domino's Mix & Match menu.
Source: Domino's Pizza

What Is Needed for Marketing to Occur

For marketing to occur, at least four factors are required: (1) two or more parties (individuals or organizations) with unsatisfied needs, (2) a desire and ability on their part to have their needs satisfied, (3) a way for the parties to communicate, and (4) something to exchange.

Two or More Parties with Unsatisfied Needs
Suppose you've developed an unmet need—a desire for a late-night meal after studying for an exam—but you don't yet know that Domino's has a location in your area. Also unknown to you is that Domino's has a special "mix & match" offer for any two or more of its menu items, just waiting to be ordered and picked up or delivered. This is an example of two parties with unmet needs: you, desiring a meal, and your local Domino's owner, needing someone to place an order.

Desire and Ability to Satisfy These Needs
Both you and the Domino's owner want to satisfy these unmet needs. Furthermore, you have the money to pay for a purchase and the time to place an order online, over the telephone, or at a Domino's location. The Domino's owner has the desire to sell its products but also the ability to do so since the items are easily made and delivered to (or picked up by) you.

A Way for the Parties to Communicate
The marketing transaction of purchasing a

Domino's pizza or one of its other products will never occur unless you are aware the product exists and you know how to make a purchase (at a street address, through a URL, or via a phone number). Similarly, Domino's won't be able to sell its products unless there's a market of potential buyers nearby. When you receive a coupon on your phone or drive by and see the Domino's store location, this communication barrier between you (the buyer) and the Domino's owner (the seller) is overcome.

Something to Exchange Marketing occurs when the transaction takes place and both the buyer and seller exchange something of value. In this case, you exchange your money ($5.99) for each item ordered from Domino's Mix & Match menu. Both you and the Domino's owner have gained and also given up something, but you are both better off because each of you has satisfied the other's unmet needs. You have the opportunity to eat Domino's food items to satisfy your hunger, but you gave up some money to do so; the Domino's owner gave up the pizza, salad, and other items but received money, which will help the owner remain in business. The ethical and regulatory foundations of this exchange process are central to marketing and are discussed in Chapter 3.

learning review

1-1. What is marketing?

1-2. Marketing focuses on _____ and _____ consumer needs.

1-3. What four factors are needed for marketing to occur?

HOW MARKETING DISCOVERS AND SATISFIES CONSUMER NEEDS

LO 1-2 Explain how marketing discovers and satisfies consumer needs.

The importance of discovering and satisfying consumer needs in order to develop and offer successful products is so critical to understanding marketing that we look at each of these two steps in detail next. Let's start by asking you to analyze the three products below.

Discovering Consumer Needs

The first objective in marketing is discovering the needs of prospective customers. Marketers often use customer surveys, concept tests, and other forms of marketing research (discussed in detail in Chapter 7) to better understand customer ideas. Many

For these three products, identify (1) what benefits the product provides buyers and (2) what factors or "showstoppers" might doom the product in the marketplace. Answers are discussed in the text.
(Left): ©Victor Virgile/Gamma-Rapho via Getty Images; *(Middle):* Source: The Coca-Cola Company; *(Right):* Source: YOYO

A wearable computer.

A no sugar soda.

A subscription service for automobiles.

firms also use "crowdsourcing" websites to solicit and evaluate ideas from customers. At LEGO Group, for example, ideas that receive 10,000 votes from site visitors are considered for possible addition to the product line. LEGO Group products that were discovered through the website include its Ghostbusters Ectomobile ambulance, its Mars Curiosity Rover, and a set based on the Minecraft video game! Sometimes, however, customers may not know or be able to describe what they need and want. Smartphones, connected homes, and electric cars are all examples of this, in which case an accurate long-term prediction of consumer needs is essential.[8]

The Challenge: Meeting Consumer Needs with New Products

While marketers are improving the ways they can generate new product ideas, experts estimate that it takes 3,000 raw ideas to generate one commercial success. Market intelligence agency Mintel estimates that 33,000 new products are introduced worldwide each month. In addition, studies of new-product launches indicate that about 40 percent of the products fail. Robert M. McMath, who has studied more than 110,000 new-product launches, has two key suggestions: (1) focus on what the customer benefit is, and (2) learn from past mistakes.[9]

The solution to preventing product failures seems embarrassingly obvious. First, find out what consumers need and want. Second, produce what they need and want, and don't produce what they don't need and want. The three products shown previously illustrate just how difficult it is to achieve new-product success, a topic covered in more detail in Chapter 9.

Without reading further, think about the potential benefits to customers and possible "showstoppers"—factors that might doom the product—for each of the three products pictured. Some of the products may come out of your past, and others may be on your horizon. Here's a quick analysis of the three products:

- *Google Glass.* In 2014 Google launched a wearable computer called Google Glass. The new product was head-mounted and similar in appearance to a pair of glasses. In addition, though, the glasses had Internet capabilities, a camera, phone, speaker, microphone, touch pad, and a heads-up display. Less than a year later Google announced that it would stop producing Google Glass. While the product was popular among technology enthusiasts it did not attract a mass market. Showstoppers included its $1,500 price tag, a general perception that it looked "nerdy," and concerns that wearing the device might violate privacy rights. Google is reportedly working on a redesigned model, however, so watch for a new Glass![10]

- *Coca-Cola Stevia No Sugar.* As consumer preferences have shifted, beverage companies have expanded their offerings to include drinks with less sugar. Soda producers, for example, have offered new products such as Pepsi True and Coca-Cola Life which are sweetened with sugar and stevia leaf extract. New products are also being developed in anticipation of the U.S. Food & Drug Administration's new Nutrition Facts label requirements, taking effect in 2020, which will provide more information about added sugars. Coca-Cola, for example, is testing Coca-Cola Stevia which will be sweetened only with stevia. A potential showstopper: In the past consumers reported that products with stevia sweetener had a bitter aftertaste. Will Coca-Cola Stevia be different? As always, as a consumer you will be the judge![11]

- *YoYo.* This pay-per-mile car subscription service hopes to disrupt the traditional car purchase and ownership experience by offering consumers access to any type of vehicle at any time at a cost lower than the $9,500 consumers spend on personal transportation each year. Selection takes place on a smartphone and the vehicle can cost as little as $0.50 per mile, which also compares favorably with car-sharing costs such as $0.96 per mile for an Uber vehicle, or $1.50 per mile for a Zipcar. What are potential showstoppers? Consumers might not value access to different types of vehicles, always driving a new vehicle, or avoiding the responsibilities of ownership.[12]

Video 1-2
Google Glass
kerin.tv/cr8e/v1-2

Video 1-3
Coca-Cola Stevia Ad
kerin.tv/cr8e/v1-3

Firms spend billions of dollars annually on marketing and technical research that significantly reduces, but doesn't eliminate, new-product failure. So meeting the changing needs of consumers is a continuing challenge for firms around the world.

Consumer Needs and Consumer Wants Should marketing try to satisfy consumer needs or consumer wants? Marketing tries to do both. Heated debates rage over this question, fueled by the definitions of needs and wants and the amount of freedom given to prospective customers to make their own buying decisions.

A *need* occurs when a person feels deprived of basic necessities such as food, clothing, and shelter. A *want* is a need that is shaped by a person's knowledge, culture, and personality. So if you feel hungry, you have developed a basic need and desire to eat something. Let's say you then want to eat a Cool Mint Chocolate Clif Bar because, based on your past experience, you know it will satisfy your hunger need. Effective marketing, in the form of creating an awareness of good products at fair prices and convenient locations, can clearly shape a person's wants.

Certainly, marketing tries to influence what we buy. A question then arises: At what point do we want government and society to step in to protect consumers? Most consumers would say they want government to protect them from harmful drugs and unsafe cars but not from candy bars and soft drinks. To protect college students, should government restrict their use of credit cards?[13] Such questions have no clear-cut answers, which is why legal and ethical issues are central to marketing. Because even psychologists and economists still debate the exact meanings of *need* and *want*, we shall use the terms interchangeably throughout the book.

As shown on the left side of Figure 1–2, discovering needs involves looking carefully at prospective customers, whether they are children buying M&M's candy, college students buying Chobani Greek Yogurt, or firms buying Xerox color copiers. A principal activity of a firm's marketing department is to scrutinize its consumers to understand what they need and want and the forces that shape those needs and wants.

What a Market Is Potential consumers make up a **market**, which is people with both the desire and the ability to buy a specific offering. All markets ultimately are people. Even when we say a firm bought a Xerox copier, we mean one or several people in the firm decided to buy it. People who are aware of their unmet needs may have the desire to buy the product, but that alone isn't sufficient. People must also have

Studying late at night for an exam and being hungry, you decide to eat a Cool Mint Chocolate Clif Bar. Is this a need or a want? The text discusses the role of marketing in influencing decisions like this one.
©McGraw-Hill Education/Evelyn Nicole Kirksey, photographer

market
People with both the desire and the ability to buy a specific offering.

FIGURE 1–2
Marketing seeks first to discover consumer needs through extensive research. It then seeks to satisfy those needs by successfully implementing a marketing program possessing the right combination of the marketing mix—the four Ps.

target market
One or more specific groups of potential consumers toward which an organization directs its marketing program.

 LO 1-3 Distinguish between marketing mix factors and environmental forces.

marketing mix
The controllable factors—product, price, promotion, and place—that can be used by the marketing manager to solve a marketing problem.

customer value proposition
The cluster of benefits that an organization promises customers to satisfy their needs.

Firms can affect some environmental forces with breakthrough products such as the Amazon Echo.
©Luke MacGregor/Bloomberg via Getty Images

the ability to buy, such as the authority, time, and money. People may even "buy" an idea that results in an action, such as having their blood pressure checked annually or switching to a reusable water bottle.

Satisfying Consumer Needs

Marketing doesn't stop with the discovery of consumer needs. Because the organization obviously can't satisfy all consumer needs, it must concentrate its efforts on certain needs of a specific group of potential consumers. This is the **target market**—one or more specific groups of potential consumers toward which an organization directs its marketing program.

The Four Ps: Controllable Marketing Mix Factors

Having selected its target market consumers, the firm must take steps to satisfy their needs, as shown on the right side of Figure 1–2. Someone in the organization's marketing department, often the marketing manager, must develop a complete marketing program to reach consumers by using a combination of four elements, often called "the four Ps"—a useful shorthand reference to them first published by Professor E. Jerome McCarthy:[14]

- *Product.* A good, service, or idea to satisfy the consumer's needs.
- *Price.* What is exchanged for the product.
- *Promotion.* A means of communication between the seller and buyer.
- *Place.* A means of getting the product to the consumer.

We'll define each of the four Ps more carefully later in the book, but for now it's important to remember that they are the elements of the **marketing mix**. These four elements are the controllable factors—product, price, promotion, and place—that can be used by the marketing manager to solve a marketing problem. For example, when a company puts a product on sale, it is changing one element of the marketing mix—namely, the price. The marketing mix elements are called *controllable factors* because they are under the control of the marketing department in an organization.

Designing an effective marketing mix also conveys to potential buyers a clear **customer value proposition**, which is a cluster of benefits that an organization promises customers to satisfy their needs. For example, Walmart's customer value proposition can be described as "help people save money so they can live better—anytime and anywhere." Michelin's customer value proposition can be summed up as "providing safety-conscious parents greater security in tires at a premium price."[15]

The Uncontrollable, Environmental Forces

While marketers can control their marketing mix factors, there are forces that are mostly beyond their control (see Figure 1–1). These are the **environmental forces** that affect a marketing decision, which consist of social, economic, technological, competitive, and regulatory forces. Examples are what consumers themselves want and need, changing technology, the state of the economy in terms of whether it is expanding or contracting, actions that competitors take, and government restrictions. Covered in detail in Chapter 3, these five forces may serve as accelerators or brakes on marketing, sometimes expanding an organization's marketing opportunities and at other times restricting them.

environmental forces
The uncontrollable forces that affect a marketing decision and consist of social, economic, technological, competitive, and regulatory forces.

Traditionally, many marketing executives have treated these environmental forces as rigid, absolute constraints that are entirely outside their influence. However, recent studies and marketing successes have shown that a forward-looking, action-oriented firm can often affect some environmental forces by achieving technological or competitive breakthroughs, such as Amazon's virtual assistant, the Echo.

THE MARKETING PROGRAM: HOW CUSTOMER RELATIONSHIPS ARE BUILT

Explain how organizations build strong customer relationships and customer value through marketing.

An organization's marketing program connects it with its customers. To clarify this link, we will first discuss the critically important concepts of customer value, customer relationships, and relationship marketing. Then we will illustrate these concepts using 3M's marketing program for its Post-it® Flag Highlighter products.

Relationship Marketing: Easy to Understand, Hard to Do

customer value
The unique combination of benefits received by targeted buyers that includes quality, convenience, on-time delivery, and both before-sale and after-sale service at a specific price.

relationship marketing
Links the organization to its individual customers, employees, suppliers, and other partners for their mutual long-term benefit.

Intense competition in today's fast-paced global markets has prompted many successful U.S. firms to focus on "customer value." Gaining loyal customers by providing unique value is the essence of successful marketing. What is new is a more careful attempt at understanding how a firm's customers perceive value and then actually creating and delivering that value to them.[16] **Customer value** is the unique combination of benefits received by targeted buyers that includes quality, convenience, on-time delivery, and both before-sale and after-sale service at a specific price. In addition, firms now actually try to place a dollar value on the purchases of loyal, satisfied customers during their lifetimes. For example, loyal Kleenex customers average 6.7 boxes a year, about $994 over 60 years in today's dollars.[17]

Research suggests that firms cannot succeed by being all things to all people. Instead, firms seek to build long-term relationships with customers by providing unique value to them. Many successful firms deliver outstanding customer value with one of three value strategies: best price, best product, or best service.[18]

With the intense competition among U.S. businesses, being seen as "best" is admittedly difficult. Still, successful firms such as Target (whose ad is shown), Starbucks, and Nordstrom have achieved great success as reflected in the mission, vision, and values statements they stress and live by:[19]

- *Best price: Target.* Target uses the brand promise of "Expect More, Pay Less®" to "make Target the preferred shopping destination for our guests by delivering outstanding value."
- *Best product: Starbucks.* Starbucks seeks "to inspire and nurture the human spirit—one person, one cup and one neighborhood at a time." Its ads remind customers that Starbucks is the "#1 Best Coffee."
- *Best service: Nordstrom.* As a leading fashion specialty retailer, Nordstrom works to "deliver the best possible shopping experience, helping our customers express their style—not just buy fashion." Nordstrom is "committed to providing our customers with the best possible service—and to improving it every day."

Remaining among the "best" is a continuing challenge for today's businesses.

A firm achieves meaningful customer relationships by creating connections with its customers through careful coordination of the product, its price, the way it is promoted, and how it is placed.

The hallmark of developing and maintaining effective customer relationships is today called **relationship marketing**, which links the organization to its individual customers, employees, suppliers, and other partners for their mutual long-term

Target provides customer value using a very specific approach. For its strategy, see the text.

Source: Target Brands, Inc.

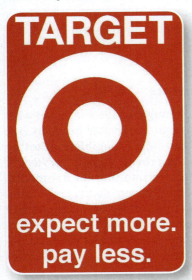

Ritz-Carlton hotels use relationship marketing concepts—tailoring the purchase experience to each individual—to create lifelong customers.

©Paul Hilton/Bloomberg/Getty Images

benefit. Relationship marketing involves a personal, ongoing relationship between the organization and its individual customers that begins before the sale and may evolve through different types of relationships after the sale.[20]

Information technology, along with cutting-edge manufacturing and marketing processes, better enable companies to form relationships with customers today. Smart, connected products, now elements of "the Internet of Everything," help create detailed databases about product usage. Then, using data analytics, or the examination of data to discover relevant patterns, companies can gain insights into how products create value for customers. For example, BMW receives data transmitted by each new vehicle it sells and General Electric collects information sent in by the jet engines it builds to help understand how customers use their products and when service may be needed. The Ritz-Carlton Hotel Company trains each of its employees to observe guest preferences and record them in the guest recognition system. In addition, the hotel's statement of values, called Gold Standards, guides employees to "build strong relationships and create Ritz-Carlton guests for life" and the website includes a variety of ways for customers to become part of its online community, including a Twitter-based concierge service.[21]

The Marketing Program and Market Segments

Effective relationship marketing strategies help marketing managers discover what prospective customers need and convert these ideas into marketable products (see Figure 1–2). These concepts must then be converted into a tangible **marketing program**—a plan that integrates the marketing mix to provide a good, service, or idea to prospective buyers. Ideally, they can be formed into **market segments**, which are relatively homogeneous groups of prospective buyers that (1) have common needs and (2) will respond similarly to a marketing action. This action might be a product feature, a promotion, or a price. As shown in Figure 1–2, in an effective organization this process is continuous: Consumer needs trigger product concepts that are translated into actual products that stimulate further discovery of consumer needs.

marketing program
A plan that integrates the marketing mix to provide a good, service, or idea to prospective buyers.

market segments
The relatively homogeneous groups of prospective buyers that (1) have common needs and (2) will respond similarly to a marketing action.

learning review

1-4. An organization can't satisfy the needs of all consumers, so it must focus on one or more subgroups, which are its _____.

1-5. What are the four marketing mix elements that make up the organization's marketing program?

1-6. What are environmental forces?

3M's Strategy and Marketing Program to Help Students Study

"How do college students *really* study?" asked David Windorski, a 3M inventor of Post-it® brand products, when thinking about adding a new item to the Post-it® line.²²

To answer this question, Windorski worked with a team of four college students. Their task was to observe and question dozens of students about their study behavior, such as how they used their textbooks, took notes, wrote term papers, and reviewed for exams. Often, they watched students highlight a passage and then mark the page with a Post-it® Note or the smaller Post-it® Flag. Windorski realized there was an opportunity to merge the functions of two products into one to help students study!

Moving from Ideas to a Marketable Highlighter Product After working on 15 or 20 models, Windorski concluded he had to build a highlighter product that would dispense Post-it® Flags because the Post-it® Notes were simply too large to put inside the barrel of a highlighter.

Hundreds of the initial highlighter prototypes with Post-it® Flags inside were produced and given to students—and also office workers—to get their reactions. This research showed users wanted a convenient, reliable cover to protect the Post-it® Flags in the highlighter. So the Post-it® Flag Highlighter with a rotating cover was born.

3M's initial product line of Post-it® Flag Highlighters and Post-it® Flag Pens included variations in color.
©McGraw-Hill Education/Mike Hruby, photographer

Adding the Post-it® Flag Pen Most of David Windorski's initial design energies had gone into his Post-it® Flag Highlighter research and development. But Windorski also considered other related products. Many people in offices need immediate access to Post-it® Flags while writing with pens. Students are a potential market for this product, too, but probably a smaller market segment than office workers.

A Marketing Program for the Post-it® Flag Highlighter and Pen After several years of research, development, and production engineering, 3M introduced its new products. Figure 1–3 outlines the strategies for each of the four marketing mix elements in 3M's program to market its Post-it® Flag Highlighters and Post-it® Flag Pens. Although similar, we can compare the marketing program for each of the two products:

- *Post-it® Flag Highlighter.* The target market shown in the orange column in Figure 1–3 is mainly college students, so 3M's initial challenge was to build student awareness of a product that they didn't know existed. The company used a mix of print ads in college newspapers and a TV ad and then relied on word-of-mouth advertising—students telling their friends about how great the product is. Gaining distribution in college bookstores was also critical. Plus, 3M charged a price to distributors that it hoped would give a reasonable bookstore price to students and an acceptable profit to distributors and 3M.

Video 1-4
3M Post-it® Flag Highlighters Ad
kerin.tv/cr8e/v1-4

MARKETING MIX ELEMENT	MARKETING PROGRAM ACTION TO REACH:			RATIONALE FOR MARKETING PROGRAM ACTION
	COLLEGE STUDENT MARKET SEGMENT	OFFICE WORKER MARKET SEGMENT		
Product strategy	Offer Post-it® Flag Highlighter to help college students in their studying	Offer Post-it® Flag Pen to help office workers in their day-to-day work activities		Listen carefully to the needs and wants of potential customer segments to use 3M technology to introduce a useful, innovative product
Price strategy	Seek retail price of about $3.99 to $4.99 for a single Post-it® Flag Highlighter or $5.99 to $7.99 for a three-pack	Seek retail price of about $3.99 to $4.99 for a single Post-it® Flag Pen; wholesale prices are lower		Set prices that provide genuine value to the customer segment being targeted
Promotion strategy	Run limited promotion with a TV ad and some ads in college newspapers and then rely on student word-of-mouth messages	Run limited promotion among distributors to get them to stock the product		Increase awareness among potential users who have never heard of this new, innovative 3M product
Place strategy	Distribute Post-it® Flag Highlighters through college bookstores, office supply stores, and mass merchandisers	Distribute Post-it® Flag Pens through office wholesalers and retailers as well as mass merchandisers		Make it easy for prospective buyers to buy at convenient retail outlets (both products) or to get at work (Post-it® Flag Pens only)

FIGURE 1–3

Marketing programs for the launch of two Post-it® brand products targeted at two target market segments.

Welcome to the most recent generation of Post-it® Flag Highlighters: the Post-it® Flag + Highlighter & Pen. The cap contains the Post-it® flags.
©McGraw-Hill Education

- *Post-it® Flag Pen.* The primary target market shown in the green column in Figure 1–3 is people working in offices. The Post-it® Flag Pens are mainly business products—bought by the purchasing department in an organization and stocked as office supplies for employees to use. So the marketing program for Post-it® Flag Pens emphasizes gaining distribution in outlets used by an organization's purchasing department.

How well did these new 3M products do in the marketplace? They have done so well that 3M bestowed a prestigious award on David Windorski and his team. And in what must be considered any inventor's dream come true, Oprah Winfrey flew Windorski to Chicago to appear on her TV show and thank him in person. She told Windorski and her audience that the Post-it® Flag Highlighter is changing the way she does things at home and at work—especially in going through potential books she might recommend for her book club. "David, I know you never thought this would happen when you were in your 3M lab . . . but I want you to take a bow before America for the invention of this . . . (highlighter). It's the most incredible invention," she said.[23]

Extending the Product Line The success of the Post-it® Flag Highlighters encouraged Windorski to continue to conduct research about how students study. He asked students, "Is it too much trouble when you're studying to grab for a 3M Post-it® Flag, then a highlighter, and then your pen?"[24] Feedback suggested there was another opportunity in the market: A 3-in-1 combination that has a highlighter on one end, a pen on the other, and 3M Post-it® Flags in the removable cap. The latest in the family of 3M product innovations is shown in the photo!

14

HOW MARKETING BECAME SO IMPORTANT

LO 1-5 Describe the characteristics of a market orientation.

To understand why marketing is a driving force in the modern global economy, let us look at (1) the evolution of the market orientation, (2) ethics and social responsibility in marketing, and (3) the breadth and depth of marketing activities.

Evolution of the Market Orientation

Marketing became the motivating force among many American firms in the 1950s, which led to the **marketing concept**—the idea that an organization should (1) strive to satisfy the needs of consumers while also (2) trying to achieve the organization's goals. General Electric probably launched the marketing concept and its focus on consumers when its 1952 annual report stated: "The concept introduces . . . marketing . . . at the beginning rather than the end of the production cycle and integrates marketing into each phase of the business."[25]

Firms such as Southwest Airlines, Marriott, and Facebook have achieved great success by putting huge effort into implementing the marketing concept, giving their firms what has been called a *market orientation*. An organization that has a **market orientation** focuses its efforts on (1) continuously collecting information about customers' needs, (2) sharing this information across departments, and (3) using it to create customer value.[26]

Focusing on Customer Relationship Management

A recent focus in the customer relationship era has been the advent of digital marketing, in which organizations and their customers develop relationships through applications (apps) and social media websites such as Facebook, Twitter, and YouTube, among others. This focus has allowed organizations to understand and market to current and prospective customers in ways that are still evolving.

An important outgrowth of this focus on the customer is the recent attention placed on **customer relationship management (CRM)**, the process of identifying prospective

marketing concept
The idea that an organization should (1) strive to satisfy the needs of consumers while also (2) trying to achieve the organization's goals.

market orientation
An organization with a market orientation focuses its efforts on (1) continuously collecting information about customers' needs, (2) sharing this information across departments, and (3) using it to create customer value.

customer relationship management (CRM)
The process of identifying prospective buyers, understanding them intimately, and developing favorable long-term perceptions of the organization and its offerings so that buyers will choose them in the marketplace and become advocates after their purchase.

Trader Joe's is consistently ranked as one of America's favorite supermarket chains. This reflects the company's focus on providing a great customer experience, as described in the text.
©Lannis Waters/ZUMA Press/Newscom

buyers, understanding them intimately, and developing favorable long-term perceptions of the organization and its offerings so that buyers will choose them in the marketplace and become advocates after their purchase.[27] This process requires the involvement and commitment of managers and employees throughout the organization[28] and a growing application of information, communication, and Internet technology, as will be described throughout this book.

The foundation of customer relationship management is really **customer experience**, which is the internal response that customers have to all aspects of an organization and its offering. This internal response includes both the direct and indirect contacts of the customer with the company. Direct contacts include the customer's contacts with the seller through buying, using, and obtaining service. Indirect contacts most often involve unplanned "touches" with the company through word-of-mouth comments from other customers, reviewers, and news reports. In terms of outstanding customer experience, Trader Joe's is high on the list. It is ranked as one of America's favorite supermarket chains by *Market Force Information* and called "America's hottest retailer" by *Fortune* magazine.

What makes the customer experience and loyalty of shoppers at Trader Joe's unique? The reasons include:

- Setting low prices, made possible by offering its own brands rather than well-known national ones.
- Offering unusual, affordable products, like Thai lime-and-chili cashews, not available from other retailers.
- Providing employee "engagement" to help customers, like actually walking them to where the roasted chestnuts are—rather than saying "aisle five."

This commitment to providing an exceptional customer experience is what gives Trader Joe's its high rankings. Recent studies support this approach, suggesting that companies must watch for differences between the experience they offer and what consumers expect at each interaction and excel at managing the complete experience from start to finish.[29]

Ethics and Social Responsibility in Marketing: Balancing the Interests of Different Groups

Today, the standards of marketing practice have shifted from an emphasis on producers' interests to consumers' interests. Guidelines for ethical and socially responsible behavior can help managers balance consumer, organizational, and societal interests.

Ethics Many marketing issues are not specifically addressed by existing laws and regulations. Should information about a firm's customers be sold to other organizations? Should online advertising that reaches young children be restricted? Should consumers be on their own to assess the safety of a product? These questions raise difficult ethical issues. Many companies, industries, and professional associations have developed codes of ethics to assist managers.

Social Responsibility While many ethical issues involve only the buyer and seller, others involve society as a whole. How a manufacturer disposes of toxic waste, for example, has potential to impact the environment and society. This situation illustrates the issue of *social responsibility*, the idea that organizations are accountable to a larger society. The well-being of society at large should also be recognized in an organization's marketing decisions. In fact, some marketing experts stress the **societal marketing concept**, the view that organizations should satisfy the needs of consumers in a way that provides for society's well-being.[30] For example, Patagonia manufactures

customer experience
The internal response that customers have to all aspects of an organization and its offering.

societal marketing concept
The view that organizations should satisfy the needs of consumers in a way that provides for society's well-being.

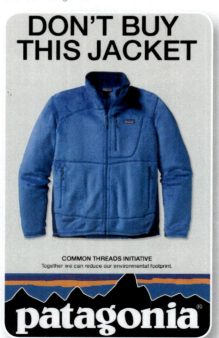

Patagonia's use of recycled plastic bottles and its commitment to extending the life of its products reflect the increasing concern among today's organizations for society's well-being.
Source: Patagonia

many of its products with polyester made from recycled plastic bottles. In addition, Patagonia's Common Threads Initiative encourages its customers to repair, trade, and eventually recycle all of its products. Patagonia says, "One of the most responsible things we can do as a company is to make high-quality stuff that lasts for years and can be repaired, so you don't have to buy more of it."

The Breadth and Depth of Marketing

Marketing today affects every person and organization. To understand this, let's analyze (1) who markets, (2) what is marketed, (3) who buys and uses what is marketed, (4) who benefits from these marketing activities, and (5) how consumers benefit.

Who Markets? Every organization markets. It's obvious that business firms involved in manufacturing (Patagonia), retailing (Trader Joe's), and providing services (Marriott) market their offerings. And nonprofit organizations such as museums, your local hospital or college, places (cities, states, countries), and even special causes (Race for the Cure) also engage in marketing. Finally, individuals such as political candidates often use marketing to gain voter attention and preference.

What Is Marketed? Goods, services, and ideas are marketed. *Goods* are physical objects, such as toothpaste, smartphones, or automobiles, that satisfy consumer needs. *Services* are intangible items such as airline trips, financial advice, or art museums. *Ideas* are thoughts about concepts, actions, or causes.

In this book, goods, services, and ideas are all considered "products" that are marketed. So a **product** is a good, service, or idea consisting of a bundle of tangible and intangible attributes that satisfies consumers' needs and is received in exchange for money or something else of value.

Strategies in marketing art museums include taking a "virtual tour" of Russia's State Hermitage Museum—courtesy of IBM.

©Izzet Keribar/Getty Images

**Video 1-5
Hermitage Tour
kerin.tv/cr8e/v1-5**

product
A good, service, or idea consisting of a bundle of tangible and intangible attributes that satisfies consumers' needs and is received in exchange for money or something else of value.

Services like those offered by art museums, hospitals, and sports teams are relying more heavily on effective marketing. For example, financial pressures have caused art museums to innovate to market their unique services—the viewing of works of art by visitors—to increase revenues. This often involves levels of creativity unthinkable several decades ago.

This creativity ranges from establishing a global brand identity by launching overseas museums to offering sit-at-home video tours. France's Louvre, home to the *Mona Lisa* painting, is developing a new satellite museum in Abu Dhabi, housed in a striking domed building.[31] Russia's world-class, 1,000-room State Hermitage Museum wanted to find a way to market itself to potential first-time visitors. So it partnered with IBM to let patrons take a "virtual tour" of its exhibits while watching on their iPads and relaxing.

Ideas are most often marketed by nonprofit organizations or the government. So The Nature Conservancy markets the cause of protecting the environment. Charities market the idea that it's worthwhile for you to donate your time or money. The Peace Corps markets to recruit qualified volunteers. And state governments in Arizona and Florida market taking a warm, sunny winter vacation in their states.

ultimate consumers
The people who use the products and services purchased for a household. Also called *consumers, buyers,* or *customers*.

organizational buyers
Those manufacturers, wholesalers, retailers, service companies, not-for-profit organizations, and government agencies that buy products and services for their own use or for resale.

Who Buys and Uses What Is Marketed? Both individuals and organizations buy and use products that are marketed. **Ultimate consumers** are the people—whether 80 years or eight months old—who use the products and services purchased for a household. In contrast, **organizational buyers** are those manufacturers, wholesalers, retailers, service companies, not-for-profit organizations, and government agencies that buy products and services for their own use or for resale. Although the terms

Marketing the idea of volunteering for the Peace Corps can benefit society.
Source: Peace Corps

utility
The benefits or customer value received by users of the product.

consumers, *buyers*, and *customers* are sometimes used for both ultimate consumers and organizations, there is no consistency on this. In this book you will be able to tell from the example whether the buyers are ultimate consumers, organizations, or both.

Who Benefits? In our free-enterprise society, there are three specific groups that benefit from effective marketing: consumers who buy, organizations that sell, and society as a whole. True competition between products and services in the marketplace ensures that consumers can find value from the best products, the lowest prices, or exceptional service. Providing choices leads to the consumer satisfaction and quality of life that we expect from our economic system.

Organizations that provide need-satisfying products with effective marketing programs—for example, Amazon, Apple, and L'Oréal—have blossomed. But competition creates problems for ineffective competitors, including the many retailers such as Toys R Us, RadioShack, and the Limited that recently filed for bankruptcy.

Finally, effective marketing benefits society.[32] It enhances competition, which both improves the quality of products and services and lowers their prices. This makes countries more competitive in world markets and provides jobs and a higher standard of living for their citizens.

How Do Consumers Benefit? Marketing creates **utility**, the benefits or customer value received by users of the product. This utility is the result of the marketing exchange process and the way society benefits from marketing. There are four different utilities: form, place, time, and possession. The production of the product or service constitutes *form utility*. *Place utility* means having the offering available where consumers need it, whereas *time utility* means having it available when needed. *Possession utility* is the value of making an item easy to purchase through the provision of credit cards or financial arrangements. Marketing creates its utilities by bridging space (place utility) and hours (time utility) to provide products (form utility) for consumers to own and use (possession utility).

learning review

1-7. What are the two key characteristics of the marketing concept?

1-8. What is the difference between ultimate consumers and organizational buyers?

LEARNING OBJECTIVES REVIEW

LO 1-1 *Define marketing and identify the diverse factors that influence marketing actions.*
Marketing is an organizational function and a set of processes for creating, communicating, and delivering value to customers and for managing customer relationships in ways that benefit the organization and its stakeholders. This definition relates to two primary goals of marketing: (*a*) discovering the needs of prospective customers and (*b*) satisfying them. Achieving these two goals also involves the four marketing mix factors largely controlled by the organization and the five environmental forces that are generally outside its control.

LO 1-2 *Explain how marketing discovers and satisfies consumer needs.*
The first objective in marketing is discovering the needs and wants of consumers who are prospective buyers and customers. This is not easy because consumers may not always

know or be able to describe what they need and want. A need occurs when a person feels deprived of basic necessities such as food, clothing, and shelter. A want is a need that is shaped by a person's knowledge, culture, and personality. Effective marketing can clearly shape a person's wants and tries to influence what he or she buys. The second objective in marketing is satisfying the needs of targeted consumers. Because an organization obviously can't satisfy all consumer needs, it must concentrate its efforts on certain needs of a specific group of potential consumers or target market—one or more specific groups of potential consumers toward which an organization directs its marketing program. It then selects its target market segment(s), which is a relatively homogeneous group of prospective buyers that (1) have common needs and (2) will respond similarly to a marketing action. Finally, the organization develops a set of marketing actions in the form of a unique marketing program to reach them.

LO 1-3 *Distinguish between marketing mix factors and environmental forces.*
Four elements in a marketing program designed to satisfy customer needs are product, price, promotion, and place. These elements are called the marketing mix, the four Ps, or the marketer's controllable variables. The marketing mix also provides a clear customer value proposition—a cluster of benefits that an offering satisfies. Environmental forces, also called uncontrollable variables, are largely beyond the organization's control. These include social, economic, technological, competitive, and regulatory forces.

LO 1-4 *Explain how organizations build strong customer relationships and customer value through marketing.*
The essence of successful marketing is to provide sufficient value to gain loyal, long-term customers. Customer value is the unique combination of benefits received by targeted buyers that usually includes quality, price, convenience, on-time delivery, and both before-sale and after-sale service. Marketers do this by using one of three value strategies: best price, best product, or best service.

LO 1-5 *Describe the characteristics of a market orientation.*
Many firms have achieved great success by putting huge effort into implementing the marketing concept—the idea that an organization should (1) strive to satisfy the needs of consumers while also (2) trying to achieve the organization's goals. Implementing the marketing concept creates a market orientation. An organization that has a market orientation focuses its efforts on (1) continuously collecting information about customers' needs, (2) sharing this information across departments, and (3) using it to create customer value.

LEARNING REVIEW ANSWERS

1-1 What is marketing?
Answer: Marketing is the activity for creating, communicating, delivering, and exchanging offerings that benefit customers, the organization, its stakeholders, and society at large.

1-2 Marketing focuses on _____ and _____ consumer needs.
Answer: discovering; satisfying

1-3 What four factors are needed for marketing to occur?
Answer: The four factors are: (1) two or more parties (individuals or organizations) with unsatisfied needs; (2) a desire and ability on their part to have their needs satisfied; (3) a way for the parties to communicate; and (4) something to exchange.

1-4 An organization can't satisfy the needs of all consumers, so it must focus on one or more subgroups, which are its _____.
Answer: target market(s)

1-5 What are the four marketing mix elements that make up the organization's marketing program?
Answer: product, price, promotion, place

1-6 What are environmental forces?
Answer: Environmental forces are the uncontrollable forces that affect a marketing decision. They consist of social, economic, technological, competitive, and regulatory forces.

1-7 What are the two key characteristics of the marketing concept?
Answer: An organization should (1) strive to satisfy the needs of consumers while also (2) trying to achieve the organization's goals.

1-8 What is the difference between ultimate consumers and organizational buyers?
Answer: Ultimate consumers are the people who use the products and services purchased for a household. Organizational buyers are those manufacturers, wholesalers, retailers, and government agencies that buy products and services for their own use or for resale.

FOCUSING ON KEY TERMS

customer experience p. 16
customer relationship management (CRM) p. 15
customer value p. 11
customer value proposition p. 10
environmental forces p. 10
exchange p. 5
market p. 9
market orientation p. 15
market segments p. 12
marketing p. 5
marketing concept p. 15
marketing mix p. 10
marketing program p. 12
organizational buyers p. 17
product p. 17
relationship marketing p. 11
societal marketing concept p. 16
target market p. 10
ultimate consumers p. 17
utility p. 18

APPLYING MARKETING KNOWLEDGE

1. What consumer wants (or benefits) are met by the following products or services? (*a*) 3M Post-it® Flag Highlighter, (*b*) Nike running shoes, (*c*) Hertz Rent-A-Car, and (*d*) Amazon online shopping.
2. Each of the four products, services, or programs in question 1 has substitutes. Respective examples are (*a*) a Bic™ highlighter, (*b*) regular tennis shoes, (*c*) an Uber or Lyft ride, and (*d*) a department store. What consumer benefits might these substitutes have in each case that some consumers might value more highly than those mentioned in question 1?
3. What are the characteristics (e.g., age, income, education) of the target market customers for the following products or services? (*a*) *National Geographic* magazine, (*b*) Chobani Greek Yogurt, (*c*) New York Giants football team, and (*d*) Facebook.
4. A college in a metropolitan area wishes to increase its evening offerings of business-related courses such as marketing, accounting, finance, and management. Who are the target market customers (students) for these courses?
5. What actions involving the four marketing mix elements might be used to reach the target market in question 4?
6. What environmental forces (uncontrollable variables) must the college in question 4 consider in designing its marketing program?
7. Does a firm have the right to "create" wants and try to persuade consumers to buy goods and services they didn't know about earlier? What are examples of "good" and "bad" want creation? Who should decide what is good and what is bad?

BUILDING YOUR MARKETING PLAN

If your instructor assigns a marketing plan for your class, we hope you will be excited—for two reasons. First, you will get insights into trying to actually "do marketing" that often go beyond what you can get by simply reading the textbook. Second, thousands of graduating students every year get their first job by showing prospective employers a "portfolio" of samples of their written work from college—often a marketing plan if they have one. This can work for you.

This "Building Your Marketing Plan" section at the end of each chapter suggests ways to improve and focus your marketing plan. You will use the sample marketing plan in Appendix A (following Chapter 2) as a guide, and this section after each chapter will help you apply those Appendix A ideas to your own marketing plan.

The first step in writing a good marketing plan is to have a business or product that enthuses you and for which you can get detailed information, so you can avoid glittering generalities. We offer these additional bits of advice in selecting a topic:

- *Do* pick a topic that has personal interest for you—a family business; a business, product, or service you or a friend might want to launch; or a student organization that needs marketing help.
- *Do not* pick a topic that is so large it can't be covered adequately or so abstract it will lack specifics.

1. Now to get you started on your marketing plan, list four or five possible topics and compare these with the criteria your instructor suggests and those shown above. Think hard, because your decision will be with you all term and may influence the quality of the resulting marketing plan you show to a prospective employer.
2. When you have selected your marketing plan topic, whether the plan is for an actual business, a possible business, or a student organization, write the "company description" in your plan, as shown in Appendix A (following Chapter 2).

VIDEO CASE 1   Chobani®: Making *Greek Yogurt* a Household Name

Video 1-6
Chobani Video Case
kerin.tv/cr8e/v1-6

"Everybody should be able to enjoy a pure, simple cup of yogurt. And that's what Chobani is," says Hamdi Ulukaya, founder and chief executive officer of Chobani, LLC, in summarizing his vision for the company.

As the winner of an Ernst & Young World Entrepreneur of the Year award, his words and success story carry great credibility.

THE IDEA

Hamdi Ulukaya came to the United States in 1994 to learn English and study business. He started a feta cheese company, Euphrates, when his visiting father complained about the quality of American feta cheese. In 2005, Kraft Foods closed its New Berlin, New York, yogurt plant. While tidying up his office, Ulukaya stumbled upon a postcard about the sale of the shuttered Kraft plant and threw it out. After sleeping on the decision, he fished it out of the wastebasket, visited the plant, and purchased it with the help of a U.S. Small Business Administration loan.

Ulukaya (center in photo) had no real experience in the yogurt business. He grew up milking sheep at his family's dairy in eastern Turkey and eating the thick, tangy yogurt of his homeland. Describing the regular yogurt he found on shelves in America, he has one comment: "Terrible!" In his view, it is too thin, too sweet, and too fake. So he decided to produce what is known as "Greek yogurt"— an authentic strained version that produces a thick texture, with high protein content and little or no fat. With the help of four former Kraft employees and yogurt master Mustafa Dogan, Ulukaya worked 18 months to perfect the recipe for Chobani Greek Yogurt.

The very first cup for sale of Ulukaya's Greek yogurt appeared on the shelves of a small grocer in Long Island, New York. The new-product launch focused on the classic "4Ps" elements of marketing mix actions: product, price, place, and promotion.

PRODUCT STRATEGY

From the start Ulukaya's Greek yogurt carried the brand name "Chobani." There was no room for error, and the product strategy for the Chobani brand focused on the separate elements of (1) the product itself and (2) its packaging.

The Chobani product strategy stresses its authentic straining process that removes excess liquid whey. This results in a thicker, creamier yogurt that yields 13 to 18 grams of protein per single-serve cup, depending on the flavor. Chobani is free of ingredients like milk protein concentrate and animal-based thickeners, which some manufacturers add to make "Greek-style" yogurts.

Chobani uses three pounds of milk to make one pound of Chobani Greek Yogurt. Some other features that make Chobani Greek Yogurt "*nothing but good*," to quote one of its advertising taglines:

- Higher in protein than regular yogurt.
- Made with real fruit and only natural ingredients.
- Preservative-free.
- No artificial flavors or artificial sweeteners.
- Contains five live and active cultures, including three probiotics.

©Diane Bondareff/Invision for Chobani/AP Images

Then, and still today, Ulukaya obsessed about Chobani's packaging of the original cups. While designing the cup, Ulukaya concluded that *not any cup* would do. He insisted on a European-style cup with a circular opening *exactly* 95 millimeters across. This made for a shorter, wider cup that was more visible on retailer's shelves. Also, instead of painted-on labels, Ulukaya chose shrink-on plastic sleeves that adhere to the cup and offer eye-popping colors.

"With our packaging people would say, 'You're making it all look different and why are you doing that?'" says Kyle O'Brien, executive vice president of sales. "If people pay attention to our cups—bright colors and all—we know we have won them, because what's inside the cup is different from anything else on the shelf."

PRICE STRATEGY

To keep control of their product, Ulukaya and O'Brien approached retailers directly rather than going through distributors. Prices were set high enough to recover Chobani's costs and give reasonable margins to retailers but not so high that future rivals could undercut its price. Today, prices remain at about $1.29 for a single-serve cup.

Source: Chobani, LLC

PLACE STRATEGY

The decision of Ulukaya and O'Brien to get Chobani Greek Yogurt into the conventional yogurt aisle of traditional supermarkets—not on specialty shelves or in health food stores—proved to be sheer genius. Today Chobani sees its Greek yogurt widely distributed in both conventional and mass supermarkets, club stores, and natural food stores. On the horizon: growing distribution in convenience and drugstores, as well as schools. Chobani is also focused on educating food service directors at schools across the United States about Greek yogurt's health benefits for schoolkids.

The Chobani growth staggers imagination. From the company's first order of 200 cases, its sales have grown to over 2 million cases per week. To increase capacity and bring new products to market faster, in 2012 Chobani opened a nearly one million square foot plant in Idaho. Built in just 326 days, it is the largest yogurt manufacturing facility in the world.

Along the way Chobani faced a strange glitch: Demand for Chobani Greek Yogurt far surpassed supply, leading to unhappy retailers with no Chobani cups to sell. Kyle O'Brien launched Operation Bear Hug. "Instead of hiding behind letters to retailers, we decided to get on a plane and to communicate with them within 24 hours about the problem and what we proposed to do about it," says O'Brien. "So we found it critical to be very transparent and open with our communication at times like that."

PROMOTION STRATEGY

In its early years Chobani had no money for traditional advertising, so it relied on word-of-mouth recommendation from enthusiastic customers. The brand harnessed consumer passion on social media channels early on and found that people loved the taste of Chobani once they tried it. So Chobani kicked off its CHOmobile tour: a mobile vehicle sampling Chobani at events across the country, encouraging consumers to taste Greek yogurt for the first time. As Chobani grew, it began to launch new promotional activities tied to (1) traditional advertising, (2) social media, and (3) direct communication with customers.

In 2011, Chobani launched its first national advertising campaign, "Real Love Stories." The only problem: apparently it was *too* successful! The resulting additional consumer demand for Chobani Greek Yogurt exceeded its production capacity, leaving retailers unhappy because of complaining consumers. What did Chobani do then? It stopped the advertising campaign and sent in another Operation Bear Hug team to communicate with retailers. Since then it has run other successful national advertising campaigns, including sponsorship of the U.S. Olympic Teams.

"Social media has been important to Chobani, which has embraced a high-touch model that emphasizes positive communication with its customers," says Sujean Lee, head of corporate affairs. Today, Chobani's Customer Loyalty Team receives about 7,000 inbound customer e-mails and phone calls a month and is able to make return phone calls to many of them. Consumers also sometimes get a handwritten note. Chobani launched its "Go Real Chobani" campaign to highlight that it is a *real* company making *real* products and engaging consumers through *real* conversations.

In addition to Facebook (www.Facebook.com/Chobani), the company interacts with its consumers through Twitter, Pinterest, Instagram, Foursquare, and other social media platforms. Chobani Kitchen (www.chobanikitchen.com) is an online resource with recipes, videos, and tips on how to use its Greek yogurt in favorite recipes.

AGGRESSIVE INNOVATION AND POSITIVE SOCIAL CHANGE

Dannon, Yoplait, and PepsiCo were shocked by the success of Chobani Greek Yogurt. Each now offers its own competing Greek yogurt. With giant competitors like these, what can Chobani do? Innovate and develop creative, new Greek yogurt products!

"Today we offer our Chobani Greek Yogurt in single-serve and multi-serve sizes, while expanding our authentic strained Greek yogurt to new occasions and forms," says Joshua Dean, vice president of brand advertising. Its recent new-product offerings include:

- Chobani Savor™—a 14-ounce squeezable package designed to position Greek yogurt as a condiment that you could use to top foods such as chili or baked potatoes.
- Chobani Kids™ tubes and pouches—made with 25 percent less sugar than other kids' yogurt products, and natural non-GMO ingredients. Sample flavor: Vanilla Chocolate Twist.
- Chobani Flip™—a 5.3-ounce, two-compartment package that lets consumers bend or "flip" mix-ins like granola or hazelnuts into the Chobani Greek Yogurt compartment. Sample flavor: Almond Coco Loco, a coconut low-fat yogurt paired with dark chocolate and honey-roasted salted almonds.
- Drink Chobani™—a smooth, drinkable yogurt with 10 grams of protein in 10 flavors.

©John Minchillo/AP Images

Chobani gives 10 percent of all profits to its Shepherd's Gift Foundation to support people and organizations working for positive, long-lasting change. The name comes from the "spirit of a shepherd," an expression in Turkey used to describe people who give without expecting anything in return. To date the foundation has supported over 50 projects—from local ones to international famine relief efforts.

WHERE TO NOW?

International operations and a unique test-market boutique in New York City give a peek at Chobani's future.

International markets provide a growth opportunity. Other countries have far greater annual per capita consumption of yogurt than the United States. For example, some Europeans eat five or six times as much on average. So while entrenched competitors exist in many foreign countries, the markets are often huge, too.

How do you test ideas for new Greek yogurt flavors? In Chobani's case, it opened what it calls a "first-of-its-kind Mediterranean yogurt bar"—called Chobani SoHo—in a trendy New York City neighborhood. Here, customers can try new yogurt creations—from Strawberry + Granola to Toasted Coconut + Pineapple. The Chobani marketing team obtains consumer feedback at Chobani SoHo, leading to potential new flavors or products in the future.

Hmmm! Ready to schedule a visit to New York City and Chobani SoHo? And then sample a creation made with Pistachio + Chocolate (plain Chobani topped with pistachios, dark chocolate, honey, oranges, and fresh mint leaves), and perhaps influence what Chobani customers will be buying in the future?[33]

Questions

1. From the information about Chobani in the case and at the start of the chapter, (*a*) who did Hamdi Ulukaya identify as the target for his first cups of Greek yogurt and (*b*) what was his initial "4Ps" marketing strategy?
2. (*a*) What marketing actions would you expect the companies selling Yoplait, Dannon, and PepsiCo yogurts to take in response to Chobani's appearance and (*b*) how might Chobani respond?
3. What are (*a*) the advantages and (*b*) the disadvantages of Chobani's Customer Loyalty Team that handles communication with customers—from phone calls and e-mails to Facebook and Twitter messages?
4. As part of building its brand, Chobani opened a unique retail store in New York City: Chobani SoHo. Why did Chobani do this?
5. (*a*) What criteria might Chobani use when it seeks markets in new countries and (*b*) what three or four countries meet these criteria?

Chapter Notes

1. David Gelles, "Chobani, The Greek Yogurt Maker, Reclaims Control of Its Finances," *The New York Times,* June 28, 2018; and "Why Chobani Is One of the Most Innovative Companies of 2017," *Fast Company,* March 2017, p. 44.
2. John Tamny, "The Story of Chobani Is about Much More Than Yogurt," *Forbes,* July 4, 2016, p. 1; and "How We Make Our Product Matters," *Chobani.com,* http://www.chobani.com/our-craft, February 12, 2017.
3. "How Chobani Dominated the Yogurt Marketing in Just 8 Years," Referral Candy, http://www.referralcandy.com/blog/chobani-marketing-strategy/; and Mark Boshnack, "Chobani Executive Touts Company's Olympic Ties," *The Daily Star,* August 12, 2016.
4. "Chobani Café Adds Flavor," *MMR,* November 28, 2016, p. 8; "Chobani Ventures beyond the Yogurt Aisle," *Drug Store News,* August, 2016, p. 102; "Chobani Launches New Greek Yogurt Product Platforms," *Plus Media Solutions,* February 11, 2015; Lauren Coleman-Lochner, "Chobani's Boutique Test Kitchen," *Bloomberg Businessweek,* October 6, 2014, p. 30; "Chobani's New York Café Doubles as Test Kitchen," *Plus Media Solutions,* October 7, 2014; and Emily Steel, "Newcomers Buy Ad Time at Big Game," *The New York Times,* January 31, 2015, p. B1.
5. Richard Robinson, "It's Time for Marketers to Start a Bonfire of the Legacies," *Marketing Week,* January 26, 2017, p. 13; David Z. Morris, "Elon Musk Is the Most Admired Leader in Technology," *Fortune,* September 8, 2016, p. 1; and "Microsoft Joins Forces with Musk on Artificial-Intelligence Deal," *Investors Business Daily,* November 15, 2016, p. 1.
6. See http://www.marketing-dictionary.org/ama (definition approved by the American Marketing Association Board of Directors, July 2013).
7. Richard P. Bagozzi, "Marketing as Exchange," *Journal of Marketing,* October 1975, pp. 32–39; and Gregory T. Gundlach and Patrick E. Murphy, "Ethical and Legal Foundations of Relational Marketing Exchanges," *Journal of Marketing,* October 1993, pp. 35–46.
8. Gordon Wyner, "Looking for Innovation in All the Right Places," *Marketing News,* January 2015, pp. 20–21; Jens Hansegard, "Lego's Plan to Find the Next Big Hit: Crowdsource It," *The Wall Street Journal,* February 25, 2015; and J. J. McCorvey, "The Crowd Can Be Harnessed—Up to a Point," *Fast Company,* October, 2014, p. 72.
9. Mintel Global New Products Database, http://www.mintel.com/global-new-products-database, accessed February 21, 2017; George Castellion and Stephen K. Markham, "Perspective: New Product Failure Rates: Influence of Argumentum ad Populum and Self-Interest," *Journal of Product Innovation Management* 30, no. 5 (2013), pp. 976–79; and Robert M. McMath and Thom Forbes, *What Were They Thinking?* (New York: Times Business, 1998), pp. 3–22.
10. Michele Chandler, "Google Glass Shatters as Social Media Accounts for Consumer Close," *Investors Business Daily,*" January 27, 2016, p. 1; Sam Frizell, "Google Glass Is Going into Hiding 'Until It Is Perfect,'" *Time.com,* February 6, 2015; and Ben Geier, "This Is Where Google Says Glass Went All Wrong," *Fortune.com,* March 23, 2015.
11. Mary Ellen Shoup, "Coca-Cola to Launch Soda Sweetened Solely by Stevia," www.beveragedaily.com, November 20, 2017; Christopher Doering, "Coca-Cola to Launch Stevia-Sweetened Soda in 2018," www.fooddive.com, November 20, 2017; and Megan Poinski, "FDA Proposes 2020 Compliance Deadline for Nutrition Facts Label," www.fooddive.com, September 29, 2017.
12. Clark Schultz, "Netflix-Type Service for Car Sharing to Launch," *Seeking Alpha,* June 7, 2016; "Former COO of Elio Motors Launches Car Subscription Service YoYo," *PR Newswire,* June 7, 2016; and Seth Parks, "Can YoYo, a Pay-per-Mile Car Subscription, Shake Up the Mobility Landscape?" www.thetruthaboutcars.com, September 19, 2016.
13. Louis DeNicola, "Credit Card Use in College after the CARD Act," *The Clearpoint Blog,* www.clearpoint.org, May 1, 2017; and "Washington: Marketing to College Student Appears to Have Declined," *Plus Media Solutions,* February 27, 2014.
14. E. Jerome McCarthy, *Basic Marketing: A Managerial Approach* (Homewood, IL: Richard D. Irwin, 1960); and Walter van Waterschool and Christophe Van den Bulte, "The 4P Classification of the Marketing Mix Revisited," *Journal of Marketing,* October 1992, pp. 83–93.
15. "Walmart CEO Outlines Growth Strategy at Annual Meeting for the Investment Community," *Walmart News Archive,* October 15, 2014, *Walmart.com;* David J. Collis and Michael G. Rukstad, "Can You Say What Your Strategy Is?" *Harvard Business Review,* April 2008, pp. 82–90; and Roger A. Kerin and Robert A. Peterson, *Strategic Marketing Problems: Cases and Comments,* 13th ed. (Upper Saddle River, NJ: Prentice Hall, 2013), p. 12.
16. Ashish Kothari and Joseph Lackner, "A Value-Based Approach to Management," *Journal of Business and Industrial Marketing* 21, no. 4, pp. 243–49; and James C. Anderson, James A. Narius, and Wouter van Rossum, "Customer Value Propositions in Business Markets," *Harvard Business Review,* March 2006, pp. 91–99.
17. V. Kumar and Werner Reinartz, "Creating Enduring Customer Value," *Journal of Marketing* 80 (November 2016), pp. 36–68; V. Kumar, *Managing Customers for Profit* (Upper Saddle River, NJ: Pearson Education, 2008); and "What's a Loyal Customer Worth?" *Fortune,* December 11, 1995, p. 182.
18. Nicolas A. Zacharias, Edwin J. Nijssen, and Ruth Maria Stock, "Effective Configurations of Value Creation and Capture Capabilities: Extending Treacy and Wiersema's Value Disciplines," *Journal of Business Research,* October 2016, pp. 4121–31; Michael Treacy and Fred D. Wiersema, *The Discipline of Market Leaders* (Reading, MA: Addison-Wesley, 1995); Michael Treacy and Fred Wiersema, "How Market Leaders Keep Their Edge," *Fortune,* February 6, 1995, pp. 88–89; and Michael Treacy, "You Need a Value Discipline—But Which One?" *Fortune,* April 17, 1995, p. 195.
19. Target, Starbucks, and Nordstrom corporate websites.
20. Johnathan Z. Zhang, George F. Watson IV, Robert W. Palmatier, and Rajiv P. Dant, "Dynamic Relationship Marketing," *Journal of Marketing,* September 2016, pp. 53–75; Robert W. Palmatier, Rajiv P. Dant, Dhruv Grewal, and Kenneth R. Evans, "Factors Influencing the Effectiveness of Relationship Marketing: A Meta-Analysis," *Journal of Relationship Marketing,* October 2006, pp. 136–53; and William Boulding, Richard Staelin, Michael Ehret, and Wesley J. Johnson, "A Customer Relationship Management Roadmap: What Is Known, Potential Pitfalls, and Where to Go," *Journal of Marketing,* October 2005, pp. 155–66.
21. Jagdish Sheth, "Revitalizing Relationship Marketing," *Journal of Services Marketing,* no. 1 (2017), pp. 6–10; Michael E. Porter and James E. Hepplemann, "How Smart, Connected Products Are Transforming Competition," *Harvard Business Review,* November 2014, pp. 65–88; Ritz-Carlton website, http://www.ritzcarlton.com/en/about/gold-standards; and Susan Foumier, Susan Dobscha, and David Glen Mick,

"Preventing the Premature Death of Relationship Marketing," *Harvard Business Review,* January–February 1998, pp. 42–51.
22. The 3M Post-it® Flag Highlighter and 3M Post-it® Flag Pen examples are based on a series of interviews and meetings with 3M inventor and researcher David Windorski from 2004 to 2011.
23. See www.oprah.com for January 15, 2008; and "Post-it® Flags Co-Sponsors Oprah's Live Web Event," *3M Stemwinder,* March 4–17, 2008, p. 3.
24. Jane, Spencer, "Lenovo Puts Style in New Laptop," *The Wall Street Journal,* January 3, 2008, p. B5.
25. *Annual Report* (New York: General Electric Company, 1952), p. 21.
26. John C. Narver, Stanley F. Slater, and Brian Tietje, "Creating a Market Orientation," *Journal of Market Focused Management,* no. 2 (1998), pp. 241–55; Stanley F. Slater and John C. Narver, "Market Orientation and the Learning Organization," *Journal of Marketing,* July 1995, pp. 63–74; and George S. Day, "The Capabilities of Market-Driven Organizations," *Journal of Marketing,* October 1994, pp. 37–52.
27. The definition of customer relationship management is adapted from Philip Kotler, Hermawan Kartajaya, and Iwan Setiawan, *Marketing 4.0* (Hoboken, NJ: Wiley, 2017); Rajendra K. Srivastava, Tasadduq A. Shervani, and Liam Fahey, "Marketing, Business Processes, and Shareholder Value: An Embedded View of Marketing Activities and the Discipline of Marketing," *Journal of Marketing,* special issue (1999), pp. 168–79; Gary F. Gebhardt, Gregory S. Carpenter, and John F. Sherry Jr., "Creating a Market Orientation: A Longitudinal, Multifirm, Grounded Analysis of Cultural Transformation," *Journal of Marketing,* October 2006, pp. 37–55; and Christopher Meyer and Andre Schwager, "Understanding Customer Experience," *Harvard Business Review,* February 2007, pp. 117–26.
28. Gebhardt et al., "Creating a Market Orientation.
29. Phil Wahba, "Is Trader Joe's Starting a Price War with Whole Foods?" *Fortune.com,* July 11, 2016; Alex Rawson, Ewan Duncan, and Conor Jones, "The Truth about Customer Experience," *Harvard Business Review,* September 2013, pp. 90–98; and Meyer and Schwager, "Understanding Customer Experience," *Havard Business Review,* February 2007, pp. 117–26.
30. Philip Kotler and Sidney J. Levy, "Broadening the Concept of Marketing," *Journal of Marketing,* January 1969, pp. 10–15; and Jim Rendon, "When Nations Need a Little Marketing," *The New York Times,* November 23, 2003, p. BU6.
31. Peter Gumbel, "Louvre, Inc." *Time,* August 11, 2008, pp. 51–52; and Stella Wai-Art Law, *A Branding Context: The Guggenheim and the Louvre,* M.A. Thesis, Columbus: The Ohio State University, 2008.
32. William L. Wilkie and Elizabeth S. Moore, "Marketing's Relationship to Society," in *Handbook of Marketing,* ed. Barton Weitz and Robin Wensley (London: Sage Publications, 2006), pp. 9–38.
33. Chobani, LLC: This case was written by William Rudelius, based on personal interviews with Chobani executives Joshua Dean, Sujean Lee, and Kyle O'Brien. Other sources include: Kate Bernot, "Chobani Hopes New Squeeze Bottles Turn Greek Yogurt into a Condiment," thetakeout.com, August 8, 2018; "The Chobani Story," MEDIA@CHOBANI.COM, 2013; Megan Durisin, "Chobani CEO: Our Success Has Nothing to Do with Yogurt," *Business Retail Insider,* May 3, 2013, p. 1; and Sarah E. Needleman, "Old Factory, Snap Decision Spawn Greek Yogurt Craze," *The Wall Street Journal,* June 21, 2012, pp. B1, B2.

2

Developing Successful Organizational and Marketing Strategies

LEARNING OBJECTIVES

After reading this chapter you should be able to:

LO 2-1 Describe three kinds of organizations and the three levels of strategy in them.

LO 2-2 Describe core values, mission, organizational culture, business, and goals.

LO 2-3 Explain why managers use marketing dashboards and marketing metrics.

LO 2-4 Discuss how an organization assesses where it is now and where it seeks to be.

LO 2-5 Explain the three steps of the planning phase of the strategic marketing process.

LO 2-6 Describe the four components of the implementation phase of the strategic marketing process.

LO 2-7 Discuss how managers identify and act on deviations from plans.

Ben and Jerry Are on a Mission: To Make Fantastic, Sustainable, World-Changing Ice Cream

Does that sound ambitious? Not if you are longtime friends Ben Cohen and Jerry Greenfield, the founders of Ben & Jerry's ice cream shops. In fact, it was the basic idea they used when they started their business!

Ben & Jerry's started in 1978 when the two men moved to Vermont to open an ice cream parlor in a renovated gas station. The venture was buoyed with enthusiasm, $12,000 in borrowed and saved money, and ideas from a $5 correspondence course in ice cream making. Their first flavor? Vanilla—because it's a universal best seller. Other flavors such as Chunky Monkey, Cherry Garcia, Peanut Butter Cup, and many others soon followed.

The ice cream flavors weren't the only extraordinary thing about the company though. Ben and Jerry embraced a concept they called "linked prosperity" which encouraged the success of all their constituents, including employees, suppliers, customers, and neighbors. They set out to achieve linked prosperity with a three-part mission statement:

- *Product Mission*: To make, distribute, and sell the finest quality all-natural ice cream.

- *Economic Mission*: To operate the company for sustainable financial growth.

- *Social Mission*: To operate the company in ways that make the world a better place.

The mission statement guided the entrepreneurs' decisions related to many aspects of the business, including purchasing practices, ingredient sourcing, manufacturing, and involvement in the community.[1]

Ben and Jerry's mission-driven approach led them to successfully implement many highly creative organizational and marketing strategies. Some examples include:

- *Free Cone Day*. One day each year Ben & Jerry's gives away free servings of ice cream to more than a million fans around the world. It's one way the company can give back to the communities it serves.

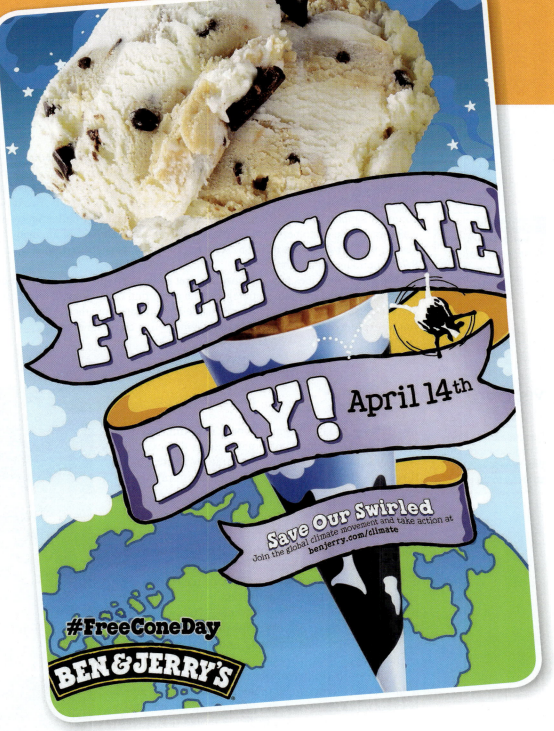

Source: Ben & Jerry's Homemade, Inc.

- *Fairtrade*. Ben & Jerry's believes that farmers who grow ingredients for their ice cream products (such as cocoa, coffee, and vanilla) should receive a fair price for their harvest. In return Fairtrade farmers agree to use sustainable farming practices, implement fair working standards, and invest in local communities.
- *B-Corp Certification*. Ben & Jerry's was one of the first companies involved in the Benefit Corporation movement, which has developed a rigorous set of principles and standards on which to evaluate companies in terms of social and environmental performance, accountability, and transparency.

- *PartnerShop Program.* PartnerShops are Ben & Jerry's scoop shops that are independently owned and operated by community-based nonprofit organizations. The shops employ youth and young adults who may face barriers to employment to help them build better lives.

As you can see, Ben & Jerry's has a strong link between its mission and its strategies. CEO Jostein Solheim explains that their purpose at Ben & Jerry's is "to be part of a global movement that makes changing the world seem fun and achievable."[2]

Today, Ben & Jerry's is owned by Unilever, which is the market leader in the global ice cream industry—one that is expected to reach $89.5 billion by 2023. Ben & Jerry's recently added a vegan line of products in four flavors, and it announced a partnership with New Belgium Brewing to produce a Chocolate Chip Cookie Dough Ale. In addition, the company supports a foundation that helps employees engage in philanthropy and supports activism. While customers love Ben & Jerry's rich premium ice cream, many buy its products to support its social mission. As a testament to its success, Ben & Jerry's has over 8.7 million fans on Facebook![3]

Chapter 2 describes how organizations set goals to provide an overall direction to their organizational and marketing strategies. The marketing department of an organization converts these strategies into plans that must be implemented and then evaluated so deviations can be exploited or corrected based on the marketing environment.

> **Video 2-1**
> **Ben & Jerry's**
> kerin.tv/cr8e/v2-1

TODAY'S ORGANIZATIONS

LO 2-1 Describe three kinds of organizations and the three levels of strategy in them.

In studying today's organizations, it is important to recognize (1) the kinds of organizations that exist, (2) what strategy is, and (3) how this strategy relates to the three levels of structure found in many large organizations.

Kinds of Organizations

An *organization* is a legal entity that consists of people who share a common mission. This motivates them to develop *offerings* (goods, services, or ideas) that create value for both the organization and its customers by satisfying their needs and wants.[4] Today's organizations are of three types: (1) for-profit organizations, (2) nonprofit organizations, and (3) government agencies.

A *for-profit organization*, often called a *business firm*, is a privately owned organization such as Target, Nike, or Brita that serves its customers to earn a profit so that it can survive. **Profit** is the money left after a for-profit organization subtracts its total expenses from its total revenues—and the reward for the risk it undertakes in marketing its offerings.

In contrast, a *nonprofit organization* is a nongovernmental organization that serves its customers but does not have profit as an organizational goal. Instead, its goals may be operational efficiency or client satisfaction. Regardless, it also must receive sufficient funds above its expenses to continue operations. Organizations like Teach For America,

> **profit**
> The money left after a for-profit organization subtracts its total expenses from its total revenues—and the reward for the risk it undertakes in marketing its offerings.

Brita is an example of a for-profit organization. Its Brita Hard-Sided Bottle is BPA-free and filters tap water. Each filter works for 300 bottles of water.
©McGraw-Hill Education

Making **Responsible Decisions**

Social Responsibility

New Types of Organizations Help Entrepreneurs Focus on Passion and Purpose

Filmmaker Pete Williams recently spent two years creating a documentary called *The New Breed* to describe the growing movement of people who are committed to using business concepts to change the world for good. These "social entrepreneurs" are using a variety of organizational models to address social needs about which they are passionate. The enterprises are sometimes organized as traditional for-profit companies with a for-purpose orientation. They can also be benefit corporations, which are for-profit organizations with legal requirements for social and environmental impact assessment. Finally, social entrepreneurs often create enterprises that are organized as nonprofit ventures. The issues they are focusing on range from health care delivery, to the cost of higher education, to agricultural efficiency.

Each year *Forbes* magazine recognizes some of the most innovative social ventures in its annual list of *30 Under 30: Social Entrepreneurs*. For example, Kelly Peeler left a Wall Street job to found NexGenVest, an organization created to help the 70 million Generation Z students navigate the financial aid and student loan market. NexGenVest customers, who are typically high school seniors and college students, contact advisors 24/7 via text message to receive personalized information and advice. Why is Peeler so passionate about this issue? Because Americans currently owe more than $1.4 trillion in student debt. In addition, Peeler believes "the next financial crisis [will be] rooted in the student loan market."

Teach For America is another example of a creative social venture. Launched by college senior Wendy Kopp, Teach For America is the national corps of outstanding recent college graduates who commit to teach for two years in urban and rural public schools and become lifelong leaders in expanding educational opportunity. Each year more than 10,000 corps members teach 750,000 students.

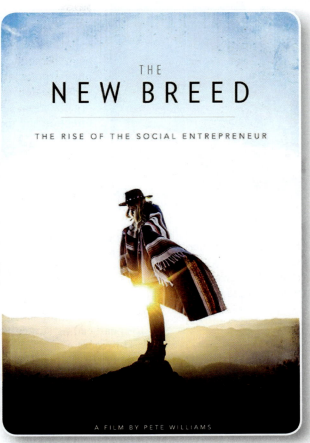

Courtesy of STAY GOLD Studios

These examples illustrate how organizations are changing to create value for a broad range of constituents by addressing the needs and challenges of society.

---

described in the Making Responsible Decisions box, seek to solve the practical needs of society and are often structured as nonprofit organizations.[5] For simplicity in the rest of the book, the terms *firm*, *company*, and *organization* are used interchangeably to cover both for-profit and nonprofit organizations.

Last, a *government agency* is a federal, state, county, or city unit that provides a specific service to its constituents. For example, the Census Bureau, a unit of the U.S. Department of Commerce, is a federal government agency that provides population and economic data.

Organizations that develop similar offerings create an *industry*, such as the computer industry or the automobile industry.[6] As a result, organizations make strategic decisions that reflect the dynamics of the industry to create a compelling and sustainable advantage for their offerings relative to those of competitors and achieve a

Prada manages a portfolio or group of businesses—including clothing, perfume, leather goods, and footwear—each of which may be viewed as a strategic business unit (SBU).
©Imaginechina via AP Images

strategy
An organization's long-term course of action designed to deliver a unique customer experience while achieving its goals.

superior level of performance.[7] Much of an organization's marketing strategy is having a clear understanding of the industry within which it competes.

What Is Strategy?

An organization has limited human, financial, technological, and other resources available to produce and market its offerings—it can't be all things to all people! Every organization must develop strategies to help focus and direct its efforts to accomplish its goals. However, the definition of strategy has been the subject of debate among management and marketing theorists. For our purpose, **strategy** is an organization's long-term course of action designed to deliver a unique customer experience while achieving its goals.[8] All organizations set a strategic direction. And marketing helps to both set this direction and move the organization there.

The Structure of Today's Organizations

Large organizations are extremely complex. They usually consist of three organizational levels whose strategies are linked to marketing, as shown in Figure 2–1.

Corporate Level The *corporate level* is where top management directs overall strategy for the entire organization. "Top management" usually means the board of directors and senior management officers with a variety of skills and experiences that are invaluable in establishing the organization's overall strategy.

The president or chief executive officer (CEO) is the highest-ranking officer in the organization and is usually a member of its board of directors. This person must possess leadership skills ranging from overseeing the organization's daily operations to spearheading strategy planning efforts that may determine its very survival.

In recent years, many large firms have changed the title of the head of marketing from vice president of marketing to chief marketing officer (CMO). These CMOs have an increasingly important role in top management and typically offer multi-industry backgrounds, cross-functional management expertise, and insightful marketing intuition as qualifications. In addition, they are increasingly called upon to bring "a strategic viewpoint, exceptional measurement and analytical capabilities, financial management rigor, and operational savviness to their role."[9]

FIGURE 2–1
The board of directors oversees the three levels of strategy in organizations: corporate, strategic business unit, and functional.

Strategic Business Unit Level Some multimarket, multiproduct firms, such as Prada and Johnson & Johnson, manage a portfolio or group of businesses. Each group is a *strategic business unit* (*SBU*), which is a subsidiary, division, or unit of an organization that markets a set of related offerings to a clearly defined target market. At the *strategic business unit level*, managers set a more specific strategic direction for their businesses to exploit value-creating opportunities. For less complex firms with a single business focus, such as Ben & Jerry's, the corporate and business unit levels may merge.

Functional Level Each strategic business unit has a *functional level*, where groups of specialists actually create value for the organization. The term *department* generally refers to these specialized functions such as marketing and finance (see Figure 2–1). At the functional level, the organization's strategic direction becomes its most specific and focused. Just as there is a hierarchy of levels within an organization, there is a hierarchy of strategic directions set by managers at each level.

A key role of the marketing department is to look outward by listening to customers, developing offerings, implementing marketing program actions, and then evaluating whether those actions are achieving the organization's goals. When developing marketing programs for new or improved offerings, an organization's senior management may form *cross-functional teams*. These consist of a small number of people from different departments who are mutually accountable to accomplish a task or a common set of performance goals. Sometimes these teams will have representatives from outside the organization, such as suppliers or customers, to assist them.

learning review

2-1. What is the difference between a for-profit and a nonprofit organization?

2-2. What are examples of a functional level in an organization?

STRATEGY IN VISIONARY ORGANIZATIONS

LO 2-2 Describe core values, mission, organizational culture, business, and goals.

To be successful, today's organizations must be forward-looking. They must anticipate future events and then respond quickly and effectively to those events. In addition, they must thrive in today's uncertain, chaotic, rapidly changing environment. A visionary organization must specify its foundation (why does it exist?), set a direction (what will it do?), and formulate strategies (how will it do it?), as shown in Figure 2–2.[10]

Organizational Foundation: Why Does It Exist?

An organization's foundation is its philosophical reason for being—why it exists. At their most basic level organizations exist to accomplish something for someone. Successful visionary organizations use this foundation to guide and inspire their employees through three elements: core values, mission, and organizational culture.

core values
The fundamental, passionate, and enduring principles of an organization that guide its conduct over time.

Core Values An organization's **core values** are the fundamental, passionate, and enduring principles that guide its conduct over time. A firm's founders or senior management develop these core values, which are consistent with their essential beliefs and character. They capture the firm's heart and soul and serve to inspire and motivate its *stakeholders*—employees, shareholders, board of directors, suppliers, distributors, creditors, unions, government, local communities, and customers. Core values also are timeless and guide the organization's conduct. The five core values at Facebook, for example, are (1) focus on impact, (2) move fast, (3) be bold, (4) be open, and (5) build social value. To be effective, an organization's core values must be communicated to and supported by its top management and employees; if not, they are just hollow words.[11]

Organizational foundation (why)
- Core values
- Mission (vision)
- Organizational culture

+

Organizational direction (what)
- Business
- Goals (objectives)
  - Long-term
  - Short-term

=

Organizational strategies (how)
- By level
  - Corporate
  - SBU
  - Functional
- By product
  - Good
  - Service
  - Idea

FIGURE 2–2
Today's visionary organizations use key elements to (1) establish a foundation and (2) set a direction using (3) strategies that enable them to develop and market their products successfully.

Video 2-2
Southwest Airlines
kerin.tv/cr8e/v2-2

mission
A statement of the organization's function in society that often identifies its customers, markets, products, and technologies. Often used interchangeably with *vision*.

organizational culture
The set of values, ideas, attitudes, and norms of behavior that is learned and shared among the members of an organization.

"Luv Goes A Long Way" ads emphasize how providing a warm, friendly experience is part of Southwest Airlines's organizational strategy.
Source: Southwest Airlines Co.

Mission By understanding its core values, an organization can take steps to define its **mission**, a statement of the organization's function in society that often identifies its customers, markets, products, and technologies. Often used interchangeably with *vision*, a *mission statement* should be clear, concise, meaningful, inspirational, and long-term.[12]

Inspiration and focus appear in the mission statements of for-profit organizations, as well as nonprofit organizations and government agencies. For example:

- *Southwest Airlines*: "Dedication to the highest quality of Customer Service delivered with a sense of warmth, friendliness, individual pride, and Company Spirit."[13]
- *American Red Cross*: "To prevent and alleviate human suffering in the face of emergencies by mobilizing the power of volunteers and the generosity of donors."[14]
- *Federal Trade Commission*: "To prevent business practices that are anticompetitive or deceptive or unfair to consumers; to enhance informed consumer choice and public understanding of the competitive process; and to accomplish this without unduly burdening legitimate business activity."[15]

Each statement exhibits the qualities of a good mission and provides a compelling picture of an envisioned future.

Recently, many organizations have added a social element to their mission statements to reflect an ideal that is morally right and worthwhile. This is what Ben & Jerry's social mission statement shows in the chapter opener. Stakeholders, particularly customers, employees, and now society, are asking organizations to be exceptional citizens by providing long-term value while solving society's problems.

Organizational Culture An organization must connect with all of its stakeholders. Thus, an important corporate-level marketing function is communicating its core values and mission to them. These activities send clear messages to employees and other stakeholders about **organizational culture**—the set of values, ideas, attitudes, and norms of behavior that is learned and shared among the members of an organization.

Organizational Direction: What Will It Do?

As shown in Figure 2–2, the organization's foundation enables it to set a direction in terms of (1) the "business" it is in and (2) its specific goals.

Business A **business** describes the clear, broad, underlying industry or market sector of an organization's offering. To help define its business, an organization looks at the set of organizations that sell similar offerings—those that are in direct competition with each other—such as "the ice cream business." The organization can then begin to answer the questions "What do we do?" or "What business are we in?"

In the first half of the 20th century, what "business" did railroad executives believe they were in? The text reveals their disastrous error.

©Digital Vision/Getty Images

Why is the definition of Uber's business changing? See the text for the answer.

Source: Uber Technologies Inc.

Professor Theodore Levitt saw that 20th-century American railroads defined their business too narrowly, proclaiming, "We are in the railroad business!" This myopic focus caused them to lose sight of who their customers were and what they needed. So railroads failed to develop strategies to compete with airlines, barges, pipelines, and trucks. As a result, many railroads merged or went bankrupt. Railroads should have realized they were in "the transportation business." Similarly, the publishing industry defined its business as being the printer of newspapers and magazines. The dramatic decline in demand for print publications, however, suggests that it should view itself as being in the information and entertainment business.[16]

With today's increased global competition, many organizations are rethinking their *business model*, the strategies an organization develops to provide value to the customers it serves. Technological innovation is often the trigger for this business model change, particularly when it is linked to consumer needs. Netflix, for example, changed its business model several times, shifting its original DVD rental model to a video streaming model, and then to an original content production model.[17] Bookstore retailer Barnes & Noble, too, is rethinking its *business model* as e-book readers like Amazon's Kindle and Apple's iPad have gained widespread popularity.[18]

Uber, the recent start-up known for its car transportation services, is continually redefining its business. The company started as a limousine service called UberCab. Soon the business was redefined as a ride-sharing service when it added UberX and UberPool apps which allowed drivers to use their own cars. The definition expanded further, to transportation, when UberRush was added to provide package delivery and UberEats was added to provide food delivery from restaurants. Today, taking a lesson from Theodore Levitt, Uber sees itself as much more than a cab service or ride-sharing service or delivery service. In fact, *Forbes* magazine simply describes Uber's business model as a "frictionless middleman."[19]

Goals Goals or **objectives** (terms used interchangeably in this book) are statements of an accomplishment of a task to be achieved, often by a specific time. Goals convert an organization's mission and business into long- and short-term performance targets. Business firms can pursue several different types of goals:

- *Profit*. Most firms seek to maximize profits—to get as high a financial return on investment (ROI) as possible.
- *Sales*. If profits are acceptable, a firm may elect to maintain or increase its sales (dollars or units) even though profits may not be maximized.
- *Market share*. **Market share** is the ratio of sales revenue of the firm to the total sales revenue of all firms in the industry, including the firm itself.
- *Quality*. A firm may seek to offer a level of quality that meets or exceeds the cost and performance expectations of its customers.
- *Customer satisfaction*. Customers are the reason the organization exists, so their perceptions and actions are of vital importance. Satisfaction can be measured with surveys or by the number of customer complaints.
- *Employee welfare*. A firm may recognize the critical importance of its employees by stating its goal of providing them with good employment opportunities and working conditions.

business
The clear, broad, underlying industry or market sector of an organization's offering.

goals
Statements of an accomplishment of a task to be achieved, often by a specific time. Also called *objectives*.

objectives
Statements of an accomplishment of a task to be achieved, often by a specific time. Also called *goals*.

market share
The ratio of sales revenue of the firm to the total sales revenue of all firms in the industry, including the firm itself.

> **Video 2-3**
> Uber Video
> kerin.tv/cr8e/v2-3

- *Social responsibility.* Firms may seek to balance the conflicting goals of stakeholders to promote their overall welfare, even at the expense of profits.

Nonprofit organizations (such as museums and hospitals) also have goals, such as to serve consumers as efficiently as possible. Similarly, government agencies set goals that seek to serve the public good.

Organizational Strategies: How Will It Do It?

As shown in Figure 2–2, the organizational foundation sets the "why" of organizations and the organizational direction sets the "what." To convert these into actual results, the organizational strategies are concerned with the "how." These organizational strategies vary in at least two ways, depending on (1) a strategy's level in the organization and (2) the offerings an organization provides to its customers.

Variation by Level Moving down the levels in an organization involves creating increasingly specific, detailed strategies and plans. So, at the corporate level, top managers may struggle with writing a meaningful mission statement; while at the functional level, the issue is who makes tomorrow's sales call.

Variation by Product Organizational strategies also vary by the organization's products. The strategy will be far different when marketing a very tangible physical good (Ben & Jerry's ice cream), a service (a Southwest Airlines flight), or an idea (a donation to the American Red Cross).

Most organizations develop a marketing plan as a part of their strategic marketing planning efforts. A **marketing plan** is a road map for the marketing actions of an organization for a specified future time period, such as one year or five years. The planning phase of the strategic marketing process (discussed later) usually results in a marketing plan that directs the marketing actions of an organization. Appendix A at the end of this chapter provides guidelines for writing a marketing plan.

> **marketing plan**
> A road map for the marketing actions of an organization for a specified future time period, such as one year or five years.

learning review

2-3. What is the meaning of an organization's mission?

2-4. What is the difference between an organization's business and its goals?

Tracking Strategic Performance with Marketing Analytics

> **LO 2-3** Explain why managers use marketing dashboards and marketing metrics.

Although marketing managers can set the strategic direction for their organizations, how do they know if they are making progress in getting there? As several industry experts have observed, "You can't manage what you don't measure."[20] One answer to this problem is the growing field of data analytics, or big data, which enables data-driven decisions by collecting data and presenting them in a visual format such as a marketing dashboard.

Car Dashboards and Marketing Dashboards A **marketing dashboard** is the visual display of the essential information related to achieving a marketing objective.[21] Today's business intelligence tools often provide real-time data to allow marketing mix changes, personalization, and evaluation of customer satisfaction. An example is when a chief marketing officer (CMO) wants to see daily what the effect of a new social media campaign is on a product's sales.[22]

> **marketing dashboard**
> The visual display of the essential information related to achieving a marketing objective.

The idea of a marketing dashboard really comes from the display of information found on a car's dashboard. On a car's dashboard, we glance at the fuel gauge and take action when our gas is getting low. With a marketing dashboard, a marketing manager glances at a graph or table to monitor key metrics and makes a decision to take action or analyze the problem further.[23]

marketing metric
A measure of the quantitative value or trend of a marketing action or result.

Dashboards, Metrics, and Plans The marketing dashboard of Sonatica, a hypothetical hardware and software firm, appears in Figure 2–3. It shows graphic displays of key performance indicators linked to Sonatica's product lines.[24] Each display in a marketing dashboard shows a **marketing metric**, which is a measure of the quantitative value or trend of a marketing action or result.[25] Choosing which marketing metrics to display is critical for a busy manager, who can be overwhelmed with irrelevant data.[26]

Today's marketers use *data visualization*, which presents information about an organization's marketing metrics graphically so marketers can quickly (1) spot deviations from plans during the evaluation phase and (2) take corrective actions.[27] This book uses data visualization in many figures to highlight in color key points described in the text. The Sonatica marketing dashboard in Figure 2–3 uses data visualization tools like a pie chart, a line or bar chart, and a map to show how parts of its business are performing as of December 2018:

- *Website Traffic Sources.* The color-coded perimeter of the pie chart shows the three main sources of website traffic (referral sites at 47 percent, search engines at 37 percent, and direct traffic at 16 percent). These three colors link to those of the circles in the column of website traffic sources. Of the 47 percent of traffic coming from referral sites, the horizontal *bullet graphs* to the right show that Sonatica's Facebook visits comprise 15 percent of total website traffic, up from a month ago (as shown by the vertical line).
- *Sales Performance by SBU.* The *spark lines* (the wavy lines in the far left column) show the 13-month trends of Sonatica's strategic business units (SBUs). For example, the trends in electronics and peripherals are generally up, causing their sales to exceed their YTD (year to date) targets. Conversely, both software and hardware sales failed to meet YTD targets, a problem quickly noted by a marketing manager seeing the red "warning" circles in their rows at the far right. This suggests that immediate corrective actions are needed for the software and hardware SBUs.

FIGURE 2–3

An effective marketing dashboard, like this one from Sonatica, a hypothetical hardware and software firm, helps managers assess a business situation at a glance.

Source: Dundas Data Visualization, Inc.

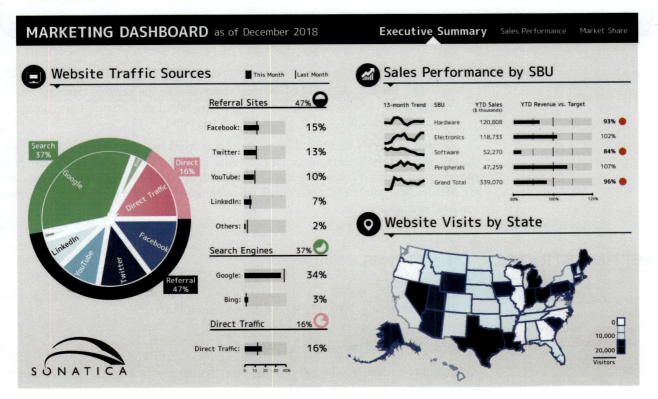

Applying Marketing Metrics

How Well Is Ben & Jerry's Doing?

As the marketing manager for Ben & Jerry's, you need to assess how it is doing within the United States in the super-premium ice cream market in which it competes. For this, you choose two marketing metrics: dollar sales and dollar market share.

Your Challenge

Scanner data from checkout counters in supermarkets and other retailers show the total industry sales of super-premium ice cream were $1.25 billion in 2018. Internal company data show you that Ben & Jerry's sold 50 million units at an average price of $5.00 per unit in 2018. A "unit" in super-premium ice cream is one pint.

Your Findings

Dollar sales and dollar market share for 2018 can be calculated using simple formulas and displayed on the Ben & Jerry's marketing dashboard as follows:

$$\text{Dollar sales (\$)} = \text{Average price} \times \text{Quantity sold}$$
$$= \$5.00 \times 50 \text{ million units}$$
$$= \$250 \text{ million}$$

$$\text{Dollar market share (\%)} = \frac{\text{Ben \& Jerry's sales (\$)}}{\text{Total industry sales (\$)}}$$
$$= \frac{\$250 \text{ million}}{\$1.25 \text{ billion}}$$
$$= 0.20 \text{ or } 20\%$$

Your dashboard displays show that from 2017 to 2018 dollar sales increased from $240 million to $250 million and that dollar market share grew from 18.4 to 20.0 percent.

Your Action

The results need to be compared with the goals established for these metrics. In addition, they should be compared with previous years' results to see if the trends are increasing, flat, or decreasing. This will lead to marketing actions.

- *Website Visits by State.* The U.S. map shows that the darker the state, the greater the number of website visits for the current month. For example, Texas has close to 20,000 visits per month, while Illinois has none.

The Ben & Jerry's dashboard in the Applying Marketing Metrics box shows how the two widely used marketing metrics of dollar sales and dollar market share can help the company assess its growth performance from 2017 to 2018. The Applying Marketing Metrics boxes in later chapters highlight other key marketing metrics and how they can lead to marketing actions.

SETTING STRATEGIC DIRECTIONS

LO 2-4 Discuss how an organization assesses where it is now and where it seeks to be.

To set a strategic direction, an organization needs to answer two difficult questions: (1) Where are we now? and (2) Where do we want to go?

A Look Around: Where Are We Now?

Asking an organization where it is at the present time involves identifying its competencies, customers, and competitors.

Lands' End's unconditional guarantee for its products highlights its focus on customers.

Source: Lands' End

Competencies Senior managers must ask the question: What do we do best? The answer involves an assessment of the organization's core *competencies*, which are its special capabilities—the skills, technologies, and resources—that distinguish it from other organizations and provide customer value. Exploiting these competencies can lead to success.[28] Competencies should be distinctive enough to provide a *competitive advantage*, a unique strength relative to competitors that provides superior returns, often based on quality, time, cost, or innovation.[29]

Customers Ben & Jerry's customers are ice cream and frozen yogurt eaters who have different preferences (form, flavor, health, and convenience). Boeing's jet airliner customers include passenger airlines such as American, United, and Southwest who serve travelers that need this type of service. Lands' End communicates a remarkable commitment to its customers and its product quality with these unconditional words:

Guaranteed. Period.®

The Lands' End website points out that this guarantee has always been an unconditional one. It reads: "If you're not satisfied with any item, simply return it to us at any time for an exchange or refund of its purchase price." But to get the message across more clearly to its customers, it created the two-word guarantee. The point is that Lands' End's strategy must provide genuine value to customers to ensure that they have a satisfying experience.[30]

Competitors In today's global marketplace, the distinctions among competitors are increasingly blurred. Lands' End started as a catalog retailer. But today, Lands' End competes with not only other clothing catalog retailers such as L.L.Bean but also traditional department stores, mass merchandisers, and specialty shops. In addition, well-known clothing brands such as Eddie Bauer now have their own chain stores. Although only some of the clothing in any of these stores may directly compete with Lands' End offerings, all of these retailers have websites to sell their offerings online. This means there's a lot of competition out there.

Growth Strategies: Where Do We Want to Go?

Knowing where the organization is at the present time enables managers to set a direction for the firm and allocate resources to move in that direction. Two techniques to aid managers with these decisions are (1) business portfolio analysis and (2) diversification analysis.

Business Portfolio Analysis Successful organizations have a portfolio or range of offerings (products and services) that possess different growth rates and market shares within the industry in which they operate. The Boston Consulting Group (BCG), an internationally known management consulting firm, has developed **business portfolio analysis**. It is a technique that managers use to quantify performance measures and growth targets to analyze their firms' SBUs as though they were a collection of separate investments.[31] The purpose of this tool is to determine which SBU or offering generates cash and which one requires cash to fund the organization's growth opportunities.

Let's assume you are filling the shoes of Apple CEO Tim Cook. Based on your knowledge of Apple products, you are currently conducting a quick analysis of four major Apple SBUs through 2020. Try to rank them from highest to lowest in terms of percentage growth in expected unit sales. We will introduce you to business portfolio analysis as we look at the possible future of the four Apple SBUs.

> **business portfolio analysis**
> A technique that managers use to quantify performance measures and growth targets to analyze their firms' strategic business units (SBUs) as though they were a collection of separate investments.

FIGURE 2–4

Boston Consulting Group (BCG) business portfolio analysis for four of Apple's consumer-related SBUs. The red arrow indicates typical movement of a product through the matrix.

All product photos: Source: Apple Inc.

The BCG business portfolio analysis requires an organization to locate the position of each of its SBUs on a growth-share matrix (see Figure 2–4). The vertical axis is the *market growth rate*, which is the annual rate of growth of the SBU's industry. The horizontal axis is the *relative market share*, defined as the sales of the SBU divided by the sales of the largest firm in the industry. A relative market share of 10× (at the left end of the scale) means that the SBU has 10 times the share of its largest competitor, whereas a share of 0.1× (at the right end of the scale) means it has only 10 percent of the share of its largest competitor.

The BCG has given specific names and descriptions to the four resulting quadrants in its growth-share matrix based on the amount of cash they generate for or require from the organization:

1. *Question marks* are SBUs with a low share of high-growth markets. They require large injections of cash just to maintain their market share, much less increase it. The name implies management's dilemma for these SBUs: choosing the right ones to invest in and phasing out the rest.
2. *Stars* are SBUs with a high share of high-growth markets that may need extra cash to finance their own rapid future growth. When their growth slows, they are likely to become cash cows.
3. *Cash cows* are SBUs that generate large amounts of cash, far more than they can use. They have dominant shares of slow-growth markets and provide cash to cover the organization's overhead and to invest in other SBUs.
4. *Dogs* are SBUs with low shares of slow-growth markets. Although they may generate enough cash to sustain themselves, they may no longer be or may not become real winners for the organization. Dropping SBUs that are dogs may be required if they consume more cash than they generate, except when relationships with other SBUs, competitive considerations, or potential strategic alliances exist.[32]

An organization's SBUs often start as question marks and go counterclockwise around Figure 2–4 to become stars, then cash cows, and finally dogs. Because an organization has limited influence on the market growth rate, its main objective is to try to change its relative dollar or unit market share. To do this, management decides

What can Apple expect in future growth of sales revenues from its iPhone products...

Source: Apple Inc.

...or its iPod devices?

Source: Apple Inc.

what strategic role each SBU should have in the future and either injects cash into or removes cash from it.

According to Interbrand, a leading brand management consulting firm, Apple has been consistently cited as one of the top global brands over the past decade in its annual Best Global Brands survey. What has made Apple so iconic is not only its revolutionary products but also its commitment to infusing the "human touch" with its technology such that its customers connect with the brand on both a cognitive *and* an emotional level. The late Steve Jobs was instrumental in creating Apple's organizational culture and core values that will continue to guide its future.[33]

Using the BCG business portfolio analysis framework, Figure 2–4 shows that the Apple picture might look this way from 2018 to 2020 for four of its SBUs:[34]

1. *Apple Watch* (wearable technology). Apple recently entered the wearable technology market with its version of a smartwatch, the Apple Watch. The watch competes with Samsung, Pebble, LG, and Motorola watches and a wide range of other wearable technologies such as Fitbit and Garmin fitness trackers. Industry analysts estimate that Apple's annual unit sales reached 18 million in 2017 and will reach 45 million watches in 2019, suggesting a 58 percent growth rate. The Apple Watch enters the market as a *question mark* and appears to be growing into a *star*.[35]

2. *iPhone* (smartphones). Apple launched its revolutionary iPhone smartphone in 2007. iPhone unit sales skyrocketed and Apple's U.S. market share is now greater than 44 percent, exceeding the market share of its largest competitor, Samsung. The smartphone market is expected to grow at an annual rate of 7 percent due to growth in India, Indonesia, and Africa. High market share and high growth suggest that Apple's iPhone is a *star*.[36]

3. *iPad/iPad mini* (tablets). Launched in 2010, iPad unit sales reached 40 percent market share by 2013—leading both Samsung's Galaxy (18 percent) and Amazon's Kindle (4 percent). Tablet sales are now declining as consumers are substituting big-screen smartphones and ultra-thin computers for tablets. For Apple, its iPad SBU is a *cash cow* (high market share in a low-growth market).[37]

4. *iPod* (music players). Apple entered the music player market with its iPod device in 2001. The product became a cultural icon, selling more that 50 million units annually until 2010 when the iPhone integrated a music player. Since 2010, sales have been declining dramatically. In 2014 Apple announced that it was discontinuing the iPod classic, and in 2017 it announced that it was discontinuing the iPod shuffle and nano. Today Apple still sells the iPod touch—although declining sales and discontinued products suggest that this SBU is entering the *dog* category.[38]

So, how did you—as Tim Cook—rank the growth opportunity for each of the four SBUs? The Apple Watch represents the highest unit growth rate at 58 percent. The iPhone SBU is likely to continue growing at 7 percent, while the iPad SBU is experiencing a decline in sales. Despite the difference in growth rates, the iPhone and iPad product lines together accounted for 76 percent of Apple's revenues in early 2018. These revenues are used to pursue growth opportunities such as the Apple HomePod, the Apple AirPods, a next-generation phone, and possibly an Apple car. Finally, long-term decline and the discontinuation of the iPod classic, shuffle, and nano may signal the beginning of the end for Apple's iPod.[39]

The primary strength of business portfolio analysis lies in forcing a firm to place each of its SBUs in the growth-share matrix, which in turn suggests which SBUs will be cash producers and cash users in the future. Weaknesses of this analysis arise from the difficulty in (1) getting the needed information and (2) incorporating competitive data into business portfolio analysis.[40]

diversification analysis
A technique that helps a firm search for growth opportunities from among current and new markets as well as current and new products.

> Video 2-4
> B&J's Chocolate Chip Cookie Dough Video
> kerin.tv/cr8e/v2-4

Diversification Analysis Diversification analysis is a technique that helps a firm search for growth opportunities from among current and new markets as well as current and new products.[41] For any market, there is both a current product (what the firm now sells) and a new product (what the firm might sell in the future). And for any product there is both a current market (the firm's existing customers) and a new market (the firm's potential customers). As Ben & Jerry's seeks to increase sales revenues, it considers all four market-product strategies shown in Figure 2–5:

- *Market penetration* is a marketing strategy to increase sales of current products in current markets, such as selling more Ben & Jerry's Chocolate Chip Cookie Dough ice cream to U.S. consumers. There is no change in either the basic product line or the markets served. Increased sales are generated by selling either more ice cream (through better promotion or distribution) *or* the same amount of ice cream at a higher price to its current customers.
- *Market development* is a marketing strategy to sell current products to new markets. For Ben & Jerry's, Brazil is an attractive new market. There is good news and bad news for this strategy: As household incomes of Brazilians increase, consumers can buy more ice cream; however, the Ben & Jerry's brand may be unknown to Brazilian consumers.
- *Product development* is a marketing strategy of selling new products to current markets. Ben & Jerry's could leverage its brand by selling children's clothing in the United States. This strategy is risky because Americans may not see the company's expertise in ice cream as extending to children's clothing.
- *Diversification* is a marketing strategy of developing new products and selling them in new markets. This is a potentially high-risk strategy for Ben & Jerry's if it decides to try to sell Ben & Jerry's branded clothing in Brazil. Why? Because the firm has neither previous production nor marketing experience from which to draw in marketing clothing to Brazilian consumers.

FIGURE 2–5
Four market-product strategies: alternative ways to expand sales revenues for Ben & Jerry's using diversification analysis.

MARKETS	PRODUCTS	
	Current	New
Current	**Market penetration** Selling more Ben & Jerry's super-premium ice cream to Americans	**Product development** Selling a new product such as children's clothing under the Ben & Jerry's brand to Americans
New	**Market development** Selling Ben & Jerry's super-premium ice cream to Brazilians for the first time	**Diversification** Selling a new product such as children's clothing under the Ben & Jerry's brand to Brazilians for the first time

learning review

2-5. What is the difference between a marketing dashboard and a marketing metric?

2-6. What is business portfolio analysis?

2-7. Explain the four market-product strategies in diversification analysis.

THE STRATEGIC MARKETING PROCESS

LO 2-5 Explain the three steps of the planning phase of the strategic marketing process.

After an organization assesses where it is and where it wants to go, management attention is focused on the strategic marketing process. The **strategic marketing process** involves the allocation of an organization's marketing mix resources to reach its target markets and achieve a competitive advantage. The process is guided by underlying principles and is divided into three phases: planning, implementation, and evaluation as shown in Figure 2–6.

strategic marketing process
The process whereby an organization allocates its marketing mix resources to reach its target markets and achieve a competitive advantage.

Principles Underlying the Strategic Marketing Process

Four principles underlie the strategic marketing process.[42] Each principle represents a fundamental assumption about customers, competitors, and organizational resources. They are:

1. *Customers are different*. Customers are not alike. Rather, important differences exist and these differences affect how customers respond to different marketing mix elements.
2. *Customers change*. Customer preferences, needs, and behavior are not static. Customer preferences, needs, and behavior change over time and circumstances and are affected by competitor actions.
3. *Competitors change and react*. The sustainability of an organization's competitive advantage is affected by the conduct of present and future competitors and how they react to an organization's actions.
4. *Organizational resources are limited*. No organization has unlimited human, technological, and financial resources. Trade-offs have to be made when capitalizing on organizational opportunities and overcoming threats to their performance.

These principles are central to the concepts, techniques, and tools applied in each phase of the strategic marketing process.

FIGURE 2–6
The strategic marketing process has three vital phases: planning, implementation, and evaluation. The figure also indicates the chapters in which these phases are discussed in the text.

> **situation analysis**
> Taking stock of where the firm or product has been recently, where it is now, and where it is headed in terms of the organization's marketing plans and the external forces and trends affecting it.

The Planning Phase of the Strategic Marketing Process

Figure 2–6 shows the three steps in the planning phase of the strategic marketing process: (1) situation (SWOT) analysis, (2) market-product focus and goal setting, and (3) the marketing program.

Step 1: Situation (SWOT) Analysis
The essence of **situation analysis** is taking stock of where the firm or product has been recently, where it is now, and where it is headed in terms of the organization's marketing plans and the external forces and trends affecting it. An effective summary of a situation analysis is a **SWOT analysis**, an acronym describing an organization's appraisal of its internal **S**trengths and **W**eaknesses and its external **O**pportunities and **T**hreats.

The SWOT analysis is based on an exhaustive study of four areas that form the foundation upon which the firm builds its marketing program:

- Identify changes and trends in the organization's industry.
- Analyze the organization's current and potential competitors.
- Assess the organization itself, including available resources.
- Research the organization's present and prospective customers.

Assume you are responsible for doing the SWOT analysis for Ben & Jerry's shown in Figure 2–7. Note that the SWOT table has four cells formed by the combination of internal versus external factors (the rows) and favorable versus unfavorable factors (the columns) that identify Ben & Jerry's strengths, weaknesses, opportunities, and threats.

The task is to translate the results of the SWOT analysis into specific marketing actions that will help the firm grow. The ultimate goal is to identify the *critical* strategy-related factors that impact the firm and then build on vital strengths, correct glaring weaknesses, exploit significant opportunities, and avoid disaster-laden threats.

The Ben & Jerry's SWOT analysis in Figure 2–7 can be the basis for these kinds of specific marketing actions. An action in each of the four cells might be:

- *Build on a strength.* Find specific efficiencies in distribution with parent-company Unilever's existing ice cream brands.

How can Ben & Jerry's develop new products and social responsibility programs that contribute to its mission? The text describes how the strategic marketing process and its SWOT analysis can help.
©McGraw-Hill Education/Evelyn Nicole Kirksey, photographer

FIGURE 2–7
Ben & Jerry's: A SWOT analysis to keep it growing. The picture painted in this SWOT analysis is the basis for management actions.

LOCATION OF FACTOR	TYPE OF FACTOR	
	Favorable	**Unfavorable**
Internal	**Strengths** • Prestigious, well-known brand name among U.S. consumers • Complements Unilever's other ice cream brands • Recognized for its social mission, values, and actions	**Weaknesses** • B&J's social responsibility actions could reduce focus • Experienced managers needed to help growth • Modest sales growth and profits in recent years
External	**Opportunities** • Growing demand for quality ice cream in overseas markets • Increasing U.S. demand for Greek-style yogurt • Many U.S. firms successfully use product and brand extensions	**Threats** • B&J customers read nutritional labels and are concerned with sugary and fatty desserts • Competes with General Mills and Nestlé brands • Increasing competition in international markets

SWOT analysis
An acronym describing an organization's appraisal of its internal **S**trengths and **W**eaknesses and its external **O**pportunities and **T**hreats.

market segmentation
Involves aggregating prospective buyers into groups, or segments, that (1) have common needs and (2) will respond similarly to a marketing action.

points of difference
Those characteristics of a product that make it superior to competitive substitutes.

- *Correct a weakness.* Recruit experienced managers from other consumer product firms to help stimulate growth.
- *Exploit an opportunity.* Develop new product lines of low-fat, low-carb frozen Greek-style yogurt flavors to respond to changes in consumer tastes.
- *Avoid a disaster-laden threat.* Focus on less risky international markets, such as Brazil and Argentina.

Step 2: Market-Product Focus and Goal Setting   Determining which products will be directed toward which customers (step 2 of the planning phase in Figure 2–6) is essential for developing an effective marketing program (step 3). This decision is often based on **market segmentation**, which involves aggregating prospective buyers into groups, or segments, that (1) have common needs and (2) will respond similarly to a marketing action. This enables an organization to focus specific marketing programs on its target market segments. The match between products and segments is often related to **points of difference**, or those characteristics of a product that make it superior to competitive substitutes. Goal setting involves specifying measurable marketing objectives to be achieved.

So step 2 in the planning phase of the strategic marketing process—deciding which products will be directed toward which customers—is the foundation for step 3, developing the marketing program.

Step 3: Marketing Program   Activities in step 2 tell the marketing manager which customers to target and which customer needs the firm's product offerings can satisfy—the *who* and *what* aspects of the strategic marketing process. The *how* aspect—step 3 in the planning phase—involves developing the program's marketing mix (the four Ps) and its budget. Figure 2–8 shows that each marketing mix element is combined to provide a cohesive marketing program.

Putting a marketing program into effect requires that the firm commit time and money to it in the form of a sales forecast (see Chapter 7) and budget that must be approved by top management.

FIGURE 2–8
The four Ps elements of the marketing mix must be blended to produce a cohesive marketing program.

> **learning review**
>
> **2-8.** What are the three steps of the planning phase of the strategic marketing process?
>
> **2-9.** What are points of difference and why are they important?

The Implementation Phase of the Strategic Marketing Process

LO 2-6 Describe the four components of the implementation phase of the strategic marketing process.

As shown in Figure 2–6, the result of the hours spent in the planning phase of the strategic marketing process is the firm's marketing plan. Implementation, the second phase of the strategic marketing process, involves carrying out the marketing plan that emerges from the planning phase. If the firm cannot execute the marketing plan—in the implementation phase—the planning phase has been a waste of time and resources.

There are four components of the implementation phase: (1) obtaining resources; (2) designing the marketing organization; (3) defining precise tasks, responsibilities, and deadlines; and (4) actually executing the marketing program designed in the planning phase.

Obtaining Resources A key task in the implementation phase of the strategic marketing process is obtaining adequate human and financial resources to execute the marketing program successfully. Small business owners often obtain funds from savings, family, friends, and bank loans. Marketing managers in existing organizations obtain these resources by getting top management to assign managerial talent and divert profits from BCG stars or cash cows.

Designing the Marketing Organization A marketing program needs a marketing organization to implement it. Figure 2–9 shows the organization chart of a typical manufacturing firm, giving some details of the marketing department's structure. Four managers of marketing activities are shown to report to the chief marketing

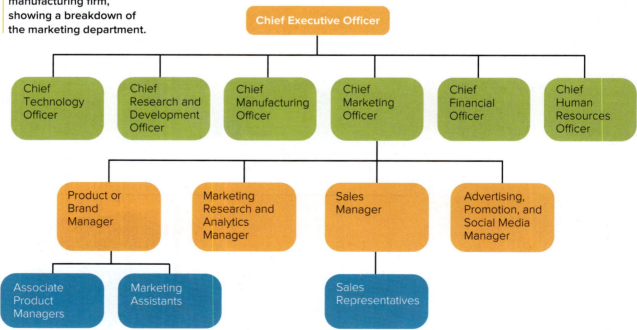

FIGURE 2–9
Organization of a typical manufacturing firm, showing a breakdown of the marketing department.

officer or CMO. Sales representatives report to the manager of sales, possibly through several regional sales managers and an international sales manager based on the size of the salesforce. The product or brand managers and their subordinates help plan, implement, and evaluate the marketing plans for their offerings. However, the entire marketing organization is responsible for converting these marketing plans into realistic marketing actions.

Defining Precise Tasks, Responsibilities, and Deadlines Successful implementation requires that team members know the tasks for which they are responsible and the deadlines for completing them. To implement the thousands of tasks on a new aircraft design, Lockheed Martin typically holds weekly program meetings. The outcome of each of these meetings is an *action item list*, an aid to implementing a marketing plan consisting of four columns: (1) the task, (2) the person responsible for completing that task, (3) the date to finish the task, and (4) what is to be delivered. Within hours of completing a program meeting, the action item list is circulated to those attending. This then serves as the starting agenda for the next meeting. Meeting minutes are viewed as secondary and backward-looking. Action item lists are forward-looking, clarify the targets, and put strong pressure on people to achieve their designated tasks by the deadline.

Suppose, for example, that you and two friends undertake a term project on the problem, "How can the college increase attendance at its performing arts concerts?" The instructor says the term project must involve a survey of a sample of students, and the written report with the survey results must be submitted by the end of the 11th week of the term. To begin, you identify all the project tasks and then estimate the time required to complete each one. To complete it in 11 weeks, your team must plan which activities can be done concurrently (at the same time) to save time.

Scheduling activities can be done efficiently with a *Gantt chart*, which is a graph of a program schedule. Figure 2–10 shows a Gantt chart—invented by Henry L. Gantt—used to schedule the class project, demonstrating how the concurrent work on several tasks enables the students to finish the project on time. Software applications such as Microsoft Project simplify the task of developing a program schedule or Gantt chart.

The key to all scheduling techniques is to distinguish tasks that *must* be done sequentially from those that *can* be done concurrently. For example, Tasks 1 and 2 that

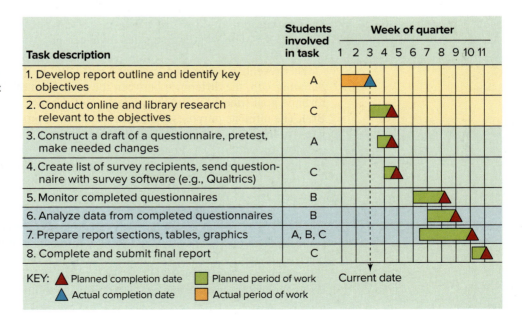

FIGURE 2–10

This Gantt chart shows how three students (A, B, and C) can schedule tasks to complete a term project on time.

are shaded yellow in Figure 2–10 *must* be done sequentially. This is because the team must agree on the outline of the project and its key objectives (Task 1) before it can begin online and library research related to the objectives (Task 2). In contrast, Tasks 6 and 7 that are shaded blue *can* be done concurrently. So writing the final report (Task 7) *can* be started before tabulating the answers to the questions (Task 6) is completed. This overlap speeds up project completion.

Executing the Marketing Program
Marketing plans are meaningless without effective execution of those plans. This requires attention to detail for both marketing strategies and marketing tactics. A **marketing strategy** is the means by which a marketing goal is to be achieved, usually characterized by a specified target market and a marketing program to reach it. The term implies both the end sought (target market) and the means or actions to achieve it (marketing program).

To implement a marketing program successfully, hundreds of detailed decisions are often required to develop the actions that comprise a marketing program for an offering. These actions, called **marketing tactics**, are detailed day-to-day operational marketing actions for each element of the marketing mix that contribute to the overall success of marketing strategies. Writing ads and setting prices for new product lines are examples of marketing tactics.

The Evaluation Phase of the Strategic Marketing Process

The evaluation phase of the strategic marketing process seeks to keep the marketing program moving in the direction set for it (see Figure 2–6). Accomplishing this requires the marketing manager to (1) compare the results of the marketing program with the goals in the written plans to identify the presence and causes of deviations and (2) act on these deviations—exploiting positive deviations and correcting negative ones.

Comparing Results with Plans to Identify Deviations
At the end of its fiscal year, which is September 30, Apple begins the evaluation phase of its strategic marketing process. Suppose you are on an Apple task force in 2009 that is responsible for making plans through 2017. You observe that extending the 2004–2009 trend of Apple's recent sales revenues (line AB in Figure 2–11) to 2017 along line BC shows an annual growth in sales revenue unacceptable to Apple's management.

Looking at potential new products in the Apple pipeline, your task force sets an aggressive annual sales growth target of 25 percent per year—the line BD in Figure 2–11. This would give sales revenues of $104 billion in 2013 and $255 billion in 2017.

This reveals a white wedge-shaped gap DBC in the figure. Planners call this the *planning gap*, the difference between the projection of the path to reach a new sales revenue goal (line BD) and the projection of the path of a plan already in place (line BC). The ultimate purpose of the firm's marketing program is to "fill in" this planning gap—in the case of your Apple task force, to move its future sales revenue line from the slow-growth line BC up to the more challenging target of line BD.

This is the essence of evaluation: comparing actual results with goals set. To reach aggressive growth targets in sales revenues, firms like Apple must continuously look for a new BCG SBU or product *cash cow* or *star*.

Acting on Deviations
When evaluation shows that actual performance differs from expectations, managers need to take immediate marketing actions—exploiting positive deviations and correcting negative ones. Comparing the explosion in Apple's actual sales revenues from 2009 to 2017 (line BE in Figure 2–11) to its target sales revenues (line BD) shows Apple's rare, world-class ability to both generate and anticipate

---

marketing strategy
The means by which a marketing goal is to be achieved, usually characterized by a specified target market and a marketing program to reach it.

marketing tactics
The detailed day-to-day operational marketing actions for each element of the marketing mix that contribute to the overall success of marketing strategies.

LO 2-7 Discuss how managers identify and act on deviations from plans.

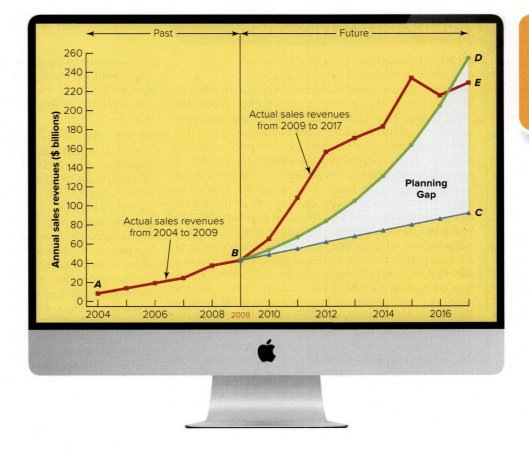

FIGURE 2–11

The evaluation phase of the strategic marketing process requires that the organization compare actual results with goals to identify and act on deviations to fill in its "planning gap." The text describes how Apple is working to fill in its planning gap

Computer: ©Joby Sessions/ MacFormat Magazine via Getty Images

consumer demand and commercialize new technologies for its revolutionary offerings. Let's consider some of its marketing actions:

- *Exploiting a positive deviation.* Favorable customer reactions to Apple's iPhone (2007) and its iPad (2010) enable it to sell the products globally and to introduce improved versions and models, such as the iPad Pro (2015) and the iPhone X (2017). Success of new versions and models also enables the introduction of new products such as the Apple Watch (2015), the Apple AirPods (2016), and the HomePod (2018).
- *Correcting a negative deviation.* As Apple's desktop PCs became dated, it moved aggressively to replace them with new iMacs and MacBooks. Also, Apple refreshed its MacBook Air (2015, 2017) and MacBook Pro (2016, 2017) lines of laptops.

As we saw earlier in the BCG business portfolio analysis of the four Apple product lines, the firm has several *stars* and *cash cows* to fill in its planning gap. We shall explore Apple's market-product strategies in more detail later in Chapters 8 and 9.

learning review

2-10. What is the implementation phase of the strategic marketing process?

2-11. How do the goals set for a marketing program in the planning phase relate to the evaluation phase of the strategic marketing process?

LEARNING OBJECTIVES REVIEW

LO 2-1 *Describe three kinds of organizations and the three levels of strategy in them.*

An organization is a legal entity that consists of people who share a common mission. It develops offerings (goods, services, or ideas) that create value for both the organization and its customers by satisfying their needs and wants. Today's organizations are of three types: for-profit organizations, nonprofit organizations, and government agencies. A for-profit organization serves its customers to earn a profit so that it can survive. Profit is the money left after a for-profit organization subtracts its expenses from its total revenues and is the reward for the risk it undertakes in marketing its offerings. A nonprofit organization is a nongovernmental organization that serves its customers but does not have profit as an organizational goal. Instead, its goals may be operational efficiency or client satisfaction. A government agency is a federal, state, county, or city unit that provides a specific service to its constituents. Most large for-profit and nonprofit organizations are divided into three levels of strategy: (*a*) the corporate level, where top management directs overall strategy for the entire organization; (*b*) the strategic business unit level, where managers set a more specific strategic direction for their businesses to exploit value-creating opportunities; and (*c*) the functional level, where groups of specialists actually create value for the organization.

LO 2-2 *Describe core values, mission, organizational culture, business, and goals.*

Organizations exist to accomplish something for someone. To give organizations direction and focus, they continuously assess their core values, mission, organizational culture, business, and goals. Today's organizations specify their foundation, set a direction, and formulate strategies—the "why," "what," and "how" factors, respectively. Core values are the organization's fundamental, passionate, and enduring principles that guide its conduct over time. The organization's mission is a statement of its function in society, often identifying its customers, markets, products, and technologies. Organizational culture is a set of values, ideas, attitudes, and norms of behavior that is learned and shared among the members of an organization. To answer the question, "What business are we in?" an organization defines its "business"—the clear, broad, underlying industry category or market sector of its offering. The organization's goals (or objectives) are statements of an accomplishment of a task to be achieved, often by a specific time. Finally, organizational strategies vary by level in the organization and by product. The strategies are often described in a marketing plan.

LO 2-3 *Explain why managers use marketing dashboards and marketing metrics.*

Marketing managers use marketing dashboards to visually display the essential information related to achieving a marketing objective. This information consists of key performance measures of a product category, such as sales or market share, known as marketing metrics, which are a measure of the quantitative value or trend of marketing actions or results. Today's marketers use data visualization to present marketing metrics graphically so they can spot deviations from plans and take corrective actions.

LO 2-4 *Discuss how an organization assesses where it is now and where it seeks to be.*

Managers of an organization ask two key questions to set a strategic direction. The first question, "Where are we now?" requires an organization to (*a*) assess its core competencies to understand how its special capabilities provide a competitive advantage; (*b*) identify its customers and how they receive genuine value and have a satisfying experience; and (*c*) analyze its competitors from a global perspective to determine the distinctions among them.

The second question, "Where do we want to go?" requires an organization to set a specific direction and allocate resources to move it in that direction. Business portfolio analysis and diversification analysis help an organization do this. Managers use business portfolio analysis to assess the organization's strategic business units (SBUs), product lines, or individual products as though they were a collection of separate investments (*cash cows, stars, question marks,* and *dogs*) to determine the amount of cash each should receive. Diversification analysis is a technique that helps a firm search for growth opportunities from among four strategies: market penetration (selling more of current products to current markets); market development (selling current products to new markets); product development (selling new products to current markets); and diversification (selling new products to new markets).

LO 2-5 *Explain the three steps of the planning phase of the strategic marketing process.*

An organization uses the strategic marketing process to allocate its marketing mix resources to reach its target markets and achieve a competitive advantage. This process is divided into three phases: planning, implementation, and evaluation. The planning phase consists of (*a*) a situation (SWOT) analysis, which involves taking stock of where the firm or product has been recently, where it is now, and where it is headed and focuses on the organization's internal factors (strengths and weaknesses) and the external forces and trends affecting it (opportunities and threats); (*b*) a market-product focus through market segmentation (grouping buyers into segments with common needs and similar responses to marketing programs) and goal setting, which in part requires creating points of difference (those characteristics of a product that make it superior to competitive substitutes); and (*c*) a marketing program that specifies the budget and actions (marketing strategies and tactics) for each marketing mix element.

LO 2-6 *Describe the four components of the implementation phase of the strategic marketing process.*

The implementation phase of the strategic marketing process carries out the marketing plan that emerges from the planning phase. It has four key components: (*a*) obtaining resources; (b) designing the marketing organization to perform product management, marketing research, sales, and advertising and promotion activities; (c) developing schedules to identify the tasks that need to be done, the time that is allocated to each one, the people responsible for each task, and the deadlines for each task—often with an action item list and Gantt chart; and (d) executing the marketing strategies, which are the means by which marketing goals are to be achieved, and their associated marketing tactics, which are the detailed day-to-day marketing actions for each element of the marketing mix that contribute to the overall success of a firm's marketing strategies. These are the marketing program actions a firm takes to achieve the goals set forth in its marketing plan.

LO 2-7 *Discuss how managers identify and act on deviations from plans.*

The evaluation phase of the strategic marketing process seeks to keep the marketing program moving in the direction that was established in the marketing plan. This requires the marketing manager to compare the results from the marketing program with the marketing plan's goals to (a) identify deviations or "planning gaps" and (b) take corrective actions to exploit positive deviations or correct negative ones.

LEARNING REVIEW ANSWERS

2-1 **What is the difference between a for-profit and a nonprofit organization?**
Answer: A for-profit organization is a privately owned organization that serves its customers to earn a profit so that it can survive. A nonprofit organization is a nongovernmental organization that serves its customers but does not have profit as an organizational goal. Instead, its goals may be operational efficiency or client satisfaction.

2-2 **What are examples of a functional level in an organization?**
Answer: The functional level in an organization is where groups of specialists from the marketing, finance, manufacturing/operations, accounting, information systems, research and development, and/or human resources departments focus on a specific strategic direction to create value for the organization.

2-3 **What is the meaning of an organization's mission?**
Answer: A mission is a clear, concise, meaningful, inspirational, and long-term statement of the organization's function in society, often identifying its customers, markets, products, and technologies. It is often used interchangeably with *vision*.

2-4 **What is the difference between an organization's business and its goals?**
Answer: An organization's business describes the clear, broad, underlying industry or market sector of an organization's offering. An organization's goals (or objectives) are statements of an accomplishment of a task to be achieved, often by a specific time. Goals convert an organization's mission and business into long- and short-term performance targets to measure how well it is doing.

2-5 **What is the difference between a marketing dashboard and a marketing metric?**
Answer: A marketing dashboard is the visual display of the essential information related to achieving a marketing objective. Each variable displayed in a marketing dashboard is a marketing metric, which is a measure of the quantitative value or trend of a marketing action or result.

2-6 **What is business portfolio analysis?**
Answer: Business portfolio analysis is a technique that managers use to quantify performance measures and growth targets to analyze their firms' SBUs as though they were a collection of separate investments. The purpose of this tool is to determine which SBU or offering generates cash and which one requires cash to fund the organization's growth opportunities.

2-7 **Explain the four market-product strategies in diversification analysis.**
Answer: The four market-product strategies in diversification analysis are: (1) Market penetration, which is a marketing strategy to increase sales of current products in current markets. There is no change in either the basic product line or the markets served. Rather, selling more of the product or selling the product at a higher price generates increased sales. (2) Market development, which is a marketing strategy to sell current products to new markets. (3) Product development, which is a marketing strategy of selling new products to current markets. (4) Diversification, which is a marketing strategy of developing new products and selling them in new markets. This is a potentially high-risk strategy because the firm has neither previous production nor marketing experience on which to draw in marketing a new product to a new market.

2-8 **What are the three steps of the planning phase of the strategic marketing process?**
Answer: The three steps of the planning phase of the strategic marketing process are: (1) Situation analysis, which involves taking stock of where the firm or product has been recently, where it is now, and where it is headed in terms of the organization's marketing plans and the external forces and trends affecting it. To do this, an organization uses a SWOT analysis, an acronym that describes an organization's appraisal of its internal **S**trengths and **W**eaknesses and its external **O**pportunities and **T**hreats. (2) Market-product focus and goal setting, which determine what products an organization will offer to which customers. This is often based on market segmentation—aggregating prospective buyers into groups or segments that have common needs and will respond similarly to a marketing action. (3) Marketing program, which is where an organization develops the marketing mix elements and budget for each offering.

2-9 **What are points of difference and why are they important?**
Answer: Points of difference are those characteristics of a product that make it superior to competitive substitutes—offerings the organization faces in the marketplace. They are important factors in the success or failure of a new product.

2-10 **What is the implementation phase of the strategic marketing process?**
Answer: The implementation phase carries out the marketing plan that emerges from the planning phase and consists of (1) obtaining resources; (2) designing the marketing organization; (3) defining precise tasks, responsibilities, and deadlines; and (4) executing the marketing program designed in the planning phase.

2-11 **How do the goals set for a marketing program in the planning phase relate to the evaluation phase of the strategic marketing process?**
Answer: The planning phase goals or objectives are used as the benchmarks with which the actual performance results are compared in the evaluation phase to identify deviations from the written marketing plans and to act on those deviations—exploiting positive ones and correcting negative ones.

FOCUSING ON KEY TERMS

business p. 32
business portfolio analysis p. 37
core values p. 31
diversification analysis p. 40
goals (objectives) p. 33
market segmentation p. 43
market share p. 33
marketing dashboard p. 34
marketing metric p. 35
marketing plan p. 34
marketing strategy p. 46
marketing tactics p. 46
mission p. 32
objectives (goals) p. 33
organizational culture p. 32
points of difference p. 43
profit p. 28
situation analysis p. 42
strategic marketing process p. 41
strategy p. 30
SWOT analysis p. 42

APPLYING MARKETING KNOWLEDGE

1. (*a*) Using Netflix as an example, explain how a mission statement gives it a strategic direction. (*b*) Create a mission statement for your own career.
2. What competencies best describe (*a*) your college or university and (*b*) your favorite restaurant?
3. Compare the advantages and disadvantages of Ben & Jerry's attempting to expand sales revenues by using (*a*) a product development strategy or (*b*) a market development strategy.
4. Select one strength, one weakness, one opportunity, and one threat from the Ben & Jerry's SWOT analysis shown in Figure 2–7. Suggest an action that a B&J marketing manager might take to address each factor.
5. What is the main result of each of the three phases of the strategic marketing process? (*a*) planning, (*b*) implementation, and (*c*) evaluation.
6. Parts of Tasks 5 and 6 in Figure 2–10 are done both concurrently and sequentially. (*a*) How can this be? (*b*) How does it help the students meet the term paper deadline? (*c*) What is the main advantage of scheduling tasks concurrently rather than sequentially?
7. The goal-setting step in the planning phase of the strategic marketing process sets quantified objectives for use in the evaluation phase. What does a manager do if measured results fail to meet objectives? Exceed objectives?

BUILDING YOUR MARKETING PLAN

1. Read Appendix A, "Building an Effective Marketing Plan." Then write a 600-word executive summary for the Paradise Kitchens marketing plan using the numbered headings shown in the plan. When you have completed the draft of your own marketing plan, write a 600-word executive summary to go in the front of your own marketing plan.
2. Using Chapter 2 and Appendix A as guides, focus your marketing plan by (*a*) writing your mission statement in 25 words or less, (*b*) listing three nonfinancial goals and three financial goals, (*c*) writing your competitive advantage in 35 words or less, and (*d*) creating a SWOT analysis table.
3. Draw a simple organization chart for your organization.

VIDEO CASE 2

IBM: Putting Smart Strategy to Work

Video 2-5
IBM Video Case
kerin.tv/cr8e/v2-5

Businesses of the world are changing the way they work and IBM has a strategy to help them. Ann Rubin, vice president of corporate marketing at IBM, explains: "IBM is in a constant state of innovation, preparing for a world that is infused with digital intelligence and a world where humans and machines work side-by-side to do things that humans simply cannot do alone." "'Let's Put Smart To Work' is our new brand platform," she continues, but "it's not just advertising, it's bigger than that. 'Let's Put Smart To Work' is an invitation. We're asking clients and partners to work with us to put smart to work to use innovative technologies to change businesses and industries and organizations."

THE NEW IBM

©Peter Probst/Alamy Stock Photo

IBM has a hundred-plus-year history of innovation. Since its early days as the Tabulating Machine Company, IBM has gone through many dramatic transformations. The company shifted from tabulation machines, to typewriters, to computers, to business services and consulting, to artificial intelligence in response to changes in technology, the global economy, and business practices. Along the way IBM developed several well-known products such as the automated teller machine (ATM), the hard disk drive, the magnetic stripe card, and the Universal Product Code (UPC). In addition, researchers at the company won four Nobel prizes and six Turing awards for contributions of lasting and major technical importance to the computer field. IBM is in the top 20 of the world's most valuable brands and in the top 50 of the world's most admired companies. Today IBM has $79 billion in sales and 380,000 employees, is ranked 34th on the *Fortune* 500, and is viewed as a cognitive solutions and cloud platform company. According to CEO Virginia Rometty, "IBM now possesses capabilities that are unmatched in our industry to address our clients' most pressing needs."

STRATEGY BASED ON VALUES

The forward-looking, visionary strategy at IBM is built on core values that are the fundamental, passionate, and enduring principles guiding its conduct. To articulate those values IBM held a global discussion event, called ValuesJam, among more than 50,000 employees. The results were three underlying values of IBM's business practices. Teresa Yoo, vice president of brand strategy and experience design, explains the outcome: "We weren't founded on or defined by a particular product or even a particular leader. It was what we believed and valued in the world, and what drove the decisions about everything that we do. So, those values have evolved over time and remain at the core of what we do. They are (1) a dedication to every client's success, (2) innovation that matters for our company and for the world, and (3) trust and personal responsibility in all our relationships."

The values influence IBM's use of strategic tools, such as portfolio analysis and SWOT analysis, in its assessment of marketplace opportunities around the globe. According to Rubin, "Using methodologies like business portfolio analysis is really important because you need to understand the opportunities in every country that you are going to and what is going to drive business in a certain area." The analysis "helps figure out what the revenue opportunity is and the growth opportunity for every one of our products in every one of our countries," she continues. Similarly, Teresa Yoo explains that "we use SWOT analysis when we're putting together a strategy for a particular brand we're building or a particular portfolio or product set. It makes a difference when you're trying to figure out what your value proposition is and you need to look at where you really stand in order to create a great strategy."

The analysis indicates fundamental changes in the business environment. IBM believes that in the near future businesses will need enterprise-strength cloud capabilities, artificial intelligence that is capable of analyzing all company and consumer data, industry-specific consulting services, and advanced cyber security. "Our brand strategy is to help IBM be easier to understand, consume, and navigate," says Yoo. "We have hundreds of products that span the whole gamut of what we do, from services to AI to cloud to research to security. So we have really focused around a few core brands that we want to be known for. They are IBM Watson for AI, IBM Cloud, IBM Security, IBM Services, and IBM Research." Overall, IBM sees these brands as the key to helping businesses become smarter businesses.

In her letter to IBM shareholders, Rometty described the trend toward smarter businesses as an "inflection point." She observed that (1) businesses are becoming smarter by leveraging intelligent digital platforms, (2) businesses are becoming smarter by making their systems and processes intelligent, and (3) businesses are becoming smarter by embedding AI and data to change how work is done, equipping themselves for an era of man + machine. The insights about the changes in businesses have led to IBM's strategy called "Let's Put Smart To Work."

THE "LET'S PUT SMART TO WORK" STRATEGY

The "Let's Put Smart To Work" initiative was launched at IBM's annual conference, called IBM Think, at which partners, clients, industry representatives, and technology leaders meet to share information about the changing business environment and business needs. IBM seeks to be an "incumbent disruptor" as it continues its transformation to the new world of enterprise technology. "The evolution of 'Let's Put Smart To Work' is the result of technologies that are fundamentally different today. They are amazing. And we are directing them more specifically to business applications," explains Yoo. We can tell clients "so let's really put it to work in your business to accomplish whatever it is that you need to get done," she adds.

The strategy touches every aspect of IBM. "'Let's Put Smart To Work'" is our rallying cry or call to action to partner with clients and to make the world a better place and to make businesses smarter," says Rubin. "IBM and our clients are putting smart to work across every industry," she adds. Industries where IBM is assisting businesses include agriculture, automotive, aviation, banking, health care, insurance, oil and gas, retail, and utilities. For example, in agriculture IBM's Watson analyzes temperature, soil pH, and other environmental factors to help farmers improve their harvest yields. In the automotive industry IBM technologies are helping combine data from IoT sensors to create better experiences for drivers in intelligent vehicles. Health care scientists are using IBM artificial intelligence to help accelerate research and find new uses for existing drugs. And in South Africa, IoT sensors are being used to monitor animal movements to help reduce rhinoceros poaching.

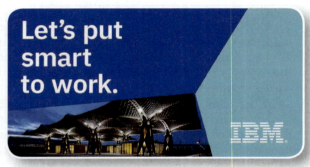

Source: IBM Corporation

MARKETING "LET'S PUT SMART TO WORK"

The IBM marketing organization includes thousands of marketing professionals located in hundreds of countries. They are all adopting an approach they call "agile marketing," which is based on improvisation, testing and data, and collaboration, and which results in speed, adaptability, and creativity. "At IBM we use agile practices, agile methodologies," says Rubin. "It's the way that you best collaborate and the way that you best iterate and the way that you best create programs and products to move forward," she adds. The general strategy and the specific elements of the agile marketing approach all come together in a marketing plan. Rubin explains, "Everything is grounded in the marketing plan, in fact, everything is grounded in our overall corporate strategy and our values, and our strategic priorities."

The marketing plan includes a variety of marketing tools. "Our marketing plan leverages all kinds of elements from traditional to emerging technologies and emerging platforms. We use traditional advertising like TV and radio and print but we have to really understand how our clients consume media," says Rubin. For example, IBM customers tend to travel a lot so IBM places a lot of out-of-home advertising in airports. Digital advertising and social media are also part of the marketing plan. "The important thing about social is understanding that every platform is different. You can't just take your TV spot and run it on Facebook and LinkedIn and Twitter and Instagram and think it's going to work. The more you look at the metrics and the data and the analytics, the more you learn those things. Then you uncover the insights and you can create the right content for the right platform," Rubin explains.

Events are also a very important part of the marketing plan. The reason, as Rubin explains, is that "it's hard to touch and feel our products so it's really important for our audience to engage with IBMers." The events give IBM managers an opportunity to engage one-on-one with their clients. Similarly, IBM sponsors events such as the Masters golf tournament, the US Open, many tennis tournaments around the world, and the Grammys, the Oscars, and the Tony awards. The reason, explains Yoo, is "the clients we are targeting tend to watch and go to those events" and the events are "an opportunity to make the technology we provide easier to understand."

THE "SMART" FUTURE

The combination of innovative technologies and changing businesses has created an exciting combination for IBM's latest transformation. Ann Rubin describes the excitement in this way: "I feel like I have the best job in IBM and frankly one of the best jobs in the marketing industry overall. The marketing industry is changing every day, so you need to keep up, but it's so exiting, there's just nothing boring about it!" So what will the future bring? Teresa Yoo's advice is, "Keep your eyes on IBM, we're working on some incredible things that are going to change the world!"[43]

Questions

1. What is IBM's "Let's Put Smart To Work" strategy?
2. How does this strategy relate to IBM's values?
3. Conduct a SWOT analysis for IBM's "Let's Put Smart To Work" initiative. What are the relevant trends to consider?
4. What marketing tools described in Chapter 2 are prominent in IBM's strategic marketing process?
5. What is "agile" marketing at IBM? Why does IBM use the agile approach?

Chapter Notes

1. "Our Values," from Ben & Jerry's website, http://www.benjerry.com/values, February 28, 2017; and "Ice Cream History Revealed! What Was Ben & Jerry's First Ice Cream Flavor?" *BusinessWire,* November 15, 2011, http://www.businesswire.com/news/home/20111115007275/en/Ice-Cream-History-Revealed!-Ben-Jerry%E2%80%99s-Ice#.VR8B7J50yM8.

2. Michal Addady, "Here's How to Get Free Ben & Jerry's Ice Cream Today," Fortune.com, April 12, 2016; Nick Craig and Scott Snook, "From Purpose to Impact," *Harvard Business Review*, May 2014, pp. 105–11; Joe Van Brussel, "Ben & Jerry's Become B-Corp Certified, Adds Credibility to Impact Investing Movement," *Huffington Post: Business,* October 23, 2012, http://www.huffingtonpost.com/2012/10/23/ben-and-jerrys-b-corp-impactinvesting_n_2005315.html; and "What Are B-Corps?" B-Corporation website, see http://www.bcorporation.net/what-are-b-corps.

3. "Global Ice Cream Market—Growth, Trends, and Forecasts (2018–2023)," Mordor Intelligence, February 2018; Michal Addady, "Ben & Jerry's Is Going Vegan," Fortune.com, February 3, 2016; and Megan Lasher, "Ben & Jerry's Is Making Chocolate Chip Cookie Dough Beer," Time.com, June 22, 2016.

4. Roger A. Kerin and Robert A. Peterson, *Strategic Marketing Problems: Cases and Comments,* 13th ed. (Upper Saddle River, NJ: Prentice Hall, 2013), p. 140.

5. Caroline Howard and Natalie Sportelli, "30 Under 30 Social Entrepreneurs," *Forbes*, December 12, 2017, p. 126; Tori Utley, "Can Business Change the World? This Filmmaker Says Yes—Through Social Entrepreneurship," *www.forbes.com*, February 28, 2018; Richard Murphy and Denielle Sachs, "The Rise of Social Entrepreneurship Suggests a Possible Future for Global Capitalism," *www.forbes.com*, May 2, 2013; and http://www.teachforamerica.org.

6. For a discussion of how industries are defined and offerings are classified, see the Census Bureau's Economic Classification Policy Committee Issues Paper #1 (http://www.census.gov/eos/www/naics/history/docs/issue_paper_1.pdf), which aggregates industries in the NAICS from a "production-oriented" view; see also the American Marketing Association definition at https://www.ama.org/resources/Pages/Dictionary.aspx?dLetter=I.

7. W. Chan Kim and Reneé Mauborgne, "Blue Ocean Strategy: From Theory to Practice," *California Management Review* 47, no. 3 (Spring 2005), p. 105; and Michael E. Porter, "What Is Strategy?" *Harvard Business Review*, November–December 1996, p. 2.

8. The definition of *strategy* reflects thoughts appearing in Porter, "What Is Strategy?" pp. 4, 8; a condensed definition of strategy is found on the American Marketing Association website, https://www.ama.org/resources/Pages/Dictionary.aspx?dLetter=S; Gerry Johnson, Kevan Scholes, and Richard Wittington, *Exploring Corporate Strategy* (Upper Saddle River, NJ: Prentice Hall, 2005), p. 10; and Costas Markides, "What Is Strategy and How Do You Know If You Have One?" *Business Strategy Review* 15, no. 2 (Summer 2004), p. 5.

9. Hal Conick, "The Evolution and Awaking of the Modern CMO," *Marketing News*, March 2017, pp. 28–37; Frank Holland, "Tomorrow's CMO Will Be Plugged into the Entire Marketing Cycle," *Adweek*, January 9, 2015, p. 1; George S. Day and Robert Malcolm, "The CMO and the Future of Marketing," *Marketing Management,* Spring 2012, pp. 34–43; Christine Moorman, "Ten Trends from the CMO Survey™," *Marketing Management,* Fall 2012, pp. 15–17; John Kador, "The View from Marketing: How to Get the Most from Your CMO," *Chief Executive,* July–August 2011, pp. 60–61; Roger A. Kerin, "Strategic Marketing and the CMO," *Journal of Marketing,* October 2005, pp. 12–13; and *The CMO Council: Biographies of Selected Advisory Board Members,* www.cmocouncil.org/advisoryboard.php.

10. Taken in part from Jim Collins and Morten T. Hansen, *Great by Choice* (New York: HarperCollins Publishers, 2011); Jim Collins and Jerry I. Porras, *Built to Last: Successful Habits of Visionary Companies* (New York: HarperCollins Publishers, 2002), p. 54; and Steve Hemsley, "How to Build a Visionary Company," *Marketing Week*, July 23, 2015, p. 1.

11. Richard Feloni, "The 5 Values Facebook Looks for in Every Employee," *Business Insider*, February 9, 2016; Collins and Porras, *Built to Last*, p. 73; Patrick M. Lencioni, "Make Your Values Mean Something," *Harvard Business Review,* July 2002, p. 6; Aubrey Malphurs, *Values-Driven Leadership: Discovering and Developing Your Core Values for Ministry,* 2nd ed. (Grand Rapids, MI: BakerBooks, 2004), p. 31; and Catherine M. Dalton, "When Organizational Values Are Mere Rhetoric," *Business Horizons* 49 (September–October 2006), p. 345.

12. Collins and Porras, *Built to Last*, pp. 94–95; and Tom Krattenmaker, "Write a Mission Statement That Your Company Is Willing to Live," *Harvard Management Communication Letter,* March 2002, pp. 3–4.

13. See https://www.southwest.com/html/about-southwest.

14. See http://www.redcross.org/about-us/mission.

15. See https://www.ftc.gov/about-ftc.

16. Amy Gallo, "A Refresher on Marketing Myopia," *Harvard Business Review,* August 22, 2016, pp. 2–5; and Theodore Levitt, "Marketing Myopia," *Harvard Business Review,* July–August 1960, pp. 45–56.

17. Stelios Kavadias, Kostas Ladas, and Christoph Loch, "The Transformative Business Model," *Harvard Business Review*, October 2016, pp. 90-98; Dan Radak, "Breaking Down the Netflix Business Model: The History and the Future of the VOD Giant," *Business 2 Community*, July 1, 2016; and Miriam Gottfried, "Eyeballs Are No Longer Enough for Netflix," *The Wall Street Journal,* January 17, 2017.

18. Jim Milliot, "What's Next for Barnes & Noble?" *Publishers Weekly*, August 22, 2016, p. 4; Jim Milliot, "E-books Gained, Online Retailers Slipped in 2014," *Publishers Weekly*, March 30, 2015, pp. 4–5; and Jeffrey A. Trachtenberg, "What's Barnes & Noble's Survival Plan?" *The Wall Street Journal*, April 18, 2014, p. B1.

19. Alan Ohnsman and Brian Solomon, "Uber's Bold Move," *Forbes*, December 30, 2016, pp. 58–74; and Adam Lashinsky, "Classifying Uber's Business Model Is a Complicated Affair," *Fortune.com*, December 5, 2016, p. 73.

20. Andrew McAfee and Erik Brynjolfsson, "Big Data: The Management Revolution," *Harvard Business Review,* October 2012, pp. 61–68.

21. The definition is adapted from Stephen Few, *Information Dashboard Design: The Effective Visual Communication of Data* (Sebastopol, CA: O'Reilly Media, Inc., 2006), pp. 2–46.

22. Pedro Hernandez, "Microsoft Enables Real-Time IoT Dashboards in Power BI," *eWeek*, February 1, 2017, p. 3; Michel Wedel and P. K. Kannan, "Marketing Analytics for Data-Rich Environments," *Journal of Marketing*, November 2016, pp. 97–121; and Koen Pauwels et al., *Dashboards & Marketing: Why, What, How and What Research Is Needed?* (Hanover, NH: Tuck School, Dartmouth, May 2008).

23. Vikal Mittal, "The Downside of Marketing Dashboards," *Marketing News*, January 2017, pp. 22–23; Few, *Information Dashboard Design;* Michael T. Krush, Raj Agnihotri, Kevin J. Trainor, and Edward L. Nowlin, "Enhancing Organizational Sensemaking: An Examination of the Interactive Effects of Sales Capabilities and Marketing Dashboards," *Industrial Marketing Management*, July 2013, pp. 824–35; Bruce H. Clark, Andrew V. Abela, and Tim Ambler, "Behind the Wheel," *Marketing Management*, May–June 2006, pp. 19–23; and Spencer E. Ante, "Giving the Boss the Big Picture," *BusinessWeek*, February 13, 2006, pp. 48–49.

24. Few, *Information Dashboard Design,* p. 13.

25. Mark Jeffery, *Data-Driven Marketing: The 15 Metrics Everyone in Marketing Should Know* (Hoboken, NJ: Wiley 2010), chapter 1; Michael Krauss, "Balance Attention to Metrics with Intuition," *Marketing News,* June 1, 2007, pp. 6–8; John Davis, *Measuring Marketing: 103 Key Metrics Every Marketer Needs* (Singapore: Wiley [Asia], 2007); and Paul W. Farris, Neil T. Bendle, Phillip E. Pfeifer, and David J. Reibstein, *Marketing Metrics,* 2nd ed. (Upper Saddle River, NJ: Wharton School Publishing, 2010).

26. David Burrows, "Too Many Metrics: The Perils of Training Marketers to Calculate ROI," *Marketing Week*, September 11, 2014, p. 42; Art Weinstein and Shane Smith, "Game Plan," *Marketing Management,* Fall 2012, pp. 24–31; Alexander Chiang, "Special Interview with Stephen Few, Dashboard and Data Visualization Expert," *Dundas Dashboard,* July 14, 2011; Stephen Few, *Now You See It* (Oakland, CA: Analytics Press, 2009), chapters 1–3; and Jacques Bughin, Amy Guggenheim Shenkan, and Mark Singer, "How Poor Metrics Undermine Digital Marketing," *The McKinsey Quarterly,* October 2008.

27. The now-classic reference on effective graphic presentation is Edward R. Tufte, *The Visual Display of Quantitative Information,* 2nd ed. (Cheshire, CT: Graphics Press, 2001); see also Few, *Information Dashboard Design*, chapters 3–5.

28. George Stalk, Phillip Evans, and Lawrence E. Shulman, "Competing on Capabilities: The New Rules of Corporate Strategy," *Harvard Business Review,* March–April 1992, pp. 57–69; and Darrell K. Rigby, *Management Tools 2007: An Executive's Guide* (Boston: Bain & Company, 2007), p. 22.

29. Roger Kerin and Robert Peterson, *Strategic Marketing Problems: Cases and Comments,* 13th ed. (Upper Saddle River, NJ: Prentice Hall, 2013), pp. 2–3; and Derek F. Abell, *Defining the Business* (Englewood Cliffs, NJ: Prentice Hall, 1980), p. 18.

30. Robert D. Hof, "How to Hit a Moving Target," *BusinessWeek,* August 21, 2006, p. 3; and Peter Kim, *Reinventing the Marketing Organization* (Cambridge, MA: Forrester, July 13, 2006), pp. 7, 9, and 17.

31. Adapted from *The Experience Curve Reviewed, IV: The Growth Share Matrix of the Product Portfolio* (Boston: The Boston Consulting Group, 1973). See also https://www.bcgperspectives.com/content/classics/strategy_the_product_portfolio (registration and login required for access).

32. Roger A. Kerin, Vijay Mahajan, and P. Rajan Varadarajan, *Contemporary Perspectives on Strategic Marketing Planning* (Boston: Allyn & Bacon, 1990), p. 52.

33. "The Best Global Brands 2016 Rankings," *Interbrand*, http://interbrand.com/best-brands/best-global-brands/2016/ranking/.

34. See the Apple press release library at http://www.apple.com/pr/library/.

35. Grace Donnelly, "Apple Is Officially Taking Over the Watch Business," *fortune.com,* February 20, 2018; Ben Lovejoy, "IDC Predicts Apple Watch Sales Will Hit 45M/Year by 2019, Still Lead Smartwatch Market," 9to5mac.com, December 2015; and Joseph Palenchar, "Apple Watch the One to Watch," *The Week in Consumer Electronics,* March 16, 2015, www.twice.com.

36. "comScore Reports June 2017 U.S. Smartphone Subscriber Market Share," *PR Newswire*, August 3, 2017; Daniel Sparks, "Apple's iPhone Has Rapidly Increased Market Share in the US," *Business Insider*, December 10, 2016; and Elad Natanson, "2016: A Pivotal Year for the Smartphone Industry," *Forbes.com*, September 12, 2016.

37. Matt Weinberger, "The World of Technology Is Changing and the iPad Is Getting Caught in the Middle," *Business Insider*, February 1, 2017; Jack Linshi, "5 Charts That Show Why the iPad's Fifth Birthday Is Bittersweet," www.time.com, April 6, 2015; "The State of the Tablet Market," *TabTimes Weekly,* April 10, 2015, http://tabtimes.com/resources/the-state-of-the-tablet-market/; and Larry Magid, "Apple's Tablets Selling Well but Market Share Slips While Samsung Grows," *Forbes*, May 1, 2013, http://www.forbes.com/sites/larrymagid/2013/05/01/apples-tablet-market-share-slips-and-samsunggrows/.

38. Anita Balakrishnan, "Apple Is Discontinuing the iPod Shuffle and Nano," CNBC, www.cnbc.com, July 27, 2017; Jason Cipriani, "The Real Reason Apple Decided to Release a New iPod Touch," *Fortune.com*, July 15, 2015; Don Reisinger, "iPod History: 10 Milestones in This Wearable Music Player's Evolution," *eWeek,* October 31, 2014; James Hall, "MP3 Players Are Dead," *Business Insider,* December 26, 2012, http://www.businessinsider.com/mp3-players-are-dead-2012-12; and Zak Islam, "Smartphones Heavily Decrease Sales of iPod, MP3 Players," *Tom's Hardware,* December 31, 2012, http://www.tomshardware.com/news/SmartphonesiPod-MP3-Players-Sales,20062.html.

39. "Share of Apple's Revenue by Product Category from the First Quarter of 2012 to the First Quarter of 2018," Statista, 2018, https://www.statista.com/statistics/382260/segments-share-revenue-of-apple/; and Martyn Casserly, "Apple Rumours & Predictions 2017," *MacWorld*, February 20, 2017.

40. Strengths and weaknesses of the BCG technique are based on Derek F. Abell and John S. Hammond, *Strategic Market Planning: Problem and Analytic Approaches* (Englewood Cliffs, NJ: Prentice Hall, 1979); Yoram Wind, Vijay Mahajan, and Donald Swire, "An Empirical Comparison of Standardized Portfolio Models," *Journal of Marketing,* Spring 1983, pp. 89–99; and J. Scott Armstrong and Roderick J. Brodie, "Effects of Portfolio Planning Methods on Decision Making: Experimental Results," *International Journal of Research in Marketing,* Winter 1994, pp. 73–84.

41. H. Igor Ansoff, "Strategies for Diversification," *Harvard Business Review,* September–October 1957, pp. 113–24.

42. Robert W. Palmatier and Shrihari Shridhar, *Marketing Strategy,* New York: Macmillan International Higher Education, 2017.
43. This case was written by Steven Hartley and Roger Kerin. Sources: Interviews with IBM executives Ann Rubin and Teresa Yoo; Thomas Haigh, "Defining American Greatness: IBM from Watson to Trump," *Communication of the ACM,* January 2018, pp. 32–37; Yagmur Simsek, "IBM Has Introduced a New Brand Platform along with a New Campaign—'Let's Put Smart To Work,'" *Digital Agency Network,* April 2018; Jason Bloomberg, "IBM Bet Company on Exponential Innovation in AI, Blockchain, and Quantum Computing," *Forbes,* March 22, 2018; "Our Values at Work," https://www.ibm.com/ibm/values/us/; Adi Ignatius, "Don't Try to Protect the Past: A Conversation with IBM CEO Ginni Rometty," *Harvard Business Review,* July–August, 2017, pp. 126–32; Avi Dan, "How Michele Peluso Is Redefining Marketing at IBM," *Forbes,* January 18, 2018; IBM 2017 Annual Report; IBM website, www.ibm.com; "The Fortune 500," *Fortune,* June 2018; "The World's Most Admired Companies," *Fortune,* January 19, 2018; and "The World's Most Valuable Brands," *Forbes,* May 23, 2018.

APPENDIX A
Building an Effective Marketing Plan

"If you have a real product with a distinctive point of difference that satisfies the needs of customers, you may have a winner," says Arthur R. Kydd, who has helped launch more than 60 start-up firms. "And you get a real feel for this in a well-written marketing or business plan," he explains.[1]

This appendix (1) describes what marketing and business plans are, including the purposes and guidelines in writing effective plans, and (2) provides a sample marketing plan.

MARKETING PLANS AND BUSINESS PLANS

After explaining the meanings, purposes, and audiences of marketing plans and business plans, this section describes some writing guidelines for them and what external funders often look for in successful plans.

Meanings, Purposes, and Audiences

A **marketing plan** is a road map for the marketing actions of an organization for a specified future time period, such as one year or five years.[2] No single "generic" marketing plan applies to all organizations and all situations. Rather, the specific format for a marketing plan for an organization depends on the following:

- *The target audience and purpose.* Elements included in a particular marketing plan depend heavily on (1) who the audience is and (2) what its purpose is. A marketing plan for an internal audience seeks to point the direction for future marketing activities and is sent to all individuals in the organization who must implement the plan or who will be affected by it. If the plan is directed to an external audience, such as friends, banks, venture capitalists, or crowdfunding sources like Kickstarter for the purpose of raising capital, it has the additional function of being an important sales document. So it contains elements such as the strategic focus, organizational structure, and biographies of key personnel that would rarely appear in an internal marketing plan. The elements of a marketing plan for each of these two audiences are compared in the two left-hand columns in Figure A–1.
- *The kind and complexity of the organization.* A neighborhood restaurant has a less detailed marketing plan than Apple, which serves international markets. The restaurant's plan would be relatively simple and directed at serving customers in a local market. In Apple's case, because there is a hierarchy of marketing plans, various levels of detail would be used—such as the entire organization, the strategic business unit, or the product/product line.
- *The industry.* Both the restaurant serving a local market and Apple, selling electronic devices globally, analyze elements of their industry. However, their geographic scopes are far different, as are the complexities of their offerings and, hence, the time periods likely to be covered by their plans. A one-year marketing plan may be adequate for the restaurant, but Apple may need a five-year planning horizon because product development cycles for complex, new electronic devices may be many years.

In contrast to a marketing plan, a **business plan** is a road map for the entire organization for a specified future period of time, such as one year or five years.[3] A key difference between a marketing plan and a business plan is that the business plan contains details on the research and development (R&D)/operations/manufacturing activities of the organization. Even for a manufacturing business, the marketing plan is probably 60 or 70 percent of the entire business plan. For firms like a small restaurant or an auto repair shop, their marketing and business plans are virtually identical. The elements of a business plan

Element of the plan	Marketing plan		Business plan	
	For internal audience (to direct the firm)	For external audience (to raise capital)	For internal audience (to direct the firm)	For external audience (to raise capital)
1. Executive summary	✓	✓	✓	✓
2. Description of company		✓		✓
3. Strategic plan/focus		✓		✓
4. Situation analysis	✓	✓	✓	✓
5. Market-product focus	✓	✓	✓	✓
6. Marketing program strategy and tactics	✓	✓	✓	✓
7. R&D and operations program			✓	✓
8. Financial projections	✓	✓	✓	✓
9. Organizational structure			✓	✓
10. Implementation plan	✓	✓	✓	✓
11. Evaluation	✓		✓	
Appendix A: Biographies of key personnel		✓		✓
Appendix B, etc.: Details on other topics	✓	✓	✓	✓

FIGURE A–1

Elements in typical marketing and business plans targeted at different audiences.

marketing plan
A road map for the marketing actions of an organization for a specified future time period, such as one year or five years.

business plan
A road map for the entire organization for a specified future period of time, such as one year or five years.

typically targeted at internal and external audiences appear in the two right-hand columns in Figure A–1.

The Most-Asked Questions by Outside Audiences

Lenders and prospective investors reading a business plan or a marketing plan that is used to seek new capital are probably the toughest audiences to satisfy. Their most-asked questions include the following:

1. Is the business or marketing idea valid?
2. Is there something unique or distinctive about the product or service that separates it from substitutes and competitors?
3. Is there a clear market for the product or service?
4. Are the financial projections realistic and healthy?
5. Are the key management and technical personnel capable, and do they have a track record in the industry within which they must compete?
6. Does the plan clearly describe how those providing capital will get their money back and make a profit?

Rhonda Abrams, author of books on writing business plans, observes, "Although you may spend five months preparing your plan, the cold, hard fact is that an investor or lender can dismiss it in less than five minutes. If you don't make a positive impression in those critical first five minutes, your plan will be rejected."[4] While her comments apply to plans seeking to raise capital, the first five questions listed above apply equally well to plans prepared for internal audiences.

Writing and Style Suggestions

There are no magic one-size-fits-all guidelines for writing successful marketing and business plans. Still, the following writing and style guidelines generally apply:[5]

- Use a direct, professional writing style. Use appropriate business terms without jargon. Present and future tenses with active voice ("I will write an effective marketing plan") are generally better than past tense and passive voice ("An effective marketing plan was written by me").

- Be positive and specific to convey potential success. At the same time, avoid superlatives ("terrific," "wonderful"). Specifics are better than glittering generalities.
- Use numbers for impact, justifying projections with reasonable quantitative assumptions, where possible.
- Use bullet points for succinctness and emphasis. As with the list you are reading, bullets enable key points to be highlighted effectively.
- Use A-level (the first level) and B-level (the second level) headings under the numbered section headings to help readers make easy transitions from one topic to another. This also forces the writer to organize the plan more carefully.
- Use visuals where appropriate. Photos, illustrations, graphs, and charts enable massive amounts of information to be presented succinctly.
- Shoot for a plan 15 to 35 pages in length, not including financial projections and appendices. An uncomplicated small business may require only 15 pages, while a high-technology start-up may require more than 35 pages.
- Use care in layout, design, and presentation. Use 11- or 12-point type (you are now reading 10-point type) in the text. Use a serif type (with "feet," like that you are reading now) in the text because it is easier to read, and sans serif (without "feet") in graphs and charts like Figure A–1. A bound report with a nice cover and a clear title page adds professionalism.

These guidelines are used, where possible, in the sample marketing plan that follows.

SAMPLE FIVE-YEAR MARKETING PLAN FOR PARADISE KITCHENS, INC.

To help interpret the marketing plan for Paradise Kitchens, Inc. that follows, we will describe the company and suggest some guidelines for interpreting the plan.[6]

Background on Paradise Kitchens, Inc.

Randall and Leah Peters have over 40 years of food industry experience with General Foods and Pillsbury, with a number of diverse responsibilities. With these backgrounds and their savings, they co-founded Paradise Kitchens, Inc. to produce and market a new line of high-quality frozen chili products.

Interpreting the Marketing Plan

The marketing plan that follows, based on an actual Paradise Kitchens plan, is directed at an external audience (see Figure A–1). For simplicity, let us assume it is early 2019, the Peters have company data through 2018, and they are developing a five-year marketing plan through 2023. Some details and dates have been altered, but the basic logic of the plan has been kept.

Notes in the margins next to the Paradise Kitchens plan fall into two categories:

1. *Substantive notes* are in blue boxes. These notes explain the significance of an element in the marketing plan and are keyed to chapter references in this textbook.
2. *Writing style, format, and layout notes* are in red boxes and explain the editorial or visual rationale for the element.

A word of encouragement: Writing an effective marketing plan is hard but also challenging and satisfying work. Dozens of the authors' students have used effective marketing plans they wrote for class in their interviewing portfolio to show prospective employers what they could do and to help them get their first job.

Color-Coding Legend

Blue boxes explain significance of marketing plan elements.

Red boxes give writing style, format, and layout guidelines.

> The Table of Contents provides quick access to the topics in the plan, usually organized by section and subsection headings.

> Seen by many experts as the single most important element in the plan, the two-page Executive Summary "sells" the plan to readers through its clarity and brevity. For space reasons, it is not shown here, but the Building Your Marketing Plan exercise at the end of Chapter 2 asks the reader to write an Executive Summary for this plan.

> The Company Description highlights the recent history and recent successes of the organization.

> The Strategic Focus and Plan sets the strategic direction for the entire organization, a direction with which proposed actions of the marketing plan must be consistent. This section is not included in all marketing plans. See Chapter 2.

> The qualitative Mission statement focuses the activities of Paradise Kitchens for the stakeholder groups to be served. See Chapter 2.

FIVE-YEAR MARKETING PLAN
Paradise Kitchens,® Inc.

Table of Contents

1. Executive Summary

2. Company Description

Paradise Kitchens,® Inc. was started by co-founders Randall F. Peters and Leah E. Peters to develop and market Howlin' Coyote® Chili, a unique line of single serve and microwavable Southwestern/Mexican style frozen chili products. The Howlin' Coyote line of chili was first introduced into the Minneapolis–St. Paul market and expanded to Denver two years later and Phoenix two years after that.

To the Company's knowledge, Howlin' Coyote is the only premium-quality, authentic Southwestern/Mexican style frozen chili sold in U.S. grocery stores. Its high quality has gained fast, widespread acceptance in its targeted markets. In fact, same-store sales doubled in the last year for which data are available. The Company believes the Howlin' Coyote brand can be extended to other categories of Southwestern/Mexican food products, such as tacos, enchiladas, and burritos.

Paradise Kitchens believes its high-quality, high-price strategy has proven successful. This marketing plan outlines how the Company will extend its geographic coverage from 3 markets to 20 markets by the year 2023.

3. Strategic Focus and Plan

This section covers three aspects of corporate strategy that influence the marketing plan: (1) the mission, (2) goals, and (3) core competency/sustainable competitive advantage of Paradise Kitchens.

Mission

The mission of Paradise Kitchens is to market lines of high-quality Southwestern/Mexican food products at premium prices that satisfy consumers in this fast-growing food segment while providing challenging career opportunities for employees and above-average returns to stockholders.

Goals

For the coming five years Paradise Kitchens seeks to achieve the following goals:

- Nonfinancial goals
  1. To retain its present image as the highest-quality line of Southwestern/Mexican products in the food categories in which it competes.
  2. To enter 17 new metropolitan markets.
  3. To achieve national distribution in two convenience store or supermarket chains by 2019 and five by 2020.
  4. To add a new product line every third year.
  5. To be among the top five chili lines—regardless of packaging (frozen or canned—in one-third of the metro markets in which it competes by 2020 and two-thirds by 2022.
- Financial goals
  1. To obtain a real (inflation-adjusted) growth in earnings per share of 8 percent per year over time.
  2. To obtain a return on equity of at least 20 percent.
  3. To have a public stock offering by the year 2020.

Core Competency and Sustainable Competitive Advantage

In terms of core competency, Paradise Kitchens seeks to achieve a unique ability to (1) provide distinctive, high-quality chilies and related products using Southwestern/Mexican recipes that appeal to and excite contemporary tastes for these products and (2) deliver these products to the customer's table using effective manufacturing and distribution systems that maintain the Company's quality standards.

To help achieve national distribution through chains, Paradise Kitchens introduced this point-of-purchase ad that adheres statically to the glass door of the freezer case.

To translate these core competencies into a sustainable competitive advantage, the Company will work closely with key suppliers and distributors to build the relationships and alliances necessary to satisfy the high taste standards of our customers.

To improve readability, each numbered section usually starts on a new page. (This is not done in this plan to save space.)

The Situation Analysis is a snapshot to answer the question "Where are we now?" See Chapter 2.

The SWOT analysis identifies strengths, weaknesses, opportunities, and threats to provide a solid foundation, which is the springboard to identify subsequent actions in the marketing plan. See Chapter 2.

Each long table, graph, or photo is given a figure number and title. It then appears as soon as possible after the first reference in the text, accommodating necessary page breaks. This avoids breaking long tables like this one in the middle. Short tables or graphs are often inserted in the text without figure numbers because they don't cause serious problems with page breaks.

Effective tables seek to summarize a large amount of information in a short amount of space.

4. Situation Analysis

This situation analysis starts with a snapshot of the current environment in which Paradise Kitchens finds itself by providing a brief SWOT (strengths, weaknesses, opportunities, threats) analysis. After this overview, the analysis probes ever-finer levels of detail: industry, competitors, company, and consumers.

SWOT Analysis

Figure 1 shows the internal and external factors affecting the market opportunities for Paradise Kitchens. Stated briefly, this SWOT analysis highlights the great strides taken by the company since its products first appeared on grocers' shelves.

Figure 1. SWOT Analysis for Paradise Kitchens

Internal Factors	Strengths	Weaknesses
Management	Experienced and entrepreneurial management and board	Small size can restrict options
Offerings	Unique, high-quality, high-price products	Many lower-quality, lower-price competitors
Marketing	Distribution in three markets with excellent consumer acceptance	No national awareness or distribution; restricted shelf space in the freezer section
Personnel	Good workforce, though small; little turnover	Big gap if key employee leaves
Finance	Excellent growth in sales revenues	Limited resources may restrict growth opportunities when compared to giant competitors
Manufacturing	Sole supplier ensures high quality	Lack economies of scale of huge competitors
R&D	Continuing efforts to ensure quality in delivered products	Lack of canning and microwavable food processing expertise

External Factors	Opportunities	Threats
Consumer/Social	Upscale market, likely to be stable; Southwestern/Mexican food category is fast-growing segment due to growth in Hispanic American population and desire for spicier foods	Premium price may limit access to mass markets; consumers value a strong brand name
Competitive	Distinctive name and packaging in its markets	Not patentable; competitors can attempt to duplicate product; others better able to pay slotting fees
Technological	Technical breakthroughs enable smaller food producers to achieve many economies available to large competitors	Competitors have gained economies in canning and microwavable food processing
Economic	Consumer income is high; convenience important to U.S. households	More households "eating out," and bringing prepared take-out into home
Legal/Regulatory	High U.S. Food & Drug Administration standards eliminate fly-by-night competitors	Mergers among large competitors being approved by government

Margin notes (left side):

The text discussion of Figure 1 (the SWOT Analysis table) elaborates on its more important elements. This "walks" the reader through the information from the vantage point of the plan's writer.

The Industry Analysis section provides the backdrop for the subsequent, more detailed analysis of competition, the company, and the company's customers. Without an in-depth understanding of the industry, the remaining analysis may be misdirected. See Chapter 2.

Sales of Mexican entrees are significant and provide a variety of future opportunities for Paradise Kitchens.

Even though relatively brief, this in-depth treatment of sales of Mexican foods in the U.S. demonstrates to the plan's readers the company's understanding of the industry within which it competes.

The Competitor Analysis section demonstrates that the company has a realistic understanding of its major chili competitors and their marketing strategies. Again, a realistic assessment gives confidence that subsequent marketing actions in the plan rest on a solid foundation. See Chapters 2, 3, 7, and 8.

In the Company's favor internally are its strengths: an experienced management team and board of directors, excellent acceptance of its product line in the three metropolitan markets within which it competes, and a strong manufacturing and distribution system to serve these limited markets. Favorable external factors include the increasing appeal of Southwestern/Mexican foods, the strength of the upscale market for the Company's products, and food-processing technological breakthroughs that make it easier for smaller food producers to compete.

Among unfavorable factors, the main weakness is the limited size of Paradise Kitchens relative to its competitors in terms of the depth of the management team, the available financial resources, and the national awareness and distribution of product lines. Threats include the danger that the Company's premium prices may limit access to mass markets and competition from the "eating-out" and "take-out" markets.

Industry Analysis: Trends in Frozen and Mexican Foods

Frozen Foods. According to recent frozen food industry reports consumers are eating out less and buying more frozen food. The reasons: as more Americans return to work they have less time to prepare meals, and there are many new, convenient, and nutritious frozen food products available in grocery stores.[7] In 2018, total sales of frozen food in supermarkets, drugstores, and mass merchandisers reached $35 billion. Prepared frozen meals, which are defined as meals or entrees that are frozen and require minimal preparation, accounted for about 39 percent of the total frozen food market.[8]

Sales of Mexican entrees now exceed $600 million. Heavy consumers of frozen meals, those who eat five or more meals every two weeks, tend to be kids, teens, and adults 35–44 years old.[9]

Mexican Foods. Currently, Mexican foods such as burritos, enchiladas, and tacos are used in two-thirds of American households. These levels of demand reflect a general trend toward spicy foods that include red chili peppers. The growing Hispanic population in the United States, over 57 million people with about $1.4 trillion in purchasing power, partly explains the increasing demand for Mexican food. Hispanic purchasing power is projected to be more than $1.7 trillion in 2020.[10]

Competitor Analysis: The Chili Market

The chili market represents over $500 million in annual sales. On average, consumers buy five to six servings annually, according to the NPD Group. The products fall primarily into two groups: canned chili (75 percent of sales) and dry chili (25 percent of sales).

Bluntly put, the major disadvantage of the segment's dominant product, canned chili, is that it does not taste very good. A taste test described in an issue of *Consumer Reports* magazine ranked 26 canned chili products "poor" to "fair" in overall sensory quality. The study concluded, "Chili doesn't have to be hot to be good. But really good chili, hot or mild, doesn't come out of a can."[11]

Company Analysis

The husband-and-wife team that co-founded Paradise Kitchens, Inc. has 44 years of experience between them in the food-processing business. Both have played key roles in the management of the Pillsbury Company. They are being advised by a highly seasoned group of business professionals, who have extensive understanding of the requirements for new-product development.

The Company now uses a single outside producer with which it works closely to maintain the consistently high quality required in its products. The greater volume has increased production efficiencies, resulting in a steady decrease in the cost of goods sold.

Customer Analysis

In terms of customer analysis, this section describes (1) the characteristics of customers expected to buy Howlin' Coyote products and (2) health and nutrition concerns of Americans today.

Customer Characteristics. Demographically, chili products in general are purchased by consumers representing a broad range of socioeconomic backgrounds. Howlin' Coyote chili is purchased chiefly by consumers who have achieved higher levels of education and whose income is $50,000 and higher. These consumers represent 50 percent of canned and dry mix chili users.

The household buying Howlin' Coyote has one to three people in it. Among married couples, Howlin' Coyote is predominantly bought by households in which both spouses work. While women are a majority of the buyers, single men represent a significant segment.

Because the chili offers a quick way to make a tasty meal, the product's biggest users tend to be those most pressed for time. Howlin' Coyote's premium pricing also means that its purchasers are skewed toward the higher end of the income range. Buyers range in age from 25 to 54 years old and often live in the western United States where spicy foods are more readily eaten.

The five Howlin' Coyote entrees offer a quick, tasty meal with high-quality ingredients.

Health and Nutrition Concerns. Coverage of food issues in the U.S. media is often erratic and occasionally alarmist. Because Americans are concerned about their diets, studies from organizations of widely varying credibility frequently receive significant attention from the major news organizations. For instance, a study of fat levels of movie popcorn was reported in all the major media. Similarly, studies on the healthfulness of Mexican food have received prominent play in print and broadcast reports. The high caloric levels of much Mexican and Southwestern-style food have been widely reported and often exaggerated. Some Mexican frozen-food competitors, such as Don Miguel, Mission Foods, Ruiz Foods, and José Olé, plan to offer or have recently offered more "carb-friendly" and "fat-friendly" products in response to this concern.

Howlin' Coyote is already lower in calories, fat, and sodium than its competitors, and those qualities are not currently being stressed in its promotions. Instead, in the space and time available for promotions, Howlin' Coyote's taste, convenience, and flexibility are stressed.

5. Market-Product Focus

This section describes the five-year marketing and product objectives for Paradise Kitchens and the target markets, points of difference, and positioning of its lines of Howlin' Coyote chilies.

Marketing and Product Objectives

Howlin' Coyote's marketing intent is to take full advantage of its brand potential while building a base from which other revenue sources can be mined—both in and out of the retail grocery business. These are detailed in four areas below:

- *Current markets.* Current markets will be grown by expanding brand and flavor distribution at the retail level. In addition, same-store sales will be grown by increasing consumer awareness and repeat purchases, thereby leading to the more efficient broker/warehouse distribution channel.
- *New markets.* By the end of Year 5, the chili, salsa, burrito, and enchilada business will be expanded to a total of 20 metropolitan areas, which represent 53 percent of the 38 major U.S. metropolitan markets. This will represent 70 percent of U.S. food store sales.
- *Food service.* Food service sales will include chili products and smothering sauces. Sales are expected to reach $693,000 by the end of Year 3 and $1.5 million by the end of Year 5.
- *New products.* Howlin' Coyote's brand presence will be expanded at the retail

level through the addition of new products in the frozen-foods section. This will be accomplished through new-product concept screening in Year 1 to identify new potential products. These products will be brought to market in Years 2 and 3.

Target Markets

The primary target market for Howlin' Coyote products is households with one to three people, where often both adults work, and with individual income typically above $50,000 per year. These households contain more experienced, adventurous consumers of Southwestern/Mexican food and want premium quality products.

To help buyers see the many different uses for Howlin' Coyote chili, recipes are even printed on the *inside* of the packages.

Points of Difference

The "points of difference"—characteristics that make Howlin' Coyote chilies unique relative to competitors—fall into three important areas:

- *Unique taste and convenience.* No known competitor offers a high-quality, "authentic" frozen chili in a range of flavors. And no existing chili has the same combination of quick preparation and home-style taste that Howlin' Coyote does.
- *Taste trends.* The American palate is increasingly intrigued by hot spices. In response to this trend, Howlin' Coyote brands offer more "kick" than most other prepared chilies.
- *Premium packaging.* Howlin' Coyote's packaging graphics convey the unique, high-quality product contained inside and the product's nontraditional positioning.

Positioning

In the past, chili products have been either convenient or tasty, but not both. Howlin' Coyote pairs these two desirable characteristics to obtain a positioning in consumers' minds as very high-quality "authentic Southwestern/Mexican tasting" chilies that can be prepared easily and quickly.

> Everything that has gone before in the marketing plan sets the stage for the marketing mix actions—the four Ps—covered in the marketing program. See Chapters 9 through 18.

> This section describes in detail three key elements of the company's product strategy: the product line, its quality and how this is achieved, and its "cutting edge" packaging. See Chapters 9 and 10.

> This Price Strategy section makes the company's price point very clear, along with its price position relative to potential substitutes. When appropriate and when space permits, this section might contain a break-even analysis. See Chapter 11.

> This "introductory overview" sentence tells the reader the topics covered in the section—in this case in-store demonstrations, recipes, and cents-off coupons. While this sentence may be omitted in short memos or plans, it helps readers see where the text is leading. These sentences are used throughout this plan. This textbook also generally uses these introductory overview sentences to aid your comprehension.

6. Marketing Program

The four marketing mix elements of the Howlin' Coyote chili marketing program are detailed below. Note that "chile" is the vegetable and "chili" is the dish.

Product Strategy

After first summarizing the product line, this section describes Howlin' Coyote's approach to product quality and packaging.

Product Line. Howlin' Coyote chili, retailing for $3.99 for an 11-ounce serving, is available in five flavors: Green Chile Chili, Red Chile Chili, Beef and Black Bean Chili, Chicken Chunk Chili, and Mean Bean Chili.

Unique Product Quality. The flavoring systems of the Howlin' Coyote chilies are proprietary. The products' tastiness is due to extra care lavished upon the ingredients during production. The ingredients used are of unusually high quality. Meats are low-fat cuts and are fresh, not frozen, to preserve cell structure and moistness. Chilies are fire-roasted for fresher taste. Tomatoes and vegetables are of select quality. No preservatives or artificial flavors are used.

Packaging. Reflecting the "cutting edge" marketing strategy of its producers, Howlin' Coyote bucks conventional wisdom in its packaging. It specifically avoids placing predictable photographs of the product on its containers. Instead, Howlin' Coyote's package shows a southwestern motif that communicates the product's out-of-the-ordinary positioning. As noted earlier, both women and men represent significant segments of actual purchasers of Howlin' Coyote Chili. The southwestern motif on the packaging is deliberately designed to appeal to both women and men.

The southwestern motif makes Howlin' Coyote's packages stand out in a supermarket's freezer case.

Price Strategy

At a $3.99 retail price for an 11-ounce package. Howlin' Coyote chili is priced comparably to the other frozen offerings but higher than the canned and dried chili varieties. However, the significant taste advantages it has over canned chilies and the convenience advantages over dried chilies justify this pricing strategy. This retail price also provides adequate margins for wholesalers and retailers in Howlin' Coyote's channel of distribution.

Promotion Strategy

Key promotion programs feature in-store demonstrations, recipes, and cents-off coupons.

> Elements of the Promotion Strategy are highlighted in terms of the three key promotional activities the company is emphasizing: in-store demonstrations, recipes, and cents-off coupons. For space reasons, the company's online strategies are not shown in the plan. See Chapters 15, 16, and 17.

> Another bulleted list adds many details for the reader, including methods of gaining customer awareness, trial, and repeat purchases as Howlin' Coyote enters new metropolitan areas.

> The Place Strategy is described here in terms of both (1) the present method and (2) the new one to be used when the increased sales volume makes it feasible. See Chapters 12 and 13.

> All the marketing mix decisions covered in the just-described marketing program have both revenue and expense effects. These are summarized in this section of the marketing plan.

> Note that this section contains no introductory overview sentence. While the sentence is not essential, many readers prefer to see it to avoid the abrupt start with Past Sales Revenues.

In-Store Demonstrations. In-store demonstrations enable consumers to try Howlin' Coyote products and discover their unique qualities. Demos will be conducted regularly in all markets to increase awareness and trial purchases.

Recipes. Because the products' flexibility of use is a key selling point, recipes are offered to consumers to stimulate use. The recipes are given at all in-store demonstrations, on the back of packages, through a mail-in recipe book offer, and in coupons sent by direct-mail or freestanding inserts.

Cents-Off Coupons. To generate trial and repeat purchase of Howlin' Coyote products, coupons are distributed in four ways:

- *In Sunday newspaper inserts*. These inserts are widely read and help generate awareness.
- *In-pack coupons*. Each box of Howlin' Coyote chili will contain coupons for $1 off two more packages of the chili. These coupons will be included for the first three months the product is shipped to a new market. Doing so encourages repeat purchases by new users.
- *Direct-mail chili coupons*. Those households that fit the Howlin' Coyote demographics described previously will be mailed coupons.
- *In-store demonstrations*. Coupons will be passed out at in-store demonstrations to give an additional incentive to purchase.

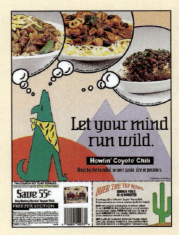

Sunday newspaper inserts encourage consumer trial and provide recipes to show how Howlin' Coyote chili can be used in summer meals.

Place (Distribution) Strategy

Howlin' Coyote is distributed in its present markets through a food distributor. The distributor buys the product, warehouses it, and then resells and delivers it to grocery retailers on a store-by-store basis. As sales grow, we will shift to a more efficient system using a broker who sells the products to retail chains and grocery wholesalers.

7. Financial Data and Projections

Past Sales Revenues

Historically, Howlin' Coyote has had a steady increase in sales revenues since its introduction in 2010. In 2014, sales jumped spectacularly, due largely to new promotion strategies. Sales have continued to rise, but at a less dramatic rate. Sales revenues appear in Figure 2.

Five-Year Projections

Five-year financial projections for Paradise Kitchens appear below. These projections reflect the continuing growth in the number of cases sold (with eight packages of Howlin' Coyote chili per case).

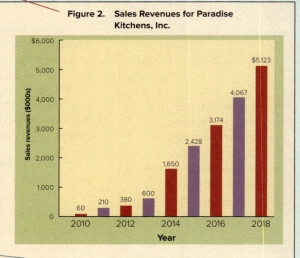

Figure 2. Sales Revenues for Paradise Kitchens, Inc.

		\multicolumn{5}{c}{Projections (000s)}			
Financial Element	Actual 2018	Year 1 2019	Year 2 2020	Year 3 2021	Year 4 2022	Year 5 2023
Cases sold (000s)	353	684	889	1,249	1,499	1,799
Net sales ($000s)	$5,123	$9,913	$12,884	$18,111	$21,733	$26,080
Gross profit ($000s)	$2,545	$4,820	$6,527	$8,831	$10,597	$12,717
Operating profit ($000s)	$339	$985	$2,906	$2,805	$3,366	$4,039

8. Organization

Paradise Kitchens's present organization appears in Figure 3. It shows the four people reporting to the President. Below this level are both the full-time and part-time employees of the Company.

Figure 3. The Paradise Kitchens Organization

At present, Paradise Kitchens operates with full-time employees in only essential positions. It now augments its full-time staff with key advisors, consultants, and subcontractors. As the firm grows, people with special expertise will be added to the staff.

9. Implementation Plan

Introducing Howlin' Coyote chilies to 17 new metropolitan markets is a complex task and requires that creative promotional activities gain consumer awareness and initial trial. Counting the three existing metropolitan markets in which Paradise Kitchens competes, by 2023 it will be in 20 metropolitan markets or 53 percent of the top 38 U.S. metropolitan markets. The anticipated rollout schedule to enter these metropolitan markets appears in Figure 4.

Figure 4. Rollout Schedule to Enter New U.S. Markets

Year	New Markets Added Each Year	Cumulative Markets	Cumulative Percentage of 38 Major U.S. Markets
Last (2018)	2	5	16
Year 1 (2019)	3	8	21
Year 2 (2020)	4	12	29
Year 3 (2021)	2	14	37
Year 4 (2022)	3	17	45
Year 5 (2023)	3	20	53

The diverse regional tastes in chili will be monitored carefully to assess whether minor modifications may be required in the chili recipes. As the rollout to new metropolitan areas continues, Paradise Kitchens will assess manufacturing and distribution trade-offs. This is important in determining whether to start new production with selected high-quality regional contract packers.

10. Evaluation

Monthly sales targets in cases have been set for Howlin' Coyote chili for each metropolitan area. Actual case sales will be compared with these targets and tactical marketing programs modified to reflect the unique sets of factors in each metropolitan area.

Appendix A. Biographical Sketches of Key Personnel

Appendix B. Detailed Financial Projections

Source: ©1996 Paradise Kitchens, Inc. All photos & ads reprinted with permission.

Appendix Notes

1. Personal interview with Arthur R. Kydd, St. Croix Management Group.
2. Examples of guides to writing marketing plans include William A. Cohen, *The Marketing Plan,* 5th ed. (New York: Wiley, 2006); and Roman G. Hiebing Jr. and Scott W. Cooper, *The Successful Business Plan: A Disciplined and Comprehensive Approach* (New York: McGraw-Hill, 2008).
3. Examples of guides to writing business plans include Rhonda Abrams, *Business Plan in a Day,* 2nd ed. (Palo Alto, CA: The Planning Shop, a Division of Rhonda, Inc., 2009); Rhonda Abrams, *The Successful Business Plan,* 5th ed. (Palo Alto, CA: The Planning Shop, a Division of Rhonda, Inc., 2010); Joseph A. Covello and Brian J. Hazelgren, *The Complete Book of Business Plans,* 2nd ed. (Naperville, IL: Sourcebooks, 2006); Joseph A. Covello and Brian J. Hazelgren, *Your First Business Plan,* 5th ed. (Naperville, IL: Sourcebooks, 2005); and Mike McKeever, *How to Write a Business Plan,* 8th ed. (Berkeley, CA: Nolo, 2007).
4. Abrams, *The Successful Business Plan,* p. 41.
5. Some of these points are adapted from ibid., pp. 41–49; others were adapted from William Rudelius, *Guidelines for Technical Report Writing* (Minneapolis: University of Minnesota, undated). See also William Strunk Jr. and E. B. White, *The Elements of Style,* 4th ed. (Needham Heights, MA: Allyn & Bacon, 2000).
6. Personal interviews with Randall F. and Leah E. Peters, Paradise Kitchens, Inc.
7. "Frozen Food Production: US Market Research Report," *IBISWorld,* June 2018; and Demitri Diakantonis, "Buyers Chew on Frozen Food Makers as Consumers Eat More Meals at Home," *Mergers & Acquisitions Report,* March 1, 2017, p. 4.
8. Frozen Food Manufacturing Industry, *Barnes Reports: 2017 U.S. Industry & Market Outlook,* NAICS 31141, p. 17; and "Frozen Food Production in the U.S.: Market Research Report," *IBISWorld,* September 2016.
9. "Frozen/Refrigerated Prepared Foods," *Progressive Grocer,* April 2015, p. 20; and Chuck Van Hyning, *NPD's National Eating Trends,* www.npdfoodworld.com.
10. Matt Weeks and Jeff Humphreys, "UGA Report: Minority Groups Driving U.S. Economy," Multicultural Economy Report press release, March 2, 2017; Jens Manuel Krogstad, "Key Facts about How the U.S. Hispanic Population Is Changing," Pew Research Center, www.pewresearch.org, September 8, 2016; and "Hispanic Influence Reaches New Heights in the U.S.," The Nielsen Company, www.nielsen.com, August 23, 2016.
11. "The Best Canned Chili: Our Taste Test Reveals There's Only One Worth Trying," *The Huffington Post,* February 7, 2014; and "This Is Chili?!" *Consumer Reports,* October 1990, p. 688.

3

Understanding the Marketing Environment, Ethical Behavior, and Social Responsibility

LEARNING OBJECTIVES

After reading this chapter you should be able to:

LO 3-1 Explain the purpose of environmental scanning.

LO 3-2 Describe social forces such as demographics and culture.

LO 3-3 Discuss how economic forces affect marketing.

LO 3-4 Describe how technological changes can affect marketing.

LO 3-5 Discuss the forms of competition that exist in a market.

LO 3-6 Explain how regulatory forces ensure competition and protect producers and consumers.

LO 3-7 Identify factors that influence ethical and unethical marketing decisions.

LO 3-8 Describe the different concepts of social responsibility.

Fortune's Businessperson of the Year: "I'm in This to Build Something Cool!"

Fortune magazine recently named Facebook CEO Mark Zuckerberg the recipient of its Businessperson of the Year award. One of the keys to Zuckerberg's success, explains *Fortune*, is his unique ability to look into the future. He sees the world as a system and works to understand how the pieces interact and are likely to change.

Zuckerberg started Facebook in his Harvard dorm room. His vision was not just to be a company, but to connect everyone in the world. Today, with 2.2 billion users, or nearly one-quarter of the world's population, Facebook is well on its way to accomplishing that vision!

Facebook's incredible success is the result of many things, including its ability to observe and adapt to a rapidly changing marketing environment. Let's take a look at the environmental forces that influence Facebook:

- *Social* forces are changing as people look for new ways to communicate, obtain information, and offer opinions. Simple online interactions that began on desktops have migrated to mobile devices and now include communication with photos, group and video chats, and instant messaging.

- *Economic* forces also influence the demand for Facebook as the cost of smartphones and wireless connectivity declines and Internet access expands throughout the globe, making social networking increasingly affordable to more and more people.

- *Technological* advances in software integration, server speed, and data storage are making Facebook increasingly fast and convenient. New enhancements such as photo editing, 3D posts, and an app development kit also increase use of Facebook.

- *Competitive* forces such as the rivalry with Google, Twitter, and Snapchat, the ability of users to easily switch platforms, and the constant threat of new social networks targeted at specific interest groups encourage rapid expansion.

©David Paul Morris/Bloomberg via Getty Images

- *Legal and regulatory* forces also influence the growth of Facebook. The company has obtained trademark and patent rights to its name and many of its features, and it provides guidelines for and responds to inquiries about a variety of topics such as privacy, data protection, protection of minors, and taxation.

Zuckerberg's rapid responses to changes in the environment and his willingness to try new things have resulted in the world's largest social network—one that is quickly connecting the world.

Facebook in the Future

Facebook's challenge now is to keep growing by continuing to respond to changes in the marketing environment. As Zuckerberg explains, Facebook needs to "think about the next big things that we want to do." For example, Zuckerberg wants Facebook to become more intuitive and to help users answer questions and solve problems. Another change will be the development of procedures for removing "inauthentic activity" (fake accounts) and enforcing custom audience targeting requirements. In the future, when users click on "why am I seeing this ad" they'll be shown exactly how advertisers got their information. Facebook also purchased virtual reality headset company Oculus VR for $2 billion in anticipation of consumer interest in VR-based communication. Facebook is currently testing augmented reality ads in Messenger with select brands. Finally, Facebook recently announced new partnerships with Major League Football and Warner Music Group and launched Community Finder, a tool to connect female entrepreneurs with their peers around the globe.[1] Chapter 17 provides additional discussion on social networks and social media.

Many businesses operate in environments where important forces change. Anticipating and responding to changes often means the difference between marketing success and failure. This chapter describes how the marketing environment has changed in the past and how it is likely to change in the future.

ENVIRONMENTAL SCANNING

LO 3-1 Explain the purpose of environmental scanning.

Changes in the marketing environment are a source of opportunities and threats to be managed. The process of continually acquiring information on events occurring outside the organization to identify and interpret potential trends is called **environmental scanning**. Environmental trends typically arise from five sources: social, economic, technological, competitive, and regulatory forces. As shown in Figure 3–1 and described later in this chapter, these forces affect the marketing activities of a firm in numerous ways.

environmental scanning
The process of continually acquiring information on events occurring outside the organization to identify and interpret potential trends.

social forces
The demographic characteristics of the population and its culture.

An Environmental Scan of Today's Marketplace

What trends might affect marketing in the future? A firm conducting an environmental scan of the marketplace might uncover a number of key trends—from the growing popularity of brand advocates, to the increasing application of virtual reality and augmented reality, to the surging scrutiny regarding the collection and use of consumer data.[2] These trends affect consumers and the organizations that serve them. Trends such as these are described in the following discussion of the five environmental forces.

SOCIAL FORCES

LO 3-2 Describe social forces such as demographics and culture.

The **social forces** of the environment include the demographic characteristics of the population and its culture. Changes in these forces can have a dramatic impact on marketing strategy.

Demographics

Describing a population according to selected characteristics such as age, gender, ethnicity, income, and occupation is referred to as **demographics**. Three key demographic characteristics include a population profile, a description of generational cohorts, and a description of racial and ethnic diversity.

FIGURE 3–1
Environmental forces affect the organization, as well as its suppliers and customers.

The Population at a Glance The most recent estimates indicate there are 7.4 billion people in the world today, and the population is likely to grow to 9.8 billion by 2050. While this growth has led to the term *population explosion*, the increases have

demographics
Describing a population according to selected characteristics such as age, gender, ethnicity, income, and occupation.

baby boomers
Includes the generation of 73 million children born between 1946 and 1964.

Generation X
Includes the 50 million people born between 1965 and 1976. Also called the *baby bust*.

Generation Y
Includes the 75 million Americans born between 1977 and 1994. Also called the *echo-boom*.

not occurred worldwide; they are primarily in the developing countries of Africa and Asia. In fact, India is predicted to have the world's largest population in 2050 with 1.7 billion people, replacing the current largest country, China, which will have a population of 1.3 billion people. World population projections show that the populations of 42 countries, including China, Japan, Ukraine, Russia, Romania, Poland, Spain, and Taiwan, will be declining.[3]

Studies of the demographic characteristics of the U.S. population suggest several important trends. Generally, the population is becoming larger, older, and more diverse. The U.S. Census Bureau estimates that the current population of the United States is approximately 328 million people. If current trends in life expectancy, birthrates, and immigration continue, by 2030 and 2050 the U.S. population will exceed 359 and 398 million people, respectively.

Generational Cohorts A major reason for the graying of America is that the 73 million **baby boomers**—the generation of children born between 1946 and 1964—are growing older. Baby boomers are retiring at a rate of 10,000 every 24 hours, and they will all be 65 or older by 2030.[4]

The baby boom cohort is followed by **Generation X**, which includes the 50 million people born between 1965 and 1976. This period is also known as the *baby bust*, because during this time the number of children born each year was declining. This is a generation of consumers who are self-reliant, supportive of racial and ethnic diversity, and better educated than any previous generation. They are not prone to extravagance and are likely to pursue lifestyles that are a blend of caution, pragmatism, and traditionalism. This generation is on the Internet more than any other generation, and they also have become the largest segment of business travelers.[5]

The generational cohort labeled **Generation Y** includes the Americans born between 1977 and 1994. This was a period of increasing births, which resulted from baby boomers having children, and it is often referred to as the *echo-boom*. Generation Y exerts influence on music, sports, computers, video games, and all forms of communication and networking. Generation Y members are interested in distinctive, memorable, and personal experiences and are very adept at managing their lives to create a work–life balance. They are strong-willed, passionate about the environment, and optimistic. This is also a group that is attracted to purposeful work where they have control. The term *millennials* is often used, with inconsistent definitions, to refer to younger members of Generation Y. The Making Responsible Decisions box describes how millennials' interest in sustainability is influencing product offerings, colleges, and employers. According

Which generational cohorts are these three advertisers trying to reach?
(Left) Source: Merrill Lynch; (Center) Source: IHG; (Right) Source: Athleta

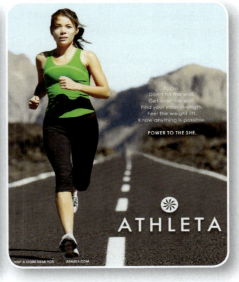

Making Responsible Decisions — Sustainability

Balancing Profits and Purpose—Millennial Style

Millennials are technologically savvy, innovative, and ambitious. In addition, they are a generation that is determined to make the world a better place. They expect brands and companies to embrace social change, corporate social responsibility, and environmental stewardship, as well as profits. This focus on a higher purpose influences their choices as consumers, as students, and as early career employees.

Some companies are taking note of millennials' interests. Procter & Gamble, for example, recently introduced fully recyclable Head & Shoulders shampoo bottles made with 25 percent recycled plastic. Similarly, Unilever has launched its Sustainable Living Plan to create "brands with purpose," Apple's new headquarters is described as "the greenest building on the planet," and Whole Foods Market makes decisions only after considering the needs of all stakeholders.

Source: Net Impact

There are approximately 17 million undergraduate millennials who expect sustainable campus communities that include LEED (Leadership in Energy and Environmental Design)–certified housing, campus transit systems, and recycling programs. Graduate students are looking for programs with sustainability electives, case studies, and potential for involvement with organizations such as Net Impact (www.netimpact.org), a nonprofit for students who want to "use business to improve the world." Sara Hochman is a typical example. She was interested in environmental issues in college, and her first job was as an environmental consultant. To make a bigger impact on her clients, she enrolled in graduate school at the University of Chicago, where she could take an elective on renewable energy and join the Energy Club.

Early career employees want "green" jobs such as social responsibility officer, corporate philanthropy manager, and sustainability database specialist. In addition they want to work at companies that advocate good corporate citizenship, responsible capitalism, and "B-Corp" status. They view themselves as part of a "positive business" movement that balances the interests of shareholders, employees, and society. Charlotte Moran, a mid-20s group marketing manager for Siemens Home Appliances, explains: "I'd find it very hard to work for a company that didn't understand its impact on the environment and didn't make an effort to change for the better."

How will your interests in being a force for good influence your education and career decisions? The world will know soon!

Generation Z
The post-millennial generation, which includes consumers born between 1995 and 2010.

multicultural marketing
Combinations of the marketing mix that reflect the unique attitudes, ancestry, communication preferences, and lifestyles of different races and ethnic groups.

culture
The set of values, ideas, and attitudes that are learned and shared among the members of a group.

Video 3-1
Colgate Super Bowl Ad
kerin.tv/cr8e/v3-1

to population estimates, millennials have recently surpassed baby boomers as the largest living generation, with 75 million people. The post-millennial generation is referred to as **Generation Z**, which includes consumers born between 1995 and 2010. They embrace the broadest definitions of diversity and inclusivity to include race, ethnicity, the LGBT community, different body types, and those with physical challenges. They lead healthy, active lifestyles, prefer a "natural" look, discover and learn online, and expect a seamless use of digital and physical aspects of the marketplace.[6]

Racial and Ethnic Diversity

A notable trend is the changing racial and ethnic composition of the U.S. population. Approximately one in three U.S. residents belongs to the following racial or ethnic groups: African American, Native American or Alaska Native, Asian American, or Native Hawaiian or Pacific Islander. While the growing size of these groups has been identified through new Census data, their economic impact on the marketplace is also very noticeable. Hispanics, African Americans, and Asian Americans spend more than $1.4 trillion, $1.2 trillion, and $891 billion each year, respectively. To adapt to this new marketplace, many companies are developing **multicultural marketing** programs, which are combinations of the marketing mix that reflect the unique attitudes, ancestry, communication preferences, and lifestyles of different races and ethnic groups.[7]

Culture

A second social force, **culture**, incorporates the set of values, ideas, and attitudes that are learned and shared among the members of a group. Because many of the elements

Diesel is making changes to appeal to women as well as men.
Source: Diesel

of culture influence consumer buying patterns, monitoring national and global cultural trends is important for marketing. Cross-cultural analysis needed for global marketing is discussed in Chapter 6.

One of the most notable cultural changes has been in the attitudes and roles of men and women in the marketplace. Some companies are moving away from traditional gender norms to avoid gender stereotypes. Target, for example, recently removed gender-based signage from its toy, entertainment, and home departments, and Disney has removed gender labels from its Halloween costumes. Fashion leader Zara introduced a line of ungendered clothing which includes sweatshirts, T-shirts, trousers, and shoes, and Calvin Klein introduced fragrance CK2 for women and men. Gender-neutral advertising is also becoming more common. Jaden Smith recently modeled Louis Vuitton's new women's line with three female models, and one of Diesel's advertising campaigns uses the tagline, "This ad is gender neutral."[8]

Another increasingly important value for consumers in the United States and around the globe is sustainability and preserving the environment. In fact, 82 percent of today's shoppers consider themselves environmentally friendly. Recent research also indicates that consumers are committed to brands with a strong link to social action. For example, Colgate's "Every Drop Counts" water conservation campaign, which included a Super Bowl ad, asks consumers to pledge to save water by turning off the faucet while brushing their teeth.[9]

learning review

3-1. Describe four generational cohorts.

3-2. Why are many companies developing multicultural marketing programs?

3-3. How are important values such as sustainability reflected in the marketplace today?

ECONOMIC FORCES

LO 3-3 Discuss how economic forces affect marketing.

The second component of the environmental scan, the **economy**, pertains to the income, expenditures, and resources that affect the cost of running a business and household. We'll consider two aspects of these economic forces: a macroeconomic view of the marketplace and a microeconomic perspective of consumer income.

economy
Pertains to the income, expenditures, and resources that affect the cost of running a business and household.

Macroeconomic Conditions

Of particular concern at the macroeconomic level is the performance of the economy based on indicators such as GDP (gross domestic product), unemployment, and price changes (inflation or deflation). In an inflationary economy, the cost to produce and buy products and services escalates as prices increase. From a marketing standpoint, if prices rise faster than consumer incomes, the number of items consumers can buy decreases. This relationship is evident in the cost of a college education. The College Board reports that since 2000 college tuition and fees have increased 160 percent (from $3,508 to $9,650) while family incomes have declined by 2 percent. The share of family income required to pay for tuition at public four-year colleges has risen from 5 percent in 2000 to 17 percent today.[10]

Periods of declining economic activity are referred to as recessions. During recessions, businesses decrease production, unemployment rises, and many consumers have less money to spend. The U.S. economy experienced recessions from 1973 to 1975, 1981 to 1982, 1990 to 1991, and in 2001. Most recently, a recessionary period began in 2007 and ended in 2009, becoming the longest in recent history.[11]

Consumer Income

The microeconomic trends in terms of consumer income are also important issues for marketers. Having a product that meets the needs of consumers may be of little value if they are unable to purchase it. A consumer's ability to buy is related to income, which consists of gross, disposable, and discretionary components.

Gross Income The total amount of money made in one year by a person, household, or family unit is referred to as **gross income** (or "money income" at the Census Bureau). While the typical U.S. household earned only about $8,700 of income in 1970, it earned about $59,039 in 2016. When adjusted for inflation, however, the income of that typical U.S. household was relatively stable. In fact, inflation-adjusted income has only increased approximately $10,400 since 1970. Approximately 51 percent of U.S. households have an annual income between $25,000 and $99,999.[12] Are you from a typical household?

Disposable Income The second income component, **disposable income**, is the money a consumer has left after paying taxes to use for necessities such as food, housing, clothing, and transportation. Thus, if taxes rise or fall faster than income, consumers are likely to have more or less disposable income. Similarly, dramatic changes in the prices of products can lead to spending adjustments. A decline in the price of gasoline, for example, often leads to increases in consumer spending in other categories. In addition, changes in home prices have a psychological impact on consumers, who tend to spend more when they feel their net worth is rising and postpone purchases when it declines. During a recessionary period, spending, debt, and the use of credit all decline.[13]

Discretionary Income The third component of income is **discretionary income**, the money that remains after paying for taxes and necessities. Discretionary income is used for luxury items such as a Cunard cruise. An obvious problem in defining discretionary versus disposable income is determining what is a luxury and what is a necessity.

---

gross income
The total amount of money made in one year by a person, household, or family unit. Also known as *money income* at the Census Bureau.

disposable income
The money a consumer has left after paying taxes to use for necessities such as food, housing, clothing, and transportation.

discretionary income
The money that remains after paying for taxes and necessities.

As consumers' discretionary income increases, so does the opportunity to indulge in the luxurious leisure travel marketed by Cunard.
Courtesy of Cunard Line

The Department of Labor monitors consumer expenditures through its annual Consumer Expenditure Survey. The most recent report indicates that consumers spend about 13 percent of their income on food, 33 percent on housing, and 3 percent on clothes. While an additional 25 percent is often spent on transportation and health care, the remainder is generally viewed as discretionary. The percentage of income spent on food and housing typically declines as income increases, which can provide an increase in discretionary income. Discretionary expenditures also can be increased by reducing savings. The Bureau of Labor Statistics observed that during the 1990s and early 2000s the savings rate declined from a long-term average of 8 percent to approximately 2 percent. That trend was reversed in 2008 when the government issued stimulus checks designed to improve the economy and, instead of spending the money, consumers saved it. Recent data on consumer expenditures indicate that the savings rate is now approximately 5.5 percent.[14]

TECHNOLOGICAL FORCES

LO 3-4 Describe how technological changes can affect marketing.

Our society is in a period of dramatic technological change. **Technology**, the third environmental force in Figure 3–1, refers to inventions or innovations from applied science or engineering research. Each new wave of technological innovation can replace existing products and companies. Maybe you've had a favorite product such as a phone or a computer replaced by an improved version. In some cases, an entire product category (think of DVDs and books) can be replaced by a completely new technology.

Technology of Tomorrow

Technological change is the result of research, so it is difficult to predict. Some of the most dramatic technological changes occurring now, however, include the following:

- Artificial intelligence capabilities will impact many marketing functions, including sales, retailing, and customer service.
- Automation will become prevalent in products ranging from autonomous cars, to delivery drones, to robots in the home and office.
- The Internet of Things (IoT) will become a reality as digital assistants such as Amazon's Alexa allow easy connectivity to all electronic devices.
- Wearable technology will take many new forms, from biometric monitors related to fitness and well-being, to visual displays for information and training, to exoskeletons to enhance personal mobility.

technology
Inventions or innovations from applied science or engineering research.

Technological change leads to new products. What products or services might be replaced by these innovations?
(Left) ©dpa picture alliance archive/Alamy Stock Photo; (Center) Source: Slack; (Right) ©Bryan Thomas/Getty Images

marketspace
An information- and communication-based electronic exchange environment mostly occupied by sophisticated computer and telecommunication technologies and digital offerings.

electronic commerce
The activities that use electronic communication in the inventory, promotion, distribution, purchase, and exchange of products and services. Also called e-commerce.

Internet of Things (IoT)
The network of products embedded with connectivity-enabled electronics.

Some of these trends in technology are already being realized in today's marketplace. IBM, for example, has partnered with Salesforce.com to use artificial intelligence to enhance Salesforce's customer service software. Amazon recently began delivery by automated drone in the United Kingdom. LG recently introduced a "connected" refrigerator that can track food expiration dates and respond to voice commands. Other technologies, such as IBM's Watson, Slack's new software, and Apple Pay, are likely to replace or become substitutes for existing products and services such as customer service representatives, e-mail, and plastic credit cards and money.[15]

Technology's Impact on Customer Value

Advances in technology have important effects on marketing. First, the cost of technology is plummeting, causing the customer value assessment of technology-based products to focus on other dimensions such as quality, service, and relationships. *PC Magazine* (www.pcmag.com) publishes an article titled "The Best Free Software" each year to tell readers about companies that give their software away, with the expectation that advertising or upgrade purchases will generate revenue. A similar approach is used by some cell phone service providers, who offer free or subsidized telephones if the consumer changes providers.[16]

Technology also provides value through the development of new products. More than 3,800 companies recently unveiled 20,000 new products at the Consumer Electronics Show held in Las Vegas. New products included wireless earbuds that translate 37 languages in real time, "wallpaper" televisions that are as thin as a credit card, and smart rings that measure the same metrics as wrist-based fitness trackers! *Better Homes and Gardens* magazine recently announced its Innovation Awards, which include anti-hacking software from Virtru, a washer and dryer combined into one unit by LG, and a 360-degree camera by Samsung. Other new products likely to be available soon include injectable health monitors that will send biometric information to a mobile monitor, such as a watch or a phone, and wireless charging systems that will send power to devices within five feet of the system.[17]

Technology Enables Data Analytics

Technology has also had a dramatic impact on the operations of marketing organizations. First, the development of online capabilities created the **marketspace**, an information- and communication-based electronic exchange environment occupied by sophisticated computer and telecommunication technologies and digital offerings.

The Internet of Things has contributed to the growth in data analytics.
©Askold Romanov/Getty Images

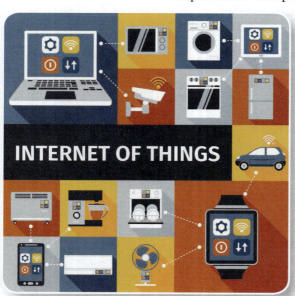

Second, these capabilities led to **electronic commerce** (e-commerce), or the activities that use electronic communication in the inventory, promotion, distribution, purchase, and exchange of products and services. Internet-based technology also allows companies to create *intranets* to communicate within the organization and *extranets* to communicate with suppliers, distributors, and other partners such as advertising agencies.

Today, technologies have advanced to allow computer chips to be placed in almost anything and to be connected to a network almost anywhere. This network of products embedded with connectivity-enabled electronics has come to be known as the **Internet of Things (IoT)**. The information generated by the Internet of Things has led to an explosion in interest in advanced analytics that can predict consumer preferences and behavior. A recent study by Forrester Research indicates that 74 percent of firms want to be "data-driven," while Wikibon Research estimates that expenditures on big data capabilities will reach $92 billion by 2026. Some experts suggest that the use of analytics is associated with success in the marketplace. Firms that have grown their revenues through analytical insights include Netflix, Google, Amazon, Dell, and eBay.[18]

COMPETITIVE FORCES

competition
The alternative firms that could provide a product to satisfy a specific market's needs.

Discuss the forms of competition that exist in a market.

The fourth component of the environmental scan, **competition**, refers to the alternative firms that could provide a product to satisfy a specific market's needs. There are various forms of competition, and each company must consider its present and potential competitors in designing its marketing strategy.

Alternative Forms of Competition

Four basic forms of competition create a continuum from pure competition to monopolistic competition to oligopoly to pure monopoly.

At one end of the continuum is *pure competition*, in which there are many sellers and each has a similar product. Companies that deal in commodities common to agribusiness (for example, wheat, rice, and grain) often are in a pure competition position in which distribution (in the sense of shipping products) is important but other elements of marketing have little impact.

In the second point on the continuum, *monopolistic competition*, many sellers compete with substitutable products within a price range. For example, if the price of coffee rises too much, consumers may switch to tea. Coupons or sales are frequently used marketing tactics.

Oligopoly, a common industry structure, occurs when a few companies control the majority of industry sales. The wireless telephone industry, for example, is dominated by four carriers that serve more than 95 percent of the U.S. market. Verizon, AT&T, Sprint, and T-Mobile have 152, 147, 75, and 53 million subscribers, respectively. Similarly, the entertainment industry in the United States is dominated by Viacom, Disney, and Time Warner, and the major firms in the U.S. defense contractor industry are Boeing, Northrop Grumman, and Lockheed Martin. Critics of oligopolies suggest that because there are few sellers, price competition among firms is not desirable because it leads to reduced profits for all producers.[19]

The final point on the continuum, *pure monopoly*, occurs when only one firm sells the product. Monopolies are common for producers of products and services considered essential to a community: water, electricity, and cable service. Typically, marketing plays a small role in a monopolistic setting because it is regulated by the state or federal government. Government control usually seeks to ensure price protection for the buyer, although deregulation in recent years has encouraged price competition in the electricity market. Concern that Microsoft's 91 percent share of the PC operating system market was a monopoly that limited consumer access to competitors' Internet browsers led to lawsuits and consent decrees from the U.S. Justice Department and investigations and fines from the European Union. A recent Federal Trade Commission investigation of Google found that although the company's market share of the online search market exceeds 70 percent, it had not harmed competition in the marketplace. An investigation by the European Union, however, is still in progress.[20]

Small Businesses as Competitors

While large companies provide familiar examples of the forms and components of competition, small businesses make up the majority of the competitive landscape for most businesses. Consider that there are approximately 28.8 million small businesses in the United States, which employ 48 percent of all private sector employees. In addition, small businesses generate 63 percent of all new jobs and 46 percent of the gross domestic product (GDP). Research has shown a strong correlation between national economic growth and the level of new small business activity in previous years.[21]

learning review

3-4. What is the difference between a consumer's disposable and discretionary income?

3-5. How does technology impact customer value?

3-6. In pure competition there are a _____ number of sellers.

REGULATORY FORCES

 LO 3-6 Explain how regulatory forces ensure competition and protect producers and consumers.

For any organization, the marketing and broader business decisions are constrained, directed, and influenced by regulatory forces. **Regulation** consists of restrictions state and federal laws place on a business with regard to the conduct of its activities. Regulation exists to protect companies as well as consumers. Much of the regulation from the federal and state levels is the result of an active political process and has been passed to ensure competition and fair business practices. For consumers, the focus of legislation is to protect them from unfair trade practices and ensure their safety.

Protecting Competition

Major federal legislation has been passed to encourage competition, which is deemed desirable because it permits the consumer to determine which competitor will succeed and which will fail. The first such law was the *Sherman Antitrust Act* (1890). Lobbying by farmers in the Midwest against fixed railroad shipping prices led to the passage of this act, which forbids (1) contracts, combinations, or conspiracies in restraint of trade and (2) actual monopolies or attempts to monopolize any part of trade or commerce. Because of vague wording and government inactivity, however, there was only one successful case against a company in the nine years after the act became law, and the Sherman Act was supplemented with the *Clayton Act* (1914). This act forbids certain actions that are likely to lessen competition, although no actual harm has yet occurred.

In the 1930s, the federal government had to act again to ensure fair competition. During that time, large chain stores appeared, such as the Great Atlantic & Pacific Tea Company (A&P). Small businesses were threatened, and they lobbied for the *Robinson-Patman Act* (1936). This act makes it unlawful to discriminate in prices charged to different purchasers of the same product, where the effect may substantially lessen competition or help to create a monopoly.

Protecting Producers and Consumers

Various federal laws are intended to protect the company while others are intended to protect the consumer. In some cases the laws are designed to protect both.

A company can protect its competitive position in new and novel products under the patent law, which gives inventors the right to exclude others from making, using, or selling products that infringe the patented invention. The federal copyright law is another way for a company to protect its competitive position in a product. The copyright law gives the author of a literary, dramatic, musical, or artistic work the exclusive right to print, perform, or otherwise copy that work. Copyright is secured automatically when the work is created. Digital technology has necessitated additional copyright legislation, called the *Digital Millennium Copyright Act* (1998), to improve protection of copyrighted digital products.[22]

Federal laws also protect consumers. Various laws address each of the four elements of the marketing mix. Product requirements, for example, are specified in laws such as

regulation
Restrictions state and federal laws place on a business with regard to the conduct of its activities.

consumerism
A grassroots movement started in the 1960s to increase the influence, power, and rights of consumers in dealing with institutions.

These products are identified by protected trademarks. Are any of these trademarks in danger of becoming generic?
©McGraw-Hill Education

Source: Federal Trade Commission

Video 3-2
Federal Trade Commission (FTC)
kerin.tv/cr8e/v3-2

Companies must meet certain requirements before they can display this logo on their websites.
Better Business Bureau. Used with permission.

the *Fair Packaging and Labeling Act* (1966), the *Child Protection Act* (1966), the *Consumer Product Safety Act* (1972), which established the Consumer Product Safety Commission to monitor product safety and establish uniform product safety standards, the *Infant Formula Act* (1980), and the *Nutritional Labeling and Education Act* (1990). Many of these laws came about because of **consumerism**, a grassroots movement started in the 1960s to increase the influence, power, and rights of consumers in dealing with institutions.

Laws also address pricing, distribution, and promotion. The *FTC Act of 1914*, for example, established the Federal Trade Commission (FTC) to monitor unfair business practices. The FTC has the power to (1) issue cease and desist orders and (2) order corrective advertising. In issuing a cease and desist order, the FTC orders a company to stop practices the commission considers unfair. With corrective advertising, the FTC can require a company to spend money on advertising to correct previous misleading promotion. Other laws, such as the *Deceptive Mail Prevention and Enforcement Act* (1999), the *Telephone Consumer Protection Act* (1991), and the *Controlling the Assault of Non-Solicited Pornography and Marketing (CAN-SPAM) Act* (2004), are designed to guide the use of direct mail, telemarketing, e-mail solicitations, and other forms of promotion.[23]

An example of a law that protects producers and consumers is the *Lanham Act* (1946), which provides for the registration of trademarks. Registration under the Lanham Act provides important advantages to a trademark owner but it does not confer ownership. A company can lose its trademark if it becomes generic, which means that it has come to be a common, descriptive word for the product. Coca-Cola, Whopper, and Xerox are registered trademarks, and competitors cannot use these names. Aspirin and escalator, however, are former trademarks that are now generic terms in the United States and can be used by anyone. Consumers benefit from the use of trademarks because it allows them to correctly identify products they want to purchase.[24]

Control through Self-Regulation

An alternative to government control is **self-regulation**, where an industry attempts to police itself. The major television networks, for example, have used self-regulation to set their own guidelines for TV ads for children's toys. These guidelines have generally worked well. There are two problems with self-regulation, however: noncompliance by members and enforcement. In addition, if attempts at self-regulation are too strong, they may violate the Robinson-Patman Act. The best-known self-regulatory group is the Better Business Bureau (BBB). This agency is a voluntary alliance of companies whose goal is to help maintain fair practices. The BBB is a nonprofit corporation that uses a Partner Code of Conduct to encourage its members to comply with its standards.[25]

self-regulation
An alternative to government control whereby an industry attempts to police itself.

There is a distinction between laws, which are society's values that are enforceable in courts, and ethics, which deal with personal and moral principles and values. The following sections discuss ethical behavior and social responsibility in marketing.

learning review

3-7. The _____ Act forbids actual monopolies, whereas the _____ Act forbids actions that are likely to lessen competition.

3-8. The Federal Trade Commission (FTC) monitors _____.

3-9. How does the Better Business Bureau encourage companies to follow its standards for commerce?

UNDERSTANDING ETHICAL MARKETING BEHAVIOR

LO 3-7 Identify factors that influence ethical and unethical marketing decisions.

Ethics are the moral principles and values that govern the actions and decisions of an individual or group.[26] They serve as guidelines on how to act rightly and justly when faced with moral dilemmas. Researchers have identified four factors that influence ethical marketing behavior.[27] Figure 3–2 presents a framework that shows these factors and their relationships.

ethics
The moral principles and values that govern the actions and decisions of an individual or group.

Societal Culture and Norms

As described previously, *culture* refers to the set of values, ideas, and attitudes that are learned and shared among the members of a group. Culture also serves as a socializing force that dictates what is morally right and just. This means that moral standards are relative to particular societies.[28] These standards often reflect the laws and regulations that affect social and economic behavior, which can create ethical dilemmas. Companies that compete in the global marketplace recognize this fact. Consider UPS, the world's largest package delivery company operating in more than 220 countries and territories worldwide.[29] According to the company's global compliance and ethics coordinator, "Although languages and cultures around the world may be different, we do not change our ethical standards at UPS. Our ethics program is global in nature." Not surprisingly, UPS is consistently ranked among the world's most ethical companies.

FIGURE 3–2
A framework for understanding ethical behavior. Each of these influences has an effect on ethical marketing behavior, as described in the text.

Business Culture and Industry Practices

Societal culture provides a foundation for understanding moral behavior in business activities. *Business cultures* "comprise the effective rules of the game, the boundaries between competitive and unethical behavior, [and] the codes of conduct in business dealings."[30] Consumers have witnessed instances where business cultures in the financial (insider trading), insurance and banking (deceptive sales practices), and defense (bribery) industries went awry. Business culture affects ethical conduct both in the exchange relationship between sellers and buyers and in the competitive behavior among sellers.

Ethics of Exchange
The exchange process is central to the marketing concept. Ethical exchanges between sellers and buyers should result in both parties being better off after a transaction.

Before the 1960s, the legal concept of *caveat emptor*—let the buyer beware—was pervasive in the American business culture. In 1962, President John F. Kennedy outlined a **Consumer Bill of Rights** that codified the ethics of exchange between buyers and sellers. These were the right (1) to safety, (2) to be informed, (3) to choose, and (4) to be heard. Consumers expect and often demand that these rights be protected, as have American businesses.

Ethics of Competition
Business culture also affects ethical behavior in competition. Two kinds of unethical behavior are most common: (1) economic espionage and (2) corruption.

Economic espionage is the clandestine collection of trade secrets or proprietary information about a company's competitors. This practice is illegal and unethical and carries serious criminal penalties for the offending individual or business. Espionage activities include illegal trespassing, theft, fraud, misrepresentation, electronic hacking, the search of a competitor's trash, and violations of written and implicit employment agreements with noncompete clauses. More than half of the largest firms in the world have uncovered espionage in some form, costing them $445 billion annually in lost sales.[31] Read the Making Responsible Decisions box to learn how Pepsi-Cola responded to an offer to obtain confidential information about its archrival's marketing plans.[32]

Corruption is a second form of unethical behavior. Corruption involves unethical conduct by a person entrusted with a position of authority, often to acquire a personal benefit. The giving and receiving of bribes, kickbacks, and gifts are the most common forms of corruption. These practices are more common in business-to-business and government marketing than in consumer marketing. In general, bribery is most evident in industries experiencing intense competition and in countries in the earlier stages of economic development or facing economic and political turmoil. According to a United Nations study, 15 percent of all companies in industrialized countries have to pay bribes to win or retain business. In Asia, this figure is 40 percent. In Eastern Europe, 60 percent of all companies must pay bribes to do business. Analysts at the World Bank estimate that the equivalent of $1 trillion is offered in bribes and kickbacks every year in the global arena.[33]

Corporate Culture and Expectations

A third influence on ethical practices is corporate culture. *Corporate culture* is the set of values, ideas, and attitudes that is learned and shared among the members of an organization. The culture of a company demonstrates itself in the dress ("We don't wear ties"), sayings ("The IBM Way"), and manner of work (team efforts) of employees. Culture is also apparent in the expectations for ethical behavior present in formal codes of ethics and the ethical actions of top management and co-workers.

Consumer Bill of Rights
An outline presented by President John F. Kennedy in 1962 that codified the ethics of exchange between buyers and sellers, including the rights to safety, to be informed, to choose, and to be heard.

Making Responsible Decisions

Ethics

Corporate Conscience in the Cola War

Suppose you are a senior executive at Pepsi-Cola and a Coca-Cola employee offers to sell you the marketing plan and sample for a new Coke product at a modest price. Would you buy it knowing Pepsi-Cola could gain a significant competitive edge in the cola war?

When this question was posed in an online survey of marketing and advertising executives, 67 percent said they would buy the plan and product sample if there were no repercussions. What did Pepsi-Cola do when this offer actually occurred? The company immediately contacted Coca-Cola, which contacted the FBI. An undercover FBI agent paid the employee $30,000 in cash stuffed in a Girl Scout cookie box as a down payment and later arrested the employee and accomplices. When asked about the incident,

©Cliff Tew

a Pepsi-Cola spokesperson said: "We only did what any responsible company would do. Competition must be tough, but must always be fair and legal."

Why did the 33 percent of respondents in the online survey say they would decline the offer? Most said they would prefer competing ethically so they could sleep at night. According to a senior advertising agency executive who would decline the offer: "Repercussions go beyond potential espionage charges. As long as we have a conscience, there are repercussions."

So what happened to the Coca-Cola employee and her accomplices? She was sentenced to eight years in prison and ordered to pay $40,000 in restitution. Her accomplices were each sentenced to five years in prison.

What does 3M's Scotchgard have to do with ethics, social responsibility, and a $200 million loss in annual sales? Read the text to find out.
©McGraw-Hill Education/Mike Hruby, photographer

Codes of Ethics A **code of ethics** is a formal statement of ethical principles and rules of conduct. It is estimated that 85 to 90 percent of U.S. companies have some sort of ethics code and one of every four large companies has corporate ethics officers. Ethics codes typically address contributions to government officials and political parties, customer and supplier relations, conflicts of interest, and accurate recordkeeping.

Ethical Behavior of Top Management and Co-workers One reason for violating ethics codes rests in the perceived behavior of top management and co-workers.[34] Observing peers and top management and gauging responses to unethical behavior play an important role in individual actions. A study of business executives reported that 63 percent had witnessed ethically troubling behavior. About 21 percent of those who reported unethical behavior were penalized, through either outright punishment or a diminished status in the company.[35] Clearly, ethical dilemmas can bring personal and professional conflict. For this reason, states have enacted laws designed to protect *whistle-blowers*, employees who report unethical or illegal actions of their employers.

Your Personal Moral Philosophy and Ethical Behavior

Ultimately, ethical choices are based on the personal moral philosophy of the decision maker. Moral philosophy is learned through the process of socialization with friends and family and by formal education. It is also influenced by the societal, business, and corporate culture in which a person finds him- or herself. Two prominent personal moral philosophies have direct bearing on marketing practice: (1) moral idealism and (2) utilitarianism.

Moral Idealism **Moral idealism** is a personal moral philosophy that considers certain individual rights or duties as universal, regardless of the outcome. This philosophy exists in the Consumer Bill of Rights and is favored by moral philosophers

code of ethics
A formal statement of ethical principles and rules of conduct.

moral idealism
A personal moral philosophy that considers certain individual rights or duties as universal, regardless of the outcome.

utilitarianism
A personal moral philosophy that focuses on "the greatest good for the greatest number" by assessing the costs and benefits of the consequences of ethical behavior.

and consumer interest groups. For example, the right to know applies to probable defects in an automobile that relate to safety.

This philosophy also applies to ethical duties. A fundamental ethical duty is to do no harm. Adherence to this duty prompted the recent decision by 3M executives to phase out production of a chemical 3M had manufactured for nearly 40 years. The substance, used in far-ranging products from pet food bags, candy wrappers, carpeting, and 3M's popular Scotchgard fabric protector, had no known harmful health or environmental effect. However, the company discovered that the chemical appeared in minuscule amounts in humans and animals around the world and accumulated in tissue. Believing that the substance could be possibly harmful in large doses, 3M voluntarily stopped its production, resulting in a $200 million loss in annual sales.[36]

Utilitarianism An alternative perspective on moral philosophy is **utilitarianism**, which is a personal moral philosophy that focuses on "the greatest good for the greatest number" by assessing the costs and benefits of the consequences of ethical behavior. If the benefits exceed the costs, then the behavior is ethical. If not, then the behavior is unethical. This philosophy underlies the economic tenets of capitalism and, not surprisingly, is embraced by many business executives and students.[37]

learning review

3-10. What rights are included in the Consumer Bill of Rights?

3-11. Economic espionage includes what kinds of activities?

3-12. What is meant by moral idealism?

UNDERSTANDING SOCIAL RESPONSIBILITY FOR SUSTAINABLE MARKETING

LO 3-8 Describe the different concepts of social responsibility.

social responsibility
The idea that organizations are part of a larger society and are accountable to that society for their actions.

As we saw in Chapter 1, the societal marketing concept stresses marketing's social responsibility by not only satisfying the needs of consumers but also providing for society's welfare. **Social responsibility** means that organizations are part of a larger society and are accountable to that society for their actions. Like ethics, agreement on the nature and scope of social responsibility is often difficult to come by, given the diversity of values present in different societal, business, and corporate cultures.

Three Concepts of Social Responsibility

There are three concepts of social responsibility: (1) profit responsibility, (2) stakeholder responsibility, and (3) societal responsibility.

Profit Responsibility *Profit responsibility* holds that companies have a simple duty: to maximize profits for their owners or stockholders. This view is expressed by Nobel Laureate Milton Friedman, who said, "There is one and only one social responsibility of business—to use its resources and engage in activities designed to increase its profits so long as it stays within the rules of the game, which is to say, engages in open and free competition without deception or fraud."[38]

Stakeholder Responsibility Criticism of the profit view has led to a broader concept of social responsibility. *Stakeholder responsibility* focuses on the obligations an organization has to those who can affect achievement of its objectives. These constituencies include consumers, employees, suppliers, and distributors. Failure to consider a company's broader constituencies when making decisions can have dire consequences. For example, Volkswagen AG was widely criticized for employing sophisticated software on selected Volkswagen, Audi, and Porsche models that impaired its diesel emission devices required by the U.S. Environmental Protection Agency.[39] Volkswagen AG executives admitted that the company engaged in emissions deception practices and agreed to pay up to $25 billion in settlement fees.[40]

Societal Responsibility An even broader concept of social responsibility has emerged in recent years. *Societal responsibility* refers to obligations that organizations have (1) to the preservation of the ecological environment and (2) to the general public. Emphasis is placed on the *triple bottom line*—recognition of the need for organizations to improve the state of people, the planet, and profit simultaneously if they are to achieve sustainable, long-term growth.[41] Marketers have embraced societal responsibility through *sustainable marketing*, which seeks to meet today's (global) economic, environmental, and social needs without compromising the opportunity for future generations to meet theirs. Green marketing, cause marketing, social audits, and sustainable development reflect this recognition.

Green marketing—marketing efforts to produce, promote, and reclaim environmentally sensitive products—takes many forms.[42] At 3M, product development opportunities emanate both from consumer research and its "Pollution Prevention Pays" (3P) program. This program solicits employee suggestions on how to reduce pollution and recycle materials. Since 1975, this program has generated over 11,000 3P projects that have eliminated more than two billion tons of air, water, and solid-waste pollutants from the environment. Levi Strauss & Co. uses eight recycled plastic bottles in each pair of Waste<Less jeans, which are composed of at least 20 percent recycled plastic. This practice has eliminated millions of discarded plastic bottles from landfills and reduced the water consumed in the manufacturing process.

Sustainable marketing efforts on behalf of the general public are becoming more common. A formal practice is **cause marketing**, which occurs when the charitable contributions of a firm are tied directly to the customer revenues produced through the promotion of one of its products.[43] This definition distinguishes cause marketing from a firm's standard charitable contributions, which are outright donations. For example, when consumers purchase selected company products, Procter & Gamble directs part of that revenue toward programs that support disadvantaged youth and provide disaster

green marketing
Marketing efforts to produce, promote, and reclaim environmentally sensitive products.

cause marketing
Occurs when the charitable contributions of a firm are tied directly to the customer revenues produced through the promotion of one of its products.

A cause marketing pioneer for more than three decades, Procter & Gamble focuses on supporting disadvantaged youth and disaster relief. A successful brand campaign in partnership with UNICEF includes the Pampers 1 Pack = 1 Vaccine initiative, protecting 300 million women and their babies against maternal and neonatal tetanus since 2006.
Source: Procter & Gamble Babycare Western Europe and Unicef

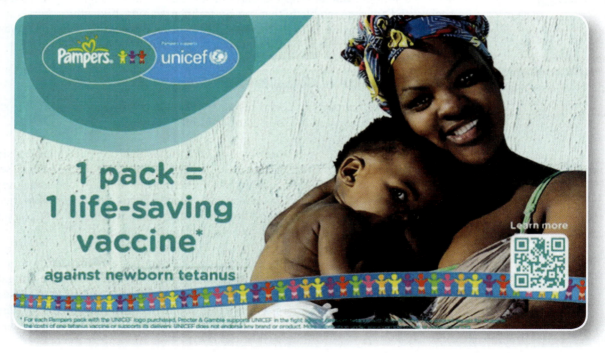

Marketing Matters > Customer Value

Will Consumers Switch Brands for a Cause? Yes, If . . .

American Express Company pioneered cause marketing when it sponsored the renovation of the Statue of Liberty. This effort raised $1.7 million for the renovation, increased card usage among cardholders, and attracted new cardholders. General Mills has raised over $780 million for schools since 1996 with its popular "Box Tops for Education" cause marketing program. It is estimated that cause marketing raised over $12 billion in 2016.

Cause marketing benefits companies as well as causes. Research indicates that 85 percent of U.S. consumers say they have a more favorable opinion of companies that support causes they care about. Also, 80 percent of consumers say they will switch to a brand or retailer that supports a good cause if the price and quality of brands or retailers are equal. In short, cause marketing may be a valued point of difference for brands and companies, all other things being equal.

For more information, including news, links, and case studies, visit the Cause Marketing Forum website at www.causemarketingforum.com.

Source: General Mills

relief. MasterCard International links usage of its card with fund-raising for institutions that combat cancer, heart disease, child abuse, drug abuse, and muscular dystrophy. Barnes & Noble promotes literacy, and Coca-Cola sponsors local Boys and Girls Clubs. Avon Products, Inc. focuses on different issues in different countries, including breast cancer, domestic violence, and disaster relief, among many others.

Cause marketing programs incorporate all three concepts of social responsibility by addressing public concerns and satisfying customer needs. They can also enhance corporate sales and profits, as described in the Marketing Matters box.[44]

Sustainable Development: Doing Well by Doing Good

sustainable development
Conducting business in a way that protects the natural environment while making economic progress.

Sustainable development involves conducting business in a way that protects the natural environment while making economic progress. Ecologically responsible initiatives such as green marketing represent one such initiative. Recent initiatives related to working conditions at offshore manufacturing sites that produce goods for U.S. companies focus on quality-of-life issues. Public opinion surveys show that 90 percent of U.S. citizens are concerned about working conditions under which products are made in Asia and Latin America. Companies such as Reebok, Nike, Liz Claiborne, Levi Strauss, and Mattel have responded by imposing codes of conduct to reduce unsafe, harsh, or abusive working conditions at offshore manufacturing facilities. Still, poor working conditions exist.[45]

Companies that evidence sustainable marketing have been rewarded for their efforts. Research has shown that these companies (1) benefit from favorable word of mouth among consumers and (2) typically outperform less responsible companies in terms of financial performance.[46]

learning review

3-13. What is meant by social responsibility?

3-14. Marketing efforts to produce, promote, and reclaim environmentally sensitive products are called _____.

3-15. What is sustainable development?

LEARNING OBJECTIVES REVIEW

LO 3-1 *Explain the purpose of environmental scanning.*
Environmental scanning is the process of continually acquiring information on events occurring outside the organization to allow marketers to identify and interpret potential trends. Environmental trends typically arise from five sources: social, economic, technological, competitive, and regulatory forces. A firm conducting an environmental scan of the marketplace might uncover key trends such as the growing popularity of brand advocates, the increasing application of virtual reality and augmented reality, and the surging scrutiny regarding the collection and use of consumer data.

LO 3-2 *Describe social forces such as demographics and culture.*
The social forces of the environment include the demographic characteristics and the culture of the population. Three key demographic characteristics include a population profile, a description of generational cohorts (baby boomers, Generation X, Generation Y, and Generation Z), and the racial and ethnic diversity of the population. Culture incorporates the set of values, ideas, and attitudes that is learned and shared among the members of a group. Notable cultural changes include the trend toward fewer differences in male and female roles and attitudes and the growing importance of values such as sustainability on consumer preferences.

LO 3-3 *Discuss how economic forces affect marketing.*
Two aspects of economic forces include macroeconomic conditions related to the marketplace and microeconomic factors such as consumer income. Indicators of marketplace conditions include GDP, unemployment, and price changes (inflation or deflation). Consumer income has gross, disposable, and discretionary components. The state of the economy and changes in income can influence consumers' ability to buy products and services.

LO 3-4 *Describe how technological changes can affect marketing.*
Technological innovations can replace existing products and services. Changes in technology can also have an impact on customer value by reducing the cost of products, improving the quality of products, and providing new products that were not previously feasible. Artificial intelligence, the Internet of Things, wearable technology, and data analytics are transforming how companies do business.

LO 3-5 *Discuss the forms of competition that exist in a market.*
There are four forms of competition: pure competition, monopolistic competition, oligopoly, and monopoly. The key components of competition include the likelihood of new competitors, the power of buyers and suppliers, and the presence of competitors and possible substitutes. While large companies are often used as examples of marketplace competitors, there are 28.8 million small businesses in the United States, which have a significant impact on the economy.

LO 3-6 *Explain how regulatory forces ensure competition and protect producers and consumers.*
Regulation exists to protect companies and consumers. Legislation that ensures a competitive marketplace includes the Sherman Antitrust Act and the Clayton Act. Companies can protect their competitive position with patent and copyright laws. Consumers are protected by laws that address each of the four elements of the marketing mix. Laws such as the Lanham Act, which provides for the registration of trademarks, benefit both companies and consumers. Self-regulation through organizations such as the Better Business Bureau provides an alternative to federal and state regulation.

LO 3-7 *Identify factors that influence ethical and unethical marketing decisions.*
Four factors (presented in Figure 3-2) influence ethical marketing behavior: (1) societal culture and norms, (2) business culture and industry practices, (3) corporate culture and expectations, and (4) personal moral philosophy and ethical behavior.

LO 3-8 *Describe the different concepts of social responsibility.*
Social responsibility means that organizations are part of a larger society and are accountable to that society for their actions. There are three concepts of social responsibility: profit responsibility, stakeholder responsibility, and societal responsibility.

LEARNING REVIEW ANSWERS

3-1 Describe four generational cohorts.
Answer: (1) Baby boomers are the generation of 73 million among the U.S. population born between 1946 and 1964. These Americans are growing older and will all be 65 or older by 2030. (2) Generation X includes the 50 million people born between 1965 and 1976. These well-educated Americans, also known as the baby-bust cohort because of declining birthrates during that time, are supportive of racial and ethnic diversity. (3) Generation Y, or millennials, are the 75 million Americans among the U.S. population born between 1977 and 1994. The rising birthrate of this "echo-boom" cohort is the result of baby boomers having children. (4) The post-millennial generation, which includes consumers born between 1995 and 2010, is referred to as Generation Z.

3-2 Why are many companies developing multicultural marketing programs?
Answer: Multicultural marketing programs consist of combinations of the marketing mix that reflect the unique attitudes, ancestry, communication preferences, and lifestyles of different races and ethnic groups. Multicultural marketing programs are being developed in response to rapid changes in the racial and ethnic diversity of the United States. The growing size of the African

American, Asian, and Hispanic populations has increased the economic impact of these groups on the marketplace.

3-3 How are important values such as sustainability reflected in the marketplace today?
Answer: Many Americans desire and practice sustainability to preserve the environment. In fact, 82 percent of today's shoppers consider themselves environmentally friendly. Consumers also prefer brands that have a strong link to social action. Colgate, for example, used a Super Bowl ad to suggest that consumers could save water by turning off the faucet while brushing their teeth.

3-4 What is the difference between a consumer's disposable and discretionary income?
Answer: Disposable income is the money a consumer has left after paying taxes to use for necessities such as food, housing, clothing, and transportation. Discretionary income is the money that remains after paying for taxes and necessities and is usually spent on luxury items.

3-5 How does technology impact customer value?
Answer: (1) The declining cost of technology allows consumers to assess the value of technology-based products on other dimensions, such as quality, service, and relationships. (2) Technology provides value through the development of new products. (3) Technology enables the collection of data used in the growing field of data analytics.

3-6 In pure competition there are a _____ number of sellers.
Answer: large

3-7 The _____ Act forbids actual monopolies, whereas the _____ Act forbids actions that are likely to lessen competition.
Answer: Sherman Antitrust; Clayton

3-8 The Federal Trade Commission (FTC) monitors _____.
Answer: unfair business practices

3-9 How does the Better Business Bureau encourage companies to follow its standards for commerce?
Answer: The Better Business Bureau (BBB) uses a Partner Code of Conduct to encourage members to comply with its standards. Companies, which join the BBB voluntarily, must agree to follow these standards before they are allowed to display the BBB Accredited Business logo.

3-10 What rights are included in the Consumer Bill of Rights?
Answer: The Consumer Bill of Rights (1962) codified the ethics of exchange between buyers and sellers. These are the rights to safety, to be informed, to choose, and to be heard.

3-11 Economic espionage includes what kinds of activities?
Answer: Economic espionage is the illegal and unethical clandestine collection of trade secrets or proprietary information about a company's competitors. This practice includes trespassing, theft, fraud, misrepresentation, wiretapping, searching of competitors' trash, and violations of written and implicit employment agreements with noncompete clauses.

3-12 What is meant by moral idealism?
Answer: Moral idealism is a personal moral philosophy that considers certain individual rights or duties as universal, regardless of the outcome; it is the philosophy embodied in the Consumer Bill of Rights and favored by consumer interest groups.

3-13 What is meant by social responsibility?
Answer: Social responsibility means that organizations are part of a larger society and are accountable to that society for their actions. It comprises three concepts: (1) profit responsibility—maximizing profits for the organization's owners or shareholders; (2) stakeholder responsibility—focusing on the obligations of the organization to those who can affect the achievement of its objectives; and (3) societal responsibility—focusing on the obligations of the organization to the preservation of the ecological environment and to the general public.

3-14 Marketing efforts to produce, promote, and reclaim environmentally sensitive products are called _____.
Answer: green marketing

3-15 What is sustainable development?
Answer: Sustainable development involves conducting business in such a way that protects the natural environment while making economic progress. Green marketing is an ecological example of such an initiative.

FOCUSING ON KEY TERMS

- baby boomers p. 75
- cause marketing p. 88
- code of ethics p. 86
- competition p. 81
- Consumer Bill of Rights p. 85
- consumerism p. 83
- culture p. 76
- demographics p. 74
- discretionary income p. 78
- disposable income p. 78
- economy p. 77
- electronic commerce p. 80
- environmental scanning p. 74
- ethics p. 84
- Generation X p. 75
- Generation Y p. 75
- Generation Z p. 76
- green marketing p. 88
- gross income p. 78
- Internet of Things (IoT) p. 80
- marketspace p. 80
- moral idealism p. 86
- multicultural marketing p. 76
- regulation p. 82
- self-regulation p. 83
- social forces p. 74
- social responsibility p. 87
- sustainable development p. 89
- technology p. 79
- utilitarianism p. 87

APPLYING MARKETING KNOWLEDGE

1. For many years Gerber has manufactured baby food in small, single-sized containers. In conducting an environmental scan, (*a*) identify three trends or factors that might significantly affect this company's future business, and (*b*) propose how Gerber might respond to these changes.

2. Describe the new features you would add to an automobile designed for consumers in the 55+ age group. In what magazines would you advertise to appeal to this target market?

3. New technologies are continuously improving and replacing existing products. Although technological

change is often difficult to predict, suggest how the following companies and products might be affected by the Internet and digital technologies: (*a*) Timex watches, (*b*) American Airlines, and (*c*) the Metropolitan Museum of Art.
4 Why would Xerox be concerned about its name becoming generic?
5 Develop a "Code of Business Practices" for a new online vitamin store. Does your code address advertising? Privacy? Use by children? Why is self-regulation important?
6 Compare and contrast moral idealism and utilitarianism as alternative personal moral philosophies.
7 How would you evaluate Milton Friedman's view of the social responsibility of a firm?

BUILDING YOUR MARKETING PLAN

Your marketing plan will include a situation analysis based on internal and external factors that are likely to affect your marketing program.

1 To summarize information about external factors, create a table and identify three trends related to each of the five forces (social, economic, technological, competitive, and regulatory) that relate to your product or service.

2 When your table is completed, describe how each of the trends represents an opportunity or a threat for your business.

Your plan should also identify any ethical or social responsibility issues related to potential stakeholders such as shareholders, suppliers, employees, customers, and society in general.

VIDEO CASE 3 Toyota: Where the Future Is Available Today

Video 3-3
Toyota Video Case
kerin.tv/cr8e/v3-3

Akio Toyoda, president of Toyota Motor Corporation, recently announced, "It's my goal to transition Toyota from an automobile company to a mobility company." What exactly does that mean? According to Jana Hartline, Mirai and Prius Prime marketing manager at Toyota, "It means that the days of traditional vehicle models are ending and the way we move is going to change in the future. We are looking at autonomous vehicles, we are looking at shared transportation, and we are looking at how we help people move across their living room and across the city. It's not just about vehicles anymore, it's about how you move people and that is what Toyota is focusing on." Welcome to the future; it's already here at Toyota!

THE COMPANY

Akio's grandfather, Kiichiro Toyoda, started the company in Japan as a manufacturer of weaving looms. Research on gasoline-powered engines led to the construction of an automobile manufacturing facility and the company's first vehicle, the "Toyopet." Subsequent vehicles included the Toyota Corolla, which is still one of the best-selling cars in the world and recently exceeded 44 million purchases in more than 150 countries. Other brands were also developed, including Lexus, Hino, Ranz, and Daihatsu.

Toyota grew to become one of the largest automobile manufacturers in the world, regularly vying for first place with Volkswagen. The company is ranked number five on *Fortune*'s list of the world's largest corporations, with sales of $254 billion and 369,000 employees. In addition, Toyota ranks ninth on the *Forbes* list of the world's most valuable brands.

What factors have contributed to the company's success? First, the Toyoda family advocates an inspiring corporate philosophy:

Seeking harmony between people, society, and the global environment, and sustainable development of society through manufacturing.

This philosophy has been supported by several statements of business values. They include The Toyota Way and The Toyota Effect.

The Toyota Way

"The corporate culture here at Toyota is guided by what we call the Toyota Way," explains Rommel Momen, Mirai manager at Toyota. "The Toyota Way is made up of two pillars, respect for people and continuous improvement," he adds. The two pillars are supported by five business practices: challenge,

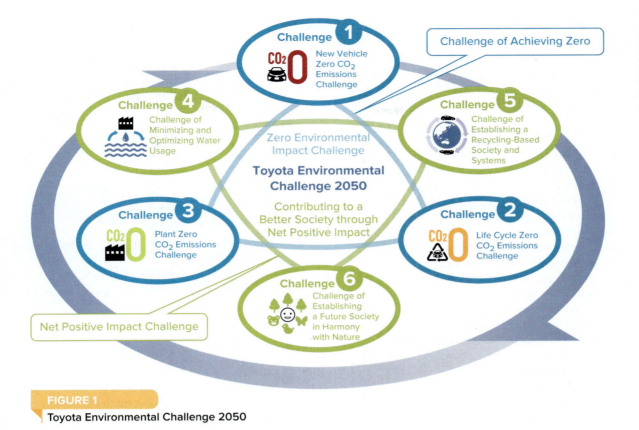

FIGURE 1
Toyota Environmental Challenge 2050

kaizen, genchi genbutsu, respect, and teamwork (see Figure 1). Momen says kaizen means "continuously improving by getting suggestions from the end user and tweaking our product to make it better and better," and genchi genbutsu means to "go look and see, go to the source, talk to the consumer, and use your own eyes, feelings, and experiences to make a great and successful product." He adds, "We try to make sure that all parties are in agreement with a strategy so that we are more cohesive, work better as a team, and show respect for people."

The Toyota Effect

The Toyota Effect describes the company's approach to creating a positive impact. According to Hartline, "The Toyota Effect is Toyota's ability to use our resources and our know-how to better society, and people, and the planet." She explains, "For example, after Superstorm Sandy, the Food Bank was having a problem fulfilling the needs of all the displaced residents, so we implemented a Toyota production system to help them package and distribute food more efficiently." Another example of the Toyota Effect is Toyota's 'Mothers of Invention' program which recognizes and supports women who are driving positive change in the world through innovation, entrepreneurship, and innovation. Toyota provides grants, networking opportunities, and access to intellectual capital as part of this program.

Today, as Toyota continues its emphasis on the environment and sustainability and transitions to a mobility company, there are a wide variety of new initiatives under way. "We have a lot of business models that we are exploring," says Hartline, "from autonomous vehicles to ride sharing." She adds, "We have all kinds of things going on around the globe where we are looking at how people are going to move from A to B in the future."

TOYOTA'S ENVIRONMENTAL CHALLENGE 2050

To guide the company's environmental efforts, Akio Toyoda launched the Toyota Environmental Challenge 2050. This global initiative seeks to reduce negative factors associated with automobiles and create a net positive impact on society and the planet. The blueprint for the future is articulated in six specific actions and includes performance benchmarks through 2050. The actions are:

1. Eliminate almost all CO_2 emissions from new Toyota vehicles.
2. Eliminate all CO_2 emissions from the manufacturing of new Toyota vehicles.

3. Eliminate all CO_2 emissions from Toyota facilities, logistics, and processes.
4. Ensure all Toyota facilities conserve and protect water resources.
5. Ensure all Toyota facilities support a recycling-based society.
6. Ensure all Toyota facilities operate in harmony with nature.

"The first three incorporate having cars that emit zero emissions, and factories that build them without any emission, and ultimately the disposal of those vehicles with zero emissions," explains Momen. "The other three incorporate the use of more biodegradable materials, the use of less water, and the overall focus to be environmentally responsible." "Corporate social responsibility means being a great steward of not just the people who work for the company but for the world," he adds.

Toyota's past efforts at sustainability have provided a good start toward these goals. The Toyota Prius, a hybrid vehicle that combines an internal combustion engine and an electric motor, for example, is the longest and best-selling vehicle of its kind on the market. "Now Toyota has 30-plus hybrid models around the globe and we are considered the hybrid leader," Hartline says. Another example of Toyota's focus on sustainability includes its investment in zero-emission and hydrogen-fueled vehicles. Hydrogen is the most abundant element in the universe and represents a future source of electricity that can be harnessed through fuel-cell technology without emitting greenhouse gases. Toyota's first hydrogen fuel-cell vehicle, the Mirai, literally means "the future."

Source: Toyota Motor Sales, U.S.A., Inc.

THE MIRAI

"Mirai is the hydrogen fuel-cell vehicle that we have on sale today," says Momen, and it represents one step toward the Toyota Environmental Challenge goals. The Mirai has a 300-mile driving range and takes only 5 minutes to refuel at a hydrogen fueling station. The technology works by mixing oxygen from the surrounding air with hydrogen stored in a tank. Then the chemical reaction creates electricity, which is used to power an electric motor. The only byproduct of the process is water, which drains out the tailpipe. Toyota has already sold more than 4,000 Mirai vehicles in California. The California Energy Commission seeks to have 5 million zero-emission vehicles, including hydrogen fuel-cell vehicles like the Mirai, on the road by 2030.

"What people don't realize about hydrogen fuel-cell technology is that when Toyota started developing the Prius, a group was also started at the same time to work on fuel-cell technology," says Hartline. "So, Toyota has been working on the development of fuel-cell technology for well over 20 years. We were looking at how we could bring this technology to market, how we could make a reliable and safe and convenient and affordable vehicle for the mass market, and that's what became the Toyota Mirai," she adds. Over the years of development, engineers have addressed issues of convenience, safety, and range to create a product that has everything consumers would expect from a Toyota vehicle.

MARKETING THE MIRAI

The many unique aspects of fuel-cell technology make the marketing planning process for the Mirai unique. Hartline offers her perspective: "Mirai is really unique right now because we're at the very beginning of this technology. It's not like marketing a Camry or a Corolla because consumers know how they work. We are trying to educate consumers about the technology and about a particular vehicle. So we worked on the marketing plan for several years prior to launch. As we developed the campaign we wanted to understand who was going to purchase the vehicle, who were our competitors, and what were the unique aspects of the vehicle. The joke at Toyota was that nothing about Mirai is normal!"

At Toyota, marketing is organized in tiers designated to specific segments. Each segment typically has specific vehicles and a senior manager, a product manager, a product planner, and brand ambassadors. Much of the marketing function is centralized at Toyota headquarters where large scale and national campaigns are managed. For example, Toyota recently ran ads during the Super Bowl that support its sponsorship of the Olympics and Paralympics. You might remember some of the ads, which feature taglines such as, "Start Your Impossible" and "Let's Go Places." Some marketing activities are also coordinated by smaller groups placed at regional locations.

Joanie Swearingen, a product planner in Vehicle Marketing and Communications at Toyota, describes some of the specific marketing activities she manages. "As a product planner," she says, "I'm interfacing with multiple event and dealer teams daily, using e-mail and our database management platform which consolidates all of our audience targeting." Swearingen adds, "So, integrated marketing is what I do each and every day." The integrated marketing programs include traditional advertising, such as the national television advertising campaigns, and many forms of social and online media. Swearingen says, "We see social media as part of online paid media," and explains, "we like to think of it holistically because the customer is seeing our communications holistically." What is her secret to success as a product planner? "I think to be successful in marketing you have to be comfortable getting uncomfortable," she reveals.

THE FUTURE OF MOBILITY AT TOYOTA

The future has many paths for Toyota. For example, the company is expanding the application of its zero-emission fuel-cell technology to heavy-duty trucks, buses, and power stations. Toyota has also invested in ride-sharing companies Uber and Grab, a self-driving car company, and the Partner Robot Group, which is developing products to assist people with visual impairments. "With all of these initiatives that we have at Toyota to try and make the environment cleaner and greener and better for everyone, we're excited and very proud to be part of this company," says Momen. Similarly, Swearingen says, "I'm really excited that I get to be part of the future and that this 'mobility for all' is just the starting point of something really great." And Hartline confirms that "Toyota is truly the mobility company for the future!"[47]

Questions

1. Describe Toyota's transition from an automobile company to a mobility company.
2. How does Toyota's corporate philosophy relate to the concepts of profit responsibility, stakeholder responsibility, and societal responsibility?
3. How does Toyota's Mirai fit with the goals of the Challenge 2050 initiative?
4. What new mobility products and services is Toyota considering for the future? What activities would you recommend for Toyota as it prepares for the future?

Chapter Notes

1. Ana Gotter, "Top Facebook Updates That You Can't Afford to Miss—July 2018 Edition," adespresso.com, July 17, 2018; Monica Maifredi, "Top Facebook Updates That You Can't Afford to Miss—March 2018 Edition," *adespresso.com,* March 21, 2018; "The 2016 Businessperson of the Year: Facebook CEO Mark Zuckerberg," *Fortune,* December 1, 2016, pp. 65–72; and Aaron Tilley, "Looking beyond Mobile, Facebook Is Getting into the Internet of Things," *Forbes.com,* March 25, 2015.
2. T. J. Kiely, "5 Digital Marketing Trends That Will Shape Your 2018," *thedrum.com,* January 12, 2018; Patricia Odell, "Top 10 Trends to Transform Digital Marketing in 2017," *Promotional Marketing,* January 20, 2017, p. 1; Hal Conick, "2017 Marketing Trends from CES," *Marketing News,* February 2017, pp. 3–4; Verne Harnish, "5 Trends to Ride in 2017," *Fortune.com,* p. 32; and Patricia Odell, "10 Disruptive Marketing Trends All Marketers Should Consider," *Promotional Marketing,* February 2, 2017, p. 1.
3. U.S. and World Population Clock, U.S. Census Bureau, August 16, 2018; and *2017 World Population Data Sheet* (Washington, DC: Population Reference Bureau, August 14, 2017).
4. Bill McPherson, "The 'Sandwich Generation' Feels the Squeeze," *Franchising World,* November 2016, pp. 55–56; and Sandra L. Colby and Jennifer M. Ortman, "The Baby Boom Cohort in the United States: 2012 to 2060," United States Census Bureau, Current Population Reports, May 2014.
5. Matthew Hennessey, "Zero Hour for Generation X," *city-journal.org,* Summer 2017; Madeline Farber, "American Airlines Dumps Gogo and Strikes Deal with ViaSat," *Fortune.com,* June 6, 2016; and Chris Matthews, "America's Most Indebted Generation, Gen X," *Fortune.com,* August 29, 2014.
6. Helena Wasserman, "Managing Millennials," *Finweek,* March 2, 2017, p. 44–45; Francine LeFrak, "How to Bridge the Gap between Profits and Purpose When Giving Back," *Forbes.com,* December 14, 2016, p. 15; Patricia Odell, "In a Nod to Millennials, Head & Shoulders Bottles Made from Beach Plastic," *Promotional Marketing,* January 26, 2017, p. 2; Richard Fry, "Millennials Overtake Baby Boomers as America's Largest Generation," Pew Research Center, April 25, 2016; Suzy Bashford, "Marketing for Good," *Marketing,* May 2015, p. 1; Alison Davis-Blake, "Educators: Teach Millennials How to Be a Force for Good," *Businessweek.com,* March 6, 2014, p. 3; "The Unilever School of Marketing for Good," *Marketing,* May 2015, p. 1; Colleen Kane, "Will Apple's New Complex Really Be the 'Greenest Building on the Planet'?" *Fortune.com,* April 29, 2015; and Andrea Van Dam, "Get Ready for Gen Z," *MMR,* June 27, 2016, p. 23–26.

7. Matt Weeks, "UGA Report: Minority Groups Driving U.S. Economy," UGA Today, March 2, 2017; and "New Census Bureau Report Analyzes U.S. Population Projections," press release, United States Census Bureau, March 3, 2015.
8. Tanya Dua, "From Coca-Cola to Barbie: The Fierce Rise of Gender-Neutral Advertising," *Digiday,* March 29, 2015; Kristina Monllos, "Brands Are Throwing Out Gender Norms to Reflect a More Fluid World," *Adweek,* October 17, 2016; Kelvin Claveria, "Ungendered: Why Forward-Thinking Marketers Are Embracing Gender Fluidity," *Visioncritical,* October 24, 2016; Sam Frizell, "Here's How Pinterest Is Trying to Attract More Men," *Time.com,* January 23, 2015, p. 1; Gillian Rich, "Can Female-Focused Lululemon Sell Yoga Pants to Men?" *Investors Business Daily,* June 14, 2013, p. 1; Elizabeth Sweet, "Guys and Dolls No More?" *The New York Times,* December 23, 2012, p. 12; and Patricia Odell, "UGG VP Marketing on Tom Brady's Impact on the Brand," *Chief Marketer,* November 29, 2012.
9. Blake Gladman, "2017: The Trends to Know," *Checkout,* January 2017, pp. 16–18; Robin M. Williams Jr., *American Society: A Sociological Interpretation,* 3rd ed. (New York: Knopf, 1970); L. Robert Kohls, "Why Do Americans Act Like That?" International Programs, San Francisco State University; Eric Pooley, David Welch, and Alan Ohnsman, "Charged for Battle," *Bloomberg Businessweek,* January 3, 2011, pp. 48–56; Edwin R. Stafford and Cathy L. Hartman, "Promoting the Value of Sustainably Minded Purchase Behaviors," *Marketing News,* January 2013, p. 28; and Katie Richards, "For Its Super Bowl Ad, Colgate Asks You to Turn the Water Off When You Brush," www.adweek.com, January 27, 2016.
10. "Tuition and Fees and Room and Board Charges over Time in Current Dollars and 2016 Dollars," College Board, http://trends.collegeboard.org/college-pricing/figures-tables/tuition-fees-room-board-time; and Bernadette D. Proctor, Jessica L. Semega, and Melissa A. Kollar, "Income and Poverty in the United States: 2015," *Current Population Reports* (Washington, DC: U.S. Census Bureau, September 13, 2016), Table A-1.
11. Azhar Iqbal and Mark Vitner, "The Deeper the Recession, the Stronger the Recovery: Is It Really That Simple?" *Business Economics,* 2011, pp. 22–31.
12. Jessica L. Semega, Kayla R. Fontenot, and Melissa A. Kollar, "Income and Poverty in the United States: 2016," Current Population Reports, United States Census Bureau, September 12, 2017, Table A-1.
13. Doug Handler and Nariman Behravesh, *U.S. Economic Environment,* IHS Economics, March 3, 2015; and Nick Timiraos and Kris Hudson, "The Demand Divide: Two-Tier Economy Reshapes U.S. Marketplace," *The Wall Street Journal,* January 29, 2015.
14. "Consumer Expenditures in 2015," U.S. Department of Labor, Bureau of Labor Statistics, August 30, 2016, Table A; and "Personal Income and Outlays," news release, U.S. Department of Commerce, Bureau of Economic Analysis, March 1, 2017.
15. Nidhi Singal, "Tech Trends 2017," *Business Today,* January 29, 2017, pp. 106–09; "5 CES Tech Trends to Look Out for in 2017," *Design Week,* January 5, 2017, p. 4; Lucy Handley, "Artificial Intelligence: A Genuine Opportunity," *Marketing Week,* May 19, 2016, pp. 33–35; Jay Greene and Ted Greenwald, "IBM, Salesforce Agree to Partner on Artificial Intelligence," *The Wall Street Journal,* March 6, 2017; Elizabeth Weise, "Amazon Delivered Its First Customer Package by Drone," *USA Today,* December 14, 2016; Adi Robertson, "LG Put WebOS and Amazon Alexa on a Fridge," *The Verge,* January 4, 2017; and Alex Davies, "Google's Self-Driving Car Company Is Finally Here," www.wired.com, December 13, 2016.
16. Eric Griffith, "The Best Free Software of 2017," *PCMag.com,* February 21, 2017; "Get Select 4G LTE Smartphones for Free When You Switch," Cricket web page, https://www.cricketwireless.com/free-cell-phones.html, accessed March 24, 2017; and Koen Pauwels and Allen Weiss, "Moving from Free to Fee: How Online Firms Market to Change Their Business Model Successfully," *Journal of Marketing,* May 2008, pp. 14–31.
17. CES website, http://www.ces.tech/Why-CES/CES-by-the-Numbers; Luke Edwards, "Best TVs of CES 2017," *www.mirrorco.uk,* January 6, 2017; Michael Sawh, "Mymanu Clik Smart Earbuds Are Coming to Translate Languages in Real Time," *www.wareable.com,* January 9, 2017; "The Best of CES 2017," *www.pcmag.com,* January 6, 2017; *Better Homes and Gardens* Editors' Choice 2017 Innovation Awards," *www.bhg.com,* 2017; and Dave Gershgorn, "The Future of Wireless Charging Is Here," *qz.com,* January 9, 2017.
18. Hal Conick, "Turning Big Data into Big Insights," *Marketing News,* January 2017, pp. 12–13; Ralph Finos, "2016–2026 Worldwide Big Data Market Forecast," *www.wikibon.com,* March 30, 2016; Marco Vriens and Patricia Kidd, "The Big Data Shift," *Marketing Insights,* November–December 2014, pp. 22–29; and Cliff Saran, "Big Data Technology Has Its Work Cut Out to Harness Web Analytics," *Computer Weekly,* May 13–19, 2014, p. 12.
19. "Number of Subscribers to Wireless Carrier in the U.S. from 1st Quarter 2013 to 2nd Quarter 2018, by Carrier (in Millions)," Statista, 2018, https://www.statista.com/statistics/283507/subscribers-to-top-wireless-carriers-in-the-us/; and "Economic Consequences of Armaments Production: Institutional Perspectives of J. K. Galbraith and T. B. Veblen," *Journal of Economic Issues,* March 1, 2008, p. 37.
20. "Desktop Operating System Market Share," *www.marketshare.com,* February 2017; Natalia Drozdiak and Sam Schechner, "Google Rebuts Antitrust Charges—Tech Firm Responds to EU Claims That It Abuses Dominance in Internet Ads, Shopping," *The Wall Street Journal,* November 4, 2016; Tom Huddelston Jr., "Google to Face Antitrust Charges in Europe," *Fortune.com,* April 29, 2015; James Kanter, "E.U. Accuses Microsoft of Violating Antitrust Deal," *The International Herald Tribune,* October 25, 2012, p. 17; and "Google Wins an Antitrust Battle," *The New York Times,* January 6, 2013, p. 10.
21. "Frequently Asked Questions," Small Business Administration, Office of Advocacy, *www.sba.gov/advocacy,* June 2016; "Small Business Trends," Small Business Administration, *www.sba.gov/content/small-business-trends;* and Kathryn Kobe, "Small Business GDP: Update 2002–2010," Small Business Administration, Office of Advocacy, January 2012.
22. "One Year Later, SOPA Activists Reignite Copyright Conversation," *CBS News,* January 18, 2013; and "Legal Roundup," *Billboard,* January 31, 2009.
23. Cotton Delo, "You Are Big Brother (But That Isn't So Bad)," *Advertising Age,* April 23, 2012, p. 1; and Ana Radelat, "Online Privacy, Postal Hikes Top List of DMA Concerns," *Advertising Age,* April 23, 2012, p. 3.
24. Dorothy Cohen, "Trademark Strategy Revisited," *Journal of Marketing,* July 1991, pp. 46–59.
25. Better Business Bureau, Partner Code of Conduct, https://www.bbb.org/en/us/partner-code-of-conduct, accessed April 3, 2018.
26. For a discussion of the definition of ethics, see Patrick E. Murphy, Gene R. Laezniak, Norman E. Bowie, and Thomas A. Klein, *Ethical Marketing: Basic Ethics in Action* (Upper Saddle River, NJ: Prentice Hall, 2005).
27. See, for example, Linda K. Trevino and Katherine A. Nelson, *Managing Business Ethics: Straight Talk about How to Get It Right,* 5th ed. (New York: Wiley, 2011).
28. Thomas Donaldson, "Values in Tension: Ethics Away from Home," *Harvard Business Review,* September–October 1996, pp. 48–62.

29. Ethisphere Institute, "2016 World's Most Ethical Companies," *www.ethisphere.com,* accessed January 3, 2017.
30. Vern Terpstra and Kenneth David, *The Cultural Environment of International Business,* 3rd ed. (Cincinnati: South-Western Publishing, 1991), p. 12.
31. "Report: Cybercrime and Espionage Costs $445 Billion Annually," *www.washingtonpost.com,* accessed January 2, 2017.
32. "Coke Employee Faces Charges in Plot to Sell Secrets," *The Wall Street Journal,* July 6, 2006, p. B6; "Do the Right Thing? Not with a Rival's Inside Info," *Advertising Age,* July 17, 2006, p. 4; and "You Can't Beat the Real Thing," *Time,* July 17, 2006, pp. 10–11.
33. "The Real Cost of Corruption," *www.forbes.com,* November 5, 2013.
34. *The 2014 National Business Ethics Survey.*
35. "The Age of the Whistleblower," *The Economist,* December 5, 2015; and *The 2014 National Business Ethics Survey.*
36. "Scotchgard Working Out Recent Stain on Its Business," *www.mercurynews.com,* accessed June 22, 2003.
37. James Q. Wilson, "Adam Smith on Business Ethics," *California Management Review,* Fall 1989, pp. 57–72.
38. Harvey S. James and Farhad Rassekh, "Smith, Friedman, and Self-Interest in Ethical Society," *Business Ethics Quarterly,* July 2000, pp. 659–74.
39. "VW Executive Is Arrested in U.S.," *The Wall Street Journal,* January 10, 2017, pp. B1, B6; "Everything You Need to Know about the VW Diesel-Emissions Scandal," *www.caranddriver.com,* December 22, 2016.
40. "Volkswagen Faces Up to Penalties," *The Wall Street Journal,* March 11–12, 2017, pp. B1, B2; and "Guide to the Volkswagen Emissions Recall," *www.consumerreports.com,* January 6, 2016.
41. Andrew W. Savitz with Karl Weber, *The Triple Bottom Line: How Today's Best Run Companies Are Achieving Economic, Social and Environmental Success* (San Francisco, CA: Jossey-Bass, 2006).
42. "3M 2015 Sustainability Report," accessed May 25, 2016; "Levi's Has a New Color for Blue Jeans: Green," *Businessweek,* October 22–October 28, 2012, pp. 26, 28; and "Walmart 2015 Global Sustainability Report," *www.walmart.com,* accessed January 30, 2016.
43. For a seminal discussion on this topic, see P. Rajan Varadarajan and Anil Menon, "Cause-Related Marketing: A Coalignment of Marketing Strategy and Corporate Philanthropy," *Journal of Marketing,* July 1988, pp. 58–74.
44. "Even as Cause Marketing Grows, 83 Percent of Consumers Still Want to See More," press release, Cone LLC, September 15, 2010; and "General Mills Celebrates 20th Birthday of Box Tops for Education with New Ways to Earn Cash for Schools," General Mills News Release, September 8, 2016.
45. "The Toll of Cheap Clothing," *Bloomberg Businessweek,* October 31–November 6, 2016, pp. 10–11.
46. "Economics—Creating Environmental Capital," *The Wall Street Journal,* March 24, 2008, Section R; Remi Trudel and June Cotte, "Does Being Ethical Pay?" *The Wall Street Journal,* May 12, 2008, p. R4; and Pete Engardio, "Beyond the Green Corporation," *BusinessWeek,* January 29, 2007, pp. 50–64.
47. This case was written by Steven Hartley and Roger Kerin. Sources: Interviews with Toyota executives Jana Hartline, Rommel Momen, and Joanie Swearingen; "Akio Toyoda, President and Member of the Board of Directors, Toyota Motor Corporation: 2018 CES Remarks," Toyota press release, January 8, 2018; Dave Leggett, "Toyota Surpasses 3,000 Mirai Hydrogen Fuel Cell Vehicle Sales in California," *Just-Auto.com,* January 27, 2018, p. 1; Darrell Etherington, "Toyota's Mobility Business Shifts into High Gear at CES," techcrunch.com, January 8, 2018; Robert Klara, "Why Toyota, the Car Company, Now Wants to Be Known More as a 'Mobility' Company," *Adweek,* November 16, 2017; Chris Martin and Lynn Doan, "This Miracle Fuel Has a Few Problems," *Bloomberg Businessweek,* March 12, 2018, pp. 23–25; "Fortune Global 500," *Fortune,* August 1, 2017, p. F1; Kurt Bandenhausen, "The World's Most Valuable Brands," *Forbes,* May 23, 2018; Brian Bremner, Craig Trudell, and Yuki Hagiwara, "Remaking Toyota," *Bloomberg Businessweek,* January 14, 2015; "Toyota Corolla: World's Most Popular Car," Toyota Global Newsroom, https://newsroom.toyota.co.jp/en/detail/62516/, September 5, 2013.

4

Understanding Consumer Behavior

LEARNING OBJECTIVES

After reading this chapter you should be able to:

LO 4-1 Describe the stages in the consumer purchase decision process.

LO 4-2 Distinguish among three variations of the consumer purchase decision process: extended, limited, and routine problem solving.

LO 4-3 Identify the major psychological influences on consumer behavior.

LO 4-4 Identify the major sociocultural influences on consumer behavior.

Enlightened Carmakers Know What Custom(h)ers and Influenc(h)ers Value

Who makes 60 percent of new-car-buying decisions? Who influences 87 percent of new-car-buying decisions? Women. Yes, women.

Women are a driving force in the U.S. automobile industry. Enlightened carmakers have hired women designers, engineers, and marketing executives to better understand and satisfy this valuable car buyer and influencer. What have they learned? While car price, reliability, and technology are important, women and men think and feel differently about car features and key elements of the new-car buying decision process and experience.

- *The sense of styling.* Women and men care about styling. For men, styling is more about a car's exterior lines and accents or "curb appeal." Women are more interested in interior design and finishes. Designs that fit their proportions, provide good visibility, offer ample storage space, and make for effortless parking are particularly important.

- *The need for speed.* Both sexes want speed, but for different reasons. Men think about how many seconds it takes to get from 0 to 60 miles per hour. Women want to feel secure that the car has enough acceleration to outrun an 18-wheeler trying to pass them on a freeway entrance ramp.

- *The substance of safety.* Safety for men is about features that help avoid an accident, such as antilock brakes and responsive steering. For women, safety is about features that help to survive an accident. These features include passenger airbags and reinforced side panels.

- *The shopping experience.* The new-car-buying experience differs between men and women in important ways. Generally, men decide up front what car they want and set out alone to find it. By contrast, women approach it as an intelligence-gathering expedition. Referred to as *CROPing,* women shoppers look for *CR*edible *OP*inions. They actively seek information and postpone a purchase decision until all options have been evaluated. Women, more

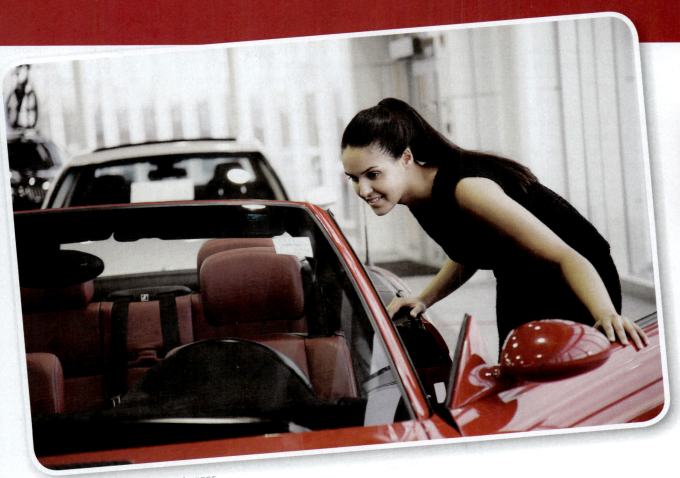
©Whisson/Jordan/Corbis/Getty Images

frequently than men, visit auto-buying websites, read car-comparison articles, and scan car advertisements. Still, recommendations of friends and relatives matter most to women. Women typically shop three dealerships before making a purchase decision—one more than men.

Carmakers have learned that women, more than men, dislike the car-buying experience—specifically, the experience of dealing with car salespeople. In contrast to many male car buyers, women do not typically revel in the gamesmanship of car buying. "Men get all excited about going out to buy a car and talk about how they're going to one-up the salesman and get a great deal," says Anne Fleming, president of www.women-drivers.com, a consumer ratings site. "I've never heard or seen any comments from women like that." In particular, women dread the price negotiations that are often involved in buying a new car. Not surprisingly, about half of women car buyers take a man with them to finalize the terms of sale.[1]

This chapter examines **consumer behavior**, the actions a person takes in purchasing and using products and services, including the mental and social processes that come before and after these actions. This chapter shows how the behavioral sciences help answer questions such as why people choose one product or brand over another, how they make these choices, and how companies use this knowledge to provide value to consumers.

> **consumer behavior**
> The actions a person takes in purchasing and using products and services, including the mental and social processes that come before and after these actions.

CONSUMER PURCHASE DECISION PROCESS AND EXPERIENCE

LO 4-1 Describe the stages in the consumer purchase decision process.

Behind the visible act of making a purchase lies an important decision process and consumer experience that must be investigated. The stages a buyer passes through in making choices about which products and services to buy is the **purchase decision process**. This process has the five stages shown in Figure 4–1: (1) problem recognition, (2) information search, (3) alternative evaluation, (4) purchase decision, and (5) postpurchase behavior.

The experience a consumer seeks (or avoids) and enjoys (or endures) at each stage of the purchase decision process often dictates whether she or he will continue or discontinue to engage in the buying process. Equally relevant, a consumer's favorable or unfavorable experience has important marketing consequences. Experience can influence consumer satisfaction, consumer loyalty, and consumer willingness to speak positively or negatively about a company, product, service, or brand.

purchase decision process
The five stages a buyer passes through in making choices about which products and services to buy: (1) problem recognition, (2) information search, (3) alternative evaluation, (4) purchase decision, and (5) postpurchase behavior.

Problem Recognition: Perceiving a Need

Problem recognition, the initial step in the purchase decision process, is perceiving a difference between a person's ideal and actual situations big enough to trigger a decision.[2] This can be as simple as finding an empty milk carton in the refrigerator; noting, as a first-year college student, that your high school clothes are not in the style that other students are wearing; or realizing that your notebook computer may not be working properly.

In marketing, advertisements or salespeople can activate a consumer's decision process by showing the shortcomings of competing (or currently owned) products or brands. For instance, an advertisement for a new-generation smartphone could stimulate problem recognition because it emphasizes "maximum use from one device."

Information Search: Seeking Value

After recognizing a problem, a consumer begins to search for information, the next stage in the purchase decision process. First, you may scan your memory for previous experiences with products or brands.[3] This action is called *internal search*. For frequently purchased products such as shampoo and conditioner, this may be enough.

In other cases, a consumer may undertake an *external search* for information.[4] This is needed when past experience or knowledge is insufficient, the perceived risk of making a wrong purchase decision is high, and the cost of gathering information is low. The primary sources of external information are (1) *personal sources,* such as relatives and friends, as well as social networking websites that the consumer trusts; (2) *public sources,* including various product-rating organizations such as *Consumer Reports,* government agencies, and TV "consumer programs"; and (3) *marketer-dominated sources,* such as information from sellers including advertising, company websites, salespeople, and point-of-purchase displays in stores.

Suppose you are considering buying a new smartphone. You will probably tap several of these information sources: friends and relatives, advertisements, brand and

FIGURE 4–1
The purchase decision process consists of five stages.

Common Selection Criteria	Brand and Model Name				
	Apple iPhone XS	HTC U12	LG G7	MotoZ2 Force	Samsung Galaxy S9
Retail price (without contract)	$999	$650	$650	$720	$720
Phone display	★★★	★★★	★★★	★★★	★★★
Audio quality	★★	★★	★★	★	★★
Text messaging	★★★	★★★	★★★	★★★	★★★
Web capability	★★★	★★★	★★★	★★★	★★★
Camera quality	★★★	★	★★	★★★	★★
Battery	★★	★★	★★	★★	★★
Composite smartphone evaluations by testing organizations	★★★ Superior	★★ Above average	★ Average		

FIGURE 4–2

Common consumer selection criteria for the evaluation of smartphones.

company websites, and stores carrying these phones (for demonstrations). You also might study the comparative evaluation of selected smartphones from independent rating agencies, such as the one shown in Figure 4–2.[5]

Alternative Evaluation: Assessing Value

The alternative evaluation stage clarifies the information gathered by (1) suggesting criteria to use for the purchase, (2) yielding brand names that might meet the criteria, and (3) developing consumer value perceptions. Given only the information shown in Figure 4–2, which selection criteria would you use in buying a smartphone? Would you use price, phone display, audio quality, text messaging, web capability, camera image quality, battery life, or some other combination of these or other criteria?

For some of you, the information provided may be inadequate because it does not contain all the factors you might consider when evaluating smartphones. These factors are a consumer's *evaluative criteria*, which represent both the objective attributes of a brand (such as display) and the subjective ones (such as prestige) you use to compare different products and brands.[6] Firms try to identify and capitalize on both types of criteria to create the best value for the money paid by you and other consumers. These criteria are often displayed in advertisements.

Consumers often have several criteria for evaluating brands. Knowing this, companies seek to identify the most important evaluative criteria that consumers use when comparing brands. For example, among the seven criteria shown in Figure 4–2, suppose you initially use three in considering smartphones: (1) a retail price under $700, (2) superior text messaging, and (3) superior web capability. These criteria establish the brands in your *consideration set*—the group of brands a consumer considers acceptable from among all the brands in the product class of which he or she is aware.[7]

Your evaluative criteria result in two brands/models in your consideration set: the HTC U12 and the LG G7. If the brand alternatives are equally attractive based on your original criteria, you might expand your list of desirable features. For example, you might decide that camera and audio quality are also important and compare the alternatives based on those criteria as well.

Shoppers routinely browse online and shop retail stores, often during the same shopping trip.
©Seb Oliver/Cultura/Getty Images

Purchase Decision: Buying Value

Having examined the alternatives in the consideration set, you are almost ready to make a purchase decision. Two choices remain: (1) from whom to buy and (2) when to buy. For a product like a smartphone, the information search process probably involved visiting retail stores, seeing different brands advertised on television and newspapers, and viewing a smartphone on a seller's website. The choice of which seller to buy from will depend on such considerations as the terms of sale, your past experience buying from the seller, and the return policy. Often a purchase decision involves a simultaneous evaluation of both product attributes and seller characteristics. For example, you might choose the second-most preferred smartphone brand at a store or website with a liberal refund and return policy versus the most preferred brand from a seller with more conservative policies.

Deciding when to buy is determined by a number of factors. For instance, you might buy sooner if one of your preferred brands is on sale or its manufacturer offers a rebate. Other factors such as the store atmosphere, pleasantness or ease of the shopping experience, salesperson assistance, time pressure, and financial circumstances could also affect whether a purchase decision is made now or postponed.[8]

Use of the Internet to gather information, evaluate alternatives, and make buying decisions adds a technological dimension to the consumer purchase decision process and buying experience. For example, 45 percent of consumers with price comparison smartphone apps routinely compare prices for identical products across different sellers at the point of purchase prior to making a purchase decision.[9]

Postpurchase Behavior: Realizing Value

After buying a product, the consumer compares it with his or her expectations and is either satisfied or dissatisfied. If the consumer is dissatisfied, marketers must determine whether the product was deficient or consumer expectations were too high. Product deficiency may require a design change. If expectations are too high, a company's advertising or the salesperson may have oversold the product's features and benefits.

Sensitivity to a customer's consumption or use experience is extremely important in a consumer's value perception. For example, research on telephone services provided by Sprint and AT&T indicates that satisfaction or dissatisfaction affects consumer value perceptions.[10] Studies show that satisfaction or dissatisfaction affects consumer communications and repeat-purchase behavior. Satisfied buyers tell three other people about their experience. In contrast, about 90 percent of dissatisfied buyers will not buy a product again and will complain to nine people.[11] Satisfied buyers also tend to buy from the same seller each time a purchase occasion arises. The financial impact of repeat-purchase behavior is significant, as described in the Marketing Matters box.[12]

Firms such as General Electric (GE), Johnson & Johnson, Coca-Cola, and British Airways focus attention on postpurchase behavior to maximize customer satisfaction and retention. These firms, among many others, now provide toll-free telephone numbers, offer liberalized return and refund policies, and engage in extensive staff training to handle complaints, answer questions, record suggestions, and solve consumer problems. For example, GE has a database that stores 750,000 answers regarding about 8,500 of its models in 120 product lines to handle 3 million calls annually. Such efforts produce positive postpurchase communications among consumers and foster relationship building between sellers and buyers.

Often a consumer is faced with two or more highly attractive alternatives, such as the choice between an LG G7 and an HTC U12. If you choose the LG G7, you might

Marketing Matters

Customer Value

How Much Is a Satisfied Customer Worth?

Customer satisfaction and experience underlie the marketing concept. But how much is a satisfied customer worth?

This question has prompted firms to calculate the financial value of a satisfied customer over time. Frito-Lay, for example, estimates that the average loyal consumer in the southwestern United States eats 21 pounds of snack chips a year. At a price of $2.50 a pound, this customer spends $52.50 annually on the company's snacks such as Lay's and Ruffles potato chips, Doritos and Tostitos tortilla chips, and Fritos corn chips. Exxon estimates that a loyal customer will spend $500 annually for its branded gasoline, not including candy, snacks, oil, or repair services purchased at its gasoline stations. Kimberly-Clark reports that a loyal customer will buy 6.7 boxes of its Kleenex tissues each year and will spend $994 on facial tissues over 60 years, in today's dollars.

These calculations have focused marketers' attention on their customers' (1) buying experience, (2) satisfaction, and (3) retention. Consider General Motors (GM), the maker of Cadillac, Chevrolet, Buick, and GMC brands. GM estimates that a retail customer is worth $276,000 over a lifetime of buying cars (11 or more), parts, and service. GM's customer retention rate is 69 percent. Also, GM estimates that its company

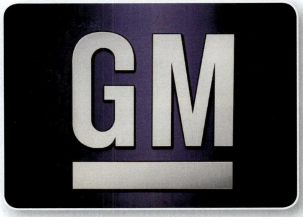
©Bill Pugliano/Getty Images

revenue increases $700 million for every percentage point that sales retention increases.

This calculation is not unique to General Motors. Research shows that a 5 percent improvement in customer retention can increase a company's profits by 70 to 80 percent.

---

think, "Should I have purchased the HTC U12?" This feeling of postpurchase psychological tension or anxiety is called *cognitive dissonance*. To alleviate it, consumers often attempt to applaud themselves for making the right choice. So after your purchase, you may seek information to confirm your choice by asking friends questions like, "Don't you like my new phone?" or by reading ads for the brand you have chosen. You might even look for negative features about the brands you didn't buy and decide that the HTC U12 smartphone did not feel right. Firms often use ads or follow-up calls from salespeople in this postpurchase behavior stage to reassure buyers that they made the right decision. For many years, Buick ran an advertising campaign with the message, "Aren't you really glad you bought a Buick?"

Consumer Involvement Affects Problem Solving

Sometimes consumers don't engage in the five-stage purchase decision process. Instead, they skip or minimize one or more stages depending on the level of **involvement**, the personal, social, and economic significance of the purchase to the consumer.[13] High-involvement purchase occasions typically have at least one of three characteristics: The item to be purchased (1) is expensive, (2) can have serious personal consequences, or (3) could reflect on one's social image. For these occasions, consumers engage in extensive information searches, consider many product attributes and brands, form attitudes, and participate in word-of-mouth communication. Low-involvement purchases, such as toothpaste and soap, barely involve most of us, but audio and video systems and automobiles are very involving.

> **involvement**
> The personal, social, and economic significance of the purchase to the consumer.

 LO 4-2 Distinguish among three variations of the consumer purchase decision process: extended, limited, and routine problem solving.

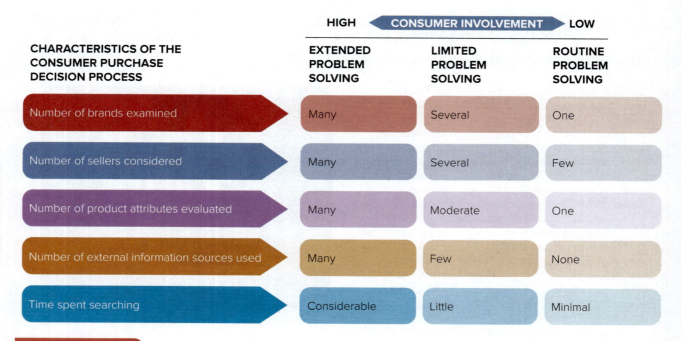

FIGURE 4–3

Comparison of problem-solving variations: extended problem solving, limited problem solving, and routine problem solving.

There are three general variations in the consumer purchase decision process based on consumer involvement and product knowledge. Figure 4–3 shows some of the important differences between the three problem-solving variations.

Extended Problem Solving In extended problem solving, each of the five stages of the consumer purchase decision process is used and considerable time and effort are devoted to the search for external information and the identification and evaluation of alternatives. Several brands are in the consideration set, and these are evaluated on many attributes. Extended problem solving exists in high-involvement purchase situations for items such as automobiles and audio systems.

Limited Problem Solving In limited problem solving, consumers typically seek some information or rely on a friend to help them evaluate alternatives. Several brands might be evaluated using a moderate number of attributes. Limited problem solving is appropriate for purchase situations that do not merit a great deal of time or effort, such as choosing a toaster or a restaurant for lunch.

Routine Problem Solving For products such as table salt and milk, consumers recognize a problem, make a decision, and spend little effort seeking external information and evaluating alternatives. The purchase process for such items is virtually a habit and typifies low-involvement decision making. Routine problem solving is typically the case for low-priced, frequently purchased grocery products.

Consumer Involvement and Marketing Strategy Low and high consumer involvement have important implications for marketing strategy. If a company markets a low-involvement product and its brand is a market leader, attention is placed on (1) maintaining product quality, (2) avoiding stockout situations so that buyers don't substitute a competing brand, and (3) using repetitive advertising messages that reinforce a consumer's knowledge or assure buyers they made the right choice. Market

What is a behavioral explanation for why Post Cereals prominently displays heart-healthy claims on its Shredded Wheat brand packaging?
©McGraw-Hill Education/Mike Hruby, photographer

challengers have a different task. They must break buying habits by using free samples, coupons, and rebates to encourage trial of their brand. Advertising messages will focus on getting their brand into a consumer's consideration set. For example, Campbell's V8 vegetable juice advertising message—"Could've Had a V8"—is targeted at consumers who routinely consider only fruit juices and soft drinks for purchase. Marketers can also link their brand attributes with high-involvement issues. Post Cereals does this by linking consumption of its whole grain cereals with improved heart health and protection against major diseases.

Marketers of high-involvement products know that their consumers constantly seek and process information about objective and subjective brand attributes, form evaluative criteria, rate product attributes of various brands, and combine these ratings for an overall brand evaluation—like the purchase decision process described in the smartphone example. Market leaders ply consumers with product information through advertising and personal selling and use social media to create online experiences for their company or brand. Market challengers capitalize on this behavior through comparative advertising that focuses on existing product attributes and often introduce novel evaluative criteria for judging competing brands. Challengers also benefit from Internet search engines such as Microsoft Bing and Google that assist buyers of high-involvement products.

Situational Influences That Affect Purchase Decisions

Often the purchase situation will affect the purchase decision process. Five *situational influences* have an impact on the purchase decision process: (1) the purchase task, (2) social surroundings, (3) physical surroundings, (4) temporal effects, and (5) antecedent states.[14]

The purchase task is the reason for engaging in the decision. The search for information and the evaluation of alternatives may differ depending on whether the purchase is a gift, which often involves social visibility, or for the buyer's own use. Social surroundings, including the other people present when a purchase decision is made, may also affect what is purchased. Consumers accompanied by children buy about 40 percent more items than consumers shopping by themselves. Physical surroundings such as décor, music, and crowding in retail stores may alter how purchase decisions are made. Temporal effects such as time of day or the amount of time available will influence where consumers have breakfast and lunch and what is ordered. Finally, antecedent states, which include the consumer's mood or the amount of cash on hand, can influence purchase behavior and choice. For example, consumers with credit cards purchase more than those with cash or debit cards.

Putting the Purchase Decision Process into Practice: Consumer Touchpoints and Consumer Journey Maps

Marketing practitioners today focus on the complete consumer purchase decision process and consumer experience.[15] Their objective is ambitious: To be present at those moments in time and place that most influence what, when, where, and how purchase decisions are triggered, information is sought and evaluated, purchase transactions are made and services are delivered, and postpurchase outcomes affect later consumer behavior. Marketers call these moments in time and place "moments of truth" because each can form or change a consumer's impression about a particular product, service, or brand.

Marketers view the purchase decision process and consumer experience through the lens of consumer touchpoints and consumer journey maps. **Consumer touchpoints**

consumer touchpoints
A marketer's product, service, or brand points of contact with a consumer from start-to-finish in the purchase decision process.

FIGURE 4–4

Apple consumer journey map and consumer touchpoints for electronic devices sold in Apple stores.

consumer journey map
A visual representation of all the touchpoints a consumer comes into contact with before, during, and after a purchase.

are a marketer's product, service, or brand points of contact with a consumer from start-to-finish in the purchase decision process. For example, consumers may see a company's offerings online, in print and digital advertisements, or in a catalog; shop for a company's products online or in a store; or call a company's customer service or technical support department. But consumer touchpoints are not always controlled by a company. Independent rating and review services and conversations with other consumers, including social media, are also touchpoints if they include reference to a company's products, services, or brands. Not surprisingly, social media posts are tracked by many marketers. Collectively, touchpoints create a consumer experience whenever consumers and companies engage to exchange information, provide service, or handle transactions.

A **consumer journey map** is a visual representation of all the touchpoints for a consumer who comes into contact with a company's products, services, or brands before, during, and after a purchase. Figure 4–4 illustrates a consumer journey map for electronic devices sold by Apple in its stores, such as smartphones, computers, and wearable technology. Representative touchpoints are shown along with the underlying consumer purchase decision process stages. A consumer journey map also shows what, when, and where different touchpoints play a central role before, during, and after a purchase. In this regard, consumer journey maps can locate and illuminate "pain points" that detract from a consumer experience. A website that is difficult to navigate is a pain point, with severe consequences. Research indicates that consumers will abandon a website that is difficult to navigate after eight seconds.

Figure 4–5 shows the many influences that affect the consumer purchase decision process. In addition to situational influences, the decision to buy a product also involves and is affected by important psychological and sociocultural influences. These two influences are covered in the remainder of this chapter. Marketing mix influences are described later in Part 4 of the book. Chapter 14 elaborates on consumer behavior in the context of online information search and buying.

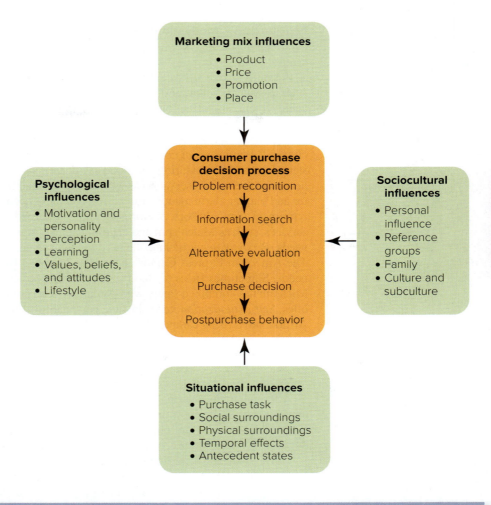

FIGURE 4–5
Influences on the consumer purchase decision process come from both internal and external sources.

4-1. What is the first stage in the consumer purchase decision process?

4-2. The brands a consumer considers buying out of the set of brands in a product class of which the consumer is aware are collectively called the _____.

4-3. What is the term for postpurchase anxiety?

PSYCHOLOGICAL INFLUENCES ON CONSUMER BEHAVIOR

LO 4-3 Identify the major psychological influences on consumer behavior.

Psychology helps marketers understand why and how consumers behave as they do. In particular, psychological concepts such as motivation and personality; perception; learning; values, beliefs, and attitudes; and lifestyle are useful for interpreting buying processes and directing marketing efforts.

Consumer Motivation and Personality

Motivation and personality are two familiar psychological concepts that have specific meanings and marketing implications. These concepts are closely related and are used to explain why people do some things and not others.

motivation
The energizing force that stimulates behavior to satisfy a need.

personality
A person's consistent behaviors or responses to recurring situations.

Video 4-1
Match.com
kerin.tv/cr8e/v4-1

Motivation Motivation is the energizing force that stimulates behavior to satisfy a need. Because consumer needs are the focus of the marketing concept, marketers try to arouse these needs.

An individual's needs are boundless. People possess physiological needs for basics such as water, shelter, and food. They also have learned needs, including self-esteem, achievement, and affection. Psychologists point out that these needs may be hierarchical; that is, once physiological needs are met, people seek to satisfy their learned needs.

Figure 4–6 shows one need hierarchy and classification scheme that contains five need classes.[16] *Physiological needs* are basic to survival and must be satisfied first. A Red Lobster advertisement featuring a seafood salad attempts to activate the need for food. *Safety needs* involve self-preservation as well as physical and financial well-being. Smoke detector and burglar alarm manufacturers focus on these needs, as do insurance companies and retirement plan advisors. *Social needs* are concerned with love and friendship. Dating services, such as Match.com and eHarmony, and fragrance companies try to arouse these needs. *Personal needs* include the need for achievement, status, prestige, and self-respect. The American Express Centurion Card and Brooks Brothers Clothiers appeal to these needs. Sometimes firms try to arouse multiple needs to stimulate problem recognition. Michelin has combined safety with parental love to promote tire replacement for automobiles. *Self-actualization needs* involve personal fulfillment. For example, a recent Under Armour advertising campaign challenged consumers to "Rule Yourself!"

Personality While motivation is the energizing force that makes consumer behavior purposeful, a consumer's personality guides and directs behavior. **Personality** refers to a person's consistent behaviors or responses to recurring situations.

Although many personality theories exist, most identify *key traits*—enduring characteristics within a person or in his or her relationships with others. Such traits include assertiveness, extroversion, compliance, dominance, and aggression, among others. These traits are inherited or formed at an early age and change little over the years. Research suggests that compliant people prefer known brand names and use more mouthwash and toilet soaps. Aggressive types use razors, not electric shavers, apply more cologne and aftershave lotions, and purchase signature goods such as Gucci and Yves St. Laurent as an indicator of status. Also, extroversion and neuroticism have been shown to be associated with impulsive buying.[17]

Personality characteristics often reveal a person's *self-concept*, which is the way people see themselves and the way they believe others see them. Marketers recognize that people have an actual self-concept and an ideal self-concept. The actual self-concept refers to how people actually see themselves. The ideal self-concept describes how people would like to see themselves.

These two self-images—actual and ideal—are reflected in the products and brands a person buys, including automobiles, home appliances and furnishings, magazines, consumer electronics, clothing, and grooming and leisure products. Frequently, these two self-images are also reflected in the stores in which a person shops. The importance of self-concept is summed up by a senior marketing executive at Lenovo, a global supplier of notebook computers: "The notebook market is getting more like cars. The car you drive reflects you, and notebooks are becoming a form of self-expression as well."[18]

FIGURE 4–6
The Maslow hierarchy of needs is based on the idea that motivation comes from a need. If a need is met, it's no longer a motivator, so a higher-level need becomes the motivator. Higher-level needs demand support of lower-level needs.

- **Self-actualization needs:** Self-fulfillment
- **Personal needs:** Status, respect, prestige
- **Social needs:** Friendship, belonging, love
- **Safety needs:** Freedom from harm, financial security
- **Physiological needs:** Food, water, shelter, oxygen

> **perception**
> The process by which an individual selects, organizes, and interprets information to create a meaningful picture of the world.

Consumer Perception

One person sees a Cadillac as a mark of achievement; another sees it as ostentatious. This is the result of **perception**—the process by which an individual selects, organizes, and interprets information to create a meaningful picture of the world.

Selective Perception Because the average consumer operates in a complex environment, the human brain attempts to organize and interpret information with a process called *selective perception,* a filtering of exposure, comprehension, and retention. *Selective exposure* occurs when people pay attention to messages that are consistent with their attitudes and beliefs and ignore messages that are inconsistent with them. Selective exposure often occurs in the postpurchase stage of the consumer decision process, when consumers read advertisements for the brand they just bought. It also occurs when a need exists—you are more likely to "see" a McDonald's advertisement when you are hungry rather than after you have eaten a pizza.

Selective comprehension involves interpreting information so that it is consistent with your attitudes and beliefs. A marketer's failure to understand this can have disastrous results. For example, Toro introduced a small, lightweight snowblower called the Snow Pup. Even though the product worked, sales failed to meet expectations. Why? Toro later found out that consumers perceived the name to mean that Snow Pup was a toy or too light to do any serious snow removal. When the product was renamed Snow Master, sales increased sharply.[19]

Selective retention means that consumers do not remember all the information they see, read, or hear, even minutes after exposure to it. This affects the internal and external information search stage of the purchase decision process. This is why furniture and automobile retailers often give consumers product brochures to take home with them when they leave the showroom.

Because perception plays an important role in consumer behavior, it is not surprising that the topic of subliminal perception is a popular item for discussion. *Subliminal perception* means that you see or hear messages without being aware of them. The presence and effect of subliminal perception on behavior is a hotly debated issue, with more popular appeal than scientific support. Indeed, evidence suggests that such messages have limited effects on behavior.[20] If these messages did influence behavior, would their use be an ethical practice? (See the Making Responsible Decisions box.)[21]

> **perceived risk**
> The anxiety felt because the consumer cannot anticipate the outcomes of a purchase but believes there may be negative consequences.

Perceived Risk Perception plays a major role in the perceived risk in purchasing a product or service. **Perceived risk** represents the anxiety felt because the consumer cannot anticipate the outcomes of a purchase but believes there may be negative consequences. Examples of possible negative consequences are the size of the financial outlay required to buy the product (can I afford $900 for those skis?), the risk of physical harm (is bungee jumping safe?), and the performance of the product (will the whitening toothpaste work?). A more abstract form is psychosocial (what will my friends say about my tattoo?).

Perceived risk affects a consumer's information search. The greater the perceived risk, the more extensive the external search stage is likely to be. For example, the average car shopper spends about 14 hours online researching cars and almost 4 hours visiting car dealerships when choosing a car.[22]

Recognizing the importance of perceived risk, companies develop strategies to reduce the consumer's perceived risk and encourage purchases. Some of these strategies and examples of firms using them include the following:

- *Obtaining seals of approval:* The Good Housekeeping Seal for Fresh Step cat litter.
- *Securing endorsements from influential people:* Colgate-Palmolive secured the endorsements of dentists to make the claim that Colgate Total toothpaste is the #1 recommended toothpaste by most dentists.

How did Colgate-Palmolive marketers allay consumers' perceived risk and change consumers' attitudes toward Colgate Total toothpaste to create a brand with over $1 billion in sales worldwide? The answers appear in the text.
©Whitebox Media/Alamy Stock Photo

Making Responsible Decisions > Ethics

The Ethics of Subliminal Messages

For over 50 years, the topic of subliminal perception and the presence of subliminal messages and images embedded in commercial communications have sparked heated debate.

The Federal Communications Commission has denounced subliminal messages as deceptive. Still, consumers spend $50 million a year for subliminal messages designed to help them raise their self-esteem, stop compulsive buying, quit smoking, or lose weight. Almost two-thirds of U.S. consumers think subliminal messages are present in commercial communications; about half are firmly convinced that this practice can cause them to buy things they don't want.

Subliminal messages are not illegal in the United States, however, and marketers are often criticized for pursuing opportunities to create these messages in both electronic and print media. A book by August Bullock, *The Secret Sales Pitch,* is devoted to this topic. Bullock identifies images and advertisements that he claims contain subliminal messages and describes techniques that can be used for conveying these messages. Do you "see" the subliminal message that is embedded in the book's cover?

Do you believe that a marketer's attempts to implant subliminal messages in electronic and print media are a deceptive practice and unethical, regardless of their intent?

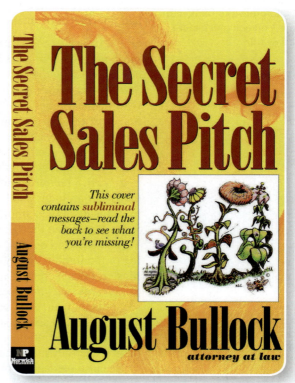

©2004 by August Bullock. All Rights Reserved. Used with permission. TheSecretSalesPitch.com

- *Providing free trials of the product:* Samples of Mary Kay's Velocity fragrance.
- *Giving extensive usage instructions:* Clairol hair coloring.
- *Providing warranties and guarantees:* Kia Motors's 10-year, 100,000-mile limited powertrain warranty.

Consumer Learning

Much consumer behavior is learned. Consumers learn which information sources to consult for information about products and services, which evaluative criteria to use when assessing alternatives, and, more generally, how to make purchase decisions. **Learning** refers to those behaviors that result from (1) repeated experience and (2) reasoning.

learning
Those behaviors that result from (1) repeated experience and (2) reasoning.

Behavioral Learning

Behavioral learning is the process of developing automatic responses to a situation built up through repeated exposure to it. Four variables are central to how consumers learn from repeated experience: drive, cue, response, and reinforcement. A *drive* is a need that moves an individual to action. Drives, such as hunger, might be represented by motives. A *cue* is a stimulus or symbol perceived by consumers. A *response* is the action taken by a consumer to satisfy the drive. *Reinforcement* is the reward. Being hungry (drive), a consumer sees a cue (a billboard), takes action (buys a sandwich), and receives a reward (it tastes great!).

Marketers use two concepts from behavioral learning theory. *Stimulus generalization* occurs when a response elicited by one stimulus (cue) is generalized to another stimulus. Using the same brand name for different products is an application of this concept,

How does this advertisement for Tylenol 8-Hour apply to cognitive learning? Read the text to find out.

Source: McNeil Consumer Healthcare Division of McNeil-PPC, Inc.

brand loyalty
A favorable attitude toward and consistent purchase of a single brand over time.

attitude
A learned predisposition to respond to an object or class of objects in a consistently favorable or unfavorable way.

beliefs
A consumer's subjective perception of how a product or brand performs on different attributes based on personal experience, advertising, and discussions with other people.

such as Tylenol Cold & Flu and Tylenol P.M. *Stimulus discrimination* refers to a person's ability to perceive differences in stimuli. Consumers' tendency to perceive all light beers as being alike led to Budweiser Light commercials that distinguished between many types of "light beers" and Bud Light.

Cognitive Learning Consumers also learn through thinking, reasoning, and mental problem solving without direct experience. This type of learning, called *cognitive learning,* involves making connections between two or more ideas or simply observing the outcomes of others' behaviors and adjusting your own accordingly. Firms also influence this type of learning. Through repetition in advertising, messages such as "1 Shade Whiter Teeth in 1 Week" link a brand (Colgate Visible White) and an idea (teeth stain removal) by showing someone using the brand and getting whiter teeth. In the same way, McNeil Consumer Heathcare links its Tylenol 8-Hour brand and an idea (pain reliever) by showing someone using the brand and finding relief.

Brand Loyalty Learning is also important to marketers because it relates to habit formation—the basis of routine problem solving. Furthermore, there is a close link between habits and **brand loyalty**, which is a favorable attitude toward and consistent purchase of a single brand over time. Brand loyalty results from the positive reinforcement of previous actions. A consumer reduces risk and saves time by consistently purchasing the same brand of shampoo and has favorable results—healthy, shiny hair. There is evidence of brand loyalty in many commonly purchased products in the United States and the global marketplace. However, the incidence of brand loyalty appears to be declining in North America, Western Europe, and Japan.[23]

Consumer Values, Beliefs, and Attitudes

Values, beliefs, and attitudes play a central role in consumer decision making and related marketing actions.

Attitude Formation An **attitude** is a "learned predisposition to respond to an object or class of objects in a consistently favorable or unfavorable way."[24] Attitudes are shaped by our values and beliefs, which are learned. Values vary by level of specificity. We speak of American core values, including material well-being and humanitarianism. We also have personal values, such as thriftiness and ambition. Marketers are concerned with both but focus mostly on personal values. Personal values affect attitudes by influencing the importance assigned to specific product attributes. Suppose thriftiness is one of your personal values. When you evaluate cars, fuel economy (a product attribute) becomes important. If you believe a specific car brand has this attribute, you are likely to have a favorable attitude toward it.

Beliefs also play a part in attitude formation. **Beliefs** are a consumer's subjective perception of how a product or brand performs on different attributes. Beliefs are based on personal experience, advertising, and discussions with other people. Beliefs about product attributes are important because, along with personal values, they create the favorable or unfavorable attitude the consumer has toward certain products, services, and brands.

Attitude Change Marketers use three approaches to try to change consumer attitudes toward products and brands, as illustrated in the following examples.[25]

1. *Changing beliefs about the extent to which a brand has certain attributes*. To allay mothers' concerns about ingredients in its mayonnaise, Hellmann's successfully communicated the product's high Omega 3 content, which is essential to human health.
2. *Changing the perceived importance of attributes*. Pepsi-Cola made freshness an important product attribute when it stamped freshness dates on its cans. Before doing so, few consumers considered cola freshness an issue. After Pepsi spent

FIGURE 4–7

The VALS framework is the visualization of the eight consumer segments. Consumers with abundant resources—psychological, emotional, and material means and capabilities—are near the top of the framework and those with minimal resources are at the bottom. Consumer groups within a motivation can be targeted together. For instance, a marketer may target Thinkers and Believers together. Do you wish to know your VALS profile? If you do, respond to the questions on the VALS Survey at www.strategicbusinessinsights.com/VALS. Simply click "VALS Survey" to get your profile. By design, the questions are for use by people whose first language is American English. If you are not a citizen of the United States or Canada, residency should allow for enough time to know the culture and its idioms. If you do not meet these conditions, your VALS type will not be accurate.

Source: www.strategicbusinessinsights.com/VALS © 2018 by Strategic Business Insights. All rights reserved. This version is for the United States only. Different frameworks are used for different countries. Used with permission.

about $25 million on advertising and promotion, a consumer survey found that 61 percent of cola drinkers believed freshness dating was an important attribute.
3. *Adding new attributes to the product.* Colgate-Palmolive included a new antibacterial ingredient, triclosan, in its Colgate Total toothpaste and spent $100 million marketing the brand. The result? Colgate Total toothpaste is now a billion-dollar-plus global brand.

Consumer Lifestyle

Lifestyle is a mode of living that is identified by how people spend their time and resources, what they consider important in their environments, and what they think of themselves and the world around them. The analysis of consumer lifestyles, called *psychographics,* provides insights into consumer needs and wants. Lifestyle analysis has proven useful in segmenting and targeting consumers for new and existing products and services (see Chapter 8).

Psychographics is a catchall label used to describe a variety of segmentations such as those based on behaviors, attitudes, activities, interests, opinions, and social values. The practice of combining psychology, lifestyle, and demographics to uncover consumer motivations for buying and using products and services is expensive. VALS™, owned and operated by Strategic Business Insights (SBI), is more than a lifestyle segmentation because VALS examines the intersection of psychology, demographics, and lifestyles.[26] Using a stand-alone survey and a proprietary algorithm, VALS measures the enduring differences between U.S. adults aged 18 and older that explain and predict consumer behavior. Eight primary segments—mindsets—are identified on the basis of motivations and resources (see Figure 4–7).

According to SBI, consumers are motivated to buy products and services and to seek life experiences that give shape, substance, and satisfaction to their lives. Different consumer groups will often exhibit different behavior; equally as often, different consumer groups will exhibit the same behavior for different reasons. The majority of consumers are driven by one of three motivations—ideals, achievement, and self-expression. Different levels of resources enhance or constrain a person's primary motivation.

The VALS resource dimension includes measures of key demographics, in addition to psychological, emotional, and material capacities such as self-confidence, curiosity, information-seeking, and risk-taking.

- *Ideals-motivated groups.* Consumers motivated by ideals are guided by knowledge and principles. High-resource *Thinkers* are the old guard. They have "ought" and "should" benchmarks for social conduct. Low-resource *Believers* are not looking to change society. They believe in right/wrong for a good life.
- *Achievement-motivated groups.* Consumers motivated by achievement look for products and services that demonstrate success to their peers or a group to which they aspire. High-resource *Achievers* have a me-first, my family-first attitude. They are anchors of the status quo. Low-resource *Strivers* live in the moment. Although they would like to better their lives, they have difficulty doing so.
- *Self-expression-motivated groups.* Consumers motivated by self-expression want to make an impact on their world. High-resource *Experiencers* are social and spontaneous. They are first in, first out of trend adoption. Low-resource *Makers* protect what they think they own. They may appear to be anti-intellectual.
- *High- and low-resource groups.* Two segments stand apart from primary motivation. High-resource *Innovators* are future oriented. They are confident enough to experiment—to try, fail, and try again. Low-resource *Survivors* are the quiet rank and file focused on meeting basic needs. They are analog, not digital.

Each segment exhibits unique media preferences. For example, Experiencers are the most likely to visit Facebook and to read fashion magazines. Makers and Achievers drive the most miles each week; therefore, they are the most likely segment to view outdoor advertising. Innovators and Thinkers are the most likely to read national newspapers. Survivors watch more hours of television in an average week compared to other groups.

learning review

4-4. The problem with the Toro Snow Pup was an example of selective _____.

4-5. What three attitude-change approaches are most common?

4-6. What does *lifestyle* mean?

SOCIOCULTURAL INFLUENCES ON CONSUMER BEHAVIOR

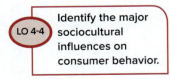
LO 4-4 Identify the major sociocultural influences on consumer behavior.

Sociocultural influences, which evolve from a consumer's formal and informal relationships with other people, also exert a significant impact on consumer behavior. They involve personal influence, reference groups, family influence, social class, culture, and subculture.

Personal Influence

A consumer's purchases are often influenced by the views, opinions, or behaviors of others. Two aspects of personal influence are very important to marketing: opinion leadership and word-of-mouth activity.

opinion leaders
Individuals who exert direct or indirect social influence over others.

word of mouth
The influencing of people during conversations.

Opinion Leadership Individuals who exert direct or indirect social influence over others are called **opinion leaders**. Opinion leaders are considered to be knowledgeable about or users of particular products and services, so their opinions influence others' choices.[27] Opinion leadership is widespread in the purchase of cars and trucks, entertainment, clothing and accessories, club membership, consumer electronics, children's toys, food, vacation destinations, and financial investments. A study by *Popular Mechanics* magazine identified 18 million opinion leaders who influence the purchases of some 85 million consumers for do-it-yourself products.

About 10 percent of U.S. adults are opinion leaders. Identifying, reaching, and influencing opinion leaders is a major challenge for companies. Some firms use music stars, actors, or sports figures as spokespersons to represent their products. Others promote their products in media believed to reach opinion leaders. Still others use more direct approaches. For example, a carmaker recently invited influential community leaders and business executives to test-drive its new models. Some 6,000 accepted the offer, and 98 percent said they would recommend their tested car. The company estimated that the number of favorable recommendations totaled 32,000.

The importance of personal influence has popularized *influencer marketing*—the practice of focusing on the identification and recruitment of influencers to advocate products, services, and brands rather than focusing exclusively on prospective buyers. Social media, notably Instagram and YouTube, are the primary platforms used in influencer marketing because they are easily and quickly shared with prospective buyers.

Word of Mouth The influencing of people during conversations is called **word of mouth**. Word of mouth is the most powerful and authentic information source for consumers because it typically involves friends viewed as trustworthy. About 75 percent of all consumer conversations about brands happen face-to-face, 15 percent happen over the phone, and 10 percent happen online.[28] According to a recent study, 67 percent of U.S. consumer product sales are directly based on word-of-mouth activity among friends, family, and colleagues.[29]

Companies use world-class athletes and music stars as spokespersons to represent their products, as in these ads featuring country music star Kelly Clarkson (for Citizen watches) and tennis star Roger Federer (for Rolex watches).
(left): Source: Citizen Watch Company of America; (right): Source: Rolex

Marketing Matters   Customer Value

BzzAgent—The Buzz Experience

Have you recently heard about a new product, movie, website, book, or restaurant from someone you know . . . or a complete stranger? If so, you may have had a word-of-mouth experience.

Marketers recognize the power of word of mouth. The challenge has been to harness that power. BzzAgent does just that. Its worldwide volunteer army of one million natural-born talkers channel their chatter toward products and services they deem authentically worth talking about, either online or in person. "Our goal is to capture honest word of mouth," says BzzAgent's founder, "and to build a network that turns passionate customers into brand evangelists."

©BzzAgent

BzzAgent's method is simple. Once a client signs on with BzzAgent, the company searches its network of "agents" for those who match the demographic and psychographic profile of the target market for a client's offering. Agents then opt-in through an invitation e-mail and receive a sample product and online training for buzz-creating strategies. Online activities, such as Facebook and Instagram posts, are completed through BzzAgent.com. Each time an agent completes an offline activity, he or she is expected to file a BzzReport describing the nature of the buzz and its effectiveness. BzzAgent moderators respond with encouragement and feedback on additional techniques, including flagging any nondisclosed content.

Agents keep the products they promote. Who are the agents? All are gregarious and genuinely like the product or service, otherwise they wouldn't participate in the BzzCampaign.

Nestlé, Procter & Gamble, Danone, L'Oréal, and Unilever are a sampling of the companies that have used BzzAgent. Are you interested in BzzAgent? Visit its website at www.bzzagent.com or www.facebook.com/bzzagent.

Video 4-2
Dove
kerin.tv/cr8e/v4-2

The power of personal influence has prompted firms to promote positive and retard negative word of mouth. For instance, "teaser" advertising campaigns are run in advance of new-product introductions to stimulate conversations. Other techniques such as advertising slogans, music, and humor also heighten positive word of mouth. Many commercials shown during the Super Bowl are created expressly to initiate conversations about the advertisements and their featured products or services the next day. Increasingly, companies recruit and deploy people to produce *buzz*—popularity created by consumer word of mouth. Read the Marketing Matters box to learn how this is done by BzzAgent.[30] Then go to the link in Video 4-2 to see BzzAgent's campaign for Dove hair care products.

Unfortunately, word of mouth can also be a source of negative information. For example, consider the damaging (and untrue) rumors that have plagued Kmart (snake eggs in clothing), Taco Bell (beef content in taco meat filling), Corona Extra beer (contamination), and Snickers candy bars in Russia (a cause of diabetes). Overcoming or neutralizing negative word of mouth is difficult and costly. However, supplying factual information, providing toll-free numbers for consumers to call the company, and giving appropriate product demonstrations have proven helpful.

The power of word of mouth is magnified by the Internet through online forums, blogs, social media, and websites. In fact, companies use special software to monitor online messages and find out what consumers are saying about their products, services, and brands. They have found that 30 percent of people spreading negative information have never owned or used the product, service, or brand and "likes" on Facebook and Instagram are sometimes gotten by fraudulent means![31]

reference groups
People to whom an individual looks as a basis for self-appraisal or as a source of personal standards.

Reference Group Influence

Reference groups are people to whom an individual looks as a basis for self-appraisal or as a source of personal standards. Reference groups affect consumer purchases because they influence the information, attitudes, and aspiration levels that help set a consumer's standards. For example, one of the first questions one asks others when planning to attend a social occasion is, "What are you going to wear?" Reference groups influence the purchase of luxury products rather than necessities—particularly when the use or consumption of a chosen brand will be highly visible to others.

Consumers have many reference groups, but three groups have clear marketing implications.[32] An *associative group* is one to which a person actually belongs, including fraternities and sororities and alumni associations. Such groups are easily identifiable and are targeted by firms selling insurance, insignia products, and charter vacations.

Associative reference groups can also form around a brand, as is the case with clubs like the HOG (Harley Owners Group), which is made up of Harley-Davidson fans. A **brand community** is a specialized group of consumers with a structured set of relationships involving a particular brand, fellow customers of that brand, and the product in use. A consumer who is a member of a brand community thinks about brand names (e.g., Harley-Davidson), the product category (e.g., motorcycles), other customers who use the brand (e.g., HOG members), and the marketer that makes and promotes the brand.

The Harley Owners Group (HOG) has over 1 million members and is a prototypical brand community. Read the text to learn about the characteristics of a brand community.
©Joseph Eid/AFP/Getty Images

An *aspiration group* is one that a person wishes to be a member of or wishes to be identified with, such as a professional society or sports team. Firms frequently rely on spokespeople or settings associated with their target market's aspiration group in their advertising.

A *dissociative group* is one that a person wishes to maintain a distance from because of differences in values or behaviors. Firms often avoid dissociative reference groups in their marketing. For example, retailer Abercrombie & Fitch once offered to pay cast members of a controversial TV reality show to *not* wear its clothing. "We understand that the show is for entertainment purposes, but believe this association is contrary to the aspirational nature of our brand, and may be distressing to many of our fans," the retailer stated.[33]

brand community
A specialized group of consumers with a structured set of relationships involving a particular brand, fellow customers of that brand, and the product in use.

Family Influence

Family influences on consumer behavior result from three sources: consumer socialization, passage through the family life cycle, and decision making within the family or household.

Consumer Socialization The process by which people acquire the skills, knowledge, and attitudes necessary to function as consumers is called *consumer socialization*.[34] Children learn how to purchase (1) by interacting with adults in purchase situations and (2) through their own purchasing and product usage experiences. Research shows that children evidence brand preferences at age two, and these preferences often last a lifetime. This knowledge prompted the licensing of the well-known Craftsman brand name to MGA Entertainment for its children's line of My First Craftsman toys and power tools, as well as Time Inc.'s *Sports Illustrated Kids* magazine and Microsoft's kid-friendly news site, MSN for Kids.

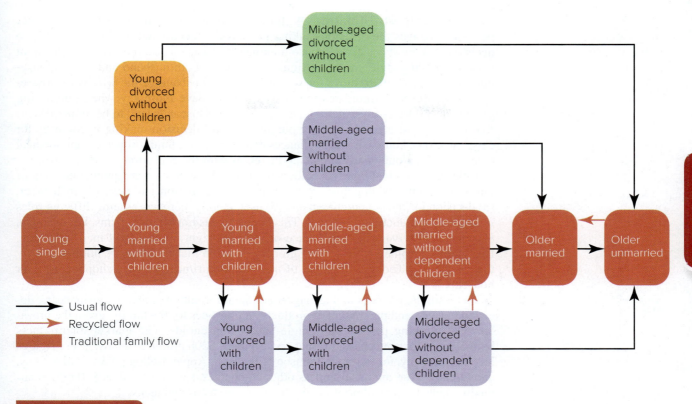

FIGURE 4–8
Modern family life-cycle stages and flows. Can you identify people you know in different stages? Do they follow the purchase patterns described in the text?

family life cycle
The distinct phases that a family progresses through from formation to retirement, each phase bringing with it identifiable purchasing behaviors.

Family Life Cycle Consumers act and purchase differently as they go through life. The concept **family life cycle** describes the distinct phases that a family progresses through from formation to retirement, each phase bringing with it identifiable purchasing behaviors.[35] Figure 4–8 illustrates the traditional progression as well as contemporary variations of the family life cycle. Today, the *traditional family*—a married couple with children younger than 18 years—constitutes just 20 percent of all U.S. households. The remaining 80 percent of U.S. households includes single parents; unmarried couples; divorced, never-married, or widowed individuals; and older married couples whose children no longer live at home.

Young singles' buying preferences are for nondurable items, including prepared foods, clothing, personal care products, and entertainment. They represent a target market for recreational travel, automobile, and consumer electronics firms. Young married couples without children are typically more affluent than young singles because usually both spouses are employed. These couples exhibit preferences for furniture, housewares, and gift items for each other. Young marrieds with children are driven by the needs of their children. They make up a sizable market for life insurance, various children's products, and home furnishings. Single parents with children are the least financially secure of households with children. Their buying preferences are often affected by a limited economic status and tend toward convenience foods, child care services, and personal care items.

Middle-aged married couples with children are typically better off financially than their younger counterparts. They are a significant market for leisure products and home improvement items. Middle-aged couples without children typically have a large amount of discretionary income. These couples buy better home furnishings, status automobiles, and financial services. Persons in the last two phases—older married and older unmarried—make up a sizable market for prescription drugs, medical services, vacation trips, and gifts for younger relatives.

Family Decision Making A third source of family influence on consumer behavior involves the decision-making process that occurs within the family.[36] Two decision-making styles exist: spouse-dominant and joint decision making. With a joint decision-making style, most decisions are made by both husband and wife. Spouse-dominant decisions are those for which either the husband or the wife is mostly responsible. Research indicates that wives tend to have more say when purchasing groceries, children's toys, clothing, and medicines. Husbands tend to be more influential in home and car maintenance purchases. Joint decision making is common for cars, vacations, houses, home appliances and electronics, family finances, and medical care. As a rule, joint decision making increases with the education of the spouses.

Roles of individual family members in the purchase process are another element of family decision making. Five roles exist: (1) information gatherer, (2) influencer, (3) decision maker, (4) purchaser, and (5) user. Family members assume different roles for different products and services. This knowledge is important to firms. For example, 89 percent of wives either influence or make outright purchases of men's clothing. Even though women are often the grocery decision makers, they are not necessarily the purchasers. Today, 31 percent of men are the primary grocery shoppers in their households.

Increasingly, preteens and teenagers are the information gatherers, influencers, decision makers, and purchasers of products and services for the family, given the prevalence of working parents and single-parent households. The market for products bought by or for preteens and teenagers surpasses $208 billion annually. These figures help explain why, for example, Johnson & Johnson, Apple, Kellogg, P&G, Nike, Sony, and Oscar Mayer, among countless other companies, spend more than $70 billion annually in electronic and print media that reach preteens and teens.

Culture and Subculture Influences

As described in Chapter 3, *culture* refers to the set of values, ideas, and attitudes that are learned and shared among the members of a group. Thus, we often refer to the American culture, the Latin American culture, or the Japanese culture. Cultural underpinnings of American buying patterns were described in Chapter 3; Chapter 6 will explore the role of culture in global marketing.

Video 4-3
Nissan Ad
kerin.tv/cr8e/v4-3

Today, 31 percent of men in the United States are the primary grocery shoppers in their households. Marketers that supply the $560 billion retail food industries are now adjusting store layouts and shelf placements to cater to men.

©Jochen Sand/Getty Images

subcultures
Subgroups within the larger, or national, culture with unique values, ideas, and attitudes.

Subgroups within the larger, or national, culture with unique values, ideas, and attitudes are referred to as **subcultures**. Various subcultures exist within the American culture. The three largest racial/ethnic subcultures in the United States are Hispanics, African Americans, and Asian Americans. Collectively, they are expected to account for more than one in four U.S. consumers and to spend about $4 trillion for products and services in 2021, which will represent almost 30 percent of the United States' total buying power.[37] Each group exhibits sophisticated social and cultural behaviors that affect buying patterns, which we describe next.

Hispanic Buying Patterns Hispanics represent the largest racial/ethnic subculture in the United States in terms of population and spending power. About 35 percent of Hispanics in the United States are immigrants, and the majority are under the age of 30. About 25 percent of Hispanics are younger than 18.

Research on Hispanic buying practices has uncovered several consistent patterns:[38]

1. Hispanics are quality and brand conscious. They are willing to pay a premium price for premium quality and are often brand loyal.
2. Hispanics prefer buying American-made products, especially those offered by firms that cater to Hispanic needs.
3. Hispanic buying preferences are strongly influenced by family and peers.
4. Hispanics consider advertising a credible product information source, and U.S. firms spend about $10 billion annually on advertising to Hispanics.
5. Convenience is not an important product attribute to Hispanic homemakers with respect to food preparation or consumption, nor is low caffeine in coffee and soft drinks, low fat in dairy products, or low cholesterol in packaged foods.

Why does ACH Food Companies, Inc. advertise its Mazola Corn Oil in Spanish? Read the text for the answer. Mazola Corn Oil,

www.mazola.com

Source: MAZOLA®, a registered trademark of ACH FOOD COMPANIES, Inc.

Despite some consistent buying patterns, marketing to Hispanics has proven to be a challenge for two reasons. First, the Hispanic subculture is diverse and composed of Mexicans, Puerto Ricans, Cubans, and others of Central and South American ancestry. Cultural differences among these nationalities often affect product preferences. For example, Goya Foods markets soups, beans, and sauces using different recipes to appeal to Puerto Ricans on the East Coast and Mexicans in the Southwest. Second, a language barrier exists, and commercial messages are frequently misinterpreted when translated into Spanish. Volkswagen learned this lesson when the Spanish translation of its "Drivers Wanted" slogan suggested "chauffeurs wanted." The Spanish slogan was changed to "*Agarra Calle,*" a slang expression that can be loosely translated as "let's hit the road."

Sensitivity to the unique needs of Hispanics by firms has paid huge dividends. For example, Metropolitan Life Insurance is the largest insurer of Hispanics. Goya Foods dominates the market for ethnic food products sold to Hispanics. Mazola Corn Oil captures two-thirds of the Hispanic market for this product category. Meredith Corporation has 6.2 million readers of its Spanish-language *People en Español* magazine.

African American Buying Patterns African Americans have the second-largest spending power of the three racial/ethnic subcultures in the United States. Consumer research on African American buying patterns has focused on similarities and differences with Caucasians. When socioeconomic status differences between African Americans and Caucasians are removed, there are more similarities than points of difference. Differences in buying patterns are greater within the African American subculture, due to levels of socioeconomic status, than between African Americans and Caucasians of similar status.

Even though similarities outweigh differences, there are consumption patterns that do differ between African Americans and Caucasians.[39] For example, African Americans spend far more than Caucasians on boys' clothing, rental goods,

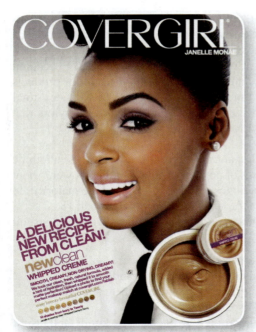

African American women represent a large market for health and beauty products. Cosmetics companies actively seek to serve this market.
Source: Procter & Gamble

smartphones, and audio equipment. African American women spend three times more on health and beauty products than Caucasian women. Furthermore, the typical African American family is five years younger than the typical Caucasian family. This factor alone accounts for some of the observed differences in preferences for clothing, music, shelter, cars, and many other products, services, and activities. Finally, it must be emphasized that, historically, African Americans have been deprived of employment and educational opportunities in the United States. Both factors have resulted in income disparities between African Americans and Caucasians, which influence purchase behavior.

Recent research indicates that while African Americans are price conscious, they are strongly motivated by quality and choice. They respond more to products and advertising that appeal to African American cultural images, as well as address their ethnic features and needs, regardless of socioeconomic status. African Americans are much more likely to tell their friends about products and services they like than the general public as a whole.

Asian American Buying Patterns Asian Americans are the fastest-growing racial/ethnic subculture in the United States. About 66 percent of Asian Americans are immigrants. Most are under the age of 30. Asian Americans tend to live in multigenerational households.

The Asian American subculture is composed of Chinese, Japanese, Filipinos, Koreans, Asian Indians, people from Southeast Asia, and Pacific Islanders. The diversity of this subculture is so great that generalizations about buying patterns of this group are difficult to make.[40] Consumer research on Asian Americans suggests that individuals and families can be divided into two groups. *Assimilated* Asian Americans are conversant in English, are highly educated, hold professional and managerial positions, and exhibit buying patterns very much like the typical American consumer. *Nonassimilated* Asian Americans are recent immigrants who still cling to their native languages and customs.

The diversity of Asian Americans, evident in language, customs, and tastes, requires marketers to be sensitive to different Asian nationalities. And, for the majority of each nationality, preserving their cultural heritage is important. As a consequence, Anheuser-Busch's agricultural products division sells eight varieties of California-grown rice, each with a different Asian label to cover a range of nationalities and tastes. The company's advertising also addresses the preferences of Chinese, Japanese, and Koreans for different kinds of rice bowls. McDonald's actively markets to Asian Americans. According to a company executive, "We recognize diversity in this market. We try to make our messages in the language they prefer to see them."

Studies show that the Asian American subculture as a whole is characterized by hard work, strong family ties, appreciation for education, and median family incomes exceeding those of any other ethnic group. This subculture is also the most entrepreneurial in the United States, as evidenced by the number of Asian-owned businesses. These qualities led Metropolitan Life Insurance to identify Asian Americans as a target for insurance following the company's success in marketing to Hispanics.

learning review

4-7. What are the two primary forms of personal influence?

4-8. Marketers are concerned with which types of reference groups?

4-9. What two challenges must marketers overcome when marketing to Hispanic consumers?

LEARNING OBJECTIVES REVIEW

LO 4-1 *Describe the stages in the consumer purchase decision process.*

The consumer purchase decision process consists of five stages: (1) problem recognition, (2) information search, (3) alternative evaluation, (4) purchase decision, and (5) postpurchase behavior. Problem recognition is perceiving a difference between a person's ideal and actual situation big enough to trigger a decision. Information search involves remembering previous purchase experiences (internal search) and external search behavior such as seeking information from other sources. Alternative evaluation clarifies the problem for the consumer by (a) suggesting the evaluative criteria to use for the purchase, (b) yielding brand names that might meet the criteria, and (c) developing consumer value perceptions. The purchase decision involves the choice of an alternative, including from whom to buy and when to buy. Postpurchase behavior involves the comparison of the chosen alternative with a consumer's expectations, which leads to satisfaction or dissatisfaction and subsequent purchase behavior. Marketing practitioners study the consumer purchase process by identifying consumer touchpoints and consumer journey maps.

LO 4-2 *Distinguish among three variations of the consumer purchase decision process: extended, limited, and routine problem solving.*

Consumers don't always engage in the five-stage purchase decision process. Instead, they skip or minimize one or more stages depending on the level of involvement—the personal, social, and economic significance of the purchase. For high-involvement purchase occasions, each of the five stages of the consumer purchase decision process is used and considerable time and effort are devoted to the search for external information and the identification and evaluation of alternatives. With limited problem solving, consumers typically seek some information or rely on a friend to help them evaluate alternatives. For low-involvement purchase occasions, consumers engage in routine problem solving. They recognize a problem, make a decision, and spend little effort seeking external information and evaluating alternatives.

LO 4-3 *Identify the major psychological influences on consumer behavior.*

Psychology helps marketers understand why and how consumers behave as they do. In particular, psychological concepts such as motivation and personality; perception; learning; values, beliefs, and attitudes; and lifestyle are useful for interpreting buying processes. Motivation is the energizing force that stimulates behavior to satisfy a need. Personality refers to a person's consistent behaviors or responses to recurring situations. Perception is the process by which an individual selects, organizes, and interprets information to create a meaningful picture of the world. Consumers filter information through selective exposure, comprehension, and retention.

Much consumer behavior is learned. Learning refers to those behaviors that result from (a) repeated experience and (b) reasoning. Brand loyalty results from learning. Values, beliefs, and attitudes are also learned and influence how consumers evaluate products, services, and brands. A more general concept is lifestyle. Lifestyle, also called psychographics, combines psychology and demographics and focuses on how people spend their time and resources, what they consider important in their environment, and what they think of themselves and the world around them.

LO 4-4 *Identify the major sociocultural influences on consumer behavior.*

Sociocultural influences, which evolve from a consumer's formal and informal relationships with other people, also affect consumer behavior. These involve personal influence, reference groups, the family, culture, and subculture. Opinion leadership and word-of-mouth behavior are two major sources of personal influence on consumer behavior. Reference groups are people to whom an individual looks as a basis for self-approval or as a source of personal standards. Family influences on consumer behavior result from three sources: consumer socialization, passage through the family life cycle, and decision making within the family or household. Finally, a person's culture and subculture have been shown to influence product preferences and buying patterns.

LEARNING REVIEW ANSWERS

4-1 What is the first stage in the consumer purchase decision process?
Answer: problem recognition—perceiving a need

4-2 The brands a consumer considers buying out of the set of brands in a product class of which the consumer is aware are collectively called the _____.
Answer: consideration set

4-3 What is the term for postpurchase anxiety?
Answer: cognitive dissonance

4-4 The problem with the Toro Snow Pup was an example of selective _____.
Answer: comprehension—consumers perceived the name to mean that Snow Pup was a toy that was too light to do any serious snow removal.

4-5 **What three attitude-change approaches are most common?**
Answer: (1) Change beliefs about the extent to which a brand has certain attributes. (2) Change the perceived importance of these attributes. (3) Add new attributes to the product.

4-6 **What does *lifestyle* mean?**
Answer: Lifestyle is a mode of living that is identified by how people spend their time and resources, what they consider important in their environment, and what they think of themselves and the world around them.

4-7 **What are the two primary forms of personal influence?**
Answer: (1) Opinion leadership—persons considered to be knowledgeable about or users of particular products and services and (2) word of mouth—the influencing of people (friends, family, and colleagues) during conversations.

4-8 **Marketers are concerned with which types of reference groups?**
Answer: Three reference groups have clear marketing implications: (1) associative groups—ones to which a person actually belongs, such as a brand community that consists of a specialized group of consumers with a structured set of relationships involving a particular brand; (2) aspiration groups—ones that people wish to be a member of or identified with; and (3) dissociative groups—ones that people wish to maintain a distance from because of differences in values or behaviors.

4-9 **What two challenges must marketers overcome when marketing to Hispanic consumers?**
Answer: (1) The diversity of nationalities among this subculture that affect product preferences and (2) the language barrier that can lead to misinterpretation or mistranslation of commercial messages when translated into Spanish.

FOCUSING ON KEY TERMS

attitude p. 111
beliefs p. 111
brand community p. 116
brand loyalty p. 111
consumer behavior p. 99
consumer journey map p. 106
consumer touchpoints p. 105
family life cycle p. 117
involvement p. 103
learning p. 110
motivation p. 108
opinion leaders p. 114
perceived risk p. 109
perception p. 109
personality p. 108
purchase decision process p. 100
reference groups p. 116
subcultures p. 119
word of mouth p. 114

APPLYING MARKETING KNOWLEDGE

1. Review Figure 4–2, which shows common smartphone attributes. Which attributes are important to you? What other attributes might you consider? Which brand would you prefer?
2. Suppose research at Panasonic reveals that prospective buyers are anxious about buying high-definition television sets. What strategies might you recommend to the company to reduce consumer anxiety?
3. Assign one or more levels of the Maslow hierarchy of needs described in Figure 4–6 to the following products: (*a*) life insurance, (*b*) cosmetics, (*c*) *The Wall Street Journal,* and (*d*) hamburgers.
4. With which stage in the family life cycle would the purchase of the following products and services be most closely identified? (*a*) bedroom furniture, (*b*) life insurance, (*c*) a Caribbean cruise, (*d*) a house mortgage, and (*e*) children's toys.

BUILDING YOUR MARKETING PLAN

To conduct a consumer analysis for the product—the good, service, or idea—in your marketing plan:

1. Identify the consumers who are most likely to buy your product—the primary target market—in terms of (*a*) their demographic characteristics and (*b*) any other kind of characteristics you believe are important.
2. Describe (*a*) the main points of difference of your product for this group and (*b*) what problem they help solve for the consumer in terms of the first stage in the consumer purchase decision process in Figure 4–1.
3. For each of the four outside boxes in Figure 4–5 (marketing mix, psychological, sociocultural, and situational influences), identify the one or two key influences with respect to your product.

This consumer analysis will provide the foundation for the marketing mix actions you develop later in your plan.

VIDEO CASE 4

Coppertone: Creating the Leading Sun Care Brand by Understanding Consumers

Video 4-4
Coppertone Video Case
kerin.tv/cr8e/v4-4

How do you create the leading sun care brand in the United States? "I would say love the consumer," explains Tracy Nunziata, marketing vice president at Coppertone. "The consumer is at the basis of everything that you're going to do, and so the more that you can understand what is going on in their minds, their behaviors, their attitudes, the more you will understand how to best market your brand and meet all of their needs," she adds.

COPPERTONE AND THE SUN CARE INDUSTRY

Coppertone has a long and interesting history of meeting the changing needs of consumers. It was developed by pharmacist Benjamin Green who observed that red petroleum was used to protect the skin of service men and women in the Air Force. He added cocoa butter and coconut oil to create Coppertone Suntan Cream—the first consumer sun care product in the United States. As Coppertone marketing director Lisa Perez explains, "Coppertone actually started off as a tanning brand. If I think back to some of the taglines the business used to use, one of the most popular was 'Tan, Don't Burn.'" Soon the company introduced the now iconic Coppertone Girl in advertising that showed a young girl surprised by a Cocker Spaniel as it tugs at her swimsuit to reveal a tan line. Little Miss Coppertone contests followed, and young celebrities such as Jodi Foster often debuted in Coppertone commercials. One of the original outdoor billboards can still be seen in Miami Beach, Florida!

As public awareness of skin care preferences increased, consumer interests shifted from tanning to protection, and Coppertone developed new products to match those interests. "What's been so great," Perez observes, is that "we've continuously evolved to meet consumer needs." For example, Coppertone created a research center that developed an objective system for measuring sun protection. This system provided the basis for the SPF (Sun Protection Factor) ratings that the Food and Drug Administration created for the sun care industry. In addition, Coppertone developed the first sunscreen product for babies, introduced the first water-resistant lotion, and launched the first continuous spray sunscreens. Coppertone has also developed the MyUV Alert™ app to provide reapplication reminders tailored to individual family members.

Today, Coppertone is the market leader with 18 percent share of an industry that has grown to $9 billion in global sales. Coppertone's success is extraordinary considering the large number of competitors in the category. Nunziata explains: "You need to understand who your competition is and what their offerings are, so understanding Neutrogena, Banana Boat, and even private-label products is essential. They all play different roles within the category, so understanding what innovations they have, how they are supporting their product, and what targets they are going after" are all important. The industry is changing also as the distinction between sun care and skin care is becoming less obvious. Many sun care products have added ingredients such as vitamin B3 and ginkgo biloba, while many skin care products now offer SPF protection, creating "multifunctional products" as a new source of competition.

THE SUN CARE PRODUCT PURCHASE DECISION PROCESS

Coppertone managers are very attentive to the path that sun care product consumers follow as they make a purchase. According to Perez, the first stage—problem recognition—begins in two ways. "First is the understanding and heightened awareness of the importance to protect their skin against sun exposure," she says. Second, is the circumstance when consumers are "going somewhere" such as the beach, the pool, or on vacation. Both situations lead consumers to conclude that they need a sun care product. Coppertone research has revealed that 80 percent of its customers decide to purchase a sun care product before they even get into a store.

After recognizing the need, sun care product customers gather information from a wide range of places. They often ask peers what they use. Consumers also go online to collect information. "They look at different brands, they look at what kind of sun protection factors they will need while using the

Source: Bayer

product," observes Nunziata. "They also search to see what are the new innovations. News is very important in this category, so they're out there searching for the best sunscreen they should be using for their different needs," she continues. To facilitate customers' information search Coppertone allocates a significant part of its marketing budget to make sure Coppertone products appear in any online searches. In addition, Coppertone uses traditional advertising, public relations activities, and announcements on its web page to ensure that new information is readily available.

The sun care product category has many options so alternative evaluation can be complicated for consumers. One of the first things consumers evaluate is the product form—spray versus lotion. Then there is a range of SPF protection levels to choose from, and a wide variety of brands. Finally, price can also be an attribute that influences the evaluation process. Coppertone is continually adding new attributes such as water resistance (Coppertone SPORT), citrus scent (Coppertone CLEARLYSheer Faces), antioxidant blends (Coppertone CLEARLYSheer AfterSun), and a portable travel size option, to match consumers' interests. Prices are frequently adjusted to ensure that Coppertone is considered by value shoppers. As Lisa Perez observes, "there are a lot of decision criteria that consumers consider."

Once consumers have examined the alternatives they can make a purchase online or in a retail store. Coppertone's website (www.coppertone.com), for example, sometimes offers links to make purchases from Walgreens, Target, Kmart, CVS, amazon.com, soap.com, and drugstore.com. If a consumer elects to go to a retail store, the Coppertone brand is also sold in food retailers such as Kroger, Safeway, and Publix, and in club stores such as Costco and Sams. As Perez describes the situation, "consumers are looking for what they want, when they want it." Because in-store personnel do not typically participate in a sun care product purchase, point-of-purchase displays are an important way for Coppertone to help consumers find the location of their product. In some cases Coppertone may partner with a retailer to provide training and information to a "beauty advisor" who works at a cosmetics counter in the store.

Nunziata believes that the postpurchase evaluation happens quickly and on two dimensions. She explains: "One, did they get burned? I think that's the biggest telltale sign of whether they are satisfied with the product. The second is how it feels. So if you have a very greasy, oily formula that's really sticky, they're not going to be happy with it." Coppertone solicits feedback about all of its products on its website and by e-mail, mail, and telephone. In addition, Coppertone's marketing activities include engagement with consumers on Facebook and Instagram and with beauty websites and bloggers. The goal is to participate in authentic conversations about the Coppertone brand.

There are many other influences on the consumer decision process. Consumers are likely to select different products, for example, in different situations such as purchases for themselves or for their children, or in different weather conditions. Similarly, psychological influences, such as outdoor and indoor lifestyles, and perceptions of health and wellness can influence sun care product preferences. Perez comments, "I think it really depends on where our consumers are in their life stage or what their lifestyle is like." Finally, sociocultural influences such as peers and reference groups are important. Coppertone has observed that female consumers are interested in their friends' product preferences particularly when it is related to skin care and cosmetics.

MARKETING AT COPPERTONE

Together, Tracy Nunziata and Lisa Perez are responsible for managing a comprehensive integrated marketing program for Coppertone products. The program includes traditional mass media such as TV and print, and a variety of social media and digital advertising outlets. In addition, the Coppertone brand is supported with many types of coupons. These include free standing inserts (FSIs) in Sunday papers, digital coupons that are available online, and instant redeemable coupons (IRCs) that consumers can find on Coppertone packaging. Another important aspect of the Coppertone marketing program is its sponsorship of the U.S. women's and U.S. men's soccer teams. In addition, Coppertone has a partnership with Disney which has led to promotions related to movies such as *Finding Dory*. Coppertone's marketing activities also include sampling, displays, and signage throughout the United States.

COPPERTONE IN THE FUTURE

Coppertone faces several unique opportunities and challenges in the future. First, demand for Coppertone products is very seasonal. In fact, the majority of Coppertone sales currently occur in just 100 days. Second, consumers have traditionally thought about Coppertone products as solutions to a particular event such as a visit to the beach or a vacation. However, as

Source: Bayer

Now and in the future Coppertone's strategies will require continued attention to understanding consumers. Perez explains: "Coppertone is a fast-moving business that's changing on a daily basis. Consumers are really on trend, they're smart, they're savvy, and they're looking for information. So, for me as a marketer, what's really important is how do I get ahead of that? And the answer is constantly evaluating trends, talking to consumers, and figuring out how we can have our marketing activities sync up and be relevant to them."[41]

Questions

1. How has an understanding of consumer behavior helped Coppertone grow in the United States and around the globe?
2. Describe the five-stage purchase decision process for a Coppertone customer.
3. What are the possible situational, psychological, and sociocultural influences on the Coppertone consumer purchase decision process?
4. What specific marketing activities does Coppertone utilize to help the company grow in the marketplace?
5. What challenges does Coppertone face in the future? What actions would you recommend related to each challenge?

consumers become more engaged in their own health and wellness, Coppertone must help consumers think about its products as a part of their everyday routine. Finally, Coppertone recently partnered with Vision Ease to launch a line of sunglasses with Coppertone polarized lenses and a line of contact lenses as part of its commitment to develop new products to meet consumers' needs.

Chapter Notes

1. "2018 U.S. Women's Car Dealership Report," *www.women-drivers.com,* February 9, 2018; "Women Just as Confident as Men about Buying Cars," *www.cbsnews,* October 25, 2016; "Women in Cars: Overtaking Men on the Fast Lane," *www.forbes.com,* May 23, 2014; and "Americans Rethinking How They Buy Cars,"*www.money.msn.com,* April 4, 2014.
2. Roger D. Blackwell, Paul W. Miniard, and James F. Engel, *Consumer Behavior,* 10th ed. (Mason, OH: South-Western Publishing, 2006).
3. For thorough descriptions of consumer expertise, see Joseph W. Alba and J. Wesley Hutchinson, "Knowledge Calibration: What Consumers Know and What They Think They Know," *Journal of Consumer Research,* September 2000, pp. 123–57.
4. For representative in-depth studies on external information search patterns, see Sungha Jang, Ashutosh Prasad, and Brian T. Ratchford, "Consumer Search of Multiple Information Sources and its Impact on Consumer Price Satisfaction," *Journal of Interactive Marketing,* November, 2017, pp. 24–40; and Joel E. Urbany, Peter R. Dickson, and William L. Wilkie, "Buyer Uncertainty and Information Search," *Journal of Consumer Research,* March 1992, pp. 452–63.
5. "Apple's Phones Get Bigger, Pricier," *The Wall Street Journal,* September 13, 2018, pp. B1, B2; "Smartphones at the Head of the Class," *Consumer Reports,* January 2018, pp. 27–29; and "Galaxy S9: Infinity Screen and Beyond," *The Wall Street Journal,* April 19, 2018, pp. B1, B4.
6. For an extended discussion on evaluative criteria, see David L. Mothersbaugh and Delbert I. Hawkins, *Consumer Behavior: Building Marketing Strategy,* 13th ed. (Burr Ridge, IL: McGraw-Hill/Irwin, 2016).
7. John A. Howard, *Buyer Behavior in Marketing Strategy,* 2nd ed. (Englewood Cliffs, NJ: Prentice Hall, 1994). For an extended discussion on consumer choice sets, see Allan D. Shocker, Moshe Ben-Akiva, Brun Boccara, and Prakesh Nedungadi, "Consideration Set Influences on Consumer Decision Making and Choice: Issues, Models, and Suggestions," *Marketing Letters,* August 1991, pp. 181–98.
8. Robert J. Donovan, John R. Rossiter, Gillian Marcoolyn, and Andrew Nesdale, "Store Atmosphere and Purchasing Behavior," *Journal of Retailing,* Fall 1994, pp. 283–94; and Eric A. Greenleaf and Donald R. Lehmann, "Reasons for Substantial Delay in Consumer Decision Making," *Journal of Consumer Research,* September 1995, pp. 186–99.
9. "Webrooming and Mobile Showrooming in 2015," *multichannelmerchant.com,* January 19, 2016.
10. Sunil Gupta and Valarie Zeithaml, "Customer Metrics and Their Impact on Financial Performance," *Marketing Science,* November–December 2006, pp. 718–39.

11. These estimates are given in Jagdish N. Sheth and Banwari Mitral, *Consumer Behavior,* 2nd ed. (Mason, OH: South-Western Publishing, 2003), p. 32.
12. Francis Buttle and Stan Maklan, *Customer Relationship Management,* 3rd ed. (London: Routledge, 2015); "Customer Retention Is Top Concern for 64% of Dealers," *www.autoremarketing.com,* May 1, 2016; and "GM at Top for Customer Loyalty," *www.thedrive.com,* January 18, 2018.
13. For an overview of research on involvement, see Wayne D. Hoyer, Deborah J. MacInnis, and Rik Pieters, *Consumer Behavior,* 7th ed. (Independence, KY: Cengage Publishing, 2018).
14. Russell Belk, "Situational Variables and Consumer Behavior," *Journal of Consumer Research,* December 1975, pp. 157–63. The examples in this section are taken from Martin Lindstrom, *buy.ology: Truth and Lies about Why We Buy* (New York: Doubleday Publishing, 2008).
15. For a thorough discussion of consumer experience and the consumer journey, see Katherine N. Lemon and Peter C. Verhoef, "Understanding Customer Experience and the Customer Journey," *Journal of Marketing,* November 2016, pp. 69–96.
16. A. H. Maslow, *Motivation and Personality* (New York: Harper & Row, 1970). For an update on this need hierarchy, see Douglas T. Kendrick et al., "Renovating the Pyramid of Needs: Contemporary Extensions Built upon Ancient Foundations," *Perspectives on Psychological Sciences* 5, no. 3 (2010), pp. 292–314.
17. Bernardo J. Carducci, *The Psychology of Personality,* 2nd ed. (Oxford, UK: Wiley, 2009), pp. 182–84; and D. Bratko, A. Butkovic, and M. Bosnjak, "Twin Study of Impulsive Buying and Its Overlap with Personality, *Journal of Individual Differences* 34, no. 1 (2013), pp. 8–14.
18. Jane Spencer, "Lenovo Puts Style in New Laptop," *The Wall Street Journal,* January 3, 2008, p. B5.
19. Julie Sedivy and Greg Carlson, *Sold on Language: How Advertisers Talk to You and What This Says about You* (New York: Wiley, 2011).
20. For further reading on subliminal perception, see Lindstrom, *buy.ology:* B. Bahrami, N. Lavie, and G. Rees, "Attentional Load Modulates Responses of Human Primary Visual Cortex to Invisible Stimuli," *Current Biology,* March 2007, pp. 39–47; and J. Karremans, W. Stroebe, and J. Claus, "Beyond Vicary's Fantasies: The Impact of Subliminal Priming and Brand Choice," *Journal of Experimental Social Psychology* 42 (2006), pp. 792–98.
21. Adrian Furnham, "Hidden Persuaders: The Psychology of Subliminal Perception," *www.psychologytoday.com,* July 20, 2015; August Bullock, *The Secret Sales Pitch* (San Jose, CA: Norwich Publishers, 2004); and Dave Lakhani, *Subliminal Persuasion* (Hoboken, NJ: Wiley, 2008).
22. "Death of a Car Salesman," *The Economist,* August 22, 2015, pp. 52–54.
23. "Deloitte Survey: Shoppers Continue to Leave National Brands," *www.prnewswire.com,* June 23, 2015; and Steve Olenski, "Is Brand Loyalty Dying a Slow and Painful Death?" *www.forbes.com,* January 7, 2013.
24. Martin Fishbein and I. Aizen, *Belief, Attitude, Intention and Behavior: An Introduction to Theory and Research* (Reading, MA: Addison-Wesley, 1975), p. 6.
25. Richard J. Lutz, "Changing Brand Attitudes through Modification of Cognitive Structure," *Journal of Consumer Research,* March 1975, pp. 49–59.
26. This discussion is based on "The VALS™ Types," *www.strategicbusinessinsights.com,* downloaded February 1, 2017.
27. This discussion is based on Ed Keller and Jon Berry, *The Influentials* (New York: Simon and Schuster, 2003); "The Kids Who Rule Toyland," *Bloomberg Businessweek,* October 23, 2017; and "For Influencers, Instagram Is the Clear-Cut Favorite," www.emarketer.com, January 30, 2018.
28. Ed Keller and Brad Fay, "Word-of-Mouth Advocacy: A New Key to Advertising Effectiveness," *Journal of Advertising Research,* December 2012, pp. 459–64.
29. "What Really Shapes the Customer Experience," *www.bcg.perspectives.com,* September 10, 2015.
30. Correspondence with Rebecca A. Hall, Marketing Manager, BzzAgent, April 28, 2017; and *www.BzzAgent.com,* downloaded April 22, 2017.
31. "Five-Star Fakes," *The Economist,* October 24, 2015, p. 64; "Amazon Targets Bogus Reviewers," *Dallas Morning News,* October 20, 2015, p. 2D; and "Why Facebook Hates and Likes Fake Likes," *www.forbes.com,* October 6, 2014.
32. Wayne D. Hoyer, Deborah J. MacInnis, and Rik Pieters, *Consumer Behavior,* 7th ed. (Independence, KY: Cengage Publishing, 2018).
33. Elizabeth Holmes, "Abercrombie and Fitch Offers to Pay 'The Situation' to Stop Wearing Its Clothes," *The Wall Street Journal,* August 16, 2011, p. B2.
34. For an extensive review on consumer socialization of children, see Deborah Roedder John, "Consumer Socialization of Children: A Retrospective Look at Twenty-Five Years of Research," *Journal of Consumer Research,* December 1999, pp. 183–213. Also see Gwen Bachmann Achenreinver and Deborah Roedder John, "The Meaning of Brand Names to Children: A Developmental Investigation," *Journal of Consumer Psychology* 13, no. 3 (2003), pp. 205–19; and Elizabeth S. Moore, William L. Wilkie, and Richard J. Lutz, "Passing the Torch: Intergenerational Influences as a Source of Brand Equity," *Journal of Marketing,* April 2002, pp. 17–37.
35. "America's Families and Living Arrangements: 2015" (Washington, DC: U.S. Department of Commerce, August 2016); "Supermarkets Lure in Male Shoppers," *The Wall Street Journal,* July 10, 2018, p. A9; and Rich Morin and D'Vera Cohn, "Women Call the Shots at Home: Public Mixed on Gender Roles in Jobs," *www.pewresearch.org,* downloaded February 4, 2011. Also see Rex Y. Du and Wagner A. Kamakura, "Household Life Cycles and Lifestyles in the United States," *Journal of Marketing Research,* February 2006, pp. 121–32.
36. David L. Mothersbaugh and Delbert I. Hawkins, *Consumer Behavior: Building Marketing Strategy,* 13th ed. (Burr Ridge, IL: McGraw-Hill/Irwin, 2016); "Food for Kids: How Children Influence Their Parents' Purchasing Decisions," *Food Products Marketing* 22, no. 5, pp. 596–609; and "62% Rise in Millennial Dads Buying Groceries: Study," progressivegrocer.com, June 13, 2016.
37. Jeffrey M. Humphreys, "The Multicultural Economy in 2018," Selig Center for Economic Growth, Terry College of Business, The University of Georgia.
38. The remainder of this discussion is based on Hoyer et al., *Consumer Behavior, Engaging the Evolving Hispanic Consumer* (New York: The Nielsen Company, 2014); and *14th Annual Hispanic Fact Pack* (New York: Advertising Age, 2018).
39. The remainder of this discussion is based on Wayne D. Hoyer, Deborah J. MacInnis, and Rik Pieters, *Consumer Behavior,* 7th ed. (Independence, KY: Cengage Publishing, 2018); and *Powerful, Growing, Influential: The African-American Consumer* (New York: The Nielsen Company, 2016).

40. The remainder of this discussion is based on *Asian-Americans Are Expanding Their Footprint in the U.S. and Making an Impact* (New York: The Nielsen Company, 2016); *"Asian American Women: Digitally Fluent with Intercultural Mindset* (New York: The Nielsen Company, 2017); and Christine Birkner, "Asian-Americans in Focus," *Marketing News,* March 2013, p. 14.

41. Coppertone: This case was written by Steven Hartley and Roger Kerin. Sources: Interviews with Coppertone executives Tracy Nunziata and Lisa Perez; information from the Coppertone website, *www.coppertone.com;* "A New Day for Sun Care," GCI Magazine, January–February 2016, pp. 32–35; "Consumers Embrace Multifunction Sun Products," *Chain Drug Review,* July 6, 2015, p. 43; Jayme Cyk, "Sun Care's New Wave," *WWB,* April 10, 2015, p. 6; Antoinette Alexander, "Raising Awareness about Sun Safety," *Drug Store News,* August 25, 2014, p. 128; Lisa Samalonis, "Sun Care: It's All about Convenience," *Beauty Packaging,* April–May 2012, p. 42–46; "Coppertone Polarized Lenses," *20/20,* 2016, p. 108; Andrew Karp, "Vision Ease Intros Coppertone Polarized Lenses in Green," *Vision Monday,* January 18, 2016, p. 27; and Mercedes M. Cardona, "Coppertone Brings Back Ad Icon for $15 Mil Effort," *Advertising Age,* February 15, 1999, p. 16.

5

LEARNING OBJECTIVES

After reading this chapter you should be able to:

LO 5-1 Distinguish among industrial, reseller, and government organizational markets.

LO 5-2 Describe the key characteristics of organizational buying that make it different from consumer buying.

LO 5-3 Explain how buying centers and buying situations influence organizational purchasing.

LO 5-4 Recognize the importance and nature of online buying in industrial, reseller, and government organizational markets.

Understanding Organizations as Customers

Organizational Buying Is Marketing, Too! Purchasing Publication Paper for JCPenney

Executives at JCPMedia, Inc. view paper differently than most people do. And for good reason. JCPMedia purchasing professionals buy over 100,000 tons of publication paper—annually.

JCPMedia is responsible for print and paper purchasing at JCPenney, one of the largest department store retailers in the United States. JCPMedia buys publication paper for JCPenney newspaper inserts and direct-mail pieces, which is a serious responsibility. Some 10 companies from around the world—including Verso Paper in the United States, Catalyst Paper Corporation in Canada, Norske Skog in Norway, and UPM-Kymmene, Inc. in Finland—supply paper to JCPenney.

"The choice of paper and suppliers is also a significant marketing decision given the sizable revenue and expense consequences," notes the Vice President–Marketing Production at JCPMedia, Inc. JCPMedia paper buyers work closely with senior JCPenney marketing executives and within budget constraints to assure that the right appearance, quality, and quantity of publication paper is purchased at the right price point for merchandise featured in the millions of JCPenney newspaper inserts and direct-mail pieces distributed every year in the United States.

In addition to paper appearance, quality, quantity, and price, JCPMedia paper buyers formally evaluate paper supplier capabilities, often by extended visits to supplier facilities in the United States, Canada, and Europe. Supplier capabilities include the capacity to deliver on-time selected grades of paper from specialty items to magazine papers, the availability of specific types of paper to meet printing deadlines, and formal programs focused on the life cycle of paper products. For example, a supplier's forestry management and sustainability practices are considered in the paper buying process. In fact, paper bought by JCPMedia is certified through the Sustainable Forestry Initiative, Forest Stewardship Council, or the Programme for the Endorsement of Forest Certification—three prominent certification programs for forest management.[1]

The next time you thumb through a JCPenney newspaper insert or direct-mail piece, take a moment to notice the paper. Considerable effort and

Courtesy of JCPenney

attention were given to its selection and purchase decision by JCPMedia paper buyers.

Purchasing paper for JCPMedia is one example of organizational buying. This chapter examines the different types of organizational buyers; key characteristics of organizational buying, including online buying; buying situations; unique aspects of the organizational buying process compared with the consumer purchase process; and some typical buying procedures and decisions in today's organizational markets.

BUSINESS-TO-BUSINESS MARKETING AND ORGANIZATIONAL BUYERS

LO 5-1 Distinguish among industrial, reseller, and government organizational markets.

Understanding organizational markets and buying behavior is a necessary prerequisite for effective business-to-business marketing. **Business-to-business marketing** is the marketing of products and services to companies, governments, or not-for-profit organizations for use in the creation of products and services that they can produce and market to others. Because over half of all U.S. business school graduates take jobs in firms that engage in business marketing, it is important to understand the characteristics of organizational buyers and their buying behavior.

business-to-business marketing
The marketing of products and services to companies, governments, or not-for-profit organizations for use in the creation of products and services that they can produce and market to others.

organizational buyers
Those manufacturers, wholesalers, retailers, service companies, not-for-profit organizations, and government agencies that buy products and services for their own use or for resale.

Organizational Buyers

Organizational buyers are those manufacturers, wholesalers, retailers, service companies, not-for-profit organizations, and government agencies that buy products and services for their own use or for resale. For example, these organizations buy computers and telephone services for their own use. However, manufacturers buy raw materials and parts that they reprocess into the finished goods they sell. Wholesalers and retailers resell the goods they buy without reprocessing them.

Organizational buyers include all buyers in a nation except ultimate consumers. These organizational buyers purchase and lease large volumes of capital equipment, raw materials, manufactured parts, supplies, and business services. In fact, because they often buy raw materials and parts, process them, and sell the upgraded product several times before it is purchased by the final organizational buyer or ultimate consumer, the total annual purchases of organizational buyers are far greater than those of ultimate consumers. IBM alone buys over $52 billion in products and services each year for its own use or resale.[2]

Organizational Markets

Organizational buyers are divided into three markets: (1) industrial, (2) reseller, and (3) government.[3] Each market is described next.

Industrial Markets There are about 7.5 million firms in the industrial, or business, market. These *industrial firms* in some way reprocess a product or service they buy before selling it again to the next buyer. This is certainly true of Corning, Inc., which transforms an exotic blend of materials to create optical fiber capable of carrying much of the telephone traffic in the United States on a single strand. It is also true (if you stretch your imagination) of a firm selling services, such as a bank that takes money from its depositors, reprocesses it, and "sells" it as loans to borrowers.

Companies that primarily sell physical goods (manufacturing; mining; construction; and farms, timber, and fisheries) represent 25 percent of all the industrial firms. The services market sells diverse services such as legal advice, auto repair, and dry cleaning. Service companies—finance, insurance, and real estate businesses; transportation, communication, and public utility firms; and not-for-profit organizations—represent 75 percent of all industrial firms.

Reseller Markets Wholesalers and retailers that buy physical products and resell them again without any reprocessing are *resellers*. In the United States there are about 1.1 million retailers and 435,000 wholesalers. In Chapters 12 and 13, you will see how manufacturers use wholesalers and retailers in their distribution ("place") strategies as channels through which their products reach ultimate consumers. In this chapter, we look at these resellers mainly as organizational buyers in terms of (1) how they make their own buying decisions and (2) which products they choose to carry.

The Orion spacecraft to be designed, developed, tested, and evaluated by Lockheed Martin Corp. is an example of a purchase by a government unit, namely, NASA. Read the text to find out how much NASA will pay for Orion's development, test flights, and its first manned mission.

Courtesy of Lockheed Martin Company

Video 5-1
NASA
kerin.tv/cr8e/v5-1

Government Markets *Government units* are the federal, state, and local agencies that buy goods and services for the constituents they serve. There are about 89,500 of these government units in the United States. These purchases include the $20.4 billion the National Aeronautics and Space Administration (NASA) intends to pay Lockheed Martin through 2023 to develop the Orion Multi-Purpose Crew Vehicle to explore asteroids and Mars.[4]

Measuring Organizational Markets

The measurement of industrial, reseller, and government markets is an important first step for a firm interested in gauging the size of one, two, or all three of these markets in the United States and around the world. This task has been made easier with the **North American Industry Classification System (NAICS)**. The NAICS provides common industry definitions for Canada, Mexico, and the United States, which makes it easier to measure economic activity in the three member countries of the North American Free Trade Agreement (NAFTA).

The NAICS groups economic activity to permit studies of market share, demand for products and services, import competition in domestic markets, and similar studies. It designates industries with a numerical code in a defined structure. A six-digit coding system is used. The first two digits designate a sector of the economy, the third digit designates a subsector, and the fourth digit represents an industry group. The fifth digit designates a specific industry and is the most detailed level at which comparable data are available for Canada, Mexico, and the United States. The sixth digit designates individual country-level national industries.

North American Industry Classification System (NAICS)
Provides common industry definitions for Canada, Mexico, and the United States, which makes it easier to measure economic activity in the three member countries of the North American Free Trade Agreement (NAFTA).

learning review

5-1. Organizational buyers are _____.

5-2. What are the three main types of organizational buyers?

CHARACTERISTICS OF ORGANIZATIONAL BUYING

LO 5-2 Describe the key characteristics of organizational buying that make it different from consumer buying.

Organizations are different from individuals, so buying for an organization is different from buying for yourself or your family. In both cases the objective in making the purchase is to solve the buyer's problem—to satisfy a need or want. However, the unique objectives and policies of an organization put special constraints on how it makes buying decisions. Understanding the characteristics of organizational buying is essential in designing effective marketing programs to reach these buyers. Key characteristics of organizational buying are listed in Figure 5–1 and discussed next.[5]

Demand Characteristics

Consumer demand for products and services is affected by their price and availability and by consumers' personal tastes and discretionary income. By comparison, industrial demand is derived. **Derived demand** means that the demand for industrial products and services is driven by, or derived from, demand for consumer products and services. For example, the demand for Weyerhaeuser's pulp and paper products is based on consumer demand for newspapers, FedEx packages, and disposable diapers. Derived demand is based on expectations of future consumer demand. For instance, Whirlpool buys parts for its washers and dryers in anticipation of consumer demand, which is affected by the replacement cycle for these products and by consumer income.

> **derived demand**
> The demand for industrial products and services that is driven by, or derived from, the demand for consumer products and services.

Size of the Order or Purchase

The size of the purchase involved in organizational buying is typically much larger than that in consumer buying. The dollar value of a single purchase made by an organization can amount to millions or billions of dollars. For example, Siemens was

FIGURE 5–1
Key characteristics and dimensions of organizational buying behavior.

CHARACTERISTICS	DIMENSIONS
Market characteristics	• Demand for industrial products and services is derived. • Few customers typically exist, and their purchase orders are large.
Product or service characteristics	• Products or services are technical in nature and purchased on the basis of specifications. • Many of the goods purchased are raw and semifinished. • Heavy emphasis is placed on delivery time, technical assistance, and postsale service.
Buying process characteristics	• Technically qualified and professional buyers follow established purchasing policies and procedures. • Buying objectives and criteria are typically spelled out, as are procedures for evaluating sellers and their products or services. • There are multiple buying influences, and multiple parties participate in purchase decisions. • There are reciprocal arrangements, and negotiation between buyers and sellers is commonplace. • Online buying over the Internet is widespread.
Marketing mix characteristics	• Direct selling to organizational buyers is the rule, and distribution is very important. • Advertising and other forms of promotion are technical in nature. • Price is often negotiated, evaluated as part of broader seller and product/service qualities, and frequently affected by quantity discounts.

Buying commercial aircraft is time-consuming, involved, and expensive. Read the text to find out how much a new Boeing 777 airplane costs.
©Karie Hamilton/Bloomberg via Getty Images

paid $1 billion to build a natural-gas-fired power plant in Texas.[6] The Boeing Company, the world's largest aerospace company, charges about $103 million for its "average" Boeing 737 commercial jetliner, $344 million for its Boeing 777, and $270 million for the Boeing 787.[7]

With so much money at stake, most organizations place constraints on their buyers in the form of purchasing policies or procedures. Buyers must often get competitive bids from at least three prospective suppliers when the order is above a specific amount, such as $5,000. When the order is above an even higher amount, such as $50,000, it may require the review and approval of a vice president or even the president of the company. Knowing how order size affects buying practices is important in determining who will participate in the purchase decision, who will make the final decision, and the length of time that will be required to arrive at a purchase agreement.

Number of Potential Buyers

Firms marketing consumer products or services often try to reach thousands or millions of individuals or households. For example, your local supermarket or bank probably serves thousands of people. Kellogg tries to reach 80 million North American households with its breakfast cereals and probably succeeds in selling to a third or half of these in any given year. Firms marketing to organizations are often restricted to far fewer buyers. Gulfstream Aerospace Corporation can sell its business jets to a few thousand organizations throughout the world, and Goodyear sells its original equipment tires to fewer than 10 car manufacturers.

Organizational Buying Objectives

Pitney Bowes is a leader in supplier diversity. The company has hundreds of diverse suppliers that account for millions of dollars in annual purchases. To learn more about companies that have successful supplier diversity, and corporate diversity overall, visit www.diversityinc.com.
Source: Pitney Bowes Inc.

Supplier Diversity Program

For business firms, the buying objective is usually to increase profits through reducing costs or increasing revenues. For example, 7-Eleven buys automated inventory systems to increase the number of products that can be sold through its convenience stores and to keep them fresh. Nissan Motor Company switched its advertising agency because it expects the new agency to devise a more effective ad campaign to help it sell more cars and increase revenues. To improve executive decision making, many firms buy advanced computer systems to process data. The objectives of nonprofit firms and government agencies are usually to meet the needs of the groups they serve.

Many companies today have broadened their buying objectives to include an emphasis on buying from minority- and women-owned suppliers and vendors. Companies such as Pitney Bowes, PepsiCo, AT&T, Coors, and JCPenney report that sales, profits, and customer satisfaction have increased because of their minority- and women-owned supplier and vendor initiatives.

Other companies include environmental sustainability initiatives. For example, Lowe's and The Home Depot no longer purchase lumber from companies that harvest timber from the world's endangered forests. Successful business marketers recognize that understanding a company's buying objectives is a necessary first step in marketing to organizations.

Organizational Buying Criteria

In making a purchase, the buying organization must weigh key buying criteria that apply to the potential supplier and what it wants to sell. *Organizational buying criteria* are the objective attributes of the supplier's products and services and the capabilities of the supplier itself. These criteria serve the same purpose as the evaluative criteria used by consumers and described in Chapter 4. The most commonly used criteria are (1) price, (2) ability to meet the quality specifications required for the item, (3) ability to meet required delivery schedules, (4) technical capability, (5) warranties and claim policies in the event of poor performance, (6) past performance on previous contracts, and (7) production facilities and capacity.[8] Suppliers that meet or exceed these criteria create customer value.

As a practical example, Figure 5–2 shows the actual buying criteria employed by organizational buyers when choosing among machine vision system products and suppliers, as well as the frequency with which these criteria are used. Interestingly, of the various selection criteria listed, a machine vision system's price is among the least frequently mentioned.[9]

Many organizational buyers today are transforming their buying criteria into specific requirements that are communicated to prospective suppliers. This practice, called *supplier development,* involves the deliberate effort by organizational buyers to build relationships that shape suppliers' products, services, and capabilities to fit a buyer's needs and those of its customers. Consider Deere & Company, the maker of John Deere farm, construction, and lawn-care equipment. Deere employs supplier-development engineers who work full-time with the company's suppliers to improve their efficiency and quality and reduce their costs. According to a Deere senior executive, "Their quality, delivery, and costs are, after all, our quality, delivery, and costs."[10]

Buyer–Seller Relationships and Supply Partnerships

Another distinction between organizational and consumer buying behavior lies in the nature of the relationship between organizational buyers and suppliers. Specifically, organizational buying is more likely to involve complex negotiations concerning delivery schedules, price, technical specifications, warranties, and claim policies. These negotiations also can last for an extended period. This was the case when the U.S. Department of Energy's Oak Ridge National Laboratory acquired an IBM Summit supercomputer at a cost of about $200 million. In terms of processing speed, the Summit can perform 200,000 trillion calculations a second![11]

Reciprocal arrangements also exist in organizational buying. *Reciprocity* is an industrial buying practice in which two organizations agree to purchase each other's products and services. The U.S. Justice Department disapproves of reciprocal buying

FIGURE 5–2

Product and supplier selection criteria for buying machine vision equipment emphasize factors other than price.

(photo): Courtesy of Keyence Corporation of America.

A machine vision inspection camera is used in the automotive industry to perform a gear inspection—in this case, to check if the notches are correctly angled and sized.

Individual selection criteria cited as most important by machine vision buyers making a product or supplier decision.

Marketing Matters

Customer Value

At Milsco Manufacturing, "Our Marketing Philosophy Is Designed to Develop Partnerships" and Deliver a Great Ride for Customers' Seats

Form, fit, and functionality are the hallmarks of a proper seating solution. Just ask the executives and engineers at Milsco Manufacturing, which produces more than 3 million seats annually in more than 200 unique variations.

Whether you are cruising the wide open spaces on your Harley-Davidson motorcycle or mowing your backyard on a John Deere lawn tractor, you're getting a comfortable ride thanks to a company you may have never heard of. Milsco is a Wisconsin-based designer and producer of seating solutions. Its customers include Harley-Davidson, John Deere, Yamaha, Caterpillar, Arctic Cat, Kubata, Toro, and Toyota, as well as numerous other well-known and respected household names in the motorcycle, power sports, agricultural, construction, marine recreation, turf care, industrial lift, golf cart, and mobility markets.

Milsco's marketing philosophy is designed to develop partnerships with its customers. The 85-year partnership between Harley-Davidson and Milsco is a case in point. Since 1934, Milsco has been the sole source of original equipment motorcycle seats and a major supplier of after-market parts and accessories, such as saddlebags, for Harley-Davidson. Milsco engineers and designers work closely with their Harley counterparts in the design of each year's new products.

In fact, Milsco partners with each of its customers to design and manufacture the most effective and functional seating solution. Every year, the company launches over 100 new products, many of which are crafted by hand, in response to new and changing customer requirements.

The next time you sit down on a Harley or a John Deere lawn tractor (or any other product involving a partnership with Milsco Manufacturing), notice the seat and remember that it was designed and manufactured for your form, fit, and functionality—and, of course, comfort.

©Lluis Gene/AFP/Getty Images

because it restricts the normal operation of the free market. However, the practice exists and can limit the flexibility of organizational buyers in choosing alternative suppliers.

Long-term contracts are also prevalent. For example, GT Advanced Technology has a multiyear, $578 million contract with Apple to supply material used in iPhone camera lenses and screens.[12]

In some cases, buyer–seller relationships evolve into supply partnerships. A *supply partnership* exists when a buyer and its supplier adopt mutually beneficial objectives, policies, and procedures for the purpose of lowering the cost or increasing the value of products and services delivered to the ultimate consumer. A classic example of a supply partnership is the one between Harley-Davidson and Milsco Manufacturing. Milsco has designed and manufactured Harley-Davidson motorcycle seats since 1934. The importance of supply partnerships for Milsco is described in the Marketing Matters box.[13]

Making Responsible Decisions | Sustainability

Sustainable Procurement for Sustainable Growth at Starbucks

Manufacturers, retailers, wholesalers, and governmental agencies are increasingly sensitive to how their buying decisions affect the environment. Concerns about the depletion of natural resources; air, water, and soil pollution; and the social consequences of economic activity have given rise to the concept of sustainable procurement. Sustainable procurement aims to integrate environmental considerations into all stages of an organization's buying process with the goal of reducing the negative impact on human health and the physical environment.

Starbucks is a pioneer and worldwide leader in sustainable procurement. The company's attention to quality coffee extends to its coffee growers located in more than 20 countries. This means that Starbucks pays coffee farmers a fair price for the beans; that the coffee is grown in an ecologically sound manner; and that Starbucks

©Jewel Samad/AFP/Getty Images

invests in the farming communities where its coffees are produced. In this way, Starbucks focuses on the sustainable growth of its suppliers.

Retailers, too, have forged partnerships with their suppliers. Walmart has such a relationship with Procter & Gamble for ordering and replenishing P&G's products in its stores. By using computerized cash register scanning equipment and direct electronic linkages to P&G, Walmart can tell P&G what merchandise is needed, along with how much, when, and to which store to deliver it on a daily basis.

Supply partnerships often include provisions for what is called *sustainable procurement*. To learn more about this buying practice and how it has been embraced at Starbucks, see the Making Responsible Decisions box.[14]

> **Video 5-2**
> Starbucks Sustainability
> kerin.tv/cr8e/v5-2

THE ORGANIZATIONAL BUYING FUNCTION AND PROCESS AND THE BUYING CENTER

organizational buying behavior
The decision-making process that organizations use to establish the need for products and services and identify, evaluate, and choose among alternative brands and suppliers.

Organizational buyers, like consumers, engage in a decision process when selecting products and services. **Organizational buying behavior** is the decision-making process that organizations use to establish the need for products and services and identify, evaluate, and choose among alternative brands and suppliers. There are important similarities and differences between the two decision-making processes. To better understand the nature of organizational buying behavior, we first describe the buying function in organizations. Next, the organizational buying process itself is detailed by comparing it with consumer buying behavior. We then describe a unique feature of organizational buying—the buying center.

The Buying Function in Organizations

The buying function in an organization is primarily responsible for facilitating the selection and purchase of products and services for the organization's own use or resale to consumers. The buying function involves gathering and screening information about products and services, prices, and suppliers, called *vendors*. The buying

STAGE IN THE BUYING DECISION PROCESS	CONSUMER PURCHASE: SMARTPHONE FOR A STUDENT	ORGANIZATIONAL PURCHASE: EARBUD HEADSET FOR A SMARTPHONE
Problem recognition	Student doesn't like the features of the smartphone now owned and desires a new one.	Marketing research and sales departments observe that competitors are improving the earbud headsets for their smartphones. The firm decides to improve the earbud headsets on its own new models, which will be purchased from an outside supplier.
Information search	Student uses personal past experience and that of friends, ads, the Internet, and *Consumer Reports* to collect information and uncover alternatives.	Design and production engineers draft specifications for earbud headsets. The purchasing department identifies suppliers of earbud headsets.
Alternative evaluation	Alternative smartphones are evaluated on the basis of important attributes desired in a phone, and several stores are visited.	Purchasing and engineering personnel visit with suppliers and assess (1) facilities, (2) capacity, (3) quality control, and (4) financial status. They drop any suppliers not satisfactory on these attributes.
Purchase decision	A specific brand of smartphone is selected, the price is paid, and the student leaves the store.	They use (1) quality, (2) price, (3) delivery, and (4) technical capability as key buying criteria to select a supplier. Then they negotiate terms and award a contract.
Postpurchase behavior	Student reevaluates the purchase decision and may return the phone to the store if it is unsatisfactory.	They evaluate suppliers using a formal vendor rating system and notify a supplier if the earbud headsets do not meet their quality standard. If the problem is not corrected, they drop the firm as a future supplier.

FIGURE 5–3

Comparing the stages in a consumer and organizational purchase decision process.

function is often responsible for the formal solicitation of bids from suppliers (vendors) and the awarding of purchasing contracts.

Individuals responsible for the selection and purchase of goods and services are typically called purchasing managers or agents, procurement managers, or sourcing managers. Their role in the organizational buying process is described below.

Stages in the Organizational Buying Process

As shown in Figure 5–3, the five stages a student might use in buying a smartphone also apply to organizational purchases. However, comparing the two columns in Figure 5–3 reveals some key differences. For example, when a manufacturer buys an earbud headset for its units from a supplier, more individuals are involved, supplier capability becomes more important, and the postpurchase evaluation behavior is more formal. The earbud headset buying decision process is typical of the steps made by organizational buyers.

The Buying Center: A Cross-Functional Group

Explain how buying centers and buying situations influence organizational purchasing.

For routine purchases with a small dollar value, a single buyer or purchasing manager often makes the purchase decision alone. In many instances, however, several people in the organization participate in the buying process. The individuals in this group,

buying center
The group of people in an organization who participate in the buying process and share common goals, risks, and knowledge important to a purchase decision.

called a **buying center**, share common goals, risks, and knowledge important to a purchase decision. For most large multistore chain resellers, such as Target, 7-Eleven convenience stores, or Safeway, the buying center is highly formalized and is called a *buying committee*. However, most industrial firms or government units use informal groups of people or call meetings to arrive at buying decisions.

The importance of the buying center requires that a firm marketing to many industrial firms and government units understand the structure, the technical and business functions represented, and the behavior of these groups.[15] Four questions provide guidance in understanding the buying center in these organizations:

1. Which individuals are in the buying center for the product or service?
2. What is the relative influence of each member of the group?
3. What are the buying criteria of each member?
4. How does each member of the group perceive our firm, our products and services, and our salespeople?

People in the Buying Center   The composition of the buying center in a given organization depends on the specific item being bought. Although a buyer or purchasing manager is almost always a member of the buying center, individuals from other functional areas are included, depending on what is to be purchased. In buying a million-dollar machine tool, the president (because of the size of the purchase) and the production vice president or manager would probably be members. For key components to be included in a final manufactured product, a cross-functional group of individuals from research and development (R&D), engineering, and quality control are likely to be added. For new word-processing software and equipment, experienced secretaries who will use the equipment would be members. Still, a major question in penetrating the buying center is finding and reaching the people who will initiate, influence, and actually make the buying decision.

Roles in the Buying Center   Researchers have identified five specific roles that an individual in a buying center can play.[16] In some purchases the same person may perform two or more of these roles.

- *Users* are the people in the organization who actually use the product or service, such as a secretary who will use a new word processor.
- *Influencers* affect the buying decision, usually by helping define the specifications for what is bought. The information technology manager would be a key influencer in the purchase of a new mainframe computer.
- *Buyers* have formal authority and responsibility to select the supplier and negotiate the terms of the contract. Senior purchasing managers perform this role at JCPMedia, as described in the chapter opening example.
- *Deciders* have the formal or informal power to select or approve the supplier that receives the contract. In routine orders the decider is usually the buyer or purchasing manager; in important technical purchases it is more likely to be someone from R&D, engineering, or quality control. The decider for a key component being incorporated in a final manufactured product might be any of these three people.
- *Gatekeepers* control the flow of information in the buying center. Purchasing personnel, technical experts, and secretaries can all keep salespeople or information from reaching people performing the other four roles.

Effective marketing to organizations requires an understanding of buying centers and their role in purchase decisions.
©monkeybusinessimages/Getty Images

Buying Situations and the Buying Center   The number of people in the buying center largely depends on

BUYING CENTER DIMENSION	BUY-CLASS SITUATION		
	NEW BUY	STRAIGHT REBUY	MODIFIED REBUY
People involved	Many	One	Two to three
Decision time	Long	Short	Moderate
Problem definition	Uncertain	Well-defined	Minor modifications
Buying objective	Good solution	Low-priced supplier	Low-priced supplier
Suppliers considered	New/present	Present	Present
Buying influence	Technical/operating personnel	Purchasing agent	Purchasing agent and others

FIGURE 5–4
The buying situation affects buying center behavior in different ways. Understanding these differences can pay huge dividends for companies that market to organizations.

buy classes
Consist of three types of organizational buying situations: straight rebuy, new buy, and modified rebuy.

the specific buying situation. Researchers who have studied organizational buying identify three types of buying situations, called **buy classes**. These buy classes vary from the routine reorder, or *straight rebuy*, to the completely new purchase, termed *new buy*. In between these extremes is the *modified rebuy*. Figure 5–4 summarizes how buy classes affect buying center tendencies in different ways. Some examples will clarify the differences.[17]

- *New buy.* Here the organization is a first-time buyer of the product or service. This involves greater potential risks in the purchase, so the buying center is enlarged to include all those who have a stake in the new buy. BMW's recent purchase of a multimillion-dollar cloud-based data management system from IBM represents a new buy.
- *Straight rebuy.* Here the buyer or purchasing manager reorders an existing product or service from the list of acceptable suppliers, probably without even checking with users or influencers from the engineering, production, or quality control departments. Office supplies and maintenance services are usually obtained as straight rebuys.
- *Modified rebuy.* In this buying situation the users, influencers, or deciders in the buying center want to change the product specifications, price, delivery schedule, or supplier. Although the item purchased is largely the same as with the straight rebuy, the changes usually necessitate enlarging the buying center to include people outside the purchasing department.

learning review

5-3. What one department is almost always represented by a person in the buying center?

5-4. What are the three types of buying situations or buy classes?

ONLINE BUYING IN BUSINESS-TO-BUSINESS MARKETING

LO 5-4 Recognize the importance and nature of online buying in industrial, reseller, and government organizational markets.

Organizational buying behavior and business-to-business marketing continue to evolve with the application of Internet technology. Organizations dwarf consumers in terms of online transactions made, average transaction size, and overall purchase volume. In fact, organizational buyers account for about 70 percent of the global dollar value of all online transactions.

Prominence of Online Buying in Organizational Markets

Online buying in organizational markets is prominent for three major reasons.[18] First, organizational buyers depend heavily on timely supplier information that describes product availability, technical specifications, application uses, price, and delivery schedules. This information can be conveyed quickly via Internet technology. Second, this technology has been shown to substantially reduce buyer order processing costs. At General Electric, online buying has cut the cost of a purchase transaction from $50 to $100 to about $5. Third, business marketers have found that Internet technology can reduce marketing costs, particularly sales and advertising expense, and broaden their potential customer base for many types of products and services.

For these reasons, online buying is popular in all three kinds of organizational markets. For example, airlines electronically order over $10.4 billion in spare parts from the Boeing Company each year. Customers of W. W. Grainger, a large U.S. wholesaler of maintenance, repair, and operating supplies, buy almost $5 billion worth of these products annually online. Supply and service purchases totaling about $50 billion each year are made online by the U.S. government.

E-Marketplaces: Virtual Organizational Markets

A significant development in organizational buying has been the creation of online trading communities, called **e-marketplaces**, that bring together buyers and supplier organizations. These online communities go by a variety of names, including *B2B exchanges* and *e-hubs,* and make possible the real-time exchange of information, money, products, and services.

E-marketplaces can be independent trading communities or private exchanges. Independent e-marketplaces act as a neutral third party and provide an Internet technology trading platform and a centralized market that enable exchanges between buyers and sellers. They charge a fee for their service and exist in settings that have one or more of the following features: (1) thousands of geographically dispersed buyers and sellers, (2) volatile prices caused by demand and supply fluctuations, (3) time sensitivity due to perishable offerings and changing technologies, and (4) easily comparable offerings between a variety of sellers.

Examples of independent e-marketplaces include Amazon Business (general business equipment and supplies), PlasticsNet (plastics), Hospital Network.com (health care supplies and equipment), and TextileWeb (garment and apparel products). Small business buyers and sellers, in particular, benefit from independent e-marketplaces. These e-marketplaces offer them an economical way to expand their customer base and reduce the cost of products and services. For example, eBay provides an electronic platform for entrepreneurs and the small business market in the United States and other countries. Read the Marketing Matters box to learn more about how eBay promotes business-to-business sales and entrepreneurship.[19]

Large companies tend to favor private exchanges that link them with their network of qualified suppliers and customers. Private exchanges focus on streamlining a company's purchase transactions with its suppliers and customers. Like independent e-marketplaces, they provide a technology trading platform and central market for buyer–seller interactions. However, unlike independent e-marketplaces, they are not a neutral third party; private exchanges represent the interests of their owners. For example, NeoGrid is an international business-to-business private exchange. It

e-marketplaces
Online trading communities that bring together buyers and supplier organizations to make possible the real-time exchange of information, money, products, and services. Also called *B2B exchanges* or *e-hubs*.

Marketing Matters   Entrepreneurship

eBay Means Business for Business-to-Business Marketing Entrepreneurs, Too!

San Jose, California–based eBay Inc. is a true Internet phenomenon. By any measure, it is the predominant person-to-person trading community in the world. But there is more.

eBay offers a trading platform for millions of small businesses in the United States engaged in business-to-business marketing and even greater numbers around the world. For example, 81 percent of small businesses on eBay Business Supply sell to five or more foreign countries. eBay Business Supply does some $4 billion per year in gross merchandise sales.

©Grzegorz Knec/Alamy Stock Photo

The eBay trading platform has proven to be a boon for small businesses. According to an eBay-commissioned survey conducted by Nielsen, 82 percent of small businesses using eBay report that it has helped their business grow and expand, 78 percent say it has helped to reduce their costs, and 79 percent say it has helped their business become more profitable.

In addition, eBay promotes entrepreneurship. According to a spokesperson from the American Enterprise Institute for Public Policy Research, "The potential for entrepreneurs to realize success through eBay is significant."

---

connects more than 250 retail customers with 80,000 suppliers. Its members include Best Buy, Campbell Soup, Costco, Safeway, Target, Tesco, and Walgreens. The Global Healthcare Exchange engages in the buying and selling of health care products for over 4,000 hospitals and more than 400 health care suppliers, such as Abbott Laboratories, GE Medical Systems, Johnson & Johnson, Medtronic USA, and McKesson Corporation in North America.

Online Auctions in Organizational Markets

Online auctions have grown in popularity among organizational buyers and business marketers. Many e-marketplaces offer this service. Two general types of auctions are common: (1) a traditional auction and (2) a reverse auction.[20] Figure 5–5 shows how buyer and seller participants and price behavior differ by type of auction. Let's look at each auction type more closely to understand the implications of each for buyers and sellers.

In a **traditional auction** a seller puts up an item for sale and would-be buyers are invited to bid in competition with each other. As more would-be buyers become involved, there is an upward pressure on bid prices. Why? Bidding is sequential. Prospective buyers observe the bids of others and decide whether or not to increase the bid price. The auction ends when a single bidder remains and "wins" the item with its highest price. Traditional auctions are often used to dispose of excess merchandise. For example, Dell Inc. sells surplus, refurbished, or closeout computer merchandise at its www.dellauction.com website.

A reverse auction works in the opposite direction from a traditional auction. In a **reverse auction**, a buyer communicates a need for a product or service and would-be suppliers are invited to bid in competition with each other. As more would-be suppliers become involved, there is a downward pressure on bid prices for the buyer's business. Why? Like traditional auctions, bidding is sequential and prospective suppliers observe the bids of others and decide whether or not to decrease the bid price. The auction ends when a single bidder remains and "wins" the business with its lowest price. Reverse auctions benefit organizational buyers by reducing the cost of their purchases. As an example, United Technologies Corp. estimates that it has saved $600 million on the purchase of $6 billion in supplies using online reverse auctions.[21]

---

traditional auction
In an e-marketplace, an online auction in which a seller puts up an item for sale and would-be buyers are invited to bid in competition with each other.

reverse auction
In an e-marketplace, an online auction in which a buyer communicates a need for a product or service and would-be suppliers are invited to bid in competition with each other.

FIGURE 5–5
Buyer and seller participants and price behavior differ by type of online auction. As an organizational buyer, would you prefer to participate in a traditional auction or a reverse auction?

(top, left): ©Jim Esposito/blend Images/Getty Images; (top, right): ©Comstock Images/Getty Images; (bottom, left): ©Comstock Images/Getty Images; (bottom, right): ©Jim Esposito/blend Images/Getty Images

Clearly, buyers welcome the lower prices generated by reverse auctions. Suppliers often favor reverse auctions because they give them a chance to capture business that they might not have otherwise had, perhaps because of a long-standing purchase relationship between the buyer and another supplier. On the other hand, suppliers say reverse auctions put too much emphasis on prices, discourage consideration of other important buying criteria, and may threaten supply partnership opportunities.[22]

learning review

5-5. What are e-marketplaces?

5-6. In general, which type of online auction creates upward pressure on bid prices and which type creates downward pressure on bid prices?

LEARNING OBJECTIVES REVIEW

LO 5-1 *Distinguish among industrial, reseller, and government organizational markets.*

There are three different organizational markets: industrial, reseller, and government. Industrial firms in some way reprocess a product or service they buy before selling it to the next buyer. Resellers—wholesalers and retailers—buy physical products and resell them again without any reprocessing. Government agencies at the federal, state, and local levels buy goods and services for the constituents they serve. The North American Industry Classification System (NAICS) provides common industry definitions for Canada, Mexico, and the United States, which facilitates the measurement of economic activity for these three organizational markets.

LO 5-2 *Describe the key characteristics of organizational buying that make it different from consumer buying.*

Seven major characteristics of organizational buying make it different from consumer buying. These include demand characteristics, the size of the order or purchase, the number of potential buyers, buying objectives, buying criteria, buyer–seller relationships and supply partnerships, and multiple buying influences within organizations. The organizational buying process itself is more formalized, more individuals are involved, supplier capability is more important, and the postpurchase evaluation behavior often includes performance of the supplier and the item purchased. Figure 5–3 details how the purchase decision process differs between a consumer and an organization.

LO 5-3 *Explain how buying centers and buying situations influence organizational purchasing.*
Buying centers and buying situations have an important influence on organizational purchasing. A buying center consists of a group of individuals who share common goals, risks, and knowledge important to a purchase decision. A buyer or purchasing manager is almost always a member of a buying center. However, other individuals may affect organizational purchasing due to their unique roles in a purchase decision. Five specific roles that a person may play in a buying center include users, influencers, buyers, deciders, and gatekeepers. The specific buying situation will influence the number of people and the different roles played in a buying center. For a routine reorder of an item—a straight rebuy situation—a purchasing manager or buyer will typically act alone in making a purchasing decision. When an organization is a first-time purchaser of a product or service—a new buy situation—a buying center is enlarged and all five roles in a buying center often emerge. A modified rebuy situation lies between these two extremes. Figure 5–4 offers additional insights into how buying centers and buying situations influence organizational purchasing.

LO 5-4 *Recognize the importance and nature of online buying in industrial, reseller, and government organizational markets.*
Organizations dwarf consumers in terms of online transactions made and purchase volume. Online buying in organizational markets is popular for three reasons. First, organizational buyers depend on timely supplier information that describes product availability, technical specifications, application uses, price, and delivery schedules. This information can be conveyed quickly via Internet technology. Second, this technology substantially reduces buyer order processing costs. Third, business marketers have found that Internet technology can reduce marketing costs, particularly sales and advertising expense, and broaden their customer base. Two developments in online buying have been the creation of e-marketplaces and online auctions. E-marketplaces provide a technology trading platform and a centralized market for buyer–seller transactions and make possible the real-time exchange of information, money, products, and services. These e-marketplaces can be independent trading communities, such as PlasticsNet, or private exchanges, such as the Global Healthcare Exchange. Online traditional and reverse auctions represent a second major development. With traditional auctions, the highest-priced bidder "wins." Conversely, the lowest-priced bidder "wins" with reverse auctions.

LEARNING REVIEW ANSWERS

5-1 Organizational buyers are _____.
Answer: Those manufacturers, wholesalers, retailers, service companies, not-for-profit organizations, and government agencies that buy products and services for their own use or for resale.

5-2 What are the three main types of organizational buyers?
Answer: (1) Industrial firms, which in some way reprocess a product or service they buy before selling it again to the next buyer; (2) resellers, which are wholesalers and retailers that buy physical products and resell them again without any reprocessing; and (3) government units, which are the federal, state, and local agencies that buy products and services for the constituents they serve.

5-3 What one department is almost always represented by a person in the buying center?
Answer: purchasing department

5-4 What are the three types of buying situations or buy classes?
Answer: (1) New buy—the organization is a first-time buyer of the product or service; (2) straight rebuy—the organization reorders an existing product or service from a list of acceptable suppliers; and (3) modified rebuy—an organization's buying center changes the product's specifications, price, delivery schedule, or supplier.

5-5 What are e-marketplaces?
Answer: E-marketplaces are online trading communities that bring together buyers and supplier organizations to make possible the real-time exchange of information, money, products, and services.

5-6 In general, which type of online auction creates upward pressure on bid prices and which type creates downward pressure on bid prices?
Answer: traditional auction; reverse auction

FOCUSING ON KEY TERMS

business-to-business marketing p. 130
buy classes p. 139
buying center p. 138
derived demand p. 132
e-marketplaces p. 140
North American Industry Classification System (NAICS) p. 131
organizational buyers p. 130
organizational buying behavior p. 136
reverse auction p. 141
traditional auction p. 141

APPLYING MARKETING KNOWLEDGE

1. Describe the major differences among industrial firms, resellers, and government units in the United States.

2. List and discuss the key characteristics of organizational buying that make it different from consumer buying.

3. What is a buying center? Describe the roles assumed by people in a buying center and what useful questions should be raised to guide any analysis of the structure and behavior of a buying center.

4. A firm that is marketing multimillion-dollar wastewater treatment systems to cities has been unable to sell a new type of system. This setback has occurred even though the firm's systems are cheaper than competitive systems and meet U.S. Environmental Protection Agency (EPA) specifications. To date, the firm's marketing efforts have been directed to city purchasing departments and the various state EPAs to get on approved bidders' lists. Talks with city-employed personnel have indicated that the new system is very different from current systems and therefore city sanitary and sewer department engineers, directors of these two departments, and city council members are unfamiliar with the workings of the system. Consulting engineers, hired by cities to work on the engineering and design features of these systems and paid on a percentage of system cost, are also reluctant to favor the new system. (*a*) What roles do the various individuals play in the purchase process for a wastewater treatment system? (*b*) How could the firm improve the marketing effort behind its new system?

BUILDING YOUR MARKETING PLAN

Your marketing plan may need an estimate of the size of the market potential or industry potential (see Chapter 7) for a particular product market in which you compete. Use these steps:

1. Define the product market precisely, such as ice cream.
2. Visit the NAICS website at www.census.gov.
3. Click "NAICS" and enter a keyword that describes your product market (e.g., ice cream).
4. Follow the instructions to find the specific NAICS code for your product market and the economic Census data that detail the dollar sales and provide the estimate of market or industry potential.

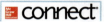

VIDEO CASE 5   Trek: Building Better Bikes through Organizational Buying

Video 5-3
Trek Video Case
kerin.tv/cr8e/v5-3

"Let me tell you a little bit about the history of Trek," says Mark Joslyn, vice president of human resources at Trek Bicycle Corporation. "It's a fantastic story," he continues proudly. "It's a story about a business that started in response to a market opportunity." That opportunity was to build bicycles with the highest-quality frames. In fact, Trek's mission was simple: "Build the best bikes in the world." To do this Trek needed to find the best raw materials from the best vendors. Michael Leighton, a Trek product manager, explains, "Our relationship with our vendors is incredibly important, and one of our recipes for success!"

THE COMPANY

Trek Bicycle was founded in 1976 by Richard Burke and Bevill Hogg. With just five employees they began manufacturing bicycles in a Wisconsin barn. From the beginning they targeted the high-quality, prestige segment of the bicycle market, using only the best materials and components for their bicycles. The first year they manufactured 900 custom-made bicycles which sold quickly. Soon, Trek exceeded its manufacturing capacity. It built a new 26,000-square-foot factory and corporate headquarters to help meet growing demand.

Trek's focus on quality meant that it was very sensitive to the materials used to manufacture the bicycles. The first models, for example, used hand-brazed steel for the frames. Then, borrowing ideas from the aerospace industry, Trek soon began making frames out of bonded aluminum. Following on the success of its aluminum bicycles, Trek began manufacturing bicycles out of carbon fiber. The idea was to be "at the front of technology," explains Joslyn.

The company also expanded its product line. Its first bikes were designed to compete directly with Japanese and Italian bicycles and included road racing models. In 1983 Trek manufactured its first mountain bike. In 1990 Trek developed a new category of bicycle—called a multitrack—that combined the speed of road bikes with the ruggedness of mountain bikes. The company also began manufacturing children's bikes, tandem bikes, BMX bikes, and models used by police departments and the U.S. Secret Service. In addition, it added a line of cycling apparel called Trek Wear and cycling accessories such as helmets. Recently, Trek also undertook an Eco Design initiative

144

to build bicycles and parts that are "green" in terms of the environmental impact of manufacturing them, how long they last, and how they can be recycled. To accommodate these production demands, Trek expanded its facilities two more times.

As Trek's popularity increased, it began to expand outside of the United States. For example, the company acquired a Swiss bicycle company called Villiger and the oldest bicycle company in Germany, Diamant. It also expanded into China, opening two stores and signing deals with 20 Chinese distributors.

Today, Trek is one of the leading manufacturers of bicycles and cycling products, with more than $800 million in sales and 2,000 employees. Trek's products are now marketed through 1,700 dealers in North America and wholly owned subsidiaries in seven countries and through distributors in 90 other countries. Its brands include Trek, Gary Fisher, and Bontrager. As a global company, Trek's mission has evolved also, and today the mission is to "help the world use the bicycle as a simple solution to complex problems." Trek employees believe that the bicycle is the most efficient form of human transportation and that it can combat climate change, ease urban congestion, and build human fitness. Their motto: "We believe in bikes." Mark Joslyn explains:

In the world today we are faced with a number of challenges. We are faced with congestion, issues with mobility, issues with the environment, and quite frankly, issues with health. We believe that the bicycle is a simple solution to all of those things. We are clearly an alternative to other forms of transportation and that's evident in the way that people are embracing cycling not just for recreation but also for transportation. And more and more, particularly in the United States, we are seeing people move to the bike as a way to get around and get to the places they need to ultimately get their life done.

ORGANIZATIONAL BUYING AT TREK

Trek's success at accomplishing its mission is the result of many important business practices, including its organizational buying process. The process begins when managers specify types of materials such as carbon fiber, component parts such as wheels and shifters, and finishing materials such as paint and decals needed to produce a Trek product. In addition, they specify quality requirements, sizing standards, and likely delivery schedules. According to Leighton, once the requirements are known, the next step is to "go to our buying center and say 'can you help us find this piece?'"

The buying center is the group of individuals who are responsible for finding the best suppliers and

©Jean Christophe Bott/Keystone/AP Images

vendors for the organization's purchases. At Trek the buying center consists of a purchasing manager, buyers who identify domestic and international sources of materials and components, and representatives from research and development, production, and quality control. The communication between the product managers and the buying center is important. "I work very closely with our buying centers to ensure that we're partnering with vendors who can supply reliable quality, and they are actually the ones who, with our quality control team, go in and say, 'yes this vendor is building product to the quality that meets Trek's standards,' and they also negotiate the pricing. Our buying center domestically is a relatively small team of people and they are focused on specific components."

When potential suppliers are identified, they are evaluated on four criteria—quality, delivery capabilities, price, and environmental impact of their production process. This allows Trek to compare alternative suppliers and to select the best match for Trek and its customers. Once a business is selected as a Trek supplier, it is continuously evaluated on elements of the four criteria. For example, current suppliers might receive scores on the number of defects in a large quantity of supplies, whether just-in-time orders made their deadlines, if target prices were maintained, and if recycled packaging was used. At Trek the tool that is used to record information about potential and existing suppliers is called a "white paper." Michael Leighton describes how this works: "Our buying center is tasked with developing what we call white papers. It's a sheet that managers can look at that shows issues and benefits related to working with these people." Every effort is made to develop long-term relationships with suppliers so that they become partners with Trek. These partnerships mean that Trek's success also contributes to the partner's success.

Trek's product managers and the buying center are involved in three types of organizational purchases. First, new buys are purchases that are made for the first time. Second, modified rebuys involve changing some aspect of a previously ordered product. Finally, straight rebuys are reorders of existing products from the list of acceptable suppliers. Leighton offers examples of each type of purchase at Trek:

> So, [for] a new buy, we work with our buying centers to find new products, something we've never done before whether it's a new saddle with a new material or a new technology that goes into the frame that damps vibration or gives a better ride. Another case might be electric bikes—maybe we are putting a motor in a bike, that's a new thing, so our buying center will help us go find those vendors. A modified rebuy is basically a saddle with a little bit different material but we are sharing some components of it, so the existing components of the saddle [are the same] but the cover is new, so it's a little bit different, but it's just the evolution of the product. A straight rebuy is looking at our strategic vision for the component further on down the line where we are just buying the same component and the volume goes up. We look at how can we make this a better business; can we save some money or can we make it more worth our while to keep buying the same product rather than buying something new.

While each of the types of purchases may occur frequently at Trek, the criteria that are used to select or evaluate a vendor may vary by the type of purchase and the type of product, making the buying process a dynamic challenge for managers.

ECO BUYING AND THE FUTURE AT TREK

One of Trek's criteria for evaluating existing and potential vendors is their environmental impact. Joslyn says it well: "We evaluate our vendors on many criteria including, increasingly, the elements that we would consider to be the 'green' part" of their offering. For example, Trek recently selected a supplier that (1) owned a quarry for extracting material, (2) used its own manufacturing facilities, and (3) used natural gas instead of coal in its production process. This was appealing to Trek because it suggested that the supplier had a "thorough understanding" of the impact of the product on the environment from start to finish.

Trek's organizational buying reflects the growing importance of its "Eco" perspective. Its bikes are becoming "smarter" as it adds electric-assist components to help them become a practical transportation alternative. Its bikes are also becoming "greener" as more low-impact materials and components are used and as packaging size and weight are reduced. Trek is also addressing the issue of recycling by building the bikes to last longer, using its dealers to help recycle tires and tubes, and funding a nonprofit organization called Dream Bikes to teach youth to fix and repair donated bikes.

> In addition to changing bikes and the way it makes them, Trek faces several other challenges as it strives to improve its organizational buying process. For example, the growing number of suppliers and vendors necessitates constant, coordinated, and real-time communication to ensure that all components are available when they are needed. In addition, changes in consumer interests and economic conditions mean that Trek must anticipate fluctuations in demand and make appropriate changes in order sizes and delivery dates. As Mark Joslyn explains, "Everything we do all the time can and should be improved. So the search for ideas inside of our business and outside of our business, always looking for ways that we can improve and bring new technology and new solutions to the marketplace, is just a core of who we are."[23]

Questions

1. What is the role of the buying center at Trek? Who is likely to comprise the buying center in the decision to select a new supplier at Trek?
2. What selection criteria does Trek utilize when it selects a new supplier or evaluates an existing supplier?
3. How has Trek's interest in the environmental impact of its business influenced its organizational buying process?
4. Provide an example of each of the three buying situations—straight rebuy, modified rebuy, and new buy—at Trek.

Chapter Notes

1. Personal correspondence with Tom Cassidy, JCPenney, January 25, 2017; and "Catalog Makes a Comeback at Penney," *The Wall Street Journal,* January 20, 2015, pp. B1, B2.
2. *Transforming Big Blue's Procurement Operations* (Sumers, NY: IBM Corporation, June 2016).
3. Figures reported in this discussion are provided by the U.S. Department of Commerce at www.commerce.gov, March 10, 2018.
4. "How NASA Is Prepping Its New Megarocket to Shoot for the Moon in 2019," www.space.com, January 5, 2018; and "Orion Update for January 2017," www.spaceflightinsider.com, January 18, 2017.
5. This list of characteristics and portions of the discussion in this section are based on Michael D. Hutt and Thomas W. Speh, *Business Marketing Management: B2B,* 12th ed. (Independence, KY: Cengage, 2017).
6. "Panda's New Power Plant Up and Running Texas," *Power Engineering,* November, 2014, pp. 23–24.
7. "Here Are the Average Prices for Boeing's 5 Major Commercial Airplanes," www.fool.com, July 10, 2017.
8. Hutt and Speh, *Business Marketing Management:* For a more expansive view on this topic, see Eric Almquist, Jamie Cleghorn, and Lori Sherer, "The B2B Elements of Value," *Harvard Business Review,* March–April 2018, pp. 72–81.
9. *Global Machine Vision Market 2018–2025* (Ann Arbor: Automated Imaging Association, September 2018).
10. This example is found in Sandy D. Jap and Jakki J. Mohr, "Leveraging Internet Technologies in B2B Relationships," *California Management Review,* Summer 2002, pp. 24–38.
11. "IBM Supercomputer Vies for No. 1," *The Wall Street Journal,* June 9–10, 2018, p. B3.
12. "Apple Signs $578M Sapphire Deal with GT Advanced Technology," *appleinsider.com,* accessed February 19, 2017.
13. "About Us," www.milsco.com, downloaded January 25, 2018; "Top Seating: Milsco," *Industry Today,* January 2018, pp. 60–69; and "Milsco Manufacturing: Easy Rider," *Industry Today,* February 2010, pp. 86–87.
14. *Starbucks Global Responsibility Report 2015,* downloaded January 5, 2017.
15. Wesley J. Johnson and Jennifer Chandler, "The Organizational Buying Center: Innovation, Knowledge Management, and Brand," in Gary L. Lilien and Rajdeep Grewal, eds., *Handbook of Business-to-Business Marketing* (Northhampton, MA: Edward Elgar Publishing, 2013), pp. 386–99.
16. These definitions are adapted from Frederick E. Webster Jr. and Yoram Wind, *Organizational Buying Behavior* (Englewood Cliffs, NJ: Prentice Hall, 1972), p. 6.
17. Jeffrey E. Lewin and Naveen Donthu, "The Influence of Purchase Situation on Buying Center Structure and Involvement: A Select Meta-Analysis of Organizational Buying Behavior Research," *Journal of Business Research,* October 2005, 1381–90. Representative studies on the buy-class framework that document its usefulness include Erin Anderson, Wujin Chu, and Barton Weitz, "Industrial Purchasing: An Empirical Exploration of the Buy-Class Framework," *Journal of Marketing,* July 1987, pp. 71–86; and Thomas W. Leigh and Arno J. Ethans, "A Script-Theoretic Analysis of Industrial Purchasing Behavior," *Journal of Marketing,* Fall 1984, pp. 22–32. Studies not supporting the buy-class framework include Donald W. Jackson, Janet E. Keith, and Richard K. Burdick, "Purchasing Agents' Perceptions of Industrial Buying Center Influences: A Situational Approach," *Journal of Marketing,* Fall 1984, pp. 75–83; R. Vekatesh, Ajay Kohli, and Gerald Zaltman, "Influence Strategies in Buying Centers," *Journal of Marketing,* October 1995, pp. 61–72; Gary L. Lilien and Anthony Wong, "An Exploratory Investigation of the Structure of the Buying Center in the Metal Working Industry," *Journal of Marketing Research,* February 1984, pp. 1–11; and Wesley J. Johnston and Thomas V. Bonoma, "The Buying Center: Structure and Interaction Patterns," *Journal of Marketing,* Summer 1981, pp. 143–56.
18. This discussion is based on "E-commerce Accounts for 56% of 2017 Revenue for Grainger," www.b2becommerceworld.com, January 24, 2018; "Feds to Ramp Up Online Purchasing Presence," www.ecommercetimes.com, January 22, 2018; and Zheng Qin, et al., *E-Commerce* (New York: Springer, 2014), p. 228.
19. "How eBay Is Trying to Expand beyond $4 Billion in B2B Sales," www.b2becommerceworld.com, June 20, 2016; "Global McKinsey Institute Report Confirms eBay, Inc. Research on Small Business Cross Border Trade," www.ebaymainstreet.com, April 24, 2014; and "Meet the eBay Millionaires," www.huffingtonpost.com, August 4, 2011.
20. This discussion is based on Robert J. Dolan and Youngme Moon, "Pricing and Market Making on the Internet," *Journal of Interactive Marketing,* Spring 2000, pp. 56–73; and Ajit Kambil and Eric van Heck, *Making Markets: How Firms Can Benefit from Online Auctions and Exchanges* (Boston: Harvard Business School Press, 2002).
21. Susan Avery, "Supply Management Is Core of Success at UTC," *Purchasing,* September 7, 2006, pp. 36–39.
22. Shawn P. Daley and Prithwiraz Nath, "Reverse Auctions for Relationship Marketers," *Industrial Marketing Management,* February 2005, pp. 157–66; and Sandy Jap, "The Impact of Online Reverse Auction Design on Buyer–Seller Relationships," *Journal of Marketing,* January 2007, pp. 146–59.
23. Trek: This case was written by Steven Hartley. Sources: "Trek Bicycle Corporation," Hoovers, 2012; "Alliance Data Signs Long-Term Extension Agreement with Trek Bicycle Corporation," *PR Newswire,* November 22, 2010; Lou Massante, "Trek Bicycle Buys Villiger, a Leader in the Swiss Market," *Bicycle Retailer & Industry News,* January 1, 2003, p. 10; "Trek Bicycle Corporation," Wikipedia, accessed September 4, 2011; and Trek website, http://www.trekbikes.com/us/en/company/believe, accessed September 4, 2012.

6

LEARNING OBJECTIVES

After reading this chapter you should be able to:

LO 6-1 Describe the nature and scope of world trade from a global perspective.

LO 6-2 Identify the major developments that have influenced world trade and global marketing.

LO 6-3 Identify the environmental forces that shape global marketing efforts.

LO 6-4 Name and describe the alternative approaches companies use to enter global markets.

LO 6-5 Explain the distinction between standardization and customization when companies craft worldwide marketing programs.

Understanding and Reaching Global Consumers and Markets

Transforming the Way India Sells and Transforming the Way India Buys: Amazon India Builds a Multibillion-Dollar Operation from the Ground up to the Cloud

"The opportunity (in India) is so large it will be measured in trillions, not billions—trillions of U.S. dollars, that is, not Indian rupees," says Diego Piacentini, Amazon's senior vice president retail operations in Asia and Europe. "But," he added, "we know that in order to win in India we need to do things we have never done in any other country. We need great people, a great platform, and honestly, a lot of money." How much money? Amazon is currently investing about $1 billion annually to build its business in India.

Amazon initiated operations in India in late 2013 when retail e-commerce totaled $2.3 billion. Amazon executives are enthusiastic about the opportunity that India represents. But doing business in India presents unique challenges.

Amazon's Awesome Opportunity in India

Why is India seen as a huge opportunity for Amazon, already the world's largest e-commerce company? Consider the following:

- India is the second most populous country in the world and the world's second-largest English-speaking country.
- India is the world's fastest-growing major economy and the total purchasing power of its economy ranks third behind China and the United States.
- India has the second-largest Internet user base in the world today and will have 850 million users in 2025.

Amazon's Awesome Challenges in India

Amazon executives admit the company's future in India is fraught with challenges to face and overcome. "What we do in India will affect Amazon's future in a very, very big way," says Amit Agarwal, the head of Amazon in India.

(left): ©Editorial/Alamy Stock Photo; (right): ©Andrey Arkusha/Shutterstock

So what challenges does Amazon India face and how has it dealt with them? Here are a few examples.

Trade Regulations. Amazon has had to modify its operating platform in India due to Indian trade regulations. Specifically, foreign companies, like Amazon, are prohibited from selling products directly to Indian consumers. Therefore, instead of Amazon buying products at wholesale prices in bulk and selling them through its online store, Amazon must rely on local manufacturers and retailers for its products. This means that Amazon stocks merchandise owned by Indian manufacturers and retailers in its distribution warehouses and provides an order fulfillment function for them. It is common for Amazon to pick up purchased items at a seller's location, pack them into boxes and bags with the Amazon logo, and deliver the goods to buyers on Amazon motorbikes. This practice often costs Amazon more money than it makes on the transaction.

Payment Systems. Barely 60 percent of Indian consumers have bank accounts. And only 12 percent have credit or debit cards. So Amazon's payment systems in India are drastically different from any the company has attempted before. About half of Indian buyers pay cash only when their purchases are delivered. In response, Amazon has partnered with thousands of small shop owners across India to act as pickup points in exchange for receiving a small commission per package.

Entrenched Competition. Amazon faces well-financed and capable domestic competitors in India. Two companies patterned after Amazon—Flipkart (owned by Walmart) and Snapdeal—already operate sizable distribution systems, advanced electronic platforms, and online stores in India. Tata Group, the largest retailer in India, has its own e-commerce platform and has linked it to thousands of its retail stores. These competitors have invested billions of dollars in their e-commerce technology and warehouses as well. And, they don't face the trade regulations imposed on Amazon as a foreign company.

Cloud Technology Expansion. Amazon expanded its cloud computing platform in India in 2017 to improve its service for Indian customers. This sizable financial and technological investment was made to address increasingly complicated server and infrastructure demands that only a localized cloud computing platform for India can provide.

Failure Is Not an Option

Despite the challenges, Amazon executives believe that failure is not an option in India. E-commerce industry analysts generally agree that India represents the last major e-commerce opportunity in the world. They expect that Indian retail e-commerce sales could reach $72 billion by 2025.

If Amazon transforms the way India sells and transforms the way India buys, as it expects to do, company executives predict that India will be the company's biggest market after the United States within a decade.[1]

This chapter describes today's complex and dynamic global marketing environment. It begins with an overview of our borderless economic world. Attention is then focused on prominent cultural, economic, and political-regulatory factors that present both an opportunity and a challenge for global marketers. Four major global market entry strategies are then detailed, including a discussion of the advantages and disadvantages of each. Finally, the task of designing, implementing, and evaluating worldwide marketing for companies is described.

DYNAMICS OF WORLD TRADE

LO 6-1 Describe the nature and scope of world trade from a global perspective.

The dollar value of world trade has roughly doubled in the past decade. Manufactured products and commodities account for 80 percent of world trade. Service industries, including telecommunications, transportation, insurance, education, banking, and tourism, represent the other 20 percent.

All nations and regions of the world do not participate equally in world trade. World trade flows reflect interdependencies among industries, countries, and regions. These flows manifest themselves in country, company, industry, and regional exports and imports. The dynamics of world trade are evolving. China is the biggest country measured by world trade. Asia is the largest region measured by world trade.[2]

Global Perspective on World Trade

The United States, China, Japan, Western Europe, and Canada together account for more than two-thirds of world trade in manufactured products and commodities. China is the world's leading exporter, followed by the United States and Germany. The United States is the world's leading importer, followed by China and Germany. China, Germany, and the United States remain well ahead of other countries in terms of imports and exports, as shown in Figure 6–1.

A global perspective on world trade views exports and imports as complementary economic flows: A country's imports affect its exports and a country's exports affect its imports. Every nation's imports arise from the exports of other nations. As the

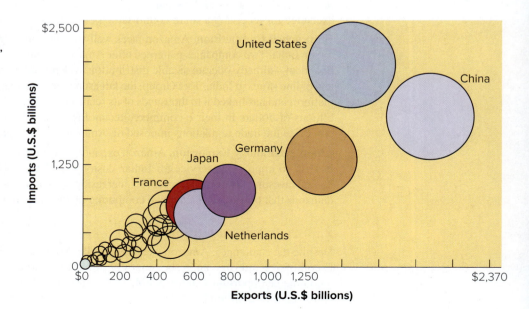

FIGURE 6–1
The United States, China, and Germany are the leaders in global merchandise trade by a wide margin. China exports more manufactured products and commodities than it imports. The United States imports more manufactured products and commodities than it exports. Read the text to learn about trends worldwide and in U.S. exports and imports.

exports of one country increase, its national output and income rise, which in turn leads to an increase in the demand for imports. This nation's greater demand for imports stimulates the exports of other countries. Increased demand for exports of other nations energizes their economic activity, resulting in higher national income, which stimulates their demand for imports. In short, imports affect exports and vice versa. This phenomenon is called the *trade feedback effect* and is one argument for free trade among nations.

Not all trade involves the exchange of money for products or services. In a world where 70 percent of all countries do not have convertible currencies or where government-owned enterprises lack sufficient cash or credit for imports, other means of payment are used. An estimated 10 to 15 percent of world trade involves **countertrade**, the practice of using barter rather than money for making global sales.

Countertrade is popular with many Eastern European nations and Asian and African countries. For example, Daimler AG agreed to sell 30 trucks to Romania in exchange for 150 Romanian-made jeeps. Daimler then sold the jeeps in Ecuador in exchange for bananas, which it brought back to Germany and sold to a German supermarket chain in exchange for cash. China's state-owned firms agreed to a $9 billion deal to build railways, hospitals, and health centers in the Democratic Republic of Congo in exchange for 10 million tons of copper and 400,000 tons of cobalt, a critical metal used in electric car batteries.

United States' Perspective on World Trade

The role of the United States in world trade can be viewed from two perspectives: (1) gross domestic product and (2) balance of trade.

Gross Domestic Product The United States has been a perennial world leader in terms of *gross domestic product* (*GDP*), which is the monetary value of all products and services produced in a country during one year. The United States is also among the world's leaders in exports due in large part to its global prominence in the aerospace, chemical, office equipment, information technology, pharmaceutical, telecommunications, and professional service industries. However, the U.S. percentage share of world exports has shifted downward over the past 40 years, whereas its percentage share of world imports has increased. Therefore, the relative position of the United States as a supplier to the world has diminished despite an absolute growth in exports. In fact, as a percentage of its GDP, U.S. exports are the lowest among industrial countries in the world. At the same time, its relative role as a marketplace for the world has increased, particularly for automobile, textile, apparel, and consumer electronics products.

Balance of Trade The difference between the monetary value of a nation's exports and imports is called the **balance of trade**. When a country's exports exceed its imports, it incurs a surplus in its balance of trade. When imports exceed exports, a deficit results. World trade trends in U.S. exports and imports are reflected in the U.S. balance of trade.

Two important things have happened in U.S. exports and imports over the past 40 years. First, imports have exceeded exports each year, indicating that the United States has a continuing balance of trade deficit. Second, the volume of both exports and imports has increased dramatically, showing why almost every American is significantly affected. The effect varies from the products they buy (Samsung smartphones from South Korea, Waterford crystal from Ireland, Louis Vuitton luggage from France) to those they sell (Cisco Systems's communication technology to Europe, Boeing aircraft to Asia, DuPont's chemicals to the Far East, Merck pharmaceuticals to Africa) and the jobs and improved standard of living that result.

World trade flows to and from the United States reflect demand and supply interdependencies for products and services among nations and industries. The four largest

---

countertrade
The practice of using barter rather than money for making global sales.

balance of trade
The difference between the monetary value of a nation's exports and imports.

importers of U.S. products and services are, in order: Canada, Mexico, China, and Japan. These individual countries purchase approximately two-thirds of U.S. exports. The four largest exporters to the United States are, in order: China, Canada, Mexico, and Japan. The United States has a balance of trade deficit with all of these four major trading partners. China alone accounts for about 40 percent of the total U.S. balance of trade deficit.

learning review

6-1. What country is the biggest as measured by world trade?

6-2. What is the trade feedback effect?

MARKETING IN A DYNAMIC GLOBAL ECONOMY

Identify the major developments that have influenced world trade and global marketing.

Global marketing has been and continues to be affected by a dynamic world economy. Five developments have significantly influenced the landscape of global marketing over the past decade:

1. Economic protectionism by individual countries.
2. Economic integration among countries.
3. Global competition among global companies for global consumers.
4. The presence of a networked global marketspace.
5. Growing prevalence of economic espionage.

Economic Protectionism by Individual Countries

protectionism
The practice of shielding one or more industries within a country's economy from foreign competition through the use of tariffs or quotas.

Protectionism is the practice of shielding one or more industries within a country's economy from foreign competition through the use of tariffs or quotas. The argument for protectionism is that it limits the outsourcing of jobs, protects a nation's political security, discourages economic dependency on other countries, and promotes development of domestic industries. The prevalence of protectionist practices has become more commonplace due to economic nationalism and populism. Setting aside the economic issues, read the Making Responsible Decisions box and decide for yourself if protectionism has an ethical dimension.[3]

Tariffs and quotas can discourage world trade, as depicted in Figure 6–2. In fact, tariffs and quotas, among other restrictive trade measures, have slowed the growth of world trade for the past decade.

tariffs
Government taxes on products or services entering a country that primarily serve to raise prices on imports.

Tariffs, which are a government tax on products or services entering a country, primarily serve to raise prices on imports. The average tariff on manufactured products in industrialized countries is 4 percent. However, wide differences exist across nations and industries. For example, European Union countries have a 10 percent tariff on cars imported from the United States, which is about four times higher than the tariff imposed by the United States on cars from the European Union.

The effect of tariffs on consumer prices is substantial. Consider U.S. rice exports to Japan. The U.S. Rice Millers' Association claims that if the Japanese rice market were opened to imports by lowering tariffs, lower prices would save Japanese consumers $6 billion annually, and the United States would gain a large share of the Japanese rice market. Tariffs imposed on bananas by European Union countries cost consumers $2 billion a year. U.S. consumers pay $5 billion annually for tariffs on imported shoes. Incidentally, 99 percent of shoes worn in the United States are imported.[4]

Making Responsible Decisions

Ethics

Global Ethics and Global Economics—The Case of Protectionism

World trade benefits from free and fair trade among nations. Nevertheless, governments of many countries continue to use tariffs and quotas to protect their various domestic industries. Why? Protectionism earns profits for domestic producers and tariff revenue for the government. There is a cost, however. Protectionist policies cost Japanese consumers between $75 billion and $110 billion annually. U.S. consumers pay about $70 billion each year in higher prices because of tariffs and other protective trade restrictions.

Sugar and textile import quotas in the United States, automobile and banana import tariffs in European countries, shoe and automobile tire import tariffs in the United States, beer import tariffs in Canada, and rice import tariffs in Japan have protected domestic industries but also interfered with world trade for these products. Regional trade agreements, such as those found in the provisions of the European Union (EU) and the North American Free Trade Agreement (NAFTA), may also pose a situation whereby member nations can obtain preferential treatment in quotas and tariffs but nonmember nations cannot.

Protectionism, in its many forms, raises an interesting global ethical question. Is protectionism, no matter how applied, an ethical practice?

©Frans Lemmens/The Image Bank/Getty Images

quota
A restriction placed on the amount of a product allowed to enter or leave a country.

A **quota** is a restriction placed on the amount of a product allowed to enter or leave a country. Quotas can be mandated or voluntary and may be legislated or negotiated by governments. Import quotas seek to guarantee domestic industries access to a certain percentage of their domestic market. For example, there is a limit on Chinese dairy products sold in India, and in Italy there is a quota on Japanese motorcycles. China has import quotas on corn, cotton, rice, and wheat.

FIGURE 6–2
How does protectionism affect world trade? Protectionism hinders world trade through tariff and quota policies of individual countries. Tariffs increase prices and quotas limit supply.

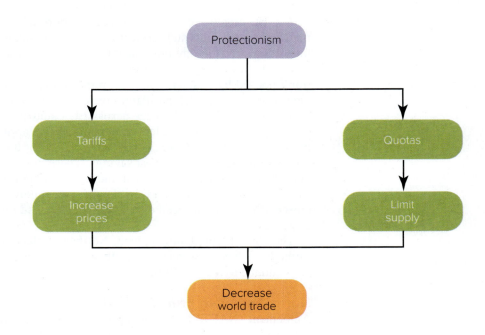

World Trade Organization (WTO)
A permanent institution that sets rules governing trade between its members through panels of trade experts who decide on trade disputes between members and issue binding decisions.

trade war
A situation in which countries try to damage each other's trade, typically by imposition of tariff and quota restrictions.

The United States also imposes quotas. For instance, U.S. sugar import quotas have existed for more than 70 years and preserve about half of the U.S. sugar market for domestic producers. American consumers pay $3 billion annually in extra food costs because of this quota. U.S. quotas on textiles are estimated to add 50 percent to the wholesale price of clothing for American consumers—which, in turn, raises retail prices.

The major industrialized nations of the world formed the **World Trade Organization (WTO)** in 1995 to address an array of world trade issues. There are 164 WTO member countries, including the United States, which account for more than 90 percent of world trade. The WTO is a permanent institution that sets rules governing trade between its members through panels of trade experts who decide on trade disputes between members and issue binding decisions.

The WTO has decided over 500 trade disputes for the purpose of mitigating trade wars between countries. A **trade war** is a situation in which countries try to damage each other's trade, typically by imposition of tariff and quota restrictions.

ECONOMIC INTEGRATION AMONG COUNTRIES

A number of countries with similar economic goals have formed transnational trade groups or signed trade agreements for the purpose of promoting free trade among member nations and enhancing their individual economies. Two of the best-known examples are the European Union (or simply EU) and the North American Free Trade Agreement (NAFTA). About 46 percent of all U.S. exports go to its free trade partners.

European Union The European Union consists of 27 member countries that have eliminated most barriers to the free flow of products, services, capital, and labor across their borders (see Figure 6–3).[5] This single market houses about 510 million consumers with a combined gross domestic product larger than that of the United States. In addition, 16 countries have adopted a common currency called the *euro*. Adoption of the euro has been a boon to electronic commerce in the EU by eliminating the need to continually monitor currency exchange rates.

The EU creates abundant marketing opportunities because firms do not need to market their products and services on a nation-by-nation basis. Rather, pan-European marketing strategies are possible due to greater uniformity in product and packaging standards; fewer regulatory restrictions on transportation, advertising, and promotion imposed by countries; and the removal of most tariffs that affect pricing practices. For example, Colgate-Palmolive Company now markets its Colgate toothpaste with one formula and package across EU countries at one price. Stanley Black & Decker—the maker of electrical hand tools, appliances, and other consumer products—now produces 8, not 20, motor sizes for the European market, resulting in production and marketing cost savings. These practices were previously impossible because of different government and trade regulations. Europeanwide distribution from fewer locations is also feasible given open borders. French tire maker Michelin closed 180 of its European distribution centers and now uses just 20 to serve all EU countries.

The United Kingdom (England, Northern Ireland, Scotland, and Wales) voted to formally withdraw from the EU, effective March 2019. The United Kingdom and the EU continue to resolve disputes related to trade.

North American Free Trade Agreement The North American Free Trade Agreement (NAFTA) lifted many trade barriers between Canada, Mexico, and the United States and created a marketplace with more than 475 million consumers.

FIGURE 6–3

The European Union in mid-2019 consists of 27 countries with about 510 million consumers. The United Kingdom formally withdrew from the European Union in March 2019.

Source: European Union www.europa.eu

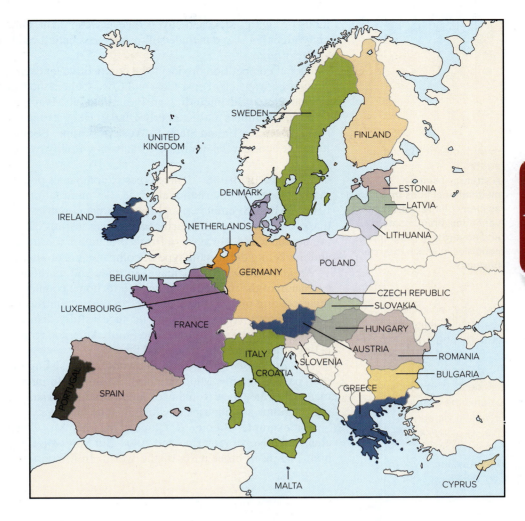

NAFTA has stimulated trade flows among member nations as well as cross-border retailing, manufacturing, and investment. For example, NAFTA paved the way for Walmart to move to Mexico and for Mexican supermarket giant Gigante and Mexican bakery giant Grupo Bimbo to move operations into the United States. Whirlpool Corporation's Canadian subsidiary stopped making washing machines in Canada and moved that operation to the United States. Whirlpool then shifted the production of kitchen ranges and compact dryers to Canada. Ford invested $60 million in its Mexico City manufacturing plant to produce smaller cars and light trucks for global sales.[6]

The United States has challenged its tariff policies with Canada and Mexico under the terms of the original NAFTA agreement and negotiated revised tariffs on trade between the countries.

Global Competition among Global Companies for Global Consumers

Economic integration among countries has created a new reality for marketers of all shapes and sizes. Today, world trade is driven by global competition among global companies for global consumers.

Global Competition
Global competition exists when firms originate, produce, and market their products and services worldwide. The automobile, pharmaceutical, apparel, electronics, aerospace, and telecommunication fields represent well-known

global competition
Exists when firms originate, produce, and market their products and services worldwide.

industries with sellers and buyers on every continent. Other industries that are increasingly global in scope include soft drinks, cosmetics, ready-to-eat cereals, snack chips, and retailing.

Global competition broadens the competitive landscape for marketers. The familiar "cola war" waged by Pepsi-Cola and Coca-Cola in the United States has been repeated around the world, including in India, China, Myanmar, and Argentina. Procter & Gamble's Pampers and Kimberly-Clark's Huggies have taken their disposable diaper rivalry from the United States to Western Europe. Boeing and Europe's Airbus vie for lucrative commercial aircraft contracts on virtually every continent.

Global Companies Three types of companies populate and compete in the global marketplace: (1) international firms, (2) multinational firms, and (3) transnational firms.[7] All three employ people in different countries, and many have administrative, marketing, and manufacturing operations (often called *divisions* or *subsidiaries*) around the world. However, a firm's orientation toward and strategy for global markets and marketing defines the type of company it is or attempts to be.

An *international firm* engages in trade and marketing in different countries as an extension of the marketing strategy in its home country. Generally, these firms market their existing products and services in other countries the same way they do in their home country. Avon, for example, successfully distributes its product line through direct selling in Asia, Europe, and South America, employing virtually the same marketing strategy used in the United States.

A *multinational firm* views the world as consisting of unique parts and markets to each part differently. Multinationals use a **multidomestic marketing strategy**, which means that they have as many different product variations, brand names, and advertising programs as countries in which they do business.

For example, Procter & Gamble markets Mr. Clean, its popular multipurpose cleaner, in North America and Asia. But you won't necessarily find the Mr. Clean brand name in other parts of the world. In Mexico and Puerto Rico, Mr. Clean is

> **multidomestic marketing strategy**
> A strategy used by multinational firms that have as many different product variations, brand names, and advertising programs as countries in which they do business.

Since opening its first international venture in Australia in 1971, Mary Kay, Inc. has expanded to more than 35 countries on five continents. This Korean ad features the company's CC Cream Sunscreen.
Courtesy of Mary Kay, Inc.

Mary Kay, Inc.
www.marykay.com

Mr. Clean has a different name in different countries and regions in the world. However, his image remains the same.
(all): Source: Procter & Gamble

global marketing strategy
A strategy used by transnational firms that employ the practice of standardizing marketing activities when there are cultural similarities and adapting them when cultures differ.

global brand
A brand marketed under the same name in multiple countries with similar and centrally coordinated marketing programs.

Maestro Limpio, and it is Don Limpio in Spain. Mr. Clean is Monsieur Propre in France and Belgium, Mastro Lindo in Italy, Pan Proper in Poland, and Mister Proper in Eastern Europe, the Middle East, and Russia.

A *transnational firm* views the world as one market and emphasizes cultural similarities across countries or universal consumer needs and wants rather than differences. Transnational marketers employ a **global marketing strategy**—the practice of standardizing marketing activities when there are cultural similarities and adapting them when cultures differ. This approach benefits marketers by allowing them to realize economies of scale from their production and marketing activities.

Global marketing strategies are popular among many business-to-business marketers such as Caterpillar and Komatsu (heavy construction equipment) and Texas Instruments, Intel, and Hitachi (semiconductors). Consumer product marketers such as Apple and Samsung (smartphones), Seiko and Swatch (watches), Coca-Cola and Pepsi-Cola (cola soft drinks), Mattel and LEGO (children's toys), Nike and Adidas (athletic shoes), Gillette (personal care products), L'Oréal and Shiseido (cosmetics), and McDonald's (quick-service restaurants) successfully execute this strategy.

Each of these companies markets a **global brand**—a brand marketed under the same name in multiple countries with similar and centrally coordinated marketing programs.[8] Global brands have the same product formulation or service concept, deliver the same benefits to consumers, and use consistent advertising across multiple countries and cultures. This isn't to say that global brands are not sometimes tailored to specific cultures or countries. However, adaptation is used only when necessary to better connect the brand to consumers in different markets.

Consider McDonald's.[9] This global marketer has adapted its proven formula of "food, fun, and families" across 119 countries on six continents. Although the Golden Arches and Ronald McDonald appear worldwide, McDonald's tailors other aspects of its marketing program. It serves beer in Germany, wine in France, and coconut, mango, and tropical mint shakes in Hong Kong. Hamburgers are made with different meat and spices in Japan, Thailand, India, and the Philippines. But McDonald's world-famous

Marketing Matters > Customer Value

The Global Teenager—A Market of Voracious Consumers

The "global teenager" market consists of 13- to 19-year-olds in Europe, North and South America, and industrialized nations of Asia, Africa, and the Pacific Rim who have experienced intense exposure to television (MTV broadcasts to 372 million households worldwide on 60 branded TV channels), movies, travel, social media, and global advertising by companies such as Apple, Sony, Nike, and Coca-Cola. The similarities among teens across these countries are greater than their differences. For example, a global study of middle-class teenagers' rooms in 25 industrialized countries indicated it was difficult, if not impossible, to tell whether the rooms were in Los Angeles, Hong Kong, Mexico City, Tokyo, Rio de Janeiro, Sydney, or Paris. Why? Teens spend about $820 billion annually for a common gallery of products: Nintendo video games, Levi's blue jeans, Nike and Adidas athletic shoes, Swatch watches, Apple and Samsung smartphones, and CoverGirl cosmetics.

©Kim Petersen/Alamy Stock Photo

Facebook, Snapchat, and Instagram are the most popular social media.

Teenagers around the world appreciate fashion and music, and they desire novelty and trendier designs and images. They also acknowledge an Americanization of fashion and culture based on another study of 6,500 teens in 26 countries. When asked what country had the most influence on their attitudes and purchase behavior, 54 percent of teens from the United States, 87 percent of those from Latin America, 80 percent of the Europeans, and 80 percent of those from Asia named the United States. This phenomenon has not gone unnoticed by parents. As one parent in India said, "Now the youngsters dress, talk, and eat like Americans."

---

french fry is standardized. Its french fry in Beijing, China, tastes like the one in Paris, France, which tastes like the one in your hometown.

Global Consumers Global competition among global companies often focuses on the identification and pursuit of global consumers, as described in the Marketing Matters box.[10] **Global consumers** consist of consumer groups living in many countries or regions of the world who have similar needs or seek similar features and benefits from products or services. Evidence suggests the presence of a global middle-income class, a youth market, and an elite segment, each consuming or using a common assortment of products and services, regardless of geographic location.

A variety of companies have capitalized on the global consumer. Whirlpool, Sony, and IKEA have benefited from the growing global middle-income class desire for kitchen appliances, consumer electronics, and home furnishings, respectively. Levi Strauss, Nike, Adidas, Coca-Cola, and Apple have tapped the global youth market. DeBeers, Rolex, Chanel, Gucci, Rolls-Royce, and Sotheby's and Christie's, the world's largest fine art and antique auction houses, cater to the elite segment for luxury products worldwide.

> **global consumers**
> Consumer groups living in many countries or regions of the world who have similar needs or seek similar features and benefits from products or services.

The Presence of a Networked Global Marketspace

The use of Internet technology as a tool for exchanging products, services, and information on a global scale is the fourth development affecting world trade. Over 4 billion businesses, educational institutions, government agencies, and households worldwide had Internet access in 2018. The broad reach of this technology attests to its potential for promoting world trade.

economic espionage
The clandestine collection of trade secrets or proprietary information about a company's competitors.

Video 6-1
Nestlé Hungary Ad
kerin.tv/cr8e/v6-1

Sweden's IKEA is capitalizing on the home-improvement trend sweeping through China. The home-furnishings retailer is courting young Chinese consumers who are eagerly updating their housing with modern, colorful, but inexpensive furniture. IKEA entered China in 1998. The company currently has 21 stores in China and plans to open another 4 to 5 stores per year through 2022.
©Imaginechina/AP Images

IKEA
www.ikea.com

A networked global marketspace enables the exchange of products, services, and information from sellers *anywhere* to buyers *anywhere* at *any time* and at a lower cost. In particular, companies engaged in business-to-business marketing have spurred the growth of global electronic commerce.[11] Ninety percent of global electronic commerce revenue arises from business-to-business transactions among a dozen countries in North America, Western Europe, and the Asia/Pacific Rim region.

Marketers recognize that the networked global marketspace offers unprecedented access to prospective buyers on every continent. Companies that have successfully capitalized on this access manage multiple country and language websites that customize content and communicate with consumers in their native tongue. Nestlé, the world's largest packaged food manufacturer, coffee roaster, and chocolate maker, is a case in point. The company operates 65 individual country websites in more than 20 languages that span five continents.

Prevalence of Economic Espionage

The dynamic global economy also has a dark side—economic espionage.[12] **Economic espionage** is the clandestine collection of trade secrets or proprietary information about a company's competitors. This practice is common in high-technology industries such as electronics, specialty chemicals, industrial equipment, aerospace, and pharmaceuticals, where technical know-how and trade secrets separate global industry leaders from followers.

It is estimated that foreign economic espionage costs U.S. firms upwards of $600 billion a year. The intelligence services of some 23 nations routinely target U.S. firms for information about research and development efforts, manufacturing and marketing plans, and customer lists. To counteract this threat, the *Economic Espionage Act* (1996) makes the theft of trade secrets by foreign entities a federal crime in the United States. This act prescribes prison sentences of up to 15 years and fines of up to $500,000 for individuals. Agents of foreign governments found guilty of economic espionage face a 25-year prison sentence and a $10 million fine.

learning review

6-3. What is protectionism?

6-4. The North American Free Trade Agreement was designed to promote free trade among which countries?

6-5. What is the difference between a multidomestic marketing strategy and a global marketing strategy?

A GLOBAL ENVIRONMENTAL SCAN

LO 6-3 Identify the environmental forces that shape global marketing efforts.

Global companies conduct continuing environmental scans of the five sets of environmental factors described earlier in Chapter 3 in Figure 3–1 (social, economic, technological, competitive, and regulatory forces). This section focuses on three kinds of uncontrollable environmental variables—cultural, economic, and political-regulatory—that affect global marketing practices in strikingly different ways than those in domestic markets.

cross-cultural analysis
The study of similarities and differences among consumers in two or more nations or societies.

values
A society's personally or socially preferable modes of conduct or states of existence that tend to persist over time.

customs
What is considered normal and expected about the way people do things in a specific country.

Cultural Diversity

Marketers must be sensitive to the cultural underpinnings of different societies if they are to initiate and consummate mutually beneficial exchange relationships with global consumers. A necessary step in this process is **cross-cultural analysis**, which involves the study of similarities and differences among consumers in two or more nations or societies.[13] A thorough cross-cultural analysis involves an understanding of and an appreciation for the values, customs, symbols, and language of other societies.

Values A society's **values** represent personally or socially preferable modes of conduct or states of existence that tend to persist over time. Understanding and working with these aspects of a society are important factors in global marketing. For example,

- McDonald's does not sell beef hamburgers in its restaurants in India because the cow is considered sacred by almost 85 percent of the population. Instead, McDonald's sells the Maharaja Mac: two all-chicken patties, special sauce, lettuce, cheese, pickles, onions on a sesame-seed bun. For the 40 percent of Indian consumers who eat no meat of any kind, McDonald's offers the McAloo Tikki burger, which features a spicy breaded potato patty, and the McPuff, a vegetable and cheese pastry.
- Germans have not been overly receptive to the use of credit cards, such as Visa or MasterCard, or the use of installment debt to purchase products and services. Indeed, the German word for debt, *schuld,* is the same as the German word for "guilt."

Cultural values become apparent in the personal values of individuals that affect their attitudes and beliefs and the importance assigned to specific behaviors and attributes of products and services. These personal values affect consumption-specific values, such as an aversion toward the use of installment debt by Germans, and product-specific values, such as the importance assigned to credit card interest rates.

Customs **Customs** are what is considered normal and expected about the way people do things in a specific country. Clearly customs can vary significantly from country to country. Consider, for example, that in France, men wear more than twice the number of cosmetics than women do and that Japanese women give Japanese men chocolates on Valentine's Day.

You will have to visit India to sample McDonald's Maharaja Mac or the McAloo Tikki burger described in the text.
Source: McDonald's

The custom of giving token business gifts is popular in many countries where they are expected and accepted. However, bribes, kickbacks, and payoffs offered to entice someone to commit an illegal or improper act on behalf of the giver for economic gain is considered corrupt in any culture.

The prevalence of bribery in global marketing has led to an agreement among the world's major exporting nations to make bribery of foreign government officials a criminal offense. This agreement is patterned after the **Foreign Corrupt Practices Act (1977)**, as amended by the *International Anti-Dumping and Fair Competition Act* (1998). These acts make it a crime for U.S. corporations to bribe an official of a foreign government or political party to obtain or retain business in a foreign country. For example, the German engineering company Siemens AG paid an $800 million fine for $1 billion in alleged bribes of government officials around the globe.[14]

> **Foreign Corrupt Practices Act (1977)**
> A law, amended by the International Anti-Dumping and Fair Competition Act (1998), that makes it a crime for U.S. corporations to bribe an official of a foreign government or political party to obtain or retain business in a foreign country.
>
> **cultural symbols**
> Things that represent ideas and concepts in a specific culture.

Cultural Symbols   **Cultural symbols** are things that represent ideas and concepts in a specific culture. Symbols and symbolism play an important role in cross-cultural analysis because different cultures attach different meanings to things. So important is the role of symbols that a field of study, called *semiotics*, has emerged that examines the correspondence between symbols and their role in the assignment of meaning for people. By adroitly using cultural symbols, global marketers can tie positive symbolism to their products, services, and brands to enhance their attractiveness to consumers. However, improper use of symbols can spell disaster. A culturally sensitive global marketer will know that:

- North Americans are superstitious about the number 13, and Japanese feel the same way about the number 4. *Shi*, the Japanese word for "four," is also the word for "death." Knowing this, Tiffany & Company sells its fine glassware and china in sets of five, not four, in Japan.
- "Thumbs-up" is a positive sign in the United States. However, in Russia and Poland, this gesture has an offensive meaning when the palm of the hand is shown, as AT&T learned. The company reversed the gesture depicted in ads, showing the back of the hand, not the palm.

Cultural symbols evoke deep feelings. Consider how executives at Coca-Cola Company's Italian office learned this lesson. In a series of advertisements directed at Italian vacationers, the Eiffel Tower, the Empire State Building, and the Tower of Pisa were turned into the familiar Coca-Cola bottle. However, when the white marble columns in the Parthenon that crowns the Acropolis in Athens were turned into Coca-Cola bottles, the Greeks were outraged. Greeks refer to the Acropolis as the "holy rock," and a government official said the Parthenon is an "international symbol

Cultural symbols evoke deep feelings. What cultural lesson did Coca-Cola executives learn when they used the Eiffel Tower in Paris, France, and the Parthenon in Athens, Greece, in a global advertising campaign? Read the text to find the answer.
(Eiffel Tower): ©Sylvain Sonnet/Photographer's Choice RF/Getty Images; *(Parthenon):* ©Antonio M. Rosario/Getty Images

of excellence" and that "whoever insults the Parthenon insults international culture." Coca-Cola apologized for the ad.[15]

What does the Nestlé Kit Kat bar have to do with academic achievement in Japan? Read the text to find out.
©CB2/ZOB/WENN/Newscom

Nestlé Company
www.nestle.com

Video 6-2
Nestlé Japan Ad
kerin.tv/cr8e/v6-2

The Mini is marketed in many countries using many languages, such as English and Italian. The Italian translation is "Stop Looking at My Rear."
(both): Source: MINI USA

Language Global marketers should know not only the native tongues of countries in which they market their products and services but also the nuances and idioms of a language. Even though about 100 official languages exist in the world, anthropologists estimate that at least 3,000 different languages are spoken. There are 24 official languages spoken in the European Union, and Canada has two official languages (English and French). Twenty major languages are spoken in India alone.

English, French, and Spanish are the principal languages used in global diplomacy and commerce. However, the best language to use to communicate with consumers is their own, as any seasoned global marketer will attest to. Brand names and messages with unintended meanings have ranged from the absurd to the obscene:

- When the advertising agency responsible for launching Pert shampoo in Canada realized that the name means "lost" in French, it substituted the brand name Pret, which means "ready."
- The Vicks brand name common in the United States is German slang for sexual intimacy; therefore, Vicks is called Wicks in Germany.

Experienced global marketers use **back translation**, where a translated word or phrase is retranslated into the original language by a different interpreter to catch errors. For example, IBM's first Japanese translation of its "Solutions for a Small Planet" advertising message yielded "Answers that make people smaller." The error was corrected. Nevertheless, unintended translations can produce favorable results. Consider Kit Kat bars marketed by Nestlé worldwide. Kit Kat is pronounced "kitto katsu" in Japanese, which roughly translates to "Surely win." Japanese teens eat Kit Kat bars for good luck, particularly when taking crucial school exams.[16]

back translation
The practice where a translated word or phrase is retranslated into the original language by a different interpreter to catch errors.

Cultural Ethnocentricity
The tendency for people to view their own values, customs, symbols, and language favorably is well known. However, the belief that aspects of one's culture are superior to another's is called *cultural ethnocentricity* and is a sure impediment to successful global marketing.

An outgrowth of cultural ethnocentricity exists in the purchase and use of products and services produced outside of a country. Global marketers are acutely aware that certain groups within countries disfavor imported products, not on the basis of price, features, or performance, but purely because of their foreign origin.

Consumer ethnocentrism is the tendency to believe that it is inappropriate, indeed immoral, to purchase foreign-made products.[17] Ethnocentric consumers believe that buying imported products is wrong because such purchases are unpatriotic, harm domestic industries, and cause domestic unemployment. Consumer ethnocentrism has been observed among a segment of the population in the United States, France, Japan, Korea, and Germany as well as other parts of Europe and Asia. Consumer ethnocentrism makes the job of global marketers more difficult.

Consumer ethnocentrism is common in many countries. This bumper sticker is just one illustration of how ethnocentric consumers express themselves in the United States.
©McGraw-Hill Education

consumer ethnocentrism
The tendency to believe that it is inappropriate, indeed immoral, to purchase foreign-made products.

Economic Considerations
Global marketing is also affected by economic considerations. Therefore, a scan of the global marketplace should include (1) an assessment of the economic infrastructure in these countries, (2) measurement of consumer income in different countries, and (3) recognition of a country's currency exchange rates.

Economic Infrastructure
The *economic infrastructure*—a country's communications, transportation, financial, and distribution systems—is a critical consideration in determining whether to try to market to a country's consumers and organizations. Parts of the infrastructure that North Americans or Western Europeans take for granted

PepsiCo has made a huge financial investment in bottling and distribution facilities in China.
©ChinaFotoPress/ZUMA Press/Newscom

PepsiCo
www.pepsico.com

can be huge problems elsewhere—not only in developing nations but even in Eastern Europe, the Indian subcontinent, and China, where such an infrastructure is assumed to be in place. For example, PepsiCo has invested $1.5 billion in transportation and manufacturing systems in China and India since 2010.

The communication infrastructures in these countries also differ. This infrastructure includes telecommunication systems and networks in use, such as telephones, cable television, broadcast radio and television, computers, satellites, and wireless telephones. In general, the communication infrastructure in many developing countries is limited or antiquated compared with that of developed countries. Not surprisingly, Amazon has invested millions of dollars in its web services in India, as described in the chapter-opening example.

Even the financial and legal system can cause problems. Formal operating procedures among financial institutions and the notion of private property are still limited. As a consequence, it is estimated that two-thirds of the commercial transactions in Russia involve nonmonetary forms of payment. The legal red tape involved in obtaining titles to buildings and land for manufacturing, wholesaling, and retailing operations also has been a huge problem. Still, the Coca-Cola Company has invested $1 billion for bottling facilities in Russia. Frito-Lay spent $60 million to build a plant outside Moscow to make Lay's potato chips.

Consumer Income and Purchasing Power A global marketer selling consumer products must also consider what the average per capita or household income is among a country's consumers and how the income is distributed to determine a nation's purchasing power. Per capita income varies greatly between nations. Average yearly per capita income in EU countries is about $35,500 and is less than $700 in some developing countries such as Liberia. A country's income distribution is important because it gives a more reliable picture of a country's purchasing power. Generally, as the proportion of middle-income households in a country increases, the greater that nation's purchasing capability tends to be.

Seasoned global marketers recognize that people in developing countries often have government subsidies for food, housing, and health care that supplement their income. So people with seemingly low incomes are actually promising customers for a variety of products. For instance, a consumer in South Asia earning the equivalent of $250 per

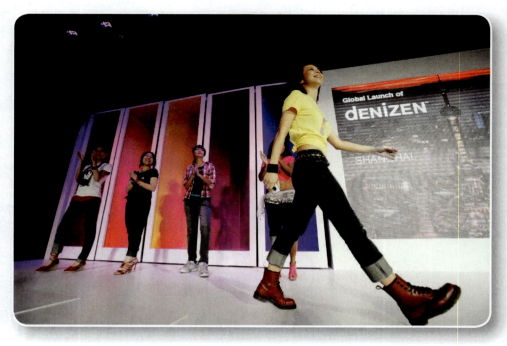

Levi Strauss & Co. launched its Denizen brand jeans in China. Created for teens and young adults in emerging markets who cannot afford Levi-branded jeans, Denizen is now sold in North America.
©Eugene Hoshiko/AP Images

Levi Strauss & Co.
www.levistrauss.com

year can afford Gillette razors. When that consumer's income rises to $1,000, a Sony television becomes affordable, and a new Volkswagen or Nissan automobile can be bought with an annual income of $10,000. In developing countries of Eastern Europe, a $1,000 annual income makes a refrigerator affordable, and $2,000 brings an automatic washer within reach—good news for Whirlpool, the world's leading manufacturer and marketer of major home appliances.

Income growth in developing countries of Asia, Latin America, and Eastern Europe stimulates world trade. The number of consumers in these countries earning the equivalent of $10,000 per year exceeds the number of consumers in the United States, Japan, and Western Europe combined. By one estimate, half of the world's population has now achieved "middle-class" status and 63 percent will achieve middle-class status by 2030.[18] For this reason, developing countries represent a prominent marketing opportunity for global companies.

Video 6-3
Denizen
kerin.tv/cr8e/v6-3

currency exchange rate
The price of one country's currency expressed in terms of another country's currency.

Currency Exchange Rates Fluctuations in exchange rates among the world's currencies are of critical importance in global marketing. Such fluctuations affect everyone, from international tourists to global companies.

A **currency exchange rate** is the price of one country's currency expressed in terms of another country's currency, such as the U.S. dollar expressed in Japanese yen, euros, Swiss francs, or the British pound. Failure to consider exchange rates when pricing products for global markets can have dire consequences. Mattel learned this lesson the hard way. The company was recently unable to sell its popular Holiday Barbie doll and accessories in some international markets because they were too expensive. Why? Barbie prices, expressed in U.S. dollars, were set without regard for how they would convert into foreign currencies and were too high for many buyers.[19]

Exchange rate fluctuations affect the sales and profits made by global companies. When foreign currencies can buy more U.S. dollars, for example, U.S. products are less expensive for the foreign customer. Short-term fluctuations, however, can have a significant effect on the profits of global companies.[20] Hewlett-Packard recently gained nearly a half million dollars of additional profit through exchange rate fluctuations in one year. On the other hand, Procter & Gamble recently lost $550 million on its operations in Russia due to devaluation of the Russian ruble.

Political-Regulatory Climate

Assessing the political and regulatory climate for marketing in a country or region of the world involves not only identifying the current climate but also determining how long a favorable or unfavorable climate will last. An assessment of a country or regional political-regulatory climate includes an analysis of its political stability and trade regulations.

Political Stability Trade among nations or regions depends on political stability. Billions of dollars in trade have been lost in the Middle East and Africa as a result of internal political strife, terrorism, and war. Losses such as these encourage careful selection of politically stable countries and regions of the world for trade.

Political stability in a country is affected by numerous factors, including a government's orientation toward foreign companies and trade with other countries. These factors combine to create a political climate that is favorable or unfavorable for marketing and financial investment in a country or region of the world. Marketing managers monitor political stability using a variety of measures and often track country risk ratings supplied by agencies such as the PRS Group, Inc. Visit the PRS Group, Inc. website at www.prsgroup.com to see political risk ratings for 100 countries, including your own. Expect to be surprised by the ranking of countries, including the United States.

Trade Regulations Countries have a variety of rules that govern business practices within their borders. These rules often serve as trade barriers. For example, Japan has some 11,000 trade regulations. Japanese car safety rules effectively require all automobile replacement parts to be Japanese and not American or European; public health rules make it illegal to sell aspirin or cold medicine without a pharmacist present. The Malaysian government has advertising regulations stating that "advertisements must not project or promote an excessively aspirational lifestyle," Sweden outlaws all advertisements to children, Iran prohibits Mattel's Barbie dolls because they are a symbol of Western decadence, and Cuba and North Korea ban Coca-Cola because of U.S. trade embargoes.

learning review

6-6. Cross-cultural analysis involves the study of _____.

6-7. When foreign currencies can buy more U.S. dollars, are U.S. products more or less expensive for a foreign consumer?

COMPARING GLOBAL MARKET-ENTRY STRATEGIES

Name and describe the alternative approaches companies use to enter global markets.

Once a company has decided to enter the global marketplace, it must select a means of market entry. Four general options exist: (1) exporting, (2) licensing, (3) joint venture, and (4) direct investment.[21] As Figure 6–4 demonstrates, the amount of financial commitment, risk, marketing control, and profit potential increases as the firm moves from exporting to direct investment.

Exporting

Exporting is producing products in one country and selling them in another country. This entry option allows a company to make the least number of changes in terms of its product, its organization, and even its corporate goals. Host countries usually do not like this practice because it provides less local employment than under alternative means of entry.

exporting
A global market-entry strategy in which a company produces products in one country and sells them in another country.

FIGURE 6–4
A firm's profit potential and control over marketing activities increase as it moves from exporting to direct investment as a global market-entry strategy. But so does a firm's financial commitment and risk. Firms often engage in exporting, licensing, and joint ventures before pursuing a direct investment strategy.

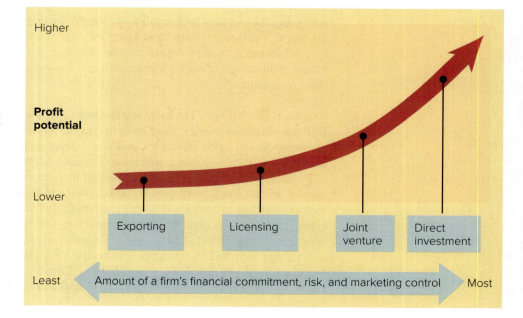

Marketing Matters > Entrepreneurship

Creative Cosmetics and Creative Export Marketing in Japan

How does a medium-sized U.S. cosmetics firm sell 1.5 million tubes of lipstick in Japan annually? Fran Wilson Creative Cosmetics can attribute its success to a top-quality product, effective advertising, and a novel export marketing program. The firm's Moodmatcher lip coloring comes in green, orange, silver, black, and six other hues that change to a shade of pink, coral, or red, depending on a woman's chemistry when it's applied.

The company does not sell to department stores. According to a company spokesperson, "Shiseido and Kanebo (two large Japanese cosmetics firms) keep all the other Japanese or import brands out of the major department stores." Rather, the company sells its Moodmatcher lipstick through a network of Japanese distributors that reach Japan's 40,000 beauty salons.

The result? The company, with its savvy Japanese distributors, accounted for 20 percent of the lipsticks exported annually to Japan by U.S. cosmetics companies.

Source: Fran Wilson, Creative Cosmetics.

©Markus Sepperer/Anzenberger/Redux

Indirect exporting is when a firm sells its domestically produced products in a foreign country through an intermediary. It has the least amount of commitment and risk but will probably return the least profit. Indirect exporting is ideal for a company that has no overseas contacts but wants to market abroad. The intermediary is often a distributer that has the marketing know-how and resources necessary for the effort to succeed. Fran Wilson Creative Cosmetics uses an indirect exporting approach to sell its products in Japan. Read the Marketing Matters box to find out how this innovative marketer and its Japanese distributors sell 20 percent of the lipsticks exported to Japan by U.S. cosmetics companies.[22]

Direct exporting is when a firm sells its domestically produced products in a foreign country without intermediaries. Companies become involved in direct exporting when they believe their volume of sales will be sufficiently large and easy to obtain, thus making intermediaries unnecessary. For example, the exporter may be approached by foreign buyers that are willing to contract for a large volume of purchases. Direct exporting involves more risk than indirect exporting for the company but also opens the door to increased profits. The Boeing Company applies a direct exporting approach. Boeing is the world's largest aerospace company and one of the largest U.S. exporters.

Even though exporting is commonly employed by large firms, it is the prominent global market-entry strategy among small- and medium-sized companies. For example, about 97 percent of U.S. firms exporting products have fewer than 500 employees. These firms account for nearly 33 percent of total U.S. merchandise exports.[23]

Licensing

Under licensing, a company offers the right to a trademark, patent, trade secret, or other similarly valued item of intellectual property in return for a royalty or a fee. The

McDonald's uses franchising as a market-entry strategy, and about two-thirds of the company's sales come from non–U.S. operations. Note that the golden arches appear prominently—one aspect of its global brand promise.
©China/Alamy Stock Photo

McDonald's
www.mcdonalds.com

> **joint venture**
> A global market-entry strategy in which a foreign company and a local firm invest together to create a local business in order to share ownership, control, and profits of the new company.

advantages to the company granting the license are low risk and a capital-free entry into a foreign country. The licensee gains information that allows it to start with a competitive advantage, and the foreign country gains employment by having the product manufactured locally. For instance, Yoplait yogurt is licensed from Sodima, a French cooperative, by General Mills for sales in the United States.

There are some serious drawbacks to this mode of entry, however. The licensor forgoes control of its product and reduces the potential profits gained from it. In addition, while the relationship lasts, the licensor may be creating its own competition. Some licensees are able to modify the product somehow and enter the market with product and marketing knowledge gained at the expense of the company that got them started. To offset this disadvantage, many companies strive to stay innovative so that the licensee remains dependent on them for improvements and successful operation. Finally, should the licensee prove to be a poor choice, the name or reputation of the company may be harmed.

A variation of licensing is *franchising*. Franchising is one of the fastest-growing market-entry strategies. Over 75,000 franchises of U.S. firms are located in countries throughout the world. Franchises include soft-drink, motel, retailing, fast-food, and car rental operations and a variety of business services. McDonald's is a premier global franchiser, with some 14,000 franchised units outside the United States.

Joint Venture

When a foreign company and a local firm invest together to create a local business, it is called a **joint venture**. These two companies share the ownership, control, and profits of the new company. For example, the Strauss Group has a joint venture with PepsiCo to market Frito-Lay's Cheetos, Doritos, and other snacks in Israel.[24]

The advantages of this option are twofold. First, one company may not have the necessary financial, physical, or managerial resources to enter a foreign market alone. The joint venture between Ericsson, a Swedish telecommunications firm, and CGCT, a French switch maker, enabled them together to beat out AT&T for a $100 million French contract. Ericsson's money and technology combined with CGCT's knowledge of the French market helped them to win the contract. Second, a government may require or strongly encourage a joint venture before it allows a foreign company to enter its market. For example, in China, international giants such as Procter & Gamble, Starbucks, and General Motors operate wholly or in part through joint ventures.

The disadvantages arise when the two companies disagree about policies or courses of action for their joint venture or when governmental bureaucracy bogs down the effort. For example, U.S. firms often prefer to reinvest earnings gained, whereas some foreign companies may want to spend those earnings. Or a U.S. firm may want to return profits earned to the United States, while the local firm or its government may oppose this—a problem faced by many potential joint ventures. The collapse of the joint venture between France's Group Danone and a local company in China is a case in point. The joint venture partners could not agree on the distribution of profits.[25]

Direct Investment

The biggest commitment a company can make when entering the global market is *direct investment*, which entails a domestic firm actually investing in and owning a foreign subsidiary or division. Examples of direct investment are Nissan's Smyrna, Tennessee, plant that produces pickup trucks and the Mercedes-Benz factory in Vance,

Alabama, that makes the M-Class sport-utility vehicle. Many U.S.-based global companies also use this mode of entry. Reebok entered Russia by creating a subsidiary known as Reebok Russia.

For many companies, direct investment often follows one of the other three market-entry strategies.[26] For example, both FedEx and UPS entered China through joint ventures with Chinese companies. Each subsequently purchased the interests of its partner and converted the Chinese operations into a division.

The advantages to direct investment include cost savings, a better understanding of local market conditions, and fewer local restrictions. Firms entering foreign markets using direct investment believe that these advantages outweigh the financial commitments and risks involved. However, sometimes they don't. U.S.-based Target Stores entered Canada in 2013 only to withdraw in 2015 after sizable operating losses and an investment of $5.7 billion; Uber departed China in 2016 after posting losses of $2 billion over two years.[27]

> **learning review**
>
> **6-8.** What mode of entry could a company follow if it has no previous experience in global marketing?
>
> **6-9.** How does licensing differ from a joint venture?

CRAFTING A WORLDWIDE MARKETING PROGRAM

Explain the distinction between standardization and customization when companies craft worldwide marketing programs.

The choice of a market-entry strategy is a necessary first step for a marketer when joining the community of global companies. The next step involves the challenging task of planning, implementing, and evaluating marketing programs worldwide.

Successful global marketers standardize global marketing programs whenever possible and customize them wherever necessary. The extent of standardization and customization is often rooted in a careful global environment scan supplemented with judgment based on experience and marketing research.

Product and Promotion Strategies

Global companies have five strategies for matching products and their promotion efforts to global markets. As Figure 6–5 shows, the strategies focus on whether a company extends or adapts its product and promotion message for consumers in different countries and cultures.

A product may be sold globally in one of three ways: (1) in the same form as in its home market, (2) with some adaptations, or (3) as a totally new product:[28]

1. *Product extension.* Selling virtually the same product in other countries is a product extension strategy. It works well for products such as Coca-Cola, Gillette razors, Sony consumer electronics, Harley-Davidson motorcycles, Nike apparel and shoes, and Apple smartphones. As a general rule, product extension seems to work best when the consumer market target for the product is alike across countries and cultures—that is, consumers share the same desires, needs, and uses for the product.

2. *Product adaptation.* Changing a product in some way to make it more appropriate for consumer preferences or a country's climate is a product adaptation strategy. Wrigley's offers grapefruit, cucumber, and tea-flavored chewing gum in China. Frito-Lay produces and markets its potato chips in Russia, but don't expect them to taste like the chips eaten in North America. Russians prefer dairy, meat, and seafood-flavored potato chips. Listerine mouthwash comes in different varieties outside the United States. There is the alcohol-free Listerine Zero,

FIGURE 6–5

Five product and promotion strategies for global marketing exist based on whether a company extends or adapts its product and promotion message for consumers in different countries and cultures. Read the text to learn how different companies employ these strategies.

popular in Muslim countries where alcohol is forbidden, and Green Tea Listerine, made especially for Asian markets. Maybelline's makeup is adapted to local skin types and weather across the globe, including an Asia-specific mascara that doesn't run during the rainy season.

3. *Product invention.* Alternatively, companies can invent totally new products designed to satisfy common needs across countries. Stanley Black & Decker did this with its Snake Light flexible flashlight. Created to address a global need for portable lighting, the product became a best seller in North America, Europe, Latin America, and Australia and became one of the most successful new products developed by Stanley Black & Decker. Similarly, Whirlpool developed a compact, automatic clothes washer specifically for households in developing countries with annual household incomes of $2,000. Called Ideale, the washer features bright colors because washers are often placed in home living areas, not hidden in laundry rooms (which don't exist in many homes in developing countries).

An identical promotion message is used for the product extension and product adaptation strategies around the world. Gillette uses the same global message for its men's toiletries: "Gillette, the Best a Man Can Get." Even though Exxon adapts its gasoline blends for different countries based on climate, the promotion message is unchanged: "Put a Tiger in Your Tank."

Global companies may also adapt their promotion message. For instance, the same product may be sold in many countries but advertised differently. As an example, L'Oréal, a French health and beauty products marketer, introduced its Golden Beauty brand of sun care products through its Helena Rubenstein subsidiary in Western Europe with a *communication adaptation strategy*. Recognizing the existence of differing cultural and buying motives related to skin care and tanning, Golden Beauty advertising features dark tanning for northern Europeans, skin protection to avoid wrinkles among Latin Europeans, and beautiful skin for Europeans living along the Mediterranean Sea, even though the products are the same.

Other companies use a *dual adaptation strategy* by modifying both their products and promotion messages. Nestlé does this with Nescafé coffee. Nescafé is marketed using different coffee blends and promotional campaigns to match consumer preferences in different countries. For example, Nescafé, the world's largest brand of coffee, generally emphasizes the taste, aroma, and warmth of shared moments in its advertising around the world. However, Nescafé is advertised in Thailand as a way to relax from the pressures of daily life.

These examples illustrate the simple rule applied by global companies: Standardize product and promotion strategies whenever possible and customize them wherever necessary. This is the art of global marketing.[29]

Video 6-4
Nescafé China
kerin.tv/cr8e/v6-4

Gillette delivers the same global message whenever possible, as shown in the Gillette for Women Venus ads from the United States, Mexico, and France.

(all): Source: Procter & Gamble

Distribution Strategy

Distribution is of critical importance in global marketing. The availability and quality of retailers and wholesalers as well as transportation, communication, and warehousing facilities are often determined by a country's stage of economic development. Figure 6–6 outlines the channel through which a product manufactured in one country must travel to reach its destination in another country. The first step involves the seller; its headquarters is the starting point and is responsible for the successful distribution to the ultimate consumer.

The next step is the channel between two nations, moving the product from one country to another. Intermediaries that can handle this responsibility include resident buyers in a foreign country, independent merchant wholesalers who buy and sell the product, or agents who bring buyers and sellers together.

Once the product is in the foreign nation, that country's distribution channels take over. These channels can be very long or surprisingly short, depending on the product line. In Japan, fresh fish go through three intermediaries before getting to a retail outlet. Conversely, shoes go through only one intermediary.

Pricing Strategy

Global companies also face many challenges in determining a pricing strategy as part of their worldwide marketing effort. Individual countries, even those with free trade agreements, may impose considerable competitive, political, and legal constraints on the pricing latitude of global companies. For example, antitrust authorities in Germany limited Walmart from selling some items below cost to lure shoppers. Without this advantage, Walmart was unable to compete against German discount stores. This, and other factors, led Walmart to leave Germany following eight years without a profit.[30]

Pricing too low or too high can have dire consequences. When prices appear too low in one country, companies can be charged with dumping, a practice subject to severe

FIGURE 6–6

Channels of distribution in global marketing are often long and complex.

penalties and fines. *Dumping* is when a firm sells a product in a foreign country below its domestic price or below its actual cost. This is often done to build a company's share of the market by pricing at a competitive level. Another reason is that the products being sold may be surplus or cannot be sold domestically and, therefore, are already a burden to the company. The firm may be glad to sell them at almost any price.

When companies price their products very high in some countries but competitively in others, they face a gray market problem. A *gray market*, also called *parallel importing*, is a situation where products are sold through unauthorized channels of distribution. A gray market comes about when individuals buy products in a lower-priced country from a manufacturer's authorized retailer, ship them to higher-priced countries, and then sell them below the manufacturer's suggested retail price through unauthorized retailers. Many well-known brands have been sold through gray markets, including Seiko watches, Chanel perfume, and Mercedes-Benz cars. Parallel importing is legal in the United States. It is illegal in the European Union.

learning review

6-10. Products may be sold globally in three ways. What are they?

6-11. What is *dumping*?

LEARNING OBJECTIVES REVIEW

LO 6-1 *Describe the nature and scope of world trade from a global perspective.*
A global perspective on world trade views exports and imports as complementary economic flows: A country's imports affect its exports and exports affects its imports. Trade flows reflect interdependencies among industries, countries, and regions.

LO 6-2 *Identify the major developments that have influenced world trade and global marketing.*
Five major developments have influenced the landscape of global marketing in the past decade. First, there has been a gradual increase of economic protectionism by individual countries, leading to tariffs and quotas. Second, economic integration and free trade among nations, reflected in the European Union and the North American Free Trade Agreement, is being challenged. Third, there exists global competition among global companies for global consumers, resulting in firms adopting global marketing strategies and promoting global brands. Fourth, a networked global marketspace has emerged using Internet technology as a tool for exchanging products, services, and information on a global scale. And finally, economic espionage has grown among countries and companies because technical know-how and trade secrets separate global industry leaders from followers.

LO 6-3 *Identify the environmental forces that shape global marketing efforts.*
Three major environmental forces shape global marketing efforts. First, there are cultural forces, including values, customs, cultural symbols, and language. Economic forces also shape global marketing efforts. These include a country's stage of economic development and economic infrastructure, consumer income and purchasing power, and currency exchange rates. Finally, political-regulatory forces in a country or region of the world create a favorable or unfavorable climate for global marketing efforts.

LO 6-4 *Name and describe the alternative approaches companies use to enter global markets.*
Companies have four alternative approaches for entering global markets. These are exporting, licensing, joint venture, and direct investment. Exporting involves producing products in one country and selling them in another country. Under licensing, a company offers the right to a trademark, patent, trade secret, or similarly valued item of intellectual property in return for a royalty or fee. In a joint venture, a foreign company and a local firm invest together to create a local business. Direct investment entails a domestic firm actually investing in and owning a foreign subsidiary or division.

LO 6-5 *Explain the distinction between standardization and customization when companies craft worldwide marketing programs.*
Companies distinguish between standardization and customization when crafting worldwide marketing programs. Standardization means that all elements of the marketing program are the same across countries and cultures. Customization means that one or more elements of the marketing program are adapted to meet the needs or preferences of consumers in a particular country or culture. Global marketers apply a simple rule when crafting worldwide marketing programs: Standardize marketing programs whenever possible and customize them wherever necessary.

LEARNING REVIEW ANSWERS

6-1 What country is the biggest as measured by world trade?
Answer: China

6-2 What is the trade feedback effect?
Answer: The phenomenon in which one country's imports affect the exports of other countries and vice versa, thus stimulating trade among countries.

6-3 What is protectionism?
Answer: Protectionism is the practice of shielding one or more industries within a country's economy from foreign competition through the use of tariffs or quotas.

6-4 The North American Free Trade Agreement was designed to promote free trade among which countries?
Answer: the United States, Canada, and Mexico

6-5 What is the difference between a multidomestic marketing strategy and a global marketing strategy?
Answer: Multinational firms view the world as consisting of unique markets. As a result, they use a multidomestic marketing strategy because they have as many different product variations, brand names, and advertising programs as countries in which they do business. Transnational firms view the world as one market. As a result, they use a global marketing strategy, which involves standardizing marketing activities when there are cultural similarities and adapting them when cultures differ.

6-6 Cross-cultural analysis involves the study of _____.
Answer: similarities and differences among consumers in two or more nations or societies.

6-7 When foreign currencies can buy more U.S. dollars, are U.S. products more or less expensive for a foreign consumer?
Answer: less expensive

6-8 What mode of entry could a company follow if it has no previous experience in global marketing?
Answer: indirect exporting through intermediaries

6-9 How does licensing differ from a joint venture?
Answer: Under licensing, a company offers the right to a trademark, patent, trade secret, or other similarly valued item of intellectual property in return for a fee or royalty. In a joint venture, a foreign company and a local firm invest together to create a local business to produce some product or service. The two companies share ownership, control, and profits of the new entity.

6-10 Products may be sold globally in three ways. What are they?
Answer: Products can be sold: (1) in the same form as in their home market (product extension); (2) with some adaptations (product adaptation); and (3) as totally new products (product invention).

6-11 What is *dumping*?
Answer: *Dumping* is when a firm sells a product in a foreign country below its domestic price or below its actual cost to produce.

FOCUSING ON KEY TERMS

back translation p. 162
balance of trade p. 151
consumer ethnocentrism p. 163
countertrade p. 151
cross-cultural analysis p. 160
cultural symbols p. 161
currency exchange rate p. 165
customs p. 160
economic espionage p. 159
exporting p. 166
Foreign Corrupt Practices Act (1977) p. 161
global brand p. 157
global competition p. 155
global consumers p. 158
global marketing strategy p. 157
joint venture p. 168
multidomestic marketing strategy p. 156
protectionism p. 152
quota p. 153
tariffs p. 152
trade war p. 154
values p. 160
World Trade Organization (WTO) p. 154

APPLYING MARKETING KNOWLEDGE

1. Explain what is meant by this statement: "Quotas are a hidden tax on consumers, whereas tariffs are a more obvious one."
2. How successful would a television commercial in Japan be if it featured a husband surprising his wife in her dressing area on Valentine's Day with a small box of chocolates containing four candies? Explain.
3. As a novice in global marketing, which global market-entry strategy would you be likely to start with? Why? What other alternatives do you have for a global market entry?
4. Coca-Cola is sold worldwide. In some countries, Coca-Cola owns the bottling facilities; in others, it has signed contracts with licensees or relies on joint ventures. When selecting a licensee in each country, what factors should Coca-Cola consider?

BUILDING YOUR MARKETING PLAN

Does your marketing plan involve reaching global customers outside the United States? If the answer is no, read no further and do not include a global element in your plan.

If the answer is yes, try to identify the following:

1. What features of your product are especially important to potential customers?
2. In which countries do these potential customers live?
3. What special marketing issues are involved in trying to reach these customers?

Answers to these questions will help you develop the more detailed marketing mix strategies described in later chapters.

VIDEO CASE 6 — Mary Kay, Inc.: Building a Brand in India

Sheryl Adkins-Green couldn't ask for a better assignment. As the newly appointed vice president of brand development at Mary Kay, Inc. she is responsible for development of the product portfolio around the world, including global initiatives and products specifically formulated for global markets. She is enthusiastic about her position, noting that "There is tremendous opportunity for growth. Even in these economic times, women still want to pamper themselves, and to look good is to feel good."

Video 6-5
Mary Kay Video Case
kerin.tv/cr8e/v6-5

Getting up to speed on her new company and her new position topped her short-term agenda. She was specifically interested in the company's efforts to date to build the Mary Kay brand in India.

THE MARY KAY WAY

Mary Kay Ash founded Mary Kay Cosmetics in 1963 with her life savings of $5,000 and the support of her 20-year-old son, Richard Rogers, who currently serves as executive chair of Mary Kay, Inc. Mary Kay, Inc. is one of the largest direct sellers of skin care and color cosmetics in the world, with more than $2.5 billion in annual sales. Mary Kay brand products are sold in more than 35 markets on five continents. The United States, China, Russia, and Mexico are the top four markets served by the company. The company's global independent sales force exceeds 2 million. About 65 percent of the company's independent sales representatives reside outside the United States.

Mary Kay Ash's founding principles were simple, time-tested, and remain a fundamental company business philosophy. She adopted the Golden Rule as her guiding principle, determining the best course of action in virtually any situation could be easily discerned by "doing unto others as you would have them do unto you." She also steadfastly believed that life's priorities should be kept in their proper order, which to her meant "God first, family second, and career third." Her work ethic, approach to business, and success have resulted in numerous awards and recognitions, including, but not limited to, the Horatio Alger American Citizen Award, recognition as one of "America's 25 Most Influential Women," and induction into the National Business Hall of Fame.

Mary Kay, Inc. engages in the development, manufacture, and packaging of skin care, makeup, spa and body, and fragrance products for men and women. It offers anti-aging, cleanser, moisturizer, lip and eye care, body care, and sun care products. Overall, the company produces more than 200 premium products in its state-of-the-art manufacturing facilities in Dallas, Texas, and Hangzhou, China. The company's approach to direct selling employs the "party plan," whereby independent sales representatives host parties to demonstrate or sell products to consumers.

GROWTH OPPORTUNITIES IN ASIA-PACIFIC MARKETS

Asia-Pacific markets represent major growth opportunities for Mary Kay, Inc. These markets for Mary Kay, Inc. include Australia, China, Hong Kong, India, Korea, Malaysia, New Zealand, the Philippines, Singapore, and Taiwan.

China accounts for the largest sales revenue outside the United States, representing about 25 percent of annual Mary Kay, Inc. worldwide sales. The company entered China in 1995 and currently has some 200,000 independent sales representatives or "beauty consultants" in that country.

Part of Mary Kay's success in China has been attributed to the company's message of female empowerment and femininity, which has resonated in China, a country where young women have few opportunities to start their own businesses. Speaking about the corporate philosophy at Mary Kay, Inc., KK Chua, president, Asia-Pacific, said, "Mary Kay's corporate objective is not only to create a market, selling skin care and cosmetics; it's all about enriching women's lives by helping women reach their full potential, find their inner beauty and discover how truly great they are."[31] This view is echoed by Sheryl Adkins-Green, who notes that the Mary Kay brand has "transformational and aspirational" associations for users and beauty consultants alike.

Mary Kay, Inc. learned that adjustments to its product line and message for women were necessary in some Asia-Pacific markets. In China, for example, the order of life's priorities—"God first, family second, and career third"—has been modified to "Faith first, family second, and career third." Also, Chinese women aren't heavy users of makeup. Therefore, the featured products include skin cream, anti-aging cream, and whitening creams. As a generalization, whitening products are popular among women in China, India, Korea, and the Philippines, where lighter skin is associated with beauty, class, and privilege.

MARY KAY, INDIA

Mary Kay, Inc. senior management believed that India represented a growth opportunity for three reasons.

First, the Indian upper and consuming classes were growing and were expected to total over 500 million individuals. Second, the population was overwhelmingly young and optimistic. This youthful population continues to push consumerism as the line between luxury and basic items continues to blur. Third, a growing number of working women have given a boost to sales of cosmetics, skin care, and fragrances in India's urban areas, where 70 percent of the country's middle-class women reside.

Senior management also believed that India's socioeconomic characteristics in 2007 were similar in many ways to China's in 1995, when the company entered that market (see Figure 1). The Mary Kay culture was viewed as a good fit with the Indian culture, which would benefit the company's venture into this market. For example, industry research has shown that continuing modernization of the country has led to changing aspirations. As a result, the need to be good looking, well-groomed, and stylish has taken on a newfound importance.

Mary Kay initiated operations in India in September 2007 with a full marketing launch in early 2008. The initial launch was in Delhi, the nation's capital and the second most populated metropolis in India, and Mumbai, the nation's most heavily populated metropolis. Delhi, with per capita income of U.S.$1,420, and Mumbai, with per capita income of $2,850, were among the wealthiest metropolitan areas in India.

According to Rhonda Shasteen, chief marketing officer at Mary Kay, Inc., "For Mary Kay to be successful in India, the company had to build a brand, build a sales force, and build an effective supply chain to service the sales force."

Building a Brand

Mary Kay, Inc. executives believed that brand building in India needed to involve media advertising; literature describing the Mary Kay culture, the Mary Kay story, and the company's image; and educational material for Mary Kay independent sales representatives. In addition, Mary Kay, Inc. became the cosmetics partner of the Miss India Worldwide Pageant. At this event, Mary Kay Miss Beautiful Skin was crowned.

Brand building in India also involved product mix and pricing. Four guidelines were followed:

1. Keep the offering simple and skin care focused for the new Indian sales force and for a new operation.
2. Open with accessibly priced basic skin care products in relation to the competition in order to establish Mary Kay product quality and value.
3. Avoid opening with products that would phase out shortly after launch.
4. Address the key product categories of Skin Care, Body Care, and Color based on current market information.

Brand pricing focused on offering accessibly priced basic skin care to the average middle-class Indian consumer between the ages of 25 and 54. This strategy, called "mass-tige pricing," resulted in product price points that were above mass but below prestige competitive product prices. Following an initial emphasis on offering high-quality, high-value products, Mary Kay introduced more technologically advanced products that commanded higher price points. For example, the company introduced the Mary Kay MelaCEP Whitening System, consisting of seven products, which was specifically formulated for Asian skin in March 2009. This system was "priced on the lower price end of the prestige category with a great value for money equation," said Hina Nagarajan, country manager for Mary Kay India.

Building a Sales Force

According to Adkins-Green, "Mary Kay's most powerful marketing vehicle is the direct selling organization," which is a key component of the brand's marketing strategy. Mary Kay relied on its Global Leadership Development Program directors and National Sales directors and the Mary Kay Sales Education staff from the United States and Canada for the initial recruitment and training of independent sales representatives in India. New independent sales representatives received 2 to 3 days of intensive training and a starter kit that included not only products, but also information pertaining to product demonstrations, sales presentations, professional demeanor, the company's history and culture, and team building.

FIGURE 1 Social and economic statistics for India in 2007 and China in 1995.

	India 2007	China 1995
Population (million)	1,136	1,198
Population age distribution (0–24; 25–49; 50+)	52%, 33%, 15%	43%, 39%, 18%
Urban population	29.2%	29.0%
Population/square mile	990	332
Gross domestic product (U.S.$ billion)	3,113	728
Per capita income (U.S.$)	$950	$399
Direct selling sales percent of total cosmetics/skin care sales	3.3%	3.0%

Courtesy of Mary Kay, Inc.

"Culture training is very important to Mary Kay (independent sales representatives) because they are going to be the messengers of Mary Kay," said Hina Nagarajan. "As a direct-selling company that offers products sold person-to-person, we recognize that there's a personal relationship between consultant and client with every sale," added Rhonda Shasteen. By late 2009, there were some 4,000 independent sales representatives in India present in some 200 cities mostly in the northern, western, and northeastern regions of the country.

Creating a Supply Chain

Mary Kay, India, imported products into India from China, Korea, and the United States. Products were shipped to regional distribution centers in Delhi and Mumbai, India, where Mary Kay Beauty Centers were located. Beauty Centers served as order pickup points for the independent sales representatives. Mary Kay beauty consultants purchased products from the company and, in turn, sold them to consumers.

LOOKING AHEAD

Mary Kay, Inc. plans to invest around $20 million in the next five years on product development, company infrastructure, and building its brand in India. "There is a tremendous opportunity for growth," says Sheryl Adkins-Green. India represents a particularly attractive opportunity. Developing the brand and brand portfolio and specifically formulating products for Indian consumers will require her attention to brand positioning and brand equity.[32]

Questions

1. Is Mary Kay an international firm, a multinational firm, or a transnational firm based on its marketing strategy? Why?
2. What global market-entry strategy did Mary Kay use when it entered India?
3. Is Mary Kay a global brand? Why or why not?

Chapter Notes

1. "The Elephant in the Room," *The Economist*, January 13, 2018, pp. 20–22; "Walmart Expands Global Footprint with Flipkart," *www.emarketer.com,* May 8, 2018; "India's Ecommerce Market Continues to Surge," *www.emarketer.com*, June 7, 2018; "Amazon Will Continue to Invest Billions in India: Jeff Bezos," *www.economictimes.indiatimes*, April 29, 2017; "Amazon to Scale Up Online Retailing in India: The Great Race," *The Economist*, March 5, 2016; Vivienne Walt, "Amazon Invades India," *Fortune*, January 1, 2016, pp. 63–71; and *Pocket World in Figures, 2018 Edition* (London: The Economist, 2018).

2. Unless otherwise indicated, all trade statistics and practices are provided by the World Trade Organization, *www.wto.org*,

downloaded May 10, 2018; U.S. Bureau of Economic Analysis, *www.bea.gov*, downloaded May 10, 2018; "Globalization Backers Face End of an Era," *The Wall Street Journal*, March 30, 2017, p. A1ff.; "Trade Deficit at Its Widest in Four Years," *The Wall Street Journal*, February 8, 2017, p. A2; "Global Economies and Consumers in 2017," *www.euromonitor.com*, March 6, 2017; "The $9B Barter Deal," *barternews.com*, February 1, 2017; and "A Fractured World: Nationalism Is Growing and Changing," *The Wall Street Journal*, January 23, 2018, pp. R1, R15.

3. Dennis R. Appleyard and Alfred J. Field, *International Economics*, 8th ed. (Burr Ridge, IL: McGraw-Hill/Irwin, 2013), Chapter 15; "Bananas: 10 Years of Import Regime in the EU," *www.eurofreshdistribution.com*, April 29, 2016; Yuri Kageyama, "Selling Rice to Japan? U.S. Plans to Try," *www.msnbc.com*, March 7, 2004; "A Shoe Tariff with a Big Footprint," *The Wall Street Journal*, November 23, 2012, p. A13; and *Economic Report of the President* (Washington, DC: U.S. Government Printing Office, 2015).

4. "Time to Put Trade above Politics," *Time*, March 7, 2015, p. 24.

5. This discussion on the European Union is based on information provided at *www.europa.eu*, downloaded March 5, 2018.

6. These examples provided by the Office of the United States Trade Representative at *www.ustr.gov*.

7. For an overview of different types of global companies and marketing strategies, see, for example, Masaaki Kotabe and Kristiaan Helsen, *Global Marketing Management*, 6th ed. (New York: Wiley, 2015); Warren J. Keegan and Mark C. Green, *Global Marketing*, 4th ed. (Upper Saddle River, NJ: Prentice Hall, 2005); and Michael Czinkota and Ilkka A. Ronkainen, *International Marketing*, 10th ed. (Mason, OH: South-Western, 2013).

8. Johnny K. Johansson and Ilkka A. Ronkainen, "The Brand Challenge," *Marketing Management*, March–April 2004, pp. 54–55.

9. Kevin Lane Keller, *Strategic Brand Management*, 4th ed. (Upper Saddle River, NJ: Prentice Hall, 2013).

10. "Number of TV Households Receiving MTV Programming Worldwide in the Fiscal Years 2007–2016," *www.statistica.com*, downloaded February 3, 2018; "These Are Teens' Favorite Brands of 2017," fortune.com, April 11, 2017; "The Most Popular Brands for China's Young Consumers," forbes.com, August 17, 2016; "Most Exciting Brands 2016: Here's Where the Indian Youth Is Today," adageindia.in, May 21, 2016; "Purchase Power of Teens Tops $819 Billion," *www.insights.mastercard.com*, November 21, 2012; and "Global Social Media Statistics for 2017," www.digitalinformationworld, February 8, 2017.

11. *Pocket World in Figures, 2018 Edition*.

12. *The Report of the Commission on the Theft of American Intellectual Property* (Seattle, WA: National Bureau of Asian Research, 2017); "2016 Cost of Data Breach Study: United States," *www.ibm.com/security/data-breach*, June 2016; "No Sign China Has Stopped Hacking U.S. Companies, Official Says," *www.bloomberg.com*, November 18, 2016; and "The Staggering Cost of Economic Espionage against the U.S.," *www.theepochtimes*, October 22, 2013.

13. For comprehensive references on cross-cultural aspects of marketing, see Paul A. Herbig, *Handbook of Cross-Cultural Marketing* (New York: Haworth Press, 1998); Jean Claude Usunier and Julie Anne Lee, *Marketing across Cultures*, 6th ed. (London: Prentice Hall Europe, 2013); and Philip K. Cateora, Mary C. Gilly, John L. Graham, and R. Bruce Money, *International Marketing*, 17th ed. (Burr Ridge, IL: McGraw-Hill/Irwin, 2016). Unless otherwise indicated, examples found in this section appear in these excellent sources.

14. "SEC Enforcement Actions: FCPA Cases," www.sec.gov, downloaded March 16, 2018.

15. Michael White, *A Short Course in International Marketing Blunders* (Novato, CA: World Trade Press, 2002).

16. Erika Fry, "How Japanese Kit Kat Got So Hot," *Fortune*, April 3, 2018, p. 12.

17. Terrence A. Shimp and Subhash Sharma, "Consumer Ethnocentrism: Construction and Validation of the CETSCALE," *Journal of Marketing Research*, August 1987, pp. 280–89. For a review of research on this topic, see Nicoletta-Theofania and George Balabanis, "Revisiting Consumer Ethnocentrism: Review, Reconceptualization, and Empirical Testing," *Journal of International Marketing*, September 2015, pp. 66–86; and A. Alsughayir, "Consumer Ethnocentrism: A Literature Review," *International Journal of Business and Management*, May 2013, pp. 50–54.

18. "These 5 Facts Explain the Unstable Global Middle Class," *www.time.com*, January 29, 2016.

19. "Mattel Plans to Double Sales Abroad," *The Wall Street Journal*, February 11, 1998, pp. A3, A11.

20. "Strong Dollar Squeezes U.S. Firms," *The Wall Street Journal*, January 28, 2015, pp. A1, A2.

21. For an extensive and recent examination of these market-entry options, see for example, Johnny K. Johansson, *Global Marketing: Foreign Entry, Local Marketing, and Global Management*, 5th ed. (Burr Ridge, IL: McGraw Hill/Irwin, 2008); A. Coskun Samli, *Entering & Succeeding in Emerging Countries: Marketing to the Forgotten Majority* (Mason, OH: South-Western, 2004); and Warren J. Keegan and Mark C. Green, *Global Marketing*, 4th ed. (Upper Saddle River, NJ: Prentice Hall, 2005).

22. Based on an interview with Pamela Viglielmo, Director of International Marketing, Fran Wilson Creative Cosmetics; and "Foreign Firms Think Their Way into Japan," *www.successstories.com/nikkei*, downloaded March 24, 2003.

23. *Small and Medium Sized Exporting Companies: Statistical Overview* (Washington, DC: International Trade Administration, April 16, 2015).

24. "About Us," *www.strauss-group.com*, downloaded March 15, 2018.

25. "Dannon Pulls Out of Disputed China Venture," *The Wall Street Journal*, October 1, 2009, p. B1.

26. Kate Gillespie and H. David Hennessey, *Global Marketing*, 4th ed. (New York: Taylor & Francis, 2016), Chapter 9.

27. "Target's New CEO Makes a Bold Decision to Leave Canada," *www.forbes.com*, January 15, 2015; and "Ride-Hailing in China," *The Economist*, August 4, 2016, p. 77.

28. This discussion is based on Kevin Lane Keller, *Strategic Brand Management*, 4th ed. (Upper Saddle River, NJ: Prentice Hall, 2013), pp. 709–10; "Adapting Listerine to a Global Market," *www.nytimes.com*, September 12, 2014; "Gum Makers Cater to Chinese Tastes," *The Wall Street Journal*, February 26, 2014, p. B9; "Global Sales of Lay's Chips Top $10 Billion in '11," *Dallas Morning News*, March 12, 2012, pp. D1, 10D; "Machines for the Masses," *The Wall Street Journal*, December 9, 2003, pp. A19, A20; "The Color of Beauty," *Forbes*, November 22, 2000, pp. 170–76; Donald R. Graber, "How to Manage a Global Product Development Process," *Industrial Marketing Management*, November 1996, pp. 483–98; and Herbig, *Handbook of Cross-Cultural Marketing*.

29. Jagdish N. Sheth and Atul Parvatiyar, "The Antecedents and Consequences of Integrated Global Marketing," *International Marketing Review* 18, no. 1 (2001), pp. 16–29. Also see D. Szymanski, S. Bharadwaj, and R. Varadarajan, "Standardization versus Adaptation of International Marketing Strategy: An Empirical Investigation," *Journal of Marketing*, October 1993, pp. 1–17.

30. "Where Wal-Mart Isn't: Four Countries the Retailer Can't Conquer," *www.businessweek.com*, October 10, 2013.

31. KK Chua, president, Asia-Pacific corporate philosophy at Mary Kay, Inc.

32. Mary Kay, India: This case was prepared by Roger A. Kerin based on company interviews.

7

LEARNING OBJECTIVES

After reading this chapter you should be able to:

LO 7-1 Identify the reason for conducting marketing research.

LO 7-2 Describe the five-step marketing research approach that leads to marketing actions.

LO 7-3 Explain how marketing uses secondary and primary data.

LO 7-4 Discuss the uses of observations, questionnaires, panels, experiments, and newer data collection methods.

LO 7-5 Explain how data analytics, data mining, and predictive modeling lead to marketing actions.

LO 7-6 Describe three approaches to developing a company's sales forecast.

Marketing Research: From Customer Insights to Actions

Hollywood Loves Marketing Research!

Black Panther, Star Wars: The Last Jedi, and *Avatar* are blockbuster movies that have attracted millions of moviegoers worldwide. The theater ticket revenues they generated each exceeded $1 billion, well above the $200+ million budgets needed to produce them. Unfortunately, not every movie has such favorable results. Movies such as *The Mummy, Blade Runner 2049,* and *47 Ronin,* for example, each lost more than $75 million. So what can studios do to try to reduce the risk that a movie will be a box-office flop? Marketing research![1]

A Film Industry Secret

Bad titles, poor scripts, temperamental stars, costly special effects, competing movies, and ever-changing consumers are just a few of the risks studio executives face. They try to reduce their risk through a largely secretive process of marketing research that involves small sample audiences selected to be representative of the larger population.

Fixing bad movie names, for example, can turn potential disasters into successful blockbusters. Many studios use title testing—a form of marketing research—to choose a name. Here are a few examples:

Video 7-1
Black Panther Movie Trailer
Kerin.tv/cr8e/v7-1

- *Atomic Blonde* originally went by the title *Coldest City*. The name was changed, though, to better match the performance of the movie's star, Charlize Theron.

- *Edge of Tomorrow,* starring Tom Cruise and Emily Blunt, first used the name of the book on which it was based, *All You Need Is Kill*. The word "kill," however, was unpopular.

- *War Dogs* started out as *Arms and the Dudes,* which was confusing and too complicated.

- *Begin Again,* with Keira Knightley and Mark Ruffalo, began as *Can a Song Save Your Life?* but test audiences didn't like that title.

©Moviestore Collection Ltd/Alamy Stock Photo

Generally, filmmakers want movie titles that are short, memorable, appealing to consumers, and without legal restrictions—the same factors that make a good brand name.[2]

Studios also try to reduce their risks with additional forms of marketing research such as:

- *Concept testing and script assessment.* These techniques are used to assess early ideas for proposed new films. In addition, because many scripts and films today

The text describes how social listening is used to help movies become a success.
Composite image: (ear) ©vvs1976/iStock/Getty Images; (thought bubble) ©Hilch/Shutterstock; (icons) ©Brilliantist Studio/Shutterstock

are part of a series such as *The Fast and the Furious, Star Wars,* and *Pirates of the Caribbean,* these forms of research can ensure that sequels are consistent with expectations created by the past movies.[3]

- *Test (or preview) screenings.* In test screenings, 300 to 400 prospective moviegoers are recruited to attend a "sneak preview" of a film before its release. After viewing the movie, the audience completes a survey to critique its title, plot, characters, music, and ending to identify improvements to make in the final edit. James Cameron, for example, used a test screening of *Titanic* to cut the length of the movie from four hours to 194 minutes, and to change the ending.[4]

- *Tracking studies.* Before an upcoming film's release, studios will ask prospective moviegoers in the target audience three questions: (1) Are you aware of the film? (2) Are you interested in seeing the film? (3) Will you see the film? Studios also use "social listening" to understand what potential moviegoers are saying on Twitter, YouTube, Tumblr, Facebook, Instagram, and other social media sites. Studios use these data to monitor a promotional campaign, forecast the movie's opening weekend box-office sales and, if necessary, add additional marketing activities to promote the film.[5]

These examples show how marketing research leads to effective marketing actions, the main topic of this chapter. Also, marketing research is often used to help a firm develop its sales forecasts, the final topic of this chapter.

THE ROLE OF MARKETING RESEARCH

 LO 7-1 Identify the reason for conducting marketing research.

Let's (1) look at what marketing research is, (2) identify some difficulties with it, and (3) describe the five steps marketers use to conduct it.

What Is Marketing Research?

Marketing research is the process of defining a marketing problem and opportunity, systematically collecting and analyzing information, and recommending actions.[6] Although imperfect, marketers conduct marketing research to reduce the risk of—and thereby improve—marketing decisions.

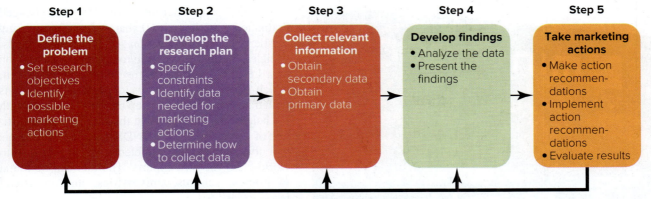

FIGURE 7–1
Five-step marketing research approach leading to marketing actions. Lessons learned from past research mistakes are fed back to improve each of the steps.

The Challenges in Doing Good Marketing Research

Whatever the marketing issue involved—whether discovering consumer tastes or setting the right price—good marketing research is challenging. For example:

- Suppose your firm is developing a product that is completely new to the marketplace, and you are charged with estimating demand for the product. How can marketing research determine if consumers will buy a product they have never seen, and never thought about, before?
- Understanding why consumers purchase some products often requires answers to personal questions. How can marketing research obtain answers that people know but are reluctant to reveal?
- Past purchase behaviors may help firms understand the influence of marketing actions. How can marketing research help people accurately remember and report their interests, intentions, and purchases?

Marketing research must overcome these difficulties and obtain the information needed so that marketers can assess what consumers want and will buy.

marketing research
The process of defining a marketing problem and opportunity, systematically collecting and analyzing information, and recommending actions.

Five-Step Marketing Research Approach

A *decision* is a conscious choice from among two or more alternatives. All of us make many such decisions daily. At work we choose from alternative ways to accomplish an assigned task. At college we choose from alternative courses. As consumers we choose from alternative brands. No magic formula guarantees correct decisions.

Managers and researchers have tried to improve the outcomes of decisions by using more formal, structured approaches to *decision making,* the act of consciously choosing from among alternatives. In this chapter, we describe a systematic marketing research approach used to collect information to improve marketing decisions and actions. This five-step approach is shown in Figure 7–1. Although our focus in this chapter is on marketing decisions, this approach provides a systematic checklist for making both business and personal decisions.

LO 7-2 Describe the five-step marketing research approach that leads to marketing actions.

STEP 1: DEFINE THE PROBLEM

Every marketing problem faces its own research challenges. For example, the marketing strategy used by LEGO Group's toy researchers and designers in Denmark illustrates the wide variations possible in collecting marketing research data to build better toys.

Marketing research helps LEGO Group identify possible marketing actions for products such as its MINDSTORMS® EV3 building system.
Source: LEGO Group

LEGO Group's definition of "toy" has changed dramatically in the past 60 years—from interlocking plastic bricks to construction sets that create figures, vehicles, buildings, and even robots. One new version of a LEGO Group toy is the MINDSTORMS® kit, which integrates electronics, computers, and robots with traditional LEGO Group bricks. Developed with the help of the Media Lab at the Massachusetts Institute of Technology, the MINDSTORMS® kit appeals to a diverse market—from elementary school kids to world-class robotics experts. The kits can be found in homes, schools, universities, and industrial laboratories.[7]

A simplified look at the marketing research for the LEGO Group's MINDSTORMS® EV3 shows the two key elements in defining a problem: setting the research objectives and identifying possible marketing actions.

Set the Research Objectives

Research objectives are specific, measurable goals the decision maker seeks to achieve in conducting the marketing research. For LEGO Group, let's assume the immediate research objective is to decide which of two new MINDSTORMS® designs should be selected for marketing.

Identify Possible Marketing Actions

measures of success
Criteria or standards used in evaluating proposed solutions to the problem.

Effective decision makers develop specific **measures of success**, which are criteria or standards used in evaluating proposed solutions to the problem. Different research outcomes, based on the measure of success, lead to different marketing actions. For LEGO Group, assume the measure of success is the total time spent with each of the two potential new MINDSTORMS® kits until a device that can do simple tricks is produced. This measure of success leads to a clear-cut marketing action: Market the kit that produces an acceptable device in the least amount of playing time.

Marketing researchers know that defining a problem is an incredibly difficult task. If the objectives are too broad, the problem may not be researchable. If they are too narrow, the value of the research results may be seriously diminished. This is why marketing researchers spend so much time defining a marketing problem precisely and writing a formal proposal that describes the research to be done.[8]

STEP 2: DEVELOP THE RESEARCH PLAN

The second step in the marketing research process requires that the researcher (1) specify the constraints on the marketing research activity, (2) identify the data needed for marketing actions, and (3) determine how to collect the data.

constraints
In a decision, the restrictions placed on potential solutions to a problem.

Specify Constraints

The **constraints** in a decision are the restrictions placed on potential solutions to a problem. Examples include the limitations on the time and money available to solve the problem.

What constraints might LEGO Group set in developing new LEGO Group MINDSTORMS® EV3 products? LEGO Group might establish the following constraints on its decision to select one of the two new designs: The decision (1) must be made in five weeks (2) using 10 teams of middle school students playing with the two alternative MINDSTORMS® kits.

Identify Data Needed for Marketing Actions

Effective marketing research studies focus on collecting data that will lead to effective marketing actions. In the MINDSTORMS® case, LEGO Group's marketers might want to know students' math skills, time spent playing video games, and so on. But that information, while nice to know, is largely irrelevant because the study should focus on collecting only those data that will help them make a clear choice between the two MINDSTORMS® designs.

Determine How to Collect Data

Determining how to collect useful marketing research data is often as important as actually collecting the data—step 3 in the process, which is discussed later. Two key elements to consider in deciding how to collect the data are (1) concepts and (2) methods.

Concepts In the world of marketing, *concepts* are ideas about products or services. To find out about consumer reactions to a potential new product, marketing researchers frequently develop a *new-product concept,* which is a picture or verbal description of a product or service the firm might offer for sale. For example, the LEGO Group designers might develop a new-product concept for a new MINDSTORMS® EV3 robot that uses a color sensor, responds to voice commands, or uses GPS navigation software.

Methods *Methods* are the approaches that can be used to collect data to solve all or part of a problem. To collect data, LEGO Group marketing researchers might use a combination of (1) observing the behavior of MINDSTORMS® users and (2) asking users questions about their opinions of the MINDSTORMS® kits. Observing people and asking them questions—the two main data collection methods—are discussed in the section that follows.

How can you find and use the methods that other marketing researchers have found successful? Information on useful methods is available in tradebooks, textbooks, and handbooks that relate to marketing and marketing research. Some periodicals and technical journals, such as the *Journal of Marketing* and the *Journal of Marketing Research,* both published by the American Marketing Association, summarize methods and techniques valuable in addressing marketing problems.

Special methods vital to marketing are (1) sampling and (2) statistical inference. For example, marketing researchers often use *sampling* by selecting a group of distributors, customers, or prospects, asking them questions, and treating their answers as typical of all those in whom they are interested. They may then use *statistical inference* to generalize the results from the sample to much larger groups of distributors, customers, or prospects to help decide on marketing actions.

learning review

7-1. What is marketing research?

7-2. What is the five-step marketing research approach?

7-3. What are constraints, as they apply to developing a research plan?

STEP 3: COLLECT RELEVANT INFORMATION

LO 7-3 Explain how marketing uses secondary and primary data.

Collecting enough relevant information to make a rational, informed marketing decision sometimes simply means using your knowledge to decide immediately. At other times it entails collecting an enormous amount of information at great expense.

Figure 7–2 shows how the different kinds of marketing information fit together. **Data**, the facts and figures related to the project, are divided into two main parts: secondary data and primary data. **Secondary data** are facts and figures that have already been recorded prior to the project at hand. As shown in Figure 7–2, secondary data are divided into two parts—internal and external secondary data—depending on whether the data come from inside or outside the organization needing the research. **Primary data** are facts and figures that are newly collected for the project. Figure 7–2 shows that primary data can be divided into observational data, questionnaire data, and other sources of data.

data
The facts and figures related to the project that are divided into two main parts: secondary data and primary data.

secondary data
Facts and figures that have already been recorded prior to the project at hand.

primary data
Facts and figures that are newly collected for the project.

Secondary Data: Internal

The internal records of a company generally offer the most easily accessible marketing information. These internal sources of secondary data may be divided into two related parts: (1) marketing inputs and (2) marketing outcomes.

Marketing input data relate to the effort expended to make sales. These range from marketing budget reports, which include advertising expenditures, to salespeople's call reports, which describe the number of sales calls per day, who was visited, and what was discussed.

Marketing outcome data relate to the results of the marketing efforts. These involve accounting records on shipments and include sales and repeat sales, often broken down by sales representative, industry, and geographic region. In addition, e-mails, phone

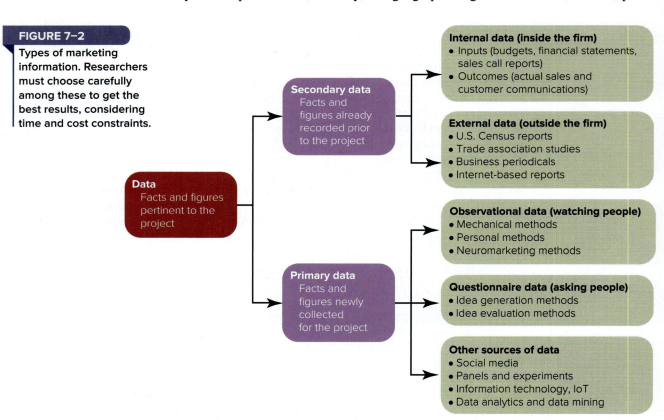

FIGURE 7–2
Types of marketing information. Researchers must choose carefully among these to get the best results, considering time and cost constraints.

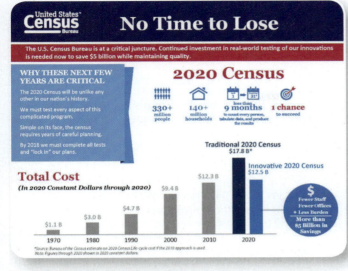

The U.S. Census provides valuable information for marketing decisions. Are you ready for the 2020 Census?
Source: U.S. Department of Commerce

Video 7-2
U.S. Census
kerin.tv/cr8e/v7-2

calls, and letters from customers can reveal both complaints and what is working well.[9]

Secondary Data: External

Published data from outside the organization are external secondary data. The U.S. Census Bureau publishes a variety of useful reports. Best known is the Census 2010, which is the most recent count of the U.S. population that occurs every 10 years. Recently, the Census Bureau began collecting data annually from a smaller number of people through the American Community Survey. Both surveys contain detailed information on American households, such as the number of people per household and the age, sex, race/ethnic background, income, occupation, and education of individuals within the household. Marketers use these data to identify characteristics and trends of ultimate consumers.

Several marketing research companies pay households and businesses to record all their purchases using a paper or electronic diary. Such *syndicated panel* data economically answer questions that require consistent data collection over time, such as, "How many times did our customers buy our products this year compared to last year?" Examples of syndicated panels that provide a standard set of data on a regular basis are the Nielsen TV ratings and J.D. Power's automotive quality and customer satisfaction surveys.

Some data services provide comprehensive information on household demographics and lifestyle, product purchases, TV viewing behavior, responses to coupon and free-sample promotions, and social media use. Their advantage is that a single firm can collect, analyze, interrelate, and present all this information. For consumer product firms such as Procter & Gamble, sales data from various channels help them allocate scarce marketing resources. As a result, they use tracking services such as IRI's InfoScan to collect product sales and coupon/free-sample redemptions that have been scanned at the checkout counters of supermarket, drug, convenience, and mass merchandise retailers.

Finally, trade associations, universities, and business periodicals provide detailed data of value to marketing researchers and planners. These data are often available online and can be identified and located using a search engine such as Google or Bing. The nearby Marketing Matters box provides examples.

Advantages and Disadvantages of Secondary Data

A general rule among marketing researchers is to obtain secondary data first and then collect primary data. Two important advantages of secondary data are (1) the tremendous time savings because the data have already been collected and published or exist internally and (2) the low cost, such as free or inexpensive Census reports. Furthermore, a greater level of detail is often available through secondary data, especially U.S. Census Bureau data.

However, these advantages must be weighed against some significant disadvantages. First, the secondary data may be out of date, especially if they are U.S. Census data collected only every 5 or 10 years. Second, the definitions or categories might not be quite right for a researcher's project. For example, the age groupings or product categories might be wrong for the project. Also, because the data have been collected for another purpose, they may not be specific enough for the project. In such cases, it may be necessary to collect primary data.

Marketing Matters

Technology

Online Databases and Internet Resources Useful to Marketers

Marketers in search of secondary data can utilize a wide variety of online databases and Internet resources. These resources provide access to articles in periodicals; statistical or financial data on markets, products, and organizations; and reports from commercial information companies.

Sources of news and articles include:

- LexisNexis Academic (www.lexisnexis.com), which provides comprehensive news and company information from domestic and foreign sources.
- *The Wall Street Journal* (www.wsj.com), *Bloomberg* (www.bloomberg.com), *CNBC* (www.cnbc.com), and *Fox Business* (www.foxbusiness.com), which provide up-to-the-minute business news and video clips about companies, industries, and trends.

Sources of statistical and financial data on markets, products, and organizations include:

- FedStats (https://fedstats.sites.usa.gov) and the Census Bureau (www.census.gov) of the U.S. Department of Commerce, which provide information on U.S. business, economic, and trade activity collected by the federal government.

Portals and search engines include:

- USA.gov (www.usa.gov), the portal to all U.S. government websites. Users can click on links to browse by topic or enter keywords for specific searches.
- Google (www.google.com), the most popular portal to the entire Internet. Users enter keywords for specific searches and then click on results of interest.

Some of these websites are accessible only if you or your educational institution have paid a subscription fee. Check with your institution's website.

---

learning review

7-4. What is the difference between secondary and primary data?

7-5. What are some advantages and disadvantages of secondary data?

LO 7-4 Discuss the uses of observations, questionnaires, panels, experiments, and newer data collection methods.

observational data
Facts and figures obtained by watching how people actually behave, using mechanical, personal, or neuromarketing data collection methods.

Primary Data: Watching People

Observing people and asking them questions are the two principal ways to collect new or primary data for a marketing study. Facts and figures obtained by watching how people actually behave is the way marketing researchers collect **observational data**. Observational data can be collected by mechanical (including electronic), personal, or neuromarketing methods.

Mechanical Methods National TV ratings, such as those of Nielsen shown in Figure 7–3, are an example of mechanical observational data collected by a "people meter." The device measures what channel and program are tuned in and who is watching. The people meter (1) is a box that is attached to a television, DVR, cable box, or satellite dish in about 30,000 households across the country; (2) has a remote control unit that is used to indicate when a viewer begins and finishes watching a TV program; and (3) stores and then transmits the viewing information to Nielsen each night. Data about TV viewing are also collected using diaries (a paper-pencil recording system).[10]

Obtaining an accurate picture of television viewing behavior is complicated, however, as audiences are increasingly delaying their viewing and watching on multiple devices. More than 70 percent of the viewing of *Better Call Saul,* for example, takes place on a delayed basis, while more than 50 percent of TV viewers watch on devices other than televisions each month. To address these issues, Nielsen introduced a cross-platform television rating system called Total Content Rating, which combines Nielsen's existing TV ratings with its new online ratings. These ratings include traditional consumer viewing of TV programs and programming that is streamed on PCs, smartphones, tablets, and video game consoles.[11]

What determines if *America's Got Talent* stays on the air? For the importance of the TV "ratings game," see the text.
©NBC/Photofest

On the basis of all these observational data, Nielsen then calculates the rating of each TV program. With 119.6 million TV households in the United States, a single rating point equals 1 percent, or 1,196,000 TV households.[12] In some situations, ratings are reported as share points, or the percentage of television households with a television in use that are tuned to the program. Because TV and cable networks sell over $68 billion annually in advertising and set advertising rates to advertisers on the basis of those data, precision in the Nielsen data is critical.[13]

A change of one percentage point in a rating can mean gaining or losing millions of dollars in advertising revenues because advertisers pay rates on the basis of the size of the audience for a TV program. So as shown by the green rows in Figure 7–3, we might expect to pay more for a 30-second TV ad on an *NFL Football* game than one on *Big Brother*. Broadcast and cable networks may change the time slot or even cancel a TV program if its ratings are consistently poor and advertisers are unwilling to pay a rate based on a higher rating.

FIGURE 7–3

Nielsen Television Index Ranking Report for network TV prime-time households for the week ending July 23, 2018. The difference of a few share points in Nielsen TV ratings affects the cost of a TV ad on a show and even whether the show remains on the air.

Rank	Program	Network	Rating	Viewers (000)
1	America's Got Talent	NBC	6.9	11,830
2	60 Minutes	CBS	4.8	7,539
3	NFL Football	NBC	4.1	6,774
4	NFL Football	NBC	4.0	6,572
5	The Big Bang Theory	CBS	3.7	5,863
6	The Bachelorette	ABC	3.7	5,479
7	Celebrity Family Feud	ABC	3.5	5,957
8	Young Sheldon	CBS	3.5	5,503
9	Big Brother-Thu	CBS	3.4	5,621
10	Big Brother-Sun	CBS	3.4	5,570

Source: Nielsen. Primetime Broadcast Programs. Viewing estimates on this page include live viewing and DVR playback on the same day, defined as 3 A.M. to 3 A.M. Ratings are the percentage of TV homes in the U.S. tuned into television.

Observational data led P&G to develop Gillette Guard razors.
©McGraw-Hill Education

Personal Methods
Watching consumers in person is another approach to collecting observational data. Procter & Gamble, for example, invests millions of dollars in observational research to identify new innovations. As several industry experts have observed, "Odds are that as you're reading this, P&G researchers are in a store somewhere observing shoppers, or even in a consumer's home." While observing consumers using its Gillette shavers in India, P&G noticed that many consumers shaved with a small cup of cold water, which caused the blades to clog. As a result, P&G introduced the Gillette Guard razor with a single blade and an easy-rinse design. Similarly, IKEA noticed that customers often stopped shopping when their baskets or carts were full, so additional shopping bags are now placed throughout IKEA stores.[14]

Another method of collecting observational data is through the use of mystery shoppers. Companies pay researchers to shop at their stores, outlets, or showrooms to obtain the point of view of actual customers. Mystery shoppers can check on the availability and pricing of products and services and on the quality of the customer service provided by employees. Supermarkets, electronics stores, banks, theme parks, and many other businesses use this technique as part of their *customer experience management* efforts, thus evaluating customer service, store cleanliness, and staff appearance and conduct. This process provides unique marketing research information that can be obtained in no other way.[15]

Ethnographic research is a specialized observational approach in which trained observers seek to discover subtle behavioral and emotional reactions as consumers encounter products in their "natural use environment," such as in their home or car.[16] For example, Kraft launched Deli Creations—sandwiches made with its Oscar Mayer meats, Kraft cheeses, and Grey Poupon mustard—after spending several months with consumers in their kitchens. Kraft discovered that consumers wanted complete, ready-to-serve meals that are easy to prepare—and it had the products to create them.[17]

Personal observation is both useful and flexible, but it can be costly and unreliable if different observers report different conclusions when watching the same event. And while observation can reveal *what* people do, it cannot easily determine *why* they do it.

Neuromarketing Methods
Marketing researchers are also utilizing neuromarketing methods to observe responses to nonconscious stimuli. Neuromarketing is a relatively new field of study that merges technologies used to study the brain with marketing's interest in understanding consumers. Aradhna Krishna, one of the foremost experts in the field, suggests that "many companies are just starting to recognize how strongly the senses affect the deepest parts of our brains." Other neuroscience tools such as eye tracking, biometric monitoring, and facial coding are also being used to complement brain studies.[18]

Neuromarketing can provide insights for many elements of a marketing program, including media options, advertising content, packaging, and labeling. Based on the results of neuromarketing studies, for example, Campbell Soup Company changed the labels of most of its soup cans. Some of the changes: Steam now rises from more vibrant images of soup; the "unemotional spoons" have disappeared; and the script logo is smaller and has been moved to the bottom of the can.[19]

"Neuromarketing" often uses a headset with sensors to measure brain waves to try to understand consumers better. For some changes made by Campbell Soup Company based on neuromarketing, see the text.
©Ronny Hartmann/picture-alliance/dpa/AP Images

Primary Data: Asking People
How many times have you responded to some kind of a questionnaire? Maybe it was a short survey at school rating your course or your professor, or perhaps it was a telephone or e-mail survey asking if you were pleased with some type of service you received. Asking consumers questions and recording their answers is the second principal way of gathering information.

We can divide this primary data collection task into (1) idea generation methods and (2) idea evaluation methods, although they sometimes overlap and each has a number of special techniques.[20] Each survey method results in valuable

questionnaire data
Facts and figures obtained by asking people about their attitudes, awareness, intentions, and behaviors.

questionnaire data, which are facts and figures obtained by asking people about their attitudes, awareness, intentions, and behaviors.

Idea Generation Methods—Coming Up with Ideas
In the past, the most common way of collecting questionnaire data to generate ideas was through an *individual interview,* which involves a single researcher asking questions of one respondent. This approach has many advantages, such as being able to probe for additional ideas using follow-up questions to a respondent's initial answers. However, this method is very expensive. Later in the chapter we'll discuss some alternatives.

General Mills sought ideas about why Hamburger Helper didn't fare well when it was introduced. Initial instructions called for cooking a half-pound of hamburger separately from the noodles or potatoes, which were later mixed with the hamburger. So General Mills researchers used a special kind of individual interview, called a *depth interview,* in which lengthy, free-flowing kinds of questions are asked to probe for underlying ideas and feelings. These depth interviews discovered that consumers (1) didn't think it contained enough meat and (2) didn't want the hassle of cooking in two different pots. The Hamburger Helper product manager changed the recipe to call for a full pound of meat and to allow users to prepare it in one dish, leading to product success.

Focus groups are informal sessions of 6 to 10 past, present, or prospective customers in which a discussion leader, or moderator, asks for opinions about the firm's products and those of its competitors, including how they use these products and special needs they have that these products don't address. Often recorded and conducted in special interviewing rooms with a one-way mirror, these groups enable marketing researchers and managers to hear and watch consumer reactions.

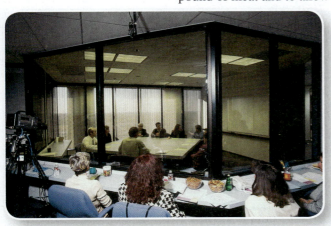

Focus groups of students and instructors were used in developing this textbook. To see the specific suggestion that may help you study, read the text.
©Spencer Grant/PhotoEdit

Video 7-3
Trend Hunter
kerin.tv/cr8e/v7-3

The informality and peer support in an effective focus group help uncover ideas that are often difficult to obtain with individual interviews. For example, to improve understanding and learning by students using this textbook, focus groups were conducted among both marketing instructors and students. Both groups recommended providing answers to each chapter's set of Learning Review questions. This suggestion was followed, so you can see the answers by going to the section at the end of the chapter or by tapping your finger on the question in the SmartBook version.

Finding "the next big thing" for consumers has caused marketing researchers to turn to some less traditional techniques. For example, "fuzzy front end" methods attempt early identification of elusive consumer tastes or trends. Trend Hunter is a firm that seeks to anticipate and track "the evolution of cool." Trend hunting (or watching) is the practice of identifying "emerging shifts in social behavior," which are driven by changes in pop culture that can lead to new products. Trend Hunter has identified about 252,000 cutting-edge ideas through its global network of 155,000 members, and it features these new ideas on its daily Trend Hunter TV broadcast via its YouTube channel (trendhuntertv).[21]

Idea Evaluation Methods—Testing an Idea
In idea evaluation, the marketing researcher tries to test ideas discovered earlier to help the marketing manager recommend marketing actions. Idea evaluation methods often involve conventional questionnaires using personal, mail, telephone, and online (e-mail or Internet) surveys of a large sample of past, present, or prospective consumers. In choosing among them, the marketing researcher balances the cost of the particular method against the expected quality of the information and the speed with which it can be obtained.

Personal interview surveys enable the interviewer to be flexible in asking probing questions or getting reactions to visual materials but are very costly. *Mail surveys* are

Wendy's spent over two years remaking its 42-year-old burger. The result: Dave's Single (also available in Double and Triple), named after Wendy's founder, Dave Thomas. See Figure 7–4 for some questions that Wendy's asked consumers in a survey to discover their fast-food preferences, behaviors, and demographics.

Source: Wendy's International, LLC

FIGURE 7–4

To obtain the most valuable information from consumers, this Wendy's survey utilizes four different kinds of questions discussed in the text.

Source: Wendy's

usually biased because those most likely to respond have had especially positive or negative experiences with the product or brand. While *telephone interviews* allow flexibility, unhappy respondents may hang up on the interviewer, even with the efficiency of computer-assisted telephone interviewing (CATI).

Increasingly, marketing researchers have begun to use *online surveys* (e-mail and Internet) to collect primary data. The reason: Most consumers have an Internet connection and an e-mail account. Marketers can embed a survey in an e-mail sent to targeted respondents. When they open the e-mail, consumers can either see the survey or click on a link to access it from a website. Marketers can also ask consumers to complete a "pop-up" survey in a separate browser window when they access an organization's website. Many organizations use this method to have consumers assess their products and services or evaluate the design and usability of their websites.

The advantages of online surveys are that the cost is relatively minimal and the turnaround time from data collection to report presentation is much quicker than the traditional methods discussed earlier. However, online surveys have serious drawbacks: Some consumers may view e-mail surveys as "junk" or "spam" and may either choose to not receive them (if they have a "spam blocker") or purposely or inadvertently delete them, unopened. For Internet surveys, some consumers have a "pop-up blocker" that prohibits a browser from opening a separate window that contains the survey; thus, they may not be able to participate in the research. For both e-mail and Internet surveys, consumers can complete the survey multiple times, creating a significant bias in the results. This is especially true for online panels. In response, research firms such as SurveyMonkey have developed sampling technology to prohibit this practice.[22]

The foundation of all research using questionnaires is developing precise questions that get clear, unambiguous answers from respondents.[23] Figure 7–4 shows a number

1. What things are most important to you when you decide to eat out at a fast-food restaurant?
_____
_____
_____

2. Have you eaten at a fast-food restaurant in the past month?
   ◉ Yes   ◉ No

3. If you answered yes to question 2, how often do you eat at a fast-food restaurant?
   ◉ Once a week or more   ◉ 2 to 3 times a month   ◉ Once a month or less

4. How important is it to you that a fast-food restaurant satisfies you on the following characteristics?
[Check the response that describes your feelings for each characteristic listed.]

Characteristic	Very Important	Somewhat Important	Important	Unimportant	Somewhat Unimportant	Very Unimportant
• Taste of food	◉	◉	◉	◉	◉	◉
• Cleanliness	◉	◉	◉	◉	◉	◉
• Price	◉	◉	◉	◉	◉	◉
• Variety of menu	◉	◉	◉	◉	◉	◉

5. For each of the characteristics listed below check the space on the scale that describes how you feel about Wendy's. Mark an X on only one of the five spaces for each characteristic listed.

Characteristic		Check the space that describes the degree to which Wendy's is . . .					
• Taste of food	Tasty	_____	_____	_____	_____	_____	Not Tasty
• Cleanliness	Clean	_____	_____	_____	_____	_____	Dirty
• Price	Inexpensive	_____	_____	_____	_____	_____	Expensive
• Variety of menu	Broad	_____	_____	_____	_____	_____	Narrow

6. Check the response that describes your agreement or disagreement with each statement listed below:

Statement	Strongly Agree	Agree	Don't Know	Disagree	Strongly Disagree
• Adults like to take their families to fast-food restaurants	◉	◉	◉	◉	◉
• Our children have a say in where the family chooses to eat	◉	◉	◉	◉	◉

7. How important are each of the following sources of information to you when selecting a fast-food restaurant at which to eat? [Check one response for each source listed.]

Source of Information	Very Important	Somewhat Important	Not at all Important
• Television	◉	◉	◉
• Newspapers	◉	◉	◉
• Radio	◉	◉	◉
• Billboards	◉	◉	◉
• Internet	◉	◉	◉
• Social networks	◉	◉	◉

8. How often do you eat out at each of the following fast-food restaurants? [Check one response for each restaurant listed.]

Restaurant	Once a Week or More	2 to 3 Times a Month	Once a Month or Less
• Burger King	◉	◉	◉
• McDonald's	◉	◉	◉
• Wendy's	◉	◉	◉

9. As head of the household, please answer the following questions about you and your household. [Check only one response for each question.]

a. What is your gender? ◉ Male ◉ Female

b. What is your marital status? ◉ Single ◉ Married ◉ Other (widowed, divorced, etc.)

c. How many children under age 18 live in your home? ◉ 0 ◉ 1 ◉ 2 ◉ 3 or more

d. What is your age? ◉ Under 25 ◉ 25–44 ◉ 45 or older

e. What is your total annual individual or household income?
◉ Less than $15,000 ◉ $15,000–$49,000 ◉ Over $49,000

of formats for questions taken from a Wendy's survey that assessed fast-food restaurant preferences among present and prospective consumers.

Question 1 is an example of an *open-ended question,* which allows respondents to express opinions, ideas, or behaviors in their own words without being forced to choose among alternatives that have been predetermined by a marketing researcher. This information is invaluable to marketers because it captures the "voice" of respondents, which is useful in understanding consumer behavior, identifying product benefits, or developing advertising messages.

In contrast, *closed-end* or *fixed alternative questions* require respondents to select one or more response options from a set of predetermined choices. Question 2 is an example of a *dichotomous question,* the simplest form of a fixed alternative question that allows only a "yes" or "no" response.

A fixed alternative question with three or more choices uses a *scale.* Question 5 is an example of a question that uses a *semantic differential scale,* a five-point scale in which the opposite ends have one- or two-word adjectives that have opposite meanings. For example, depending on the respondent's opinion regarding the cleanliness of Wendy's restaurants, he or she would check the left-hand space on the scale, the right-hand space, or one of the three other intervening points. Question 6 uses a *Likert scale,* in which the respondent indicates the extent to which he or she agrees or disagrees with a statement.

The questionnaire in Figure 7–4 provides valuable information to the marketing researcher at Wendy's. Questions 1 to 8 inform him or her about the respondent's likes and dislikes in eating out, frequency of eating out at fast-food restaurants generally and at Wendy's specifically, and sources of information used in making decisions about fast-food restaurants. Question 9 gives details about the respondent's personal or household characteristics, which can be used in trying to segment the fast-food market, a topic discussed in Chapter 8.

Marketing research questions must be worded precisely so that all respondents interpret the same question similarly. For example, in a question asking whether you eat at fast-food restaurants regularly, the word *regularly* is ambiguous. Two people might answer "yes" to the question, but one might mean "once a day" while the other means "once or twice a month." However, each of these interpretations suggests that dramatically different marketing actions be directed to these two prospective consumers.

The high cost of using personal interviews in homes has increased the use of *mall intercept interviews,* which are personal interviews of consumers visiting shopping centers. These face-to-face interviews reduce the cost of personal visits to consumers in their homes while providing the flexibility to show respondents visual cues such as ads or actual product samples. A disadvantage of mall intercept interviews is that the people interviewed may not be representative of the consumers targeted, giving a biased result.

Electronic technology has revolutionized traditional concepts of interviews or surveys. Today, respondents can walk up to a kiosk in a shopping center, read questions off a screen, and key their answers into a computer on a touch screen. Fully automated telephone interviews exist in which respondents key their replies on a touch-tone telephone.

Primary Data: Other Sources

Four other methods of collecting primary data exist that overlap somewhat with the methods just discussed. These involve using (1) social media, (2) panels and experiments, (3) information technology, and (4) data analytics and data mining. Social media and panels and experiments are discussed below. Information technology, data analytics, and data mining are discussed in the next section, Step 4: Develop Findings.

Social Media
Facebook, Twitter, and other social media are revolutionizing the way today's marketing research is done. In developing a new potato chip flavor,

Carmex's Facebook account allows it to respond to consumers' comments and to follow daily consumer experiences. For how it uses social media marketing research, see the Applying Marketing Metrics box.
Source: Carmex/Facebook

Frito-Lay substituted Facebook research for its usual focus groups. Visitors to its Facebook Page were polled, allowing them to suggest new flavors, three of which appeared in supermarkets. All they had to do was click a "Vote" button to show their preferences. And Estée Lauder asked social media users to vote on which discontinued shades to bring back.[24]

Carma Laboratories, Inc., the maker of Carmex lip balm, is a third-generation, family-owned business with a history of accessibility to customers. In fact, founder Alfred Woelbing personally responded to every letter he received from customers. Today, Carma Labs relies on social media programs to help promote its products.[25]

One opportunity for Carmex (www.mycarmex.com) is to conduct marketing research using social media listening tools to understand the nature of online lip balm conversations. The nearby Applying Marketing Metrics box shows how Carmex uses marketing metrics to assess its social media programs for its line of products. Data have been modified to protect proprietary information.

Carmex uses several social media metrics, such as *conversation velocity, share of voice,* and *sentiment*.[26] These metrics are tracked by electronic search engines that comb the Internet for consumers' behaviors and "brand mentions" to calculate share of voice and determine whether these brand mentions appear to be "positive," "neutral," or "negative" in order to calculate "sentiment." A widely used Facebook metric measures the number of *likes,* a term that refers to the number of Facebook users opting in to a brand's messages and liking the brand.

Marketing researchers increasingly want to glean information from sites to "mine" their raw consumer-generated content in real time. However, when relying on this consumer-generated content, the sample of individuals from whom this content is gleaned may not be statistically representative of the marketplace.[27]

Panels and Experiments Two special ways that observations and questionnaires are sometimes used are panels and experiments.

Marketing researchers often want to know if consumers change their behavior over time, so they take successive measurements of the same people. A *panel* is a sample of consumers or stores from which researchers take a series of measurements. For example, the NPD Group collects data about consumer purchases such as apparel, food, and electronics from its online Consumer Panel, which consists of nearly 2 million individuals worldwide. So a firm like General Mills can count the frequency of consumer purchases to measure switching behavior from one brand of its breakfast cereal (Wheaties) to another (Cheerios) or to a competitor's brand (Kellogg's Special K). A disadvantage of panels is that the marketing research firm needs to recruit new members continually to replace those who drop out. These new recruits must match the characteristics of those they replace to keep the panel representative of the marketplace.

To discover how McDonald's used test markets to help develop its delivery service, see the text.
Source: McDonald's

An *experiment* involves obtaining data by manipulating factors under tightly controlled conditions to test cause and effect. The interest is in whether changing one of the independent variables (a cause) will change the behavior of the dependent variable that is studied (the result). In marketing experiments, the independent variables of interest—sometimes called the marketing *drivers*—are often one or more of the marketing mix

Applying Marketing Metrics
Are the Carmex Social Media Programs Working Well?

As a marketing consultant to Carmex, you've just been asked to assess its social media activities for its lip balm product line.

Carmex has recently launched new social media programs and promotions to tell U.S. consumers more about its line of lip balm products. These include Facebook and Twitter contests that allow Carmex fans and followers to win free samples by connecting with Carmex. A creative "Carmex Kiss" widget allows users to upload their photo and to send an animated kiss to a friend.

Your Challenge

To assess how the Carmex social media programs are doing, you choose these five metrics: (1) Carmex conversation velocity—total Carmex mentions on the Internet; (2) Facebook fans—the number of Facebook users in a time period who have liked Carmex's Facebook brand page; (3) Twitter followers—the number of Twitter users in a time period who follow Carmex's Twitter feed; (4) Carmex share of voice—Carmex mentions on the Internet as a percentage of mentions of all major lip balm brands; and (5) Carmex sentiment—the percentage of Internet Carmex share-of-voice mentions that are (*a*) positive, (*b*) neutral, or (*c*) negative.

Your Findings

Analyzing the marketing dashboard here, you reach these conclusions. First, the number of both Facebook fans and Twitter followers for Carmex is up significantly for 2018 compared to 2017, which is good news. Second, the Carmex share of voice of 35 percent is good, certainly relative to the 48 percent for the #1 brand ChapStick. But especially favorable is Carmex's 12 percent increase in share of voice compared to a year ago. Third, the Carmex sentiment dashboard shows 80 percent of the mentions are positive, and only 5 percent are negative. Even more significant is that positive mentions are up 23 percent over last year.

Your Actions

You conclude that Carmex's social media initiatives are doing well. Your next step is to probe deeper into the data to see which ones—such as free samples or the Carmex Kiss—have been especially effective in triggering the positive results and build on these successes in the future.

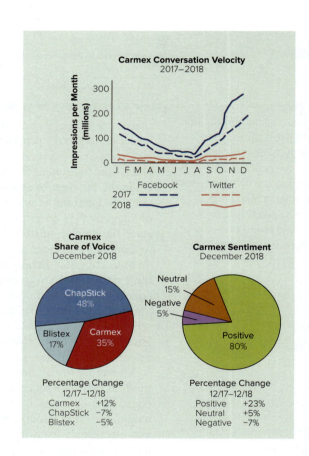

elements, such as a product's features, price, or promotion (like advertising messages or coupons). The ideal dependent variable usually is a change in the purchases (incremental unit or dollar sales) of individuals, households, or organizations. Food companies often use *test markets,* which offer a product for sale in a small geographic area to help evaluate potential marketing actions. McDonald's, for example, tested its delivery service in three Florida cities to assess consumer interest before deciding to expand. Recently, McDonald's expanded delivery to 20,000 of its restaurants.[28]

A potential difficulty with experiments is that outside factors (such as actions of competitors) can distort the results of an experiment and affect the dependent variable (such as sales). A researcher's task is to identify the effect of the marketing variable of interest on the dependent variable when the effects of outside factors in an experiment might hide it.

Advantages and Disadvantages of Primary Data

Compared with secondary data, primary data have the advantages of being more flexible and more specific to the problem being studied. The main disadvantages are that primary data are usually far more costly and time-consuming to collect than secondary data.

---

learning review

7-6. What is the difference between observational data and questionnaire data?

7-7. Which type of survey provides the greatest flexibility for asking probing questions: mail, telephone, or personal interview?

7-8. What is the difference between a panel and an experiment?

STEP 4: DEVELOP FINDINGS

Mark Twain once observed, "Collecting data is like collecting garbage. You've got to know what you're going to do with the stuff before you collect it." So, marketing data have little more value than garbage unless they are analyzed carefully and translated into information and findings, step 4 in the marketing research approach.[29]

Analyze the Data

Analyzing marketing data today often involves very sophisticated and complex methods. Examples of this include big data, data analytics, artificial intelligence, data mining, and predictive modeling, which are discussed first, followed by a detailed example of analyzing sales of Tony's Pizza.

LO 7-5 Explain how data analytics, data mining, and predictive modeling lead to marketing actions.

information technology Includes all of the computing resources that collect, store, and analyze data.

Big Data, Data Analytics, and Artificial Intelligence *Big data* is a broad term generally used to describe large amounts of data collected from a variety of sources and analyzed with an increasingly sophisticated set of technologies. **Information technology** includes all of the computing resources that collect, store, and analyze the data. Marketing researchers have observed that today we live in an era of data deluge. The challenge facing managers is not data collection or even storage but how to efficiently transform the huge amount of data into useful information. This transformation is accomplished through the use of data analytics. Products such as Yahoo!'s Hadoop and Google's Bigtable are examples of the analytical tools available for people often referred to as data scientists. Their work is also creating a new field of marketing research that focuses on *data visualization,* or the presentation of the results of the analysis.

Today, marketers obtain data from many sources such as barcode scanners at checkout counters, online tracking software on computers and tablets, and usage histories on your telephone. In fact, the growth of the Internet of Things (IoT) now allows data collection from almost any device a consumer might use. Marketing managers use a combination of data, technology, and analytics to convert the data into useful information that answer marketing questions and lead to effective marketing actions. An organization that accomplishes this successfully is often referred to as an *intelligent enterprise.*[30]

As shown in Figure 7–5, the elements of an intelligent marketing enterprise platform interact to facilitate the work of the marketing researcher or data scientist. The top half of the figure shows how big data are created through a sophisticated communication network that collects data from internal and external sources. These data are stored, organized, and managed in databases. Collectively, these databases form a data

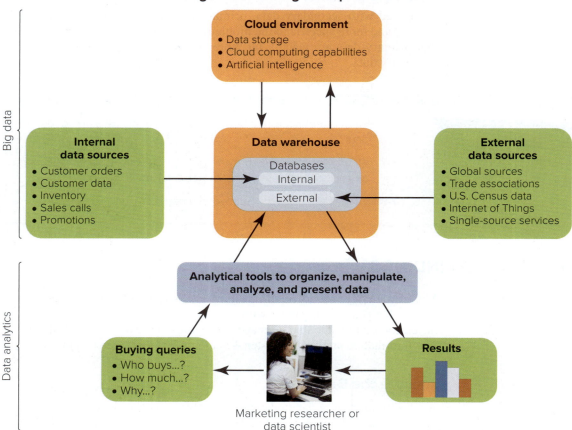

FIGURE 7–5

How marketing researchers and managers use an intelligent enterprise platform to turn data into action.

Photo: ©Todd Warnock/ Lifesize/Getty Images

data mining
The practice of examining large databases to find statistical relationships between consumer purchasing patterns.

warehouse. Data storage (and computing) may also take place in "the Cloud," which is simply a collection of servers accessed through an Internet connection. Large databases are also subject to *artificial intelligence* platforms which undertake reasoning and common sense tasks to allow computers to "behave" intelligently. IBM, Tesla, and Amazon, for example, are using artificial intelligence to operate Watson, guide self-driving cars, and make purchase recommendations, respectively.[31]

As shown at the bottom of Figure 7–5, data analytics consists of several elements. Marketers use computers to specify important marketing queries or questions and to access the databases in the warehouse (or the Cloud). Analytical tools are used to organize and manipulate the data to identify any managerial insights that may exist. The results are then presented using tables and graphics for easier interpretation. When accessing a database, marketers can use sensitivity analysis to ask "what if" questions to determine how hypothetical changes in product or brand drivers—the factors that influence the buying decisions of a household or organization—can affect sales.

Traditional marketing research typically involves identifying possible drivers and then collecting data. For example, we might collect data to test the hypothesis that increasing couponing (the driver) during spring will increase trials by first-time buyers (the result).

Data Mining and Predictive Modeling In contrast, **data mining** is the practice of examining large databases to find statistical relationships between consumer purchasing patterns. Some of these are common sense: Since many consumers buy peanut butter and grape jelly together, why not run a joint promotion between Skippy

Making Responsible Decisions

Ethics

No More Personal Secrets: The Downside of Data Mining and Predictive Modeling

Amazon, Google, Yahoo!, eBay, YouTube, reputation.com, . . . yes . . . and Facebook and Twitter, too!

The common denominator for all these is their sophisticated data mining techniques that reveal an incredible amount of personal information about almost anyone. *Time* journalist Joel Stein, using both online and offline sources, discovered how easily outsiders could find his Social Security number and then found a number of other things about himself—some correct, some not.

For example, his data mining effort revealed that he likes hockey, rap, rock, parenting, recipes, clothes and beauty products, and movies. He makes most of his purchases online, averaging only $25 per purchase. He uses Facebook, LinkedIn, Pandora, and StumbleUpon. He bought his house in November, which is when his home insurance is up for renewal. His dad's wife has a traffic ticket.

And, some sources predicted that he is an 18- to 19-year-old woman! For the record, Mr. Stein is not a teen and he is a male.

OK, OK, sometimes data mining and predictive modeling errors occur!

These data are collected many ways—from tracking devices (like cookies, discussed in Chapter 14) on websites, to apps downloaded on a cell phone, PC, or tablet device that reveal a user's contact list and location, to techniques that aggregate data from multiple online sources.

These personal details have huge benefits for marketers, but do they invade a consumer's privacy? Data mining and predictive modeling now enable companies to target individual consumers and facilitate the design of personalized product offerings. This involves using not only demographics such as age and gender but also "likes," past buying habits, social media used, brands bought, TV programs watched, stores visited, and so on.

Want to do some sleuthing yourself? Download Ghostery at www.ghostery.com. It tells you all the companies grabbing your data when you visit a website.

At 10 P.M., what is this man likely to buy besides these diapers? For the curious answer that data mining reveals, see the text.
©Brent Jones

predictive modeling Based on statistical models that use data mining and probability analysis to foretell outcomes.

peanut butter and Welch's grape jelly? But would you have expected that men buying diapers in the evening sometimes buy a six-pack of beer too? Supermarkets discovered this when they mined purchase data from checkout scanners. So they placed diapers and beer near each other, then placed potato chips between them—and increased sales on all three items!

Refinements in data mining and data analytics now permit marketers to actually foresee consumer behavior using **predictive modeling**—statistical models that use data mining and probability analysis to foretell outcomes. These models contain a number of predictors, or variables, that affect the likelihood of future results.

As an example, Target Stores has used data mining to identify 25 products that, when bought together or over time, predict a woman's likelihood of being pregnant as well as her child's expected due date. To determine the probability of pregnancy, a woman's purchase patterns, coupled with available demographic data, are linked to published baby registries. Predictive modeling shows that certain items are purchased in the first trimester, others in the second trimester, and still others in the third trimester, including the baby's due date. For good measure, the buying of blue or pink blankets indicates a high probability of the child's gender. Armed with this knowledge, Target is able to send product ads and coupons to mothers-to-be appropriate for each stage in her pregnancy.[32]

For how much data mining and predictive modeling can reveal about you and your purchasing behavior and a look at the ethical issues involved, see the Making Responsible Decisions box.[33]

How are sales doing? To see how marketers at Tony's Pizza assessed this question and the results, read the text.
©McGraw-Hill Education

Analyzing Sales of Tony's Pizza Schwan's Company (formerly known as The Schwan Food Company) produces 3 million frozen pizzas a day under brand names that include Tony's and Red Baron. Let's see how Teré Carral, the marketing manager for the Tony's brand, might address a market segment question. We will use hypothetical data to protect Tony's proprietary information.

Teré is concerned about the limited growth in the Tony's brand over the past four years. She hires a consultant to collect and analyze data to explain what's going on with her brand and to recommend ways to improve its growth. Teré asks the consultant to put together a proposal that includes the answers to two key questions:

1. How are Tony's sales doing on a household basis? For example, are fewer households buying Tony's pizzas, or is each household buying fewer Tony's pizzas? Or both?
2. What factors might be contributing to Tony's very flat sales over the past four years?

Facts uncovered by the consultant are vital. For example, is the average household consuming more or less Tony's pizza than in previous years? Is Tony's flat sales performance related to a specific factor? With answers to these questions Teré can take actions to address the issues in the coming year.

Present the Findings

Findings should be clear and understandable from the way the data are presented. Managers are responsible for *actions*. Often it means delivering the results in clear pictures and, if possible, in a single page.

The consultant gives Teré the answers to her questions using the marketing dashboards in Figure 7–6, a creative way to present findings graphically. Let's look over Teré's shoulder as she interprets these findings:

- Figure 7–6A, *Annual Sales*—This shows the annual growth of Tony's Pizza is stable but virtually flat from 2015 through 2018.
- Figure 7–6B, *Average Annual Sales per Household*—Look closely at this graph. At first glance, it seems like sales in 2018 are *half* what they were in 2015, right? But be careful to read the numbers on the vertical axis. They show that household purchases of Tony's pizzas have been steadily declining over the past four years, from an average of 3.4 pizzas per household in 2015 to 3.1 pizzas per household in 2018. (Significant, but hardly a 50 percent drop.) Now the question is, if Tony's annual sales are stable, yet the average individual household is buying fewer Tony's pizzas, what's going on? The answer is, more households are buying pizzas—it's just that each household is buying fewer Tony's pizzas. That households aren't choosing Tony's is a genuine source of concern. But again, here's a classic example of a marketing problem representing a marketing opportunity. The number of households buying pizza is *growing,* and that's good news for Tony's.
- Figure 7–6C, *Average Annual Sales per Household, by Household Size*—This chart starts to show a source of the problem: Even though average sales of pizza to households with only one or two people are stable, households with three or four people and those with five or more are declining in average annual pizza consumption. Which households tend to have more than two people? Answer: Households *with children.* Therefore, we should look more closely at the pizza-buying behavior of households with children.

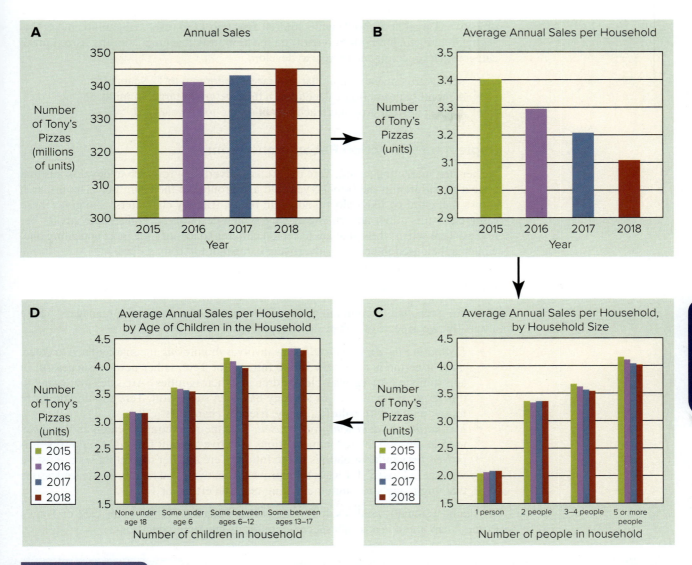

FIGURE 7–6

These marketing dashboards present findings to Tony's marketing manager that will lead to recommendations and actions.

Source: Teré Carral, Tony's Pizza.

- Figure 7–6D, *Average Annual Sales per Household, by Age of Children in the Household*—The real problem that emerges is the serious decline in average consumption in the households with younger children, especially in households with children in the 6-to-12-year-old age group.

Identifying a sales problem in households with children 6 to 12 years old is an important discovery, as Tony's sales are declining in a market segment that is known to be one of the heaviest in buying pizzas.

STEP 5: TAKE MARKETING ACTIONS

Effective marketing research doesn't stop with findings and recommendations—someone has to identify the marketing actions, put them into effect, and monitor how the decisions turn out, which is the essence of step 5.

Make Action Recommendations

Teré Carral, the marketing manager for Tony's Pizza, meets with her team to convert the marketing research findings into specific marketing recommendations with a clear objective: Target households with children ages 6 to 12 to reverse the trend among this segment and gain strength in one of the most important segments in the frozen pizza category. Her recommendation is to develop:

- An advertising campaign that will target children 6 to 12 years old.
- A monthly promotion calendar with this age group target in mind.
- A special event program reaching children 6 to 12 years old.

Implement the Action Recommendations

As her first marketing action, Teré undertakes advertising research to develop ads that appeal to children in the 6-to-12-year-old age group and their families. The research shows that children like colorful ads with funny, friendly characters. She gives these research results to her advertising agency, which develops several sample ads for her review. Teré selects three that are tested on children to identify the most appealing one, which is then used in her next advertising campaign for Tony's Pizza.

Evaluate the Results

Evaluating results is a continuing way of life for effective marketing managers. There are really two aspects of this evaluation process:

- *Evaluating the decision itself.* This involves monitoring the marketplace to determine if action is necessary in the future. For Teré, is her new ad successful in appealing to 6-to-12-year-old children and their families? Are sales increasing to this target segment? If this strategy has been successful, Teré should add more follow-up ads with colorful, funny, friendly characters.
- *Evaluating the decision process used.* Was the marketing research and analysis used to develop the recommendations effective? Was it flawed? Could it be improved for similar situations in the future? Teré and her marketing team must be vigilant in looking for ways to improve the analysis and results—to learn lessons that might apply to future marketing research efforts at Tony's.

Again, systematic analysis does not guarantee success. But, as in the case of Tony's Pizza, it can improve a firm's success rate for its marketing decisions.

learning review

7-9. In the marketing research for Tony's Pizza, what is an example of (*a*) a finding and (*b*) a marketing action?

7-10. In evaluating marketing actions, what are the two dimensions on which they should be evaluated?

SALES FORECASTING TECHNIQUES

LO 7-6 Describe three approaches to developing a company's sales forecast.

Forecasting or estimating potential sales is often a key goal in a marketing research study. Good sales forecasts are important for a firm as it schedules production. The term **sales forecast** refers to the total sales of a product that a firm expects to sell during a specified time period under specified environmental conditions and its own marketing efforts. For example, Betty Crocker might develop a sales forecast of 4 million cases of cake mix for U.S. consumers in 2019, assuming consumers' dessert preferences remain constant and competitors don't change prices.

Three main sales forecasting techniques are often used: (1) judgments of the decision maker, (2) surveys of knowledgeable groups, and (3) statistical methods.

sales forecast
The total sales of a product that a firm expects to sell during a specified time period under specified environmental conditions and its own marketing efforts.

Judgments of the Decision Maker

Probably 99 percent of all sales forecasts are simply the judgment of the person who must act on the results of the forecast—the individual decision maker. *A direct forecast* involves estimating the value to be forecast without any intervening steps. Examples appear daily: How many quarts of milk should I buy? How much money should I withdraw at the ATM?

A *lost-horse forecast* involves starting with the last known value of the item being forecast, listing the factors that could affect the forecast, assessing whether they have a positive or negative impact, and making the final forecast. The technique gets its name from how you'd find a lost horse: Go to where it was last seen, put yourself in its shoes, consider those factors that could affect where you might go (to the pond if you're thirsty, the hayfield if you're hungry, and so on), and go there.

For example, New Balance recently introduced its Fresh Foam Zante, a shoe with an optimal balance between cushioning and stability. It is designed to be a lighter, better fitting, and functionally enhanced shoe. Suppose a New Balance marketing manager in early 2019 needs to make a sales forecast through 2021. She would take the known value of 2018 sales and list positive factors (Road Shoe of the Year Award, positive wear-tester comments) and the negative factors (increased competition, slow economic growth) to arrive at the final sales forecast.

How might a marketing manager for the New Balance Zante running shoe create a sales forecast through 2021? Read the text to find out.
©McGraw-Hill Education

Surveys of Knowledgeable Groups

If you wonder what your firm's sales will be next year, ask people who are likely to know something about future sales. Two common groups that are surveyed to develop sales forecasts are prospective buyers and the firm's salesforce.

A *survey of buyers' intentions forecast* involves asking prospective customers if they are likely to buy the product during some future time period. For industrial products with few prospective buyers, this can be effective. There are only a few hundred customers in the entire world for Boeing's large airplanes, so Boeing surveys them to develop its sales forecasts and production schedules.

A *salesforce survey forecast* involves asking the firm's salespeople to estimate sales during a forthcoming period. Because these people are in contact with customers and are likely to know what customers like and dislike, there is logic to this approach. However, salespeople can be unreliable forecasters—painting too rosy a picture if they are enthusiastic about a new product or too grim a forecast if their sales quota and future compensation are based on it.

Statistical Methods

The best-known statistical method of forecasting is *trend extrapolation,* which involves extending a pattern observed in past data into the future. When the pattern is described with a straight line, it is *linear trend extrapolation*. Suppose that in early 2000 you were a sales forecaster for the Xerox Corporation and had actual sales data running from 1988 to 1999 (see Figure 7–7). Using linear trend extrapolation, you draw a line to fit the past sales data and project it into the future to give the forecast values shown for 2000 through 2020.

If in 2018 you want to compare your forecasts with actual results, you are in for a surprise—illustrating the strength and weakness of trend extrapolation. Trend extrapolation assumes that the underlying relationships in the past will continue into the future, which is the basis of the method's key strength: simplicity. If this assumption

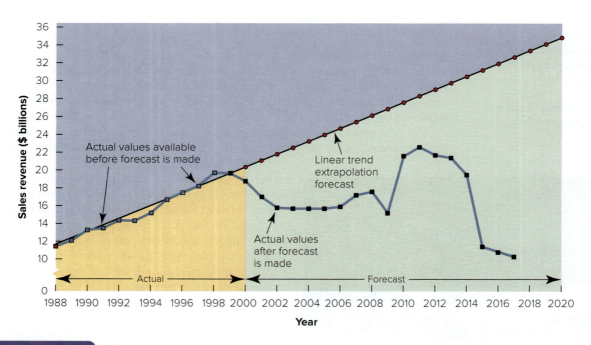

FIGURE 7–7
Linear trend extrapolation of sales revenues at Xerox, made at the start of 2000.

proves correct, you have an accurate forecast. However, if this proves wrong, the forecast is likely to be wrong. In this case, your forecasts from 2000 through 2017 were too high, as shown in Figure 7–7, largely because of fierce competition in the photocopying industry.

learning review

7-11. What are the three kinds of sales forecasting techniques?

7-12. How do you make a lost-horse forecast?

LEARNING OBJECTIVES REVIEW

LO 7-1 *Identify the reason for conducting marketing research.*
To be successful, products must meet the wants and needs of potential customers. So marketing research reduces risk by providing the vital information to help marketing managers understand those wants and needs and translate them into marketing actions.

LO 7-2 *Describe the five-step marketing research approach that leads to marketing actions.*
Marketing researchers engage in a five-step decision-making process to collect information that will improve marketing decisions. The first step is to define the problem, which requires setting the research objectives and identifying possible marketing actions. The second step is to develop the research plan, which involves specifying the constraints, identifying data needed for marketing decisions, and determining how to collect the data. The third step is to collect the relevant information, which includes considering pertinent secondary data (both internal and external) and primary data (by observing and questioning consumers) as well as using information technology and data mining to trigger marketing actions. The fourth step is to develop findings from the marketing research data collected. This involves analyzing the data and presenting the findings of the research. The fifth and last step is to take marketing actions, which involves making and implementing the action recommendations and then evaluating the results.

LO 7-3 *Explain how marketing uses secondary and primary data.*
Secondary data have already been recorded prior to the start of the project and consist of two parts: (*a*) internal secondary data, which originate from within the organization, such as sales reports and customer comments; and (*b*) external secondary data, which are created by other organizations,

such as the U.S. Census Bureau (which provides data on the country's population, manufacturers, retailers, and so on) or business and trade publications (which provide data on industry trends, market size, etc.). Primary data are collected specifically for the project and are obtained by either observing or questioning people.

LO 7-4 *Discuss the uses of observations, questionnaires, panels, experiments, and newer data collection methods.*
Marketing researchers observe people in various ways, such as electronically using Nielsen people meters to measure TV viewing behavior or personally using mystery shoppers or ethnographic techniques. A recent electronic innovation is neuromarketing—using brain scanning to record the responses of a consumer's brain to marketing stimuli like packages or TV ads. Questionnaires involve asking people questions (*a*) in person using interviews or focus groups or (*b*) via a questionnaire using a telephone, print, e-mail, Internet, or social media survey. A cross tabulation is often used with questionnaire data to analyze the relationships among two or more variables to lead to marketing actions. Panels involve a sample of consumers or stores that are repeatedly measured through time to see if their behaviors change. Experiments, such as test markets, involve measuring the effect of marketing variables such as price or advertising on sales. Collecting data from social networks like Facebook or Twitter is increasingly important because users can share their opinions about products and services with countless "friends" around the globe.

LO 7-5 *Explain how data analytics, data mining, and predictive modeling lead to marketing actions.*
Marketing researchers have observed that today we live in an era of data deluge. Information technology enables this massive amount of marketing data to be stored, accessed, and processed. Transforming the data into useful information is accomplished through the use of data analytics, which uses specific queries or questions to guide the analysis. In contrast, data mining is the extraction of hidden information from the databases to find statistical relationships. Predictive modeling uses data mining and probability analysis to make marketing decisions and actions.

LO 7-6 *Describe three approaches to developing a company's sales forecast.*
One approach to developing a sales forecast uses the subjective judgments of the decision maker, such as in direct or lost-horse forecasts. A direct forecast involves estimating the value to be forecast without any intervening steps. A lost-horse forecast starts with the last known value of the item being forecast and then lists the factors that could affect the forecast, assesses whether they have a positive or negative impact, and makes the final forecast. Surveys of knowledgeable groups, a second method, involve obtaining information such as the intentions of potential buyers or estimates provided by the salesforce. Statistical methods involving extending a pattern observed in past data into the future are a third approach. The best-known statistical method is linear trend extrapolation.

LEARNING REVIEW ANSWERS

7-1 What is marketing research?
Answer: Marketing research is the process of defining a marketing problem and opportunity, systematically collecting and analyzing information, and recommending actions to reduce the risk of and thereby improve marketing decisions.

7-2 What is the five-step marketing research approach?
Answer: The five-step marketing research approach provides a systematic checklist for making marketing decisions and actions. The five steps are: (1) define the problem; (2) develop the research plan; (3) collect relevant information (data); (4) develop findings; and (5) take marketing actions.

7-3 What are constraints, as they apply to developing a research plan?
Answer: Constraints in a decision are the restrictions placed on potential solutions to a problem, such as time and money. These set the parameters for the research plan—due dates, budget, and so on.

7-4 What is the difference between secondary and primary data?
Answer: Secondary data are facts and figures that have already been recorded prior to the project at hand, whereas primary data are facts and figures that are newly collected for the project.

7-5 What are some advantages and disadvantages of secondary data?
Answer: Advantages of secondary data are the time savings, the low cost, and the greater level of detail that may be available. Disadvantages of secondary data are that the data may be out of date, unspecific, or have definitions, categories, or age groupings that are wrong for the project.

7-6 What is the difference between observational data and questionnaire data?
Answer: Observational data are facts and figures obtained by watching, either mechanically or in person, how people actually behave. Questionnaire data are facts and figures obtained by asking people about their attitudes, awareness, intentions, and behaviors.

7-7 Which type of survey provides the greatest flexibility for asking probing questions: mail, telephone, or personal interview?
Answer: personal interview (or individual/depth interview)

7-8 What is the difference between a panel and an experiment?
Answer: A panel is a sample of consumers or stores from which researchers take a series of measurements. An experiment involves obtaining data by manipulating factors under tightly controlled conditions to test cause and effect, such as changing a variable in a customer purchase decision (marketing drivers) and seeing what happens (increase/decrease in unit or dollar sales).

7-9 In the marketing research for Tony's Pizza, what is an example of (*a*) a finding and (*b*) a marketing action?
Answer: (*a*) Figure 7-6A depicts annual sales from 2015 to 2018; the finding is that annual sales are relatively flat, rising only 5 million units over the four-year period. (*b*) Figure 7-6D shows a finding (the decline in pizza consumption in households with younger children) that leads to a recommendation to develop an ad targeting children 6 to 12 years old (the marketing action).

7-10 In evaluating marketing actions, what are the two dimensions on which they should be evaluated?

Answer: There are two aspects marketers use to evaluate the results of marketing actions: (1) evaluate the decision itself, which involves monitoring the marketplace to determine if action is necessary in the future; and (2) evaluate the decision process used to determine (a) whether the marketing research and analysis used to develop the recommendations were effective or flawed in some way and (b) whether the process could be improved for similar situations in the future.

7-11 What are the three kinds of sales forecasting techniques?

Answer: They are: (1) judgments of the decision maker who acts on the results of a sales forecast; (2) surveys of knowledgeable groups, those who are likely to know something about future sales; and (3) statistical methods such as trend extrapolation, which involves extending a pattern observed in past data into the future.

7-12 How do you make a lost-horse forecast?

Answer: To make a lost-horse forecast, begin with the last known value of the item being forecast, list the factors that could affect the forecast, assess whether they have a positive or negative impact, and then make the final forecast.

FOCUSING ON KEY TERMS

constraints p. 182
data p. 184
data mining p. 196
information technology p. 195
marketing research p. 180
measures of success p. 182
observational data p. 186
predictive modeling p. 197
primary data p. 184
questionnaire data p. 189
sales forecast p. 200
secondary data p. 184

APPLYING MARKETING KNOWLEDGE

1. Suppose your dean of admissions is considering surveying high school seniors about their perceptions of your school to design better informational brochures for them. What are the advantages and disadvantages of doing (a) telephone interviews and (b) an Internet survey of seniors requesting information about the school?

2. Wisk detergent decides to run a test market to see the effect of coupons and in-store advertising on sales. The index of sales is shown in the nearby table.
What are your conclusions and recommendations?

3. Nielsen obtains ratings of local TV stations in small markets by having households fill out diary questionnaires. These give information on (a) who is watching TV and (b) the program being watched. What are the limitations of this questionnaire method?

4. The format in which information is presented is often vital. (a) If you were a harried marketing manager and queried your information system,

Element in Test Market	Weeks before Coupon	Week of Coupon	Week after Coupon
Without in-store ads	100	144	108
With in-store ads	100	268	203

would you rather see the results in tables or charts and graphs? (b) What are one or two strengths and weaknesses of each format?

5. (a) Why might a marketing researcher prefer to use secondary data rather than primary data in a study? (b) Why might the reverse be true?

6. Which of the following variables would linear trend extrapolation be more accurate for? (a) Annual population of the United States or (b) annual sales of cars produced in the United States by Ford. Why?

BUILDING YOUR MARKETING PLAN

To help you collect the most useful data for your marketing plan, develop a three-column table:

1. In column 1, list the information you would ideally like to have to fill holes in your marketing plan.

2. In column 2, identify the source for each bit of information in column 1, such as doing an Internet search, talking to prospective customers, looking at internal data, and so forth.

3. In column 3, set a priority on information you will have time to spend collecting by ranking each item: 1 = most important; 2 = next most important; and so forth.

VIDEO CASE 7

Carmex® (A): Leveraging Facebook for Marketing Research

"What makes social media 'social' is its give and take," says Jeff Gerst of Bolin Marketing, who manages the Carmex® social media properties. By "give" Gerst is referring to the feedback consumers send on social media; "take" is what they receive—such as news and coupons. "For Carmex, Facebook isn't just a way to share coupons or the latest product news, but it is also a marketing research resource. We have instantaneous access to the opinions of our consumers."

> **Video 7-4**
> **Carmex (A)**
> **Video Case**
> kerin.tv/cr8e/v7-4

"While some people think of social media as 'free,' that is not true. However, almost everything in social media can be faster and cheaper than in the offline world," adds Dane Hartzell, general manager of Bolin Digital. "Many platforms have been prebuilt and we marketers only need to modify them slightly."

CARMEX AND ITS PRODUCT LINE

Although Carmex has been making lip balm since 1937, only in recent years has it made serious efforts to stress growth and become more competitive. For example, Carmex has:

- Extended its lip balm products into new flavors and varieties.
- Expanded into nearly 30 international markets.
- Developed the Carmex Moisture Plus line of premium lip balms for women.
- Launched a line of skin care products, its first venture outside of lip care.

Carmex has used social media tools in developing all of these initiatives, but the focus of this case is how Carmex might use Facebook marketing research to grow its lip balm varieties in the United States.

FACEBOOK MARKETING RESEARCH: TREND SPOTTING

Brands can leverage Facebook and all social media platforms to test what topics and themes its audience engages with the most as well as validate concepts and ideas. Carmex recently identified the growing trend of consumers seeking product customization. Carmex combined research with Facebook engagement data, which helped to validate consumer interest and led it to develop two new lines of limited-edition lip balm products.

©McGraw-Hill Education

The first line was a set of three different Carmex "City Sticks" featuring New York, Chicago, and Las Vegas versions of the Carmex lip balm stick with recognizable landmarks from each city on them. The brand partnered with Walgreens to exclusively sell the "City Sticks" in each of the three cities. During this time Carmex leveraged its social media channels on Facebook and Instagram to solicit photos of fans holding up their favorite style of Carmex in front of a landmark in their own city. Carmex then used these photos to help it decide on new locations for future limited-edition "City Sticks."

Carmex's second line of new products was four fashion-forward "glamorous" designs of Carmex Moisture Plus. Carmex researched current design trends in the women's fashion industry to come up with the four different styles, and it had seen good engagement from its Facebook community on "fashion themed" posts, which helped validate the concept. The four styles were: "Chic," a black and white houndstooth; "Fab," with bright purple circles; "Adventurous," a leopard print; and "Whimsical," with blue, orange, green, and pink intertwined ribbons. The first announcement of the new line was to Carmex Facebook fans.

with Carmex. Anytime a liker posts a comment on the Carmex Wall, likes its status, or replies to one of its posts, the engagement level increases.

The easiest way for Carmex to grow the number of "likes" on its Facebook Page is through contests and promotions. If it gives away prizes, people will be drawn to its site and its likes will increase. However, these people may not actually be fans of the Carmex product so at the end of the promotion, they may "unlike" Carmex or they may remain fans but not engage with the Carmex Page at all.

"One of the biggest challenges facing Facebook Community Managers for brands is how to grow your likes without hurting the level of engagement," says Holly Matson, director of experience planning at Bolin Marketing.

"Depending on how we go about conducting the research," Gerst adds, "we can drive engagement with our existing Facebook community, we can use this as an opportunity to grow our Facebook community or, potentially, we could do both." The benefits of this Carmex Facebook strategy are twofold: (1) narrowing the number of flavors to be researched from three to two and (2) enhancing the connections with the Carmex Facebook community.

FACEBOOK MARKETING RESEARCH: TWO KEY METRICS

"We have three potential new flavors and we can only put two into quantitative testing," explains Jeff Gerst to his team. "So we have two goals in doing marketing research on this. One is to use Facebook to help us determine which two flavors we should move forward with. The second goal is to drive our Facebook metrics."

The two key Facebook metrics the Carmex marketing team has chosen to help narrow the flavor choices from three to two are "likes" and "engagement." "Likes" are the number of new "likers" to the brand's Facebook Page. This metric measures the size of the brand's Facebook audience. In contrast, "engagement" measures how active its Facebook audience is

HOW THE METRICS MIGHT BE USED

Carmex's Facebook activity can benefit (1) by using a poll to increase engagement, (2) by launching a contest to increase the number of likers, and (3) by trying to increase both engagement and likers through combining a poll with a contest.

The "Engagement" Strategy: Use a Poll

Let's look at two ways to use the engagement strategy showing actual Facebook screens. First, Carmex can post a somewhat open-ended question on its Facebook Wall, such as, "Which Carmex lip balm flavor would you most like to see next: Watermelon, Green Apple, or Peach Mango?" (Figure 1). However, consumers are less likely to respond to a question if they have to type in a response and have their name attached to it.

FIGURE 1
Facebook Open-Ended Poll Question

Courtesy Jeff Gerst of Bolin Marketing

FIGURE 2

Facebook Fixed-Alternative Poll Question

Carmex
Which Carmex lip balm flavor would you most like to see next?
- Watermelon
- Green Apple
- Peach Mango

Courtesy Jeff Gerst of Bolin Marketing

Alternatively, Carmex can post the same question on its Wall as a fixed-alternative poll question (Figure 2). Then consumers need only click on a flavor to vote; this is quick, anonymous, and will drive more people to vote, where more votes means more engagement. Within five minutes Carmex will have several dozen votes and, by the end of a business day, Carmex can very easily have over 500 responses.

In this scenario, the consumers are content because they are able to engage with a brand they like and have their opinions heard. Carmex is content because it has engaged hundreds of its fans on its Facebook Page, and it gains results that are very helpful in deciding which flavors to put into testing. This scenario gets an answer quickly and drives fan engagement with existing fans but does not drive new likers to the Carmex Facebook Page.

The "Likes" Strategy: Use a Contest

If Carmex wants to grow the size of its Facebook community, which means the number of its brand page "likes," it can adopt a different strategy. Carmex can announce a contest where, if consumers "like" Carmex on Facebook and share a comment, they will be entered to win three limited-edition flavors. The chance to win limited-edition flavors is exciting to Carmex enthusiasts, and a contest like this will draw new consumers to the page. Carmex can ask the winners to review the limited-edition flavors and see if there is a consensus on which flavors should move on to quantitative testing. Setting up a contest, developing official rules, promoting the contest through Facebook ads, and fulfilling a contest can be costly and time-consuming.

The Combined Strategy: Use Poll and Contest

Carmex can also choose to layer these two strategies into a combined strategy where it runs the limited-edition flavor contest to promote new likes and meanwhile posts the poll question on its Facebook Wall to drive engagement.

REACHING A DECISION

Figure 3 shows the potential results from the three Facebook strategies being considered—the poll only, the contest only, or both strategies together. Assume the Carmex marketing team has sought your help in selecting a strategy and needs your answers to the questions below.[34]

FIGURE 3

Potential Results from Three Possible Facebook Strategies

FACEBOOK STRATEGY	POTENTIAL IMPACT ON...		
	Increased "Engagement"	Increased "Likes"	Cost
Poll Only	High	Low	Low
Contest Only	Low	High	Moderate
Poll + Contest	High	High	Moderate to High

Favorable   Neutral   Unfavorable

Courtesy Jeff Gerst of Bolin Marketing

Questions

1. What are the advantages and disadvantages for the Carmex marketing team in collecting data to narrow the flavor choices from three to two using (*a*) an online survey of a cross section of Internet households or (*b*) an online survey of Carmex Facebook likers?
2. (*a*) On a Facebook brand page, what are "engagement" and "likes" really measuring? (*b*) For Carmex, which is more important and why?
3. (*a*) What evokes consumers' "engagement" on a brand page on Facebook? (*b*) What attracts consumers to "like" a brand page on Facebook?
4. (*a*) What are the advantages of using a fixed-alternative poll question on Facebook? (*b*) When do you think it would be better to use an open-ended question?
5. (*a*) If you had a limited budget and two weeks to decide which two flavors to put into quantitative testing, would you choose a "poll only" or a "contest only" strategy? Why? (*b*) If you had a sizable budget and two months to make the same decision, which scenario would you choose? Why?

Chapter Notes

1. "Worldwide Grosses," Box Office Mojo, http://www.boxoffice mojo.com/alltime/world/, accessed March 29, 2017; and Tim Dirks, "Greatest Box-Office Bombs, Disasters and Film Flops of All-Time," AMC Filmsite, http://www.filmsite.org/greatestflops.html, 2017.
2. Hilary Lewis, "8 Movies with Major Title Changes," *Hollywood Reporter,* August 26, 2016; Rachel Dodes, "Movies: What's in a Name?" *The Wall Street Journal,* October 19, 2012, p. D1; and John Horn, "Studios Play Name Games," *Star Tribune,* August 10, 1997, p. F11.
3. Kathryn Lunte, "Screening Success: Marketing Research for Movies," *Film and Digital Media,* https://filmanddigitalmedia wordpress.com/?s=screening+success, February 28, 2015.
4. Rudie Obias, "11 Movies That Changed Because of Test Audiences," *mentalfloss.com,* April 4, 2016; and Willow Bay, "Test Audiences Have Profound Effect on Movies," *CNN Newsstand & Entertainment Weekly,* September 28, 1998.
5. Natalie Robehmed, "How Hollywood Monitors Social Media to Help Movies Make Money," *www.forbes.com,* April 30, 2015; Brooks Barnes, "Hollywood Tracks Social Media Chatter to Target Hit Films," *The New York Times,* www.nytimes.com, December 7, 2014; and Carl Diorio, "Tracking Projections: Box Office Calculations an Inexact Science," *Variety,* May 24, 2001.
6. A lengthier, expanded definition is found on the American Marketing Association's website. See https://www.ama.org/AboutAMA/Pages/Definition-of-Marketing.aspx; and for a researcher's comments on this and other definitions of marketing research, see Lawrence D. Gibson, "Quo Vadis, *Marketing Research?*" *Marketing Research,* Spring 2000, pp. 36–41.
7. Lindsay Kolowich, "Building a Playful Brand, Brick by Brick: The History of Lego Marketing," *Hubspot,* August 10, 2015; Parmy Olson, "Gadgets We Love: LEGO Mindstorms EV3," *www.forbes.com,* December 2, 2014, p. 1; and Harry McCracken, "Build-A-Bot," *Time,* January 21, 2013, pp. 52–53.
8. Lawrence D. Gibson, "Defining Marketing Problems," *Marketing Research,* Spring 1998, pp. 4–12; and Martin Meister, "How to Define a Marketing Research Problem," *Business Insights Review,* July 11, 2012.
9. David A. Aaker, V. Kumar, George S. Day, and Robert P. Leone, *Marketing Research,* 10th ed. (Hoboken, NJ: Wiley, 2010), pp. 114–16.
10. "TV Ratings," Nielsen website, http://www.nielsen.com/us/en/solutions/measurement/television.html, accessed April 3, 2017; Miriam Gottfried, "Nielsen Isn't Leaving the Living Room Soon," *The Wall Street Journal,* January 20, 2015, p. C8; and Meg James, "Nielsen 'People Meter' Changed the TV Ratings Game 25 Years Ago," *Los Angeles Times,* August 31, 2012.
11. Jason Lynch, "Here Are the TV Shows and Networks People Watch Live Most and Least Often," *www.adweek.com,* October 7, 2016; Jeanine Poggi, "TV's New Ratings Aren't What Advertisers Want," *Advertising Age,* January 23, 2017, p. 36; "For the First Time, More Than Half of Americans Will Watch Streaming TV," *eMarketer,* February 3, 2016; George Winslow, "Researchers Tackle Cross-Platform Measurement," *Broadcasting & Cable,* September 15, 2014, p. 22; and Jeanine Poggi, "The CMO's Guide to Fall TV Ratings," *Advertising Age,* September 29, 2014, p. 40.
12. "Nielsen Estimates 119.6 Million TV Homes in the U.S. for the 2017–18 TV Season," The Nielsen Company website, http://www.nielsen.com/us/en/insights/news/2017/nielsen-estimates-119-6-million-us-tv-homes-2017-2018-tv-season.html.
13. "Zenith's 2018 U.S. Spending Forecast," *Advertising Age, Marketing Fact Pack,* December 18, 2017, p. 14.
14. Suhit Anantula, "How Gillette Learned Design-Led Consumer Research from P&G," *Humanomics,* March 2, 2015; Bruce Brown and Scott Anthony, "How P&G Tripled Its Innovation Success Rate," *Harvard Business Review,* June 2011, p. 64–72; and "Observe and Learn from Consumers," *Managing People at Work,* April 2011, p. 4.
15. Elka Torpey, "Mystery Shopper," *Career Outlook,* February 2016, p. 1; and Jim Dudlicek, "Mystery Machine," *Progressive Grocer,* May 2015, p. 10.
16. "How to Use Ethnography for In-Depth Consumer Insight," *Marketing Week,* May 22, 2014, p. 4; and Gavin Johnson and Melinda Rea-Holloway, "Ethnography: How to Know If It's Right for Your Study," *Alert! Magazine,* Marketing Research Association, 47, no. 2 (February 2009), pp. 1–4.
17. Kenneth Chang, "Enlisting Science's Lessons to Entice More Shoppers to Spend More," *The New York Times,* September 19, 2006, p. D3; and Janet Adamy, "Cooking Up Changes at Kraft Foods," *The Wall Street Journal,* February 20, 2007, p. B1.
18. Zach Brooke, "Marketing's Mind Readers," *Marketing News,* January, 2017, pp. 38–41; Kyle Hilton, "The Science of Sensory Marketing," *Harvard Business Review,* March 2015, pp. 28–29; Roger Dooley, "Nielsen Doubles Down on Neuro," *Forbes,* June 3, 2015; Aradhna Krishna, *Customer Sense* (New York: Palgrave Macmillan, 2013); Lluis Martinez-Ribes, "The Power of the Senses," http://www.martinez-ribes.com/

19. Jack Neff, "Neuromarketing Exits the 'Hype Cycle,' Starts Shaping TV Commercials," *Advertising Age,* April 18, 2016, p. 17; and Ilan Brat, "The Emotional Quotient of Soup Shopping," *The Wall Street Journal,* February 17, 2010, p. B6.
20. For a more complete discussion of questionnaire methods, see Joseph F. Hair Jr., Mary Wolfinbarger, Robert P. Bush, and David J. Ortinau, *Essentials of Marketing Research,* 3rd ed. (New York: McGraw-Hill/Irwin, 2013), Chapters 4 and 8.
21. See www.trendhunter.com/about-trend-hunter.
22. "What Is Online Research?" Marketing Research Association at http://www.marketingresearch.org/?q=node/221. See also *www.surveymonkey.com.*
23. For more discussion on wording questions effectively, see Gilbert A. Churchill Jr., Tom J. Brown, and Tracy A. Suter, *Basic Marketing Research,* 7th ed. (Mason, OH: South-Western, Cengage Learning, 2010), pp. 289–307.
24. Stephanie Clifford, "Social Media Act as a Guide for Marketers," *The New York Times,* July 31, 2012, pp. A1, A3; and Noam Cohen, "The Breakfast Meeting: Social Media as Focus Group," *The New York Times,* July 31, 2012, p. A3.
25. Jeff Gerst of Bolin Marketing provided the Carmex example, with the permission of Carma Laboratories, Inc.
26. Mark Jeffery, *Data-Driven Marketing: The 15 Metrics Everyone in Marketing Should Know* (Hoboken, NJ: Wiley, 2010), pp. 156–86.
27. Gordon Wyner, "The Uncertain Future of Market Research," *Marketing News,* June 2017, pp. 18–19; Douglas D. Bates, "The Future of Qualitative Research Is Online," *Alert! Magazine,* Marketing Research Association 47, no. 2 (February 2009); Jack Neff, "The End of Consumer Surveys?" *Advertising Age,* September 15, 2008; Jack Neff, "Marketing Execs: Researchers Could Use a Softer Touch," *Advertising Age,* January 27, 2009; Bruce Mendelsohn, "Social Networking: Interactive Marketing Lets Researchers Reach Consumers Where They Are," *Alert! Magazine,* Marketing Research Association 46, no. 4 (April 2008); Toby, "Social Media Research: Interview with Joel Rubinson of ARF: Part 1," *Diva Marketing Blog,* February 16, 2009; and Toby, "Social Media Research: Interview with Joel Rubinson of ARF: Part 2," *Diva Marketing Blog,* February 23, 2009.
28. Bill Peters, "Happy Meals on Wheels: McDonald's Touts '3-Mile' Delivery Advantage," *Investors Business Daily,* March 1, 2107, p. 1; and Kate Samuelson, "These Cities Will Be the First to Get McDonald's Delivery Service," *www.fortune.com,* December 16, 2016.
29. The step 4 discussion was written by David Ford and Don Rylander of Ford Consulting Group, Inc.; the Tony's Pizza example was provided by Teré Carral of Tony's Pizza.
30. Janakiraman Moorthy, Rangin Lahiri, Neelanjan Biswas, Dipyaman Sanyal, Jayanthi Ranjan, Krishnadas Nanath, and Pulak Ghosh, "Big Data: Prospects and Challenges," *Vikalpa,* January–March, 2015, pp. 74–96; Karthik Kambatla, Giorgos Kollias, Vipin Kumar, and Ananth Grama, "Trends in Big Data Analytics," *Journal of Parallel and Distributed Computing,"* January 2014, pp. 2561–73; Steve LaValle, Eric Lesser, Rebecca Shockley, Michael S. Hopkins, and Nina Kruschwitz, "Big Data, Analytics and the Path from Insights to Value," *Sloan Management Review,* Winter 2011, pp. 21–31; and "Big Data: Before You Start Restricting It, Be Aware of All the Opportunities," *The Wall Street Journal,* November 19, 2012, p. R10.
31. Hal Conick, "The Past, Present and Future of AI in Marketing," *Marketing News,* January 2017, pp. 26-35.
32 "Target Using Predictive Analytics to Increase Value Capture," HBS Digital Innovation and Transformation", November 22, 2015, https://digit.hbs.org/submission/target-using-predictive-analytics-to-increase-value-capture/.
33. "How Social Media Data Mining Could Shape the Products of Tomorrow," *www.phys.org,* February 15, 2017; Joni R. Jackson, "Big Data: Goldmine or Minefield," *AMA Winter Conference Proceedings,* 2016, p. 41; Joel Stein, "Your Data, Yourself," *Time,* March 21, 2011, pp. 39–46; Ryan Flinn, "The Big Business of Sifting through Social Media Data," *Bloomberg Businessweek,* October 25–October 31, 2010, pp. 20–22; and Michael Lev-Ram, "The Hot New Gig in Tech," *Fortune,* September 5, 2011, p. 29.
34. Carmex: This case was written by Jeff Gerst of Bolin Marketing.

8

LEARNING OBJECTIVES

After reading this chapter you should be able to:

LO 8-1 Explain what market segmentation is and when to use it.

LO 8-2 Identify the five steps involved in segmenting and targeting markets.

LO 8-3 Recognize the bases used to segment consumer and organizational (business) markets.

LO 8-4 Develop a market-product grid to identify a target market and recommend resulting marketing actions.

LO 8-5 Explain how marketing managers position products in the marketplace.

Market Segmentation, Targeting, and Positioning

Segmentation Rules in the Kingdom of Happiness!

In his book *Delivering Happiness,* Zappos founder Tony Hsieh describes his career as an entrepreneur and venture capitalist. His philosophy is to balance profits, passion, and purpose to create a unique company culture and an extraordinary customer experience. If you have purchased a pair of shoes online you may be one of millions of people who agree that the Zappos experience delivers great shoes and happiness![1]

Zappos's Secret to Success

Zappos began with the idea of creating a website that would offer the best selection of shoes. The key to the success of the new venture was Hsieh's segmentation strategy: Focus on people who like to use mobile technology and who will shop for and buy shoes online. While this focus on the segment of online shoe buyers generated more than $1 billion in annual sales, the Zappos vision soon evolved to include consumers of anything in the one-third of all retail transactions that are likely to occur online. The segmentation strategy also evolved as Zappos implemented behavioral segmentation to match relevant products from other categories based on past shoe purchases. Some recommendations are even based on the type of device consumers use to shop.[2]

In addition to a huge selection of shoes and personalized recommendations of other products, Zappos provides 24-hour customer service with no wait times, as well as free shipping and free returns. Pamela Leo, a New Jersey customer, says "With Zappos I can try the shoes in the comfort of my own home . . . it's fabulous."[3]

Delivering WOW Customer Service

"We try to spend most of our time on stuff that will improve customer-service levels," Hsieh explains. This customer-service obsession for its market segment of online customers means that all new Zappos.com employees go through four

©Brad Swonetz/Redux

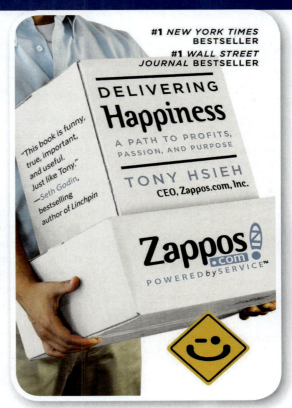
Source: Grand Central Publishing

weeks of customer-loyalty training. Hsieh offers $2,000 to anyone completing the training who wants to leave Zappos.com, and another $1,000 per year up to $5,000. The theory: If you take the money, you're not right for Zappos.com. Few take the money![4]

Ten "core values" are the foundation for the Zappos.com culture, brand, and business strategies. Some examples:[5]

#1. Deliver WOW through service.
#3. Create fun and a little weirdness.
#6. Build open and honest relationships with communication.

The other Zappos.com core values appear on its website: www.zappos.com. Hsieh's interest in the company culture also led him to implement a stucture called "holocracy," which emphasizes self-management by eliminating traditional hierarchical reporting lines and replacing them with "work circles."[6]

The Zappos.com strategy illustrates successful market segmentation and targeting, the first topics in this chapter. The chapter concludes with the topic of positioning the organization, product, or brand.

WHY SEGMENT MARKETS?

 LO 8-1 Explain what market segmentation is and when to use it.

A business firm segments its markets so it can respond more effectively to the wants of groups of potential buyers and thus increase its sales and profits. Not-for-profit organizations also segment the clients they serve so they can satisfy client needs more effectively while achieving the organization's goals. Let's describe (1) what market segmentation is and (2) when to segment markets, sometimes using the Zappos.com segmentation strategy as an example.

What Market Segmentation Means

People have different needs and wants, even though it would be easier for marketers if they didn't. **Market segmentation** involves aggregating prospective buyers into groups, or segments, that (1) have common needs and (2) will respond similarly to a marketing action. As defined in Chapter 1, *market segments* are the relatively homogeneous groups of prospective buyers that result from the market segmentation process. Each market segment consists of people who are relatively similar to each other in terms of their consumption behavior.

The existence of different market segments has caused firms to use a marketing strategy of **product differentiation**. This strategy involves a firm using different marketing mix actions, such as product features and advertising, to help consumers perceive the product as being different and better than competing products. The perceived differences may involve physical features, such as size or color, or nonphysical ones, such as image or price.

> **market segmentation**
> Involves aggregating prospective buyers into groups, or segments, that (1) have common needs and (2) will respond similarly to a marketing action.
>
> **product differentiation**
> A marketing strategy that involves a firm using different marketing mix actions to help consumers perceive a product as being different and better than competing products.

Segmentation: Linking Needs to Actions The process of segmenting a market and selecting specific segments as targets is the link between the various buyers' needs and the organization's marketing program, as shown in Figure 8–1. Market segmentation is only a means to an end: It leads to tangible marketing actions that can increase sales and profitability.

Market segmentation first stresses the importance of grouping people or organizations in a market according to the similarity of their needs and the benefits they are looking for in making a purchase. Second, such needs and benefits must be related to specific marketing actions that the organization can take, such as providing a new product or offering a special promotion.

> **Video 8-1**
> Zappos Video
> kerin.tv/cr8e/v8-1

The Zappos.com Segmentation Strategy The Zappos.com target customer segment originally consisted of people who wanted to (1) have a wide selection of shoes, (2) shop online in the convenience of their own homes, and (3) receive quick delivery and free returns. Zappos's actions include offering a huge inventory of shoes using an online selling strategy and providing overnight delivery. These actions have enabled Zappos.com to create a positive customer experience and generate repeat purchases. Zappos's success in selling footwear has enabled it to add lines of clothing, handbags, accessories (such as sunglasses), and housewares to reach new segments of buyers.

FIGURE 8–1
Market segmentation links market needs to an organization's marketing program—its specific marketing mix actions designed to satisfy those needs.

Identify market needs
Benefits in terms of:
- Product features
- Expense
- Quality
- Savings in time and convenience

→ **Link needs to actions**
Take steps to segment and target markets

→ **Execute marketing program actions**
A marketing mix of:
- Product
- Price
- Promotion
- Place (distribution)

Zappos.com is reaching new market segments with new products and edgy, attention-getting ads.
Source: Zappos.com, Inc.

market-product grid
A framework to relate the market segments of potential buyers to products offered or potential marketing actions.

With millions of customers and more than 5,000 calls daily to Zappos's service center, its executives believe the speed with which a customer receives an online purchase plays a big role in gaining repeat customers.[7] The company continues to stress this point of difference of providing the absolute best service among online sellers.

Using Market-Product Grids How do you sleep—on your side, your back, or your stomach? These are really the key market segments of sleepers. Sleep researchers have discovered that you'll probably get a better night's sleep if you have the right firmness of pillow under your head. Using this research, we can develop the market-product grid shown in Figure 8–2.[8]

A **market-product grid** is a framework to relate the market segments of potential buyers to products offered or potential marketing actions. The market-product grid in Figure 8–2 shows the different market segments for bed pillows—side, back, and stomach sleepers—in the horizontal rows. The product offerings—the pillows—appear in the vertical columns and are based on three different pillow firmnesses—firm, medium, and soft.

Marketing research reveals the size of each sleeper segment, as shown by both the percentages and the circles in Figure 8–2. This tells pillow manufacturers the relative importance of each of the three market segments, which is critical information when scheduling production. It also emphasizes the importance of firm pillows, a product targeted at the side sleeper market segment. As Figure 8–2 shows, this segment is almost three times the size of the other two combined. Therefore, meeting the needs of this market segment with the right firmness of pillow is especially important.

When and How to Segment Markets

One-size-fits-all mass markets—like that for Tide laundry detergent 40 years ago—no longer exist. The marketing officer at Procter & Gamble, which markets Tide, says, "Every one of our brands is targeted." Due to slow economic growth, the size of the middle-income market is shrinking. In response, P&G has begun implementing a new segmentation strategy: Offer different products to reach (1) high-income and (2) low-income families.[9]

A business goes to the trouble and expense of segmenting its markets when it expects that this extra effort will increase its sales, profit, and return on investment. When expenses are greater than the potentially increased sales from segmentation, a firm should not attempt to segment its market. Three specific segmentation strategies

FIGURE 8–2
This market-product grid shows the kind of sleeper that is targeted for each of the bed pillow products. The sizes of the circles show that side sleepers are the dominant market segment and that they prefer firm pillows.

MARKET SEGMENTS	BED PILLOW PRODUCTS		
	Firm Pillows	Medium Pillows	Soft Pillows
Side sleepers	●		
Back sleepers		●	
Stomach sleepers			●

These *different* covers for the *same* magazine issue show a very effective market segmentation strategy. For which strategy it is and why it works, see the text.

Source: Street & Smith's Yearbooks

that illustrate this point are (1) one product and multiple market segments, (2) multiple products and multiple market segments, and (3) segments of one, or mass customization.

One Product and Multiple Market Segments

When an organization produces only a single product or service and attempts to sell it to two or more market segments, it avoids the extra costs of developing and producing additional versions of the product. In this case, the incremental costs of taking the product into new market segments are typically those of a separate promotional campaign or a new channel of distribution.

Magazines are single products frequently directed at two or more distinct market segments. The annual *Street & Smith's Baseball* uses 15 different covers featuring a baseball star from each of its regions in the United States. Yet each regional issue has the same magazine content.

Other examples of a single offering for multiple segments include books, movies, and many services. Book series such as *Harry Potter, The Twilight Saga, Divergent,* and *The Hunger Games* have phenomenal success in part due to their publishers' creativity in marketing to preteen, teen, and adult segments. Movies have a similar challenge, particularly since different segments are reached through different channels such as movie theaters, streaming services, and pay-per-view cable channels. Finally, services such as Disney's resorts offer the same basic experience to at least three distinct segments—children, parents, and grandparents. Although separate advertising, promotion, and distribution for these offerings can be expensive, these expenses are minor compared with the costs of producing a different version of the offerings for each segment.[10]

Multiple Products and Multiple Market Segments

For an example of multiple products aimed at multiple market segments, consider the products of Ford Motor Company. Each of its different lines of cars, SUVs, trucks, crossovers, and hybrids are targeted at a different type of customer. Producing these different vehicles is clearly more expensive than producing only a single vehicle. But this strategy is very effective *if* it meets customers' needs better, doesn't reduce quality or increase price, and adds to Ford's sales revenues and profits.

Unfortunately, this product differentiation strategy in the auto industry has a huge potential downside: The proliferation of different brands, models, and options can raise prices and reduce quality. Several years ago Ford offered vehicles under a variety of brand names, including Ford, Lincoln, Mercury, Jaguar, Aston Martin, Volvo, and Land Rover. In addition, each of the brands offered different models and many options for each model, which often meant thousands of combinations were possible. The huge number of combinations led to limited production volume, which increased prices.[11]

Today Ford is pursuing a different strategy. The company has discontinued or sold all of its brands except Ford and Lincoln and reduced the number of models offered. In addition, it now offers many options but only in packages. Although there are fewer choices, Ford's simplified product line provides two benefits to consumers: (1) lower prices because producing a higher volume is more efficient and (2) higher quality because of the ability to debug fewer basic designs.[12]

Segments of One: Mass Customization

American marketers are rediscovering today what their ancestors running the corner general store knew a century ago: Each customer has unique needs and wants and desires special tender loving care. Economies of scale in manufacturing and marketing during the past century made mass-produced products so affordable that most customers were willing to compromise their individual tastes and settle for standardized products. Today's Internet ordering and flexible manufacturing and marketing processes have made *mass customization* possible, which means tailoring products or services to the tastes of individual customers on a high-volume scale.

Mass customization is the next step beyond *build-to-order* (BTO), which involves manufacturing a product only when there is an order from a customer. Apple uses BTO systems that trim work-in-progress inventories and shorten delivery times to customers. To do this, Apple restricts its computer manufacturing line to only a few basic models that can be assembled in four minutes. This gives customers a good choice with quick delivery. But even this system falls a bit short of total mass customization because customers do not have an unlimited number of features from which to choose.

The Segmentation Trade-Off: Synergies versus Cannibalization

The key to successful product differentiation and market segmentation strategies is finding the ideal balance between satisfying a customer's individual wants and achieving *organizational synergy,* the increased customer value achieved through performing organizational functions such as marketing or manufacturing more efficiently. The "increased customer value" can take many forms: more products, improved quality of existing products, lower prices, easier access to products through improved distribution, and so on. So the ultimate criterion for an organization's marketing success is that customers should be better off as a result of the increased synergies.

The organization should also achieve increased revenues and profits from the product differentiation and market segmentation strategies it uses. When the increased customer value involves adding new products or a new chain of stores, the product differentiation–market segmentation trade-off raises a critical issue: Are the new products or new chain simply stealing customers and sales from the older, existing ones? This is known as *cannibalization.*

Marketers increasingly emphasize a two-tier, "Tiffany/Walmart" strategy. Many firms now offer different variations of the same basic offering to high-end and low-end segments. Gap Inc.'s Banana Republic chain sells blue jeans for $58, whereas its Old Navy stores sell a slightly different version for $22.

ANN INC.'s LOFT chain tries to reach younger, value-conscious women with a casual lifestyle, while its Ann Taylor chain targets more sophisticated and relatively affluent women. For the potential dangers of this two-segment strategy, see the text.
©Goran Bogicevic/Alamy Stock Photo

Unfortunately, the lines between customer segments can often blur and lead to problems. For example, consider the competition within the ANN INC. organization between stores in its two chains—Ann Taylor and LOFT. The Ann Taylor chain targets "successful, relatively affluent, fashion-conscious women," while its sister chain, LOFT, targets "value-conscious women who want a casual lifestyle at work and home." The LOFT stores wound up stealing sales from the Ann Taylor chain. The result: More than 100 stores from both chains were closed.[13] Both chains are now aggressively targeting their

The smaller Walmart Neighborhood Market format offers convenient locations to discount shoppers.
©Scott Olson/Getty Images

customers by stressing online sales and opening new factory outlets—Ann Taylor Factory and LOFT Outlet stores.

Walmart has been opening Walmart Neighborhood Market stores that are about one-third the size of its supercenters. These smaller stores are intended to compete for the segments that shop at discount chains such as Dollar General. Walmart Neighborhood Markets are designed to meet a range of needs by offering fresh produce, health and beauty supplies, household items, gasoline, and a pharmacy. Walmart currently has 700 of the small format stores and plans to open 20 new stores this year. Will its own Tiffany/Walmart strategy—or perhaps "Walmart/Dollar General" strategy—prove successful or lead to cannibalization of the larger stores? Watch for new stores near you during the next few years to determine the answer.[14]

learning review

8-1. Market segmentation involves aggregating prospective buyers into groups that have two key characteristics. What are they?

8-2. In terms of market segments and products, what are the three market segmentation strategies?

STEPS IN SEGMENTING AND TARGETING MARKETS

LO 8-2 Identify the five steps involved in segmenting and targeting markets.

Figure 8–3 identifies the five-step process used to segment a market and select the target segments on which an organization wants to focus. Segmenting a market requires both detailed analysis and large doses of common sense and managerial judgment. So market segmentation is both science and art!

For the purposes of our discussion, assume that you have just purchased a Wendy's restaurant. Your Wendy's is located next to a large urban university, one that offers both day and evening classes. Your restaurant offers the basic Wendy's fare: hamburgers, chicken and deli sandwiches, salads, french fries, and Frosty desserts. Even though you are part of a chain that has some restrictions on menu and decor, you are free to set your hours of business and to develop local advertising. How can market segmentation help? In the sections that follow, you will apply the five-step process for segmenting and targeting markets to arrive at marketing actions for your Wendy's restaurant.

Step 1: Group Potential Buyers into Segments

It's not always a good idea to segment a market. Grouping potential buyers into meaningful segments involves meeting some specific criteria that answer the questions, "Would segmentation be worth doing?" and "Is it possible?" If so, a marketer must find specific variables that can be used to create these various segments.

FIGURE 8–3
The five key steps in segmenting and targeting markets link the market needs of customers to the organization's marketing program.

A local Wendy's restaurant—like yours!
©Reed Saxon/AP Images

Criteria to Use in Forming the Segments A marketing manager should develop market segments that meet five essential criteria:[15]

- *Simplicity and cost-effectiveness of assigning potential buyers to segments.* A marketing manager must be able to put a market segmentation plan into effect. This means identifying the characteristics of potential buyers in a market and then cost-effectively assigning them to a segment.
- *Potential for increased profit.* The best segmentation approach is the one that maximizes the opportunity for future profit and return on investment (ROI). If this potential is maximized without segmentation, don't segment. For nonprofit organizations, the criterion is the potential for serving clients more effectively.
- *Similarity of needs of potential buyers within a segment.* Potential buyers within a segment should be similar in terms of common needs that, in turn, lead to common marketing actions, such as product features sought or advertising media used.
- *Difference of needs of buyers among segments.* If the needs of the various segments aren't very different, combine them into fewer segments. A different segment usually requires a different marketing action that, in turn, means greater costs. If increased sales don't offset extra costs, combine segments and reduce the number of marketing actions.
- *Potential of a marketing action to reach a segment.* Reaching a segment requires a simple but effective marketing action. If no such action exists, don't segment.

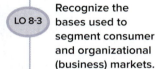

LO 8-3 Recognize the bases used to segment consumer and organizational (business) markets.

This MicroFridge appliance includes everything from a small refrigerator, freezer, and microwave oven to a smoke sensor and a charging station for laptops and mobile phones. To which market segment might this appeal? The answer appears in the text.
Source: Intirion Corporation

Ways to Segment Consumer Markets Four general bases of segmentation can be used to segment U.S. consumer markets. These four segmentation bases are (1) *geographic segmentation,* which is based on where prospective customers live or work (region, city size); (2) *demographic segmentation,* which is based on some *objective* physical (gender, race), measurable (age, income), or other classification attribute (birth era, occupation) of prospective customers; (3) *psychographic segmentation,* which is based on some *subjective* mental or emotional attributes (personality), aspirations (lifestyle), or needs of prospective customers; and (4) *behavioral segmentation,* which is based on some observable actions or attitudes by prospective customers—such as where they buy, what benefits they seek, how frequently they buy, and why they buy. Some examples are:

- *Geographic segmentation: Region.* Campbell Soup Company found that its canned nacho cheese sauce, which could be heated and poured directly onto nacho chips, was too spicy for Americans in the East and not spicy enough for those in the West and Southwest. The result: Campbell's plants in Texas and California now produce a hotter nacho cheese sauce to serve their regions better.
- *Demographic segmentation: Household size.* More than half of all U.S. households are made up of only one or two persons, so Campbell Soup Company packages meals with only one or two servings for this market segment.
- *Psychographic segmentation: Lifestyle.* Nielsen's lifestyle segmentation is based on the belief that "birds of a feather flock together." Thus, people of similar lifestyles tend to live near one another, have similar interests, and buy similar offerings. This is of great value to

marketers. Nielsen PRIZM® classifies every household in the United States into 1 of 66 unique market segments.
- *Behavioral segmentation: Product features.* Understanding what features are important to different customers is a useful way to segment markets because it can lead directly to specific marketing actions, such as a new product, an ad campaign, or a distribution channel. For example, college dorm residents frequently want to keep and prepare their own food to save money or have a late-night snack. However, their dorm rooms are often woefully short of space. Micro-Fridge understands this and markets a combination microwave, refrigerator, freezer, smoke sensor, and charging station appliance targeted to these students.
- *Behavioral segmentation: Usage rate.* **Usage rate** is the quantity consumed or patronage—store visits—during a specific period. It varies significantly among different customer groups. Airlines have developed frequent-flyer programs to encourage passengers to use the same airline repeatedly to create loyal customers. This technique, sometimes called *frequency marketing,* focuses on usage rate. One key conclusion emerges about usage: In market segmentation studies, some measurement of usage by, or sales obtained from, various segments is central to the analysis.

> **usage rate**
> The quantity consumed or patronage (store visits) during a specific period. *Frequency marketing focuses on usage rate.*

The Aberdeen Group analyzed which segmentation bases were used by the 20 percent most profitable organizations of the 220 surveyed. From highest to lowest, these were the segmentation bases they used:

- Geographic bases—88 percent.
- Behavioral bases—65 percent.
- Demographic bases—53 percent.
- Psychographic bases—43 percent.

The top 20 percent often use more than one of these bases in their market segmentation studies, plus measures such as purchase histories and usage rates of customers.[16]

Simmons continuously surveys over 25,000 adults each year to obtain quarterly, projectable usage rate data from the U.S. national population for more than 500 consumer product categories and 8,000-plus brands. Its purpose is to discover how the products and services they buy and the media they use relate to their behavioral, psychographic, and demographic characteristics.

Usage rate is sometimes referred to in terms of the **80/20 rule**, a concept that suggests 80 percent of a firm's sales are obtained from 20 percent of its customers. The percentages in the 80/20 rule are not really fixed at exactly 80 percent and 20 percent, but they suggest that a small fraction of customers provides most of a firm's sales.

> **80/20 rule**
> A concept that suggests 80 percent of a firm's sales are obtained from 20 percent of its customers.

Patronage of Fast-Food Restaurants
As part of its survey, Simmons asked adults which fast-food restaurant(s) was (were) (1) the sole or only restaurant, (2) the primary one, or (3) one of several secondary ones they patronized. As a Wendy's restaurant owner, the information depicted in Figure 8–4 should give you some ideas in developing a marketing program for your local market. For example, the Wendy's bar graph in Figure 8–4 shows that your sole (0.6 percent) and primary (10.5 percent) user segments are somewhat behind Burger King and far behind McDonald's. Thus, your challenge is to look at these two competitors and devise a marketing program to win customers from them.

The nonusers part of the Wendy's bar graph in Figure 8–4 shows that 14.9 percent of adult Americans don't go to fast-food restaurants in a typical month and are really nonprospects—unlikely to ever patronize any fast-food restaurant. However, 58.0 percent of nonusers are prospects who may be worth a targeted marketing program. These adults use the product category (fast food) but do not yet patronize Wendy's. New menu items or promotional strategies may succeed in converting these prospects into users that patronize Wendy's.

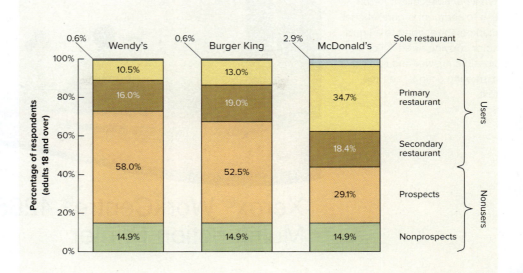

FIGURE 8–4

Comparison of various kinds of users and nonusers for Wendy's, Burger King, and McDonald's fast-food restaurants. This figure gives Wendy's restaurants a snapshot of its customers compared to those of its major competitors.

Source: Simmons National Consumer Survey Spring 2014 Adult Survey OneView^SM Crosstabulation Report, Simmons Research LLC, 2017.

Variables to Use in Forming Segments for Wendy's To analyze your Wendy's customers, you need to identify which variables to use to segment them. Because the restaurant is located near a large urban university, the most logical starting point for segmentation is really behavioral: Are the prospective customers students or nonstudents?

To segment the students, you could try a variety of (1) geographic variables, such as city or zip code; (2) demographic variables, such as gender, age, year in school, or college major; or (3) psychographic variables, such as personality or needs. But none of these variables really meets the five criteria listed previously—particularly, the fifth criterion about leading to a doable marketing action to reach the various segments. The behavioral basis of segmentation for the "students" segment really combines two variables: (1) where students live and (2) when they are on campus. This results in four "student" segments:

- Students living in dormitories (residence halls, sororities, fraternities).
- Students living near the university in apartments.
- Day commuter students living outside the area.
- Night commuter students living outside the area.

The three main segments of "nonstudents" include:

- Faculty and staff members who work at the university.
- People who live in the area but aren't connected with the university.
- People who work in the area but aren't connected with the university.

People in each of these nonstudent segments aren't quite as similar as those in the student segments, which makes them harder to reach with a marketing program or action. Think about (1) whether the needs of all these segments are different and (2) how various advertising media can be used to reach these groups effectively.

Ways to Segment Organizational (Business) Markets A number of variables can be used to segment organizational (business) markets. For example, a product manager at Xerox responsible for its new line of multifunction color printers (MFPs) might use these segmentation bases and corresponding variables:

- *Geographic segmentation: Statistical area.* Firms located in a metropolitan statistical area might receive a personal sales call, whereas those in a micropolitan statistical area might be contacted by telephone.

What variables might Xerox use to segment organizational markets to respond to a firm's color copying needs? For the possible answer and related marketing actions, see the text.

Source: Xerox

- *Demographic segmentation: NAICS code.* Firms categorized by the North American Industry Classification System (NAICS) code as manufacturers that deal with customers throughout the world might have different document printing needs than retailers or lawyers serving local customers.
- *Demographic segmentation: Number of employees.* The size of the firm is related to the volume of digital documents produced, so firms with varying numbers of employees might be specific target markets for different Xerox MFPs.
- *Behavioral segmentation: Usage rate.* Similar to this segmentation variable for consumer markets, features are often of major importance in organizational markets. So Xerox can target organizations needing fast printing, copying, faxing, and scanning in color—the benefits and features emphasized in the ad for its Xerox WorkCentre 4265 Multifunction Printer.

learning review

8-3. The process of segmenting and targeting markets is a bridge between which two marketing activities?

8-4. What is the difference between the demographic and behavioral bases of market segmentation?

Step 2: Group Products to Be Sold into Categories

Video 8-2
Dave's Hot 'N Juicy Ad
kerin.tv/cr8e/v8-2

What does your Wendy's restaurant sell? Of course you are selling individual products such as Frostys, hamburgers, and fries. But for marketing purposes you're really selling combinations of individual products that become a "meal." This distinction is critical, so let's discuss both (1) individual Wendy's products and (2) groupings of Wendy's products.

MARKET SEGMENT		PRODUCT OR INNOVATION								
GENERAL	GROUP WITH NEED	HOT 'N JUICY HAMBURGER (1969)	DRIVE-THRU (1970)	BAKED POTATO (1983)	SUPER VALUE MEALS (1989)	FRESH-MADE SALADS (2002)	BACONATOR® (2007)	CHILI CHEESE FRIES (2012)	MY WENDY'S MOBILE APP (2015)	SOUTHWEST CHICKEN SANDWICH (2018)
GENDER	Male	P	P	P	P	S	P	P	P	P
	Female			P		P		P	P	P
NEEDS	Price/Value				P	S				
	Health-Conscious			S		P				P
	Convenience	S	P	P		S		P	P	S
	Meat Lovers	P			S		S			
UNIVERSITY AFFILIATION	Affiliated (students, faculty, staff)	P	S	P	P	P	S	P	P	P
	Nonaffiliated (residents, workers)	S	P	S	S	S	P	S	S	S

Key: P = Primary market   S = Secondary market

FIGURE 8–5

Wendy's new products and other innovations target specific market segments based on a customer's gender, needs, or university affiliation.

Photos: Source: Wendy's International, LLC

Individual Wendy's Products When Dave Thomas founded Wendy's in 1969, he offered only four basic items: "Hot 'N Juicy" hamburgers (now called Dave's hamburgers), Frosty Dairy Desserts (Frostys), french fries, and soft drinks. Since then, Wendy's has introduced many new products and innovations to compete for customers' fast-food dollars. Some of these are shown in Figure 8–5. New products include baked potatoes, fresh-made salads, the Baconator, chili cheese fries, and a Southwest Avocado Chicken Sandwich. But there are also nonproduct innovations to increase consumer convenience like drive-thru services and the Wendy's mobile app.

Figure 8–5 also shows that each product or innovation is not targeted equally to all market segments based on gender, needs, or university affiliation. The cells in Figure 8–5 labeled "P" represent Wendy's primary target market segments when it introduced each product or innovation. The boxes labeled "S" represent the secondary target market segments that also bought these products or used these innovations. In some cases, Wendy's discovered that large numbers of people in a segment not originally targeted for a particular product or innovation bought or used it anyway.

Groupings of Wendy's Products: Meals Finding a means of grouping the products a firm sells into meaningful categories is as important as grouping customers into segments. If the firm has only one product or service, this isn't a problem. But when it has many, these must be grouped in some way so buyers can relate to them. This is why department stores and supermarkets are organized into product groups, with the departments or aisles containing related merchandise. Likewise, manufacturers organize products into groupings in the catalogs they send to customers.

What are the product groupings for your Wendy's restaurant? It could be the item purchased, such as hamburgers, salads, Frostys, and french fries. This is where judgment—the qualitative aspect of marketing—comes in. Customers really buy an eating experience—a meal occasion that satisfies a need at a particular time of day. So the product groupings that make the most marketing sense are the five "meals" based on the time of day consumers buy them: breakfast, lunch, between-meal snack, dinner, and after-dinner snack. These groupings are more closely related to the way purchases are actually made and permit you to market the entire meal, not just your individual items such as french fries or hamburgers.

Step 3: Develop a Market-Product Grid and Estimate the Size of Markets

LO 8-4 Develop a market-product grid to identify a target market and recommend resulting marketing actions.

As noted earlier in the chapter, a market-product grid is a framework to relate the market segments of potential buyers to products offered or potential marketing actions by an organization. In a complete market-product grid analysis, each cell in the grid can show the estimated market size of a given product sold to a specific market segment. Let's first look at forming a market-product grid for your Wendy's restaurant and then estimate market sizes.

Forming a Market-Product Grid for Wendy's Developing a market-product grid means identifying and labeling the markets (or horizontal rows) and product groupings (or vertical columns), as shown in Figure 8–6. From our earlier discussion, we've chosen to divide the market segments into students versus nonstudents, with subdivisions of each. The columns—or "products"—are really the meals (or eating occasions) customers enjoy at the restaurant.

Estimating Market Sizes for Wendy's Now the size of the market in each cell (the unique market-product combination) of the market-product grid must be estimated. For your Wendy's restaurant, this involves estimating the sales of each kind of meal expected to be sold to each student and nonstudent market segment.

The market size estimates in Figure 8–6 vary from a large market ("3") to no market at all ("0") for each cell in the market-product grid. These may be simple guesstimates if you don't have the time or money to conduct formal marketing research (as discussed in Chapter 7). But even such crude estimates of the size of specific markets using a

FIGURE 8–6
A market-product grid for your Wendy's fast-food restaurant next to an urban university. The numbers in the grid show the estimated size of the market in each cell, which leads to selecting the shaded target market.

MARKET SEGMENTS		PRODUCT OR INNOVATION				
General	Where They Live	Break-fast	Lunch	Between-Meal Snack	Dinner	After-Dinner Snack
Student	Dormitory	0	1	3	0	3
	Apartment	1	3	3	1	1
	Day Commuter	0	3	2	1	0
	Night Commuter	0	0	1	3	2
Nonstudent	Faculty or Staff	0	3	1	1	0
	Live in Area	0	1	2	2	1
	Work in Area	1	3	0	1	0

Key: 3 = Large market; 2 = Medium market; 1 = Small market; and 0 = No market

Wendy's has been aggressive in introducing new menu items—such as its Asiago Ranch Chicken Club—to appeal to fast-food customers.
Source: Wendy's International, LLC

market-product grid are helpful in determining which target market segments to select and which product groupings to offer.

Step 4: Select Target Markets

A firm must take care to choose its target market segments carefully. If it picks too narrow a set of segments, it may fail to reach the volume of sales and profits it needs. If it selects too broad a set of segments, it may spread its marketing efforts so thinly that the extra expense exceeds the increased sales and profits.

Criteria to Use in Selecting the Target Segments Two kinds of criteria in the market segmentation process are those used to (1) divide the market into segments (discussed earlier) and (2) actually pick the target segments. Even experienced marketing executives often confuse them. Five criteria can be used to select the target segments for your Wendy's restaurant:

- *Market size*. The estimated size of the market in the segment is an important factor in deciding whether it's worth going after. There is really no market for breakfasts among dormitory students with meal plans, so you should not devote any marketing effort toward reaching this tiny segment. In your market-product grid (Figure 8–6), this market segment is given a "0" to indicate there is no market.
- *Expected growth*. Although the size of the market in the segment may be small now, perhaps it is growing significantly or is expected to grow in the future. Sales of fast-food meals eaten outside the restaurants are projected to exceed those eaten inside. And Wendy's has been shown to be the fast-food leader in average time to serve a drive-thru order—faster than McDonald's. This speed and convenience is potentially very important to night commuters in adult education programs.
- *Competitive position*. Is there a lot of competition in the segment now or is there likely to be in the future? The less the competition, the more attractive the segment is. For example, if the college dormitories announce a new policy of "no meals on weekends," this segment is suddenly more promising for your restaurant. Wendy's recently introduced the "My Wendy's" mobile app for ordering and making payments at its restaurants to keep up with a similar service at Burger King.
- *Cost of reaching the segment*. A segment that is inaccessible to a firm's marketing actions should not be pursued. For example, the few nonstudents who live in the area may not be reachable with ads in newspapers or other media. As a result, you should not waste money trying to advertise to them.
- *Compatibility with the organization's objectives and resources*. If your Wendy's restaurant doesn't yet have the cooking equipment to make breakfasts and has a policy against spending more money on restaurant equipment, then don't try to reach the breakfast segment. As is often the case in marketing decisions, a particular segment may appear attractive according to some criteria and very unattractive according to others.

Choose the Wendy's Segments Ultimately, a marketing executive has to use these criteria to choose the segments for special marketing efforts. As shown in Figure 8–6, let's assume you've written off the breakfast product grouping for two reasons: It's too small a market and it's incompatible with your objectives and resources. In terms of competitive position and cost of reaching the segment, you focus on the four student segments and *not* the three nonstudent segments (although you're certainly not going to turn their business away!). This combination of market-product segments—your target market—is shaded in Figure 8–6.

Step 5: Take Marketing Actions to Reach Target Markets

The purpose of developing a market-product grid is to trigger marketing actions to increase sales and profits. This means that someone must develop and execute an action plan in the form of a marketing program.

Your Immediate Wendy's Segmentation Strategy With your Wendy's restaurant you've already reached one significant decision: There is a limited market for breakfast, so you won't open for business until 10:00 A.M. In fact, Wendy's first attempt at a breakfast menu was a disaster and was discontinued in 1986. However, that strategy has changed yet again with a limited breakfast menu now being offered in some locations.

Another essential decision is where and what meals to advertise to reach specific market segments. An ad in the student newspaper could reach all the student segments, but it might be too expensive. If you choose three segments for special attention (Figure 8–7), advertising actions to reach them might include:

- *Day commuters* (an entire market segment). Run ads inside commuter buses and put flyers under the windshield wipers of cars in parking lots used by day commuters. These ads and flyers promote all the meals at your restaurant to the day commuter segment of students, a horizontal orange row through the product groupings or "meals" in your market-product grid.
- *Between-meal snacks* (directed to all four student market segments). To promote eating during this downtime for your restaurant, offer "Ten percent off all purchases between 2:00 and 4:30 P.M. during spring semester." This ad promotes a single meal to all four student segments, a vertical blue column through the market-product grid.
- *Dinners to night commuters* (selecting a unique market-product combination). The most focused of all three campaigns, this strategy promotes a single meal to the single segment of night commuter students shaded green. The campaign uses flyers placed under the windshield wipers of cars in night parking lots. To encourage eating dinner at Wendy's, offer a free Frosty with the coupon when the person buys a meal between 5 and 8 P.M. using the drive-thru window.

FIGURE 8–7
Advertising actions to market various meals to a range of possible market segments of students.

MARKET SEGMENTS	PRODUCT GROUPINGS: MEAL OCCASION			
Behavioral: Where They Live	Lunch	Between-Meal Snack	Dinner	After-Dinner Snack
Dormitory Students	1	3	0	3
Apartment Students	3	3	1	1
Day Commuter Students	3	2	1	0
Night Commuter Students	0	1	3	2

Ads in buses; flyers under windshield wipers of cars in parking lots

Ad campaign: "10% off all purchases between 2:00 and 4:30 P.M. during spring semester"

Ad on flyer under windshield wipers of cars in night parking lots: "Free Frosty with this coupon when you buy a drive-thru meal between 5:00 and 8:00 P.M."

Key: 3 = Large market; 2 = Medium market; 1 = Small market; and 0 = No market

Depending on how your advertising actions work, you can repeat, modify, or drop them and design new campaigns for other segments you deem are worth the effort. This advertising example is just a small piece of a complete marketing program for your Wendy's restaurant.

Keeping an Eye on Competition Competitors will not be sitting still, so in running your Wendy's you must be aware of their strategies as well. McDonald's, for example, continues to expand its popular all-day breakfast menu. In addition, McDonald's is testing sustainable beef, slushies in three flavors, and a mobile ordering and payment platform. Meanwhile, Burger King tested Mac n' Cheetos in response to a trend of blending fast food with well-known snack foods, and it replaced its Tendercrisp chicken sandwich with a Crispy Chicken sandwich in response to consumer comments on social media.[17]

There's always plenty of competition in the hamburger business. Five Guys Burgers and Fries has grown to more than 1,500 outlets.
©ZUMA Press/Alamy Stock Photo

Even new hamburger chains are popping up. In 1986, a Virginia husband-and-wife team started the Five Guys Burgers and Fries hamburger restaurant and 15 years later had only five restaurants in the Washington, D.C., area. But from 2003 to 2018, Five Guys exploded, with more than 1,500 locations nationwide and another 1,500 new restaurants planned. Some of its points of difference: simple menu and decor, modest prices, only fresh ground beef (none frozen), and a trans-fat-free menu (cooking with peanut oil). But who's keeping track? The Big Three of McDonald's, Burger King, and Wendy's certainly are.[18]

In addition to competition from traditional hamburger chains like Five Guys, all three are responding aggressively to reach the new "fast-casual" market segment. These customers want healthier food and lower prices in sit-down restaurants—a market segment being successfully targeted by fast-casual restaurants like Chipotle Mexican Grill, Noodles and Company, and Panera Bread.[19]

Finally, a new source of competition is emerging from a variety of chains that aren't necessarily classified as restaurants at all. These include convenience store chains like 7-Eleven, coffee shops like Starbucks, smoothie outlets like Jamba Juice, and gas stations with prepared and reheatable packaged food.[20] Many of these outlets are now selling food items and trying to gain market share from the Big Three.

Future Strategies for Your Wendy's Restaurant Changing customer tastes and competition mean you must alter your strategies when necessary. This involves looking at (1) what Wendy's headquarters is doing, (2) what competitors are doing, and (3) what might be changing in the area served by your restaurant.

Wendy's recently introduced aggressive new marketing programs that include:[21]

- Advertising its use of fresh beef that has not been frozen; switching to eggs from cage-free hens; and testing new menu items such as a Spicy Sriracha Chicken sandwich.
- Increasing convenience for customers by adding more than 1,000 self-service ordering kiosks; and testing home delivery in several markets, including India, Dubai, and Manila.
- Becoming the official hamburger of the NCAA and kicking off the campaign with TV ads, a Wendy's food truck tour, and social media promotions during March Madness.

The Wendy's strategy has been remarkably successful, replacing Burger King as the #2 burger chain in terms of sales behind McDonald's, and it has reported growth in average sales per store during a period when McDonald's has experienced declining demand. In addition, a recent *Consumer Reports* survey of the best and worst fast-food restaurants in America ranked Wendy's burgers higher than McDonald's, Burger King, and three other burger chain options.[22]

With these corporate Wendy's plans and new actions from competitors, maybe you'd better rethink your market segmentation decisions on hours of operation. Also, if new businesses have moved into your area, what about a new strategy to reach people that work in the area? Or you might consider a new promotion for the night owls and early birds—the 12 A.M. to 5 A.M. customers.

Apple's Ever-Changing Segmentation Strategy

Steve Jobs and Steve Wozniak didn't realize they were developing today's multibillion-dollar PC industry when they invented the Apple I in a garage on April Fool's Day in 1976. However, when the Apple II was displayed at a computer trade show in 1977, consumers loved it and Apple Computer was born. Typical of young companies, Apple focused on its products and had little concern for its markets. Its creative, young engineers were often likened to "Boy Scouts without adult supervision."[23] Yet in 1984 the new Apple Macintosh revolutionized computers, and its 1984 Super Bowl TV ad is generally recognized as the best TV ad in history.

Steve Jobs detailed his vision for a reincarnated Apple by describing a new market segmentation strategy that he called the "Apple Product Matrix." This strategy consisted of developing two general types of computer products (desktops and laptops) targeted at two market segments—the consumer and professional sectors.

In most segmentation situations, a single product does not fit into an exclusive market niche. Rather, product lines and market segments overlap. So Apple's market segmentation strategy enables it to offer different products to meet the needs of different market segments, as shown in the Marketing Matters box.

Market-Product Synergies: A Balancing Act

Recognizing opportunities for key synergies—that is, efficiencies—is vital to success in selecting target market segments and making marketing decisions. Market-product grids illustrate where such synergies can be found. How? Let's consider Apple's market-product grid in the Marketing Matters box and examine the difference between marketing synergies and product synergies shown there.

> Video 8-3
> **Apple's 1984 Super Bowl Ad**
> kerin.tv/cr8e/v8-3

How has Apple moved from its 1977 Apple II to today's iMac? The Marketing Matters box provides insights.
©SSPL/Getty Images

What market-product synergies does Apple's iMac satisfy? Read the text to find out.
Source: Apple Inc.

- *Marketing synergies*. Running horizontally across the grid, each row represents an opportunity for efficiency in terms of a market segment. Were Apple to focus on just one group of consumers, such as the medium/large business segment, its marketing efforts could be streamlined. Apple would not have to spend time learning about the buying habits of students or college faculty. So it could probably create a single ad to reach the medium/large business target segment (the yellow row), highlighting only those products it would need to worry about developing: the Mac Pro, the MacBook Pro, the iMac, the MacBook Air, and the Mac Mini. Although clearly not Apple's strategy today, new firms often focus only on a single customer segment.

- *Product synergies*. Running vertically down the market-product grid, each column represents an opportunity for efficiency in research and development (R&D) and production. If Apple wanted to simplify its product line, reduce R&D and production expenses, and manufacture only one computer, which might it choose? Based on the market-product grid, Apple might do well to focus on the iMac (the orange column), because every segment purchases it.

Marketing Matters

Technology

Apple's Segmentation Strategy—Camp Runamok No Longer

Camp Runamok was the nickname given to Apple in its early years because the innovative company had no coherent series of product lines directed at identifiable market segments. Today, Apple has targeted its various lines of Macintosh computers at specific market segments, as shown in the accompanying market-product grid.

The market-product grid shifts as a firm's strategy changes, so the one here is based on Apple's current computer products. The grid suggests the market segmentation strategy Apple is using to compete in the digital age.

MARKETS		COMPUTER PRODUCTS				
SECTOR	SEGMENT	Mac Pro	MacBook Pro	iMac	MacBook Air	Mac Mini
CONSUMER	Individuals			✓	✓	✓
	Small/home office		✓	✓	✓	
	Students			✓	✓	✓
	Teachers		✓	✓		
PROFESSIONAL	Medium/large business	✓	✓	✓	✓	✓
	Creative	✓	✓	✓		
	College faculty		✓	✓	✓	
	College staff			✓	✓	

Photos: Source: Apple Inc.

Marketing synergies often come at the expense of product synergies because a single customer segment will likely require a variety of products, each of which will have to be designed and manufactured. The company saves money on marketing but spends more on production. Conversely, if product synergies are emphasized, marketing will have to address the concerns of a wide variety of consumers, which costs more time and money. Marketing managers responsible for developing a company's product line must balance both product and marketing synergies as they try to increase the company's profits.

learning review

8-5. What factor is estimated or measured for each of the cells in a market-product grid?

8-6. What are some criteria used to decide which segments to choose for targets?

8-7. How are marketing and product synergies different in a market-product grid?

POSITIONING THE PRODUCT

LO 8-5 Explain how marketing managers position products in the marketplace.

When a company introduces a new product, a decision critical to its long-term success is how prospective buyers view it in relation to those products offered by its competitors. **Product positioning** refers to the place a product occupies in consumers' minds based on important attributes relative to competitive products. By understanding where consumers see a company's product or brand today, a marketing manager can seek to change its future position in their minds. This requires **product repositioning**, or *changing* the place a product occupies in a consumer's mind relative to competitive products.

product positioning
The place a product occupies in consumers' minds based on important attributes relative to competitive products.

product repositioning
Changing the place a product occupies in a consumer's mind relative to competitive products.

Two Approaches to Product Positioning

Marketers follow two main approaches to positioning a new product in the market. *Head-to-head positioning* involves competing directly with competitors on similar product attributes in the same target market. Using this strategy, Dollar Rent A Car competes directly with Avis and Hertz.

Differentiation positioning involves seeking a less-competitive, smaller market niche in which to locate a brand. McDonald's tried to appeal to the health-conscious segment with its low-fat McLean Deluxe hamburger to avoid competing directly with Wendy's and Burger King. But this item was eventually dropped from the menu.

Writing a Positioning Statement

Marketing managers often convert their positioning ideas for the offering into a succinct written positioning statement. Ideally, the statement identifies the target market and needs satisfied, the product (service) class or category in which the organization's offering competes, and the offering's unique benefits or attributes provided. The positioning statement is used not only internally within the marketing department but also outside the organization, for example in working with research and development engineers or advertising agencies.[24] Here is the Volvo positioning statement for the North American market:

> *For upscale American families, who desire a carefree driving experience (target market and need), Volvo is a premium-priced automobile (product category) that offers the utmost in safety and dependability (benefits).*

This positioning statement directs Volvo's North American marketing strategy and focuses it product development efforts, such as the inclusion of side door airbags in its automobiles. The statement also directs Volvo's marketing communications message. So Volvo advertising stresses safety and dependability—the two benefits that underlie its award-winning "Volvo for life" slogan.

Product Positioning Using Perceptual Maps

A key to positioning a product or brand effectively is discovering the perceptions in the minds of potential customers by taking four steps:

1. Identify the important attributes for a product or brand class.
2. Discover how target customers rate competing products or brands with respect to these attributes.
3. Discover where the company's product or brand is on these attributes in the minds of potential customers.
4. Reposition the company's product or brand in the minds of potential customers.

perceptual map
A means of displaying in two dimensions the location of products or brands in the minds of consumers to enable a manager to see how they perceive competing products or brands, as well as the firm's own product or brand.

As shown in Figure 8–8, from these data it is possible to develop a **perceptual map**, a means of displaying in two dimensions the location of products or brands in

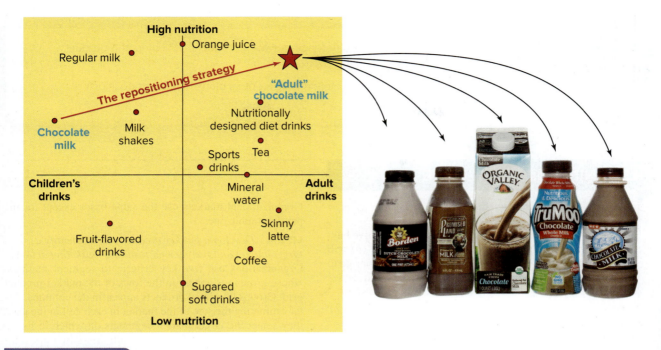

FIGURE 8–8

The strategy American dairies are using to reposition chocolate milk to reach adults: Have adults view chocolate milk as both more nutritional and more "adult."

photo: ©McGraw-Hill Education

the minds of consumers. This enables a manager to see how consumers perceive competing products or brands, as well as the firm's own product or brand.

A Perceptual Map to Reposition Chocolate Milk for Adults

Recently, U.S. dairies decided to reposition chocolate milk in the minds of American adults to increase its sales. This is how dairies repositioned chocolate milk for American adults using the four steps listed above:

1. *Identify the important attributes (or scales) for adult drinks.* Research reveals the key attributes adults use to judge various drinks are (*a*) low versus high nutrition and (*b*) children's drinks versus adult drinks, as shown by the two axes in Figure 8–8.
2. *Discover how adults see various competing drinks.* Locate various adult drinks on these axes, as shown in Figure 8–8.
3. *Discover how adults see chocolate milk.* Figure 8–8 shows adults see chocolate milk as moderately nutritious (on the vertical axis) but as mainly a child's drink (on the horizontal axis).
4. *Reposition chocolate milk to make it more appealing to adults.* What actions did U.S. dairies take to increase sales? They repositioned chocolate milk to the location of the red star shown in the perceptual map in Figure 8–8.

More "zip" for chocolate milk? The text and Figure 8–8 describe how American dairies have successfully repositioned chocolate milk to appeal to adults.

©McGraw-Hill Education

The dairies' arguments are nutritionally powerful. For women, chocolate milk provides calcium, critically important in female diets. And dieters get a more filling, nutritious beverage than with a soft drink for about the same calories. The result: Chocolate milk sales increased dramatically, much of it because of adult consumption.[25] Part of this is due to giving chocolate milk "nutritional respectability" for adults, but another part is due to the innovative packaging that enables many new chocolate milk containers to fit in a car's cup holders.

learning review

8-8. What is the difference between product positioning and product repositioning?

8-9. Why do marketers use perceptual maps in product positioning decisions?

LEARNING OBJECTIVES REVIEW

LO 8-1 *Explain what market segmentation is and when to use it.*
Market segmentation involves aggregating prospective buyers into groups that (*a*) have common needs and (*b*) will respond similarly to a marketing action. Organizations go to the expense of segmenting their markets when it increases their sales, profits, and ability to serve customers better.

LO 8-2 *Identify the five steps involved in segmenting and targeting markets.*
Step 1 is to group potential buyers into segments. Buyers within a segment should have similar characteristics to each other and respond similarly to marketing actions like a new product or a lower price. Step 2 involves putting related products to be sold into meaningful groups. In step 3, organizations develop a market-product grid with estimated sizes of markets in each of the market-product cells of the resulting table. Step 4 involves selecting the target market segments on which the organization should focus. Finally, step 5 involves taking marketing mix actions—often in the form of a marketing program—to reach the target market segments.

LO 8-3 *Recognize the bases used to segment consumer and organizational (business) markets.*
The four bases used to segment consumer markets are: geographic, demographic, psychographic, and behavioral. Organizational markets use the same bases except for the psychographic one.

LO 8-4 *Develop a market-product grid to identify a target market and recommend resulting marketing actions.*
Organizations use five key criteria to segment markets, whose groupings appear in the rows of the market-product grid. Groups of related products appear in the columns. After estimating the size of the market in each cell in the grid, they select the target market segments on which to focus. They then identify marketing mix actions—often in a marketing program—to reach the target market most efficiently.

LO 8-5 *Explain how marketing managers position products in the marketplace.*
Marketing managers often locate competing products on two-dimensional perceptual maps to visualize the products in the minds of consumers. They then try to position new products or reposition existing products in this space to attain maximum sales and profits.

LEARNING REVIEW ANSWERS

8-1 Market segmentation involves aggregating prospective buyers into groups that have two key characteristics. What are they?
Answer: The groups should (1) have common needs and (2) respond similarly to a marketing action.

8-2 In terms of market segments and products, what are the three market segmentation strategies?
Answer: The three market segmentation strategies are: (1) one product and multiple market segments; (2) multiple products and multiple market segments; and (3) "segments of one," or mass customization—the next step beyond build-to-order.

8-3 The process of segmenting and targeting markets is a bridge between which two marketing activities?
Answer: identifying market needs and executing the marketing program

8-4 What is the difference between the demographic and behavioral bases of market segmentation?
Answer: Demographic segmentation is based on some objective physical (gender, race), measurable (age, income), or other classification attribute (birth era, occupation) of prospective customers. Behavioral segmentation is based on some observable actions or attitudes by prospective customers—such as where they buy, what benefits they seek, how frequently they buy, and why they buy.

8-5 What factor is estimated or measured for each of the cells in a market-product grid?
Answer: Each cell in the grid shows the estimated market size of a given product sold to a specific market segment.

8-6 What are some criteria used to decide which segments to choose for targets?
Answer: Possible criteria include market size, expected growth, competitive position, cost of reaching the segment, and compatibility with the organization's objectives and resources.

8-7 How are marketing and product synergies different in a market-product grid?
Answer: Marketing synergies run horizontally across a market-product grid. Each row represents an opportunity for efficiency in the marketing efforts to a market segment. Product synergies

run vertically down the market-product grid. Each column represents an opportunity for efficiency in research and development (R&D) and production. Marketing synergies often come at the expense of product synergies because a single customer segment will likely require a variety of products, each of which will have to be designed and manufactured. The company saves money on marketing but spends more on production. Conversely, if product synergies are emphasized, marketing will have to address the concerns of a wide variety of consumers, which costs more time and money.

8-8 What is the difference between product positioning and product repositioning?

Answer: Product positioning refers to the place a product occupies in consumers' minds based on important attributes relative to competitive products. Product repositioning involves changing the place a product occupies in a consumer's mind relative to competitive products.

8-9 Why do marketers use perceptual maps in product positioning decisions?

Answer: Perceptual maps are a means of displaying in two dimensions the location of products or brands in the minds of consumers. Marketers use perceptual maps to see how consumers perceive competing products or brands as well as their own product or brand. Then they can develop marketing actions to move their product or brand to the ideal position.

FOCUSING ON KEY TERMS

80/20 rule 218
market segmentation 212
market-product grid 213
perceptual map 228
product differentiation 212
product positioning 228
product repositioning 228
usage rate 218

APPLYING MARKETING KNOWLEDGE

1. What variables might be used to segment these consumer markets? (*a*) lawn mowers, (*b*) frozen dinners, (*c*) dry breakfast cereals, and (*d*) soft drinks.
2. What variables might be used to segment these industrial markets? (*a*) industrial sweepers, (*b*) photocopiers, (*c*) production control systems, and (*d*) car rental agencies.
3. In Figure 8–6, the dormitory market segment includes students living in college-owned residence halls, sororities, and fraternities. What market needs are common to these students that justify combining them into a single segment in studying the market for your Wendy's restaurant?
4. You may disagree with the estimates of market size given for the rows in the market-product grid in Figure 8–6. Estimate the market size, and give a brief justification for these market segments: (*a*) dormitory students, (*b*) day commuters, and (*c*) people who work in the area.
5. Suppose you want to increase revenues for your fast-food restaurant even further. Referring to Figure 8–7, what advertising actions might you take to increase revenues from (*a*) dormitory students, (*b*) dinners, and (*c*) after-dinner snacks consumed by night commuter students?
6. Locate these drinks on the perceptual map in Figure 8–8: (*a*) cappuccino, (*b*) beer, and (*c*) soy milk.

BUILDING YOUR MARKETING PLAN

Your marketing plan needs a market-product grid to (*a*) focus your marketing efforts and (*b*) help you create a forecast of sales for the company. Use these steps:

1. Define the market segments (the rows in your grid) using the bases of segmentation used to segment consumer and organizational markets.
2. Define the groupings of related products (the columns in your grid).
3. Form your grid and estimate the size of the market in each market-product cell.
4. Select the target market segments on which to focus your efforts with your marketing program.
5. Use the information and the lost-horse forecasting technique (discussed in Chapter 7) to make a sales forecast (company forecast).
6. Draft your positioning statement.

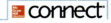

VIDEO CASE 8

Prince Sports, Inc.: Tennis Racquets for Every Segment

Video 8-4
Prince Sports Video Case
kerin.tv/cr8e/v8-4

"Over the last decade we've seen a dramatic change in the media to reach consumers," says Linda Glassel, vice president of sports marketing and brand image of Prince Sports, Inc.

PRINCE SPORTS IN TODAY'S CHANGING WORLD

"Today—particularly in reaching younger consumers—we're now focusing so much more on social marketing and social networks, be it Facebook, Twitter, or internationally with Hi5, Bebo, and Orkut," she adds.

Linda Glassel's comments are a snapshot look at what Prince Sports faces in the changing world of tennis in the 21st century.

Prince Sports is a racquet sports company whose portfolio of brands includes Prince (tennis, squash, and badminton), Ektelon (racquetball), and Viking (platform/paddle tennis). Its complete line of tennis products alone is astounding: more than 150 racquet models; more than 50 tennis strings; over 50 footwear models; and countless types of bags, apparel, and other accessories.

Prince prides itself on its history of innovation in tennis—including inventing the first "oversize" and "longbody" racquets, the first "synthetic gut" tennis string, and the first "Natural Foot Shape" tennis shoe. Its challenge today is to continue to innovate to meet the needs of all levels of tennis players.

"One favorable thing for Prince these days is the dramatic growth in tennis participation—higher than it's been in many years," says Nick Skally, senior marketing manager. A recent study by the Sporting Goods Manufacturers Association confirms this point: Tennis participation in the United States was up 43 percent—the fastest-growing traditional individual sport in the country.

TAMING TECHNOLOGY TO MEET PLAYERS' NEEDS

Every tennis player wants the same thing: to play better. But they don't all have the same skills, or the same ability to swing a racquet fast. So adult tennis players fall very broadly into three groups, each with special needs:

- *Those with shorter, slower strokes.* They want maximum power in a lightweight frame.
- *Those with moderate to full strokes.* They want the perfect blend of power and control.
- *Those with longer, faster strokes.* They want greater control with less power.

To satisfy all these needs in one racquet is a big order.

"When we design tennis racquets, it involves an extensive amount of market research on players at all levels," explains Tyler Herring, global business director for performance tennis racquets. Prince's research led it to introduce its breakthrough O^3 technology. "Our O^3 technology solved an inherent contradiction between racquet speed and sweet spot," he says. Never before had a racquet been designed that simultaneously delivers faster racquet speed with a dramatically increased "sweet spot." The "sweet spot" in a racquet is the middle of the frame that gives the most power and consistency when hitting. Recently, Prince introduced its latest evolution of the O^3 platform called EXO^3. Its newly patented design suspends the string bed from the racquet frame—thereby increasing the sweet spot by up to 83 percent while reducing frame vibration up to 50 percent.

SEGMENTING THE TENNIS MARKET

"The three primary market segments for our tennis racquets are our performance line, our recreational line, and our junior line," says Herring. He explains that within each of these segments Prince makes difficult design trade-offs to balance (1) the price a player is willing to pay, (2) what playing features (speed versus spin, sweet spot versus control, and so on) they want, and (3) what technology can be built into the racquet for the price point.

Within each of these three primary market segments, there are at least two subsegments—sometimes overlapping! Figure 1 gives an overview of Prince's market segmentation strategy and identifies sample racquet models. The three right-hand columns show the design variations of length, unstrung weight, and head size. The figure shows the complexities Prince faces in converting its technology into a racquet with physical features that satisfy players' needs.

MARKET SEGMENTS			PRODUCT FEATURES IN RACQUET			
Main Segments	Subsegments	Segment Characteristics (Skill level, age)	Brand Name	Length (Inches)	Unstrung Weight (Ounces)	Head Size (Sq. in.)
Performance	Precision	For touring professional players wanting great feel, control, and spin	EXO^3 Ignite 95	27.0	11.8	95
	Thunder	For competitive players wanting a bigger sweet spot and added power	EXO^3 Red 95	27.25	9.9	105
Recreational	Small head size	For players looking for a forgiving racquet with added control	AirO Lightning MP	27.0	9.9	100
	Larger head size	For players looking for a larger sweet spot and added power	AirO Maria Lite OS	27.0	9.7	110
Junior	More experienced young players	For ages 8 to 15; somewhat shorter and lighter racquets than high school or adult players	AirO Team Maria 23	23.0	8.1	100
	Beginner	For ages 5 to 11; much shorter and lighter racquets; tennis balls with 50% to 75% less speed for young beginners	Air Team Maria 19	19.0	7.1	82

FIGURE 1
Prince targets racquets at specific market segments.

DISTRIBUTION AND PROMOTION STRATEGIES

"Prince has a number of different distribution channels—from mass merchants like Walmart and Target, to sporting goods chains, to smaller specialty tennis shops," says Nick Skally. For the large chains, Prince contributes co-op advertising for its in-store circulars, point-of-purchase displays, in-store signage, consumer brochures, and even "space planograms" to help the retailer plan the layout of Prince products in its tennis area. Prince aids for small tennis specialty shops include a supply of demo racquets, detailed catalogs, posters, racquet and string guides, merchandising fixtures, and hardware, such as racquet hooks and footwear shelves, in addition to other items. Prince also provides these shops with "player standees," which are corregated life-size cutouts of professional tennis players.

Prince reaches tennis players directly through its website (www.princetennis.com), which gives product information, tennis tips, and the latest tennis news. Besides using social networks like Facebook and Twitter, Prince runs ads in regional and national tennis publications and develops advertising campaigns for online sites and broadcast outlets.

In addition to its in-store activities, advertising, and online marketing, Prince invests heavily in its Teaching Pro

©Consumer Trends/Alamy Stock Photo

program. These sponsored teaching pros receive all the latest product information, demo racquets, and equipment from Prince, so they can truly be Prince ambassadors in their community. Aside from their regular lessons, instructors and teaching professionals hold local "Prince Demo events" around the country to give potential customers a hands-on opportunity to see and try various Prince racquets, strings, and grips.

Prince also sponsors over 100 professional tennis players who appear in marquee events such as the four Grand Slam tournaments (Wimbledon and the Australian, French, and U.S. Opens). TV viewers can watch Russia's Maria Sharapova walk onto a tennis court carrying a Prince racquet bag or France's Gaël Monfils hit a service ace using his Prince racquet.

Where is Prince headed in the 21st century? "As a marketer, one of the biggest challenges is staying ahead of the curve," says Glassel. And she stresses, "It's learning, it's studying, it's talking to people who understand where the market is going."[26]

Questions

1. In the 21st century what trends in the environmental forces (social, economic, technological, competitive, and regulatory) (*a*) work for and (*b*) work against success for Prince Sports in the tennis industry?
2. Because sales of Prince Sports in tennis-related products depends heavily on growth of the tennis industry, what marketing activities might it use in the United States to promote tennis playing?
3. What promotional activities might Prince use to reach (*a*) recreational players and (*b*) junior players?
4. What might Prince do to gain distribution and sales in (*a*) mass merchandisers like Target and Walmart and (*b*) specialty tennis shops?
5. In reaching global markets outside the United States (*a*) what are some criteria that Prince should use to select countries in which to market aggressively, (*b*) what three or four countries meet these criteria best, and (*c*) what are some marketing actions Prince might use to reach these markets?

Chapter Notes

1. Aimee Groth, *The Kingdom of Happiness: Inside Tony Hsieh's Zapponean Utopia* (New York: Touchstone, 2017); Tony Hsieh, *Delivering Happiness* (New York: Hatchette Book Group, 2010); and information from the "About Zappos" section of the Zappos.com website.
2. Greg Bensinger, "How We Shop: Shoppers' Move to Apps Changes Game for Retailers," *The Wall Street Journal,* April 14, 2106, p. B1; Deborah L. Cowles, Jan P. Owens, and Kristen L Walker, "Ensuring a Good Fit: Fortifying Zappos' Customer Service and User Experience," *International Journal of Integrated Marketing Communications,* Fall 2013, pp. 57–66; and Amanda Green, "Know Thy Customer: Behavioral Tracking Brings New Granularity to Segmentation," *On the Beat,* October 19, 2011, p. 11.
3. Susan Adams, "Seven Lessons from the Failure of Shoes.com," *Forbes.com,* March 17, 2017; Chris Paradixo, "Improving Customer Experience with Digital Marketing," *Insurance Advocate,* December 22, 2104, p. 18; and quoted in Kimberly Weisal, "A Shine in Their Shoes," *BusinessWeek,* December 5, 2005, p. 84.
4. Dan Percival, "Why Zappos Pays People to Quit," medium.com, August 1, 2017; and Duff McDonald, "Zappos.com: Success through Simplicity," *CIO-Insight,* November 10, 2006.
5. Jon Wolske, "Ten Core Values Drive Zappos," *Credit Union Magazine,* July 2014, p. 12; Jena McGregor, "Zappos' Secret: It's an Open Book," *Bloomberg Businessweek,* March 23 and 30, 2009, p. 62; and Jeffrey M. O'Brien, "The 10 Commandments of Zappos," *Fortune,* January 22, 2009; see http://money.cnn.com/2009/01/21/news/companies/obrien_zappos10.fortune and www.Zappos.com.
6. Elaine Low, "At Amazon's Zappos, CEO Tony Hsieh Delivers on Being Different," *Investors Business Daily,* August 6, 2016, p. 18; Jennifer Reingold, "The Zappos Experiment," *Fortune,* March 15, 2016, pp. 206–14; and Motoko Rich, "Why Is This Man Smiling?" *The New York Times,* April 10, 2011, pp. ST1, ST10.
7. Dan Pontefract, "What Is Happening at Zappos?" *www.Forbes.com,* May 11, 2015; and Natalie Zmuda, "Marketer of the Year: Zappos," *Advertising Age,* October 20, 2008, p. 36.
8. Eric N. Berkowitz, Roger A. Kerin, and William Rudelius, *Marketing* (St. Louis, MO: Times Mirror/Mosby College Publishing, 1986), pp. 189–91; Sleep Research Institute, the National Sleep Foundation, and the International Sleep Products Association (March 20, 2007); and Frederick G. Crane, Roger A. Kerin, Steven W. Hartley, and William Rudelius, *Marketing,* 8th Canadian ed. (Toronto, Canada: McGraw-Hill Ryerson Ltd., 2011), pp. 229–32.
9. Ellen Byron, "As Middle Class Shrinks, P&G Aims High and Low," *The Wall Street Journal,* September 12, 2011, pp. A1, A16; Ellen Byron, "P&G Puts Spotlight on Newer Products," *The Wall Street Journal,* October 21, 2010, pp. B1, B2; Anthony Bianco, "The Vanishing Mass Market," *BusinessWeek,* July 12, 2004, pp. 61–65; and Geoff Colvin, "Selling P&G," *Fortune,* September 17, 2007, pp. 163–69.
10. John Patrick Pullen, "Hey, Millennials: Here's Where You Can Stream Your Favorite Movies," *Time.com,* April 29, 2015; John Stone, "Disney's Grand Adventure," *Travel Agent,* November 17, 2014, pp. 38, 40; and Jeffrey A. Trachtenberg and Ann Paul Sonne, "Rowling Casts E-Book Spell," *The Wall Street Journal,* June 24, 2011, pp. B1, B2.
11. Jason Lancaster, "What Makes Luxury Cars So Expensive?" *The Huffington Post,* May 19, 2015; and Kathleen Kerwin and Keith Naughton, "Remaking Ford," *BusinessWeek,* October 11, 1999, pp. 132–142.
12. Gordon Wyner, "Why Segment?" *Marketing News,* June 2016, pp. 24–25; Doug DeMuro, "Buying a Car: Why Do So Many Options Come in Packages," *www.autotrader.com,* June 2015; "Company Timeline," Ford website, https://corporate.ford.com/history.html; J. P. Donlon, "The Road Ahead," *Chief Executive,* July–August 2011, pp. 31–37; and "Epiphany in Dearborn," *The Economist,* December 11, 2010, pp. 72–74.

13. Trefis Team, "What's Driving Ann Taylor's Store Count?" *Forbes,* July 17, 2014; 2010 *Ann Taylor Annual Report;* and selected press releases.
14. "Neighborhood Markets Show Ability to Drive Sales," *MMR,* December 19, 2016, p. 59; "Discounters Aim to Extend Reach with Small Formats," *Chain Drug Review,* April 27, 2015, p. 75; and Jonathan Hipp, "The Strategy behind Walmart Neighborhood Market Stores," *GlobeSt.com,* http://www.globest.com/blogs/netleaseinsider/netlease/TheStrategy-Behind-Walmart-Neighborhood-Market-Stores-358653–1.html, June 5, 2015.
15. The relation of these criteria to implementation is discussed in Jacqueline Dawley, "Making Connections: Enhance the Implementation of Value of Attitude-Based Segmentation," *Marketing Research,* Summer 2006, pp. 16–22.
16. Ian Michiels, "Customer Analytics: Segmentation beyond Demographics," *The Aberdeen Group,* August 2008, p. 11.
17. Beth Kowitt, "McDonald's Is Exploring a New Menu Item: Sustainable Beef," *www.fortune.com,* February 27, 2017; William White, "McDonald's New Menu Items 2017: McD Slushies Debut at 6,000 Locations," *www.investorplace.com,* April 12, 2017; Leonie Roderick, "International Bulletin: McDonald's Tests Mobile Ordering," *Marketing Week,* March 16, 2017, p. 1; Austen Hufford, "McDonald's to Expand All-Day Breakfast Menu," *The Wall Street Journal,* July 6, 2016; and Haley Peterson, "Burger King Is Fixing a Huge Weakness in Its Menu after Customers Called It 'Disgusting,'" *Business Insider,* March 2, 2017.
18. Beth Mattson-Teig, "Burger Battle," *Shopping Center Today,* February, 2017, pp. 20–21; Jack Dickey and Bill Saporito, "Beefed Up," *Time,* February 23, 2015, pp. 56–62; and "About Us," Five Guys Burger and Fries website, http://www.fiveguys.com/about-us.aspx, accessed April 23, 2017.
19. Nick Setyan, "Supply Outpacing Demand in Fast Casual and Casual Dining Restaurants," *Wall Street Transcript,* March 24, 2017, pp. 12–14; Justin Fox, "The Once but Not Future Burger," *Bloomberg Businessweek,* May 4, 2015, pp. 14–15; Julie Jargon, "Fast Food Aspires to Move Up the Food Chain," *The Wall Street Journal,* October 11, 2012, p. B11; and Josh Sanburn, "Fast-Casual Nation," *Time,* April 23, 2012, pp. 60–61.
20. Kerry Close, "McDonald's Is Making a Power Move to Compete with Starbucks," *Money,* March 10, 2016; Keith O'Brien, "Supersize," *The New York Times Magazine,* May 6, 2012, pp. 44–48; and "A Look Ahead: 2011–Fast Food," *Advertising Age,* January 20, 2011, p. 4.
21. Maureen Morrison, "Wendy's Has a Beef with Rivals' Frozen Burgers," *Advertising Age,* February 8, 2016, p. 6; Michal Addady, "Wendy's Announces Plans to Use Cage-Free Eggs," *Fortune.com,* January 21, 2016; Michal Addady, "Wendy's Is Now Serving a Sriracha-Inspired Sandwich," *Fortune.com,* December 8, 2016; "Wendy's All Set to Deliver Burgers at Your Doorstep," *FRPT Retail Snapshot,* September 21, 2015; Jed Graham, "Wendy's Serves Up Big Kiosk Expansion as Wage Hikes Hit Fast Food," *Investors Business Daily,* June 11, 2016, p. 1; and Patricia Odell, "Wendy's NCAA Partnership Kicks Off 3 Weeks of Madness," *Promotional Marketing,* March 15, 2017.
22. "Wendy's FY2016 Results Show Impact of Optimization Efforts," *QSRweb.com,* March 1, 2017, p. 39; Maggie McGrath, "As U.S. Sales Slump, Burger King Sees Whopper of an Opportunity Abroad," *Forbes.com,* October 24, 2016; Dan Mitchell, "Here Is What's Going On with All Your Favorite Fast Food Chains," *Time.com,* May 7, 2015; and "Best Fast-Food Restaurant Buying Guide," *Consumer Reports,* April 7, 2016.
23. Glen Sanford and the discussion of Apple's segmentation strategies through the years is based on information from its website, www.apple.com and www.apple-history.com/history.html.
24. Much of the discussion about positioning and perceptual maps is based on Roger A. Kerin and Robert A. Peterson, *Strategic Marketing Problems: Cases and Comments,* 13th ed. (Upper Saddle River, NJ: Prentice Hall, 2013), pp. 146–47; Orville C. Walker Jr. and John W. Mullins, *Marketing Strategy: A Decision-Focused Approach,* 8th ed. (Burr Ridge, IL: McGraw-Hill Education, 2014), p. 202; and "Volvo for Life," http://businessscandinavia.org/volvo-for-life, June 5, 2016.
25. Kimberly J. Decker, "Chocolate Milk Helps Dairy Industry Recover," *Dairy Foods,* October 2016, pp. 32–36; John Sheperd, "Nestle Launches Nesquik Protein Plus for Adults," *Aroq-Just-food.com,* September 30, 2016, p. 4; and Nicholas Zamiska, "How Milk Got a Major Boost by Food Panel," *The Wall Street Journal,* August 30, 2004, pp. B1, B5.
26. Prince Sports: This case was written by William Rudelius and is based on personal interviews with Linda Glassel, Tyler Herring, and Nick Skally.

9

LEARNING OBJECTIVES

After reading this chapter you should be able to:

LO 9-1 Recognize the various terms that pertain to products and services.

LO 9-2 Identify the ways in which consumer and business products and services can be classified.

LO 9-3 Describe four unique elements of services.

LO 9-4 Explain the significance of "newness" in new products and services as it relates to the degree of consumer learning involved.

LO 9-5 Describe the factors contributing to the success or failure of a new product or service.

LO 9-6 Explain the purposes of each step of the new-product development process.

Developing New Products and Services

Apple: The World-Class New-Product Machine

How does a company become the most admired *and* financially valuable organization in the world? Just look to Apple Inc. and its legendary product innovations that have touched the lives of people on every continent for 40 years.

Apple's New-Product Development Successes

Apple's new-product successes, orchestrated by its late co-founder, Steve Jobs, revolutionized five different industries: personal computing, music, smartphones, tablet computing, and digital publishing. A sampling of Apple's market-changing innovations includes:

- Apple II—the first commercial personal computer (1977).
- Macintosh—the first personal computer with a mouse and a graphical user interface (1984).
- iPod—the first and most successful MP3 music player (2001).
- iPhone—the world's best multitouch smartphone and media player with more than 1 million apps (2007).
- iPad (2010) and iPad mini (2012)—the thin tablet devices that allow users to read books, newspapers, magazines, and even textbooks.
- CarPlay—a device that allows you to use your iPhone while driving your car to make calls, listen to music, and access messages by voice or touch (2014).
- Apple Watch—a smartwatch that is a market share leader in wearable technology (2015).
- Apple AirPods—wireless Bluetooth earbuds that revolutionized the headphone market (2017).
- HomePod—a Siri-powered premium speaker and smart home hub (2018).

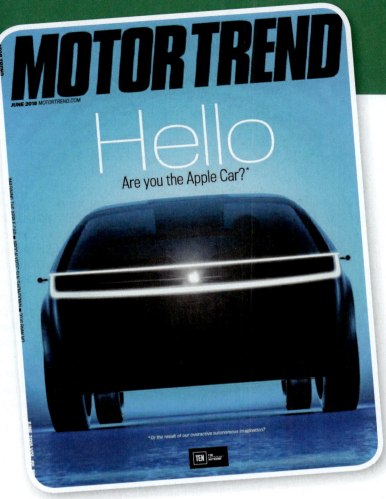

Source: Motor Trend

Apple's New-Product Development Stumbles

But Apple has stumbled at times too in its relentless pursuit of innovation. Examples of notable failures are:

- Apple III (1980) and Apple Lisa (1983)—two products intended for business users that failed due to design flaws. Each product was discontinued four years after introduction.

- Apple Newton (1987)—a personal digital assistant (PDA) that featured handwriting recognition software. Newton was discontinued 10 years later because of its limited battery life and hard-to-read screen.

- Macintosh Portable (1989)—Apple's first attempt to create a battery-powered portable computer. Its high price, coupled with an "un-portable" weight of 16 pounds, led to its demise two years later.

- "Hockey Puck" Mouse (1998)—the first commercially released Apple Mouse to use a USB connection. The mouse's round shape made it difficult to hold and use. It was discontinued in 2000.

These examples illustrate that new-product development is a challenge, even for Apple. Apple learned from each stumble and applied valuable insights from its failures to produce subsequent successes. In short, when a new-product development effort fails, Apple fails wisely. For example, the Macintosh was born from the failure of

Apple Lisa. Apple's iPhone was a direct result of Apple's failed original music phone, produced in conjunction with Motorola.

The Next Chapter in Apple's Story: An Apple-Enabled iCar?

What major innovation is next on Apple's product development horizon? A car? Yes, an Apple-enabled iCar may debut by 2020 with a list price of $55,000.

According to industry insiders, Apple has assembled a team of automotive, design, and computer software engineers to become a player in the automotive industry. The team has the task of applying expertise that Apple has honed in developing its iPhones—in areas such as batteries, sensors, and hardware-software integration—to the next generation of automobiles.

Details on Apple's development efforts are sketchy. It is thought that Apple will partner with an existing car manufacturer to build the actual car. Apple is currently testing its technology on Lexus sport-utility vehicles and Volkswagen vans. The car will have distinctive features: the ability to work with other Apple devices and autonomous capability, including driving, parking, and braking. Expect to learn more about Apple's plans and progress at its newly registered Internet domain name, www.AppleCar, when it goes live.

Independent automotive engineers have provided *Motor Trend* magazine with their conceptualization of what an Apple-enabled iCar might look like. These features are vividly displayed in a recent issue of the magazine, which is also available online. Is the image shown on the *Motor Trend* magazine cover what you might expect from Apple's design engineers?

The life of an organization depends on how it conceives, produces, and markets *new* products and services. This chapter describes the nature of products and services, highlights why new products succeed or fail, and details the new-product development process. Chapter 10 will discuss how organizations manage *existing* products, services, and brands.[1]

WHAT ARE PRODUCTS AND SERVICES?

LO 9-1 Recognize the various terms that pertain to products and services.

The essence of marketing is in developing products and services to meet buyer needs. A **product** is a good, service, or idea consisting of a bundle of tangible and intangible attributes that satisfies consumers' needs and is received in exchange for money or something else of value. Let's clarify the meanings of goods, services, and ideas.

A Look at Goods, Services, and Ideas

A *good* has tangible attributes that a consumer's five senses can perceive. For example, the Apple Watch can be touched and its features can be seen and heard. A good also may have intangible attributes consisting of its delivery or warranties and embody more abstract concepts, such as becoming healthier or wealthier. Goods also can be divided into nondurable goods and durable goods. A *nondurable* good is an item consumed in one or a few uses, such as food products and fuel. A *durable* good is one that usually lasts over many uses, such as appliances, cars, and smartphones. This classification method also provides direction for marketing actions. For example, nondurable goods, such as Wrigley's gum, rely heavily on consumer advertising. In contrast, costly durable goods, such as cars, generally emphasize personal selling.

Services are intangible activities or benefits that an organization provides to satisfy consumers' needs in exchange for money or something else of value. Services have become a significant part of the U.S. economy and often augment products. For example, a product is Apple's iPhone and Verizon is a wireless network service provider.

Finally, in marketing, an *idea* is a thought that leads to a product or action, such as a concept for a new invention or for getting people out to vote.

Nondurable goods like chewing gum are easily consumed and rely on consumer advertising.
©McGraw-Hill Education/Mike Hruby, photographer

238

Throughout this book, *product* generally includes not only physical goods but services and ideas as well. When *product* is used in its narrower meaning of "goods," it should be clear from the example or sentence.

Classifying Products

LO 9-2 Identify the ways in which consumer and business products and services can be classified.

Two broad categories of products widely used in marketing relate to the type of user. **Consumer products** are products purchased by the ultimate consumer, whereas **business products** (also called *B2B products* or *industrial products*) are products organizations buy that assist in providing other products for resale. Some products can be considered both consumer and business items. For example, an Apple iMac computer can be sold to consumers for personal use or to business firms for office use. Each classification results in different marketing actions. Viewed as a consumer product, the iMac would be sold through Apple's retail stores or directly from its online store. As a business product, an Apple salesperson might contact a firm's purchasing department directly and offer discounts for large volume purchases.

Consumer Products   The four types of consumer products shown in Figure 9–1 differ in terms of (1) the effort the consumer spends on the decision, (2) the attributes used in making the purchase decision, and (3) the frequency of purchase. **Convenience products** are items that the consumer purchases frequently, conveniently, and with a minimum of shopping effort. **Shopping products** are items for which the consumer compares several alternatives on criteria such as price, quality, or style. **Specialty products** are items that the consumer makes a special effort to search out and buy. **Unsought products** are items that the consumer does not know about or knows about but does not initially want.

Figure 9–1 shows how each type of consumer product stresses different marketing mix actions, degrees of brand loyalty, and shopping effort. But how a consumer product is classified depends on the individual. One consumer may view a smartphone as a shopping product and visit several stores and websites before deciding on a brand, whereas another consumer may view a smartphone as a specialty product and make a special effort to buy only an iPhone.

Business Products   A major characteristic of business products is that their sales are often the result of *derived demand;* that is, sales of business products frequently result (or are derived) from the sale of consumer products. For example, as consumer demand for General Motors cars (a consumer product) increases, the company may increase its demand for paint spraying equipment (a business product).

Business products may be classified as components or support products. *Components* are items that become part of the final product. These include raw materials such as lumber, as well as assemblies such as a Toyota car engine. *Support products* are items used to assist in producing other products and services. These include:

- *Installations,* such as buildings and fixed equipment.
- *Accessory equipment,* such as tools and office equipment.
- *Supplies,* such as stationery, paper clips, and brooms.
- *Industrial services,* such as maintenance, repair, and legal services.

Strategies to market business products reflect both the complexities of the product involved (paper clips versus private jets) and the buy-class situations discussed in Chapter 5.

Classifying Services

Services can be classified according to whether they are delivered by (1) people or equipment, (2) business firms or nonprofit organizations, or (3) government agencies.

---

product
A good, service, or idea consisting of a bundle of tangible and intangible attributes that satisfies consumers' needs and is received in exchange for money or something else of value.

services
Intangible activities or benefits that an organization provides to satisfy consumers' needs in exchange for money or something else of value.

consumer products
Products purchased by the ultimate consumer.

business products
Products organizations buy that assist in providing other products for resale. Also called *B2B products* or *industrial products*.

convenience products
Items that the consumer purchases frequently, conveniently, and with a minimum of shopping effort.

shopping products
Items for which the consumer compares several alternatives on criteria such as price, quality, or style.

specialty products
Items that the consumer makes a special effort to search out and buy.

unsought products
Items that the consumer does not know about or knows about but does not initially want.

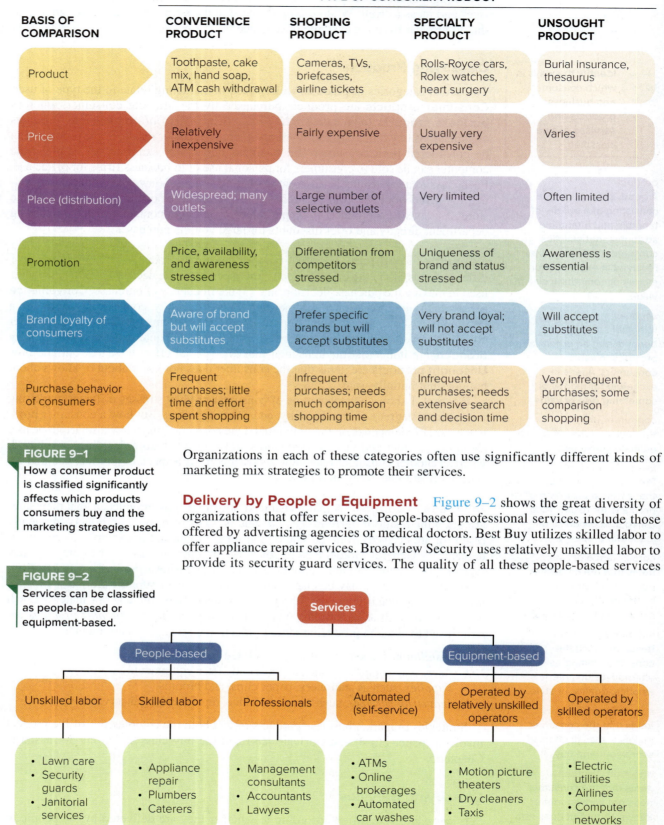

FIGURE 9–1
How a consumer product is classified significantly affects which products consumers buy and the marketing strategies used.

FIGURE 9–2
Services can be classified as people-based or equipment-based.

Organizations in each of these categories often use significantly different kinds of marketing mix strategies to promote their services.

Delivery by People or Equipment Figure 9–2 shows the great diversity of organizations that offer services. People-based professional services include those offered by advertising agencies or medical doctors. Best Buy utilizes skilled labor to offer appliance repair services. Broadview Security uses relatively unskilled labor to provide its security guard services. The quality of all these people-based services

Southwest Airlines is an example of an equipment-based service.
©PSL Images/Alamy Stock Photo

can vary significantly depending on the abilities of the person delivering the service.

Figure 9–2 also suggests that equipment-based services do not have the marketing concern of inconsistent quality because employees generally do not have direct contact when providing the service to consumers. Instead, consumers usually receive these automated services without interacting with any service employees, such as doing self check-in at Southwest Airlines, watching a movie at a local theater, or using Schwab's online stock trading platform.

Delivery by Business Firms or Nonprofit Organizations As discussed in Chapter 2, privately owned companies must make profits to survive, whereas nonprofit organizations seek to satisfy clients and be efficient. The kinds of services each offers affect their marketing activities. Recently, many nonprofit organizations, such as The American Red Cross, have used marketing to improve their communications and better serve those in need.

Delivery by Government Agencies Governments at the federal, state, and local levels provide a broad range of services. These organizations also have adopted many marketing practices used by business firms. For example, the United States Postal Service website, www.usps.com, operates much like an online retailer and its delivery practices are designed to allow it to compete with UPS, FedEx, and DHL in the U.S. and global package delivery business.

The Uniqueness of Services

Four unique elements distinguish services from goods. These are *intangibility, inconsistency, inseparability,* and *inventory*—referred to as the **four I's of services**.

LO 9-3 Describe four unique elements of services.

four I's of services
The four unique elements that distinguish services from goods: intangibility, inconsistency, inseparability, and inventory.

Intangibility Being intangible, services can't be touched or seen before the purchase decision. Instead, services tend to be a performance rather than an object, which makes them much more difficult for consumers to evaluate. To help consumers assess and compare services, marketers try to make them tangible or show the benefits of using the service. For example, American Airlines attempts to make the benefits of flying on its airline more tangible by running an ad showing and emphasizing the comfort of its reclining seats.

Inconsistency Services depend on the people who provide them. As a result, their quality varies with each person's capabilities and day-to-day job performance. Inconsistency is more of a problem in services than it is with tangible goods. Tangible products can be good or bad in terms of quality, but with modern production lines, their quality will at least be consistent. On the other hand, the Philadelphia Phillies baseball team may have great hitting and pitching one day and the next day lose by 10 runs. Organizations attempt to reduce inconsistency through standardization and training.

Inseparability Inseparability means that the consumer cannot distinguish the service provider from the service itself. For example, the quality of large lectures at your university or college may be excellent, but if you don't get your questions answered, find the advising services poor, or do not receive adequate library assistance, you may not be satisfied with the entire educational experience delivered. Therefore, you probably won't separate your perception of the "educational experience"—the service itself—from all the people delivering the educational services for that institution.

idle production capacity
Occurs when the service provider is available but there is no demand for the service.

Inventory Many goods have inventory handling costs that relate to their storage, perishability, and movement. With services, these costs are more subjective and are related to **idle production capacity**, which is when the service provider is available but there is no demand for the service. For a service, inventory cost involves paying the service provider along with any needed equipment. If a physician is paid to see patients but no one schedules an appointment, the idle physician's salary must be paid regardless of whether the service was performed. In service businesses that pay employees a commission, such as a part-time sales associate at The Home Depot, the sales associate's work hours can be reduced to lower Home Depot's idle production capacity.

Today, many businesses find it useful to distinguish between their core product—either a good or a service—and supplementary services. U.S. Bank has both a core service (a checking account) and supplementary services, such as deposit assistance, parking, drive-throughs, and ATMs. Supplementary services often allow service providers to differentiate their offerings from those of competitors to add value for consumers.

Assessing and Improving Service Quality

Once a consumer tries a service, how is it evaluated? Primarily by comparing expectations about a service to the actual experience a consumer has with the service. Differences between the consumer's expectations and his or her actual experiences are identified through *gap analysis*. This analysis asks consumers to assess their expectations and experiences on dimensions of service quality. For airline customers, three dimensions of service quality and the kinds of questions airline customers might ask to evaluate them are as follows:

- Reliability—Is my flight on time?
- Tangibility—Are the gate, the plane, and the baggage area clean?
- Responsiveness—Are the flight attendants willing to answer my questions?

Expectations are influenced by word-of-mouth communications, personal needs, past experiences, and promotional activities, while actual experiences are determined by the way an organization delivers its service.[2] What if someone is dissatisfied and complains? Research suggest that customers who experience a "service failure" will increase their satisfaction if the service provider makes a sincere attempt to address the complaint.[3]

For services in which consumers are simply observers—such as music concerts, zoos, or art museums—conducting marketing research to improve service quality is especially difficult. As shown in the photo, the Detroit Institute of Arts (DIA) observes and interviews visitors to make its galleries more appealing. It discovered that visitors were often confused by the museum's panels—the written descriptions next to the art. So it made the panels more user-friendly by:

- Moving them closer to the art.
- Reducing the maximum word count from 250 to 150.
- Increasing readability by breaking up blocks of text with bullet points, subheadings, color, and graphics.

The result: These changes have significantly increased the "readership" of these descriptive panels, some of which in the past were read by only 2 percent of gallery visitors. To further engage patrons, the DIA now offers augmented reality tours in its art galleries.[4]

Product Classes, Forms, Items, Lines, and Mixes

Most organizations offer a range of products and services to consumers. Each set of offerings can be categorized according to the *product class* or industry to which they belong, like the iPad, which is classified as a tablet device. Products can exist in various *product forms* within a product class (see Chapters 2 and 10). A **product item**

product item
A specific product that has a unique brand, size, or price.

For how the Detroit Institute of Arts uses direct observation and interviews to measure the results of its marketing actions, see the text.
©Fabrizio Costantini

◀ 'The Meeting of David and Abigail' by Peter Paul Rubens. It is one of the gallery's big draws.

Matt Sikora, the museum's director of evaluation, with his hand-held computer. ▼

▲ After noticing that visitors overlooked the gallery summary panel, the museum moved it next to this Rubens.

Museum visitor from ▶ Youngstown, OH.

product line
A group of product or service items that are closely related because they satisfy a class of needs, are used together, are sold to the same customer group, are distributed through the same outlets, or fall within a given price range.

product mix
Consists of all the product lines offered by an organization.

| Video 9-1 |
| Crapola |
| kerin.tv/cr8e/v9-1 |

What company cheerfully tells its customers to "Have a crappy day"? Read the text to find out about this "tasty" offering!
Source: Brainstorm Bakery

is a specific product that has a unique brand, size, or price. For example, Ultra Downy softener for clothes comes in different forms (liquid for the washer and sheets for the dryer) and load sizes (40, 60, etc.). Each of the different product items represents a separate *stock keeping unit* (*SKU*), which is a unique identification number that defines an item for ordering or inventory purposes.

A **product line** is a group of product or service items that are closely related because they satisfy a class of needs, are used together, are sold to the same customer group, are distributed through the same outlets, or fall within a given price range. Nike's product lines include shoes and clothing, whereas the Mayo Clinic's service lines consist of inpatient hospital care and outpatient physician services. Each product line has its own marketing strategy.

The "Crapola Granola" product line started as an edgy party joke from Brian and Andrea Strom, owners of tiny Brainstorm Bakery. The dried **CR**anberries and **AP**ples gran**OLA**—hence the "Crapola" name—also contains nuts and five organic grains sweetened with maple syrup and honey. Its package promises that Crapola "Makes Even Weird People Regular."

Crapola is sold in retail outlets in the Midwest, California, and Oregon as well as online at www.crapola.us. Currently, the company offers other recipes: "Number Two," "Colon-ial Times," and "Kissapoo." These product line extensions enable both consumers and retailers to simplify their buying decisions. So a family liking Crapola might buy another product in the line. With a broader product line, the Stroms may obtain distribution in supermarket chains, which strive to increase efficiencies by dealing with fewer suppliers.[5]

Many firms offer a **product mix**, which consists of all of the product lines offered by an organization. For example, Cray Inc. has a small product mix of three lines (supercomputers, storage systems, and a "data appliance") that are mostly sold to governments and large businesses. Procter & Gamble, however, has a large product mix that includes product lines such as beauty and grooming (Crest toothpaste and Gillette razors) and household care (Downy fabric softener, Tide detergent, and Pampers diapers).

learning review

9-1. What are the four main types of consumer products?

9-2. What are the four I's of services?

9-3. What is the difference between a product line and a product mix?

NEW PRODUCTS AND WHY THEY SUCCEED OR FAIL

LO 9-4 Explain the significance of "newness" in new products and services as it relates to the degree of consumer learning involved.

New products are the lifeblood of a company and keep it growing, but the financial risks can be large. Before discussing how new products reach the market, we'll begin by looking at *what* a new product is.

What Is a New Product?

The term *new* is difficult to define. Was Sony's PlayStation 5 *new* when there was already a PlayStation 4? Perhaps—because the PlayStation 5, Nintendo's Wii U, and Microsoft's Xbox One X all positioned their consoles as entertainment "hubs" rather than just game consoles. What does *new* mean for new-product marketing? Newness from several points of view are discussed next.

Newness Compared with Existing Products If a product is functionally different from existing products, it can be defined as new. Sometimes this newness is revolutionary and creates a whole new industry, as was the case with the Apple smartphone. At other times, more features are added to an existing product to try to appeal to more customers. And as smart TVs, smartphones, smart cars, smartwatches, and tablet devices become more sophisticated, consumers' lives can get far more complicated. This proliferation of extra features—sometimes called product "feature bloat"—overwhelms many consumers and creates an unintended consequence: namely, consumer "feature fatigue." The Marketing Matters box describes the causes of feature bloat and the effect of feature fatigue.[6]

Newness from the Consumer's Perspective A second way to define new products is in terms of their effects on consumption. This approach classifies new products according to the degree of learning required by the consumer, as shown in Figure 9–3.

FIGURE 9–3
The degree of "newness" in a new product affects the amount of learning effort consumers must exert to use the product and the resulting marketing strategy.

BASIS OF COMPARISON	CONTINUOUS INNOVATION	DYNAMICALLY CONTINUOUS INNOVATION	DISCONTINUOUS INNOVATION
	LOW ← Degree of New Consumer Learning Needed → HIGH		
Definition	Requires no new learning by consumers	Disrupts consumer's normal routine but does not require totally new learning	Requires new learning and consumption patterns by consumers
Examples	New improved shaver, detergent, and toothpaste	Electric toothbrush, LED HDTVs, and smartphones	Wireless router, digital video recorder, and electric car
Marketing strategy	Gain consumer awareness and wide distribution	Advertise points of difference and benefits to consumers	Educate consumers through product trial and personal selling

Marketing Matters

Customer Value

Too Much of a Good Thing: Feature Bloat and Feature Fatigue in New-Product Development

Adding more features to a product to satisfy more consumers seems like a no-brainer strategy for success. Right?

Feature Bloat

In fact, most marketing research with potential buyers of a product shows that while they *say* they want more features, in actuality they are overwhelmed with the mind-boggling complexity—or "feature bloat"—of some new products. *Feature bloat* is the tendency for some product developers to add unnecessary features or functionality to a product that are not of any benefit to most consumers and unnecessarily add to the cost of the product.

For example, consumers today can purchase a single product that functions as a cell phone, game console, calculator, text-messaging device, wireless Internet connection, digital camera, MP3 player, and global positioning system. The addition of each feature allows product developers to make claim to a new product . . . and rightly so!

Feature Fatigue

But, research shows that while feature bloat can increase the capability of a new product (relative to existing products) and encourage a purchase, the actual usage experience after purchase can result in consumer dissatisfaction, or feature fatigue. According to researchers at the University of Maryland, *feature fatigue* occurs because "consumers give more weight to capability and less weight to usability before use (of the product) than after use (of the product), they tend to choose overly complex products that do not maximize their satisfaction when they use them."

A common result of feature fatigue is annoyance and a reduced likelihood of repurchase and consumer retention. This phenomenon has been observed in the domain of wearable technology, including digital watches and smart glasses. The figure shows the feature bloat to feature fatigue trajectory from a consumer's point of view. The critical tipping point occurs when the addition of another feature annoys rather than engages a consumer.

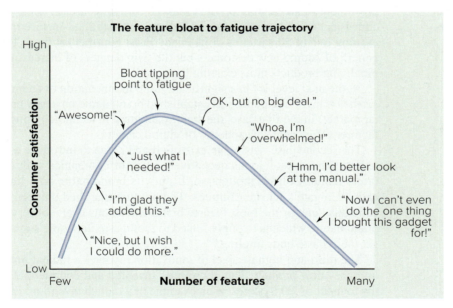

With a *continuous innovation,* consumers don't need to learn new behaviors. Toothpaste manufacturers can add new attributes or features like "whitens teeth" or "removes plaque" when they introduce a new or improved product, such as Colgate Total Advanced Gum Defense toothpaste. But the extra features in the new toothpaste do not require buyers to learn new tooth-brushing behaviors, so it is a continuous innovation. The benefit of this simple innovation is that effective marketing mainly depends on generating awareness, not re-educating customers.

With a *dynamically continuous innovation,* only minor changes in behavior are required. Procter & Gamble's Swiffer WetJet all-in-one mopping solution is a successful dynamically continuous innovation. Its novel design eliminates mess, elbow grease, and heavy lifting of floor cleaning materials without requiring any substantial behavioral change. So the marketing strategy here is to educate prospective buyers on the product's benefits, advantages, and proper use. Procter & Gamble did this with Swiffer. The result? A billion dollars in annual sales.

A *discontinuous innovation* involves making the consumer learn entirely new consumption patterns to use the product. Have you bought a "smart home" gadget from Amazon or Google that controls household systems like security, heating, and lighting? Congratulations if you successfully installed it yourself! Best Buy's Geek Squad and Amazon's Smart Home Services have a thriving business installing and activating these gadgets because they can be complicated to set up and operate appropriately.[7] Marketing efforts for discontinuous innovations usually involve not only gaining initial consumer awareness but also educating consumers on both the benefits and proper use of the innovative product.

Newness in Legal Terms The U.S. Federal Trade Commission (FTC) advises that the term *new* be limited to use with a product up to six months after it enters regular distribution. The difficulty with this suggestion is in the interpretation of the term *regular distribution*.

The text describes the potential benefits and dangers of an incremental innovation such as Purina's Elegant Medleys, its restaurant-inspired food for cats.
Source: Nestlé

Newness from the Organization's Perspective Successful organizations view newness and innovation in their products at three levels. The lowest level, which usually involves the least risk, is a *product line extension*. This is an incremental improvement of an existing product line the company already sells. For example, Purina added its "new" line of Elegant Medleys, a "restaurant-inspired food for cats," to its existing line of 50 varieties of its Fancy Feast gourmet cat food. This has the potential benefit of adding new customers but the twin dangers of increasing expenses and cannibalizing products in its existing line.

At the next level is (1) a significant jump in innovation or technology or (2) a *brand extension* involving putting an established brand name on a new product in an unfamiliar market. In the first case, the significant jump in technology might be when a manufacturer offers new smartphones or digital cameras.

The second case—using an existing brand name to introduce a new product into an unfamiliar market—looks deceptively easy for companies with a powerful, national brand name. Colgate thought so. It puts its brand name on a line of frozen dinners called Colgate's Kitchen Entrees. The product line died quickly. A marketing expert calls this "one of the most bizarre brand extensions ever," observing that the Colgate brand name, which is strongly linked to toothpaste in people's minds, does not exactly get their "taste buds tingling."[8]

The third and highest level of innovation involves a radical invention, a truly revolutionary new product. The 3D printer, invented and commercialized by Chuck Hull, the founder of 3D Systems, is an example of a radical invention. Effective new-product development in firms exists at all three levels.

Why Products and Services Succeed or Fail

We all know the giant product and service successes—such as Apple's iPhone and Netflix. Yet the thousands of product failures every year that slide quietly into oblivion cost American businesses billions of dollars. Ideally, a new product or service needs a precise **protocol**, a statement that, before product development begins, identifies (1) a well-defined target market; (2) specific customers' needs, wants, and preferences; and (3) what the product will be and do to satisfy consumers.

Research reveals how difficult it is to produce a single commercially successful new product, especially among consumer packaged goods (CPG) that appear on

protocol
A statement that, before product development begins, identifies (1) a well-defined target market; (2) specific customers' needs, wants, and preferences; and (3) what the product will be and do to satisfy consumers.

supermarket shelves one month and are gone forever a few months later. Most American families buy the same 150 items over and over again—making it difficult to gain buyers for new products. So less than 3 percent of new consumer packaged goods exceed first-year sales of $50 million—the benchmark of a successful CPG launch.[9]

To learn marketing lessons and convert potential failures to successes, we can analyze why new products fail and then study several failures in detail. As we go through the new-product development process later in the chapter, we can identify ways such failures might have been avoided—admitting that hindsight is clearer than foresight.

LO 9-5 Describe the factors contributing to the success or failure of a new product or service.

Marketing Reasons for New-Product Failures Both marketing and nonmarketing factors contribute to new-product failures. Using the research results from several studies on new-product success and failure, we can identify the critical marketing factors—which sometimes overlap—that often separate new-product winners and losers:[10]

1. *Insignificant point of difference.* Research shows that a distinctive point of difference is the single most important factor for a new product to defeat competing ones—having superior characteristics that deliver unique benefits to the user. Consider General Mills's launch of Fingos, a sweetened cereal flake about the size of a corn chip, with a $34 million promotional budget. Consumers were supposed to snack on them dry, but they didn't.[11] The point of difference was not important enough to get consumers to stop eating competing snacks such as popcorn and potato chips.

2. *Incomplete market and product protocol before product development starts.* Without this protocol, firms try to design a vague product for a phantom market. Developed by Kimberly-Clark, Avert Virucidal tissues contained vitamin C derivatives scientifically designed to kill cold and flu germs when users sneezed, coughed, or blew their noses into them. The product failed in test marketing. People didn't believe the claims and were frightened by the "cidal" in the brand name, which they connected to words like *suicidal*. A big part of Avert's failure was its lack of a product protocol that clearly defined how it would satisfy consumer wants and needs.[12]

The Keurig Kold cold beverage maker produced great-tasting carbonated drinks. So why did it fail? Read the text to find out.
©Suzanne Kreiter/The Boston Globe via Getty Images

3. *Not satisfying customer needs on critical factors.* Overlapping somewhat with point 1, this factor stresses that problems on one or two critical factors can kill the product, even though the general quality is high. Consider the failure of Kold made by Keurig Green Mountain, Inc. The company discontinued its Kold-brand countertop soda machine that allowed users to make chilled Coca-Cola, Dr Pepper, and other carbonated beverages at home. Despite making a great-tasting cold carbonated drink, Kold didn't deliver on other factors consumers considered critical. The machine was too large to fit on most kitchen countertops, the time necessary to produce the drink was too long, and the price was too high. Kold was priced at $370 and the cost per 8-ounce drink was $1.25.[13]

The Hewlett-Packard Tablet was late in its introduction and a generation behind in functionality compared to the Apple iPad 2. The result? Discontinuance two months after its introduction.
©David Paul Morris/Bloomberg via Getty Images

4. *Bad timing.* This results when a product is introduced too soon, too late, or when consumer tastes and preferences are shifting dramatically. Bad timing gives new-product managers nightmares. Hewlett-Packard, for example, introduced its HP Tablet a few years after Apple launched its original iPad, about the same time Apple introduced its next-generation iPad 2 that featured multiple apps. Hewlett-Packard was late and its HP Tablet was significantly behind in apps compared to the iPad 2. Failure to deliver a product that satisfied consumer preferences in a timely manner caused Hewlett-Packard to abandon its HP Tablet two months after its launch.

What dog or cat wouldn't want to drink vitamin-enriched, carbonated bottled water? As it happens, we may never know. Due to a lack of demand by their human companions, the product was short-lived on supermarket shelves.
©Patrick Farrell/KRT/Newscom

5. *No economical access to buyers.* Grocery products provide an example of this factor. Today's mega-supermarkets carry more than 60,000 different SKUs. With about 40,000 new consumer packaged goods (food, beverage, health and beauty aids, household, and pet items) introduced annually in the United States, the cost to gain access to retailer shelf space is huge. Because shelf space is judged in terms of sales per square foot, Thirsty Dog! (a zesty, beef-flavored, vitamin-enriched, mineral-loaded, lightly carbonated bottled water for your dog) must displace an existing product on the supermarket shelves, a difficult task with the high sales-per-square-foot demands of these stores. Thirsty Dog! and its companion product Thirsty Cat! failed to generate enough sales to meet these requirements.

6. *Poor execution of the marketing mix: brand name, package, price, promotion, distribution.* Somewhere in the marketing mix there can be a showstopper that kills the product. Introduced by Gunderson & Rosario, Inc., Garlic Cake was supposed to be served as an hors d'oeuvre with sweet breads, spreads, and meats, but somehow the company forgot to tell this to potential consumers. Garlic Cake died because consumers were left to wonder just what a Garlic Cake is and when on earth a person would want to eat it.

7. *Too little market attractiveness.* The ideal is a large target market with high growth and real buyer need. But often the target market is too small or competitive to warrant the huge expenses necessary to reach it. OUT! International's Hey! There's A Monster In My Room spray was designed to rid scary creatures from a kid's bedroom and had a bubble-gum fragrance. While a creative and cute product, the brand name probably kept the kids awake at night more than their fear of the monsters because it implied the monster was still hiding in the bedroom. Also, was this a real market?

8. *Poor product quality.* This factor often results when a product is not thoroughly tested. The costs to an organization for poor quality can be staggering and include the labor, materials, and other expenses to fix the problem—not to mention the lost sales, profits, and market share that usually result. Consider self-balancing scooters, commonly referred to as "hoverboards." After gaining widespread attention with the media, as well as popularity with teens, hoverboards made by a variety of manufacturers were found to catch fire or explode. Needless to say, hoverboard sales suffered greatly as a result.[14]

Product quality has hampered the commercial potential of hoverboards. Sales plummeted after product safety issues were discovered.
©B Christopher/Alamy Stock Photo

Simple marketing research could have revealed the problems in these new-product disasters. Developing successful new products may sometimes involve luck, but more often it involves having a product that really meets a need and has significant points of difference over competitive products.

Organizational Inertia in New-Product Failures

Organizational problems and attitudes can also cause new-product disasters. Two key ones are:

- *Encountering "groupthink" in task force and committee meetings.*[15] Someone in the new-product planning team meeting knows or suspects the product concept is a dumb idea. But that person is afraid to speak up for fear of being cast as a "negative thinker" or "not a team player" and then ostracized from real participation in the group. Do you think someone on the Life Savers new-product team suspected a Life Savers soda wasn't a good idea but

Applying Marketing Metrics

Which States Are Underperforming?

In 2015, you started your own company to sell a nutritious, high-energy snack you developed. It is now January 2019. As a marketer, you ask yourself, "How well is my business growing?"

Your Challenge

The snack is sold in all 50 states. Your goal is 10 percent annual growth. To begin 2019, you want to quickly solve any sales problems that occurred during 2018. You know that states whose sales are stagnant or in decline are offset by those with greater than 10 percent growth.

Studying a table of the sales and percentage change versus a year ago in each of the 50 states would work but it also would be very time-consuming. A good graphic is better. You choose the following marketing metric, where "sales" are measured in units:

$$\text{Annual \% sales change} = \frac{(2018 \text{ Sales} - 2017 \text{ Sales}) \times 100}{2017 \text{ Sales}}$$

You want to act quickly to improve sales. In your map, growth that is greater than 10 percent is green, 0 to 10 percent growth is orange, and decline is red. Notice that you (1) picked a metric and (2) made your own rules that green is good, orange is bad, and red is very bad.

Your Findings

You see that sales growth in the northeastern states is weaker than the 10 percent target, and sales are actually declining in many of the states.

Annual Percentage Change in Unit Volume, by State

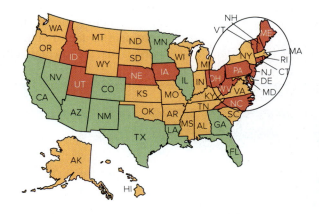

Your Action

Marketing is often about grappling with sales shortfalls. You'll need to start by trying to identify and correct the problems in the largest volume states that are underperforming—in this case in the northeastern United States.

You'll want to do marketing research to see if the problem starts with (1) an external factor involving consumer tastes or (2) an internal factor such as a breakdown in your distribution system.

---

was afraid to speak up? Probably yes, but they didn't, and the soda failed. In the same way, a strong public commitment to a new product by its key advocate may make it difficult to kill the product even when new negative information comes to light. Groupthink can be minimized when team leaders encourage team members to challenge assumptions, express constructive dissent, and offer alternatives.

- *Avoiding the "NIH problem."* A great idea is a great idea, regardless of its source. Yet in the bureaucracy that can occur in large organizations, ideas from outside often get rejected simply because they come from outside—what has been termed the "not-invented-here (NIH) problem." Forward-looking companies attempt to deal with this problem by embracing the policy of open innovation. **Open innovation** consists of practices and processes that encourage the use of external as well as internal ideas and internal as well as external collaboration when conceiving, producing, and marketing new products and services. Approaches to open innovation are highlighted in the description of the new-product development process discussed shortly.

> **open innovation**
> Practices and processes that encourage the use of external as well as internal ideas and internal as well as external collaboration when conceiving, producing, and marketing new products and services.

These organizational problems can contribute to the eight marketing reasons for new-product failures described above.

How Applying Marketing Metrics Can Monitor New-Product Performance

The Applying Marketing Metrics box illustrates how marketers measure actual market performance versus the goals set in new-product planning. In the scenario described, you have developed a new snack and set a goal of 10 percent annual growth. You have chosen a marketing metric of "annual % sales change" to measure the annual growth rate from 2017 and 2018 for each of the 50 states.

Your special concerns are the states shown in red, where sales have actually declined. As shown in the box, having identified the northeastern United States as a problem region, you can now conduct in-depth marketing research to lead to corrective actions. For example, is the decline in sales in this region due to an external factor, such as consumer preference? Perhaps consumers in the northeastern United States prefer more regional snack tastes or think your snack is too sweet. Or perhaps the problem is due to your own internal marketing strategy, such as poor distribution, prices that are too high, or ineffective advertising.

learning review

9-4. What kind of innovation would an improved electric toothbrush be?

9-5. Why can an "insignificant point of difference" lead to new-product failure?

9-6. What marketing metric might you use in a marketing dashboard to discover which states have weak sales?

THE NEW-PRODUCT DEVELOPMENT PROCESS

Explain the purposes of each step of the new-product development process.

new-product development process
The seven stages an organization goes through to identify opportunities and convert them into salable products or services.

To develop new products efficiently, companies such as General Mills and 3M use a specific sequence of steps to make their products ready for market. Figure 9–4 shows the **new-product development process**, the seven stages an organization goes through to identify opportunities and convert them into salable products or services. Today many firms use a formal Stage-Gate® process to evaluate whether the results at each stage of the new-product development process are successful enough to warrant proceeding to the next stage. If problems in a stage can't be corrected, the project doesn't proceed to the next stage and product development is killed.[16]

Stage 1: New-Product Strategy Development

For companies, **new-product strategy development** is the stage of the new-product development process that defines the role for a new product in terms of the firm's overall objectives. During this stage, the firm uses both a SWOT analysis (Chapter 2) and environmental scanning (Chapter 3) to assess its strengths and weaknesses relative to the trends it identifies as opportunities or threats. The outcome not only defines the

FIGURE 9–4
Carefully using the seven stages in the new-product development process increases the chances of new-product success.

250

new-product strategy development
The stage of the new-product development process that defines the role for a new product in terms of the firm's overall objectives.

vital "protocol" for each new-product idea but also identifies the strategic role it might serve in the firm's business portfolio.

Occasionally a firm's Stage 1 activities can be blindsided by a revolutionary new product or technology that completely disrupts its business, sometimes called a "disruptive innovation." For example:

- *Wikipedia*. This free and community-edited online encyclopedia caused Encyclopedia Britannica to cease print production after 244 years.
- *Digital photography*. Even though they were invented by Kodak, digital cameras made film and film cameras obsolete by the mid-2000s and drove Kodak into bankruptcy. Kodak did not actively market its digital cameras because it wanted to protect its film business.

Clearly, a firm's new-product strategy development must be on the lookout for innovative products or technology that might disrupt its plans.

New-product development for services, such as buying a stock or airline ticket or watching a National Football League game, is often difficult. Why? Because services are intangible and performance-oriented. Nevertheless, service innovations can have a huge impact on our lives. For example, the online brokerage firm E*TRADE revolutionized the financial services industry through its online investment trading.

Stage 2: Idea Generation

idea generation
The stage of the new-product development process that develops a pool of concepts to serve as candidates for new products, building upon the previous stage's results.

Idea generation, the second stage of the new-product development process, involves developing a pool of concepts to serve as candidates for new products, building upon the previous stage's results. Many forward-looking organizations have discovered that they are not generating enough useful new-product ideas. One internal approach for getting ideas within the firm is to train employees in the art and science of asking specific, probing questions. The goal in generating new-product ideas and strategies is to move from "what is" questions that describe the present situation to "what if" questions that focus on solutions and marketing actions.[17] The following discussion suggests methods of generating new-product ideas both internally and externally, the latter often using open innovation.

Video 9-2
Life Is Good
kerin.tv/cr8e/v9-2

Suggestions from Employees and Friends Businesses often get successful new-product ideas from employees who ask the "what if" question. For example, a janitor at a Frito-Lay manufacturing plant asked himself, "What if I put chili on a Cheeto?" He then tinkered with a spicy and hot chili-powder recipe at home in his kitchen and asked senior Frito-Lay executives to taste his flavor. The result? Flamin' Hot Cheetos became one of the best-selling snack products in the company's history. As for the janitor, Richard Montanez, he is now an executive vice president at the company.[18]

The breakthrough for the Life Is Good T-shirt business started with a keg party the company founders, brothers Bert and John Jacobs, had with friends. At their parties the brothers often posted drawings with sayings for possible T-shirt ideas on their living room wall and asked their friends to jot down their reactions on the drawings.[19] At one party the drawing of a smiling, beret-wearing stick figure with the phrase "Life is good" got the most favorable comments. They named the character "Jake," printed 48 T-shirts with a smiling Jake and the words "Life is good," and sold out in less than an hour at a local street fair. Today Life Is Good, with its positive, upbeat messages, has $100 million in annual sales. The company sells Life Is Good T-shirts, hats, and other items for men, women, children, and pets in 4,500 retail stores and online in 30 countries.[20]

Brothers John and Bert Jacobs are constantly looking for positive, upbeat messages to print on their Life Is Good T-shirts.
©Michael Dwyer/AP Images

Customer and Supplier Suggestions Firms ask their salespeople to talk to customers and ask their purchasing personnel to talk to suppliers to discover new-product ideas. Whirlpool gets ideas from customers on ways to standardize components so that it can cut the number of different product platforms to reduce costs. Business researchers tell firms to actively involve customers and suppliers in the new-product development process. This means the focus should be on what the new product will actually do for them rather than simply what they want.

A. G. Lafley, former CEO of Procter & Gamble (P&G), gave his executives a *revolutionary* thought: "Look outside the company for solutions to problems rather than insisting P&G knows best." When he ran P&G's laundry detergent business, he had to redesign the laundry boxes so they were easier to open. Why? While consumers *said* P&G's laundry boxes were "easy to open," cameras they agreed to have installed in their laundry rooms showed they opened the boxes with *screwdrivers!*[21]

Video 9-3
P&G's Tide Pods Ad
kerin.tv/cr8e/v9-3

With a $150 million marketing budget, P&G launched Tide Pods, a revolutionary three-chamber liquid dose of detergent that cleans, fights stains, and brightens. P&G describes Tide Pods as "its biggest laundry innovation in more than a quarter century." P&G says the Tide Pods product has produced the highest consumer-satisfaction scores the company has ever seen for a new laundry product. Following its successful new-product launch, however, P&G redesigned its packaging after discovering that some children thought the pods were candy and tried to eat them. How successful has Tide Pods been for P&G? After its first year, the product garnered a 73 percent share of the "unit dose" segment of the detergent market on estimated sales of $500 million—making it one of the company's most successful product launches![22]

Procter & Gamble's new Tide Pods launch shows how it has improved both planning and implementation by involving consumers earlier in its innovation activities.
©McGraw-Hill Education/Mike Hruby, photographer

"Crowdsourcing" is another creative idea generation method if an R&D marketing team wants ideas from 10,000 or 20,000 customers or suppliers. *Crowdsourcing* involves generating insights leading to actions based on ideas from massive numbers of people. This open innovation practice requires a precise question to focus the idea generation process. Dell Technologies used crowdsourcing to develop an online site to generate 13,464 ideas for new products as well as website and marketing improvements, of which 402 were implemented.[23]

Research and Development Laboratories Another source of new products is a firm's own research and development laboratories. Apple's sleek, cutting-edge designs for the iPad, iPhone, iMac, Apple Watch, and AirPods came out of its Apple Industrial Design Group, guided by its chief design officer, Jonathan Ive. What is the secret to Apple's world-class ability to convert vague concepts into tangible products? An action-item list from every meeting that focuses on *who* does *what* by *when*![24]

Professional R&D and innovation laboratories that are *outside* the walls of large corporations are also sources of open innovation and can provide new-product ideas. IDEO is a world-class new-product development firm that uses "design thinking," which involves incorporating human behavior as well as building upon the ideas of others in the innovation-design process. As the most prolific and influential design firm in the world, IDEO has created thousands of new products for its clients. Brainstorming sessions conducted at IDEO can generate 100 new ideas in an hour!

IDEO designs include developing the standing Crest Neat Squeeze toothpaste dispenser and improving the original Apple mouse. Recently, Fresh Express asked IDEO to design an innovative single-serve package for salads. IDEO's solution: A five-section package—one large section for the salad greens and four smaller ones for proteins, dressings, and so on—with each section sealed in plastic (see the photo).[25]

An IDEO innovation: A five-section, single-serve package for salads. Visit IDEO's website (www.ideo.com) to view its recent innovations.
Source: IDEO

Competitive Products Analyzing the competition can lead to new-product ideas. General Motors targeted Tesla Motors as a reference for its Chevrolet Bolt—a $30,000 all-electric vehicle. The Bolt is capable of driving 200 miles in a single charge and features a hatchback design to look more like a crossover vehicle. According to a General Motors executive, the Bolt will "completely shake up the status quo for electric vehicles as the first affordable long-range EV in the market." The Bolt was designed to be a direct competitor to Tesla's Model 3 priced at $35,000.[26]

Smaller Firms, Universities, and Inventors

Many firms look for outside visionaries that have inventions or innovative ideas that can become products. Some sources and outcomes of this open innovation strategy include:[27]

Inventor Aaron Krause has the distinction of introducing the most successful new product on the TV reality show *Shark Tank*.
©John Ziomek/Courier-Post via USA TODAY NETWORK

Crowdfunder Kickstarter.com enabled Pebble to develop and market one of the first commercially successful smartphone-connected smartwatches two years before the Apple Watch.
©Neil Godwin/T3 Magazine via Getty Images

- *Smaller, nontraditional firms.* Small technology firms and even small, nontraditional firms in adjacent industries provide creative advances. General Mills partnered with Weight Watchers to develop Progresso Light soups, the first consumer packaged product in any grocery category to carry the Weight Watchers endorsement.
- *Universities.* Many universities have technology transfer centers that often partner with businesses to commercialize faculty inventions. The first-of-its-kind carbonated yogurt Go-Gurt Fizzix was launched as a result of General Mills partnering with Brigham Young University to license the university's patent to put the "fizz" into yogurt.
- *Inventors.* Many lone inventors and entrepreneurs develop brilliant new-product ideas—like Aaron Krause's Scrub Daddy. This sponge, in the shape of a smiley face, changes its texture in water: hard in cold, soft in hot. Scrub Daddy was pitched on the TV reality show *Shark Tank* and became the most successful product introduced on the program, with total revenues surpassing $100 million.

Early-stage financing is almost always a problem for inventors and those starting a new business because of the risk involved. *Crowdfunding* is a way to gather an online community of supporters to financially rally around a specific project that is unlikely to get resources from traditional sources such as banks or venture capital firms. For example, Kickstarter.com raised $1.2 million for start-up SmartThings to introduce a product that allows users to monitor their homes by remote control. But its biggest crowdfunding success was for the Pebble smartwatch with iPhone and Android smartphone integration. More than 70,000 backers contributed over $30 million to develop and market this product between 2012 and 2016. Nevertheless, Pebble became insolvent in 2016 and its assets were acquired by Fitbit. If you are interested in crowdfunding projects, you should know that for every $10 pledged, about $1 goes toward failed projects. The average Kickstarter donor gives $25.[28]

Great ideas can come from almost anywhere—a central idea behind open innovation. The challenge is recognizing and implementing them.

Stage 3: Screening and Evaluation

screening and evaluation
The stage of the new-product development process that internally and externally evaluates new-product ideas to eliminate those that warrant no further effort.

Screening and evaluation is the stage of the new-product development process that internally and externally evaluates new-product ideas to eliminate those that warrant no further effort.

Internal Approach In this approach to screening and evaluation, a firm's employees evaluate the technical feasibility of a proposed new-product idea to determine whether it meets the objectives defined in the new-product strategy development stage. For example, 3M scientists develop many world-class innovations in the company's labs. A recent innovation was its microreplication technology—one that has 3,000 tiny

Marketing Matters

Technology

Was the Google Glass Half Full or Half Empty?

How did the Google Glass morph from being one of *Time* magazine's best inventions of the year in 2012 to an embarrassing flop in 2015? Perhaps, Google's product development team failed to ask three simple questions: How would consumers perceive Google Glass? Who would use it? and How would it be used?

Google Glass resembled a pair of eyeglasses with a small screen visible to the wearer (see the photo). Its notable features included a touchpad that allowed the wearer to "see" current and past events, such as phone calls, photos, and updates, and a camera to take pictures and record video. The sound, video, and graphics accessed through the screen created an *augmented reality* that overlaid the physical, real-world environment at the same time.

Google started selling a prototype (not the finished product) to 8,000 qualified "Glass Explorers" in April 2013 for $1,500. The intent was to collect feedback on the device and then quickly update and fix problems before a planned launch of the product in May 2014 for the same price. Unfortunately, by releasing Google Glass widely, and charging $1,500, the public believed the device to be a finished product, not a prototype. It quickly became apparent that the prototype suffered from a short battery life, poor sound quality, and distorted images.

The technical problems could be fixed. But Google Glass had more severe problems—all of which related to incomplete concept testing. For example, Google never really understood how consumers would perceive the device. Was it simply a "cool" geeky gadget or wearable, chic eyeglass technology for a broader audience? How would wearers use the technology? As it happened, users immediately embraced the photo and video capabilities, and Google Glass wearers were thrown out of clubs and banned from theaters because of privacy and intellectual property concerns. More troubling, Google Glass wearers were derisively called "Glassholes."

The result? Google Glass was withdrawn from the market in January 2015. A new version of Google Glass, called Glass Enterprise Edition, was introduced in 2018 for use by tech workers at a price of $1,828. Stay tuned on its success.

©Seth Wenig/AP Images

---

gripping "fingers" per square inch. An internal assessment showed 3M that this technology could be used to improve the gripping of both batting and work gloves.

Organizations that develop service-dominated offerings need to ensure that employees have the commitment and skills to meet customer expectations and sustain customer loyalty—an important criterion in screening a new-service idea. This is the essence of *customer experience management* (*CEM*), which is the process of managing the entire customer experience within the company. Marketers must consider employees' interactions with customers so that the new services are consistently delivered and experienced, clearly differentiated from other service offerings, and relevant and valuable to the target market.

External Approach Firms that take an external approach to screening and evaluation use *concept tests,* external evaluations with consumers that consist of preliminary testing of a new-product idea rather than an actual finished product. Generally, these tests are more useful with minor modifications of existing products than with new, innovative products with which consumers are not familiar.

Concept tests rely on written descriptions of the product but may be augmented with sketches, mockups, or promotional literature. Key questions for concept testing include: How does the customer perceive the product? Who would use it? and How would it be used? Failure to address these questions can lead to disastrous results. Consumer response to Google Glass is a case in point, as detailed in the Marketing Matters box.[29]

learning review

9-7. What is the new-product strategy development stage in the new-product development process?

9-8. What are the main sources of new-product ideas?

9-9. How do internal and external screening and evaluation approaches differ?

Stage 4: Business Analysis

business analysis
The stage of the new-product development process that specifies the features of the product and the marketing strategy needed to bring it to market and make financial projections.

Business analysis specifies the features of the product or service and the marketing strategy needed to bring it to market and make financial projections. This is the last checkpoint before significant resources are invested to create a *prototype*—a full-scale operating model of the product or service. The business analysis stage assesses the total "business fit" of the proposed new product with the company's mission and objectives—from whether the product or service can be economically produced to the marketing strategy needed to have it succeed in the marketplace.

This process requires not only detailed sales and profit financial projections but also assessments of the marketing and product synergies related to the company's existing operations. Will the new product require a lot of new equipment or technology to produce it or can it be made using existing machines? Will the new product cannibalize sales of existing products or will it increase revenues by reaching new market segments? Can the new product be protected with patents or copyrights?

Carmakers in North America, Europe, and Asia had to address these and other questions when the initial business analysis for driverless vehicles began a decade ago. The business analysis included R&D and manufacturing expenditures, investments in the acquisition of technology, and production scheduling and product marketing timelines.

Stage 5: Development

development
The stage of the new-product development process that turns the idea on paper into a prototype.

Development is the stage of the new-product development process that turns the idea on paper into a prototype. This results in a demonstrable, producible product that involves not only manufacturing the product efficiently but also performing laboratory and consumer tests to ensure the product meets the standards established for it in the protocol.

The Cruise AV is designed to operate safely on its own, with no driver, steering wheel, pedals, or other manual controls when it goes on the road in 2019 or 2020.
Source: General Motors

Google's driverless car initiative is an extreme example of the complexity of the Stage 5 development process for a durable consumer good. The Google development team relies on a fleet of vehicles as test models, among them the Toyota Prius and the Lexus RX 450h. Google's driverless cars have completed over 3 million miles of driving. These miles are "driven" by a nonhuman driver with an impressive driving record behind the wheel and a Google engineer in the passenger seat. A spinning, roof-mounted laser range finder and sophisticated software navigated the streets of San Francisco and the curvy Pacific Coast Highway.

In 2017, the Google driverless car became part of Waymo, a subsidiary of Google's parent company, Alphabet. Waymo will not commercialize the vehicle itself but intends to market the self-driving technology to carmakers, such as Fiat Chrysler. But there is more to the story. General Motors will introduce the Cruise AV, the first mass-produced self-driving car built from the ground up in 2019 or 2020. This car will have no steering wheel, gas or brake pedals, or other manual controls.[30]

Stage 6: Market Testing

market testing
The stage of the new-product development process that exposes actual products to prospective consumers under realistic purchase conditions to see if they will buy.

Market testing is the stage of the new-product development process that involves exposing actual products to prospective consumers under realistic purchase conditions to see if they will buy. If the budget permits, consumer packaged goods firms often do this by *test marketing,* which involves offering a product for sale on a limited basis in a defined area for a specific time period. The three main kinds of test markets are (1) standard, (2) controlled, and (3) simulated.[31] Because standard test markets are so time-consuming and expensive and can alert competitors to a firm's plans, some firms skip test markets entirely or use controlled or simulated test markets.

Standard Test Markets
In a *standard test market,* a company develops a product and then attempts to sell it through normal distribution channels in a number of test-market cities. Test-market cities must be demographically representative of markets targeted for the new product, have cable TV systems that can deliver different ads to different homes, and have retailers with checkout counter scanners to measure sales. A distinguishing feature of a standard test market is that the producer sells the product to distributors, wholesalers, and retailers, just as it would do for other products.

Depending on the results of a test market, companies will take one of three actions. If the results don't meet expectations, a product is discontinued. If the results are favorable, a full-fledged national product introduction may be undertaken. Alternatively, a company may choose to undertake a *regional rollout,* in which a product is introduced sequentially into geographical areas to allow production levels and marketing activities to build up gradually to support the product.

Controlled Test Markets
A *controlled test market* involves contracting the entire test program to an outside service. The service pays retailers for shelf space and can therefore guarantee a specified percentage of the test product's potential distribution volume. IRI is a leader in supplying controlled test markets to consumer packaged goods firms like General Mills. Its service uses demographically representative cities to track sales made to a panel of households. In some cases the effectiveness of different TV commercials and other direct-to-consumer promotions can be measured.

Consumer products, such as those from General Mills, often use controlled test markets to assess the likely success of new-product, promotional, or pricing strategies.
Courtesy of Bolin Marketing

Simulated Test Markets
To save time and money, companies often turn to *simulated (or laboratory) test markets (STMs),* a technique that somewhat replicates a full-scale test market. STMs are often run in shopping malls, to find consumers who use the product class being tested. Next, qualified participants are shown the product or the product concept and asked about usage, reasons for purchase, and important product attributes. They then see the company's and competitors' ads for the test product. Finally, participants are given money and allowed to

choose between buying the firm's product or the products of competitors in a real or simulated store environment.

Stage 7: Commercialization

commercialization
The stage of the new-product development process that positions and launches a new product in full-scale production and sales.

Finally, the product is brought to the point of **commercialization**—the stage of the new-product development process that positions and launches a new product in full-scale production and sales. This is the most expensive stage for most new products. If competitors introduce a product that leapfrogs the firm's own new product or if cannibalization of its own existing products appears significant, the firm may halt the new-product launch. Companies can face disasters at the commercialization stage, regardless of whether they are selling business products or consumer products. Examples are Boeing's 787 Dreamliner and Burger King's french fries, which are discussed next.

Takeaway new-product lesson from the Boeing 787 Dreamliner: "Innovation . . . can get messy." See the text for details.
©KiyoshiOta/Bloomberg via Getty Images

The Boeing 787 Dreamliner Experience When Boeing announced the design for its Boeing 787 Dreamliner commercial airplane, its technical advances would mean the plane would burn 20 percent less fuel and cost 30 percent less to maintain than present airliners. Boeing invested billions of dollars in the 787's development, and airlines subsequently placed orders for almost 1,300 Dreamliners. But there is more to the story.

As the Dreamliner entered its commercialization stage, airlines around the world began taking deliveries. But with all the new technology in the Dreamliner, the new airplane was plagued by technical nightmares—even after extensive testing. Its wings, made with plastic-reinforced carbon fiber instead of aluminum, proved difficult to produce and attach to the fuselage. And the Dreamliner's new "high-tech skin" failed to dissipate lightning like the old aluminum skin. But an even more serious problem arose: Lithium-ion batteries, which provide electrical power, caught fire on two Dreamliner aircraft, prompting regulators to ground all Dreamliners in service around the world. Perhaps *The Wall Street Journal* gave the best new-product lesson from the Boeing 787 Dreamliner example: "Innovation—for all its value—doesn't come as easily as a catchphrase. It can get messy."[32]

To discover the downs and ups of commercializing a new product, see the text discussion of Burger King's multiyear search for a french fry recipe that can compete with McDonald's.
©McGraw-Hill Education/Mike Hruby, photographer

Burger King's French Fries: The Complexities of Commercialization McDonald's french fries are considered the gold standard against which all other fries in the fast-food industry are measured. But that didn't deter Burger King in taking on McDonald's fries. The company spent millions of R&D dollars developing a french fry designed to retain heat longer and add crispiness.

The result was a thick-cut french fry. It had a new "coating" on the outside to create a "crispy, golden-brown deliciousness" while retaining the heat longer—for at least 10 minutes—because 75 percent of customers eat their fries "on the go" in their cars, offices, or homes. Burger King also launched the largest TV advertising campaign in its history to promote the new fries. The launch turned into a disaster. The reason: Except under ideal conditions, the new fry proved too complicated to get right day after day in Burger King restaurants.

Then, Burger King introduced its "Satisfries" as the french fries in its kids meals. These were intended to help address concerns about nutrition for and obesity in children. Satisfries had about 20 percent fewer calories and 25 percent less fat than its regular fries. But Burger King's effort failed. Burger King discontinued its Satisfries at most of its restaurants because it couldn't communicate a meaningful point of difference to its customers and Satisfries cost more than its regular fries.[33]

learning review

9-10. How does the development stage of the new-product development process involve testing the product inside and outside the firm?

9-11. What is a test market, and what are the three kinds?

9-12. What is the commercialization of a new product?

LEARNING OBJECTIVES REVIEW

LO 9-1 *Recognize the various terms that pertain to products and services.*
A product is a good, service, or idea consisting of a bundle of tangible and intangible attributes that satisfies consumers and is received in exchange for money or something else of value.

A good has tangible attributes that a consumer's five senses can perceive and intangible ones such as warranties; a laptop computer is an example. Goods also can be divided into nondurable goods, which are consumed in one or a few uses, and durable goods, which usually last over many uses.

Services are intangible activities or benefits that an organization provides to satisfy consumer needs in exchange for money or something else of value, such as an airline trip. An idea is a thought that leads to a product or action, such as eating healthier foods.

LO 9-2 *Identify the ways in which consumer and business products and services can be classified.*
Classified by type of user, the major distinctions are consumer products, which are products purchased by the ultimate consumer, and business products, which are products that assist an organization in providing other products for resale.

Consumer products can be classified further based on the effort involved in the purchase decision process, marketing mix attributes used in the purchase, and the frequency of purchase: (*a*) convenience products are items that consumers purchase frequently and with a minimum of shopping effort; (*b*) shopping products are items for which consumers compare several alternatives on selected criteria; (*c*) specialty products are items that consumers make special efforts to seek out and buy; and (*d*) unsought products are items that consumers either do not know about or do not initially want.

Business products can be broken down into (*a*) components, which are items that become part of the final product, such as raw materials or parts, and (*b*) support products, which are items used to assist in producing other goods and services and include installations, accessory equipment, supplies, and industrial services.

Services can be classified in terms of whether they are delivered by (*a*) people or equipment, (*b*) business firms or nonprofit organizations, or (*c*) government agencies.

Firms can offer a range of products, which involve decisions regarding the product item, product line, and product mix.

LO 9-3 *Describe four unique elements of services.*
The four unique elements of services—the four I's—are intangibility, inconsistency, inseparability, and inventory. Intangibility refers to the tendency of services to be a performance that cannot be held or touched, rather than an object. Inconsistency is a characteristic of services because they depend on people to deliver them, and people vary in their capabilities and in their day-to-day performance. Inseparability refers to the difficulty of separating the deliverer of the services (hairstylist) from the service itself (hair salon). Inventory refers to the need to have service production capability when there is service demand.

LO 9-4 *Explain the significance of "newness" in new products and services as it relates to the degree of consumer learning involved.*
From the important perspective of the consumer, "newness" is often seen as the degree of learning that a consumer must engage in to use the product. With a continuous innovation, no new behaviors must be learned. With a dynamically continuous innovation, only minor behavioral changes are needed. With a discontinuous innovation, consumers must learn entirely new consumption patterns.

LO 9-5 *Describe the factors contributing to the success or failure of a new product or service.*
A new product or service often fails for these marketing reasons: (1) insignificant points of difference, (2) incomplete market and product protocol before product development starts, (3) a failure to satisfy customer needs on critical factors, (4) bad timing, (5) no economical access to buyers, (6) poor product quality, (7) poor execution of the marketing mix, and (8) too little market attractiveness.

LO 9-6 *Explain the purposes of each step of the new-product development process.*
The new-product development process consists of seven stages a firm uses to develop salable products or services: (1) *New-product strategy development* involves defining the

role for the new product within the firm's overall objectives. (2) *Idea generation* involves developing a pool of concepts from consumers, employees, basic R&D, and competitors to serve as candidates for new products. (3) *Screening and evaluation* involves evaluating new-product ideas to eliminate those that are not feasible from a technical or consumer perspective. (4) *Business analysis* involves defining the features of the new product, developing the marketing strategy and marketing program to introduce it, and making a financial forecast. (5) *Development* involves not only producing a prototype product but also testing it in the lab and with consumers to see that it meets the standards set for it. (6) *Market testing* involves exposing actual products to prospective consumers under realistic purchasing conditions to see if they will buy the product. (7) *Commercialization* involves positioning and launching a product in full-scale production and sales with a specific marketing program.

LEARNING REVIEW ANSWERS

9-1 What are the four main types of consumer products?
Answer: They are: (1) convenience products—items that the consumer purchases frequently, conveniently, and with a minimum of shopping effort; (2) shopping products—items for which the consumer compares several alternatives on criteria such as price, quality, or style; (3) specialty products—items that the consumer makes a special effort to search out and buy; and (4) unsought products—items that the consumer does not know about or knows about but does not initially want.

9-2 What are the four I's of services?
Answer: The four I's of services are: (1) intangibility, which means that they can't be held, touched, or seen; (2) inconsistency, which means that their quality varies with each person's capabilities and day-to-day job performance; (3) inseparability, which means that the consumer cannot (and does not) separate the deliverer of the service from the service itself; and (4) inventory, which means that inventory carrying costs are more subjective and are related to idle production capacity—when the service provider is available but there is no demand for the service.

9-3 What is the difference between a product line and a product mix?
Answer: A product line is a group of product or service items that are closely related because they satisfy a class of needs, are used together, are sold to the same customer group, are distributed through the same outlets, or fall within a given price range. The product mix consists of all the product lines offered by an organization.

9-4 What kind of innovation would an improved electric toothbrush be?
Answer: continuous innovation—no new learning is required by consumers

9-5 Why can an "insignificant point of difference" lead to new-product failure?
Answer: The new product must have superior characteristics that deliver unique benefits to the user; compared to competitors, its benefits must be sufficient enough to motivate a change in consumption behavior. Without these points of difference, the product will probably fail.

9-6 What marketing metric might you use in a marketing dashboard to discover which states have weak sales?
Answer: The marketing metric—annual percentage change in unit volume by state—will help identify those states that are underperforming.

9-7 What is the new-product strategy development stage in the new-product development process?
Answer: New-product strategy development is the first stage of the new-product process that defines the role for a new product in terms of the firm's overall objectives. During this stage, the firm uses both a SWOT analysis and environmental scanning to assess its strengths and weaknesses relative to the trends it identifies as opportunities or threats. The outcome not only defines the vital "protocol" for each new-product idea but also identifies the strategic role it might serve in the firm's business portfolio.

9-8 What are the main sources of new-product ideas?
Answer: Many firms obtain ideas externally using open innovation, in which an organization finds and executes creative new-product ideas by developing strategic relationships with outside individuals and organizations. Some of these sources include employee and co-worker suggestions; customer and supplier suggestions (either directly, through the firm's salesforce or purchasing department or through crowdsourcing—soliciting ideas via the Internet from large numbers of people); R&D laboratories (both internal to the firm and professional innovation firms such as IDEO); competitive products (analyzing their points of difference that lead to a competitive advantage for them); and smaller, nontraditional technology firms, university technology transfer centers that partner with business firms to commercialize faculty inventions, and lone inventors or entrepreneurs.

9-9 How do internal and external screening and evaluation approaches differ?
Answer: In internal screening, company employees evaluate the technical feasibility of new-product ideas to determine whether they meet the objectives defined in the new-product strategy development stage. For services, employees are assessed to determine whether they have the commitment and skills to meet customer expectations and sustain customer loyalty. In external screening, evaluation consists of preliminary concept testing of the new-product idea (not the actual product itself) using written descriptions, sketches, mockups, or promotional literature with consumers.

9-10 How does the development stage of the new-product development process involve testing the product inside and outside the firm?
Answer: Development is the stage of the new-product process that turns the idea on paper into a prototype—a demonstrable, producible product that can be efficiently manufactured. Internally, laboratory tests are done to see if the product achieves the physical, quality, and safety standards set for it. Externally, market testing is done to expose actual products to prospective consumers under realistic purchase conditions to see if they will buy.

9-11 What is a test market, and what are the three kinds?
Answer: Test marketing involves offering a product for sale on a limited basis in a defined area for a specific time period. The three main kinds of test markets are: (1) standard, (2) controlled, and (3) simulated. In a standard test market, a city (or cities) is

selected that is viewed as being demographically representative of the markets targeted for the new product. Standard test markets must have both cable TV systems that can deliver different ads to different homes and retailers with checkout counter scanners to measure sales results. In a controlled test market, the firm contracts the entire test program to an outside service, which pays retailers for shelf space to guarantee a specified percentage of the test product's potential distribution volume. In a simulated (or laboratory) test market (STM), the firm attempts to replicate a full-scale test market by creating a fictitious storefront in a shopping mall and exposing prospective customers to the product (or concept) and ads from both it and its competitors to see if they will buy.

9-12 **What is the commercialization of a new product?**
Answer: Commercialization, the most expensive stage for most new products, is the last stage of the new-product development process. It involves positioning and launching a new product in full-scale production and sales.

FOCUSING ON KEY TERMS

business analysis p. 255
business products p. 239
commercialization p. 257
consumer products p. 239
convenience products p. 239
development p. 255
four I's of services p. 241
idea generation p. 251
idle production capacity p. 241

market testing p. 256
new-product development process p. 250
new-product strategy development p. 250
open innovation p. 249
product p. 239
product item p. 242
product line p. 243

product mix p. 243
protocol p. 246
screening and evaluation p. 253
services p. 239
shopping products p. 239
specialty products p. 239
unsought products p. 239

APPLYING MARKETING KNOWLEDGE

1 Products can be classified as either consumer or business products. How would you classify the following products? (*a*) Johnson's baby shampoo, (*b*) a Black & Decker two-speed drill, and (*c*) an arc welder.

2 Are Nature Valley granola bars and Eddie Bauer hiking boots convenience, shopping, specialty, or unsought products?

3 Based on your answer to question 2, how would the marketing actions differ for each product and the classification to which you assigned it?

4 In terms of the behavioral effect on consumers, how would a computer, such as an Apple iMac, be classified? In light of this classification, what actions would you suggest to the manufacturers of these products to increase their sales in the market?

5 What methods would you suggest to assess the potential commercial success of the following new products? (*a*) a new, improved ketchup; (*b*) a three-dimensional television system that has taken the company 10 years to develop; and (*c*) a new children's toy on which the company holds a patent.

6 Concept testing is an important step in the new-product development process. Outline the concept tests for (*a*) an electrically powered car and (*b*) a new loan payment system for automobiles that is based on a variable interest rate. What are the differences in developing concept tests for products as opposed to services?

BUILDING YOUR MARKETING PLAN

In fine-tuning the product strategy for your marketing plan, do these two things:

1 Develop a simple three-column table in which (*a*) market segments of potential customers are in the first column and (*b*) the one or two key points of difference of the product to satisfy the segment's needs are in the second column.

2 In the third column of your table, write ideas for specific new products for your business in each of the rows in your table.

VIDEO CASE 9

GoPro: Making All of Us Heroes with Exciting New Products

GoPro CEO Nick Woodman and his college friends loved to surf. It was a passion. As GoPro Vice President of Brand Integrity, Justin Wilkenfeld, explains, "We would run down to the beach to surf every day, trying to balance that with going to classes." The passion turned into a great new product idea when Woodman was surfing in Australia and wanted to capture the experience but couldn't get photographers close enough to obtain good photos. The result was the first GoPro camera which attached to a wrist strap. "The idea was that you could capture that experience hands-free and really focus on enjoying your passion as opposed to worrying about what's on the other side of a screen," Wilkenfeld says.

> Video 9-4
> GoPro Video Case
> kerin.tv/cr8e/v9-4

Chances are that you've viewed some of the millions of videos created by surfers, snowboarders, rock stars, hockey players, parents, sky divers, scuba divers, pilots, and just about anyone with a passion for their life. In fact, GoPro estimates that more than 1 billion minutes of GoPro video are viewed each year, just on YouTube! Woodman and his friends call it "The GoPro Movement."

"Joining the GoPro movement is all about joining the GoPro community around the world," says Wilkenfeld. "This is a group of passionate people that live a big life and love to experience things." GoPro's success at attracting customers from around the world is supported by its commitment to developing new products that meet their needs. According to Wilkenfeld, "One of the biggest challenges of developing technology is getting ahead of the consumer and developing things that you think they are going to need."

©GoPro, Inc.

THE COMPANY

GoPro's history of new-product development is truly inspirational, particularly when the current product line is compared to the first offering. As Kelly Baker, Director of Media Relations, explains, "The first product out on the market was in this big, kind of clunky, plastic housing attached to your wrist that you could flip up and down. It captured images on 35mm film that you would take into a pharmacy or photography studio and get your pictures printed." That product was replaced by the Digital HERO camera which was powered by one AAA battery and provided silent 10-second VGA videos.

Other new products soon followed. GoPro added audio capabilities, wide-angle lenses, and time lapse features. In addition, mountable versions that included Helmet HERO, Motorsports HERO, and Surf HERO expanded its market beyond the wrist-camera positioning. The biggest shift in popularity, however, occurred when GoPro added the HD HERO featuring 1080p images. Complementary products such as removable battery packs, video editing tools, a GoPro app, and Wi-Fi remote controls were also added to the product line.

As the popularity of GoPro products grew so did the company, leading to its IPO on the Nasdaq stock exchange. According to Baker, "the most impressive statistics are the growth in employees and the growth in sales." Today the company has more than 1,300 employees and $1.5 billion in sales.

THE PRODUCT DEVELOPMENT PROCESS AT GOPRO

The stream of new products is essential to GoPro. "What's special for GoPro is that we're a company built on passion and, ultimately, on the shoulders of our consumers," remarks Wilkenfeld. Generally, the company follows a rigorous sequence of steps or stages to maintain its offerings for consumers.

The first stage, new-product strategy development, reflects GoPro's environmental scanning efforts. Initially Woodman and his friends observed the social trend toward sharing experiences. This trend was facilitated through its cameras and the growth of social media. GoPro also recognized a growing interest in capturing unique situations and camera angles where the use of other cameras such as smartphones isn't feasible. To build on this trend the company announced a developer program that allows third-party companies to build GoPro-compatibility into their products. BMW, for example, created an application that combines GoPro video with telemetry data and location data to add value for its customers, while Fisher-Price is planning to build GoPro mounts into its Jumperoo and Walker products to provide a child's perspective.

The second stage is idea generation, which is the result of several distinct activities at GoPro. "When we're developing new products there are two different sources—one being just a crazy idea that an engineer or Nick or somebody on the team has, and then there is a more formulaic approach," say Wilkenfeld. Both approaches work well at GoPro, where employees are so passionate about GoPro they are constantly thinking of new ideas and where an open innovation perspective encourages ideas from consumers, retailers, and a team of amateur and professional athletes. GoPro even offers awards for the best content submitted to its website—in a variety of categories such as action, adventure, music, animals, family, travel, and science—where new and creative ideas are often found.

Screening and evaluation involves an assessment of each idea to determine if it warrants further effort. Although this stage assesses a variety of quantitative requirements of new technologies, GoPro is also careful to assess qualitative aspects of new ideas. "If you are all about the data and you're completely data-driven, then you're only going to be doing things that the consumer is asking you to do, and you're not exploring and experimenting and really coming up with ideas that the customer didn't necessarily know that they needed or wanted," Wilkenfeld explains.

Once an idea is approved, GoPro begins its business analysis step, which involves building a "business case" for the idea. One of the key considerations in this step is the potential for cannibalization. For example, when GoPro introduced its HERO Session camera at a price much lower than other GoPro models it had to consider the possibility of cannibalizing sales of its own products. The amount of time needed to reach break-even points and the likely timing for competitors to respond to new products must also be considered. "Lifecycles are definitely a consideration," says Wilkenfeld.

GoPro begins to turn the idea into a prototype in the development stage. The team often produces a prototype with 3D printers to check the aesthetics and the dimensions of new products. Once the final design is determined, functional prototypes are developed. Wilkenfeld explains, "Our product teams test early prototypes to see if the functionality is there, if it's a viable product to take to market, before we get too far down the path."

Once production-quality prototypes are available, GoPro begins stage six, market testing. The first element of the testing engages GoPro's employees. According to Wilkenfeld, "We have a program every Thursday called Live It, Eat It, Love It which is about living the brand." Employees go out and test GoPro products to provide feedback to the product development teams. A second element of the testing process sends prototypes to social media advocates, professional photographers, athletes, and past consumers to identify final changes to the products.

Changes from market testing lead to the final stage of the new-product development process, commercialization. At this point a good marketing plan is important. According to Wilkenfeld, "To be successful at the launch of a new product you've got to be very cognizant of what the right levers are to pull and what the audiences are, with digital marketing specifically." Stephanie Miller, senior manager of the GoPro Social Team, agrees: "Social media play a huge role in the go-to-market strategies for product releases and product launches. First and foremost, it starts with using social as a listening tool to understand the macro climate and key business trends that we are going to be launching the product into."

Providing its customers with a steady stream of new products means that the new-product development process is an ongoing activity at GoPro. The process varies for different types of products, though. "The typical product development life cycle is really going to depend on the type of product," explains Wilkenfeld. "You have products that could take a few months turnaround time, and then you have products that could take a couple of years, it really just depends on the complexity of the product," he adds. Although GoPro's success has certainly been related to the products it develops, there is also another element to its success. Wilkenfeld smiles and explains that to be successful "you also have to market the products!"

MARKETING AT GOPRO

As you might expect, GoPro is also exceptional at marketing. The fast-moving industry and highly engaged customers necessitate a comprehensive toolbox of marketing activities. Kelly Baker explains,

©GoPro, Inc.

"Consumers want to believe in brands that they feel are authentic and organic in their category. GoPro is about being passionate and exciting and engaging and living a big life and I think that comes across as genuine to our users."

GoPro's marketing activities include traditional media such as print ads in *Outside Magazine* and even a Super Bowl ad. In addition, GoPro uses social media, sponsorships, and an increasing emphasis on content marketing. Stephanie Miller manages all social media channels, including Facebook, Instagram, Twitter, Pinterest, Periscope, and YouTube. "GoPro has a fantastically large social audience. We are over 22 million strong around the world, and we have a presence in over 17 countries," explains Miller. It's not easy, though. Miller describes the situation: "What we share on Facebook could be different than what we share on Twitter, which could differ from our Instagram strategy. It's a very fine-tuned approach."

Video 9-5
GoPro Super Bowl Ad
kerin.tv/cr8e/v9-5

Sponsorships are also a large part of GoPro's marketing program. Baker and her team maintain a roster of about 140 athletes from a wide variety of sports. For example, Kelly Slater (surfing), Chris Cole (skateboarding), Sage Kotsenburg (snowboarding), Lindsay Vonn (skiing), and many others are sponsored by GoPro. "GoPro's athlete sponsorship program often starts very organically, meaning we look for athletes that are already using our camera," Baker explains.

"We want people that are heroes in the sport and in their community" because "we know that is going to make them a wonderful ambassador for our brand," she adds.

A relatively new part of GoPro's marketing program is the growth of content marketing—the creation and distribution of content (e.g., videos, web pages, podcasts, infographics, etc.) for a specific audience. For example, GoPro often buys the rights to self-shot videos with inspiring content, edits them, and posts them to its own channels for additional distribution. Yara Khakbaz, executive producer at GoPro, observes that user-generated content (UGC) and "storytelling" are a unique and powerful aspect of GoPro's program. This new emphasis is the result of additional attention to new target markets. GoPro started with extreme sports enthusiasts, of course, and then added professional markets such as movie directors and producers, and then moms and families, and now travel and adventure enthusiasts. All of these markets are interested in telling their own interesting and powerful stories. As Khakbaz explains, content marketing is "really about building our audience and inspiring our users and our consumers to continue capturing and sharing their stories." "These genuine moments, that raw authenticity, is GoPro," she adds.

The future promises much more authenticity and excitement from GoPro. New products such as the Fusion (a 360-degree video camera) and apps for Cloud connectivity and virtual reality are in development. "GoPro has really helped enable modern storytelling in ways that we didn't even dream of, and what makes it so special for us is that we're constantly validated by people using our products," says Wilkenfeld. "That's what I love about it, is that it's an inspirational place to work."[34]

Questions

1. What are the points of difference, or unique attributes, for GoPro products?
2. What are GoPro's primary target markets? How does content marketing influence these markets?
3. Describe the new-product development process used at GoPro. What are the similarities and differences to the process described in Figure 9-4?
4. Which of the eight reasons for new-product failure did GoPro avoid to ensure the success of its products?
5. Identify one new-product idea you would suggest that GoPro evaluate.

Chapter Notes

1. "Apple iCar Release Date Rumors, Features and Images," www.macworld.co.uk, March 6, 2018; "Apple Car Races to Catch Up," *The Wall Street Journal,* April 25, 2017, pp. B1, B4; "Apple Gears Up for Self-Driving Push," *The Wall Street Journal,* April 15–16, 2017, pp. A1, A4; "The Apple Car, as Imagined by *Motor Trend,*" www.wsj.com, April 14, 2016; "Apple Reveals Storming Apple Watch Success in Best-Ever Quarter," www.forbes.com, January 7, 2018; and "Has Apple Lost Its Design Mojo?" *Fortune,* January 1, 2018, pp. 46–55.
2. Valerie A. Zeithaml, Mary Jo Bitner, and Dwayne D. Gremler, *Services Marketing,* 7th ed. (New York: McGraw-Hill Education, 2017).
3. Anna S. Mattila, "Do Women Like Options More Than Men? An Examination in the Context of Service Recovery," *Journal of Services Marketing,* no. 7 (2010), pp. 499–508; Leslie M. Fine, "Service Marketing," *Business Horizons,* May–June 2008, pp. 163–168; and James G. Maxham III and Richard G. Netermeyer, "A Longitudinal Study of Complaining Customers' Evaluations of Multiple Service Failures and Recovery Efforts," *Journal of Marketing,* October 2002, pp. 57–71.
4. Isaac Arnsdorf, "The Museum Is Watching You," *The Wall Street Journal,* August 18, 2010, pp. D1, D2; and "Like Pokemon Go for Art Lovers, Lumin Brings Augmented Reality to DIA," *www.freep.com,* January 21, 2017.
5. www.crapola.us, retrieved March 20, 2018; "On the Run with Crapola Granola," *Star Tribune,* January 14, 2013, p. D2; and James Norton, "Brian and Andrea Strom of Crapola Granola," *Heavy Table,* January 16, 2013.
6. Debora Viana Thompson, Rebecca W. Hamilton, and Roland Rust, "Feature Fatigue: When Product Capabilities Become Too Much of a Good Thing," *Journal of Marketing Research,* November 2005, pp. 431–42; Ronald T. Rust, Debora Viana Thompson, and Rebecca W. Hamilton, "Defeating Feature Fatigue," *Harvard Business Review,* February 2006, pp. 98–107; Rebecca W. Hamilton, Roland T. Rust, and Chekitan S. Dev, "Which Features Increase Customer Retention," *MIT Sloan Management Review,* Winter 2017, pp. 41–50; and "eMarketer Releases New Report on Declining Interest in Wearables," *emarketer.com,* March 17, 2017.
7. "Amazon Is Quietly Rolling Out Its Own Geek Squad to Set Up Gadgets in Your Home," *www.recode.net,* July 30, 2017.
8. Unless otherwise noted, the examples described in this section appear in "The 25 Biggest Product Flops of All Time," www.walletpop.com/photos/top-25-biggest-product-flops-of-all-time, accessed March 21, 2018; and Zac Frank and Tania Khadder, "The 20 Worst Product Failures," www.saleshq.monster.com/news/articles/2655-the-20-worst-product-failures, accessed March 21, 2018.
9. Joan Schneider and Julie Hall, "Why Most Product Launches Fail," *Harvard Business Review,* April 2011, pp. 21–23.
10. Robert G. Cooper, "New Products: What Separates the Winners from the Losers?" in *The PDMA Handbook of New Product Development,* Kenneth B. Kahn, ed. (New York: Wiley, 2013), pp. 3–34; and Merle Crawford and Anthony Di Benedetto, *New Products Management,* 11th ed. (New York: McGraw-Hill/Irwin, 2015). The examples described in this section come from these sources unless otherwise indicated.
11. Martin Gitlin and Topher Ellis, *The Great American Cereal Book: How Breakfast Got Its Crunch* (New York: Harry N. Abrams, Inc., 2011).
12. The Avert Virucidal tissues and Garlic Cake examples discussed later are described in Robert M. McMath and Thom Forbes, *What Were They Thinking?* (New York: Random House, 1998).
13. "Keurig Will Stop Selling Its $370 Kold Soda Machine," *www.fortune.com,* June 7, 2016.
14. "Hoverboards Recalled for Fire Risk," *The Wall Street Journal,* July 7, 2016, p. B3.
15. The remaining discussion is based on D. Deichmann, L. Rozentale, and R. Barnhorn, "Open Innovation Generates Great Ideas, So Why Aren't Companies Adopting Them?" hbr.org, December 20, 2017; "The 25 Biggest Product Flops of All Time," www.walletpop.com/photos/top-25-biggest-product-flops-of-all-time, accessed March 21, 2017; "Innovation as a Team Wins, Study Finds," *The Wall Street Journal,* August 9, 2018, p. B6; and Cass Sunstein and Reid Hastie, *Wiser: Getting beyond Groupthink to Make Groups Smarter* (Boston: Harvard Business Review Press, 2015).
16. Robert G. Cooper, "The Stage-Gate Idea-to-Launch Process—Update: What's New and NexGen Systems," *Journal of Product Innovation Management,* May 2008, pp. 213–32; and Robert G. Cooper and Anita F. Summer, "Agile-Stage-Gate: New Idea-to-Launch Method for Manufactured New Products Is Faster, More Responsive," *Industrial Marketing Management,* November 2016, pp. 167–180.
17. Hal B. Greyersen, Jeff Dyer, and Clayton M. Christensen, "Why Ask Why?" *ChiefExecutive.Net,* January–February 2012, pp. 40–43.
18. "Flamin' Hot Cheetos: How a Frito-Lay Janitor Created One of the Most Popular Snacks," washingtonpost.com, February 23, 2018.
19. Dinah Eng, "Life Is Good in the T-shirt Business," *Fortune,* May 19, 2014, pp. 39–42.
20. www.lifeisgood.com; and "Life Is Good's $100 Million Ad-Free Global Success Story," www.cnbc.com, May 19, 2015.
21. Sarah Ellison, "P&G Chief's Turnaround Recipe: Find Out What Women Want," *The Wall Street Journal,* June 1, 2005, pp. A1, A16.
22. Jack Neff, "Tide Pods Winning $7 Billion Detergent Wars by Defining Value," *Advertising Age,* December 18, 2012; Dale Buss, "P&G Awash in Success of Tide Pods Despite Wrinkles Along the Way," *Brandchannel,* December 18, 2012; Emily Glazer, "Tide Rides Convenience Wave," *The Wall Street Journal,* February 23, 2012, p. 138; and Emily Glazer, "P&G to Alter Tide Pods Packaging," *The Wall Street Journal,* May 26–27, 2012, p. B3.
23. Barry Bayus, "Crowdsourcing New Product Ideas over Time: An Analysis of the Dell IdeaStorm Community," *Management Science,* January 2013, pp. 226–44.
24. "Rethinking Apple's Recipe for Success," www.nytimes.com, May 26, 2016; and Adam Lashinsky, "Inside Apple," *Fortune,* May 23, 2011, p. 128.
25. Charlie Rose, "How to Design Breakthrough Inventions," *CBS 60 Minutes,* air date January 6, 2013.
26. www.tesla.com, March 1, 2017; and "With Electric Cars, GM Targets Tesla," *The Wall Street Journal,* January 15, 2015, p. B2.
27. Kevin J. Boudreau and Karim R. Lakhani, "Using the Crowd as an Innovation Partner," hbr.org, April 2013; Peter Erickson, "One Food Company's Foray into Open Innovation," *PDMA Visions Magazine,* June 2008, pp. 12–14; and Stephen Key, "Want to Invent Best-Selling Products? Innovate Like the Founder of Scrub Daddy," www.inc.com, September 25, 2017.
28. "The Biggest Crowdfunding Campaigns: Where Are They Now?" *The Wall Street Journal,* May 1, 2018, pp. R1, R2; and "A Concise History of the Smartwatch," bloombergbusiness.com, January 8, 2018.

29. "Google Glass: What Went Wrong," *www.cnn.com,* January 20, 2015; "The Reason Why Google Glass, Amazon Fire Phone, and Segway All Failed," *www.forbes.com,* February 12, 2015; "Google Glass Gets a New Direction," *www.wsj.com,* January 15, 2015; and "Google Glass 2.0 Is a Startling Second Act," *www.wired.com,* July 18, 2017.
30. "GM Is Leading the Self-Driving Car Race While Tesla Lags Far Behind, Report Says," *www.fastcompany.com,* January 16, 2018.
31. Tom J. Brown, Tracy A. Suter, and Gilbert A. Churchill, *Basic Marketing Research,* 8th ed. (Mason, OH: South-Western, Cengage Learning, 2013).
32. Daniel Michaels, "Innovation Is Messy Business," *The Wall Street Journal,* January 24, 2013, pp. B1, B2; Christopher Drew, "Dreamliner Troubles Put Boeing on Edge," *The New York Times,* January 20, 2013; and "Probe of Boeing 787 Battery Fire Expands," *The Wall Street Journal,* January 24, 2013.
33. Maureen Morrison, "Burger King Adds Satisfries Meals," *www.adage.com,* March 23, 2014; "Burger King Stores Discontinue Satisfries and Sales Sizzle," *www.bloombergbusiness.com,* August 13, 2014; and "The French Fry Wars: Burger King Cooks Up a New Recipe," *The Miami Herald,* December 12, 2011.
34. GoPro: This case was written by Steven Hartley and Roger Kerin. Sources: Interviews with GoPro executives Justin Wilkenfeld, Yara Khakbaz, Kelly Baker, and Stephanie Miller; "We Are GoPro: A Guide to the DNA of Our Brand," GoPro, 2016; Aleksandra Gjorgievska, "GoPro Hires Veteran Apple Designer Seeking to Spur Growth," *www.bloomberg.com,* April 13, 2016; Chris Morris, "GoPro Buys Pair of Video Editing Apps," *www.fortune.com,* March 1, 2016; Ardath Albee, "Get Your Fans to Share Their Love: What Every Brand Can Learn from GoPro," *www.contentmarketinginstitute.com,* September 1, 2015; Travis Hoium, "GoPro Finally Starting to 'Get It,'" *www.fool.com,* April 18, 2016; and Marco della Cava, "Google, GoPro Bring Virtual Reality to the Masses with Jump," *USA Today,* May 28, 2015.

10

LEARNING OBJECTIVES

After reading this chapter you should be able to:

LO 10-1 Explain the product life-cycle concept.

LO 10-2 Identify ways that marketing executives manage a product's life cycle.

LO 10-3 Recognize the importance of branding and alternative branding strategies.

LO 10-4 Describe the role of packaging and labeling in the marketing of a product.

LO 10-5 Recognize how the four Ps framework is expanded in the marketing of services.

Managing Successful Products, Services, and Brands

Gatorade: Bringing Science to Sweat for More Than 50 Years

Why is the thirst for Gatorade unquenchable? Look no further than constant product innovation and masterful brand management.

Like Kleenex in the tissue market and Jell-O among gelatin desserts, Gatorade is synonymous with sports drinks. Concocted in 1965 at the University of Florida as a rehydration beverage for the school's football team, the drink was coined "Gatorade" by an opposing team's coach after watching his team lose to the Florida Gators in the Orange Bowl. The name stuck, and a new beverage product class was born. Stokely-Van Camp, Inc. bought the Gatorade formula in 1967 and commercialized the product.

Creating the Gatorade Brand

The Quaker Oats Company acquired Stokely-Van Camp in 1983 and quickly increased Gatorade sales through a variety of means. More flavors were added. Multiple package sizes were offered using different containers. Distribution expanded from convenience stores and supermarkets to mass merchandisers such as Walmart. Consistent advertising effectively conveyed the product's unique performance benefits and links to athletic competition. Global expansion was vigorously pursued.

Today, Gatorade is a global brand and is sold in more than 80 countries. It is also the official sports drink of NASCAR, the National Football League, Major League Baseball, the National Basketball Association, the National Hockey League, Major League Soccer, and the Women's National Basketball Association.

Masterful brand management spurred Gatorade's success. Gatorade entered the bottled-water category with Propel Fitness Water, a lightly flavored water fortified with vitamins, in 1999. The Gatorade Performance Series was introduced in 2001, featuring an Energy Bar, Energy Drink, and a Nutritional Shake.

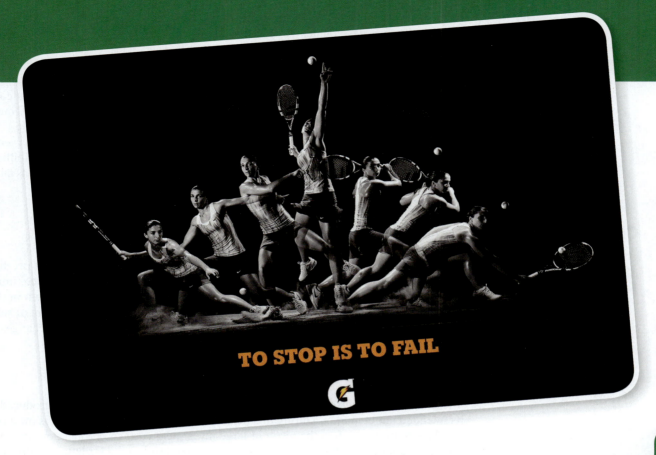

Source: PepsiCo

Building the Gatorade Brand

Brand development accelerated after PepsiCo bought Quaker Oats and the Gatorade brand in 2001. Gatorade Endurance Formula was created for serious runners, construction workers, and other people doing long, sweaty workouts. A low-calorie Gatorade called G2 appeared in 2008.

In 2009, Gatorade executives unleashed a bevy of enhanced beverages in bold new packaging. "Just like any good athlete, Gatorade is taking it to the next level," said Gatorade's chief marketing officer. "Whether you're in it for the win, for the thrill or for better health, if your body is moving, Gatorade sees you as an athlete, and we're inviting you into the brand." According to a company announcement, "The new Gatorade attitude would be most visible through a total packaging redesign." For example, Gatorade Thirst Quencher now displays the letter *G* front and center along with the brand's iconic bolt. "For Gatorade, G represents the heart, hustle, and soul of athleticism and will become a badge of pride for anyone who sweats, no matter where they're active."

Continuing product development efforts guided the creation of the G Series of products in 2010 and 2011. At the time, Gatorade underwent a brand repositioning during which it developed different Gatorade products targeted at different types of athletes. These lines

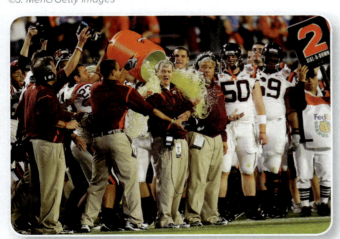

Gatorade's marketing performance is a direct result of continuous product improvement and masterful brand management as defined by the "Gatorade bath."
©J. Meric/Getty Images

Video 10-1
Gatorade Ad
kerin.tv/cr8e/v10-1

included the traditional G Series for athletes and the G Series Endurance for extreme sports athletes. Product development within these lines continues today as evidenced by the launch of new Gatorade chews, bars, powders, shakes, and yogurt. Organic Gatorade was introduced in 2016. Gatorade Flow, a hydrating drink with fewer calories, was launched in 2017.

Gatorade introduced a microchip-fitted "smart cap" bottle and sweat patch that communicate digitally and provide athletes and fitness buffs constant updates on how much they should drink in 2018.[1]

The marketing of Gatorade illustrates continuous product development and masterful brand management in a dynamic marketplace. Gatorade remains a vibrant multibillion-dollar brand more than 50 years after its creation. This chapter shows how the actions taken by Gatorade executives exemplify those made by successful marketers.

CHARTING THE PRODUCT LIFE CYCLE

LO 10-1 Explain the product life-cycle concept.

product life cycle
Describes the stages a new product goes through in the marketplace: introduction, growth, maturity, and decline.

Products, like people, are viewed as having a life cycle. The concept of the **product life cycle** describes the stages a new product goes through in the marketplace: introduction, growth, maturity, and decline (Figure 10–1).[2] The two curves shown in this figure, total industry sales revenue and total industry profit, represent the sum of sales revenue and profit of all firms producing the product. The reasons for the changes in each curve and the marketing decisions involved are detailed next.

Introduction Stage

The introduction stage of the product life cycle occurs when a product is introduced to its intended target market. During this period, sales grow slowly and profit is minimal. The lack of profit is often the result of large investment costs in product development, such as the millions of dollars spent by Gillette to develop the Gillette Fusion razor shaving system. The marketing objective for the company at this stage is to create consumer awareness and stimulate *trial*—the initial purchase of a product by a consumer.

Companies often spend heavily on advertising and other promotion tools to build awareness and stimulate product trial among consumers in the introduction stage. For example, Gillette budgeted $200 million in advertising to introduce the Fusion shaving system to male shavers. The result? Over 60 percent of male shavers became aware of the new razor within six months and 26 percent tried the product.[3]

Advertising and promotion expenditures in the introduction stage are often made to stimulate *primary demand,* the desire for the product class rather than for a specific brand, since there are few competitors with the same product. As more competitors launch their own products and the product progresses along its life cycle, company attention is focused on creating *selective demand,* the preference for a specific brand.

Other marketing mix variables also are important at this stage. Gaining distribution can be a challenge because channel intermediaries may be hesitant to carry a new product. Also, a company often restricts the number of variations of the product to ensure control of product quality. As an example, the original Gatorade came in only one flavor—lemon-lime.

During introduction, pricing can be either high or low. A high initial price may be used as part of a *skimming* strategy to help the company recover the costs of development as well as capitalize on the price insensitivity of early buyers. A master of this strategy is 3M. According to a 3M manager, "We hit fast, price high, and get the heck out when the me-too products pour in."[4] High prices tend to attract competitors eager to enter the market because they see the opportunity for profit. To discourage competitive entry, a company can price low, referred to as *penetration pricing*. This pricing strategy helps build unit volume, but a company must closely monitor costs. These and other pricing techniques are covered in Chapter 11.

The success of the Gillette Fusion shaving system can be understood using product life-cycle concepts, as discussed in the text.
©McGraw-Hill Education/Mike Hruby, photographer

FIGURE 10–1

How stages of the product life cycle relate to a firm's marketing objectives and marketing mix actions.

Figure 10–2 charts the stand-alone fax machine product life cycle for business use in the United States from the early 1970s to early 2019.[5] Sales grew slowly in the 1970s and early 1980s after Xerox pioneered the first portable fax machine. Fax machines were first sold direct to businesses by company salespeople and were premium priced. The average price for a fax machine in 1980 was a hefty $12,700, or about $39,000 in today's dollars! Those fax machines were primitive by today's standards. They contained mechanical parts, not electronic circuitry, and offered few features seen in today's models.

Several product classes are in the introductory stage of the product life cycle today. These include smart TVs and all-electric-powered automobiles.

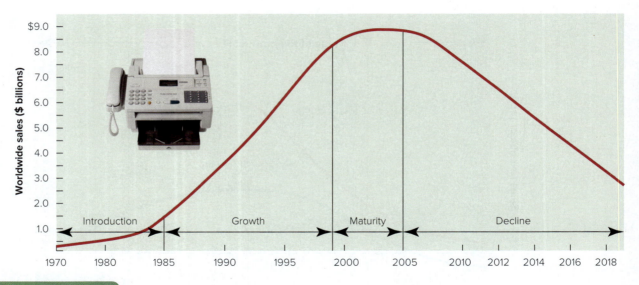

FIGURE 10–2

Product life cycle for the stand-alone fax machine for business use: 1970–2019. All four product life-cycle stages appear: introduction, growth, maturity, and decline.

(photo): ©Getty Images

Growth Stage

The growth stage of the product life cycle is characterized by rapid increases in sales. It is in this stage that competitors appear. For example, Figure 10–2 shows the dramatic increase in fax machine sales from 1986 to 1998. The number of companies selling fax machines also increased, from 1 in the early 1970s to 7 manufacturers in 1983, which sold 9 brands. By 1998 there were some 25 manufacturers and 60 brands from which to choose.

The result of more competitors and more aggressive pricing is that profit usually peaks during the growth stage. For instance, the average price for a fax machine plummeted from $3,300 in 1985 to $500 in 1995. At this stage, advertising shifts emphasis to stimulating selective demand; product benefits are compared with those of competitors' offerings for the purpose of gaining market share.

Product sales in the growth stage grow at an increasing rate because of new people trying or using the product and a growing proportion of *repeat purchasers*—people who tried the product, were satisfied, and bought again. For the Gillette Fusion razor, over 60 percent of men who tried the razor adopted the product permanently. For successful products, the ratio of repeat to trial purchases grows as the product moves through the life cycle. Durable fax machines meant that replacement purchases were rare. However, it became common for more than one machine to populate a business as the machine's use became more widespread.

Changes appear in the product in the growth stage. To help differentiate a company's brand from competitors, an improved version or new features are added to the original design and product proliferation occurs. Changes in fax machines included (1) models with built-in telephones; (2) models that used plain, rather than thermal, paper for copies; and (3) models that integrated e-mail.

In the growth stage, it is important to broaden distribution for the product. In the retail store, for example, this often means that competing companies fight for display and shelf space. Expanded distribution in the fax industry is an example. Early in the growth stage, just 11 percent of office machine dealers carried this equipment. By the mid-1990s, over 70 percent of these dealers sold fax equipment, and distribution was expanded to other stores selling electronic equipment, such as Best Buy and Office Depot.

Numerous product classes or industries are in the growth stage of the product life cycle today. Examples include e-book readers and 3D printers.

Electric automobiles like the Chevrolet Bolt made by General Motors are in the introductory stage of the product life cycle. By comparison, 3D printers are in the growth stage of the product life cycle. Each product faces unique challenges based on its product life-cycle stage.
(left): ©Samuel Corum/Anadolu Agency/Getty Images; (right): ©Tomacco/iStock/Getty Images

General Motors Company
www.gm.com

Maturity Stage

The maturity stage is characterized by a slowing of total industry sales or product class revenue. Also, marginal competitors begin to leave the market. Most consumers who would buy the product are either repeat purchasers of the item or have tried and abandoned it. Sales increase at a decreasing rate in the maturity stage as fewer new buyers enter the market. Profit declines due to fierce price competition among many sellers, and the cost of gaining new buyers at this stage rises.

Marketing attention in the maturity stage is often directed toward holding market share through further product differentiation and finding new buyers and uses. For example, Gillette modified its Fusion shaving system with the addition of Fusion ProGlide, a five-blade shaver with an additional blade on the back for trimming. Fax machine manufacturers developed Internet-enabled multifunctional models with new features such as scanning, copying, and color reproduction. They also designed fax machines suitable for small and home businesses, which today represent a substantial portion of sales. Still, a major consideration in a company's strategy in this stage is to control overall marketing cost by improving promotional and distribution efficiency.

Fax machines entered the maturity stage in the late 1990s. At the time, about 90 percent of industry sales were captured by five producers (Hewlett-Packard, Brother, Sharp, Epson, and Samsung), reflecting the departure of marginal competitors. By 2004, some 200 million stand-alone fax machines were installed throughout the world, sending more than 120 billion faxes annually.

Numerous product classes and industries are in the maturity stage of their product life cycle. These include carbonated soft drinks and presweetened breakfast cereals.

Decline Stage

The decline stage occurs when sales drop. Fax machines entered this stage in early 2005 and the average price for a fax machine had sunk below $100. There are 46 million fax machines installed throughout the world today, sending about 20 billion faxes in 2017. Frequently, a product enters this stage not because of any wrong strategy on the part of companies, but because of environmental changes. For example, digital music pushed compact discs into decline in the recorded music industry. Will Internet

Marketing Matters > Customer Value

Will E-mail Spell Extinction for Fax Machines?

Technological substitution that creates value for customers often causes the decline stage in the product life cycle. Will e-mail replace fax machines?

This question has been debated for years. Even though e-mail continues to grow with broadening Internet access, millions of fax machines are still sold each year. Industry analysts estimated that the number of e-mail mailboxes worldwide would be 5.2 billion in 2018. However, the phenomenal popularity of e-mail has not brought fax machines to extinction. Why? The two technologies do not directly compete for the same messaging applications.

E-mail is used for text messages. Faxing is predominately used for communicating formatted documents by business users, notably doctors and other health care providers concerned about Internet security. Fax usage is expected to increase through 2020, even though unit sales of fax machines have declined on a worldwide basis. Internet technology and e-mail may eventually replace facsimile technology and paper and make fax machines extinct, but not soon.

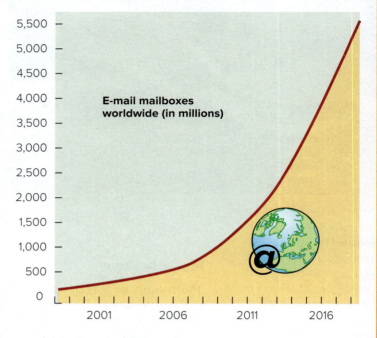

---

technology and e-mail make fax machines extinct anytime soon? The Marketing Matters box offers one perspective on this question that may surprise you.[6]

Numerous product classes or industries are in the decline stage of their product life cycle. Two prominent examples include analog TVs and desktop personal computers.

Products in the decline stage tend to consume a disproportionate share of management and financial resources relative to their future worth. A company will follow one of two strategies to handle a declining product: deletion or harvesting.

Deletion Product *deletion,* or dropping the product from the company's product line, is the most drastic strategy. Because a residual core of consumers still consume or use a product even in the decline stage, product elimination decisions are not taken lightly. For example, Sanford Corporation continues to sell its Liquid Paper correction fluid for use with typewriters in the era of word-processing equipment.

Harvesting A second strategy, *harvesting,* is when a company retains the product but reduces marketing costs. The product continues to be offered, but salespeople do not allocate time in selling nor are advertising dollars spent. The purpose of harvesting is to maintain the ability to meet customer requests. Coca-Cola, for instance, still sells Tab, its first diet cola, to a small group of die-hard fans. According to Coke's CEO, "It shows you care. We want to make sure those who want Tab, get Tab."[7]

Three Aspects of the Product Life Cycle

Some important aspects of product life cycles are (1) their length, (2) the shape of their sales curves, and (3) the rate at which consumers adopt products.

Length of the Product Life Cycle There is no set time that it takes a product to move through its life cycle. As a rule, consumer products have shorter life cycles than business products. For example, many new consumer food products such as Frito-Lay's Baked Lay's potato chips move from the introduction stage to maturity in 18 months. The availability of mass communication vehicles informs consumers quickly and shortens life cycles. Technological change shortens product life cycles as new-product innovation replaces existing products. For instance, smartphones have largely replaced digital cameras in the amateur photography market.

Shape of the Life-Cycle Curve The product life-cycle sales curve shown in Figure 10–1 is the *generalized life cycle,* but not all products have the same shape to their curve. In fact, there are several life-cycle curves, each type suggesting different marketing strategies. Figure 10–3 shows the shape of life-cycle sales curves for four different types of products: high-learning, low-learning, fashion, and fad products.

A *high-learning product* is one for which significant customer education is required and there is an extended introductory period (Figure 10–3A). It may surprise you, but personal computers had this life-cycle curve. Consumers in the 1980s had to learn the benefits of owning the product or be educated in a new way of performing familiar tasks. Convection ovens for home use required consumers to learn a new way of cooking and alter familiar recipes used with conventional ovens. As a result, these ovens spent years in the introductory period.

In contrast, sales for a *low-learning product* begin immediately because little learning is required by the consumer and the benefits of purchase are readily understood (Figure 10–3B). This product often can be easily imitated by competitors, so the marketing strategy is to broaden distribution quickly. In this way, as competitors rapidly enter, most retail outlets already have the innovator's product. It is also important to have the manufacturing capacity to meet demand. A successful low-learning product is Gillette's Fusion razor. This product achieved $1 billion in worldwide sales in less than three years and remains the best-selling razor in the world.

A *fashion product* (Figure 10–3C) is a style of the times. Life cycles for fashion products frequently appear in women's and men's apparel. Fashion products are introduced, decline, and then seem to return. The length of the cycles may be months,

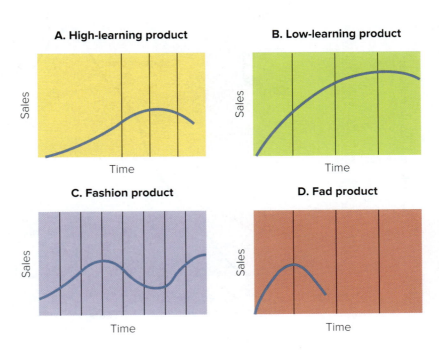

FIGURE 10–3

Alternative product life-cycle curves based on product types. Note the long introduction stage for a high-learning product compared with a low-learning product. Read the text for an explanation of the different product life-cycle curves.

years, or decades. Consider women's hosiery. Product sales have been declining for years. Women consider it more fashionable to not wear hosiery—bad news for Hanes brands, the leading marketer of women's sheer hosiery. According to an authority on fashion, "Companies might as well let the fashion cycle take its course and wait for the inevitable return of pantyhose."[8]

A *fad product* experiences rapid sales on introduction and then an equally rapid decline (Figure 10–3D). These products are typically novelties and have a short life cycle. They include fidgit spinners, car tattoos described as the first removable and reusable graphics for automobiles, and vinyl dresses and fleece bikinis made by a Minnesota clothing company.[9]

The Product Level: Class and Form The product life cycle shown in Figure 10–1 is a total industry or generalized product class sales curve. Yet, in managing a product it is often important to distinguish among the multiple life cycles (class and form) that may exist.

Product class refers to the entire product category or industry, such as prerecorded music. **Product form** pertains to variations of a product within the product class. For prerecorded music, product form exists in the technology used to provide the music, such as cassette tapes, compact discs, and digital music downloading and streaming. Figure 10–4 shows the life cycles for these three product forms and demonstrates the impact of technological innovation on sales.[10]

The Product Life Cycle and Consumer Behavior The life cycle of a product depends on sales to consumers. Not all consumers rush to buy a product in the introductory stage, and the shapes of the life-cycle curves indicate that most sales occur after the product has been on the market for some time. In essence, a product diffuses, or spreads, through the population, a concept called the *diffusion of innovation*.[11]

Some people are attracted to a product early. Others buy it only after they see their friends or opinion leaders with the item. Figure 10–5 shows the consumer population divided into five categories of product adopters based on when they adopt a new

> **product class**
> Refers to the entire product category or industry.
>
> **product form**
> Pertains to variations of a product within the product class.

FIGURE 10–4
Prerecorded music product life cycles by product form illustrate the effect of technological innovation on sales. Compact discs replaced cassette tapes, and digital music and streaming replaced compact discs in 2015. Do you even remember the cassette tape?

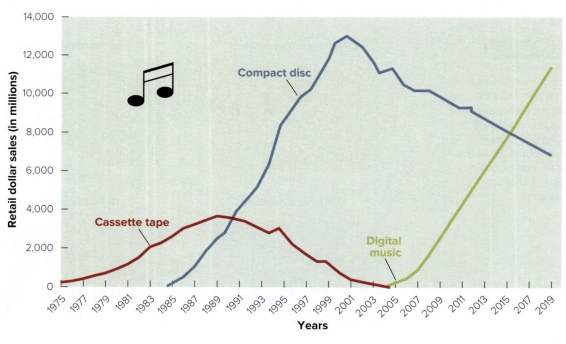

FIGURE 10–5

Five categories and profiles of product adopters. For a product to be successful, it must be purchased by innovators and early adopters.

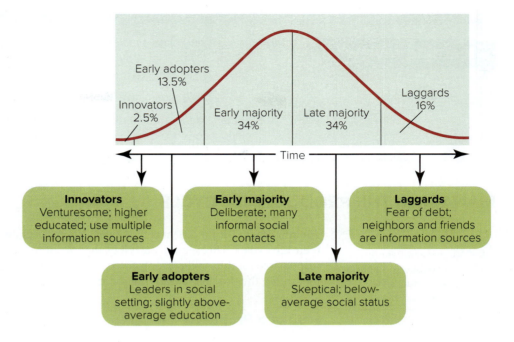

product. Brief profiles accompany each category. For any product to be successful, it must be purchased by innovators and early adopters. This is why manufacturers of new pharmaceuticals try to gain adoption by respected hospitals, clinics, and physicians. Once accepted by innovators and early adopters, successful new products move on to the early majority, late majority, and laggard categories.

Several factors affect whether a consumer will adopt a new product or not. Common reasons for resisting a product in the introduction stage are *usage barriers* (the product is not compatible with existing habits), *value barriers* (the product provides no incentive to change), *risk barriers* (physical, economic, or social), and *psychological barriers* (cultural differences or image).[12]

These factors help to explain the slow adoption of all-electric-powered automobiles in the United States. Less than 1 percent of cars sold in 2018 were all-electric-powered vehicles. Industry analysts cite the usage barrier for disappointing sales. They note that prospective buyers believe these cars are not compatible with existing driving habits. Analysts also mention a value barrier. Consumers have not recognized the superiority of all-electric cars over vehicles with internal combustion engines. Third, a risk barrier exists in large measure due to buyer uncertainty about the actual cost of all-electric-powered car ownership. According to one auto industry analyst, "The innovators and early adopters have purchased all-electric vehicles, but mainstream consumers have not followed." Not surprisingly, all-electric-powered automobiles remain in the introductory stage of the product life cycle.[13]

Companies attempt to overcome these barriers in numerous ways. For example, manufacturers of all-electric-powered automobiles provide low-cost leasing options to overcome usage, value, and risk barriers. Other companies provide warranties, money-back guarantees, extensive usage instructions, demonstrations, and free samples to stimulate initial trial of new products. For instance, software developers offer demonstrations downloaded from the Internet. Skin care consumers can browse through the Skin Advisor site at www.olay.com to find out how certain skin care products will look based on a selfie submitted by the consumer. Free samples are one of the most popular means to gain consumer trial. In fact, 71 percent of consumers consider a sample to be the best way to evaluate a new product.[14]

learning review

10-1. Advertising plays a major role in the _____ stage of the product life cycle, and _____ plays a major role in the maturity stage.

10-2. How do high-learning and low-learning products differ?

10-3. What are the five categories of product adopters in the diffusion of innovations?

MANAGING THE PRODUCT LIFE CYCLE

 LO 10-2 Identify ways that marketing executives manage a product's life cycle.

An important task for a firm is to manage its products through the successive stages of their life cycles. This section describes the role of the product manager, who is usually responsible for this, and presents three ways to manage a product through its life cycle: modifying the product, modifying the market, and repositioning the product.

Role of a Product Manager

The product manager, sometimes called a *brand manager,* manages the marketing efforts for a close-knit family of products or brands. The product manager style of marketing organization is used by consumer goods firms, including General Mills and PepsiCo, and by technology companies such as Intel and Hewlett-Packard.

All product managers are responsible for managing existing products through the stages of the life cycle. Some are also responsible for developing new products. Product managers' marketing responsibilities include developing and executing a marketing program for the product line described in an annual marketing plan and approving ad copy, media selection, and package design.

Product managers also engage in extensive data analysis related to their products and brands. Sales, market share, and profit trends are closely monitored. Managers often supplement these data with two measures: (1) a category development index (CDI) and (2) a brand development index (BDI). These indexes help to identify strong and weak market segments (usually demographic or geographic segments) for specific consumer products and brands and provide direction for marketing efforts. The calculation, visual display, and interpretation of these two indexes for Hawaiian Punch are described in the Applying Marketing Metrics box.

Modifying the Product

product modification Involves altering one or more of a product's characteristics, such as its quality, performance, or appearance, to increase the product's value to customers and increase sales.

Product modification involves altering one or more of a product's characteristics, such as its quality, performance, or appearance, to increase the product's value to customers and increase sales. Wrinkle-free and stain-resistant clothing made possible by nanotechnology revolutionized the men's and women's apparel business and stimulated industry sales of casual pants, shirts, and blouses. A common approach to product modification to increase a product's value to consumers is called *product bundling*—the sale of two or more separate products in one package. For example, Microsoft Office is sold as a bundle of computer software, including Word, Excel, and PowerPoint.

New features, packages, or scents can be used to change a product's characteristics and give the sense of a revised product. Procter & Gamble revamped Pantene shampoo and conditioner with a new vitamin formula and relaunched the brand with a multimillion-dollar advertising and promotion campaign. The result? Pantene, a brand first introduced in the 1940s, remains a top-selling shampoo and conditioner in the United States in an industry with more than 1,000 competitors.

Applying Marketing Metrics

Knowing Your CDI and BDI

Where are sales for my product category and brand strongest and weakest? Data related to this question are displayed in a marketing dashboard using two indexes: (1) a category development index (CDI) and (2) a brand development index (BDI).

Your Challenge

You have joined the marketing team for Hawaiian Punch, the top fruit punch drink sold in the United States. The brand has been marketed to mothers with children under 13 years old. The majority of Hawaiian Punch sales are in gallon and 2-liter bottles. Your assignment is to examine the brand's performance and identify growth opportunities for the Hawaiian Punch brand among households that consume prepared fruit drinks (the product category).

Your marketing dashboard displays a category development index and a brand development index provided by a syndicated marketing research firm. Each index is based on the calculations below:

$$\text{Category Development Index (CDI)} = \frac{\text{Percent of a product category's total U.S. sales in a market segment}}{\text{Percent of the total U.S. population in a market segment}} \times 100$$

$$\text{Brand Development Index (BDI)} = \frac{\text{Percent of a brand's total U.S. sales in a market segment}}{\text{Percent of the total U.S. population in a market segment}} \times 100$$

A CDI over 100 indicates above-average product category purchases by a market segment. A number under 100 indicates below-average purchases. A BDI over 100 indicates a strong brand position in a segment; a number under 100 indicates a weak brand position.

You are interested in CDI and BDI displays for four household segments that consume prepared fruit drinks: (1) households without children; (2) households with children 6 years old or under; (3) households with children aged 7 to 12; and (4) households with children aged 13 to 18.

Your Findings

The BDI and CDI metrics displayed below show that Hawaiian Punch is consumed by households with children, and particularly households with children under age 12. The Hawaiian Punch BDI is over 100 for both segments—not surprising since the brand is marketed to these segments. Households with children 13 to 18 years old evidence high fruit drink consumption with a CDI over 100. But Hawaiian Punch is relatively weak in this segment, with a BDI under 100.

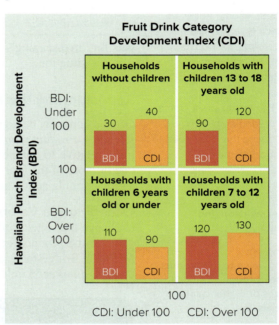

Your Action

An opportunity for Hawaiian Punch exists among households with children 13 to 18 years old—teenagers. You might propose that Hawaiian Punch be repositioned for teens. In addition, you might recommend that Hawaiian Punch be packaged in single-serve cans or bottles to attract this segment, much like soft drinks. Teens might also be targeted for advertising and promotions.

Modifying the Market

With **market modification** strategies, a company tries to find new customers, increase a product's use among existing customers, or create new use situations.

Finding New Customers
As part of its market modification strategy, LEGO Group is offering a new line of products to attract consumers outside of its traditional market. Known for its popular line of construction toys for young boys, LEGO Group

---

market modification
Strategies by which a company tries to find new customers, increase a product's use among existing customers, or create new use situations.

has introduced a product line for young girls called LEGO Friends. Harley-Davidson has tailored a marketing program to encourage women to take up biking, thus doubling the number of potential customers for its motorcycles.

Increasing a Product's Use Promoting more frequent usage has been a strategy of Campbell Soup Company. Because soup consumption rises in the winter and declines during the summer, the company now advertises more heavily in warm months to encourage consumers to think of soup as more than a cold-weather food. Similarly, the Florida Orange Growers Association advocates drinking orange juice throughout the day rather than for breakfast only.

Creating a New Use Situation Finding new uses for an existing product has been the strategy behind Gillette, the world leader for men's shaving products. The company now markets its Gillette Body line of razors, blades, and shaving gels for "manscaping"—the art of shaving body hair in areas below the neckline—a new use situation.

Harley-Davidson redesigned some of its motorcycle models to feature smaller hand grips, a lower seat, and an easier-to-pull clutch lever to create a more comfortable ride for women. According to Genevieve Schmitt, founding editor of WomenRidersNow.com, "They realize that women are an up-and-coming segment and that they need to accommodate them."
©Gary Gardiner/Bloomberg via Getty Images

Harley-Davidson, Inc.
www.harley-davidson.com

trading up
Adding value to the product (or line) through additional features or higher-quality materials.

trading down
Reducing a product's number of features, quality, or price.

Video 10-2
Gillette Ad
kerin.tv/cr8e/v10-2

Repositioning the Product

Often a company decides to reposition its product or product line in an attempt to bolster sales. *Product repositioning* changes the place a product occupies in a consumer's mind relative to competitive products. A firm can reposition a product by changing one or more of the four marketing mix elements. Four factors that trigger the need for a repositioning action are discussed next.

Changing the Value Offered In repositioning a product, a company can decide to change the value it offers buyers and trade up or down. **Trading up** involves adding value to the product (or line) through additional features or higher-quality materials. Michelin, Bridgestone, and Goodyear have done this with a "run-flat" tire that can travel up to 50 miles at 55 miles per hour after suffering total air loss. Dog food manufacturers, such as Ralston Purina, also have traded up by offering super-premium foods based on "life-stage nutrition." Mass merchandisers, such as Target and Walmart, can trade up by adding a designer clothes section to their stores.

Gillette razors, blades, and gels have been adapted for shaving men's body hair in areas below the neckline. This new use situation for its shaving products is called "manscaping."
Source: Procter & Gamble

Trading down involves reducing a product's number of features, quality, or price. For example, airlines have added more seats, thus reducing legroom, and limited meal service by offering only snacks on most domestic flights. Trading down also exists when companies engage in *downsizing*—reducing the package content without changing package size and maintaining or increasing the package price. Companies are criticized for this practice, as described in the Making Responsible Decisions box.[15]

Reacting to a Competitor's Position One reason to reposition a product is because a competitor's

Making Responsible Decisions

Ethics

Consumer Economics of Downsizing—Get Less, Pay More

For more than 30 years, Starkist put 6.5 ounces of tuna into its regular-sized can. Today, Starkist puts 6.125 ounces of tuna into its can but charges the same price. Frito-Lay (Doritos and Lay's snack chips), PepsiCo (Tropicana orange juice), and Häagen-Dazs (ice cream) have whittled away at package contents 5 to 10 percent while maintaining their products' package sizes, dimensions, and prices.

Procter & Gamble recently kept its retail price on its jumbo pack of Pampers and Luvs diapers, but reduced the number of diapers per pack from 140 to 132. Similarly, Unilever reduced the number of Popsicles in each package from 24 to 20 without changing the package price. Georgia-Pacific reduced the content of its Brawny paper towel six-roll pack by 20 percent without lowering the price.

©McGraw-Hill Education

Consumer advocates charge that downsizing the content of packages while maintaining prices is a subtle and unannounced way of taking advantage of consumer buying habits. They also say downsizing is a price increase in disguise and a deceptive, but legal, practice. Some manufacturers argue that this practice is a way of keeping prices from rising beyond psychological barriers for their products. Other manufacturers say prices are set by individual stores, not by them.

Is downsizing an unethical practice if manufacturers do not inform consumers that the package contents are less than they were previously?

---

entrenched position is adversely affecting sales and market share. New Balance, Inc. successfully repositioned its athletic shoes to focus on fit, durability, and comfort rather than competing head-on against Nike on performance and Adidas on fashion. The company offers an expansive range of shoes and networks with podiatrists, not sports celebrities.

Reaching a New Market   When Unilever introduced iced tea in Britain, sales were disappointing. British consumers viewed it as leftover hot tea, not suitable for drinking. The company made its tea carbonated and repositioned it as a cold soft drink to compete as a carbonated beverage and sales improved. Johnson & Johnson effectively repositioned its St. Joseph aspirin from a product for infants to an adult low-strength aspirin to reduce the risk of heart problems or strokes.

Catching a Rising Trend   Changing consumer trends can also lead to product repositioning. Growing consumer interest in foods that offer health and dietary benefits is an example. Many products have been repositioned to capitalize on this trend. Quaker Oats makes the FDA-approved claim that oatmeal, as part of a low-saturated-fat, low-cholesterol diet, may reduce the risk of heart disease. Calcium-enriched products, such as Kraft American cheese and Uncle Ben's Calcium Plus rice, emphasize healthy bone structure for children and adults. Weight-conscious consumers have embraced low-fat and low-calorie diets in growing numbers. Today, most food and beverage companies offer reduced-fat and low-calorie versions of their products.

learning review

10-4. How does a product manager manage a product's life cycle?

10-5. What does "creating a new use situation" mean in managing a product's life cycle?

10-6. Explain the difference between trading up and trading down in product repositioning.

BRANDING AND BRAND MANAGEMENT

LO 10-3 Recognize the importance of branding and alternative branding strategies.

branding
A marketing decision in which an organization uses a name, phrase, design, symbols, or combination of these to identify its products and distinguish them from those of competitors.

brand name
Any word, device (design, sound, shape, or color), or combination of these used to distinguish a seller's products or services.

brand personality
A set of human characteristics associated with a brand name.

Video 10-3
Dr Pepper Ad
kerin.tv/cr8e/v10-3

brand equity
The added value a brand name gives to a product beyond the functional benefits provided.

A basic decision in marketing products is **branding**, in which an organization uses a name, phrase, design, symbols, or combination of these to identify its products and distinguish them from those of competitors. A **brand name** is any word, device (design, sound, shape, or color), or combination of these used to distinguish a seller's products or services. Well-known devices used to distinguish brands apart from a name include symbols (the Nike swoosh), logos (the white apple used by Apple), and characters (Charlie the Tuna for Starkist).

A *trademark* identifies that a firm has legally registered its brand name or trade name so the firm has its exclusive use, thereby preventing others from using it. For example, Coca-Cola and Procter & Gamble have trademarked hashtags (#) that make reference to their brands. In the United States, trademarks are registered with the U.S. Patent and Trademark Office and protected under the *Lanham Act*. A well-known trademark can help a company advertise its offerings to customers and develop their brand loyalty. Consider Kylie and Kendall Jenner, cast members of the reality television show *Keeping Up with the Kardashians*. They filed to have their first names trademarked for use in "entertainment, fashion, and pop culture." Their filing was withdrawn after entertainer Kylie Minogue objected.[16]

Consumers may benefit most from branding. Recognizing competing products by distinct trademarks allows them to be more efficient shoppers. Consumers can recognize and avoid products with which they are dissatisfied, while becoming loyal to other, more satisfying brands. As discussed in Chapter 4, brand loyalty often eases consumers' decision making by eliminating the need for an external search.

Brand Personality and Brand Equity

Product managers recognize that brands offer more than product identification and a means to distinguish their products from those of competitors.[17] Successful and established brands take on a **brand personality**, a set of human characteristics associated with a brand name. Research shows that consumers assign personality traits to products—traditional, romantic, rugged, sophisticated, rebellious—and choose brands that are consistent with their own or desired self-image.

Marketers can and do imbue a brand with a personality through advertising that depicts a certain user or usage situation and conveys emotions or feelings associated with the brand. For example, personality traits linked with Coca-Cola are all-American and real; with Pepsi, young and exciting; and with Dr Pepper, nonconforming and unique. The traits often linked to Harley-Davidson are masculinity, defiance, and rugged individualism.

Brand name importance to a company has led to a concept called **brand equity**, the added value a brand name gives to a product beyond the functional benefits provided. This added value has two distinct advantages. First, brand equity provides a competitive advantage. The Sunkist brand implies quality fruit. The Disney name defines children's entertainment. A second advantage is that consumers are often willing to pay a higher price for a product with brand equity. Brand equity, in this instance, is represented by the premium a consumer will pay for one brand over another when the functional benefits provided are identical. Gillette razors and blades, Bose audio systems, Duracell batteries, Cartier jewelry, and Louis Vuitton luggage all enjoy a price premium arising from brand equity.

Creating Brand Equity Brand equity doesn't just happen. It is carefully crafted and nurtured by marketing programs that forge strong, favorable, and unique customer associations and experiences with a brand. Brand equity resides in the minds of consumers and results from what they have learned, felt, seen, and heard about a brand over time. Marketers recognize that brand equity is not easily or quickly

The strong brand equity for the Reebok brand name permits the company to charge premium prices for its products.
Source: Reebok

achieved. Rather, it arises from a sequential building process consisting of four steps (see Figure 10–6).[18]

- The first step is to develop positive brand awareness and an association of the brand in consumers' minds with a product class or need to give the brand an identity. Gatorade and Kleenex have achieved this in the sports drink and facial tissue product classes, respectively.
- Next, a marketer must establish a brand's meaning in the minds of consumers. Meaning arises from what a brand stands for and has two dimensions—a functional, performance-related dimension and an abstract, imagery-related dimension. Nike has done this through continuous product development and improvement and its links to peak athletic performance in its advertising.
- The third step is to elicit the proper consumer responses to a brand's identity and meaning. Here attention is placed on how consumers think and feel about a

FIGURE 10–6
The customer-based brand equity pyramid shows the four-step building process that forges strong, favorable, and unique customer associations with a brand.

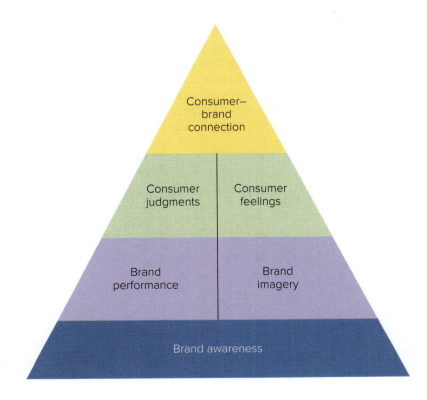

brand. Thinking focuses on a brand's perceived quality, credibility, and superiority relative to other brands. Feeling relates to the consumer's emotional reaction to a brand. Michelin elicits both responses for its tires. Not only is Michelin thought of as a credible and superior-quality brand, but consumers also acknowledge a warm and secure feeling of safety, comfort, and self-assurance without worry or concern about the brand.

- The final, and most difficult, step is to create a consumer–brand connection evident in an intense, active loyalty relationship between consumers and the brand. A deep psychological bond characterizes a consumer–brand connection and the personal identification customers have with the brand. Brands that have achieved this status include Harley-Davidson, Apple, and eBay.

Valuing Brand Equity Brand equity also provides a financial advantage for the brand owner.[19] Successful, established brand names, such as Gillette, Louis Vuitton, Nike, Gatorade, and Apple, have an economic value in the sense that they are intangible assets. The Apple brand name alone is valued at $183 billion. The recognition that brands are assets is apparent in the decision to buy and sell companies. For instance, when Procter & Gamble bought the Gillette Company for $57 billion, the Gillette brand name alone was valued at $24 billion, or 42 percent of the company's purchase price!

Brands alone can be bought and sold by a company. For example, Triarc Companies bought the Snapple brand from Quaker Oats for $300 million and sold it three years later to Cadbury Schweppes for $900 million. This example illustrates that brands, unlike physical assets that depreciate with time and use, can appreciate in value when effectively marketed. However, brands can lose value when they are not managed properly. Consider the purchase and sale of Lender's Bagels. Kellogg bought the brand for $466 million only to sell it to Aurora Foods for $275 million three years later following deteriorating sales and profits.

Financially lucrative brand licensing opportunities arise from brand equity.[20] **Brand licensing** is a contractual agreement whereby one company (licensor) allows its brand name(s) or trademark(s) to be used with products or services offered by another company (licensee) for a royalty or fee. For example, the National Football League (NFL) and the National Basketball Association (NBA) each earn about $3.5 billion annually by licensing team names and logos for merchandise. The Peanuts brand characters, including Charlie Brown, Snoopy, and Lucy, generate almost $100 million annually in licensing fees.

Successful brand licensing requires careful marketing analysis to ensure a proper fit between the licensor's brand and the licensee's products. World-renowned designer Ralph Lauren earns over $2.5 billion each year by licensing his Ralph Lauren, Polo, and Chaps brands for dozens of products, including paint by Glidden, furniture by Henredon, footwear by Rockport, eyewear by Luxottica, and fragrances by L'Oréal.[21] Kleenex diapers, Bic perfume, and Domino's fruit-flavored bubble gum are a few examples of poor matches and licensing failures.

> **brand licensing**
> A contractual agreement whereby one company (licensor) allows its brand name(s) or trademark(s) to be used with products or services offered by another company (licensee) for a royalty or fee.

Picking a Good Brand Name

We take brand names such as Red Bull, iPad, Android, and Axe for granted, but it is often a difficult and expensive process to pick a good name. Companies will spend between $25,000 and $100,000 to identify and test a new brand name. Six criteria are mentioned most often when selecting a good brand name.[22]

- *The name should suggest the product benefits.* For example, Accutron (watches), Easy Off (oven cleaner), Glass Plus (glass cleaner), Cling-Free (antistatic cloth for drying clothes), Chevrolet Bolt and Spark (electric cars), and Tidy Bowl (toilet bowl cleaner) all clearly describe the benefits of purchasing the product.

Ralph Lauren has a long-term licensing agreement with Luxottica Group, S.p.A. of Milan for the design, production, and worldwide distribution of prescription frames and sunglasses under the Ralph Lauren brand. The agreement is an ideal fit for both companies. Ralph Lauren is a leader in the design, marketing, and distribution of premium lifestyle products. Luxottica is the global leader in the premium and luxury eyewear sector.
©Rebecca Sapp/WireImage for Mediaplacement/Getty Images

Luxottica Group, S.p.A.
www.luxottica.com

Ralph Lauren Corporation
www.ralphlauren.com

- *The name should be memorable, distinctive, and positive.* In the auto industry, when a competitor has a memorable name, others quickly imitate. When Ford named a car the Mustang, the Pinto and Bronco soon followed. The Thunderbird name led to the Phoenix, Eagle, Sunbird, and Firebird from other car companies.
- *The name should fit the company or product image.* Sharp is a name that can apply to audio and video equipment. Bufferin, Excedrin, Anacin, and Nuprin are scientific-sounding names, good for analgesics. Eveready, Duracell, and DieHard suggest reliability and longevity—two qualities consumers want in a battery.
- *The name should have no legal or regulatory restrictions.* Legal restrictions produce trademark infringement suits, and regulatory restrictions arise through the improper use of words. For example, the U.S. Food and Drug Administration discourages the use of the word *heart* in food brand names. This restriction led to changing the name of Kellogg's Heartwise cereal to Fiberwise, and Clorox's Hidden Valley Ranch Take Heart Salad Dressing had to be modified to Hidden Valley Ranch Low-Fat Salad Dressing. Increasingly, brand names need a corresponding website address on the Internet. This further complicates name selection because over 250 million domain names are already registered globally.
- *The name should be simple and emotional.* Examples that illustrate the former include Bold laundry detergent, Axe deodorant and body spray, and Bic pens; examples illustrating the latter include Joy and Obsession perfumes and Caress soap, shower gel, and lotion.
- *The name should have favorable phonetic and semantic associations in other languages.* In the development of names for international use, having a non-meaningful brand name has been considered a benefit. A name such as Exxon does not have any prior impressions or undesirable images among a diverse world population of different languages and cultures. The 7UP name is another matter. In Shanghai, China, the phrase means "death through drinking" in the local dialect. Sales have suffered as a result.

Branding Strategies

Companies can choose from among several different branding strategies, including multiproduct branding, multibranding, private branding, and mixed branding (see Figure 10–7).

FIGURE 10–7
Alternative branding strategies present both advantages and disadvantages to marketers. See the text for details.

multiproduct branding
A branding strategy in which a company uses one name for all its products in a product class.

multibranding
A branding strategy that involves giving each product a distinct name when each brand is intended for a different market segment.

What branding concept is American Express using with its multicolored cards?
©Peter Jobst/Alamy Stock Photo

Multiproduct Branding Strategy With **multiproduct branding**, a company uses one name for all its products in a product class. This approach is sometimes called *family branding* or *corporate branding* when the company's name is used. For example, Microsoft, Samsung, Gerber, and Sony engage in corporate branding—the company's trade name and brand name are identical. Church & Dwight uses the Arm & Hammer family brand name for all its products featuring baking soda as the primary ingredient.

There are several advantages to multiproduct branding. Capitalizing again on brand equity, consumers who have a good experience with the product will transfer this favorable attitude to other items in the product class with the same name. Therefore, this brand strategy makes possible *product line extensions,* the practice of using a current brand name to enter a new market segment in its product class.

Campbell Soup Company employs a multiproduct branding strategy with soup line extensions. It offers regular Campbell's soup, home-cooking style, and chunky varieties and more than 100 soup flavors. This strategy can result in lower advertising and promotion costs because the same name is used on all products, thus raising the level of brand awareness. A risk with line extension is that sales of an extension may come at the expense of other items in the company's product line. Line extensions work best when they provide incremental company revenue by taking sales away from competing brands or attracting new buyers.

Some multiproduct branding companies employ *subbranding,* which combines a corporate or family brand with a new brand, to distinguish a part of its product line from others. Consider American Express. It has applied subbranding with its American Express Green, Gold, Platinum, Blue, and Centurion black charge cards, with unique service offerings for each. Similarly, Porsche successfully markets its higher-end Porsche Carrera and its lower-end Porsche Boxster.

A strong brand equity also allows for *brand extension:* the practice of using a current brand name to enter a different product class. For instance, equity in the Huggies family brand name has allowed Kimberly-Clark to successfully extend its name to a full line of baby and toddler toiletries. This brand extension strategy generates $500 million in annual sales globally for the company. Honda's established name for motor vehicles has extended easily to snowblowers, lawn mowers, snowmobiles, and business jets.

Co-branding opportunities also arise from a strong brand equity. *Co-branding* is the practice of pairing two or more strong brands to facilitate the marketing of a joint product or service for their mutual benefit. For example, companies use component or ingredient branding (Dell computers with Intel processors, or Hershey's chocolate with Betty Crocker cupcake mix), joint venture branding (Citibank and American Airlines credit cards), and sponsorships

What branding concept is illustrated by this pairing of the Hershey's and Betty Crocker brands?
©Keith Homan/Alamy Stock Photo

(AT&T, Mercedes-Benz, and IBM co-sponsor the annual Masters Golf Tournament).

However, there is a risk with excessive brand extensions, subbrands, and co-brands. Marketing experts claim that too many uses for one brand name can dilute the meaning of a brand for consumers and harm its brand equity. *Brand dilution* occurs when consumers no longer associate a brand with a specific product or service or start thinking less favorably about the brand.[23]

Multibranding Strategy   Alternatively, a company can engage in **multibranding**, which involves giving each product a distinct name. Multibranding is a useful strategy when each brand is intended for a different market segment. Procter & Gamble makes Camay soap for those concerned with soft skin and Safeguard for those who want deodorant protection. Stanley Black & Decker markets its line of tools for the do-it-yourself (DIY) household segment with the Black & Decker name but uses the DeWalt name for its professional tool line.

Multibranding is applied in a variety of ways. Some companies array their brands on the basis of price–quality segments. Marriott International offers 18 hotel and resort brands, each suited for a particular traveler experience and budget. To illustrate, Marriott EDITION hotels and Vacation Clubs offer luxury amenities at a premium price. Marriott and Renaissance hotels offer medium- to high-priced accommodations. Courtyard hotels and TownePlace Suites appeal to economy-minded travelers, whereas the Fairfield Inn is for those on a very low travel budget.

For how Kimberly-Clark has used a brand extension strategy to leverage its Huggies brand equity among mothers, see the text.
©McGraw-Hill Education/Mike Hruby, photographer

Kimberly-Clark Corporation
www.kimberly-clark.com

Other multibrand companies introduce new product brands as defensive moves to counteract competition. Called *fighting brands*, their chief purpose is to confront competitor brands.[24] For instance, Frito-Lay introduced Santitas brand tortilla chips to go head-to-head against regional tortilla chip brands that were biting into sales of its flagship Doritos and Tostitos brand tortilla chips. Ford launched its Fusion brand to halt the defection of Ford owners who were buying competitors' midsize cars. According to Ford's car group marketing manager, "Every year we were losing around 50,000 people from our products to competitors' midsize cars. We were losing Mustang, Focus, and Taurus owners. Fusion was our interceptor."[25]

Compared with the multiproduct strategy, advertising and promotion costs tend to be higher with multibranding. The company must generate awareness among consumers and retailers for each new brand name without the benefit of any previous impressions. The advantages of this strategy are that each brand is unique to each market segment and there is no risk that a product failure will affect other products in the line. Still, some large multibrand firms have found that the complexity and expense of implementing this strategy can outweigh the benefits. For example, Procter & Gamble has pruned about 100 of its brands through product deletion and sales to other companies over the past four years.[26]

private branding
A branding strategy used when a company manufactures products but sells them under the brand name of a wholesaler or retailer. Also called *private labeling* or *reseller branding*.

Private Branding Strategy   A company uses **private branding**, often called *private labeling* or *reseller branding*, when it manufactures products but sells them under the brand name of a wholesaler or retailer. Rayovac, Paragon Trade Brands, and ConAgra Foods are major suppliers of private-label alkaline batteries, diapers, and grocery products, respectively. Costco, Amazon, Walmart, and Kroger are large retailers that have their own brand names. Private branding is popular because it typically produces high profits for manufacturers and resellers. Consumers also buy them. It is estimated that one of every five items purchased at U.S. supermarkets, drugstores, and mass merchandisers bears a private brand.[27]

Stanley Black & Decker uses a multibranding strategy to reach different market segments. It markets its tool line for the do-it-yourself (DIY) household segment using the Black & Decker name, but it uses the DeWalt name for professionals.

(left): Source: The Black & Decker Corporation; (right): Source: DEWALT

Black & Decker
www.stanleyblackanddecker.com

mixed branding
A branding strategy where a firm markets products under its own name(s) and that of a reseller because the segment attracted to the reseller is different from its own market.

Mixed Branding Strategy A fourth branding strategy is **mixed branding**, where a firm markets products under its own name(s) and that of a reseller because the segment attracted to the reseller is different from its own market. Diverse companies such as Del Monte, Whirlpool, and Dial produce private brands of pet foods, home appliances, and soap, respectively.

PACKAGING AND LABELING PRODUCTS

 Describe the role of packaging and labeling in the marketing of a product.

packaging
A component of a product that refers to any container in which it is offered for sale and on which label information is conveyed.

label
An integral part of the package that typically identifies the product or brand, who made it, where and when it was made, how it is to be used, and package contents and ingredients.

The **packaging** component of a product refers to any container in which it is offered for sale and on which label information is conveyed. A **label** is an integral part of the package and typically identifies the product or brand, who made it, where and when it was made, how it is to be used, and package contents and ingredients. To a great extent, the customer's first exposure to a product is the package and label, and both are an expensive and important part of marketing strategy. For Pez Candy, Inc., the central element of its marketing strategy is the character-head-on-a-stick plastic container that dispenses a miniature candy tablet. For more on how packaging creates customer value for Pez Candy, see the Marketing Matters box.[28]

Creating Customer Value and Competitive Advantage through Packaging and Labeling

Packaging and labeling cost U.S. companies about 15 cents of every dollar spent by consumers for products.[29] Despite their cost, packaging and labeling are essential because both provide important benefits for the manufacturer, retailer, and ultimate consumer. Packaging and labeling also can provide a competitive advantage.

Communication Benefits A major benefit of packaging is the label information it conveys to the consumer, such as directions on how, where, and when to use the product and the source and composition of the product, which is needed to satisfy legal requirements of product disclosure. For example, the labeling system for packaged and processed foods in the United States provides a uniform format for nutritional and dietary information. Many packaged foods contain informative recipes to promote usage of the product. Campbell Soup estimates that the green bean casserole recipe on its cream of mushroom soup can accounts for $20 million in soup sales each year![30] Other

Marketing Matters

Customer Value

Creating Customer Value through Packaging—Pez Heads Dispense More Than Candy

Customer value can assume numerous forms. For Pez Candy, Inc. (www.pez.com), customer value manifests itself in some 450 Pez character candy dispensers. Each refillable dispenser ejects tasty candy tablets in a variety of flavors that delight preteens and teens alike in more than 80 countries—including China, which it entered in 2017.

Pez was formulated in 1927 by Austrian food mogul Eduard Haas III and successfully sold in Europe as an adult breath mint. The name *Pez*, which comes from the German word for "peppermint," *pfefferminz*, was originally packaged in a hygienic, headless plastic dispenser. Pez first appeared in the United States in 1953 with a headless dispenser, marketed to adults. After conducting extensive marketing research, Pez was repositioned with fruit flavors, repackaged with licensed character heads on top of the dispenser, and remarketed as a children's product in the mid-1950s. Since then, most top-level licensed characters and hundreds of other characters have become Pez heads. Consumers buy about 80 million Pez dispensers and 3 billion Pez tablets a year in the United States alone, and company sales growth exceeds that of the candy industry as a whole.

The unique Pez package dispenses a "use experience" for its customers beyond the candy itself, namely, fun. And fun translates into a 98 percent awareness level for Pez among teenagers and an 89 percent awareness level among mothers with children. Pez has not advertised its product for years. With that kind of awareness, who needs advertising?

©Blank Archives/Getty Images

information consists of seals and symbols, either government-required or commercial seals of approval (such as the Good Housekeeping Seal).

Functional Benefits Packaging often plays a functional role—providing storage, convenience, or protection or ensuring product quality. Stackable food containers are one example of how packaging can provide functional benefits. For example, beverage companies have developed lighter and easier ways to stack products on shelves and in refrigerators. Examples include Coca-Cola beverage packs designed to fit neatly onto refrigerator shelves and Ocean Spray Cranberries's rectangular juice bottles that allow 10 units per package versus 8 of its former round bottles.

The convenience dimension of packaging is increasingly important. Kraft Miracle Whip salad dressing, Heinz ketchup, and Skippy Squeez'It peanut butter are sold in squeeze bottles; microwave popcorn has been a major market success; and Chicken of the Sea tuna and Folgers coffee are packaged in single-serving portions. Nabisco offers portion-control package sizes for the convenience of weight-conscious consumers. It offers 100-calorie packs of Oreos, Cheese Nips, and other products in individual pouches.

Consumer protection is another important function of packaging, including the development of tamper-resistant containers. Today, companies commonly use safety seals or pop-tops that reveal previous opening. Consumer protection through labeling exists in "open dating," which states the expected shelf life of the product.

For the functional benefits provided by Pringles's cylindrical packaging, see the text.
©McGraw-Hill Education/Mike Hruby, photographer

Functional features of packaging also can affect product quality. Pringles, with its cylindrical packaging, offers uniform chips, minimal breakage, and for some consumers, a better value than chips packaged in flex-bags.

Perceptual Benefits   A third component of packaging and labeling is the perception created in the consumer's mind. Package and label shape, color, and graphics distinguish one brand from another, convey a brand's positioning, and build brand equity. According to the director of marketing for L'eggs hosiery, "Packaging is important to the positioning and equity of the L'eggs brand."[31] Why? Packaging and labeling have been shown to enhance brand recognition and facilitate the formation of strong, favorable, and unique brand associations.

Successful marketers recognize that changes in packages and labels can update and uphold a brand's image in the customer's mind. Pepsi-Cola has embarked on a packaging change to uphold its image among teens and young adults, introducing new package graphics that change every few weeks to reflect different themes, such as sports, music, fashion, and cars.

Because labels list a product's source, brands competing in the global marketplace can benefit from "country of origin or manufacture" perceptions, as described in Chapter 6. Consumers tend to hold stereotypes about country-product pairings that they judge "best"—English tea, French perfume, Italian leather, and Japanese electronics—which can affect a brand's image. Increasingly, Chinese firms are adopting the English language and Roman letters for their brand labels sold in China. This is being done because of a common perception in many Asian countries that "things Western are good."[32]

Packaging has been a major element of L'eggs hosiery positioning since its launch in 1969.
©McGraw-Hill Education/Mike Hruby, photographer

Hanes Brands, Inc.
www.leggs.com

Packaging and Labeling Challenges and Responses

Package and label designers face four challenges. They are (1) the continuing need to connect with customers; (2) environmental concerns; (3) health, safety, and security issues; and (4) cost reduction.

Connecting with Customers   Packages and labels must be continually updated to connect with customers. The challenge lies in creating aesthetic and functional design features that attract customer attention and deliver customer value in their use. If done right, the rewards can be huge. For example, the marketing team responsible for Kleenex tissues converted its standard rectangular box into an oval shape with colorful seasonal graphics. Sales soared with this aesthetic change in packaging. After months of in-home research, Kraft product managers discovered that consumers often transferred Chips Ahoy! cookies to jars for easy access and to avoid staleness. The company solved both problems by creating a patented resealable opening on the top of the bag. The result? Sales of the new package doubled that of the old package.

Environmental Concerns   Because of widespread global concern about the growth of solid waste and the shortage of viable landfill sites, the amount, composition, and disposal of packaging material continue to receive much attention. For example, PepsiCo, Coca-Cola, and Nestlé have decreased the amount of plastic in their beverage bottles to reduce solid waste. Recycling packaging material is another major thrust. Procter & Gamble now uses recycled cardboard in over 70 percent of its paper packaging. Its Spic and Span liquid cleaner is packaged in 100 percent recycled material. Other firms, such as Walmart, are emphasizing the use of less packaging material. Over the past decade, the company has worked with its 600,000 global suppliers to reduce overall packaging and shipping material by 5 percent.

Health, Safety, and Security Issues   A third challenge involves the growing health, safety, and security concerns of packaging materials. Today, most consumers believe companies should make sure products and their packages are safe and secure, regardless of the cost, and companies are responding in numerous ways. Most butane lighters sold today, like those made by Scripto, contain a child-resistant safety latch to prevent misuse and accidental fire. Childproof caps on pharmaceutical products and household cleaners and sealed lids on food packages are now common. New packaging technology and materials that extend a product's *shelf life* (the time a product can be stored) and prevent spoilage continue to be developed.

Cost Reduction   About 80 percent of packaging material used in the world consists of paper, plastics, metal, and glass. As the cost of these materials rises, companies are constantly challenged to find innovative ways to cut packaging costs while delivering value to their customers. Many food and personal care companies have replaced bottles and cans with sealed plastic or foil pouches. Pouches cut packaging costs by 10 to 15 percent.[33]

THE MARKETING OF SERVICES

 Recognize how the four Ps framework is expanded in the marketing of services.

We conclude the chapter with a brief discussion of the marketing mix for services. As such, it is necessary to expand the four Ps framework to include people, physical environment, and process. This framework is called the **seven Ps of services marketing**.[34]

Product (Service)

To a large extent, the concepts of the product component of the marketing mix apply equally well to Cheerios (a product) and to American Express (a service). Yet there are two aspects of the product–service element of the mix that warrant special attention when dealing with services: exclusivity and brand name.

Chapter 9 pointed out that one favorable dimension in a new product is its ability to be patented. However, services cannot be patented. Hence the creator of a successful quick-service restaurant chain could quickly discover the concept being copied by others. Domino's Pizza has seen competitors, such as Pizza Hut, copy the quick delivery advantage that originally propelled the company to success.

Because services are intangible and, therefore, more difficult to describe, the brand name or identifying logo of the service organization is particularly important in consumer decisions. Brand names help make the abstract nature of services more concrete. Service marketers apply branding concepts in the same way as product marketers. Recall that American Express has applied subbranding with its different color charge cards, with unique service offerings for each.

Price

In the service industries, *price* is referred to in various ways. The terms used vary, depending upon whether the services are provided by hospitals (charges); consultants, lawyers, physicians, or accountants (fees); airlines (fares); or hotels (rates). Regardless of the term used, price plays two essential roles: (1) to affect consumer perceptions and (2) to be used in capacity management. Because of the intangible nature of services, price can indicate the quality of the service. Would you wonder about the quality of a $100 surgery? Studies show that when there are few cues by which to judge the quality of a product or service, consumers use price.

The capacity management role of price is also important to movie theaters, airlines, restaurants, and hotels. Many service businesses use **off-peak pricing**, which consists of charging different prices during different seasons of the year and different times of the day or days of the week to reflect variations in demand for the service. Airlines offer seasonal discounts and movie theaters offer matinee prices.

seven Ps of services marketing
An expanded marketing mix concept for services that includes the four Ps (product, price, promotion, and place or distribution) as well as people, physical environment, and process.

off-peak pricing
Charging different prices during different seasons of the year and different times of the day or during different days of the week to reflect variations in demand for the service.

Place (Distribution)

Place or distribution is a major factor in developing a service marketing strategy because of the inseparability of services from the producer. Historically, little attention has been paid to distribution in services marketing. But as competition grows, the value of convenient distribution is being recognized. Hairstyling chains such as Cost Cutters Family Hair Care, tax preparation offices such as H&R Block, and accounting firms such as PricewaterhouseCoopers all use multiple locations for the distribution of services. In the banking industry, customers of participating banks using the Cirrus system can access any one of thousands of automated teller machines (ATMs) throughout the United States. The Internet now provides global coverage for travel services, banking, entertainment, and many other information-based services.

Promotion

The purpose of promotion for services, specifically advertising, is to show the benefits of using the service. It is valuable to stress availability, location, consistent quality, and efficient, courteous service. Also, services must be concerned with their image. Promotional efforts, such as Merrill Lynch's use of the bull in its ads, contribute to image and positioning strategies. In general, promotional concerns of services are similar to those of products. Another form of promotion, *publicity,* plays a major role in the promotional strategy of nonprofit services and some professional organizations. Nonprofit organizations such as public school districts, the Chicago Symphony Orchestra, religious organizations, and hospitals use publicity to disseminate their messages. Because of the heavy reliance on publicity, many services use *public service announcements* (*PSAs*). PSAs are free and nonprofit groups tend to rely on them as the foundation of their media plan. However, the timing and location of a PSA are under the control of the medium, not the organization. Thus, the nonprofit service group cannot control who sees the message or when the message is delivered.

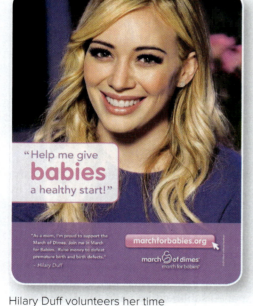

Hilary Duff volunteers her time to the March of Dimes to raise funds to give babies a healthy start in life in the March for Babies PSA. March for Babies has raised more than $2.3 billion to support infant-related research, education, and vaccines.
Source: March of Dimes

March of Dimes
www.marchforbabies.com

People

Many services depend on people for the creation and delivery of the customer service experience. The nature of the interaction between employees and customers strongly influences customers' perceptions of the service experience. Customers will often judge the quality of the experience based on the performance of the people providing the service. Still, as a National Football League executive admitted, "Even though we are in the experience business, we can't guarantee a win every time."[35]

Companies such as Disney, Southwest Airlines, and Starbucks diligently manage the experience they offer customers. They integrate their activities to connect with customers at each contact point to move beyond customer relationships to customer loyalty. Zappos.com, an online retailer, requires that all employees complete a four-week customer loyalty training program to deliver one of the company's core concepts—"Deliver WOW through service."

Physical Environment

The appearance of the environment in which the service is delivered and where the firm and customer interact can influence the customer's perception of the service. The physical evidence of the service includes all the tangibles surrounding the service: the buildings, landscaping, vehicles, furnishings, signage, brochures, and equipment. Service firms need to systematically and carefully manage physical evidence to convey the proper impression of the service to the customer. This is sometimes referred to as impression, or evidence, management. For many services, the physical environment provides an opportunity for the firm to send consistent and strong messages about the nature of the service to be delivered.

Process

Process refers to the actual procedures, mechanisms, and flow of activities by which the service is created and delivered. The actual creation and delivery steps that the customer experiences provide customers with evidence on which to judge the service. These steps involve not only "what" gets created but also "how" it is created. Grease Monkey believes that it has the right process in the vehicle oil change and fluid exchange service business. Customers do not need appointments, stores are open six days per week, the service is completed in 15–20 minutes, and a waiting room allows customers to read or work while the service is being completed.

Most services have a limited capacity due to the inseparability of the service from the service provider and the perishable nature of services. For example, a patient must be in the hospital at the same time as the surgeon to "buy" an appendectomy, and only one patient can be helped at that time. Similarly, no additional surgery can be performed tomorrow because of an unused operating room or an available surgeon today—the service capacity is lost if it is not used. So the service component of the marketing mix must be integrated with efforts to influence consumer demand. This is referred to as **capacity management**. Service organizations must manage the availability of the offering so that (1) demand matches capacity over the duration of the demand cycle (for example, one day, week, month, or year), and (2) the organization's assets are used in ways that will maximize its return on investment.

> **capacity management**
> Integrating the service component of the marketing mix with efforts to influence consumer demand.

learning review

10-7. What is the difference between a line extension and a brand extension?

10-8. Explain the role of packaging in terms of perception.

10-9. How do service businesses use off-peak pricing?

LEARNING OBJECTIVES REVIEW

LO 10-1 *Explain the product life-cycle concept.*
The product life cycle describes the stages a new product goes through in the marketplace: introduction, growth, maturity, and decline. Product sales growth and profitability differ at each stage, and marketing managers have marketing objectives and marketing mix strategies unique to each stage based on consumer behavior and competitive factors. In the introductory stage, the need is to establish primary demand, whereas the growth stage requires selective demand strategies. In the maturity stage, the need is to maintain market share; the decline stage necessitates a deletion or harvesting strategy. Some important aspects of product life cycles are (*a*) their length, (*b*) the shape of the sales curves, and (*c*) the rate at which consumers adopt products.

LO 10-2 *Identify ways that marketing executives manage a product's life cycle.*
Marketing executives manage a product's life cycle in three ways. First, they can modify the product itself by altering its characteristics, such as product quality, performance, or appearance. Second, they can modify the market by finding new customers for the product, increasing a product's use among existing customers, or creating a new use situation for the product. Finally, they can reposition the product using any one or a combination of marketing mix elements. Four factors trigger a repositioning action. They include reacting to a competitor's position, reaching a new market, catching a rising trend, and changing the value offered to consumers.

LO 10-3 *Recognize the importance of branding and alternative branding strategies.*

A basic decision in marketing products is branding, in which an organization uses a name, phrase, design, symbols, or a combination of these to identify its products and distinguish them from those of its competitors. Product managers recognize that brands offer more than product identification and a means to distinguish their products from competitors. Successful and established brands take on a brand personality and acquire brand equity—the added value a given brand name gives to a product beyond the functional benefits provided—that is crafted and nurtured by marketing programs that forge strong, favorable, and unique consumer associations with a brand. A good brand name should suggest the product benefits, be memorable, fit the company or product image, be free of legal restrictions, and be simple and emotional. Companies can and do employ several different branding strategies. With multiproduct branding, a company uses one name for all its products in a product class. A multibranding strategy involves giving each product a distinct name. A company uses private branding when it manufactures products but sells them under the brand name of a wholesaler or retailer. Finally, a company can employ mixed branding, where it markets products under its own name(s) and that of a reseller.

LO 10-4 *Describe the role of packaging and labeling in the marketing of a product.*

Packaging and labeling play numerous roles in the marketing of a product. The packaging component of a product refers to any container in which it is offered for sale and on which label information is conveyed. Manufacturers, retailers, and consumers acknowledge that packaging and labeling provide communication, functional, and perceptual benefits. Contemporary packaging and labeling challenges include (1) the continuing need to connect with customers, (2) environmental concerns, (3) health, safety, and security issues, and (4) cost reduction.

LO 10-5 *Recognize how the four Ps framework is expanded in the marketing of services.*

The four Ps framework also applies to services with some adaptations. Because services cannot be patented, unique offerings are difficult to protect. In addition, because services are intangible, brands and logos (which can be protected) are particularly important. The inseparability of production and consumption of services means that capacity management is important to services. The intangible nature of services makes price an important indication of service quality. Distribution has become an important marketing tool for services, and electronic distribution allows some services to provide global coverage. In recent years, service organizations have increased their promotional activities. Finally, the performance of people, the appearance of the physical environment, and the process involved in delivering a service are recognized as central to the customer experience.

LEARNING REVIEW ANSWERS

10-1 Advertising plays a major role in the _____ stage of the product life cycle, and _____ plays a major role in the maturity stage.
Answer: introductory; product differentiation

10-2 How do high-learning and low-learning products differ?
Answer: A high-learning product requires significant customer education and there is an extended introductory period. A low-learning product requires little customer education because the benefits of purchase are readily understood, resulting in immediate sales.

10-3 What are the five categories of product adopters in the diffusion of innovations?
Answer: The five categories of product adopters based on the diffusion of innovation are: (1) innovators—2.5 percent; (2) early adopters—13.5 percent; (3) early majority—34 percent; (4) late majority—34 percent; and (5) laggards—16 percent.

10-4 How does a product manager manage a product's life cycle?
Answer: A product manager shepherds a product through its life cycle by (1) modifying the product, which involves altering one or more of its characteristics to increase its value to customers and thus increase sales; (2) modifying the market, which involves finding new customers, increasing a product's use among existing customers, or creating new use situations; and (3) repositioning the product, which involves changing the place it occupies in consumers' minds relative to competitive products.

10-5 What does "creating a new use situation" mean in managing a product's life cycle?
Answer: Creating a new use situation means finding new uses or applications for an existing product.

10-6 Explain the difference between trading up and trading down in product repositioning.
Answer: Trading up involves adding value to the product (or line) through additional features or higher-quality materials. Trading down involves reducing the number of features, quality, or price or downsizing—reducing the content of packages without changing package size and maintaining or increasing the package price.

10-7 What is the difference between a line extension and a brand extension?
Answer: A line extension uses a current brand name to enter a new market segment in its product class, whereas a brand extension uses a current brand name to enter a completely different product class.

10-8 Explain the role of packaging in terms of perception.
Answer: A package's shape, color, and graphics distinguish one brand from another, convey a brand's positioning, and build brand equity.

10-9 How do service businesses use off-peak pricing?
Answer: Service businesses charge different prices during different times of the day or days of the week to reflect variations in demand for the service.

FOCUSING ON KEY TERMS

brand equity p. 280
brand licensing p. 282
brand name p. 280
brand personality p. 280
branding p. 280
capacity management p. 291
label p. 286
market modification p. 277
mixed branding p. 286
multibranding p. 285
multiproduct branding p. 284
off-peak pricing p. 289
packaging p. 286
private branding p. 285
product class p. 274
product form p. 274
product life cycle p. 268
product modification p. 276
seven Ps of services marketing p. 289
trading down p. 278
trading up p. 278

APPLYING MARKETING KNOWLEDGE

1. Listed here are three different products in various stages of the product life cycle. What marketing strategies would you suggest to these companies? (*a*) Canon digital cameras—maturity stage, (*b*) Hewlett-Packard tablet computers—growth stage, and (*c*) handheld manual can openers—decline stage.
2. It has often been suggested that products are intentionally made to break down or wear out. Is this strategy a planned product modification approach?
3. The product manager of GE is reviewing the penetration of trash compactors in American homes. After more than two decades in existence, this product is in relatively few homes. What problems can account for this poor acceptance? What is the shape of the trash compactor life cycle?
4. For years, Ferrari has been known as a manufacturer of expensive luxury automobiles. The company plans to attract the major segment of the car-buying market that purchases medium-priced automobiles. As Ferrari considers this trading-down strategy, what branding strategy would you recommend? What are the trade-offs to consider with your strategy?

BUILDING YOUR MARKETING PLAN

For the product offering in your marketing plan,

1. Identify (*a*) its stage in the product life cycle and (*b*) key marketing mix actions that might be appropriate, as shown in Figure 10–1.
2. Develop (*a*) branding and (*b*) packaging strategies, if appropriate for your offering.

VIDEO CASE 10 Justin's: Managing a Successful Product with Passion

"If you don't start somewhere, you'll never end up anywhere," explains Justin Gold, entrepreneur and founder of the Justin's brand of organic nut butters and peanut butter cups. It was this mantra that helped Gold turn his passion for good-tasting organic food into his now-famous brand and a growing portfolio of successful products. In fact, the Justin's website proclaims that Justin's is "Making a Butter World!"

Video 10-4
Justin's Video Case
kerin.tv/cr8e/v10-4

THE COMPANY

The idea for better nut butter came from Gold's personal experiences. "I'm an active vegetarian and I was mountain biking, running, and skiing," he explains. The combination meant that nut butter was a staple in his diet. "I was curious," he adds, "why is it that peanut butter is only available in two flavors—smooth and crunchy? Why can't you flavor a peanut butter?" So, Justin bought a basic food processor and natural ingredients and began experimenting at home in his

Courtesy of Justin's

kitchen. He filled jars with his new flavors, and to deter his roommates from eating them he labeled the jars "Justin's." That simple decision was the beginning of the brand name for his products and for the company!

Everyone who tried the homemade nut butters encouraged Justin to start selling them. As a result he created a business plan based on research about consumers and advice from a network of mentors. According to Gold, "As an entrepreneur you basically think about things in four sections—sales, marketing, operations, and finance." The first sales of the product were through a farmer's market, and popularity there led to distribution in select retailers, including Whole Foods. The big breakthrough, however, came when Justin decided to package nut butter in a squeeze pack. The packages were placed next to the jars on the shelf in the stores, and consumers would buy them as a trial size and then come back and buy a jar. "That squeeze pack really put us on the map as an innovator in the nut butter category," says Gold. "It set us apart from all the competitors out there because we had a point of differentiation."

Justin's continued to grow and was ranked in the Top 15 on the *Inc.* Fastest Growing Companies list for the Food and Beverage category. In addition, Justin was recognized as Entrepreneur of the Year by Ernst and Young. Three key values have contributed to the company's success. They include:

- *Passion* for natural and organic foods.
- *Consciousness* of sustainable and environmentally friendly practices and concern for the community.
- *Product* quality based on production innovation, nutrition, and amazing taste.

Eventually Justin decided that he needed a partner to continue the company's growth. Justin's was sold to Hormel Foods Corporation, a multinational manufacturer and marketer of consumer-branded food products, including Skippy peanut butter. "We felt that they were the perfect partner for us, we felt that Hormel was buying into our values and our mission," says Gold.

Today Justin's product line includes 10 flavors of nut butters, eight variations of nut butter cups, four types of snack packs, and a cookbook titled *Justin My Kitchen*. In addition to the initial distribution through Whole Foods stores, retail partners now include Safeway, Costco, Target, REI, Natural Grocers, King Soopers, Sprouts, and Walmart. Online retailers also include Amazon.com, Jet.com, and Thrivemarket.com. Sales have grown to include millions of jars and squeeze packs of nut butter! Recently, Justin's received a Most Innovative New Product Award from the National Confectioners Association for its new Organic White Chocolate Mini Peanut Butter Cups.

PRODUCT AND BRAND MANAGEMENT AT HORMEL

Hormel's acquisition of Justin's provided the growing nut butter company with a variety of resources. First, the acquisition provided Justin's with access to national distribution channels in the food industry. Second, it provided access to a wide variety of suppliers to ensure that many of the ingredients of Justin's existing and future products could be organic. Finally, Hormel provided sophisticated brand management expertise.

Lisa Selk, CEO of another Hormel acquisition, CytoSport, and the previous marketing director of Skippy brand peanut butter, describes the brand management orientation. "Hormel is a $9 billion company. We have a long legacy of developing brands and creating great products for American consumers and across the globe. We have 35 number one or two brands and over 20,000 employees in our company. We have passion around all of our brands," she says. The company has developed an organizational brand structure that utilizes a variety of management tools to ensure the success of the brands.

The product life cycle, for example, provides guidance for many of Hormel's brand managers as some products have a long history with the 120-year-old company while other products are much newer to the marketplace. "If you think about the product life cycle of Skippy, it's definitely a mature product and brand," explains Selk. "The typical marketing strategy for a mature brand is mass media reminder messages. It is really about how many impressions you can get across TV, print, social, and digital spaces." Product managers can guide their brands through the product life cycle by modifying the product, modifying the market, and repositioning the product. Skippy, for example, is using these approaches by creating PB Bites, finding new consumers through online channels, and positioning the product as a source of protein.

Hormel also uses a combination of branding strategies. A multiproduct branding strategy, using one name for many products, is applied to products such as Hormel Bacon, Hormel Chili, Hormel Deli Meats, and Hormel Pepperoni. A multibranding strategy, using a distinct name for each product, is also used by Hormel for many of its brands such as Jennie-O, Muscle Milk, Skippy, and Justin's. The combination of products and brands creates a portfolio that must be managed. As Selk observes, "We have a long legacy of developing brands and creating great products for American consumers."

Another important brand management tool is package design and labeling. "Design is extremely important in the early development of a product," explains Selk, "because you cannot change during its life cycle." The package design helps consumers identify the product and they become accustomed to searching for the familiar appearance on the shelf. Occasionally small changes are warranted, however. According to Selk, "Benefits are going to change." For example, "Protein is one of those things that consumers are looking for in their daily diet so we're calling out how many grams of protein on the front of the package," she continues. The label also provides essential information, particularly as regulations about nutritional facts change.

Courtesy of Justin's

MARKETING AT JUSTIN'S

There are many traditional and unique aspects to the marketing organization at Justin's. "Marketing at Justin's is organized on two paths," explains Mike Guanella, president of Justin's. "We have the brand managers who own all elements of the product line, all the four Ps, and we have master brand managers who own all of the communications that touch on all elements of the brand, not just the products," he continues. The brand managers serve in a traditional role by assuming responsibility for developing and executing the specific elements of the marketing program, while the master brand managers provide a creative solution to communication activities that influence the entire brand name.

Justin's brand managers are typically responsible for a category such as nut butters or butter cups. "The brand manager owns a specific product line, either spreads or confection, and they would own all elements of that brand, the decision making around strategy, and tactics," says Guanella. "Think about the brand manager being the hub of all the spokes that come out to deliver a product to the market. Our brand managers own every element of the four Ps from our promotional strategy, to everyday pricing, to working with our sales team." The master brand managers must take a broader perspective. According to Guanella, "Our master brand managers own elements that cut across all our product lines." For example, "Our website and our media campaigns focus on Justin's as a master brand as opposed to specific product lines."

The brand managers and master brand managers work together on new and existing products. New products are developed and typically launched in the natural food retailer channel with samples, demos, and event marketing. As the products grow, their distribution is expanded to conventional retailer channels with traditional promotion. Finally, "some of our products are approaching the mature phase," says Guanella, which becomes "an opportunity to refresh those products with different flavor offerings or different size offerings."

THE FUTURE

The team at Justin's is very excited about the future. Lisa Selk observes that "as a marketer the best feeling you can have is to create a product and put it on the shelf and watch it be consumed by people." Mike Guanella comments, "I work for a company that makes products that I love and does it in a meaningful way. A company that's focused on sustainability and corporate responsibility. It's the perfect combination. I love what I do!" And as Justin himself discloses, "at Justin's we call it the Nuthouse because you want to go somewhere where you're not only working but you love to come to work and you feel like you're making a difference!"[36]

Questions

1. How are passion, consciousness, and product quality part of the product management process at Justin's?
2. How does the stage of the product life cycle influence marketing decisions at Hormel and Justin's?
3. What roles are served by the brand managers and master brand managers of Justin's products and brands?
4. Describe the branding strategies used by Hormel and how Justin's products fit into the Hormel product line.
5. How are sustainability and corporate responsibility considerations likely to influence the future at Justin's?

Chapter Notes

1. David Robertson, "How Gatorade Invented New Products by Revisiting Old Ones," hbr.org, August 17, 2017; "Gatorade Taps into Tech-Thirsty Consumers," *The Wall Street Journal,* March 11, 2016, pp. B1, B2; "PepsiCo Introduces Organic Gatorade," *www.adage.com,* August 30, 2016; "How Gatorade Plans to Reinvent Sports Drinks Again," *www.fastcompany.com,* January 11, 2016; "Gatorade's New Selling Point: We're Necessary Performance Gear," *www.adage.com,* January 2, 2012; Darren Rovell, *First in Thirst: How Gatorade Turned the Science of Sweat into a Cultural Phenomenon* (New York: AMACOM, 2005); and *www.Gatorade.com.*
2. For an extended discussion of the generalized product life cycle, see Donald R. Lehmann and Russell S. Winer, *Product Management,* 5th ed. (Burr Ridge, IL: McGraw-Hill, 2008).
3. *Gillette Fusion Case Study* (New York: Datamonitor, June 6, 2008). All subsequent references to Gillette Fusion are based on this case study and "Men's Shaving in the U.S.," *www.statista.com,* accessed April 1, 2017.
4. Orville C. Walker Jr. and John W. Mullins, *Marketing Management: A Strategic Decision-Making Approach,* 8th ed. (Burr Ridge, IL: McGraw-Hill/Irwin, 2014), p. 209.
5. Portions of this discussion on the fax machine product life cycle are based on Jonathan Coopersmith, *Faxed: The Rise and Fall of the Fax Machine* (Baltimore: Johns Hopkins University Press, 2015); "Why Fax Won't Die," *www.fastcompany.com,* February 10, 2015; Kurt Wagner, "Why the Fax Machine Refuses to Die," *www.CNNMoney,* May 15, 2013; and "Global Fax Machine

Market 2017: Industry Size, Growth, Trends, Demand and Analysis," *www.technologynewsextra,* March 24, 2017.

6. "Fax Machines Are Still Common in Medicine," cnbc.com, February 10, 2018; *Email Statistics Report, 2014–2018* (Palo Alto, CA: The Radicati Group, 2016); and "Why Fax Won't Die."
7. Kate MacArthur, "Coke Energizes Tab, Neville Isdell's Fave," *Advertising Age,* August 29, 2005, pp. 3, 21.
8. "Hosiery Sales Hit Major Snag," *Dallas Morning News,* December 18, 2006, p. 50.
9. Arthur Asa Berger, *Ads, Fads, and Consumer Culture: Advertising's Impact on American Character and Society,* 5th ed. (Lanham, MD: Rowman & Littlefield, 2015).
10. *Year-End Marketing Reports on U.S. Recorded Music Shipments* (New York Recording Industry Association of America).
11. Everett M. Rogers, *Diffusion of Innovations,* 5th ed. (New York: Free Press, 2003).
12. Jagdish N. Sheth and Banwari Mittal, *Consumer Behavior: A Managerial Perspective,* 2nd ed. (Mason, OH: South-Western, 2003).
13. "Will Electric Vehicles Replace Gas-Powered Ones?" *The Wall Street Journal,* November 14, 2017, pp. R5–R6; and "Car Makers Race to Go Electric Cheaply," *The Wall Street Journal,* February 24–25, 2018, p. B2.
14. "When Free Samples Become Saviors," *The Wall Street Journal,* August 14, 2001, pp. B1, B4.
15. Pierre Chandon, "Research: Customers Notice When Products Shrink More Than When They Get Bigger," *hbr.org,* March 7, 2017; "Supermarket Products Get Smaller . . . but Prices Stay the Same," *www.theguardian.com,* April 19, 2017; and "Same Package, Same Price, Less Product," *The Wall Street Journal,* June 12, 2015, pp. B1, B2.
16. "Kylie and Kendall Jenner File to Trademark Their Names," *www.huffingtonpost.com,* May 4, 2015; and "We Came to an Agreement and It's All Fine, *www.standard.co.uk,* March 29, 2018.
17. This discussion is based on Kevin Lane Keller, *Strategic Brand Management,* 4th ed. (Upper Saddle River, NJ: Prentice Hall, 2013). Also see Kevin Lane Keller, "Reflections on Customer-Based Brand Equity: Perspectives, Progress, and Priorities," *AMS Review,* June 2016, pp. 1–16.
18. Keller, *Strategic Brand Management.*
19. This discussion is based on "Apple Heads the World's Most Valuable Brands of 2018 at $183 billion," forbes.com, May 23, 2018; "Untouchable Intangibles," *The Economist,* August 30, 2014, p. 58; John Deighton, "How Snapple Got Its Juice Back," *Harvard Business Review,* January 2002, pp. 47–53; and "Breakfast King Agrees to Sell Bagel Business," *The Wall Street Journal,* September 28, 1999, pp. B1, B6. Also see Vithala R. Rao, Manoj K. Agarwal, and Denise Dahlhoff, "How Is Manifest Branding Strategy Related to the Value of a Corporation?" *Journal of Marketing,* October 2004, pp. 125–41.
20. The examples in this section are taken from "The Global Top 150 Licensors," *License!Global,* May 2018, pp. T3ff; and "Its the Great White North, Charlie Brown," *The Wall Street Journal,* May 27–28, 2017, p. A11.
21. "The Global Top 150 Licensors," pp. T3ff.
22. Marc Fetscherin et al., "In China? Pick Your Brand Name Carefully," *Harvard Business Review,* September 2012, p. 26; Beth Snyder Bulik, "What's in a (Good) Product Name? Sales," *Advertising Age,* February 2, 2009, p. 10; and Keller, *Strategic Brand Management.*
23. Ibid.
24. Mark Ritson, "Should You Launch a Fighter Brand?" *Harvard Business Review,* October 2009, pp. 87–94.
25. "Rides," *Dallas Morning News,* September 30, 2005, p. 8D.
26. "P&G Brand Divestitures Will Be Bigger Than Original Targets," *www.adage.com,* February 19, 2015; and "Procter & Gamble Growth Remains Elusive for Its New Chief," *www.bloomberg.com,* April 26, 2017.
27. *Store Brand Facts* (New York: Private Label Manufacturers Association, 2018).
28. *www.pez.com,* downloaded September 1, 2018; Shawn Peterson, *PEZ: From Austrian Invention to American Icon* (Charleston, SC: The History Press, 2016); and "So Sweet: William and Kate PEZ Dispensers," *www.today.msnbc.com,* March 30, 2012.
29. "Market Statistics," *www.Packaging-Gateway.com,* downloaded March 25, 2016.
30. "Green Bean Casserole Turns 50," *Dallas Morning News,* November 19, 2005, p. 10D.
31. "Iconic L'eggs Sheer Energy Egg Package Returns," *Package World,* March 6, 2014, pp. 16–17.
32. "Here Comes the Modern Chinese Consumer," *www.mckinsey.com,* March 2016.
33. *2018 State of the U.S. Flexible Packaging Industry* (Annapolis, MD: Flexible Packaging Association, 2018).
34. This discussion is based on Valerie A. Zeithaml, Mary Jo Bitner, and Dwayne D. Gremler, *Services Marketing: Integrating Customer Focus across the Firm,* 7th ed. (Burr Ridge, IL: McGraw-Hill/Irwin, 2017).
35. Quoted in Johny K. Johansson and Kurt A. Carlson, *Contemporary Brand Management* (Thousand Oaks: Sage, 2015), at p. 12.
36. This case was written by Steven Hartley and Roger Kerin. Sources: Interviews with Justin's executives Justin Gold, Mike Guanella, and Lisa Selk; Elaine Low, "Natural Foods Are Mainstream, but Startups Now Face a Big Choice," *Investors Business Daily,* March 12, 2018; "Hormel Foods Corporation Appoints Lisa Selk as Chief Executive Officer, CytoSport, Inc.," *PR Newswire,* August 18, 2017; Danielle Romano, "Welcome to the Latest & Greatest," *Convenience Store News,* June 2018; "Hormel Foods Launches New Justin's Nut Butter Cups," *FoodBev Media,* June 21, 2018; "Hormel Foods Announces Closing of Acquisition of Justin's LLC and COO Appointment," company press release, May 31, 2016; Robin D. Schatz, "How to Go from Farmer's Market to Whole Foods," *Inc.,* July–August 2013; and Justin's website, www.justins.com.

11

LEARNING OBJECTIVES

After reading this chapter you should be able to:

LO 11-1 Describe the nature and importance of pricing and the approaches used to select an approximate price level.

LO 11-2 Explain what a demand curve is and the role of revenues in pricing decisions.

LO 11-3 Explain the role of costs in pricing decisions and describe how combinations of price, fixed cost, and unit variable cost affect a firm's break-even point.

LO 11-4 Recognize the objectives a firm has in setting prices and the constraints that restrict the range of prices a firm can charge.

LO 11-5 Describe the steps taken in setting a final price.

Pricing Products and Services

VIZIO, Inc.—Building a Smart TV Brand at a Great Value

Can you name the largest U.S.-based TV maker? Stumped? It's VIZIO, Inc., an entrepreneurial Irvine, California, company. The VIZIO brand was created by William Wang, VIZIO's co-founder, who was born in Taiwan, immigrated to the United States at age 13, and learned the English language watching television.

In 2002, Wang was struck by an ad for a $10,000 flat-panel HDTV set and immediately saw an opportunity. Instead of marketing these sets as luxury items, Wang thought he could make and market an HDTV that would be affordable for the average customer.

Like many entrepreneurs, he borrowed money from friends and family and mortgaged his home. Within a year, he and his partners delivered the company's first VIZIO HDTV to Costco for distribution through that company's stores. VIZIO HDTVs are now sold through Costco, Walmart, BJ's Wholesale, Best Buy, Sam's Club, and Target stores nationwide, along with authorized online partners such as Amazon. VIZIO has sold more than 50 million HDTVs since its founding.

VIZIO's ability to deliver affordable HDTVs to the average customer is based on a novel strategy. VIZIO didn't invest in expensive manufacturing facilities but instead relied on contract manufacturers to build its products. Product development and marketing specialists in the United States handle product design and marketing. "The whole goal is to ensure that we have the right product at the right time and the right price and really drive a seamless end-to-end value chain," says a company spokesperson.

"Consumers want to save money without sacrificing quality or technology," says VIZIO's chief technology officer, who emphasizes that VIZIO's strategy is to make affordable products with innovative features. He adds, "We're far from the cheapest brand on the market at present. Everybody deserves the latest technology, too."

VIZIO's visionary commitment to delivering high-quality technology at a great value to consumers is evident by its pioneering role in launching smart TVs a decade ago. Smart TVs make it possible for viewers to watch content from the Internet directly on their TVs, for a more interactive TV watching experience. VIZIO is the smart TV market leader in North America.

Source: Vizio, Inc.

Source: Vizio, Inc.

Video 11-1
VIZIO
kerin.tv/cr8e/v11-1

VIZIO's powerful and profitable value-based pricing strategy clearly resonates with consumers. VIZIO is frequently ranked "Highest in Customer Satisfaction" with HDTVs by J.D. Power and Associates. VIZIO has the second-largest market share for televisions and smart televisions in the United States.[1]

Welcome to the fascinating—and intense—world of pricing. This chapter describes the important factors organizations consider when they go about setting prices for their products and services.

NATURE AND IMPORTANCE OF PRICE

LO 11-1 Describe the nature and importance of pricing and the approaches used to select an approximate price level.

The price paid for products and services goes by many names. You pay *tuition* for your education, *rent* for an apartment, *interest* on a bank credit card, and a *premium* for car insurance. Your dentist or physician charges you a *fee,* a professional or social organization charges *dues,* and airlines charge a *fare.* In business, an executive is given a *salary,* a salesperson receives a *commission,* and a worker is paid a *wage.* And what you pay for clothes or a haircut is termed a *price*.

Among all marketing and operations factors in a business firm, price has a unique role. It is the place where all other business decisions come together. The price must be "right"—in the sense that customers must be willing to pay it; it must generate enough sales dollars to pay for the cost of developing, producing, and marketing the product; *and* it must earn a profit for the company. Small changes in price can have big effects on both the number of units sold and company profit.

What Is a Price?

From a marketing viewpoint, **price (P)** is the money or other considerations (including other products and services) exchanged for the ownership or use of a product or service. For example, Wilkinson Sword has exchanged some of its knives for advertising used to promote its razor blades. This practice of exchanging products and services for other products and services rather than for money is called **barter**. Barter transactions account for billions of dollars annually in domestic and international trade. In the United States alone, $12 billion of products and services are traded every year without any money changing hands.[2]

price (P) The money or other considerations (including other products and services) exchanged for the ownership or use of a product or service.

barter The practice of exchanging products and services for other products and services rather than for money.

The Price Equation

For most products, money is exchanged. However, the amount paid is not always the same as the list, or quoted, price because of discounts, allowances, and extra fees. Today's pricing tactic involves using "special fees" and "surcharges." This practice is driven by consumers' zeal for low prices combined with the ease of making price comparisons on the Internet. Buyers are more willing to pay extra fees than a higher list price, so sellers use add-on charges as a way of having the consumer pay more without raising the list price.

All the factors that increase or decrease the final price of an offering help construct a "price equation," which is shown for a few products in Figure 11–1. These are key considerations if you want to buy a 2019 Bugatti Chiron Sport.[3] This all-wheel car accelerates from 0 to 60 mph in just 2.4 seconds. With its 1,500-horsepower engine, top speed is electronically limited—limited!—to 261mph! The aerodynamic body is made out of carbon fiber to safely handle the speed.

Are you interested in trading in your 2008 Mini-Cooper (shown on the right) for a 2019 Bugatti Chiron Sport (shown on the left), the world's most expensive car? Read the text to find out the true cost of purchasing a new car.

(left): ©CTK/Alamy Stock Photo; (right): ©Drive Images/Alamy Stock Photo

FIGURE 11–1

The "price" a buyer pays can take different names depending on what is purchased, and it can change depending on the price equation.

Calculating a Final Price The Bugatti Chiron Sport U.S. list price is a cool $3 million, give or take a dollar or two. But the dealer has agreed to give you a trade-in allowance of $7,000 based on the trade-in value for your 2008 Mini-Cooper two-door sedan that is in good condition. And your great-uncle has offered to give you a 5-year interest-free loan. Other charges include: (1) an import duty of $55,000; (2) a gas-guzzler tax of $7,000; (3) a sales tax of $225,000; (4) an auto registration fee of $5,000 to the state; and (5) a $54,000 destination charge to ship the car to you from France.

Applying the price equation shown in Figure 11–1 to your Bugatti Chiron purchase, your final price is:

$$\begin{aligned}
\text{Final price} &= [\text{List price}] - [\text{Allowances}] + [\text{Extra fees}] \\
&= [\$3{,}000{,}000] - [\$7{,}000] \\
&\quad + [\$55{,}000 + \$7{,}000 + \$225{,}000 + \$5{,}000 + \$54{,}000] \\
&= \$3{,}000{,}000 - \$7{,}000 + \$346{,}000 \\
&= \$3{,}339{,}000
\end{aligned}$$

Note that your final price is $339,000 more than the list price! Are you still interested in buying? If so, put yourself on the waiting list.

Price as an Indicator of Value

From a consumer's standpoint, price is often used to indicate value when it is compared with perceived benefits, such as the quality or durability of a product or service. Specifically, **value** is the ratio of perceived benefits to price, or[4]

$$\text{Value} = \frac{\text{Perceived benefits}}{\text{Price}}$$

This relationship shows that for a given price, as perceived benefits increase, value increases. Not surprisingly, if you're used to paying $7.99 for a medium frozen cheese pizza, wouldn't a large one at the same price be more valuable? Conversely, for a given price, value decreases when perceived benefits decrease. The reduced contents in many consumer packaged products sold in supermarkets without a comparable drop in price decreases value to consumers.

value
The ratio of perceived benefits to price; or Value = (Perceived benefits ÷ Price).

Marketing Matters

Customer Value

Does Spirit Airlines Engage in Value Pricing? For Some Yes, for Others No

Does Spirit Airlines engage in value pricing? Well, it depends on what benefits certain passengers seek and the price they are willing to pay.

The U.S. Department of Transportation reports that Spirit Airlines fares are, on average, 40 percent lower than other airlines for the same trip. What benefits do passengers get for this low fare? A seat that will not recline on an airplane that will get you to your intended destination faster than a car or bus. Do you want a boarding pass, a beverage, room in an overhead bin for luggage, or an assigned or aisle seat? You will pay separately for those benefits, which will increase the price you pay to get to your destination.

So, does Spirit Airlines engage in value pricing? The answer is yes for those who wish to get to their destination as cheaply as currently possible. For others, no. They expect to get more (benefits) for what they give (fare). Not surprisingly, Spirit Airlines consistently ranks highest among U.S. airlines for complaints (e.g., on-time, performance, legroom), except fares. In response to passenger complaints, a company spokesperson summed up Spirit Airlines's view on value pricing, saying Spirit Airlines won't "add cost for things that most customers don't value as much as our low fares just to reduce the complaints of a few customers. Doing that would raise prices for everyone, compromising our commitment to what our customers have continuously told us they truly value—the lowest possible price."

©Sam Pollitt/Alamy Stock Photo

value pricing
The practice of simultaneously increasing product and service benefits while maintaining or decreasing price.

profit equation
Profit = Total revenue − Total cost; or Profit = (Unit price × Quantity sold) − (Fixed cost + Variable cost).

Using Value Pricing

Creative marketers engage in **value pricing**, the practice of simultaneously increasing product and service benefits while maintaining or decreasing price. For some products, price influences consumers' perception of overall quality and ultimately its value to them.[5] In a survey of home furnishing buyers, 84 percent agreed with the statement: "The higher the price, the higher the quality."[6] For example, Kohler introduced a walk-in bathtub that is safer for children and older adults. Although priced higher than conventional step-in bathtubs, the product is successful because buyers are willing to pay a bit more for what they perceive as the value of extra safety.

In this context, "value" involves the judgment by a consumer of the worth of a product or service relative to substitutes that satisfy the same need. Through the process of comparing the costs and benefits of substitute items, a "reference value" emerges. For many consumers, the posted airfares of competing airlines serving the same cities become reference values. Based on airfare alone, Spirit Airlines usually offers the lowest price. But value assessments also include benefits received at a given price. Read the Marketing Matters box and decide whether or not Spirit Airlines offers value pricing.[7]

Price in the Marketing Mix

Pricing is a critical decision made by a marketing executive because price has a direct effect on a firm's profits. This is apparent from a firm's **profit equation**, where:

Profit = Total revenue − Total cost
= (Unit price × Quantity sold) − (Fixed cost + Variable cost)

What makes this relationship even more complicated is that price affects the quantity sold, as illustrated with demand curves later in this chapter. Furthermore, since the quantity sold usually affects a firm's costs because of efficiency of production, price also indirectly affects costs. Thus, pricing decisions influence both total revenue (sales) and total cost, which makes pricing one of the most important decisions marketing executives face.

COMMON PRICING APPROACHES

A key for a marketing manager setting a final price for a product or service is to find an approximate price level to use as a reasonable starting point. Four common approaches to helping find this approximate price level are (1) demand-oriented, (2) cost-oriented, (3) profit-oriented, and (4) competition-oriented (see Figure 11–2). Although these approaches are discussed separately below, some of them overlap, and a seasoned marketing manager will consider several in selecting an approximate price level.

Demand-Oriented Pricing Approaches

Demand-oriented approaches weigh factors underlying expected customer tastes and preferences more heavily than cost, profit, and competition factors when selecting a price level.

Skimming Pricing A firm introducing a new or innovative product can use **skimming pricing**, setting the highest initial price that customers who really desire the product are willing to pay. These customers are not very price sensitive because they weigh the new product's price, quality, and ability to satisfy their needs against the same characteristics of substitutes. As the demand of these customers is satisfied, the firm lowers the price to attract another, more price-sensitive segment. Thus, skimming pricing gets its name from skimming successive layers of "cream," or customer segments, as prices are lowered in a series of steps.

Skimming pricing is an effective strategy when (1) enough prospective customers are willing to buy the product immediately at the high initial price to make these sales profitable, (2) the high initial price will not attract competitors, (3) lowering price has only a minor effect on increasing the sales volume and reducing the unit costs, and (4) customers interpret the high price as signifying high quality. These four conditions are most likely to exist when the new product is protected by patents or copyrights or its uniqueness is understood and valued by consumers. Microsoft, for example, adopted a skimming strategy for its Xbox One X video game console in 2018 since many of these conditions applied. The Xbox One X was priced about $100 more than Sony's PlayStation 4 Pro and $200 more than the Nintendo Switch.

Penetration Pricing Setting a low initial price on a new product to appeal immediately to the mass market is **penetration pricing**, the exact opposite of skimming pricing. Amazon consciously chose a penetration strategy when it introduced its new generation Amazon Kindle Fire tablet computer at $49.99. The average price of competitive models was $323.[8]

skimming pricing
Setting the highest initial price that customers really desiring the product are willing to pay when introducing a new or innovative product.

penetration pricing
Setting a low initial price on a new product to appeal immediately to the mass market.

FIGURE 11–2
Four approaches for selecting an approximate price level.

Select an approximate price level

Demand-oriented approaches
- Skimming
- Penetration
- Prestige
- Odd-even
- Bundle

Cost-oriented approaches
- Standard markup
- Cost-plus

Profit-oriented approaches
- Target profit
- Target return on sales
- Target return on investment

Competition-oriented approaches
- Customary
- Above, at, or below market
- Loss leader

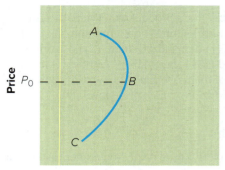

FIGURE 11–3

For prestige pricing, the demand curve for high-quality products bought by status-conscious consumers is backward sloping.

Video 11-2
Rolex Ad
kerin.tv/cr8e/v11-2

prestige pricing
Setting a high price so that quality- or status-conscious consumers will be attracted to the product and buy it.

odd-even pricing
Setting prices a few dollars or cents under an even number.

bundle pricing
The marketing of two or more products in a single package price.

Which pricing strategy is used by DIRECTV? Read the text to find out which one and why.
Source: DIRECTV

The conditions favoring penetration pricing are the reverse of those supporting skimming pricing: (1) many segments of the market are price sensitive, (2) a low initial price discourages competitors from entering the market, and (3) unit production and marketing costs fall dramatically as production volumes increase. A firm using penetration pricing may (1) maintain the initial price for a time to gain profit lost from its low introductory level or (2) lower the price further, counting on the new volume to generate the necessary profit.

In some situations, penetration pricing may follow skimming pricing. A company might initially price a product high to attract price-insensitive consumers and recoup initial research and development costs and introductory promotional expenditures. Once this is done, penetration pricing is used to appeal to a broader segment of the population and increase market share.[9]

Prestige Pricing Consumers may use price as a measure of the quality or prestige of an item so that as price is lowered beyond some point, demand for the item actually falls. **Prestige pricing** involves setting a high price so that quality- or status-conscious consumers will be attracted to the product and buy it. As shown in Figure 11–3, the demand curve for prestige pricing slopes downward and to the right between points A and B but turns back to the left between points B and C because demand is actually reduced between points B and C. From A to B, buyers see the lowering of price as a bargain and buy more; from B to C, they become dubious about the quality and prestige and buy less. A marketing manager's pricing strategy here is to stay above price P_0 (the initial price).

Rolls-Royce cars, Chanel perfume, Cartier jewelry, Lalique crystal, and Swiss watches, such as Rolex, have an element of prestige pricing in them and may sell worse at lower prices than at higher ones.[10] The recent success of Swiss watchmaker TAG Heuer is an example. The company quadrupled the average price of its watches and its sales volume jumped sevenfold.[11] Recently, Energizer learned that buyers of high-performance alkaline batteries tend to link a lower price with lower quality. The Marketing Matters box describes the pricing lesson learned by Energizer.[12]

Odd-Even Pricing Apple priced its iPhone XS model at $999, Sears offers a Craftsman radial saw for $899.99, and the suggested retail price for the Gillette Fusion shaving system is $11.99. Why not simply price these items at $1,000, $900 and $12, respectively? These firms are using **odd-even pricing**, which involves setting prices a few dollars or cents under an even number. The presumption is that consumers see the iPhone XS as priced at "something over $900" rather than "about $1,000." In theory, demand increases if the price drops from $1,000 to $999. There is some evidence to suggest this does happen. However, research suggests that overuse of odd-ending prices tends to mute its effect on demand.[13]

Bundle Pricing A frequently used demand-oriented pricing practice is **bundle pricing**—the marketing of two or more products in a single package price. For example, Delta Air Lines offers vacation packages that include airfare, car rental, and lodging. Bundle pricing is based on the idea that consumers value the package more than the individual items. This is due to benefits received from not having to make separate purchases and enhanced satisfaction from one item given the presence of another. This is the idea behind McDonald's Extra Value Meal and AT&T and DIRECTV's TV, phone, and Internet bundles. Moreover, bundle pricing often provides a lower total cost to buyers and lower marketing costs to sellers.

Cost-Oriented Pricing Approaches

With cost-oriented approaches, a price setter stresses the cost side of the pricing problem, not the demand side. Price is set by looking

Marketing Matters

Customer Value

Energizer's Lesson in Price Perception—Value Lies in the Eye of the Beholder

Battery manufacturers are as tireless as a certain drum-thumping bunny in their efforts to create products that perform better, last longer, and, not incidentally, outsell the competition. The commercialization of new alkaline battery technology at a price that creates value for consumers is not always obvious or easy. Just ask the marketing executives at Energizer about their experience with pricing Energizer Advanced Formula and Energizer e^2 AA alkaline batteries.

When Duracell launched its high-performance Ultra brand AA alkaline battery with a 25 percent price premium over standard Duracell batteries, Energizer quickly countered with its own high-performance battery—Energizer Advanced Formula. Believing that consumers would not pay the premium price, Energizer priced its Advanced Formula brand at the same price as its standard AA alkaline battery, expecting to gain market share from Duracell. It did not happen. Why? According to industry analysts, consumers associated Energizer's low price with inferior quality in the high-performance segment. Instead of gaining market share, Energizer lost market share to Duracell and Rayovac, the number three battery manufacturer.

Having learned its lesson, Energizer subsequently released its e^2 high-performance battery, this time priced 4 percent higher than Duracell Ultra and about 50 percent higher than Advanced Formula. The result? Energizer recovered lost sales and market share. The lesson learned? Value lies in the eye of the beholder.

©Joe Marino/Bill Cantrell/UPI/Newscom

What standard markups are used for the soft drinks, candy, and popcorn at your local movie theater? Read the text to find out.
©andresr/E+/Getty Images

standard markup pricing
Adding a fixed percentage to the cost of all items in a specific product class.

cost-plus pricing
Summing the total unit cost of providing a product or service and adding a specific amount to the cost to arrive at a price.

at the production and marketing costs and then adding enough to cover direct expenses, overhead, and profit.

Standard Markup Pricing Managers of supermarkets and other retail stores have such a large number of products that estimating the demand for each product as a means of setting price is impossible. Therefore, they use **standard markup pricing**, which entails adding a fixed percentage to the cost of all items in a specific product class. This percentage markup varies depending on the type of retail store (such as furniture, clothing, or grocery) and the product involved. High-volume products usually have smaller markups than low-volume products.

Supermarkets such as Kroger and Safeway have different markups for staple items and discretionary items. The markup on staple items such as sugar, flour, and dairy products varies from 10 percent to 23 percent. Markups on discretionary items like snack foods and candy range from 27 percent to 47 percent. These markups must cover all of the expenses of the store, pay for overhead costs, and contribute something to profits. Although these markups may appear very large, they result in only a 1 percent profit on sales revenue, assuming the supermarket is operating efficiently.

By comparison, consider the markups on snacks and beverages purchased at your local movie theater. The markup is 593 percent on soft drinks, 104 percent on candy bars, and 806 percent on popcorn. These markups might sound high, but consider the consequences. "If we didn't charge as much for concessions as we did, a movie ticket would cost $20," says the CEO of Regal Entertainment, the largest U.S. theater chain.[14]

Cost-Plus Pricing Many manufacturing, professional services, and construction firms use a variation of standard markup pricing. **Cost-plus pricing** involves summing the total unit cost of providing a product or service and adding a specific amount to the

How was the price of the Rock and Roll Hall of Fame and Museum determined? Read the text to find out.
©Stan Rohrer/Alamy Stock Photo

cost to arrive at a price. Cost-plus pricing generally assumes two forms. With *cost-plus percentage-of-cost pricing,* a fixed percentage is added to the total unit cost. This is often used to price one- or few-of-a-kind items, as when an architectural firm charges a percentage of the construction costs of, say, the $92 million Rock and Roll Hall of Fame and Museum in Cleveland, Ohio.

In buying highly technical, few-of-a-kind products such as hydroelectric power plants or space satellites, governments have found that general contractors are reluctant to specify a formal, fixed price for the procurement. Therefore, they use *cost-plus fixed-fee pricing,* which means that a supplier is reimbursed for all costs, regardless of what they turn out to be, but is allowed only a fixed fee as profit that is independent of the final cost of the project. For example, suppose the National Aeronautics and Space Administration agreed to pay Lockheed Martin $4 billion as the cost for its Orion lunar spacecraft and agreed to a $6.5 billion fee for providing the lunar spacecraft. Even if Lockheed Martin's cost increased to $7 billion for the lunar spacecraft, its fee would remain at $6.5 billion.

Cost-plus pricing is the most commonly used method to set prices for business products. Increasingly, however, this method is finding favor among business-to-business marketers in the service sector. For example, the rising cost of legal fees has prompted some law firms to adopt a cost-plus pricing approach. Rather than billing business clients on an hourly basis, lawyers and their clients agree on a fixed fee based on expected costs plus a profit for the law firm. Many advertising agencies now use this approach. Here, the client agrees to pay the agency a fee based on the cost of its work plus some agreed-on profit, which is often a percentage of total cost.

Profit-Oriented Pricing Approaches

A price setter may choose to balance both revenues and costs to set price using profit-oriented approaches. These might either involve setting a target of a specific dollar volume of profit or expressing this target profit as a percentage of sales or investment.

The Caplow Company specializes in high-quality custom framing of fine art and photography as well as antique frame restoration for its customers. Read the text to find out how it would apply target profit pricing approaches and break-even analysis later in the chapter.
©Jane Westerlund

Target Profit Pricing   A firm that sets an annual target of a specific dollar volume of profit is using a **target profit pricing** approach. As the owner of The Caplow Company, a picture framing shop, suppose you decide to use target profit pricing to establish a price for a typical framed picture. First, you need to make some assumptions, such as:

- Variable cost is a constant $22 per unit.
- Fixed cost is a constant $26,000.
- Demand is insensitive to price up to $60 per unit.
- A target profit of $7,000, at an annual volume of 1,000 units (framed pictures).

You can then calculate price as follows:

$$\text{Profit} = \text{Total revenue} - \text{Total cost}$$
$$\text{Profit} = (P \times Q) - [FC + (UVC \times Q)]$$
$$\$7{,}000 = (P \times 1{,}000) - [\$26{,}000 + (\$22 \times 1{,}000)]$$
$$\$7{,}000 = 1{,}000P - (\$26{,}000 + \$22{,}000)$$
$$1{,}000P = \$7{,}000 + \$48{,}000$$
$$P = \$55$$

target profit pricing
Setting an annual target of a specific dollar volume of profit.

target return-on-sales pricing
Setting a price to achieve a profit that is a specified percentage of the sales volume.

target return-on-investment pricing
Setting a price to achieve an annual target return on investment (ROI).

customary pricing
Setting a price that is dictated by tradition, a standardized channel of distribution, or other competitive factors.

above-, at-, or below-market pricing
Setting a market price for a product or product class based on a subjective feel for the competitors' price or market price as the benchmark.

Note that a critical assumption is that this higher average price for a framed picture will not cause the demand to fall.

Target Return-on-Sales Pricing A shortcoming with target profit pricing is that although it is simple and the target involves only a specific dollar volume, there is no benchmark of sales or investment used to show how much of the firm's effort is needed to achieve the target. Firms such as supermarket chains often use **target return-on-sales pricing** to set typical prices that will give them a profit that is a specified percentage, say, 1 percent, of the sales volume. This price method is often used because of the difficulty in establishing a benchmark of sales or investment to show how much of a company's efforts is needed to achieve the target.

Target Return-on-Investment Pricing Large, publicly owned corporations such as General Motors and many public utilities set annual return-on-investment (ROI) targets, such as an ROI of 10 percent. **Target return-on-investment pricing** is a method of setting prices to achieve this target. For example, an electric or natural gas utility may decide to seek a 10 percent ROI. If its investment in plant and equipment is $50 billion, it would need to set the price of electricity or natural gas at a level that results in $5 billion a year in profit.

Competition-Oriented Pricing Approaches

Rather than emphasize demand, cost, or profit factors, a price setter can stress what "the market" is doing by using competition-oriented approaches.

Customary Pricing For some products where tradition, a standardized channel of distribution, or other competitive factors dictate the price, **customary pricing** is used. For example, tradition prevails in the pricing of Swatch watches. The $50 customary price for the basic model has changed little in 10 years. Candy bars offered through standard vending machines have a customary price of $1. A significant departure from this price may result in a loss of sales for the manufacturer. Hershey changes the amount of chocolate in its candy bars depending on the price of raw chocolate rather than varying its customary retail price so that it can continue selling through vending machines.

Above-, At-, or Below-Market Pricing For most products, it is difficult to identify a specific market price for a product or product class. Still, marketing managers often have a subjective feel for the competitors' price or market price. Using this benchmark, they then may deliberately choose a strategy of **above-, at-, or below-market pricing**.

Among watch manufacturers, Rolex takes pride in emphasizing that it makes one of the most expensive watches you can buy, a clear example of above-market pricing. Manufacturers of national brands of clothing such as Hart Schaffner & Marx and Christian Dior and retailers such as Neiman Marcus deliberately set premium prices for their products.

Revlon cosmetics and Arrow brand shirts are generally priced "at market." As such, they also provide a reference price for competitors that use above- and below-market pricing.

A number of firms use below-market pricing. Manufacturers and retailers that offer private brands of products ranging from peanut butter to shampoo deliberately set prices for these products about 8 to 10 percent below the prices of nationally branded competitive products such as Skippy peanut butter and Vidal Sassoon shampoo. Below-market pricing also exists in business-to-business marketing. Hewlett-Packard, for instance, initially priced its office personal computers below those of competitors to promote a value image among corporate buyers.[15]

Has Red Bull's price premium among energy-drink brands sold in convenience stores increased or decreased? The Applying Marketing Metrics box answers this question.
©McGraw-Hill Education/Mike Hruby, photographer

Applying Marketing Metrics
Are Red Bull Prices Above, At, or Below the Market?

How would you determine whether a firm's retail prices are above, at, or below the market? You might visit retail stores and record what prices retailers are charging for products or brands. However, this laborious activity can be simplified by combining dollar market share and unit volume market share measures to create a "price premium" display on your marketing dashboard.

Your Challenge

Red Bull is the leading energy-drink brand in the United States in terms of dollar market share and unit market share (see the table). Company marketing executives have research showing that Red Bull has a strong brand equity. What they want to know is whether the brand's price premium resulting from its brand equity has eroded due to heavy price discounting in the convenience store channel. The convenience store channel accounts for 60 percent of energy-drink sales.

A price premium is the percentage by which the actual price charged for a specific brand exceeds (or falls short of) a benchmark established for a similar product or basket of products. As such, a price premium shows whether a brand is priced above, at, or below the market. This premium is calculated as follows:

$$\text{Price premium (\%)} = \frac{\text{Dollar sales market share for a brand}}{\text{Unit volume market share for a brand}} - 1$$

Your Findings

Using 2016 energy-drink brand market share data for U.S. convenience stores, the Red Bull price premium was 1.152, or 15.2 percent, calculated as follows: (38 percent ÷ 33 percent) − 1 = 0.152. Red Bull's average price was 15.2 percent higher than the average price for energy-drink brands sold in convenience stores. Red Bull's price premium based on 2015 brand market share data was 1.121, or 12.1 percent, calculated as follows: (37 percent ÷ 33 percent) − 1 = 0.121. Red Bull's price premium has increased relative to its competitors, notably Monster Energy and Rockstar. The price premiums for Red Bull and these two competitive brands for 2015 and 2016 are displayed in the marketing dashboard.

Your Action

Red Bull has maintained its price premium while retaining its unit volume share, which is not only favorable news for the brand but also evidence of price discounting by other brands. Clearly, the company's brand-building effort, reflected in sponsorships and a singular focus on brand attributes valued by consumers, should be continued.

Brand	Dollar Sales Market Share 2016	Dollar Sales Market Share 2015	Unit Volume Market Share 2016	Unit Volume Market Share 2015
Red Bull	38%	37%	33%	33%
Monster	18	17	19	18
Rockstar	7	8	8	9
Other brands	37	38	40	40
	100%	100%	100%	100%

Companies use a "price premium" to assess whether their products and brands are priced above, at, or below the market. An illustration of how the price premium measure is calculated, displayed, and interpreted appears in the Applying Marketing Metrics box.[16]

Loss-Leader Pricing For a special promotion, retail stores deliberately sell a product below its customary price to attract attention to it. The purpose of this **loss-leader pricing** is not to increase sales but to attract customers in hopes they will buy other products as well, particularly the discretionary items with large markups. For example, supermarkets often use milk and bananas as loss leaders.

> **loss-leader pricing**
> Deliberately selling a product below its customary price, not to increase sales, but to attract customers' attention to it in hopes that they will buy other products with large markups as well.

learning review

11-1. Value is _____.

11-2. What circumstances in pricing a new product might support skimming or penetrating pricing?

ESTIMATING DEMAND AND REVENUE

LO 11-2 Explain what a demand curve is and the role of revenues in pricing decisions.

Basic to setting a product's price is the extent of customer demand for it. Marketing executives must also translate this estimate of customer demand into estimates of revenues the firm expects to receive.

Estimating Demand

How much will you pay for a frozen cheese pizza you can pop in the oven for a quick dinner while you are studying for a marketing exam? $6? $8? $10? And what are some of the factors affecting this decision? Your preference for pizza compared to other quick-service food? The ease with which you can call Domino's or your local Chinese restaurant for an already-prepared meal delivered to your residence? How much money you have available in your credit card account while you're thinking about the tuition payment that's due next month? All these factors affect demand.

To illustrate the fundamentals of estimating demand, let's assume you are a consultant to the marketing manager at Red Baron® pizza and your job is to start analyzing the demand for its Red Baron frozen cheese pizzas. In the process, you'll have to consider what the demand curve for frozen cheese pizza might look like, how it affects Red Baron's sales revenues, and the price elasticity of demand.

> **demand curve**
> A graph that relates the quantity sold and price, showing the maximum number of units that will be sold at a given price.

The Demand Curve A **demand curve** is a graph that relates the quantity sold and price, showing the maximum number of units that will be sold at a given price. Based on secondary research you conducted regarding the annual demand for Red Baron frozen cheese pizza, you are able to construct the demand curve D_1 in Figure 11–4A. Note the following relationship: As price falls, more people decide to buy Red Baron frozen cheese pizza, which increases its unit sales. But price is not the complete story when estimating demand. Economists emphasize three other key factors that influence demand for a product:

1. *Consumer tastes.* As we saw in Chapter 3, these depend on many forces such as demographics, culture, and technology. Because consumer tastes can change quickly, up-to-date marketing research is essential to estimate demand. For example, if research by nutritionists concludes that some pizzas are healthier (because they are now gluten-free or vegetarian), demand for them will probably increase.

What key factors affect the demand for Red Baron frozen cheese pizzas? Read the text to find out.

©McGraw-Hill Education/Mike Hruby, photographer

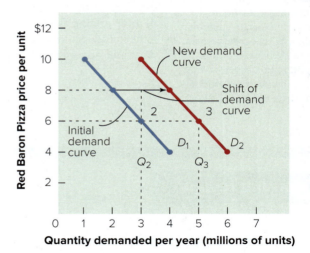

FIGURE 11–4

Demand curves for Red Baron frozen cheese pizza showing the effect on annual sales (quantity demanded per year) by change in price caused by (A) a movement along the demand curve and (B) a shift of the demand curve.

2. *Price and availability of similar products.* If the price of a competitor's pizza that is a substitute for yours—like Tombstone® pizza—falls, more people will buy it; its demand will rise and the demand for yours will fall. Other low-priced dinners are also substitutes for pizza. For example, if you want something fast so you can study, you could call Domino's and order a pizza for home delivery. So, as the price of a substitute falls or its availability increases, the demand for your Red Baron frozen cheese pizza will fall.

3. *Consumer income.* In general, as real consumers' incomes increase (allowing for inflation), demand for a product will also increase. So, if you get a scholarship and have extra cash for discretionary spending, you might eat more Red Baron frozen cheese pizzas and fewer peanut butter and jelly sandwiches to satisfy your appetite.

The first two factors influence what consumers *want* to buy, and the third factor affects what they *can* buy. Along with price, these are often called *demand factors*, or factors that determine consumers' willingness and ability to pay for products and services. As discussed in Chapters 7 and 9, it can be challenging to estimate demand for new products, especially because consumer likes and dislikes are often so difficult to read clearly.

Movement along versus Shift of a Demand Curve

The demand curve D_1 for Red Baron frozen cheese pizzas in Figure 11–4A shows that as its price is lowered from $8 (point 1) to $6 (point 2), the quantity sold (demanded) increases from 2 million (Q_1) to 3 million (Q_2) units per year. This is an example of a *movement along a demand curve* and it assumes that other factors (consumer tastes, price and availability of substitutes, and consumers' incomes) remain unchanged.

What if some of these factors do change? For example, if advertising causes more people to want Red Baron frozen cheese pizzas, demand will increase. Now the initial demand curve, D_1 (the blue line in Figure 11–4B), no longer represents the demand. Instead, the new demand curve, D_2 (the red line in Figure 11–4B) represents the new demand for Red Baron frozen cheese pizzas. Economists call this a *shift in the demand curve*—in this case, a shift to the right from D_1 to D_2. This increased demand means that more Red Baron frozen cheese pizzas are wanted for a given price. At a price of $6 (point 3), the demand is 5 million units per year (Q_3) on D_2 rather than 3 million units per year (Q_2) on D_1.

Price Elasticity of Demand

price elasticity of demand
The percentage change in quantity demanded relative to a percentage change in price.

With a downward-sloping demand curve, marketing managers are especially interested in how sensitive consumer demand and the firm's revenues are to changes in the product's price. This can be conveniently measured by **price elasticity of demand**, or the percentage change in quantity demanded relative to a percentage change in price. Price elasticity of demand (E) is expressed as follows:

$$\text{Price elasticity of demand (E)} = \frac{\text{Percentage change in quantity demanded}}{\text{Percentage change in price}}$$

Because quantity demanded usually decreases as price increases, price elasticity of demand is usually a negative number. However, for the sake of simplicity and by convention, elasticity figures are shown as positive numbers. Finally, price elasticity of demand assumes two forms discussed here: elastic demand and inelastic demand.

Elastic demand exists when a 1 percent decrease in price produces more than a 1 percent increase in quantity demanded, thereby actually increasing total revenue. This results in a price elasticity that is greater than 1 with elastic demand. In other words, a product with elastic demand is one in which a slight decrease in price results in a relatively large increase in demand or units sold. The reverse is also true; with elastic demand, a slight increase in price results in a relatively large decrease in demand. So marketers may cut price to increase consumer demand, the units sold, and total revenue for a product with elastic demand, depending on what competitors' prices are.

Inelastic demand exists when a 1 percent decrease in price produces less than a 1 percent increase in quantity demanded, thereby actually decreasing total revenue. This results in a price elasticity that is less than 1 with inelastic demand. So a product with inelastic demand means that slight increases or decreases in price will not significantly affect the demand, or units sold, for the product. The concern for marketers is that while lowering price will increase the quantity sold, total revenue will actually fall.

Fundamentals of Estimating Revenue

total revenue (TR)
The total money received from the sales of a product.

Whereas economists may talk about "demand curves," marketing executives are more likely to speak in terms of "revenue generated." Demand curves lead directly to an essential revenue concept critical to pricing decisions: **total revenue (TR)**, or the total money received from the sale of a product. Total revenue (TR) equals the unit price (P) times the quantity sold (Q). Using this equation, let's recall The Caplow Company and assume our annual demand has improved so we can set a price of $120 per picture framed and sell 400 pictures per year. So,

$$\begin{aligned} TR &= P \times Q \\ &= \$120 \times 400 \\ &= \$48,000 \end{aligned}$$

This combination of price and quantity sold annually will give us a total revenue of $48,000 per year. Is that good? It depends on whether you are making a profit. Alas, total revenue is only part of the profit equation that we saw earlier:

$$\text{Total profit} = \text{Total revenue} - \text{Total cost}$$

The next section covers the other part of the profit equation: cost.

learning review

11-3. What three key factors are necessary when estimating consumer demand?

11-4. Price elasticity of demand is _____.

DETERMINING COST, VOLUME, AND PROFIT RELATIONSHIPS

LO 11-3 Explain the role of costs in pricing decisions and describe how combinations of price, fixed cost, and unit variable cost affect a firm's break-even point.

Whereas revenues are the monies received by the firm from selling its products or services to customers, costs or expenses are the monies the firm pays out to its employees and suppliers. Marketing managers often use break-even analysis to relate revenues and costs, topics covered in this section.

The Importance of Controlling Costs

Understanding the role and behavior of costs is critical for all marketing decisions, particularly pricing decisions. Four cost concepts are important in pricing decisions: *total cost, fixed cost, variable cost,* and *unit variable cost* (see Figure 11–5).

Many firms go bankrupt because their costs get out of control, causing their **total cost (TC)**—the sum of their fixed costs and variable costs—to exceed their total revenue over an extended period of time. So firms constantly try to control their fixed costs, such as insurance and executive salaries, and reduce the variable costs in their manufactured items, say by having production done outside the United States. This is why sophisticated marketing managers make pricing decisions that balance both revenues and costs.

total cost (TC)
The total expense incurred by a firm in producing and marketing a product. Total cost is the sum of fixed cost and variable cost.

Break-Even Analysis

Break-even analysis is a technique that analyzes the relationship between total revenue and total cost to determine profitability at various levels of output. Figure 11–6 provides the data needed to conduct a break-even analysis for The Caplow Company introduced earlier in the chapter. The *break-even point* (BEP) is the quantity at which total revenue and total cost are equal. Profit then comes from all units sold beyond the BEP. In terms of the definitions in Figure 11–5:

break-even analysis
A technique that analyzes the relationship between total revenue and total cost to determine profitability at various levels of output.

$$\text{BEP}_{\text{Quantity}} = \frac{\text{Fixed cost}}{\text{Unit price} - \text{Unit variable cost}} = \frac{\text{FC}}{\text{P} - \text{UVC}}$$

Calculating a Break-Even Point
Suppose you are the owner of The Caplow Company and you wish to identify how many picture frames you must sell to cover your fixed cost at a given price. Let's assume demand for your pictures is strong, so the average price customers are willing to pay for each picture is $120. Also, suppose your fixed cost (FC) is $32,000 (real estate taxes, interest on a bank loan, etc.) and unit

FIGURE 11-5
Fundamental concepts about "costs," which are the monies the firm pays out to its employees and suppliers.

> **Total cost (TC)** is the total expense incurred by a firm in producing and marketing a product. Total cost is the sum of fixed cost and variable cost.
>
> **Fixed cost (FC)** is the sum of the expenses of the firm that are stable and do not change with the quantity of a product that is produced and sold. Examples of fixed costs are rent on the building, executive salaries, and insurance.
>
> **Variable cost (VC)** is the sum of the expenses of the firm that vary directly with the quantity of a product that is produced and sold. For example, as the quantity sold doubles, the variable cost doubles. Examples are the direct labor and direct materials used in producing the product and the sales commissions that are tied directly to the quantity sold. As mentioned above,
> TC = FC + VC
>
> **Unit variable cost (UVC)** is expressed on a per unit basis, or $\text{UVC} = \frac{\text{VC}}{\text{Q}}$

Quantity of Pictures Sold (Q)	Price per Picture (P)	Total Revenue (TR = P × Q)	Unit Variable Cost (UVC)	Total Variable Cost (VC = UVC × Q)	Fixed Cost (FC)	Total Cost (TC = FC + VC)	Profit (TR − TC)
0	$120	$0	$40	$0	$32,000	$32,000	($32,000)
400	$120	$48,000	$40	$16,000	$32,000	$48,000	$0
800	$120	$96,000	$40	$32,000	$32,000	$64,000	$32,000
1,200	$120	$144,000	$40	$48,000	$32,000	$80,000	$64,000
1,600	$120	$192,000	$40	$64,000	$32,000	$96,000	$96,000
2,000	$120	$240,000	$40	$80,000	$32,000	$112,000	$128,000

FIGURE 11–6
Calculating a break-even point for The Caplow Company shows that its profit starts at 400 picture frames sold per year.

variable cost (UVC) for a picture is now $40 (labor, glass, frame, and matting). Your break-even quantity (BEP) is 400 pictures, as follows:

$$\text{BEP}_{\text{Quantity}} = \frac{\$32,000}{\$120 - \$40}$$

$$\text{BEP}_{\text{Quantity}} = 400 \text{ pictures}$$

Developing a Break-Even Chart The row shaded in orange in Figure 11–6 shows that the break-even quantity at a price of $120 per picture is 400 picture frames. At less than 400 picture frames, The Caplow Company incurs a loss, and at more than 400 pictures, it makes a profit. Figure 11–7 depicts a graphic presentation of the break-even analysis, called a *break-even chart*. It shows that total revenue (line DE) and total cost (line AC) intersect and are equal at a quantity of 400 picture frames sold, which is the break-even point (F) at which profit is exactly $0. Can the company do better? If The Caplow Company can increase the quantity sold annually to 2,000 picture frames,

FIGURE 11–7
This break-even chart for The Caplow Company shows the break-even point at 400 picture frames and a sizable profit at 2,000 picture frames.

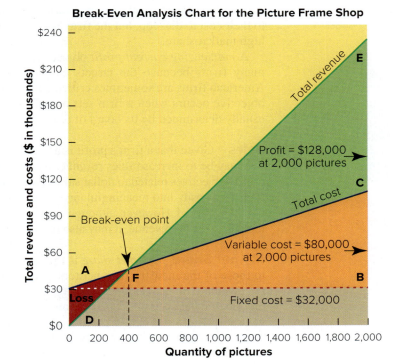

the graph in Figure 11–7 shows it could earn an annual profit of $128,000 ($240,000 − $112,000 or line EC), shown by the row shaded in green in Figure 11–6.

> **learning review**
>
> **11-5.** What is the difference between fixed costs and variable costs?
>
> **11-6.** What is a break-even point?

PRICING OBJECTIVES AND CONSTRAINTS

Recognize the objectives a firm has in setting prices and the constraints that restrict the range of prices a firm can charge.

pricing objectives
Specifying the role of price in an organization's marketing and strategic plans.

With such a variety of alternative pricing strategies available, a marketing manager must consider the pricing objectives and constraints that will narrow the range of choices. While pricing objectives frequently reflect corporate goals, pricing constraints often relate to conditions existing in the marketplace.

Identifying Pricing Objectives

Pricing objectives involve specifying the role of price in an organization's marketing and strategic plans. To the extent possible, these pricing objectives are carried to lower levels in the organization, such as in setting objectives for marketing managers responsible for an individual brand. These objectives may change depending on the financial position of the company as a whole, the success of its products, or the segments in which it is doing business. H. J. Heinz, for example, has specific pricing objectives for its Heinz Ketchup brand that vary by country.

Profit Three different objectives relate to a firm's profit, which is often measured in terms of return on investment (ROI) or return on assets (ROA). These objectives have different implications for pricing strategy. One objective is *managing for long-run profits,* in which companies—such as many Japanese car or South Korean HDTV manufacturers—forgo immediate profit by developing quality products to penetrate competitive markets over the long term. Products are priced relatively low compared to their cost to develop, but the firm expects to make greater profits later because of its high market share.

A *maximizing current profit* objective, such as for a quarter or year, is common in many firms because the targets can be set and performance measured quickly. American firms are sometimes criticized for this short-run orientation. A *target return* objective occurs when a firm sets a profit goal (such as 20 percent for pretax ROI), usually determined by its board of directors.

Sales Given that a firm's profit is high enough for it to remain in business, an objective may be to increase sales revenue, which can lead to increases in market share and profit. Objectives related to dollar sales revenue or unit sales have the advantage of being translated easily into meaningful targets for marketing managers responsible for a product line or brand. However, although cutting the price of one product in a firm's line may increase its sales revenue, it may also reduce the sales revenue of related products.

Market Share *Market share* is the ratio of the firm's sales revenues or unit sales to those of the industry (competitors plus the firm itself). Companies often pursue a market share objective when industry sales are relatively flat or declining. For example, Boeing has set its prices to maintain its 60 percent share of the commercial airline market to compete with Airbus. As a result, it sometimes incurs losses. Although increased market share is a primary goal of some firms, others see it as a means to other ends: increasing sales and profits.

Unit Volume Many firms use *unit volume,* the quantity produced or sold, as a pricing objective. These firms often sell multiple products at very different prices and need to match the unit volume demanded by customers with price and production capacity. Using unit volume as an objective can be counterproductive if a volume objective is achieved, say, by drastic price cutting that drives down profit.

Survival In some instances, profits, sales, and market share are less important objectives of the firm than mere survival. For example, RadioShack, an electronics retailer, faced survival problems because it couldn't compete with the prices promoted by other retailers. The company enacted a price-matching program and advertised large discounts on its merchandise to raise cash and hopefully stave off bankruptcy. These efforts failed and RadioShack declared bankruptcy in 2017.

Social Responsibility A firm may forgo higher profit on sales and follow a pricing objective that recognizes its obligations to customers and society in general. For example, Gerber supplies a specially formulated product free of charge to children who cannot tolerate foods containing cow's milk.

Identifying Pricing Constraints

Factors that limit the range of prices a firm may set are **pricing constraints**. Consumer demand for the product clearly affects the price that can be charged. Other constraints on price vary from factors within the organization to competitive factors outside the organization.

pricing constraints
Factors that limit the range of prices a firm may set.

Demand for the Product Class, Product, and Brand The number of potential buyers for a product class (cars), product (sports cars), and brand (Bugatti Chiron Sport) clearly affects the price a seller can charge. Generally, the greater the demand for a product, or brand, the higher the price that can be set. For example, the New York Mets set different ticket prices for their games based on the appeal of their opponent—prices are higher when they play the New York Yankees and lower when they play the Pittsburgh Pirates.

Newness of the Product: Stage in the Product Life Cycle The newer a product and the earlier it is in its life cycle, the higher is the price that can usually be charged. Are you willing to spend $40,000 for an LG 98-inch 3D OLED HD Smart TV? The high initial price is possible because of patents and limited competition early in its product life cycle. By the time you read this, the price probably will be much lower.

What is the cost of producing and marketing designer denim jeans? You might be surprised at how much a specialty retailer makes.
©Amanda Edwards/Getty Images

Cost of Producing and Marketing the Product Another profit consideration for marketers is to ensure that firms in their channels of distribution make an adequate profit. Without profits for channel members, a marketer is cut off from its customers. Of the $200 a customer spends for a pair of designer denim jeans, 50 percent of each dollar spent by a customer goes to a specialty retailer to cover its costs and profit. The other 50 percent goes to the marketer (34 percent) and manufacturers and suppliers (16 percent).[17] So, the next time you buy a $200 pair of designer denim jeans, remember that $100 goes to the specialty retailer that stocked, displayed, and sold the jeans to you.

Competitors' Prices When Apple introduced its iPad, it was not only unique and in the introductory stage of its product life cycle but also the first commercially successful tablet device sold. As a result, Apple had great latitude in setting a price. Now, with a wide range of competition in tablets from Samsung's Galaxy Note, Lenovo's Think Pad, and others, Apple's pricing latitude is less broad.

Legal and Ethical Considerations Setting a final price is clearly a complex process. The task is further complicated by legal and ethical issues. Four pricing practices that have received special scrutiny are described below:

- *Price fixing.* A conspiracy among firms to set prices for a product is termed price fixing. Price fixing is illegal under the Sherman Act. When two or more competitors collude to explicitly or implicitly set prices, this practice is called *horizontal price fixing.* For example, six foreign vitamin companies recently pled guilty to price fixing in the human and animal vitamin industry and paid the largest fine in U.S. history: $335 million.[18] *Vertical price fixing* involves controlling agreements between independent buyers and sellers (a manufacturer and a retailer) whereby sellers are required to not sell products below a minimum retail price.
- *Price discrimination.* The Clayton Act as amended by the Robinson-Patman Act prohibits price discrimination—the practice of charging different prices to different buyers for goods of like grade and quality. However, not all price differences are illegal; only those that substantially lessen competition or create a monopoly are deemed unlawful.
- *Deceptive pricing.* Price deals that mislead consumers fall into the category of deceptive pricing. Deceptive pricing is outlawed by the Federal Trade Commission. *Bait and switch* is an example of deceptive pricing. This occurs when a firm offers a very low price on a product (the bait) to attract customers to a store. Once in the store, the customer is persuaded to purchase a higher-priced item (the switch) using a variety of tricks, including (1) degrading the promoted item and (2) not having the promised item in stock or refusing to take orders for it.
- *Predatory pricing.* Predatory pricing is the practice of charging a very low price for a product with the intent of driving competitors out of business. Once competitors have been driven out, the firm raises its prices. Proving the presence of this practice has been difficult and expensive because it must be shown that the predator explicitly attempted to destroy a competitor and the predatory price was below the defendant's average cost.

learning review

11-7. What is the difference between pricing objectives and pricing constraints?

11-8. Explain what bait and switch is and why it is an example of deceptive pricing.

SETTING A FINAL PRICE

Describe the steps taken in setting a final price.

The final price set by the marketing manager serves many functions. It must be high enough to cover the cost of providing the product or service *and* meet the objectives of the company. Yet it must be low enough that customers are willing to pay it. But not too low, or customers may think they're purchasing an inferior product. Dizzy yet? Setting price is one of the most difficult tasks the marketing manager faces, but three generalized steps are useful to follow.

Step 1: Select an Approximate Price Level

Before setting a final price, the marketing manager must understand the market environment, the features and customer benefits of the particular product, and the goals of the firm. A balance must be struck between factors that might drive a price higher (such as a profit-oriented approach) and other forces (such as increased competition from substitutes) that may drive a price down.

Marketing managers consider pricing objectives and constraints first, then choose among the general pricing approaches—demand-, cost-, profit-, or competition-oriented—to arrive at an approximate price level. This price is then analyzed in terms of cost, volume, and profit relationships. Break-even analyses may be run at this point, and finally, if this approximate price level "works," it is time to take the next step: setting a specific list or quoted price.

Step 2: Set the List or Quoted Price

A seller must decide whether to follow a one-price or flexible-price policy.

One-Price Policy A *one-price policy,* also called *fixed pricing,* is setting one price for all buyers of a product or service. CarMax uses this approach in its stores and features a "no haggle, one price" price for cars. Some retailers have married this policy with a below-market approach. Dollar Value Stores and 99¢ Only Stores sell everything in their stores for $1 or less. Family Dollar Stores sell everything for $2.

Dynamic Price Policy In contrast, a *dynamic price policy,* or *flexible-price policy,* involves setting different prices for products and services depending on individual buyers and purchase situations in light of demand, cost, and competitive factors. Dell Technologies uses dynamic pricing as it continually adjusts prices in response to changes in its own costs, competitive pressures, and demand from its various personal computer segments (home, small business, corporate, etc.). "Our flexibility allows us to be [priced] different even within a day," says a Dell spokesperson.[19]

Dynamic pricing is not without its critics because of its discriminatory potential. One frequent criticism of dynamic pricing lies in the realm of "surge" pricing, which occurs when a company raises the price of its products or services if there is a spike in demand. Read the Making Responsible Decisions box to learn about the ethics and economics of surge pricing used by Uber and Lyft and decide where you stand on the practice.[20]

Step 3: Make Special Adjustments to the List or Quoted Price

When you pay $1 for a bag of M&M's in a vending machine or receive a quoted price of $50,000 from a contractor to renovate a kitchen, the pricing sequence ends with the last step just described: setting the list or quoted price. But when you are a manufacturer of M&M's candies and sell your product to dozens or hundreds of wholesalers and retailers in your channel of distribution, you may need to make a variety of special adjustments to the list or quoted price. Wholesalers also must adjust the list or quoted prices they set for retailers. Two adjustments to the list or quoted price are (1) discounts and (2) allowances.

Discounts *Discounts* are reductions from list price that a seller gives a buyer as a reward for some activity of the buyer that is favorable to the seller. Four kinds of discounts are especially important in marketing strategy: (1) quantity, (2) seasonal, (3) trade (functional), and (4) cash.

- *Quantity discounts.* To encourage customers to buy larger quantities of a product, firms at all levels in the channel of distribution offer quantity discounts, which are reductions in unit costs for a larger order. For example, an instant photocopying service might set a price of 10 cents a copy for 1 to 24 copies, 9 cents a copy for 25 to 99 copies, and 8 cents a copy for 100 copies or more.
- *Seasonal discounts.* To encourage buyers to stock inventory earlier than their normal demand would require, manufacturers often use seasonal discounts.

Video 11-3
CarMax Ad
kerin.tv/cr8e/v11-3

Making Responsible Decisions | Ethics

The Ethics and Economics of Surge Pricing

Uber and Lyft have changed the way local taxi service operates. Using independent drivers and driver-owned vehicles, both companies serve as middlemen using digital technology to provide on-demand transportation services to consumers. Nevertheless, Uber and Lyft customers often complain about the practice of "surge" or "prime-time" pricing used by these companies during periods of peak demand. From a classical economics perspective, this form of dynamic pricing makes sense based on supply and demand relationships. Fare increases in periods of high demand—a shift in the demand curve to the right—in turn increase the supply of drivers available for passengers.

©Imaginechina/AP Images

From an ethical perspective, supporters of surge or prime-time pricing argue from a utilitarian view that this type of pricing increases the supply of drivers and more people get a ride. Remember from Chapter 3 that utilitarianism focuses on "the greatest good for the greatest number" by assessing the costs and benefits of the behavior, in this case, dynamic pricing.

Critics of surge or prime-time pricing argue that this practice is flagrant price gouging by Uber and Lyft. Where do you stand on the economics versus ethics debate related to surge or prime-time pricing?

Manufacturers provide a variety of discounts to assist channel members, such as clothing retailers, that offer "Buy One, Get One Free" promotions.
©DBurke/Alamy Stock Photo

A firm such as Toro that manufactures lawn mowers and snow throwers offers seasonal discounts to encourage wholesalers and retailers to stock up on lawn mowers in January and February and snow throwers in July and August—five or six months before the seasonal demand by ultimate consumers.

- *Trade (functional) discounts.* To reward wholesalers and retailers for marketing functions they will perform in the future, a manufacturer often gives trade, or functional, discounts. These reductions off the list or base price are offered to resellers in the channel of distribution on the basis of (1) where they are in the channel and (2) the marketing activities they are expected to perform in the future.
- *Cash discounts.* To encourage retailers to pay their bills quickly, manufacturers offer them cash discounts. Cash discounts are typically expressed as a percentage off the list price.

Allowances Allowances—like discounts—are reductions from list or quoted prices to buyers for performing some activity.

- *Trade-in allowances.* A new-car dealer can offer a substantial reduction in the list price of that new Toyota Camry by offering you a trade-in allowance of $2,500 for your Kia Rio. A trade-in allowance is a price reduction given when a used product is part of the payment on a new product. Trade-ins are an effective way to lower the price a buyer has to pay without formally reducing the list price.
- *Promotional allowances.* Sellers in the channel of distribution can qualify for promotional allowances for undertaking certain advertising or selling activities to promote a product. Various types of allowances include an actual cash payment or an extra amount of "free goods" (as with a free case of pizzas to a retailer for every dozen cases purchased). Frequently, a portion of these savings is passed on to the consumer by retailers.

Some companies, such as Procter & Gamble, have chosen to reduce promotional allowances for retailers by using everyday low pricing. *Everyday low pricing (EDLP)* is the practice of replacing promotional allowances with lower manufacturer list prices. EDLP promises to reduce the average price to consumers while minimizing promotional allowances that cost manufacturers billions of dollars every year.

learning review

11-9. What are the three steps in setting a final price?

11-10. What is the purpose of (*a*) quantity discounts and (*b*) promotional allowances?

LEARNING OBJECTIVES REVIEW

LO 11-1 *Describe the nature and importance of pricing and the approaches used to select an approximate price level.*

Price is the money or other considerations (such as barter) exchanged for the ownership or use of a product or service. Although price typically involves money, the amount exchanged is often different from the list or quoted price because of incentives (rebates, discounts, etc.), allowances (trade), and extra fees (finance charges, surcharges, etc.).

Demand, cost, profit, and competition influence the initial consideration of the approximate price level for a product or service. Demand-oriented pricing approaches stress consumer demand and revenue implications of pricing and include five types: skimming, penetration, prestige, odd-even, and bundle pricing. Cost-oriented pricing approaches emphasize the cost aspects of pricing and include two types: standard markup and cost-plus pricing. Profit-oriented pricing approaches focus on a balance between revenues and costs to set a price and include three types: target profit, target return-on-sales, and target return-on-investment pricing. And finally, competition-oriented pricing approaches stress what competitors or the marketplace are doing and include three types: customary; above-, at-, or below-market; and loss-leader pricing.

LO 11-2 *Explain what a demand curve is and the role of revenues in pricing decisions.*

A demand curve is a graph relating the quantity sold and price, which shows the maximum number of units that will be sold at a given price. Three demand factors affect price: (*a*) consumer tastes, (*b*) price and availability of substitute products, and (*c*) consumer income. These demand factors determine consumers' willingness and ability to pay for products and services. Assuming these demand factors remain unchanged, if the price of a product is lowered or raised, then the quantity demanded for it will increase or decrease, respectively. The demand curve relates to a firm's total revenue, which is the total money received from the sale of a product, or the price of one unit times the quantity of units sold.

LO 11-3 *Explain the role of costs in pricing decisions and describe how combinations of price, fixed cost, and unit variable cost affect a firm's break-even point.*

Four important costs impact a firm's pricing decisions: (*a*) total cost, or total expenses, the sum of the fixed costs and variable costs incurred by a firm in producing and marketing a product; (*b*) fixed cost, the sum of the expenses of the firm that are stable and do not change with the quantity of a product that is produced and sold; (*c*) variable cost, the sum of the expenses of the firm that vary directly with the quantity of a product that is produced and sold; and (*d*) unit variable cost, the variable cost expressed on a per unit basis.

Break-even analysis is a technique that analyzes the relationship between total revenue and total cost to determine profitability at various levels of output. The break-even point is the quantity at which total revenue and total cost are equal. Assuming no change in price, if the costs of a firm's product increase due to higher fixed costs (manufacturing or advertising) or variable costs (direct labor or materials), then its break-even point will be higher. And if total cost is unchanged, an increase in price will reduce the break-even point.

LO 11-4 *Recognize the objectives a firm has in setting prices and the constraints that restrict the range of prices a firm can charge.*

Pricing objectives specify the role of price in a firm's marketing strategy and may include profit, sales revenue, market share, unit volume, survival, or some socially responsible price level. Pricing constraints that restrict a firm's pricing flexibility include demand, product newness, production and marketing costs, prices of competitive substitutes, and legal and ethical considerations.

LO 11-5 *Describe the steps taken in setting a final price.*

Three common steps marketing managers often use in setting a final price are (1) select an approximate price level as a starting point; (2) set the list or quoted price, choosing between a one-price policy or a flexible-price policy; and (3) modify the list or quoted price by considering discounts and allowances.

LEARNING REVIEW ANSWERS

11-1 Value is _____.
Answer: the ratio of perceived benefits to price; or Value = (Perceived benefits ÷ Price)

11-2 What circumstances in pricing a new product might support skimming or penetration pricing?
Answer: Skimming pricing is an effective strategy when: (1) enough prospective customers are willing to buy the product immediately at the high initial price to make these sales profitable; (2) the high initial price will not attract competitors; (3) lowering the price has only a minor effect on increasing the sales volume and reducing the unit costs; and (4) customers interpret the high price as signifying high quality. These four conditions are most likely to exist when the new product is protected by patents or copyrights or its uniqueness is understood and valued by consumers. The conditions favoring penetration pricing are the reverse of those supporting skimming pricing: (1) many segments of the market are price sensitive; (2) a low initial price discourages competitors from entering the market; and (3) unit production and marketing costs fall dramatically as production volumes increase. A firm using penetration pricing may (1) maintain the initial price for a time to gain profit lost from its low introductory level or (2) lower the price further, counting on the new volume to generate the necessary profit.

11-3 What three key factors are necessary when estimating consumer demand?
Answer: consumer tastes, price and availability of similar products, and consumer income.

11-4 Price elasticity of demand is _____.
Answer: the percentage change in the quantity demanded relative to a percentage change in price.

11-5 What is the difference between fixed costs and variable costs?
Answer: Fixed cost is the sum of the expenses of the firm that are stable and do not change with the quantity of a product that is produced and sold. Variable cost is the sum of the expenses of the firm that vary directly with the quantity of a product that is produced and sold.

11-6 What is a break-even point?
Answer: A break-even point (BEP) is the quantity at which total revenue and total cost are equal.

11-7 What is the difference between pricing objectives and pricing constraints?
Answer: Pricing objectives specify the role of price in an organization's marketing and strategic plans. Pricing constraints are factors that limit the range of prices a firm may set.

11-8 Explain what bait and switch is and why it is an example of deceptive pricing.
Answer: Bait and switch is the practice of offering a very low price on a product (the bait) to attract customers to a store. Once in the store, the customer is persuaded to purchase a higher-priced item (the switch) using a variety of tricks, including (1) degrading the promoted item and (2) not having the promised item in stock or refusing to take orders for it.

11-9 What are the three steps in setting a final price?
Answer: They are: (1) select an appropriate price level; (2) set the list or quoted price; and (3) make special adjustments to the list or quoted price.

11-10 What is the purpose of (*a*) quantity discounts and (*b*) promotional allowances?
Answer: Quantity discounts are used to encourage customers to buy larger quantities of a product. Promotional allowances are used to encourage sellers in the channel of distribution to undertake certain advertising or selling activities to promote a product.

FOCUSING ON KEY TERMS

above-, at-, or below-market pricing p. 307
barter p. 300
break-even analysis p. 312
bundle pricing p. 304
cost-plus pricing p. 305
customary pricing p. 307
demand curve p. 309
loss-leader pricing p. 309
odd-even pricing p. 304
penetration pricing p. 303
prestige pricing p. 304
price (P) p. 300
price elasticity of demand p. 311
pricing constraints p. 315
pricing objectives p. 314
profit equation p. 302
skimming pricing p. 303
standard markup pricing p. 305
target profit pricing p. 306
target return-on-investment pricing p. 307
target return-on-sales pricing p. 307
total cost (TC) p. 312
total revenue (TR) p. 311
value p. 301
value pricing p. 302

APPLYING MARKETING KNOWLEDGE

1. How would the price equation apply to the purchase price of (*a*) gasoline, (*b*) an airline ticket, and (*c*) a checking account?
2. Under what conditions would a camera manufacturer adopt a skimming price approach for a new product? A penetration approach?
3. What are some similarities and differences between skimming pricing, prestige pricing, and above-market pricing?
4. Touché Toiletries Inc. has developed an addition to its Lizardman Cologne line tentatively branded Ode d'Toade Cologne. Unit variable costs are 45 cents for a 3-ounce bottle, and heavy advertising expenditures in the first year would result in total fixed costs of $900,000. Ode d'Toade Cologne is priced at $7.50 for a 3-ounce bottle. How many bottles of Ode d'Toade must be sold to break even?
5. What would be your response to the statement "Profit maximization is the only legitimate pricing objective for the firm"?

BUILDING YOUR MARKETING PLAN

In starting to set a final price:
1. List two pricing objectives and three pricing constraints.
2. Think about your customers and competitors and set three possible prices.
3. Assume a fixed cost and unit variable cost and (*a*) calculate the break-even points and (*b*) plot a break-even chart for the three prices specified in step 2.

VIDEO CASE 11
Carmex (B): Setting the Price of the Number One Lip Balm

Video 11-4
Carmex (B)
Video Case
kerin.tv/cr8e/v11-4

"Carmex is dedicated to providing consumers with superior lip balm formulas—that heal, sooth and protect—while ensuring lips remain healthy and hydrated," exclaims Paul Woelbing, president of Carma Laboratories, Inc.

It's an ambitious mission, but the company has been extraordinarily successful with its 75-year-old product. Woelbing and his management team at Carma Laboratories can attribute their success to a strong brand, a loyal customer base, a growing product line, financial strength, and an exceptional talent for setting prices that achieve company objectives and still provide value to customers. Even during the recession and periods of slow growth the company has been successful. "In a rough economy, shopping habits change," Woelbing says. "People buy smaller quantities more frequently, but they still need personal care products."

THE COMPANY

Carmex was created by Paul's grandfather, Alfred Woelbing, in his kitchen in Wauwatosa, Wisconsin, in 1937. Alfred had an entrepreneurial spirit and experimented with ingredients such as camphor, menthol, phenol, lanolin, salicylic acid, and cocoa seed butter to make the new product. The name didn't have any meaning other than Alfred liked the sound of "Carma," and "ex" was a popular suffix for many brands at the time. He packaged the balm in small glass jars and sold the product for 25 cents from the trunk of his car by making personal sales calls to pharmacies in Wisconsin, Illinois, and Indiana. From the beginning, price and value were important to the product's success. If pharmacies weren't initially interested in Carmex, Alfred would leave a dozen jars for free. The samples would sell quickly and soon the pharmacies would place orders for more!

©McGraw-Hill Education

©McGraw-Hill Education

As the company grew, Alfred's son, Don, joined the business and helped add new products to the company's offerings. For example, in the 1980s Carmex made its first significant packaging change by also offering the balm in squeezable tubes. In the 1990s Carmex became available in stick form, which had been used by two of Carma's major competitors—ChapStick and Blistex. In the 2000s Carmex became available in mint, cherry, and strawberry flavors. The company also expanded into larger manufacturing facilities, added a new distribution center, and hired its first marketing experts.

Today, the company is led by Alfred's grandsons, Paul and Eric Woelbing, who continue to manage the company to new levels of success. They appeared on *The Oprah Winfrey Show* to announce the sale of their billionth jar of Carmex. The governor of Wisconsin declared a Carmex commemoration day to celebrate its 75th anniversary. NBA all-star LeBron James became a promotional partner. In addition, *Pharmacy Times* magazine recently named Carmex the number one pharmacist-recommended brand of lip balm for the 15th consecutive year. "We are honored to receive this unprecedented acknowledgement," said Woelbing.

Industry observers estimate that Carma Labs holds approximately 10 percent of the lip balm market. The company distributes its products through major drug, food, and mass merchant retailers, convenience stores, and online in more than 25 countries around the world. The company's most recent products—Carmex Healing Cream and Carmex Hydrating Lotion—represent a significant step from lip care to skin care. The expanded product line, multichannel distribution, growing volume, international trade, and direct competition make pricing decisions even more important today than when Alfred started the business many years ago.

SETTING PRICES OF CARMEX PRODUCTS

"There are many factors that go into what results in the retail price in the store," explains Kirk Hodgdon of Bolin Marketing. As one of the marketing experts who helps Carma Labs with advertising, marketing research, and pricing decisions, Hodgdon uses information about consumer demand, production and material costs, profit goals, and competition to help Woelbing and Carmex retailers arrive at specific prices. The many factors often overlap and lead to different prices for different products, channels, and target markets. "It's a challenge!" says Hodgdon.

Source: Carma Labs Inc.

Consumers' tastes and preferences, for example, influence the price of Carmex products. Bolin director of marketing, Alisa Allen, explains: "Consumers will tell you that they love Carmex because it's a great value. That doesn't necessarily mean that it's the absolute lowest price. It means that it does so much; they pay a dollar and they get all kinds of benefits from the product above and beyond what they would expect." A single jar of original formula Carmex may sell for $0.99 at mass retailers such as Walmart and Target, and between $1.59 and $1.79 in drug and food retailers such as Walgreens and Kroger. These prices are a good indication of how important it is to understand consumers when setting prices. "There are magic price points for consumers," says Allen, "Any time you can drop a penny off, the consumer responds to that price."

Carmex has also introduced a premium lip balm product, Carmex Moisture Plus, at a retail price between $2.49 and $2.99. Moisture Plus is a lip balm that is packaged in a sleek silver tube, offers a slant tip like lipstick, and is targeted toward women. The formula offers women a satin gloss shine and includes vitamin E and aloe for richer moisturization. The upscale package and additional product benefits help Carmex Moisture Plus command a higher price than the traditional Carmex jar and tube.

The cost of the ingredients that make up the Carmex lip balm formulas, the packaging, the manufacturing equipment, and the staffing are also factored into the price of the products. Volumes are a key driver of the cost of packaging and ingredients. For example, Carmex purchases up to 12 million yellow tubes each year for the traditional product and 2 million sticks each year for the newer Moisture Plus product. The difference in quantities leads to a lower price for the traditional yellow tubes. Similarly, ingredient suppliers, label suppliers, and box suppliers all provide discounts for larger quantities. It is also more efficient for Carmex's manufacturing facility to make a large batch of traditional formula than it is to make a small batch of Moisture Plus. Carmex has also reduced its costs with efforts such as its new eco-friendly Carmex jar which holds the same amount of lip balm but uses 20 percent less plastic, eliminating 35 tons of raw material costs and the related shipping costs!

Carmex also considers retailer margins when it sets its prices. According to Allen, "We typically sell our product to two types of retailers." There are everyday low price (EDLP) retailers such as Walmart, and high-low retailers such as Walgreens. EDLP retailers offer consumers the lowest price every day without discounting through promotions. High-low retailers charge consumers a higher price, but they occasionally discount the product through special promotions that Carmex often supports with "marketing discretionary funds." Carmex typically offers its products at different prices to EDLP and high-low retailers to allow each retailer to achieve its profit margin goals and to account for Carmex's promotion expenditures. When the additional expenditures are considered, however, the cost to both types of retailers is similar.

Finally, Carmex considers competitors' prices when setting its prices. Burt's Bees, ChapStick, Blistex, and many other brands offer lip balm products and consumers often compare their prices to the price of Carmex. "We have found through research that it is extremely important that the price gap is not too great," explains Allen. "If that gap becomes too wide consumers will leave the Carmex brand and purchase a competitor's product." When Carmex was preparing to launch its premium Moisture Plus product it conducted a thorough analysis of similar products to ensure that Moisture Plus was in an acceptable price range.

CARMEX IN THE FUTURE

The original, and now legendary, Carmex formula and packaging will continue into the future with occasional changes to its pricing practices. New products, however, are on the horizon and likely to challenge the perceptions of the traditional products and prices in the Carmex line. Carmex Moisture Plus products, for example, will be offered in limited edition designs that ask consumers "Which personality are you?" Paul Woelbing explains the new approach:

> Lip care is an important component of a daily beauty regimen and consumers need a product they can rely on that protects and serves as an important foundation. The goal of the new Carmex Moisture Plus line is to offer our consumers a hard-working lip balm line that represents and reflects their unique style.

Some of the new styles include: *Chic* in houndstooth, *Fab* in a groovy retro look, *Adventurous* in a leopard print, and *Whimsical* in an art deco design.

"We are so excited about the future of Carmex," says Hodgdon. "We are planning new products, we have new plans for retailers, and the future is nothing but bright!"[21]

Questions

1 Which of the four approaches to setting a price does Carmex use for its products? Should one approach be used exclusively?

2 Why do many Carmex product prices end in 9? What type of pricing is this called? What should happen to demand when this approach is used?

3 Should cost be a factor in Carmex's prices? What do you think is a reasonable markup for Carmex and for its retailers?

4 What is the difference between an EDLP retailer and a high-low retailer? Why does Carmex charge them different prices?

5 Conduct an online search of lip balm products and compare the price of a Carmex product with three similar products from competitors. How do you think the competitors are setting their prices?

Chapter Notes

1. "The Vizio Story," www.vizio.com, downloaded May 15, 2018; "Share of Smart TVs by Manufacturer," statista.com, downloaded April 12, 2018; "eEco Is Calling Off Purchase of Vizio," *The Wall Street Journal*, April 11, 2017, p. B4; VIZIO, Inc. Form S-1 Registration Statement (Washington, DC: U.S. Securities and Exchange Commission, July 24, 2015); and "How Vizio Conquered TV," www.fortune.com, July 25, 2012.

2. "Rise of the Barter Economy," www.bloomberg.com, April 26, 2012.

3. "2019 Bugatti Chiron Sport: Lightweight and Tuned to Handle," roadandtrack.com, March 6, 2018.

4. Adapted from Kent B. Monroe, *Pricing: Making Profitable Decisions*, 3rd ed. (New York: McGraw-Hill, 2003).

5. Numerous studies have examined the price-quality-value relationship. See, for example, Jacob Jacoby and Jerry C. Olsen, eds., *Perceived Quality* (Lexington, MA: Lexington Books, 1985); William D. Dodds, Kent B. Monroe, and Dhruv Grewal, "Effects of Price, Brand, and Store Information on Buyers' Product Evaluations," *Journal of Marketing Research*, August 1991, pp. 307–19; and Roger A. Kerin, Ambuj Jain, and Daniel Howard, "Store Shopping Experience and Consumer Price-Quality-Value Perceptions," *Journal of Retailing*, Winter 1992, pp. 235–45. For a thorough review of the price-quality-value relationship, see Valerie A. Zeithaml, "Consumer Perceptions of Price, Quality, and Value," *Journal of Marketing*, July 1998, pp. 2–22.

6. Roger A. Kerin and Robert A. Peterson, "Haverwood Furniture, Inc. (A)," *Strategic Marketing Problems: Cases and Comments*, 13th ed. (Upper Saddle River, NJ: Prentice Hall, 2013), pp. 294–305.

7. "The Best and Worst U.S. Airlines Based on Price vs. Performance," www.forbes.com, March 7, 2018; "How Low-Cost Airlines Alter the Economics of Flying," www.msn.com, September 2, 2017; "America's Least Favorite Airline (hint: it's not United)," www.money.com, April 25, 2017; "The Best and Worst Airlines of the Year," www.fortune.com, April 4, 2016; "Spirit Named 2015 Value Airline of the Year," www.airtransportworld.com, February 25, 2015; and "Spirit Airlines Sees All Those Passenger Complaints as Mere Misunderstandings," www.bloombergbusiness.com, April 18, 2014.

8. "Amazon Tablet Market Share Surges, Thanks to Its Low-Cost Slates," *Investor's Business Daily*, March 3, 2016, p. 6.

9. The conditions favoring skimming versus penetration pricing are described in Kent B. Monroe, *Pricing: Making Profitable Decisions*, 3rd ed. (Burr Ridge, IL: McGraw-Hill/Irwin, 2003).

10. Jean-Noel Kapferer, *The New Strategic Brand Management: Advanced Insights and Strategic Thinking*, 5th ed. (London: Kogan Page Ltd., 2012).

11. Jean-Noel Kapferer, *Kapferer on Luxury: How Luxury Brands Can Grow Yet Remain Rare* (London: Kogan Page Ltd., 2015).

12. "Premium AA Alkaline Batteries," *Consumer Reports*, March 21, 2002, p. 54; Kemp Powers, "Assault and Batteries," *Forbes*, September 4, 2000, pp. 54, 56; and "Razor Burn at Gillette," *BusinessWeek*, June 18, 2001, p. 37.

13. "The Psychological Difference between $12.00 and $11.67," www.theatlantic.com, January 30, 2015. For further reading on odd-even pricing, see Mark Stiving and Russell S. Winer, "An Empirical Analysis of Price Endings with Scanner Data," *Journal of Consumer Research*, June 1997, pp. 57–67; and Robert M. Schindler, "Patterns of Rightmost Digits Used in Advertised Prices: Implications for Nine-Ending Effects," *Journal of Consumer Research*, September 1997, pp. 192–201.

14. "We Did the Math: Here's How Much Movie Theaters Mark Up Your Popcorn and Snacks," www.businessinsider.com, April 26, 2015; and "What Popcorn Prices Mean for Movies," *Advertising Age*, May 19, 2008, p. 4.

15. "In Lean Times, Big Companies Make a Grab for Market Share," *The Wall Street Journal*, September 5, 2003, pp. A1, A6.

16. "2016 Convenience Store Sales Data," www.cspdailynews.com, April 21, 2017.

17. Christina Binkley, "How Can Jeans Cost $300?" *The Wall Street Journal*, July 7, 2011, pp. D1, D2.

18. "Six Vitamin Firms Agree to Settle Price-Fixing Suit," *The Wall Street Journal*, October 11, 2000, p. B10.

19. "The Promise and Perils of Dynamic Pricing," *Knowledge@Wharton*, February 26, 2016.

20. "Uber Starts Charging What It Thinks You're to Pay," www.bloomberg.com, May 29, 2017: "Pricing the Surge," www.economist.com, May 29, 2014; and "The Price Is Right or Uber Will Raise It," www.bloombergview.com, May 19, 2015.

21. Carmex (B): This case was written by Steven Hartley and Alisa Allen. Sources: Kristen Scheuing, "The Man Behind Carmex," *Wisconsin Trails*, March–April 2011; "Carmex and Carma Laboratories: *Pharmacy Times* Names Carmex Number One Recommended Lip Balm," *IndiaPharma News*, June 21, 2013; "New Lip Balm Offers Sun Protection While Drenching Lips in Moisture," *Postmedia Breaking News*, May 21, 2013; Carma Laboratories website, www.mycarmex.com, accessed September 2, 2013; and interviews with Bolin Media personnel.

12

LEARNING OBJECTIVES

After reading this chapter you should be able to:

LO 12-1 Explain what is meant by a marketing channel of distribution and why intermediaries are needed.

LO 12-2 Distinguish among traditional marketing channels, electronic marketing channels, and different types of vertical marketing systems.

LO 12-3 Describe factors that marketing executives consider when selecting and managing a marketing channel.

LO 12-4 Explain what supply chain and logistics management are and how they relate to marketing strategy.

Managing Marketing Channels and Supply Chains

Eddie Bauer: The "Brick, Click, and Flip" Pick for the Active Outdoor Enthusiast

Are you an "active outdoor enthusiast"? If so, Eddie Bauer is the outdoor lifestyle apparel and gear company and brand for you.

Eddie Bauer is an iconic and authentic outdoor lifestyle brand with a 100-year heritage. It can trace its origins to Eddie Bauer, its founder and legendary sportsman, merchant, and apparel designer. He started his company in 1920 in Seattle, Washington, with a promise: "To give you such outstanding quality, value, service, and guarantee that we may be worthy of your high esteem & trade." This promise is now *The Eddie Bauer Creed* and still guides the company.

Eddie Bauer's Multichannel Marketing Strategy

But there is more to Eddie Bauer than the promise of premium-quality products, great value, and superb service. Eddie Bauer has the distinction of being one of the first companies to fully implement a "brick, click, and flip" multichannel strategy. This strategy features an integrated mix of retail stores ("brick"), a website ("click"), and seasonal catalogs ("flip") that responds to where, when, and how its customers wish to browse and buy Eddie Bauer outdoor lifestyle apparel and gear.

Equally important, every effort is made to ensure that customers' apparel and gear shopping and purchase experience is the same across its retail store, website, and catalog marketing channels. According to an Eddie Bauer marketing manager, "We don't distinguish between channels because it's all Eddie Bauer to our customers." Company executives recognize that a "brick, click, and flip" multichannel strategy relies on measuring customer satisfaction across its store, website (www.eddiebauer.com), and catalog consumer touchpoints to better manage, maintain, and improve them.

Eddie Bauer integrates purchasing data from each of its channels to provide insights into evolving customer needs, preferences, and perceived value. This practice often illuminates unique product and market opportunities. For example, Eddie Bauer's CEO recently noted that when the company examined data from its website channel it uncovered that Eddie Bauer had at least 20,000 customers in *(top): ©Bonnie Kamin/PhotoEdit, Inc.; (bottom, left): Source: Eddie Bauer, LLC; (bottom, right): ©McGraw-Hill Education/Mike Hruby, photographer*

New York City and thousands more in adjacent areas. This led to opening a retail store in downtown Manhattan, the most densely populated borough of New York City.

Supply Chain Dynamics at Eddie Bauer

Eddie Bauer executives understand and effectively manage supply chain dynamics common with its "brick, click, and flip" multichannel strategy. These executives are responsible for a vast network of apparel and gear suppliers for its 370 Eddie Bauer stores in the United States and Canada and its website and catalog operations.

Managing a multichannel supply chain is a complex task due to the starkly different objectives and priorities of retail stores and online and catalog operations. For example, the supply chain for retail stores focuses on efficiently keeping the products most desired by customers displayed on store shelves, with rapid replenishment from distribution centers. For online and catalog operations, the focus is on providing wider product assortments and even customized products that are shipped from a central distribution center or a supplier's inventory.

Eddie Bauer has mastered the delicate balance between effectiveness and efficiency in managing its multichannel marketing channel supply chain.[1]

This chapter first focuses on marketing channels of distribution and why they are an important component in the marketing mix. It then shows how such channels benefit consumers and the sequence of firms that make up a marketing channel. Finally, it describes factors that influence the choice and management of marketing channels, including channel conflict and cooperation.

The chapter concludes with a discussion of logistics and supply chain management. In particular, attention is placed on the necessary alignment between supply chain management and marketing strategy and the trade-offs managers make between total distribution costs and customer service.

NATURE AND IMPORTANCE OF MARKETING CHANNELS

LO 12-1 Explain what is meant by a marketing channel of distribution and why intermediaries are needed.

Reaching prospective buyers, either directly or indirectly, is a prerequisite for successful marketing. At the same time, buyers benefit from distribution systems used by companies.

What Is a Marketing Channel of Distribution?

You see the results of distribution every day. You may have purchased Lay's potato chips at a 7-Eleven convenience store, a book online through Amazon.com, and Levi's jeans at a Kohl's department store. Each of these items was brought to you by a marketing channel of distribution, or simply a **marketing channel**, which consists of individuals and firms involved in the process of making a product or service available for use or consumption by consumers or industrial users.

Marketing channels can be compared to a pipeline through which water flows from a source to a terminus. Marketing channels make possible the flow of products and services from a producer, through intermediaries, to a buyer. Intermediaries go by various names (see Figure 12–1) and perform various functions. Some intermediaries purchase items from the seller, store them, and resell them to buyers. For example, Celestial Seasonings produces specialty teas and sells them to food wholesalers. The wholesalers then sell these teas to supermarkets and grocery stores, which, in turn, sell them to consumers. Other intermediaries such as brokers and agents represent sellers but do not actually take title to products—their role is to bring a seller and buyer together. Century 21 real estate agents are examples of this type of intermediary.

marketing channel Consists of individuals and firms involved in the process of making a product or service available for use or consumption by consumers or industrial users.

How Customer Value Is Created by Intermediaries

The importance of intermediaries is made even clearer when we consider the functions they perform and the value they create for buyers.

Important Functions Performed by Intermediaries
Intermediaries make possible the flow of products from producers to ultimate consumers by performing three basic functions (see Figure 12–2). Intermediaries perform a *transactional function* when they buy and sell products or services. But an intermediary such as a wholesaler

FIGURE 12–1
Terms used for marketing intermediaries vary in specificity and use in consumer and business markets.

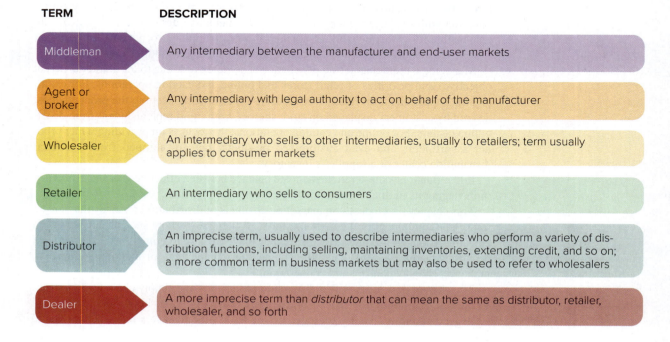

TERM	DESCRIPTION
Middleman	Any intermediary between the manufacturer and end-user markets
Agent or broker	Any intermediary with legal authority to act on behalf of the manufacturer
Wholesaler	An intermediary who sells to other intermediaries, usually to retailers; term usually applies to consumer markets
Retailer	An intermediary who sells to consumers
Distributor	An imprecise term, usually used to describe intermediaries who perform a variety of distribution functions, including selling, maintaining inventories, extending credit, and so on; a more common term in business markets but may also be used to refer to wholesalers
Dealer	A more imprecise term than *distributor* that can mean the same as distributor, retailer, wholesaler, and so forth

TYPE OF FUNCTION	ACTIVITIES RELATED TO FUNCTION
Transactional function	• *Buying*: Purchasing products for resale or as an agent for supply of a product • *Selling*: Contacting potential customers, promoting products, and seeking orders • *Risk taking*: Assuming business risks in the ownership of inventory that can become obsolete or deteriorate
Logistical function	• *Assorting*: Creating product assortments from several sources to serve customers • *Storing*: Assembling and protecting products at a convenient location to offer better customer service • *Sorting*: Purchasing in large quantities and breaking into smaller amounts desired by customers • *Transporting*: Physically moving a product to customers
Facilitating function	• *Financing*: Extending credit to customers • *Grading*: Inspecting, testing, or judging products and assigning them quality grades • *Marketing information and research*: Providing information to customers and suppliers, including competitive conditions and trends

FIGURE 12–2
Marketing channel intermediaries perform these fundamental functions, each of which consists of different activities.

also performs the function of sharing risk with the producer when it stocks merchandise in anticipation of sales. If the stock is unsold for any reason, the intermediary—not the producer—suffers the loss.

The logistics of a transaction (described at length later in this chapter) involve the details of preparing and getting a product to buyers. Gathering, sorting, and dispersing products are some of the *logistical functions* of the intermediary—imagine the several books required for a literature course sitting together on one shelf at your college bookstore! Finally, intermediaries perform *facilitating functions* that, by definition, make a transaction easier for buyers. For example, Macy's issues credit cards to consumers so they can buy now and pay later.

All three functions must be performed in a marketing channel, even though each channel member may not participate in all three. Channel members often negotiate which specific functions they will perform and for what price.

Consumer Benefits Consumers also benefit from intermediaries. Having the products and services you want, when you want them, where you want them, and in the form you want them is the ideal result of marketing channels.

In more specific terms, marketing channels help create value for consumers through the four utilities described in Chapter 1: time, place, form, and possession. *Time utility* refers to having a product or service when you want it. For example, FedEx provides next-morning delivery. *Place utility* means having a product or service available where consumers want it, such as having a Chevron gas station located on a long stretch of lonely highway. *Form utility* involves enhancing a product or service to make it more appealing to buyers. Consider the importance of bottlers in the soft-drink industry. Coca-Cola and Pepsi-Cola manufacture the flavor concentrate (cola, lemon-lime) and sell it to bottlers—intermediaries—which then add sweetener and the concentrate to carbonated water and package the beverage in bottles and cans, which are then sold to retailers. *Possession utility* entails efforts by intermediaries to help buyers take possession of a product or service, such as having airline tickets delivered by a travel agency.

learning review

12-1. What is meant by a marketing channel?

12-2. What are the three basic functions performed by intermediaries?

MARKETING CHANNEL STRUCTURE AND ORGANIZATION

LO 12-2 Distinguish among traditional marketing channels, electronic marketing channels, and different types of vertical marketing systems.

A product can take many routes on its journey from a producer to buyers. Marketers continually search for the most efficient route from the many alternatives available. As you'll see, there are some important differences between the marketing channels used for consumer products and business products.

Marketing Channels for Consumer Products and Services

Figure 12–3 shows the four most common marketing channels for consumer products and services. It also shows the number of levels in each marketing channel, as evidenced by the number of intermediaries between a producer and ultimate buyers. As the number of intermediaries between a producer and buyer increases, the channel is viewed as increasing in length. Thus, the producer → wholesaler → retailer → consumer channel is longer than the producer → consumer channel.

Direct Channel Channel A represents a *direct channel* because the producer and the ultimate consumers deal directly with each other. Many products and services are distributed this way. Many insurance companies sell their services using a direct channel and branch sales offices. The Schwan's Company of Marshall, Minnesota, the largest direct-to-home provider of foods in the United States, uses route sales representatives who sell from refrigerated trucks. Because there are no intermediaries with a direct channel, the producer performs all channel functions.

Indirect Channel The remaining three channel forms in Figure 12–3 are *indirect channels* because intermediaries are inserted between the producer and consumers and perform numerous channel functions. Channel B, with a retailer added, is most common when a retailer is large and can buy in large quantities from a producer or when the cost of inventory makes it too expensive to use a wholesaler. Automobile manufacturers such as Toyota use this channel, and a local car dealer acts as a retailer. Why is there no wholesaler? So many variations exist in the product that it would be impossible for a wholesaler to stock all the models required to satisfy buyers; in addition, the cost of maintaining an inventory would be too high. However, large retailers such as Target, 7-Eleven, Safeway, and The Home Depot buy in sufficient quantities to make it cost effective for a producer to deal with only a retail intermediary.

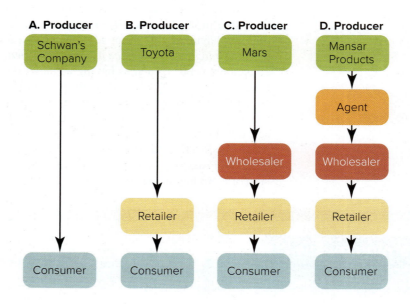

FIGURE 12–3

Common marketing channels for consumer products and services differ by the kind and number of intermediaries involved.

What kind of marketing channel does IBM use for its Watson supercomputer—an artificially intelligent computer system capable of answering questions in natural language? Read the text to find out.

©Ben Hider/Getty Images

Adding a wholesaler in Channel C is most common for low-cost, low-unit value items that are frequently purchased by consumers, such as candy, confectionary items, and magazines. For example, Mars sells case quantities of its line of candies to wholesalers, who then break down (sort) the cases so that individual retailers can order in boxes or much smaller quantities.

Channel D, the most indirect channel, is employed when there are many small manufacturers and many small retailers; in this type of channel, an agent is used to help coordinate a large supply of the product. Mansar Products, Ltd. is a Belgian producer of specialty jewelry that uses agents to sell to wholesalers in the United States, who then sell to many small independent jewelry retailers.

Marketing Channels for Business Products and Services

The four most common channels for business products and services are shown in Figure 12–4. In contrast with channels used for consumer products, business channels typically are shorter and rely on one intermediary or none at all because business users are fewer in number, tend to be more concentrated geographically, and buy in larger quantities.

Direct Channel Channel A in Figure 12–4, represented by IBM's large, mainframe computer business, is a direct channel. Firms using this channel maintain their own salesforce and perform all channel functions. This channel is employed when buyers are large and well-defined, the sales effort requires extensive negotiations, and the products are of high unit value and require hands-on expertise in terms of installation or use. Not surprisingly, IBM's Watson supercomputer, priced at $3 million, is sold and delivered directly to buyers.

Indirect Channel Channels B, C, and D in Figure 12–4 are indirect channels with one or more intermediaries between the producer and the industrial user. In Channel B, an industrial distributor performs a variety of marketing channel functions, including selling, stocking, delivering a full product assortment, and financing. In many ways, industrial distributors are like wholesalers in consumer channels. Caterpillar uses 500 industrial distributors to sell its construction and mining equipment in over

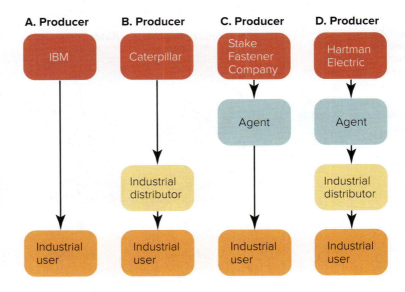

FIGURE 12–4

Common marketing channels for business products and services differ by the kind and number of intermediaries involved.

180 countries. In addition to selling, Caterpillar distributors stock 40,000 to 50,000 parts and service equipment using highly trained technicians.

Channel C introduces a second intermediary, an agent, who serves primarily as the independent selling arm of producers and represents a producer to industrial users. For example, Stake Fastener Company, a producer of industrial fasteners, has an agent call on industrial users rather than employing its own salesforce.

Channel D is the longest channel and includes both agents and industrial distributors. For instance, Hartman Electric, a producer of electric products, uses agents to call on electrical distributors who sell to industrial users.

Internet Marketing Channels

These common marketing channels for consumer and business products and services are not the only routes to the marketplace. *Internet marketing channels* also make products and services available for consumption or use by consumers or organizational buyers. A unique feature of these channels is that they combine electronic and traditional intermediaries to create time, place, form, and possession utility for buyers.

Figure 12–5 shows the Internet marketing channels for books (Amazon.com), automobiles (Autobytel.com), reservation services (Orbitz.com), and personal computers (Dell.com). Are you surprised that they look a lot like common consumer product marketing channels? An important reason for the similarity resides in the channel functions detailed in Figure 12–2. Electronic intermediaries can and do perform transactional and facilitating functions effectively and at a relatively lower cost than traditional intermediaries because of efficiencies made possible by digital technology. But electronic intermediaries are incapable of performing elements of the logistical function, particularly for products such as automobiles. This function remains with traditional intermediaries or with the producer, as is evident with Dell Inc. and its direct channel.

Many services can be distributed through electronic marketing channels, such as car rental reservations marketed by Alamo.com, financial securities by E-Trade.com, and insurance by Esurance.com. However, many other services, such as health care and auto repair, still involve traditional intermediaries.

Direct and Multichannel Marketing

Many firms also use direct and multichannel marketing to reach buyers. *Direct marketing channels* allow consumers to buy products by interacting with various advertising media without a face-to-face meeting with a salesperson. Direct marketing channels include mail-order selling, direct-mail sales, catalog sales, telemarketing, interactive media, and televised home shopping (e.g., the Home Shopping Network). Some firms

FIGURE 12–5

Consumer Internet marketing channels look much like those for consumer products and services. Read the text to learn why.

Ethan Allen successfully engages in multichannel marketing through its 300 design centers in the United States and Canada, its website, and its catalogs.
(left): ©Rob Crandall/Alamy Stock Photo; (center): Source: Ethan Allen Global, Inc.; (right): Source: Ethan Allen Global, Inc.

sell products almost entirely through direct marketing. These firms include L.L.Bean (apparel) and Newegg.com (consumer electronics). Marketers such as Nestlé, in addition to using traditional channels composed of wholesalers and retailers, also employ direct marketing through catalogs and telemarketing to reach more buyers.

Multichannel marketing, sometimes called *omnichannel marketing*, is the *blending* of different communication and delivery channels that are *mutually reinforcing* in attracting, retaining, and building relationships with consumers who shop and buy in traditional intermediaries and online. Multichannel marketing seeks to integrate a firm's electronic marketing and delivery channels. Few companies have truly mastered multichannel marketing. Not surprisingly, improving multichannel marketing practices is considered a top priority among marketers.[2]

Multichannel marketing has been found to leverage the value-adding capabilities of different channels. For example, retail stores leverage their physical presence by allowing customers to pick up their online orders or return or exchange nonstore purchases at a nearby store if they wish. At JCPenney, for instance, over 90 percent of its online returns are brought to one of its stores. Catalogs can serve as shopping tools for online purchasing, as they do for store purchasing. Websites can help consumers do their homework before visiting a store. As described in the chapter-opening example, Eddie Bauer has done this. While its retail stores still account for the majority of its sales revenue, its website accounts for 35 to 40 percent of company sales.[3]

multichannel marketing
The blending of different communication and delivery channels that are mutually reinforcing in attracting, retaining, and building relationships with consumers who shop and buy in traditional intermediaries and online.

Dual Distribution and Strategic Channel Alliances

In some situations, producers use **dual distribution**, an arrangement whereby a firm reaches different buyers by employing two or more different types of channels for the same basic product. For example, GE sells its large appliances directly to home and apartment builders but uses retail stores, including Lowe's home centers, to sell to consumers. In some instances, firms pair multiple channels with a multibrand strategy (see Chapter 10). This is done to minimize cannibalization of the firm's family brand and differentiate the channels. For example, Hallmark sells its Hallmark greeting cards through Hallmark stores and select department stores and its Ambassador brand of cards through discount and drugstore chains.

dual distribution
An arrangement whereby a firm reaches different buyers by employing two or more different types of channels for the same basic product.

An innovation in marketing channels is the use of *strategic channel alliances*, whereby one firm's marketing channel is used to sell another firm's products. Strategic alliances are popular in global marketing, where the creation of marketing channel relationships is expensive and time-consuming. For example, Kroger, the largest U.S supermarket chain, recently partnered with Alibaba, China's largest e-commerce marketer, to sell Kroger's organic private-branded food products. General Mills and Nestlé

Video 12-1
Honey Nut Cheerios Ad
kerin.tv/cr8e/v12-1

Marketing Matters > Customer Value

Nestlé and General Mills—Cereal Partners Worldwide

Can you say Nestlé Cheerios *miel amandes?* Millions in France start their day with this European equivalent of General Mills's Honey Nut Cheerios, made possible by Cereal Partners Worldwide (CPW). CPW is a strategic alliance designed from the start to be a global business. It combines the cereal manufacturing and marketing capability of U.S.-based General Mills with the worldwide distribution clout of Swiss-based Nestlé. The photo shows Nestlé's Trix cereal (not General Mills) sold in China.

From its headquarters in Switzerland, CPW first launched General Mills cereals under the Nestlé label in France, the United Kingdom, Spain, and Portugal in 1991. Today, CPW competes in more than 130 international markets.

The General Mills–Nestlé strategic channel alliance also increased the ready-to-eat cereal worldwide market share of these companies, which are already rated as the two best-managed firms in the world. CPW currently accounts for more than 10 percent of the nearly $30 billion worldwide hot- and cold-cereal market, with more than $4 billion in annual revenue.

©picture alliance/Daniel Kalker/Newscom

have an extensive alliance that spans about 140 international markets from Mexico to China. Read the Marketing Matters box so you won't be surprised when you are served Nestlé (not General Mills) Cheerios when traveling outside North America.[4]

Vertical Marketing Systems

The traditional marketing channels described so far represent a loosely knit network of independent producers and intermediaries brought together to distribute products and services. However, other channel arrangements exist for the purpose of improving efficiency in performing channel functions and achieving greater marketing effectiveness. These arrangements are called vertical marketing systems. **Vertical marketing systems** are professionally managed and centrally coordinated marketing channels designed to achieve channel economies and maximum marketing impact.[5] Figure 12–6 depicts the three major types of vertical marketing systems: corporate, contractual, and administered.

vertical marketing systems
Professionally managed and centrally coordinated marketing channels designed to achieve channel economies and maximum marketing impact.

Corporate Systems The combination of successive stages of production and distribution under a single ownership is a *corporate vertical marketing system.* For example, a producer might own the intermediary at the next level down in the channel. This practice, called *forward integration,* is exemplified by Ralph Lauren, which manufactures clothing and also owns apparel shops. Other examples of forward integration include Goodyear, Apple, and Sherwin-Williams. Alternatively, a retailer might own a manufacturing operation, a practice called *backward integration.* For example, Kroger supermarkets operate manufacturing facilities that produce everything from aspirin to cottage cheese for sale under the Kroger label. Tiffany & Co., the exclusive jewelry retailer, manufactures about half of the fine jewelry items for sale through its over 250 specialty stores and boutiques worldwide.

Companies seeking to reduce distribution costs and gain greater control over supply sources or resale of their products pursue forward and backward integration. However,

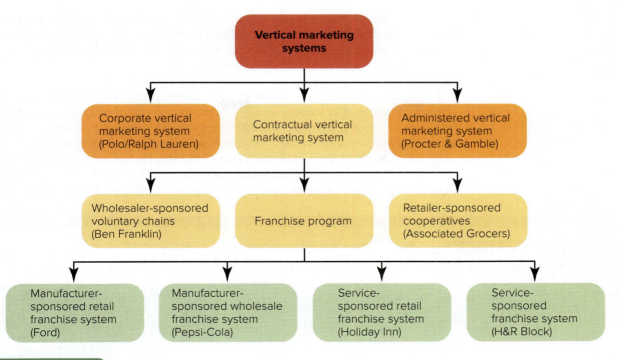

FIGURE 12–6

There are three major types of vertical marketing systems—corporate, contractual, and administered. Contractual systems are the most popular for reasons described in the text.

both types of integration increase a company's capital investment and fixed costs. For this reason, many companies favor contractual vertical marketing systems to achieve channel efficiencies and marketing effectiveness.

Contractual Systems Under a *contractual vertical marketing system,* independent production and distribution firms integrate their efforts on a contractual basis to obtain greater functional economies and marketing impact than they could achieve alone. Contractual systems are the most popular among the three types of vertical marketing systems.

Three variations of contractual systems exist. *Wholesaler-sponsored voluntary chains* involve a wholesaler that develops a contractual relationship with small, independent retailers to standardize and coordinate buying practices, merchandising programs, and inventory management efforts. With the organization of a large number of independent retailers, economies of scale and volume discounts can be achieved to compete with chain stores. IGA and Ben Franklin variety and craft stores represent wholesaler-sponsored voluntary chains. *Retailer-sponsored cooperatives* exist when small, independent retailers form an organization that operates a wholesale facility cooperatively. Member retailers then concentrate their buying power through the wholesaler and plan collaborative promotional and pricing activities. Examples of retailer-sponsored cooperatives include Associated Grocers and Ace Hardware.

The most visible variation of contractual systems is franchising. *Franchising* is a contractual arrangement between a parent company (a franchisor) and an individual or firm (a franchisee) that allows the franchisee to operate a certain type of business under an established name and according to specific rules.

Four types of franchise arrangements are most popular. *Manufacturer-sponsored retail franchise systems* are prominent in the automobile industry, where a manufacturer such as Ford licenses dealers to sell its cars subject to various sales and service conditions. *Manufacturer-sponsored wholesale franchise systems* exist in the soft-drink industry. For example, Pepsi-Cola licenses wholesalers (bottlers) that purchase concentrate from Pepsi-Cola and then carbonate, bottle, promote, and distribute its products to retailers and restaurants. *Service-sponsored retail franchise systems* are used by firms that have designed a unique approach for performing a service and wish to profit by selling the franchise to others. Holiday Inn, Avis, and McDonald's represent this type of franchising approach. *Service-sponsored franchise systems* exist when franchisors license individuals or firms to dispense a service under a trade name and according to specific guidelines. Examples include Snelling and Snelling, Inc. employment services and H&R Block tax services.

Administered Systems In comparison, *administered vertical marketing systems* achieve coordination at successive stages of production and distribution by the size and influence of one channel member rather than through ownership. Procter & Gamble, given its broad product assortment ranging from disposable diapers to detergents, is able to obtain cooperation from supermarkets in displaying, promoting, and pricing its products. Walmart obtains cooperation from manufacturers in terms of product specifications, price levels, and promotional support due to its position as the world's largest retailer.

> **learning review**
>
> **12-3.** What is the difference between a direct and an indirect channel?
>
> **12-4.** Why are channels for business products typically shorter than channels for consumer products?
>
> **12-5.** What is the principal distinction between a corporate vertical marketing system and an administered vertical marketing system?

MARKETING CHANNEL CHOICE AND MANAGEMENT

LO 12-3 Describe factors that marketing executives consider when selecting and managing a marketing channel.

Marketing channels not only link a producer to its buyers but also provide the means through which a firm implements various elements of its marketing strategy. Therefore, choosing a marketing channel is a critical decision.

Factors Affecting Channel Choice and Management

Marketing executives consider three questions when choosing a marketing channel and intermediaries:

1. Which channel and intermediaries will provide the best coverage of the target market?
2. Which channel and intermediaries will best satisfy the buying requirements of the target market?
3. Which channel and intermediaries will be the most profitable?

Target Market Coverage Achieving the best coverage of the target market requires attention to the *density*—that is, the number of stores in a geographical area—and type of intermediaries to be used at the retail level of distribution. Three degrees of distribution density exist: intensive, exclusive, and selective.

Intensive distribution means that a firm tries to place its products and services in as many outlets as possible. Intensive distribution is usually chosen for convenience products or services such as candy, fast food, newspapers, and soft drinks. For example, Coca-Cola's retail distribution objective is to place its products "within an arm's reach of desire." Cash, yes cash, is distributed intensively by Visa. It operates over 1.8 million automated teller machines in more than 200 countries.

Exclusive distribution is the extreme opposite of intensive distribution because only one retailer in a specific geographical area carries the firm's products. Exclusive distribution is typically chosen for specialty products or services, such as some women's fragrances and men's and women's apparel and accessories. Gucci, one of the world's leading luxury products companies, uses exclusive distribution in the marketing of its Yves Saint Laurent, Sergio Rossi, Boucheron, Opium, and Gucci brands.

intensive distribution
A level of distribution density whereby a firm tries to place its products and services in as many outlets as possible.

exclusive distribution
A level of distribution density whereby only one retailer in a specific geographical area carries the firm's products.

Retailers and industrial distributors prefer exclusive distribution for two reasons. First, it limits head-to-head competition for an identical product. Second, it provides a point of difference for a retailer or distributor. For instance, luxury retailer Saks Inc. seeks exclusive product lines for its stores. According to the company CEO, "It's incumbent on us not to be just a place where you can buy the big brands. Those brands are still critical—the Chanels, the Pradas, the Guccis—but even with those brands, we need to find things unique to us."[6]

Selective distribution lies between these two extremes and means that a firm selects a few retailers in a specific geographical area to carry its products. Selective distribution weds some of the market coverage benefits of intensive distribution to the control over resale evident with exclusive distribution. For example, Dell Technologies chose selective distribution when it decided to sell selected products through U.S. retailers along with its direct channel.[7] According to Michael Dell, the company CEO, "There were plenty of retailers who said, 'sell through us,' but we didn't want to show up everywhere." The company now sells a limited range of its products through Walmart, Sam's Club, Best Buy, and Costco. Dell's decision was consistent with current trends. Today, selective distribution is the most common form of distribution intensity.

The growth of online buying has lessened, but not eliminated, the role of geography in determining target market coverage. The continued importance of geography in target market coverage is evident in multichannel marketing where a retail presence is important. This topic is explored further in Chapter 1 in the discussion on multichannel marketing and the popularity of cross-channel shopping.

Buyer Requirements A second consideration in channel choice is gaining access to channels and intermediaries that satisfy at least some of the interests buyers might want fulfilled when they purchase a firm's products or services. These interests fall into four broad categories: (1) information, (2) convenience, (3) variety, and (4) pre- or postsale services. Each relates to customer experience.

Information is an important requirement when buyers have limited knowledge or desire specific data about a product or service. Properly chosen intermediaries communicate with buyers through in-store displays, demonstrations, and personal selling. Apple has opened about 500 retail outlets staffed with highly trained personnel to communicate how its products can better satisfy each customer's needs.

Convenience has multiple meanings for buyers, such as proximity or driving time to a retail outlet. For example, 7-Eleven stores, with more than 50,000 outlets worldwide, many of which are open 24 hours a day, satisfy this interest for buyers. Candy and snack-food firms benefit by gaining display space in these stores. For other consumers, convenience means a minimum of time and hassle. Jiffy Lube, which promises to change engine oil and filters quickly, appeals to this aspect of convenience. For Internet shoppers, convenience means that websites must be easy to locate and navigate, and image downloads must be fast. A commonly held view among website developers is the "eight second rule": Consumers will abandon their efforts to enter or navigate a website if download time exceeds eight seconds.[8]

Variety reflects buyers' interest in having numerous competing and complementary items from which to choose. Variety is evident in the breadth and depth of products and brands carried by intermediaries, which enhances their attraction to buyers. Thus, manufacturers of pet food and supplies seek distribution through pet superstores such as Petco and PetSmart, which offer a wide array of pet products and services.

Pre- or postsale services provided by intermediaries are an important buying requirement for products such as large household appliances that require delivery, installation, and credit. Therefore, Whirlpool seeks dealers that provide such services.

> **selective distribution**
> A level of distribution density whereby a firm selects a few retailers in a specific geographical area to carry its products.

Which buying requirements are satisfied by Jiffy Lube? Read the text to find out.
©David McNew/Getty Images

Applying Marketing Metrics
Channel Sales and Profit at Charlesburg Furniture

Charlesburg Furniture is one of 1,000 wood furniture manufacturers in the United States. The company sells its furniture through furniture store chains, independent furniture stores, and department store chains, mostly in the southern United States. The company has traditionally allocated its marketing funds for cooperative advertising, in-store displays, and retail sales support on the basis of dollar sales by channel.

Your Challenge
As the vice president of sales and marketing at Charlesburg Furniture, you have been asked to review the company's sales and profit in its three channels and recommend a course of action for 2018. The question: Should Charlesburg Furniture continue to allocate its marketing funds on the basis of channel dollar sales or profit?

Your Findings
Charlesburg Furniture tracks the sales and profit from each channel (and individual customer) and the three-year trend of sales by channel on its marketing dashboard. This information is displayed in the marketing dashboards below.

Your Action
Charlesburg Furniture should consider abandoning the practice of allocating marketing funds solely on the basis of channel sales volume. The importance of independent furniture stores to Charlesburg's profitability warrants further spending, particularly given this channel's favorable sales trend. Doubling the percentage allocation for marketing funds for this channel may be too extreme, however. Charlesburg Furniture might also consider the longer-term role of department store chains as a marketing distribution channel.

Several findings stand out. Furniture store chains and independent furniture stores account for 85.2 percent of Charlesburg Furniture sales and 93 percent of company profit. These two channels also evidence growth as measured by annual percentage change in sales. By comparison, the annual percentage sales growth of department store chains has declined, recording negative growth in 2017. This channel accounts for 14.8 percent of company sales and 7 percent of company profit.

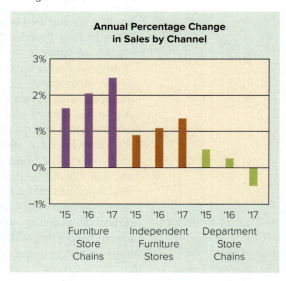

Profitability The third consideration in choosing a channel is profitability, which is determined by the margins earned (revenue minus cost) for each channel member and for the channel as a whole. Channel cost is the critical dimension of profitability. These costs include distribution, advertising, and selling expenses associated with different types of marketing channels. The extent to which channel members share these costs determines the margins received by each member and by the channel as a whole.

Companies routinely monitor the performance of their marketing channels. Read the Applying Marketing Metrics box to see how Charlesburg Furniture views the sales and profit performance of its marketing channels.

Managing Channel Relationships: Conflict and Cooperation

Unfortunately, because channels consist of independent individuals and firms, there is always the potential for disagreements concerning who performs which channel functions, how profits are allocated, which products and services will be provided by whom, and who makes critical channel-related decisions. These channel conflicts necessitate measures for dealing with them.

Sources of Conflict in Marketing Channels

Channel conflict arises when one channel member believes another channel member is engaged in behavior that prevents it from achieving its goals. Two types of conflict occur in marketing channels: vertical conflict and horizontal conflict.

Vertical conflict occurs between different levels in a marketing channel—for example, between a manufacturer and a wholesaler or retailer or between a wholesaler and a retailer. Three sources of vertical conflict are most common.[9] First, conflict arises when a channel member bypasses another member and sells or buys products direct, a practice called **disintermediation**. For example, conflict occurred when American Airlines decided to terminate its relationship with Orbitz and Expedia, two online ticketing and travel sites, and sell directly through AA Direct Connect. Second, conflict occurs due to disagreements over how profit margins are distributed among channel members. This happened when Amazon and the Hachette Book Group, the third-largest trade book and educational publisher, engaged in a seven-month dispute about how e-book revenue should be divided between the two companies. A third conflict situation arises when manufacturers believe wholesalers or retailers are not giving their products adequate attention. For example, Newell Brands, Inc. stopped shipping its popular Sharpie brand pens and markers to Office Depot because it believed Office Depot was not spending what the two companies agreed on for showcasing and marketing Sharpies.

Horizontal conflict occurs between intermediaries at the same level in a marketing channel, such as between two or more retailers (Target and Kmart) or two or more wholesalers that handle the same manufacturer's brands. Two sources of horizontal conflict are common.[10] First, horizontal conflict arises when a manufacturer increases its distribution coverage in a geographical area. For example, a franchised Cadillac dealer in Chicago might complain to General Motors that another franchised Cadillac dealer has located too close to its dealership. Second, dual distribution causes conflict when different types of retailers carry the same brands. When independent Goodyear tire dealers learned that Goodyear Tire Company decided to sell its brands through Sears, Walmart, and Sam's Club, many dealers switched to competing tire makers. Likewise, when Under Armour began selling its athletic wear to department stores, sporting goods retailers became irate and began promoting their own store brands over Under Armour products.

Securing Cooperation in Marketing Channels
Conflict can have destructive effects on the workings of a marketing channel so it is necessary to secure cooperation among channel members. One means is through a *channel captain,* a channel member that coordinates, directs, and supports other channel members. Channel captains can be producers, wholesalers, or retailers. P&G assumes this role because it has a strong consumer following in brands such as Crest, Tide, and Pampers. Therefore, it can set policies or terms that supermarkets will follow. McKesson, a pharmaceutical drug wholesaler, is a channel captain because it coordinates and supports the product

Channel conflict is sometimes visible to consumers. Read the text to learn what type of channel conflict has antagonized this independent Goodyear tire dealer.
©Joe & Kathy Heiner/Lindgren & Smith, Inc.

channel conflict
Arises when one channel member believes another channel member is engaged in behavior that prevents it from achieving its goals.

disintermediation
A source of channel conflict that occurs when a channel member bypasses another member and sells or buys products direct.

flow from numerous small drug manufacturers to drugstores and hospitals nationwide. Walmart is a retail channel captain because of its strong consumer image, number of outlets, online presence, and purchasing volume.

A firm becomes a channel captain because it is the channel member with the ability to influence the behavior of other members. Influence can take four forms. First, economic influence arises from the ability of a firm to *reward* other members given its strong financial position or customer franchise. Microsoft Corporation and Walmart have such influence. *Expertise* is a second source of influence. For example, American Hospital Supply helps its customers (hospitals) manage inventory and streamline order processing for hundreds of medical supplies. Third, *identification* with a particular channel member can create influence for that channel member. For instance, retailers may compete to carry the Ralph Lauren line, or clothing manufacturers may compete to be carried by Neiman Marcus, Nordstrom, or Bloomingdale's. In both instances, the desire to be identified with a channel member gives that firm influence over others. Finally, influence can arise from the *legitimate right* of one channel member to direct the behavior of other members. This situation is likely to occur in contractual vertical marketing systems where a franchisor can legitimately direct how a franchisee behaves.

> **learning review**
>
> **12-6.** What are the three questions marketing executives consider when choosing a marketing channel and intermediaries?
>
> **12-7.** What are the three degrees of distribution density?

LOGISTICS AND SUPPLY CHAIN MANAGEMENT

LO 12-4 Explain what supply chain and logistics management are and how they relate to marketing strategy.

logistics
Those activities that focus on getting the right amount of the right products to the right place at the right time at the lowest possible cost.

A marketing channel relies on logistics to make products available to consumers and industrial users. **Logistics** involves those activities that focus on getting the right amount of the right products to the right place at the right time at the lowest possible cost. The performance of these activities is *logistics management,* the practice of organizing the cost-effective flow of raw materials, in-process inventory, finished goods, and related information from point of origin to point of consumption to satisfy *customer requirements.*

Three elements of this definition deserve emphasis. First, logistics deals with decisions needed to move a product from the source of raw materials to consumption—that is, the *flow* of the product. Second, those decisions have to be *cost effective.* Third, while it is important to drive down logistics costs, there is a limit: A firm needs to drive down logistics costs as long as it can deliver expected *customer service,* which means satisfying customer requirements.

The role of management is to see that customer needs are satisfied in the most cost-effective manner. When properly done, the results are spectacular. Consider Procter & Gamble. The company set out to meet consumer needs more effectively by collaborating with its suppliers and retailers to ensure that the right products reached store shelves at the right time and at a lower cost. The effort was judged a success when, during an 18-month period, P&G's retail customers posted a $65 million savings in logistics costs and customer service increased. When done improperly, disaster can result. KFC in the United Kingdom is an example. The company switched food distributors to reduce costs only to find that it couldn't deliver chickens on time or in sufficient quantities to its stores. KFC had to close 80 percent of its stores for the better part of a week due to no chickens.[11]

Companies today recognize that getting the right items needed for consumption or production to the right place at the right time in the right condition at the right cost is often beyond their individual capabilities and control. Instead, collaboration, coordination, and information sharing among manufacturers, suppliers, and distributors are necessary to create a seamless flow of products and services to customers. This perspective is represented in the concept of a supply chain and the practice of supply chain management.

Supply Chains versus Marketing Channels

A **supply chain** refers to the various firms involved in performing the activities required to create and deliver a product or service to consumers or industrial users. It differs from a marketing channel in terms of the firms involved. A supply chain includes suppliers that provide raw material inputs to a manufacturer as well as the wholesalers and retailers that deliver finished products to consumers. The management process is also different.

Supply chain management is the integration and organization of information and logistics activities *across firms* in a supply chain for the purpose of creating and delivering products and services that provide value to consumers. The relation among marketing channels, logistics management, and supply chain management is shown in Figure 12–7. An important feature of supply chain management is its application of sophisticated information technology that allows companies to share and operate systems for order processing, transportation scheduling, and inventory and facility management.

Sourcing, Assembling, and Delivering a New Car: The Automotive Supply Chain

All companies are members of one or more supply chains. A supply chain is essentially a series of linked suppliers and customers in which every customer is, in turn, a supplier to another customer until a finished product reaches the ultimate consumer. Even the simplified supply chain diagram for carmakers shown in Figure 12–8 illustrates how complex a supply chain can be.[12] A carmaker's supplier network includes thousands of firms that provide the 2,000 functional components, 30,000 parts, and 10 million lines of software code in a typical automobile. They provide items ranging from raw materials, such as steel and rubber, to components, including transmissions, tires, brakes, and seats, to complex subassemblies such as chassis and suspension systems that make for a smooth, stable ride. The process of coordinating and scheduling the flow of materials and components for their assembly into actual automobiles by carmakers is heavily dependent on logistical activities, including transportation, order processing, inventory control, materials handling, and information technology. A central link is the carmaker's supply chain manager, who is responsible for translating customer requirements into actual orders and arranging for delivery dates and financial arrangements for automobile dealers.

supply chain
The various firms involved in performing the activities required to create and deliver a product or service to consumers or industrial users.

FIGURE 12–7
Relating logistics management and supply chain management to supplier networks and marketing channels.

FIGURE 12–8

The automotive supply chain includes thousands of firms that provide the functional components, software codes, and parts in a typical car.

Photos: © McGraw-Hill Education/Mike Hruby, photographer

Logistical aspects of the automobile marketing channel are also an important part of the supply chain. Major responsibilities include transportation (which involves the selection and oversight of external carriers—trucking, airline, railroad, and shipping companies—for cars and parts to dealers), the operation of distribution centers, the management of finished goods inventories, and order processing for sales. Supply chain managers also play an important role in the marketing channel. They work with car dealer networks to ensure that the right mix of automobiles is delivered to each location. In addition, they make sure that spare and service parts are available so that dealers can meet the car maintenance and repair needs of consumers. All of this is done with the help of information technology that links the entire automotive supply chain. What does all of this cost? It is estimated that logistics costs represent 25 to 30 percent of the retail price that you pay for a new car.

Supply Chain Management and Marketing Strategy

Video 12-2
IBM
kerin.tv/cr8e/v12-2

The automotive supply chain illustration shows how information and logistics activities are integrated and organized across firms to create and deliver a car to you, the consumer. What's missing from this illustration is the linkage between a specific company's supply chain and its marketing strategy. Just as companies have different marketing strategies, they also design and manage supply chains differently. The goals to be achieved by a firm's marketing strategy determine whether its supply chain needs to be more responsive or efficient in meeting customer requirements.

Aligning a Supply Chain with Marketing Strategy There are a variety of supply chain configurations, each of which is designed to perform different tasks well. Marketers today recognize that the choice of a supply chain follows from a clearly defined marketing strategy and involves three steps:[13]

1. *Understand the customer.* To understand the customer, a company must identify the needs of the customer segment being served. These needs, such as a desire for a low price or convenience of purchase, help a company define the relative importance of efficiency and responsiveness in meeting customer requirements.
2. *Understand the supply chain.* Second, a company must understand what a supply chain is designed to do well. Supply chains range from those that emphasize being responsive to customer requirements and demand to those that emphasize efficiency with a goal of supplying products at the lowest possible delivered cost.
3. *Harmonize the supply chain with the marketing strategy.* Finally, a company needs to ensure that what the supply chain is capable of doing well is consistent with the targeted customer's needs and its marketing strategy. If a mismatch exists between what the supply chain does particularly well and a company's marketing strategy, the company will need to either redesign the supply chain to support the marketing strategy or change the marketing strategy. Read the Marketing Matters box to learn how IBM overhauled its complete supply chain to support its marketing strategy.

Marketing Matters

Customer Value

IBM's Watson Supply Chain—Delivering a Total Solution for Its Customers

IBM is one of the world's great business success stories because of its ability to reinvent itself to satisfy shifting customer needs in a dynamic global marketplace. The company's transformation of its supply chain using artificial intelligence provided by Watson, its path-breaking supercomputer, is a case in point.

IBM has built a single integrated supply chain that can handle raw material procurement, manufacturing, logistics, customer support, order entry, and customer fulfillment across all of IBM—something that has never been done before. Why would IBM undertake this task? According to IBM's former CEO, Samuel J. Palmisano, "You cannot hope to thrive in the IT industry if you are a high-cost, slow-moving company. Supply chain is one of the new competitive battle-grounds. We are committed to being the most efficient and productive player in our industry."

©Peter Probst/Alamy Stock Photo

The task is not easy. IBM's supply chain management organization works out of 360 locations in 64 countries, tracking more than 1.5 million in assets for both IBM and its clients. The organization also deals with about 17,000 suppliers in 100 countries. Yet with surprising efficiency, IBM's supply chain is linked from raw material sourcing to postsales support.

Today, IBM is uniquely poised to configure and deliver a tailored mix of hardware, software, and service to provide a total solution for its customers using Watson. Watson is IBM's supercomputer that combines artificial intelligence and sophisticated software and is now being used to improve the performance of its supply chain. Not surprisingly, IBM's supply chain is heralded as one of the best in the world!

©Kristoffer Tripplaar/Alamy Stock Photo

How are these steps applied and how are efficiency and responsiveness considerations built into a supply chain? Let's look at how two well-known companies—Dell Technologies and Walmart—have harmonized their supply chain and marketing strategy.[14]

Dell: A Responsive Supply Chain The Dell Technologies marketing strategy primarily targets customers who desire having the most up-to-date computer systems customized to their needs. These customers are also willing to (1) wait to have their customized computer system delivered in a few days, rather than picking out a model at a retail store, and (2) pay a reasonable, though not the lowest, price in the marketplace. Given Dell's customer segment, the company has the option of adopting an efficient or responsive supply chain.

An efficient supply chain may use inexpensive, but slower, modes of transportation, emphasize economies of scale in its production process by reducing the variety of system configurations offered, and limit its assembly and inventory storage facilities to a single location. If Dell opted only for efficiency in its supply chain, it would be difficult to satisfy its target customers' desire for rapid delivery and a wide variety of customizable products.

Dell instead has opted for a responsive supply chain. It relies on more expensive express transportation for receipt of components from suppliers and delivery of finished products to customers. The company achieves product variety and manufacturing efficiency by designing common platforms across several products and using common components. Also, Dell has invested heavily in information technology to link itself with suppliers and customers.

©R Heyes Design/Alamy Stock Photo

Walmart: An Efficient Supply Chain Now let's consider Walmart. Walmart's marketing strategy is to be a reliable, lower-price retailer for a wide variety of mass consumption consumer goods. This strategy favors an efficient supply chain designed to deliver products to 245 million consumers each week at the lowest possible cost. Efficiency is achieved in a variety of ways. For instance, Walmart keeps relatively low inventory levels, and most of it is stocked in stores available for sale, not in warehouses gathering dust. The low inventory arises from Walmart's use of *cross-docking*—a practice that involves unloading products from suppliers, sorting products for individual stores, and quickly reloading products onto its trucks for a particular store. No warehousing or storing of products occurs, except for a few hours or, at most, a day. In fact, Walmart fines suppliers who deliver products early! Cross-docking allows Walmart to operate only a small number of distribution centers relative to its vast network of Walmart stores, Supercenters, Neighborhood Markets, Marketside stores, and Sam's Clubs, which contributes to efficiency.

Walmart has invested much more than its competitors in information technology to operate its supply chain. The company feeds information about customer requirements and demand from its stores back to its suppliers, which manufacture only what is being demanded. This large investment has improved the efficiency of Walmart's supply chain and made it responsive to customer needs.

Three lessons can be learned from these two examples. First, there is no one best supply chain for every company. Second, the best supply chain is the one that is consistent with the needs of the customer segment being served and complements a company's marketing strategy. And finally, supply chain managers need to be prepared to make trade-offs between efficiency and responsiveness on various elements of a company's supply chain.

TWO CONCEPTS OF LOGISTICS MANAGEMENT IN A SUPPLY CHAIN

The objective of logistics management in a supply chain is to minimize total logistics costs while delivering the appropriate level of customer service.

Total Logistics Cost Concept

total logistics cost
The expenses associated with transportation, materials handling and warehousing, inventory, stockouts (being out of inventory), order processing, and return products handling.

For our purposes, **total logistics cost** includes expenses associated with transportation, materials handling and warehousing, inventory, stockouts (being out of inventory), order processing, and return products handling. Note that many of these costs are interrelated so that changes in one will impact the others. For example, if a company attempts to reduce its transportation costs by shipping in larger quantities, it will increase its inventory levels. While larger inventory levels will increase inventory costs, they should also reduce stockouts. It is important, therefore, to study the impact on all of the logistics decision areas when considering a change.

Customer Service Concept

customer service
The ability of logistics management to satisfy users in terms of time, dependability, communication, and convenience.

Because a supply chain is a *flow,* the end of it—or *output*—is the service delivered to customers. Within the context of a supply chain, **customer service** is the ability of logistics management to satisfy users in terms of time, dependability, communication, and convenience. As suggested by Figure 12–9, a supply chain manager's key task is to balance these four customer service factors against six total logistics cost factors.

Time In a supply chain setting, time refers to *order cycle* or *replenishment* time for an item, which means the time between the ordering of an item and when it is received and ready for use or sale. The various elements that make up the typical order cycle include recognition of the need to order, order transmittal, order processing, documentation, and transportation. A current emphasis in supply chain management is to reduce order cycle time so that the inventory levels of customers may be minimized. Another emphasis is to make the process of reordering and receiving products as simple as possible, often through inventory systems called *quick response* and *efficient consumer response* delivery systems. For example, at Saks Fifth Avenue, point-of-sale scanner technology records each day's sales. When stock falls below a minimum level, a

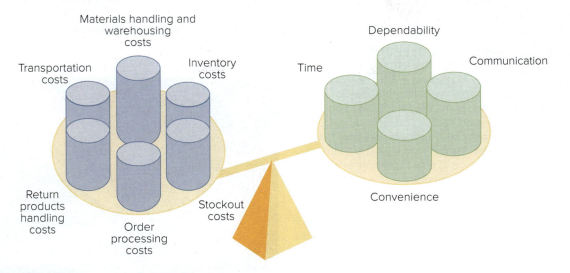

FIGURE 12–9

Supply chain managers balance total logistics cost factors against customer service factors.

replenishment order is automatically produced. Vendors such as Donna Karan (DKNY) receive the order, which is processed and delivered within 48 hours.[15]

Dependability Dependability is the consistency of replenishment. This is important to all firms in a supply chain—and to consumers. How often do you return to a store if it fails to have in stock the item you want to purchase? Dependability can be broken into three elements: consistent lead time, safe delivery, and complete delivery. Consistent service allows planning (such as appropriate inventory levels), whereas inconsistencies create surprises. Intermediaries may be willing to accept longer lead times if they know about them in advance and can thus make plans.

Communication Communication is a two-way link between the buyer and supplier that helps in monitoring service and anticipating future needs. Status reports on orders are a typical example of communication between the buyer and seller.

Convenience The concept of convenience for a supply chain manager means that there should be a minimum of effort on the part of the buyer in doing business with the seller. Is it easy for the customer to order? Are the products available from many outlets? Will the seller arrange all necessary details, such as transportation? This customer service factor has promoted the use of **vendor-managed inventory (VMI)**, whereby the *supplier* determines the product amount and assortment a customer (such as a retailer) needs and automatically delivers the appropriate items.

Campbell Soup's system illustrates how VMI works.[16] Every morning, retailers electronically inform the company of their demand for all Campbell products and the inventory levels in their distribution centers. Campbell uses that information to forecast future demand and determine which products need replenishment based on upper and lower inventory limits established with each retailer. Trucks leave the Campbell shipping plant that afternoon and arrive at the retailer's distribution centers with the required replenishments the same day.

> **vendor-managed inventory (VMI)**
> An inventory management system whereby the supplier determines the product amount and assortment a customer (such as a retailer) needs and automatically delivers the appropriate items.
>
> **reverse logistics**
> A process of reclaiming recyclable and reusable materials, returns, and reworks from the point of consumption or use for repair, remanufacturing, redistribution, or disposal.

CLOSING THE LOOP: REVERSE LOGISTICS

The flow of products in a supply chain does not end with the ultimate consumer or industrial user. Companies today recognize that a supply chain can work in reverse. **Reverse logistics** is a process of reclaiming recyclable and reusable materials, returns, and reworks from the point of consumption or use for repair, remanufacturing,

Making Responsible Decisions > Sustainability

Reverse Logistics and Green Marketing Go Together at Hewlett-Packard: Recycling e-Waste

About 50 megatons (1 megaton = 1 million tons) of electronics and electronic equipment find their way to landfills around the world annually. In 2018, Americans alone discarded over 400 million analog TV sets and computer monitors and Japanese consumers trashed more than 610 million cell phones. The result? Landfills are seeping lead, chromium, mercury, and other toxins prevalent in digital debris into the environment.

Fortunately, Hewlett-Packard has taken it upon itself to act responsibly and address this issue through its highly regarded reverse logistics program. Hewlett-Packard has recycled computer and printer hardware since 1987 and is an industry leader in this practice. The company's recycling service is available today in more than 73 countries, regions, and territories. Hewlett-Packard has recycled about 3 billion pounds of used electronic products and supplies to be refurbished for resale or donation or for recovery of materials.

The recycling effort at Hewlett-Packard is also part of the company's product development program. Among other initiatives in this program, emphasis is placed on product and

Source: Hewlett-Packard Development Company, L.P.

packaging changes to reduce reverse supply chain and environmental costs. For example, more than 75 percent of the company's ink cartridges and 24 percent of its LaserJet toner cartridges are now manufactured with recycled plastic.

---

redistribution, or disposal. The effect of reverse logistics can be seen in the reduced waste in landfills and lowered operating costs for companies. The Making Responsible Decisions box describes the successful reverse logistics initiative at Hewlett-Packard.[17]

Companies such as Motorola and Nokia (return and reuse of mobile phones) and Caterpillar, Xerox, and IBM (remanufacturing and recycling) have implemented acclaimed reverse logistics programs. Other firms have enlisted third-party logistics providers such as UPS, FedEx, and Penske Logistics to handle this process along with other supply chain functions. GNB Technologies, Inc., a manufacturer of lead-acid batteries for automobiles and boats, has outsourced much of its supply chain activity to UPS Supply Chain Services.[18] The company contracts with UPS to manage its shipments between plants, distribution centers, recycling centers, and retailers. This includes movement of both new batteries and used products destined for recycling and covers both truck and railroad shipments. This partnership, along with the initiatives of other battery makers, has paid economic and ecological dividends. By recycling 90 percent of the lead from used batteries, manufacturers have kept the demand for new lead in check, thereby holding down costs to consumers. Also, solid waste management costs and the environmental impact of lead in landfills are reduced.

> Video 12-3
> UPS
> kerin.tv/cr8e/v12-3

learning review

12-8. What is the principal difference between a marketing channel and a supply chain?

12-9. The choice of a supply chain involves what three steps?

12-10. A manager's key task is to balance which four customer service factors against which six logistics cost factors?

LEARNING OBJECTIVES REVIEW

LO 12-1 *Explain what is meant by a marketing channel of distribution and why intermediaries are needed.*

A marketing channel of distribution, or simply a marketing channel, consists of individuals and firms involved in the process of making a product or service available for use or consumption by consumers or industrial users. Intermediaries make possible the flow of products from producers to buyers by performing three basic functions. The transactional function involves buying, selling, and risk taking because intermediaries stock merchandise in anticipation of sales. The logistical function involves the gathering, storing, and dispensing of products. The facilitating function assists producers in making products and services more attractive to buyers. The performance of these functions by intermediaries creates time, place, form, and possession utility for consumers.

LO 12-2 *Distinguish among traditional marketing channels, electronic marketing channels, and different types of vertical marketing systems.*

Traditional marketing channels describe the route taken by products and services from producers to buyers. This route can range from a direct channel with no intermediaries, because a producer and the ultimate consumer deal directly with each other, to indirect channels where intermediaries (agents, wholesalers, distributors, or retailers) are inserted between a producer and consumer and perform numerous channel functions. Electronic marketing channels employ the Internet to make products and services available for consumption or use by consumer or business buyers. Vertical marketing systems are professionally managed and centrally coordinated marketing channels designed to achieve channel economies and maximum marketing impact. There are three major types of vertical marketing systems (VMSs). A corporate VMS combines successive stages of production and distribution under a single ownership. A contractual VMS exists when independent production and distribution firms integrate their efforts on a contractual basis to obtain greater functional economies and marketing impact than they could achieve alone. An administered VMS achieves coordination at successive stages of production and distribution by the size and influence of one channel member rather than through ownership.

LO 12-3 *Describe factors that marketing executives consider when selecting and managing a marketing channel.*

Marketing executives consider three questions when selecting and managing a marketing channel and intermediaries. (1) Which channel and intermediaries will provide the best coverage of the target market? Marketers typically choose one of three levels of market coverage: intensive, selective, or exclusive distribution. (2) Which channel and intermediaries will best satisfy the buying requirements of the target market? These buying requirements fall into four categories: information, convenience, variety, and pre- or postsale services. (3) Which channel and intermediaries will be the most profitable? Here marketers look at the margins earned (revenues minus cost) for each channel member and for the channel as a whole.

LO 12-4 *Explain what supply chain and logistics management are and how they relate to marketing strategy.*

A supply chain refers to the various firms involved in performing the various activities required to create and deliver a product or service to consumers or industrial users. Supply chain management is the integration and organization of information and logistics across firms for the purpose of creating value for consumers. Logistics involves those activities that focus on getting the right amount of the right products to the right place at the right time at the lowest possible cost. Logistics management includes the coordination of the flows of both inbound and outbound products, an emphasis on making these flows cost effective, and customer service. A company's supply chain follows from a clearly defined marketing strategy. The alignment of a company's supply chain with its marketing strategy involves three steps. First, a supply chain must reflect the needs of the customer segment being served. Second, a company must understand what a supply chain is designed to do well. Supply chains range from those that emphasize being responsive to customer requirements and demands to those that emphasize efficiency with the goal of supplying products at the lowest possible delivered cost. Finally, a supply chain must be consistent with the targeted customer's needs and the company's marketing strategy. The Dell and Walmart examples in the chapter illustrate how this alignment is achieved by two market leaders.

LEARNING REVIEW ANSWERS

12-1 What is meant by a marketing channel?
Answer: A marketing channel consists of individuals and firms involved in the process of making a product or service available for use or consumption by consumers or industrial users.

12-2 What are the three basic functions performed by intermediaries?
Answer: Intermediaries perform transactional, logistical, and facilitating functions.

12-3 What is the difference between a direct and an indirect channel?
Answer: A direct channel is one in which a producer of consumer or business products and services and ultimate consumers or industrial users deal directly with each other. In an indirect channel, intermediaries are inserted between the producer and ultimate consumers or industrial users and perform numerous channel functions.

12-4 Why are channels for business products typically shorter than channels for consumer products?
Answer: Business channels are typically shorter than consumer channels because business users are fewer in number, tend to be more concentrated geographically, and buy in larger quantities.

12-5 What is the principal distinction between a corporate vertical marketing system and an administered vertical marketing system?
Answer: A corporate vertical marketing system combines successive stages of production and distribution under a single

ownership. An administered vertical marketing system achieves coordination by the size and influence of one channel member rather than through ownership.

12-6 What are the three questions marketing executives consider when choosing a marketing channel and intermediaries?
Answer: The three questions to consider when choosing a marketing channel and intermediaries are: (1) Which will provide the best coverage of the target market? (2) Which will best satisfy the buying requirements of the target market? (3) Which will be the most profitable?

12-7 What are the three degrees of distribution density?
Answer: intensive; exclusive; selective

12-8 What is the principal difference between a marketing channel and a supply chain?
Answer: A marketing channel consists of individuals and firms involved in the process of making a product or service available for use or consumption by consumers or industrial users. A supply chain differs from a marketing channel in terms of membership. It includes suppliers who provide raw materials to a manufacturer as well as the wholesalers and retailers—the marketing channel—that deliver the finished goods to ultimate consumers.

12-9 The choice of a supply chain involves what three steps?
Answer: (1) Understand the customer. (2) Understand the supply chain. (3) Harmonize the supply chain with the marketing strategy.

12-10 A manager's key task is to balance which four customer service factors against which six logistics cost factors?
Answer: The four customer service factors are time, dependability, communication, and convenience. The logistics cost factors are transportation costs, materials handling and warehousing costs, inventory costs, stockout costs (being out of inventory), order processing costs, and return products handling costs.

FOCUSING ON KEY TERMS

channel conflict p. 337
customer service p. 342
disintermediation p. 337
dual distribution p. 331
exclusive distribution p. 334
intensive distribution p. 334
logistics p. 338
marketing channel p. 326
multichannel marketing p. 331
reverse logistics p. 343
selective distribution p. 335
supply chain p. 339
total logistics cost p. 342
vendor-managed inventory (VMI) p. 343
vertical marketing systems p. 332

APPLYING MARKETING KNOWLEDGE

1. A distributor for Celanese Chemical Company stores large quantities of chemicals, blends these chemicals to satisfy the requests of customers, and delivers the blends to a customer's warehouse within 24 hours of receiving an order. What utilities does this distributor provide?

2. Suppose the president of a carpet manufacturing firm has asked you to look into the possibility of bypassing the firm's wholesalers (who sell to carpet, department, and furniture stores) and selling direct to these stores. What caution would you voice on this matter, and what type of information would you gather before making this decision?

3. What type of channel conflict is likely to be caused by dual distribution, and what type of conflict can be reduced by direct distribution? Why?

4. How does the channel captain idea differ among corporate, administered, and contractual vertical marketing systems with particular reference to the use of the different forms of influence available to firms?

5. List the customer service factors that would be vital to buyers in the following types of companies: (*a*) manufacturing, (*b*) retailing, (*c*) hospitals, and (*d*) construction.

BUILDING YOUR MARKETING PLAN

Does your marketing plan involve selecting channels and intermediaries? If the answer is "no," read no further and do not include this element in your plan. If the answer is "yes":

1. Identify which channel and intermediaries will provide the best coverage of the target market for your product or service.

2. Specify which channel and intermediaries will best satisfy the important buying requirements of the target market.

3. Determine which channel and intermediaries will be the most profitable.

4. Select your channel(s) and intermediary(ies).

5. If inventory is involved, (*a*) identify the three or four major kinds of inventory needed for your organization (retail stock, finished products, raw materials, supplies, and so on), and (*b*) suggest ways to reduce their costs.

6. (*a*) Rank the four customer service factors (time, dependability, communication, and convenience) from most important to least important from your customers' point of view, and (*b*) identify actions for the one or two factors that are the most important in regard to your product or service.

VIDEO CASE 12

Amazon: Delivering the Earth's Biggest Selection!

"The secret is we are on our seventh generation of fulfillment centers and we have gotten better every time," explains Jeff Bezos, CEO of Amazon.com, Inc. The global online retailer is a pioneer of fast, convenient, low-cost shopping that has attracted millions of consumers. Of course, while Amazon has changed the way many people shop, the company still faces the traditional and daunting task of creating a seamless flow of deliveries to its customers—often millions of times each day.

Video 12-4
Amazon Video Case
kerin.tv/cr8e/v12-4

THE COMPANY

Bezos started Amazon.com with a simple idea: Use the Internet to transform book buying into the fastest, easiest, and most enjoyable shopping experience possible. The company was incorporated in 1994 and launched its website in July 1995. At the forefront of a huge growth of dot-com businesses, Amazon pursued a get-big-fast business strategy. Sales grew rapidly and Amazon began adding products and services other than books. In fact, Amazon soon set its goal on being "Earth's most customer-centric company, where customers can find and discover virtually anything they might want to buy online."

Today Amazon.com continues to grow by providing low prices, vast selection, and convenience. Its selection of products covers a broad range of categories including: Books; Movies, Music & Games; Electronics & Computers; Home, Garden & Tools; Beauty, Health & Grocery; Toys; Clothing, Shoes & Jewelry; Sports & Outdoors; and Automotive & Industrial. In addition, Amazon offers digital music, an app store for Android, Amazon Cloud Drive, Kindle e-readers, Kindle Fire tablets, Amazon Fire TV, and the Amazon Fire phone. Other services allow customers to:

- Search for a product or brand using all or part of its name.
- Place orders with one click using the "Buy Now with 1-Click" button on the website and the "Mobile 1-Click" button for phones.
- Receive personalized recommendations based on past purchases through opt-in e-mails.

These products and services have attracted millions of people around the globe. Further, the company's growth has made Amazon.com, along with its international sites in Australia, Brazil, Canada, China, France, Germany, India, Italy, Japan, Mexico, Spain, and the United Kingdom, the world's largest online retailer.

Amazon's e-commerce platform is also used by more than 2 million small businesses, retail brands, and individual sellers. For example, programs such as Selling on Amazon, Fulfillment by Amazon, Amazon Webstore, and Checkout by Amazon allow small businesses to use Amazon's e-commerce platform to facilitate sales. Online retailers store their products at Amazon's fulfillment centers and when they sell a product, Amazon ships it! Amazon.com also operates retail websites for brands such as bebe, Marks & Spencer, Lacoste, and AOL's Shop@AOL. Individual sellers use the Amazon network to reach millions of potential customers. These business partnerships all contribute to Amazon's sales, which now exceed $75 billion.

Bezos defines Amazon by its "big ideas, which are customer centricity, putting the customer at the center of everything we do, and invention—we like to pioneer, we like to explore." Amazon's success is also the

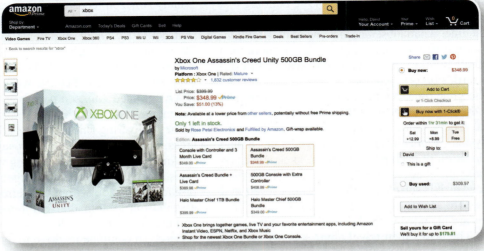

Source: Amazon.com, Inc.

result of an intense focus on cost and efficiency that leads to lower prices. More specifically, Amazon is exceptional at managing the elements of its supply chain, which make up one of the most complex and expensive aspects of the company's business.

SUPPLY CHAIN AND LOGISTICS MANAGEMENT AT AMAZON.COM

What happens after an order is submitted on Amazon's website but before it arrives at the customer's door? A lot. Amazon.com maintains huge distribution, or "fulfillment," centers where it keeps inventory of millions of products. This is one of the key differences between Amazon.com and some of its competitors—it actually stocks products. Bezos describes how they have improved: "Years ago, I drove the Amazon packages to the post office every evening in the back of my Chevy Blazer. My vision extended so far that I dreamed we might one day get a forklift. Fast-forward to today and we have 96 fulfillment centers." So Amazon must manage the flow of products from its 15 million-plus suppliers to its U.S. and international fulfillment centers with the flow of customer orders from the fulfillment centers to individuals' homes or offices.

The process begins with the suppliers. Amazon collaborates with its suppliers to increase efficiencies and improve inventory turnover. For example, Amazon uses software to forecast purchasing patterns by region, which allows it to give its suppliers better information about delivery dates and volumes. After the products arrive at the fulfillment center they are scanned and placed on shelves in what often appear to be haphazard locations. That is, books may be on the same shelf next to toys and kitchen utensils. Dave Clark, vice president of worldwide operations and customer service at Amazon, explains: "If you look at how these items fit in the bin, they are optimized to utilize the available space, we have computers and algorithms that tell people the areas of the building that have the most space to put the product that's coming in at that time." Clark observes that one of its 1-million-square-foot fulfillment centers (the size of more than 20 football fields) represents a "physical manifestation of earth's biggest selection."

At the same time, Amazon has been improving the part of the process that sorts the products into the individual orders. Once an order is placed in the computer system, sophisticated software generates a map of the location of each product and a "pick ambassador" walks the aisles to select the products. Each item is scanned as it is selected so that inventory levels and locations are always up-to-date. Packers ensure that all items are included in the box before it is taped and labeled. The boxes then travel along a conveyor belt and are diverted into groups based on the delivery location. A network of trucks and regional postal hubs then conclude the process with delivery of the order. Amazon actually uses more trucks than planes!

The success of Amazon's logistics and supply chain management activities may be most evident during the year-end holiday shopping season. Amazon received orders for 36.8 million items on Cyber Monday (the Monday following Thanksgiving), including orders for Xbox and PlayStation gaming consoles that reached more than 1,000 units per minute. During the entire holiday season Amazon shipped orders to 185 countries. Well over 99 percent of the orders were shipped and delivered on time.

CONTINUOUS IMPROVEMENT AT AMAZON

In a recent letter to Amazon shareholders Bezos reported that Amazon employees are "always asking how do we make this better?" He also described the Amazon Kaizen program (named for the Japanese term meaning "change for the better") and how it is used to streamline processes and reduce defects and waste. As a result there are many new changes and improvements under way at Amazon, many of which are related to its supply chain and logistics management approach.

One example of a new service at Amazon is Amazon Fresh, its online, same-day-delivery service for groceries. The service has been in trial stage in Seattle for several years and recently expanded to Los Angeles and San Francisco. The success of the service in these cities is likely to influence how quickly Amazon expands into other cities. Another new service at Amazon is based on its agreement with the United States Postal Service to offer Sunday delivery to select cities. The demand for this service in the trial cities will also influence how quickly it is rolled out to other cities. Finally Amazon received a lot of attention when it revealed that it is developing unmanned aerial drones that could fly small shipments to customers within 30 minutes. "We can carry objects up to 5 pounds which covers 86 percent of the items that we deliver," explains Bezos. The Federal Aviation Administration (FAA) granted Amazon permission to fly drones experimentally in early 2015. Expect to see Amazon drones delivering shipments as early as 2020 in some areas, assuming final FAA approvals on this practice.

Amazon.com has come a long way since 1995. Its logistics and supply chain management activities have provided Amazon with a cost-effective and efficient distribution system that combines automation and communication technology with superior customer service. To continue its drive to increase future sales, profits, and customer service, Amazon continues to use its inventive spirit to encourage innovation. According to Bezos, "What we are doing is challenging and fun—we get to work in the future."[19]

Questions

1 How do Amazon.com's logistics and supply chain management activities help the company create value for its customers?

2 What systems did Amazon develop to improve the flow of products from suppliers to Amazon fulfillment centers? What systems improved the flow of orders from the fulfillment centers to customers?

3 Why will logistics and supply chain management play an important role in the future success of Amazon.com?

Chapter Notes

1. *www.eddiebauer.com,* accessed August 18, 2018; "Eddie Bauer CEO Offers Inside Tour of Epic Turnaround Campaign," presentation at the University of Washington Foster School of Business, March 16, 2017; "A Lost Eddie Bauer Returns to Its Roots Outdoors," *www.forbes.com,* November 10, 2016; and "Eddie Bauer in Early Stages of Turnaround," www.*wwd.com,* February 15, 2014.

2. "How to Make Marketing Channel Marketing Work," *www.emarketer.com,* June 16, 2016.

3. "A Lost Eddie Bauer Returns to Its Roots Outdoor."

4. *General Mills 2017 Annual Report* (General Mills, Inc.: Golden Valley, MN, 2018); General Mills with Nestlé Is Trying to Make Cereal More Popular Overseas," *www.startribune,* May 15, 2015; "Cereal Marketers Race for Global Bowl Domination," *Advertising Age,* August 20, 2012, pp. 12–13; and "General Mills Reports Fiscal 2014 Third-Quarter Results," General Mills press release, March 19, 2014.

5. For an overview of vertical marketing systems, see Lou Pelton, Martha Cooper, David Strutton, and James R. Lumpkin, *Marketing Channels,* 3rd ed. (Burr Ridge, IL: McGraw-Hill/Irwin, 2005).

6. Rachel Dodes, "Saks to Add Exclusive Lines," *The Wall Street Journal,* February 25, 2010, p. B2.

7. "Dell Treads Carefully into Selling PCs in Stores," *The Wall Street Journal,* January 3, 2008, p. B1.

8. "8-second rule," www.pcmag.com/encyclopedia/term, accessed May 1, 2018.

9. "American Airlines Yanks Its Flights off Travel Sites," *www.USAtoday.com,* December 23, 2010; "Amazon, Hachette Reach a Truce," *The Wall Street Journal,* November 14, 2014, pp. B1, B2; and "Sales Took Back Seat in Sharpie Spat," *The Wall Street Journal,* March 27, 2018, p. B4.

10. For an extensive discussion on channel member conflict and influence, see Robert W. Palmatier, Louis W. Stern, and Adel I. El-Ansary, *Marketing Channel Strategy,* 8th ed. (Upper Saddle River, NJ: Prentice Hall, 2015), Chapters 10 and 11. The examples in this section come from this source and "Under Armour Does Itself Harm," *The Wall Street Journal,* August 18, 2017, p. B12.

11. These examples are from David Simchi-Levi, Philip Kaminsky, and Edith Simchi-Levi, *Designing and Managing the Supply Chain,* 4th ed. (Burr Ridge, IL: McGraw-Hill/Irwin, 2011); and "At KFC, a Bucketful of Trouble," *Bloomberg Businessweek,* March 5, 2018, pp. 20–21.

12. Patrick Burnson, "Auto Industry Supply Chain Managers Should Take Hard Look at Analytics," *Supply Chain Management,* October 2015, pp. 3–7; and John Paul MacDuffie and Takahiro Fujimoto, "Why Dinosaurs Will Keep Ruling the Automobile Industry," *Harvard Business Review,* June 2010, pp. 23–25.

13. Portions of this discussion are based on Sunil Chopra and Peter Meindl, *Supply Chain Management: Strategy, Planning, and Operations,* 6th ed. (Upper Saddle River, NJ: Prentice Hall, 2016), Chapters 1–3.

14. Theodore Stank et al., *The Supply Chain Game Changers* (Upper Saddle River, NJ: Pearson and FT Press, 2017); Dave Blanchard, "Top 25 Supply Chains of 2016," *www.industryweek.com,* June 6, 2016; "The 2014 Supply Chain Top 25: Leading the Decade," *Supply Chain Management Review,* September–October, 2014, pp. 8–17; "Walmart Will Punish Its Suppliers for Delivering Early," *www.msn.com,* July 12, 2017; and Sunil Chopra and Peter Meindl, *Supply Chain Management: Strategy, Planning, and Operations,* 6th ed. (Upper Saddle River, NJ: Prentice Hall, 2016).

15. "Retailers Aim to Turn Minutes into Millions," *The Wall Street Journal,* December 19, 2012, pp. B1, B2; and Christina Passariello, "Logistics Are in Vogue with Designers," *The Wall Street Journal,* June 27, 2008, p. B1.

16. Stank et al., *The Supply Chain Game Changers.*

17. "Dead, But Not Forgotten," *Fortune,* September 15, 2017, p. 38; "Product Return and Recycling," *www.hp.com,* May 10, 2018; and "Designed for Their Demise," *The Wall Street Journal,* June 8, 2016, p. R4.

18. Doug Bartholomew, "IT Delivers for UPS," *Industry Week,* August 2002, pp. 35–36.

19. Amazon: This case was written by Steven Hartley. Sources: Tim Worstall, "Both Amazon and WalMart Are Really Logistics Companies, Not Retailers," *www.Forbes.com,* April 11, 2014; Dan Mitchell, "Next Up for Disruption: The Grocery Business," *www.Fortune.com,* April 4, 2014; Mae Anderson, "Amazon's Bezos Outlines Grocery, Drone Plans," *Businessweek.com,* April 10, 2014; Jeff Bercovici, "The Same-Day War: Amazon, Google and Walmart Race to Bring Your Groceries," *Forbes,* May 5, 2014; Brad Stone, "Why Amazon's Going Up in the Air," *Bloomberg Businessweek,* December 9–15, 2013, pp. 12–13; "Record-Setting Holiday Season for Amazon Prime," Amazon press release, December 26, 2013; "Company Info: Overview," http://phx.corporate-ir.net/phoenix. zhtml?c=176060&p=irol-mediaKit; Jeff Bezos, "2013 Letter to Shareholders," http://phx.corporate-ir.net/phoenix. zhtml?c=97664&p=irol-reportsannual; "Amazon's Jeff Bezos Looks to the Future," *60 Minutes* episode, December 1, 2013; and Mark Veverka, "The World's Best Retailer," *Barron's,* March 30, 2009.

13

Retailing and Wholesaling

LEARNING OBJECTIVES

After reading this chapter you should be able to:

LO 13-1 Identify retailers in terms of the utilities they provide.

LO 13-2 Explain the alternative ways to classify retail outlets.

LO 13-3 Describe the many methods of nonstore retailing.

LO 13-4 Specify the retailing mix actions used to implement a retailing strategy.

LO 13-5 Explain changes in retailing with the wheel of retailing and the retail life-cycle concepts.

LO 13-6 Describe the types of firms that perform wholesaling activities and their functions.

Smart Stores Are Changing the Customer Journey!

If you have embraced the many new digital technologies that are changing our lives today, and you like shopping, prepare yourself for an awesome treat. The combination of technology and retailing is creating a new way to change and improve the customer journey—the smart store!

Smart stores use a variety of technical solutions to enhance the in-store experience. For example, retailers are beginning to use an organizational version of the Internet of Things (IoT) to connect everyone and everything in a store. In addition, smart stores are adding point-of-purchase displays that use biometric scanners to detect when a customer approaches and activate a customized video based on their personal characteristics. Similarly, virtual reality and 3D modeling tools allow customers to see visual depictions of products, such as appliances or furniture, in settings like their home. Potential benefits of the combination of these smart store technologies include better inventory, faster decision making, and higher customer satisfaction.

Smart stores are also incorporating wearable technology, such as smartwatches, into the shopping experience. Smartwatches can provide information about deals, the location of products, and which checkout lanes are faster. Target and Kohl's, for example, send messages about special offers to Apple Watch wearers who are near their stores. Once shoppers are in the store, their watches direct them toward sale items and alert them when they are near a selected product. Some grocery stores send notifications to shopping apps such as List Ease, which was developed by mobile marketing company InMarket, to guide shoppers to groceries on their list. "Think of it as a list on your wrist," explains InMarket's Dave Heinzinger. Similarly, Apple Watch users who "like" a recipe on cooking app Epicurious are directed to the ingredients needed to make the meal!

Smartphones are also part of the new smart store experience. Valpak has created an app to provide access to coupons for stores within a 25-mile radius of their location. Similarly, loyalty card apps are eliminating the need to carry, and find, the cards by storing the barcodes and providing them for display when needed. Even more dramatic is the growing use of near field communication (NFC) (top):©Jiraroj Praditcharoenkul/Alamy Stock Photo; (bottom, left):©Bebeto Matthews/AP Images; (bottom, right):©Zapp2Photo/Shutterstock

Video 13-1
Apple Watch
kerin.tv/cr8e/v13-1

products such as Apple Pay, Android Pay, and PayPal's mobile wallet, which permit consumers to pay by holding a device near a payment terminal. In the case of an Apple Watch wearer, simply moving the watch near the scanner initiates a payment from the shopper's credit card.

Finally, smart glasses, which resemble a pair of eyeglasses but with a small display screen visible to the wearer, are becoming part of the smart store experience. The glasses use image and voice recognition capabilities to allow relevant information to be displayed on the screen. While consumers can use the glasses to assist them with shopping, retail clerks, salespeople, and technicians can also use the glasses to check manuals for technical information, verify stock inventories, place orders, or even check out customers from anywhere in the store. In the near future, smart contact lenses also will be available to consumers and retailers.[1]

These are just a few examples of the many exciting changes occurring in retailing today. This chapter examines the critical role of retailing in the marketplace and the challenging decisions retailers face as they strive to create value for customers.

What types of products will consumers buy on their smartphone, from catalogs, television, or the Internet? In what type of store will consumers look for products they don't buy directly? How important is the location of the store? Will customers expect services such as alterations, delivery, installation, or repair? What price should be charged for each product? These are difficult and important questions that are an integral part of retailing. In the channel of distribution, retailing is where the customer meets the product. It is through retailing that exchange (a central aspect of marketing) occurs. **Retailing** includes all activities involved in selling, renting, and providing products and services to ultimate consumers for personal, family, or household use.

> **retailing**
> All activities involved in selling, renting, and providing products and services to ultimate consumers for personal, family, or household use.

THE VALUE OF RETAILING

Identify retailers in terms of the utilities they provide.

Retailing is an important marketing activity. Not only do producers and consumers meet through retailing actions, but retailing also creates customer value and has a significant impact on the economy. To consumers, the value of retailing is in the form of utilities provided (see Figure 13–1). Retailing's economic value is represented by the people employed in retailing as well as by the total amount of money exchanged in retail sales.

Consumer Utilities Offered by Retailing

The utilities provided by retailers create value for consumers. Time, place, form, and possession utilities are offered by most retailers in varying degrees, but one utility is often emphasized more than others. Look at Figure 13–1 to see how well you can match the retailer with the utility being emphasized in the description.

FIGURE 13–1 Which utilities are best provided by these retailers?

Aeon is one of the largest retailers outside the United States.
©Rodrigo Reyes Marin/AFLO/Newscom

Providing mini banks in supermarkets, as Wells Fargo does, puts the bank's products and services close to the consumer, providing place utility. By providing financing or leasing and taking used cars as trade-ins, CarMax makes the purchase easier and provides possession utility. Form utility—production or alteration of a product—is offered by Ralph Lauren through its online *The Polo Custom Shop* program, which offers shirts that meet each customer's specifications. Finding the right sporting equipment during the off-season is the time utility provided by Dick's Sporting Goods. Many retailers offer a combination of the four basic utilities. Some supermarkets, for example, offer convenient locations (place utility); are open 24 hours a day (time utility); customize purchases in the bakery, deli, and florist (form utility); and allow several payment and credit options (possession utility).

The Global Economic Impact of Retailing

Retailing is important to the U.S. and global economies. Five of the 40 largest businesses in the United States are retailers (Walmart, Costco, The Home Depot, Target, and Lowe's). Walmart's $500 billion in annual sales in 2017 surpassed the gross domestic product of all but 23 countries for that same year. Walmart, Home Depot, Target, and Lowe's together have more than 3.3 million employees—more than the combined populations of Jacksonville, Florida; Austin, Texas; Tulsa, Oklahoma; and San Jose, California.[2] Many types of retailers, including food stores, automobile dealers, and general merchandise outlets, are also significant contributors to the U.S. economy.[3]

Outside the United States large retailers include Aeon in Japan, Carrefour in France, Metro Group in Germany, and Tesco in Britain.[4] In emerging economies such as China and Mexico, a combination of local and global retailers is evolving. Walmart, for example, has more than 6,300 stores outside the United States, including stores in Argentina, Brazil, China, India, Japan, Mexico, and the United Kingdom. Despite the presence of these large retailers, however, most international markets are dominated by local retailers.[5]

Video 13-2
CarMax
kerin.tv/cr8e/v13-2

form of ownership
Distinguishes retail outlets based on whether independent retailers, corporate chains, or contractual systems own the outlet.

learning review

13-1. When Ralph Lauren makes shirts to a customer's exact preferences, what utility is provided?

13-2. Two measures of the impact of retailing in the global economy are _____ and _____.

CLASSIFYING RETAIL OUTLETS

 LO 13-2 Explain the alternative ways to classify retail outlets.

For manufacturers, consumers, and the economy, retailing is an important component of marketing that has several variations. Because of the large number of alternative forms of retailing, it is easier to understand the differences among retail institutions by recognizing that outlets can be classified in several ways. First, **form of ownership** distinguishes retail outlets based on whether independent retailers, corporate chains, or

Making Responsible Decisions

Sustainability

How Green Is Your Retailer? The Rankings Are Out!

In a recent Nielsen survey of consumers from 60 countries, 55 percent of the respondents said they are willing to pay more for products and services provided by companies that are committed to positive social and environmental impact. In response, many retailers are "going green" and developing comprehensive and sophisticated business practices that reflect a new focus on social and environmental responsibility. The trend has become so important that *Newsweek* evaluates eight indicators of environmental performance to provide annual "green rankings" of large companies.

The U.S. Green Retail Association offers guidance for retailers who are getting started at implementing new practices and also provides a third-party certification that recognizes a commitment to "green" values. Some practices are intuitive and simple, such as encouraging the use of reusable shopping bags, installing LED lighting, and using nontoxic cleaning products. Many retailers are even using recyclable materials for credit and gift cards, rather than plastic. Other practices, such as reducing CO_2 emissions with economical delivery vehicles, using rainwater for landscape maintenance, or finding alternative uses for landfill waste, require a larger effort. Very often, however, these environmental initiatives also have financial benefits. When The Home Depot switched light displays to compact fluorescent (CFL) and LED light bulbs, painted the roofs of stores white, and installed solar panels, it reduced its energy use by 20 percent.

Shopping malls are adopting the practices also. In Syracuse, New York, for example, Destiny USA mall

Source: Newsweek, LLC

implemented water harvesting, air quality protection, landfill reclamation, and energy conservation practices to become the largest LEED (Leadership in Energy and Environmental Design) certified retail building in the world. Similarly, Walgreens became the first retailer to construct a Net Zero Energy store by using solar panels, wind turbines, daylight harvesting, and energy efficient building materials. To expand retailers' sustainability practices even further, some states such as California are adding "zero-waste" laws which require actions such as composting restaurant waste.

Do sustainability practices such as these influence your purchase decisions? If the answer is yes, you may want to review the green rankings at http://www.newsweek.com/search/site/green. Are your favorite retailers "green"?

---

level of service
Describes the degree of service provided to the customer from three types of retailers: self-, limited-, and full-service.

merchandise line
Describes how many different types of products a store carries and in what assortment.

contractual systems own the outlet. Second, **level of service** is used to describe the degree of service provided to the customer. Three levels of service are provided by self-, limited-, and full-service retailers. Finally, the type of **merchandise line** describes how many different types of products a store carries and in what assortment. The alternative types of outlets are discussed in greater detail in this section. For many consumers today, retail outlets are also evaluated in terms of their environmentally friendly, or green, activities, in addition to their level of service and merchandise line. The Making Responsible Decisions box gives examples of the green activities of several retailers.[6]

Form of Ownership

There are three general forms of retail ownership—independent retailer, corporate chain, and contractual systems.

Independent Retailer One of the most common forms of retail ownership is the independent business owned by an individual. Independent retailers account for most of the 3.7 million retail establishments in the United States and include hardware stores, convenience stores, clothing stores, and electronics stores. In addition, there are 90,600 furniture stores, 113,500 gas stations, and 278,700 car dealerships. For the independent retailer, the advantage of this form of ownership is simple: The owner is the boss. For customers, the independent store can offer convenience, personal service, and lifestyle compatibility.[7]

©R Heyes Design/Alamy Stock Photo

Corporate Chain A second form of ownership, the corporate chain, involves multiple outlets under common ownership. Macy's, Inc., for example, operates 670 Macy's department stores in 45 states. Macy's also owns 38 Bloomingdale's, which compete with other chain stores such as Saks Fifth Avenue and Neiman Marcus. Finally, Macy's recently acquired Bluemercury, which includes 124 specialty beauty and spa services stores.

In a chain operation, centralization in decision making and purchasing is common. Chain stores have advantages in dealing with manufacturers, particularly as the size of the chain grows. A large chain can bargain with a manufacturer to obtain good service or volume discounts on orders. Target's large volume makes it a strong negotiator with manufacturers of most products. For consumers, the buying power of chains translates into lower prices compared with other types of stores. Consumers also benefit in dealing with chains because there are multiple outlets with similar merchandise and consistent management policies.

Retailing has become a high-tech business for many large chains. Walmart, for example, has developed a sophisticated inventory management and cost control system that allows rapid price changes for each product in every store. In addition, retailers are implementing pioneering new technologies such as Cloud-based Internet-of-Things (IoT) platforms combined with radio frequency identification (RFID) tags to improve the quality of information available about the shopping experience in their stores.

Contractual Systems Contractual systems involve independently owned stores that band together to act like a chain. Recall that in Chapter 12, we discussed three kinds of contractual vertical marketing systems: retailer-sponsored cooperatives, wholesaler-sponsored voluntary chains, and franchises (see Figure 12–6). One retailer-sponsored cooperative is Associated Grocers, which consists of neighborhood grocers that all agree with several other independent grocers to buy their goods directly from food manufacturers. In this way, members can take advantage of volume discounts commonly available to chains and also give the impression of being a large chain, which may be viewed more favorably by some consumers. Wholesaler-sponsored voluntary chains such as Independent Grocers Alliance (IGA) try to achieve similar benefits.

In a franchise system, an individual or firm (the franchisee) contracts with a parent company (the franchisor) to set up a business or retail outlet. The franchisor usually assists in selecting the location, setting up the store or facility, advertising, and training personnel. The franchisee usually pays a one-time franchise fee and an annual royalty, usually tied to the franchise's sales. There are two general types of franchises: *business-format franchises,* such as McDonald's, 7-Eleven, Subway, and Anytime Fitness, and *product-distribution franchises,* such as a Ford dealership or a Coca-Cola distributor. In business-format franchising, the franchisor provides step-by-step procedures for most aspects of the business and guidelines for the most likely decisions a franchisee will face. In product-distribution franchising, the franchisor provides a few general guidelines and the franchisee is much more independent.

Jimmy John's Gourmet Sandwiches is a popular business-format franchisor.
©ZUMA Press/Alamy Stock Photo

Franchise fees paid to the franchisor can range from $15,000 for a Subway franchise to $75,000 for a Hampton Inn hotel franchise. When the fees are combined with other costs such as real estate and equipment, however, the total investment can be much higher. Franchisees also pay an ongoing royalty fee that ranges from 5.5 percent for a Domino's Pizza franchise to 30 percent for an H&R

Block tax preparation franchise. By selling franchises, an organization reduces the cost of expansion but loses some control. A good franchisor, however, will maintain strong control of the outlets in terms of delivery and presentation of merchandise and try to enhance recognition of the franchise name.[8]

Level of Service

Although most customers have little reason to notice form of ownership differences among retailers, they are typically aware of differences in terms of level of service. In some department stores, such as T.J. Maxx, very few services are provided. Some grocery stores encourage customers to bring reusable bags and to bag their groceries themselves. In contrast, outlets such as Neiman Marcus provide a wide range of customer services, from gift wrapping to wardrobe consultation.

Redbox provides a service without clerks.
©Ross Dettman/AP Images

Self-Service Self-service requires that customers perform many functions during the purchase process. Warehouse clubs such as Costco, for example, are usually self-service, with all nonessential customer services eliminated. Many gas stations, supermarkets, and airlines today also have self-service lanes and terminals. Movie and game retailer Redbox has 41,500 kiosks throughout the United States—and operates without a single clerk. New forms of self-service are being developed at convenience stores, fast-food restaurants, and even coffee shops! At Zipcar you sign up, receive a Zipcard, book a car online, walk to a car, scan your card across a reader on the windshield to open the door, and drive away! In general, the trend is toward retailing experiences that make customers co-creators of the value they receive. A recent survey showed that airline terminals with automated kiosks reduce the wait time for travelers by 22 percent. Seeing these improvements, banks are trying to change ATMs from being simple cash dispensers to serving as smart self-service devices.[9]

Limited Service Limited-service outlets provide some services, such as credit and merchandise return, but not others, such as clothing alterations. General merchandise stores such as Walmart, Kmart, and Target are usually considered limited service outlets. Customers are responsible for most shopping activities, although salespeople are available in departments such as consumer electronics, jewelry, and lawn and garden.

Full Service Full-service retailers, which include most specialty stores and department stores, provide many services to their customers. Neiman Marcus, Nordstrom, and Saks Fifth Avenue, for example, all rely on better service to sell more distinctive, higher-margin goods and to retain their customers. Nordstrom offers a wide variety of services, including on-site alterations and tailoring; free exchanges and easy returns; gift cards; credit cards through Nordstrom Bank; a 7-days-a-week customer service line; a live chat line with beauty, design, and wedding specialists; online shopping with in-store pickup; catalogs; and a four-level loyalty program called Nordstrom Rewards. During the next few years the company plans to spend $4.3 billion on additional services and improvements such as an in-store return capability for online purchases, personalized offers to rewards program members, and "smart" fitting rooms. The full-service orientation has helped Nordstrom earn the title of most popular retailer for five consecutive years in an annual industry survey.[10]

Type of Merchandise Line

Retail outlets also vary by their merchandise lines, the key distinction being the breadth and depth of the items offered to customers (see Figure 13–2). *Depth of product line* means the store carries a large assortment of each item, such as a shoe store that offers running shoes, dress shoes, and children's shoes. *Breadth of product line* refers to the variety of different items a store carries, such as appliances and books.

FIGURE 13–2
Stores vary in terms of the breadth and depth of their merchandise lines.

Depth of Product Line Stores that carry a considerable assortment (depth) of a related line of items are limited-line stores. Dick's Sporting Goods stores carry considerable depth in sports equipment ranging from weight-lifting accessories to running shoes. Stores that carry tremendous depth in one primary line of merchandise are single-line stores. Victoria's Secret, a nationwide chain, carries great depth in women's lingerie. Both limited- and single-line stores are often referred to as *specialty outlets*.

Specialty discount outlets focus on one type of product, such as electronics (Best Buy), office supplies (Staples), or books (Barnes & Noble), at very competitive prices. These outlets are referred to in the trade as *category killers* because they often dominate the market. Best Buy, for example, is the largest consumer electronics retailer, with more than 1,000 stores; Staples operates more than 1,200 office supply stores; and Barnes & Noble is the largest book retailer. Interesting trends in this form of retailing include the use of price matching to compete with online retailers, improved websites and mobile apps, and shipping directly from any store with inventory rather than just warehouses.[11]

Staples is the category killer in office supplies because it dominates the market in that category.
©McGraw-Hill Education

scrambled merchandising
Offering several unrelated product lines in a single store.

Breadth of Product Line Stores that carry a broad product line, with limited depth, are referred to as *general merchandise stores*. For example, large department stores such as Dillard's, Macy's, and Neiman Marcus carry a wide range of different types of products but not unusual sizes. The breadth and depth of merchandise lines are important decisions for a retailer. Traditionally, outlets carried related lines of goods. Today, however, **scrambled merchandising**, offering several unrelated product lines in a single store, is common. For example, the modern drugstore carries food, cosmetics, magazines, paper products, toys, small hardware items, and pharmaceuticals. Supermarkets sell flowers, DVDs, and pharmaceuticals, in addition to selling groceries.

learning review

13-3. Centralized decision making and purchasing are an advantage of _____ ownership.

13-4. What are some examples of new forms of self-service retailers?

13-5. A shop for big men's clothes carries pants in sizes 40 to 60. Would this be considered a broad or a deep product line?

NONSTORE RETAILING

LO 13-3 Describe the many methods of nonstore retailing.

Most of the retailing examples discussed thus far in the chapter, such as corporate chains, department stores, and limited- and single-line specialty stores, involve store retailing. Many retailing activities today, however, are not limited to sales in a store. Nonstore retailing occurs outside a retail outlet through activities that involve varying

Vending machines offer a variety of products. Which types of products are most common in a vending machine? For the answer, see the text.
©David Brewster/MCT/Newscom

levels of customer and retailer involvement. The six forms of nonstore retailing are automatic vending, direct mail and catalogs, television home shopping, online retailing, telemarketing, and direct selling.

Automatic Vending

Nonstore retailing includes vending machines, or *v-commerce,* which make it possible to serve customers when and where stores cannot. Machine maintenance, operating costs, and location leases can add to the cost of the products, so prices in vending machines are often higher than those in stores. About 40 percent of the products sold from vending machines are cold beverages, another 38 percent are candy and snacks, and 7 percent are food. Many new types of products are quickly becoming available in vending machines. Best Buy now uses vending machines to sell mobile phone and computer accessories, digital cameras, flash drives, and other consumer electronics products in airports, hospitals, and businesses. Similarly, HealthyYOU Vending manufactures machines designed to distribute healthy drinks, snacks, and entrées in offices, health clubs, hospitals, schools, and colleges. The 4.5 million vending machines currently in use in the United States generate more than $20.9 billion in annual sales.[12]

Direct Mail and Catalogs

Video 13-3
IKEA
kerin.tv/cr8e/v13-3

Direct-mail and catalog retailing has been called "the store that comes to the door." It is attractive for several reasons. First, it can eliminate the cost of a store and clerks. Dell, for example, is one of the largest computer and information technology retailers, and it does not have any stores. Second, direct mail and catalogs improve marketing efficiency through segmentation and targeting, and they create customer value by providing a fast and convenient means of making a purchase. Finally, many catalogs now serve as an element of a multichannel strategy designed to encourage consumers to visit a website, a social media page, or even a store. Online retailers such as Zappos, Amazon, and eBay, for example, now offer catalogs. The average U.S. household today receives 19 direct-mail items or catalogs each week. The Data and Marketing Association estimates that 100 million adults make a catalog purchase each year. Direct-mail and catalog retailing is popular outside the United States, also. Furniture retailer IKEA delivered 213 million copies of its catalog in 17 languages for 28 countries last year.[13]

Specialty catalogs appeal to market niches. They create value by providing a fast and convenient way to shop.
(left): Source: Inter IKEA Systems B.V.; (center): Source: Crate and Barrel; (right): Source: L.L.Bean Inc.

Several factors have had an impact on direct-mail and catalog retailing in recent years. The influence of large retailers such as IKEA, Crate & Barrel, L.L.Bean, and others has been positive as their marketing activities have increased the number and variety of products consumers purchase through direct mail and catalogs. Higher paper costs and increases in postage rates, the growing interest in do-not-mail legislation, the concern for "green" mailings and catalogs, and the possibility of the U.S. Postal Service reducing delivery to five days, however, have caused direct-mail and catalog retailers to search for ways to provide additional customer value. One approach has been to focus on proven customers rather than prospective customers. Another successful approach used by many catalog retailers is to send specialty catalogs to market niches identified in their databases. L.L.Bean, for example, has developed an individual catalog for fly-fishing enthusiasts.[14]

Television Home Shopping

Television home shopping is a form of nonstore retailing that takes place when consumers watch a shopping channel on which products are displayed; orders are then placed over the telephone or via the Internet. Currently, the three largest programs are QVC, HSN, and Evine. QVC ("quality, value, convenience") broadcasts live 24 hours each day, 364 days a year, and reaches 360 million homes in the United States, the United Kingdom, Germany, Japan, Italy, and China. The company generates sales of $8.7 billion from its 60 million customers by offering more than 770 products each week. The television home shopping channels offer apparel, jewelry, cooking and home improvement products, electronics, toys, and even food. The channels are facing new competition as YouTube begins to stream live shows, such as *Today's Shopping Choice*, a 24-hour, 7-days-a-week broadcast.[15]

Television home shopping programs serve millions of customers each year. See the text to learn how they are attracting new customers.
Source: QVC, Inc.

In the past, television home shopping programs attracted mostly 35- to 64-year-old women. To attract a younger audience, QVC has invited celebrities onto the show. For example, Heidi Klum has been on the show promoting her jewelry collection, and Kim, Khloe, and Kourtney Kardashian have been hosts selling their apparel line. Broadcasting events, such as the Red Carpet Style show at the Four Seasons Hotel in Beverly Hills, also help attract new customers. In addition, QVC supports its television program with retail stores, a website, mobile apps, text alerts, and the recently purchased flash sale shopping portal Zulily. Similarly, Home Shopping Network (HSN) now offers a multiplatform shopping experience. Some experts suggest that television shopping programs are becoming a modern version of door-to-door retailing by combining elements of reality TV programs, talk shows, and infomercials.[16]

Online Retailing

Online retailing allows consumers to seek, evaluate, and order products through the Internet. For many consumers, the advantages of this form of retailing are the 24-hour access, the ability to comparison shop, in-home privacy, and variety.

Today, traditional and online retailers—"bricks and clicks"—are melding to improve consumer value and shopping experiences for customers. For example, Walmart (www.walmart.com) offers its Store Pickup service that allows customers to place an order online and pick it up at a Walmart store. In addition, Walmart now offers free two-day shipping to consumers' homes on more than two million items when the order includes $35 or more on selected items. Online retail sales are projected to account for 17.5 percent of global retail sales and 14 percent of U.S. retail sales in 2021.[17]

Online retailing manifests itself in a variety of ways. Consumers can become members of an online discount service like www.netmarket.com. This service offers

Shopping "bots" like mysimon.com find the best prices for products specified by consumers. Read the text to learn more!

Source: CBS Interactive Inc.

thousands of products and hundreds of brand names at very low prices to its subscribers. Another way to engage in online retailing is to use a shopping "bot" such as www.mysimon.com. This site searches the Internet for a product specified by the consumer and provides a report listing retailers with the best prices. Consumers can also use the Internet to patronize online malls (www.shopzilla.com) and retailers (such as www.gap.com and www.barnesandnoble.com), buy directly from manufacturers (www.dell.com), and visit travel agencies (www.travelocity.com). Another way is to participate in online auctions such as www.ebay.com, where 169 million buyers from 190 markets bid on more than 1 billion listings.[18]

One of the biggest problems online retailers face is that more than 75 percent of online shoppers abandon their shopping cart without completing a purchase. A common reason shoppers leave a site is because they are comparison shopping. One way online retailers are addressing this issue is to offer consumers a comparison of competitors' offerings. At Allbookstores.com, for example, consumers can use a "comparison engine" to compare prices with Amazon.com, Barnesandnoble.com, and as many as 25 other bookstores. Experts suggest that online retailers should think of their websites as dynamic billboards if they are to attract and retain customers; they should be easy to use, customizable, and facilitate interaction to enhance the online customer experience.[19] For example, BMW, Mercedes, and Jaguar encourage website visitors to "build" a vehicle by selecting interior and exterior colors, packages, and options; view the customized virtual car; and then use Facebook, Twitter, or e-mail to share the configuration with friends.

Online retailing has evolved to include social shopping options, including *intermediaries,* such as Groupon and LivingSocial, which match consumers with merchants; *marketplaces,* such as Storenvy, which provide a self-service advertising site; and *aggregators,* such as Yipit, which crawl the Web to find deals to list on their own sites. Many consumers also use online resources as price comparison sites, which influence their offline shopping at local stores.[20]

Chapter 14 describes online retailing in greater depth. Topics include website design, consumer behavior in an online environment, and the prevalence of the traditional and online "bricks and clicks" approach to multichannel marketing.

Telemarketing

telemarketing
Using the telephone to interact with and sell directly to consumers.

Another form of nonstore retailing, called **telemarketing**, involves using the telephone to interact with and sell directly to consumers. Compared with direct mail, telemarketing is often viewed as a more efficient means of targeting consumers. Insurance companies, brokerage firms, and newspapers have often used this form of retailing as a way to cut costs but still maintain access to their customers. According to the Data and Marketing Association, more than 40 percent of businesses use telemarketing as a means of reaching consumers.[21]

The telemarketing industry has gone through dramatic changes as a result of legislation related to telephone solicitations. Issues such as consumer privacy, industry standards, and ethical guidelines have encouraged discussion among consumers, Congress, the Federal Trade Commission (FTC), and businesses. As a result, legislation created the National Do Not Call Registry (www.donotcall.gov) for consumers who do not want to receive telephone calls related to company sales efforts. Currently, there are more than 221 million phone numbers on the registry. Companies that use telemarketing have adapted by adding compliance software to ensure that numbers on the list are not called. Currently the FTC and industry leaders are discussing measures to curb robocalls, or the use of autodialers to deliver a prerecorded message.[22]

Direct Selling

©McGraw-Hill Education/Mark Dierker, photographer

Direct selling, sometimes called door-to-door retailing, involves direct sales of products and services to consumers through personal interactions and demonstrations in their home or office. A variety of companies, including familiar names such as Avon, Fuller Brush, Mary Kay Cosmetics, and World Book, have created an industry with more than $36 billion in U.S. sales and $184 billion worldwide by providing consumers with personalized service and convenience. In the United States, there are more than 20 million direct salespeople working full time and part time in a variety of product categories, including wellness, home durables, and personal care.[23]

Growth in the direct-selling industry is the result of two trends. First, many direct-selling retailers are expanding into markets outside the United States. Avon, for example, has 6 million sales representatives in 80 countries. More than one-third of Amway's $8.8 billion in sales now comes from China and 90 percent comes from outside the United States. Similarly, other retailers such as Herbalife and Electrolux are rapidly expanding into new markets.[24] Direct selling is likely to continue to grow in markets where the lack of effective distribution channels increases the importance of door-to-door convenience and the lack of consumer knowledge about products and brands increases the need for a person-to-person approach.

The second trend in the direct-selling industry is the growing number of companies that are using direct selling to reach consumers who prefer one-on-one customer service and a social shopping experience rather than online shopping or shopping in big discount stores. The Direct Selling Association reports that the number of companies using direct selling is increasing. Pampered Chef, for example, has 60,000 independent sales reps who sell the company's products at in-home "Cooking Shows." Interest among potential sales representatives is growing because direct selling offers more independence and control of their work activities. Millennials, in particular, have observed that they can create a lifestyle that doesn't require a traditional nine-to-five routine.[25]

> **retailing mix**
> The activities related to managing the store and the merchandise in the store, which include retail pricing, store location, retail communication, and merchandise.

learning review

13-6. Successful catalog retailers often send _____ catalogs to _____ markets identified in their databases.

13-7. How are retailers increasing consumer interest and involvement in online retailing?

13-8. Where are direct-selling retail sales growing? Why?

RETAILING STRATEGY

> **LO 13-4** Specify the retailing mix actions used to implement a retailing strategy.

This section describes how a retailer develops and implements a retailing strategy. In developing a retailing strategy, managers work with the **retailing mix**, which includes activities related to managing the store and the merchandise in the store. The retailing mix is similar to the marketing mix and includes retail pricing, store location, retail communication, and merchandise (see Figure 13–3).

Retail Pricing In setting prices for merchandise, retailers must decide on the markup, markdown, and timing for markdowns. The *markup* refers to how much should be added to the cost the retailer paid for a product to reach the final selling price. Retailers decide on the *original markup,* but by the time the product is sold, they end up with a *maintained markup*. The original markup is the difference between retailer cost and initial selling price. When products do not sell as quickly as anticipated,

FIGURE 13–3
Retailing strategy is related to store positioning and the retailing mix. Note the similarity between the retailing mix and the marketing mix.

©Ian Dagnall/Alamy Stock Photo

At off-price retail stores like T.J. Maxx, prices are low but selection may be unpredictable.
©Tim Boyle/Bloomberg via Getty Images

their price is reduced. The difference between the final selling price and retailer cost is the maintained markup, which is also called the *gross margin*.

Discounting a product, or taking a *markdown,* occurs when the product does not sell at the original price and an adjustment is necessary. Often new models or styles force the price of existing models to be marked down. Discounts may also be used to increase store traffic or demand for complementary products.[26] For example, retailers might take a markdown on the price of cake mix to generate frosting purchases.

The *timing* of a markdown can be important. Many retailers take a markdown as soon as sales fall off to free up valuable selling space and cash. However, other stores delay markdowns to discourage bargain hunters and maintain an image of quality. There is no clear answer, but retailers must consider how the timing might affect future sales. Research indicates that frequent promotions increase consumers' ability to remember regular prices.[27]

Although most retailers plan markdowns, many retailers use price discounts as part of their regular merchandising policy. Walmart and The Home Depot, for example, emphasize consistently low prices and eliminate most markdowns with a strategy often called *everyday low pricing* (EDLP). Walmart is also developing a strategy it calls EDLP 2.0, which enables consumers to reduce their price through product bundling and payment and shipping options.[28] Because consumers often use price as an indicator of product quality, however, the brand name of the product and the image of the store become important decision factors in these situations.[29] Another strategy, *everyday fair pricing,* is advocated by retailers that may not offer the lowest price but try to create value for customers through service and the total buying experience. Research indicates that price-matching and price-beating guarantees allow retailers such as online auctions to support higher prices.[30] Consumers often use the prices of *benchmark* or *signpost* items, such as a can of Coke, to form an overall impression of a store's prices.[31] In addition, price is the most likely factor to influence consumers' assessment of merchandise value.[32] When store prices are based on rebates, retailers must be careful to avoid negative consumer perceptions if the rebate processing time is long (e.g., six weeks).[33]

Off-price retailing is a retail pricing practice that is used by retailers such as T.J. Maxx, Burlington, and Ross Stores. *Off-price retailing* involves selling brand-name merchandise at lower than regular prices. The difference between the off-price retailer and a discount store is that off-price merchandise is bought by the retailer from manufacturers with excess inventory at prices below wholesale prices. The discounter, however, buys at full wholesale prices but takes less of a markup than

Off 5th provides an outlet for excess merchandise from Saks Fifth Avenue.
©Paul Sakuma/AP Images

traditional department stores. Because of this difference in the way merchandise is purchased by the retailer, selection at an off-price retailer is unpredictable, and searching for bargains has become a popular activity for many consumers. "It's more like a sport than it is like ordinary shopping," says Christopher Boring of Columbus, Ohio, owner of Retail Planning Associates.[34] Savings to the consumer at off-price retailers are reportedly as high as 70 percent off the prices of a traditional department store. Variations of off-price retailing include outlet stores, such as Gap Factory Store and Off 5th (an outlet for Saks Fifth Avenue), and warehouse clubs, such as Sam's Club and Costco. A growing form of competition for warehouse clubs are online membership clubs such as Amazon Prime.[35]

Store Location A second aspect of the retailing mix involves choosing a location and deciding how many stores to operate. Department stores, which started downtown in most cities, have followed customers to the suburbs, and in recent years more stores have been opened in large regional malls. Most stores today are near several others in one of four settings: the central business district, the regional center, the community shopping center, the strip mall, or the power center.

The *central business district,* the oldest retail setting, is usually located in the community's downtown area. Until the regional outflow to the suburbs, it was the major shopping area, but the suburban population has grown at the expense of the downtown shopping area. Consumers often view central business district shopping as less convenient because of lack of parking, higher crime rates, and exposure to the weather. Many cities such as Louisville, Denver, and San Antonio have implemented plans to revitalize shopping in their central business districts by attracting new offices, entertainment, and residents to downtown locations.

©David Paul Morris/Bloomberg via Getty Images

Regional shopping centers consist of 50 to 150 stores that typically attract customers who live or work within a 5- to 10-mile range. These large shopping areas often contain two or three *anchor stores,* which are well-known national or regional stores such as Nordstrom, Saks Fifth Avenue, and Bloomingdale's. The largest variation of a regional center in North America is the West Edmonton Mall in Alberta, Canada. This shopping center is a conglomerate of more than 800 stores, the world's largest indoor amusement park, more than 100 restaurants, a movie complex, and two hotels, all of which attract 30 million visitors each year.[36]

Not every suburban store is located in a shopping mall. Many neighborhoods have clusters of stores, referred to as a *strip mall,* to serve people who are within a 5- to 10-minute drive. Gas station, hardware, laundry, grocery, and pharmacy outlets are commonly found in a strip mall. Unlike the larger shopping centers, the composition of these stores is usually unplanned. A variation of the strip mall is called the *power center,* which is a huge shopping strip with multiple anchor (or national) stores such as T.J. Maxx, Ulta, Ross Dress for Less, or Pier 1 Imports. Power centers combine the convenience of location provided by strip malls with the power of national stores. These large strip malls often have two to five anchor stores and contain a supermarket, which brings the shopper to the power center on a weekly basis.[37]

The many retailing formats described previously in this chapter represent an exciting menu of choices for creating customer value in the marketplace. Each format allows retailers to offer unique benefits and meet the particular needs of various customer groups. While each format has many successful applications, retailers in the future are likely to combine many of the formats to offer a broader spectrum of benefits and

Amazon is opening physical stores where consumers can shop and pick up orders.
©Timothy A. Clary/AFP/Getty Images

multichannel retailers
Retailers that utilize and integrate a combination of traditional store formats and nonstore formats such as catalogs, television home shopping, and online retailing.

shopper marketing
The use of displays, coupons, product samples, and other brand communications to influence shopping behavior in a store.

shopping experience
A consumer's perception of an encounter with a store's physical environment, personnel, and policies and procedures.

category management
An approach to managing the assortment of merchandise in which a manager is assigned the responsibility for selecting all products that consumers in a market segment might view as substitutes for each other, with the objective of maximizing sales and profits in the category.

experiences and to appeal to different segments of consumers.[38] These **multichannel retailers** will utilize and integrate a combination of traditional store formats and nonstore formats such as catalogs, television home shopping, and online retailing. Barnes & Noble, for example, created Barnesandnoble.com to compete with Amazon.com.

Similarly, Office Depot has integrated its store, catalog, and Internet operations, and Amazon has opened physical stores in six states, with more coming soon. Recent research suggests that retailers can increase profitability by encouraging their online shoppers to visit their stores.[39]

Retail Communication A retailer's communication activities can play an important role in positioning a store and creating its image. The typical elements of communication and promotion are discussed in Chapter 16 (advertising, sales promotion, and public relations), Chapter 17 (social media), and Chapter 18 (personal selling); however, the message communicated by the many other elements of the retailing mix is also important.

Deciding on the image of a retail outlet is an important retailing mix factor that has been widely recognized and studied since the late 1950s. Pierre Martineau described *image* as "the way in which the store is defined in the shopper's mind," partly by its functional qualities and partly by an aura of psychological attributes.[40] In this definition, *functional* refers to mix elements such as price ranges, store layouts, and breadth and depth of merchandise lines. The *psychological attributes* are the intangibles such as a sense of belonging, excitement, style, or warmth. Image has been found to include impressions of the corporation that operates the store, the category or type of store, the product categories in the store, the brands in each category, merchandise and service quality, and the marketing activities of the store.[41]

Closely related to the concept of image is the store's atmosphere, or ambience. Many retailers believe that sales are affected by layout, color, lighting, music, scent,[42] and other elements of the retail environment. This concept leads many retailers to use **shopper marketing**—the use of displays, coupons, product samples, and other brand communications to influence shopping behavior in a store. Shopper marketing can also influence behavior in an online shopping environment and when shoppers use smartphone apps to identify shopping needs or make purchase decisions.[43] In creating the right image and atmosphere, a retail store tries to attract a target audience and fortify beliefs about the store, its products, and the shopping experience in the store. **Shopping experience** is a consumer's perception of an encounter with a store's physical environment, personnel, and policies and procedures. Research shows that the caliber and kind of shopping experience delivered by retailers is a major source of retailer differentiation.[44] While store image perceptions can exist independently of shopping experiences, consumers' shopping experiences influence their perceptions of a store.[45] In addition, the physical surroundings of the retail environment influence a store's employees.[46]

Merchandise Management The final element of the retailing mix is the merchandise offering. Managing the breadth and depth of the product line requires retail buyers who are familiar with both the needs of the target market and the alternative products available from the many manufacturers that might be interested in having a product available in the store. A popular approach to managing the assortment of merchandise today is called **category management**. This approach assigns a manager the responsibility for selecting all products that consumers in a market segment might view as substitutes for each other, with the objective of maximizing sales and profits in the category. For example, a category manager might be responsible for shoes in a department store or paper products in a grocery store. As such, he or she would consider trade deals, order costs, and the between-brand effects of price range changes to determine brand assortment, order quantities, and prices. In addition, category managers must consider the impact of the location and assortment of other product categories if they share limited space (e.g., the checkout aisle) in a store.[47]

Applying Marketing Metrics
Why Apple Stores May Be the Best in the United States!

How effective is my retail format compared to other stores? How are my stores performing this year compared to last year? Information related to these questions is often displayed in a marketing dashboard using two measures: (1) sales per square foot and (2) same-store sales growth.

Your Challenge

You have been assigned to evaluate the Apple Store retail format. The store's simple, inviting, and open atmosphere has been the topic of discussion among many retailers. To allow an assessment of Apple Stores, use *sales per square foot* as an indicator of how effectively retail space is used to generate revenue and *same-store sales growth* to compare the increase in sales of stores that have been open for the same period of time. The calculations for these two indicators are:

$$\text{Sales per square foot} = \frac{\text{Total sales}}{\text{Selling area in square feet}}$$

$$\text{Same-store sales growth} = \frac{\text{Store sales in year 2} - \text{Store sales in year 1}}{\text{Store sales in year 1}}$$

Your Findings

You decide to collect sales information for Target, Neiman Marcus, Best Buy, Tiffany, and Apple Stores to allow comparisons with other successful retailers. The information you collect allows the calculation of *sales per square foot* and *same-store sales growth* for each store. The results are then easy to compare in the graphs below.

Your Action

The results of your investigation indicate that Apple Stores' sales per square foot ($4,798) are higher than any of the comparison stores. In addition, Apple's same-store sales growth rate (22 percent) is higher than all of the other retailers. You conclude that the elements of Apple's format are very effective and even indicate that Apple may currently be the best retailer in the United States.

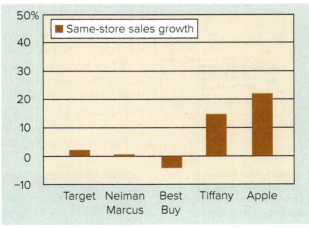

Retailers have a variety of marketing metrics that can be used to assess the effectiveness of a store or retail format. First, there are measures related to customers, such as the number of transactions per customer, the average transaction size per customer, the number of customers per day or per hour, and the average length of a store visit. Second, there are measures related to the stores and the products, such as level of inventory, number of returns, inventory turnover, inventory carrying cost, and average number of items per transaction. Finally, there are financial measures, such as gross margin, sales per employee, return on sales, and markdown percentage.[48] The two most popular measures for retailers are *sales per square foot* and *same-store sales growth*. The Applying Marketing Metrics box describes the calculation of these measures for Apple Stores.[49]

learning review

13-9. How does original markup differ from maintained markup?

13-10. A huge shopping strip mall with multiple anchor stores is a(n) _____ center.

13-11. What is a popular approach to managing the assortment of merchandise in a store?

THE CHANGING NATURE OF RETAILING

Explain changes in retailing with the wheel of retailing and the retail life-cycle concepts.

Retailing is the most dynamic aspect of a channel of distribution. New types of retailers are always entering the market, searching for a new position that will attract customers. The reason for this continual change is explained by two concepts: the wheel of retailing and the retail life cycle. In addition, changes in retailing are being facilitated by big data and new advanced forms of analytics.

The Wheel of Retailing

wheel of retailing
A concept that describes how new forms of retail outlets enter the market.

The **wheel of retailing** describes how new forms of retail outlets enter the market.[50] Usually they enter as low-status, low-margin stores such as a drive-in hamburger stand with no indoor seating and a limited menu (Figure 13–4, box 1). Gradually these outlets add fixtures and more embellishments to their stores (in-store seating, plants, and chicken sandwiches as well as hamburgers) to increase the attractiveness for customers. With these additions, prices and status rise (box 2). As time passes, these outlets add still more services and their prices and status increase even further (box 3). These retail outlets now face some new form of retail outlet that again appears as a low-status, low-margin operator (box 4), and the wheel of retailing turns as the cycle starts to repeat itself.

When Ray Kroc bought McDonald's in 1955, it opened shortly before lunch and closed just after dinner, and it offered a limited menu for the two meals without any inside seating for customers. Over time, the wheel of retailing has led to new products and services. In 1975, McDonald's introduced the Egg McMuffin and turned breakfast into a fast-food meal. Today, McDonald's offers an extensive menu, including oatmeal and premium coffee, and it provides seating and services such as wireless Internet

Video 13-4
McDonald's
kerin.tv/cr8e/v13-4

FIGURE 13–4

The wheel of retailing describes how retail outlets change over time. Read the text to find out the position of McDonald's and Checkers on the wheel of retailing.

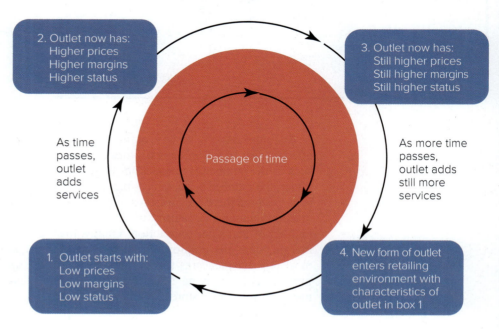

connections and kid-friendly PlayPlaces. For the future, McDonald's is testing new food products, including snow crab on a sourdough bun, garlic fries, and fresh-beef Quarter Pounders, and new services, such as self-serve kiosks, mobile ordering, and table service.[51]

These changes are leaving room for new forms of outlets such as Checkers Drive-In Restaurants. The Checkers chain opened fast-food stores that offered only basics—burgers, fries, and cola, a drive-thru window, and no inside seating—and now has more than 800 stores. The wheel is turning for other outlets, too—Boston Market has added pickup, delivery, and full-service catering to its original restaurant format, and it also provides Boston Market meal solutions through supermarket delis and Boston Market frozen meals in the frozen food sections of groceries. For still others, the wheel has come full circle. Taco Bell is now opening small, limited-offering outlets in gas stations, discount stores, or "wherever a burrito and a mouth might possibly intersect."[52]

The wheel of retailing is also evident in retail outlets outside the restaurant industry. Discount stores were a major new retailing form in the 1960s and priced their products below those of department stores. As prices in discount stores rose in the 1980s, they found themselves overpriced compared with a new form of retail outlet—the warehouse club. Today, off-price retailers and factory outlets are offering prices even lower than warehouse clubs.

Outlets such as Checkers enter the wheel of retailing as low-status, low-margin stores.
©McGraw-Hill Education/Mark Dierker, photographer

The Retail Life Cycle

Similar to the product life cycle for products, retail outlets experience a process of growth and decline that is described by the **retail life cycle**.[53] Figure 13–5 shows the stages of the retail life cycle and where various forms of retail outlets are currently positioned along its spectrum. *Early growth* is the stage of emergence of a retail outlet, with a sharp departure from existing competition. Market share rises gradually, although profits may be low because of start-up costs. In the next stage, *accelerated development,* both market share and profit achieve their greatest growth rates. Usually multiple outlets are established as companies focus on the distribution element of the retailing mix. In this stage, some later

retail life cycle
The process of growth and decline that retail outlets, like products, experience, consisting of the early growth, accelerated development, maturity, and decline stages.

FIGURE 13–5
The retail life cycle describes stages of growth and decline for retail outlets.

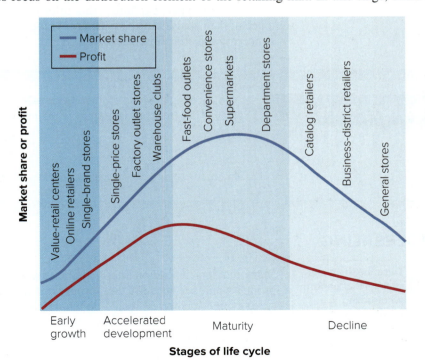

competitors may enter. Wendy's, for example, appeared on the hamburger chain scene almost 20 years after McDonald's had begun operation. The key goal for the retailer in this stage is to establish a dominant position in the fight for market share.

The battle for market share is usually fought before the *maturity stage,* and some competitors drop out of the market. In the war among hamburger chains, Jack in the Box, Gino's Hamburgers, and Burger Chef used to be more dominant outlets. In the maturity stage, new retail forms enter the market (such as Fatburger and In-N-Out Burger in the hamburger chain industry), stores try to maintain their market share, and price discounting occurs.

The challenge facing retailers is to delay entering the *decline stage,* in which market share and profit fall rapidly. Specialty apparel retailers such as Gap, Benetton, and Ann Taylor have noticed a decline in market share after years of growth, department stores such as Macy's and Sears have closed hundreds of locations, and retailers such as Toys"R"Us, The Limited, Gander Mountain, RadioShack, and many others have closed or filed for bankruptcy. To prevent further decline, retailers will need to find ways of improving the in-store experience and discouraging their customers from moving to e-commerce options.[54]

Data Analytics

Data analytics has been described as the "new science of retailing." Data now available from the use of wearable technology (described earlier in this chapter) and the growth of multichannel marketing complement the substantial amounts of data already collected through scanner and loyalty card systems. The combination of these data sources has the potential to enable a new, comprehensive, and integrated analytical tool for retailers. In fact, a survey of 418 managers in eight industries indicated that firms in the retail industry have the most to gain from deploying customer analytics.

The use of data analytics can benefit retailers in at least three ways. First, understanding how consumers use multiple channels, information sources, and payment options can help retailers predict shopping behavior. Second, detailed customer-specific data allow merchants to provide personalized, real-time messaging and promotions. Finally, tracking customer needs allows retailers to offer innovative products, maintain optimal inventory levels, and manage prices to remain competitive and profitable. As one retailing expert explains, "this information is invaluable." The growing importance of data analytics is also increasing the attention to statistical techniques, privacy concerns, and ethical issues.[55]

learning review

13-12. Using the wheel of retailing, describe the characteristics of a new retail form that has just entered the market.

13-13. Market share is usually fought out before the _____ stage of the retail life cycle.

13-14. What is the "new science of retailing"?

WHOLESALING

LO 13-6 Describe the types of firms that perform wholesaling activities and their functions.

Many retailers depend on intermediaries that engage in wholesaling activities—selling products and services for the purposes of resale or business use. There are several types of intermediaries, including wholesalers and agents (described briefly in Chapter 12), as well as manufacturers' sales offices, that are important to understand as part of the retailing process.

Merchant Wholesalers

merchant wholesalers
Independently owned firms that take title to the merchandise they handle.

Merchant wholesalers are independently owned firms that take title to the merchandise they handle. They go by various names, including *industrial distributor*. Most firms engaged in wholesaling activities are merchant wholesalers.

Merchant wholesalers are classified as either full-service or limited-service wholesalers, depending on the number of functions performed. Two major types of full-service wholesalers exist. *General merchandise* (or *full-line*) *wholesalers* carry a broad assortment of merchandise and perform all channel functions. This type of wholesaler is most prevalent in the hardware, drug, and clothing industries. However, these wholesalers do not maintain much depth of assortment within specific product lines. *Specialty merchandise* (or *limited-line*) *wholesalers* offer a relatively narrow range of products but have an extensive assortment within the product lines carried. They perform all channel functions and are found in the health foods, automotive parts, and seafood industries.

Four major types of limited-service wholesalers exist. *Rack jobbers* furnish the racks or shelves that display merchandise in retail stores, perform all channel functions, and sell on consignment to retailers, which means they retain the title to the products displayed and bill retailers only for the merchandise sold. Familiar products such as hosiery, toys, housewares, and health and beauty items are sold by rack jobbers. *Cash and carry wholesalers* take title to merchandise but sell only to buyers who call on them, pay cash for merchandise, and furnish their own transportation for merchandise. They carry a limited product assortment and do not make deliveries, extend credit, or supply market information. This type of wholesaler is common in electric supplies, office supplies, hardware products, and groceries.

Drop shippers, or *desk jobbers,* are wholesalers that own the merchandise they sell but do not physically handle, stock, or deliver it. They simply solicit orders from retailers and other wholesalers and have the merchandise shipped directly from a producer to a buyer. Drop shippers are used for bulky products such as coal, lumber, and chemicals, which are sold in extremely large quantities. *Truck jobbers* are small wholesalers that have a small warehouse from which they stock their trucks for distribution to retailers. They usually handle limited assortments of fast-moving or perishable items that are sold for cash directly from trucks in their original packages. Truck jobbers handle products such as bakery items, dairy products, and meat.

Agents and Brokers

Courtesy of Manufacturers' Agents National Association

manufacturers' agents
Agents who work for several producers and carry noncompetitive, complementary merchandise in an exclusive territory. Also called *manufacturers' representatives*.

Unlike merchant wholesalers, agents and brokers do not take title to merchandise and typically perform fewer channel functions. They make their profit from commissions or fees paid for their services, whereas merchant wholesalers make their profit from the sale of the merchandise they own.

Manufacturers' agents and selling agents are the two major types of agents used by producers. **Manufacturers' agents**, or *manufacturers' representatives,* work for several producers and carry noncompetitive, complementary merchandise in an exclusive territory. Manufacturers' agents act as a producer's sales arm in a territory and are principally responsible for the transactional channel functions, primarily selling. They are used extensively in the automotive supply, footwear, and fabricated steel industries. The Manufacturers' Agents National Association (MANA) facilitates the process of matching manufacturers' representatives with logical products and companies.

By comparison, *selling agents* represent a single producer and are responsible for the entire marketing function of that producer. They design promotional plans, set prices, determine distribution policies, and make recommendations on product strategy. Selling agents are used by small producers in the textile, apparel, food, and home furnishings industries.

brokers
Independent firms or individuals whose principal function is to bring buyers and sellers together to make sales.

Brokers are independent firms or individuals whose principal function is to bring buyers and sellers together to make sales. Brokers, unlike agents, usually have no continuous relationship with the buyer or seller but negotiate a contract between two parties and then move on to another task. Brokers are used extensively by producers of seasonal products (such as fruits and vegetables) and in the real estate industry.

A unique broker that acts in many ways like a manufacturer's agent is a food broker, representing buyers and sellers in the grocery industry. Food brokers differ from conventional brokers because they act on behalf of producers on a permanent basis and receive a commission for their services. For example, Nabisco uses food brokers to sell its candies, margarine, and Planters peanuts, but it sells its line of cookies and crackers directly to retail stores.

Manufacturers' Branches and Offices

Unlike merchant wholesalers, agents, and brokers, manufacturers' branches and sales offices are wholly owned extensions of the producer that perform wholesaling activities. Producers assume wholesaling functions when there are no intermediaries to perform these activities, customers are few in number and geographically concentrated, or orders are large or require significant attention. A *manufacturer's branch office* carries a producer's inventory and performs the functions of a full-service wholesaler. A *manufacturer's sales office* does not carry inventory, typically performs only a sales function, and serves as an alternative to agents and brokers.

learning review

13-15. What is the difference between merchant wholesalers and agents?

13-16. Under what circumstances do producers assume wholesaling functions?

LEARNING OBJECTIVES REVIEW

LO 13-1 *Identify retailers in terms of the utilities they provide.*
Retailers provide time, place, form, and possession utilities. Time utility is provided by stores with convenient time-of-day (e.g., open 24 hours) or time-of-year (e.g., seasonal sports equipment available all year) availability. Place utility is provided by the number and location of the stores. Possession utility is provided by making a purchase possible (e.g., financing) or easier (e.g., delivery). Form utility is provided by producing or altering a product to meet the customer's specifications (e.g., custom-made shirts).

LO 13-2 *Explain the alternative ways to classify retail outlets.*
Retail outlets can be classified by their form of ownership, level of service, and type of merchandise line. The forms of ownership include independent retailers, corporate chains, and contractual systems that include retailer-sponsored cooperatives, wholesaler-sponsored voluntary chains, and franchises. The levels of service include self-service, limited-service, and full-service outlets. Stores classified by their merchandise line include stores with depth, such as sporting goods specialty stores, and stores with breadth, such as large department stores.

LO 13-3 *Describe the many methods of nonstore retailing.*
Nonstore retailing includes automatic vending, direct mail and catalogs, television home shopping, online retailing, telemarketing, and direct selling. The methods of nonstore retailing vary by the level of involvement of the retailer and the level of involvement of the customer. Vending, for example, has low involvement, whereas both the consumer and the retailer have high involvement in direct selling.

LO 13-4 *Specify the retailing mix actions used to implement a retailing strategy.*
Retailing mix actions are used to manage a retail store and the merchandise in a store. The mix variables include price, store location, communication activities, and merchandise. Two common forms of assessment for retailers are sales per square foot and same-store growth.

LO 13-5 *Explain changes in retailing with the wheel of retailing and the retail life-cycle concepts.*
The wheel of retailing concept explains how retail outlets typically enter the market as low-status, low-margin stores. Over time, stores gradually add new products and services, thus increasing their prices, status, and margins and leaving

an opening for new low-status, low-margin stores. The retail life cycle describes the process of growth and decline for retail outlets through four stages: early growth, accelerated development, maturity, and decline.

LO 13-6 *Describe the types of firms that perform wholesaling activities and their functions.*
There are three types of firms that perform wholesaling functions. (1) Merchant wholesalers are independently owned and take title to merchandise. They include general merchandise wholesalers, specialty merchandise wholesalers, rack jobbers, cash and carry wholesalers, drop shippers, and truck jobbers. Merchant wholesalers can perform a variety of channel functions. (2) Agents and brokers do not take title to merchandise and primarily perform marketing functions. (3) Manufacturers' branches, which may carry inventory, and sales offices, which perform sales functions, are wholly owned by the producer.

LEARNING REVIEW ANSWERS

13-1 When Ralph Lauren makes shirts to a customer's exact preferences, what utility is provided?
Answer: form utility—involves the production or alteration of a product

13-2 Two measures of the impact of retailing in the global economy are _____ and _____.
Answer: (1) the total annual sales (4 of the 40 largest businesses in the United States are retailers); and (2) the number of employees working at large retailers

13-3 Centralized decision making and purchasing are an advantage of _____ ownership.
Answer: corporate chain

13-4 What are some examples of new forms of self-service retailers?
Answer: New forms of self-service are being developed at warehouse clubs, gas stations, supermarkets, airlines, convenience stores, fast-food restaurants, and even coffee shops.

13-5 A shop for big men's clothes carries pants in sizes 40 to 60. Would this be considered a broad or a deep product line?
Answer: deep product line; the range of sizes relates to the assortment of a product item (pants) rather than the variety of product lines (pants, shirts, shoes, etc.)

13-6 Successful catalog retailers often send _____ catalogs to _____ markets identified in their databases.
Answer: specialty; niche

13-7 How are retailers increasing consumer interest and involvement in online retailing?
Answer: Retailers have improved the online retailing experience by adding experiential or interactive activities to their websites, allowing customers to "build" virtual products by customizing their purchases. Also, to minimize consumers leaving a website to compare prices and shipping costs on other sites, some firms now offer shoppers the ability to compare competitors' offerings.

13-8 Where are direct-selling retail sales growing? Why?
Answer: Direct-selling retailers are (1) expanding into global markets outside the United States and (2) reaching consumers who prefer one-on-one customer service and a social shopping experience rather than shopping online or at big discount stores.

13-9 How does original markup differ from maintained markup?
Answer: The original markup is the difference between retailer cost and initial selling price, whereas maintained markup is the difference between the final selling price and retailer cost, which is also called the gross margin.

13-10 A huge shopping strip mall with multiple anchor stores is a(n) _____ center.
Answer: power

13-11 What is a popular approach to managing the assortment of merchandise in a store?
Answer: category management

13-12 Using the wheel of retailing, describe the characteristics of a new retail form that has just entered the market.
Answer: a low-status, low-margin, low-price outlet

13-13 Market share is usually fought out before the _____ stage of the retail life cycle.
Answer: maturity

13-14 What is the "new science of retailing"?
Answer: Data analytics has been described as the new science of retailing. The use of data analytics can benefit retailers by predicting shopping behavior, allowing personalized messaging, and suggesting innovative products.

13-15 What is the difference between merchant wholesalers and agents?
Answer: Merchant wholesalers are independently owned firms that take title to the merchandise they handle and make their profit from the sale of merchandise they own. Agents do not take title to merchandise, typically perform fewer channel functions, and make their profit from commissions or fees paid for their services.

13-16 Under what circumstances do producers assume wholesaling functions?
Answer: Producers assume wholesaling functions when there are no intermediaries to perform these activities, customers are few in number and geographically concentrated, or orders are large or require significant attention.

FOCUSING ON KEY TERMS

brokers p. 370
category management p. 364
form of ownership p. 353
level of service p. 354
manufacturers' agents p. 369
merchandise line p. 354
merchant wholesalers p. 369
multichannel retailers p. 364
retail life cycle p. 367
retailing p. 352
retailing mix p. 361
scrambled merchandising p. 357
shopper marketing p. 364
shopping experience p. 364
telemarketing p. 360
wheel of retailing p. 366

APPLYING MARKETING KNOWLEDGE

1. Discuss the impact of the growing number of dual-income households on (*a*) nonstore retailing and (*b*) the retail mix.
2. In retail pricing, retailers often have a maintained markup. Explain how this maintained markup differs from original markup and why it is so important.
3. What are the similarities and differences between the product and retail life cycles?
4. How would you classify Walmart in terms of its position on the wheel of retailing versus that of an off-price retailer?
5. Develop a chart to highlight the role of each of the four main elements of the retailing mix across the four stages of the retail life cycle.
6. Breadth and depth are two important components in distinguishing among types of retailers. Discuss the breadth and depth implications of the following retailers discussed in this chapter: (*a*) Nordstrom, (*b*) Walmart, (*c*) L.L.Bean, and (*d*) Best Buy.
7. According to the wheel of retailing and the retail life cycle, what will happen to factory outlet stores?
8. The text discusses the development of online retailing in the United States. How does the development of this retailing form agree with the implications of the retail life cycle?
9. Comment on this statement: "The only distinction among merchant wholesalers and agents and brokers is that merchant wholesalers take title to the products they sell."

BUILDING YOUR MARKETING PLAN

Does your marketing plan involve using retailers? If the answer is "no," read no further and do not include a retailing element in your plan. If the answer is "yes":

1. Use Figure 13–3 to develop your retailing strategy by (*a*) selecting a position in the retail positioning matrix and (*b*) specifying the details of the retailing mix.
2. Develop a positioning statement describing the breadth of the product line (broad versus narrow) and value added (low versus high).
3. Describe an appropriate combination of retail pricing, store location, retail communication, and merchandise assortment.
4. Confirm that the wholesalers needed to support your retailing strategy are consistent with the channels and intermediaries you selected in Chapter 12.

VIDEO CASE 13: Mall of America®: America's Biggest Mall Knows the Secret to Successful Retailing!

The secret to success at Mall of America is continually creating "new experiences for our guests," explains Jill Renslow, senior vice president of business development and marketing. "We want to make not only our locals, but also our tourists have a unique experience every time they come and visit," she adds.

Video 13-5
Mall of America Video Case
kerin.tv/cr8e/v13-5

That's an ambitious undertaking for any retailer, but it is particularly challenging for Mall of America because it attracts more than 40 million guests each year. To create new experiences the mall uses a combination of constantly changing retail offerings, entertainment options, and special attractions. From new stores, to musical acts, to celebrity book signings, to fashion shows, and even two appearances by Taylor Swift, Mall of America has become the "Hollywood of the Midwest." "The key truly is being fresh and exciting," says Renslow.

THE BIG IDEA FOR A BIG MALL

The concept of a huge mall was the result of several trends. First, covered shopping centers began to replace downtown main-street shopping areas in the United States. Second, retail developers observed that casinos were adding nongambling activities to attract entire families. Taking their cue from Las Vegas, a Canadian family, the Ghermezians, built the West Edmonton Mall as a destination venue with shopping, restaurants, hotels, and a theme park. The success of the West Edmonton Mall led to the search for another location for the destination mall concept, and soon Mall of America was under construction in Minneapolis, Minnesota!

According to Dan Jasper, vice president of communications at Mall of America, the Ghermezians are a "wonder family that are visionaries." "They dream really big dreams, and they bring them to reality; they did that in Edmonton with the West Edmonton Mall, and they did that here in Minnesota with Mall of America," he explains. Today Mall of America is the largest mall in the United States with 4.8 million square feet of shopping and entertainment space. And it's getting bigger! "We're opening our new grand front entrance and that will bring us to 5.5 million square feet, making us by far not only the busiest, not only the most successful, but the largest, most massive mall in the nation," says Jasper.

Executives at Mall of America face several important challenges. First, they must keep a huge and diverse portfolio of retailers and attractions in the mall. Second, they must attract millions of visitors each year. Finally, they must increase its marketing and social media presence in the marketplace. The combination of these three activities is essential to the mall's continued success. This is particularly true at a time when e-commerce and online shopping are growing in popularity.

MANAGING THE MALL

The size of Mall of America is difficult to comprehend. There are more than four miles of store front in an area the size of 88 football fields. Three anchor stores—Macy's, Nordstrom, and Sears—are complemented by more than 500 specialty stores. The diversity of the retail offerings is equally amazing. The types of stores range from familiar names such as Banana Republic, Apple, and True Religion to unique stores such as Brickmania, which offers custom LEGO® building kits, and Games by James, which offers thousands of board games and puzzles. According to Renslow, "That's what's special about Mall of America, that's what attracts people from around the world."

To encourage entrepreneurs to come to the mall there is a specialty leasing program that offers the new retailers an affordable entry-level lease in exchange for flexibility related to their location. Mike Pohl, owner of the ACES Flight Simulation store, is one example of the unique businesses the program attracts. "I decided to locate at Mall of America because it's the single biggest retail location in the country," Pohl explains. "There are 40 million people who come here every year, and it's primarily an entertainment mall compared to a traditional mall, so it was a wonderful match for ACES," he adds.

Mall of America also includes more than 20 restaurants, the House of Comedy for touring comedians, and an American Girl store with a doll hair salon and party facilities. The 14 theaters at Mall of America include a 200-seat 3D theater equipped with D-BOX Motion Code seats and a 148-seat theater for guests aged 21 and older.

Additional unique features of Mall of America include:

- Nickelodeon Universe®, a seven-acre theme park with more than 20 attractions and rides, including a roller coaster, Ferris wheel, and a water chute in a skylighted area with more than 400 trees.
- Sea Life® Minnesota aquarium, where visitors can see jellyfish, stingrays, and sea turtles, snorkel with tropical fish, or even SCUBA with sharks!
- Two connected-access hotels including a 342-room JW Marriott and a 500-room Radisson Blu.
- The Chapel of Love, which offers custom weddings and wedding packages and has performed more than 5,000 weddings in the mall!

Regular events and activities include the Art + Style Series, Toddler Tuesdays, the Mall Stars program for people who want to walk and exercise in the Mall, and the Mall of America Music Series. Mall of America also hosts corporate events for organizations with large groups. There are more than 12,000 free parking spaces available to accommodate any size group!

THE MARKET

From its opening day, visitors have been going to Mall of America at the extraordinary rate of 10,000 visitors per day. This is possible because the mall attracts shoppers from more than 18 states—including Minnesota, Wisconsin, Kentucky, Michigan, Ohio, and Pennsylvania—and from more than 11 countries—including Canada, Great Britain, France, Mexico, Germany, Scandinavia, Italy, the Netherlands, Japan, China, and Spain. The mall has worked closely with airlines and other partners to

©Steve Skjold/Alamy Stock Photo

©Alvis Upitis/Alamy Stock Photo

offer "Shop 'Til You Drop" packages that bring shoppers from around the world.

As Renslow explains: "Mall of America shoppers are literally from ages 3 to 83, which is a great opportunity for us but also a challenge. We need to be able to make sure that we communicate with each one of our guests. So we focus on the local market, which makes up 60 percent of our shoppers, and we also focus on our tourists who are 40 percent of our shoppers, and we have different messages to those different audiences." Another key target audience for the mall includes young women. Unmarried women have disposable income and like to travel, and married women are the primary purchase decision makers in their households and often bring their spouses, children, and girlfriends to the mall.

MARKETING, SOCIAL MEDIA, AND MALL OF AMERICA

Another key to Mall of America's success has been its ability to manage its presence in the marketplace. According to Sarah Schmidt, public relations manager for Mall of America, "A typical campaign for Mall of America includes TV, radio, and print and we also include social media campaigns." A recent campaign called "The Scream Collector," for example, started with a TV ad and then followed up with progress reports on billboards. Another campaign created a blizzard in the mall. The "blizzard was a tweet-powered blizzard where guests had to tweet #twizzard, and once it hit a certain number of tweets it started snowing in the mall," Schmidt says.

Social media provide an important element in Mall of America campaigns. Dan Jasper explains, "Mall of America is at the forefront of social media and digital technology within the retail industry; for shopping malls nobody has us beat." The mall has created a communication hub that integrates social media, texting, phone, and security all in a single system. "What that allows us to do is to speak with one voice, and to give real-time answers, suggestions, and advice to consumers," he says.

What is in the future for Mall of America? According to Jasper the answer is an even bigger mall. "In the coming years we're going to double the size of Mall of America," he says. So, prepare yourself for an even more extraordinary retailing experience![56]

Questions

1. What is the key to success at Mall of America?
2. What trends contributed to the idea for the Mall of America? How did it get started?
3. What challenges does Mall of America face as it strives to continue its success?
4. What specific actions has Mall of America taken to address each challenge?

Chapter Notes

1. "Apple Pay Leads the Way in Merchant Acceptance," www.mobilpaymentstoday.com, February 27, 2017; "Smart Stores," www.designretailonline.com, June 2016, p. 8; Pat Dermody, "Mobile Alters Customer Journey," *MMR*, March 7, 2016, p. 8; Bob Violino, "Wearable Device Market to More Than Double over Next Five Years," www.information-management.com, October 6, 2016; Roy Hessel, "What's Next for Smart Glasses?" *Retail Tech*, campfire-capital.com, November 4, 2016; Clare O'Connor, "Here's What Shopping with Apple Watch Will Look Like," *www.Forbes.com*, March 13, 2015; Samuel Mueller, "Wearable Technology and Its Impact on Retail," www.wearabletechworld.com, April 14, 2015; Lisa Johnson, "First Look: Apple Watch Tech & Retail Apps,"*www.twice.com*, May 4, 2015; "Retailers in Sync with Latest Developments in Technology," *MMR*, May 25, 2015, p. 42; "Study: Wearable Technology Will Upend Retail," www.chainstoreage.com, November 2014; and "Valpak at Forefront of Technology," Valpak press release, www.valpak.com, April 22, 2015.

2. "The Fortune 500," *Fortune*, June 1, 2018, p. F-1; "GDP," The World Bank, data.worldbank.org, accessed September 8, 2018; "Annual Estimates of the Resident Population for Incorporated Places of 50,000 or More, Ranked by July 1, 2017, Population," American FactFinder, U.S. Census Bureau, factfinder.census.gov; and *The World Factbook* (Washington, DC: Central Intelligence Agency), www.cia.gov.

3. "Estimated Annual Sales of U.S. Retail and Food Service Firms by Kind of Business," 2015 Annual Retail Trade Report (Washington, DC: U.S. Department of Commerce, Bureau of the Census, March 6, 2017).

4. Corinne Jurney, "The World's Largest Public Companies," *Forbes*, May 24, 2017.

5. "Our Locations," Walmart website, http://corporate.walmart.com/our-story/our-locations, accessed May 28, 2017; and Marcel Corstjens and Rajiv Lal, "Retail Doesn't Cross Borders," *Harvard Business Review*, April 2012, pp. 104–11.

6. Edmund Mander, "When Going Green Gets Rough," *Shopping Centers Today*, January 2017, p. 12; Derrick Teal, "Retailers Going Green," *EDC*, November 2014, pp. 28–33; Leslie Eaton, "Wal-Mart and the Green Consumer," *The Wall Street Journal*, March 31, 2015, p. R6; "Global Consumers Are Willing to Put Their Money Where Their Heart Is," press release, Nielsen, June 17, 2014; "From One Generation to the Next," *Home Depot 2014 Sustainability Report*; and Edwin R. Stafford and Cathy L. Hartman, "Promoting the Value of Sustainably Minded Purchase Behaviors," *Marketing News*, January 2013, p. 28.

7. "The Economic Impact of the U.S. Retail Industry," PricewaterhouseCoopers and the National Retail Federation, 2014, p. 12; and "Retail Trade—Establishments, Employees, and Payroll," *County Business Patterns*, U.S. Census Bureau, July 2010, Table 1048.

8. "2017 Franchise 500" *Entrepreneur*, http://www.entrepreneur.com/franchise500.

9. Antonella Comes, "Unlocking the Potential of Self-Service with Smart ATMs," *ATMmarketplace.com*, April 4, 2017; "Automated Kiosks Reduce Time Waiting at Airport," *Travel Agent*, April 20, 2015, p. 5; "When Customer Service Becomes Self-Service," *Consumer Reports*, September 2014, pp. 33–35; "The Next Generation of Retailing Driven by Automated, Self-Service Solutions," *Market News Publishing*," February 4, 2013; and "Apartment Complex Readies for Automated C-Store," *States News Service*, September 10, 2012.

10. "Nordstom Most Popular Retailer, Reveals Survey," *RetailCustomerExperience.com*, March 1, 2017, p. 49; Phil Wahba, "Nordstrom's Multi-Billion Dollar Plan for e-Commerce Domination," www.Fortune.com, March 3, 2015; "Wealthy Customers Sing Praises of Shopping Experiences at Bergdorf, Nordstrom and Barneys," *Marketwire*, February 5, 2013; Megan Conniff, "Customer Service Is Changing, and So Is Nordstrom," www.Shop.org, September 12, 2012; and Michael A. Wiles, "The Effect of Customer Service on Retailers' Shareholder Wealth: The Role of Availability and Reputation Cues," *Journal of Retailing*, 2007, pp. 19–31.

11. Miriam Gottfried, "How to Fight Amazon.com, Best Buy-Style," *The Wall Street Journal Online*, November 20, 2016; "Best Buy Adopts Price-Matching in U.S., Big Box Retailer Takes on Amazon, Apple," *The Toronto Star*, February 20, 2013, p. B2; John Ewoldt, "Big-Box Retailers Take on Internet," *StarTribune*, November 18, 2012, p. 1A; and Michael Shedlock, "Big-Box Retailers Reconsider Size," *Mish's Global Economic Trend Analysis*, March 5, 2011.

12. Emily Refermat, "State of the Vending Industry Annual Report," *Automatic Merchandiser*, June/July 2016; "No Time to Shop for Your Valentine? From Flowers to Caviar, a Vending Machine Can Save the Day," *Targeted News Service*, February 11, 2013; Jill Becker, "Vending Machines for All Your Needs," www.CNN.com, August 15, 2012; Jackie Crosby, "Vending Machine Variety Goes beyond Snack Food Offerings," *Los Angeles Times*, January 18, 2011, p. B2; and Carlie Kollath, "Veggies in Vending Machines?" *Biz Buzz*, April 6, 2011.

13. "Sustainability Report," IKEA Group, 2016; "About IKEA Catalogue," http://www.ikea.com/ms/en_JP/customer_service/faq/help/about_ikea/ikea_catalogue.html; "Trends from 2017 DMA Statistical Fact Book," Direct Mail Statistics, Data & Marketing Association, thedma.org, accessed September 19, 2017; *Statistical Fact Book* (New York: Direct Marketing Association, 2010), pp. 4, 33; and David Kaplan, "Catalogs Thinner but Still Carry Weight, Retailers Use Them to Draw Consumers to Stores, Web or Social Media Sites," *The Houston Chronicle*, November 28, 2010, p. 1.

14. "How Much Will Postal Cuts Hurt?" *Advertising Age*, February 11, 2013, p. 3; Ira Teinowitz and Nat Ives, "No Day Is a Good Day for No Mail," *Advertising Age*, February 9, 2009, p. 8; "A Zip-Code Screen for Catalog Customers," *The Wall Street Journal*, June 24, 2008, p. B1; and Richard H. Levey, "It's All about Me," *Direct*, November 1, 2008.

15. Bridget McCrea, "The 'Amazon-ing' of Home Shopping," *Response*, November 2016, pp. 32–36; and "Fact Sheet" from the QVC website, http://www.qvc.com/AboutQVCFacts.content.html, accessed May 30, 2017.

16. Paul Ziobro, "Is There Time for QVC in the Age of Amazon?" *The Wall Street Journal*, January 9, 2017; Bianca Carneiro, "Mum Camila McConaughey Outshines Supermodels Miranda Kerr and Heidi Klum at QVC's Red Carpet Style Event," *Mail Online*, February 23, 2013; Jordan Zakarin, "Inside QVC: The Semi-Scripted Reality of the $8 Billion Business Next Door," *The Hollywood Reporter*, December 17, 2012; and Elizabeth Holmes, "The Golden Age of TV Shopping," *The Wall Street Journal*, November 11, 2010, p. D1.

17. "E-commerce Share of Total Global Retail Sales from 2015–2021" and "E-commerce Share of Total Retail Sales in United States from 2013 to 2021," statista.com, April 18, 2018.

18. "Who We Are," eBay website, https://www.ebayinc.com/our-company/who-we-are/, accessed May 31, 2017.

19. Stephan Serrano, "Complete List of Cart Abandonment Statistics: 2006–2018," barilliance.com, February 28, 2018; Chang Hee Park, "Online Purchase Paths and Conversion Dynamics Across Multiple Websites," *Journal of Retailing*, September 2017, pp. 253–65; and Susan Rose, Moira Clark, Phillip Samouel, and Neil Hair, "Online Customer Experience in e-Retailing: An Empirical Model of Antecedents and Outcomes," *Journal of Retailing* 2 (2012), pp. 308–22.

20. Onur H. Bodur, Noreen M. Klein, and Neeraj Arora, "Online Price Search: Impact of Price Comparison Sites on Offline Price Evaluations," *Journal of Retailing,* March 2015, pp. 125–39.
21. "Marketing Vehicle Frequency," *Statistical Fact Book* (New York: Direct Marketing Association, 2015), p. 24.
22. Leonard Klie, "Apple, Google, Verizon, and Others Join Fight Against Robocalls," *Customer Relationship Management,* November 2016, p. 18; "FTC Issues FY 2012 National Do Not Call Registry Data Book," *Federal Trade Commission Documents and Publications,* October 16, 2012; and Nate Anderson, "Do Not Call List Tops 200 Million, Some Scammers Still Ignore It," www.wired.com, July 31, 2010.
23. Sharon Terlep, "Avon Ladies, Backed by Private Equity, Aim to Reconquer Middle America," *The Wall Street Journal,* March 21, 2017; *Direct Selling in 2015: An Overview,* Direct Selling Association, 2016, http://www.dsa.org/docs/default-source/research/dsa_2015factsheetfinal.pdf?sfvrsn=8; and "Direct Selling USA—Pinpoint Growth Sectors and Identify Factors Driving Change," *M2 Presswire,* April 12, 2011.
24. "Amway Reports 2016 Sales of $8.8 Billion USD," news release, *globalnews.amway.com,* February 8, 2017; Phil Wahba, "Amway Boss Defends Direct Selling, Touts 'Made in the USA,'" *www.Fortune.com,* December 11, 2014; "Herbalife Plans Expansion of Manufacturing Capabilities in China," *Asia Pacific Biotech News,* September 2014, p. 22; and "Amway Says China Sales Increase to 27.1b Yuan," *China Daily,* February 21, 2013.
25. Sissi Wang, "Paying to Party," *Canadian Business,* October 2015, pp. 99–101; Virginia Bridges, "In a Slow Economy, Some Try the Direct Approach," *The Virginian-Pilot,* February 17, 2013, p. K1; and "Company Facts," The Pampered Chef website, http://www.pamperedchef.com/company-facts, accessed June 2, 2017.
26. Dinesh K. Gauri, Brian Ratchford, Joseph Pancras, and Debabrata Talukdar, "An Empirical Analysis of the Impact of Promotional Discounts on Store Performance," *Journal of Retailing,* September 2017, pp. 283–303; and Francis J. Mulhern and Robert P. Leon, "Implicit Price Bundling of Retail Products: A Multiproduct Approach to Maximizing Store Profitability," *Journal of Marketing,* October 1991, pp. 63–76.
27. Marc Vanhuele and Xavier Dreze, "Measuring the Price Knowledge Shoppers Bring to the Store," *Journal of Marketing,* October 2002, pp. 72–85.
28. "Walmart Enables Customers to Play a Role in EDLP 2.0," *MMR,* December 19, 2016, p. 59; "Are Sales a Thing of the Past?" *Newstex, www.jennstrathman.com,* January 10, 2013; and Gwen Ortmeyer, John A. Quelch, and Walter Salmon, "Restoring Credibility to Retail Pricing," *Sloan Management Review,* Fall 1991, pp. 55–66.
29. "On Sale! But Does Inexpensive Mean Cheap?" *www.Futurity.org,* November 27, 2012; Rajneesh Suri, Jane Zhen Cai, Kent B. Monroe, and Mrugank V. Thakor, "Retailers' Merchandise Organization and Price Perceptions," *Journal of Retailing* 1 (2012), pp. 168–79; and William Dodds, "In Search of Value: How Price and Store Name Information Influence Buyers' Product Perceptions," *Journal of Consumer Marketing,* Spring 1991, pp. 15–24.
30. Ernan Haruvy, "Measuring the Impact of Price Guarantees on Bidding in Consumer Online Auctions," *Journal of Retailing,* March 2016, pp. 96–108; Stephanie Clifford, "Stores Bend to Cost-Savvy Shoppers: Experiments in Pricing Move Away from Usual Markups and Discounts," *The International Herald Tribune,* March 29, 2012, p. 18; and Leonard L. Berry, "Old Pillars of New Retailing," *Harvard Business Review,* April 2001, pp. 131–37.
31. Eric Anderson and Duncan Simester, "Mind Your Pricing Cues," *Harvard Business Review,* September 2003, pp. 96–103.
32. Julie Baker, A. Parasuraman, Dhruv Grewal, and Glenn B. Voss, "The Influence of Multiple Store Environment Cues on Perceived Merchandise Value and Patronage Intentions," *Journal of Marketing,* April 2002, pp. 120–41.
33. Hyeong Min Kim, "Consumers' Responses to Price Presentation Formats in Rebate Advertisements," *Journal of Retailing* 4 (2006), pp. 309–17.
34. Rita Koselka, "The Schottenstein Factor," *Forbes,* September 28, 1992, pp. 104, 106.
35. "Warehouse Clubs & Superstores," *Hoover's, www.hoovers.com,* June 2, 2017; and "After Four Decades, Club Format Still a Hit," *MMR,* May 22, 2017, p. 101.
36. "About WEM," West Edmonton Mall website, http://www.wem.ca/about-wem/overview, accessed June 2, 2017.
37. John Tennant, "Power Centers Boom in Secondary Markets," *Shopping Center Business,* September 21, 2016, p. 70; and "Power Centers Lead U.S. Sectors," *Shopping Centers Today,* July 2014, p. 58.
38. "A Business Survival Guide to Multi-Channel Retail," *www.Business2Community.com,* December 3, 2012; Umut Konus, Peter C. Verhoef, and Scott A. Neslin, "Multichannel Shopper Segments and Their Covariates," *Journal of Retailing,* December 2008, p. 398; and Robert A. Peterson and Sridhar Balasubramanian, "Retailing in the 21st Century: Reflections and Prologue to Research," *Journal of Retailing,* Spring 2002, pp. 9–16.
39. "How to Make the Most of Omnichannel Retailing," *Harvard Business Review,* July–August 2016, pp. 22–23; "5 Reasons Why Amazon Is Experimenting with Physical Stores," *www.Fortune.com,* May 24, 2017, p. 2; Tom Banks, "Amazon Launches First Physical Store," *Design Week,* February 4, 2015, p. 4; Judith Rosen, "Amazon at Your Campus: The Next-Generation Campus Store," *www.publishersweekly.com,* May 25, 2015, pp. 5–6; Koen Pauwels and Scott A. Neslin, "Building with Bricks and Mortar: The Revenue Impact of Opening Physical Stores in a Multichannel Environment," *Journal of Retailing,* June 2015, pp. 182–97; "PWC's Annual Survey of Online Shoppers Debunks 10 Myths of Multichannel Retailing," *PR Newswire,* February 6, 2013; and Lawrence A. Crosby, "Multi-Channel Relationships," *Marketing Management,* Summer 2011, pp. 12–13.
40. Pierre Martineau, "The Personality of the Retail Store," *Harvard Business Review,* January–February 1958, p. 47.
41. Julie Baker, Dhruv Grewal, and A. Parasuraman, "The Influence of Store Environment on Quality Inferences and Store Image," *Journal of the Academy of Marketing Science,* Fall 1994, pp. 328–39; Howard Barich and Philip Kotler, "A Framework for Marketing Image Management," *Sloan Management Review,* Winter 1991, pp. 94–104; Susan M. Keaveney and Kenneth A. Hunt, "Conceptualization and Operationalization of Retail Store Image: A Case of Rival Middle-Level Theories," *Journal of the Academy of Marketing Science,* Spring 1992, pp. 165–75; James C. Ward, Mary Jo Bitner, and John Barnes, "Measuring the Prototypicality and Meaning of Retail Environments," *Journal of Retailing,* Summer 1992, p. 194; and Dhruv Grewal, R. Krishnan, Julie Baker, and Norm Burin, "The Effect of Store Name, Brand Name and Price Discounts on Consumers' Evaluations and Purchase Intentions," *Journal of Retailing,* Fall 1998, pp. 331–52. For a review of the store image literature, see Mary R. Zimmer and Linda L. Golden, "Impressions of Retail Stores: A Content Analysis of Consumer Images," *Journal of Retailing,* Fall 1988, pp. 265–93.
42. Andreas Herrmann, Manja Zidansek, David E. Sprott, and Eric R. Spangenberg, "The Power of Simplicity: Processing Fluency and the Effects of Olfactory Cues on Retail Sales," *Journal of Retailing* 1 (2013), pp. 30–43.
43. Jack Neff, "Shopper Marketing's New Frontier: e-Commerce," *Advertising Age,* March 14, 2011, p. 14; Andrew Adam Newman,

"Taking Pickles out of the Afterthought Aisle," *The New York Times,* April 26, 2011, p. 3; Piet Levy, "Snack Attack," *Marketing News,* February 28, 2011, p. 12; Yong Jian Wang, Michael S. Minor, and Jie Wei, "Aesthetics and the Online Shopping Environment: Understanding Consumer Responses," *Journal of Retailing* 87, no. 1 (2011), pp. 46–58; and Els Breugelmans and Katia Campo, "Effectiveness of In-Store Displays in a Virtual Store Environment," *Journal of Retailing* 87, no. 1 (2011), pp. 75–89.

44. "Retail Consumer Research 2016," www.accenture.com, November 2016.

45. Jans-Benedict Steenkamp and Michel Wedel, "Segmenting Retail Markets on Store Image Using a Consumer-Based Methodology," *Journal of Retailing,* Fall 1991, p. 300; Philip Kotler, "Atmospherics as a Marketing Tool," *Journal of Retailing* 49 (Winter 1973–74), p. 61; and Roger A. Kerin, Ambuj Jain, and Daniel L. Howard, "Store Shopping Experience and Consumer Price-Quality-Value Perceptions," *Journal of Retailing,* Winter 1992, pp. 376–97.

46. Mary Jo Bitner, "Servicescapes: The Impact of Physical Surroundings on Customers and Employees," *Journal of Marketing,* April 1992, pp. 57–71.

47. Sungtak Hong, Kanishka Misra, and Naufel J. Vilcassim, "The Perils of Category Management: The Effect of Product Assortment on Multicategory Purchase Incidence," *Journal of Marketing,* September 2016, pp. 34–52; Joseph M. Hall, Praveen K. Kopale, and Aradhna Krishna, "Retailer Dynamic Pricing and Ordering Decisions: Category Management versus Brand-by-Brand Approaches," *Journal of Retailing* 86, no. 2 (2010), pp. 172–83; and "Category Management Professionals Can Benefit from Integration of Leading Category and Space Management Suite with Comprehensive and Accurate Product Information," *BusinessWire,* April 28, 2011.

48. Kevin Peters, "How I Did It: Office Depot's President on How 'Mystery Shopping' Helped Spark a Turnaround," *Harvard Business Review,* November 2011, pp. 47–50; and John Davis, *Measuring Marketing* (Singapore: Wiley, 2007), p. 46.

49. Phil Wahba, "Apple Extends Its Lead in the Nation's Top 10 Retailers by Sales," *Fortune.com,* March 23, 2015; Tom Webb, "Retail Ramifications: Best Buy and Apple Seem a Perfect Pair—Except for Apple's Store Ambitions," *St. Paul Pioneer Press,* February 19, 2011; Paul W. Farris, Neil T. Bendle, Phillip E. Pfeifer, and David J. Reibstein, *Marketing Metrics* (Philadelphia: Wharton School Publishing, 2006), p. 106; Jerry Useem, "Simply Irresistible," *Fortune,* March 19, 2007, pp. 107–12; "Apple 2.0," www.blogs.business2.com/apple/the_evil_empire/index.html; Steve Lohr, "Apple, a Success at Stores, Bets Big on Fifth Avenue," *The New York Times,* May 19, 2006; Jim Dalrymple, "Inside the Apple Stores," *MacWorld,* June 2007, pp. 16–17; John Davis, *Measuring Marketing* (Singapore: Wiley, 2007), pp. 280–81; and Retailsails 2011 Chain Store Productivity Report, September 23, 2011, http://www.retailsails.com/, accessed October 7, 2011.

50. The wheel of retailing theory was originally proposed by Malcolm P. McNair, "Significant Trends and Developments in the Postwar Period," in *Competitive Distribution in a Free, High-Level Economy and Its Implications for the University,* ed. A. B. Smith (Pittsburgh: University of Pittsburgh Press, 1958), pp. 1–25; also see Stephen Brown, "The Wheel of Retailing—Past and Future," *Journal of Retailing,* Summer 1990, pp. 143–49; and Malcolm P. McNair and Eleanor May, "The Next Revolution of the Retailing Wheel," *Harvard Business Review,* September–October 1978, pp. 81–91.

51. "McDonald's Tests Crab on Sourdough," *www.QSRweb.com,* March 1, 2017, p. 56; Bill Peters, "McDonald's Will Serve Fresh-Beef Quarter Pounders," *Investors Business Daily,* March 30, 2017, p. 20; "Bronx McDonald's Introduces Self-Service Kiosks," *www.KioskMarketplace.com,* February 1, 2017, p. 1; and Johnathan Maze, "McDonald's Adds Mobile Ordering, Table Service," *Nation's Restaurant News,* December 12, 2016, pp. 46–47.

52. "Our Story," Checkers website, http://checkerscompany.com/our_story, accessed June 12, 2015; "Story," Boston Market website, http://www.bostonmarket.com/ourStory/index.jsp?page=story, accessed June 12, 2015; and Bill Saporito and Ronald B Lieber, "What's for Dinner?" *Fortune,* April 15, 1995, pp. 50–64.

53. William R. Davidson, Albert D. Bates, and Stephen J. Bass, "Retail Life Cycle," *Harvard Business Review,* November–December 1976, pp. 89–96.

54. Hal Conick, "The End of Retail (As We Knew It)," *Marketing News,* September 2017, pp. 40–47; and Anne Marie Doherty, "Who Will Weather Economic Storms on the High Street?" *The Western Mail,* January 1, 2009, p. 29.

55. Eric T. Bradlow, Manish Gangwar, Praveen Kopalle, and Sudhir Voleti, "The Role of Big Data and Predictive Analytics in Retailing," *Journal of Retailing,* March 2017, pp. 79–95; Rachit Khare, "Are You Sitting on a Data Goldmine? What All Retail Brands Need to Know," *www.RetailCustomerExperience.com,* May 25, 2017; Frank Germann, Gary L. Lilien, Lars Fiedler, and Matthias Kraus, "Do Retailers Benefit from Deploying Customer Analytics?" *Journal of Retailing,* December 2014, pp. 587–93; "New Analytics Technology Puts Hong Kong's Fashion Retailers in the Fast Lane," *Network World Asia,* June/July 2014, p. 36; Murali Nadarajah, "Deck the Halls with Analytics," *Retail-Merchandiser.com,* November/December 2014, p. 17; and Marshall Fisher and Ananth Raman, "The New Science of Retailing: How Analytics Are Transforming the Supply Chain and Improving Performance," *Retail Merchandiser,* May/June 2010, p. 6.

56. Mall of America: This case was written by Steven Hartley. Sources: Jennifer Latson, "Why America's Biggest Mall Is Getting Bigger," *www.Time.com,* August 12, 2015; Samuel Greengard, "Mall of America Increases Its Social Presence," *CIO Insight,* July 28, 2015, p. 2; "This Is How You Resurrect America's Dying Malls," *www.Time.com,* April 15, 2014, p. 1; "JW Mall of America Hotel Set to Open in November," *Travel Weekly,* April 9, 2015, p. 17; Erika Fry, "Why Mall of America Is Expanding as Many Retailers Implode," *www.Fortune.com,* March 10, 2014; "Mall of America Marks 20 Years," *Women's Wear Daily,* November 5, 2012, p. 8; Jerry Gerlach and James Janke, "The Mall of America as a Tourist Attraction," *Focus,* Summer 2001, p. 32; and the Mall of America website, http://www.mallofamerica.com/.

14

Implementing Interactive and Multichannel Marketing

LEARNING OBJECTIVES

After reading this chapter you should be able to:

LO 14-1 Describe what interactive marketing is and how it creates customer value, customer relationships, and customer experiences.

LO 14-2 Explain why certain types of products and services are particularly suited for interactive marketing.

LO 14-3 Describe why consumers shop and buy online and how marketers influence online purchasing behavior.

LO 14-4 Define cross-channel consumers and the role of multichannel marketing in reaching these consumers.

Seven Cycles Delivers Just One Bike. Yours.

"One Bike. Yours." is the company tagline for Seven Cycles, Inc., located in Watertown, Massachusetts. And for good reason.

Seven Cycles is the world's largest custom bicycle frame builder. The company produces a broad range of road, mountain, cyclocross, tandem, touring, single-speed, and commuter bikes annually, and no two bikes are exactly alike. This feat is all the more impressive because Seven Cycles has sold over 30,000 custom-made bicycles since its founding 20 years ago. Custom bikes do come at a premium, with prices starting at around $4,000.

At Seven Cycles, attention is focused on each customer's unique cycling experience through the optimum fit, function, performance, and comfort of his or her very own bike. According to one satisfied customer, "Getting a Seven is more of a creation than a purchase."

While Seven Cycles does offer stock frames in more than 200 sizes, each is still built to order and a full 95 percent of the bicycle frames that Seven ships are completely custom made. Customized elements include frame size, frame geometry, tubing diameters, and wall thickness, as well as countless options such as cable routing, water bottle mounts, paint color, and decal color. Every custom option is available at no additional charge and the number of combinations is virtually infinite.

The marketing success of Seven Cycles is due to its state-of-the-art custom-built carbon, titanium, and steel bicycle frames. But as Rob Vandermark, company founder and president, says, "Part of our success is that we are tied to a business model that includes the Internet."

Seven uses its multilanguage (English, German, Swedish, Italian, Chinese, Japanese, Korean, and Flemish) website (www.sevencycles.com) to let customers get deeply involved in the frame-building process and the selection of components to outfit their complete bike. It enables customers to collaborate on the design of their own bike using the company's Custom Kit fitting system, which considers the rider's size, aspirations, and riding habits. Then customers can monitor their bike's progress through the development and production process by clicking "Where's My Frame?" on the Seven Cycles website.

seven 7 cycles

(both photos): Courtesy of Seven Cycles, Inc.

This customization process and continuous feedback make for a collaborative relationship between Seven Cycles and its nearly 200 authorized retailers in the United States. Some 30 international distributors and customers in 40 countries account for about 40 percent of the company's bike sales. "Our whole process is designed to keep the focus on the rider the bike is being built for, so it ends up being a very different and more interactive experience than most people are used to. That experience is a large part of the value we sell, above and beyond the bike," explains Jennifer Miller, co-founder and chief financial officer at Seven Cycles.

In addition to the order process, website visitors can peruse weekly news stories and learn about new product introductions to get a unique perspective on the business. They can read employee biographies online to learn more about the people who build the bikes. The website also offers a retailer-specific section as a 24/7 repository of updated information for the company's channel partners.

Beyond the website, current Seven owners can interact with the company on the Seven Cycles blog to learn about its activities and products. Seven Cycles also uses its company Facebook Page, Instagram, and Twitter to post brief and timely updates and build a stronger sense of community around the brand.[1]

This chapter describes how companies design and implement interactive marketing programs. It begins by explaining how Internet technology can create customer value, build customer relationships, and produce customer experiences in novel ways. Next, it describes how Internet technology affects and is affected by consumer behavior and marketing practices. Finally, the chapter shows how marketers integrate and leverage their communication and delivery channels to implement multichannel marketing programs to better serve cross-channel consumers.

CREATING CUSTOMER VALUE, RELATIONSHIPS, AND EXPERIENCES IN MARKETSPACE

LO 14-1 Describe what interactive marketing is and how it creates customer value, customer relationships, and customer experiences.

Consumers and companies populate two market environments today. One is the traditional *marketplace.* Here buyers and sellers engage in face-to-face exchange relationships in a material environment characterized by physical facilities (stores and offices) and mostly tangible objects. The other is the *marketspace,* an Internet-enabled digital environment characterized by face-to-screen exchange relationships and electronic images and offerings.

Marketing Challenges in Two Environments

The existence of two market environments is a boon for consumers. Many consumers browse and buy in both market environments. More are expected to do so in the future as mobile devices, notably smartphones, expand their capabilities.

About 90 percent of Internet users aged 15 and older have shopped online in the United States. They are expected to buy over $500 billion worth of products and services in 2022 (excluding travel, automobile, and prescription drugs).[2]

Nevertheless, marketing in two market environments poses significant challenges for companies based on their origin in the traditional marketplace and digital marketspace. In fact, the challenge of marketing in two environments has revolutionized marketing channel and supply chain systems and traditional retailing.

Legacy Companies   Legacy companies that trace their origins to the traditional marketplace, such as Procter & Gamble, Walmart, and General Motors, are continually challenged to define the nature and scope of their marketspace presence. These companies consistently refine the role of digital technology in attracting, retaining, and building consumer relationships to improve their competitive positions in the traditional marketplace while also bolstering their marketspace presence. Other companies with marketplace origins have chosen not to participate in the marketspace. Luxury fashion designs, for the most part, don't sell their products online. According to the founder of Prada, "We think that, for luxury, it's not right. Personally, I'm not interested."[3] Not surprisingly, over 90 percent of luxury fashion merchandise is sold exclusively through retail stores.

Internet Companies   On the other hand, companies with marketspace origins, including Amazon.com, Google, eBay, E*TRADE, and others, are challenged to continually refine, broaden, and deepen their marketspace presence. At the same time, these companies, and other companies, must consider what role, if any, the traditional marketplace will play in their future. For example, eyeglass online retailer Warby Parker, online mattress seller Casper Sleep, clothing online retailer Bonobos, jewelry online retailer Blue Nile and, yes, Amazon, have opened physical showrooms that give shoppers an opportunity to experience the company's products in person before purchasing them online.

Regardless of origin, a company's success in achieving a meaningful marketspace presence hinges largely on (1) its ability to design and execute a marketing program that capitalizes on the unique value creation and (2) the relationship-building capabilities of digital technology in delivering a favorable customer experience.

Creating Customer Value in Marketspace

Why has the marketspace captured the eye and imagination of marketers worldwide? Recall that marketing creates time, place, form, and possession utilities, thereby creating value for consumers. Marketers believe that the possibilities for customer value creation are greater in the digital marketspace than in the physical marketplace.

Consider place and time utility. In marketspace, the provision of direct, on-demand information is possible from marketers *anywhere* to customers *anywhere, at any time.* Why? Operating hours and geographical constraints do not exist in marketspace. For example, Recreational Equipment, Inc. (www.rei.com), an outdoor gear marketer, reports that 35 percent of its orders are placed between 10:00 P.M. and 7:00 A.M., long after and before retail stores are open for business. Similarly, a U.S. consumer from Chicago can access Marks & Spencer (www.marks-and-spencer.co.uk), the well-known British department store, to shop for clothing as easily as a person living near London's Piccadilly Square. Cross-border sales will account for 20 percent of worldwide online sales in 2022.[4]

Possession utility—getting a product or service to consumers so they can own or use it—is accelerated in marketspace. Airline, car rental, and lodging electronic reservation systems such as Orbitz (www.orbitz.com) allow comparison shopping for the lowest fares, rents, and rates and almost immediate access to and confirmation of travel arrangements and accommodations.

The greatest marketspace opportunity for marketers, however, lies in its potential for creating form utility. Communication capabilities in marketspace invite consumers to tell marketers specifically what their requirements are, making customization of a product or service to fit their exact needs possible. Today, 35 percent of online consumers are interested in customizing product features or in purchasing build-to-order products that use their specifications.[5] At Seven Cycles, customers can arrange for a custom-made bike to fit their specifications, as described in the chapter-opening example.

Seven Cycles offers form utility by creating customized bikes for customers in over 40 countries.
Courtesy of Seven Cycles, Inc.

Seven Cycles, Inc.
www.sevencycles.com

Interactivity, Individuality, and Customer Relationships in Marketspace

Marketers benefit from two unique capabilities of digital technology that promote and sustain customer relationships. One is *interactivity*; the other is *individuality*.[6] Both capabilities are important building blocks for buyer–seller relationships. For these relationships to occur, companies interact with their customers by listening and responding to their needs. Marketers must also treat customers as individuals and empower them to (1) influence the timing and extent of the buyer–seller interaction and (2) have a say in the kind of products and services they buy, the information they receive, and in some cases, the prices they pay.

Internet-enabled digital technology allows for interaction, individualization, and customer relationship building to be carried out on a scale never before available and makes interactive marketing possible. **Interactive marketing** involves two-way buyer–seller electronic communication in which the buyer controls the kind and amount of information received from the seller. Interactive marketing is characterized by sophisticated choiceboard and personalization systems that transform information supplied by customers into customized responses to their individual needs.

Mars, Inc. uses choiceboard technology to decorate M&M's candies with personal photos and messages.
©McGraw-Hill Education

Mars, Inc.
www.mymms.com

Video 14-1
My M&M's®
kerin.tv/cr8e/v14-1

interactive marketing
Two-way buyer–seller electronic communication in which the buyer controls the kind and amount of information received from the seller.

choiceboard
An interactive, Internet-enabled system that allows individual customers to design their own products and services by answering a few questions and choosing from a menu of product or service attributes (or components), prices, and delivery options.

collaborative filtering
A process that automatically groups people with similar buying intentions, preferences, and behaviors and predicts future purchases.

Choiceboards A **choiceboard** is an interactive, Internet-enabled system that allows individual customers to design their own products and services by answering a few questions and choosing from a menu of product or service attributes (or components), prices, and delivery options. Customers today design their own computers with Dell's online configurator, style their own athletic shoe at www.reebok.com, assemble their own investment portfolios with Schwab's mutual fund evaluator, build their own bicycle at www.sevencycles.com, and decorate M&M's with photos of themselves and unique messages at www.mymms.com. Because choiceboards collect precise information about the preferences and behavior of individual buyers, a company becomes more knowledgeable about a customer and better able to anticipate and fulfill that customer's needs.

Most choiceboards are essentially transaction devices. However, companies have expanded the functionality of choiceboards using collaborative filtering technology. **Collaborative filtering** is a process that automatically groups people with similar buying intentions, preferences, and behaviors and predicts future purchases. For example, say two people who have never met buy largely the same music over time. Collaborative filtering software is programmed to reason that these two buyers might have similar musical tastes: If one buyer likes a particular music, then the other will like it as well. The outcome? Collaborative filtering gives marketers the ability to make a dead-on sales recommendation to a buyer in *real time*. You see collaborative filtering applied each time you view a selection at Amazon.com and see "Customers who bought this (item) also bought. . . ." About 35 percent of Amazon's revenue comes from its product recommendations.

Personalization Choiceboards and collaborative filtering are marketer-initiated efforts to provide customized responses to the needs of individual buyers. By comparison, personalization systems are typically buyer-initiated efforts. **Personalization** is the consumer-initiated practice of generating content on a marketer's website that is custom tailored to an individual's specific needs and preferences. Today, one-half of the largest online retailers in the United States use sophisticated personalization systems based on data mining results and predictive modeling techniques described in Chapter 7.[7]

Sunglass Hut is a case in point. When a shopper visits its website (www.sunglasshut.com) and clicks on a pair of sunglasses, a "see similar styles" option is shown. This

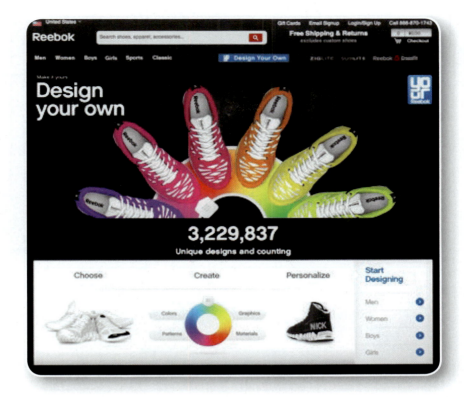

Reebok uses choiceboard technology to create customized athletic shoes for its customers.

Courtesy of Reebok International Ltd.

Reebok
www.reebok.com

personalization
The consumer-initiated practice of generating content on a marketer's website that is custom tailored to an individual's specific needs and preferences.

permission marketing
The solicitation of a consumer's consent (called "opt-in") to receive e-mail and advertising based on personal data supplied by the consumer.

option uses image recognition and artificial intelligence technology to show other sunglasses that might be suitable choices for the shopper. So instead of suggesting what the shopper might want based on what other people have purchased, which is the case with choiceboards and collaborative filtering, the shopper is shown items that fit his or her preferences and features.

Personalization techniques are welcome by consumers. Still, companies acknowledge the need to balance a consumer's desire to be catered to on a one-to-one basis and concerns about intrusion. Research shows that about 40 percent of consumers feel "slightly creepy" when personalization technology correctly reads and anticipates their needs.[8]

An important aspect of personalization is a buyer's willingness to have tailored communications brought to his or her attention. Obtaining this approval is called **permission marketing**—the solicitation of a consumer's consent (called *opt-in*) to receive e-mail and advertising based on personal data supplied by the consumer. Permission marketing is a proven vehicle for building and maintaining customer relationships, provided it is properly used.

Companies that successfully employ permission marketing adhere to three rules.[9] First, they make sure opt-in customers receive only information that is relevant and meaningful to them. Second, their customers are given the option to *opt-out,* or change the kind, amount, or timing of information sent to them. Finally, their customers are assured that their name or buyer profile data will not be sold or shared with others. This assurance is important because a significant portion of adult Internet users are concerned about the privacy of their personal information and wish to protect it.[10]

Creating a Compelling Online Customer Experience

A continuing challenge for companies is the design and execution of marketing programs that capitalize on the unique customer value-creation capabilities of Internet technology. Companies realize that applying this technology to create time, place, form, and possession utility is just a starting point for creating a meaningful marketspace presence. Today, the quality of the customer experience delivered by a company is the standard by which a meaningful marketspace presence is measured.

FIGURE 14–1

Seven website design elements that drive customer experience.

(photo): ©NetPhotos/Alamy Stock Photo

From an interactive marketing perspective, *customer experience* is defined as the sum total of the interactions that a customer has with a company's website, from the initial look at a home page through the entire purchase decision process.[11] Seven fundamental website design elements contribute to a customer experience. These elements are context, content, community, customization, communication, connection, and commerce. Each is described below and summarized in Figure 14–1.

Context   *Context* refers to a website's aesthetic appeal and the functional look and feel of the site's layout and visual design. A functionally oriented website focuses largely on the company's offering, be it products, services, or information. Deal-oriented travel websites, such as Priceline.com, tend to be functionally oriented with an emphasis on destinations, scheduling, and prices. In contrast, beauty websites, such as Revlon.com, are more aesthetically oriented. As these examples suggest, context conveys the core consumer benefit provided by the company's offerings.

Content   *Content* applies to all digital information on a website, including the presentation form—text, video, audio, and graphics. Content relevance and presentation along with context dimensions combine to engage a website visitor and provide a platform for the five remaining design elements. The importance of content in website design is reflected in the mantra "Content is king."

Customization   Website *customization* is the ability of a site to modify itself to, or be modified by and for, each individual user. Customization involves moving items around to reflect a consumer's priorities or selecting topics of interest to them. This design element is prominent in websites that offer personalized content, such as My eBay and My Amazon.

Connection   The *connection* element is the network of linkages between a company's website and other sites. These links are embedded in the website; appear as

Travelocity pays close attention to creating a favorable customer experience by employing all seven website design elements.

Source: Travelocity

Travelocity
www.travelocity.com

highlighted words, a picture, or graphic; and allow a user to effortlessly visit other sites with a mouse click. For example, companies routinely display links to their Facebook, Instagram, and Twitter accounts. Connection is a major design element for informational websites such as *The New York Times*. Users of NYTimes.com can access the book review section and link to Barnes & Noble to order a book or browse related titles without ever visiting a store.

Communication *Communication* refers to the dialogue that unfolds between the website and its users. Consumers now expect that communication to be interactive and individualized in real time, much like a personal conversation. Many websites enable a user to talk directly with a customer representative while shopping the site. However, an increasing number of websites use *chatbots*—sophisticated computer programs that mimic human conversation using artificial intelligence.

Community In addition, many company websites encourage user-to-user communications hosted by the company to create virtual communities, or simply *community*. This design element is popular because it has been shown to enhance customer experience and build favorable buyer–seller relationships. Examples of communities range from the Pampers Village hosted by Procter & Gamble (www.pampers.com) to the Harley Owners Group (HOG) sponsored by Harley-Davidson (www.harley-davidson.com).

Commerce The seventh design element is *commerce*—the website's ability to conduct sales transactions for products and services. Online transactions are quick and simple in well-designed websites.

Most websites do not include every design element. Although every website has context and content, they differ in the use of the remaining five elements. Why? Websites have different purposes. For example, only websites that emphasize the actual sale of products and services include the commerce element. Websites that are used primarily for advertising and promotion purposes emphasize the communication and connection elements.

Companies use a broad array of measures to assess website performance. For example, the amount of time per month visitors spend on their website, or "stickiness," is used to gauge customer experience.[12] Read the Applying Marketing Metrics box to learn how stickiness is measured and interpreted at one of the largest automobile dealerships in the United States.[13]

learning review

14-1. The consumer-initiated practice of generating content on a marketer's website that is custom tailored to an individual's specific needs and preferences is called _____.

14-2. What are the seven website design elements that companies use to produce a customer experience?

Applying Marketing Metrics

Sizing Up Site Stickiness at Sewell Automotive Companies

Automobile dealerships have invested significant time, effort, and money in their websites. Why? Car browsing and shopping on the Internet is now commonplace.

Dealerships commonly measure website performance by tracking visits, visitor traffic, and "stickiness"—the amount of time per month visitors spend on their website. Website design, easy navigation, involving content, and visual appeal combine to enhance the interactive customer experience and website stickiness.

To gauge stickiness, companies monitor the average time spent per unique monthly visitor (in minutes) on their websites. This is done by tracking and displaying the average visits per unique monthly visitor and the average time spent per visit, in minutes, in their marketing dashboards. The relationship is as follows:

Average Time Spent per Unique Monthly Visitor (minutes) =
$\begin{pmatrix} \text{Average Visits per} \\ \text{Unique Monthly Visitor} \end{pmatrix} \times \begin{pmatrix} \text{Average Time Spent} \\ \text{per Visit (minutes)} \end{pmatrix}$

Your Challenge

As the manager responsible for Sewell.com, the Sewell Automotive Companies' website, you have been asked to report on the effect that recent improvements in the company's website have had on the amount of time per month visitors spend on the website. Sewell ranks among the largest U.S. automotive dealerships and is a recognized customer service leader in the automotive industry. Its website reflects the company's commitment to an unparalleled customer experience at its family of dealerships.

Your Findings

Examples of monthly marketing dashboard traffic and time measures are displayed below for June 2017, three months before the website improvements were made (green arrow), and June 2018, after the improvements were made (red arrow).

The average time spent per unique monthly visitor increased from 8.5 minutes in June 2017 to 11.9 minutes in June 2018—a sizable jump. The increase is due primarily to the upturn in the average time spent per visit from 7.1 minutes to 8.5 minutes. The average number of visits also increased, but the percentage change was much less.

Your Action

Improvements in the website have noticeably "moved the needle" on average time spent per unique monthly visitor. Still, additional action may be required to increase average visits per unique monthly visitor. These actions might include an analysis of Sewell's web advertising program, search engine initiatives with Google, links to automobile manufacturer corporate websites, and broader print and electronic media advertising.

Average Time Spent per Unique Monthly Visitor (minutes)

Average Visits per Unique Monthly Visitor

Average Time Spent per Visit (minutes)

ONLINE CONSUMER BEHAVIOR AND MARKETING OPPORTUNITIES AND PRACTICES

Who are online consumers, and what do they buy? Why, when, and how do they choose to shop and purchase products and services in the digital marketspace rather than (or in addition to) the traditional marketplace? Answers to these questions have a direct bearing on marketing practices.

Who Is the Online Consumer?

online consumers
The subsegment of all Internet users who employ this technology to research products and services and make purchases.

Online consumers are the subsegment of all Internet users who employ this technology to research products and services and make purchases. As a group, online consumers are equally likely to be women and men and tend to be better educated, younger, and more affluent than the general U.S. population. Even though online shopping and buying is popular, a small percentage of online consumers still account for a disproportionate share of online retail sales in the United States. It is estimated that 20 percent of online consumers account for 69 percent of total consumer online sales. Also, while women and men shop online with equal frequency, men tend to spend more per purchase transaction than women.[14]

What Consumers Buy Online

LO 14-2 Explain why certain types of products and services are particularly suited for interactive marketing.

Much still needs to be learned about online consumer purchase behavior. Although research has documented the most frequently purchased products and services bought online, marketers also need to know *why* these items are popular.

Five broad product classes or categories account for almost 70 percent of online consumer buying today and for the foreseeable future, as shown in Figure 14–2.[15] One product category consists of items for which product information is an important part of the purchase decision but prepurchase trial is not necessarily critical. Items such as computers, computer accessories, and consumer electronics are examples.

A second kind of product contains items that can be delivered digitally, including computer software, books, music, and video. Unique items, such as apparel accessories and home furnishings, represent a third group.

A fourth kind of product or service includes items that are regularly purchased and where convenience is very important. These include health care and personal care items. A final grouping consists of highly standardized products and services for which information about price is important. Automotive products and casual apparel are examples.

Why Consumers Shop and Buy Online

LO 14-3 Describe why consumers shop and buy online and how marketers influence online purchasing behavior.

Why do consumers shop and buy online? Marketers emphasize the customer value-creation possibilities, the importance of interactivity, individuality, and relationship building, and the ability to produce a compelling customer experience. However, consumers typically refer to six reasons why they shop and buy online: convenience, choice, customization, communication, cost, and control (Figure 14–3).

Convenience Online shopping and buying is *convenient*. Consumers can visit Walmart at www.walmart.com to scan and order from among thousands of displayed

FIGURE 14–2
Five product categories account for about 70 percent of U.S. online retail sales today—a trend that is projected to continue in the future.

2018: Percent of Online Retail Sales	Product Category	2021: Percent of Online Retail Sales
20.8%	Apparel & accessories	22.9%
18.7%	Computer & accessories	18.3%
11.9%	Automobile & auto parts	12.2%
9.4%	Books, music, and video	9.3%
8.1%	Health & personal care	8.1%

NOTE: Online retail sales exclude airline travel, event tickets, and prescription drugs.

FIGURE 14–3

Why do consumers shop and buy online? Read the text to learn how convenience, choice, customization, communication, cost, and control result in a favorable customer experience.

(photo): ©Fuse/Getty Images

bots
Electronic shopping agents or robots that search websites to compare prices and product or service features.

eight-second rule
A view that customers will abandon their efforts to enter and navigate a website if download time exceeds eight seconds.

customerization
The growing practice of not only customizing a product or service but also personalizing the marketing and overall shopping and buying interaction for each customer.

products without fighting traffic, finding a parking space, walking through long aisles, and standing in store checkout lines. Alternatively, online consumers often use **bots**, electronic shopping agents or robots that search websites to compare prices and product or service features. In either instance, an online consumer has never ventured into a store. However, for convenience to remain a source of customer value creation, websites must be easy to locate and navigate, and image downloads must be fast.

A commonly held view among online marketers is the **eight-second rule**: Customers will abandon their efforts to enter and navigate a website if download time exceeds eight seconds. Furthermore, the more clicks and pauses between clicks required to access information or make a purchase, the more likely it is a customer will exit a website.

Choice *Choice,* the second reason consumers shop and buy online, has two dimensions. First, choice exists in the product or service selection offered to consumers. Buyers desiring selection can avail themselves of more than 1 billion websites worldwide for almost anything they want. For instance, online buyers of consumer electronics can shop individual manufacturers such as Bose (www.bose.com) and QVC.com, a general merchant that offers more than 100,000 products.

Choice assistance is the second dimension. Here, choiceboard and personalization technologies invite customers to engage in an electronic dialogue with marketers for the purpose of making informed choices. Choice assistance is one of the reasons for the continued success of Zappos.com. The company offers an online chat room that enables prospective buyers to ask questions and receive answers in real time. In addition, carefully designed search capabilities permit consumers to review products by brand and particular items.

Customization Even with a broad selection and choice assistance, some customers prefer one-of-a-kind items that fit their specific needs. *Customization* arises from Internet-enabled capabilities that make possible a highly interactive and individualized information and exchange environment for shoppers and buyers. Remember the earlier Reebok, Schwab, Dell, and Seven Cycles examples? To varying degrees, online consumers also benefit from **customerization**—the practice of not only customizing a product or service but also personalizing the marketing and overall shopping and buying interaction for each customer.[16]

Customerization seeks to do more than offer consumers the right product, at the right time, and at the right price. It combines choiceboard and personalization systems

Zappos.com is successful because it meets all the requirements necessary for consumers to shop and buy online. In less than 10 years, the company has posted significant annual sales of shoes, apparel, bags, accessories, housewares, and jewelry.
Source: Zappos.com

Zappos.com
www.zappos.com

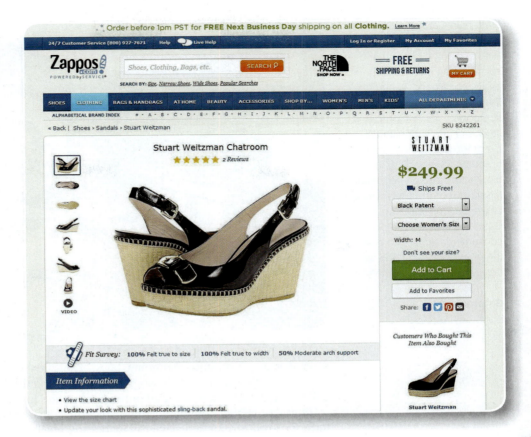

to expand the exchange environment beyond a transaction and makes shopping and buying an enjoyable, personal experience.

Communication Online consumers particularly welcome the *communication* capabilities of Internet-enabled technologies. This communication can take three forms: (1) marketer-to-consumer e-mail notifications, (2) consumer-to-marketer buying and service requests, and (3) consumer-to-consumer chat rooms and instant messaging, in addition to social networking websites such as Twitter and Facebook.

Communication has proven to be a double-edged sword for online consumers. On the one hand, the interactive communication capabilities increase consumer convenience, reduce information search costs, and make choice assistance and customization possible. Communication also promotes the development of company-hosted and independent **web communities**—websites that allow people to congregate online and exchange views on topics of common interest. For instance, Coca-Cola hosts MyCoke.com, and iVillage.com is an independent web community for women and includes topics such as career management, personal finances, parenting, relationships, beauty, and health.

Web logs, or blogs, are another form of communication. A *blog* is a web page that serves as a publicly accessible personal journal for an individual or organization. Blogs are popular because they provide online forums on a wide variety of subjects ranging from politics to car repair. Companies such as Hewlett-Packard, PepsiCo, and Harley-Davidson routinely monitor blogs and social media posts to gather customer insights.[17]

On the other hand, communications can take the form of electronic junk mail or unsolicited e-mail, called **spam**. In fact, 60 percent of e-mail messages in the world are spam.[18] The prevalence of spam has prompted many online services to institute policies and procedures to prevent spammers from spamming their subscribers, and

web communities
Websites that allow people to congregate online and exchange views on topics of common interest.

spam
Communications that take the form of electronic junk mail or unsolicited e-mail.

Staffers in Gatorade's "Mission Control" room in Chicago, Illinois, monitor Internet and social media outlets, such as Facebook and Twitter, 24 hours a day. Whenever someone uses Twitter to say he or she is drinking a Gatorade or mentions the brand on Facebook or in a blog, it pops up on-screen at Mission Control. In this way, conversations featuring Gatorade provide useful consumer insights into how the brand is viewed and used.
©Clayton Hauck Photography

Gatorade
www.gatorade.com

several states have anti-spamming laws. The 2004 CAN-SPAM (Controlling the Assault of Non-Solicited Pornography and Marketing) Act restricts information collection and unsolicited e-mail promotions on the Internet.

Internet-enabled communication capabilities also make possible *buzz,* a popular term for word-of-mouth behavior in marketspace. Chapter 4 described the importance of word of mouth in consumer behavior. Internet technology has magnified its significance. According to Jeff Bezos, the founder of Amazon.com, "If you have an unhappy customer on the Internet, he doesn't tell his six friends, he tells his 6,000 friends!"[19] Buzz is particularly influential for toys, cars, sporting goods, movies, apparel, consumer electronics, pharmaceuticals, health and beauty products, and health care services. Some marketers have capitalized on this phenomenon by creating buzz through viral marketing.

Viral marketing is an Internet-enabled promotional strategy that encourages individuals to forward marketer-initiated messages to others via e-mail, social networking websites, and blogs. There are three approaches to viral marketing. First, marketers can embed a message in the product or service so that customers hardly realize they are passing it along. The classic example is Hotmail, which was one of the first companies to provide free, Internet-based e-mail. Each outgoing e-mail message had the tagline: "Get Your Private, Free Email from MSN Hotmail." This effort produced more than 350 million users.

Second, marketers can make the website content so compelling that viewers want to share it with others. Careerbuilder.com has done this with its Monk-e-mail site, which allows users to send personalized, private-themed e-cards for all occasions. More than 100 million Monk-e-mails have been sent in the past decade. Finally, marketers can offer incentives (discounts, sweepstakes, or free merchandise). For example, Burger King asked, "What do you love more, your friend or the Whopper?" in its Whopper Sacrifice campaign. Facebook users were asked to "unfriend" 10 people from their Facebook friends list in exchange for a free burger.[20]

Cost Consumer *cost* is a fifth reason for online shopping and buying. Many popular items bought online can be purchased at the same price or cheaper than in retail stores.[21] Lower prices also result from sophisticated software that permits **dynamic pricing**, the practice of changing prices for products and services in real time in

---

viral marketing
An Internet-enabled promotional strategy that encourages individuals to forward marketer-initiated messages to others via e-mail, social networking websites, and blogs.

> Video 14-2
> Frito-Lay
> kerin.tv/cr8e/v14-2

dynamic pricing
The practice of changing prices for products and services in real time in response to supply and demand conditions.

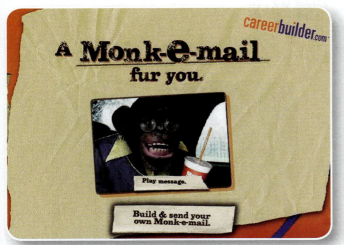

Careerbuilder.com, an online career placement company, has produced a great viral marketing success with its Monk-e-mail featuring talking monkeys. People can stylize their monkeys by choosing headgear, clothes, glasses, backgrounds, and other features. They can also record a message using one of four monkey voices or their own voice. Monk-e-mail can be sent to friends or posted on Twitter.
Source: Careerbuilder.com

CareerBuilder
www.careerbuilder.com

cookies
Computer files that a marketer can download onto the computer and mobile phone of an online shopper who visits the marketer's website.

behavioral targeting
Uses information provided by cookies to direct online advertising from marketers to those online shoppers whose behavioral profiles suggest they would be interested in such advertising.

response to supply and demand conditions. As described in Chapter 11, dynamic pricing is a form of flexible pricing and can often result in lower prices. It is typically used for pricing time-sensitive items such as airline seats, scarce items found at art or collectible auctions, and out-of-date items such as last year's models of computer equipment and accessories.

A consumer's cost of external information search, including time spent and often the hassle of shopping, is also reduced. Greater shopping convenience and lower external search costs are two major reasons for the popularity of online shopping and buying among women—particularly those who work outside the home.

Control The sixth reason consumers prefer to buy online is the *control* it gives them over their shopping and purchase decision process. Online shoppers and buyers are empowered consumers. They deftly use Internet technology to seek information, evaluate alternatives, and make purchase decisions on their own time, terms, and conditions. For example, studies show that automobile shoppers spend an average of 11 hours researching cars online before setting foot in a showroom.[22] The result of these activities is a more informed and discerning shopper.

Even though consumers have many reasons for shopping and buying online, a segment of Internet users refrains from making purchases for privacy and security reasons. These consumers are concerned about a rarely mentioned seventh C—cookies.

Cookies are computer files that a marketer can download onto the computer and mobile phone of an online shopper who visits the marketer's website. Cookies allow the marketer's website to record a user's visit, track visits to other websites, and store and retrieve this information in the future. Cookies also contain visitor information such as expressed product preferences, personal data, passwords, and credit card numbers.

Cookies make possible customized and personal content for online shoppers. They also make possible the practice of behavioral targeting for marketers. **Behavioral targeting** uses information provided by cookies to direct online advertising from marketers to those online shoppers whose behavioral profiles suggest they would be interested in such advertising. A controversy surrounding cookies is summed up by an authority on the technology: "At best cookies make for a user-friendly web world: like a salesclerk who knows who you are. At worst, cookies represent a potential loss of privacy."[23] Read the Making Responsible Decisions box to learn more about privacy and security issues in the digital marketspace.[24]

When and Where Consumers Shop and Buy Online

Shopping and buying also happen at different times in marketspace than in the traditional marketplace.[25] About 80 percent of online retail sales occur Monday through Friday. The busiest shopping day is Wednesday. By comparison, 35 percent of retail store sales are registered on the weekend. Saturday is the most popular shopping day. Monday through Friday online shopping and buying often occur during normal work hours—some 30 percent of online consumers say they visit websites from their place of work, which partially accounts for the sales level during the workweek.

Favorite websites for workday shopping and buying include those featuring event tickets, auctions, online periodical subscriptions, flowers and gifts, consumer electronics, and travel. Websites offering health and beauty items, apparel and accessories, and music and video tend to be browsed and bought from a consumer's residence.

Making Responsible Decisions

Ethics

Who Is Responsible for Internet Privacy and Security?

Privacy and security are two key reasons consumers are leery of online shopping and buying. A recent Pew Internet & American Life Project poll reported that 76 percent of online consumers have privacy and security concerns about the Internet. And, 73 percent of online consumers consider it an invasion of privacy if a search engine tracks their activity to personalize future search results. Even more telling, many have stopped shopping a website or forgone an online purchase because of these concerns. Industry analysts estimate that over $30 million in e-commerce sales are lost annually because of privacy and security concerns among online shoppers.

Consumer concerns are not without merit. According to the Federal Trade Commission, 46 percent of fraud complaints are Internet-related, costing consumers $560 million. In addition, consumers lose millions of dollars each year due to identity theft resulting from breaches in company security systems.

A percolating issue is whether the U.S. government should pass more stringent Internet privacy and security laws. About 70 percent of online consumers favor such action. Companies, however, favor self-regulation. For example, TRUSTe (www.truste.com) awards its trademark to company websites that comply with standards of privacy protection and disclosure. Still, consumers are ultimately

©Brain light/Alamy Stock Photo

responsible for using care and caution when engaging in online behavior, including e-commerce. Consumers have a choice of whether or not to divulge personal information and are responsible for monitoring how their information is being used.

What role should the U.S. government, company self-regulation, and consumer vigilance play in dealing with privacy and security issues in the digital marketspace?

How Consumers Shop and Buy Online

social commerce
The use of social networks for browsing and buying.

subscription commerce
The payment of a fee to have products and services delivered on a recurring schedule.

How online consumers shop and buy has evolved with changing technology. The majority of online consumers prefer using their laptop and desktop computers (60 percent). Six percent prefer their tablet computer. Five percent prefer their smartphones for shopping and buying. And 29 percent of online consumers have no particular preference and use multiple devices for shopping and buying.[26]

With evolving technology, notably the prevalence of smartphones and social media platforms, online shopping and buying has become more social. Today, about 75 percent of online consumers rely on social media for product and service ideas, referrals, and reviews. And an increasing number of these consumers are making purchases on social media without going to a company's website to conduct business. The use of social networks for browsing and buying is called **social commerce**. Facebook, Twitter, and Pinterest have taken the lead in promoting social commerce.

Today, 15 percent of online consumers rely on subscriptions to shop and buy online.[27] **Subscription commerce** involves the payment of a fee to have products and services delivered on a recurring schedule. Amazon Prime and Netflix represent two prominent examples. Convenience, lower prices, and greater personalization have fueled the popularity of subscription commerce.

learning review

14-3. What are the six reasons consumers prefer to shop and buy online?

14-4. What is the eight-second rule?

CROSS-CHANNEL CONSUMERS AND MULTICHANNEL MARKETING

LO 14-4 Define cross-channel consumers and the role of multichannel marketing in reaching these consumers.

Consumers often shop and buy in both online and offline environments. Individuals who move effortlessly between these environments have given rise to the cross-channel consumer and the importance of multichannel marketing.

Who Is the Cross-Channel Consumer?

Cross-channel consumers are online consumers who shop online but buy offline, or shop offline but buy online. They differ from exclusive online consumers and exclusive offline consumers (see Figure 14–4). These distinctions will vary by the products or services shopped and bought.[28] For example, e-books are shopped and purchased by exclusive online consumers. Expensive, custom-made furniture and home furnishings are typically shopped and purchased by an exclusive offline consumer.

cross-channel consumer
An online consumer who shops online but buys offline, or shops offline but buys online.

Showrooming Cross-channel consumers who shop offline but buy online engage in **showrooming**—the practice of examining products in a store and then buying them online for a cheaper price. While obtaining a lower price is a primary motivation for showrooming, showroomers often gather additional product information, look for online promotions or deals, and check product reviews and ratings on social media. About three-fourths of online consumers have engaged in showrooming for one or more products. Consumer electronics and home appliances are the most popular showrooming product categories.

showrooming
The practice of examining products in a store and then buying them online for a cheaper price.

Webrooming Cross-channel consumers who shop online but buy offline engage in **webrooming**—the practice of examining products online and then buying them in a store. While lower price is again a significant motivator for webrooming, webroomers cite other factors as well: avoiding shipping costs, gaining immediate possession of a product, and allowing for easier returns. About 80 percent of online consumers have engaged in webrooming for one or more products. Automobiles and auto parts, apparel (including shoes), and home office equipment are popular webrooming product categories.

webrooming
The practice of examining products online and then buying them in a store.

Recent research indicates that 6 in 10 webroomers have showroomed while 9 in 10 showroomers have webroomed. Cross-channel consumers overall account for a significant amount of online activity and sales. Retail sales from cross-channel consumers is estimated to be about five times greater than from online-only retail sales.

Implementing Multichannel Marketing

The prominence of cross-channel consumers has focused increased attention on multichannel marketing. Recall from Chapter 12 that *multichannel marketing* is the blending

FIGURE 14–4
Cross-channel consumers engage in "showrooming" and "webrooming" depending on how they shop and buy online and offline.

of different communication and delivery channels that are mutually reinforcing in attracting, retaining, and building relationships with consumers who shop and buy in the traditional marketplace and the digital marketspace—the cross-channel consumer.

Efforts to implement multichannel marketing involve three steps. First, it is necessary to document cross-channel consumer behavior. Second, marketers should employ communication and delivery channels that are mutually reinforcing in attracting, retaining, and building relationships with their current and potential consumers. Finally, companies should monitor and measure multichannel marketing performance.

Document the Cross-Channel Consumer Journey Marketers have found that the identification of consumer journey maps and consumer touchpoints are invaluable for multichannel marketing to succeed. As described in Chapter 4, consumer journey maps and consumer touchpoints detail the time and place consumers and companies (brands) engage to exchange information, provide service, or handle buying transactions.

Figure 14–5 sketches a generic multichannel marketing consumer journey map. Three insights can be gained from such a map. First, the map identifies the communication and delivery channels engaged by cross-channel consumers. Second, the map shows the links between communication and delivery channels across the prepurchase, purchase, and postpurchase phases of the consumer purchase decision process. Finally, the map highlights consumer touchpoints that are outside the control of the company, such as comparison websites and social media. These touchpoints can form or change a cross-channel consumer's impression about a particular product, service, brand, or company.

Employ Channels That Are Mutually Reinforcing in Attracting, Retaining, and Building Relationships with Consumers There is no one best approach to multichannel marketing. The configuration of communication and delivery channels employed depends on the channels used by current and potential consumers

FIGURE 14–5
Illustrative Cross-Channel Consumer Journey Map

of a company's products, brands, and services and their information-gathering and purchase preferences. It also depends on how different channels mutually reinforce one another in attracting, retaining, and building relationships with consumers. This is done by conveying a consistent customer experience through consumer touchpoints and messages across channels.

For example, as described earlier in this chapter, many companies that originally built their businesses online now operate retail stores and showrooms. They are now multichannel marketers. Similarly, the Clinique Division of Esteé Lauder Companies, which built its business in traditional department stores, reports that 80 percent of current customers who visit its website (www.clinique.com) later purchase a Clinique product at a department store. Equally important, 37 percent of non-Clinique consumers make a Clinique purchase after visiting the company's website.[29]

Monitor and Measure Multichannel Marketing Performance The third step in implementing multichannel marketing is monitoring and measuring performance. This step has proven difficult for marketers for two reasons. First, the magnitude of data corresponding to which channel(s) each consumer accesses during each stage in the purchase decision process has made data difficult to assemble and integrate. Second, the task of assigning the proportional credit to each channel and consumer touchpoint across all online and offline channels for a desired consumer action is extremely complex.

Nevertheless, progress has been made in monitoring and measuring performance.[30] For example, companies routinely track their website visitors who buy in retail stores or in catalogs. Google, which monitors online shopping behavior across the Web, now applies statistical methods to measure the extent to which online advertising leads to store purchases for individual companies. Still, a comprehensive approach to monitor and measure a company's multichannel marketing performance across channels and consumer touchpoints remains elusive.

Despite the challenges, the popularity of multichannel marketing is apparent in its growing impact on online retail sales.[31] Fully 70 percent of U.S. online retail sales are made by companies that practice multichannel marketing.

learning review

14-5. A cross-channel consumer is _____.

14-6. Efforts to implement multichannel marketing involve what three steps?

LEARNING OBJECTIVES REVIEW

LO 14-1 *Describe what interactive marketing is and how it creates customer value, customer relationships, and customer experiences.*

Interactive marketing involves two-way buyer–seller electronic communication in a computer-mediated environment in which the buyer controls the kind and amount of information received from the seller. It creates customer value by providing time, place, form, and possession utility for consumers. Customer relationships are created and sustained through two unique capabilities of Internet technology: interactivity and individuality. From an interactive marketing perspective, customer experience represents the sum total of the interactions that a customer has with a company's website, from the initial look at a home page through the entire purchase decision process. Companies produce a customer experience through seven website design elements: context, content, community, customization, communication, connection, and commerce.

LO 14-2 *Explain why certain types of products and services are particularly suited for interactive marketing.*
Certain product and service classes seem to be particularly suited for interactive marketing. One category consists of items for which product information is an important part of the purchase decision but prepurchase trial is not necessarily critical. A second category contains items that can be digitally delivered. Unique items represent a third category. A fourth category includes items that are regularly purchased and where convenience is very important. A fifth category consists of highly standardized items for which information about price is important.

LO 14-3 *Describe why consumers shop and buy online and how marketers influence online purchasing behavior.*
There are six reasons consumers shop and buy online. They are convenience, choice, customization, communication, cost, and control. Marketers have capitalized on these reasons through a variety of means. For example, they provide choice assistance using choiceboard and collaborative filtering technology, which also provides opportunities for customization. Company-hosted web communities and viral marketing practices capitalize on the communications dimensions of digital technologies. Dynamic pricing provides real-time responses to supply and demand conditions, often resulting in lower prices for consumers. Permission marketing is popular given consumer interest in control.

LO 14-4 *Define cross-channel consumers and the role of multichannel marketing in reaching these consumers.*
A cross-channel consumer is an online consumer who shops online but buys offline (called webrooming), or shops offline but buys online (called showrooming). These cross-channel consumers are reached through multichannel marketing. Multichannel marketing continues to grow in popularity, despite the challenges involved in measuring multichannel marketing performance across channels and touchpoints.

LEARNING REVIEW ANSWERS

14-1 The consumer-initiated practice of generating content on a marketer's website that is custom tailored to an individual's specific needs and preferences is called _____.
Answer: personalization

14-2 What are the seven website design elements that companies use to produce a customer experience?
Answer: From an interactive marketing perspective, customer experience is defined as the sum total of the interactions that a customer has with a company's website, from the initial look at a home page through the entire purchase decision process. Companies produce a customer experience through seven website design elements, which are: (1) context—a website's aesthetic appeal and functional look and feel reflected in site layout and visual design; (2) content—all digital information on a website, including the text, video, audio, and graphics; (3) community—the user-to-user communications hosted by the company to create virtual communities; (4) customization—the ability of a site to modify itself to, or be modified by, each individual user; (5) communication—the dialogue that unfolds between the website and its users; (6) connection—the network of linkages between a company's site and other sites; and (7) commerce—the website's ability to conduct sales transactions for products and services. Most websites do not include every design element. Although every website has context and content, they differ in the use of the remaining five elements.

14-3 What are the six reasons consumers prefer to shop and buy online?
Answer: The six reasons consumers prefer to shop and buy online are: convenience, choice, customization, communication, cost, and control. A reason consumers avoid shopping and buying online is the security threat posed by cookies.

14-4 What is the eight-second rule?
Answer: The eight-second rule is a view that customers will abandon their efforts to enter and navigate a website if download time exceeds eight seconds.

14-5 A cross-channel consumer is _____.
Answer: A cross-channel consumer is an online consumer who shops online but buys offline or who shops offline but buys online.

14-6 Efforts to implement multichannel marketing involve what three steps?
Answer: The three steps are: (1) document cross-channel consumer behavior; (2) employ channels that are mutually reinforcing in attracting, retaining, and building relationships with consumers; and (3) monitor and measure multichannel marketing performance.

FOCUSING ON KEY TERMS

behavioral targeting p. 391
bots p. 388
choiceboard p. 382
collaborative filtering p. 382
cookies p. 391
cross-channel consumer p. 393
customerization p. 388
dynamic pricing p. 390
eight-second rule p. 388
interactive marketing p. 382
online consumers p. 386
permission marketing p. 383
personalization p. 383
showrooming p. 393
social commerce p. 392
spam p. 389
subscription commerce p. 392
viral marketing p. 390
web communities p. 389
webrooming p. 393

APPLYING MARKETING KNOWLEDGE

1. Have you made an online purchase? If so, why do you think so many people who have access to the Internet are not also online buyers? If not, why are you reluctant to do so? Do you think that electronic commerce benefits consumers even if they don't make a purchase?
2. Like the traditional marketplace, the digital marketspace offers marketers opportunities to create time, place, form, and possession utility. How do you think Internet-enabled technology rates in terms of creating these values? Take a shopping trip at a virtual retailer of your choice (don't buy anything unless you really want to). Then compare the time, place, form, and possession utility provided by the virtual retailer to that provided by a traditional retailer in the same product category.
3. Visit Amazon.com (www.amazon.com) or Barnes & Noble (www.barnesandnoble.com). As you tour the website, think about how shopping for books online compares with a trip to your university bookstore to buy books. Specifically, compare and contrast your shopping experiences with respect to convenience, choice, customization, communication, cost, and control.
4. You are planning to buy a new car so you visit www.edmunds.com. Based on your experience visiting that site, do you think you will enjoy more or less control in negotiating with the dealer when you actually purchase your vehicle?
5. Visit the website for your university or college. Based on your visit, would you conclude that the site is a transactional site or a promotional site? Why? How would you rate the site in terms of the six website design elements that affect customer experience?

BUILDING YOUR MARKETING PLAN

Does your marketing plan involve a marketspace presence for your product or service? If the answer is "no," read no further and do not include this element in your plan. If the answer is "yes," then attention must be given to developing a website in your marketing plan. A useful starting point is to:

1. Describe how each website element—context, content, community, customization, communication, connection, and commerce—will be used to create a customer experience.
2. Identify a company's website that best reflects your website conceptualization.

VIDEO CASE 14   Pizza Hut and imc²: Becoming a Multichannel Marketer

It's no surprise that Pizza Hut is the world's largest pizza chain, with more than 10,000 restaurants in 100 countries. But did you know that Pizza Hut has become one of the top U.S. Internet retailers?

According to Brian Niccol, Pizza Hut's chief marketing officer (CMO), "We've done what many would say is impossible. We successfully built an online business in three years that produces hundreds of millions of dollars in annual revenue. Today, Pizza Hut is a category leader in the interactive and emerging marketplace." So how did the company do it? Pizza Hut simply revolutionized the quick serve restaurant (QSR) world through a multichannel marketing approach that created a customer experience and a customer engagement platform that was second to none.

Source: Pizza Hut, Inc.

THE RETAIL PIZZA BUSINESS

With three national competitors dominating the marketplace, the pizza business is very competitive. Even customers who could be considered heavy users of a particular brand regularly purchase from competitors on the basis of timing, pricing, and convenience.

In general, Pizza Hut's most frequent customers (and likely those of the other two major competitors)

video 14-3
Pizza Hut
Video Case
kerin.tv/cr8e/v14-3

can be divided into two categories: (1) families, primarily time-starved mothers, looking for a quick and simple mealtime solution; and (2) young adult males who fuel their active lifestyle with one of the world's most versatile and convenient foods (no cooking, no utensils, no cleanup, and leftovers are perfect for breakfast). While these two groups could not be more dissimilar on the surface, value and convenience are important for both groups. Cost-conscious mothers look for a good quality product and a hassle-free eating experience. Deal-seeking young adult males seek more of the food they love with less time and cash invested in the process.

The importance of the take-home and delivery segment of the U.S. pizza market is illustrated by the fact that Pizza Hut's principal national competitors focus exclusively on this aspect of the business. Most take-home and delivery sales are ordered before a customer enters the restaurant. In addition, a growing number of retail pizza customers had become comfortable ordering pizza online. Pizza ordering, as it turned out, was an ideal product for the digital world. People understood the basic menu, generally knew that they could customize their order in a variety of ways, and were accustomed to not being in the store when ordering. Brand retail presence and established customer delivery networks also made the shift to online ordering easier for national pizza chains than other national quick serve restaurants. But, as Pizza Hut understood, there is still an incredible level of complexity in making something truly sophisticated simple and easy for the customer.

CREATING A PLAN OF ACTION

For the most part, the intent of online ordering for the pizza business was to make transactions with the customer easier and cheaper for the brand. Pizza Hut recognized the opportunity to engage people with its brand and with other people directly and do something special—namely, build sustainable relationships with its customers and enable Pizza Hut to engage people in a more meaningful and profitable way. In short, Pizza Hut set about to reinvent the retail pizza business by breaking away from a transactional platform to an efficient and powerful customer engagement platform by reaching out to customers' kitchens and couches to offer a better mealtime ordering, delivery, and dining experience.

Pizza Hut selected imc^2 as one of its lead agencies to plan a comprehensive interactive strategy that focused first on the redesign of the Pizza Hut corporate website (including redefining the customer experience online and across all of the brand's touchpoints) and then on a series of progressively sophisticated and industry-leading customer engagement strategies. imc^2 brought 15 years of experience in interactive marketing and brand engagement to the assignment.

PIZZAHUT.COM, CUSTOMER EXPERIENCE, AND BRAND ENGAGEMENT

Pizza Hut and imc^2 executives agreed that the strategy for reinventing the retail pizza business would involve

Source: Pizza Hut, Inc.

developing opportunities for customers to engage with the brand by using the right technologies to enable and encourage interaction. A new website was necessary to better address all major design elements. How Pizza Hut and imc^2 executed these design elements not only created value for its customers but also served as a basis for differentiation in the retail pizza business. Let's look at these design elements and PizzaHut.com's performance.

The Pizza Hut website was completely redesigned to support nationwide online ordering (including all franchise locations for the first time) and is updated frequently to keep up with the company's fast-paced marketing strategy and ambitious product innovation rollout schedule. Since promotions are an important expectation in pizza purchasing and speak to the brand's consumers in a language that clearly connects with their desire for value, the website *context* and *content* balance the ability to shop for a deal with quick and easy ordering access for people who arrive at PizzaHut.com ready to purchase. The site presents a number of Pizza Hut's current offers in the central viewing window as well as through the rolling navigation directly underneath the main content. Primary navigation for information, such as the menu, locations, and nutrition facts, are displayed horizontally across the top of the rotating content.

Website *customization* is achieved in several ways, but the primary utility is to simplify ordering. For customers who have already registered, there are several personalization options, including rapid ordering called *Express Checkout*—a feature that's based on saved preferences similar to a "playlist." For example, if you have a group of friends that likes to watch movies together, you might create an order named *Movie Night* that has your group's favorite pizzas. Using the *Express Checkout* option accessible directly on the home page, you can select *Movie Night,* quickly review the order, click the "submit" button, and the pizzas are on their way, relying on saved delivery and payment options through a stored *cookie* (a piece of digital code that is used to identify previous visitors) to speed the transaction. With this type of functionality, you can think of convenience as an investment that creates loyalty and somewhat insulates the brand against switching down the line when customers would have to register with and learn a competitor's system, and where access to their favorite features might not be available.

Website *content* and *communications* are integrated with the company's overall communications programs—including traditional media—with product innovations, promotions, and special events shared across platforms. True to the brand, communications are fun and energetic, matching bold images and vibrant color with a smart, clever, and lighthearted voice. One noteworthy example includes an April Fools' Day rebranding of the company as "Pasta Hut" to coincide with the launch of the brand's innovative line of Tuscani Pastas. This campaign included online support in the form of display media (banner ads) and the temporary rebranding of PizzaHut.com as PastaHut.com with special imagery and copy supporting the name change. Not only did the brand get plenty of coverage in the press, but it deepened the connection with customers by showing a willingness to be spontaneous and fun, inviting people to play along with the joke.

Pizza Hut's integrated marketing communications approach enables the company to easily test and incorporate other items and brands under the larger corporate umbrella, such as the WingStreet operation and the pasta extension. This demonstrates the brand's ability to stretch the QSR concept way beyond its pizza roots and suggests the kind of direction the company may pursue in the future.

PizzaHut.com and the brand's other online assets are all about getting the world's favorite pizza and signature products into the hands and stomachs of customers. Since *commerce* is a huge consideration on the site, there are multiple pathways for ordering, including several onsite methods, a Facebook app (the first national pizza chain to produce an ordering application for the world's leading social networking site), a branded desktop widget, mobile ordering (also known as Total Mobile Access, which includes both a WAP [wireless application protocol] site and text ordering), and a sophisticated and simple iPhone app that lets customers build and submit their order visually. Additional revenue streams can also be quickly built online, as demonstrated by the eGift Card program conceived and implemented by imc^2.

Realizing that it did not make sense for the company or its customers to create a *community* on the site, Pizza Hut tapped into Facebook to achieve results in a very cost-effective manner. With approximately 1 million fans and the first of its kind Facebook ordering application, the brand can efficiently engage a huge group of people in a very natural way without disrupting their daily routine. Again, the brand understands that if you make something convenient, you can increase trust while securing greater transactional loyalty. Pizza Hut's program to identify a summer

Source: Pizza Hut, Inc.

intern, or *Twintern,* responsible for monitoring and encouraging dialogue on Twitter and other social media networks is another example of how the brand is building on existing platforms and making effective use of the massive social marketing infrastructure.

PizzaHut.com connects mobile, desktop, social networks, and other digital gateways to complement traditional media and its retail presence. So when Pizza Hut thinks about the *connection* design element, it includes more than just linking to other websites online. Rather, it provides a comprehensive approach to creating a seamless customer experience wherever and whenever people want to engage with the brand.

PERFORMANCE MEASUREMENT AND OUTCOMES

Pizza Hut diligently measures the performance of PizzaHut.com. The company created a customized marketing dashboard that allows the Pizza Hut management team to monitor various aspects of the brand's marketing program and provides an almost constant stream of fresh information that it can use to optimize engagement with people or tweak various aspects of performance.

The results have been remarkable, but understand that due to the highly competitive nature of the industry, they are fluid and represent only a moment in time. Consider, for example:

1. PizzaHut.com dominates the pizza category with number one rankings in website traffic and search volume. According to comScore, a global leader in digital analytics and measurement, the Pizza Hut site achieves the most traffic per online dollars spent in the pizza category.
2. PizzaHut.com has become one of the top Internet retailers in the United States.
3. Pizza Hut's iPhone app had more than 100,000 downloads in the first two weeks after release.

WHAT'S NEXT

So what's next for PizzaHut.com? While the brand has made huge gains in a very short time period, staying on top in the rapidly evolving digital marketplace requires constant attention. Pizza Hut envisions that its online business will surpass the $1 billion mark and that digital transactions will lead all revenue within a decade.

While understandably protective of the company's future strategy, Pizza Hut CMO Niccol has ambitious goals and he's not joking when he deadpans, "I want Pizza Hut to become the Amazon of food service and be pioneers for the digital space. I do not want us to be a brick-and-mortar company that just dabbles in the space." The transition to something along the lines of the Amazon model suggests that the brand might further evolve its identity as a pizza business and stretch or completely redefine the QSR model.

Most brands that want to grow in the evolving economy will have to think and plan long term and be able to act swiftly as marketplace conditions change. imc^2 Chief Marketing Officer Ian Wolfman, when assessing the future of marketing, sums up the opportunity neatly: "Our agency believes that marketing's current transformation will result in a complete reorientation of how brands and companies engage with their consumers and other stakeholders. Brands that thrive will be those, like Pizza Hut, that can efficiently build sustainable relationships with people—relationships that have both high trust and high transactions" (see Figure 1). He goes on to explain that "brands taking a longer view have an unexpected advantage over traditional models that often focus too tightly on hitting near-term quarterly targets." Referring to research his agency has done on the subject, Wolfman points out that the most successful brands in the future will likely be those that resonate with people on a deeply emotional level and operate with a clearly defined sense of purpose.

Pizza Hut, with its focus on digitally enabled customer convenience and category innovation, is ideally positioned to connect with people on a level that builds trust and increases transactions. Referring to the initial time investment, however modest, that

FIGURE 1

customers have to make in registering with the system and enabling various devices, Niccol sees the landscape as very promising for brands that put their customers' interests and preferences first. "If we do our job right—creating authentic engagement and making it convenient and valuable for people to interact with the brand—the numbers follow."[32]

Questions

1 What kind of website is PizzaHut.com?
2 How does PizzaHut.com incorporate the seven website design elements?
3 How are choiceboard and personalization systems used in the PizzaHut.com website?

Chapter Notes

1. Interview with John Lewis, account executive and marketing manager at Seven Cycles, Inc.; *www.sevencycles.com,* April 20, 2018; "Seven Cycles Celebrates 20th Anniversary," *bicycleretailer.com,* February 2, 2017; and "Made in Massachusetts: Seven Cycles," www.wcvb.com/article/made-in-massachusetts-seven-cycles, January 12, 2016.
2. "U.S. Online Retail Forecast: 2017–2022," *www.forrester.com,* March 22, 2018.
3. "Transaction Denied," *Bloomberg Businessweek,* July 13, 2014, p. 90.
4. "For Many Retailers, the Lure of Cross-Border Ecommerce Is Profit," emarketer.com, March 25, 2018.
5. Rupal Parekh, "Personalized Products Please but Can They Create Profit?" *Advertising Age,* May, 21, 2013, p. 4.
6. Rafi A. Mohammed, Robert J. Fisher, Bernard J. Jaworski, and Gordon J. Paddison, *Internet Marketing: Building Advantage in a Networked Economy,* 2nd ed. (Burr Ridge, IL: McGraw-Hill/Irwin, 2004).
7. "Models Will Run the World," *The Wall Street Journal,* August 20, 2018, p. A17; and "Recommended Just for You: The Power of Personalization," *www.forbes.com,* May 13, 2017.
8. "Consumers Don't Want Personalization to Get Too Personal," emarketer.com, April 14, 2018.
9. "Consumers Love Personalized Offers, but Only If They Opt In," emarketer.com, May 16, 2018; Manfred Kraft, Christine M. Arden, and Peter Verhoef, "Permission Marketing and Privacy Concerns: Why Do Customers (Not) Grant Permissions?" *Journal of Interactive Marketing* 39 (2017), pp. 39–54; and "Is This Really Opting-in?" *Advertising Age,* October 3, 2016, pp. 4ff.
10. Kelly D. Martin and Patrick E. Murphy, "The Role of Data Privacy in Marketing," *Journal of the Academy of Marketing Science,* March 2017, pp. 135–55.
11. This discussion is drawn from Jeffrey F. Rayport and Bernard J. Jaworski, *e-Commerce,* 2nd ed. (Burr Ridge, IL: McGraw-Hill/Irwin, 2004); and *The Essential Guide to Best Practices in eCommerce* (Portland, OR: Webtrends, Inc., 2006).
12. Larry Freed, *Innovating Analytics* (Hoboken, NJ: Wiley, 2013).
13. This example and its data are provided courtesy of The Sewell Automotive Companies.
14. *The Truth about Online Consumers: 2017 Global Online Consumer Report,* KPMG White Paper, January 2017.
15. "U.S. E-commerce Performance StatPack," *www.emarketer.com,* January 30, 2018.
16. Jerry Wind and Arvind Ranaswamy, "Customerization: The Next Wave in Mass Customization," *Journal of Interactive Marketing,* Winter 2001, pp. 13–32.
17. Valerie Bauerkin, "Gatorade's Mission: Sell More Drinks," *The Wall Street Journal,* September 14, 2010, p. B6; and Tom Hayes and Michael S. Malone, "Marketing in the World of the Web," *The Wall Street Journal,* November 29–30, 2008, p. A13. Also see Kate Fitzgerald, "Blogs Fascinate, Frighten Marketers Eager to Tap Loyalists," *Advertising Age,* March 5, 2007, p. S–4.
18. "Global Spam Volume as a Percentage of Total E-mail Traffic," www.statista.com, April 2018.
19. Quoted in Judy Strauss, Adel El-Ansary, and Raymond Frost, *E-Marketing,* 5th ed. (Upper Saddle River, NJ: Prentice Hall, 2009), p. 357.
20. Victoria Taylor, "The Best-Ever Social Media Campaigns," *www.forbes.com,* August 17, 2017.
21. "Showrooming Hits Luxury Fashion," *The Wall Street Journal,* April 10, 2014, pp. B1, B2.
22. "Say Goodbye to the Car Salesman," *The Wall Street Journal,* November 21, 2013, pp. B1, B2; and "Death of a Car Salesman," *The Economist,* August 22, 2015, pp. 52–53.
23. "Cookies Cause Bitter Backlash," *The Wall Street Journal,* September 20, 2010, pp. B1, B2.
24. "Be Afraid, Be Very Afraid," *Advertising Age,* January 8, 2018, pp. 17–19; "How Dirty Is Your Data?" *www.forresterresearch.com,* May 3, 2016; "Terms and Conditions," *Marketing News,* November 2014, pp. 35–41; "Consumers Want Consent in Data Mining of Personal Info," *Dallas Morning News,* June 5, 2015, pp. D1, D6; and "2017 Internet Crime Report," *www.ic3.gov.*
25. "Online Shopping Part of the Office Routine," *Dallas Morning News,* December 13, 2015, p. 2D; and Kathleen Kim, "More Employers Letting Employees Shop Online at Work," *www.inc.com,* November 14, 2012.
26. "How Consumers across the Globe Use Multiple Devices to Shop and Buy," *www.emarketer.com,* July 20, 2016.
27. "The Subscription Addiction," *The Economist,* April 7, 2018, p. 58.
28. This discussion is based on the following sources: Sonja Gensler, Scott Neslin, and Peter Verhoef, "The Showrooming Phenomenon: It's More Than Just about Price," *Journal of Interactive Marketing,* May 2017, 29–43; "Survey Shows Boost in Web Shopping," *The Wall Street Journal,* June 8, 2016, p. B5; and "Webrooming and Showrooming in 2015," *multichannelmerchant.com,* January 19, 2015.
29. "The Global House of Prestige Beauty," *The Estee Lauder Companies 2016 Annual Report,* March 2017.
30. "How to Make Multichannel Marketing Work," *www.emarketer.com,* June 10, 2016; and "Now Google Can Tell If Its Ads Send Us to Stores," *Dallas Morning News,* May 24, 2017.
31. "Clicks to Bricks," *DMNews,* March, 2017, pp. 26–30.
32. Source: Pizza Hut: This case was prepared by Pizza Hut and imc[2] and Roger A. Kerin for exclusive use in this text.

15

LEARNING OBJECTIVES

After reading this chapter you should be able to:

LO 15-1 Discuss integrated marketing communications and the communication process.

LO 15-2 Describe the promotional mix and the uniqueness of each component.

LO 15-3 Select the promotional approach appropriate to a product's target audience, life-cycle stage, and channel strategies.

LO 15-4 Describe the elements of the promotion decision process.

LO 15-5 Explain the value of direct marketing for consumers and sellers.

Integrated Marketing Communications and Direct Marketing

Sometimes Taco Bell Leads to Wedding Bells!

Taco Bell's customers are independent, a little cult-like, and definitely interested in a "cool" factor. So when Taco Bell's chief marketing officer, Marisa Thalberg, heard that some customers were adding Taco Bell to their wedding festivities, she added more excitement to the mix by creating the Love & Tacos Contest!

The contest asked entrants to submit a photo or video on Instagram or Twitter telling their Taco Bell love story and using the hashtag "#loveandtacoscontest." Consumers voted online to select the top 10 entries, and then Taco Bell judges selected the winning couple to receive an all-expenses-paid trip to get married at Taco Bell's new restaurant in Las Vegas. There was also a Happily Ever After sweepstakes where people could enter to be a guest at the winning couple's wedding. Other marketing activities related to the "love" theme include a partnership with pop-up wedding and elopement provider Flora Pop and a new menu item—a $600 wedding package. The package, available to all Las Vegas store customers, contains a Taco Bell garter and bow tie, a taco sauce packet wedding bouquet, just-married T-shirts, champagne flutes, and a Cinnabon Delights wedding cake.

Taco Bell also uses many other forms of promotion to keep its customers engaged and to communicate its value price positioning. Television, radio, outdoor, and cinema ads are common, as well as news releases and public relations support. You might remember it introduced the Quesalupa with its "Bigger Than Everything" television ad on the Super Bowl. Taco Bell also recently modified some of its advertising to emphasize that it uses only antibiotic-free chicken and cage-free eggs—attributes that are important to its millennial audience. Special promotions include collaborations with Sony to give Taco Bell diners the chance to win PlayStation VR headsets, controllers, and a game gift card; with the NBA to give away free tacos to all store visitors when an away team "steals" a game in the league finals; and with Airbnb to offer a free night in a Taco Bell converted into a living space to promote its Steak DoubleDilla. Taco Bell even revised its 20-year-old logo to a simpler version that it thinks will connect better with young diners.

Of course social media play an important role in Taco Bell campaigns also. Taco Tales, for example, are a series of videos posted on Taco Bell's YouTube

Source: Taco Bell IP Holder, LLC.

channel about the things fans have done to eat at a Taco Bell. Episode 2, titled *Race Thru*, has more than 1.5 million views! Similarly, The Taco Bell Clip Show posts content ranging from Taco Bell wedding proposals to sauce packet trick shots to drive-thru pranks. Taco Bell's Facebook page and Twitter account have 9.8 million and 1.8 million followers, respectively.[1]

Taco Bell's successful marketing campaigns demonstrate the opportunity for engaging potential customers and the importance of integrating the various elements

promotional mix
The combination of one or more communication tools used to: (1) inform prospective buyers about the benefits of the product, (2) persuade them to try it, and (3) remind them later about the benefits they enjoyed by using the product.

integrated marketing communications (IMC)
The concept of designing marketing communications programs that coordinate all promotional activities—advertising, personal selling, sales promotion, public relations, and direct marketing—to provide a consistent message across all audiences.

communication
The process of conveying a message to others that requires six elements: a source, a message, a channel of communication, a receiver, and the processes of encoding and decoding.

of a marketing communication program. Promotion represents the fourth element in the marketing mix. The promotional element consists of five communication tools, including advertising, personal selling, sales promotion, public relations, and direct marketing. The combination of one or more of these communication tools is called the **promotional mix**. All of these tools can be used to (1) inform prospective buyers about the benefits of the product, (2) persuade them to try it, and (3) remind them later about the benefits they enjoyed by using the product. In the past, marketers often viewed these communication tools as separate and independent. The advertising department, for example, often designed and managed its activities without consulting departments or agencies that had responsibility for sales promotion or public relations. The result was often an overall communication effort that was uncoordinated and, in some cases, inconsistent. Today, the concept of designing marketing communications programs that coordinate all promotional activities—advertising, personal selling, sales promotion, public relations, and direct marketing—to provide a consistent message across all audiences is referred to as **integrated marketing communications (IMC)**. This coordination is increasingly important as new media options, interactions between traditional and contemporary media, and shifting consumer communication patterns all make optimal communication more challenging. In addition, by taking the consumer journey and consumer expectations into consideration, IMC is a key element in a company's customer experience management strategy.[2]

This chapter provides an overview of the communication process, a description of the promotional mix elements, several tools for integrating the promotional mix, and a process for developing a comprehensive promotion program. One of the promotional mix elements, direct marketing, is also discussed in this chapter. Chapter 16 covers advertising, sales promotion, and public relations; Chapter 17 covers social media; and Chapter 18 discusses personal selling.

THE COMMUNICATION PROCESS

LO 15-1 Discuss integrated marketing communications and the communication process.

Communication is the process of conveying a message to others, and it requires six elements: a source, a message, a channel of communication, a receiver, and the processes of encoding and decoding[3] (see Figure 15–1). The *source* may be a company or person who has information to convey. The information sent by a source, such as a description of a new smartphone, forms the *message*. The message is conveyed by

FIGURE 15–1
The communication process consists of six key elements. See the text to learn about factors that influence the effectiveness of the process.

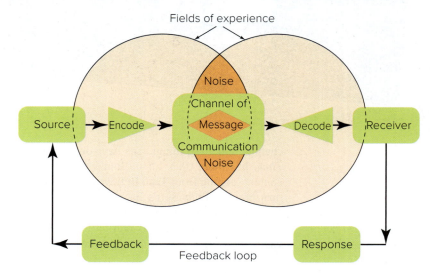

How would you decode this ad? What message is The North Face trying to send?
Source: The North Face

The North Face
www.thenorthface.com

Video 15-1
The North Face
kerin.tv/cr8e/v15-1

means of a *channel of communication* such as a salesperson, advertising media, or public relations tools. Consumers who read, hear, or see the message are the *receivers*.

Encoding and Decoding Messages

Encoding and decoding are essential to communication. *Encoding* is the process of having the sender transform an idea into a set of symbols. *Decoding* is the reverse, or the process of having the receiver take a set of symbols, the message, and transform the symbols into an idea. Look at the North Face advertisement: Who is the source, and what is the message?

Decoding is performed by the receivers according to their own frame of reference: their attitudes, values, and beliefs.[4] The North Face is the source and the advertisement is the message, which appeared in *Wired* magazine (the channel). How would you interpret (decode) this advertisement? The picture and text in the advertisement show that the source's intention is to generate interest in its product with the headline "Never Stop Exploring"—a statement the source believes will appeal to the readers of the magazine.

The process of communication is not always a successful one. Errors in communication can happen in several ways. The source may not adequately transform the abstract idea into an effective set of symbols, a properly encoded message may be sent through the wrong channel and never make it to the intended receiver, the receiver may not properly transform the set of symbols into the correct abstract idea, or finally, feedback may be so delayed or distorted that it is of no use to the sender. Although communication appears easy to perform, truly effective communication can be very difficult.

For the message to be communicated effectively, the sender and receiver must have a mutually shared *field of experience*—a similar understanding and knowledge they apply to the message. Figure 15–1 shows two circles representing the fields of experience of the sender and receiver, which overlap in the message. Some of the better-known message problems have occurred when U.S. companies have taken their messages to cultures with different fields of experience. Many misinterpretations are merely the result of bad translations. For example, KFC made a mistake when its "finger-lickin' good" slogan was translated into Mandarin Chinese as "eat your fingers off"![5]

Feedback

Figure 15–1 shows a line labeled *feedback loop,* which consists of a response and feedback. A *response* is the impact the message had on the receiver's knowledge, attitudes, or behaviors. *Feedback* is the sender's interpretation of the response and indicates whether the message was decoded and understood as intended. Chapter 16 reviews approaches called *pretesting,* which ensure that messages are decoded properly.

Noise

Noise includes extraneous factors that can work against effective communication by distorting a message or the feedback received (Figure 15–1). Noise can be a simple error, such as a printing mistake that affects the meaning of a newspaper advertisement or the use of words or pictures that fail to communicate the message clearly. Noise can also occur when a salesperson's message is misunderstood by a prospective buyer, such as when a salesperson's accent, use of slang terms, or communication style make hearing and understanding the message difficult.

learning review

15-1. What six elements are required for communication to occur?

15-2. A difficulty for U.S. companies advertising in international markets is that the audience does not share the same _____.

15-3. A misprint in a newspaper ad is an example of _____.

THE PROMOTIONAL ELEMENTS

Describe the promotional mix and the uniqueness of each component.

To communicate with consumers, a company can use one or more of five promotional alternatives: advertising, personal selling, public relations, sales promotion, and direct marketing. Figure 15–2 summarizes the distinctions among these five elements. Three of these elements—advertising, sales promotion, and public relations—are often said to use *mass selling* because they are used with groups of prospective buyers. In contrast, personal selling uses *customized interaction* between a seller and a prospective buyer. Personal selling activities include face-to-face, telephone, and interactive electronic communication. Direct marketing also uses messages customized for specific customers. Digital and social media influence each of these promotional elements and are covered in detail in Chapter 17.

Magazines are a mass media outlet for advertising.
©Elnur Amikishiyev/Alamy Stock Photo

Advertising

Advertising is any paid form of nonpersonal communication about an organization, product, service, or idea by an identified sponsor. The *paid* aspect of this definition is important because the space for the advertising message normally must be bought. A full-page, four-color ad in *Time* magazine, for example, costs $254,200. An occasional exception is the public service announcement, where the advertising time or space is donated. The *nonpersonal* component of advertising is also important. Advertising involves mass media (such as TV, radio, and magazines), which are nonpersonal and do not have an immediate feedback loop as does personal selling. So before the message is sent, marketing research plays a valuable role; for example, it determines that the target market will actually see the medium chosen and that the message will be understood.

There are several advantages to a firm using advertising in its promotional mix. It can be attention-getting—as with the Sony PS4 ad shown later in this section—and also communicate specific product benefits to prospective buyers. By paying for the advertising space, a company can control *what* it wants to say and, to some extent, to *whom* the message is sent. Advertising also allows the

FIGURE 15–2
Each of the five elements of the promotional mix has strengths and weaknesses.

advertising
Any paid form of nonpersonal communication about an organization, product, service, or idea by an identified sponsor.

personal selling
The two-way flow of communication between a buyer and seller, often in a face-to-face encounter, designed to influence the purchase decision of a person or group.

company to decide *when* to send its message (which includes how often). The nonpersonal aspect of advertising also has its advantages. Once the message is created, the same message is sent to all receivers in a market segment. If the pictorial, text, and brand elements of an advertisement are properly pretested, an advertiser can ensure the ad's ability to capture consumers' attention and trust that the same message will be decoded by all receivers in the market segment.[6]

Advertising has some disadvantages. As shown in Figure 15–2 and discussed in depth in Chapter 16, the costs to produce and place a message are significant, and the lack of direct feedback makes it difficult to know how well the message was received.

Personal Selling

The second major promotional alternative is **personal selling**, which is the two-way flow of communication between a buyer and seller designed to influence the purchase decision of a person or group. Unlike advertising, personal selling is usually face-to-face communication between the sender and receiver. Why do companies use personal selling?

There are important advantages to personal selling, as summarized in Figure 15–2. A salesperson can control to *whom* the presentation is made, reducing the amount of *wasted coverage* or communication with consumers who are not in the target audience. The personal component of selling has another advantage in that the seller can see or hear the potential buyer's reaction to the message. If the feedback is unfavorable, the salesperson can modify the message.

public relations
A form of communication management that seeks to influence the feelings, opinions, or beliefs held by customers, prospective customers, stockholders, suppliers, employees, and other publics about a company and its products or services.

Video 15-2
McDonald's
kerin.tv/cr8e/v15-2

publicity
A nonpersonal, indirectly paid presentation of an organization, product, or service.

The flexibility of personal selling can also be a disadvantage. Different salespeople can change the message so that no consistent communication is given to all customers. The high cost of personal selling is probably its major disadvantage. On a cost-per-contact basis, it is generally the most expensive of the five promotional elements.

Public Relations

Public relations is a form of communication management that seeks to influence the feelings, opinions, or beliefs held by customers, prospective customers, stockholders, suppliers, employees, and other publics about a company and its products or services.[7] Many tools, such as special events, lobbying efforts, annual reports, press conferences, social media (including Facebook and Twitter), and image management, may be used by a public relations department, although publicity often plays the most important role.[8] **Publicity** is a nonpersonal, indirectly paid presentation of an organization, product, or service. It can take the form of a news story, editorial, or product announcement. A difference between publicity and both advertising and personal selling is the "indirectly paid" dimension. With publicity a company does not pay for space in a mass medium (such as television or radio) but attempts to get the medium to run a favorable story on the company. In this sense, there is an indirect payment for publicity in that a company must support a public relations staff.

An advantage of publicity is credibility. When you read a favorable story about a company's product (such as a glowing restaurant review), there is a tendency to believe it. Travelers throughout the world have relied on Lonely Planet's guides such as *Italy*. These books describe out-of-the-way, inexpensive restaurants and hotels, giving invaluable publicity to these establishments. Such businesses do not (nor can they) buy a mention in the guide. Publicity is particularly effective when consumers lack prior knowledge of the product or service.[9]

The disadvantage of publicity relates to the lack of the user's control over it. A company can invite media to cover an interesting event such as a store opening or a new-product release, but there is no guarantee that a story will result, that it will be positive, or that the target audience will receive the message. Social media such as Facebook, Twitter, and topic-specific blogs have grown dramatically and allow public discussions of almost any company activity. Many public relations departments now focus on facilitating and responding to online discussions. McDonald's, for example, replies to tweets on its customer service Twitter account, which has more than 3.5 million followers. Generally, publicity is an important element of most promotional campaigns, although the lack of control means that it is rarely the primary element. Research

Which three elements of the promotional mix are represented by the Sony PS4 ad, the Lonely Planet's travel guide to Italy, and M&M's sweepstakes? Read the text to find out.
Sources: (left): Sony Corporation of America; (center): Lonely Planet; (right): Mars, Incorporated

McDonald's facilitates online discussions with Twitter.
Source: McDonald's/Twitter

sales promotion
A short-term inducement of value offered to arouse interest in buying a product or service.

direct marketing
A promotional alternative that uses direct communication with consumers to generate a response in the form of an order, a request for further information, or a visit to a retail outlet.

©MarsBars/E+/Getty Images

Video 15-3
Data & Marketing Association
kerin.tv/cr8e/v15-3

related to the sequence of IMC elements, however, indicates that publicity followed by advertising with the same message increases the positive response to the message.[10]

Sales Promotion

A fourth promotional element is **sales promotion**, a short-term inducement of value offered to arouse interest in buying a product or service. Used in conjunction with advertising or personal selling, sales promotions are offered to intermediaries as well as to ultimate consumers. Coupons, rebates, samples, contests, and sweepstakes, such as the M&M's promotion pictured earlier, are just a few examples of sales promotions discussed later in this chapter.

The advantage of sales promotions is that the short-term nature of these programs (such as a coupon or sweepstakes with an expiration date) often stimulates sales for their duration. Offering value to the consumer in terms of a cents-off coupon or rebate may increase store traffic from consumers who are not store-loyal.[11]

Sales promotions cannot be the sole basis for a campaign because gains are often temporary and sales drop off when the deal ends. Advertising support is needed to convert the customer who tried the product because of a sales promotion into a long-term buyer. If sales promotions are conducted continuously, they lose their effectiveness. Customers begin to delay purchase until a coupon is offered, or they question the product's value. Some aspects of sales promotions also are regulated by the federal government.[12] These issues are reviewed in detail in Chapter 16.

Direct Marketing

Another promotional alternative, **direct marketing**, uses direct communication with consumers to generate a response in the form of an order, a request for further information, or a visit to a retail outlet. The communication can take many forms, including face-to-face selling, direct mail, catalogs, telephone solicitations, direct response advertising (on television and radio and in print), and online marketing.[13] Like personal selling, direct marketing often consists of interactive communication. It also has the advantage of being customized to match the needs of specific target markets. Messages can be developed and adapted quickly to facilitate one-to-one relationships with customers.

While direct marketing has been one of the fastest-growing forms of promotion, it has several disadvantages. First, most forms of direct marketing require a comprehensive and up-to-date database with information about the target market. Developing and maintaining the database can be expensive and time-consuming. In addition, growing concern about privacy has led to a decline in response rates among some customer groups. The importance of data in direct marketing efforts, however, is emphasized by the Data & Marketing Association, which advocates "innovative and responsible use of data-driven marketing." Companies with successful direct marketing programs are sensitive to these issues and often use a combination of direct marketing alternatives together, or direct marketing combined with other promotional tools, to increase value for customers.

learning review

15-4. Explain the difference between advertising and publicity when both appear on television.

15-5. Cost per contact is high with the _____ element of the promotional mix.

15-6. Which promotional element should be offered only on a short-term basis?

INTEGRATED MARKETING COMMUNICATIONS—DEVELOPING THE PROMOTIONAL MIX

Select the promotional approach appropriate to a product's target audience, life-cycle stage, and channel strategies.

A firm's promotional mix is the combination of one or more of the promotional tools it chooses to use. In putting together the promotional mix, a marketer must consider two issues. First, the balance of the elements must be determined. Should advertising be emphasized more than personal selling? Should a promotional rebate be offered? Would public relations activities be effective? Several factors affect such decisions: the target audience for the promotion, the stage of the product's life cycle, the characteristics of the product, the decision stage of the buyer, and even the channel of distribution. Second, because the various promotional elements are often the responsibility of different departments, coordinating a consistent promotional effort is necessary. A promotional planning process designed to ensure integrated marketing communications (IMC) can facilitate this goal.

The Target Audience

Promotional programs are directed to the ultimate consumer, to an intermediary (retailer, wholesaler, or industrial distributor), or to both. Promotional programs directed to buyers of consumer products often use mass media because the number of potential buyers is large. Personal selling is used at the place of purchase, generally the retail store. Direct marketing may be used to encourage first-time or repeat purchases. Combinations of many media alternatives are a necessity for some target audiences today. The Marketing Matters box describes how today's college students can be reached through mobile marketing programs.[14]

Advertising directed to business buyers is used selectively in trade publications such as *Restaurant Business* magazine for buyers of restaurant equipment and supplies. Because business buyers often have specialized needs or technical questions, personal selling is particularly important. The salesperson can provide information and the necessary support after the sale.

Intermediaries are often the focus of promotional efforts. As with business buyers, personal selling is the major promotional ingredient. The salespeople assist intermediaries in making a profit by coordinating promotional campaigns sponsored by the manufacturer and providing marketing advice and expertise. Intermediaries' questions often pertain to the allowed markup, merchandising support, and return policies.

Publications such as Restaurant *Business reach business* buyers.
Source: Winsight, LLC

The Product Life Cycle

All products have a product life cycle (see Chapter 10), and the composition of the promotional mix changes over the four life-cycle stages, as shown in Figure 15–3.

- *Introduction stage.* Providing information to consumers in an effort to increase their level of awareness is the primary promotional objective in the introduction stage of the product life cycle. In general, all the promotional mix elements are used at this time.

Marketing Matters

Technology

Hey Marketers, College Students Are Digital and Mobile!

College students represent an attractive target market for many businesses today for several reasons. First, they are early adopters shaping spending habits that could lead them to become lifelong customers. Second, experts estimate that their annual spending power is $545 billion. Finally, the freshman class of 2025 is expected to be the largest ever, with more than 2.5 million students. The challenge for marketers is that students are tech-savvy, hyper-connected, and demanding. In an effort to reach students with their offerings, marketers are tailoring their activities to match the segment's unique combination of characteristics.

College students consist of "digital natives" who have grown up with technology. They have and use laptop computers, high-definition televisions, game consoles, tablet PCs, and smartphones. In fact, a recent study of university and college students found that 86 percent of new college students own a smartphone. They access Facebook, Twitter, YouTube, and Instagram; they download apps, coupons, and information 24/7; and they communicate with e-mail, text messages, and blogs. For many businesses, these facts suggest that marketing through cell phones, or mobile marketing, will be an essential element in integrated marketing communications campaigns in the future.

Several guidelines help ensure the success of mobile marketing. First, it is important to create a mobile-ready app that is flashy, fun, and has the potential to "go viral." In addition, successful mobile apps should help shoppers make price comparisons and match product characteristics to their needs, preferences, and lifestyles. Communication must be short (140 characters on Twitter!), honest, authentic, and transparent about the purpose and value of the brand. Finally, mobile marketing campaigns should facilitate multitasking. According to one expert, marketers "should picture students looking at text and images while traveling on a bus, rushing to a lecture, or out socializing."

Examples of successful mobile marketing campaigns include MTV's use of a Twitter jockey to provide messages to its viewers, Starbucks's mobile app to make payments easier, and Warner Bros.'s use of Snapchat to reach millennials with short games and video teasers about its new movies.

Watch for other brands that use mobile marketing as part of their campaigns to reach college students in the future.

Source: Warner Bros. Entertainment Inc./Snapchat

FIGURE 15–3

The product life cycle illustrates how promotional objectives and activities change over the four stages.

Stage of product life cycle	Introduction	Growth	Maturity	Decline
Promotional objective	To inform	To persuade	To remind	To phase out
Promotional activity	• Publicity in magazines • Advertising • Salesforce calling on intermediaries • Sales promotion in form of free samples	• Personal selling to intermediaries • Advertising to differentiate a product from competing brands	• Reminder advertising • Sales promotion in form of discounts, coupons, and events • Limited personal selling • Direct-mail reminders	• Little money spent on promotion

push strategy
Directing the promotional mix to channel members to gain their cooperation in ordering and stocking the product.

- *Growth stage.* The primary promotional objective in the growth stage is to persuade the consumer to buy the product. Advertising is used to communicate brand differences, and personal selling is used to solidify the channel of distribution.
- *Maturity stage.* In the maturity stage, the need is to maintain existing buyers. Advertising's role is to remind buyers of the product's existence. Sales promotion, in the form of discounts, coupons, and events, is important in maintaining loyal buyers.
- *Decline stage.* The decline stage in the product life cycle is usually a period of phaseout for the product, and little money is spent on the promotional mix.

Channel Strategies

Chapter 12 discussed the channel flow from a producer to intermediaries to consumers. Achieving control of the channel is often difficult for the manufacturer, and promotional strategies can assist in moving a product through the channel of distribution. This is where a manufacturer has to make an important decision about whether to use a push strategy or a pull strategy—or both—in its channel of distribution.[15]

Push Strategy Figure 15–4A shows how a manufacturer uses a **push strategy**, directing the promotional mix to channel members to gain their cooperation in ordering and stocking the product. In this approach, personal selling and sales promotions play major roles. Salespeople call on wholesalers to encourage orders and provide sales assistance. Sales promotions, such as case discount allowances (e.g., 20 percent off the regular case price), are offered to stimulate demand. By pushing the product through the channel, the goal is to get channel members to push it to their customers.

Why does this ad suggest readers should "Ask your doctor about the pill that starts with f"? For the answer, see the text.
Source: AstraZeneca

Ford Motor Company, for example, provides support and incentives for its 3,238 Ford dealers. Through a multilevel program, Ford provides incentives to reward dealers for meeting sales goals. Dealers receive an incentive when they are near a goal, another when they reach a goal, and an even larger one if they exceed sales projections. Ford also offers some dealers special incentives for maintaining superior facilities or improving customer service. All of these actions are intended to encourage Ford dealers to "push" the Ford products through the channel to consumers.[16]

Pull Strategy In some instances, manufacturers face resistance from channel members who do not want to order a new product or increase inventory levels of an existing

FIGURE 15–4
Push and pull strategies direct the promotional mix to different points in the channel of distribution.

pull strategy
Directing the promotional mix at ultimate consumers to encourage them to ask the retailer for a product.

brand. As shown in Figure 15–4B, a manufacturer may then elect to implement a **pull strategy** by directing its promotional mix at ultimate consumers to encourage them to ask the retailer for a product. Seeing demand from ultimate consumers, retailers order the product from wholesalers and thus the item is pulled through the intermediaries. Pharmaceutical companies, for example, now spend more than $3.8 billion annually on *direct-to-consumer* prescription drug advertising, to complement traditional personal selling and free samples directed only at doctors.[17] The strategy is designed to encourage consumers to ask their doctor for a specific drug by name—pulling it through the channel. Successful campaigns, such as the print ad for farxiga, which says, "Ask your doctor about the pill that starts with f," can have dramatic effects on the sales of a product.

learning review

15-7. Promotional programs can be directed to _____, _____, or both.

15-8. Describe the promotional objective for each stage of the product life cycle.

15-9. Explain the differences between a push strategy and a pull strategy.

DEVELOPING AN INTEGRATED MARKETING COMMUNICATIONS PROGRAM

LO 15-4 Describe the elements of the promotion decision process.

Because media costs are high, promotion decisions must be made carefully, using a systematic approach. Paralleling the planning, implementation, and evaluation steps described in the strategic marketing process (Chapter 2), the promotion decision process is divided into (1) developing, (2) executing, and (3) assessing the promotion program (see Figure 15–5).

Identifying the Target Audience

The first step in developing the promotion program involves identifying the *target audience,* the group of prospective buyers toward which a promotion program will be directed. To the extent that time and money permit, the target audience for the promotion program is the target market for the firm's product, which is identified from primary and secondary sources of marketing information. The more a firm knows about its target audience—including demographics, interests, preferences, media use, and purchase behaviors—the easier it is to develop a promotional program. A firm might use a profile based on gender, age, and income, for example, to place ads during specific TV programs or in particular magazines. Similarly, a firm might use *online*

FIGURE 15–5
The promotion decision process includes planning, implementation, and evaluation.

behavioral targeting—collecting information about your web-browsing behavior to personalize the banner and display ads that you will see as you surf the Web. Behavioral targeting is discussed in more detail in Chapter 14.[18]

Specifying Promotion Objectives

After the target audience has been identified, a decision must be reached on what the promotion should accomplish. Consumers can be said to respond in terms of a customer path, or a **hierarchy of effects**, which is the sequence of stages a prospective buyer goes through from initial awareness of a product to eventual action. The five stages are:

- *Awareness*—the consumer's ability to recognize and remember the product or brand name.
- *Interest*—an increase in the consumer's desire to learn about some of the features of the product or brand.
- *Evaluation*—the consumer's appraisal of the product or brand on important attributes.
- *Trial*—the consumer's actual first purchase and use of the product or brand.
- *Adoption*—through a favorable experience on the first trial, the consumer's repeated purchase and use of the product or brand.

> **hierarchy of effects**
> The sequence of stages a prospective buyer goes through from initial awareness of a product to eventual action that includes awareness, interest, evaluation, trial, and adoption of the product.

These steps can serve as guidelines for developing promotion objectives. For a totally new product, the sequence applies to the entire product category, but for a new brand competing in an established product category, it applies to the brand itself. Marketers often use the term *consumer touchpoints,* as discussed in Chapter 4, to designate where, when, and how a customer or prospective buyer comes in contact with a product or brand message. In addition, the popularity of social media sometimes leads to an "advocacy" stage where loyal consumers recommend brands they have adopted.[19]

Although sometimes an objective for a promotion program involves several steps in the hierarchy of effects, it often focuses on a single stage. Regardless of what the specific objective might be, from building awareness to increasing repeat purchases, promotion objectives should possess three important qualities. They should (1) be designed for a well-defined target audience, (2) be measurable, and (3) cover a specified time period.

Setting the Promotion Budget

After setting the promotion objectives, a company must decide how much to spend. The promotion expenditures needed to reach U.S. households are enormous. Five U.S. advertisers—Comcast, P&G, AT&T, Amazon, and General Motors—each spend a total of more than $3 billion annually on promotion.[20] Determining the ideal amount for the budget is difficult because there is no precise way to measure the exact results of spending promotion dollars. However, several methods can be used to set the promotion budget.[21]

©Peter Probst/Alamy Stock Photo

- *Percentage of sales*. In the percentage of sales budgeting approach, the amount of money spent on promotion is a percentage of past or anticipated sales. A common budgeting method, this approach is often stated in terms such as, "Our promotion budget for this year is 3 percent of last year's gross sales."[22] See the Applying Marketing Metrics box for an application of the promotion-to-sales ratio to the restaurant industry.[23]
- *Competitive parity*. Competitive parity budgeting matches the competitor's absolute level of spending or the proportion per point of market share.[24]
- *All you can afford*. The all-you-can-afford budgeting method allows money to be spent on promotion only after all other budget items—such as manufacturing costs—are covered.[25]

Applying Marketing Metrics
How Much Should You Spend on IMC?

Integrated marketing communications (IMC) programs coordinate a variety of promotion alternatives to provide a consistent message across audiences. The amount spent on the various promotional elements, or on the total campaign, may vary depending on the target audience, the type of product, where the product is in the product life cycle, and the channel strategy selected. Managers often use the promotion-to-sales ratio on their marketing dashboard to assess how effective the IMC program expenditures are at generating sales.

Your Challenge

As a manager at Dunkin' Donuts, you've been asked to assess the effectiveness of all promotion expenditures during the past year. The promotion-to-sales ratio can be used to make year-to-year comparisons of a company's promotional programs, to compare the effectiveness of a company's program with competitors' programs, or to make comparisons with industry averages. You decide to calculate the promotion-to-sales ratio for Dunkin' Donuts. In addition, to allow a comparison, you decide to make the same calculation for two of your competitors—Starbucks and Panera Bread—and for the entire restaurant chain industry. The ratio is calculated as follows:

Promotion-to-sales ratio =
Total promotion expenditures ÷ Total sales

Your Findings

The information needed for these calculations is readily available from trade publications and annual reports. The following graph shows the promotion-to-sales ratio for Dunkin' Donuts, Starbucks, Panera Bread, and the entire restaurant chain industry. Dunkin' Donuts spent $130 million on its promotion program to generate $7.85 billion in sales for a ratio of 1.65 (percent). In comparison, Starbucks's ratio was .57, Panera's ratio was 1.12, and the industry average was 1.23.

Your Action

Dunkin' Donuts's promotion-to-sales ratio is higher than both of its competitors and higher than the industry average. This suggests that the current mix of promotional activities and the level of expenditures may not be creating an effective IMC program. In the future, you will want to monitor the factors that may influence the ratio.

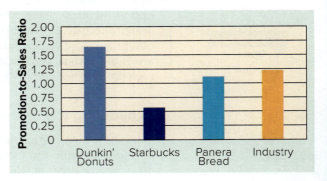

- *Objective and task.* The best approach to budgeting is objective and task budgeting, whereby the company (1) determines its promotion objectives, (2) outlines the tasks it will undertake to accomplish those objectives, and (3) determines the promotion cost of performing those tasks.[26]

Selecting the Right Promotional Tools

Once a budget has been determined, the combination of the five basic IMC tools—advertising, personal selling, sales promotion, public relations, and direct marketing—can be specified. While many factors provide direction for selection of the appropriate mix, the large number of possible combinations of the promotional tools means that many combinations can achieve the same objective. Therefore, an analytical approach and experience are particularly important in this step of the promotion decision process. The specific mix can vary from a simple program using a single tool to a comprehensive program using all forms of promotion.

The Olympic Games have become a very visible example of a comprehensive integrated communications program. Because the Games are repeated every two years, the promotion is continuous during "on" and "off" years. Included in the program are advertising campaigns, personal selling efforts by the Olympic committee and organizers, sales promotion activities such as product tie-ins and sponsorships, public relations programs managed by the host cities, online and social media communication, and direct marketing efforts targeted at a variety of audiences, including governments, organizations, firms, athletes, and individuals.[27] At this stage in the development of the promotion program, it is also important to assess the relative importance of the various tools. While it may be desirable to utilize and integrate several forms of promotion, one may deserve special emphasis. The Olympics, for example, place primary importance on public relations and publicity.

This logo for the 2020 Summer Olympics in Tokyo, Japan, is part of a comprehensive IMC program.
Source: International Olympic Committee

Video 15-4
Olympics
kerin.tv/cr8e/v15-4

Designing the Promotion

The central element of a promotion program is the promotion itself. Advertising consists of advertising copy and the artwork that the target audience is intended to see or hear. Personal selling efforts depend on the characteristics and skills of the salesperson. Sales promotion activities consist of the specific details of inducements such as coupons, samples, and sweepstakes. Public relations efforts are readily seen in tangible elements such as news releases, and direct marketing actions depend on written, verbal, and electronic forms of delivery. The design of the promotion will play a primary role in determining the message that is communicated to the audience. This design activity is frequently viewed as the step requiring the most creativity. Successful designs are often the result of a creative process that includes obtaining insight regarding consumers' interests and purchasing behavior, idea generation, and validation of the ideas using pretesting techniques. All of the promotion tools have many design alternatives. Advertising, for example, can utilize fear, humor, attractiveness, or other themes in its appeal. Similarly, direct marketing can be designed for varying levels of personal or customized appeals. One of the challenges of IMC is to design each promotional activity to communicate the same message.[28]

Scheduling the Promotion

Once the design of each of the promotional program elements is complete, it is important to determine the most effective timing of their use. The promotion schedule describes the order in which each promotional tool is introduced and the frequency of its use during the campaign.

The Walt Disney Company and Lucasfilm, for example, use a schedule of promotional tools for their movies. To generate interest in *Star Wars: The Last Jedi,* the companies teamed up with YouTube to stream more than 30 hours of live events from the Star Wars Convention, which included a panel of the film's actors, including Daisy Ridley and Mark Hamill; a tribute to the late Carrie Fisher; and the release of the first trailer for the movie. The trailer, a photo gallery, and a production announcement were posted to the Lucasfilm website, starwars.com, along with episodes of the *Star Wars Show*. Actors from the film made promotional appearances on television talk shows and were highlighted in several magazine cover stories. Disney then revealed the packaging for a line of toys and products featuring movie characters Rey, Finn, and Poe. The campaign culminated with a celebration called Force Friday where collectibles, books, and apparel went on sale. The results of the movie release were record box office sales in the United States and worldwide![29]

What promotional tools did Disney use to support the release of *Star Wars: The Last Jedi*? Read the text to find out.
©Walt Disney Studios Motion Pictures/Photofest

Overall, the scheduling of the various promotions was designed to generate interest, bring consumers into theaters, and then encourage additional purchases after seeing the movie. Several factors such as seasonality and competitive promotion activity can also influence the promotion schedule. Businesses such as ski resorts, airlines, and professional sports teams are likely to reduce their promotional activity during the off-season. Similarly, restaurants, retail stores, and health clubs are likely to increase their promotional activity when new competitors enter the market.

EXECUTING AND ASSESSING THE PROMOTION PROGRAM

As shown earlier in Figure 15–5, the ideal execution of a promotion program involves pretesting each design before it is actually used to allow for changes and modifications to improve its effectiveness. Similarly, posttests are recommended to evaluate the impact of each promotion and the contribution of the promotion toward achieving the program objectives. The most sophisticated pretest and posttest procedures have been developed for advertising and are discussed in Chapter 16.

Testing procedures for sales promotion and direct marketing efforts currently focus on comparisons of different designs or the responses of different segments. To fully benefit from IMC programs, companies must create and maintain a test-result database that allows comparisons of the relative impact of the promotional tools and their execution options in varying situations. Information from the database will allow informed design and execution decisions and provide support for IMC activities during internal reviews by financial or administrative personnel. The San Diego Padres baseball team, for example, developed a database of information relating attendance to its integrated campaign, which included a new logo, special events, merchandise sales, and a loyalty program.

©PSL Images/Alamy Stock Photo

Carrying out the promotion program can be expensive and time-consuming. One researcher estimates that "an organization with sales less than $10 million can successfully implement an IMC program in one year, one with sales between $200 million and $500 million will need about three years, and one with sales between $2 billion and $5 billion will need five years." In addition, firms with a market orientation are more likely to implement an IMC program, and firms with support from top management have more effective IMC programs.[30] To facilitate the transition, approximately 200 integrated marketing communications agencies are in operation. In addition, some of the largest agencies are adopting approaches that embrace "total communications solutions."

Media agency PHD, which recently won *Advertising Age* magazine's Media Agency of the Year award, for example, is part of a global network of 4,000 people in more than 80 countries who deliver "smart strategic thinking and creative innovation for the world's leading brands." In fact, the agency website proclaims that it offers services "across all online and offline media," including direct response, mobile, social, ethnic, and international media. PHD's clients include Volkswagen, Hyatt, Google, Delta, KAYAK, GlaxoSmithKline, and Carnival. One of its integrated campaigns, for Flonase nasal spray, included the development of an Allergy Tracker, a partnership with the Weather Channel, access to the tracker through smartphones and desktops, promotion on Facebook and Twitter, and online advertising on retailer sites such as Target and Walgreens. The campaign resulted in 4.3 million viewers per month, 10 million minutes of tracker use in 12 months, and sales growth of 11.2 percent. While many agencies may still be specialists, the trend today is clearly toward an integrated perspective that includes all forms of promotion. Agencies can accomplish this by including account managers, channel experts, media specialists, and planning personnel in their campaign design efforts.[31]

Video 15-5
PHD Media
kerin.tv/cr8e/v15-5

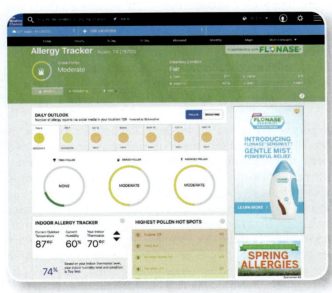

Read the text to learn how an integrated campaign helped Flonase increase sales.
Source: GSK/The Weather Company, LLC

An important factor in developing successful IMC programs is to create a process that facilitates their design and use. A tool used to evaluate a company's current process is the IMC audit. The audit analyzes the internal communication network of the company; identifies key audiences; evaluates customer databases; assesses messages in recent advertising, public relations releases, packaging, websites, e-mail and social media communication, signage, sales promotions, and direct mail; and determines the IMC expertise of company and agency personnel.[32] This process is becoming increasingly important as consumer-generated media such as blogs, RSS (rich site summary), podcasts, and social networks become more popular and as the use of search engines increases. Now, in addition to ensuring that traditional forms of communication are integrated, companies must be able to monitor consumer content, respond to inconsistent messages, and even answer questions from individual customers. According to Professor Judy Franks, marketers should also be cognizant of consumers she calls "accelerators." These individuals easily move content from medium to medium—from TV to YouTube to a mobile phone text message, for example—without any influence or control from the message source.[33]

learning review

15-10. What are the stages of the hierarchy of effects?

15-11. What are the four approaches to setting the promotion budget?

15-12. How have advertising agencies changed to facilitate the use of IMC programs?

DIRECT MARKETING

LO 15-5 Explain the value of direct marketing for consumers and sellers.

Direct marketing takes many forms and utilizes a variety of media. Several forms of direct marketing—direct mail and catalogs, television home shopping, telemarketing, and direct selling—were discussed as methods of nonstore retailing in Chapter 13. In addition, interactive marketing is discussed in detail in Chapter 14. Finally, although advertising is discussed in Chapter 16, a form of advertising—direct response advertising—is an important form of direct marketing. In this section, the growth of direct marketing, its value for consumers and sellers, and key global, technological, and ethical issues are discussed.

The Growth of Direct Marketing

Facebook is one of many activities in JCPenney's direct marketing campaign.
Source: JCPenney

The increasing interest in customer relationship management is reflected in the dramatic growth of direct marketing. The ability to customize communication efforts and create one-to-one interactions is appealing to most marketers, particularly those with IMC programs, because it leads to more favorable attitudes from the recipients. While many direct marketing methods are not new, the ability to design and use them has increased with the availability of customer information databases and new printing technologies. In recent years, direct marketing growth has outpaced total economic growth. Direct marketing expenditures exceed $146 billion and are growing at a rate of 9 percent.[34]

Most direct marketing campaigns use several methods. JCPenney, for example, is one company that has integrated its direct marketing activities. The company begins a campaign by sending coupons to customers through e-mail and text messages. Consumers also receive direct-mail postcards and "Look Books" that invite them to visit the company's e-commerce website www.jcpenney.com or mobile commerce site https://m.jcpenney.com. A special social commerce app is also available for purchases on JCPenney's Facebook "Fan" Page. Many companies also integrate their direct marketing with other forms of promotion. Porsche, for example, recently launched television ads to change consumer perceptions of its cars and supported the campaign with direct-mail brochures, a mobile application, and an online video contest. As part of its campaign, Porsche parked its cars in the driveways of selected homes, took photos, and then created customized cards for delivery to each of the homes! Mobile direct marketing sales and social network direct marketing sales are growing at 33 percent and 20 percent, respectively—the fastest of all direct marketing tools.[35]

The Value of Direct Marketing

One of the most visible indicators of the value of direct marketing for consumers is its increasing level of use in its various forms. For example, in the past year, each household received 19 direct-mail items per week, of which approximately 30 percent were read; more than 114 million people made purchases online; and consumers spent more than $76 billion on products available through mobile (smartphone, smartwatch, and tablet) offers. In addition, 57 percent of social media users say that they are more likely to purchase a product after seeing a positive post.

For consumers, direct marketing offers a variety of benefits, including: They don't have to go to a store; they can usually shop 24 hours a day; buying direct saves time; they avoid hassles with salespeople; they can save money; it's fun and entertaining; and it offers more privacy than in-store shopping. Many consumers also believe that direct marketing provides excellent customer service. Toll-free telephone numbers, customer service representatives with access to information regarding purchasing preferences, overnight delivery services, and unconditional guarantees all help create value for direct marketing customers. At Landsend.com, when customers need assistance they can click the "Live Help" icon to receive help from a sales representative on the phone or through online chat or online video until the correct product is found. "It's like we were walking down the aisle in a store!" says one Lands' End customer.[36]

Banana Republic uses direct mail to motivate people to visit its stores.
Source: Banana Republic

The value of direct marketing for sellers can be described in terms of the responses it generates. **Direct orders** are the result of offers that contain all the information necessary for a prospective buyer to make a decision to purchase and complete the transaction. Online retailer Zulily.com, for example, asks customers to create a list of their favorite brands and then sends them a message and a link to make the purchase when the brands are on sale. **Lead generation** is the result of an offer designed to generate interest in a product or service and a request for additional information. Four Seasons Hotels now sells private residences in several of its properties and sends direct mail to prospective residents asking them to request additional information on the telephone or through a website. Finally, **traffic generation** is the outcome of an offer designed to motivate people to visit a business. The Home Depot, for example, uses an opt-in e-mail alert to announce special sales that attract consumers to the store. Similarly, Banana Republic uses direct mail to generate traffic in its stores.[37]

Technological, Global, and Ethical Issues in Direct Marketing

The information technology and databases described in Chapter 7 are key elements in any direct marketing program. Databases are the result of organizations' efforts to create profiles of customers so that direct marketing tools, such as e-mail and catalogs, can be directed at specific customers. While most companies try to keep records of their customers' past purchases, many other types of data are needed to use direct marketing to develop one-to-one relationships with customers. Some data, such as lifestyles, media use, and demographics, are best collected from the consumer. Other types of data, such as price, quantity, and brand, are best collected from the businesses where purchases are made. New integrated marketing databases match consumers' postal addresses, telephone numbers, e-mail addresses, and device IDs. In addition, many businesses are beginning to match their customer records with Facebook profiles, Twitter following behavior, and Google search activity.[38]

Increases in printing and postage rates have also increased the importance of information related to the cost of direct marketing activities. For example, the Data &

direct orders
The result of direct marketing offers that contain all the information necessary for a prospective buyer to make a decision to purchase and complete the transaction.

lead generation
The result of a direct marketing offer designed to generate interest in a product or service and a request for additional information.

traffic generation
The outcome of a direct marketing offer designed to motivate people to visit a business.

Making Responsible Decisions — Ethics

What Is the Future of Your Privacy?

In 2003, the Federal Trade Commission opened the National Do Not Call Registry to give Americans a tool for maintaining their privacy on home and cellular telephone lines. More than 70 percent of all Americans registered. Since then, several state legislatures have also passed laws to create do-not-call lists for automated (robo) telephone calls. In addition, new discussions about privacy related to mail and computer use are now taking place.

Generally, the question being debated is, "What information is private?" Are telephone numbers, addresses of residences, and online activities private or public information? Proponents of a do-not-mail registry argue that, like telephone calls, citizens should be able to stop unsolicited mail. Proponents of do-not-track regulations suggest that website owners who use cookies to collect information about consumers' shopping habits should do so only with a consumer's consent. Marketers counter that consumers who share this information are more likely to receive messages and advertising that better match their interests.

The Data & Marketing Association currently advocates several solutions. First, it has created DMAchoice, an online tool to help consumers manage the types of mail and e-mail they receive. Second, the organization endorses a self-regulatory program for online behavioral advertising (OBA) that encourages advertisers to include an "Ad Choices" icon in the corner of online ads to allow consumers to opt out of having data collected about their online activities. The program is part of an advertising coalition called the Digital Advertising Alliance. Moving beyond self-regulation, the European Union recently passed the *E-Privacy Directive* to provide explicit laws for website owners. And in the United States, the Senate is evaluating the Do Not Track Online Act, although it did not receive support from the FCC. These guidelines and regulations, of course, have huge implications for advertisers, portals such as Facebook and Google, and consumers.

What is your opinion? What types of information should be private? Can we find a balance between self-regulation and legislation?

Source: Courtesy of Direct Advertising Alliance

Marketing Association estimates that e-mail advertising expenditures outperform social media advertising by a ratio of 3-to-1. Similarly, catalog businesses have found they can reduce the cost of printing by using innovations such as soy-based ink and recycled paper, and they can reduce postage fees through database list analysis. Related to postage fees, many direct marketers are assessing the potential impact of the USPS plan for a five-day mail delivery cycle.[39]

Direct marketing faces several challenges and opportunities in global markets today. Many countries, including the United Kingdom, Australia, the European Union, and Japan, have requirements for a mandatory "opt-in"—that is, potential customers must give permission to be included on a list for direct marketing solicitations. In addition, the mail, telephone, and Internet systems in many countries are not as well developed as they are in the United States. The need for improved reliability and security in these countries has slowed the growth of direct mail, while the dramatic growth of mobile phone penetration has created an opportunity for direct mobile marketing campaigns. Another issue for global direct marketers is payment. The availability of credit and credit cards varies throughout the world, creating the need for alternatives such as C.O.D. (cash on delivery), bank deposits, and online payment accounts such as PayPal and Venmo.[40]

Global and domestic direct marketers both face challenging ethical issues today. Concerns about privacy, for example, have led to various attempts to provide guidelines that balance consumer and business interests. The European Union passed a consumer privacy law, called the *Data Protection Directive,* after several years of discussion with the Federation of European Direct Marketing and the UK's Direct Marketing Association. A new version of the law, called the *General Data Protection Regulation* (*GDPR*), addresses new developments such as social networks and Cloud computing. The GDPR was passed in 2016 and is scheduled to take effect in 2018.

Video 15-6
Ad Choices
kerin.tv/cr8e/v15-6

In the United States, the Federal Trade Commission and many state legislatures have also been concerned about privacy. Several bills that call for a do-not-mail registry similar to the Do Not Call Registry are being discussed. Similarly, there are growing concerns about the web "tracking" tools used by direct marketers to segment consumers and match them with advertising. The Making Responsible Decisions box describes some of the issues under consideration.[41]

learning review

15-13. The ability to design and use direct marketing programs has increased with the availability of _____ and _____.

15-14. What are the three types of responses generated by direct marketing activities?

LEARNING OBJECTIVES REVIEW

LO 15-1 *Discuss integrated marketing communications and the communication process.*

Integrated marketing communications is the concept of designing marketing communications programs that coordinate all promotional activities—advertising, personal selling, sales promotion, public relations, and direct marketing—to provide a consistent message across all audiences. The communication process conveys messages with six elements: a source, a message, a channel of communication, a receiver, and encoding and decoding. The communication process also includes a feedback loop and can be distorted by noise.

LO 15-2 *Describe the promotional mix and the uniqueness of each component.*

There are five promotional alternatives. Advertising, sales promotion, and public relations are mass selling approaches, whereas personal selling and direct marketing use customized messages. Advertising can have high absolute costs but reaches large numbers of people. Personal selling has a high cost per contact but provides immediate feedback. Public relations is often difficult to obtain but is very credible. Sales promotion influences short-term consumer behavior. Direct marketing can help develop customer relationships, although maintaining a database can be very expensive.

LO 15-3 *Select the promotional approach appropriate to a product's target audience, life-cycle stage, as well as stages of the buying decision and channel strategies.*

The promotional mix depends on the target audience. Programs for consumers, business buyers, and intermediaries might emphasize advertising, personal selling, and sales promotion, respectively. The promotional mix also changes over the product life-cycle stages. During the introduction stage, all promotional mix elements are used. During the growth stage advertising is emphasized, while the maturity stage utilizes sales promotion and direct marketing. Little promotion is used during the decline stage. Finally, the promotional mix can depend on the channel strategy. Push strategies require personal selling and sales promotions directed at channel members, while pull strategies depend on advertising and sales promotion directed at consumers.

LO 15-4 *Describe the elements of the promotion decision process.*

The promotional decision process consists of three steps: planning, implementation, and evaluation. The planning step consists of six elements: (1) identifying the target audience, (2) specifying the objectives, (3) setting the budget, (4) selecting the right promotional elements, (5) designing the promotion, and (6) scheduling the promotion. The implementation step includes pretesting. The evaluation step includes posttesting.

LO 15-5 *Explain the value of direct marketing for consumers and sellers.*

The value of direct marketing for consumers is indicated by its increasing level of use. For example, during the past year, more than 114 million people made purchases online. The value of direct marketing for sellers can be measured in terms of three types of responses: direct orders, lead generation, and traffic generation.

LEARNING REVIEW ANSWERS

15-1 **What six elements are required for communication to occur?**
Answer: The six elements required for communication to occur are: (1) a source, which is a company or person who has information to convey; (2) a message, which is the information sent; (3) a channel of communication, which is how the information is conveyed; (4) a receiver, which is the consumer who reads, hears, or sees the message; and the processes of (5) encoding, in which the sender transforms the idea into a set of symbols; and (6) decoding, in which the receiver takes the symbols, or the message, and transforms it back into an idea.

15-2 A difficulty for U.S. companies advertising in international markets is that the audience does not share the same _____.
Answer: field of experience, which is a similar understanding and knowledge that is applied to a message

15-3 A misprint in a newspaper ad is an example of _____.
Answer: noise—the extraneous factors that distort a message

15-4 Explain the difference between advertising and publicity when both appear on television.
Answer: Since advertising space on TV is paid for, a firm can control what it wants to say and to whom and how often the message is sent over a broadcast, cable, satellite, or local TV network. Since publicity is an indirectly paid presentation of a message about a firm or its products or services, the firm has little control over what is said to whom or when. Instead, it can only suggest to the TV medium that it run a favorable story about the firm or its offerings.

15-5 Cost per contact is high with the _____ element of the promotional mix.
Answer: personal selling

15-6 Which promotional element should be offered only on a short-term basis?
Answer: sales promotion

15-7 Promotional programs can be directed to _____, _____, or both.
Answer: the ultimate consumer; the intermediary (retailer, wholesaler, or industrial distributor)

15-8 Describe the promotional objective for each stage of the product life cycle.
Answer: Introduction—to inform consumers of the product's existence; Growth—to persuade consumers to buy the product; Maturity—to remind consumers that the product still exists; and Decline—to phase out the product.

15-9 Explain the differences between a push strategy and a pull strategy.
Answer: In a push strategy, a firm directs the promotional mix to channel members to gain their cooperation in ordering and stocking the product. In a pull strategy, a firm directs the promotional mix at ultimate consumers to encourage them to ask retailers for the product, who then order it from wholesalers or the firm itself.

15-10 What are the stages of the hierarchy of effects?
Answer: The five stages of the hierarchy of effects are awareness, interest, evaluation, trial, and adoption.

15-11 What are the four approaches to setting the promotion budget?
Answer: The four approaches to setting the promotion budget are percentage of sales, competitive parity, all you can afford, and objective and task.

15-12 How have advertising agencies changed to facilitate the use of IMC programs?
Answer: Some agencies have adopted: (1) a total communications solutions approach; (2) an integrated perspective that includes all forms of promotion; (3) an IMC audit to analyze the internal communication network of the company to identify key audiences; evaluate customer databases; assess messages contained in recent advertising, press releases, packaging, websites, social media, direct marketing, etc.; and determine the IMC expertise of company and agency personnel; and (4) strategies to monitor consumer content, respond to inconsistent messages, and answer questions from individual customers.

15-13 The ability to design and use direct marketing programs has increased with the availability of _____ and _____.
Answer: customer information databases; new printing technologies

15-14 What are the three types of responses generated by direct marketing activities?
Answer: They are: (1) direct orders, the result of offers that contain all the information necessary for a prospective buyer to make a decision to purchase and complete the transaction; (2) lead generation, the result of an offer designed to generate interest in a product or service and a request for additional information; and (3) traffic generation, the outcome of an offer designed to motivate people to visit a business.

FOCUSING ON KEY TERMS

advertising p. 406
communication p. 404
direct marketing p. 409
direct orders p. 419
hierarchy of effects p. 414
integrated marketing communications (IMC) p. 404
lead generation p. 419
personal selling p. 407
promotional mix p. 404
public relations p. 408
publicity p. 408
pull strategy p. 413
push strategy p. 412
sales promotion p. 409
traffic generation p. 419

APPLYING MARKETING KNOWLEDGE

1. After listening to a recent sales presentation, Mary Smith signed up for membership at the local health club. On arriving at the facility, she learned there was an additional fee for racquetball court rentals. "I don't remember that in the sales talk; I thought they said all facilities were included with the membership fee," complained Mary. Describe the problem in terms of the communication process.

2. Develop a matrix to compare the five elements of the promotional mix on three criteria—to *whom* you deliver the message, *what* you say, and *when* you say it.
3. Explain how the promotional tools used by an airline would differ if the target audience were (*a*) consumers who travel for pleasure and (*b*) corporate travel departments that select the airlines to be used by company employees.
4. Suppose you introduced a new consumer food product and invested heavily both in national advertising (pull strategy) and in training and motivating your field salesforce to sell the product to food stores (push strategy). What kinds of feedback would you receive from both the advertising and your salesforce? How could you increase both the quality and quantity of each?
5. Fisher-Price Company, long known as a manufacturer of children's toys, has introduced a line of clothing for children. Outline a promotional plan to get this product introduced in the marketplace.
6. Many insurance companies sell health insurance plans to companies. In these companies the employees pick the plan, but the set of offered plans is determined by the company. Recently, Blue Cross Blue Shield, a health insurance company, ran a television ad stating, "If your employer doesn't offer you Blue Cross Blue Shield coverage, ask why." Explain the promotional strategy behind the advertisement.
7. Identify the sales promotion tools that might be useful for (*a*) Tastee Yogurt, a new brand introduction; (*b*) 3M self-sticking Post-it® Notes; and (*c*) Wrigley's Spearmint gum.
8. Design an integrated marketing communications program—using each of the five promotional elements—for Rhapsody, the online music service.
9. BMW recently introduced its first sports activity vehicle, the X6, to compete with other popular crossover vehicles such as the Mercedes-Benz GLE-Class. Design a direct marketing program to generate (*a*) leads, (*b*) traffic in dealerships, and (*c*) direct orders.
10. Develop a privacy policy for database managers that provides a balance of consumer and seller perspectives. How would you encourage voluntary compliance with your policy? What methods of enforcement would you recommend?

BUILDING YOUR MARKETING PLAN

To develop the promotion strategy for your marketing plan, follow the steps suggested in the planning phase of the promotion decision process described in Figure 15–5.

1. You should (*a*) identify the target audience, (*b*) specify the promotion objectives, (*c*) set the promotion budget, (*d*) select the right promotion tools, (*e*) design the promotion, and (*f*) schedule the promotion.
2. Also specify the pretesting and posttesting procedures needed in the implementation and evaluation phases.
3. Finally, describe how each of your promotion tools is integrated to provide a consistent message.

VIDEO CASE 15   Taco Bell: Using IMC to Help Customers Live Más!

"Every touch point is considered," explains Stephanie Perdue, Taco Bell's senior director of marketing, "from the posters in the restaurants down to the packaging, and all of the different media channels." Stephanie is describing the integrated marketing communications (IMC) approach used by Taco Bell, the nation's leading Mexican-style quick service restaurant. IMC is one of the key factors that has contributed to the extraordinary success of the food chain, which serves more than 36 million customers each week!

Video 15-7
Taco Bell Video Case
kerin.tv/cr8e/v15-7

THE COMPANY

The story behind Taco Bell and its success is fascinating. After World War II, a young marine named Glen Bell returned to his home state of California with an entrepreneurial spirit and an observation that people were hungry for fast, good food. He opened his first restaurant, Bell's Burgers, based on the simple concept that customers might want to walk up and get their food from a service window. Not far away, two brothers named McDonald were operating their new restaurant using a "drive-in" concept. For several years, Bell and the McDonald brothers enjoyed friendly competition as pioneers of the growing fast-food industry. However, when the burger restaurant market became crowded with competitors, Bell decided to try something new—tacos!

Tacos were new to most Americans so Bell experimented with many concepts. First he developed a crunchy taco shell and opened a restaurant called Taco Tia. His marketing activities consisted of handing out sombreros and having Mariachis play outside the restaurant. Next, Bell started another restaurant, El Taco, with a group of celebrity partners. Finally, after a friend suggested that Glen should use his name in his business, the first Taco Bell was opened in Downey, California.

©David Paul Morris/Bloomberg via Getty Images

Taco Bell grew quickly and as Bell began opening additional locations he decided that the restaurants should resemble the appearance of California's historic missions. With the help of an architect he created an inviting design based on an adobe-like exterior with a red clay-tile roof. The name and logo utilized a mission-style bell, a version of which is still in use today. Through franchises and additional corporate locations Taco Bell soon reached from coast to coast.

Today Taco Bell is a subsidiary of Yum! Brands, which also owns and operates KFC, Pizza Hut, and WingStreet. Taco Bell now has more than 6,500 locations and $1.5 billion in sales. Many locations are co-branded with KFC, Pizza Hut, and Long John Silver's stores. Taco Bell also operates Taco Bell Express locations in convenience stores, truck stops, shopping malls, and airports.

INTEGRATED MARKETING COMMUNICATIONS AT TACO BELL

From its beginning, Taco Bell has used very creative promotional activities. For example, when the Mir space station was about to reenter the Earth's atmosphere, Taco Bell placed a target in the Pacific Ocean and announced that every person in the United States would receive a free taco if any piece of the falling space station hit the target. Similarly, in its "Steal a Base, Steal a Taco" promotion, Taco Bell promises to give everyone a free taco if any player steals a base in the World Series. While the space station did not hit the target, several players have stolen bases in the World Series, leading to free tacos for everyone! Taco Bell has also offered special promotions with Mountain Dew, partnered with the NBA as its official fast food, and created videos for movie-theater advertising.

You might remember some of Taco Bell's past advertising campaigns, such as "Yo quiero Taco Bell," "Grand Taste. Loco Value," or "Get it at The Bell." The more recent "Think Outside the Bun" campaign was designed for millennials. Then as that group changed, Taco Bell executives recognized that they had an opportunity to reposition the chain. Tracee Larocca, brand creative director at Taco Bell, explains, "We realized there was a big opportunity as the culture shifted from 'food as fuel' to 'food as experience.'" Taco Bell considered many new taglines, such as "Keep Life Spicy" and "Hunger for Más," and eventually developed the "Live Más" campaign. As campaigns and positioning change, integrated marketing becomes increasingly important. According to Larocca, "as the brand's creative director, my job is to make sure that all of our communications have the same look, tone, and feel across all platforms, making sure we maintain consistency in our brand voice no matter what we're doing internally or externally."

Advertising Age magazine recently named Taco Bell the winner of its Marketer of the Year award for its extraordinary use of integrated marketing in the launch of its Doritos Locos Tacos. The new product went through three years of development and 45 prototypes before its launch, which led to sales of 100 million units in its first 10 weeks. Taco Bell allocates approximately 70 percent of its budget to traditional media, 20 percent to digital media, and 10 percent to new media where it can "explore." The traditional media budget included a Super Bowl ad utilizing the "Live Más" theme. "It was all about a mindset and not necessarily an age range or a demographic," explains Larocca. The ad, called "Forever Young," showed "a group of old people breaking out of a retirement home and having a great night on the town," she adds.

The social media component of the campaign included Facebook, Twitter, Vine, Snapchat, and Instagram. The Twitter campaign, for example, included a Hometown Tweet-off where anyone could send a tweet saying why a Taco Bell truck should visit their hometown. Similarly, Taco Bell posted pictures to Facebook and watched the responses in the comments and the "likes." Some of the new media budget was used to try things such as Taco Bell's own video channels for Web and mobile, and a live stream to a billboard in Times Square. As Rob Poetsch, director of public affairs and engagement, observed about the Doritos Locos Tacos launch, "for the first time, we had a fully integrated plan that engaged all of our constituents."

THE FUTURE AT TACO BELL

Taco Bell continues to develop new products, brand concepts, and promotions. For example, naked egg tacos, Cinnabon Delights, and the breakfast Crunchwrap are new additions to the menu. In addition, a new brand concept called Taco Bell Cantina, which is testing its first locations in Chicago and San Francisco, will offer "tapas-style" appetizers for customers to share, and beer and wine in an urban setting. In addition, Taco Bell announced its plan to award $10 million in Live Más Scholarships by 2022 to "innovators, creators and dreamers" aged 16–24. All of these activities are contributing to the company's continued growth. Yum! Brands expects Taco Bell's domestic sales to double by 2021![42]

Questions

1. What factors contributed to Taco Bell's early success?
2. Which of the promotional elements described in Figure 15–2 were used by Taco Bell in its Doritos Locos Tacos campaign?
3. How does Taco Bell ensure the continued success of the food chain?

Chapter Notes

1. Patricia Odell, "Taco Bell—Cult-Like and Performing Weddings," *Promotional Marketing,* February 16, 2017, p. 2; "Taco Bell Puts Wedding on Vegas Menu," *QSRweb.com,* March 1, 2017, p. 49; Mahita Gajanan, "Taco Bell Will Give Away Free Tacos for the NBA Finals," *Money.com*; Patty Odell, "Taco Bell Shifts Marketing Strategy Says CMO Marisa Thalberg," *Promotional Marketing,* April 6, 2017, p. 2; "Taco Bell TV Spot Puts Breakfast on Front Burner," *QSRweb.com,* March 1, 2017, p. 75; "Airbnb and Taco Bell Join Forces on a Sleepover," *Event Marketer,* December 2016, p. 17; Jessica Wohl, "Taco Bell Campaigns Aim to Elevate the Value Pitch," *Advertising Age,* September 26, 2016, p. 42; Patricia Odell, "Taco Bell Looks to Social Fans for Video Content Inspiration," *Promotional Marketing,* December 20, 2016; Jenni Romaniuk, "Are You Ready for the Next Big Thing?" *Journal of Advertising Research,* December 2012, pp. 397–99; and "How to Engage Your Audience on Social Media," *www.Business2Community.com,* March 28, 2013.

2. Rajeev Batra and Kevin Lane Keller, "Integrating Marketing Communications: New Findings, New Lessons, and New Ideas," *Journal of Marketing,* November 2016, pp. 122–145; Sita Mishra and Sushma Muralie, "Managing Dynamism of IMC—Anarchy to Order," *Journal of Marketing and Communication,* September 2010, pp. 29–37; Philip J. Kitchen, Ilchul Kim, and Don E. Schultz, "Integrated Marketing Communications: Practice Leads Theory," *Journal of Advertising Research,* December 2008, pp. 531–46; and Bob Liodice, "Essentials for Integrated Marketing," *Advertising Age,* June 9, 2008, p. 26.

3. Wilbur Schramm, "How Communication Works," in *The Process and Effects of Mass Communication,* Wilbur Schramm, ed. (Urbana: University of Illinois Press, 1955), pp. 3–26.

4. E. Cooper and M. Jahoda, "The Evasion of Propaganda," *Journal of Psychology* 22 (1947), pp. 15–25; H. Hyman and P. Sheatsley, "Some Reasons Why Information Campaigns Fail," *Public Opinion Quarterly* 11 (1947), pp. 412–23; and J. T. Klapper, *The Effects of Mass Communication* (New York: Free Press, 1960), Chapter VII.

5. "Mistakes in Advertising," on the Learn English website, http://www.learnenglish.de/mistakes/HorrorMistakes.htm, accessed March 18, 2013; and Bianca Bartz, "International Ads Lost in Translation," TrendHunter Marketing website, http://www.trendhunter.com/trends/advertising-bloopers-international-ads-lost-in-translation, accessed March 18, 2013.

6. Rik Pieters and Michel Wedel, "Attention Capture and Transfer in Advertising: Brand, Pictorial, and Text-Size Effects," *Journal of Marketing,* April 2004, pp. 36–50.

7. Adapted from American Marketing Association, Resource Library Dictionary, http://www.marketingpower.com/layouts/Dictionary.aspx?dLetter=P, accessed March 18, 2013.

8. Dave Folkens, "3 Ways Social Media Is Changing Public Relations," *Online Marketing Blog,* February 17, 2011; Michael Bush, "How Social Media Is Helping the Public-Relations Sector Not Just Survive, but Thrive," *Advertising Age,* August 23, 2010, p. 1; David Robinson, "Public Relations Comes of Age," *Business Horizons* 49 (2006), pp. 247–56; and Dick Martin, "Gilded and Gelded: Hard-Won Lessons from the PR Wars," *Harvard Business Review,* October 2003, pp. 44–54.

9. Martin Eisend and Franziska Kuster, "The Effectiveness of Publicity versus Advertising: A Meta-Analytic Investigation of Its Moderators," *Journal of the Academy of Marketing Science,* December 2011, pp. 906–21; and Joan Stewart, "Pros and Cons of Free Publicity in Newspapers, Magazines," *www.Business2Community.com,* January 30, 2013.

10. "The Public Relations Metamorphosis: Social Media Is Here to Stay," *www.Business2Community.com,* December 21, 2012; Piet Levy, "CSR Take Responsibility," *Marketing News,* May 30, 2010, p. 20; Jooyoung Kim, Hye Jin Yoon, and Sun Young Lee, "Integrating Advertising and Publicity: A Theoretical Examination of the Effects of Exposure Sequence, Publicity Valence, and Product Attribute Consistency," *Journal of Advertising,* Spring 2010, p. 97; and Marsha D. Loda and Barbara Carrick Coleman, "Sequence Matters: A More Effective Way to Use Advertising and Publicity," *Journal of Advertising Research* 45 (December 2005), pp. 362–71.

11. Kusum L. Ailawadi, Scott A. Neslin, and Karen Gedenk, "Pursuing the Value-Conscious Consumer: Store Brands versus National Brand Promotions," *Journal of Marketing,* January 2001, pp. 71–89.

12. Nikki Hopewell, "The Rules of Engagement: A Bevy of Rules and Best Practices Govern Promotions and Contests," *Marketing News,* June 1, 2008, p. 6; and Gerard Prendergast, Yi-Zheng Shi, and Ka-Man Cheung, "Behavioural Response to Sales Promotion Tools," *International Journal of Advertising* 24 (2005), pp. 467–86.

13. Adapted from American Marketing Association, Resource Library Dictionary, http://www.marketingpower.com/layouts/Dictionary.aspx?dLetter=D, accessed March 18, 2013.

14. Todd Spangler, "Warner Bros. 'King Arthur' Movie Get First Snapchat-Sponsored Puzzle-Game Lens," *Variety,* January 20, 2017; Brielle Jaekel, "Warner Bros. Teases New Film with Short Snippet on Snapchat," *Mobile Marketer,* March 21, 2016; Bill McCarthy, "Back-to-School 2016: Capturing the College Student's Dollar," *ShopperTrak,* August 26, 2016; Baiyun Chen, Ryan Seilhamer, Luke Bennett, and Sue Bauer, "Students' Mobile Learning Practices in Higher Education: A Multi-Year Study," *Educausereview,* June 22, 2015; Richard Fry, "Class of 2025 Expected to Be the Biggest, Most Diverse Ever," *www.pewresearch.org,* September 11, 2015; Paul Jacobs, "3 Tips for Marketing to College Students," *Promotional Marketing,* May 26, 2015, p. 1; "Top 5 Brands Using Mobile Marketing Successfully," *www.Business2Community.com,* March 11, 2013; "Mysteries and Myths of Millennials in Social Media," *www.Business2Community.com,* July 21, 2012; Stuart Elliott, "In an Upgrade, Google Adds to Its Model for Mobile Marketing," *The New York Times,* March 7, 2013, p. 3; "Tailoring Your Mobile Strategy to the New Millennials," *VentureBeat,* July 18, 2012; Antje Cockrill, Mark M. Goode, and Amy White, "The Bluetooth Enigma: Practicalities Impair Potential," *Journal of Advertising Research,* March 2011, pp. 298–312; and Thomas Pardee, "Media-Savvy Gen Y Finds Smart and Funny Is 'New Rock-N-Roll,'" *Advertising Age,* October 11, 2010, p. 17.

15. "Push vs. Pull Strategies," *Daily News,* May 3, 2011; "Question: Should B2B Be Focusing All Its Efforts on 'Pull' Marketing Therefore Turning Its Back on 'Push' Marketing Techniques?" *B2B Marketing Magazine,* September 2009; and Michael Levy, John Webster, and Roger Kerin, "Formulating Push Marketing Strategies: A Method and Application," *Journal of Marketing,* Winter 1983, pp. 25–34.

16. Michael Martinex, "Ford Plans Regional Incentives for Dealers," *Automotive News,* March 20, 2017, p. 4; "Working with Ford Dealers," Sustainability Report 2015/16, http://corporate.ford.com/microsites/sustainability-report-2015-16/people-dealers.html; Bradford Wernle, "Quality, Market Share, Leasing Top Ford Dealers' Agenda," *Automotive News,* February 10, 2013; and Jamie LaReau, "Ford Dealers Revamp Pay Plans, Some Efforts Resemble Stair-Step Programs," *Automotive News,* February 14, 2011.

17. "Is Online Pharm DTC Ad Spend Continuing Its Downward Slide?" *Pharma Marketing Blog,* April 2, 2014, *www.pharmamkting.blogspot.com*; Beth Snyder Bulik, "Ad Spending: 15 Years of DTC," *Advertising Age Insights White Paper,* October 17, 2011; Sheng Yuan, "Public Response to Direct-to-Consumer Advertising of Prescription Drugs," *Journal of Advertising Research,* March 2008, pp. 30–41; and Fusun F. Gonul, Franklin Carter, Elina Petrova, and Kannan Srinivasan, "Promotion of Prescription Drugs and Its Impact on Physicians' Choice Behavior," *Journal of Marketing,* July 2001, pp. 79–90.

18. Sophie C. Boerman, Sanne Kruikemeier, and Frederik J. Zuiderveen Borgesius, "Online Behavioral Advertising: A Literature Review and Research Agenda," *Journal of Advertising,* no. 3, 2017, pp. 363–76; Don E. Shultz, Martin P. Block, and Kaylan Raman, "Understanding Consumer-Created Media Synergy," *Journal of Marketing Communications,* July 2012, pp. 173–87; "Why Behavioral Targeting Is Effective," *www.Business2Community.com,* January 15, 2013; Lauren Drell, "4 Ways Behavioral Targeting Is Changing the Web," *Mashable,* April 26, 2011; and adapted from American Marketing Association, Resource Library Dictionary, http://www.marketingpower.com/_layouts/Dictionary.aspx?dLetter=B, accessed April 2, 2013.

19. Philip Kotler, Hermawan Kartajaya, and Iwan Setiawan, *Marketing 4.0* (Hoboken, NJ: Wiley, 2017); Robert J. Lavidge and Gary A. Steiner, "A Model for Predictive Measurement of Advertising Effectiveness," *Journal of Marketing,* October 1961, p. 61; and C. H. Patti, S. W. Hartley, M. M. van Dessel and D. W. Baack, "Improving Integrated Marketing Communications Practices: A Comparison of Objectives and Results," *Journal of Marketing Communications* 23, no. 4 (2017), pp. 351–70.

20. "Leading National Advertisers," *Advertising Age Fact Pack,* June 25, 2018, p. 6.

21. George S. Low and Jakki J. Mohr, "Setting Advertising and Promotion Budgets in Multi-Brand Companies," *Journal of Advertising Research,* January–February 1999, pp. 67–78; Don E. Schultz and Anders Gronstedt, "Making Marcom an Investment," *Marketing Management,* Fall 1997, pp. 41–49; and J. Enrique Bigne, "Advertising Budget Practices: A Review," *Journal of Current Issues and Research in Advertising,* Fall 1995, pp. 17–31.

22. John Philip Jones, "Ad Spending: Maintaining Market Share," *Harvard Business Review,* January–February 1990, pp. 38–42; and Charles H. Patti and Vincent Blasko, "Budgeting Practices of Big Advertisers," *Journal of Advertising Research* 21 (December 1981), pp. 23–30.

23. "U.S. Market Leaders," *Advertising Age,* June 27, 2016, p. 20.

24. Brenda Marlin, "Adding It Up: You Can Save Time by Trying One of Three Short-Cut Approaches to an Annual Budget," *ABA Banking,* October 1, 2007, p. 36; James A. Shroer, "Ad Spending: Growing Market Share," *Harvard Business Review,* January–February 1990, pp. 44–48; and Jeffrey A. Lowenhar and John L. Stanton, "Forecasting Competitive Advertising Expenditures," *Journal of Advertising Research* 16, no. 2 (April 1976), pp. 37–44.

25. Daniel Seligman, "How Much for Advertising?" *Fortune,* December 1956, p. 123.

26. James E. Lynch and Graham J. Hooley, "Increasing Sophistication in Advertising Budget Setting," *Journal of Advertising Research* 30 (February–March 1990), pp. 67–75.

27. "The Olympic Brand Maintains Its Global Strength and Recognition," *States News Service,* February 12, 2013; Graham Ruddock, "London Olympics Sponsors Are Already into Their Stride," *The Daily Telegraph,* May 6, 2011, p. 8; "The Olympics Come but Once Every Two Years," *Marketing News,* November 1, 2008, p. 12; "Olympics Will Bring Online Opportunities for Many Brands," *Revolution,* July 14, 2008, p. 13; and Don E. Schultz, "Olympics Get the Gold Medal in Integrating Marketing Event," *Marketing News,* April 27, 1998, pp. 5, 10.

28. S. Turnbull and C. Wheeler, "The Advertising Creative Process: A Study of UK Agencies," *Journal of Marketing Communications* 2 (2017), pp. 176–94; "It's Time to Take an Integrated Marketing Approach," *www.Business2Community.com,* January 22, 2013; "Integrated Marketing: One Message, Many Media," *Marketing Week,* September 18, 2008, p. 31; and Cornelia Pechman, Guangzhi Zhao, Marvin E. Goldberg, and Ellen Thomas Reibling, "What to Convey in Antismoking Advertisements for Adolescents: The Use of Protection Motivation Theory to Identify Effective Message Themes," *Journal of Marketing,* April 2003, pp. 1–18.

29. Elaine Low, "Force Friday II Will Unveil 'Star Wars: The Last Jedi' Toys," *Investors Business Daily,* February 16, 2017; Rachel King, "Disney and Lucasfilm Reveal the First Trailer for 'Star Wars: The Last Jedi,'" *www.Fortune.com,* May 1, 2017, p. 195; and Matt Liebl, "'Star Wars: The Last Jedi' Product Packing Reveals a Much Different Rey," *www.Gamezone.com,* February 16, 2017.

30. Sabine A. Einwiller and Michael Boenigk, "Examining the Link between Integrated Communication Management and Communication Effectiveness in Medium-Sized Enterprises," *Journal of Marketing Communications,* December 2012, pp. 335–61; and Mike Reid, "Performance Auditing of

Integrated Marketing Communication (IMC) Actions and Outcomes," *Journal of Advertising* 34 (Winter 2005), p. 41.

31. Lindsay Stein, "Media Agency of the Year: PHD," *Advertising Age,* January 23, 2017, p. 28; and PHD website, http://www.phdmedia.com/north-america/our-work/, accessed June 7, 2017.

32. "Integrated Marketing: The Benefits of Integrated Marketing," *Marketing Week,* September 18, 2008, p. 33; and Tom Duncan, "Is Your Marketing Communications Integrated?" *Advertising Age,* January 24, 1994, p. 26.

33. Don E. Schultz, "The Media Circuits Evolution," *Marketing News,* March 30, 2011, p. 11; "Integrated Marketing: Digital Fuels Integration Boom," *Marketing Week,* December 11, 2008, p. 27; Don E. Schultz, "IMC Is Do or Die in New Pull Marketplace," *Marketing News,* August 15, 2006, p. 7; and Don E. Schultz, "Integration's New Role Focuses on Customers," *Marketing News,* September 15, 2006, p. 8.

34. Ginger Conlon, "2016 Will Be a Growth Year in Marketing Spending," *www.dmnews.com,* February 1, 2016; *Statistical Fact Book 2015* (New York: Direct Marketing Association, 2015); Tae Hyun Baek and Mariko Morimoto, "Stay Away from Me," *Journal of Advertising,* Spring 2012, pp. 59–76; and *Statistical Fact Book 2012* (New York: Direct Marketing Association, 2012), pp. 5, 16.

35. "Direct Mail Strategy: JCPenney's New Postcard Campaign," *www.Business2Community.com,* April 18, 2012; Cindy Waxer, "Automotive Brands Are Test-Driving New Marketing Strategies," *DMNews,* October 2012; "JCPenney America's Shopping Destination This Christmas," *Business Wire,* November 10, 2010; "JCPenney Kicks Off Christmas Gift Program," *Wireless News,* November 16, 2010; Alex Palmer, "JCPenney Launches Facebook e-Commerce Store," *DMNews,* December 15, 2010; Tim Peterson, "Porsche Launches Integrated Campaign to Shift Consumer Perception," *DMNews,* March 25, 2011; and *Statistical Fact Book 2012* (New York: Direct Marketing Association, 2012), p. 5.

36. *Statistical Fact Book 2015*; *Statistical Fact Book 2012,* pp. 24, 67; and "Six Ways Lands' End Makes Online Shopping a Joy," *PR Newswire,* November 21, 2007.

37. Daniela Forte, "Why Large Retailers Are Acquiring Flash Sale Sites," *www.multichannelmerchant.com,* June 20, 2016; and Theresa Howard, "E-mail Grows as Direct-Marketing Tool: They're Quicker to Make, Cheap to Send," *USA Today,* November 28, 2008, p. 5B.

38. Evan Neufeld, "Cross-Device and Cross-Channel Identity Measurement Issues and Guidelines," *Journal of Advertising Research,* March 2017, pp. 109–17; Cotton Delo, "Facebook Testing Effort to Match Offline Purchases to Online Profiles," *Advertising Age,* February 25, 2013, p. 6; Michael Learmonth, "Facebook Goes the Route of Direct Marketing, While Twitter Plays It Safe with Focus on User Interests," *Advertising Age,* September 10, 2012, p. 20; and "Infogroup Targeting Solution Launches Sapphire™, a New Integrated Marketing Database," *GlobeNewswire,* August 7, 2012.

39. Sapna Maheshwari and Matt Townsend, "BC-E-MAIL-MARKETING-RETA," *Postmedia Breaking News,* March 14, 2013; "A-Catalog-Printer.com Uses Revolutionary Soy Ink Technology to Help the Environment and Reduce Costs of Printing," *SBWire,* March 22, 2013; Charley Howard, "Help USPS Help You: 3 Ways to Cut Mail Costs through Workshare Discounts," http://www.targetmarketingmag.com/article/3-ways-cut-mail-costs-throughworkshare-discounts-417119/1#, February 2011; and "How Much Will Postal Cuts Hurt?" *Advertising Age,* February 11, 2013, p. 3.

40. "Companies Opposing Anti-Spam Laws," *The Toronto Star,* February 9, 2013, p. B5; Beth Negus Viveiros, "New Bill Takes Permission Beyond Opt-In in EU," *Chief Marketer,* April 19, 2011; "China: New Media Blossoming as Business Models Revamp," *BBC Monitoring World Media,* December 9, 2008; "The Data Dilemma," *Marketing Direct,* February 6, 2007, p. 37; and Marc Nohr, "South Africa—A Worthy Contender," *Marketing Direct,* March 5, 2007, p. 20.

41. Sean Michael Kerner, "What FCC's Move Against 'Do Not Track' Means," *eWeek,* November 9, 2015; "Protecting Your Identity and Your Privacy," *Targeted News Service,* March 1, 2013; "The Do Not Track Online Act Was Reintroduced in Congress," *The Business Insider,* March 1, 2013; "Online Behavioral Advertising," in the DMA OBA Guidelines, Direct Marketing Association website, http://thedma.org/issues/dma-oba-guidelines, accessed April 6, 2013; Don E. Shultz, "The Bugaboo of Behaviors," *Marketing Management,* Summer 2011, pp. 10–11; "Cell Phones Now Protected by the Do Not Call List," *States News Service,* May 16, 2011; Jonathan Brunt, "'Do Not Mail' Can't Gain Traction," *Spokesman Review,* May 5, 2010, p. 7; "DMA: 'Do Not Track Online Act' Is Unnecessary," *States News Service,* May 9, 2011; "DMA Updates Its 'Guidelines for Ethical Business Practice,'" *States News Service,* May 25, 2011; Martin Courtney and Tony Lock, "Keep It Safe, Keep It Legal," *Computing,* May 26, 2011; Siobhain Butterworth, "Cookie Law Shambles Really Takes the Biscuit," *Guardian Unlimited,* May 27, 2011; and Lara O'Reilly, "New Cookie Law: What You Need to Know," *Marketing Week,* May 26, 2011.

42. Taco Bell: This case was written by Steven Hartley. Sources: Samantha Scelzo, "I Tried the Naked Egg Taco from Taco Bell and Had the Most Sophisticated Experience," *Mashable,* www.mashable.com, August 17, 2017; "August Was a Big Month for the Taco Bell Foundation's Live Más Scholarship," press release, www.tacobell.com, September 20, 2017; Maureen Morrison, "In Breakfast Wars, Taco Bell's Bold Marketing Pays Off with Big Sales," *Advertising Age,* July 28, 2014, p. 6; "Taco Bell Serving Alcohol in Wicker Park Officially Opens Tuesday," WLS-TV, September 22, 2015; Maureen Morrison, "Taco Bell's New Concept: Designer Tacos in California," *Advertising Age,* April 28, 2014, p. 4; Vanessa Wong, "Taco Bell's Secret Recipe for New Products," *Bloomberg Businessweek,* June 2–8, 2014, pp. 18–20; Maureen Morrison, "Marketer of the Year 2013," *Advertising Age,* September 2, 2013, p. 15; Mark Brandau, "Yum Plans to Double U.S. Taco Bell Sales," *Restaurant News,* May 22, 2013; "The Glen Bell Legacy," www.tacobell.com/static_files/TacoBell/StaticAssets/documents/GlenBellLegacy.pdf; "Taco Bell," http://www.yum.com/brands/tb.asp; and interviews with Taco Bell executives.

16

Advertising, Sales Promotion, and Public Relations

LEARNING OBJECTIVES

After reading this chapter you should be able to:

LO 16-1 Explain the differences between product advertising and institutional advertising and the variations within each type.

LO 16-2 Describe the steps used to develop, execute, and evaluate an advertising program.

LO 16-3 Explain the advantages and disadvantages of alternative advertising media.

LO 16-4 Discuss the strengths and weaknesses of consumer-oriented and trade-oriented sales promotions.

LO 16-5 Recognize public relations as an important form of communication.

Fantasy Is Becoming Reality for Advertisers!

Just a few years ago virtual reality (VR) and augmented reality (AR) technologies were primarily the domain of video game companies and hard-core gamers. Not anymore. Today, more than 20 million people have tried the technologies and advertisers are thrilled!

Advertisers are facing an increasingly challenging environment where ad blocking, a surplus of media, and changing viewing behaviors are reducing the effectiveness of traditional advertising. In addition, consumers want less intrusive advertising and fewer irrelevant ads. According to Helen Mussard, vice president of global marketing for Vibrant Media, when consumers "choose to engage with an ad, it has to be relevant to them personally and has to be a worthwhile use of their time."

VR and AR technologies offer advertisers a way to provide unique, immersive experiences to consumers. Virtual reality is a 360-degree computer-simulated audio and video experience created with headsets that look a little like ski goggles. Augmented reality is a live view of a physical, real-world environment with computer-generated images added to the view. Perhaps you remember the location-based AR game Pokémon Go, one of the first augmented reality success stories. Experts predict that by 2020 more than 154 million people will use these technologies. In addition, a recent survey indicates that 67 percent of media planners want more VR and AR ads implemented into digital marketing campaigns.

So how will virtual reality and augmented reality work for businesses? According to Alex Lirtsman, co-founder of digital marketing agency ReadySetRocket, "It's the ultimate way a car company can showcase their latest car, a retailer can provide a view of their Fashion Week event, a travel destination can showcase activities, or any advertiser can truly take a 30-second spot to the next level."

Many technology companies offer headset options, ranging from Google's Daydream View (which requires a smartphone) to Sony's VR headset, to Facebook's Oculus Rift, to HTC's Vive. The cost ranges from $79 for a viewer to $800 for a headset with a high-resolution display. While current sales of these products are approximately $700 million, experts suggest that sales will reach $150 billion in just a few years.

Source: McDonald's

Source: Lowe's

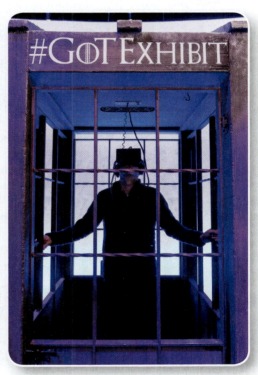

©Ray Tang/REX/Shutterstock

Several companies have already implemented virtual reality campaigns. McDonald's, for example, introduced Happy Goggles in Sweden, which lets you refold a Happy Meal box into a virtual reality viewer for children. Lowe's created Holoroom, a tool that allows customers to virtually step into model kitchens or bathrooms using an Oculus Rift headset. The TV series *Game of Thrones* created a VR experience where users ascend a 700-foot ice wall, and Marriott hotels created an experience that "teleports" people to London or Maui.

advertising
Any paid form of nonpersonal communication about an organization, product, service, or idea by an identified sponsor.

Video 16-1
Virtual Reality
kerin.tv/cr8e/v16-1

While some of this sounds like enthusiasm for new gadgets, advertisers are preparing for a substantial new medium. According to film director Chris Milk, "From an advertising perspective, it's a very powerful tool. Advertisers are looking for two main things: penetrating people's consciousness and getting their undivided attention. With virtual reality, you have their undivided attention because they can't see or hear anything else." Results of initial studies indicate that the technology appeals to younger, tough-to-reach consumers in the 12–34 age group, and that new VR and AR campaigns lead to 2,700 percent higher brand recall![1]

The growth of virtual reality is just one of the many exciting changes occurring in the field of advertising today and illustrates the importance of advertising as one of the five promotional mix elements in marketing communications programs. This chapter describes three of the promotional mix elements—advertising, sales promotion, and public relations. Direct marketing was covered in Chapter 15, and personal selling is covered in Chapter 18.

TYPES OF ADVERTISEMENTS

LO 16-1 Explain the differences between product advertising and institutional advertising and the variations within each type.

Chapter 15 described **advertising** as any paid form of nonpersonal communication about an organization, product, service, or idea by an identified sponsor. As you scan ads on your smartphone, look through any magazine, watch television, listen to the radio, or browse the Internet, the variety of advertisements you see or hear may give you the impression that they have few similarities. Advertisements are prepared for different purposes, but they basically consist of two types: product advertisements and institutional advertisements.

Product Advertisements

Focused on selling a product or service, **product advertisements** take three forms: (1) pioneering (or informational), (2) competitive (or persuasive), and (3) reminder. Look at the ads below for Mercedes-Benz, Progressive, and Duracell to determine the type and objective of each ad.

Used in the introductory stage of the product life cycle, *pioneering* advertisements tell people what a product is, what it can do, and where it can be found. The key objective of a pioneering advertisement (such as the Mercedes-Benz ad introducing its self-driving car) is to inform the target market. Informational ads, particularly those with specific message content, have been found to be interesting, convincing, and effective.[2]

Advertising that promotes a specific brand's features and benefits is *competitive*. The objective of these messages is to persuade the target market to select the firm's

Product advertisements take three forms—pioneering, competitive, or reminder—depending on their objective. See if you can correctly identify the ads shown here.
Sources: Left: Mercedes-Benz USA, LLC; Middle: Progressive Casualty Insurance Company; Right: Duracell Inc.

product advertisements
Advertisements that focus on selling a product or service and which take three forms: (1) pioneering (or informational), (2) competitive (or persuasive), and (3) reminder.

institutional advertisements
Advertisements designed to build goodwill or an image for an organization rather than promote a specific product or service.

brand rather than that of a competitor. An increasingly common form of competitive advertising is *comparative* advertising, which shows one brand's strengths relative to those of competitors.[3] The Progressive ad, for example, highlights its competitive rates compared to other auto insurers. Studies indicate that comparative ads attract more attention and increase the perceived quality of the advertiser's brand although their impact may vary by product type, message content, and audience gender.[4] Firms that use comparative advertising need marketing research to provide legal support for their claims.[5]

Reminder advertising is used to reinforce previous knowledge of a product. The Duracell ad reminds consumers not to forget that those Christmas toys will need batteries. Reminder advertising is good for products that have achieved a well-recognized position and are in the mature phase of their product life cycle. Another type of reminder ad, *reinforcement,* is used to assure current users they made the right choice. For example, consider the tagline used in Dial soap advertisements: "Aren't you glad you use Dial? Don't you wish everybody did?"

Institutional Advertisements

The objective of **institutional advertisements** is to build goodwill or an image for an organization rather than promote a specific product or service. Institutional advertising has been used by companies such as Texaco, Pfizer, and IBM to build confidence in the company name.[6] Often this form of advertising is used to support the public relations plan or counter adverse publicity. Four alternative forms of institutional advertisements are often used:

1. *Advocacy* advertisements state the position of a company on an issue. Chevron's "We Agree" campaign placed ads stating its position on issues such as renewable energy, protecting the planet, and community development. Another form of advocacy advertisement is used when organizations make a request related to a particular action or behavior, such as a request by Coca-Cola to recycle.
2. *Pioneering institutional* advertisements, like the pioneering ads for products discussed earlier, are used for announcements about what a company is, what it can do, or where it is located. Recent Bayer ads stating "We cure more headaches than you think" are intended to inform consumers that the company produces many products in addition to aspirin. Whole Foods uses pioneering institutional ads to inform people about its new Responsibly Grown rating system.
3. *Competitive institutional* advertisements promote the advantages of one product class over another and are used in markets where different product classes compete for the same buyers. America's milk processors and dairy farmers use their "Milk Life" campaign to increase demand for milk as it competes against other beverages.
4. *Reminder institutional* advertisements, like reminder ads for products, simply bring the company's name to the attention of the target market again. The Army branch of the U.S. military sponsors a campaign to remind potential recruits of the opportunities available in the Army.

Video 16-2
Chevron
kerin.tv/cr8e/v16-2

A competitive institutional ad by dairy farmers tries to increase demand for milk.
Source: America's Milk Companies

---

learning review

16-1. What is the difference between pioneering and competitive ads?

16-2. What is the purpose of an institutional advertisement?

DEVELOPING THE ADVERTISING PROGRAM

LO 16-2 Describe the steps used to develop, execute, and evaluate an advertising program.

The promotion decision process described in Chapter 15 can be applied to each of the promotional elements. Advertising, for example, can be managed by following the three steps (developing, executing, and evaluating) of the process.

Identifying the Target Audience

To develop an effective advertising program, advertisers must identify the target audience. All aspects of an advertising program are likely to be influenced by the characteristics of the prospective consumer. Understanding the lifestyles, attitudes, and demographics of the target market is essential. Mountain Dew, for example, is targeted at millennial males, while Kraft's Crystal Light Liquid is targeted at calorie-conscious women. Both campaigns emphasize advertising techniques that match their target audiences. To appeal to millennial males, Mountain Dew launched its "Do the Dew" campaign, featuring professional skateboarder Sean Malto, on Facebook, Twitter, Snapchat, and Instagram. Meanwhile, to attract calorie-conscious women, Crystal Light began providing nutritional information on Target.com and offering a free T-shirt with purchase.

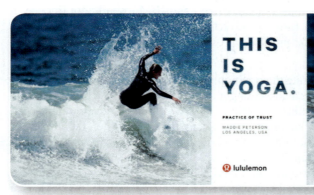

Lululemon places its ads to reach current and potential new customers.
Source: Lululemon Athletica

Similarly, the placement of the advertising depends on the audience. When Lululemon introduced its "This Is Yoga" campaign featuring "healthy lifestyle" apparel it included a mix of social media, digital channels, billboards, and in-store merchandising. In addition, video ads on Sling TV featuring popular athletes, such as Olympic gold medalist Kerri Walsh Jennings and surfer Maddie Peterson, were placed to reach current and potential consumers. Even scheduling can depend on the audience. Nike schedules advertising, sponsorships, deals, and endorsements to correspond with the Olympics to appeal to amateur, college, and professional athletes.[7]

Specifying Advertising Objectives

The guidelines for setting promotion objectives described in Chapter 15 also apply to setting advertising objectives. This step helps advertisers with other choices in the promotion decision process, such as selecting media and evaluating a campaign. Advertising with an objective of creating awareness, for example, would be better matched with a magazine than a directory such as the yellow pages. The Association of Magazine Media believes objectives are so important that it created an awards program to recognize magazine advertising campaigns that demonstrate both creative excellence and effectiveness in meeting campaign objectives. Similarly, the Advertising Research Foundation sponsors research forums to advance the practice of measuring and evaluating the effectiveness of advertising and marketing communication.[8]

Setting the Advertising Budget

In 1990, advertisers paid $700,000 to place a 30-second ad during the Super Bowl. By 2018, the cost of placing a 30-second ad during Super Bowl LII was $5 million. The escalating cost is related to the number of viewers: 103 million people watched the game. In addition, the audience is attractive to advertisers because research indicates it is equally split between men and women; these viewers are likely to engage brands on social media before and after the game; and they look forward to watching the ads during the game. The ads are effective too: Pepsi ads led to 3,932,000 views on its website; Weathertech

Do you remember this Amazon ad from the Super Bowl?
Source: Amazon.com, Inc.

Video 16-3
Amazon Super Bowl Ad
kerin.tv/cr8e/v16-3

increased customer engagement by 225%; and a study of movies released after their Super Bowl ads showed an increase of $8.4 million in opening weekend revenue. As a result, the Super Bowl attracts both new advertisers, such as Monster headphones, Pringles, Kraft, and Intuit, and regular advertisers such as Anheuser-Busch and Coca-Cola. Amazon's "Alexa Loses Her Voice" ad about celebrities filling in for Alexa when she temporarily loses her voice received the highest rating from the *USA Today* Ad Meter.[9]

Designing the Advertisement

An advertising message usually focuses on the key benefits of the product that are important to a prospective buyer in making trial and adoption decisions. The message depends on the general form or appeal used in the ad and the actual words included in the ad.

Message Content Most advertising messages are made up of both informational and persuasive elements. These two elements are so intertwined that it is sometimes difficult to tell them apart. For example, basic information such as the product name, benefits, features, and price can be presented in a way that tries to attract attention and encourage purchase. On the other hand, even the most persuasive advertisements have to contain at least some basic information to be successful.

Information and persuasive content can be combined in the form of an appeal to provide a basic reason for the consumer to act. Although the marketer can use many different types of appeals, common advertising appeals include fear, sex, and humor.

Fear appeals suggest to the consumer that he or she can avoid some negative experience through the purchase and use of a product or service, a change in behavior, or a reduction in the use of a product. Examples with which you may be familiar include automobile safety ads that depict an accident or injury; political candidate endorsements that warn against the rise of other, unpopular ideologies; or social cause ads warning of the serious consequences of drug and alcohol use. Insurance companies often try to show the negative effects on the relatives of those who die prematurely without carrying enough life or mortgage insurance. Food producers encourage the purchase of low-carb, low-fat, and high-fiber products as a means of reducing weight, lowering cholesterol levels, and preventing a heart attack. The MeNotMeth organization has run a series of ads that use fear appeals in headlines such as: "I lost ME to METH." The image shows a distressed young man looking into the camera.

Read the text to learn why AG uses a sex appeal in its advertising.
Source: AG Adriano Goldschmied

When using fear appeals, the advertiser must be sure that the appeal is strong enough to get the audience's attention and concern but not so strong that it will lead them to tune out the message. Research suggests that overly threatening messages have a negative effect on the intention to adapt behavior. In fact, research on antismoking ads indicates that stressing the severity of long-term health risks may actually enhance smoking's allure among youth.[10]

In contrast, *sex appeals* suggest to the audience that the product will increase the attractiveness of the user. Sex appeals can be found in almost any product category, from automobiles to toothpaste. Consumers, however, are redefining what is acceptable use of sex appeals. There is growing interest in positive messages about female and male roles, and views on gender identity are changing. Abercrombie & Fitch, for example, has moved away from overly "sexualized" campaigns, and brands such as Zara, Guess, and Mattel's Barbie are using gender neutral ads. The contemporary lifestyle brand AG designs its advertising to communicate its "chic, sophisticated, classic" positioning for men and women. Studies indicate that sex appeals generate a greater response than other appeals, and they increase attention by helping advertising stand out in today's cluttered media environment. Unfortunately, sexual content does not always lead to changes in recall, recognition, or purchase intent. Experts suggest that sexual content is most effective when there is a strong fit between the use of a sex appeal in the ad and the image and positioning of the brand.[11]

Humorous appeals imply either directly or subtly that the product is more fun or exciting than competitors' offerings. As with fear and sex appeals, the use of humor is widespread in advertising and can be found in many product categories. You may have smiled at the popular Geico ads that use a talking gecko, or a group of robbers ordering a getaway car with an app, or a group of pigeons on a wire talking about Geico. These ads use humor to differentiate the company from its competitors. Geico has also created viral videos and posted them on video-sharing websites such as YouTube, where millions of viewers watch them within days.[12] You may have a favorite humorous ad character, such as the Energizer battery bunny, the Old Spice man, the AFLAC duck, or Travelocity's gnome. Advertisers believe that humor improves the effectiveness of their ads, although some studies suggest that humor wears out quickly, losing the interest of consumers. Another problem with humorous appeals is that their effectiveness may vary across cultures if used in a global campaign.[13]

Video 16-4
Anomaly
kerin.tv/cr8e/v16-4

The "Wake Up the Silent Home" campaign helped Anomaly win *Advertising Age*'s Agency of the Year award.
Source: Sonos, Inc.

Creating the Actual Message Copywriters are responsible for creating the text portion of the message in advertisements. Translating the copywriter's ideas into an actual advertisement is a complex process. Designing quality artwork, layout, and production for advertisements is costly and time-consuming. The American Association of Advertising Agencies reports that a high-quality, 30-second TV commercial typically costs about $354,000 to produce. One reason for the high cost is that as companies have developed global campaigns, the need to shoot commercials in several locations has increased. In addition, advertisers frequently also need content for websites, online video channels, and digital place-based media, often as episodic series, to complement traditional commercials.[14]

Advertising agency Anomaly was recently designated *Advertising Age* magazine's Agency of the Year for its "work in data analytics, intellectual property and multicultural insights." Examples of the agency's approach include the "Be Heard" campaign for Beats by Dre, which includes 23 of the world's top athletes from 11 countries and 12 sports; the "It's Not What We Listen To, It's

Who We Are" campaign for YouTube Music; the "Food as It Should Be" campaign for Panera Bread; and the "Wake Up the Silent Home" campaign describing the Sonos speaker brand as the cure for the "silent home" epidemic caused by cell phone use. Anomaly was also recognized by *Fast Company* magazine as one of the World's Top 10 Most Innovative Companies in Advertising. In fact, the agency's website offers the definition of its name—deviation or departure from the normal—to describe its approach to advertising.[15]

learning review

16-3. Describe three common forms of advertising appeals.

16-4. _____ are responsible for creating the text portion of the messages in advertisements.

Selecting the Right Media

Video 16-5
Beats by Dre
kerin.tv/cr8e/v16-5

Every advertiser must decide where to place its advertisements. The alternatives are the *advertising media,* the means by which the message is communicated to the target audience. Newspapers, magazines, radio, and TV are examples of advertising media. Media selection is related to the target audience, type of product, nature of the message, campaign objectives, available budget, and the costs of the alternative media. Figure 16–1 shows the distribution of the $249 billion spent on advertising by medium.[16]

In deciding where to place advertisements, a company has several media to choose from and a number of alternatives, or vehicles, within each medium. Often advertisers use a mix of media forms and vehicles to maximize the exposure of the message to the target audience while at the same time minimizing costs. These two conflicting goals are of central importance to media planning.

Because advertisers try to maximize the number of individuals in the target market exposed to the message, they must be concerned with reach. *Reach* is the number of different people or households exposed to an advertisement. The exact definition of reach sometimes varies among alternative media. Newspapers often use reach to describe their total circulation or the number of different households that buy the paper.

FIGURE 16–1

Television, direct mail, and Internet account for more than 75 percent of all advertising expenditures ($ in millions).

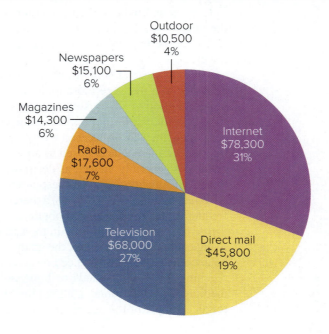

Applying Marketing Metrics
What Is the Best Way to Reach 1,000 Customers?

Marketing managers must choose from many advertising options as they design a campaign to reach potential customers. Because there are so many media alternatives (television, radio, magazines, etc.) and multiple options within each medium, it is important to monitor the efficiency of advertising expenditures on your marketing dashboard.

Your Challenge

As the marketing manager for a company about to introduce a new soft drink into the U.S. market, you are preparing a presentation in which you must make recommendations for the advertising campaign. You have observed that competitors use magazine ads, newspaper ads, and even Super Bowl ads! To compare the cost of some of the alternatives you decide to use one of the most common measures in advertising: cost per thousand impressions (CPM). The CPM is calculated as follows:

$$\text{CPM} = \left(\frac{\text{Cost of ad}}{\text{Audience size}}\right) \times 1{,}000$$

Your challenge is to determine the most efficient use of your advertising budget.

Your Findings

Your research department helps you collect cost and audience size information for three options: full-page color ads in *Time* magazine and the *USA Today* newspaper, and a 30-second television ad during the Super Bowl. With this information you are able to calculate the cost per thousand impressions for each alternative.

Media Alternative	Cost of Ad	Audience Size	Cost per Thousand Impressions
Time (magazine)	$ 254,200	2,000,000	$127
USA Today (newspaper)	$ 242,600	852,955	$284
Super Bowl (television)	$5,000,000	103,000,000	$ 49

Your Action

Based on the calculations for these options, you see that there is a large variation in the cost of reaching 1,000 potential customers (CPM) and also in the absolute cost of the advertising. Although advertising during the Super Bowl has the lowest CPM, $49 for each 1,000 impressions, it also has the largest absolute cost! Your next step will be to consider other factors such as your total available budget, the profiles of the audiences each alternative reaches, and whether the type of message you want to deliver is better communicated in print or on television.

Television and radio stations, in contrast, describe their reach using the term *rating*—the percentage of households in a market that are tuned to a particular TV show or radio station. In general, advertisers try to maximize reach in their target market at the lowest cost.

Although reach is important, advertisers are also interested in exposing their target audience to a message more than once. This is because consumers often do not pay close attention to advertising messages, some of which contain large amounts of relatively complex information. When advertisers want to reach the same audience more than once, they are concerned with *frequency,* the average number of times a person in the target audience is exposed to a message or advertisement. Like reach, greater frequency is generally viewed as desirable. Studies indicate that with repeated exposure to advertisements consumers respond more favorably to brand extensions.[17]

When reach (expressed as a percentage of the total market) is multiplied by frequency, an advertiser will obtain a commonly used reference number called *gross rating points* (*GRPs*). To obtain the appropriate number of GRPs to achieve an advertising campaign's objectives, the media planner must balance reach and frequency. The balance will also be influenced by cost. *Cost per thousand* (*CPM*) refers to the cost of reaching 1,000 individuals or households with the advertising message in a given medium (*M* is the Roman numeral for 1,000). See the Applying Marketing Metrics box for an example of the use of CPM in media selection.

LO 16-3 Explain the advantages and disadvantages of alternative advertising media.

Different Media Alternatives

Figure 16–2 summarizes the advantages and disadvantages of the major advertising media, which are described in more detail below. For detailed coverage of direct mail, refer to Chapter 15.

Television Television is a valuable medium because it communicates with sight, sound, and motion. Print advertisements alone could never give you the sense of a sports car accelerating from a stop or cornering at high speed. In addition, television reaches more than 96 percent of all households—118.4 million, including households that receive programming delivered over the Internet. There are also many opportunities for out-of-home TV viewing, as televisions are present in many bars, hotels, offices, airports, and college campuses.[18]

Several aspects of traditional television viewing are changing. First, research at the Nielsen Company indicates that the amount of time allocated to television viewing is increasing. American viewers now spend 41 hours each week watching television programming on multiple screens, including traditional TVs, computers, tablets, and smartphones. In addition, viewers are increasingly time shifting their viewing with

FIGURE 16–2
Advertisers must consider the advantages and disadvantages of the many media alternatives.

MEDIUM	ADVANTAGES	DISADVANTAGES
Television	Reaches extremely large audience; uses picture, print, sound, and motion for effect; can target specific audiences	High cost to prepare and run ads; short exposure time and perishable message; difficult to convey complex information
Radio	Low cost; can target specific local audiences; ads can be placed quickly; can use sound, humor, and intimacy effectively	No visual element; short exposure time and perishable message; difficult to convey complex information
Magazines	Can target specific audiences; high-quality color; long life of ad; ads can be clipped and saved; can convey complex information	Long time needed to place ad; relatively high cost; competes for attention with other magazine features
Newspapers	Excellent coverage of local markets; ads can be placed and changed quickly; ads can be saved; quick consumer response; low cost	Ads compete for attention with other newspaper features; short life span; poor color
Yellow Pages	Excellent coverage of geographic segments; long use period; available 24 hours/365 days	Proliferation of competitive directories in many markets; difficult to keep up to date
Internet	Video and audio capabilities; animation can capture attention; ads can be interactive and link to advertiser	Animation and interactivity require large files and more time to load; effectiveness is still uncertain
Outdoor	Low cost; local market focus; high visibility; opportunity for repeat exposures	Message must be short and simple; low selectivity of audience; criticized as a traffic hazard
Direct mail	High selectivity of audience; can contain complex information and personalized messages; high-quality graphics	High cost per contact; poor image (junk mail)

DVRs, DVDs, subscription services such as Netflix, and Internet options such as Hulu and Apple TV. In fact, the availability of streaming services has led to two trends: canceling pay-TV services, or "cord-cutting," and watching multiple episodes of a series in a short period of time, or "binge watching." Technologies are changing, too. In recent years, many consumers have purchased high-definition televisions. The future, however, will include 4K, 8K, OLED, QLED, and glassless 3D televisions, which are four to eight times as sharp as high-definition television, can convert ordinary television into 3D, offer voice-activated and motion controls, and allow the viewer to watch two programs simultaneously.[19]

Television's major disadvantage is cost: The price of a prime-time, 30-second ad can range from $699,602 to run on *Sunday Night Football*, to $239,782 to run on *Modern Family*, to $76,143 to run on *MacGyver*. Because of these high charges, many advertisers choose less expensive "spot" ads, which run between programs, or 15-second ads, rather than investing in ads that run the more traditional length of 30 or 60 seconds. In fact, approximately 44 percent of all TV ads are now 15 seconds long. Recent studies suggest that the placement of an ad within a program, and longer ads relative to other ads in a sequence of ads, may influence the ad's effectiveness. In addition, there is some indication that advertisers are shifting their interest to live events rather than programs that might be watched on a DVR days later.[20]

Another popular form of television advertising is the infomercial. **Infomercials** are program-length (30-minute) advertisements that take an educational approach to communication with potential customers. You may remember seeing infomercials for Life-Lock, NutriBullet, ThighMaster, and OxiClean products. Infomercials are increasingly popular because they can be both informative and entertaining, and because the average cost of a 30-minute block of television time is only $425. The industry generates more than $250 billion in annual sales and has facilitated the long-term success of many products. The Total Gym infomercials featuring Chuck Norris and Christie Brinkley, for example, have led to more than $1 billion in sales![21]

infomercials
Program-length (30-minute) advertisements that take an educational approach to communication with potential customers.

Radio The United States has more than 15,500 broadcast radio stations. These stations consist of approximately 4,660 AM stations and 10,860 FM stations. In addition, there are thousands of webcast Internet radio stations. The major advantage of radio is that it is a segmented medium. For example, the American Forces Network, the Family Life Network, Business Talk Radio, and the Performance Racing Network are all listened to by different market segments. Satellite radio service SiriusXM offers more than 175 commercial-free, digital, coast-to-coast channels to consumers for a monthly fee, and Internet radio services such as Pandora, Spotify, and SoundCloud offer personalized channels to each listener. The large number of media options today has reduced the amount of time spent listening to radio, although radio still reaches 91 percent of all adults weekly. Millennials listen to radio an average of 9.9 hours each week, making radio an important medium for businesses with college students and recent graduates as a target market.[22]

A disadvantage of radio is that it has limited use for products that must be seen. Another problem is the ease with which consumers can tune out a commercial by switching stations. Radio is also a medium that competes for people's attention as they do other activities, such as driving, working, or relaxing. Radio listening time reaches its peak during the morning drive time (7 to 8 A.M.), remains high during the day, and then begins to decline in the afternoon (after 4 P.M.) as people return home and start evening activities.[23]

Magazines Magazines have become a very specialized medium. In fact, there are currently more than 7,293 consumer magazines. Some 237 new magazines were introduced last year, including *Airbnbmag*, a

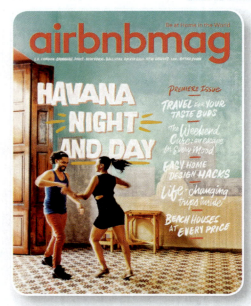

Magazines such as *Airbnbmag* appeal to narrowly defined segments such as travelers who use Airbnb's home-sharing service.
Source: Airbnb, Inc.

magazine about travel destinations that are frequently searched on Airbnb's home-sharing service; *Cre@te,* a magazine designed to inspire readers to use science, technology, and engineering to make great projects at home; and *Milk Street,* a magazine about an approach called "new home cooking" with a twist—no ads! Many publishers are also adding digital versions of existing magazines. *Skateboarder,* for example, can now also be read on the magazine's website, an iPad, or a smartphone. Some magazines, such as *Auto Trader* and *Computer Weekly,* are dropping their print format to offer only an online version. Finally, magazines such as *Good Housekeeping* and *Elle* are adding voice user interface (VUI) versions of their publications so the content will be available on voice assistant devices such as Amazon's Alexa and Apple's Siri.[24]

The marketing advantage of this medium is the great number of special-interest publications that appeal to narrowly defined segments. Runners read *Runner's World,* sailors buy *Yachting,* gardeners subscribe to *Garden Design,* and children peruse *Sports Illustrated for Kids.* Popular categories of magazines include arts and antiques, fashion, travel, cooking, automobiles, sports, and health. Each magazine's readers often represent a unique profile. Take the *Rolling Stone* reader, who tends to listen to music more than most people. SiriusXM Satellite Radio knows an ad in *Rolling Stone* is reaching the desired target audience. In addition, recent studies comparing advertising in different media suggest that magazine advertising is perceived to be more "inspirational" than other media.[25]

The cost of advertising in national magazines is a disadvantage, but many national publications publish regional and even metro editions, which reduces the absolute cost and wasted coverage. *Time,* for example, publishes well over 400 editions, including Latin American, Canadian, Asian, South Pacific, European, and U.S. editions.

Newspapers Newspapers are an important local medium with excellent reach potential. Daily publication allows advertisements to focus on specific current events, such as a 24-hour sale. Local retailers often use newspapers as their sole advertising medium. Newspapers are rarely saved by the purchaser, however, so companies are generally limited to ads that call for an immediate customer response (although customers can clip and save ads they select). Companies also cannot expect newspapers to offer the same quality color reproduction available in most magazines.

National advertising campaigns rarely include this medium except in conjunction with local distributors of their products. In these instances, both parties often share the advertising costs using a cooperative advertising program, which is described later in this chapter. Another exception is the use of newspapers such as *The Wall Street Journal* and *USA Today,* which have national print circulation of more than 1,099,000 and 852,000 readers, respectively. One newspaper, *Metro,* offers a global audience of 18 million daily readers in Boston, New York, Philadelphia, and 100 cities in Europe, North and South America, and Asia. Today, hundreds of newspapers, including *The New York Times, The Wall Street Journal,* the *Chicago Sun-Times,* and the *San Francisco Chronicle,* offer online versions of their printed newspapers.[26]

Yellow Pages Yellow pages represent an advertising media alternative comparable to outdoor advertising in terms of expenditures—about $8 billion in the United States. According to the Local Search Association, 40 percent of U.S. consumers turn to print yellow pages at least once a year and 25 percent use online yellow pages (desktop, tablet, and mobile) each month. One reason for this high level of use is that yellow pages directories reach almost all households. Yellow pages are a "directional" medium because they direct consumers to where purchases can be made after other media have created awareness and demand. One disadvantage faced by yellow pages today is the proliferation of directories. DexYP (*Real Yellow Pages*) and Hibu (*Yellowbook*) now produce competing directories for many cities, neighborhoods, and ethnic groups.[27]

©Shaul Schwarz/Getty Images

Print yellow pages are used more than 11 billion times each year. See the text for advantages and disadvantages of this media alternative.
©studiomode/Alamy Stock Photo

Internet The Internet represents a relatively new medium for many advertisers, although it has already attracted a wide variety of industries and is the largest medium in terms of advertising expenditures. Online advertising is similar to print advertising in that it offers a visual message. It has additional advantages, however, because it can also use the audio and video capabilities of the Internet. There are a variety of online advertising options. The most popular options are paid search, display (banner) ads, classified ads, and video. Online advertising also has the unique feature of being interactive. Called *rich media,* these interactive ads have drop-down menus, built-in games, or search engines to engage viewers. Online advertising also offers an opportunity to reach younger consumers who have developed a preference for online communication.

Classified ads, such as those on Craigslist, and video ads also contribute to the growth of online advertising by providing many of the advantages and characteristics of other media such as yellow pages, magazines, newspaper, and television. Video ads also have the benefit of "going viral" when people share the ads with friends. The widespread availability of Internet access and the popularity of smartphones means that online advertising also provides the unique characteristic of being mobile. In fact, **mobile marketing** now includes the broad set of interactive messaging options that enable organizations to communicate and engage with consumers through any mobile device. Recent research indicates that the location data available from mobile devices can substantially increase the effectiveness of mobile marketing efforts.[28]

> **mobile marketing**
> The broad set of interactive messaging options that enable organizations to communicate and engage with consumers through any mobile device.

comScore's service can provide an assessment of the effectiveness of a website by measuring its impact on the digital audience.

Courtesy of comScore, Inc.; (tape measure): ©Kim Hall/Getty Images

Another disadvantage to online advertising is the difficulty of measuring impact. Several companies are testing methods of tracking where viewers go on their computer in the days and weeks after seeing an ad. Nielsen's online rating service, for example, measures actual Internet use through meters installed on the computers of 500,000 individuals in 20 countries. Measuring the relationship between online and offline behavior is also important. Research by comScore, which studied 139 online ad campaigns, revealed that online ads didn't always result in a "click," but they increased the likelihood of a purchase by 17 percent and they increased visits to the advertiser's website by 40 percent.[29] The Making Responsible Decisions box describes how click fraud is increasing the necessity of assessing online advertising effectiveness.[30]

Outdoor A very effective medium for reminding consumers about your product is outdoor advertising, such as the scoreboard at at your favorite stadium. The most common form of outdoor advertising, called *billboards,* often results in good reach and frequency and has been shown to increase purchase rates, particularly when the billboards provide useful information in an entertaining way, in relevant locations.[31] The visibility of this medium is good supplemental reinforcement for well-known products, and it is a relatively low-cost, flexible alternative. Also, a company can buy space in a specific, targeted geographical market. A disadvantage to billboards, however, is that no opportunity exists for lengthy advertising copy. Also, a good billboard site depends on traffic patterns and sight lines. If you have ever lived in a metropolitan area, chances are you might have seen another form of outdoor advertising, *transit advertising.* This medium includes messages on the interior and exterior of buses, subway and light-rail cars, and taxis.

Outdoor advertising can be an effective medium for reminding consumers about a product.

©Bhubeth Bhajanavorakul/Shutterstock

Other Media As traditional media have become more expensive and cluttered, advertisers have been attracted to a variety of nontraditional advertising options called out-of-home advertising, or *place-based media.* Messages are placed in locations that attract a specific target audience such as bus stops, airports, doctors' offices, health clubs, theaters (where ads are played on the screen before the movies are shown), grocery stores, storefronts, and even the bathrooms of bars, restaurants, and nightclubs. Soon there will be advertising on video screens on gas pumps, ATMs, and in elevators, and increasingly it will be interactive.

Making Responsible Decisions

Ethics

Who Is Responsible for Preventing Click Fraud?

Spending on Internet advertising now exceeds $78 billion as many advertisers shift their budgets from print and TV to the Internet. For most advertisers one advantage of online advertising is that they pay only when someone clicks on their ad. Unfortunately, the growth of the medium has led to "click fraud," which is the deceptive clicking of ads solely to increase the amount advertisers must pay. There are several forms of click fraud. One method is the result of Paid-to-Read (PTR) websites that recruit and pay members to simply click on ads. Another method is the result of "clickbots," which are software programs that produce automatic clicks on ads, sometimes through mobile devices. The activity is difficult to detect and stop. Google, for example, recently discovered 41 apps with hidden "adware" that had been downloaded 36 million times over a one-year period. Experts estimate that up to 20 percent of clicks may be the result of fraud and may be costing advertisers as much as $6.5 billion each year!

Investigations of the online advertising industry have discovered a related form of click fraud that occurs when legitimate website visitors click on ads without any intention of looking at the site. As one consumer explains, "I always try and remember to click on the ad banners once in a while to try and keep the sites free." Stephen Dubner calls this "webtipping"!

©Aleksandra H. Kossowska/Shutterstock

As the Internet advertising industry grows, it will become increasingly important to resolve the issue of click fraud. Consumers, advertisers, websites that carry paid advertising, and the large web portals are all involved in a complicated technical, legal, and social situation. The advertising industry's Media Ratings Council has suggested a possible solution: that 50 percent of a display ad must be in view for one second to be an impression that brands pay for. Some advertisers such as Unilever, however, require 100 percent viewability. Similarly, some advertisers are now requesting "smart-pricing," which means that they pay less if the click does not lead to a consumer action such as a purchase or an information request.

Who should lead the way in the effort to find a solution to click fraud? What actions do you suggest for the advertising industry, websites, and consumers?

Out-of-home advertising such as this outdoor display is becoming interactive to engage consumers.
©Roman Tiraspolsky/Shutterstock

The $2.5 billion industry has attracted advertisers such as AT&T and JCPenney, which use in-store campaigns, and Geico, Sprint, and FedEx, which use out-of-home advertising to reach mobile professionals in health clubs, airports, and hotels. Research suggests that creative use of out-of-home advertising, such as preshow theater ads, enhances consumer recall of the ads.[32]

Scheduling the Advertising

There is no correct schedule to advertise a product, but three factors must be considered. First is the issue of *buyer turnover,* which is how often new buyers enter the market to buy the product. The higher the buyer turnover, the greater the amount of advertising required. A second issue in scheduling is the *purchase frequency*; the more frequently the product is purchased, the less repetition is required. Finally, companies must consider the *forgetting rate,* the speed with which buyers forget the brand if advertising is not seen.

Setting schedules requires an understanding of how the market behaves. Most companies tend to follow one of three basic approaches:

1. *Continuous (steady) schedule.* When seasonal factors are unimportant, advertising is run at a continuous or steady schedule throughout the year.

2. *Flighting (intermittent) schedule.* Periods of advertising are scheduled between periods of no advertising to reflect seasonal demand.
3. *Pulse (burst) schedule.* A flighting schedule is combined with a continuous schedule because of increases in demand, heavy periods of promotion, or introduction of a new product.

For example, products such as breakfast cereals have a stable demand throughout the year and would typically use a continuous schedule of advertising. In contrast, products such as snow skis and suntan lotions have seasonal demands and receive flighting-schedule advertising during the seasonal demand period. Some products such as toys or automobiles require pulse-schedule advertising to facilitate sales throughout the year and during special periods of increased demand (such as holidays or new car introductions). Some evidence suggests that pulsing schedules are superior to other advertising strategies.[33] In addition, research indicates the effectiveness of a particular ad wears out quickly and, therefore, many alternative forms of a commercial may be more effective.[34]

learning review

16-5. You see the same ad in *Time* and *Fortune* magazines and on billboards and TV. Is this an example of reach or frequency?

16-6. Why has the Internet become a popular advertising medium?

16-7. Describe three approaches to scheduling advertising.

EXECUTING THE ADVERTISING PROGRAM

Executing the advertising program involves pretesting the advertising copy and actually carrying out the advertising program. John Wanamaker, the founder of Wanamaker's Department Store in Philadelphia, remarked, "I know half my advertising is wasted, but I don't know what half." By evaluating advertising efforts, marketers can try to ensure that their advertising expenditures are not wasted.[35] Evaluation is done usually at two separate times: before and after the advertisements are run in the actual campaign. Several methods used in the evaluation process at the stages of idea formulation and copy development are discussed below.

Pretesting the Advertising

To determine whether the advertisement communicates the intended message or to select among alternative versions of the advertisement, **pretests** are conducted before the advertisements are placed in any medium.

Portfolio Tests Portfolio tests are used to test copy alternatives. The test ad is placed in a portfolio with several other ads and stories, and consumers are asked to read through the portfolio. Afterward, subjects are asked for their impressions of the ads on several evaluative scales, such as from "very informative" to "not very informative."

Jury Tests Jury tests involve showing the ad copy to a panel of consumers and having them rate how they liked it, how much it drew their attention, and how attractive they thought it was. This approach is similar to the portfolio test in that consumer reactions are obtained. However, unlike the portfolio test, a test advertisement is not hidden within other ads.

pretests
Tests conducted before an advertisement is placed in any medium to determine whether it communicates the intended message or to select among alternative versions of the advertisement.

Theater Tests Theater testing is the most sophisticated form of pretesting. Consumers are invited to view new television shows or movies in which test commercials are also shown. Viewers register their feelings about the advertisements either on handheld electronic recording devices used during the viewing or on questionnaires afterward.

Carrying Out the Advertising Program

The responsibility for actually carrying out the advertising program can be handled by one of three types of agencies. The *full-service agency* provides the most complete range of services, including marketing research, media selection, copy development, artwork, and production. The most common form of compensation for an agency is a fee-based model, although recent surveys by the Association of National Advertisers (ANA) indicate that there may be a shift away from this method. Another form of compensation is a commission-based model which pays a percentage of the value of media costs. Finally, advertisers that have implemented integrated marketing communication approaches have utilized incentive-based models. These plans typically link compensation to specific performance goals. The use of incentive-based models may be declining also, however, because they can become very complex with traditional and digital marketing elements.

Limited-service agencies specialize in one aspect of the advertising process, such as providing creative services to develop the advertising copy, buying previously unpurchased media (media agencies), or providing Internet services (Internet agencies). Limited-service agencies that deal in creative work are compensated by a contractual agreement for the services performed. Finally, *in-house agencies* made up of the company's own advertising staff may provide full services or a limited range of services.

posttests
Tests conducted after an advertisement has been shown to the target audience to determine whether it accomplished its intended purpose.

ASSESSING THE ADVERTISING PROGRAM

The advertising decision process does not stop with executing the advertising program. The advertisements must be evaluated to determine whether they are achieving their intended objectives, and results may indicate that changes must be made in the advertising program.

Posttesting the Advertising

An advertisement may go through **posttests** after it has been shown to the target audience to determine whether it accomplished its intended purpose. Five approaches common in posttesting are discussed here.[36]

The Starch test uses aided recall to evaluate an ad on four dimensions. See the text to learn more.
Courtesy of GfK North America

Aided Recall After being shown an ad, respondents are asked whether their previous exposure to it was through reading, viewing, or listening. The Starch test shown in the accompanying photo uses aided recall to determine the percentage of those who (1) remember seeing a specific ad (*noted*), (2) saw or read any part of the ad identifying the product or brand (*associated*), (3) read any part of the ad's copy (*read any*), and (4) read at least half of the ad (*read most*). Elements of the ad are then tagged with the results, as shown in the photo.[37]

Unaided Recall The unaided recall approach involves asking respondents a question such as, "What ads do you remember seeing yesterday?" without any prompting to determine whether they saw or heard advertising messages.

Attitude Tests Attitude tests involve asking respondents questions to measure changes in their attitudes after an advertising campaign. For example, they might be asked whether they now have a more favorable attitude toward the product advertised. Recent research suggests that attitudes can be influenced by many factors, including the increasingly popular use of co-creation to develop consumer-generated ads.[38]

Inquiry Tests Inquiry tests involve offering additional product information, product samples, or premiums to an ad's readers or viewers. Ads generating the most inquiries are presumed to be the most effective.

Sales Tests Sales tests involve studies such as controlled experiments (e.g., using radio ads in one market and newspaper ads in another and comparing the results) and consumer purchase tests (measuring retail sales that result from a given advertising campaign). The most sophisticated experimental methods today allow a manufacturer, a distributor, or an advertising agency to manipulate an advertising variable (such as schedule or copy) through cable systems and observe subsequent sales effects by monitoring data collected from checkout scanners in supermarkets.[39]

Making Needed Changes

Results of posttesting the advertising copy are used to reach decisions about changes in the advertising program. If the posttest results show that an advertisement is doing poorly in terms of awareness, cost efficiency, or sales, it may be dropped and other ads run in its place in the future. On the other hand, sometimes an advertisement may be so successful it is run repeatedly or used as the basis for a larger advertising program.

learning review

16-8. Explain the difference between pretesting and posttesting advertising copy.

16-9. What is the difference between aided and unaided recall posttests?

SALES PROMOTION

Discuss the strengths and weaknesses of consumer-oriented and trade-oriented sales promotions.

Sales promotion is a key element of the promotional mix today; it now accounts for more than $82 billion in annual expenditures. In a recent forecast by Zenith Media Services, sales promotion expenditures accounted for 18 percent of all promotional spending.[40] The large allocation of marketing expenditures to sales promotion reflects the trend toward integrated marketing communications programs, which often include a variety of sales promotion elements. Selection and integration of the many promotion techniques require a good understanding of the advantages and disadvantages of each kind of sales promotion. Sales promotions can have a positive influence on brand loyalty, perceptions of quality, purchase intentions, and sales.[41] The two major kinds of sales promotions, consumer-oriented and trade-oriented, are discussed below.

Consumer-Oriented Sales Promotions

consumer-oriented sales promotions
Sales tools used to support a company's advertising and personal selling directed to ultimate consumers. Also called *consumer promotions*.

Directed to ultimate consumers, **consumer-oriented sales promotions**, or simply *consumer promotions,* are sales tools used to support a company's advertising and personal selling. A variety of consumer-oriented sales promotion tools may be used, including coupons, deals, premiums, contests, sweepstakes, samples, loyalty programs, point-of-purchase displays, rebates, and product placements.

Coupons
Coupons are sales promotions that usually offer a discounted price to the consumer, which encourages trial. Approximately 321 billion coupons worth $550 billion are distributed in the United States each year. More than 93 percent of all coupons are distributed as freestanding inserts in newspapers. Research indicates that consumer use of coupons is steady at approximately 80 percent. Consumers redeemed 2.5 billion of the coupons last year, for a savings of approximately $3.4 billion.

Companies that have increased their use of coupons include Procter & Gamble, Nestlé, and Kraft, while the top retailers for coupon redemption were Walmart, Kroger, and Target. The number of coupons generated at Internet sites (e.g., www.valpak.com and www.coupon.com) and on mobile phones has been increasing as well, although they account for less than 1 percent of all coupons. The redemption rate for online coupons—approximately 12 percent—however, is substantially higher than other forms of coupons. Daily deal sites like Groupon.com and LivingSocial.com have helped fuel the growth in couponing. Today, coupons are available in almost every product category and they are used by men and women of all ages.[42]

Coupons encourage trial by offering a discounted price. See the text to learn if coupons increase sales.
©McGraw-Hill Education/Mike Hruby, photographer

Coupons are often far more expensive than the face value of the coupon; a 25-cent coupon can cost three times that after paying for the advertisement to deliver it, dealer handling, clearinghouse costs, and redemption. In addition, misredemption, or attempting to redeem a counterfeit coupon or a valid coupon when the product was not purchased, should be added to the cost of the coupon. The Coupon Information Corporation estimates that companies pay out refunds worth hundreds of millions of dollars each year as a result of coupon fraud. Recent growth in coupon fraud has marketers considering adding holograms and visual aids to help cashiers identify valid coupons.[43]

Deals
Deals are short-term price reductions, commonly used to increase trial among potential customers or to retaliate against a competitor's actions. For example, if a rival manufacturer introduces a new cake mix, the company responds with a "two packages for the price of one" deal. This short-term price reduction builds up the stock on the kitchen shelves of cake mix buyers and makes the competitor's introduction more difficult.

Premiums
A promotion tool often used with consumers is the premium, which consists of merchandise offered free or at a significant savings over its retail price. This latter type of premium is called self-liquidating because the cost charged to the consumer covers the cost of the item. McDonald's, for example, used a free premium in a promotional partnership with Nintendo during the release of the Nintendo Switch console. Collectible toys that portrayed one of eight Super Mario characters were given away free with the purchase of a Happy Meal. What are the most popular premiums? According to the Promotional Products Association International, the top premiums are apparel, writing instruments, shopping bags, cups and mugs, and desk accessories. By offering a premium, companies encourage customers to return frequently or to use more of the product. Research suggests that deal-prone consumers and value seekers are attracted to premiums.[44]

Contests
Contests are another sales promotion tool used with consumers. Contests encourage consumers to apply their skill or analytical or creative thinking to try to win a prize. This form of promotion has been growing as requests for videos, photos, and essays are a good match with the trend toward consumer-generated content. For example, Nabisco sponsored the Oreo Creation Contest, asking people to submit their ideas for the next cookie flavor on its social media platforms. A panel of judges then

Nabisco's Oreo Creation Contest offered a $500,000 prize and a trip to New York City.
Source: Nabisco

selected the finalists based on taste appeal, creativity, and originality. The three highest-scoring submissions were produced and placed in the market for voting by the public. The winner received a trip to New York City and was awarded a $500,000 prize! If you like contests, you can enter online now at websites such as www.contestbee.com.[45]

Sweepstakes Sweepstakes are sales promotions that require participants to submit some kind of entry but are purely games of chance requiring no analytical or creative effort by the consumer. Popular sweepstakes include the HGTV "Dream Home Giveaway," which receives more than 90 million entries each year, and McDonald's Monopoly, which offers a grand prize of $1 million.[46]

Two variations of sweepstakes are popular now. First are sweepstakes that offer products that consumers value as prizes. Mars Chocolate, for example, created a sweepstakes where consumers enter a UPC code from M&M's products for a chance to win one of five Toyota automobiles. Pepsi created a similar sweepstakes called "Pepsi Fire" that allows consumers to use Snapchat to submit codes from bottles of Pepsi and Pepsi Fire to win prizes.

The second type of sweepstakes offers an "experience" as the prize. For example, one of television's most popular series, *The Voice*, and Nissan sponsored a sweepstakes for a chance to win a trip for two to the season finale of *The Voice* in Los Angeles. Similarly, for each of the past five years, People Entertainment Network has sponsored the Oscars Fan Experience Sweepstakes for a chance to win a trip to the Oscars in Hollywood.

Federal laws, the Federal Trade Commission, and state legislatures have issued rules covering sweepstakes, contests, and games to regulate fairness, ensure that the chance for winning is represented honestly, and guarantee that the prizes are actually awarded. Several well-known sweepstakes created by Publishers Clearing House and *Reader's Digest* have paid fines and agreed to new sweepstakes guidelines in response to regulatory scrutiny.[47]

Samples Another common consumer sales promotion is sampling, which is offering the product free or at a greatly reduced price. Often used for new products, sampling puts the product in the consumer's hands. A trial size is generally offered that is smaller than the regular package size. If consumers like the sample, it is hoped they will remember and buy the product. Taco Bell has offered free tacos nationwide several times in the past to encourage customers to try new products. Recently, Taco Bell gave away free Doritos Locos tacos because the Golden State Warriors "stole" an away game in the NBA finals. The taco has become the company's most successful new product. Similarly, Ben & Jerry's offers a complimentary scoop of ice cream on "Free Cone Day." Some consumers watch for free samples online at sites such as www.freesamples.org. According to Stacy Fisher, who started trying free samples in college and now blogs about them, free samples are "a great way to try new things and save money."[48]

Loyalty Programs Loyalty programs are a sales promotion tool used to encourage and reward repeat purchases by acknowledging each purchase made by a consumer and offering a premium as purchases accumulate. The most popular loyalty programs today are credit card reward programs. More than 75 percent of all cards offer incentives for use of their card. Citibank, for example, offers "Thank You" points for using Citi credit or debit cards. The points can be redeemed for books, music, gift cards,

Ben & Jerry's free samples encourage customers to try new flavors, while the Plenti loyalty program rewards frequent customers at participating businesses.
Sources: Left: Ben & Jerry's Homemade, Inc.; Right: ©McGraw-Hill Education

product placement
A consumer sales promotion tool that uses a brand-name product in a movie, television show, video game, or a commercial for another product.

Point-of-purchase displays help increase consumers' attention in a store.
©McGraw-Hill Education

cash, travel, and special limited time rewards. Airlines, retailers, hotels, and grocery stores also offer popular loyalty programs. Specialty retailers such as Bed, Bath and Beyond and Best Buy have enhanced their reward programs to add value to their offerings as they compete with low-cost merchandise. A new rewards program, called Plenti, lets you earn points with several stores and businesses such as Macy's, Mobil, and Rite Aid. There are now more than 3.3 billion loyalty program memberships, for an average of 29 for each household in the United States, with point balances exceeding $50 billion.[49]

Point-of-Purchase Displays In a store aisle, you often encounter a sales promotion called a point-of-purchase display. These product displays take the form of advertising signs, which sometimes actually hold or display the product, and are often located in high-traffic areas near the cash register or the end of an aisle. The point-of-purchase display with signage for the movie *Pacific Rim: Uprising* is designed to maximize the consumer's attention to DVDs and provide storage for the products. Annual expenditures on point-of-purchase promotion are expected to grow as point-of-purchase becomes integrated with all forms of promotion.

Rebates Another consumer sales promotion tool, the cash rebate, offers the return of money based on proof of purchase. For example, T-Mobile recently offered a $325 rebate to any Pixel smartphone owner who would switch his or her mobile service from Verizon. When a rebate is offered on lower-priced items, the time and trouble of mailing in a proof of purchase to get the rebate check often means that many buyers never take advantage of it. However, this "slippage" is less likely to occur with frequent users of rebate promotions. In addition, online consumers are more likely to take advantage of rebates.[50]

Product Placements A final consumer promotion tool, **product placement**, involves the use of a brand-name product in a movie, television show, video game, or commercial for another product. It was Steven Spielberg's placement of

Product placement can take many forms today. Are you familiar with this example from the movie *Black Panther*?
©Walt Disney Studios Motion Pictures/Photofest

Hershey's Reese's Pieces in *E.T. the Extra Terrestrial* that first brought a lot of interest to the candy. Similarly, when Tom Cruise wore Bausch and Lomb's Ray-Ban sunglasses in *Risky Business* and its Aviator glasses in *Top Gun*, sales skyrocketed from 100,000 pairs to 7,000,000 pairs in five years. After *Toy Story*, Etch-A-Sketch sales increased 4,500 percent and Mr. Potato Head sales increased 800 percent.

More recently you might remember seeing products from Lexus in *Black Panther*; Under Armour in *Baywatch*; Stella Artois in *La La Land*; and, of course, Lego in *The Lego Batman Movie*. Which brand has the highest level of product placement in films? It's Ford, with placement in 31 of the top 50 films. And which film has the most product placements? *The Fate of the Furious,* with 109 identifiable brands and products.

The annual value of all product placements has grown to an estimated $6 billion as consumer resistance to traditional advertising has led advertisers to try new forms of promotion. Complaints that product placement has become excessive have led the Federal Communications Commission to begin developing guidelines for TV product placements. Meanwhile, the British government recently passed a law allowing product placement only if a bold "P" logo is shown before and after the program. Research suggests that a product placement disclosure such as this may lead to less favorable attitudes toward the products.[51]

Trade-Oriented Sales Promotions

Trade-oriented sales promotions, or simply *trade promotions,* are sales tools used to support a company's advertising and personal selling directed to wholesalers, retailers, or distributors. Some of the sales promotions just reviewed are used for this purpose, but three other common approaches are targeted uniquely to these intermediaries: (1) allowances and discounts, (2) cooperative advertising, and (3) training of distributors' salesforces.

trade-oriented sales promotions
Sales tools used to support a company's advertising and personal selling directed to wholesalers, distributors, or retailers. Also called *trade promotions*.

Allowances and Discounts Trade promotions often focus on maintaining or increasing inventory levels in the channel of distribution. An effective method for encouraging such increased purchases by intermediaries is the use of allowances and discounts. However, overuse of these price reductions can lead to retailers changing their ordering patterns in the expectation of such offerings. Although there are many variations that manufacturers can use with discounts and allowances, three common approaches are the merchandise allowance, the case allowance, and the finance allowance.[52]

Reimbursing a retailer for extra in-store support or special featuring of the brand is a *merchandise allowance*. Performance contracts between the manufacturer and trade member usually specify the activity to be performed, such as a picture of the product in a newspaper with a coupon good at only one store. The merchandise allowance then consists of a percentage deduction from the list case price ordered during the promotional period. Allowances are not paid by the manufacturer until it sees proof of performance (such as a copy of the ad placed by the retailer in the local newspaper).

A second common trade promotion, a *case allowance,* is a discount on each case ordered during a specific time period. These allowances are usually deducted from the invoice. A variation of the case allowance is the "free goods" approach, whereby retailers receive some amount of the product free based on the amount ordered, such as 1 case free for every 10 cases ordered.[53]

A final trade promotion, the *finance allowance,* involves paying retailers for financing costs or financial losses associated with consumer sales promotions. This trade promotion is regularly used and has several variations. One type is the floor stock protection program—manufacturers give retailers a case allowance price for products in their warehouse, which prevents shelf stock from running down during the promotional period. Also common are freight allowances, which compensate retailers that transport orders from the manufacturer's warehouse.

Cooperative Advertising Resellers often perform the important function of promoting the manufacturer's products at the local level. One common sales promotional activity is to encourage both better quality and greater quantity in the local advertising efforts of resellers through **cooperative advertising**. These are programs by which a manufacturer pays a percentage of the retailer's local advertising expense for advertising the manufacturer's products.

Usually, the manufacturer pays a percentage, often 50 percent, of the cost of advertising up to a certain dollar limit, which is based on the amount of the manufacturer's products purchased by the retailer. In addition to paying for the advertising, the manufacturer often furnishes the retailer with a selection of different ad executions, sometimes suited for several different media. A manufacturer may provide, for example, several different print layouts as well as a few broadcast ads for the retailer to adapt and use.[54]

Training of Distributors' Salesforces One of the many functions the intermediaries perform is customer contact and selling for the producers they represent. Both retailers and wholesalers employ and manage their own sales personnel. A manufacturer's success often rests on the ability of the reseller's salesforce to represent its products. Thus, it is in the best interest of the manufacturer to help train the reseller's salesforce.

Because the reseller's salesforce is often less sophisticated and knowledgeable about the products than the manufacturer might like, training can increase their sales performance. Training activities include producing manuals and brochures to educate the reseller's salesforce. The salesforce then uses these aids in selling situations. Other activities include national sales meetings sponsored by the manufacturer and field visits to the reseller's location to inform and motivate the salesperson to sell the products. Manufacturers also develop incentive and recognition programs to motivate a reseller's salespeople to sell their products.

> **cooperative advertising**
> Advertising programs whereby a manufacturer pays a percentage of the retailer's local advertising expense for advertising the manufacturer's products.

> **publicity tools**
> Methods of obtaining nonpersonal presentation of an organization, product, or service without direct cost, such as news releases, news conferences, and public service announcements (PSAs).

learning review

16-10. What is the difference between a coupon and a deal?

16-11. Which trade promotion tool is used to encourage the local advertising efforts of resellers?

PUBLIC RELATIONS

Recognize public relations as an important form of communication.

As noted in Chapter 15, public relations is a form of communications management that seeks to influence the image of an organization and its products and services. In developing a public relations campaign, several **publicity tools**—methods of obtaining nonpersonal presentation of an organization, product, or service without direct cost—are available to the public relations director. Many companies frequently use the *news*

Emma Stone receives publicity for her movies by visiting programs such as The Tonight Show Starring Jimmy Fallon.
©Theo Wargo/NBC/Stringer/Getty Images

release, consisting of an announcement regarding changes in the company or the product line. The objective of a news release is to inform a newspaper, radio station, or other medium of an idea for a story.

A second common publicity tool is the *news conference.* Representatives of the media are all invited to an informational meeting, and advance materials regarding the content are sent. This tool is often used when new products are introduced or significant changes in corporate structure and leadership are being made.

Nonprofit organizations rely heavily on *public service announcements (PSAs),* which are free space or time donated by the media. For example, the charter of the American Red Cross prohibits any local chapter from advertising, so to solicit blood donations local chapters often depend on PSAs on radio or television to announce their needs.

learning review

16-12. What is a news release?

16-13. What type of publicity tool is used most often by nonprofit organizations?

LEARNING OBJECTIVES REVIEW

LO 16-1 *Explain the differences between product advertising and institutional advertising and the variations within each type.*

Product advertisements focus on selling a good or service and take three forms: Pioneering advertisements tell people what a product is, what it can do, and where it can be found; competitive advertisements persuade the target market to select the firm's brand rather than a competitor's; and reminder advertisements reinforce previous knowledge of a product. Institutional advertisements are used to build goodwill or an image for an organization. They include advocacy advertisements, which state the position of a company on an issue, and pioneering, competitive, and reminder advertisements, which are similar to the product ads but focus on the institution.

LO 16-2 *Describe the steps used to develop, execute, and evaluate an advertising program.*

The promotion decision process can be applied to each of the promotional elements. The steps to develop an advertising program include the following: identify the target audience, specify the advertising objectives, set the advertising budget, design the advertisement, create the message, select the media, and schedule the advertising. Executing the program requires pretesting, and evaluating the program requires posttesting.

LO 16-3 *Explain the advantages and disadvantages of alternative advertising media.*

Television advertising reaches large audiences and uses picture, print, sound, and motion; its disadvantages, however, are that it is expensive and perishable. Radio advertising is inexpensive and can be placed quickly, but it has no visual element and is perishable. Magazine advertising can target specific audiences and can convey complex information, but it takes a long time to place the ad and is relatively expensive. Newspapers provide excellent coverage of local markets and can be changed quickly, but they have a short life span and poor color. Yellow pages advertising reaches most households and is used frequently; its disadvantage, however, is that there is a proliferation of directories. Internet advertising can be interactive, but its effectiveness is difficult to measure. Outdoor advertising provides repeat exposures, but its message must be very short and simple. Direct mail can be targeted at very selective audiences, but its cost per contact is high.

LO 16-4 *Discuss the strengths and weaknesses of consumer-oriented and trade-oriented sales promotions.*

Coupons encourage retailer support but may delay consumer purchases. Deals reduce consumer risk but also reduce perceived value. Premiums offer consumers additional merchandise they want, but they may be purchasing only for the premium. Contests create involvement but require creative thinking. Sweepstakes encourage repeat purchases, but sales drop after the sweepstakes. Samples encourage product trial but are expensive. Loyalty programs help create loyalty but are expensive to run. Displays provide visibility but are difficult to place in retail space. Rebates stimulate demand but are easily copied. Product placements provide a positive message in a noncommercial setting that is difficult to control. Trade-oriented sales promotions include (a) allowances and discounts, which increase purchases but may change retailer ordering patterns; (b) cooperative advertising, which encourages local advertising; and (c) salesforce training, which helps increase sales by providing the salespeople with product information and selling skills.

LO 16-5 *Recognize public relations as an important form of communication.*

Public relations activities usually focus on communicating positive aspects of the business. A frequently used public relations tool is publicity. Publicity tools include news releases and news conferences. Nonprofit organizations often use public service announcements.

LEARNING REVIEW ANSWERS

16-1 **What is the difference between pioneering and competitive ads?**
Answer: Pioneering (or informational) ads, used in the introductory stage of the product life cycle, tell people what a product is, what it can do, and where it can be found. The key objective of a pioneering ad is to inform the target market. Competitive (or persuasive) ads promote a specific brand's features and benefits to persuade the target market to select the firm's brand rather than that of a competitor. A form of a competitive ad is the comparative ad that shows one brand's strengths relative to those of competitors.

16-2 **What is the purpose of an institutional advertisement?**
Answer: The purpose of an institutional advertisement is to build goodwill or an image for an organization rather than a specific offering. This form of advertising is often used to support the public relations plan or counter adverse publicity.

16-3 **Describe three common forms of advertising appeals.**
Answer: The three common forms of advertising appeals are: (1) fear appeals, which suggest to the consumer that he or she can avoid some negative experience through the purchase and use of a product or service, a change in behavior, or a reduction in the use of a product; (2) sex appeals, which suggest to the audience that the product will increase the attractiveness of the user; and (3) humorous appeals, which imply either directly or subtly that the product is more fun or exciting than competitors' offerings.

16-4 _____ **are responsible for creating the text portion of the messages in advertisements.**
Answer: Copywriters

16-5 **You see the same ad in *Time* and *Fortune* magazines and on billboards and TV. Is this an example of reach or frequency?**
Answer: This is an example of frequency—reaching the same audience more than once.

16-6 **Why has the Internet become a popular advertising medium?**
Answer: The Internet offers a visual message, can use both audio and video, is interactive through rich media, and tends to reach younger consumers.

16-7 **Describe three approaches to scheduling advertising.**
Answer: The three approaches to scheduling advertising are: (1) a continuous (steady) schedule, which is when advertising is run at a continuous or steady schedule throughout the year because seasonal factors are unimportant; (2) a flighting (intermittent) schedule, which is when periods of advertising are scheduled between periods of no advertising to reflect seasonal demand; and (3) a pulse (burst) schedule, which is when a flighting schedule is combined with a continuous schedule because of increase in demand, heavy periods of promotion, or introduction of a new product.

16-8 **Explain the difference between pretesting and posttesting advertising copy.**
Answer: Pretests are conducted before ads are placed in any medium to determine whether they communicate the intended message or to select among alternative versions of the ad. Posttests are conducted after the ads are shown to the target audience to determine whether they accomplished their intended purpose.

16-9 **What is the difference between aided and unaided recall posttests?**
Answer: Aided and unaided recall posttests are conducted after the ads are shown to the target audience. Aided recall involves showing an ad to respondents who then are asked if their previous exposure to it was through reading, viewing, or listening. Aided recall is used to determine the percentage of those who (1) remember seeing a specific magazine ad (noted), (2) saw or read any part of the ad identifying the product or brand (seen-associated), (3) read any part of the ad's copy (read some), and (4) read at least half of the ad (read most). Unaided recall involves specifically asking respondents if they remember an ad without any prompting to determine if they saw or heard its message.

16-10 **What is the difference between a coupon and a deal?**
Answer: Coupons and deals are consumer-oriented sales promotion tools used to support a company's advertising and personal selling. A coupon usually offers a discounted price to encourage trial. A deal is a short-term price reduction used to increase trial among potential customers or to retaliate against a competitor's actions.

16-11 **Which trade promotion tool is used to encourage the local advertising efforts of resellers?**
Answer: Cooperative advertising, a promotion program by which a manufacturer pays a percentage of a retailer's advertising expense, is used to encourage both better quality and greater quantity in the local advertising efforts of resellers.

16-12 **What is a news release?**
Answer: A news release is a publicity tool that consists of an announcement regarding changes in the company or the product line to inform the media of an idea for a story.

16-13 **What type of publicity tool is used most often by nonprofit organizations?**
Answer: public service announcements (PSAs)

FOCUSING ON KEY TERMS

advertising p. 430
consumer-oriented sales promotions p. 444
cooperative advertising p. 449
infomercials p. 438
institutional advertisements p. 431
mobile marketing p. 440
posttests p. 443
pretests p. 442
product advertisements p. 430
product placement p. 447
publicity tools p. 449
trade-oriented sales promotions p. 448

APPLYING MARKETING KNOWLEDGE

1. How does competitive product advertising differ from competitive institutional advertising?
2. Suppose you are the advertising manager for a new line of children's fragrances. Which form of media would you use for this new product?
3. You have recently been promoted to be director of advertising for the Timkin Tool Company. In your first meeting with Mr. Timkin, he says, "Advertising is a waste! We've been advertising for six months now and sales haven't increased. Tell me why we should continue." Give your answer to Mr. Timkin.
4. A large life insurance company has decided to switch from using a strong fear appeal to a humorous approach. What are the strengths and weaknesses of such a change in message strategy?
5. Some national advertisers have found that they can have more impact with their advertising by running a large number of ads for a period and then running no ads at all for a period. Why might such a flighting schedule be more effective than a continuous schedule?
6. Which medium has the lowest cost per thousand (CPM)?

Medium	Cost of Ad	Audience Size
TV show	$5,000	25,000
Magazine	2,200	6,000
Newspaper	4,800	7,200
FM radio	420	1,600

7. Each year, managers at Bausch and Lomb evaluate the many advertising media alternatives available to them as they develop their advertising program for contact lenses. What advantages and disadvantages of each alternative should they consider? Which media would you recommend to them?
8. What are two advantages and two disadvantages of the advertising posttests described in the chapter?
9. Federated Banks is interested in consumer-oriented sales promotions that would encourage older adults to direct deposit their Social Security checks with the bank. Evaluate the sales promotion options, and recommend two of them to the bank.
10. How can public relations be used by automobile manufacturers following recall notices related to faulty airbag inflators?

BUILDING YOUR MARKETING PLAN

To augment your promotion strategy from Chapter 15:

1. Use Figure 16–2 to select the advertising media you will include in your plan by analyzing how combinations of media (e.g., television and Internet advertising, radio and yellow pages advertising) can complement each other.
2. Select your consumer-oriented sales promotion activities.
3. Specify which trade-oriented sales promotions and public relations tools you will use.

VIDEO CASE 16

Google, Inc.: The Right Ads at the Right Time

"So what we did, in essence, is we said advertising should be useful to a consumer just as much as the organic search results, and we don't want people just to buy advertising and be able to show an ad if it's irrelevant to the consumer's need," says Richard Holden, director of product management at Google. To accomplish this, Google developed a "Quality Score" model to predict how effective an ad will be. The model uses many factors such as click-through rates, advertiser history, and keyword performance to develop a score for each advertisement. "Essentially, what we're trying to do is predict ahead, before we actually show an ad, how a consumer will react to that ad, and our interest is in showing fewer ads, not more ads; just the right ads at the right time," Holden continues. The Google advertising model has revolutionized the advertising industry, and it continues to improve every day!

Video 16-6
Google Video Case
kerin.tv/cr8e/v16-6

©grzegorz knec/Alamy Stock Photo

THE COMPANY

Google began in 1996 as a research project for Stanford computer science students Larry Page and Sergey Brin. They started with a simple idea—that a search engine based on the relationships between websites would provide a better ranking than a search engine based only on the number of times a key term appeared on a website. The success of their model led to rapid growth, and the founders moved the company from their dorm room, to a friend's garage, to offices in Palo Alto, California, and eventually to its current location, known as the Googleplex, in Mountain View, California. In 2000, Google began selling advertising as a means of generating revenue. Its advertising model allowed advertisers to bid on search words and pay for each "click" by a search-engine user. The ads were required to be simple and text-based so that the search result pages remained uncluttered and the search time was as fast as possible.

Page and Brin's first search engine was called "BackRub" because their technique was based on relationships, or backlinks, between websites. The name quickly changed, however. The name "Google" is a misspelling of the word "googol," which is a mathematical term for a 1 followed by 100 zeros. Page and Brin used the name in the original domain, www.google.stanford.edu, to reflect their interest in organizing the immense amount of information available on the Web. The domain name, of course, became www.google.com and eventually Webster's dictionary added the verb "google" with the definition "to use the Google search engine to obtain information on the Internet." The name has become so familiar that *Advertising Age* recently reported that Google is "the world's most powerful brand"!

Today, Google receives several hundred million inquiries each day as it pursues its mission: to organize the world's information and make it universally accessible and useful. The company is a subsidiary of Alphabet Inc. which generates more than $100 billion in annual revenue and has more than 80,000 employees. As Google has grown, it has developed 10 guidelines that represent the corporate philosophy. They are:

1. Focus on the user and all else will follow.
2. It's best to do one thing really, really well.
3. Fast is better than slow.
4. Democracy on the Web works.
5. You don't need to be at your desk to need an answer.
6. You can make money without doing evil.
7. There's always more information out there.
8. The need for information crosses all borders.
9. You can be serious without a suit.
10. Great just isn't good enough.

Using these guidelines, Google strives to continually improve its search engine. "The perfect search engine," explains Google co-founder Larry Page, "would understand exactly what you mean and give back exactly what you want."

ONLINE ADVERTISING

Google generates revenue by offering online advertising opportunities—next to search results or on specific web pages. The company always distinguishes ads from the search results or the content of a web page and it never sells placement in the search results. This approach ensures that Google website visitors always know when someone has paid to put a message in front of them. The advantage of online advertising is that it is measurable and allows immediate assessment of its effectiveness. As Gopi Kallayil, product marketing manager, explains: "There is a very high degree of measurability and trackability that you get through on-line advertising." In addition, he says, "With online advertising you can actually track the value of every single dollar that you spend, understand which particular customers the ad reached, and what they did after they received the advertising message."

The online advertising market has grown from its initial focus on simple text ads to a much larger set of options. There are five key categories of online advertising. They are:

- Search: 47%
- Display: 35%
- Classified: 10%
- Referral: 7%
- E-mail: 1%

Google is the dominant provider of online search requests and receives more than 60 percent of the search advertising revenue. The fastest-growing advertising category, however, is display advertising, where Yahoo! and Microsoft are established providers. Google believes that there is an opportunity to grow its display advertising sales by making the ads useful information instead of visual clutter. According to Google co-founder Sergey Brin, "It's like search-matching people with information they want. It just happens to be promotional."

Several improvements in technology and business practice tools contributed to Google's success. First, Google developed its patented PageRank™ algorithm, which evaluates the entire link structure of the Web and uses the link structure to determine which pages are most important. Then the process uses hypertext-matching analysis to determine which pages are relevant to a specific search. A combination of the importance and the relevance of web pages provides the search results—in just a fraction of a second. Second, Google developed two business practice tools—AdWords and AdSense—to help (1) advertisers create ads, and (2) content providers generate advertising revenue. Both tools have become essential elements of Google's advertising model.

AdWords

To help advertisers place ads on their search-engine results, Google developed an online tool called AdWords. Advertisers can use AdWords to create ad text, select target keywords, and manage their account. The process allows advertisers to reach targeted audiences. Frederick Vallaeys, an AdWords evangelist, explains: "One of my favorite things about AdWords is the fact that it really helps you find the right customer at the right time and show them the right message. With AdWords you can very specifically target your market because you're targeting them at a time when they do a search on Google. At that time they've told you a keyword, you know exactly what they're looking for, and here is your opportunity as a marketer to give them the exact answer to what they've just told you they wanted to find." Google has found that text ads that are relevant to the person reading them have much higher response ("click-through") rates than ads that are not targeted.

AdWords is also easy for any advertiser to use. Large or small businesses can simply open an account with a credit card and have ads appear within minutes. "When AdWords rolled out their self-service product, it really was one of the first times when it was very easy for a small business to put their ad up on the Internet on a search engine and compete on a level playing field alongside *Fortune* 1000 companies," says Vallaeys. Google has an experienced sales and service team available to help any advertiser select appropriate keywords, generate ad copy, and monitor campaign performance. The team is dedicated to helping its advertisers improve click-through rates because high click-through rates are an indication that ads are relevant to a user's interests. Methods of improving advertising performance include changing the keywords and rewriting copy. Because there is no limit to the number of keywords that an advertiser can select and each keyword can be matched with different ad copy, the potential for many very customer-specific options is high.

Another advantage of Google's AdWords program is that it allows advertisers to easily control costs. The ads appear as a "Sponsored Link" next to search results each time the Google search engine matches the search request with the ad's keywords and Quality Score, although the advertiser is not charged unless someone "clicks" on the link. In a traditional advertising model, advertisers were charged using a CPM (cost-per-thousand) approach, which charged for the impressions made by an ad. According to Holden, the Google model "transformed that to what we call a CPC, or a cost-per-click model, and this is a model that an advertiser, instead of paying for an impression, only pays when somebody actually clicks on that ad and is delivered to their website. So, in effect, they may be getting the benefit from impressions being shown, but we're not actually charging them anything unless there's a definite lead being delivered to their website." Google also offers advertisers real-time analytical services to allow assessment of and changes to any component of an advertising campaign.

AdSense

The AdSense program was designed for website owners as a tool for placing ads next to their web page content rather than next to search results. Currently, thousands of website managers use AdSense to place ads on their sites and generate revenue. Google applies the same general philosophy to matching ads with websites as it does to matching ads to search requests. By delivering ads that precisely target the content on the site's pages, Google believes the advertising enhances the experience for visitors to the website. In this way advertisers, website publishers, and information seekers all benefit.

AdSense is one of the tools Google is using to pursue its goal of increasing its display advertising business. Yahoo! and Microsoft's Bing are leaders in display advertising because they can put ads on their own websites such as Yahoo! Finance and MSN Money. To provide additional outlets for display ads, Google recently purchased YouTube. In addition, Google purchased DoubleClick, an advertising exchange where websites put space up for auction and ad agencies bid to place ads for their clients. Google is also trying to make it easy for anyone to create a display ad by introducing a new tool called Display Ad Builder. Some experts observe that because Google is so dominant at search advertising, its future growth will depend on success in display advertising.

GOOGLE'S FUTURE STRATEGY

How will Google continue its success? One possibility is that it will begin to try to win advertising away from the U.S. TV industry. While this is a new type of advertising requiring creative capabilities and relationships with large advertising agencies, Google has dedicated many of its resources to becoming competitive for television advertising expenditures. For example, Google recently helped Volvo develop a campaign that included a YouTube ad and Twitter updates. Google is also likely to develop new websites, establish blogs, and build relationships with existing sites.

Another opportunity for Google will be mobile telephone advertising. There are currently more than 5.4 billion mobile phones in use, and 1.9 billion of those are Internet-capable. Just as Google's search engine provides a means to match relevant information with consumers, phones offer a chance to provide real-time and location-specific information. Some of the challenges in mobile advertising will be facilitating the use of augmented reality, virtual reality, social media, emoji ad messaging, and 360-degree video ads. Google believes its new Pixel phone and its Android operating system will also help.

Finally, as Google pursues its mission it will continue to expand throughout the world. Search results are already available in more than 40 languages, and volunteers are helping with many others. It is obvious that Google is determined to "organize the world's information" and make it "accessible and useful."[55]

Questions

1 Describe several unique characteristics about Google and its business practices.
2 What is Google's philosophy about advertising? How can less advertising be preferred to more advertising?
3 Describe the types of online advertising available today. Which type of advertising does Google currently dominate? Why?
4 How can Google be successful in the display advertising business? What other areas of growth are likely to be pursued by Google in the future?

Chapter Notes

1. Erik J. Martin, "How Virtual and Augmented Reality Ads Improve Consumer Engagement," www.econtentmag.com, May–June 2017, pp. 4–8; Chris Daniels, "Virtual Reality: How PR Can Make the VR Opportunity Real," www.prweek.com, January–February 2017, p. 20; George Slefo, "Only 8% of Brands Intend to Use Virtual Reality for Advertising," www.adage.com, February 8, 2017; Jeanine Poggi, "The CMO's Guide to Virtual Reality," *Advertising Age,* May 16, 2016, p. 30; "Making Sense of Virtual Reality's Role in Branding," *Advertising Age,* October 17, 2016, p. 6; Dan Kedmey, "Virtually Real," *Time,* February 9, 2015, p. 12; Maria Minsker, "Facebook Gets Real about Virtual Reality," *Customer Relationship Management,* March 2015, p. 16; Michelle Castillo, "How Virtual Reality Could Revolutionize Ads in the Sports Industry," *Adweek,* May 22, 2015, p. 1; Rae Ann Fera, "Get the Most Out of VR," *Marketing Magazine,* January 2015, p. 18; Ann-Christine Diaz, "Grab Your Headset: Producers Plunge into Virtual Reality," *Advertising Age,* February 9, 2015, p. 26; Madeline Berg, "From HDR to Virtual Reality: Inside the Future of Entertainment," *Forbes.com,* June 10, 2015; and John Gaudiosi, "How Augmented Reality and Virtual Reality Will Generate $150 Billion in Revenue by 2020," *Fortune.com,* April 29, 2015.
2. Karen V. Fernandez and Dennis L. Rosen, "The Effectiveness of Information and Color in Yellow Pages Advertising," *Journal of Advertising,* Summer 2000, p. 61; and David A. Aaker and Donald Norris, "Characteristics of TV Commercials Perceived as Informative," *Journal of Advertising Research* 22, no. 2 (April–May 1982), pp. 61–70.
3. Larry D. Compeau and Dhruv Grewal, "Comparative Price Advertising: An Integrative Review," *Journal of Public Policy &*

Marketing, Fall 1998, pp. 257–73; and William Wilkie and Paul W. Farris, "Comparison Advertising: Problems and Potentials," *Journal of Marketing,* October 1975, pp. 7–15.

4. Chingching Chang, "The Relative Effectiveness of Comparative and Noncomparative Advertising: Evidence for Gender Differences in Information-Processing Strategies," *Journal of Advertising,* Spring 2007, p. 21; Jerry Gotlieb and Dan Sarel, "The Influence of Type of Advertisement, Price, and Source Credibility on Perceived Quality," *Journal of the Academy of Marketing Science,* Summer 1992, pp. 253–60; and Cornelia Pechmann and David Stewart, "The Effects of Comparative Advertising on Attention, Memory, and Purchase Intentions," *Journal of Consumer Research,* September 1990, pp. 180–92.

5. Kathy L. O'Malley, Jeffrey J. Bailey, Chong Leng Tan, and Carl S. Bozman, "Effects of Varying Web-Based Advertising-Substantiation Information on Attribute Beliefs and Perceived Product Quality," *Academy of Marketing Studies Journal* (2007), p. 19; Bruce Buchanan and Doron Goldman, "Us vs. Them: The Minefield of Comparative Ads," *Harvard Business Review,* May–June 1989, pp. 38–50; Dorothy Cohen, "The FTC's Advertising Substantiation Program," *Journal of Marketing,* Winter 1980, pp. 26–35; and Michael Etgar and Stephen A. Goodwin, "Planning for Comparative Advertising Requires Special Attention," *Journal of Advertising* 8, no. 1 (Winter 1979), pp. 26–32.

6. David W. Schumann, Jan M. Hathcote, and Susan West, "Corporate Advertising in America: A Review of Published Studies on Use, Measurement, and Effectiveness," *Journal of Advertising,* September 1991, p. 35; Lewis C. Winters, "Does It Pay to Advertise in Hostile Audiences with Corporate Advertising?" *Journal of Advertising Research,* June–July 1988, pp. 11–18; and Robert Selwitz, "The Selling of an Image," *Madison Avenue,* February 1985, pp. 61–69.

7. Lucy Britner, "PepsiCo Goes Mobile with Latest Global Mountain Dew Campaign," *Aroq-justdrinks.com,* January 14, 2017; "Crystal Light: Seasonal Promotions, *motherhaus.com*; John Kell, "Lululemon Turns to Vice Media for Big Ad Push," *fortune.com,* May 15, 2017; Patty Odell, "Lululemon This Is Yoga Marks First Global Brand Campaign," *Promotional Marketing,* May 18, 2017; Ashley Ross, "Why Models Are Addicted to This Fitness Trend," *Time.com,* May 7, 2015; "New Crystal Light Liquid Drink Mix Frees You from the Choice between Taste or Calories," *PR Newswire,* February 11, 2013; Katie Smith, "US: Nike in Uniform Deal with International Olympic Committee," *Just-Style Global News,* October 17, 2012; and Shareen Pthak, "How Nike Ambushed the Olympics with This Neon Shoe," *Advertising Age,* August 20, 2012, p. 1.

8. See the Advertising Research Foundation website, *http://thearf.org/advancing-marketingforum.php,* accessed May 4, 2013.

9. Alan Siegel, "Amazon Edges NFL in Ad Meter Even Closer Than Super Bowl LII," *USA Today,* www.admeter.usatoday.com, February 5, 2018; "TV Viewership of the Super Bowl in the United States, *Statista,* https://www.statista.com/statistics/216526/super-bowl-us-tv-viewership/; E. Jay Zarett, "How Much Do Super Bowl Commercials Cost in 2018?," www.sportingnews.com, February 4, 2018; Ahley Rodriquez, "Here Are All the Super Bowl Commercials in This Year's Game—From Big Tech to the Big Names," www.qz.com, February 2, 2018; Peter R. Orszag, "Some Super Bowl TV Ads Are Worth the Price," *Chicago Tribune,* February 1, 2018; Zak Stambor, "What Was the Impact of Retailers' Super Bowl Ads?" digitalcommerce360.com, February 7, 2018; Harlan E. Spotts, Scott C. Purvis, and Sandeep Patnaik, "How Digital Conversations Reinforce Super Bowl Advertising," *Journal of Advertising Research,* December 2014, pp. 454–68; and Rama Ylkur, Chuck Tomkovick, and Patty Traczyk, "Super Bowl Effectiveness: Hollywood Finds the Games Golden," *Journal of Advertising Research,* March 2004, pp. 143–59.

10. Sarah De Meulenaer, Patrick De Pelsmacker, and Nathalie Dens, "Have No Fear: How Individuals Differing in Uncertainty Avoidance, Anxiety, and Chance Belief Process Health Risk Messages," *Journal of Advertising* 44, no. 2 (2015), pp. 114–25; Ioni Lewis, Barry Watson, Richard Tay, and Katherine M. White, "The Role of Fear Appeals in Improving Driver Safety," *The International Journal of Behavioral Consultation and Therapy,* June 22, 2007, p. 203; Cornelia Pechmann, Guangzhi Zhao, Marvin E. Goldberg, and Ellen Thomas Reibling, "What to Convey in Antismoking Advertisements for Adolescents: The Use of Protection Motivation Theory to Identify Effective Message Themes," *Journal of Marketing,* April 2003, pp. 1–18; and John F. Tanner Jr., James B. Hunt, and David R. Eppright, "The Protection Motivation Model: A Normative Model of Fear Appeals," *Journal of Marketing,* July 1991, pp. 36–45.

11. Jacob Hornik, Chezy Ofir, and Matti Rachamim, "Advertising Appeals, Moderators, and Impact on Persuasion," *Journal of Advertising Research,* September 2017, pp. 305–18; Doug Lloyd, "Does Sex Still Sell in 2016?" *campaignlive.com,* September 9, 2016; Samantha Grossman,"This Video Urges the Advertising Industry to Stop Treating Women Like Objects," *Time.com,* January 26, 2016; Kristina Monllos, "Brands Are Throwing Out Gender Norms to Reflect a More Fluid World," *adweek.com,* October 17, 2016; and Sanjay Putrevu, "Consumer Responses toward Sexual and Nonsexual Appeals: The Influence of Involvement, Need for Cognition (NFC), and Gender," *Journal of Advertising,* Summer 2008, p. 57.

12. Rupal Parekh, "With Strong Work for Walmart and Geico, Martin Agency Is Creating a New Specialty: Making Marketers Recession-Proof," *Advertising Age,* January 19, 2009, p. 30; and Louis Llovio, "Geico Gecko's Viral Videos," *Richmond Times Dispatch,* March 28, 2009, p. B-9.

13. Thomas W. Cline and James J. Kellaris, "The Influence of Humor Strength and Humor-Message Relatedness on Ad Memorability: A Dual Process Model," *Journal of Advertising,* Spring 2007, p. 55; Yong Zhang and George M. Zinkham, "Responses to Humorous Ads," *Journal of Advertising,* Winter 2006, p. 113; and Yih Hwai Lee and Elison Ai Ching Lim, "What's Funny and What's Not: The Moderating Role of Cultural Orientation in Ad Humor," *Journal of Advertising,* Summer 2008, p. 71.

14. Nikki Gilliland, "Four Examples of Brands Using an Episodic Content Marketing Strategy," *Econsultancy.com,* June 23, 2016; "Results of 4A's 2011 Television Production Cost Survey," *4A's Bulletin,* January 22, 2013 (New York: American Association of Advertising Agencies); and "Washington: Results of 4A's 2011 Television Production Cost Survey," *Plus Media Solutions,* January 23, 2013.

15. E. J. Schultz, "Agency of the Year," *Advertising Age,* January 23, 2017, p. 6; Gabrie Beltron, "The World's Top 10 Most Innovative Companies in Advertising," *Adweek,* February 13, 2014; and Anomaly website, *www.anomaly.com,* accessed June 12, 2017.

16. "U.S. Spending Forecast," Marketing Fact Pack 2018, *Advertising Age,* December 18, 2017, p. 14.

17. Vicki R. Lane, "The Impact of Ad Repetition and Ad Content on Consumer Perceptions of Incongruent Extensions," *Journal of Marketing,* April 2000, pp. 80–91.

18. "Rise of the 'Zero TV' Home: Ratings Altered to Take into Account the People Who Only Watch Online," *Mail Online,* April 8, 2013; and "Nielsen Estimates More Than 118.4 Million TV Homes in the U.S.," Insights, Nielsen website, *www.nielsen.com,* August 26, 2016.

19. J. C. Lupis, "The State of Traditional TV," *marketingcharts.com,* April 24, 2017; Max Langridge and Rik Henderson,

"Best of CES 2017," *pocket-lint.com,* January 10, 2017; Christopher Ingrahm, "Americans Are Watching More TV and Working Less," *Washington Post,* June 28, 2016; Aaron Pressman, "More Than One in Five Households Has Dumped the Goliath," *fortune.com,* April 5, 2016; "Millennials Lead Way among Cord-Cutters," *twice.com,* June 20, 2016; David A. Schweidel and Wendy W. Moe, "Binge Watching and Advertising," *Journal of Marketing,* September 2016, pp. 1–19; and "Free to Move between Screens: The Cross-Platform Report," The Nielsen Company (New York), March 2013.

20. "Cost for a 30-Second Commercial," *Marketing Fact Pack 2018,* December 18, 2017, pp. 18–19; Yongick Jeong, "The Impact of the Length of Preceding and Succeeding Ads on Television Advertising Effectiveness," *Journal of Marketing Communications* 23, no. 4 (2017), pp. 385–99; "How Many Minutes of Commercials Are Shown in an Average TV Hour?" *tvweek.com,* May 13, 2014; Emily Fredrix, "TV Commercials Shrink to Match Attention Spans," *USA Today,* October 30, 2010; Kate Newstead and Jenni Romaniuk, "Cost per Second: The Relative Effectiveness of 15- and 30-Second Television Advertisements," *Journal of Advertising Research,* 2009, pp. 68–76; and Srinivasan Swaminathan and Robert Kent, "Second-by-Second Analysis of Advertising Exposure in TV Pods," *Journal of Advertising Research,* March 2013, pp. 91–100.

21. T. L. Stanley, "As Seen On TV!" *Adweek,* December 5, 2016, p. 10; "Jordan Witney's Program Rankings: Top 10 Infomercials," *Response,* May 2017, p. 14; "10 Best-Selling Infomercial Products," *Gizmodo,* May 1, 2013; "All the Info on Infomercials," *www.Backstage.com,* November 18, 2010; and Herb Weisbaum, "ConsumerMan: Busting Infomercial Myths," *www.MSNBC.com,* December 16, 2010.

22. "Broadcast Station Totals," News, Federal Communications Commission, April 11, 2017; and "Average Weekly Reach" and "Radio Reaches Millennials," *Why Radio Fact Sheet,* Radio Advertising Bureau, December 2016.

23. "Top-Rated Hours," in *State of the Media: Audio Today,* February 2016, Nielsen, p. 10.

24. *Magazine Media Factbook 2016/17* (New York: The Association of Magazine Media), pp. 86–87; "What a Marvelous May for New Launches: 68 Total—20 with Promised Frequency," Launch Monitor, *mrmagazine.com,* June 12, 2017; Patty Odell, "Airbnb, The Digital Disruptor, Launches a Print Magazine," *Promotional Marketing,* May 9, 2017, p. 1; Steve Smith, "Magazines Learn a New Language," *Media Industry Newsletter,* February 6, 2017, p. 2; "*Skateboarder* Magazine Changes the Game with Innovative Digital-First Platform," *States News Service,* April 16, 2013; and Rebecca Clancy, "*Auto Trader* Print Edition to Stop as Focus Shifts to Digital," *The Telegraph,* May 7, 2013.

25. "U.S. Print Magazines Launches by Category," *Magazine Media Factbook 2016/17,* The Association of Magazine Media, 2016; and "Magazines Mean Engagement," *Magazine Media Factbook 2012/13* (New York: The Association of Magazine Media), p. 14.

26. "General Advertising Rate Card," *The Wall Street Journal,* January 3, 2017; "Media Kit," *USA Today,* June 13, 2017; and "About Us," *Metro* website, http://www.metro.us, June 13, 2017.

27. "U.S. Spending Forecast," *Marketing Fact Pack,* December 18, 2017, p. 14; Anne Kadet, "Yellow Pages Hang On in Digital Age," *The Wall Street Journal,* June 17, 2016; Mary Beth Quirk, "Yes, People Do Still Really Use the Yellow Pages," *consumerist.com,* June 17, 2016; Gene Marks, "Do People Still Use the Yellow Pages? The Answer May Surprise You," *inc.com,* January 28, 2015; "Can Yellow Pages Make a Come Back?" *Zacks Investment Research,* March 21, 2013; and see National Yellow Pages Consumer Choice & Opt-Out Site, *https://www.yellowpagesoptout.com/homepage.*

28. "Share of Search Queries Handled by Leading U.S. Search Engine Providers," *statista.com,* April 2017; Peter Pal Zubcsek, Zsolt Katona, and Miklos Sarvary, "Predicting Mobile Advertising Response Using Consumer Colocation Networks," *Journal of Marketing,* July 2017, pp. 109–26; Jan H. Schumann, Florian von Wangenheim, and Nicole Groene, "Targeted Online Advertising: Using Reciprocity Appeals to Increase Acceptance among Users of Free Web Services," *Journal of Marketing,* January 2014, pp. 59–75; "10 Ways to Improve the Banner Ad Design and Enhance the Click Through Rate," *Tech and Techie,* May 6, 2013; "'Banner Blindness' Now a Major Marketing Concern," *Bulldog Reporter's Daily Dog,* March 29, 2013; and Thales Teixeira, "The New Science of Viral Ads," *Harvard Business Review,* March 2012, pp. 25–27. The definition of mobile marketing is adapted from the Mobile Marketing Association definition, see http://www.mmaglobal.com/news/mma-updates-definition-mobile-marketing, November 17, 2009.

29. See "Guidelines, Standards & Best Practices," at the Interactive Advertising Bureau website, http://www.iab.net/guidelines; "IAB Releases New Standard Ad Unit Portfolio," press release, International Advertising Bureau, February 26, 2012; "Online Measurement," Nielsen website, http://www.nielsen.com/us/en/nielsen-solutions/nielsen-measurement/nielsen-onlinemeasurement.html; and Abbey Klaassen, "Why the Click Is the Wrong Metric for Online Ads," *Advertising Age,* February 23, 2009, p. 4.

30. Thomas Fox-Brewster, "Google Just Killed What Might Be the Biggest Android Ad Fraud Ever," *Forbes.com,* May 26, 2017; Keith Weed, "We Must Beat Fraud and Demand 100% Viewability," *Marketingweek.com,* March 2017, p. 22; Tim Bourgeois, "Techniques for Combating Digital Ad Fraud, Transparency, and Viewability," *EContent,* May–June 2017, p. 23; Keith Weed, "Three Things All Marketers Can Do to Eliminate Ad Fraud," *Marketing Week,* September 22, 2016, p. 13; Christopher Heine, "What Counts as an Online Ad View? A Standard Is Nearing, but the Fight's Not Over," *Adweek,* February 27, 2015, p. 1; Robert Lemos, "Ad Networks a Digital Paradise for Cyber-Criminals, Researchers Find," *eWeek,* November 11, 2014, p. 1; "Why We Need to Pivot in the Fight against Ad Fraud," *VentureBeat,* April 18, 2013; and Benjamin Edelman, "Pitfalls and Fraud in Online Advertising Metrics," *Journal of Advertising Research,* July 2014, pp. 127–32.

31. George R. Franke and Charles R. Taylor, "Public Perceptions of Billboards: A Meta-Analysis," *Journal of Advertising* 46, no.3 (2017), pp. 395–410; and Arch G. Woodside, "Outdoor Advertising as Experiments," *Journal of the Academy of Marketing Science* 18 (Summer 1990), pp. 229–37.

32. "Clear Channel Outdoor Holdings Releases 'Out-of-Home Advertising and the Retail Industry' Report," *Professional Services Close-Up,* January 25, 2011; Andrew Hampp, "What's New with Outdoor Ads, and What's This Digital Out-of-Home I Keep Hearing About?" *Advertising Age,* September 27, 2010, p. 48; "The Year Ahead for...Outdoor," *Campaign,* January 9, 2009, p. 28; Andrew Hampp, "Digital Out of Home, That's Those Pixilated Billboards, Right?" *Advertising Age,* March 30, 2009; Andrew Hampp, "Out of Home That Stood Out," *Advertising Age,* December 15, 2008, p. 22; and Daniel W. Baack, Rick T. Wilson, and Brian D. Till, "Creativity and Memory Effects," *Journal of Advertising,* Winter 2008, p. 85.

33. Sehoon Park and Minhi Hahn, "Pulsing in a Discrete Model of Advertising Competition," *Journal of Marketing Research,* November 1991, pp. 397–405.

34. Peggy Masterson, "The Wearout Phenomenon," *Marketing Research,* Fall 1999, pp. 27–31; and Lawrence D. Gibson,

"What Can One TV Exposure Do?" *Journal of Advertising Research,* March–April 1996, pp. 9–18.

35. Rik Pieters, Michel Wedel, and Rajeev Batra, "The Stopping Power of Advertising: Measure and Effects of Visual Complexity," *Journal of Marketing,* September 2010, pp. 48–60; Rob Norton, "How Uninformative Advertising Tells Consumers Quite a Bit," *Fortune,* December 26, 1994, p. 37; and "Professor Claims Corporations Waste Billions on Advertising," *Marketing News,* July 6, 1992, p. 5.

36. The discussion of posttesting is based on William F. Arens, Michael F. Weigold, and Christian Arens, *Contemporary Advertising,* 12th ed. (New York: McGraw-Hill Irwin, 2009), pp. 228–30.

37. "ROI Metric Available in MRI Starch Syndicated," Mediamark Research & Intelligence, www.mediamark.com, accessed April 23, 2009.

38. Debora V. Thompson and Prashant Malaviya, "Consumer-Generated Ads: Does Awareness of Advertising Co-Creation Help or Hurt Persuasion?" *Journal of Marketing,* May 2013, pp. 33–47; David A. Aaker and Douglas M. Stayman, "Measuring Audience Perceptions of Commercials and Relating Them to Ad Impact," *Journal of Advertising Research* 30 (August–September 1990), pp. 7–17; and Ernest Dichter, "A Psychological View of Advertising Effectiveness," *Marketing Management* 1, no. 3 (1992), pp. 60–62.

39. David Krugel, "Television Advertising Effectiveness and Research Innovation," *Journal of Consumer Marketing,* Summer 1988, pp. 43–51; and Laurence N. Gold, "The Evolution of Television Advertising Sales Measurement: Past, Present, and Future," *Journal of Advertising Research,* June–July 1988, pp. 19–24.

40. "U.S. Spending Forecast," *Marketing Fact Pack 2018,* December 18, 2017, p. 14.

41. Fernando de Oliveira Santini, Valter Afonso Vieira, Claudio Hoffmann Sampaio, and Marcelo Gattermann Perin, "Meta-Analysis of the Long- and Short-Term Effects of Sales Promotions on Consumer Behavior," *Journal of Promotion Management* 22, no. 3 (2016), pp. 425–42; Magid M. Abraham and Leonard M. Lodish, "Getting the Most Out of Advertising and Promotion," *Harvard Business Review,* May–June 1990, pp. 50–60; Steven W. Hartley and James Cross, "How Sales Promotion Can Work for and against You," *Journal of Consumer Marketing,* Summer 1988, pp. 35–42; and Robert D. Buzzell, John A. Quelch, and Walter J. Salmon, "The Costly Bargain of Trade Promotion," *Harvard Business Review,* March–April 1990, pp. 141–49.

42. "Valassis 2016 Coupon Savings Report Reveals Rise in Annual Coupon Incentives," press release, Valassis, September 26, 2016; "2016 Coupon Scoreboard," Valassis, 2016; "Coupon Facts Report Reveals Evolving Media Mix and Marketing Strategies," press release, Valassis, February 25, 2014; "Coupon Savings Report," Valassis, 2016; "2014 Annual NCH Coupon Facts," NCH Marketing Services, 2014; "Coupon Use Hits 40-Year Low," couponsinthenews.com, February 1, 2016; Charlie Brown, "Marketers' Coupon Strategies Deliver Increased Consumer Savings in 2014 While Staying within Budgets," *Annual Topline View CPG Coupon Facts,* NCH Marketing Services, 2015; "2012 NCH Consumer Survey: Demographic Profile of Coupon Users," NCH Marketing Services, 2012; Claudia Buck, "Coupon Industry: No Scissors Required," *The State Journal-Register,* February 24, 2013, p. 40; and "How Mobile Coupons Are Driving an Explosion in Mobile Commerce," *The Business Insider,* May 22, 2013.

43. "What Is Coupon Fraud?" The Coupon Information Corporation, http://www.couponinformationcenter.com, accessed June 14, 2017; Josh Elledge, "Coupon Fraud Hurts Us All," *Grand Rapids Press,* April 19, 2011, p. B1; and Amy Johannes, "Flying the Coup," *Promo,* July 1, 2008, p. 28.

44. Ryan Kilpatrick, "Nintendo Toys Are Coming Back to McDonald's Happy Meals," *Fortune.com,* April 27, 2017; "The Influence of Promotional Products on Consumer Behavior," Promotional Product Association International, November 2012; Amy Johannes, "Premium Connections," *Promo,* October 2008, p. 34; and Gerard P. Prendergast, Alex S. L. Tsang, and Derek T. Y. Poon, "Predicting Premium Proneness," *Journal of Advertising Research,* June 2008, p. 287.

45. Patty Odell, "Oreo Launches $500,000 #MyOreo Creation Contest," *Promotional Marketing,* May 10, 2017; Patty Odell, "The Wonder Vault Surprises Contest Entrants," *Promotional Marketing,* June 6, 2017; and "User Content Offers a New Perspective," *PR Week,* February 23, 2009, p. 21.

46. "Congratulations to Kathy of Alabama," HGTV Dream Home 2015, HGTV website, www.hgtv.com; and "The Monopoly Game at McDonald's Returns Sept. 30," McDonald's website, http://news.mcdonalds.com/US/releases/The-MONOPOLY-Game-at-McDonald%E2%80%99s-Returns-Sept-30, September 14, 2014.

47. Tanya Dua, "Pepsi Is Putting Snapchat Barcodes on Million of Soda Bottles," digiday.com, May 23, 2107; Kate Hogan, "Want a Ticket to the Oscars? People Can Hook You Up!" people.com, November 21, 2016; "Nissan Voice Sweepstakes 2015," *The Daily Jackpot,* sweeps.thedailyjackpot.com, December 18, 2014; and "Mars Chocolate North America Launches 5 Characters, 5 Cars Promotion," *Travel & Leisure Close-Up,* June 20, 2011.

48. Kate Taylor, "Taco Bell Is Giving Away Free Food on Tuesday," *Business Insider,* June 13, 2017; Elana Ashanti Jefferson, "Sample Hunters Offer Advice for Trying—Before You Buy," *Denver Post,* July 16, 2012, p. 3C; and Schuyler Velasco, "Ben & Jerry's Free Cone Day," *The Christian Science Monitor,* April 9, 2013.

49. Tom Hoffman, "How Valuable Is a Loyalty Program?" *Customer Strategist,* Peppers & Rogers Group, April 1, 2015; David Moin, "Macy's in New Plenti Program," *Women's Wear Daily,* March 18, 2015, p. 2–1; Jeff Berry, "The 2015 Colloquy Loyalty Census," *Colloquy,* February 2015; and Kara McGuire, "Retailers Work to Make Shopping Its Own Reward," *Star Tribune,* December 19, 2010, p. 1A.

50. Todd R. Weiss, "T-Mobile Tries to Lure Google Pixel Owners With $325 Rebates," *eWeek,* October 28, 2016; Nathalia Dens, Patrick De Pelsmacker, Marijke Wouters, and Nathalia Purnawirawan, "Do You Like What You Recognize?" *Journal of Advertising,* Fall 2012, pp. 35–53; "The Case for Rebates," *Chief Marketer,* July 1, 2011; and Marvin A. Jolson, Joshua L. Wiener, and Richard B. Rosecky, "Correlates of Rebate Proneness," *Journal of Advertising Research,* February–March 1987, pp. 33–43.

51. Dominic Artzrouni, "Product Placement in Movies: 2017 Annual Review," Concave Brand Tracking, April 11, 2018; Huan Chen and Ye Wang, "Product Placement in Top-Grossing Hollywood Movies: 2001–2012, *Journal of Promotion Management,* No. 6, 2016, pp. 835–52; Abe Sauer, "Announcing the 2015 Brandcameo Product Placement Awards," *brandchannel,* February 20, 2015; and Sophie C. Boerman, Eva A. van Reijmersdal, and Peter C. Neijens, "Using Eye Tracking to Understand the Effect of Brand Placement Disclosure Types in Television Programs," *Journal of Advertising,* 44, no. 3 (2015), pp. 196–7.

52. This discussion is drawn particularly from John A. Quelch, *Trade Promotions by Grocery Manufacturers: A Management Perspective* (Cambridge, MA: Marketing Science Institute, August 1982).

53. Michael Chevalier and Ronald C. Curhan, "Retail Promotions as a Function of Trade Promotions: A Descriptive Analysis," *Sloan Management Review* 18 (Fall 1976), pp. 19–32.
54. G. A. Marken, "Firms Can Maintain Control over Creative Co-op Programs," *Marketing News,* September 28, 1992, pp. 7, 9.
55. Google, Inc.: This case was written by Steven Hartley. Sources: "IAB Releases New Ad Portfolio with Flexible Ad Sizes in Alignment with LEAN Principles," press release, Interactive Advertising Bureau, July 20, 2017; "2 Billion Consumers Worldwide to Get Smart(phones) by 2016," emarketer, December 11, 2014; Jessica E. Vascellaro, "Google Decides to Find Its Creative Side," *The Wall Street Journal,* October 7, 2009; Robert D. Hof, "Google's New Ad Weapon," *BusinessWeek,* June 22, 2009, p. 52; Maria Bartiromo, "Eric Schmidt on Where Google Is Headed," *BusinessWeek,* August 17, 2009, p. 11; "Why Microsoft-Yahoo Deal Could Be Good for Google," *Advertising Age,* August 10, 2009, p. 10; Peter Burrow, "Apple and Google: Another Step Apart," *BusinessWeek,* August 17, 2009, p. 24; Jeff Jarvis, "How the Google Model Could Help," *BusinessWeek,* February 9, 2009, p. 32; Abbey Klaasen, "Google Says Print Ads Isn't the Answer for Newspapers," *Advertising Age,* January 26, 2009, p. 17; Matthew Creamer, "Recession Doesn't Dent Total Value of Top 100 Brands," *Advertising Age,* April 27, 2009; "The 500 Largest U.S. Corporations," *Fortune,* May 4, 2009, p. F-1; "ComScore Releases August 2009 U.S. Search Engine Rankings," *www.comscore.com,* October 10, 2009; interviews with Google personnel; and information contained on the Google website (*www.google.com*).

17

Using Social Media and Mobile Marketing to Connect with Consumers

LEARNING OBJECTIVES

After reading this chapter you should be able to:

LO 17-1 Define social media and describe how they have transformed marketing communications.

LO 17-2 Identify the four major social media and describe how brand managers integrate them into marketing actions.

LO 17-3 Describe the characteristics of a social media marketing program, including selecting social media and choosing social media content.

LO 17-4 Compare the performance measures of social media linked to costs (inputs) versus revenues (outputs).

LO 17-5 Identify the cause of the convergence of the real and digital worlds and how this will affect the future of social media.

Mobile Moments Will Soon Include a Nice Ride!

Consumers experience 150–200 "mobile moments" each day. These are the mobile marketing communications that smartphone users are exposed to through social media, messaging, or e-mail. Although marketers use the term "mobile" to refer to the portability of phones, the term will soon take on new meaning as connected cars—cars with Internet access—make "mobile" even more mobile!

You many have already seen some of the initial connected cars, which have smartphone-enabled dashboards, voice recognition software, and large screens. Car manufacturers, however, are quickly adding new benefits for consumers. Mary Bara, chair and CEO of General Motors, observes that "the auto industry will change more in the next five to ten years than it has in the past 50." GM, for example, recently launched a coupon distribution service which sends offers to cars based on their location and proximity to local merchants.

Gas stations are obvious merchants that will benefit from connected cars. Convenience stores are also getting involved. The convenience store channel is very attractive to busy millennials, who are focused on convenience and eager to find a good deal—particularly if it might be supported by information from a social network. Almost one-half of convenience store retailers already offer mobile apps, which will allow real-time special advertising offers as they begin to sync with the Internet-connected car systems.

Advertising through the Internet has been growing dramatically and just recently became the largest medium, reaching $69 billion and exceeding TV advertising expenditures. While Internet advertising to desktops has been substantial, Internet advertising to mobile devices has been the primary area of growth. In fact, 61 percent of Internet advertising expenditures are now targeted at mobile devices. Phones, tablets, and cars have several channels through which ads can be received. First, social media channels such as Facebook and Twitter receive push notifications when the app has been set to receive messages. Second, e-mail continues to be the backbone of many mobile marketing campaigns. Finally, messaging apps such as WhatsApp, Talk, Facebook Messenger, WeChat,

Background: ©Pozdeyev Vitaly/Shutterstock; Icons: ©Hilch/Shutterstock

and Slack allow consumers to chat with company representatives, ask questions, and obtain personalized recommendations. These messaging options, when combined with Internet bots, are becoming a new form of shopping known as *conversational commerce*.

What can you expect in the future as connected cars and conversational commerce grow? A new, convenient, integrated path for the evolving customer journey. IBM, for example, recently created a partnership with BMW to provide a Cloud computing platform for 8.5 million connected vehicles. The service will allow consumers to interact with dealerships, auto insurers, repair shops, and many other businesses. Watch for other new offerings ranging from connected motorcycles, to autonomous cars, to buy buttons in messaging apps![1]

This chapter defines social media, describes four widely used social media, explains how organizations use them in developing marketing strategies, and considers where social media are headed in the future.

UNDERSTANDING SOCIAL MEDIA

LO 17-1 Define social media and describe how they have transformed marketing communications.

Defining *social media* is challenging, but it's necessary to help a brand or marketing manager select the right one. This section defines social media, classifies social media, and describes why and how social media have transformed marking communications.

What Are Social Media?

This section defines social media and classifies the countless social media available to assist marketing managers in choosing among them.

Defining Social Media Social media represent a unique blending of technology and social interaction to create a communal experience and personal value for users. **Social media** are online media where users submit comments, photos, and videos—often accompanied by a feedback process to identify "popular" topics. Most social media involve a genuine online conversation among people about a subject of mutual interest, one built on their personal thoughts and experiences. However, other social media sites involve games and virtual worlds in which the online interaction includes playing a game, completing a quest, controlling an avatar, and so on. Business firms also refer to social media as "consumer-generated media." A single social media site with millions of users interacting with each other, like Facebook, Twitter, and LinkedIn, is referred to as a *social network*.

The term "social media" is sometimes used interchangeably with the terms "Web 2.0" and "Web 3.0" and "user-generated content"—concepts that are the foundation of today's social media. Web 2.0 and Web 3.0 identify technological functionalities that make possible today's high degree of interactivity among users. Web 2.0 includes functionalities that permit people to collaborate and share information online. Web 3.0, now in its early application stages, includes additional functionalities that allow personalization and customization to each individual based on location, interests, and needs. It integrates new features such as Cloud computing, big data, the Internet of Things, security solutions, and privacy protection.[2]

social media
Online media where users submit comments, photos, and videos—often accompanied by a feedback process to identify "popular" topics.

The next-generation Web, Web 3.0, will be customized to each individual. Read the text to learn how!
©Wright Studio/Shutterstock

User-generated content (UGC) refers to any form of online media content that is publicly available and created by consumers or end users. The term "user-generated content" (also referred to as *consumer-generated content*) includes video, blogs, discussion forum posts, digital images, audio files, and related content. To qualify as UGC, content must satisfy three basic criteria:[3]

1. It is published either on a publicly accessible website or on a social media site, so it is not simply an e-mail.
2. It shows a significant degree of original or creative effort, so it is more than simply posting a newspaper article on a personal blog without editing or comments.
3. It is consumer-generated by an individual outside of a professional or commercial organization.

Today, about 80 percent of the content appearing on social media is user-generated.[4]

user-generated content (UGC)
The various forms of online media content that are publicly available and created by consumers or end users. Also called *consumer-generated content*.

Classifying Social Media Most of us would probably say that Facebook, Twitter, LinkedIn, and YouTube are well-known social media. But marketing managers trying to reach potential customers need a system to classify the more than 400 specialized and diverse social media to select the best among them. Kaplan and Haenlein have proposed a classification system for marketers based on two factors:[5]

1. *Media richness.* This involves the degree of acoustic, visual, and personal contact between two communication partners—face-to-face communications, say, being higher in media richness than telephone or e-mail communications. The

462

How do marketing managers choose the best social media sites to reach their target markets? As a first step, the text describes how social media can be classified and how they differ from traditional media.
©Anatolii Babii/Alamy Stock Photo

higher the media richness and quality of presentation, the greater the social influence that communication partners have on each other's behavior.

2. *Self-disclosure.* In any type of social interaction, individuals want to make a positive impression to achieve a favorable image with others. This favorable image is affected by the degree of self-disclosure about a person's thoughts, feelings, likes, and dislikes—where greater self-disclosure is likely to increase one's influence on those reached.

Figure 17–1 uses these two factors of media richness and self-disclosure to position a number of social media sites in two-dimensional space. For example, Wikipedia is a collaborative project that is low on both self-disclosure and media richness. LinkedIn, on the other hand, contains detailed career and résumé information for business networking and is high in self-disclosure but only moderate in media richness.

Marketing managers look carefully at the positioning of the social media shown in Figure 17–1 when selecting those to use in their plans. For example, LinkedIn, positioned in the Social Networking Sites segment in Figure 17–1, is a professional networking service with 500 million members in 200 countries. LinkedIn recently generated $2.3 billion in annual revenue from advertising, recruiter fees, and subscriptions. LinkedIn's customers include companies such as Citigroup, Microsoft, Chevron, Hewlett-Packard, and Volkswagen, which promote their companies' career opportunities to people with specific job titles, and individuals who are seeking a job or building a professional network.[6]

Why and How Social Media Transformed Marketing Communications

Consumers receive information, news, and education from print (newspapers, magazines) and electronic (radio, television) media. These traditional media remain important elements in a company's marketing communications effort. Studies indicate that social media can complement and augment these traditional media when they are focused on brand-building, customer acquisition, and customer advocacy.

FIGURE 17–1

A sample of social media, classified by media richness and self-disclosure. Note that in moving from words to photos, videos, and animation, media richness increases. Also, in moving from very impersonal messages to highly personal ones, self-disclosure increases.

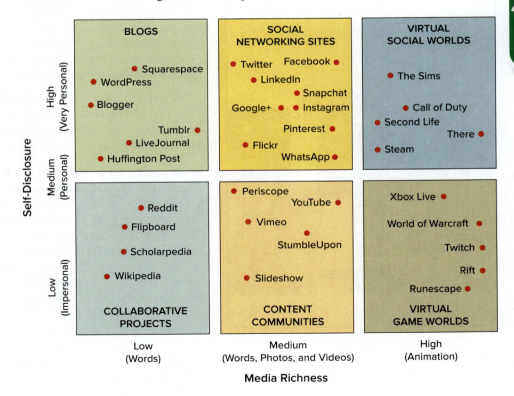

Comparing Social and Traditional Media A comparison of traditional and social media is necessary to understand why social media have transformed marketing communications. Important similarities and differences are described below:[7]

See the text for a comparison of social and traditional media.
©McGraw-Hill Education

- *Ability to reach both large and niche audiences.* Both kinds of media can be designed to reach either a mass market or specialized segments.
- *Expense and access.* Messages and ads in traditional media like newspapers or television generally are expensive to produce and have restricted access by individuals. Also, traditional media are typically owned privately or by the government in some countries. In contrast, messages on social media are generally accessible everywhere, are available to anyone with a smartphone, a computer, or a tablet device, and can be produced cheaply.
- *Training and number of people involved.* Producing traditional media typically requires specialized skills and training and often involves teams of people. In contrast, sending messages on social media requires only limited skills, so practically anyone can post a message that includes words and images.
- *Time to delivery.* Traditional media can involve days or even months of continuing effort to deliver the communication, and time lags can be extensive. In contrast, individuals using social media can post virtually instantaneous content.
- *Permanence.* Traditional media, once created, cannot be altered. For example, once a magazine article is printed and distributed, it cannot be changed. But social media message content can be altered almost instantaneously by comments or editing.
- *Credibility and social authority.* Individuals and organizations can establish themselves as "experts" in their given field, thereby becoming "influencers" in that field. For example, *The New York Times* has immense credibility among newspaper media. But with social media, a sender often simply begins to participate in the "conversation," hoping that the quality of the message will establish credibility with the receivers, thereby enhancing the sender's influence.

Clearly, the reach, cost, investment, timeliness, flexibility, and influence of social media explain *why* they have transformed marketing communications. *How* social media have changed marketing communications is discussed next.

Emergence of Influencer Marketing Social media have changed how marketing communications are targeted and spurred the emergence of influencer marketing. **Influencer marketing** is the practice of focusing on the identification and recruitment of influencers to advocate a company's products, services, and brands rather than focusing exclusively on prospective buyers.

Influencer marketing is based on the concept of personal influence; namely, a consumer's purchases are often influenced by the views, opinions, or behavior of others (see Chapter 4). Influencer marketing applies this behavioral concept to social media in the presence of social networks and user-generated content. A perfect marriage!

The identification of influencers on social media is based, in large part, on the number of followers an influencer has on social networking sites such as Facebook, Instagram, and Twitter and

Kendall Jenner has close to 100 million Instagram followers. Read the text to learn how many followers she, her sisters, and mother likely have on social media.
Source: Instagram

influencer marketing
The practice of focusing on the identification and recruitment of influencers to advocate a company's products, services, and brands rather than focusing exclusively on prospective buyers.

content community sites such as YouTube.[8] The number of followers, in turn, is often attributed to an influencer's *perceived* credibility, knowledgeability, authenticity, and reliability in providing relevant content to his or her audience. In short, social media influencers are trusted by their followers.

The recruitment of social media influencers involves partnering with individuals who are willing and able to effectively engage their followers with a product, service, or brand. These influencers are often compensated. They are paid outright, given free products or services, and reimbursed for their expenses in creating and posting content. It is estimated that 75 percent of large U.S. companies will spend $101 billion on influencer marketing initiatives in 2020.[9]

Social media influencers exist within specific categories. For example, the Kardashians (Kim, Kourtney, and Khloe) and Jenners (Kris, Kylie, and Kendall) are prominent influencers in the fashion, fitness, entertainment, beauty, and pop culture categories. Their combined worldwide social media followers likely exceed 500 million people.

learning review

17-1. What are social media?

17-2. In classifying social media, what do we mean by (*a*) media richness and (*b*) self-disclosure?

17-3. Compare traditional media and social media in terms of time required to deliver the communication.

A LOOK AT FOUR IMPORTANT SOCIAL MEDIA

LO 17-2 Identify the four major social media and describe how brand managers integrate them into marketing actions.

Facebook, Twitter, LinkedIn, and YouTube are four widely used options in the world of social media. So marketing managers need a special understanding of these four platforms as they integrate social media into their marketing strategies to supplement the traditional media they already use. This section briefly compares, defines, and explains each of these four major social media and shows how brand managers can use them. Because of its importance, Facebook merits more detailed coverage.

Comparing Four Social Media

Figure 17–2 compares four major social media (Facebook, Twitter, LinkedIn, and YouTube) from the point of view of a brand manager.[10] Facebook can increase brand exposure by enabling convenient user posting of links, photos, and videos. Twitter makes it easy to place brand messages and gain online customer support. While primarily a powerful network in helping users find jobs, LinkedIn has also found a niche in helping small businesses network to reach potential customers, as well as filling its traditional role of connecting job seekers and jobs. YouTube's videos make it especially useful in explaining a complex product.

Mark Zuckerberg and Sheryl Sandberg are CEO and COO of Facebook, a social network that connects over 2.2 billion users.
©Zef Nikolla/Facebook via Bloomberg/Getty Images

Facebook

Facebook is the first choice among people seeking to create and maintain online connections with others by using photos, videos, and short text entries. Facebook has also enhanced its capabilities with its recent aquisitions of Instagram (photo sharing), WhatsApp (messaging), and Oculus (virtual reality). With more than 2.2 billion active users—one in every four people on the planet—Facebook is truly the 900-pound gorilla among all social media.

BASIS OF COMPARISON	SOCIAL MEDIA			
	facebook	twitter	LinkedIn	YouTube
Male–Female Breakdown (U.S.)	47% male, 53% female	48% male, 53% female	56% male, 44% female	50% male, 50% female
Brand Exposure	Powerful for gaining brand exposure through convenient user posting of links, photos, and videos.	Consistent placement of brand messages is easy with applications like HootSuite and TweetCastor. Sponsored tweets promote brands.	Free opportunities exist, like Business Pages and LinkedIn Influencer posts. Paid Sponsored Updates provide added reach.	Powerful in gaining attention and explaining a complex product, and branding. Channels unite users on content and heighten viewership.
Customer Communication	Great for people who like your brand and want to share their opinions. Leads all social networks for this.	Twitter is powerful for gaining online customer support. Engaging one-on-one is simple and easy to track.	Half of those using social media for customer service use a LinkedIn Company Page while 40% do so with LinkedIn Groups.	YouTube gains user's ready attention in attracting customer support. Easy to allow responses to user comments and ratings.
Traffic to Website	Is the traffic leader through rewording engaging content with better news feed placement. But its share of referred visits is falling.	Referral traffic from Twitter is growing faster than any other social network. Photos and videos make tweets even more clickable.	LinkedIn generates referrals—though less than many other social networks—but can be valuable for B2B and business development.	YouTube is an important source of traffic. Get traffic back to user's site by adding a hyperlink in the video description.

Facebook logo: ©Craig Ruttle/AP Images; Twitter logo: ©Ingvar Björk/Alamy Stock Photo; LinkedIn logo: ©Kristoffer Tripplaar/Alamy Stock Photo; YouTube logo: ©TP/Alamy Stock Photo

FIGURE 17–2
How brand managers can use four social media in developing their marketing strategies.

Facebook
A website where users may create a personal profile, add other users as friends, and exchange comments, photos, videos, and "likes" with them.

Facebook: An Overview Facebook is a website where users may create a personal profile, add other users as friends, and exchange comments, photos, videos, and "likes" with them. Facebook users today can keep friends and family updated on what they are thinking, doing, and feeling. In addition, users may chat with friends and create and join common-interest groups, and businesses can create Facebook Pages as a means of advertising and building relationships with customers. Facebook is open to anyone age 13 and older.

CEO Mark Zuckerberg and COO Sheryl Sandberg have managed Facebook through incredible growth. To understand the magnitude of the company, consider that Facebook:

- Grows by 8 people per second, or 7,246 people every 15 minutes.
- Processes 300 million photos, 5.7 billion likes, and 730 million comments each day.
- Has 85 percent of its users living outside the United States and Canada.
- Generates revenue from more than 2.5 million advertisers.

Half of all Facebook users have more than 200 friends in their network, and 18- to 29-year-olds have 300![11]

Facebook in a Brand Manager's Strategy Facebook Business Pages were created as a method for brand managers to generate awareness for their product, service, or brand within Facebook. They allow brand managers to promote their business on Facebook, separate from their private and personal profiles. Done well, these are magnets for feedback. Additionally, Facebook Business Page information is generally public and cataloged by search engines so brand managers can identify influencers within their customer base.

To generate new customers and increase traffic to their Facebook Pages, brand managers can use paid ads and sponsored stories within the Facebook advertising platform. An advantage of these Facebook ads is that the content can migrate into Facebook conversations among friends—to the delight of advertisers.

The marketing challenge for an organization's Facebook Page is to post content that will generate the best response. Brand managers, however, have observed that some people do not want sponsored content on their feeds. To engage fans in a conversation on Facebook, research suggests the following guidelines:[12]

- *Be creative* in using links, photos, and videos.
- *Make it familiar, but with a twist*. Focus content strategy on imagery and messaging that is familiar to fans—punctuated with something unique. Aflac uses its Aflac Duck—the well-known "spokes-duck"—to treat fans to Aflac Duck commercials, virtual Duck gifts, and supplemental insurance offers.
- *Keep it fresh*. Redbox uses frequent posts to keep fans informed about its latest film releases.
- *Learn users' passions and let them guide content*. Taco Bell polls users to see which menu item they'd like featured in the following week's menu profile photo.

Gaining meaningful user loyalty enables a company to target promotional offers to its online fans, who typically represent about 5 percent of their customer base. Data indicate that users who "like" a brand are more likely to make a purchase because they are loyal customers. Other indicators, such as views and clicks, are also important measures of engagement.[13]

Mobile Marketing at Facebook

Keeping 2 billion users happy is a tall order—even for Facebook. As the most common method of accessing Facebook shifts from computers to mobile smartphones, the company is continually making changes to its mobile capabilities. As CEO Mark Zuckerberg explains: "Moving from just being a single service to a family of world-class apps to help people share in different ways is the biggest shift in our strategy to connect people in many years."[14] Some recent examples include:

- *New Privacy Protections*. In response to increasing concern about privacy and the use of personal data, Facebook has several new privacy protections. For example, users are now asked to review how Facebook uses their data and are given the option to opt out of targeting based on personal profile information. In addition, Facebook will now limit the ads that can be displayed to teenagers and offer rewards for reports of data abuses.[15]
- *Dating Feature*. Facebook has introduced a new feature called "Dating" that will compete with dating apps such as Tinder and Bumble. The new service allows Facebook users to create separate profiles from their main Facebook accounts and also uses a dedicated inbox that allows only text-based messages when chatting for the first time.[16]
- *Live streaming*. In response to a growing interest in video, Facebook has added a service to allow users to broadcast up to four hours of live streaming video. The service, called Facebook Live, is a feature that lets users share activities and events with their followers and friends live. Followers can receive notifications when a user begins a live broadcast.[17]
- *E-mail marketing for Facebook app*. In a program called Custom Audiences, Facebook helps advertisers target customers as they scroll through Facebook's mobile app by matching e-mail addresses provided by the advertisers with the e-mail addresses it has for many of its users. Facebook also identifies "look-alikes," people who are similar to an advertiser's customers, for targeted ads. Currently, more than half of Facebook's sales revenues come from mobile devices.[18]

What other changes will Facebook make as part of its mobile marketing strategy? Perhaps only Mark Zuckerberg knows!

Twitter

Now that "tweets" have become part of our everyday language, it's apparent that Twitter has entered the mainstream of American life. Worldwide, Twitter now has over 336 million active monthly users who post 500 million tweets per day.[19]

Wendy's used Twitter to engage a customer in a conversation that involved millions of people and broke a world record!

Wendy's: ©Ken Wolter/Shutterstock; Phone: Source: Twitter

Twitter
A website that enables users to send and receive "tweets," messages up to 280 characters long.

Twitter: An Overview **Twitter** is a website that enables users to send and receive *tweets*, messages up to 280 characters long. Twitter is based on the principle of "followers." So when you choose to follow another Twitter user, that user's tweets appear in reverse chronological order on your Twitter page. Twitter also offers a live video feature by clicking on the camera icon when you see the "What's happening?" message.

Because of its short message length, the ease of posting, receiving, and forwarding ("retweeting") tweets, and its convenience on a smartphone, Twitter can be a good form of communication for consumers and brands. Wendy's uses Twitter as an important tool in its social media program to communicate brand messages to its followers. As part of Wendy's social media outreach, the brand is active on Twitter with daily messages, retweets, and replies.

Teenager Carter Wilkerson, for example, asked Wendy's how many retweets it would take to receive free chicken nuggets for a year. Wendy's response led to more than 3 million retweets, a new world record for the most retweeted tweet (breaking the previous record held by Ellen DeGeneres), and a year's supply of nuggets!

Beyond sending and receiving messages, Wendy's relies on Twitter as a listening device. Wendy's social media team monitors mentions of Wendy's on Twitter to see what people are saying. If there are product concerns, Wendy's can reach out to consumers to make sure their concerns are quickly addressed.

Twitter in a Brand Manager's Strategy With the 280-character limit on tweets, brand managers cannot expect extensive comments on their brands. But they can use social media management tools like TweetDeck or HootSuite to see what Twitter users are saying—good and bad—about both their own brands and competitive ones. They can then respond to the negative comments and retweet the positive ones. Managers can also use interactive video and live video features on Twitter to get users engaged with their brands.

Brand managers can utilize several strategies for listening to and interacting with current and potential consumers using Twitter. For example, they can:[20]

- Generate brand buzz by developing an official Twitter profile, recruiting followers, and showing photos and videos of their products.
- Follow the Twitter profiles that mention their product and monitor what is being said, responding to user criticisms to develop happier customers.
- Tweet and video stream on topics that provide information of value to their consumers.

As with Facebook, Twitter can actively engage customers if done creatively. To further enhance this engagement, Twitter recently announced that it is creating a 24-hour streaming video channel with partners such as MLB, the NFL, and Viacom. According to CEO Jack Dorsey, Twitter wants "to be the first place that anyone hears of anything going on that matters to them."[21]

LinkedIn

Unlike Facebook and Twitter, the LinkedIn site's main purpose is professional networking and job searching.

LinkedIn
A business-oriented website that lets users post their professional profiles to connect to a network of businesspeople, who are also called *connections*.

LinkedIn: An Overview
LinkedIn is a business-oriented website that lets users post their professional profiles to connect to a network of businesspeople. These businesspeople are also called *connections*. This social network has over 500 million registered members who conduct 6 billion professionally oriented searches annually. Because of its popularity, LinkedIn has postings for more than 10 million jobs and data on more than 9 million companies. LinkedIn's international presence, too, is staggering—it is used in over 200 countries and 24 languages. LinkedIn was recently acquired by Microsoft for $26 billion![22]

LinkedIn in a Brand Manager's Strategy
Marketing managers can use LinkedIn to promote their brand in subtle ways. This is done mainly for business-to-business (B2B) image building and networking with other professionals. Using LinkedIn Groups, managers can join groups of professionals in the same industry or with similar interests to share ideas, content, and job information and to demonstrate the organization's capabilities in particular areas.

According to a recent survey of small business owners, 41 percent see LinkedIn as potentially beneficial to their company—more than twice that for Facebook, Twitter, or YouTube.[23] LinkedIn recently streamlined its research process for finding qualified employees so that an employer can type its needs into the LinkedIn "search box" and receive a summary that includes people, jobs, groups, and companies. In addition, it has added a Job Matching feature to help recruiters find better matches for open positions. Brand managers also use LinkedIn for business development to identify sales leads and locate vendors.[24] Sales representatives often use LinkedIn to see the profiles of purchasing personnel or managers with whom they are meeting.

College students can use the LinkedIn Profile Checklist to build an attention-getting profile page.
Source: LinkedIn

LinkedIn in a College Senior's Job Search
Of growing importance, LinkedIn has over 40 million students and recent college graduates as members. College career centers and the LinkedIn student link (http://university.linkedin.com/linkedin-for-students) give key ideas for building an attention-getting LinkedIn profile for students in search of jobs:[25]

- Write an informative, short, memorable profile headline.
- Include a clear, simple, recent photo of just yourself. According to experts, your profile is more likely to be viewed if you have a photo.
- Create a professional summary—concisely giving your education, qualifications, goals, relevant work experience, and extracurricular activities.
- Fill the Skills & Expertise section with keywords and phrases the recruiters use in their searches.
- Include recommendations from people who know you well—supervisors, colleagues, instructors, and advisors.
- Set your LinkedIn profile to "public" and create a unique URL (www.linkedin.com/in/JohnSmith) that you also include in your résumé.

Finally, in your LinkedIn profile avoid these 10 most overused buzzwords: responsible, strategic, creative, effective, patient, expert, organizational, driven, innovative, and analytical.[26]

YouTube

The ability of YouTube to reach its audience stretches the imagination. Think about this: YouTube's one and a half billion users (1) make four billion views per day, (2) upload 300 hours of video each minute, and (3) generate 50 percent of YouTube's traffic from mobile devices.[27]

YouTube
A video-sharing website in which users can upload, view, and comment on videos.

YouTube: An Overview   **YouTube** is a video-sharing website, owned by Google, in which users can upload, view, and comment on videos. YouTube uses streaming video technology to display user-generated video content that includes movie and TV clips, music videos, and original videos developed by amateurs. While most of the content is uploaded by amateurs, many companies offer material on the site through a YouTube channel.

YouTube redesigns its home page periodically to provide a more organized structure to steer users to "channels," rather than simply encouraging them to browse like in the past. Recently, YouTube also redesigned the format for its YouTube channels. These channels serve as home pages for organizations and individuals and allow them to upload their own videos, as well as post and share videos created by others.

What are the most-watched videos on YouTube? They are Luis Fonsi's "Despacito," Wiz Khalifa's "See You Again," and Ed Sheeran's "Shape of You," with 5.5 billion, 3.7 billion, and 3.7 billion views, respectively. All of these artists have a YouTube channel that aggregates their music and other videos they have uploaded for fans and other users to view.[28]

YouTube in a Brand Manager's Strategy   YouTube offers a great opportunity for a brand manager to produce and show a video that explains the benefits of a complex product. Since YouTube is owned by Google, it incorporates a search engine, so users interested in a specific topic can find it easily. In terms of cost advantages, while a brand manager must pay the cost of creating a video, launching a new channel on YouTube is free. YouTube also offers a program to help small businesses create video ads and buy and manage key words for their video ads on the website. For insight regarding new ways online video is becoming part of marketing strategies, see the Marketing Matters box.[29]

For how OK Go has used "Obsession" (12 million views) on YouTube to gain fans, licensees, live shows, and sponsors, see the text.
Source: OK Go

OK Go is an American rock band that has used YouTube to win fans, licensees, and sponsors for its music. OK Go's YouTube music videos—what it calls "treadmill videos"—are the foundation for its success. One of its first music videos, "This Too Shall Pass," won several awards and has accumulated 59 million views. One of its most recent music videos, "Obsession," had 12 million views in just five months. OK Go is an example of musicians using YouTube to achieve music success, a route far different than trying to attract attention from a music label company.[30]

Guidelines for marketing and promoting a brand using YouTube videos include:[31]

- Exploit visual aspects of your message, perhaps sacrificing product messages to tell a more entertaining story.
- Create a branded channel rich in key words to improve the odds of the video showing up in user searches. Select a viral title.
- Target viewers by using YouTube's insights and analytics research to reveal the number of views, the number of visits to your website, and what key words are driving user visits.

Of special interest to brand managers: YouTube recently started offering advertisers the option of targeting YouTube ads based on people's Google search histories. In the past, targeting was based on the videos people had watched.[32]

learning review

17-4. How is user-generated content presented by someone using Facebook?

17-5. What are some ways brand managers use Facebook to converse with a brand's fans? How does Facebook facilitate mobile marketing activities?

17-6. How can brand managers use YouTube to converse with customers? What is a new form of mobile marketing using online video?

Marketing Matters

Technology

Vloggers Are the New Power Players, Worldwide!

The online advertising world is changing. Recent studies indicate that nearly half of all web video ads are never seen. To further complicate the situation, it is increasingly difficult to hold the attention of the millennial and Gen Z audiences. One possible answer is that YouTube has stopped supporting 30-second unskippable ads, in favor of shorter, 6-second ads. It is video bloggers, or *vloggers,* however, who may be the secret to successful online advertising!

Marketers have observed that vloggers are becoming the online version of traditional celebrities. Zoe 'Zoella' Sugg, for example, started posting videos about cosmetics as a teenager and today has 12 million subscribers to her YouTube channel. Her audience attracts a variety of advertisers and brand collaborations, particularly since the audience is very young. Similarly, Felix Kjellberg, known online as PewDiePie, began a YouTube channel about video games in college and today has 62 million subscribers. His videos have attracted more than 14 billion views and he was recently named one of *Time* magazine's most influential people of the year.

The influence of vloggers has become so substantial that *Forbes* magazine now publishes a list of the 30 Top Power Players on social media. The list includes influencers in three categories—beauty, fitness, and home—who are ranked on audience size, propensity for virality, and engagement. The members of the list are from eight different countries and between them they have 250 million social media followers from around the globe!

Watch for your favorite brands to partner with influential vloggers like these sometime soon!

VIDEO 17-1
Zoella: Life, Beauty & Chats
kerin.tv/cr8e/v17-1

SOCIAL MEDIA MARKETING PROGRAMS AND CUSTOMER ENGAGEMENT

LO 17-3 Describe the characteristics of a social media marketing program, including selecting social media and choosing social media content.

Experienced marketing managers understand how to use traditional media to generate sales for their brand. Some are successful, and others are less so. But many of these same managers will admit that understanding social media dynamics is a challenge and they are not often sure how to use them most effectively for their brands.

A **social media marketing program** is that portion of a company's integrated marketing communications effort designed to create and deliver online media content that attracts viewer attention and encourages readers to share it with their social network. Its purpose is to reach "active consumers" who will become "influentials" and be "delighted" with a brand and its message. These consumers will then become "evangelists" who will communicate with their online friends and the company about the joys of using a brand. Social media marketing program success depends on whether it creates and sustains **customer engagement**—the degree and depth of brand-focused interactions a customer chooses to perform online with his or her social network.

This section looks at (1) how to select social media, (2) the kind of social media content that is created, and (3) how to measure the results of social media programs. The section closes by describing Carmex's "Shot Seen 'Round the World" promotion. The ultimate dream for a brand manager, this Carmex–LeBronJames.com promotion went viral on YouTube!

social media marketing program
That portion of a company's integrated marketing communications effort to create and deliver compelling online media content that attracts viewer attention and encourages readers to share it with their social network.

customer engagement
The degree and depth of brand-focused interactions a customer chooses to perform online with his or her friends.

Selecting Social Media

In using social media, a brand manager tries to select and use one or more of the options from the hundreds that exist. This often entails assessing (1) the characteristics of the website's visitors and (2) the number of users or unique visitors to the website.

Audience Data Available for Social Media Both marketing research organizations and the social media themselves provide user profile data for the social media to help brand managers choose among them. As presented earlier, the top row of Figure 17–2 shows a recent profile of the U.S. male–female audience breakdown for four major social media. As shown in the figure, Facebook users are 53 percent female and 47 percent male, while LinkedIn users are 44 percent female and 56 percent male, important differences to brand managers allocating promotion budgets.

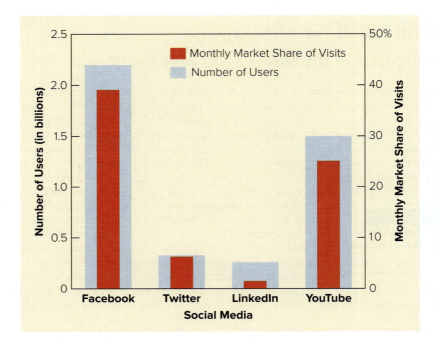

FIGURE 17–3

The number of users and monthly market share of visits for four social media sites: Facebook, Twitter, LinkedIn, and YouTube.

Recent Activity on the Four Social Media Figure 17–3 compares the number of users and the monthly market share of visits for Facebook, Twitter, LinkedIn, and YouTube websites. Number of users is a measure of the size of the audience. Market share is an indication of the use of the website relative to the other sites. In terms of the number of users, Facebook and YouTube have 1.5 billion or more users, although Facebook's market share is more than 50 percent larger. Similarly, Twitter and LinkedIn have between 250 and 350 million users but Twitter has a higher market share, indicating more frequent use.[33]

Selecting Social Media Content

Marketers have a variety of social media content options from which to choose. The choice of social media content is first dependent on the content's intended purpose. Is it intended to be promotional, entertaining, or educational or to serve another purpose? Second, how will social media content complement the overall integrated marketing communications effort in creating and sustaining customer engagement? Third, how will the social media content be best conveyed in different social media? Finally, content choice is also based on the characteristics of the one or more market segments a marketer wants to reach with social media. This starts with demographic characteristics like geographic region, gender, age range, and education. Additional factors like relationship status and user interests are often included as well.

Different Types of Social Media Content Social media marketing experts typically identify seven types of social media content used by companies to create and sustain customer engagement.[34] Elements of each are described below.

- *Educational Content.* This content includes infographics, FAQs, tips and tricks, and how-to posts.
- *Inspirational Content.* This content includes quotes, amazing facts or trivia, personal stories of triumph, and inspirational images.
- *Interactive Content.* This content includes quizzes and games, polls, virtual reality, and contests.
- *Connecting Content.* This content includes stories, behind-the-scenes images, and posts that thank fans or ask for opinions and feedback.

- *Promotional Content.* This content includes promotions, coupons, discounts, customer testimonials, and webinars.
- *Newsworthy Content.* This content includes the latest developments regarding a brand and topical coverage about an industry, product, or service.
- *Entertaining Content.* This content includes puzzles, viral videos, jokes, and comics.

Companies commonly use hashtags (#) to showcase product, brand, and service social media content to create customer awareness and engagement and user generated content as part of an integratated marketing communications program. Hashtags originated on Twitter, but are used in other social media as well with increasing frequency. A successful example is Purina's #PetsAtWork. This hashtag encouraged people to post workplace pet photos and stories which in turn increased visits to Purina.com visits by 34 percent.

Creative Development, Execution, and Delivery of Social Media Content

The quality of social media content is based largely on its creative development, execution, and delivery. The success of PepsiCo's "Friend Finder" YouTube video is an example.

Video 17-2
Pepsi MAX
kerin.tv/cr8e/v17-2

Building on its highly successful "Uncle Drew" and "Test Drive" videos and TV ads, PepsiCo used its entertaining "Friend Finder" video to promote its Pepsi MAX beverage—a zero-calorie cola. The video begins with the observation that one-third of all people lose their friends at music festivals and then goes on to show people at a festival who have lost their friends. They then download the Pepsi MAX "Friend Finder" app and follow drones to find their friends!

"Friend Finder" was a huge hit for Pepsi MAX, with more than 5 million views on YouTube. Even better, the video reinforced the brand's global "Live For Now" tagline emphasized in its integrated marketing communications effort. As a product in the mature stage of its product life cycle, Pepsi MAX used its entertaining social media content to make its diet beverage relevant to a younger target audience. The video captured the viewer's attention by replacing some product messaging with entertainment. The Pepsi MAX success is consistent with recent studies that suggest social interactions play a key role in driving repeat purchases.[35]

In choosing to use a social media campaign like this Pepsi MAX video on YouTube, brand managers were able to make its diet beverage relevant to a younger target audience.
Source: PepsiCo

Measuring the Results of Social Media Marketing Programs

LO 17-4 Compare the performance measures of social media linked to costs (inputs) versus revenues (outputs).

Performance measures for social media marketing programs can be divided into (1) those linked to inputs or costs (Figure 17–4) and (2) those tied to the outputs or revenues resulting from social media. Clearly, the ideal performance measure for both conventional and social media is one that ties actual sales revenues to the cost of the ad or other promotion. With the growth of social media, marketing and brand managers are being challenged to connect the cost of these new social media promotions to the sales they generate. The result has been an emergence of many new performance measures, often requiring a whole new language.

Performance Measures Linked to Inputs or Costs

Figure 17–4 shows three performance measures for social media linked mainly to inputs or costs. Moving down the list of measures shown in Figure 17–4, one starts with a measure tied only to costs (cost per thousand, or CPM), then moves to a measure of interest in a product (cost per click, or CPC), and finally moves to a measure linked more closely

Performance Measure	Costs to Advertisers	Who Provides It	Who Uses It	An Assessment Advantages	An Assessment Disadvantages
Cost per thousand (CPM)	"I will pay $0.50 for every 1,000 times this ad loads, up to $100 per month."	Small websites that sell ads directly (may be using a third-party service)	Advertisers who simply want to build "awareness"	Simple to use	Impressions don't always lead to sales
Cost per click (CPC)	"I will pay $1 for every visitor who clicks on this ad and goes from your website to mine."	Most websites use this method—executed by a third party like Google/AdWords	Advertisers who want to pay for success, but may not be able to track sales from advertisement to purchase	I pay only for a visitor who has expressed an interest in my ad	Ads may not display if they are a poor fit for the viewing audience
Cost per action (CPA)	"I will pay $5 for every purchase that originates from an ad on your site."	Usually executed through third parties; Google AdSense offers this feature	Sophisticated advertisers who want to pay for success	I pay only for what works	Similar to CPC but harder to track and more expensive per action

FIGURE 17–4

Performance measures for social media linked mainly to inputs or costs, as seen by a brand manager.

to the sales revenues generated from the social media ad or action (cost per action, or CPA).

The cost per thousand (CPM) measure ties to the number of times the ad loads and a user might see it—but it does not indicate whether the user has actually reacted to it. This measure is roughly equivalent to the CPM for traditional media discussed in Chapter 16. The cost per click (CPC) measure gives the rate the advertiser pays, say to Facebook, every time a visitor clicks on the ad and jumps from that page to the advertiser's website. Finally, the cost per action (CPA) measure ties loosely to actual sales—for example, paying $5 for every purchase that originates from an ad, say, on the Facebook site. By summing up the revenues from all these purchases, a difficult task, this CPA measure most closely ties the cost of the social media ad to the sales revenues generated by the ad.

Performance Measures Linked to Outputs or Revenues Many of the measures for evaluating how a brand manager's social media marketing program is doing reflect the two-way communications present in social media. These measures often tie to output results in terms of "fans," "friends," "followers," or "visitors" to a social media site, which can be a first step to estimating the sales revenue generated. From a brand manager's viewpoint, here are some of the frequently used Facebook measures, moving from the more general to the more specific:

- *Users/members*. Individuals who have registered on a social networking site by completing the process involved, such as providing their name, user ID (usually an e-mail address), and password, as well as answering a few questions (date of birth, gender, etc.).
- *Fans*. The number of people who have opted in to a brand's messages through a social media platform at a given time.
- *Share of voice*. The brand's share or percentage of all the online social media chatter related to, say, its product category or a topic.
- *Page views*. The number of times a Facebook Page is loaded in a given time period.
- *Visitors*. The total number of visitors to a Facebook Page in a given time period; if someone visits three times in one day, she is counted three times.
- *Unique visitors*. The total number of unique visitors to a Facebook Page in a given time period; if someone visits three times in one day, he is counted only once.
- *Average page views per visitor*. Page views divided by visitors in a given time period.

- *Interaction rate.* The number of people who interact with a Post ("like," make a comment, and so on) divided by the total number of people seeing the Post.
- *Click-through rate (CTR).* Percentage of recipients who have clicked on a link on the Page to visit a specific site.
- *Fan source.* Where a social network following comes from—with fans coming from a friend being more valuable than those coming from an ad.

Note that while sales revenues resulting from social media do not appear in these measures, as we move down the list, the measures are often more specific than comparable ones used in traditional media. This is because it is far simpler to electronically track the social media users who click on a website or ad than it is to track consumers who watch, listen to, or read traditional media.

Specialized Focus for Other Social Media One of the advantages of social media is that communities can form around ideas and commonalities, regardless of the physical location of their members. While major social media sites such as Facebook or YouTube may garner the majority of the traffic, smaller media like Pinterest may be more successful for some products and services.

Pinterest, a virtual pinboard and content-sharing social network, allows people to "pin" or share images of their favorite things, such as clothing, craft ideas, home décor, and recipes. Pinterest members create customized, themed "boards" and categorize their images as "Odds & Ends," "Food," "Knitting," and so on. These images are shared with other members of the Pinterest community. Members can also share their pinned images on Facebook and Twitter.[36]

Pinterest has over 150 million users, 80 percent of whom are women—with 75 percent of daily traffic coming through mobile applications.[37] As a result, it has become a major sales driver for retailers and manufacturers that target women. In using Pinterest, brand managers can post images of their company's products on their Pinterest board and link them back to their websites.

Pinterest allows users to "pin" or share images of favorite interests on its site, which is useful for brand managers promoting their companies' products.
Source: Pinterest

Carmex Goes Viral with Luck and a LeBron James Bear Hug

Brand managers dream about their stars aligning—having their social media promotions go viral and reaping millions of dollars worth of free brand exposure. Carmex lip balm had this experience!

Video 17-3
Carmex
kerin.tv/cr8e/v17-3

The Background As noted earlier in the chapter, Carmex has a partnership with LeBronJames.com. It started when the firm found out that LeBron James of the National Basketball Association uses Carmex in his pregame routine.

The Half-Court Hero Contest As part of their partnership, Carmex created the "Carmex and LeBronJames.com 'Half-Court Hero'" promotion. The promotion featured an online entry form and weekly prizes leading up to a grand prize drawing for one lucky winner to travel to the game and have the chance to take a half-court shot worth $75,000. The "Hero" part meant that if the winner hit the shot—made the basket—Carmex would also donate $75,000 to the LeBron James Family Foundation and the Boys and Girls Clubs of America.

Michael Drysch was the lucky winner and walked to center court in front of a sold-out crowd of 20,000 fans. Michael carefully aligned himself just left of center court, took two steps, and launched a one-handed hook shot.

The Shot

Nothing but Net!

LeBron's Bear Hug

The Shot: Nothing but Net! LeBron's Bear Hug Achieving a brand manager's wildest dream! The text describes how the Carmex "shot seen 'round the world" achieved this dream—including 33 million YouTube viewers.
Courtesy of Altus Business Development, Inc.

Nothing but net!! And $75,000 richer!

The crowd erupted as Michael turned and pumped his fist. But before he could celebrate any further, LeBron himself came running out of his team's huddle to bear hug Michael to the ground in a moment of pure jubilation.

The "Shot Seen 'Round the World" Goes Viral

Instantly, the footage of Half-Court Hero winner Michael Drysch's incredible hook shot and the celebratory bear hug from LeBron James went viral online. NBATV interviewed him side-by-side with James after the game. It was the #1 Play of the Day on ESPN's SportsCenter. The Carmex brand team immediately arranged a public relations tour for Michael Drysch that included a trip to New York City for appearances on *Good Morning America, Inside Edition, CNN Early Start,* and dozens of local radio shows.

Meanwhile, the Carmex marketing team kept Carmex's social media accounts and website updated throughout the weekend with Twitter and Facebook Posts from the public relations tour. Within three months, Carmex's Half-Court Hero shot had been seen by over 30 million YouTube viewers and became the most-watched video of all time on the National Basketball Association's YouTube page. In all, the promotion earned Carmex over 500 million media impressions across TV, print, online, and social media.[38]

The Carmex experience is a classic "textbook example" of matching social media content and social media influencers. Its social media content was inspirational, promotional, interactive, connecting, and entertaining. The partnership with LeBron James—the most popular NBA player on social media, with more than 100 million Facebook, Twitter, and Instagram followers—was ideal.[39]

Michael Drysch receives his reward for sinking his unlikely hook shot in the "Carmex and LeBronJames.com 'Half-Court Hero'" promotion. Also benefiting were the LeBron James Family Foundation and the Boys and Girls Clubs of America!
Courtesy of Altus Business Development, Inc.

learning review

17-7. What are the seven kinds of social media content?

17-8. Stated simply, how can an advertiser on Facebook expect to generate sales?

17-9. What did the Carmex team do to exploit its incredible good fortune after seeing Michael Drysch make his "Half-Court Hero" shot?

THE FUTURE: CONVERGENCE AND MOBILITY

LO 17-5 Identify the cause of the convergence of the real and digital worlds and how this will affect the future of social media.

Trends in marketing's use of social media reflect what scientists call "mirror worlds" or "smart systems" that are really the convergence of the real and digital worlds. A *smart system* is a computer-based network that triggers actions by sensing changes in the real or digital world. This section discusses: (1) the convergence of real and digital worlds; (2) how this convergence links social media to marketing actions; and (3) where all this *may* be headed in *your* future.

The Convergence of Real and Digital Worlds

Saying that our physical and virtual worlds are converging sounds like science fiction. This convergence of real and digital worlds is the result of a proliferation of interlinked social commerce technologies, databases and algorithms, and apps. A look at several of these elements helps explain this real world–digital world convergence and what it means for marketing.

Social Commerce Technologies Social media and digital technologies are converging to change the way companies engage consumers and the way consumers communicate, shop, and pay for products and services. Snapchat, for example, recently released a link to an augmented reality image of Michael Jordan, which showed the basketball player wearing the newest model of sneakers. Users could then "walk around" Jordan, view the product, and tap into the Snap Store to make a purchase. The sneakers sold out in 23 minutes![40]

Databases and Algorithms As discussed in Chapters 7 and 8, finding prospective customers often involves market segmentation that requires databases searched with exotic algorithms—models used to query, organize, manipulate, and present data. The owners of these databases, among them Google and Facebook, must make them as useful as possible to potential advertisers in order to succeed. Among databases, Google is the hands-down winner—indexing 47 billion unique web pages. Its search engine now gives results in answers to research queries in photos, facts, and "direct answers," and not just the "blue links" of website addresses.[41]

Facebook entered Google's territory by announcing its own search engine algorithm. Facebook users can conduct their own queries about people, places, photos, and interests. An example is "Restaurants recommended by friends." This lets Facebook give advertisers real value in the "likes" found on its site. For example, a small chocolate retail shop in New York City can target young parents who buy lots of organic food products.[42] So it's not difficult to see how a casual "like" for a brand by a user in a database's "digital world" can converge into an actual "real-world" purchase by the user through a very targeted promotion planned by a brand manager.

Apps The apps for smartphones are accelerating the convergence of the real and digital worlds. **Apps** (or *mobile apps* or *applications*) are small, downloadable software programs that run on smartphones and tablet devices. When Apple launched its iPhone, it didn't expect smartphone apps to be very important. Wrong! Apple's App Store currently offers more than 2 million apps either free or for sale, and Google Play

Read the text to learn about augmented reality on Snapchat!
Source: Snapchat/Nike

apps
Small, downloadable software programs that can run on smartphones and tablet devices. Also called *mobile apps* or *applications*.

Video 17-4
Clash of Clans
kerin.tv/cr8e/v17-4

The text describes the strategy Candy Crush Saga uses to link the technical power of the *digital world* to the human psychology of its players in the *real world*.
©IanDagnall Computing/Alamy Stock Photo

offers more than 3 million apps for users of Android devices. With the wide array of apps to choose from, today's consumers typically spend two hours a day using about eight apps.[43]

Many apps are video games. Angry Birds, for example, has been downloaded more than 3 billion times since its release, which is one reason Angry Birds–themed products now range from mascara to toys and entertainment parks. The popularity of the game is declining though as it enters the decline stage of its product life cycle (PLC).[44] The video games Farmville, Temple Run, QuizUp, 4Pics1Word, and Fruit Ninja also reveal the short PLC for these apps in today's tough competitive environment.

Enter Clash of Clans and Candy Crush Saga video games. These and other successful new video games exploit the real world–digital world convergence. Today's successful new video games (1) build on a huge personal-rewards psychology for players; (2) can be played on the small smartphone screens; (3) top the most-downloaded charts of Apple iOS, Google, Android, and Facebook; and (4) often use a "freemium strategy"—where the download is free but users pay for extra features, such as for ways to speed up the game.

Time magazine analyzes how designers of the Candy Crush video game use its key elements to link the *digital world* of Candy Crush to the personal *real-world* satisfactions and rewards of its players:[45]

- *It's better with friends.* Users can give—and get—extra lives using Facebook.
- *It never ends.* There are over 500 levels, and designers add more almost every week.
- *It makes the player feel special.* The game gives positive feedback for nearly every click and tap.
- *It lets a player—sort of—cheat.* Players can pay for power-ups to skip past wait times.
- *It's challenging.* Increasingly varied puzzles often take multiple attempts to complete.

The Candy Crush app has now been installed over 500 million times across Facebook, iOS, and Android devices.

Even Angry Birds has changed its strategy from charging a download cost to using a freemium strategy with its recently launched Angry Birds 2. Sound easy to build an app? Maybe. But hundreds of creative apps die a quiet death each year!

Mobile Marketing: Tightening Links to Marketing Actions

The convergence of the real and digital worlds has also contributed to the growth of *mobile marketing,* or the broad set of interactive messaging options that are used to communicate through personal mobile devices.[46] This continuous connection present in mobile marketing has led to important smartphone apps, such as:

- *Price-comparison searches.* Scan product bar codes or QR codes and research 500,000 stores, synchronizing searches between your computer and your smartphone.
- *Location-based promotions.* Use your GPS-enabled smartphone for location check-ins to receive discounts at stores such as JCPenney.
- *Loyalty programs.* Win loyalty points for walking into stores like Target or Macy's and receive discounts from them.

The number of smartphone shopping searches and purchases has exploded in recent years, causing huge opportunities and challenges for conventional brick-and-mortar retailers.

The clear point of difference in mobile marketing is its unique ability to empower users by connecting with them individually and continuously—learning about their likes and personal characteristics and sharing this information with online friends and (often) marketers selling products. This socially networked world will lead to connected users having more direct interactions with sellers.

The convergence of social media, smartphones, tablet devices, and new apps will lead to companies having a more dynamic interaction with their customers. But is this an unqualified success for buyers? Consider the following perspectives.

A Consumer Purchase Where Sensors Have Some Control

A vending machine scans your face to identify your age and gender and changes its display and—in the future—may give you a quantity discount for buying two of your favorite candy bars (it knows about your Facebook "likes") while showing an electronic dinner coupon for a nearby restaurant if you appear between 7:00 and 9:00 P.M. this evening. The results of the candy and dinner offer are directly measurable for marketers. While it offers unusual convenience, does this buying situation start to interfere with your personal privacy?

Too busy to visit your grocery store this week? If you are in South Korea or China, you can shop on the wall of your subway station with your smartphone—and have your purchases delivered to your door!
©Imaginechina/AP Images

A Consumer Purchase Where the Buyer Controls All

Some cities in South Korea and China are on the leading edge of virtual supermarket shopping. Tesco Home Plus, a global supermarket chain, provides a quick spur-of-the-moment opportunity for grocery shopping. Shoppers use their smartphones to scan images on the wall of a subway station to buy Tesco's grocery products while waiting for their train. They use the smartphone app to pay for the groceries, which are delivered to their door right after they get home.[47] In this example, buyers achieve great convenience—probably an unqualified success.

On Privacy: How Much "Convergence" Is Too Much?

Smart systems are fine up to a point. For example, most of us are comfortable letting convergence find us a timely deal at a local restaurant using a location-based app on our smartphone. It may even be all right if Google's Search, Maps, Photos, Gmail, and YouTube services provide information about our geographical inquiries, recreational preferences, past travel activities, and financial circumstances to an algorithm that suggests an "ideal vacation plan."

Facebook's recent disclosures about a data breach for 87 million Facebook users, however, has many people contemplating the use and security of personal information. In fact, smartphones, smart cars and houses, and personal digital assistants, combined with the growing number of other connected devices (e.g., watches, refrigerators, luggage, etc.), create the potential to monitor almost all behaviors. Some numbers and facts related to privacy include:

- 2,000-plus. Estimated number of times the online activity of an average Internet user is tracked every day.
- 3,500. Number of indicators used by Acxiom Corp., a leading data broker, to predict brand affinity, preferences, and behavior.
- 2.5 billion. Approximate number of addressable consumers in the Acxiom global database.

About 68 percent of Internet users today feel that privacy laws don't protect them adequately. So 86 percent of them have used privacy technologies to take online steps to remove or mask their digital data.[48]

The future? Data privacy continues to be a topic of discussion and regulation around the globe. In 2018 the General Data Protection Regulation (GDPR) became the new legal framework governing the use of data across EU markets. In the United States, the discussion continues to try to determine the appropriate balance of the interests of consumers and businesses.

learning review

17-10. What is an example of how the real (physical) and digital (virtual) worlds are converging?

17-11. What are apps and why are they important?

17-12. Can personal privacy become a problem as the real and digital worlds converge with smart systems?

LEARNING OBJECTIVES REVIEW

LO 17-1 *Define social media and describe how they have transformed marketing communications.*

Social media are online media where users submit comments, photos, and videos, often accompanied by a feedback process to identify "popular" topics. The reach, cost, investment, timeliness, flexibility, and influence of social media has transformed marketing communications, including the practice of influencer marketing.

LO 17-2 *Identify the four major social media and describe how brand managers integrate them into marketing actions.*

The four major social media sites are Facebook, Twitter, LinkedIn, and YouTube. Facebook is a social network where users create a personal profile, add other users as "friends," and exchange comments, photos, videos, and "likes" with them. To increase traffic to a Facebook Page, brand managers can use paid ads and sponsored stories. Twitter enables users to send and receive "tweets," messages up to 280 characters long. For Twitter, brand managers can use monitoring programs to track what people are saying about their organization's brand. LinkedIn lets users post their personal profiles to a network of businesspeople. LinkedIn can be used to create a company profile to share brand information and career opportunities with LinkedIn users and to demonstrate the company's expertise and professionalism. YouTube is a video-sharing website where users can upload, view, and comment on videos. YouTube also allows marketers to create a brand channel to promote a product, show ads for it, and have viewers comment on it.

LO 17-3 *Describe the characteristics of a social media marketing program, including selecting social media and choosing social media content.*

A social media marketing program is that portion of a company's integrated marketing communications effort designed to create and deliver online media content that attracts viewer attention and encourages readers to share it with their social network. Selecting social media entails assessing (1) the characteristics of the website's visitors and (2) the number of users or unique visitors to the website. Choosing specific social media content from among the many options available depends on its intended purpose.

LO 17-4 *Compare the performance measures of social media linked to costs (inputs) versus revenues (outputs).*

Performance measures linked to costs (inputs) include (1) cost per thousand (similar to the CPM for a print ad), which is the number of times an ad is displayed to a user; (2) cost per click (CPC), which gives the rate the advertiser pays each time a visitor clicks on the ad and then jumps to the advertiser's web page; and (3) cost per action (CPA), which is the amount paid for every purchase that originates from an ad on a social media site. Examples of performance measures linked to revenues (outputs) include (1) users/members that have registered on social media websites; (2) the number of unique monthly users viewing the website at a given time; (3) page views, or the number of times a specific web page is loaded; and (4) visitors, or the total number of users viewing a particular web page during a specified time period.

LO 17-5 *Identify the cause of the convergence of the real and digital worlds and how this will affect the future of social media.*

The convergence of the real and digital worlds in social media is the result of the proliferation of interlinked smartphones, tablet devices, sensors, special identification tags, databases, algorithms, apps, and other elements. This convergence will allow consumers and marketers to increase the exchange of personal and product-related information with each other. For consumers, however, this could lead to a loss of privacy and possible exploitation by unscrupulous marketers.

LEARNING REVIEW ANSWERS

17-1 What are social media?

Answer: Social media are online media where users submit comments, photos, and videos—often accompanied by a feedback process to identify "popular" topics. Business firms also refer to social media as "consumer-generated media." A single social media site with millions of users interacting with each other, like Facebook, is a *social network*.

17-2 In classifying social media, what do we mean by (*a*) media richness and (*b*) self-disclosure?

Answer: Social media can be classified based on two factors: (*a*) Media richness involves the degree of acoustic, visual, and personal contact between two communication partners. (*b*) Self-disclosure involves the degree to which an individual shares his or her thoughts, feelings, likes, and dislikes when engaged in a social interaction.

17-3 **Compare traditional media and social media in terms of time required to deliver the communication.**
Answer: Traditional media can involve days or even months of continuing effort to deliver the communication, and time lags can be extensive. In contrast, individuals using social media can post virtually instantaneous content.

17-4 **How is user-generated content presented by someone using Facebook?**
Answer: User-generated content (UGC) refers to the various forms of online media content that are publicly available and created by end users. Facebook users create a personal profile, add other users as friends, and exchange comments, photos, videos, and "likes" with them. Additionally, users may chat with friends and create and join common-interest groups.

17-5 **What are some ways brand managers use Facebook to converse with a brand's fans? How does Facebook facilitate mobile marketing activities?**
Answer: A brand manager can create awareness for a product, service, or brand by creating a Facebook Page for it. To generate new customers and increase traffic to their Facebook Pages, brand managers can use paid ads and sponsored stories within the Facebook advertising platform. The marketing challenge for a Facebook Page is to post and create the content that will generate the best response. Facebook facilitates mobile marketing with new initiatives, such as Facebook Live, Instant Articles, Moments, and Custom Audiences.

17-6 **How can brand managers use YouTube to converse with customers? What is a new form of mobile marketing using online video?**
Answer: YouTube allows brand managers to create an actual brand channel to host their advertisements and other video clips that can explain or demonstrate complex products. YouTube can also link to a brand's website. YouTube, because it is a visual medium, allows a brand manager to entertain as well as inform users about the brand. A new form of mobile marketing is the use of vloggers (video bloggers) to reach online audiences.

17-7 **What are the seven kinds of social media content?**
Answer: The seven kinds of social media content are: educational, inspirational, interactive, connecting, promotional, newsworthy, and entertaining.

17-8 **Stated simply, how can an advertiser on Facebook expect to generate sales?**
Answer: The brand manager composes a title, ad copy, and images or photos for an ad to be placed on Facebook. A website address links the ad to the brand's website or its Facebook Page. To encourage and produce new sales that can be tracked, the brand manager might also link the ad to a coupon code or some other promotional offer.

17-9 **What did the Carmex team do to exploit its incredible good fortune after seeing Michael Drysch make his "Half-Court Hero" shot?**
Answer: At an NBA basketball game, Michael Drysch did the impossible and made Carmex's Half-Court Hero basketball shot. Instantly, the footage of Half-Court Hero winner Michael Drysch's incredible hook shot went viral online. The Carmex brand team immediately arranged a public relations tour for Drysch that included a trip to New York City for appearances on several TV and radio shows. Meanwhile, the Carmex marketing team kept Carmex's social media accounts and website updated throughout the weekend with Twitter and Facebook posts from the public relations tour. Within three months, Carmex's Half-Court Hero shot had been seen by over 20 million YouTube viewers.

17-10 **What is an example of how the real (physical) and digital (virtual) worlds are converging?**
Answer: The convergence of real and digital worlds is the result of a proliferation of interlinked smartphones, tablet devices, sensors, special identification tags, databases, algorithms, apps, and other elements. In addition, apps for smartphones are accelerating the convergence of the real and digital worlds as they make the devices more productive and provide users with entertainment. Finally, marketers can tailor specific messages to targeted users by using their personal data and preferences so that they can order products and services as a result of receiving these offers.

17-11 **What are apps and why are they important?**
Answer: Apps are small, downloadable software programs that run on smartphones and tablet devices. They are speeding up the convergence of the real (physical) and digital (virtual) worlds. Many apps are related to social media, such as programs for (1) price-comparison searches; (2) loyalty programs; (3) location-based promotions; and (4) entertainment, such as video games, music, and so on.

17-12 **Can personal privacy become a problem as the real and digital worlds converge with smart systems?**
Answer: The convergence of social media, smartphones, tablet devices, and new apps will lead to companies having a more dynamic interaction with their customers. This convergence allows for the collection of users' personal data, preferences, and behaviors, which allows marketers to tailor offerings based on these data. The issue is, do we want others to know all this information about us?

FOCUSING ON KEY TERMS

apps p. 477
customer engagement p. 471
Facebook p. 466
influencer marketing p. 464
LinkedIn p. 469
social media p. 462
social media marketing program p. 471
Twitter p. 468
user-generated content (UGC) p. 462
YouTube p. 470

APPLYING MARKETING KNOWLEDGE

1 In your new job as a retail store manager you decide to add mobile marketing to your promotional campaign. Describe how ads directed at connected cars could increase sales in your store.

2 You and three college friends have decided to launch an online business selling clothes college students wear—T-shirts, shorts, sweats, and so on. You plan to use Facebook ads. What "likes" or

interests do (*a*) college men and (*b*) college women have that might help you in planning your Facebook strategy?

3. You are about to graduate from college and want a job in marketing research or sales. Go to the LinkedIn site, register, and determine what information you would put on your LinkedIn profile to help you find a new job.

4. What is the significance of user-generated content when contrasted with social media and traditional media?

5. You are a brand manager for a sneaker manufacturer like Nike or New Balance and you are trying to use Facebook to reach (*a*) college-aged women and (*b*) men over 55 years of age. What three or four "likes" or interests would you expect each segment to have when you try to reach it with Facebook?

6. In measuring the results of social media, what are the (*a*) advantages and (*b*) disadvantages of performance measures linked directly to revenues versus costs?

BUILDING YOUR MARKETING PLAN

Remembering the target market segments you identified in Chapter 8 for your marketing plan:

1. (*a*) Identify which one of the four social media described in the chapter would be most useful and (*b*) give your reasons. Would you consider other social media like Pinterest? Why or why not?

2. Briefy describe (*a*) how you would use this website to try to increase sales of your products and (*b*) why you expect target market customers to respond to it.

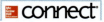

VIDEO CASE 17   Body Glove: Helping Consumers Do What They Love!

How did Body Glove® become one of the most recognizable outdoor sports brands in the world? Well, the story begins in Missouri, where twin brothers, Bob and Bill Meistrell, taught themselves to swim in a pond on their family farm. Their interest in water led them to California where they opened the Dive N' Surf sports shop in Redondo Beach with $1,800 they borrowed from their mother. They grew the business with a simple philosophy of quality products, great customer service, and a fair price. The real secret to their success, though, may have been their personal approach to business and life. Billy Meistrell, son and nephew of the founders, explains, "I constantly heard my dad and uncle say, 'Do what you love and love what you do!'"

Video 17-5
Body Glove Video Case
kerin.tv/cr8e/v17-5

THE BODY GLOVE BRAND

The combination of their approach to business and being pioneers in diving and surfing was a powerful business model for the Meistrell brothers. According to Billy, "their work was their playground, and with that came so much passion and creativity that they developed many new products which gave everybody a much richer lifestyle in the water." One of their first innovations, for example, was the result of using the insulation from the back of a refrigerator, neoprene, to create the first practical wetsuit, which they called the Dive N' Surf Thermocline. The name, however, was difficult to explain so they began discussing potential new brand names. An observation that the wetsuit "fit like a glove" led to the now famous name Body Glove!

The brothers realized there was a lot of potential in their idea and decided they needed help. They turned to their CPA, Russ Lesser, who eventually became president of Body Glove. One of the first things that Lesser did was recommend that they get into the wholesale business. He helped arrange the purchase of a factory and the business started to grow. "We started manufacturing wetsuits," explains Lesser, "and that helped create the whole surf lifestyle." The popularity of the brand soon allowed Body Glove to pursue licensing agreements for many other products, including bathing suits. "That's when Body Glove really took off," says Lesser, "the new bathing suits hit every fashion magazine in the world." "Now we have a whole variety of watersports products. We have wet suits, we have boogie boards, we have surfboards, we have fins, masks, and snorkels, and we have all sorts of apparel," he adds. Annual sales in the United States soon approached $200 million.

Taking Body Glove to global markets was the next step and they needed a partner that could facilitate the growth. "We were approached by Marquee Brands who wanted to expand into the licensing business," says Lesser, and eventually Marquee acquired a majority position in the company. "I think it's a good match because they have the capital to expand and to market and they also have contacts around the world," he continues.

Today, Body Glove represents a classic success story. "Two young men with no money and no family connections created a company with millions of dollars of sales revenue and also created thousands of jobs," observes Lesser. The brand has a global following and the iconic Body Glove Hand Logo is one of the most recognized in sporting goods and watersports. In addition, the company continues its heritage as the third generations of the Meistrell families continue their involvement in the management of the brand, particularly the marketing activities.

MARKETING AT BODY GLOVE

The marketing function at Body Glove includes a senior executive at Marquee Brands, a marketing director, a brand director, and a team of marketing staff. Together they create annual marketing plans designed to grow the brand. According to Jenna Meistrell, brand director at Body Glove, "Every year we sit with our internal team and develop a marketing plan for the following year." "We set direction for the business by looking at all of our various product categories in different markets and figure out which categories need support," she adds. Each plan uses a combination of traditional and contemporary marketing tools.

"Traditional marketing will always be important to us," says Jenna. "We maintain print advertisements in *Surfer* magazine, *Wake* magazine, and *Outside, Elle, and Vogue,*" she continues. Body Glove also uses out-of-home advertising such as advertising in Times Square and billboards near popular outdoor sports locations. The advertising always communicates a message that builds on the Body Glove heritage. Jenna explains, "Every year we try to do a new campaign and this year our campaign is 'Do What You Love.' The campaign is important to us because we almost use it as our mission statement. It's the foundation of the company, ensuring that our consumers are outside doing what they love and it is a great marketing campaign because it applies easily to all of our product categories."

Other marketing tools also play an important role in Body Glove's marketing plans. Distribution channels, for example, are being expanded. There are now more than 200 Body Glove stores in Southeast Asia, and a new partnership in Europe will provide distribution in more than 1,000 specialty and department stores. In addition, Body Glove has always had a team of sponsored athletes from the surfing, diving, and wakeboarding communities who serve as brand ambassadors. The company even produced three feature-length films—the Drop Zone series—which follow the company's sponsored athletes on watersports adventures. And of course there are a variety of sales promotion tools such as foam hands with the Body Glove logo, license plate frames, and bumper stickers. When Billy Meistrell drives a Body Glove vehicle, people stop him and ask for stickers!

SOCIAL MEDIA AT BODY GLOVE

To reach the growing market of Body Glove consumers around the globe, social media is playing an increasing role in the company's marketing. Nick Meistrell, director of marketing at Body Glove, explains: "We all know that content is king in this age, through digital and through social, you have to be generating some valuable content to be relevant among consumers and people that are attracted to your brand." There are a lot of social media options available today and Nick tries to use many of them. "I look at a 360-degree approach, I want to hit consumers through every possible outlet," he says.

What are some of the popular options today? Nick offers his perspective:

- *Facebook.* We look at Facebook as a platform to launch new products and really drive some click-through to our website and our e-commerce page. It can give consumers an experience and communicate the lifestyle, not just push product.
- *Twitter.* Twitter used to be a platform for us to tell consumers about new things we are doing. Today, however, it has become a customer service tool. Twitter is the foundation for our customer service function and is used more than the customer service link on our website. We get customer service inquiries on Twitter every day!

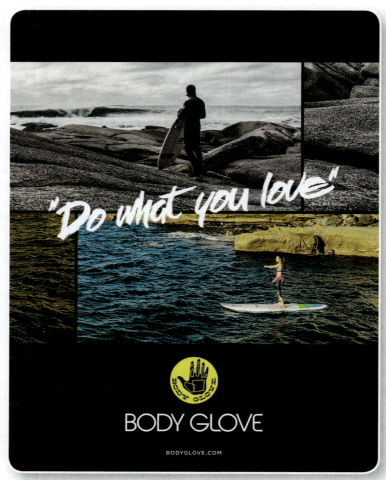

Source: Body Glove

- *LinkedIn*. LinkedIn is a great platform for us to look for new talent when we are hiring. It is also a good way to talk about all the great stuff we are doing at Body Glove and to interact with other businesses and like-minded businesspeople.
- *YouTube*. YouTube is a huge platform for our brand. Content is king and we feel it is a great outlet to show our content. We have a great subscription base that is constantly hungry for new content. We also look at it as the new platform for commercials. So, instead of buying traditional commercials for television, we are buying our commercial space on YouTube to strategically target the right consumer.
- *Instagram*. Instagram is also a huge part of our marketing program. In this digital age you must generate organic, relevant content. Instagram is a great platform to show new content from photos and videos.
- *Pinterest*. We have so many unique products under our umbrella that can appeal to many types of consumers and Pinterest is a great place to post and see them. People love sharing moods and feelings about those products on Pinterest.

Each platform is unique and can accomplish different marketing objectives. Each platform is evolving and changing quickly, also. As Nick observes, "You have to stay cutting edge and stay up-to-date on all the relevant things that are happening out there."

One important aspect of social media is that it is increasingly accessed from mobile devices. "At the end of the day, 67 percent of our consumers now get their information online, mainly through a mobile device," Nick explains. Another aspect of social media that is changing is the ability to assess its effectiveness. "We find that it's really relevant to use the analytics built into each platform because each platform offers its own unique tools. When we are measuring our digital activity we look at impressions, we look at click-through rates, we look at cost per impression, and we look at revenue generated through our e-commerce platform."

THE FUTURE

Body Glove continues its support of conservation efforts that help preserve the environment, such as its participation in the Earth's Oceans Foundation. In addition, Body Glove has a variety of exciting new initiatives under way. In terms of new products, Body Glove recently introduced Body Glove Airstream Earbuds, Body Glove shoes for men and women, and an inflatable stand up paddleboard. The company also began a "Create Happiness" campaign to support a yoga and fitness initiative, and it announced a partnership with FlowRider to promote surf simulation machines. The team at Body Glove is very excited about the future. Billy smiles as he reflects, "There is no company that has put more people in the water and made so many families have a fun lifestyle than Body Glove!"

So, the next time you are in or near the water, watch for Body Glove to help you "do what you love"![49]

Questions

1. How does Body Glove's heritage and philosophy contribute to its success?
2. Which of the criteria mentioned in Chapter 10 help explain why changing the brand name to Body Glove was a good decision?
3. Describe Body Glove's use of traditional marketing tools.
4. What social media platforms does Body Glove use to communicate with its customers today?
5. Why are social media and mobile marketing an increasingly important part of Body Glove's marketing plan?

Chapter Notes

1. Sam Del Rowe, "How to Succeed at Mobile Marketing," *Customer Relationship Management,* January 2017, pp. 27–29; Joe Stanganelli, "Mobile Is Critical for In-Store Retail," *dmnews.com,* March 2017, p. 4; Renee M. Covino, "Marketing to Today's Mobile Consumer," *Convenience Store News,* May 2017, pp. 60–64; Jonathan Bacon, "How Connected Cars Are Driving Innovation," *Marketing Week,* January 21, 2016; Chester Dawson, "IBM Pairs with BMW to Market Connected Car Services," *The Wall Street Journal,* June 4, 2017; "Mobiles Share of Internet Ad Spending," Mobile Fact Pack, *Advertising Age,* October 17, 2016, p. 5; "Connecting with the Cosmos: The Total Audience Media Universe," *Newswire,* Nielsen, March 19, 2015; and Marc de Swaan Arons, Frank van den Driest, and Keith Weed, "The Ultimate Marketing Machine," *Harvard Business Review,* July–August 2014, pp. 55–63.

2. Tuck Siong Chung, Michel Wedel, and Roland T. Rust, "Adaptive Personalization Using Social Networks," *Journal of the Academy of Marketing Science,* 2016, pp. 66–87; Russell Newman, Victor Chang, Robert John Walters, and Gary Brian Wills, "Web 2.0—The Past and the Future," *International Journal of Information Management,* April 6, 2016; and Guy Levy-Yurista, "Web 3.0 and Tomorrow's IoT: Human Identity Delivers the 'Internet of Me,'" *http://insights.wired.com,* December 16, 2015.

3. "Participative Web and User-Created Content: Web 2.0 and Social Networking" (Paris: Organization for Economic Co-operation and Development, 2007); and Jason Daley, "Tearing Down the Walls," *Entrepreneur,* December 2010, pp. 57–60.

4. "116 Amazing Social Media Statistics and Facts," brandwatch.com, June 15, 2018.

5. Andreas M. Kaplan and Michael Haenlein, "Users of the World, Unite! The Challenges and Opportunities of Social Media," *Business Horizons* 53, no. 1 (2010), pp. 62–64.

6. Annual Report 2017, Microsoft, p. 25; "LinkedIn Fact Sheet," https://press.linkedin.com/content/dam/press/docs/linkedin-company-fact-sheet-12-08-16.pdf, May 17, 2017; and Michael Sebastian, "LinkedIn Sells Nearly Half a Billion Dollars in Ads Last Year," www.adage.com, February 5, 2015.

7. Lisette de Vries, Sonja Gensler, and Peter S. H. Leeflang, "Effects of Traditional Advertising and Social Messages on Brand-Building Metrics and Customer Acquisition," *Journal of Marketing,* September 2017, pp. 1–15; V. Kumar, JeeWon Brianna Choi, and Mallik Greene, "Synergistic Effects of Social Media and Traditional Marketing on Brand Sales: Capturing the Time-Varying Effects," *Journal of the Academy of Marketing Science,* 2017, pp. 268–88; and Chiranjeev Kohli, Rajneesh Suri, and Anuj Kapoor, "Will Social Media Kill Branding?" *Business Horizons* 58 (2015), pp. 35–44.

8. Duncan Brown and Nick Hayes, *Influencer Marketing: Who Really Influences Your Customers,* Oxford, UK: Elsevier/Butterworth-Heinemann, 2008.

9. "Clean Break," *Advertising Age,* October 1, 2018, p. 30; "Want to Try Influencer Marketing? Be Careful," *forbes.com,* May 22, 2018.

10. Salman Aslam, "Facebook by the Numbers: Stats, Demographics, & Fun Facts," omnicoreagency.com, January 24, 2017; "Number of Active Twitter Users in the United States from 2010 to 2014, by Gender," *statista.com,* 2017; Dara Fontein, "Top LinkedIn Demograhics That Matter to Social Media Marketers," hootsuite.com, January 5, 2017; and "The Latest YouTube Stats on Audience Demographics: Who's Tuning In," thinkwithgoogle.com, June 17, 2017. Figure 17–2 is adapted from "The CMO's Guide to the 2014 Social Landscape." See *http://visual.ly/cmos-guide-2014-social-landscape.*

11. Dan Shewan, "21 Amazing Facebook Facts You Didn't Know," wordstream.com, December 17, 2017; Kit Smith, "Marketing: 47 Facebook Statistics for 2016," *brandwatch.com,* May 12, 2016; and "Stats," *newsroom.fb.com,* June 17, 2017.

12. Douglas Holt, "Branding in the Age of Social Media," *Harvard Business Review,* March 2016, pp. 40–50; and "Top 10 Ways to Engage Fans on Facebook," Buddy Media, Inc., 2010.

13. Juanito Galindo, "2018: What Is the Current Value of a Facebook "Like" for Brands?" medium.com, January 3, 2018; and Ashish Kumar, Ram Bezawada, Rishika Rishika, Ramkumar Janakirarman, and P. K. Kannan, "From Social to Sale: The Effects of Firm-Generated Content in Social Media on

Customer Behavior," *Journal of Marketing,* January 2016, pp. 7–25.

14. Deepa Seetharaman, "Facebook to Enhance Messenger App," *The Wall Street Journal,* March 26, 2015, p. B8.
15. "Top Facebook Updates That You Can't Afford to Miss—April 2018 Edition," adespresso.com, April 23, 2018.
16. Louise Matsakis, "Facebook's New 'Dating' Feature Could Crush Apps Like Tinder," Wired.com, May 1, 2018.
17. Ross Grogan, "Facebook Live: The New Branding Tool," *Shoot,* May–June 2017, p. 3; and Lauren Johnson, "Facebook Live," *Adweek,* March 20, 2017, p. 20.
18. Rolfe Winkler and Jack Marshall, "Google Imitates Facebook with E-mail Marketing," *The Wall Street Journal,* April 15, 2015, p. B4.
19. "Q1 2018 Letter to Shareholders," Twitter website, April 25, 2018; David Sayce, "Number of Tweets per Day?" *dsayce.com,* November 2016; and Twitter website, *https://about.twitter.com/company,* June 18, 2017.
20. Rachel Gee, "How Twitter's Advertising Is Moving beyond 140 Characters," *Marketing Week,* October 20, 2016; and Thomas Lee, "Social-Media Bees Create Target Buzz," *Star Tribune,* April 13, 2013, pp. A1, A6.
21. Todd Spangler, "Twitter Pushes Live-Video Deals with MLB, NFL, Viacom, BuzzFeed, Live Nation, WNBA and More," *Variety,* May 1, 2017; Garett Sloane, "Twitter Aims to Tame the Lions," *Advertising Age,* June 12, 2017, p. 4; and Kurt Wagner, "Twitter Is Replacing the Moments Tab with a New Explore Tab Instead," *recode.net,* January 26, 2017.
22. Barb Darrow, "LinkedIn Claims Half a Billion Users," *fortune.com,* April 24, 2017, p. 35; and Meenakshi Chaudhary, "LinkedIn by the Numbers: 2017 Statistics," *linkedin.com,* April 5, 2017.
23. Steve Bygott, "Top 5 Tips for Better Branding on LinkedIn," *Best's Review,* June 2017, p. 10; and "LinkedIn Is Trying to Quicken Its Pulse," *Bloomberg Businessweek,* April 22–April 28, 2013, pp. 32–33.
24. Pedro Hernandez, "LinkedIn's Job-Matching Feature Goes Mobile," *eWeek,* May 17, 2017, p. 6.
25. Amy Segelin, "7 Ways to Get Recruiters to Notice You on LinkedIn," *fortune.com,* May 16, 2017; and "Building a Great Student Profile," LinkedIn for Students. See http://university.linkedin.com/linkedin-for-students.html.
26. Kolby Goodman, "Stand above the Rest," *Diary of Alpha Kappa Psi,* Spring 2014, pp. 12–14.
27. YouTube website, https://www.youtube.com/yt/press/statistics.html; Craig Smith, "By the Numbers: 90+ Amazing YouTube Statistics," *DMR Digital Marketing Ramblings,* June 8, 2015; and Amanda Axvig, Vice President of Marketing, AOI Marketing, Inc.
28. Grant Pardee and Kristen Hubby, "The 25 Most-Viewed YouTube Videos of All Time," *The Daily Dot,* January 8, 2017.
29. Clare O'Connor, "Forbes Top Influencers: Meet the 30 Power Players Making a Fortune on Social Media," *forbes.com,* April 10, 2017; Clare O'Connor, "14 Big-Time Brands Paying Social Influencers to Spread Their Message," *forbes.com,* April 10, 2017; Clare O'Connor, "Forbes Top Influencers: How Zoe 'Zoella' Sugg Makes Millions from YouTube Beauty Tutorials," *forbes.com,* April 10, 2017; and Rachel Gee, "Why YouTube's Move to Ditch 30-Second Unskippable Ads Makes It 'More Powerful,'" *Marketing Week,* February 21, 2017.
30. Robin Hilton, "OK Go's New Video for 'The One Moment' Is Another Mind-Blower," *npr.org,* November 23, 2016; Jonah Weiner, "Video Makes the Radio Star," *Bloomberg Businessweek,* April 1–April 7, 2013, pp. 75–77; and Amanda Axvig, Vice President of Marketing, AOI Marketing, Inc.
31. Shalini Bisht, "How to Do Effective YouTube Marketing," *Kartrocket.com,* February 15, 2017.
32. Garett Sloane, "Advertisers Can Now Target YouTube Ads Based on People's Google Search Histories," *Advertising Age,* January 20, 2017.
33. "Most Popular Social Networks Worldwide as of April 2018, Rank by Number of Active Users," in Social Media Usage in the United States, www.statista.com, 2018; and Priit Kallas, "Top 10 Social Networking Sites by Market Share Statistics (November 2017), dreamgrow.com, December 4, 2017.
34. This discussion is based on Vinay Koshy, "7 Types of Social Media Content," https://maximzessocial business.com, accessed, May 13, 2018; Melissa S. Barker et al., *Social Media Marketing: A Strategic Approach,* 2nd ed. (Boston, MA: Cengage Learning, 2017); and "Purina Launches Inaugural Pets at Work Report," Company Press Release, June 20, 2017.
35. Christian de Looper, "Pepsi's Friend Finder Blimp Will Help You Find Your Lost Friends at a Music Festival," *Tech Times,* August 25, 2015; Sheila Shayon, "Pepsi Continues to Bask in Branded Content Glory with Top YouTube Views," *Brand Channel,* April 8, 2013; and Kamer Toker-Yildiz, Minakshi Trivedi, Jeonghye Choi, and Sue Ryung Chang, "Social Interactions and Monetary Incentives in Driving Consumer Repeat Behavior," *Journal of Marketing Research,* June 2017, pp. 364–80.
36. Mae Anderson, "A Look at Why Social Media Site Pinterest Is Catnip to Retailers and Shoppers Alike," *Star Tribune,* April 25, 2014.
37. Salman Aslam, "Pinterest by the Numbers: Stats, Demographics & Fun Facts," *omnicoreagency.com,* January 23, 2017.
38. The Carmex "Half-Court Hero" example was written by Patrick Hodgdon, Manager of Digital Marketing, Bolin Marketing.
39. "Team LeBron Beats Team Curry in Social Media Value Faceoff," forbes.com, February, 18, 2018.
40. Ann-Marie Alcantara, "Snapchat's Ecommerce Strategy Hit a New High When It Sold Out the New Air Jordans in Minutes," adweek.com, February 22, 2018.
41. "The Size of the World Wide Web (The Internet)," *worldwidewebsize.com,* June 20, 2017.
42. Evelyn M. Rusli, "Buy Signal: Facebook Widens Data Targeting," *The Wall Street Journal,* April 10, 2013, p. B4.
43. Sam Costello, "How Many Apps Are in the App Store?" lifewire.com, April 7, 2018; and Artyom Dogtiev, "App Download and Usage Statistics," businessofapps.com, May 3, 2018.
44. Andy Robertson, "'Angry Birds 2' Arrives 6 Years and 3 Billion Downloads after First Game," *forbes.com,* July 16, 2015; Juhana Rossi, "Angry Birds' Maker Perches for Global Growth Take-off," *The Wall Street Journal,* April 4, 2013, p. B4; Spencer E. Ante, "Rovio Mines Video with 'Angry Birds Toons,'" *The Wall Street Journal,* March 12, 2013, p. B6; and John Gaudiosi, "Rovio Execs Explain What Angry Birds Toons Channel Opens Up to Its 1.7 Billion Gamers," *Forbes,* March 13, 2013. See http://www.forbes.com/sites/johngaudiosi/2013/03/11/rovio-execs-explain-what-angry-birds-toons-channel-opens-up-to-its-1-7-billion-gamers.

45. Daniel Engher, "Why Is Candy Crush So Addictive?" *Popular Science,* July 17, 2015.
46. Andreas M. Kaplan, "If You Love Something, Let It Go Mobile: Mobile Marketing and Mobile Social Media 4×4," *Business Horizons* 55, no. 2 (2012), pp. 129–39.
47. Martin Petit D'Meurville, Kimberley Pham, and Courney Trin, "Shop on the Go," *Business Today,* February 15, 2015, pp. 113–16.
48. Christopher Mims, "Privacy Is Dead. Here's What Comes Next," *The Wall Street Journal*, May 6, 2018; and David Pierce, "How to Keep Google from Owning Your Online Life," *The Wall Street Journal,* May 8, 2018.
49. This case was written by Steven Hartley and Roger Kerin. Sources: Interviews with Body Glove executives Billy Meistrell, Nick Meistrell, Jenna Meistrell, and Russ Lesser; Kailee Bradstreet, "Body Glove Aims to 'Create Happiness' through Its Yoga Tour and New Fitness Initiative," adventuresportsnetwork.com, May 30, 2018; "New Audio Innovations from Body Glove: For People on the Move," memebum.com, July 2, 2018; "Body Glove Makes Waves with FlowRider," shop-eat-surf.com, May 8, 2018; Jim Harris,"On the Waves," Retail-Merchandiser.com, November/December 2017; "Marquee Brands: The Sky's the Limit," licensemag.com, August 2017; Kailee Bradstreet, "Body Glove Expands Distribution into Europe," adventuresportsnetwork.com, April 5, 2018; "Marquee Brands Acquires Body Glove," *PR Newswire,* November 2, 2016; Meghan Flynn, "Ultimate in Watersports," *Retail Merchandiser,* March/April, 2011; Frank Gromling, *Fits Like a Glove: The Bill & Bob Meistrell Story* (Flagler Beach, Florida: Ocean Publishing, 2013); Marquee Brands website, marqueebrands.com.

18

Personal Selling and Sales Management

LEARNING OBJECTIVES

After reading this chapter you should be able to:

 Discuss the nature and scope of personal selling and sales management in marketing.

 Identify the different types of personal selling.

 Explain the stages in the personal selling process.

Describe the major functions of sales management.

Meet Today's Sales Professional

Have you been considering sales as a career opportunity? If so, then consider Lindsey Smith as a role model.

Lindsey Smith began her career representing Molecular Imaging Products within the Medical Diagnostics Division of GE Healthcare Americas. She joined the company eleven years ago right out of college with a BBA degree. The epitome of today's sales professional, she lists integrity, motivation, trust and relationship building, and a team orientation as just a few of the ingredients necessary for a successful sales career today.

As a sales professional, she recognizes the importance of constantly updating and refining her product knowledge, analytical and communication skills, and strategic thinking about opportunities to more fully satisfy each customer's clinical, economic, and technical requirements. And for good reason. Her customer contacts include physicians (radiologists, neurologists, and cardiologists), medical technologists, nurses, and health care provider CEOs, CFOs, and other administrators.

Lindsey Smith's selling orientation and customer relationship philosophy rest on four pillars:

1. *A commitment to creating value for clients.* Lindsey believes "every sales call and client interaction should create value for both the customer and the company."
2. *Seek to serve clients as a trusted consultant.* Lindsey emphasizes "being a resource for my customers by providing novel solutions for them."
3. *Reinforce the company's competitive advantage.* Lindsey continually reinforces GE Healthcare Americas's competitive advantage: "I emphasize my company's value proposition and showcase the company's product innovation, solutions, and service."
4. *Regard challenges as opportunities.* Lindsey says, "I consider challenges as opportunities to provide innovative solutions and resources to customers and to build client trust and long-term relationships."

Lindsey Smith's approach to selling and customer relationships has served her customers and her well. She is among the company's top revenue producers and

©Hillsman Stuart Jackson

has a long list of loyal customers. Not surprisingly, Ms. Smith has been a recipient of the company's Commercial Excellence Award in six of the last eight years.

In 2014, Lindsey Smith was named senior client director at GE Healthcare Americas. This position is responsible for the entire GE Healthcare Americas company portfolio, including medical technology, health care consulting, information technology, service operations, and finance solutions for one of GE's largest strategic health care systems. This position also involves management of 75 commercial and operations personnel.[1]

This chapter describes the scope and significance of personal selling and sales management in marketing and creating value for customers. It first highlights the many forms of personal selling. Next, the major steps in the selling process are outlined with an emphasis on building buyer–seller relationships.

The chapter then focuses on salesforce management and its critical role in achieving a company's broader marketing objectives. Three major salesforce management functions are then detailed. They are sales plan formulation, sales plan implementation, and salesforce evaluation. Finally, technology's persuasive influence on how selling is done and how salespeople are managed is described.

SCOPE AND SIGNIFICANCE OF PERSONAL SELLING AND SALES MANAGEMENT

Chapter 15 described personal selling and management of the sales effort as being part of the firm's promotional mix. Although it is important to recognize that personal selling is a useful vehicle for communicating with present and potential buyers, it is much more.

Nature of Personal Selling and Sales Management

LO 18-1 Discuss the nature and scope of personal selling and sales management in marketing.

Personal selling involves the two-way flow of communication between a buyer and seller, often in a face-to-face encounter, designed to influence the purchase decision of a person or group. However, personal selling also takes place over the telephone and through video teleconferencing and Internet-enabled links between buyers and sellers.

Personal selling remains a highly human-intensive activity despite the use of technology. Accordingly, the people involved must be managed. **Sales management** involves planning the selling program and implementing and evaluating the personal selling effort of the firm. The tasks involved in managing personal selling include setting objectives; organizing the salesforce; recruiting, selecting, training, and compensating salespeople; and evaluating the performance of individual salespeople.

personal selling
The two-way flow of communication between a buyer and seller, often in a face-to-face encounter, designed to influence the purchase decision of a person or group.

sales management
Planning the selling program and implementing and evaluating the personal selling effort of the firm.

Selling Happens Almost Everywhere

"Everyone lives by selling something," wrote author Robert Louis Stevenson a century ago. This is particularly true for manufacturing sales personnel, real estate brokers, stockbrokers, and salesclerks who work in retail stores. In reality, however, virtually every occupation that involves customer contact has an element of personal selling. For example, attorneys, accountants, bankers, and company personnel recruiters perform sales-related activities, whether or not they acknowledge it.

Could this be a salesperson in the operating room? Read the text to find out why Medtronic salespeople visit hospital operating rooms.
©Radius Images/Getty Images

Medtronic
www.medtronic.com

Personal Selling in Marketing and Entrepreneurship

> **Video 18-1**
> **Cambridge Sales**
> kerin.tv/cr8e/v18-1

Personal selling serves three major roles in a firm's overall marketing effort. First, salespeople are the critical link between the firm and its customers. This role requires that salespeople match company interests with customer needs to satisfy both parties in the exchange process. Second, salespeople *are* the company in a consumer's eyes. They represent what a company is or attempts to be and are often the only personal contact a customer has with the company. For example, as acknowledged by IBM's former chief executive officer, the company's 40,000-strong salesforce is "our face to the client."[2] Third, personal selling may play a dominant role in a firm's marketing program. This situation typically arises when a firm uses a push marketing strategy, described in Chapter 15. Avon, for example, pays almost 40 percent of its total sales dollars for selling expenses.

Personal selling also has been shown to be critical to successful entrepreneurial efforts for three reasons.[3] First, selling a business concept to potential investors is an entrepreneur's first sales effort. Second, selling the business concept to prospective employees necessary for the success of the venture is essential. Finally, the more traditional sales art of convincing customers to buy one's product or service, getting referrals, and building professional networks is necessary. In short, highly successful entrepreneurs have a great sales talent.

Creating Customer Solutions and Value through Salespeople: Relationship Selling

As the critical link between the firm and its customers, salespeople can create customer value in many ways. For instance, by being close to the customer, salespeople can identify creative solutions to customer problems. Salespeople at Medtronic, Inc., the world leader in the heart pacemaker market, are in the operating room for more than 90 percent of the procedures performed with their product and are on call 24 hours a day. "It reflects the willingness to be there in every situation, just in case a problem arises—even though nine times out of ten the procedure goes just fine," notes a satisfied customer.[4]

Salespeople can create value by easing the customer buying process. This happened at TE Connectivity, a producer of electrical products. Salespeople and customers had a difficult time getting product specifications and performance data on the company's 70,000 products quickly and accurately. The company now has all of its information on its website, which can be downloaded instantly by salespeople and customers.

Customer value is also created by salespeople who follow through after the sale. At Jefferson Smurfit Corporation, a multibillion-dollar supplier of packaging products, one of its salespeople juggled production from three of the company's plants to satisfy an unexpected demand for boxes from General Electric. This person's action led to the company being given GE's Distinguished Supplier Award.

> **relationship selling**
> The practice of building ties to customers based on a salesperson's attention and commitment to customer needs over time.

Customer value creation is made possible by **relationship selling**, the practice of building ties to customers based on a salesperson's attention and commitment to customer needs over time. Relationship selling involves mutual respect and trust among buyers and sellers. It focuses on creating long-term customers and long-run customer value, not a one-time sale. In this regard, senior sales executives consider building long-term relationships with customers to be the most important activity affecting sales performance.[5]

Relationship selling represents another dimension of *customer relationship management*, first introduced in Chapter 1. The concept emphasizes the importance of first learning about customer needs and wants and then tailoring solutions to customer problems as a means to customer value creation. Recent research suggests that a salesperson may have a genetic predisposition to create customer value. See the Marketing Matters box for details.[6]

Marketing Matters > Customer Value

Science and Selling: Is Customer Value Creation in Your Genes?

Is a predisposition to create customer value in your genes? Are you a born salesperson? Recent research by University of Michigan Marketing Professor Richard P. Bagozzi and his colleagues offers a novel insight into this question that may or may not surprise you.

Their research identifies a genetic marker, the 7R variant of the DRD_4 gene, that is correlated with a salesperson's predisposition or willingness to interact with customers and learn about their problems in order to meet their needs. The researchers also found that the presence of the A1 variant of the DRD_2 gene is correlated with a predisposition or tendency to try to persuade customers to buy a given product rather than listen to their needs.

These two different genetic markers help explain the difference between a salesperson's customer orientation versus sales orientation. A customer orientation is guided by ideas such as, "I try to align customers who have problems with products that will help them solve their problems," where the aim is to satisfy mutual needs and the hope is to build a long-term relationship.

In contrast, a sales orientation is driven by notions such as, "I try to sell customers all I can convince them to buy, even if I think it is more than a wise customer should buy." In this case, the motivation is to satisfy one's own short-term interests and not necessarily the needs of the customer.

Faced with a selling situation, do you have a sales orientation or a customer orientation? Customer value creation may be in your genes!

©Dimitri Otis/Photographer's Choice/Getty Images

learning review

18-1. What is personal selling?

18-2. What is involved in sales management?

THE MANY FORMS OF PERSONAL SELLING

LO 18-2 Identify the different types of personal selling.

Personal selling assumes many forms based on the amount of selling done and the amount of creativity required to perform the sales task. Broadly speaking, three types of personal selling exist: order taking, order getting, and customer sales support activities. While some firms use only one of these types of personal selling, others use a combination of all three.

order taker
Processes routine orders or reorders for products that were already sold by the company.

Order-Taking Salespeople

Typically, an **order taker** processes routine orders or reorders for products that were already sold by the company. The primary responsibility of order takers is to preserve an ongoing relationship with existing customers and maintain sales.

Two types of order takers exist. *Outside order takers* visit customers and replenish inventory stocks of resellers, such as retailers or wholesalers. For example, Frito-Lay salespeople call on supermarkets, convenience stores, and other establishments to ensure that the company's line of snack products (such as Lay's potato chips and Doritos and Tostitos tortilla chips) is in adequate supply. In addition, outside order takers often provide assistance in arranging displays.

Inside order takers, also called *order clerks* or *salesclerks,* typically answer simple questions, take orders, and complete transactions with customers. Many retail clerks are inside order takers. Inside order takers are often employed by companies that use *inbound telemarketing,* the use of toll-free telephone numbers that customers can call to obtain information about products or services and make purchases. In business-to-business settings, order taking arises in straight rebuy situations as described in Chapter 5.

Order takers generally do little selling in a conventional sense. They engage in modest problem solving with customers. They often represent products that have few options, such as magazine subscriptions and highly standardized industrial products. Inbound telemarketing is also an essential selling activity for more "customer service" driven firms, such as Dell Technologies. At these companies, order takers undergo extensive training so that they can better assist callers with their purchase decisions.

Order-Getting Salespeople

order getter
Sells in a conventional sense and identifies prospective customers, provides customers with information, persuades customers to buy, closes sales, and follows up on customers' use of a product or service.

An **order getter** sells in a conventional sense and identifies prospective customers, provides customers with information, persuades customers to buy, closes sales, and follows up on customers' use of a product or service. Like order takers, order getters can be inside (an automobile salesperson) or outside (a Xerox salesperson).

Order getting involves a high degree of creativity and customer empathy and is typically required for selling complex or technical products with many options, so considerable product knowledge and sales training are necessary. In modified rebuy or new-buy purchase situations in business-to-business selling, an order getter acts as a problem solver who identifies how a particular product may satisfy a customer's need. Similarly, in the purchase of a service, such as insurance, an insurance agent can provide a mix of plans to satisfy a buyer's needs depending on income, stage of the family's life cycle, and investment objectives.

Order getting is not a 40-hour-per-week job. Industry research shows that outside order getters, or field service representatives, often work over 50 hours per week. As shown in Figure 18–1, 36 percent of an average field sales representative's time is actually spent selling by phone or face-to-face. Another 15 percent is devoted to generating leads and researching customer accounts. The remainder of a sales representative's workweek is occupied by administrative tasks, meetings, service calls, travel, training, and customer follow-up.[7]

Order getting by outside salespeople is also expensive.[8] It is estimated that the average cost of a single field sales call on a business customer is about $500, factoring in the salesperson's compensation, benefits, and travel-and-entertainment expenses. This cost illustrates why outbound telemarketing is popular. *Outbound telemarketing* is the practice of using the telephone rather than personal visits to contact current and prospective customers. A much lower cost per sales call (from $20 to $25) and little or no field expense accounts for its widespread appeal.

Customer Sales Support Personnel

Customer sales support personnel augment the selling effort of order getters by performing a variety of services. For example, *missionary salespeople* do not directly solicit orders but rather concentrate on performing promotional activities and

FIGURE 18–1

How do outside order-getting salespeople spend their time each week? You might be surprised after reading the text.

(photos: top-left): ©Asia Images/Getty Images; (top-right): ©Tetra Images/Getty Images; (bottom-left): ©Susan Van Etten/PhotoEdit, Inc; (bottom-right): ©Stanley Fellerman/Corbis

team selling
The practice of using an entire team of professionals in selling to and servicing major customers.

introducing new products. They are used in the pharmaceutical industry, where they encourage physicians to prescribe a firm's product. Actual sales are made through wholesalers or directly to pharmacists who fill prescriptions. *Sales engineers* specialize in identifying, analyzing, and solving customer problems. These salespeople bring know-how and technical expertise to the selling situation but often do not actually sell products and services. Sales engineers are popular in selling business products such as chemicals and heavy equipment.

Many firms engage in cross-functional **team selling**, the practice of using an entire team of professionals in selling to and servicing major customers.[9] Team selling is used when specialized knowledge is needed to satisfy the different interests of individuals in a customer's buying center. A selling team might consist of a salesperson, a sales engineer, a service representative, and a financial executive, each of whom would deal with a counterpart in the customer's firm.

Selling teams take different forms. In *conference selling,* a salesperson and other company resource people meet with buyers to discuss problems and opportunities. In *seminar selling,* a company team conducts an educational program for a customer's technical staff, describing state-of-the-art developments. IBM and Xerox pioneered cross-functional team selling in working with prospective buyers. Since then, other firms have embraced this practice to create and sustain value for their customers, as described in the Marketing Matters box.[10]

learning review

18-3. What is the principal difference between an order taker and an order getter?

18-4. What is team selling?

Marketing Matters   Customer Value

Creating and Sustaining Customer Value through Cross-Functional Team Selling

The day of the lone salesperson calling on a customer is rapidly becoming history. Today, 75 percent of companies employ cross-functional teams of professionals to work with customers to improve relationships, find better ways of doing things, and, of course, create and sustain value for their customers.

Xerox and IBM pioneered cross-functional team selling, but other firms have been quick to follow as they spotted the potential to create and sustain value for their customers. Recognizing that corn growers needed a herbicide they could apply less often, a DuPont team of chemists, sales and marketing executives, and regulatory specialists created just the right product that recorded sales of $57 million in its first year. Procter & Gamble uses teams of marketing, sales, advertising, computer systems, and supply chain personnel to work with its major retailers, such as Walmart, to identify ways to develop, promote, and deliver products. Pitney Bowes, Inc., which produces sophisticated computer systems that weigh, rate, and track packages for firms such as UPS and FedEx, also uses sales teams to meet customer needs. These teams consist of sales personnel, "carrier management specialists," and engineering and administrative executives who continually find ways to improve the technology involved in shipping goods across town and around the world.

Efforts to create and sustain customer value through cross-functional team selling have become a necessity as customers seek greater value for their money. According to the vice president for procurement of a *Fortune* 500 company, "Today, it's not just getting the best price but getting the best value—and there are a lot of pieces to value."

©blickwinkel/Alamy Stock Photo

THE PERSONAL SELLING PROCESS: BUILDING CUSTOMER RELATIONSHIPS

LO 18-3 Explain the stages in the personal selling process.

Selling, and particularly order getting, is a complicated activity that involves building buyer–seller relationships. Although the salesperson–customer interaction is essential to personal selling, much of a salesperson's work occurs before this meeting and continues after the sale itself. The **personal selling process** consists of six stages: (1) prospecting, (2) preapproach, (3) approach, (4) presentation, (5) close, and (6) follow-up (see Figure 18–2).

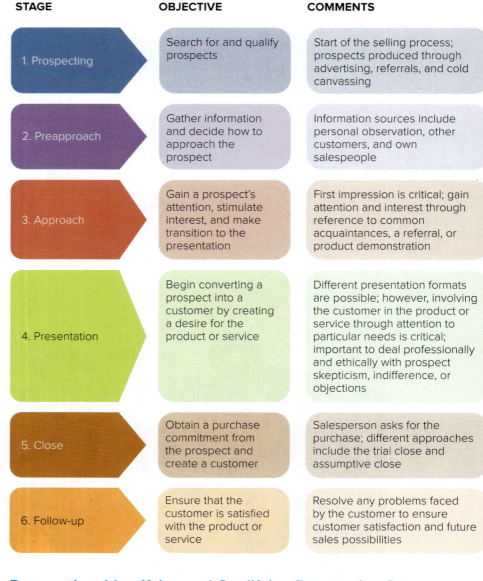

FIGURE 18–2
Stages and objectives of the personal selling process. Each stage is critical for successful selling and building a customer relationship.

personal selling process
Sales activities occurring before, during, and after the sale itself, consisting of six stages: (1) prospecting, (2) preapproach, (3) approach, (4) presentation, (5) close, and (6) follow-up.

Prospecting: Identifying and Qualifying Prospective Customers

Personal selling begins with the *prospecting* stage—the search for and qualification of potential customers. There are three types of prospects. A *lead* is the name of a person who may be a possible customer. A *prospect* is a customer who wants or needs the product. If an individual wants the product, can afford to buy it, and is the decision maker, this person is a *qualified prospect*.

Leads and prospects are generated using several sources. For example, advertising may contain a coupon or a toll-free number to generate leads. Some companies use exhibits at trade shows, professional meetings, and conferences to generate leads or prospects. Staffed by salespeople, these exhibits are used to attract the attention of prospective buyers and share information. Others utilize the Internet for generating leads and prospects. Today, salespeople are using websites, e-mail, and social networks, such as LinkedIn, to connect to individuals and companies that may be interested in their products or services.

Another approach for generating leads is through *cold canvassing* or *cold calling*, either in person or by telephone. This approach simply means that a salesperson may open a directory, pick a name, and contact that individual or business. Despite its high refusal rate, cold canvassing can be successful.[11] However, cold canvassing is frowned

Trade shows are a popular source for leads and prospects. Companies like TSNN provide comprehensive trade show information.
©Urbanmyth/Alamy Stock Photo

TSNN
www.tsnn.com

upon in some cultures. For example, in most Asian and Latin American societies, personal visits, based on referrals, are expected.

Cold canvassing is often criticized by U.S. consumers and is now regulated. Research shows that a large majority of U.S. consumers consider this practice to be an intrusion on their privacy, rude, and distasteful.[12] The *Telephone Consumer Protection Act* (1991) contains provisions to curb abuses such as early morning or late night calling. Additional federal regulations require more complete disclosure regarding solicitations, include provisions that allow consumers to avoid being called at any time through the Do Not Call Registry, and impose fines for violations. For example, satellite television provider Dish Network was fined $280 million for making 66 million calls to consumers who had put their telephone numbers on the Do Not Call Registry.[13]

Preapproach: Preparing for the Sales Call

Once a salesperson has identified a qualified prospect, preparation for the sale begins with the preapproach. The *preapproach* stage involves obtaining further information on the prospect and deciding on the best method of approach. Knowing how the prospect prefers to be approached and what the prospect is looking for in a product or service is essential, regardless of industry or cultural setting.

For instance, a Merrill Lynch stockbroker will need information on a prospect's discretionary income, investment objectives, and preference for discussing brokerage services over the telephone or in person. For business product companies such as Texas Instruments, the preapproach involves identifying the buying role of a prospect (for example, influencer or decision maker), important buying criteria, and the prospect's receptivity to a formal or informal presentation. Identifying the best time to contact a prospect is also important. Northwestern Mutual Life Insurance Company suggests that the following are the best times to call on people in different occupations: dentists before 9:30 A.M., lawyers between 11:00 A.M. and 2:00 P.M., and college professors between 7:00 and 8:00 P.M.

The preapproach stage is especially important in international selling, where customs dictate appropriate protocol. In many South American countries, for example, buyers expect salespeople to be punctual for appointments. However, prospective buyers are routinely 30 minutes late. South Americans take negotiating seriously and prefer straightforward presentations, but a hard-sell approach will not work.[14]

Successful salespeople recognize that the preapproach stage should never be short-changed. Their experience coupled with research on customer complaints indicates that failure to learn as much as possible about the prospect is unprofessional and the ruin of a sales call.

Approach: Making the First Impression

The *approach* stage involves the initial meeting between the salesperson and the prospect, where the objectives are to gain the prospect's attention, stimulate interest, and build the foundation for the sales presentation itself and the basis for a working relationship. The first impression is critical at this stage, and it is common for salespeople to begin the conversation with a reference to common acquaintances, a referral, or even the product or service itself. Which tactic is taken will depend on the information obtained in the prospecting and preapproach stages.

The approach stage is very important in international settings.[15] In many societies outside the United States, considerable time is devoted to nonbusiness talk designed to establish a rapport between buyers and sellers. For instance, it is common for two or three meetings to occur before business matters are discussed in the Middle East and Asia. Gestures are also very important. The initial meeting between a salesperson and a prospect in the United States customarily begins with a firm handshake. Handshakes also apply in France, but they are gentle, not firm. Forget the handshake in Japan. An appropriate bow is expected. What about business cards? Business cards should be printed in English on one side and the language of the prospective customer on the other. Knowledgeable U.S. salespeople know that their business cards should be handed to Asian customers using both hands, with the name facing the receiver. In Asia, anything involving a person's name demands respect.

How business cards are exchanged with Asian customers is very important. Read the text to learn the appropriate protocol in the approach stage of the personal selling process.
©Phillip Jarrell/Taxi/Getty Images

Presentation: Tailoring a Solution for a Customer's Needs

The *presentation* stage is at the core of the order-getting selling process, and its objective is to convert a prospect into a customer by creating a desire for the product or service. Three major presentation formats exist: (1) stimulus-response format, (2) formula selling format, and (3) need-satisfaction format.

Stimulus-Response Format

The **stimulus-response presentation** format assumes that given the appropriate stimulus by a salesperson, the prospect will buy. With this format the salesperson tries one appeal after another, hoping to hit the right button. A counter clerk at McDonald's is using this approach when he or she asks whether you'd like an order of french fries or a dessert with your meal. The counter clerk is engaging in what is called *suggestive selling*. Although useful in this setting, the stimulus-response format is not always appropriate, and for many products a more formalized format is necessary.

Formula Selling Format

The **formula selling presentation** format is based on the view that a presentation consists of information that must be provided in an accurate, thorough, and step-by-step manner to inform the prospect. A popular version of this format is the *canned sales presentation*, which is a memorized,

stimulus-response presentation
A sales presentation format that assumes that given the appropriate stimulus by a salesperson, the prospect will buy.

formula selling presentation
A sales presentation format that consists of information that must be provided in an accurate, thorough, and step-by-step manner to inform the prospect.

need-satisfaction presentation
A sales presentation format that emphasizes probing and listening by the salesperson to identify the needs and interests of prospective buyers.

adaptive selling
A need-satisfaction presentation format that involves adjusting the presentation to fit the selling situation, such as knowing when to offer solutions and when to ask for more information.

consultative selling
A need-satisfaction presentation format that focuses on problem identification, where the salesperson serves as an expert on problem recognition and resolution.

standardized message conveyed to every prospect. Used frequently by firms in telephone and door-to-door selling of consumer products (for example, Kirby vacuum cleaners), this approach treats every prospect the same, regardless of differences in needs or preferences for certain kinds of information.

Canned sales presentations can be advantageous when the differences between prospects are unknown or with novice salespeople who are less knowledgeable about the product and selling process than experienced salespeople. Although it guarantees a thorough presentation, it often lacks flexibility and spontaneity. More important, it does not provide for feedback from the prospective buyer—a critical component in the communication process and the start of a relationship.

Need-Satisfaction Format The stimulus-response and formula selling formats share a common characteristic: The salesperson dominates the conversation. By comparison, the **need-satisfaction presentation** format emphasizes probing and listening by the salesperson to identify the needs and interests of prospective buyers. Once these are identified, the salesperson tailors the presentation to the prospect and highlights product benefits that may be valued by the prospect. The need-satisfaction format, which emphasizes problem solving and customer solutions, is most consistent with the marketing concept and its focus on relationship building.

Two selling styles are common with this format.[16] **Adaptive selling** involves adjusting the presentation to fit the selling situation, such as knowing when to offer solutions and when to ask for more information. Sales research and practice show that knowledge of the customer and sales situation are key ingredients for adaptive selling. Many consumer service firms such as brokerage and insurance firms and consumer product firms like Rockport, AT&T, and Gillette effectively apply this selling style.

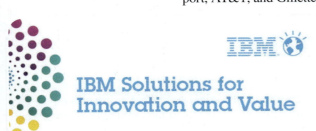

IBM is a leader in consultative selling with its focus on developing novel solutions that create customer value.
Source: IBM Corporation

Consultative selling focuses on problem identification, where the salesperson serves as an expert on problem recognition and resolution. With consultative selling, problem solution options are not simply a matter of choosing from an array of existing products or services. Rather, novel solutions often arise, thereby creating unique value for the customer.

Upselling and cross-selling is possible when a salesperson is viewed as an expert on problem recognition and resolution. *Upselling* is the practice of introducing a higher-end product solution than the one in question. *Cross-selling* is the practice of proposing related or complementary products and services. In both types of selling, the underlying intent is to create greater value for customers.

Consultative selling is prominent in business-to-business marketing. Johnson Controls's Automotive Systems Group, IBM's Global Services, DHL Worldwide Express, GE Healthcare, and Xerox offer customer solutions through their consultative selling style. According to a senior Xerox sales executive, "Our business is no longer about selling boxes. It's about selling digital, networked-based information management solutions, and this requires a highly customized and consultative selling process. So we look for consultative and business-savvy salespeople." But what does a customer solution really mean? The Marketing Matters box offers a unique answer.[17]

Handling Objections A critical concern in the presentation stage is handling objections. *Objections* are excuses for not making a purchase commitment or decision. Some objections are valid and are based on the characteristics of the product or service or price. However, many objections reflect prospect skepticism or indifference. Whether valid or not, experienced salespeople know that objections do not put an end to the

Marketing Matters > Customer Value

Imagine This...Putting the Customer into Customer Solutions!

Solutions to problems are what companies are looking for from suppliers. At the same time, suppliers focus on customer solutions to differentiate themselves from competitors. So what is a customer solution and what does it have to do with selling?

Sellers view a solution as a customized and integrated combination of products and services for meeting a customer's business needs. But what do buyers think? From a buyer's perspective, a solution is one that (1) meets their requirements, (2) is designed to uniquely solve their problem, (3) can be implemented, and (4) ensures follow-up.

This insight arose from a field study conducted by three researchers at Emory University. Their in-depth study also yielded insight into what an effective customer solution offers. According to one buyer interviewed in their study:

They (the supplier) make sure that their sales and marketing guys know what's going on. The sales and technical folks know what's going on, and the technical and support guys know what's going on with me. All these guys are in the loop, and it's not a puzzle for them.

So what does putting the customer into customer solutions have to do with selling? Three things stand out. First, considerable time and effort is necessary to fully understand a specific customer's requirements. Second, effective customer solutions are based on relationships among sellers and buyers. And finally, consultative selling is central to providing novel solutions for customers, thereby creating value for them.

Selling solutions has an added benefit to those companies that engage in this practice. Their dollar return on the sales effort is improved.

©Frank Herholdt/Stone/Getty Images

---

presentation. Rather, techniques can be used to deal with objections in a courteous, ethical, and professional manner. The following six techniques are the most common:[18]

1. *Acknowledge and convert the objection.* This technique involves using the objection as a reason for buying. For example, a prospect might say, "The price is too high." The reply: "Yes, the price is high because we use the finest materials. Let me show you...."
2. *Postpone.* The postpone technique is used when the objection will be dealt with later in the presentation: "I'm going to address that point shortly. I think my answer would make better sense then."
3. *Agree and neutralize.* Here a salesperson agrees with the objection, then shows that it is unimportant. A salesperson would say, "That's true. Others have said the same. But, they thought that issue was outweighed by other benefits."
4. *Accept the objection.* Sometimes the objection is valid. Let the prospect express such views, probe for the reason behind it, and attempt to stimulate further discussion on the objection.
5. *Denial.* When a prospect's objection is based on misinformation and clearly untrue, it is wise to meet the objection head on with a firm denial.
6. *Ignore the objection.* This technique is used when it appears that the objection is a stalling mechanism or is clearly not important to the prospect.

Each of these techniques requires a calm, professional interaction with the prospect and is most effective when objections are anticipated in the preapproach stage. Handling objections is a skill requiring a sense of timing, appreciation for the prospect's state of mind, and adeptness in communication. Objections also should be handled ethically. Lying or misrepresenting product or service features are clearly unethical practices.

Close: Asking for the Customer's Order or Business

The *closing* stage in the selling process involves obtaining a purchase commitment from the prospect. This stage is the most important and the most difficult because the salesperson must determine when the prospect is ready to buy. Telltale signals indicating a readiness to buy include body language (prospect reexamines the product or contract closely), statements ("This equipment should reduce our maintenance costs"), and questions ("When could we expect delivery?").

The close itself can take several forms. Three closing techniques are used when a salesperson believes a buyer is about ready to make a purchase: (1) trial close, (2) assumptive close, and (3) urgency close. A *trial close* involves asking the prospect to make a decision on some aspect of the purchase: "Would you prefer the blue or gray model?" An *assumptive close* entails asking the prospect to consider choices concerning delivery, warranty, or financing terms under the assumption that a sale has been finalized. An *urgency close* is used to commit the prospect quickly by making reference to the timeliness of the purchase: "The low interest financing ends next week," or "That is the last model we have in stock." Of course, these statements should be used only if they accurately reflect the situation; otherwise, such claims would be unethical. When a prospect is clearly ready to buy, the final close is used, and a salesperson asks for the order.

The closing stage involves obtaining a purchase commitment from the prospect. Read the text to learn how the close itself can take several forms.

©Purestock/GettyImages

Follow-up: Solidifying the Customer Relationship

The selling process does not end with the closing of a sale; rather, professional selling requires customer follow-up. One marketing authority equated the follow-up with courtship and marriage by observing, "The sale merely consummates the courtship. Then the marriage begins. How good the marriage is depends on how well the relationship is managed."[19] The *follow-up* stage includes making certain the customer's purchase has been properly delivered and installed and addressing any difficulties experienced with the use of the item. Attention to this stage of the selling process solidifies the buyer–seller relationship. Research shows that the cost and effort to obtain repeat sales from a satisfied customer is roughly half of that necessary to gain a sale from a new customer.[20] In short, today's satisfied customers become tomorrow's qualified prospects or referrals.

learning review

18-5. What are the six stages in the personal selling process?

18-6. What is the distinction between a lead and a qualified prospect?

18-7. Which presentation format is most consistent with the marketing concept? Why?

THE SALES MANAGEMENT PROCESS

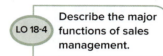

LO 18-4 Describe the major functions of sales management.

Selling must be managed if it is going to contribute to a firm's marketing objectives. Although firms differ in the specifics of how salespeople and the selling effort are managed, the sales management process is similar across firms. Sales management consists of three interrelated functions: (1) sales plan formulation, (2) sales plan implementation, and (3) salesforce evaluation (see Figure 18–3).

Sales Plan Formulation: Setting Direction

Formulating the sales plan is the most basic of the three sales management functions. According to the vice president of the Harris Corporation, a global communications company, "If a company hopes to implement its marketing strategy, it really needs a detailed sales planning process."[21] The **sales plan** is a statement describing what is to be achieved and where and how the selling effort of salespeople is to be deployed. Sales plan formulation involves three tasks: (1) setting objectives, (2) organizing the salesforce, and (3) developing account management policies.

sales plan
A statement describing what is to be achieved and where and how the selling effort of salespeople is to be deployed.

Setting Objectives Setting objectives is central to sales management because this task specifies what is to be achieved. In practice, objectives are set for the total salesforce and for each salesperson.

Selling objectives can be output related and focus on dollar or unit sales volume, number of new customers added, or profit. Alternatively, they can be input related and emphasize the number of sales calls and selling expenses. Output- and input-related objectives are used for the salesforce as a whole and for each salesperson. A third type of objective that is behaviorally related is typically specific for each salesperson and includes his or her product knowledge, customer service satisfaction ratings, and selling and communication skills.

Increasingly, firms are also emphasizing knowledge of competition as an objective since salespeople are calling on customers and should see what competitors are doing. In fact, 85 percent of companies encourage their salespeople to gather competitive intelligence.[22] But should salespeople explicitly ask their customers for information about competitors? Read the Making Responsible Decisions box to see how salespeople view this practice.[23]

Whatever objectives are set, they should be precise and measurable and specify the time period over which they are to be achieved. Once established, these objectives serve as performance standards for the evaluation of the salesforce, the third function of sales management.

Organizing the Salesforce Organizing a selling organization is the second task in formulating the sales plan. Companies organize their salesforce on the basis of (1) geography, (2) customer, or (3) product.

A *geographical sales organization* is the simplest structure, where the United States, or indeed the globe, is first divided into regions and each region is divided into districts or territories. Salespeople are assigned to each district with defined

FIGURE 18–3
The sales management process involves sales plan formulation, sales plan implementation, and salesforce evaluation.

Sales plan formulation
- Setting objectives
- Organizing the salesforce
- Developing account management policies

Sales plan implementation
- Salesforce recruitment and selection
- Salesforce training
- Salesforce motivation and compensation

Salesforce evaluation
- Quantitative assessment
- Behavioral evaluation

Making Responsible Decisions > Ethics

The Ethics of Asking Customers about Competitors

Salespeople are a valuable source of information about what is happening in the marketplace. By working closely with customers and asking good questions, salespeople often have firsthand knowledge of customer problems and wants. They also are able to spot the activities of competitors. However, should salespeople explicitly ask customers about competitor strategies such as pricing practices, product development efforts, and trade and promotion programs?

Gaining knowledge about competitors by asking customers for information is a ticklish ethical issue. Research indicates that 25 percent of U.S. salespeople engaged in business-to-business selling consider this practice unethical, and their companies have explicit guidelines for this practice.

It is also noteworthy that Japanese salespeople consider this practice to be more unethical than do U.S. salespeople. Do you believe that asking customers about competitor strategies and practices is unethical? Why or why not?

©Color Day Production/Getty Images

---

geographical boundaries and call on all customers and represent all products sold by the company. An advantage of this structure is that it can minimize travel time, expenses, and duplication of selling effort. However, if a firm's products or customers require specialized knowledge, then a geographical structure is unsuitable.

When different types of buyers have different needs, a *customer sales organization* is used. In practice this means that a different salesforce calls on each separate type of buyer or marketing channel. For example, Konica switched from a geographical to a marketing channel structure with different sales teams serving specific retail channels: mass merchandisers, photo specialty outlets, and food and drugstores. The rationale for this approach is that more effective, specialized customer support and knowledge are provided to buyers. However, this structure often leads to higher administrative costs and some duplication of selling effort, because several salesforces are used to represent the same products.

An important variation of the customer organizational structure is **key account management**—the practice of using team selling to focus on important customers to build mutually beneficial, long-term, cooperative relationships.[24] Key account management involves teams of sales, service, and often technical personnel who work with purchasing, manufacturing, engineering, logistics, and financial executives in customer organizations. This approach, which often assigns company personnel to a customer account, results in "customer specialists" who can provide exceptional service. Procter & Gamble uses this approach with Walmart, as does Stanley Black & Decker with The Home Depot.

When specific knowledge is required to sell certain types of products, then a *product sales organization* is used. For example, Maxim Steel has a salesforce that sells drilling pipe to oil companies and another that sells specialty steel products to manufacturers. The advantage of this structure is that salespeople can develop expertise with technical characteristics, applications, and selling methods associated with a particular product or family of products. However, this structure produces high administrative costs and duplication of selling effort, because two company salespeople may call on the same customer.

In short, there is no one best sales organization for all companies in all situations.[25] Rather, the organization of the salesforce should reflect the marketing strategy of the firm. Each year about 10 percent of U.S. firms change their sales organizations to implement new marketing strategies.

key account management
The practice of using team selling to focus on important customers to build mutually beneficial, long-term, cooperative relationships.

Frito-Lay uses a geographical sales organization to service its retail accounts.
©David Goldman/AP Images for Frito Lay

account management policies
Policies that specify whom salespeople should contact, what kinds of selling and customer service activities should be engaged in, and how these activities should be carried out.

Developing Account Management Policies The third task in formulating a sales plan involves developing **account management policies** specifying whom salespeople should contact, what kinds of selling and customer service activities should be engaged in, and how these activities should be carried out. These policies might state which individuals in a buying organization should be contacted, the amount of sales and service effort that different customers should receive, and the kinds of information salespeople should collect before or during a sales call.

An example of an account management policy in Figure 18-4 shows how different accounts or customers can be grouped according to level of opportunity and the firm's competitive sales position.[26] When specific account names are placed in each cell, salespeople clearly see which accounts should be contacted, with what kind of selling and service activity, and how to deal with them. Accounts in cells 1 and 2 might have high frequencies of personal sales calls and increased time spent on a call. Cell 3 accounts will have lower call frequencies, and cell 4 accounts might be contacted through telemarketing or direct mail rather than in person. For example, Union Pacific Railroad put its 20,000 smallest accounts on a telemarketing program. A subsequent survey of these accounts indicated that 84 percent rated Union Pacific's sales effort "very effective" compared with 67 percent before the switch.

Sales Plan Implementation: Putting the Plan into Action

The sales plan is put into practice through the tasks associated with sales plan implementation. Whereas sales plan formulation focuses on "doing the right things," implementation emphasizes "doing things right." The three major tasks involved in implementing a sales plan are (1) salesforce recruitment and selection, (2) salesforce training, and (3) salesforce motivation and compensation.

Salesforce Recruitment and Selection Effective recruitment and selection of salespeople is one of the most crucial tasks of sales management. It entails finding people who match the type of sales position required by a firm. Recruitment and selection practices will differ greatly between order-taking and order-getting sales positions, given the differences in the demands of these two jobs. Therefore, recruitment

FIGURE 18–4
An account management policy grid grouping customers according to level of opportunity and the firm's competitive sales position.

	Competitive position of sales organization	
	High	**Low**
Account opportunity level — High	**1** *Attractiveness:* Accounts offer a good opportunity because they have high potential and the sales organization has a strong position. *Account management policy:* Accounts should receive a high level of sales calls and service to retain and possibly build accounts.	**3** *Attractiveness:* Accounts may offer a good opportunity if the sales organization can overcome its weak position. *Account management policy:* Emphasize a heavy sales organization position or shift resources to other accounts if a stronger sales organization position is impossible.
Account opportunity level — Low	**2** *Attractiveness:* Accounts are somewhat attractive because the sales organization has a strong position, but future opportunity is limited. *Account management policy:* Accounts should receive a moderate level of sales and service to maintain the current position of the sales organization.	**4** *Attractiveness:* Accounts offer little opportunity, and the sales organization position is weak. *Account management policy:* Consider replacing personal calls with telephone sales or direct mail to service accounts. Consider dropping the account if unprofitable.

and selection begin with a carefully crafted job analysis and job description followed by a statement of job qualifications.

A *job analysis* is a study of a particular sales position, including how the job is to be performed and the tasks that make up the job. Information from a job analysis is used to write a *job description*, a written document that describes job relationships and requirements that characterize each sales position. It explains (1) to whom a salesperson reports, (2) how a salesperson interacts with other company personnel, (3) the customers to be called on, (4) the specific activities to be carried out, (5) the physical and mental demands of the job, and (6) the types of products and services to be sold.

The job description is then translated into a statement of job qualifications, including the aptitudes, knowledge, skills, and a variety of behavioral characteristics considered necessary to perform the job successfully. Qualifications for order-getting sales positions often mirror the expectations of buyers: (1) imagination and problem-solving ability, (2) strong work ethic, (3) honesty, (4) intimate product knowledge, (5) effective communication and listening skills, and (6) attentiveness reflected in responsiveness to buyer needs and customer loyalty and follow-up. Firms use a variety of methods for evaluating prospective salespeople. Personal interviews, reference checks, and background information provided on application forms are the most frequently used methods.[27]

Successful selling also requires a high degree of emotional intelligence. **Emotional intelligence** is the ability to understand one's own emotions and the emotions of people with whom one interacts on a daily basis. These qualities are important for adaptive selling and often spell the difference between effective and ineffective order-getting salespeople.[28] Are you interested in what your emotional intelligence might be? Read the Marketing Matters box and test yourself.

emotional intelligence
The ability to understand one's own emotions and the emotions of people with whom one interacts on a daily basis.

Salesforce Training Whereas the recruitment and selection of salespeople is a one-time event, salesforce training is an ongoing process that affects both new and seasoned salespeople.[29] Sales training covers much more than selling practices. For

Marketing Matters — Technology

What Is Your Emotional Intelligence? You Might Be Surprised.

A person's success at work depends on many talents, including intelligence and technical skills. Recent research indicates that an individual's emotional intelligence or EI is also important, if not more important!

Evidence suggests that emotional intelligence is two times more important in contributing to performance than intellect and expertise alone. Emotional intelligence has five dimensions: (1) self-motivation skills; (2) self-awareness, or knowing one's own emotions; (3) the ability to manage one's emotions and impulses; (4) empathy, or the ability to sense how others are feeling; and (5) social skills, or the ability to handle the emotions of other people.

What is your emotional intelligence? Visit the website at https://globalleadershipfoundation.com/geit/eitest.html and answer 40 short questions to learn how you score on certain emotional intelligence dimensions and obtain additional insights.

Courtesy of DTS International

example, IBM Global Services salespeople, who sell consulting and various information technology services, take at least two weeks of in-class and Internet-based training on both consultative selling and the technical aspects of the business.

Training new salespeople is an expensive process. Salespeople in the United States receive employer-sponsored training annually at a cost of over $15 billion per year. On-the-job training is the most popular type of training, followed by individual instruction taught by experienced salespeople. Formal classes, seminars taught by professional sales trainers, and computer-based training are also popular.

Salesforce Motivation and Compensation A sales plan cannot be successfully implemented without motivated salespeople. Research on salesperson motivation suggests that (1) a clear job description, (2) effective sales management practices, (3) a personal need for achievement, and (4) proper compensation, incentives, or rewards will produce a motivated salesperson.[30]

The importance of compensation as a motivating factor means that close attention must be given to how salespeople are financially rewarded for their efforts. Salespeople are paid using one of three plans: (1) straight salary, (2) straight commission, or (3) a combination of salary and commission. Under a *straight salary compensation plan*, a salesperson is paid a fixed fee per week, month, or year. With a *straight commission compensation plan,* a salesperson's earnings are directly tied to the sales or profit generated. For example, an insurance agent might receive a 2 percent commission of $2,000 for selling a $100,000 life insurance policy. A *combination compensation plan* contains a specified salary plus a commission on sales or profit generated.

Each compensation plan has its advantages and disadvantages.[31] A straight salary plan is easy to administer and gives management a large measure of control over how salespeople allocate their efforts. However, it provides little incentive to expand sales volume. This plan is used when salespeople engage in many nonselling activities, such as account or customer servicing. A straight commission plan provides the maximum amount of selling incentive but can discourage salespeople from providing customer service. This plan is common when nonselling activities are minimal. Combination plans are most preferred by salespeople and attempt to build on the advantages of salary and commission plans while reducing the potential shortcomings of each. Most companies use combination plans today.

Nonmonetary rewards are also given to salespeople for meeting or exceeding objectives. These rewards include trips, honor societies, distinguished salesperson awards, and letters of commendation. Some unconventional rewards include the new pink Cadillacs, Buicks, BMWs, and jewelry given by Mary Kay Cosmetics to outstanding salespeople.[32]

Effective recruitment, selection, training, motivation, and compensation programs combine to create a productive salesforce. Ineffective practices often lead to costly salesforce turnover. The expense of replacing and training a new salesperson, including the cost of lost sales, can be high. Also, new recruits are often less productive than seasoned salespeople.[33]

Mary Kay, Inc. offers unique nonmonetary rewards, including cars, to recognize its successful sales consultants. The color pink used by Mary Kay, Inc. on its cars is unique to the company.
Courtesy of Mary Kay, Inc.

Mary Kay Cosmetics, Inc.
www.marykay.com

Salesforce Evaluation: Measuring Results

The final function in the sales management process involves evaluating the salesforce. It is at this point that salespeople are assessed as to whether sales objectives were met and account management policies were followed. Both quantitative and behavioral measures are used to tap different selling dimensions.

Quantitative Assessments
Quantitative assessments are based on input- and output-related objectives set forth in the sales plan. Input-related measures focus on the actual activities performed by salespeople such as those involving sales calls, selling expenses, and account management policies. The number of sales calls made, selling expense related to sales made, and the number of reports submitted to superiors are frequently used input measures.

Output measures often appear in a sales quota. A **sales quota** contains specific goals assigned to a salesperson, sales team, branch sales office, or sales district for a stated time period. Dollar or unit sales volume, last year/current year sales ratio, sales of specific products, new accounts generated, and profit achieved are typical goals. The time period can range from one month to one year.

sales quota
Specific goals assigned to a salesperson, sales team, branch sales office, or sales district for a stated time period.

Behavioral Evaluation
Behavioral measures are also used to evaluate salespeople. These include assessments of a salesperson's attitude, attention to customers, product knowledge, selling and communication skills, appearance, and professional demeanor. Even though these assessments are sometimes subjective, they are frequently considered and are, in fact, inevitable, in salesperson evaluation. Why? These factors are often important determinants of quantitative outcomes.

About 60 percent of U.S. companies now include customer satisfaction as a behavioral measure of salesperson performance. The relentless focus on customer satisfaction by Eastman Chemical Company salespeople contributed to the company being named a recipient of the prestigious Malcolm Baldrige National Quality Award.[34] Eastman surveys its customers with multiple versions of its customer satisfaction questionnaire delivered in nine languages. Some 25 performance items are studied, including on-time and correct delivery, product quality, pricing practice, and sharing of market information. Salespeople review the results with customers. Eastman salespeople know that "the second most important thing they have to do is get their customer satisfaction surveys out to and back from customers," says Eastman's sales training director. "Number one, of course, is getting orders."

Increasingly, companies are using marketing dashboards to track salesperson performance for evaluation purposes. An illustration appears in the Applying Marketing Metrics box.

Customer Relationship Management Systems and Technology

Personal selling and sales management have undergone a revolution with the use of customer relationship management (CRM) systems and technology. In fact, the convergence of computer, information, communication, and Internet technologies has transformed the selling and sales management function in many companies. CRM systems and technology consolidate customer and sales information in a single database so that salespeople and sales managers can more easily access, analyze, and manage a company's relationship with individual customers or accounts. These systems and technologies are designed with the goal of improving business relationships with customers, creating value for customers, assisting in new customer acquisition and current customer retention, and achieving profitable sales growth for companies.[35]

Customer relationship management systems and technologies are tailored to the needs of companies. As a rule, these systems and technologies automate workflow processes and focus on salesforce automation, marketing automation, and customer service and support automation.

Customer relationship management (CRM) systems and technology combine computer, information, communication, and Internet technologies to transform the selling and sales management function. U.S. companies spend upwards of $37 billion each year on CRM applications.
©shironosov/iStock/Getty Images

Salesforce Automation
The most basic application of CRM systems and technologies, and the one most applicable to selling and sales management, is salesforce

Applying Marketing Metrics

Tracking Salesperson Performance at Moore Chemical & Sanitation Supply, Inc.

Moore Chemical & Sanitation Supply, Inc. (MooreChem) is a large midwestern supplier of cleaning chemicals and sanitary products. MooreChem sells to janitorial companies that clean corporate and professional office buildings.

MooreChem recently installed a sales and account management planning software package that included a dashboard for each of its sales representatives. Salespeople had access to their dashboards as well. These dashboards included seven metrics—sales revenue, gross margin, selling expense, profit, average order size, new customers, and customer satisfaction. Each metric was gauged to show actual salesperson performance relative to target goals.

Your Challenge

As a newly promoted district sales manager at MooreChem, your responsibilities include tracking each salesperson's performance in your district. You are also responsible for directing the sales activities and practices of district salespeople.

In anticipation of a performance review with one of your salespeople, Brady Boyle, you review his dashboard for the previous quarter. This information can be used to provide a constructive review of his performance.

Your Findings

Brady Boyle's quarterly performance is displayed below. Boyle has exceeded targeted goals for sales revenue, selling expenses, and customer satisfaction. All of these metrics show an upward trend. He has met his target for gaining new customers and average order size. But, Boyle's gross margin and profit are below targeted goals. These metrics evidence a downward trend as well. Brady Boyle's mixed performance requires a constructive and positive correction.

Your Action

Brady Boyle should already know how his performance compares with targeted goals. Remember, Boyle has access to his dashboard. Recall that he has exceeded his sales target, but is considerably under his profit target. Boyle's sales trend is up, but his profit trend is down.

You will need to focus attention on Boyle's gross margin and selling expense results and trend. Boyle, it seems, is spending time and money selling lower-margin products that produce a targeted average order size. It may very well be that Boyle is actually expending effort selling more products to his customers. Unfortunately, the product mix yields lower gross margins, resulting in a lower profit.

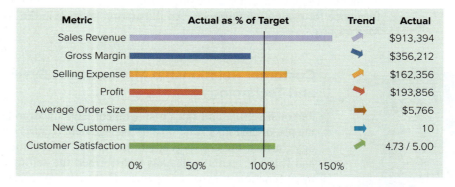

---

salesforce automation (SFA)
The use of various technologies to make the sales function more effective and efficient.

automation. **Salesforce automation (SFA)** is the use of various technologies to make the selling function more effective and efficient. Examples of salesforce automation include computer hardware and software for account development and analysis (including an account's purchase history and preferences); time management; order processing, delivery, and follow-up; proposal generation; and product and sales training. Its application is designed to free time for salespeople to be with customers building relationships, designing solutions. and providing service.

Sales presentation hardware and software are another application. For example, Toshiba America Medical Systems salespeople use laptop computers with capabilities to provide interactive presentations for their computerized tomography (CT) and magnetic resonance imaging (MRI) scanners. The computer technology allows the customer to see elaborate three-dimensional animations, high-resolution scans, and video

Toshiba America Medical Systems salespeople have found salesforce automation to be an effective sales presentation tool and training device.

(both): Source: Toshiba America Medical Systems

Toshiba America Medical Systems

www.toshiba.com

clips of the company's products in operation as well as narrated testimonials from satisfied customers. Toshiba has found this application to be effective for both sales presentations and salesforce training.

Marketing Automation A more sophisticated combination of CRM systems and technology is marketing automation. *Marketing automation* applies systems and technologies to provide intelligence to salespeople. It is used to identify qualified prospects from leads, provide support for preparing an appropriate preapproach and approach strategy for a customer, track the customer buying process, and identify opportunities for upselling and cross-selling a company's products and services to new and existing customers.

Marketing automation emphasizes sophisticated analytical techniques and computer software. For example, these techniques use tracking codes in social media, e-mail, and websites to track the behavior of anyone showing an interest in a product or service to gain a measure of intent to buy. Customer leads and prospects are scored, based on their activities, and automatically sent highly targeted product and service information through social media and e-mail. If you've ever researched a product or service online and shortly thereafter received messages from suppliers of that product or service, you've seen marketing automation at work.

Customer Service and Support Automation The third most prominent application of customer relationship management processes and technology is customer service and support automation. *Customer service and support automation* consists of processes and technologies that supply customers with information about postsale activities, including installation, repair, replacement, and replenishment, and technical expertise pertaining to products. Two features of successful customer service and support automation are the availability of "live chat" opportunities and the ability to provide a single source for customer problem solving. Both features attempt to overcome customer frustration with having to contact multiple service and support personnel to solve any, and all, problems.

Customer relationship management processes and technology are clearly changing how selling is done and how salespeople are managed. U.S. companies spend upwards of $37 billion annually on CRM applications. These applications promise to boost selling productivity, improve customer relationships, and decrease selling and customer service costs. Nevertheless, one-half of senior sales and marketing executives in the United States believe that CRM processes and technologies have not yet achieved their full potential.[36]

learning review

18-8. What are the three types of selling objectives?

18-9. What three factors are used to organize sales organizations?

18-10. How is emotional intelligence tied to adaptive selling?

LEARNING OBJECTIVES REVIEW

LO 18-1 *Discuss the nature and scope of personal selling and sales management in marketing.*

Personal selling involves the two-way flow of communication between a buyer and seller, often in a face-to-face encounter, designed to influence the purchase decision of a person or group. Sales management involves planning the selling program and implementing and controlling the personal selling effort of the firm. The scope of selling and sales management is apparent in three ways. First, virtually every occupation that involves customer contact has an element of personal selling. Second, selling plays a significant role in a company's overall marketing effort. Salespeople occupy a boundary position between buyers and sellers; they *are* the company to many buyers and account for a major cost of marketing in a variety of industries. Salespeople also can create value for customers. Finally, through relationship selling, salespeople play a central role in tailoring solutions to customer problems as a means to customer value creation.

LO 18-2 *Identify the different types of personal selling.*

Three types of personal selling exist: (*a*) order taking, (*b*) order getting, and (*c*) customer sales support activities. Each type differs from the others in terms of actual selling done and the amount of creativity required to perform the sales task. Order takers process routine orders or reorders for products that were already sold by the company. They generally do little selling in a conventional sense and engage in only modest problem solving with customers. Order getters sell in a conventional sense and identify prospective customers, provide customers with information, persuade customers to buy, close sales, and follow up on customers' use of a product or service. Order getting involves a high degree of creativity and customer empathy and is typically required for selling complex or technical products with many options. Customer sales support personnel augment the sales effort of order getters by performing a variety of services. Sales support personnel are prominent in cross-functional team selling, the practice of using an entire team of professionals in selling to and servicing major customers.

LO 18-3 *Explain the stages in the personal selling process.*

The personal selling process consists of six stages: (1) prospecting, (2) preapproach, (3) approach, (4) presentation, (5) close, and (6) follow-up. Prospecting involves the search for and qualification of potential customers. The preapproach stage involves obtaining further information on the prospect and deciding on the best method of approach. The approach stage involves the initial meeting between the salesperson and prospect. The presentation stage involves converting a prospect into a customer by creating a desire for the product or service. The close involves obtaining a purchase commitment from the prospect. The follow-up stage involves making certain that the customer's purchase has been properly delivered and installed and addressing any difficulties experienced with the use of the item.

LO 18-4 *Describe the major functions of sales management.*

Sales management consists of three interrelated functions: (*a*) sales plan formulation, (*b*) sales plan implementation, and (*c*) salesforce evaluation. Sales plan formulation involves setting objectives, organizing the salesforce, and developing account management policies. Sales plan implementation involves salesforce recruitment and selection; training; and motivation and compensation. Salesforce evaluation involves the use of quantitative and behavioral measures to assess the performance of the salesforce. Finally, customer relationship management systems and technologies are becoming increasingly important in sales management, boosting selling productivity, improving customer relationships, and decreasing selling and customer service costs.

LEARNING REVIEW ANSWERS

18-1 What is personal selling?

Answer: Personal selling involves the two-way flow of communication between a buyer and seller, often in a face-to-face encounter, designed to influence the purchase decision of a person or group.

18-2 What is involved in sales management?

Answer: Sales management involves planning the selling program and implementing and evaluating the personal selling effort of the firm. The tasks involved in managing personal selling include setting objectives; organizing the salesforce; recruiting, selecting, training, and compensating salespeople; and evaluating the performance of individual salespeople.

18-3 What is the principal difference between an order taker and an order getter?

Answer: An order taker processes routine orders or reorders for products that were already sold by the company. The primary responsibility of order takers is to preserve an ongoing relationship with existing customers and maintain sales. An order getter sells in a conventional sense and identifies prospective customers, provides customers with information, persuades customers to buy, closes sales, and follows up on customers' use of a product or service. Order getting involves a high degree of creativity, customer empathy, considerable product knowledge, and sales training.

18-4 What is team selling?

Answer: Team selling is the practice of using an entire team of professionals in selling to and servicing major customers. Team selling is used when specialized knowledge is needed to satisfy the different interests of individuals in a customer's buying center.

18-5 What are the six stages in the personal selling process?

Answer: The six stages in the personal selling process are: (1) prospecting—searching for qualified potential customers; (2) preapproach—obtaining further information on prospects and deciding on the best method of approach; (3) approach—setting up the first meeting between the salesperson and the prospect to gain his/her attention, stimulate interest, and establish a foundation for the relationship and eventual sales presentation; (4) presentation—converting a prospect into a customer by creating a desire for the offering; (5) close—obtaining a purchase commitment from the prospect; and (6) follow-up—delivering, installing, and/or resolving any difficulties with the purchase.

18-6 **What is the distinction between a lead and a qualified prospect?**
Answer: A lead is the name of a person who may be a possible customer, whereas a qualified prospect is an individual who wants the product, can afford to buy it, and is the decision maker.

18-7 **Which presentation format is most consistent with the marketing concept? Why?**
Answer: The need-satisfaction presentation format emphasizes probing and listening by the salesperson to identify the needs and interests of prospective buyers and then tailors the presentation to the prospect and highlights product benefits. This is consistent with the marketing concept and its focus on relationship building.

18-8 **What are the three types of selling objectives?**
Answer: The three types of selling objectives are: (1) output-related (dollars or unit sales, number of new customers, profit); (2) input-related (number of sales calls, selling expenses); and (3) behavior-related (product and competitive knowledge, customer service satisfaction ratings, selling and communication skills).

18-9 **What three factors are used to organize sales organizations?**
Answer: The three factors used to organize sales organizations are (1) geography, (2) customer, or (3) product.

18-10 **How is emotional intelligence tied to adaptive selling?**
Answer: Emotional intelligence is the ability to understand one's own emotions and the emotions of people with whom one interacts on a daily basis. Evidence suggests that emotional intelligence is two times more important in contributing to performance than intellect and expertise alone. Emotional intelligence has five dimensions: (1) self-motivation skills; (2) self-awareness, or knowing one's own emotions; (3) the ability to manage one's emotions and impulses; (4) empathy, or the ability to sense how others are feeling; and (5) social skills, or the ability to handle the emotions of other people. These qualities are important for adaptive selling.

FOCUSING ON KEY TERMS

account management policies p. 504
adaptive selling p. 499
consultative selling p. 499
emotional intelligence p. 505
formula selling presentation p. 498
key account management p. 503
need-satisfaction presentation p. 499
order getter p. 493
order taker p. 492
personal selling p. 490
personal selling process p. 495
relationship selling p. 491
sales management p. 490
sales plan p. 502
sales quota p. 507
salesforce automation (SFA) p. 508
stimulus-response presentation p. 498
team selling p. 494

APPLYING MARKETING KNOWLEDGE

1. Jane Dawson is a new sales representative for the Charles Schwab brokerage firm. In searching for clients, Jane purchased a mailing list of subscribers to *The Wall Street Journal* and called them all regarding their interest in discount brokerage services. She asked if they have any stocks and if they have a regular broker. Those people without a regular broker were asked their investment needs. Two days later, Jane called back with investment advice and asked if they would like to open an account. Identify each of Jane Dawson's actions in terms of the personal selling process.

2. For the first 50 years of business, the Johnson Carpet Company produced carpets for residential use. The salesforce was structured geographically. In the past five years, a large percentage of carpet sales have been to industrial users, hospitals, schools, and architects. The company also has broadened its product line to include area rugs, Oriental carpets, and wall-to-wall carpeting. Is the present salesforce structure appropriate, or would you recommend an alternative?

3. Where would you place each of the following sales jobs on the order-taker/order-getter continuum shown below? (a) Burger King counter clerk, (b) automobile insurance salesperson, (c) Hewlett-Packard computer salesperson, (d) life insurance salesperson, and (e) shoe salesperson.

Order taker —————————————— Order getter

4. Listed here are two different firms. Which salesforce compensation plan would you recommend for each firm, and what reasons would you give for your recommendations? (a) A newly formed company that sells lawn care equipment on a door-to-door basis directly to consumers; and (b) the Nabisco Company, which sells heavily advertised products in supermarkets by having the salesforce call on these stores and arrange shelves, set up displays, and make presentations to store buying committees.

5. Suppose someone said to you, "The only real measure of a salesperson is the amount of sales produced." How might you respond?

BUILDING YOUR MARKETING PLAN

Does your marketing plan involve a personal selling activity? If the answer is "no," read no further and do not include a personal selling element in your plan. If the answer is "yes":

1 Identify the likely prospects for your product or service.
2 Determine what information you should obtain about the prospect.
3 Describe how you would approach the prospect.
4 Outline the presentation you would make to the prospect for your product or service.
5 Develop a sales plan, focusing on the organizational structure you would use for your salesforce (geographic, product, or customer).

VIDEO CASE 18

Xerox: Building Customer Relationships through Personal Selling

"I'm like the quarterback of the team. I manage 250 accounts, and anything from billing issues, to service issues, to selling the products. I'm really the face to the customer," says Alison Capossela, a Washington, DC–based Xerox sales representative.

Video 18-2
Xerox Video Case
kerin.tv/cr8e/v18-2

As the primary company contact for Xerox customers, Alison is responsible for developing and maintaining customer relationships. To accomplish this she uses a sophisticated selling process that requires many activities, from making presentations, to attending training sessions, to managing a team of Xerox personnel, to monitoring competitors' activities. The face-to-face interactions with customers, however, are the most rewarding for Capossela. "It's an amazing feeling; the more they challenge me the more I fight back. It's fun!" she explains.

THE COMPANY

Xerox Corporation's mission is to "help people find better ways to do great work by constantly leading in document technologies, products, and services that improve customers' work processes and business results." To accomplish this mission Xerox employs 130,000 people in 160 countries. Xerox is the world's leading document management enterprise and a *Fortune* 500 company.

Xerox offers a wide range of products and services. These include printers, copiers and fax machines, multifunction and network devices, high-speed color presses, digital imaging and archiving products and services, and supplies such as toner, paper, and ink. The entire company is guided by customer-focused and employee-centered core values (e.g., "We succeed through satisfied customers") and a passion for innovation, speed, and adaptability.

THE SELLING PROCESS AT XEROX

A decade ago, Xerox began a shift to a consultative selling model that focused on helping customers solve their business problems rather than just placing more equipment in their office. The shift meant that sales reps needed to be less product-oriented and more relationship- and value-oriented. Xerox wanted to be a provider of total solutions.

Today, Xerox has more than 8,000 sales professionals throughout the world who spend a large amount of their day developing customer relationships. Capossela explains: "Fifty percent of my day is spent with my customers, 25 percent is following up with phone calls or e-mails, and another 25 percent involves preparing proposals." The approach has helped Xerox attract new customers and keep existing customers.

The sales process at Xerox typically follows the six stages of the personal selling process identified in Figure 18–2: (1) Xerox identifies potential clients through responses to advertising, referrals, and telephone calls; (2) the salesforce prepares for a presentation by familiarizing themselves with the potential client and its document needs; (3) a Xerox sales representative approaches the prospect and suggests a meeting and presentation; (4) as the presentation begins, the salesperson summarizes relevant information about potential solutions Xerox can offer, states what he or she hopes to get out of the meeting, explains how the products and services work, and reinforces the benefits of working with Xerox; (5) the salesperson engages in an action close (gets a signed document or a firm confirmation of the sale); and then (6) the salesperson continues to meet and communicate with the client to provide assistance and monitor the effectiveness of the installed solution.

Xerox sales representatives also use the selling process to maintain relationships with existing customers. In today's competitive environment it is not unusual to have customers who have been approached by competitors or who are required to obtain more than one bid before renewing a contract. Xerox has teams of people who collect and analyze information about competitors and their products. The information is sent out to sales reps or offered to them through workshops and seminars. The most difficult competitors are the ones that have also invested in customer relationships. The selling process allows Xerox to continually react and respond to new information and take advantage of opportunities in the marketplace.

THE SALES MANAGEMENT PROCESS AT XEROX

The Xerox salesforce is divided into four geographic organizations: North America, which includes the United States and Canada; Europe, which includes 17 countries; Global Accounts, which manages large accounts that operate in multiple locations; and Developing Markets, which includes all other geographic territories that may require Xerox products and services. Within each geographic area, the majority of Xerox products and services are typically sold through its direct salesforce. Xerox also utilizes a variety of other channels, including value-added resellers, independent agents, dealers, systems integrators, telephone, and Internet sales channels.

Motivation and compensation are important aspects of any salesforce. At Xerox there is a passion for winning that provides a key incentive for sales reps. Compensation also plays an important role. In addition, Xerox has a recognition program called the President's Club where the top performers are awarded a five-day trip to one of the top resorts in the world. The program has been a huge success and has now been offered for more than 30 years.

Perhaps the most well-known component of Xerox's sales management process is its sales representative recruitment and training program. "For recruitment, Xerox looks for seasoned businesspeople who can talk to customers," says Kevin Warren, president of United States customer operations at Xerox. "Our value proposition is that we take care of document management to help run your business," Warren explains. "So we look for consultative and business-savvy salespeople."

On the training front, Xerox developed the "Create and Win" program to help sales reps learn the consultative selling approach. The components of the program consist of interactive training sessions and distance-learning webinars. Every new sales representative at Xerox receives eight weeks of training development in the field and at the Xerox Corporate University in Virginia. "The training program is phenomenal!" according to Capossela. The training and its focus on the customer is part of the Xerox culture outside of the sales organization also. Every senior executive at Xerox is responsible for working with at least one customer. They also spend a full day every month responding to incoming customer calls and inquiries.

WHAT IS IN THE FUTURE FOR THE XEROX SALESFORCE?

The recent growth and success at Xerox is creating many opportunities for the company and its sales representatives. For example, Xerox is accelerating the development of its top salespeople. Mentors are used to provide advice for day-to-day issues and long-term career planning. In addition, globalization has become such an important initiative at Xerox that experienced and successful sales representatives are quickly given opportunities to manage large global accounts.

Source: Xerox

Xerox is also moving toward an approach that empowers sales representatives to make decisions about how to handle accounts. The large number of Xerox customers means there are a variety of different corporate styles, and the sales reps are increasingly the best qualified to manage the relationship. This approach is just one more example of Xerox's commitment to customers and creating customer value.[37]

Questions

1 How does Xerox create customer value through its personal selling process?
2 How does Alison Capossela provide solutions for Xerox customers?
3 Why is the Xerox training program so important to the company's success?

Chapter Notes

1. Interview with Lindsey Smith, GE Healthcare Americas, March 6, 2016.
2. Jessi Hempel, "IBM's All-Star Salesman," *www.cnnmoney.com,* September 26, 2008.
3. Jim Clifton and Sangeeta Bharadwaj Badal, *Entrepreneural Strengths Finder* (New York: Gallup Press, 2014); and Meghan Casserly, "The Five Sales Tactics Every Entrepreneur Must Master," *forbes.com,* January 30, 2013.
4. "Guess Who Else Is in on the Operation?" *The Dallas Morning News,* November 27, 2016.
5. Mark W. Johnson and Greg W. Marshall, *Contemporary Selling: Building Relationships, Creating Value,* 5th ed. (New York: Routledge, 2016).
6. Richard P. Bagozzi et al., "Genetic and Neurological Foundations of Customer Orientation: Field and Experimental Evidence," *Journal of the Academy of Marketing Science,* September 2012, pp. 639–58; and "Does Your Salesperson Have the Right Genes?" *Harvard Business Review,* April 2013, p. 24.
7. "Why Sales Reps Spend So Little Time Selling," forbes.com, February 15, 2017; "Top-Five Focus Areas for Improving Sales Effectiveness Initiatives," *www.accenture.com,* downloaded May 5, 2017.
8. "The New Willy Loman Survives by Staying Home," *Bloomberg Businessweek,* January 14–January 20, 2013, pp. 16–17.
9. For an overview of team selling, see Eli Jones, Andrea Dickson, Lawrence B. Chonko, and Joseph P. Cannon, "Key Accounts and Team Selling: A Review, Framework, and Research Agenda," *Journal of Personal Selling & Sales Management,* Spring 2005, pp. 181–98.
10. Eric Baron, *Innovative Team Selling* (New York: Wiley, 2013); and "Team Selling Works!" *www.sellingpower.com,* March 24, 2013.
11. Scott Sterns, "Cold Calls Have Yet to Breathe Their Last Gasp," *The Wall Street Journal,* December 14, 2006, p. D2.
12. Jim Edwards, "Dinner, Interrupted," *BrandWeek,* May 26, 2003, pp. 28–32.
13. "Those Pesky Unwanted Calls Won't Go Away," *The Wall Street Journal,* September 9–10, 2017, p. A2.
14. Paul A. Herbing, *Handbook of Cross-Cultural Marketing* (New York: Haworth Press, 1998).
15. Philip R. Cateora, Mary C. Gilly, John L. Graham, and R. Bruce Money, *International Marketing,* 17th ed. (Burr Ridge, IL: McGraw-Hill/Irwin, 2016).
16. This discussion is based on Mark W. Johnston and Greg W. Marshall, *Contemporary Selling: Building Relationships, Creating Value,* 5th ed. (New York: Routledge, 2016).
17. Kapil R. Tuli, Ajay K. Kohli, and Sundar G. Bharadwaj, "Rethinking Customer Solutions: From Product Bundles to Relational Processes," *Journal of Marketing,* July 2007, pp. 1–17. Also, see Stefan Worm, Sundar G. Bharadwaj, Wolfgang Ulaga, and Werner J. Reinartz, "When and Why Do Customer Solutions Pay Off in Business Markets?" *Journal of the Academy of Marketing Science,* July 2017, pp. 490–512; and Wolfgang Ulaga and Ajay Kohli, "The Role of a Solutions Salesperson: Reducing Uncertainty and Fostering Adaptiveness," *Industrial Marketing Management,* February 2018, pp. 161–68.
18. For an extensive discussion of objections, see Charles M. Futrell, *Fundamentals of Selling,* 13th ed. (Burr Ridge, IL: McGraw-Hill/Irwin, 2014), chapter 12.
19. Theodore Levitt, *The Marketing Imagination* (New York: Free Press, 1983), p. 111.
20. Stephen B. Castleberry and John F. Tanner Jr., *Selling: Building Partnerships,* 9th ed. (Burr Ridge, IL: McGraw-Hill, 2014).
21. *Management Briefing: Sales and Marketing* (New York: Conference Board, October 1996), pp. 3–4.
22. Christopher Murphy, *Competitive Intelligence: Gathering, Analyzing, and Putting It to Work* (New York: Routledge, 2016).
23. Joel LeBon, *Competitive Intelligence and the Sales Force* (New York: Business Expert Press, 2013); and Douglas E. Hughes, Joel LeBon, and Adam Rapp, "Gaining and Leveraging Customer-Based Competitive Intelligence: The Pivotal Role of Social Capital and Salesperson Adaptive Selling Skills," *Journal of the Academy of Marketing Science,* January 2013, pp. 91–110.
24. Eli Jones, Andrea Dickson, Lawrence B. Chonko, and Joseph P. Cannon, "Key Accounts and Team Selling: A Review, Framework, and Research Agenda," *Journal of Personal Selling & Sales Management,* Spring 2005, pp. 181–98. Also see, Arun Sharma, "Success Factors in Key Accounts," *Journal of Business & Industrial Marketing* 21, no. 3 (2006), pp. 141–50.
25. William L. Cron and David W. Cravens, "Sales Force Strategy," in Robert A. Peterson and Roger A. Kerin, eds., *Wiley International Encyclopedia of Marketing: Volume 1—Marketing Strategy* (West Sussex, UK: Wiley, 2011), pp. 197–207.
26. This discussion is based on William L. Cron and Thomas E. DeCarlo, *Dalrymple's Sales Management,* 10th ed. (Hoboken, NJ: Wiley, 2009).
27. René Y. Darmon, *Leading the Sales Force* (New York: Cambridge University Press, 2007).
28. Jeb Blount, *Sales EQ: How Ultra High Performance Salespeople Leverage Sales-Specific Emotional Intelligence to Close the Complex Deal* (Hoboken, NJ: Wiley, 2017); Richard D. McFarland, Joseph C. Rode, and Tassadduq A. Shirvani, "A Contingency Model of Emotional Intelligence in Professional Selling," *Journal of the Academy of Marketing Science,* January 2016, pp. 108–18; "Look for Employees with High EQ over IQ," *forbes.com,* March 18, 2013; and Blair Kidwell, David M. Hardesty, Brian R. Murtha, and Shibin Sheng, "Emotional Intelligence in Marketing Exchanges," *Journal of Marketing,* January 2011, pp. 78–93.
29. Rosann L. Spiro, Gregory A. Rich, and William J. Stanton, *Management of a Sales Force,* 12th ed. (Burr Ridge, IL: McGraw-Hill/Irwin, 2008), chapter 7; and Thomas L. Powers, Thomas E. DeCarlo, and Gouri Gupte, "An Update on the Status of Sales Management Training," *Journal of Personal Selling & Sales Management,* Fall 2010, pp. 319–26.
30. Rushana Khusainova, Ad de Jong, Nick Lee, Greg Marshall, and Sohn Rudd, "(Re)defining Salesperson Movivation: Current Status, Main Challenges, and Research Directions," *Journal of Personal Selling & Sales Management* Winter 2018, pp. 2–29; and Thomas Steenburgh and Michael Ahearne, "Motivating Salespeople: What Really Works," *Harvard Business Review,* July–August 2012, pp. 71–75.
31. This discussion is based on Mark W. Johnston and Greg W. Marshall, *Sales Force Management,* 11th ed. (Burr Ridge, IL: McGraw-Hill/Irwin, 2014), chapter 11; and Andris Zoltners, Prabhakant Sinha, and Sally E. Lorimer, *The Complete Guide to Sales Force Incentive Compensation* (New York: AMACOM, 2006).
32. *www.MaryKay.com,* accessed June 5, 2018.
33. Jeffrey E. Lewin and Jeffrey K. Sager, "The Influence of Personal Characteristics and Coping Strategies on Salespersons' Turnover Intentions," *Journal of Personal Selling & Sales Management,* Fall 2010, pp. 355–70; and René Y. Darmon, "The Concept of Salesperson Replacement Value: A Sales

Force Turnover Management Tool," *Journal of Personal Selling & Sales Management,* Summer 2008, pp. 211–32.

34. James R. Evans, *Quality and Performance Excellence,* 7th ed. (Mason, OH: Cengage, 2014).

35. Don Peppers and Martha Rogers, *Managing Customer Experience and Relationships,* 3rd ed. (Hoboken, NJ: Wiley, 2017); and Francis Buttle and Stan Maklan, *Customer Relationship Management: Concepts and Technologies,* 3rd ed. (New York: Routledge, 2017).

36. "Top-Five Focus Areas for Improving Sales Effectiveness Initiatives," *www.accenture.com,* accessed May 5, 2017.

37. Xerox: This case was written by Steven Hartley and Roger Kerin. Sources: Interview with Alison Capossela, Xerox Corporation; "A Day in the Life of a Xerox Employee in Sales," *xerox.com/jobs,* accessed October 1, 2017; and company background and data available on the Xerox website, *www.xerox.com.*

APPENDIX B

PLANNING A CAREER IN MARKETING

GETTING A JOB: THE PROCESS OF MARKETING YOURSELF

Getting a job is usually a lengthy process, and it is exactly that—a *process* that involves careful planning, implementation, and evaluation. You may have everything going for you: a respectable grade point average (GPA), relevant work experience, several extracurricular activities, superior communication skills, and demonstrated leadership qualities. Despite these, you still need to market yourself systematically and aggressively; after all, even the best products lie dormant on retailers' shelves unless marketed effectively. As authors Reid Hoffman and Ben Casnocha suggest, think of finding your first job as "The Startup of You!"

The process of getting a job involves the same activities marketing managers use to develop key brand characteristics and introduce successful products into the marketplace.[1] The only difference is that you are marketing yourself, not a product. You need to conduct marketing research by analyzing your personal qualities (performing a self-audit) and by identifying job opportunities.

Based on your research results, select a target market—those job opportunities that are compatible with your interests, goals, skills, and abilities—and design a marketing mix around that target market. *You* are the "product"; you must decide how to "position" and "brand" yourself in the job market.[2]

The price component of the marketing mix is the salary range and job benefits (such as health and life insurance, vacation time, and retirement benefits) that you hope to receive. Promotion involves communicating with prospective employers through written and electronic correspondence (advertising) and job interviews (personal selling). The place element focuses on how to reach prospective employers—at the career services office, job fairs, or online, for example.

This appendix will assist you in career planning by (1) providing information about careers in marketing and (2) outlining a job search process.

CAREERS IN MARKETING

The diversity of marketing opportunities is reflected in the many types of marketing jobs, including product management, marketing research, and public relations. While many of these jobs are found at traditional employers such as manufacturers, retailers, and advertising agencies, there are also many opportunities in a variety of other types of organizations.

Professional services such as law, accounting, and consulting firms, for example, have a growing need for marketing expertise. Similarly, nonprofit organizations such as universities, the performing arts, museums, and government agencies are developing marketing functions. Event organizations such as athletic teams, golf and tennis tournaments, and the Olympics are also new and visible sources of marketing jobs.

The diversity of marketing jobs is also changing because of changes in the marketing discipline. The growth of digital marketing, mobile marketing, and

©photobooth/Shutterstock

social media has created a variety of new jobs including data analysts, content marketing specialists, and social media managers. The growth of multichannel and omnichannel marketing has led to the need for channel integration specialists. The increasing involvement and engagement of consumers has required public relations personnel to become social networking experts and consumer-generated content managers. Other specialties in demand now include customer relations management (CRM), customer experience management (CEM), multicultural marketing, and digital marketing.[3]

Examples of companies that have opportunities for graduates with degrees in marketing include Amazon, AT&T, Capital One, Comcast, JPMorgan, Marriott, Nordstrom, PepsiCo, PwC, REI, and Shutterfly.[4] Most of these career opportunities offer a chance to work with interesting people on stimulating and rewarding problems. One product manager comments, "I love marketing as a career because there are different challenges every day."[5]

Recent studies of career paths and salaries suggest that marketing careers can also provide excellent opportunities for advancement and substantial pay. For example, one of every four chief executive officers (CEOs) held positions in marketing before becoming CEO.[6] Similarly, reports of average starting salaries of college graduates indicate that salaries in marketing compare favorably with those in many other fields. The average starting salary of new marketing undergraduates in 2018 was $62,634, compared with $53,722 for journalism majors and $51,150 for advertising majors.[7] The future is likely to be even better. The U.S. Department of Labor reports that employment of advertising, promotion, and marketing managers is expected to grow at a rate of 10 percent through 2026. This growth is being spurred by the introduction of new products to the marketplace and the growing need to "manage digital media campaigns, which often target customers through the use of websites, social media, and live chats."[8]

Figure B–1 describes marketing occupations in seven major categories: product management and physical distribution; sales; nonprofit marketing; global marketing; advertising and promotion; retailing; and marketing research. One of these may be right for you. Additional sources of marketing career information are provided at the end of this appendix.

Video B-1
Careers
kerin.tv/cr8e/vB-1

Product Management and Physical Distribution

Many organizations assign one manager the responsibility for a particular product. For example, Procter & Gamble (P&G) has separate managers for Tide, Cheer, Gain, and Bold. Product or brand managers are involved in all aspects of a product's marketing program, such as marketing research, sales, sales promotion, advertising, and pricing, as well as manufacturing. Managers of similar products typically report to a category manager, or marketing director, and may be part of a *product management team* to encourage interbrand cooperation.[9]

Several other jobs related to product management (see Figure B–1) deal with physical distribution issues such as storing the manufactured product (inventory), moving the product from the firm to the customers (transportation), and engaging in many other aspects of the manufacture and sale of goods. Prospects for these jobs are likely to increase as a wider range of products and technologies lead to increased demand. In addition, as manufacturers cut costs, they are increasingly shifting more responsibilities to wholesalers.[10]

Product or brand managers are involved in all aspects of a product's marketing program.
©Dibyangshu Sarkar/AFP/Getty Images

Advertising and Promotion

Advertising positions are available in three kinds of organizations: advertisers, media companies, and agencies. Advertisers include manufacturers, retail stores, service firms, and many other types of companies. Often they have an advertising department

PRODUCT MANAGEMENT AND PHYSICAL DISTRIBUTION

Product development manager creates a road map for new products by working with customers to determine their needs and with designers to create the product.

Product or brand manager is responsible for integrating all aspects of a product's marketing program, including research, sales, sales promotion, advertising, and pricing.

Supply chain manager oversees the part of a company that transports products to consumers and handles customer service.

Operations manager supervises warehousing and other physical distribution functions and often is directly involved in moving products on the warehouse floor.

Inventory control manager forecasts demand for products, coordinates production with plant managers, and tracks shipments to keep customers supplied.

Physical distribution specialist is an expert in the transportation and distribution of products and also evaluates the costs and benefits of different types of transportation.

SALES

Direct or retail salesperson sells directly to consumers in the salesperson's office, the consumer's home, or a retailer's store.

Trade salesperson calls on retailers or wholesalers to sell products for manufacturers.

Industrial or semitechnical salesperson sells supplies and services to businesses.

Complex or professional salesperson sells complicated or custom-designed products to businesses. This requires understanding of the product technology.

Customer service manager maintains good relations with customers by coordinating the sales staff, marketing management, and physical distribution management.

NONPROFIT MARKETING

Marketing manager develops and directs marketing campaigns, fund-raising, and public relations.

GLOBAL MARKETING

Global marketing manager is an expert in world-trade agreements, international competition, cross-cultural analysis, and global market-entry strategies.

ADVERTISING AND PROMOTION

Account executive maintains contact with clients while coordinating the creative work among artists and copywriters. Account executives work as partners with the client to develop marketing strategy.

Media buyer deals with media sales representatives in selecting advertising media and analyzes the value of media being purchased.

Copywriter works with art director in conceptualizing advertisements and writes the text of print or radio ads or the storyboards of television ads.

Art director handles the visual component of advertisements.

Sales promotion manager designs promotions for consumer products and works at an ad agency or a sales promotion agency.

Public relations manager develops written or video messages for the public and handles contacts with the press.

Digital marketing manager develops and executes the e-business marketing plan and manages all aspects of the advertising, promotion, and content for the online business.

Social media marketing manager plans and manages the delivery of marketing messages through all social media and monitors and responds to the feedback received.

RETAILING

Buyer selects products a store sells, surveys consumer trends, and evaluates the past performance of products and suppliers.

Store manager oversees the staff and services at a store.

MARKETING RESEARCH

Project manager coordinates and oversees market studies for a client.

Account executive serves as a liaison between client and marketing research firm, like an advertising agency account executive.

Marketing research analyst/Data scientist analyzes consumer data to identify preferences, behavior patterns, and user profiles to create and evaluate marketing programs.

Competitive intelligence researcher uses new information technologies to monitor the competitive environment.

Marketing database manager is responsible for collection and maintenance of data and information, support of the data analytics and decision support systems, and timely and accurate report generation.

Source: Adapted from Lila B. Stair and Leslie Stair, Careers in Marketing (New York: McGraw-Hill, 2008); and David W. Rosenthal and Michael A. Powell, Careers in Marketing, ©1984, pp. 352–54.

FIGURE B–1
Seven major categories of marketing occupations.

responsible for preparing and placing their own ads. Advertising careers are also possible with the media: television, radio stations, magazines, and newspapers. Finally, advertising agencies offer job opportunities through their use of account management, research, media, and creative services.

Growing interest in integrated marketing programs has increased opportunities for sales promotion managers, public relations managers, and Internet marketing managers. These positions require an understanding of the potential synergy of all promotional tools. Responsibilities include the design and implementation of sweepstakes, sampling programs, events and partnerships, newsletters, press releases and conferences, e-mail promotions, web-content management, and permission marketing campaigns. In addition, as advertisers increase search marketing budgets, the number of search marketing positions is increasing. Finally, many companies have decided that they need social media managers to ensure that messages can be sent to and received from the millions of people now on Facebook, Twitter, and other social media websites.[11]

Retailing

There are two separate career paths in retailing: merchandise management and store management. The key position in merchandising is that of a buyer, who is responsible for selecting merchandise, guiding the promotion of the merchandise, setting prices, bargaining with wholesalers, training the salesforce, and monitoring the competitive environment. The buyer must also be able to organize and coordinate many critical activities under severe time constraints. In contrast, store management involves the supervision of personnel in all departments and the general management of all facilities, equipment, and merchandise displays. In addition, store managers are responsible for the financial performance of each department and for the store as a whole. Typical positions beyond the store manager level include district manager, regional manager, and divisional vice president.[12]

Retailers such as Nordstrom offer careers in merchandise management and store management.
Source: Nordstrom, Inc.

Most starting jobs in retailing are trainee positions. A trainee is usually placed in a management training program and then given a position as an assistant buyer or assistant department manager. Advancement and responsibility can be achieved quickly because there is a shortage of qualified personnel in retailing and because superior performance of an individual is quickly reflected in sales and profits—two visible measures of success. In addition, the growth of omnichannel retailing and social media have created new opportunities such as website management, online merchandise procurement, and mobile retailing.[13]

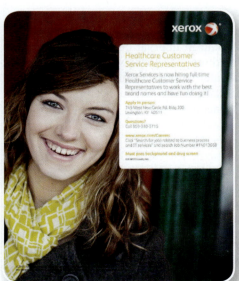

Xerox is well known for its sales career opportunities.
Courtesy of Xerox Corporation

Sales

College graduates from many disciplines are attracted to sales positions because of the increasingly professional nature of selling jobs and the many opportunities they can provide. A selling career offers benefits that are hard to match in any other field: (1) the opportunity for rapid advancement (into management or to new territories and accounts); (2) the potential for extremely attractive compensation; (3) personal satisfaction, feelings of accomplishment, and increased self-confidence; and (4) independence—salespeople often have almost complete control over their time and activities.

Employment opportunities in sales occupations are found in a wide variety of organizations, including insurance agencies, retailers, and financial service firms. In addition, many salespeople work as manufacturers' representatives for organizations that have selling responsibilities for several manufacturers.[14] Activities in sales jobs include *selling duties,* such as prospecting for customers, demonstrating the product, or quoting prices; *sales-support duties,* such as handling complaints and helping solve technical problems; and *nonselling duties,* such as preparing

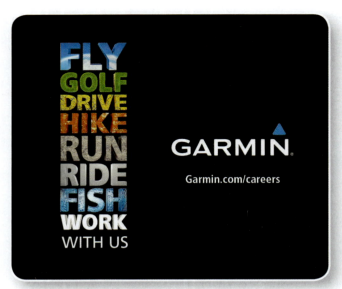

Garmin is an example of a company that encourages students to think about a career and the culture of the company.
Source: Garmin

reports, attending sales meetings, and monitoring competitive activities. Salespeople who can deal with these varying activities and have empathy for customers are critical to a company's success. According to *Bloomberg Businessweek,* "Great salespeople feel for their customers. They understand their needs and pressures; they get the challenges of their business. They see every deal through the customer's eyes."[15]

Marketing Research

Marketing researchers play important roles in many organizations today. In fact, *U.S. News & World Report* suggests that marketing research analyst positions are the number one job in business. They are responsible for obtaining, analyzing, and interpreting data to facilitate making marketing decisions. This means marketing researchers are basically problem solvers. Success in the area requires not only an understanding of statistical analysis, research methods, and programming, but also a broad base of marketing knowledge, writing and verbal presentation skills, and an ability to communicate with colleagues and clients. According to Stan Sthanunathan, vice president of marketing strategy and insights at Coca-Cola, a researcher's job "is to bring out opportunities."[16] Individuals who are inquisitive, methodical, analytical, and solution-oriented find the field particularly rewarding.

The responsibilities of the men and women currently working in the marketing research industry include defining the marketing problem, designing the questions, selecting the sample, collecting and analyzing the data, and, finally, reporting the results of the research. These jobs are available in three kinds of organizations. *Marketing research consulting firms* contract with large companies to provide research about their customers, products, or services.[17] *Advertising agencies* may provide research services to help clients with questions related to advertising and promotional problems. Finally, some companies have an *in-house research staff* to design and execute their research projects. Online marketing research, which is likely to become the most common form of marketing research in the near future, requires an understanding of new tools such as dynamic scripting, response validation, intercept sampling, instant messaging surveys, and online consumer panels.[18]

Accenture places thousands of consultants throughout the world.
©Delane B. Rouse/AP Images

International Careers

Many of the careers just described can be found in international settings—in large multinational U.S. corporations, small- to medium-size firms with export business, and franchises. The international consulting firm Accenture, for example, has thousands of consultants around the world. Similarly, many franchises such as 7-Eleven, which has 46,100 locations outside of North America, are rapidly expanding outside the United States.[19] The changes in the European Union, Brazil, Russia, India, China, and other growing markets are likely to provide many opportunities for international careers.

Several methods of gaining international experience are possible. For example, some companies may alternate periods of work at domestic locations with assignments outside the United States. In addition, working for a firm with headquarters outside the United States at one of its local offices may be appealing. In many organizations, international

520

experience has become a necessity for promotion and career advancement. "If you are going to succeed, an expatriate assignment is essential," says Eric Kraus of Gillette Co. in Boston.[20]

THE JOB SEARCH PROCESS

Activities you should consider during your job search process include assessing yourself, identifying job opportunities, preparing your résumé and related correspondence, and going on job interviews.

Assessing Yourself

You must know your product—you—so that you can market yourself effectively to prospective employers. Consequently, a critical first step in your job search is conducting a self-inquiry or self-assessment. This activity involves understanding your interests, abilities, personality, preferences, and individual style. You must be confident that you know what work environment is best for you, what makes you happy, the balance you seek between personal and professional activities, and how you can be most effective at reaching your goals. This process helps ensure that you are matching your profile to the right job, or as business consultant and author Jim Collins explains, "Finding the right seat on the bus."[21]

©Stuart Miles/Shutterstock

A self-analysis, in part, entails identifying your strengths and weaknesses. To do so, draw a vertical line down the middle of a sheet of paper and label one side of the paper "strengths" and the other side "weaknesses." Based on your answers to the questions, record your strong and weak points in their respective columns. Ideally, this cataloging should be done over a few days to give you adequate time to reflect on your attributes. In addition, you might seek input from others who know you well (such as parents, close relatives, friends, professors, or employers) and can offer more objective viewpoints. Finally, to help identify additional strengths, you might purchase a copy of the very popular book *StrengthsFinder 2.0* by Tom Rath. A hypothetical list of strengths and weaknesses is shown in Figure B–2.

Personality and vocational interest tests, provided by many colleges and universities, can give you other ideas about yourself. After tests have been administered and scored, test takers meet with testing service counselors to discuss the results. Test results generally suggest jobs for which students have an inclination. The most common tests at the college level are the Strong Interest Inventory and the Campbell Interest and Skill Survey. Some counseling centers and career coaches also use the Myers-Briggs® Type Indicator personality inventory and the Peoplemap™ assessments to help identify professions you may enjoy.[22] If you have not already done so, you may wish to see whether your school offers such testing services.

FIGURE B–2

Hypothetical list of a job candidate's strengths and weaknesses.

Strengths	Weaknesses
I am a good problem solver.	I have minimal work experience.
I have good communication skills.	I have a mediocre GPA.
I work well with others.	I have poor technical skills.
I am honest and dependable.	I will not relocate.
I am willing to travel.	I procrastinate unless there is a deadline.

Identifying Your Job Opportunities

To identify and analyze the job market, you must conduct some marketing research to determine what industries *and* companies offer promising job opportunities that relate to the results of your self-analysis. Several sources that can help in your search are discussed next.

Campus career centers are excellent sources of job information.
©GIPhotoStock Z/Alamy Stock Photo

Career Services Office Your campus career services office is an excellent source of job information. Personnel in that office can (1) inform you about which companies will be recruiting on campus; (2) alert you to unexpected job openings; (3) advise you about short-term and long-term career prospects; (4) offer advice on résumé construction; (5) assess your interviewing strengths and weaknesses; and (6) help you evaluate a job offer. Career services offices are also expanding to help students connect with companies that might not recruit on campus.[23] In addition, the office usually contains a variety of written materials focusing on different industries and companies and tips on job hunting.

Online Career and Employment Services Many companies no longer make frequent on-campus visits. Instead, they may use the many online services available to advertise an employment opportunity or to search for candidate information. The National Association of Colleges and Employers, for example, maintains a site called NACElink Network (www.nacelink.com). Similarly, Monster (www.monster.com) and Careerbuilder (www.careerbuilder.com) are on-line databases of employment ads, candidate résumés, and other career-related information. Some of the information resources include career guidance, a cover letter library, occupational profiles, résumé templates, and networking services.[24] Employers may contact students directly when the candidate's qualifications meet their specific job requirements.

Monster.com is a popular employment website where students can match their skills and interests with job openings.
Source: Monster Worldwide

Library The public or college library can provide you with reference material that, among other things, describes successful firms and their operations, defines the content of various jobs, and forecasts job opportunities. For example, *Fortune* publishes a list of the 1,000 largest U.S. and global companies and their respective sales and profits, and Dun & Bradstreet publishes directories of more than 26 million companies in the United States. The *Occupational Outlook Handbook* is an annual publication of the U.S. Department of Labor that provides projections for specific job prospects, as well as information pertaining to those jobs. A librarian can indicate reference materials that will be most pertinent to *your* job search.

Advertisements Help-wanted advertisements provide an overview of what is happening in the job market. Local newspapers (particularly Sunday editions), college newspapers, trade publications (such as *Marketing News* or *Advertising Age*), and business magazines contain classified advertisement sections that generally have job opening announcements, often for entry-level positions. Reviewing the want ads can help you identify what kinds of positions are available and their requirements and job titles, which firms offer certain kinds of jobs, and levels of compensation.

Employment Agencies An employment agency can make you aware of several job opportunities very quickly because of its large number of job listings available through computer databases. Many agencies specialize in a particular field (such as sales and marketing). The advantages of using an agency include that it (1) reduces the cost of a job search by bringing applicants and employers together, (2) often has exclusive job listings available only by working through the agency, (3) performs much of the job search for you, and (4) tries to find a job that is compatible with your qualifications and interests.[25] In the past, some employment agencies have engaged in questionable business practices, so check with the Better Business Bureau (www.bbb.org) or your business contacts to determine the quality of the various agencies.

Personal Contacts and Networking An important source of job information that students often overlook is their personal contacts. People you know often may know of job opportunities, so you should advise them that you're looking for a job. Relatives and friends might aid your job search. Instructors you know well and business contacts can provide a wealth of information about potential jobs and even help arrange an interview with a prospective employer. They may also help arrange *informational interviews* with employers that do not have immediate openings. These interviews allow you to collect information about an industry or an employer and give you an advantage if a position does become available. Creating and maintaining a network of professional contacts is one of the most important career-building activities you can undertake.[26] There are many popular social networking sites available to job seekers. LinkedIn, for example, has 500 million users, including recruiters. Other sites include Plaxo, Twitter, Jobster, Facebook, Craigslist, MyWorkster, VisualCV, and Jobfox. While social networks offer an opportunity to connect with a global community of professionals, experts advise that users should always be thoughtful, respectful, and unpretentious when posting on these platforms.[27]

©Kristoffer Tripplaar/Alamy Stock Photo

State Employment Office State employment offices have listings of job opportunities in their state and counselors to help arrange a job interview for you. Although state employment offices perform functions similar to employment agencies, they differ in listing only job opportunities in their state and providing their services free of charge.

Direct Contact Another means of obtaining job information is direct contact—personally communicating to prospective employers (either by mail, e-mail, or in person) that you would be interested in pursuing job opportunities with them. Often you may not even know whether jobs are available in these firms. If you correspond with the companies in writing, a letter of introduction and an attached résumé should serve as your initial form of communication. One way to make direct contact with companies is to attend a career or job fair. These events allow many employers, recruiters, and prospective job seekers to meet in one location.[28] Your goals in direct contact are to create a positive impression and, ultimately, to arrange a job interview.

Writing Your Résumé

A résumé is a document that communicates to prospective employers who you are. An employer reading a résumé is looking for a snapshot of your qualifications to decide if you should be invited to a job interview. It is imperative that you design a résumé that presents you in a favorable light and allows you to get to that next important step.[29] Personnel in your career services office can provide assistance in designing your résumé.

The Résumé Itself

A well-constructed résumé generally contains up to nine major sections: (1) identification (name, address, telephone number, and e-mail address); (2) job or career objective; (3) educational background; (4) honors and awards; (5) work experience or history; (6) skills or capabilities (that pertain to a particular kind of job for which you may be interviewing); (7) extracurricular activities; (8) personal interests; and (9) personal references.[30] If possible, you should include quantitative information about your accomplishments and experience, such as "increased sales revenue by 20 percent" for the year you managed a retail clothing store.

There are several other important considerations as you prepare your résumé. First, remember that your résumé is a marketing tool and its purpose is to present you for a particular job or role. Therefore, anticipate that you will have more than one version of your résumé, or more likely, a customized résumé for each job opportunity you are considering. Second, although traditional printed versions of résumés can be created with visually appealing fonts and graphics, a simpler, digital version of your résumé is also a necessity. A digital résumé should use a popular font (e.g., Times New Roman) and relatively large font size (e.g., 10–14 pt.) and avoid italic text, shading, or underlining. Finally, your résumé should accommodate employers who use applicant tracking software (ATS) to search for keywords. You should identify potential keywords for each job posting and include them within your experience, accomplishments, and education descriptions.[31]

Related to the use of technology, video résumés are becoming increasingly popular as a means for job seekers to communicate their personality to employers with job opportunities in customer-facing roles such as sales and public relations. In addition, don't forget that many employers may visit social networking sites such as LinkedIn and Facebook or they may simply "Google" your name, to see what comes up. Review your online profiles and photos before you start your job search to provide a positive and accurate image![32]

The Cover Letter

The letter accompanying a résumé, or cover letter, serves as the job candidate's introduction. As a result, it must gain the attention and interest of the reader or it will fail to give the incentive to examine the résumé carefully. In designing a letter to accompany your résumé, address the following issues:[33]

- Address the letter to a specific person.
- Identify the position for which you are applying and how you heard of it.
- Indicate why you are applying for the position.
- Summarize your most significant credentials and qualifications.
- Refer the reader to the enclosed résumé.
- Request a personal interview, and advise the reader when and where you can be reached.

As a general rule, nothing works better than an impressive cover letter and good academic credentials.

Interviewing for Your Job

The job interview is a conversation between a prospective employer and a job candidate that focuses on determining whether the employer's needs can be satisfied by the candidate's qualifications. The interview is a "make or break" situation: If the interview goes well, you have increased your chances of receiving a job offer; if it goes poorly, you probably will be eliminated from further consideration.

Preparing for a Job Interview

To be successful in a job interview, you must prepare for it so you can exhibit professionalism and indicate to a prospective employer that you are serious about the job. When preparing for the interview, several critical activities need to be performed.

Before the interview, gather facts about the industry, the prospective employer, and the job. Relevant information might include the general description for the occupation; the firm's products or services; the firm's size, number of employees, and financial and competitive position; the requirements of the position; and the name and personality of the interviewer. Obtaining this information will provide you with additional insight into the firm and help you formulate questions to ask the interviewer. This information might be gleaned, for example, from corporate annual reports, *The Wall Street Journal,* Moody's manuals, Standard & Poor's *Register of Corporations,*

FIGURE B–3	Interviewer Questions
Anticipate questions frequently asked by interviewers and practice how you might respond.	1. What do you consider to be your greatest strengths and weaknesses? 2. What do you see yourself doing in 5 years? In 10 years? 3. What are three important leadership qualities that you have demonstrated? 4. What jobs have you enjoyed the most? The least? Why? 5. Why do you want to work for our company?

Directors, and Executives, The Directory of Corporate Affiliations, selected issues of *Bloomberg Businessweek,* or trade publications. In addition, you should look at comments on the company review website Glassdoor. You should also study the LinkedIn profiles, Twitter feeds, and blogs of the people you'll be meeting. If information is not readily available, you could call the company and indicate that you wish to obtain some information about the firm before your interview.[34]

Preparation for the job interview should also involve role playing or pretending that you are in the "hot seat" being interviewed. Before role playing, anticipate questions interviewers may pose and how you might address them (see Figure B–3). Do not memorize your answers, though, because you want to appear spontaneous, yet logical and intelligent. Nonetheless, it is helpful to practice how you might respond to the questions. In addition, develop questions you might ask the interviewer that are important and of concern to you (see Figure B–4). Asking good questions can make you stand out from other candidates. "It's an opportunity to show the recruiter how smart you are," comments one recruiter.[35]

Before the job interview you should attend to several details. Know the exact time and place of the interview; write them down—do not rely on your memory. If your initial interview is a video interview, test your Internet connection, software (e.g., Skype), camera, and lighting.[36] Get the full company name straight. Find out what the interviewer's name is and how to pronounce it. Have a notepad and a pen at the interview in case you need to record anything. Make certain that your appearance is clean, neat, professional, and conservative. And be punctual; arriving tardy to a job interview gives you an appearance of being unreliable.

View the interview as a conversation between the prospective employer and you.
©White Packert/The Image Bank/Getty Images

Succeeding in Your Job Interview You have done your homework, and at last the moment arrives and it is time for the interview. Although you may experience some apprehension, view the interview as a conversation between the prospective employer and you. Both of you are in the interview to look over the other party, to see whether there might be a good match. When you meet the interviewer, greet him or her by name, be cheerful, smile, and maintain good eye contact (in the case of a video interview, look at the camera!). Take your lead from the interviewer at the outset. Sit down after the interviewer has offered you a seat. Sit up straight in your chair, and look alert and interested at all times. Appear relaxed, not tense. Be enthusiastic.

FIGURE B–4	Interviewee Questions
Interviewees should develop questions about topics that are important to them.	1. What is the company's promotion policy? 2. Describe the typical first-year assignment for this job. 3. How is an employee evaluated? 4. Why do you enjoy working for your firm? 5. How much responsibility would I have in this job?

During the interview, be yourself. If you try to behave in a manner that is different from the real you, your attempt may be transparent to the interviewer or you may ultimately get the job but discover that you aren't suited for it. However, remember that the interview is not the time to tweet, text, or take a telephone call.[37] In addition to assessing how well your skills match those of the job, the interviewer will probably try to assess your long-term interest in the firm.

As the interview comes to a close, leave it on a positive note. Thank the interviewer for his or her time and the opportunity to discuss employment opportunities. If you are still interested in the job, express this to the interviewer. The interviewer will normally tell you what the employer's next step is—probably a visit to the company.[38] Rarely will a job offer be made at the end of the initial interview. If it is and you want the job, accept the offer; if there is any doubt in your mind about the job, however, ask for time to consider the offer.

Following Up on Your Job Interview   After your interview, send a thank-you note to the interviewer and indicate whether you are still interested in the job. If you want to continue pursuing the job, polite persistence may help you get it. The thank-you note is a gesture of appreciation and a way of maintaining visibility with the interviewer. (Remember the adage "Out of sight, out of mind.") Even if the interview did not go well, the thank-you note may impress the interviewer so much that his or her opinion of you changes. Also, although e-mail is a common form of communication today, it is often viewed as less personal than a letter or telephone call, so be confident that e-mail is preferred before using it to correspond with the interviewer.[39]

As you conduct your follow-up, be persistent but polite. If you are too eager, one of two things could happen to prevent you from getting the job: The employer might feel that you are a nuisance and would exhibit such behavior on the job, or the employer may perceive that you are desperate for the job and thus are not a viable candidate.

Handling Rejection   You have put your best efforts into your job search. You developed a well-designed résumé and prepared carefully for the job interview. Even the interview appears to have gone well. Nevertheless, a prospective employer may send you a rejection letter. ("We are sorry that our needs and your superb qualifications don't match.") Although you will probably be disappointed, not all interviews lead to a job offer because there normally are more candidates than there are positions available.

If you receive a rejection letter, you should think back through the interview. What appeared to go right? What went wrong? Perhaps personnel from your career services office can shed light on the problem, particularly if they are accustomed to having interviewers rate each interviewee. Try to learn lessons to apply in future interviews. Keep interviewing and gaining interview experience; your persistence will eventually pay off.

SELECTED SOURCES OF MARKETING CAREER INFORMATION

The following is a selected list of marketing information sources that you should find useful during your academic studies and professional career.

Business and Marketing Publications

Virgil L. Burton, *Encyclopedia of Business Information Sources,* 34th ed. (Detroit, MI: Gale Group, 2017). A bibliographic guide to over 25,000 citations covering more than 1,100 primary subjects of interest to business personnel.

John A. Davis, *Measuring Marketing: The 100+ Essential Metrics Every Marketer Needs,* 3rd Edition, (Boston: Walter de Gruyter Inc., 2018). This book offers readers an informative guide to important analytical tools and marketing metrics needed to quantify success in today's dynamic business world.

Hoover's Handbook of World Business (Austin, TX: Mergent, Inc., 2017). A detailed source of information about companies outside the United States, including firms from Canada, Europe, Japan, China, India, and Taiwan.

Marketing Dictionary (American Marketing Association). This online resource contains definitions of marketing phrases and terms and is continually adding new terms to keep marketers up to date. See https://www.ama.org/resources/Pages/Dictionary.aspx.

Jadish Sheth and Naresh Malhotra, eds., *International Encyclopedia of Marketing* (West Sussex, UK: Wiley, 2011). This six-volume reference contains 360 entries from over 500 global experts. Entries are arranged alphabetically within each subject volume, and each volume carries an index.

Career Planning Publications

Richard N. Bolles, *What Color Is Your Parachute? 2019: A Practical Manual for Job-Hunters and Career-Changers* (Berkeley, CA: Ten Speed Press, 2018). A companion workbook is also available. See www.jobhuntersbible.com.

Reid Hoffman and Ben Casnocha, *The Start-Up of You: Adapt to the Future, Invest in Yourself, and Transform Your Career* (New York: Crown Publishing Group, 2012).

Sheryl Sandberg, *Lean In for Graduates* (New York: Knopf, 2014).

Louis R. VanArsdale and Jessica Li, *Government Jobs in America* (New York: Community Publications, and Government Job News, 2018).

Martin Yate, *Knock 'em Dead: The Ultimate Job Search Guide* (Holbrook, MA: Adams Media Corporation, 2017).

Websites: Resources on job searches, résumé writing, interviewing, and U.S. and international job postings:

www.glassdoor.com
www.careerbuilder.com
www.monster.com
www.indeed.com

Selected Periodicals

Advertising Age, Crain Communications, Inc. (weekly). See www.adage.com. (subscription rate: $2.10 per week)

Bloomberg Businessweek, McGraw-Hill Companies (weekly). See www.businessweek.com. (subscription rate: $25 for 12 weeks)

Journal for the Advancement of Marketing Education, Marketing Management Association. See http://www.mmaglobal.org/publications/jame/, open source.

Journal of International Marketing, American Marketing Association (quarterly). See www.marketingpower.com. (subscription rates: $155 print; $185 print and online)

Journal of Marketing, American Marketing Association (quarterly). See www.marketingpower.com. (subscription rates: $190 print; $220 print and online)

Journal of Marketing Education, Sage Publications (three times per year). See www.sagepub.com. (subscription rate: $134)

Journal of Marketing Research, American Marketing Association (bimonthly). See www.marketingpower.com. (subscription rates: $190 print; $220 print and online)

Journal of Personal Selling and Sales Management, American Marketing Association (quarterly). See www.jpssm.org. (subscription rate: $106)

Journal of Public Policy and Marketing, American Marketing Association (semiannually). See www.marketingpower.com. (subscription rates: $110 print; $140 print and online)

Journal of Retailing, Elsevier Science Publishing (quarterly). See www.elsevier.com. (subscription rate: $209)

Marketing Education Review, CTC Press (three times per year). See www.marketingeducationreview.com. (subscription rate: $72 print; $232 print and online)

Marketing News, American Marketing Association (biweekly). See www.marketingpower.com. (subscription rates: $80)

Professional and Trade Associations

American Advertising Federation
1101 Vermont Ave. N.W., Suite 500
Washington, DC 20005-6306
(202) 898-0089
www.aaf.org

American Marketing Association
130 E. Randolph St., 22nd Floor
Chicago, IL 60601
(800) AMA-1150 or (312) 542-9000
www.ama.org

ANA Business Marketing
708 Third Ave., 33rd Floor
New York, NY 10017
(212) 697-5950
www.marketing.org

Data & Marketing Association
1333 Broadway, #301
New York, NY 10018
(212) 768-7277
www.thedma.org

International Franchise Association
1900 K Street N.W., Suite 700
Washington, DC 20005
(202) 628-8000
www.franchise.org

Marketing Science Institute
1000 Massachusetts Ave.
Cambridge, MA 02138-5396
(617) 491-2060
www.msi.org

Mobile Marketing Association
41 E. 11th St. 11th Floor
New York, NY 10003
(646) 257-4515
www.mmaglobal.com

National Retail Federation
1101 New York Ave. N.W.
Washington, DC 20005
(202) 783-7971
www.nrf.com

Public Relations Society of America
120 Wall St., 21st Floor
New York, NY 10005
(212) 460-1400
www.prsa.org

Sales and Marketing Executive International
P.O. Box 1390
Suma, WA 98295-1390
(312) 893-0751
www.smei.org

Society for Marketing Professional Services
123 North Pitt St., Suite 400
Alexandria, VA 22314
(703) 549-6117
www.smps.org

Appendix Notes

1. David Hagenbuch, "The Three C's of Personal Branding," *Marketing News,* July 2017, pp. 52–53; Reid Hoffman and Ben Casnocha, *The Startup of You* (New York: Crown Publishing, 2012); Joann S. Lublin, "The Year Ahead: Your 'Personal Brand' May Need Some Work," *The Wall Street Journal,* January 2, 2014, p. B4; Catherine Kaputa, *You Are a Brand! How Smart People Brand Themselves for Business Success* (Boston, MA: Nicholas Brealey Publishing, 2010); Diane Brady, "Creating Brand You," *Bloomberg Businessweek,* August 22, 2007, pp. 72–73; and Denny E. McCorkle, Joe F. Alexander, and Memo F. Diriker, "Developing Self-Marketing Skills for Student Career Success," *Journal of Marketing Education,* Spring 1992, pp. 57–67.

2. Debra Wheatman, "Seven Tips for Conducting a Targeted Career Campaign," *Marketing News,* January 2015, p. 62; Morag Cuddeford-Jones, "Managing a Marketing Career Is Academic," *Marketing Week,* January 16, 2013; Linda J. Popky, *Marketing Your Career: Positioning, Packaging and Promoting Yourself for Success* (Woodside Business Press, 2009); Marianne E. Green, "Marketing Yourself: From Student to Professional," *Job Choices for Business & Liberal Arts Students,* 50th ed., 2007, pp. 30–31; and Joanne Cleaver, "Find a Job through Self-Promotion," *Marketing News,* January 31, 2000, pp. 12, 16.

3. Sarah Steimer, "The Complete Job-Seekers Guide (From A to Z)," *Marketing News,* May 2018, pp. 24–33; Gordon Wyner, "Navigating a Marketing Career," *Marketing News,* March 2017, pp. 24–25; and Michelle Boggs, "Hiring Trends for the Year Ahead," *Marketing News,* April 2015, p. 63.

4. *Job Outlook 2018: College Hiring to Increase by 4 Percent,* naceweb.org (Bethlehem, PA: National Association of Colleges and Employers), November 15, 2017; *www.Monster.com,* accessed April 13, 2018; and Michael Bush and Sarah Lewis-Kulin, "100 Best Companies to Work For," *Fortune,* March 1, 2018, pp. 53–78.

5. Nicholas Basta, "The Wide World of Marketing," *BW's Guide to Careers,* February–March 1984, pp. 70–72.

6. Hal Conick, "Study Finds One Quarter of CEOs Have a Marketing or Sales Background," *Marketing News,* February 18, 2017; Anjali Bansal, David S. Daniel, John T. Mitchell, and Patrick B. Walsh, "The CEO Today: Sharing Leadership at the Top," *Research & Insight,* SpencerStuart, March 2013, http://www.spencerstuart.com/research/articles/1642/; Jonathan Harper and Frank Birkel, "From CMO to CEO: The Route to the Top," *Research & Insight,* SpencerStuart, December 2009, http://www.spencerstuart.com/research/articles/1329/; and "Leading CEOs: A Statistical Snapshot of S&P 500 Leaders," *Research & Insight,* SpencerStuart, December 2008, http://www.spencerstuart.com/research/ceo/975/.

7. Salary Survey (Bethlehem, PA: National Association of Colleges and Employers, Winter 2018), pp. 9, 13.

8. Bureau of Labor Statistics, U.S. Department of Labor, "Advertising, Promotions, and Marketing Managers," *Occupational Outlook Handbook, Advertising, Promotions, and Marketing Managers,* on the Internet at https://www.bls.gov/ooh/management/advertising-promotions-and-marketing-managers.htm, accessed April 13, 2018.

9. Matthew Creamer, "P&G Primes Its Pinpoint Marketing," *Advertising Age,* May 7, 2007.

10. "Wholesale and Manufacturing Sales Representatives," *Occupational Outlook Handbook,* 2014–15 ed. (Washington, DC: U.S. Department of Labor), http://www.bls.gov/ooh/sales/wholesale-and-manufacturing-sales-representatives.htm#tab-6, accessed July 14, 2015.

11. "13 Professional Skills for a Rewarding Career in Digital Marketing," *Business2Community.com,* January 9, 2013; Sarah Lundy, "Job Opportunities Multiply in Social Media: With More People Connecting Online, Businesses Rush to Join the Party," *Buffalo News,* January 10, 2011, p. C1; Duane Forrester, "Search Can Offer Jobs, Decent Salaries," *Advertising Age,* May 26, 2008, p. 28; and Tanya Lewis, "Talent in Demand," *PRWeek Career Guide,* 2006, pp. 4–6.

12. Ellen Davis, "The Increasing Scope of Retail Careers" *Stores Magazine,* July 31, 2014, p. 73; and Roslyn Dolber, *Opportunities in Retailing Careers* (New York: McGraw-Hill, 2008).

13. Anne Roggeveen and Lauren Beitelspacher, "Educating the Retailers of Tomorrow: An Overview of *Journal of Marketing Education* Special Issue on Retailing," *Journal of Marketing Education,* April 2018, pp. 3–5; Peter Coy, "Help Wanted," *Bloomberg Businessweek,* May 11, 2009, pp. 40–46; and "The Way We'll Work," *Time,* May 25, 2009, pp. 39–50.

14. "Wholesale and Manufacturing Sales Representatives," *Occupational Outlook Handbook,* 2014–15 ed. (Washington, DC: U.S. Department of Labor), http://www.bls.gov/ooh/sales/wholesale-and-manufacturing-sales-representatives.htm, accessed July 14, 2015.

15. Jack and Suzy Welch, "Dear Graduate . . . To Stand Out among Your Peers, You Have to Overdeliver," *Bloomberg Businessweek,* June 19, 2006, p. 100.

16. Carol Shea, "Career Advice for New Marketing Researchers," *Marketing News,* July 2015, p. 61; Piet Levy, "10 Minutes with Stan Sthanunathan, Vice President of Marketing Strategy and Insights, The Coca-Cola Co.," *Marketing News,* February 28, 2011, p. 34; and Edmund Hershberger and Madhav N. Segal, "Ads for MR Positions Reveal Desired Skills," *Marketing News,* February 1, 2007, p. 28.

17. Zach Brooke, "An Internal Success Story," *Marketing News,* August 2017, pp. 52–54; Nielsen company website, http://www.nielsen.com/us/en/about-us.html; and "Market Research Analyst," in Les Krantz, ed., *Jobs Rated Almanac,* 6th ed. (New York: St. Martin's Press, 2002).

18. Deborah L. Vence, "In an Instant, More Researchers Use IM for Fast, Reliable Results," *Marketing News,* March 1, 2006, p. 53; and Joshua Grossnickle and Oliver Raskin, "What's Ahead on the Internet," *Marketing Research,* Summer 2001, pp. 9–13.

19. "2015 Franchise 500," *Entrepreneur* website, *www.entrepreneur.com,* accessed July 14, 2015.
20. Lisa Bertagnoli, "Marketing Overseas Excellent for Career," *Marketing News,* June 4, 2001, p. 4.
21. Barbara Flood, "Turbo Charge Your Job Search, Job Searching and Career Development Tips," *Information Outlook,* May 1, 2007, p. 40.
22. Barbara Flood, "Turbo Charge Your Job Search, Job Searching and Career Development Tips," *Information Outlook,* May 1, 2007, p. 40.
23. "More MBA Grads Take the Road Less Traveled," *Bloomberg Businessweek,* April 18–24, 2011, p. 53.
24. Susan Adams, "Secrets of Making the Most of Job Search Websites," *Forbes.com,* January 15, 2014, p. 13; and Francine Russo, "The New Online Job Hunt," *Time,* October 3, 2011, pp. B14–B16.
25. Ronald B. Marks, *Personal Selling: A Relationship Approach,* 6th ed. (New York: Pearson, 1996).
26. Chris Farrell, "It's Not What Grads Know, It's Who They Know," *Bloomberg Businessweek,* June 18, 2012, pp. 9–10; Sima Dahl, "A New Job Is No Excuse to Ease Up on Networking," *Marketing News,* February 28, 2011, p. 4; Leonard Felson, "Undergrad Marketers Must Get Jump on Networking Skills," *Marketing News,* April 8, 2001, p. 14; Wayne E. Baker, *Networking Smart* (New York: McGraw-Hill, 1994); and Piet Levy, "AMA Chapters across the Country Are Increasingly Using Job Boards, Networking Events and Other Techniques to Help Members in This Economy," *Marketing News,* March 15, 2009, p. 14.
27. Hal Conick, "6 Moves That Can Make (or Break) Your Career on Twitter," *Marketing News,* April 2018, pp. 50–51; Jessica Schaeffer, "How to Use Social Media to Scope Your Next Job," *Marketing News,* April–May 2017, pp. 65–66; and "Careers in Marketing: Utilizing Social Networking to Improve Your Job Prospects," *CareerAlley,* July 22, 2012.
28. Stacie Garlieb, "How to Fare Well at a Job Fair," *Marketing News,* May 2014, p. 60; and "Stand Out at the Career Fair," *Job Choices for Business & Liberal Arts Students: 2009,* 52nd ed. (Bethlehem, PA: National Association of Colleges and Employers, 2008), pp. 22–23.
29. Amy Diepenbrock, "Will Your Resume Open the Door to an Interview?" *Job Choices for Business & Liberal Arts Students, 2011,* National Association of Colleges and Employers, p. 31; and Marianne E. Green, "Marketing Yourself: From Student to Professional," *Job Choices for Business & Liberal Arts Students: 2009* (Bethlehem, PA: National Association of Colleges and Employers, 2008), pp. 28–29.
30. Marianne E. Green, "Resume Writing: Sell Your Skills to Get the Interview!" *Job Choices for Business & Liberal Arts Students,* 50th ed., 2007, pp. 39–47.
31. Sarah Steimer, "Are Creative Resumes Risky for Marketers?" *Marketing News,* January 2017, p. 53; Debra Wheatman, "Resume Trends Worth Following," *Marketing News,* July 2014, p. 63; Karla Ahern and Naomi Keller, "Expert Advice: Your Resume Questions Answered," *Marketing News,* September 2014, p. 61; and Sima Dahl, "Social Media and Your Job Search: How the Age of the Referral May Impact Your Career," *Marketing News,* September 30, 2012, p. 6.
32. Zach Brooke, "New Year, New Headshot," *Marketing News,* March 2018, pp. 57–58; Hal Conick, "6 Ways to Make (or Break) Your Career on Twitter," *Marketing News,* May 2016, pp. 52–53; Lydia Stockdale, "How to Make a Great Video CV," *The Guardian,* February 27, 2014; and Robert Klara, "These Guys Want to Clean Up Your Reputation," *Adweek,* March 3, 2014, p. 22–23.
33. Charlotte Rogers, "Badge of Honour," *marketingweek.com,* March 2017, pp. 12–13; William J. Banis, "The Art of Writing Job-Search Letters," *Job Choices for Business and Liberal Arts Students,* 50th ed., 2007, pp. 32–38; and Arthur G. Sharp, "The Art of the Cover Letter," *Career Futures* 4, no. 1 (1992), pp. 50–51.
34. Zach Brooke, "How to Make Glassdoor Work for You," *Marketing News,* June 2017, pp. 88–89; Lindsey Pollak, "The 10 Commandments of Social Media Job Seeking," *Job Choices for Business & Liberal Arts Students, 2011,* National Association of Colleges and Employers, p. 20; Alison Damast, "Recruiters' Top 10 Complaints," *Bloomberg Businessweek,* April 26, 2007; and Marilyn Moats Kennedy, "'Don't List' Offers Important Tips for Job Interviews," *Marketing News,* March 15, 2007, p. 26.
35. Tom Gimbel, "How to Stand Out as a Marketing Job Applicant," *Marketing News,* February 2017, pp. 61–62; Sima Dahl, "Where Do You See Yourself in Five Years?" *Marketing News,* November 15, 2010, p. 4; and Dana James, "A Day in the Life of a Corporate Recruiter," *Marketing News,* April 10, 2000, pp. 1, 11.
36. Meghan Casserly, "'You Look Like a Convict' and the Most Common Pitfalls of Interviewing over Skype," *Forbes.com,* October 3, 2012.
37. Paul Davidson, "Managers to Millennials: Job Interview No Time to Text," *USA Today,* April 29, 2013.
38. Robert M. Greenberg, "The Company Visit—Revisited," *NACE Journal,* Winter 2003, pp. 21–27.
39. Mary E. Scott, "High-Touch vs. High-Tech Recruitment," *NACE Journal,* Fall 2002, pp. 33–39.

GLOSSARY

above-, at-, or below-market pricing Setting a market price for a product or product class based on a subjective feel for the competitors' price or market price as the benchmark. p. 307

account management policies Policies that specify whom salespeople should contact, what kinds of selling and customer service activities should be engaged in, and how these activities should be carried out. p. 504

adaptive selling A need-satisfaction presentation format that involves adjusting the presentation to fit the selling situation, such as knowing when to offer solutions and when to ask for more information. p. 499

advertising Any paid form of nonpersonal communication about an organization, product, service, or idea by an identified sponsor. pp. 406, 430

apps Small, downloadable software programs that can run on smartphones and tablet devices. Also called *mobile apps* or *applications*. p. 477

attitude A "learned predisposition to respond to an object or class of objects in a consistently favorable or unfavorable way." p. 111

baby boomers Includes the generation of 73 million children born between 1946 and 1964. p. 75

back translation The practice where a translated word or phrase is retranslated into the original language by a different interpreter to catch errors. p. 162

balance of trade The difference between the monetary value of a nation's exports and imports. p. 151

barter The practice of exchanging products and services for other products and services rather than for money. p. 300

behavioral targeting Uses information provided by cookies to direct online advertising from marketers to those online shoppers whose behavioral profiles suggest they would be interested in such advertising. p. 391

beliefs A consumer's subjective perception of how a product or brand performs on different attributes based on personal experience, advertising, and discussions with other people. p. 111

bots Electronic shopping agents or robots that search websites to compare prices and product or service features. p. 388

brand community A specialized group of consumers with a structured set of relationships involving a particular brand, fellow customers of that brand, and the product in use. p. 116

brand equity The added value a brand name gives to a product beyond the functional benefits provided. p. 280

brand licensing A contractual agreement whereby one company (licensor) allows its brand name(s) or trademark(s) to be used with products or services offered by another company (licensee) for a royalty or fee. p. 282

brand loyalty A favorable attitude toward and consistent purchase of a single brand over time. p. 111

brand name Any word, device (design, sound, shape, or color), or combination of these used to distinguish a seller's products or services. p. 280

brand personality A set of human characteristics associated with a brand name. p. 280

branding A marketing decision in which an organization uses a name, phrase, design, symbols, or combination of these to identify its products and distinguish them from those of competitors. p. 280

break-even analysis A technique that analyzes the relationship between total revenue and total cost to determine profitability at various levels of output. p. 312

brokers Independent firms or individuals whose principal function is to bring buyers and sellers together to make sales. p. 370

bundle pricing The marketing of two or more products in a single package price. p. 304

business The clear, broad, underlying industry or market sector of an organization's offering. p. 32

business analysis The stage of the new-product development process that specifies the features of the product and the marketing strategy needed to bring it to market and make financial projections. p. 255

business plan A road map for the entire organization for a specified future period of time, such as one year or five years. p. 56

business portfolio analysis A technique that managers use to quantify performance measures and growth targets to analyze their firms' strategic business units (SBUs) as though they were a collection of separate investments. p. 37

business products Products organizations buy that assist in providing other products for resale. Also called *B2B products* or *industrial products*. p. 239

business-to-business marketing The marketing of products and services to companies, governments, or not-for-profit organizations for use in the creation of products and services that they can produce and market to others. p. 130

buy classes Consist of three types of organizational buying situations: straight rebuy, new buy, and modified rebuy. p. 139

buying center The group of people in an organization who participate in the buying process and share common goals, risks, and knowledge important to a purchase decision. p. 138

capacity management Integrating the service component of the marketing mix with efforts to influence consumer demand. p. 291

category management An approach to managing the assortment of merchandise in which a manager is assigned the responsibility for selecting all products that consumers in a market segment might view as substitutes for each other, with the objective of maximizing sales and profits in the category. p. 364

cause marketing Occurs when the charitable contributions of a firm are tied directly to the customer revenues produced through the promotion of one of its products. p. 88

channel conflict Arises when one channel member believes another channel member is engaged in behavior that prevents it from achieving its goals. p. 337

choiceboard An interactive, Internet-enabled system that allows individual customers to design their own products and services by answering a few questions and choosing from a menu of product or service attributes (or components), prices, and delivery options. p. 382

code of ethics A formal statement of ethical principles and rules of conduct. p. 86

collaborative filtering A process that automatically groups people with similar buying intentions, preferences, and behaviors and predicts future purchases. p. 382

commercialization The stage of the new-product development process that positions and launches a new product in full-scale production and sales. p. 257

communication The process of conveying a message to others that requires six elements: a source, a message, a channel of communication, a receiver, and the processes of encoding and decoding. p. 404

competition The alternative firms that could provide a product to satisfy a specific market's needs. p. 81

constraints In a decision, the restrictions placed on potential solutions to a problem. p. 182

consultative selling A need-satisfaction presentation format that focuses on problem identification, where the salesperson serves as an expert on problem recognition and resolution. p. 499

consumer behavior The actions a person takes in purchasing and using products and services, including the mental and social processes that come before and after these actions. p. 99

Consumer Bill of Rights An outline presented by President John F. Kennedy in 1962 that codified the ethics of exchange between buyers and sellers, including the rights to safety, to be informed, to choose, and to be heard. p. 85

consumer ethnocentrism The tendency to believe that it is inappropriate, indeed immoral, to purchase foreign-made products. p. 163

consumer journey map A visual representation of all the touchpoints a consumer comes into contact with before, during, and after a purchase. p. 106

consumer products Products purchased by the ultimate consumer. p. 239

consumer touchpoints A marketer's product, service, or brand points of contact with a consumer from start-to-finish in the purchase decision process. p. 105

consumer-oriented sales promotions Sales tools used to support a company's advertising and personal selling directed to ultimate consumers. Also called *consumer promotions*. p. 444

consumerism A grassroots movement started in the 1960s to increase the influence, power, and rights of consumers in dealing with institutions. p. 83

convenience products Items that the consumer purchases frequently, conveniently, and with a minimum of shopping effort. p. 239

cookies Computer files that a marketer can download onto the computer and mobile phone of an online shopper who visits the marketer's website. p. 391

cooperative advertising Advertising programs whereby a manufacturer pays a percentage of the retailer's local advertising expense for advertising the manufacturer's products. p. 449

core values The fundamental, passionate, and enduring principles of an organization that guide its conduct over time. p. 31

cost-plus pricing Summing the total unit cost of providing a product or service and adding a specific amount to the cost to arrive at a price. p. 305

countertrade The practice of using barter rather than money for making global sales. p. 151

cross-channel consumer A consumer who shops online but buys offline, or shops offline but buys online. p. 393

cross-cultural analysis The study of similarities and differences among consumers in two or more nations or societies. p. 160

cultural symbols Things that represent ideas and concepts in a specific culture. p. 161

culture The set of values, ideas, and attitudes that are learned and shared among the members of a group. p. 76

currency exchange rate The price of one country's currency expressed in terms of another country's currency. p. 165

customary pricing Setting a price that is dictated by tradition, a standardized channel of distribution, or other competitive factors. p. 307

customer engagement The degree and depth of brand-focused interactions a customer chooses to perform online with his or her friends. p. 471

customer experience The internal response that customers have to all aspects of an organization and its offering. p. 16

customer relationship management (CRM) The process of identifying prospective buyers, understanding them intimately, and developing favorable long-term perceptions of the organization and its offerings so that buyers will choose them in the marketplace and become advocates after their purchase. p. 15

customer service The ability of logistics management to satisfy users in terms of time, dependability, communication, and convenience. p. 342

customer value The unique combination of benefits received by targeted buyers that includes quality, convenience, on-time delivery, and both before-sale and after-sale service at a specific price. p. 11

customer value proposition The cluster of benefits that an organization promises customers to satisfy their needs. p. 10

customerization The growing practice of not only customizing a product or service but also personalizing the marketing and overall shopping and buying interaction for each customer. p. 388

customs What is considered normal and expected about the way people do things in a specific country. p. 160

data The facts and figures related to the project that are divided into two main parts: secondary data and primary data. p. 184

data mining The practice of examining large databases to find statistical relationships between consumer purchasing patterns p. 196

demand curve A graph that relates the quantity sold and price, showing the maximum number of units that will be sold at a given price. p. 309

demographics Describing a population according to selected characteristics such as age, gender, ethnicity, income, and occupation. p. 74

derived demand The demand for industrial products and services that is driven by, or derived from, the demand for consumer products and services. p. 132

development The stage of the new-product development process that turns the idea on paper into a prototype. p. 255

direct marketing A promotional alternative that uses direct communication with consumers to generate a response in the form of an order, a request for further information, or a visit to a retail outlet. p. 409

direct orders The result of direct marketing offers that contain all the information necessary for a prospective buyer to make a decision to purchase and complete the transaction. p. 419

discretionary income The money that remains after paying for taxes and necessities. p. 78

disintermediation A source of channel conflict that occurs when a channel member bypasses another member and sells or buys products direct. p. 337

disposable income The money a consumer has left after paying taxes to use for necessities such as food, housing, clothing, and transportation. p. 78

diversification analysis A technique that helps a firm search for growth opportunities from among current and new markets as well as current and new products. p. 40

dual distribution An arrangement whereby a firm reaches different buyers by employing two or more different types of channels for the same basic product. p. 331

dynamic pricing The practice of changing prices for products and services in real time in response to supply and demand conditions. p. 390

e-marketplaces Online trading communities that bring together buyers and supplier organizations to make possible the real-time exchange of information, money, products, and services. Also called *B2B exchanges* or *e-hubs*. p. 140

economic espionage The clandestine collection of trade secrets or proprietary information about a company's competitors. p. 159

economy Pertains to the income, expenditures, and resources that affect the cost of running a business and household. p. 77

eight-second rule A view that customers will abandon their efforts to enter and navigate a website if download time exceeds eight seconds. p. 388

80/20 rule A concept that suggests 80 percent of a firm's sales are obtained from 20 percent of its customers. p. 218

electronic commerce The activities that use electronic communication in the inventory, promotion, distribution, purchase, and exchange of products and services. Also called *e-commerce*. p. 80

emotional intelligence The ability to understand one's own emotions and the emotions of people with whom one interacts on a daily basis. p. 505

environmental forces The uncontrollable forces that affect a marketing decision and consist of social, economic, technological, competitive, and regulatory forces. p. 10

environmental scanning The process of continually acquiring information on events occurring outside the organization to identify and interpret potential trends. p. 74

ethics The moral principles and values that govern the actions and decisions of an individual or group. p. 84

exchange The trade of things of value between buyer and seller so that each is better off after the trade. p. 5

exclusive distribution A level of distribution density whereby only one retailer in a specific geographical area carries the firm's products. p. 334

exporting A global market-entry strategy in which a company produces products in one country and sells them in another country. p. 166

Facebook A website where users may create a personal profile, add other users as friends, and exchange comments, photos, videos, and "likes" with them. p. 466

family life cycle The distinct phases that a family progresses through from formation to retirement, each phase bringing with it identifiable purchasing behaviors. p. 117

Foreign Corrupt Practices Act (1977) A law, amended by the International Anti-Dumping and Fair Competition Act (1998), that makes it a crime for U.S. corporations to bribe an official of a foreign government or political party to obtain or retain business in a foreign country. p. 161

form of ownership Distinguishes retail outlets based on whether independent retailers, corporate chains, or contractual systems own the outlet. p. 353

formula selling presentation A sales presentation format that consists of information that must be provided in an accurate, thorough, and step-by-step manner to inform the prospect. p. 498

four I's of services The four unique elements that distinguish services from goods: intangibility, inconsistency, inseparability, and inventory. p. 241

Generation X Includes the 50 million people born between 1965 and 1976. Also called the *baby bust*. p. 75

Generation Y Includes the 75 million Americans born between 1977 and 1994. Also called the *echo-boom*. p. 75

Generation Z The post-millennial generation, which includes consumers born between 1995 and 2010. p. 76

global brand A brand marketed under the same name in multiple countries with similar and centrally coordinated marketing programs. p. 157

global competition Exists when firms originate, produce, and market their products and services worldwide. p. 155

global consumers Consumer groups living in many countries or regions of the world who have similar needs or seek similar features and benefits from products or services. p. 158

global marketing strategy A strategy used by transnational firms that employ the practice of standardizing marketing activities when there are cultural similarities and adapting them when cultures differ. p. 157

goals Statements of an accomplishment of a task to be achieved, often by a specific time. Also called *objectives*. p. 33

green marketing Marketing efforts to produce, promote, and reclaim environmentally sensitive products. p. 88

gross income The total amount of money made in one year by a person, household, or family unit. Also known as *money income* by the Census Bureau. p. 78

hierarchy of effects The sequence of stages a prospective buyer goes through from initial awareness of a product to eventual action that includes awareness, interest, evaluation, trial, and adoption of the product. p. 414

idea generation The stage of the new-product development process that develops a pool of concepts to serve as candidates for new products, building upon the previous stage's results. p. 251

idle production capacity Occurs when the service provider is available but there is no demand for the service. p. 241

influencer marketing The practice of focusing on the identification and recruitment of influencers to advocate a company's products, services, and brands rather than focusing exclusively on prospective buyers. p. 464

infomercials Program-length (30-minute) advertisements that take an educational approach to communication with potential customers. p. 438

information technology Includes all of the computing resources that collect, store, and analyze data. p. 195

institutional advertisements Advertisements designed to build goodwill or an image for an organization rather than promote a specific product or service. p. 431

integrated marketing communications (IMC) The concept of designing marketing communications programs that coordinate all promotional activities—advertising, personal selling, sales promotion, public relations, and direct marketing—to provide a consistent message across all audiences. p. 404

intensive distribution A level of distribution density whereby a firm tries to place its products and services in as many outlets as possible. p. 334

interactive marketing Two-way buyer–seller electronic communication in which the buyer controls the kind and amount of information received from the seller. p. 382

Internet of Things (IoT) The network of products embedded with connectivity-enabled electronics. p. 80

involvement The personal, social, and economic significance of the purchase to the consumer. p. 103

joint venture A global market-entry strategy in which a foreign company and a local firm invest together to create a local business in order to share ownership, control, and profits of the new company. p. 168

key account management The practice of using team selling to focus on important customers to build mutually beneficial, long-term, cooperative relationships. p. 503

label An integral part of the package that typically identifies the product or brand, who made it, where and when it was made, how it is to be used, and package contents and ingredients. p. 286

lead generation The result of a direct marketing offer designed to generate interest in a product or service and a request for additional information. p. 419

learning Those behaviors that result from (1) repeated experience and (2) reasoning. p. 110

level of service Describes the degree of service provided to the customer from three types of retailers: self-, limited-, and full-service. p. 354

LinkedIn A business-oriented website that lets users post their professional profiles to connect to a network of businesspeople, who are also called *connections*. p. 469

logistics Those activities that focus on getting the right amount of the right products to the right place at the right time at the lowest possible cost. p. 338

loss-leader pricing Deliberately selling a product below its customary price, not to increase sales, but to attract customers' attention to it in hopes that they will buy other products with large markups as well. p. 309

manufacturers' agents Agents who work for several producers and carry noncompetitive, complementary merchandise in an exclusive territory. Also called *manufacturers' representatives*. p. 369

market People with both the desire and the ability to buy a specific offering. p. 9

market modification Strategies by which a company tries to find new customers, increase a product's use among existing customers, or create new use situations. p. 277

market orientation An organization with a market orientation focuses its efforts on (1) continuously collecting information about customers' needs, (2) sharing this information across departments, and (3) using it to create customer value. p. 15

market segmentation Involves aggregating prospective buyers into groups, or segments, that (1) have common needs and (2) will respond similarly to a marketing action. p. 212

market segments The relatively homogeneous groups of prospective buyers that (1) have common needs and (2) will respond similarly to a marketing action. p. 12

market share The ratio of sales revenue of the firm to the total sales revenue of all firms in the industry, including the firm itself. p. 33

market testing The stage of the new-product development process that exposes actual products to prospective consumers under realistic purchase conditions to see if they will buy. p. 256

market-product grid A framework to relate the market segments of potential buyers to products offered or potential marketing actions. p. 213

marketing The activity, set of institutions, and processes for creating, communicating, delivering, and exchanging offerings that have value for customers, clients, partners, and society at large. p. 5

marketing channel Consists of individuals and firms involved in the process of making a product or service available for use or consumption by consumers or industrial users. p. 326

marketing concept The idea that an organization should (1) strive to satisfy the needs of consumers while also (2) trying to achieve the organization's goals. p. 15

marketing dashboard The visual display of the essential information related to achieving a marketing objective. p. 34

marketing metric A measure of the quantitative value or trend of a marketing action or result. p. 35

marketing mix The controllable factors—product, price, promotion, and place—that can be used by the marketing manager to solve a marketing problem. p. 10

marketing plan A road map for the marketing actions of an organization for a specified future time period, such as one year or five years. pp. 34, 56

marketing program A plan that integrates the marketing mix to provide a good, service, or idea to prospective buyers. p. 12

marketing research The process of defining a marketing problem and opportunity, systematically collecting and analyzing information, and recommending actions. p. 180

marketing strategy The means by which a marketing goal is to be achieved, usually characterized by a specified target market and a marketing program to reach it. p. 46

marketing tactics The detailed day-to-day operational marketing actions for each element of the marketing mix that contribute to the overall success of marketing strategies. p. 46

marketspace An information- and communication-based electronic exchange environment mostly occupied by sophisticated computer and telecommunication technologies and digital offerings. p. 80

measures of success Criteria or standards used in evaluating proposed solutions to the problem. p. 182

merchandise line Describes how many different types of products a store carries and in what assortment. p. 354

merchant wholesalers Independently owned firms that take title to the merchandise they handle. p. 369

mission A statement of the organization's function in society that often identifies its customers, markets, products, and technologies. Often used interchangeably with *vision*. p. 32

mixed branding A branding strategy where a firm markets products under its own name(s) and that of a reseller because the segment attracted to the reseller is different from its own market. p. 286

mobile marketing The broad set of interactive messaging options that enable organizations to communicate and engage with consumers through any mobile device. p. 440

moral idealism A personal moral philosophy that considers certain individual rights or duties as universal, regardless of the outcome. p. 86

motivation The energizing force that stimulates behavior to satisfy a need. p. 108

multibranding A branding strategy that involves giving each product a distinct name when each brand is intended for a different market segment. p. 285

multichannel marketing The blending of different communication and delivery channels that are mutually reinforcing in attracting, retaining, and building relationships with consumers who shop and buy in traditional intermediaries and online. p. 331

multichannel retailers Retailers that utilize and integrate a combination of traditional store formats and nonstore formats such as catalogs, television home shopping, and online retailing. p. 364

multicultural marketing Combinations of the marketing mix that reflect the unique attitudes, ancestry, communication preferences, and lifestyles of different races and ethnic groups. p. 76

multidomestic marketing strategy A strategy used by multinational firms that have as many different product variations, brand names, and advertising programs as countries in which they do business. p. 156

multiproduct branding A branding strategy in which a company uses one name for all its products in a product class. p. 284

need-satisfaction presentation A sales presentation format that emphasizes probing and listening by the salesperson to identify the needs and interests of prospective buyers. p. 499

new-product development process The seven stages an organization goes through to identify opportunities and convert them into salable products or services. p. 250

new-product strategy development The stage of the new-product development process that defines the role for a new product in terms of the firm's overall objectives. p. 250

North American Industry Classification System (NAICS) Provides common industry definitions for Canada, Mexico, and the United States, which makes it easier to measure economic activity in the three member countries of the North American Free Trade Agreement (NAFTA). p. 131

objectives Statements of an accomplishment of a task to be achieved, often by a specific time. Also called *goals*. p. 33

observational data Facts and figures obtained by watching how people actually behave, using mechanical, personal, or neuromarketing data collection methods. p. 186

odd-even pricing Setting prices a few dollars or cents under an even number. p. 304

off-peak pricing Charging different prices during different seasons of the year and different times of the day or during different days of the week to reflect variations in demand for the service. p. 289

online consumers The subsegment of all Internet users who employ this technology to research products and services and make purchases. p. 386

open innovation Practices and processes that encourage the use of external as well as internal ideas and internal as well as external collaboration when conceiving, producing, and marketing new products and services. p. 249

opinion leaders Individuals who exert direct or indirect social influence over others. p. 114

order getter Sells in a conventional sense and identifies prospective customers, provides customers with information, persuades customers to buy, closes sales, and follows up on customers' use of a product or service. p. 493

order taker Processes routine orders or reorders for products that were already sold by the company. p. 492

organizational buyers Those manufacturers, wholesalers, retailers, service companies, not-for-profit organizations, and government agencies that buy products and services for their own use or for resale. pp. 17, 130

organizational buying behavior The decision-making process that organizations use to establish the need for products and services and identify, evaluate, and choose among alternative brands and suppliers. p. 136

organizational culture The set of values, ideas, attitudes, and norms of behavior that is learned and shared among the members of an organization. p. 32

packaging A component of a product that refers to any container in which it is offered for sale and on which label information is conveyed. p. 286

penetration pricing Setting a low initial price on a new product to appeal immediately to the mass market. p. 303

perceived risk The anxiety felt because the consumer cannot anticipate the outcomes of a purchase but believes there may be negative consequences. p. 109

perception The process by which an individual selects, organizes, and interprets information to create a meaningful picture of the world. p. 109

perceptual map A means of displaying in two dimensions the location of products or brands in the minds of consumers to enable a manager to see how they perceive competing products or brands, as well as the firm's own product or brand. p. 228

permission marketing The solicitation of a consumer's consent (called "opt-in") to receive e-mail and advertising based on personal data supplied by the consumer. p. 383

personal selling The two-way flow of communication between a buyer and seller, often in a face-to-face encounter, designed to influence the purchase decision of a person or group. pp. 407, 490

personal selling process Sales activities occurring before, during, and after the sale itself, consisting of six stages: (1) prospecting, (2) preapproach, (3) approach, (4) presentation, (5) close, and (6) follow-up. p. 495

personality A person's consistent behaviors or responses to recurring situations. p. 108

personalization The consumer-initiated practice of generating content on a marketer's website that is custom tailored to an individual's specific needs and preferences. p. 383

points of difference Those characteristics of a product that make it superior to competitive substitutes. p. 43

posttests Tests conducted after an advertisement has been shown to the target audience to determine whether it accomplished its intended purpose. p. 443

predictive modeling Based on statistical models that use data mining and probability analysis to foretell outcomes. p. 197

prestige pricing Setting a high price so that quality- or status-conscious consumers will be attracted to the product and buy it. p. 304

pretests Tests conducted before an advertisement is placed in any medium to determine whether it communicates the intended message or to select among alternative versions of the advertisement. p. 442

price (P) The money or other considerations (including other products and services) exchanged for the ownership or use of a product or service. p. 300

price elasticity of demand The percentage change in quantity demanded relative to a percentage change in price. p. 311

pricing constraints Factors that limit the range of prices a firm may set. p. 315

pricing objectives Specifying the role of price in an organization's marketing and strategic plans. p. 314

primary data Facts and figures that are newly collected for the project. p. 184

private branding A branding strategy used when a company manufactures products but sells them under the brand name of a wholesaler or retailer. Also called *private labeling* or *reseller branding*. p. 285

product A good, service, or idea consisting of a bundle of tangible and intangible attributes that satisfies consumers' needs and is received in exchange for money or something else of value. p. 17, 239

product advertisements Advertisements that focus on selling a product or service and which take three forms: (1) pioneering (or informational), (2) competitive (or persuasive), and (3) reminder. p. 430

product class Refers to the entire product category or industry. p. 274

product differentiation A marketing strategy that involves a firm using different marketing mix actions to help consumers perceive a product as being different and better than competing products. p. 212

product form Pertains to variations of a product within the product class. p. 274

product item A specific product that has a unique brand, size, or price. p. 242

product life cycle Describes the stages a new product goes through in the marketplace: introduction, growth, maturity, and decline. p. 268

product line A group of product or service items that are closely related because they satisfy a class of needs, are used together, are sold to the same customer group, are distributed through the same outlets, or fall within a given price range. p. 243

product mix Consists of all the product lines offered by an organization. p. 243

product modification Involves altering one or more of a product's characteristics, such as its quality, performance, or appearance, to increase the product's value to customers and increase sales. p. 276

product placement A consumer sales promotion tool that uses a brand-name product in a movie, television show, video game, or a commercial for another product. p. 447

product positioning The place a product occupies in consumers' minds based on important attributes relative to competitive products. p. 228

product repositioning Changing the place a product occupies in a consumer's mind relative to competitive products. p. 228

profit The money left after a for-profit organization subtracts its total expenses from its total revenues—and the reward for the risk it undertakes in marketing its offerings. p. 28

profit equation Profit = Total revenue − Total cost; or Profit = (Unit price × Quantity sold) − (Fixed cost + Variable cost). p. 302

promotional mix The combination of one or more communication tools used to: (1) inform prospective buyers about the benefits of the product, (2) persuade them to try it, and (3) remind them later about the benefits they enjoyed by using the product. p. 404

protectionism The practice of shielding one or more industries within a country's economy from foreign competition through the use of tariffs or quotas. p. 152

protocol A statement that, before product development begins, identifies: (1) a well-defined target market; (2) specific customers' needs, wants, and preferences; and (3) what the product will be and do to satisfy consumers. p. 246

public relations A form of communication management that seeks to influence the feelings, opinions, or beliefs held by customers, prospective customers, stockholders, suppliers, employees, and other publics about a company and its products or services. p. 408

publicity A nonpersonal, indirectly paid presentation of an organization, product, or service. p. 408

publicity tools Methods of obtaining nonpersonal presentation of an organization, product, or service without direct cost, such as news releases, news conferences, and public service announcements (PSAs). p. 449

pull strategy Directing the promotional mix at ultimate consumers to encourage them to ask the retailer for a product. p. 413

purchase decision process The five stages a buyer passes through in making choices about which products and services to buy: (1) problem recognition, (2) information search, (3) alternative evaluation, (4) purchase decision, and (5) postpurchase behavior. p. 100

push strategy Directing the promotional mix to channel members to gain their cooperation in ordering and stocking the product. p. 412

questionnaire data Facts and figures obtained by asking people about their attitudes, awareness, intentions, and behaviors. p. 189

quota A restriction placed on the amount of a product allowed to enter or leave a country. p. 153

reference groups People to whom an individual looks as a basis for self-appraisal or as a source of personal standards. p. 116

regulation Restrictions state and federal laws place on a business with regard to the conduct of its activities. p. 82

relationship marketing Links the organization to its individual customers, employees, suppliers, and other partners for their mutual long-term benefit. p. 11

relationship selling The practice of building ties to customers based on a salesperson's attention and commitment to customer needs over time. p. 491

retail life cycle The process of growth and decline that retail outlets, like products, experience, consisting of the early growth, accelerated development, maturity, and decline stages. p. 367

retailing All activities involved in selling, renting, and providing products and services to ultimate consumers for personal, family, or household use. p. 352

retailing mix The activities related to managing the store and the merchandise in the store, which include retail pricing, store location, retail communication, and merchandise. p. 361

reverse auction In an e-marketplace, an online auction in which a buyer communicates a need for a product or service and would-be suppliers are invited to bid in competition with each other. p. 141

reverse logistics A process of reclaiming recyclable and reusable materials, returns, and reworks from the point of consumption or use for repair, remanufacturing, redistribution, or disposal. p. 343

sales forecast The total sales of a product that a firm expects to sell during a specified time period under specified environmental conditions and its own marketing efforts. p. 200

sales management Planning the selling program and implementing and evaluating the personal selling effort of the firm. p. 490

sales plan A statement describing what is to be achieved and where and how the selling effort of salespeople is to be deployed. p. 502

sales promotion A short-term inducement of value offered to arouse interest in buying a product or service. p. 409

sales quota Specific goals assigned to a salesperson, sales team, branch sales office, or sales district for a stated time period. p. 507

salesforce automation (SFA) The use of various technologies to make the sales function more effective and efficient. p. 508

scrambled merchandising Offering several unrelated product lines in a single store. p. 357

screening and evaluation The stage of the new-product development process that internally and externally evaluates new-product ideas to eliminate those that warrant no further effort. p. 253

secondary data Facts and figures that have already been recorded prior to the project at hand. p. 184

selective distribution A level of distribution density whereby a firm selects a few retailers in a specific geographical area to carry its products. p. 335

self-regulation An alternative to government control whereby an industry attempts to police itself. p. 83

services Intangible activities or benefits that an organization provides to satisfy consumers' needs in exchange for money or something else of value. p. 239

seven Ps of services marketing An expanded marketing mix concept for services that includes the four Ps (product, price, promotion, and place or distribution) as well as people, physical environment, and process. p. 289

shopper marketing The use of displays, coupons, product samples, and other brand communications to influence shopping behavior in a store. p. 364

shopping experience A consumer's perception of an encounter with a store's physical environment, personnel, and policies and procedures. p. 364

shopping products Items for which the consumer compares several alternatives on criteria such as price, quality, or style. p. 239

showrooming The practice of examining products in a store and then buying them online for a cheaper price. p. 393

situation analysis Taking stock of where the firm or product has been recently, where it is now, and where it is headed in terms of the organization's marketing plans and the external forces and trends affecting it. p. 42

skimming pricing Setting the highest initial price that customers really desiring the product are willing to pay when introducing a new or innovative product. p. 303

social commerce The use of social networks for browsing and buying. p. 392

social forces The demographic characteristics of the population and its culture. p. 74

social media Online media where users submit comments, photos, and videos—often accompanied by a feedback process to identify "popular" topics. p. 462

social media marketing program That portion of a company's integrated marketing communications effort to create and deliver compelling online media content that attracts viewer attention and encourages readers to share it with their social network. p. 471

social responsibility The idea that organizations are part of a larger society and are accountable to that society for their actions. p. 87

societal marketing concept The view that organizations should satisfy the needs of consumers in a way that provides for society's well-being. p. 16

spam Communications that take the form of electronic junk mail or unsolicited e-mail. p. 389

specialty products Items that the consumer makes a special effort to search out and buy. p. 239

standard markup pricing Adding a fixed percentage to the cost of all items in a specific product class. p. 305

stimulus-response presentation A sales presentation format that assumes that given the appropriate stimulus by a salesperson, the prospect will buy. p. 498

strategic marketing process The process whereby an organization allocates its marketing mix resources to reach its target markets and achieve a competitive advantage. p. 41

strategy An organization's long-term course of action designed to deliver a unique customer experience while achieving its goals. p. 30

subcultures Subgroups within the larger, or national, culture with unique values, ideas, and attitudes. p. 119

supply chain The various firms involved in performing the activities required to create and deliver a product or service to consumers or industrial users. p. 339

sustainable development Conducting business in a way that protects the natural environment while making economic progress. p. 89

SWOT analysis An acronym describing an organization's appraisal of its internal **S**trengths and **W**eaknesses and its external **O**pportunities and **T**hreats. p. 42

target market One or more specific groups of potential consumers toward which an organization directs its marketing program. p. 10

target profit pricing Setting an annual target of a specific dollar volume of profit. p. 306

target return-on-investment pricing Setting a price to achieve an annual target return on investment (ROI). p. 307

target return-on-sales pricing Setting a price to achieve a profit that is a specified percentage of the sales volume. p. 307

tariffs Government taxes on products or services entering a country that primarily serve to raise prices on imports. p. 152

team selling The practice of using an entire team of professionals in selling to and servicing major customers. p. 494

technology Inventions or innovations from applied science or engineering research. p. 79

telemarketing Using the telephone to interact with and sell directly to consumers. p. 360

total cost (TC) The total expense incurred by a firm in producing and marketing a product. Total cost is the sum of fixed cost and variable cost. p. 312

total logistics cost The expenses associated with transportation, materials handling and warehousing, inventory, stockouts (being out of inventory), order processing, and return products handling. p. 342

total revenue (TR) The total money received from the sales of a product. p. 371

trade war A situation in which countries try to damage each other's trade, typically by imposition of tariff and quota restrictions. p. 154

trade-oriented sales promotions Sales tools used to support a company's advertising and personal selling directed to wholesalers, distributors, or retailers. Also called *trade promotions*. p. 448

trading down Reducing a product's number of features, quality, or price. p. 278

trading up Adding value to the product (or line) through additional features or higher-quality materials. p. 278

traditional auction In an e-marketplace, an online auction in which a seller puts an item up for sale and would-be buyers are invited to bid in competition with each other. p. 141

traffic generation The outcome of a direct marketing offer designed to motivate people to visit a business. p. 419

Twitter A website that enables users to send and receive "tweets," messages up to 280 characters long. p. 468

ultimate consumers The people who use the products and services purchased for a household. Also called *consumers, buyers,* or *customers*. p. 17

unsought products Items that the consumer does not know about or knows about but does not initially want. p. 239

usage rate The quantity consumed or patronage (store visits) during a specific period. *Frequency marketing* focuses on usage rate. p. 218

user-generated content (UGC) The various forms of online media content that are publicly available and created by consumers or end users. Also called *consumer-generated content*. p. 462

utilitarianism A personal moral philosophy that focuses on "the greatest good for the greatest number" by assessing the costs and benefits of the consequences of ethical behavior. p. 87

utility The benefits or customer value received by users of the product. p. 18

value The ratio of perceived benefits to price; or Value = (Perceived benefits ÷ Price). p. 301

value pricing The practice of simultaneously increasing product and service benefits while maintaining or decreasing price. p. 302

values A society's personally or socially preferable modes of conduct or states of existence that tend to persist over time. p. 160

vendor-managed inventory (VMI) An inventory management system whereby the supplier determines the product amount and assortment a customer (such as a retailer) needs and automatically delivers the appropriate items. p. 343

vertical marketing systems Professionally managed and centrally coordinated marketing channels designed to achieve channel economies and maximum marketing impact. p. 332

viral marketing An Internet-enabled promotional strategy that encourages individuals to forward marketer-initiated messages to others via e-mail, social networking websites, and blogs. p. 390

web communities Websites that allow people to congregate online and exchange views on topics of common interest. p. 389

webrooming The practice of examining products online and then buying them in a store. p. 393

wheel of retailing A concept that describes how new forms of retail outlets enter the market. p. 366

word of mouth The influencing of people during conversations. p. 114

World Trade Organization (WTO) A permanent institution that sets rules governing trade between its members through panels of trade experts who decide on trade disputes between members and issue binding decisions. p. 154

YouTube A video-sharing website in which users can upload, view, and comment on videos. p. 470

NAME INDEX

A

Aaker, David A., 208, 455, 458
Abela, Andrew V., 54
Abell, Derek F., 54
Abraham, Magid M., 458
Abrams, Rhonda, 53, 70
Adams, Susan, 234, 529
Adamy, Janet, 208
Addady, Michal, 53, 235
Adkins-Green, Sheryl, 174, 175, 176
Agarwal, Amit, 148
Agarwal, Manoj K., 297
Agnihotri, Raj, 54
Ahearne, Michael, 514
Ahern, Karla, 529
Ailawadi, Kusum L., 425
Aizen, I., 126
Alba, Joseph W., 125
Albee, Ardath, 265
Alcantara, Ann-Marie, 486
Alexander, Antoinette, 127
Alexander, Joe F., 528
Allen, Alisa, 322, 323
Almquist, Eric, 147
Alsughayir, A., 177
Ambler, Tim, 54
Anantula, Suhit, 208
Anderson, Eric, 376
Anderson, Erin, 147
Anderson, James C., 24
Anderson, Mae, 349, 486
Anderson, Nate, 376
Ansoff, H. Igor, 54
Ante, Spencer E., 54, 486
Anthony, Scott, 208
Appleyard, Dennis R., 177
Arden, Christine M., 401
Arens, Christian, 458
Arens, William F., 458
Armstrong, J. Scott, 54
Arnsdorf, Isaac, 264
Arons, Marc de Swaan, 485
Arora, Neeraj, 376
Artzrouni, Dominic, 458
Ash, Mary Kay, 174
Aslam, Salman, 485, 486
Avery, Susan, 147
Axvig, Amanda, 486

B

Baack, D. W., 426
Bachmann, Gwen, 126
Back, Daniel W., 457
Bacon, Jonathan, 485
Badal, Sangeeta Bharadwaj, 514
Baek, Tae Hyun, 427
Bagozzi, Richard P., 24, 492, 514
Bahrami, B., 126
Bailey, Jeffrey J., 456
Baker, Julie A., 376
Baker, Kelly, 261, 262–263, 265
Baker, Wayne E., 529
Balabanis, George, 177
Balakrishnan, Anita, 54
Balasubramanian, Sridhar, 376
Bandenhausen, Kurt, 97
Banis, William J., 529
Banks, Tom, 376
Bansal, Anjali, 528
Bara, Mary, 460
Barich, Howard, 376
Barker, Melissa S., 486
Barnes, Brooks, 208
Barnes, John, 376
Barnhorn, R., 264
Baron, Eric, 514
Bartholomew, Doug, 349
Bartiromo, Maria, 459
Bartz, Bianca, 425
Bashford, Suzy, 95
Bass, Stephen J., 377
Basta, Nicholas, 528
Bates, Albert D., 377
Bates, Douglas D., 209
Batra, Rajeev, 425, 458
Bauer, Eddie, 324
Bauer, Sue, 426
Bauerkin, Valerie, 401
Bay, Willow, 208
Bayus, Barry, 264
Becker, Jill, 375
Behravesh, Nariman, 96
Beitelspacher, Lauren, 528
Belk, Russell, 126
Bell, Glen, 423–424
Beltron, Garbrie, 456
Ben-Akiva, Moshe, 125
Bendle, Neil T., 54, 377, 527
Bennett, Luke, 426
Bensinger, Greg, 234
Bercovici, Jeff, 349
Berg, Madeline, 455
Berger, Arthur Asa, 297
Berkowitz, Eric N., 234
Bernot, Kate, 25
Berry, Jeff, 458
Berry, Jon, 126
Berry, Leonard L., 376
Bertagnoli, Lisa, 529
Bezawada, Ram, 485
Bezos, Jeff, 347, 348, 349, 390
Bharadwaj, Sundar G., 177, 514
Bianco, Anthony, 234
Bigne, J. Enrique, 426
Binkley, Christina, 323
Birkel, Frank, 528
Birkner, Christine, 127
Bisht, Shalini, 486
Biswas, Neelanjan, 209
Bitner, Mary Jo, 264, 297, 376, 377
Blackwell, Roger D., 125
Blanchard, Dave, 349
Blasko, Vincent, 426
Block, Martin P., 426
Bloomberg, Jason, 55
Blount, Jeb, 514
Blunt, Emily, 178
Boccara, Brun, 125
Bodur, Onur H., 376
Boenigk, Michael, 426
Boerman, Sophie C., 426, 458
Boggs, Michelle, 528
Bolles, Richard N., 527
Bonoma, Thomas V., 147
Borgesius, Frederik J. Zuiderveen, 426
Boring, Christopher, 363
Boshnack, Mark, 23
Bosnjak, M., 126
Boudreau, Kevin J., 264
Boulding, William, 24
Bowie, Norman E., 96
Boyle, Brady, 508
Bozman, Carl S., 456
Bradlow, Eric T., 377
Bradstreet, Kailee, 487
Brady, Diane, 528
Brandau, Mark, 427
Brat, Ilan, 209
Bratko, D., 126
Bremmer, Brian, 97
Breugelmans, Els, 377
Bridges, Virginia, 376
Brin, Sergey, 453, 454
Brinkley, Christie, 438
Britner, Lucy, 456
Brodie, Roderick J., 54
Brooke, Zach, 208, 528, 529
Brown, Bruce, 208
Brown, Charlie, 458
Brown, Duncan, 485
Brown, Stephen, 377
Brown, Tom J., 209, 265

Brunt, Jonathan, 427
Brynjolfsson, Erik, 53
Buchanan, Bruce, 456
Buck, Claudia, 458
Bughin, Jacques, 54
Bulik, Beth Snyder, 297, 426
Bullock, August, 110, 126
Burdick, Richard K., 147
Burin, Norm, 376
Burke, Richard, 144
Burnson, Patrick, 349
Burrow, Peter, 459
Burrows, David, 54
Burton, Virgil L., 527
Bush, Michael, 425, 528
Bush, Robert P., 209
Buss, Dale, 264
Butkovic. A., 126
Butterworth, Siobhain, 427
Buttle, Francis, 126, 515
Buzzell, Robert D., 458
Bygott, Steve, 486
Byron, Ellen, 234

C

Cameron, James, 180
Campo, Katia, 377
Cannon, Joseph P., 514
Capossela, Alison, 512, 513, 515
Cardona, Mercedes M., 127
Carducci, Bernardo J., 126
Carlson, Greg, 126
Carlson, Kurt A., 297
Carneiro, Bianca, 375
Carpenter, Gregory S., 25
Carral, Teré, 198, 199–200, 209
Carter, Franklin, 426
Casnocha, Ben, 516, 527, 528
Casserly, Meghan, 514, 529
Cassidy, Tom, 147
Castellion, George, 24
Castillo, Michelle, 455
Castleberry, Stephen B., 514
Cateora, Philip K., 177, 514
Chandler, Jennifer, 147
Chandler, Michelle, 24
Chandon, Pierre, 297
Chang, Chingching, 456
Chang, Kenneth, 208
Chang, Sue Ryung, 486
Chang, Victor, 485
Chaudhary, Meenakshi, 486
Chen, Baiyun, 426
Chen, Huan, 458
Chevalier, Michael, 459
Chiang, Alexander, 54
Choi, JeeWon Brianna, 485

Choi, Jeonghye, 486
Chonko, Lawrence B., 514
Chopra, Sunil, 349
Christensen, Clayton M., 264
Chu, Wujin, 147
Chua, K. K., 174, 177
Chung, Tuck Siong, 485
Churchill, Gilbert A., Jr., 209, 265
Cipriani, Jason, 54
Clancy, Rebecca, 457
Clark, Bruce H., 54
Clark, Dave, 348
Clark, Moira, 375
Clarkson, Kelly, 114
Claus, J., 126
Claveri, Kelvin, 96
Cleghorn, Jamie, 147
Clever, Joanne, 528
Clifford, Stephanie, 209, 376
Cline, Thomas W., 456
Close, Kerry, 235
Cockrill, Antje, 426
Cohen, Ben, 26
Cohen, Dorothy, 96, 456
Cohen, Noam, 209
Cohen, William A., 70
Cohn, D'Vera, 126
Colby, Sandra L., 95
Cole, Chris, 263
Coleman, Barbara Carrick, 425
Coleman-Lochner, Lauren, 24
Collins, Jim, 53, 521
Collis, David J., 24
Colvin, Geoff, 234
Comes, Antonella, 375
Compeau, Larry D., 455
Conick, Hal, 53, 95, 96, 209, 377, 528, 529
Conlon, Ginger, 427
Conniff, Megan, 375
Cook, Tim, 37, 39
Cooper, E., 425
Cooper, Martha, 349
Cooper, Robert G., 264
Cooper, Scott W., 70
Coopersmith, Jonathan, 296
Corstjens, Marcel, 375
Costello, Sam, 486
Cotte, June, 97
Courtney, Martin, 427
Covello, Joseph A., 70
Covino, Renee M., 485
Cowles, Deborah L., 234
Coy, Peter, 528
Craig, Nick, 53
Crane, Frederick G., 234
Cravens, David W., 514
Crawford, Merle, 264
Creamer, Matthew, 459, 528

Cron, William L., 514
Crosby, Jackie, 375
Crosby, Lawrence A., 376
Cross, James, 458
Cruise, Tom, 178, 448
Cuddeford-Jones, Morag, 528
Curhan, Ronald C., 459
Cyk, Jayme, 127
Czinkota, Michael, 177

D

D'Meurville, Martin Petit, 487
Dahl, Sima, 529
Dahlhoff, Denise, 297
Daley, Jason, 485
Daley, Shawn P., 147
Dalrymple, Jim, 377
Dalton, Catherine M., 53
Damast, Alison, 529
Dan, Avi, 55
Daniel, David S., 528
Daniels, Chris, 455
Dant, Rajiv P., 24
Darmon, René Y., 514
Darrow, Barb, 486
David, Kenneth, 97
Davidson, Paul, 529
Davidson, William R., 377
Davies, Alex, 96
Davis, Ellen, 528
Davis, John, 54, 377
Davis-Blake, Alison, 95
Dawley, Jacqueline, 235
Dawson, Chester, 485
Day, George S., 24, 53, 208
De Looper, Christian, 486
De Meulenaer, Sarah, 456
De Pelsmacker, Patrick, 456, 458
De Vries, Lisette, 485
Dean, Joshua, 22, 25
DeCarlo, Thomas E., 514
Decker, Kimberly J., 235
DeGeneres, Ellen, 468
Deichmann, D., 264
Deighton, John, 297
Del Rowe, Sam, 485
Dell, Michael, 335
Della Cava, Marco, 265
Delo, Cotton, 96, 427
DeMuro, Doug, 234
DeNicola, Louis, 24
Dens, Nathalia, 456, 458
Dermody, Pat, 375
Dev, Chekitan S., 264
Diakantonis, Demitri, 70
Diaz, Ann-Christine, 455
DiBenedetto, Anthony, 264

Dichter, Ernest, 458
Dickey, Jack, 235
Dickson, Andrea, 514
Dickson, Peter R., 125
Diepenbrock, Amy, 529
Diorio, Carl, 208
Diriker, Memo F., 528
Dirks, Tim, 208
Doan, Lynn, 97
Dobscha, Susan, 24
Dodds, William D., 323, 376
Dodes, Rachel, 208, 349
Doering, Christopher, 24
Dogan, Mustafa, 21
Dogtiev, Artyom, 486
Doherty, Anne Marie, 377
Dolan, Robert J., 147
Dolber, Roslyn, 528
Donaldson, Thomas, 96
Donlon, J. P., 234
Donnelly, Grace, 54.
Donovan, Robert J., 125
Donthu, Naveen, 147
Dooley, Roger, 208
Dorsey, Jack, 468
Drell, Lauren, 426
Drew, Christopher, 265
Dreze, Xavier, 376
Drozdiak, Natalia, 96
Drysch, Michael, 475–476
Du, Rex Y., 126
Dua, Tanya, 96, 458
Dubner, Stephen, 441
Dudlicek, Jim, 208
Duncan, Ewan, 25
Duncan, Tom, 427
Durisin, Megan, 25
Dyer, Jeff, 264

E

Eaton, Leslie, 375
Edelman, Benjamin, 457
Edwards, Jim, 514
Edwards, Luke, 96
Ehret, Michael, 24
Einwiller, Sabine, A., 426
Eisend, Martin, 425
El-Ansary, Adel I., 349, 401
Elledge, Josh, 458
Elliott, Stuart, 426
Ellis, Topher, 264
Ellison, Sarah, 264
Eng, Dinah, 264
Engardio, Pete, 97
Engel, James F., 125
Engher, Daniel, 487
Eppright, David R., 456

Erickson, Peter, 264
Etgar, Michael, 456
Ethans, Arno J., 147
Etherington, Darrell, 97
Evans, James R., 515
Evans, Kenneth R., 24
Evans, Phillip, 54
Ewoldt, John, 375

F

Fahey, Liam, 25
Fallon, Jimmy, 450
Farber, Madeline, 95
Farrell, Chris, 529
Farris, Paul W., 54, 377, 456, 527
Fay, Brad, 126
Federer, Roger, 114
Feloni, Richard, 53
Felson, Leonard, 529
Fera, Rae Ann, 455
Fernandez, Karen V., 455
Fetscherin, Marc, 297
Few, Stephen, 53, 54
Fiedler, Lars, 377
Field, Alfred J., 177
Fine, Leslie M., 264
Finos, Ralph, 96
Fishbein, Martin, 126
Fisher, Carrie, 416
Fisher, Marshall, 377
Fisher, Robert J., 401
Fisher, Stacy, 446
Fitzgerald, Kate, 401
Fleming, Anne, 99
Flinn, Ryan, 209
Flood, Barbara, 529
Flynn, Meghan, 487
Folkens, Dave, 425
Fonsi, Luis, 470
Fontein, Dara, 485
Fontenot, Kayla R., 96
Forbes, Thom, 24, 264
Ford, David, 209
Forrester, Duane, 528
Forte, Daniella, 427
Foster, Jodi, 123
Foumier, Susan, 24
Fox, Justin, 235
Fox-Brewster, Thomas, 457
Frank, Zac, 264
Franke, George R., 457
Fredrix, Emily, 457
Freed, Larry, 401
Friedman, Milton, 87
Frizell, Sam, 24, 96
Frost, Raymond, 401
Fry, Erika, 177, 377

Fry, Richard, 95, 426
Fujimoto, Takahiro, 349
Furnham, Adrian, 126
Futrell, Charles M., 514

G

Gajanan, Mahita, 425
Galbraith, J. K., 96
Galindo, Juanito, 485
Gallo, Amy, 53
Gangwar, Manish, 377
Gantt, Henry L., 45
Garlieb, Stacie, 529
Gaudiosi, John, 455, 486
Gauri, Dinesh K., 376
Gebhardt, Gary F., 25
Gedenk, Karen, 425
Gee, Rachel, 486
Geier, Ben, 24
Gelles, David, 24
Gensler, Sonja, 401, 485
Gerlach, Jerry, 377
Germann, Frank, 377
Gershgorn, Dave, 96
Gerst, Jeff, 205, 206, 209
Ghermezians, 372
Ghosh, Pulak, 209
Gibson, Lawrence D., 208
Gillespie, Kate, 177
Gilliland, Nikki, 456
Gilly, Mary C., 177, 514
Gimbel, Tom, 529
Gitlin, Martin, 264
Gjurgievska, Aleksandra, 265
Gladman, Blake, 96
Glassel, Linda, 232, 234, 235
Glazer, Emily, 264
Gold, Justin, 293, 294, 296, 297
Gold, Laurence N., 458
Goldberg, Marvin E., 426, 456
Golden, Linda L., 376
Goldman, Doron, 456
Gonul, Fusun F., 426
Goode, Mark M., 426
Goodman, Kolby, 486
Goodwin, Stephen A., 456
Gotlieb, Jerry, 456
Gotter, Ana, 95
Gottfried, Miriam, 53, 208, 375
Graber, Donald R., 177
Graham, Jed, 235
Graham, John L., 177, 514
Grama, Ananth, 209
Green, Amanda, 234
Green, Benjamin, 123
Green, Marianne E., 528, 529
Green, Mark C., 177

Greenberg, Robert M., 529
Greene, Jay, 96
Greene, Mallik, 485
Greenfield, Jerry, 26
Greengard, Samuel, 377
Greenleaf, Eric A., 125
Greenwald, Ted, 96
Gremler, Dwayne D., 264, 297
Grewal, Dhruv, 24, 323, 376, 455
Grewal, Rajdeep, 147
Greyerson, Hal B., 264
Grifffith, Eric, 96
Groene, Nicole, 457
Grogan, Ross, 486
Gromling, Frank, 487
Gronstedt, Anders, 426
Grossman, Samantha, 456
Grossnickle, Joshua, 528
Groth, Aimee, 234
Guanella, Mike, 295, 296, 297
Guangzhi Zhao, 426
Gumbel, Peter, 25
Gundlach, Gregory T., 24
Gupta, Sunil, 125
Gupte, Gouri, 514

H

Haas, Eduard, III, 287
Haenlein, Michael, 462, 485
Hagenbuch, David, 528
Hagiwara, Yuki, 97
Hahn, Minhi, 457
Haigh, Thomas, 55
Hair, Joseph F., Jr., 209
Hair, Neil, 375
Hall, James, 54
Hall, Joseph M., 377
Hall, Julie, 264
Hall, Rebecca A., 126
Hamil, Mark, 416
Hamilton, Rebecca W., 264
Hammond, John S., 54
Hampp, Andrew, 457
Handler, Doug, 96
Handley, Lucy, 96
Hansegard, Jens, 24
Hansen, Morten T., 53
Hardesty, David M., 514
Harnish, Verne, 95
Harper, Jonathan, 528
Harris, Jim, 487
Hartley, Steven W., 55, 97, 127, 147, 234, 265, 297, 323, 349, 377, 426, 427, 458, 459, 515
Hartline, Jana, 92, 93, 94, 95, 97
Hartman, Cathy L., 96, 375
Hartzell, Dane, 205

Haruvy, Ernan, 376
Hastie, Reid, 264
Hathcote, Jan M., 456
Hawkins, Delbert I., 125, 126
Hayes, Nick, 485
Hayes, Tom, 401
Hazelgren, Brian J., 70
Heine, Christopher, 457
Heinzinger, Dave, 350
Helsen, Kristiaan, 177
Hempel, Jessi, 514
Hemsley, Steve, 53
Henderson, Rik, 456
Hennessey, H. David, 177
Hennessey, Matthew, 95
Hepplemann, James, 24
Herbig, Paul A., 177, 514
Hernandez, Pedro, 53, 486
Herring, Tyler, 232, 235
Herrmann, Andreas, 376
Hershberger, Edmund, 528
Hessel, Roy, 375
Hiebing, Roman G., Jr., 70
Hilton, Kyle, 208
Hilton, Robin, 486
Hipp, Jonathan, 235
Hoard, Charley, 427
Hochman, Sarah, 76
Hodgdon, Kirk, 322, 323
Hodgdon, Patrick, 486
Hof, Robert D., 54., 459
Hoffman, Reid, 516, 527, 528
Hoffman, Tom, 458
Hogan, Kate, 458
Hogg, Bevill, 144
Hoium, Travis, 265
Holden, Richard, 453, 454
Holland, Frank, 53
Holmes, Elizabeth, 126, 375
Holt, Douglas, 485
Hong, Sungtak, 377
Hooley, Graham J., 426
Hopewell, Nikki, 425
Hopkins, Michael S., 209
Horn, John, 208
Hornik, Jacob, 456
Howard, Caroline, 53
Howard, Daniel L., 323, 377
Howard, John A., 125
Howard, Theresa, 427
Hoyer, Wayne D., 126
Hsieh, Tony, 210–211, 234
Hubby, Kristen, 486
Huddleston, Tom, Jr., 96
Hudson, Kris, 96
Hufford, Austen, 235
Hughes, Douglas E., 514
Hull, Chuck, 246
Humphreys, Jeffrey M., 70, 126

Hunt, James B., 456
Hunt, Kenneth A., 376
Hutchinson, J. Wesley, 125
Hutt, Michael D., 147
Hyman, H., 425

I

Ignatius, Adi, 55
Ingrahm, Christopher, 457
Iqbal, Azhar, 96
Islam, Zak, 54
Ive, Jonathan, 252
Ives, Nat, 375

J

Jackson, Donald W, 147
Jackson, Joni R., 209
Jacobs, Bert, 251
Jacobs, John, 251
Jacobs, Paul, 426
Jacoby, Jacob, 323
Jaekel, Brielle, 426
Jahoda, M., 425
Jain, Ambuj, 323, 377
James, Dana, 529
James, Harvey S., 97
James, LeBron, 321, 475–476
James, Meg, 208
Janakirarman, Ramkumar, 485
Jang, Sungha, 125
Janke, James, 377
Jap, Sandy D., 147
Jargon, Julie, 235
Jarvis, Jeff, 459
Jasper, Dan, 372, 374
Jaworski, Bernard J., 401
Jefferson, Elana Ashanti, 458
Jeffery, Mark, 54, 209
Jenner, Kendall, 280, 464, 465
Jenner, Kris, 465
Jenner, Kylie, 280, 465
Jeong, Yongick, 457
Jobs, Steve, 39, 226, 236
Johannes, Amy, 458
Johansson, Johnny K., 177, 297
John, Deborah Roedder, 126
Johnson, Gavin, 208
Johnson, Gerry, 53
Johnson, Lauren, 486
Johnson, Lisa, 375
Johnston, Mark W., 514
Johnston, Wesley J., 24, 147
Jolson, Marvin A., 458
Jones, Conor, 25
Jones, Eli, 514

Jones, John Philip, 426
Jong, Ad de, 514
Jordan, Michael, 477
Joslyn, Mark, 144, 145, 146
Jurney, Corinne, 375

K

Ka-Man Cheung, 425
Kadet, Anne, 457
Kador, John, 53
Kageyama, Yuri, 177
Kahn, Kenneth B., 264
Kallas, Priit, 486
Kallayil, Gopi, 454
Kamakura, Wagne A, 126
Kambatla, Karthik, 209
Kambil, Ajit, 147
Kaminsky, Philip, 349
Kane, Colleen, 95
Kannan, P. K., 53, 485
Kanter, James, 96
Kapferer, Jean-Noe, 323
Kaplan, Andreas M., 462, 485, 487
Kaplan, David, 375
Kapoor, Anuj, 485
Kaputa, Catherine, 528
Kardashian, Khloe, 359, 465
Kardashian, Kim, 359, 465
Kardashian, Kourtney, 359, 465
Karp, Andrew, 127
Karremans, J., 126
Kartajaya, Hermawan, 25, 426
Katoma, Zsolt, 457
Kavadias, Stelios, 53
Keaveney, Susan M., 376
Kedmey, Dan, 455
Keegan, Warren J., 177
Keith, Janet E., 147
Kell, John, 456
Kellaris, James J., 456
Keller, Ed, 126
Keller, Kevin Lane, 177, 297, 425
Keller, Naomi, 529
Kendrick, Douglas T., 126
Kennedy, John F., 85
Kennedy, Marilyn Moats, 529
Kent, Robert, 457
Kerin, Roger A., 24, 53, 54., 55, 97, 127, 177, 234, 235, 265, 297, 323, 377, 401, 426, 487, 514, 515
Kerner, Sean Michael, 427
Kerwin, Kathleen, 234
Key, Stephen, 264
Khadder, Tania, 264
Khakbaz, Yara, 263, 265
Khalifa, Wiz, 470
Khare, Rachit, 377

Khusainova, Rushana, 514
Kidd, Patricia, 96
Kidwell, Blair, 514
Kiely, T. J., 95
Kilpatrick, Ryan, 458
Kim, Hyeong Min, 376
Kim, Ilchul, 425
Kim, Jooyoung, 425
Kim, Kathleen, 401
Kim, Peter, 54.
Kim, W. Chan, 53
King, Rachel, 426
Kitchen, Philip J., 425
Kjellberg, Felix, 471
Klaassen, Abbey, 457, 459
Klapper, J. T., 425
Klara, Robert, 97, 529
Klein, Noreen M., 376
Klein, Thomas A., 96
Klie, Leonard, 376
Klum, Heidi, 359
Knightley, Keira, 178
Kobe, Kathryn, 96
Kohli, Ajay K., 147, 514
Kohli, Chiranjeev, 485
Kohls, L. Robert, 96
Kollar, Melissa A., 96
Kollath, Carlie, 375
Kollias, Giorgos, 209
Kolowich, Lindsay, 208
Konus, Umut, 376
Kopale, Praveen K., 377
Kopp, Wendy, 29
Koselka, Rita, 376
Koshy, Vinay, 486
Kotabe, Masaaki, 177
Kothari, Ashish, 24
Kotler, Philip, 25, 376, 377, 426
Kowitt, Beth, 235
Kraft, Manfred, 401
Krantz, Les, 528
Krattenmaker, Tom, 53
Kraus, Eric, 521
Kraus, Matthas, 377
Krause, Aaron, 253
Krauss, Michael, 54
Krishna, Aradhna, 188, 208, 377
Krishnan, R., 376
Kroc, Ray, 366
Krogstad, Jens Manuel, 70
Krugel, David, 458
Kruikemeier, Sanne, 426
Kruschwwitz, Nina, 209
Krush, Michael T., 54
Kumar, Ashish, 485
Kumar, V., 485
Kumar, Vipin, 24, 208, 209
Kuster, Franziska, 425
Kydd, Arthur R., 56, 70

L

Lackner, Joseph, 24
Laczniak, Gene R., 96
Ladas, Kostas, 53
Lahiri, Rangin, 209
Lakhani, Dave, 126
Lakhani, Karim R., 264
Lal, Rajiv, 375
Lancaster, Jason, 234
Lane, Vicki R., 456
Langridge, Max, 456
LaReau, Jamie, 426
Larocca, Tracee, 424
Lasher, Megan, 53
Lashinsky, Adam, 53, 264
Latson, Jennifer, 377
LaValle, Steve, 209
Lavidge, Robert J., 426
Lavie, N., 126
Learmonth, Michael, 427
LeBon, Joel, 514
Lee, Julie Anne, 177
Lee, Nick, 514
Lee, Sujean, 22, 25
Lee, Sun Young, 425
Lee, Thomas, 486
Lee, Yih Hwai, 456
Leeflang, Peter S. H., 485
LeFrak, Francine, 95
Leggett, Dave, 97
Lehmann, Donald R., 125, 296
Leiber, Ronald B., 377
Leigh, Thomas W., 147
Leighton, Michael, 144, 145, 146
Lemon, Katherine N., 126
Lemos, Robert, 457
Lencioni, Patrick M., 53
Leo, Pamela, 210
Leone, Robert P., 208, 376
Lesser, Eric, 209
Lesser, Russ, 482–483, 487
Lev-Ram, Michael, 209
Levey, Richard H., 375
Levitt, Theodore, 33, 53, 514
Levy, Michael, 426
Levy, Piet, 377, 425, 528, 529
Levy, Sidney J., 25
Levy-Yurista, Guy, 485
Lewin, Jeffrey E., 147, 514
Lewis, Hilary, 208
Lewis, Ioni, 456
Lewis, John, 401
Lewis, Tanya, 528
Lewis-Kulin, Sarah, 528
Li, Jessica, 527
Liebl, Matt, 426
Lilien, Gary L., 147, 377
Lim, Elison Ai Ching, 456

Lindstrom, Martin, 126, 209
Linshi, Jack, 54
Liodice, Bob, 425
Lirtsman, Alex, 428
Llovio, Louis, 456
Lloyd, Doug, 456
Loch, Christoph, 53
Lock, Tony, 427
Loda, Marsha D., 425
Lodish, Leonard M., 458
Lohr, Steve, 377
Lorimer, Sally E., 514
Lovejoy, Ben, 54.
Low, Elaine, 234, 297, 426
Low, George S., 426
Lowenhar, Jeffrey A., 426
Lublin, Joann S., 528
Lumpkin, James R., 349
Lundy, Sarah, 528
Lunte, Kathryn, 208
Lupis, J. C., 456
Lutz, Richard J., 126
Lynch, James E., 426
Lynch, Jason, 208

M

MacArthur, Kate, 297
MacDuffie, John Paul, 349
MacInnis, Deborah J., 126
Magid, Larry, 54
Mahajan, Vijay, 54
Maheshwari, Sapna, 427
Maifredi, Monica, 95
Maklan, Stan, 126, 515
Malaviya, Prashant, 458
Malcolm, Robert, 53
Malone, Michael S., 401
Malphurs, Audrey, 53
Malto, Sean, 432
Mander, Edmund, 375
Marcoolyn, Gillian, 125
Marken, G. A., 459
Markham, Stephen K., 24
Markides, Costas, 53
Marks, Gene, 457
Marks, Ronald B., 529
Marlin, Brenda, 426
Marshall, Greg W., 514
Marshall, Jack, 486
Martin, Chris, 97
Martin, Dick, 425
Martin, Erik J., 455
Martin, Kelly D., 401
Martineau, Pierre, 364, 376
Martinex, Michael, 426
Martinez-Ribes, Lluis, 208
Maslow, Abraham H., 126
Massante, Lou, 147

Masterson, Peggy, 457
Matsakis, Louise, 486
Matson, Holly, 205
Matthews, Chris, 95
Mattila, Anna S., 264
Mattson-Teig, Beth, 235
Mauborgne, Renée, 53
Maxham, James G., III, 264
May, Eleanor, 377
Maze, Johnathan, 377
McAfee, Andrew, 53
McCarthy, Bill, 426
McCarthy, E. Jerome, 10, 24
McCorkle, Denny E., 528
McCorvey, J., 24
McCracken, Harry, 208
McCrea, Bridget, 375
McDonald brothers, 423–424
McDonald, Duff, 234
McFarland, Richard D., 514
McGrath, Maggie, 235
McGregor, Jena, 234
McGuire, Kara, 458
McKeever, Mike, 70
McMath, Robert M., 8, 24, 264
McNair, Malcolm P., 377
McPherson, Bill, 95
Meindl, Peter, 349
Meister, Martin, 208
Meistrell, Bill, 482, 483, 485, 487
Meistrell, Bob, 482
Meistrell, Jenna, 483, 487
Meistrell, Nick, 483, 484, 487
Mendelsohn, Bruce, 209
Meyer, Christopher, 25
Michaels, Daniel, 265
Michiels, Ian, 235
Mick, David Glen, 24
Milk, Chris, 430
Miller, Jennifer, 379
Miller, Stephanie, 262, 263, 265
Milliot, Jim, 53
Mims, Christopher, 487
Miniard, Paul W., 125
Minogue, Kylie, 280
Minor, Michael S., 377
Minsker, Maria, 455
Mirchell, Dan, 235
Mishra, Sita, 425
Misra, Kanishka, 377
Mitchell, Dan, 349
Mitchell, John T., 528
Mitral, Banwari, 126, 297
Mittal, Vikal, 54
Moe, Wendy W., 457
Mohammed, Rafi A., 401
Mohr, Jakki J., 147, 426
Moin, David, 458
Momen, Rommel, 92, 93, 94, 95, 97
Money, R. Bruce, 177, 514

Monfils, Gaël, 234
Monllos, Kristina, 96, 456
Monroe, Kent B., 323, 376
Montanez, Richard, 251
Moon, Youngme, 147
Moore, Elizabeth S., 25, 126
Moorman, Christine, 53
Moorthy, Janakiraman, 209
Moran, Charlotte, 76
Morimoto, Mariko, 427
Morin, Rich, 126
Morris, Chris, 265
Morris, David Z., 23
Morrison, Maureen, 235, 265, 427
Mothersbaugh, David L., 125, 126
Mueller, Samuel, 375
Mulhern, Francis J., 376
Mullins, John W., 235, 296
Muralie, Sushma, 425
Murphy, Christopher, 514
Murphy, Patrick E., 24, 96, 401
Murphy, Richard, 53
Murtha, Brian R., 514
Musk, Elon, 5
Mussard, Helen, 428

N

Nadarajah, Murlai, 377
Nagarajan, Hina, 175, 176
Nanath, Krishnadas, 209
Narius, James A, 25
Narver, John C., 24
Natanson, Elad, 54
Nath, Prithwiraz, 147
Naughton, Keith, 234
Nedungadi, Prakesh, 125
Needleman, Sarah E., 25
Neff, Jack, 209, 264, 376
Neijens, Peter C., 458
Nelson, Katherine A., 96
Nesdale, Andrew, 125
Neslin, Scott, 401
Neslin, Scott A., 376, 425
Netermeyer, Richard G., 264
Neufeld, Evan, 427
Newman, Russell, 485
Newstead, Kate, 457
Niccol, Brian, 397, 400, 401
Nijssen, Edwin J., 24
Nohr, Marc, 427
Norris, Chuck, 438
Norris, Donald, 455
Norton, James, 264
Norton, Rob, 458
Nowlin, Edward L., 54
Nunziata, Tracy, 123, 124, 127

O

O'Brien, Jeffrey M., 234
O'Brien, Kyle, 21, 22, 25
O'Connor, Clare, 375, 486
O'Malley, Kathy L., 456
O'Reilly, Lara, 427
Obias, Rudie, 208
Odell, Patricia, 95, 96, 235, 425, 456, 457, 458
Ofir, Chezy, 456
Ohnsman, Alan, 53, 96
OK Go, 470
Olenski, Steve, 126
Olsen, Jerry C., 323
Orszag, Peter R., 456
Ortineau, David J., 209
Ortman, Jennifer M., 95
Ortmeyer, Gwen, 376
Owens, Jan P., 234

P

Paddison, Gordon J., 401
Page, Larry, 453
Palenchar, Joseph, 54.
Palmatier, Robert W., 24, 55, 349
Palmer, Alex, 427
Palmisano, Samuel J., 341
Pancras, Joseph, 376
Paradixo, Chris, 234
Parasuraman, A., 376
Pardee, Grant, 486
Pardee, Thomas, 426
Parekh, Rupal, 401, 456
Park, Chang Hee, 375
Park, Schoon, 457
Parks, Seth, 24
Parvatiyar, Atul, 177
Passariello, Christina, 349
Patniak, Sandeep, 456
Patti, Charles H., 426
Pauwels, Koen, 53, 96, 376
Pechman, Cornelia, 426, 456
Peeler, Kelly, 29
Pelton, Lou, 349
Peppers, Don, 515
Percival, Dan, 234
Perdue, Stephanie, 423
Perez, Lisa, 123, 124, 125, 127
Perin, Marcelo Gattermann, 458
Peters, Bill, 209, 377
Peters, Kevin, 377
Peters, Leah E., 58, 59, 70
Peters, Randall F., 58, 59, 70
Peterson, Haley, 235
Peterson, Maddie, 432
Peterson, Robert A., 24, 53, 54., 235, 323, 376, 514
Peterson, Shawn, 297
Peterson, Tim, 427
Petrova, Elina, 426
PewDiePie, 471
Pfeifer, Phillip E., 54, 377, 527
Pham, Kimberley, 487
Piacentini, Diego, 148
Pierce, David, 487
Pieters, Rik, 126, 425, 458
Poelson, Rob, 424
Poetsch, Rob, 402
Poggi, Jeanine, 208, 455
Pohl, Mike, 373
Poinski, Megan, 24
Pollak, Lindsey, 529
Pontefract, Dan, 234
Pooley, Eric, 96
Poon, Derek T. Y., 458
Popky, Linda J., 528
Porras, Jerry I., 53
Porter, Michael E., 24, 53
Powers, Kemp, 323
Powers, Thomas L., 514
Prasad, Ashutosh, 125
Prendergast, Gerald P., 425, 458
Pressman, Aaron, 457
Proctor, Bernadette D., 96
Pthak, Shareen, 456
Pullen, John Patrick, 234
Purnawirawan, Nathalia, 458
Purvis, Scott C., 456
Putrevu, Sanjay, 456

Q

Qin, Zheng, 147
Quelch, John A., 376, 458
Quirk, Mary Beth, 457

R

Rachamim, Matti, 456
Radak, Dan, 53
Radelat, Ana, 96
Raman, Ananth, 377
Raman, Kaylan, 426
Ranaswamy, Arvind, 401
Ranjan, Jayanthi, 209
Rao, Vithala R., 297
Rapp, Adam, 514
Raskin, Oliver, 528
Rassekh, Farhad, 97
Ratchford, Brian T., 125, 376
Rath, Tom, 521
Rawson, Alex, 25
Rayport, Jeffrey F., 401
Rea-Holloway, Melinda, 208
Rees, G., 126
Refermat, Emily, 375
Reibling, Ellen Thomas, 426, 456
Reibstein, David J., 54, 377, 527
Reid, Mike, 426
Reinartz, Werner J., 24, 514
Reingold, Jennifer, 234
Reisinger, Don, 54
Rendon, Jim, 25
Renslow, Jill, 372, 373, 374
Rich Gregory A., 514
Rich, Gillian, 96
Rich, Motoko, 234
Richards, Katie, 96
Ridley, Daisy, 416
Rigby, Darrell K., 54
Rishika, Rishika, 485
Ritson, Mark, 297
Robehmed, Natalie, 208
Robertson, Adi, 96
Robertson, Andy, 486
Robertson, David, 296
Robinson, David, 425
Robinson, Joel, 209
Robinson, Richard, 24
Rode, Joseph C., 514
Roderick, Leonie, 235
Rodriguez, Ahley, 456
Rogers, Charlotte, 529
Rogers, Everett M., 297
Rogers, Martha, 515
Roggeveen, Anne, 528
Romaniuk, Jenni, 425, 457
Romano, Danielle, 297
Rometty, Ginni, 55
Rometty, Virginia, 51
Ronkainen, Ilkka A., 177
Rose, Charlie, 264
Rose, Susan, 375
Rosecky, Richard B., 458
Rosen, Dennis L., 455
Rosen, Judith, 376
Ross, Ashley, 456
Rossi, Juhanna, 486
Rossiter, John R., 125
Rovell, Darren, 296
Rozentale, L., 264
Rubin, Ann, 50, 51, 52, 55
Ruddock, Graham, 426
Rudd, Sohn, 514
Rudelius, William, 25, 70, 234, 235
Ruffalo, Mark, 178
Rukstad, Michael G., 24
Rusli, Evelyn M., 486
Russo, Francine, 529
Rust, Roland T., 264, 485
Rylander, Don, 209

S

Sachs, Denielle, 53
Sager, Jeffrey K., 514
Salmon, Walter J., 376, 458
Samalonis, Lisa, 127
Samli, A. Coskun, 177
Samouel, Phillip, 375
Sampaio, Claudio Hoffmann, 458
Samuelson, Kate, 209
Sanburn, Josh, 235
Sandberg, Sheryl, 466, 527
Sanford, Glen, 235
Santini, Fernando de Oliveira, 458
Sanyal, Dipyaman, 209
Saporito, Bill, 235, 377
Saran, Cliff, 96
Sarel, Dan, 456
Sarvary, Miklos, 457
Sauer, Abe, 458
Savitz, Andrew W., 97
Sawh, Michael, 96
Sayce, David, 486
Scelzo, Samantha, 427
Schaeffer, Jessica, 529
Schamm, Wilbur, 425
Schatz, Robin D., 297
Schechner, Sam, 96
Scheuing, Kristen, 323
Schindler, Robert M., 323
Schmidt, Sarah, 374
Schmitt, Genevieve, 278
Schneider, Joan, 264
Scholes, Kevan, 53
Schultz, Clark, 24
Schultz, Don E., 425, 426, 427
Schultz, E. J., 456
Schumann, David W., 456
Schumann, Jan H., 457
Schwager, Andre, 25
Schweidel, David A., 457
Scott, Mary E., 529
Sebastian, Michael, 485
Sedivy, Julie, 126
Seetharaman, Depa, 486
Segal, Madhav N., 528
Segelin, Amy, 486
Seilhamer, Ryan, 426
Seligman, Daniel, 426
Selk, Lisa, 295, 296, 297
Selwitz, Robert, 456
Semega, Jessica L., 96
Serrano, Stephan, 375
Setiawan, Iwan, 25, 426
Setyan, Nick, 235
Sharapova, Maria, 234
Sharma, Arun, 514
Sharma, Subhash, 177
Sharp, Arthur G., 529

Shasteen, Rhonda, 175, 176
Shayon, Sheila, 486
Shea, Carol, 528
Sheatsley, P., 425
Shedlock, Michael, 375
Sheeran, Ed, 470
Sheng, Shibin, 514
Shenkan, Amy Guggenheim, 54
Sheperd, John, 235
Sherer, Lori, 147
Sherry, John F., Jr., 24, 25
Shervani, Tasadduq A., 25
Sheth, Jagdish N., 24, 126, 177, 297
Shewan, Dan, 485
Shimp, Terence A., 177
Shirvani, Tassadduq A., 514
Shocker, Allan D., 125
Shockley, Rebecca, 209
Shoup, Mary Ellen, 24
Shridhar, Shrihari, 55
Shroer, James A., 426
Shulman, Lawrence E., 54
Siegel, Alan, 456
Simchi-Levi, David, 349
Simchi-Levi, Edith, 349
Simester, Duncan, 376
Simsek, Yagmur, 55
Singal, Nidhi, 96
Singer, Mark, 54
Sinha, Prabhakant, 514
Skally, Nick, 232, 233, 235
Slater, Kelly, 263
Slater, Stanley F., 25
Slefo, George, 455
Sloane, Garett, 486
Smith, A. B., 377
Smith, Jaden, 77
Smith, Katie, 456
Smith, Kit, 485
Smith, Lindsey, 488, 489, 514
Smith, Shane, 54
Smith, Steve, 457
Snook, Scott, 53
Solheim, Jostein, 28
Solomon, Brian, 53
Sonne, Ann Paul, 234
Spangenberg, Eric R., 376
Spangler, Todd, 426, 486
Sparks, Daniel, 54
Speh, Thomas W., 147
Spencer, Jane, 25, 126
Spielberg, Steven, 447–448
Spiro, Rosann L., 514
Sportelli, Natalie, 53
Spotts, Harlan E., 456
Sprott, David E., 376
Srinivasan, Kannan, 426
Srivastava, Rajendra K., 25
Staelin, Richard, 24
Stafford, Edwin R., 96, 375

Stair, Leslie, 518
Stair, Lila B., 518
Stalk, George, 54
Stambor, Zak, 456
Stanganelli, Joe, 485
Stank, Theodore, 349
Stanley, T. L., 457
Stanton, John L., 426
Stanton, William J., 514
Stayman, Douglas M., 458
Steel, Emily, 23
Steenburgh, Thomas, 514
Steenkamp, Jans-Benedict, 377
Steimer, Sarah, 528, 529
Stein, Joel, 197
Stein, Lindsay, 427
Steiner, Gary A., 426
Stern, Louis W., 349
Sterns, Scott, 514
Stevenson, Robert Louis, 490
Stewart, David, 456
Stewart, Joan, 425
Sthanunathan, Stan, 520
Stiving, Mark, 323
Stock, Ruth Maria, 24
Stockdale, Lydia, 529
Stone, Brad, 349
Stone, Emma, 450
Stone, John, 234
Strauss, Judy, 401
Stroebe, W., 126
Strom, Andrea, 243
Strom, Brian, 243
Strunk, William, Jr., 70
Strutton, David, 349
Sugg, Zoe "Zoella," 471
Summer, Anita F., 264
Sunstein, Cass, 264
Suri, Rajneesh, 376, 485
Suter, Tracy A., 209, 265
Swaminathan, Srinivasan, 457
Swearingen, Joanie, 95, 97
Sweet, Elizabeth, 96
Swift, Taylor, 372
Swire, Donald, 54
Szymanski, D., 177

T

Talukdar, Debabrata, 376
Tamny, John, 24
Tan, Chong Leng, 456
Tanner, John F., Jr., 456, 514
Tay, Richard, 456
Taylor, Charles R., 457
Taylor, Kate, 458
Taylor, Victoria, 401
Teal, Derrick, 375
Teinowitz, Ira, 375

Teixeira, Thales, 457
Tennant, John, 376
Terlep, Sharon, 376
Terpstra, Vern, 97
Thakor, Mrugank V., 376
Thalberg, Marisa, 402, 425
Theron, Charlize, 178
Thomas, Dave, 190, 221
Thompson, Debora Viana, 264, 458
Tietje, Brian, 24
Till, Brian D., 457
Tilley, Aaron, 95
Timiraos, Nick, 96
Toker-Yildiz, Kamer, 486
Tomkovick, Chuck, 456
Torpey, Elka, 208
Townsend, Matt, 427
Toyoda, Akio, 92
Toyoda, Kiichiro, 92
Trachtenberg, Jeffrey A., 53, 234
Traczyk, Patty, 456
Trainor, Kevin J., 54
Treacy, Michael, 24
Trevino, Linda K., 96
Trin, Courtney, 487
Trivedi, Minakshi, 486
Trudel, Remi, 97
Trudell, Craig, 97
Tsang, Alex S. L., 458
Tufte, Edward R., 54
Tuli, Kapil R., 514
Turnbull, S., 426
Twain, Mark, 195

U

Ulaga, Wolfgang, 514
Ulukaya, Hamdi, 2, 3, 4, 20, 21, 22
Urbany, Joel E., 125
Useem, Jerry, 377
Usunier, Jean Claude, 177
Utley, Tori, 53

V

Vallaeys, Frederick, 454
Van Brussel, Joe, 53
Van Dam, Andrea, 95
Van den Bulte, Christophe, 24
Van den Driest, Frank, 485
Van Dessel, M. M., 426
Van Heck, Eric, 147
Van Hyning, Chuck, 70
Van Reijmersdal, Eva A., 458
Van Rossum, Wouter, 24
Van Wagenheim, Florian, 457
Van Waterschool, Walter, 24
VanArsdale, Louis R., 527

Vandermark, Rob, 378
Vanhuele, Marc, 376
Varadarajan, P. Rajan, 54., 97
Varadarajan, R., 177
Vascellaro, Jessica E., 459
Veblen, T. B., 96
Vekatesh, R., 147
Velasco, Schuyler, 458
Vence, Deborah L., 528
Verhoef, Peter C., 126, 376, 401
Veverka, Mark, 349
Vieira, Valter Alfonso, 458
Viglielmo, Pamela, 177
Vilcassim, Naufel J., 377
Violino, Bob, 375
Vitner, Mark, 96
Viveiros, Beth Negus, 427
Voleti, Sudhir, 377
Vonn, Lindsay, 263
Voss, Glenn B., 376
Vriens, Marco, 96

W

Wagner, Kurt, 486
Wahba, Phil, 25, 375, 376, 377
Wai-Art Law, Stella, 25
Walker, Kristen L., 234
Walker, Orville C., Jr., 235, 296
Walsh, Kerri, 432
Walsh, Patrick B., 528
Walt, Vivienne, 176
Walters, Robert John, 485
Wanamaker, John, 442
Wang, Sissi, 376
Wang, William, 298
Wang, Ye, 458
Wang, Yong Jian, 377
Ward, James C, 376
Warren, Kevin, 513
Wasserman, Helena, 95
Watson, Barry, 456
Watson, George F., IV, 24
Waxer, Cindy, 427
Webb, Tom, 377
Weber, Karl, 97
Webster, Frederick E., Jr., 147
Webster, John, 426
Wedel, Michel, 53, 377, 425, 458, 485
Weed, Keith, 457, 485
Weeks, Matt, 70, 96
Wei, Jie, 377
Weigold, Michael F., 458
Weinberger, Matt, 54
Weiner, Jonah, 486
Weinstein, Art, 54
Weisal, Kimberly, 234
Weisbaum, Herb, 457
Weise, Elizabeth, 96

Weiss, Allen, 96
Weiss, Todd R., 458
Weitz, Barton, 25, 147
Welch, David, 96
Welch, Jack, 528
Welch, Suzy, 528
Wensley, Robin, 25
Wernle, Bradford, 426
West, Susan, 456
Wheatman, Debra, 528, 529
Wheeler, C., 426
White, Amy, 426
White, E. B., 70
White, Katherine M., 456
White, Michael, 177
White, William, 235
Wiener, Joshua L., 458
Wiersema, Fred D., 24
Wiles, Michael A., 375
Wilkenfeld, Justin, 261, 262, 263, 265
Wilkerson, Carter, 468
Wilkie, William L., 25, 125, 126, 456
Williams, Robin M., Jr., 96
Wills, Gary Brian, 485
Wilson, James Q., 97
Wilson, Rick T., 457
Wind, Jerry, 401
Wind, Yoram, 54, 147
Windorski, David, 13, 14, 25
Winer, Russell S., 296, 323
Winkler, Rolfe, 486
Winslow, George, 208
Winters, Lewis C., 456
Wittington, Richard, 53
Woelbing, Alfred, 193, 321
Woelbing, Don, 321
Woelbing, Eric, 321
Woelbing, Paul, 321, 322
Wohl, Jessica, 425
Wolfinbarger, Mary, 209
Wolfman, Ian, 40
Wolske, Jon, 234
Wong, Anthony, 147
Wong, Vanessa, 427
Woodman, Nick, 261, 262
Woodside, Arch G., 457
Worm, Stefan, 514
Worstall, Tim, 349
Wouters, Marijke, 458
Wozniak, Steve, 226
Wyner, Gordon, 24, 209, 234, 528

Y

Yate, Martin, 527
Yi-Zheng, Shi, 425
Ylkur, Rama, 456
Yoo, Teresa, 51, 52, 55

Yoon, Hye Jin, 425
Yuan, Sheng, 426

Z

Zacharias, Nicolas A., 24
Zakarin, Jordan, 375
Zaltman, Gerald, 147
Zamiska, Nicholas, 235
Zarett, E. Jay, 456
Zeithaml, Valerie A., 125, 264, 297, 323
Zhang, Johathan Z., 24
Zhang, Yong, 456
Zhao, Guangzhi, 456
Zhen, Jane, 376
Zidansek, Manja, 376
Zimmer, Mary R., 376
Zinkham, George M., 456
Ziobro, Paul, 375
Zmuda, Natalie, 234
Zoltners, Andris, 514
Zubcsek, Peter Pal, 457
Zuckerberg, Mark, 72, 73, 95, 466, 467

COMPANY/PRODUCT INDEX

A

AA Direct Connect, 337
Abbott Laboratories, 141
Abercrombie and Fitch, 116, 434
Aberdeen Group, 218
Ace Hardware, 333
ACES Flight Simulation, 373
ACH Food Companies, Inc., 119
Acxiom Corporation, 479
Adidas, 157, 158, 279, 357
Aeon, 353
AFLAC duck, 434, 467
AG, 434
Airbnb, 402, 438–439
Airbus, 156, 314
Alibaba, 331
Allbookstores.com, 360
Allergy Tracker, 417
Alphabet, Inc., 255, 453
Amazon, 18, 58, 80, 81, 196, 197, 285, 294, 303, 326, 330, 337, 360, 364, 380, 382, 390, 414, 433, 517
    business model, 347–348
    continuous improvement, 348–349
    logistics management, 348
    product line, 347
    supply chain management, 348
Amazon Alexa, 79, 439
Amazon Business, 140
Amazon Echo, 10, 11
Amazon India
    failure not an option, 149–150
    opportunities, 148–149
Amazon Kindle, 33, 39, 303
Amazon Prime, 363
Amazon's Smart Home Services, 246
Ambassador cards, 331
American Airlines, 37, 241, 284, 337
American Enterprise Institute, 141
American Express cards, 284
American Express Centurion Card, 108
American Express Company, 89, 289
American Forces Network, 438
American Girl, 373
American Hospital Supply, 338
American Red Cross, 32, 34, 241, 450
Amway, 361
Anacin, 283
Android, 253
Android Pay, 351
Angry Birds, 478
Anheuser-Busch, 120, 433
Annie's yogurt, 4

ANN INC.'S LOFT, 215
ANN LOFT Outlet stores, 216
Ann Taylor chain, 215–216, 368
Ann Taylor Factory outlets, 216
Anomaly, 434, 435
Anytime Fitness, 35
Apple, Inc., 4, 18, 33, 37–38, 39, 46, 56, 118, 135, 157, 158, 169, 215, 239, 244, 246, 252, 280, 282, 304, 315, 332
    consumer journey map, 106
    exploiting/correcting deviations, 47
    new-product failures, 237–238
    new-product successes, 236
    segmentation strategy, 227
Apple AirPods, 39, 47, 236, 252
Apple-Enabled Car, 238
Apple HomePod, 39
Apple II, 236
Apple III, 237
Apple Industrial Design Group, 252
Apple Lisa, 239
Apple Macintosh, 226
Apple Newton, 237
Apple Pay, 79, 80, 351
Apple's App Sore, 477
Apple's Siri, 439
Apple Stores, 365, 373
Apple TV, 438
Apple Watch, 38, 39, 47, 236, 238, 252, 351
Arctic Cat, 135
Arm & Hammer, 284
Arrow shirts, 307
Associated Grocers, 35, 333
Aston Martin, 214
AT&T, 81, 102, 133, 161, 168, 285, 304, 414, 441, 499, 517
Audi, 88
Aurora Foods, 282
Autobytel.com, 330
Avert Virucidal, 247
Aviator glasses, 448
Avis, 228, 333
Avon, 361, 491

B

Baked Lay's potato chips, 273
Banana Boat, 123
Banana Republic, 215, 373, 419
Barbie dolls, 165, 166, 434
Barnes & Noble, 33, 89, 357, 364, 385

barnesandnoble.com, 360
Bausch and Lomb, 448
Bayer, 431
Beats, 434
Bebo, 232
Bed, Bath and Beyond, 447
Bell's Burgers, 423
Ben & Jerry's, 31, 32, 34, 37, 40, 446, 447
    marketing metrics, 36
    mission, 26–28
    SWOT analysis, 42–43
    and Unilever, 28
Benetton, 368
Ben Franklin stores, 333
Best Buy, 58, 141, 240, 246, 270, 298, 335, 357, 365, 447
Betty Crocker, 200, 284, 285
Bic, 282, 283
BJ's Wholesale, 298
Blistex, 321, 322
Bloomberg, 186
Bloomingdale's, 338, 363
Blue Nile, 380
BMW, 12, 139, 262, 360, 461, 506
BMX bikes, 144
Body Glove
    brand, 482–483
    marketing, 483
    social media use, 483–484
Body Glove Airstream Earbuds, 485
Body Glove shoes, 485
Boeing Company, 37, 81, 133, 140, 151, 156, 167, 201, 314
Boeing jetliners, 133
Boeing 787 Dreamliner, 257
Bold detergent, 283, 517
Bolin Digital, 205
Bolin Marketing, 205, 206, 322
Bonobos, 380
Bontrager, 145
Bose, 388
Boston Market, 367
Boucheron, 334
Boys and Girls Clubs of America, 89, 475
Brainstorm Bakery, 243
Brawny paper towels, 279
Brita Hard-Sided Bottle, 28
British Airways, 102
Broadview Security, 240
Bronco, 283
Brooks Brother Clothiers, 108
Budweiser Light, 111
Bufferin, 283

549

Bugatti Chiron Sport, 300–301, 315
Buick, 103, 506
Bumble, 467
Burger Chef, 368
Burger King, 218, 219, 225, 226, 228, 390
   French fries problem, 257–58
Burlington, 362
Burt's Bees, 322
Business Talk Radio, 438
BzzAgent, 115

C

Cadbury Schweppes, 282
Cadillac, 103, 337, 340, 506
Calvin Klein, 77
Camay soap, 285
Campbell Soup Company, 141, 188, 217, 278, 284, 286, 343
Campbell's V8, 105
Candy Crush Saga, 478
Capital One, 517
Caplow Company, 306
   revenue estimation, 311–313
CareerBuilder, 390, 391, 522
Caress soap, 283
Carma Laboratories, 193, 321, 322
CarMax, 317, 352, 353
Carmex, 193, 471
   Facebook for marketing research, 205–207
   half-court hero contest, 475–476
   marketing metrics, 194
   price setting, 321–323
Carmex Healing Cream, 321
Carmex Hydrating Lotion, 321
Carmex Kiss, 194
Carmex-LeBronJames.com, 471
Carmex Moisture Plus, 205, 206, 322
Carnival, 417
CarPlay, 236
Carrefour, 353
Cartier, 280, 304
Casper Sleep, 380
Catalyst Paper Corporation, 128
Caterpillar, 135, 157, 328–330, 344
Cause Marketing Forum, 89
CC Cream, 156
Celestial Seasonings, 326
Century 21, 326
Cereal Partners Worldwide, 332
CGCT, 168
Chanel, 158, 172, 304, 335
Chaps brands, 282
ChapStick, 194, 321, 322
Charlesburg Furniture, 336
Checkers Drive-in Restaurants, 367

Cheer, 517
Cheerios, 193, 289
Cheese Nips, 287
Cheetos, 168
Chevrolet, 103, 340
Chevrolet Bolt, 252–253, 271, 282
Chevron, 327, 431, 463
Chicago Symphony Orchestra, 290
Chicken of the Sea, 287
Chipotle Mexican Grill, 225
Chips Ahoy!, 288
Chobani Flip, 3
Chobani Food Incubator, 4
Chobani Greek Yogurt, 9
   customer value, 2–4
   innovation, 22–23
   marketing by, 20–23
   place strategy, 22
   price strategy, 21
   product development, 21
   product strategy, 21
   promotion, 22
Chobani Kitchen, 22
Chobani Savor, 3
Chobani SoHo, 23
CHOmobile, 3
Christian Dior, 307
Christie's, 158
Church & Dwight, 284
Cinnabon Delights, 402
Cirrus system, 290
Cisco Systems, 151
Citibank, 284, 446
Citigroup, 463
Citizen watches, 114
CK2, 77
Clairol, 110
Clash of Clans, 478
Cling-Free, 282
Clinique, 395
Clorox, 283
CNBC, 186
Coca-Cola, 7, 83, 247
Coca-Cola Company, 35, 89, 102, 156, 157, 158, 161, 162, 163, 166, 169, 272, 280, 287, 288, 327, 334, 389, 431, 433, 520
   cola wars, 86
Coca-Cola Life, 8
Coca-Cola Stevia No Sugar, 8
Coke, 362
Colgate-Palmolive Company, 77, 109, 112, 154
Colgate's Kitchen Entrees, 246
Colgate toothpaste, 154
Colgate Total Advanced Gum Defense toothpaste, 245
Colgate Visible White, 111
Comcast, 414, 517
Community Finder, 73

comScore, 400, 440
ConAgra Foods, 285
Converse, 357
Cool Mint Chocolate Clif Bar, 9
Coors, 133
Coppertone
   future of, 124–125
   marketing, 124
   purchase decision process, 123–124
   sun care industry, 123
Coppertone CLEARLYSheer, 124
Coppertone CLEARLYSheer AfterSun, 124
Coppertone SPORT, 124
Coppertone Suntan Cream, 123
Corning, Inc., 130
Corona Extra, 115
Costco, 124, 141, 285, 294, 298, 335, 353, 356, 363
Cost Cutters Family Hair Care, 290
coupon.com, 445
Coupon Information Corporation, 445
Courtyard hotels, 285
CoverGirl, 120, 158
Craftsman radial saw, 304
Craigslist, 440, 523
Crapola Granola, 243
Crate & Barrel, 58
Cray Inc., 243
Crest Neat Squeeze toothpaste, 252
Crest toothpaste, 243, 337
Cruise AV, 255, 256
Cunard, 78
CVS, 124

D

Daihatsu, 92
Daimler AG, 151
Dannon, 2, 4, 22
Danone, 115
Data and Marketing Association, 58, 360, 409, 419–420
DeBeers, 158
Deere & Company, 134
Dell.com, 330
Dell Technologies, 58, 81, 141, 252, 284, 317, 330, 382, 388, 493
   supply chain, 341
Del Monte, 286
Delta Air Lines, 304, 417
Destiny USA, 354
DeWalt, 285, 286
Dex YP, 439
DHL Worldwide Express, 241, 499
Dial soap, 286, 431
Diamant, 145
Dick's Sporting Goods, 352, 353, 357
DieHard, 283

Diesel, 77
Digital Advertising Alliance, 420
Digital HERO, 261
Dillard's, 357
Direct Selling Association, 361
DIRECTV, 304
Dish Network, 497
Disney; see Walt Disney Company
Dive N' Surf, 482
DKNY, 343
Dollar General, 216
Dollar Value Stores, 317
Domino's Pizza, 6–7, 35, 289, 309
Domio's fruit-flavored bubble gum, 282
Don Limpio, 157
Don Miguel, 64
Donna Karan, 343
Doritos, 103, 168, 279, 285, 493
Doritos Locos, 446
DoubleClick, 455
Dove hair care products, 115
Downy fabric softener, 243
Dream Bikes, 145
Drink Chobani, 3
Dr Pepper, 247, 280
Dunkin' Donuts, 415
DuPont, 151, 495
Duracell, 280, 283, 430, 431
Duracell Ultra brand AA alkaline batteries, 305

E

Eagle, 283
Earth's Oceans Foundation, 485
Eastman Chemical Company, 507
Easy Off, 282
ebay.com, 360
eBay Inc., 5, 58, 81, 140, 197
   business-to-business marketing, 141
Eddie Bauer, 37, 331
   mulichannel marketing strategy, 324–325
   supply chain, 325
eHarmony, 108
Ektelon, 232
Electrolux, 361
Elegant Medleys, 246
Encyclopaedia Britannica, 251
Energizer, 304, 305
Energizer Advanced Formula, 305
Energizer bunny, 434
Energizer e^2 AA alkaline batteries, 305
Epson, 271
Ericsson, 168
Ernst and Young, 294
ESPN, 476
Estée Lauder Companies, 193, 395
Esurance, 330

Etch-A-Sketch, 448
Ethan Allen, 331
E*TRADE, 251, 330, 380
Eveready, 283
Evine, 359
Excedrin, 283
Excel, 276
Expedia, 337
Exxon, 103, 170, 283

F

Facebook, 2, 4, 15, 31, 35, 52, 113, 115, 124, 158, 180, 192, 193, 194, 232, 233, 263, 360, 389, 390, 392, 399, 403, 408, 411, 417, 418, 419, 424, 432, 460, 462, 464, 465–467, 469, 471, 472, 474, 475, 476, 477, 479, 519, 523, 524
   and Body Glove, 483
   company history, 72
   compared to other social media, 466
   environmental forces influencing, 72–73
   for marketing research, 205–207
Facebook Messenger, 460
Fage, 4
Family Dollar Stores, 317
Family Life Network, 438
Fancy Feast, 246
Farmville, 478
Fatburger, 368
FedEx, 169, 241, 327, 344, 441, 495
Fiat Chrysler, 256
Fingos, 247
Firebird, 283
Fisher-Price, 262
Fitbit, 39, 253
Five Guys Burgers and Fries, 225
Flamin' Hot Cheetos, 251
Flipkart, 149
Flonase, 417
Flora Pop, 402
Florida Orange Growers Association, 278
Florsheim, 357
FlowRider, 485
Folgers, 287
Ford Focus, 285
Ford Fusion, 285
Ford Motor Company, 4, 155, 214, 283, 285, 340, 412, 448
   divestments by, 215
Ford Taurus, 285
Forrester Research, 80
4Pics1Word, 478
Four Seasons Hotel, Beverly Hills, 359
Four Seasons Hotels, 419
Foursquare, 22
Fox Business, 186

Fran Wilson Creative Cosmetics, 167
Fresh Express, 252
Fresh Foam Zante, 201
Fresh Step cat litter, 109
Frigidaire, 357
Frito-Lay, 163, 168, 169, 193, 251, 273, 279, 285, 504
Fritos, 103
Fruit Ninja, 478
Fuller Brush, 361

G

Gain, 517
Games by James, 373
Gander Mountain, 368
gap.com, 360
Gap Factory Store, 363
Gap Inc., 215, 368
Garlic Cake, 248
Garmin, 39, 520
Gary Fisher, 145
Gatorade, 281, 282, 390
   brand management, 266–268
Gatorade Flow, 268
Gatorade Performance Series, 266–267
Gatorade Thirst Quencher, 267
Geek Squad, 246
GE Healthcare, 499
GE Healthcare Americas, 488, 489
Geico, 434, 441
General Electric, 12, 15, 102, 140, 331, 357, 491
General Electric Medical Systems, 141
General Mills, 4, 89, 168, 189, 193, 247, 253, 256, 276
   alliance with Nestlé, 331–332
General Motors, 103, 168, 239, 252–253, 256, 271, 307, 337, 340, 380, 414, 460
Georgia-Pacific, 279
Gerber, 284, 315
Ghostbusters Ectomobile, 8
Ghostery, 197
Gillette body line of razors, 278
Gillette Company, 157, 165, 169, 170, 171, 268, 278, 282, 499, 521
Gillette Fusion, 268, 270, 273, 304
Gillette Fusion ProGlide, 271
Gillette Guard razors, 188
Gillette razors, 243, 280
Gino's Hamburgers, 368
Glassdoor, 525
Glass Enterprise Edition, 254
Glass Plus, 282
GlaxoSmithKline, 417
Glidden, 282
Global Healthcare Exchange, 141
GMC automobile, 103

551

GNB Technologies, Inc., 344
Go-Gurt Fizzix, 253
Golden Beauty sun care, 170
Golden State Warriors, 446
Goodyear Tire Company, 133, 278, 332, 337
Google, Inc., 72, 81, 105, 185, 186, 197, 246, 380, 386, 395, 417, 419, 428, 470, 477
   online advertising, 453–455
Google Glass, 8, 254
Google Play, 477–478
Google's Bigtable, 195
Google's driverless car, 255
Google Search, 479
GoPro
   marketing, 262–263
   new-product development, 261–262
Goya Foods, 119
Grab, 95
Grease Monkey, 291
Great Atlantic & Pacific Tea Company, 82
Green Tea Listerine, 170
Grey Poupon, 188
Group Danone, 168
Groupon, 360, 445
Grupo Bimbo, 155
G Series Endurance, 268
G Series Gatorade, 268
GT Advanced Technology, 135
Gucci, 108, 334, 335
Guess, 434
Gulfstream Aerospace Corporation, 133
Gunderson & Rosario, Inc., 248

H

H. J. Heinz Company, 314
Häagen-Dazs, 279
Hallmark, 331
Hamburger Helper, 189
Hampton Inn, 35
H&R Block, 290, 355–356
Hanes Brands, 274, 288
Harley-Davidson, 116, 169, 278, 280, 282, 385, 389
   and Milsco Manufacturing, 135
Harris Corporation, 502
Hartman Electric, 329–330
Hart Schaffner & Marx, 307
Hatchette Book Group, 337
Hawaiian Punch, 276, 277
Head & Shoulders, 76
HealthyYOU Vending, 58
Heinz Ketchup, 287, 314
Helena Rubinstein, 170
Hellmann's, 111
Helmet HERO, 261

Henredon, 282
Herbalife, 361
HERO Session camera, 262
Hershey Company, 284, 307, 448
Hertz, 228
Hewlett-Packard, 165, 271, 272, 276, 307, 389, 463
   recycling program, 344
HGTV, 446
Hibu, 439
Hidden Valley Low-Fat Salad Dressing, 283
Hidden Valley Ranch Take Heart Salad Dressing, 283
Hi5, 232
Hino, 92
Hitachi, 157
Hockey Puck mouse, 237
Holiday Barbie, 165
Holiday Inn, 333
Home Depot, 133, 242, 353, 354, 362, 419, 503
HomePod, 236
Home Shopping Network, 330, 359
Honda, 284
HootSuite, 468
Hormel Bacon, 294
Hormel Chili, 294
Hormel Deli Meats, 294
Hormel Foods Corporation, 294, 295
Hormel Pepperoni, 294
Hospital health care supplies, 140
Hotmail, 390
HTC, 428
HTC U12, 101, 102–103
Huggies, 156, 285
Hulu, 438
Hyatt, 417
Hyperloop, 5

I

IBM, 17, 80, 85, 130, 139, 162, 196, 285, 328, 340, 344, 431, 461, 491, 494, 495
   events sponsored by, 52
   smart strategy, 50–52
IBM Cloud, 51
IBM Global Services, 499, 506
IBM Research, 51
IBM Security, 51
IBM Services, 51
IBM Summit Supercomputer, 134
IBM Watson, 51, 52, 79, 80, 328, 341
Ideale clothes washer, 170
IDEO, 252
IGA; see Independent Grocers Alliance
IKEA, 58, 158, 159, 188
iMac, 47, 226, 239, 252

imc^2 agency, and Pizza Hut, 398–399
Independent Grocers Alliance, 333, 355
InMarket, 350
In-N-Out Burger, 368
Instagram, 22, 114, 115, 124, 158, 180, 263, 385, 402, 424, 432, 464, 465
   and Body Glove, 484
Intel Corporation, 157, 276
Interbrand, 39
Intuit, 433
iPad, 17, 33, 38, 39, 47, 236, 242, 252, 315, 439
iPad Pro, 47
iPad 2, 272
iPhone, 38, 39, 47, 135, 236, 246, 252, 253
iPhone X, 47
iPhone XS, 101, 304
iPod, 38, 39, 236
IRI, 256
   InfoScan, 185
iVillage.com, 389

J

J.D. Power and Associates, 185, 299
Jack in the Box, 368
Jaguar, 214, 360
Jamba Juice, 225
JCPenney, 128–129, 133, 331, 418, 441, 478
JCPMedia Inc., 138
   as organizational buyer, 128–129
Jefferson Smurfit Corporation, 491
Jell-O, 266
Jennie-O, 294
Jet.com, 294
Jiffy Lube, 335
Jimmy John's, 35
Jobfox, 523
John Deere products, 134, 135
Johnson & Johnson, 31, 102, 118, 141, 279
Johnson Controls's Automotive Systems Group, 499
Jose Olé, 64
Joy perfume, 283
JPMorgan, 517
Jumperoo, 262
Justin's, product management, 293–296
JW Marriott hotel, 373

K

Kanebo, 167
KAYAK, 417
Kellogg, 118, 133, 282
Kellogg's Fiberwise, 283
Kellogg's Heartwise, 283

Kellogg Special K, 193
Keurig Green Mountain, Inc., 247
Keurig Kold, 2247
KFC, 338, 405, 424
Kia Motors, 110
Kia Rio, 318
Kickstarter.com, 56, 253
Kimberly-Clark, 103, 156, 247, 284, 285
King Soopers, 294
Kirby vacuum cleaners, 499
Kit Kat bars, 162
Kleenex, 11, 103, 266, 281, 282, 288
Kmart, 115, 124, 337, 356
Kodak, 251
Kohler, 302
Kohl's, 350
Komatsu, 157
Konica, 503
Kraft American cheese, 279
Kraft Foods, 21, 188, 288, 433, 445
Kraft Miracle Whip, 287
Kraft's Crystal Light Liquid, 432
Kroger, 124, 285, 305, 322, 331, 445
Kubata, 135

L

L.L.Bean, 37, 58, 331
Lalique, 304
Land Rover, 214
Lands' End, 37, 419
Lay's potato chips, 103, 163, 326, 493
Lay's snack chips, 279
LeBron James Family Foundation, 475
L'eggs, 288
LEGO Group, 8, 157, 373, 448
    marketing research, 181–183
    market modification, 277–278
Lender's Bagels, 282
Lenovo, 108
Lenovo Think Pad, 315
Levi's jeans, 326
Levi Strauss & Company, 88, 89, 158, 163
LexisNexis Academic, 186
Lexus, 92, 340, 448
Lexus RX 450h, 255
LG Corporation, 39, 80
LG G7, 101, 102
LG 98-inch 3D OLED HD Smart TV, 315
LG Signature 77-inch TV, 4
Life Is Good T-shirts, 251
LifeLock, 438
Life Savers soda, 248–249
Limited, The, 18, 368
Lincoln, 214, 215, 340

LinkedIn, 52, 197, 462, 463, 465, 468–469, 471, 472, 496, 523, 524, 525
    and Body Glove, 484
    compared to other social media, 466
Liquid Paper, 272
List Ease, 350
Listerine, 169
Listerine Zero, 169
LivingSocial, 360, 445
Liz Claiborne, 89
Local Search Association, 439
Lockheed Martin, 81, 131, 306
Lonely Planet, 408
Long John Silver's stores, 424
L'Oréal, 18, 115, 157, 170, 282
Louis Vuitton, 77, 151, 280, 282
Lowe's, 133, 331, 429
Lucasfilm, 416
Lululemon, 432
Luvs, 279
Luxottica S.p.A., 282, 283
Lyft, 317, 318

M

MacBook Air, 47, 226
MacBook Pro, 47, 226
Macintosh, 236
Macintosh Portable, 237
Mac Mini, 226
Mac Pro, 226
Macy's, Inc., 35, 327, 357, 368, 373, 447, 478
Major League Baseball, 266, 468
Major League Football, 73
Major League Soccer, 266
M&M's, 9, 382, 408, 409, 446
Mansar Products, Ltd., 328, 329
March of Dimes, 290
Marks & Spencer, 381
Marquee Brands, 483
Marriott EDITION hotels and Vacation Clubs, 285
Marriott Hotels, 15, 17, 429, 517
Marriott International, 285
Mars, Inc., 328, 382
Mars Chocolate, 446
Mars Curiosity Rover, 8
Mary Kay Cosmetics, Inc., 156, 361, 506
    in Asia-Pacific markets, 174
    business model, 174
Mary Kay India, 174–176
    brand-building, 175
    building salesforce, 175–176
    supply chain, 176
Mary Kay MelaCEP Whitening System, 175
Mary Kay's Velocity fragrance, 110

MasterCard International, 89, 161
Mastro Lindo, 157
Match.com, 108
Mattel, 89, 157, 165, 166, 434
Maxim Steel, 503
Maybelline, 170
Mayo Clinic, 243
Mazola oil, 119
McDonald's, 35, 109, 120, 157–158, 160, 168, 193, 194, 218, 219, 223, 225, 226, 228, 304, 333, 366, 367, 368, 408, 409, 429, 445, 446, 498
McKesson Corporation, 141, 337
McNeil Consumer Healthcare, 111
Media Ratings Council, 441
Medtronic, Inc., 141, 491
Mercedes-Benz, 168–169, 172, 285, 360, 4301
Merck, 151
Mercury, 214, 340
Meredith Corporation, 119
Merrill Lynch, 290, 497
Metro Group, 353
Metropolitan Life Insurance, 119, 120
MGA Entertainment, 116
Michelin, 10, 154, 278, 282
MicroFridge, 218
Microsoft Bing, 105, 185, 455
Microsoft Corporation, 81, 116, 284, 338, 454, 463
Microsoft Office, 276
Microsoft Project, 45
Microsoft Word, 276
Microsoft Xbox One X, 244, 303
Milsco Manufacturing, and Harley-Davidson, 135
MINDSTORMS EV3, 182, 183
Minecraft video game, 8
Mini-Cooper, 162, 300–301
Mirai, 92, 94–95
Mission Foods, 64
Mister Proper, 157
Mobil, 447
Molecular Imaging Products, 488
Monk-e-mail, 390, 391
Monsieur Propre, 157
Monster.com, 522
Monster Energy, 308
Monster headphones, 433
Moodmatcher lipstick, 167
Moore Chemical & Sanitation Supply, Inc., 507
Motorola, 39, 344
Motorsports HERO, 261
Moto Z2 Force, 101
Mountain Dew, 424, 432
Mr. Clean, 156–157
MSN for Kids, 116
MSN Money, 455
MTV, 411

Muscle Milk, 294
Mustang, 283, 285
My Amazon, 384
My eBay, 384
My First Craftsman toys, 116
MyWorkster, 523

N

Nabisco, 287, 370, 445–446
NACElink Network, 522
NASCAR, 266
National Basketball Association, 266, 282, 402, 424, 446, 476
National Football League, 251, 266, 282, 290, 468
National Hockey League, 266
Natural Grocers, 294
Nature Conservancy, 17
NBATV, 476
Neiman Marcus, 35, 307, 338, 356, 357, 365
NeoGrid, 140–141
Nescafé, 170
Nestlé, 115, 159, 162, 170, 288, 331, 445
  alliance with General Mills, 331–332
Netflix, 33, 81, 246, 438
Net Impact, 76
netmarket.com, 359
Neuralink, 5
Neutragena, 123
New Balance, Inc., 201, 279
New Belgium Brewing, 28
Newegg.com, 331
Newell Brands, Inc., 337
New York Mets, 315
New York Yankees, 315
NexGenVest, 29
Nickeldeon Universe, 373
Nielsen Company, 141, 437, 440
Nielsen lifestyle segmentation, 217
Nielsen PRIZM, 218
Nielsen Television Index Ranking Report, 187
Nielsen TV ratings, 185, 186
Nike, 28, 89, 118, 157, 158, 169, 243, 279, 280, 281, 282, 357, 432
99¢ Only Stores, 317
Nintendo, 158
Nintendo Switch, 303, 445
Nintendo Wii U, 244
Nissan Motor Company, 133, 165, 446
Nissan Smyrna, 168
Nokia, 344
Noodles and Company, 225
Nordstrom, 11, 338, 356, 363, 373, 517, 519
Nordstrom Bank, 356
Norske Skog, 128

North Face, 405
Northrup Grumman, 81
Northwestern Mutual Life Insurance Company, 497
NPD Group, 193
Nuprin, 283
NutriBullet, 438

O

Obsession perfume, 283
Ocean Spray Cranberries, 287
Oculus, 465
Oculus Rift, 428–429
Oculus VR, 73
Off 5th, 363
Office Depot, 270, 337, 364
Old Navy, 215
Old Spice, 434
OpenAI, 5
Opium, 334
Orbitz.com, 330, 337, 381
Oreos, 287, 445–446
Organic Gatorade, 268
Organic White Chocolate Mini Peanut Butter Cups, 295
Orkut, 232
Oscar Mayer, 118, 188
OUT! International's Hey! There's a Monster In My Room, 248
OxiClean, 438

P

Pampered Chef, 361
Pampers, 88, 156, 243, 279, 337
Panasonic, 357
Pandora, 197, 438
Panera Bread, 225, 415, 435
Pan Proper, 157
Pantene, 276
Paradise Kitchens, Inc.
  background, 58
  business model, 59
  company analysis, 63
  competitor analysis, 62–63
  core competency, 60
  customer analysis, 63–64
  financial data, 67–68
  goals, 60
  implementation plan, 69
  industry analysis, 62
  marketing and product objectives, 64–65
  marketing program, 66–67
  organizational structure, 68–69
  points of difference, 65
  positioning, 65

situation analysis, 61–64
strategic focus and plan, 59
sustainable competitive advantage, 60
SWOT analysis, 61–62
target market, 65
Paragon Trade Brands, 285
Partner Robot Group, 95
Patagonia, 16, 17
PayPal, 5, 351, 420
Pebble smartwatch, 253
Penske Logistics, 344
People Entertainment Network, 446
PepsiCo, 22, 111–112, 133, 156, 157, 163, 168, 267, 279, 280, 288, 327, 333, 389, 432, 446, 473, 517
  cola wars, 86
Pepsi-Cola, 85
Pepsi MAX, 473
PepsiTrue, 10
Performance Racing Network, 438
Periscope, 263
Pert shampoo, 162
Petco, 335
PetsAtWork, 473
PetSmart, 335
Pez Candy, Inc., 286
  packaging, 287
Pfizer, 431
PHD agency, 417
Philadelphia Phillies, 241
Phoenix, 283
Pier 1 Imports, 363
Pinterest, 22, 263, 392, 475
  and Body Glove, 484
Pinto, 283
Pitney Bowes, 133
Pittsburgh Pirates, 315
Pixel smartphone, 447, 455
Pizza Hut, 289, 424
  customer experience, 398–399
  multichannel marketing, 397–401
Planters peanuts, 370
PlasticsNet, 140
Plaxo, 523
Pokémon Go, 428
Polo, 282
Polo Custom Shop, 352, 353
Porsche, 88, 284, 418–419
Porsche Boxster, 284
Porsche Carrera, 284
Post Cereals, 105
Post-it Flag Highlighter, 11, 13–14
Post-it Flag Pens, 13–14
Post-it Flags, 13
Post-it Notes, 13
PowerPoint, 276
Prada, 30, 31, 335, 380
Pret, 162

Priceline.com, 384
PricewaterhouseCoopers, 290, 517
Prince Sports, Inc., market segments, 232–234
Pringles, 433
Prius Prime, 92
Procter & Gamble, 76, 88, 115, 118, 136, 156, 165, 168, 185, 188, 213, 243, 245–246, 252, 276, 279, 280, 282, 285, 288, 319, 334, 337, 338, 380, 385, 414, 445, 495, 503, 517
Progressive, 430, 431
Progresso Light soups, 253
Promotional Products Association International, 445
Propel Fitness Water, 266
PRS Group, Inc., 165
Publishers Clearing House, 446
Publix, 124
Purina, 246, 473

Q

Quaker Oats Company, 266, 267, 279, 282
Quiz Up, 478
QVC, 359, 388

R

RadioShack, 18, 315, 368
Radisson Blu, 373
Ralph Lauren Corporation, 282, 283, 332, 338, 352, 353
Ralston Purina, 278
Ranz, 92
Ray-Ban, 448
Rayovac, 285, 305
Reader's Digest, 446
ReadySetRocket, 428
Recreational Equipment, Inc., 294, 381, 517
Red Baron, 198, 309, 310
Redbox, 356
Red Bull, 282, 308
Red Lobster, 108
Reebok, 33, 89, 169, 388
Reebok Russia, 169
Reese's Pieces, 448
Regal Entertainment, 305
REI; *see* Recreational Equipment, Inc.
Renaissance hotels, 285
Revlon, 307, 384
Rite Aid, 447
Ritz-Carlton Hotel Company, 12
Rockport, 282, 499
Rockstar, 308
Rolex, 114, 158, 304, 307

Rolls-Royce, 158, 304
Ross Stores, 362, 363
Ruffles potato chips, 103
Ruiz Foods, 64

S

Safeway, 124, 138, 141, 294, 305
Saks Fifth Avenue, 35, 342, 356, 363
Saks Inc., 335
Salesforce.com, 80
Sam's Club, 124, 298, 335, 337, 342, 363
Samsung, 39, 80, 157, 271, 284
Samsung Galaxy, 39
Samsung Galaxy Note, 315
Samsung Galaxy S9, 101
San Diego Padres, 417
Sanford Corporation, 272
Santitas, 285
Schwab, 241, 382, 388
Schwan Food Company, 198, 328
Scotchgard, 86, 87
Scripto, 289
Scrub Daddy, 253
Sea Life Minnesota, 373
Sears, 304, 337, 368, 373
Seiko, 157, 172
Sergio Rossi, 334
Seven Cycles, Inc., 381, 388
  customization, 378–379
  interactive marketing, 378–379
  multichannel marketing, 378–379
7-Eleven stores, 35, 133, 138, 225, 326, 335, 520
7 Up, 283
Sewell Automotive Companies, 386
Sharp, 271, 283
Sharpie brand pens, 337
Sherwin-Williams, 332
Shiseido, 167
shopzilla.com, 360
Shredded Wheat, 105
Shutterfly, 517
Siemens AG, 132, 161
Simmons, 218
Sirius XM Satellite Radio, 438, 439
Skin Advisor, 275
Skippy peanut butter, 196–197, 294, 307
Skippy Squeez' It peanut butter, 287
Skype, 525
Slack, 79, 80, 461
Sling TV, 432
Smapchat, 158
Smart Things, 253
Smooth Yogurt, 3
Snake Light flexible flashlight, 170
Snapchat, 72, 411, 424, 432

Snapdeal, 149
Snapple, 282
SnapStore, 477
Snelling and Snelling, Inc., 334
Snickers, 115
Snow Master, 109
Snow Pup, 109
Sodima, 168
Solar City, 5
Sonatica, 35
Sonos, Inc., 434
Sony Corporation, 118, 158, 165, 169, 284, 428
Sony PlayStation, 402
Sony PlayStation 5, 244
Sony PlayStation 4, 244, 303, 406, 408
Sotheby's, 158
SoundCloud, 438
Southwest Airlines, 15, 32, 34, 37, 241, 290
SpaceX, 5
Sperry boat shoes, 357
Spic and Span, 288
Spirit Airlines pricing policy, 302
Sporting Goods Manufacturers Association, 232
Spotify, 438
Sprint, 81, 102, 441
Sprouts, 294
St. Joseph aspirin, 279
Stake Fastener Company, 329–330
Stanley Black & Decker, 154, 170, 285, 286, 503
Staples, 357
Starbucks, 11, 168, 225, 290, 411, 415
  sustainable procurement, 136
Starkist, 279, 280
Stella Artois, 448
Stokely-Van Camp, 266
Strategic Business Insights, 112
Strauss Group, 168
StumbleUpon, 197
Subway, 35
Sunbird, 283
Sunglass Hut, 382
Sunkist, 280
Surf HERO, 261
SurveyMonkey, 190
Swatch watches, 157, 307
Swifter WetJet, 245–246

T

Tab, 272
Tabulating Machine Company, 51
Taco Bell, 115, 367, 446, 467
  integrated marketing communications, 402–403, 424
Talk, 460

Target Stores, 11, 28, 35, 77, 124, 138, 141, 169, 197, 233, 278, 294, 298, 322, 337, 350, 353, 356, 365, 445, 478
Tata Group, 149
Teach for America, 29
TE Connectivity, 491
Temple Run, 478
Tesco, 141, 353
Tesco Home Plus, 479
Tesla Model 3, 253
Tesla Motors, 5, 196, 252–253
Texaco, 431
Texas Instruments, 157, 497
TextileWeb, 140
ThighMaster, 438
Thirsty Cat!, 248
Thirsty Dog!, 248
3D Systems, 246
3M Corporation, 11, 87, 88, 253–254, 268
   marketing program, 13–14
Thrivemarket, 294
Thunderbird, 283
Tide, 213, 243, 337, 517
Tide Pods, 252
Tidy Bowl, 282
Tiffany & Company, 161, 332, 365
Time Inc., 116
Time Warner, 81
Tinder, 467
TJ Maxx, 356, 362, 363
T-Mobile, 81, 447
Tombstone pizza, 310
Tony's Pizza, 195
   marketing actions, 199–200
   sales analysis, 198–199
Toro, 109, 135, 318
Toshiba America Medical Systems, 507–508
Tostitos, 103, 285, 493
Total Gym, 438
Total toothpaste, 109, 112
TownePlace Suites, 285
Toyota Camry, 96, 318
Toyota Corolla, 92, 96
Toyota Motor Corporation, 135, 239, 328, 340, 446
   background, 92
   environmental challenge, 93–94
   Mirai production and marketing, 94–95
   mission, 92–93
Toyota Prius, 96, 255
Toys "R" Us, 18, 368
Trader Joe's, 15–16
Travelocity, 360, 385, 434
Trek Bicycle Corporation
   company history, 144–145
   eco buying, 146–147
   organizational buying at, 145–146

Trend Hunter, 189
Triarc Companies, 282
True Religion, 373
TRUSTe, 392
TSNN, 497
TweetDeck, 468
Twitter, 2, 12, 15, 22, 52, 72, 180, 192, 232, 233, 263, 360, 385, 389, 392, 402, 403, 408, 411, 417, 419, 424, 432, 455, 460, 462, 464, 465, 467–468, 469, 472, 473, 475, 476, 519, 523, 525
   and Body Glove, 483
   compared to other social media, 466
Tylenol Cold & Flu, 111
Tylenol 6-Hour, 111
Tylenol P.M., 111

U

U.S. Rice Millers' Association, 152
Uber, 8, 33, 95, 169, 317, 318
Uber Eats, 33
UberPool, 33
UberRush, 33
Uber X, 33
Ulta, 363
Ultra Downy, 243
Uncle Ben's Calcium Plus rice, 279
Under Armour, 108, 337, 448
Unilever, 28, 115, 279, 441
Union Pacific Railroad, 504
United Airlines, 37
United Parcel Service, 84, 169, 241, 344, 495
United Parcel Service Supply Chain Services, 344
United States Postal Service, 241, 359, 420
United Technologies, 141
UPM-Kymmene, Inc., 128
U.S. Bank, 242

V

valpak.com, 445
Venmo, 420
Verizon, 81, 238, 447
Viacom, 81, 468
Vibrant Media, 428
Victoria's Secret, 357
Vidal Sassoon, 307
Viking, 232
Villiger, 145
Vine, 424
Virtru, 80
Visa, 161, 334
Vision Ease, 125
VisualCV, 523

Vive, 428
VIZIO, Inc. pricing policy, 298–299
Volkswagen AG, 88, 92, 119, 165, 417, 463
Volvo, 214, 228, 455

W

W. W. Grainger, 140
Walgreens, 124, 141, 206, 322, 354, 417
Walker products, 262
Wall Street Journal, The 186
Walmart, 10, 35, 136, 149, 171, 233, 266, 278, 285, 288, 294, 298, 322, 334, 335, 337, 338, 353, 356, 359, 362, 380, 387, 445, 495, 503
   supply chain, 341–342
Walmart Neighborhood Markets, 216, 342
Walmart Supercenters, 342
Walt Disney Company, 77, 81, 124, 214, 280, 290, 416
Wanamaker's Department Store, 442
Warby Parker, 380
Warner Brothers, 411
Warner Music Group, 73
Waterford crystal, 151
Waymo, 255
Weather Channel, 417
Weathertech, 432–433
WeChat, 460
Weight Watchers, 253
Welch's grape jelly, 197
Wells Fargo, 352, 353
Wendy's, 216, 217, 218, 228, 368, 468
   market segmentation, 219–226
Wendy's survey, 190–191
Weyerhaeuser, 132
WhatsApp, 460, 465
Wheaties, 193
Whirlpool Corporation, 132, 155, 165, 170, 286, 335, 357
Whole Foods Markets, 76, 294, 431
Whopper, 83
Wikibon Research, 80
Wikipedia, 463
Wilkinson Sword, 300
Wing Street, 424
Women's National Basketball Association, 266
World Book, 361
Wrigley's gum, 169, 238

X

Xerox Color WorkCentre 4265 Multifunction Printer, 220
Xerox Corporate University, 513

Xerox Corporation, 9, 83, 201, 202, 219–220, 269, 344, 493, 494, 495, 499, 519
   building customer relationships, 512–513

Y

Yahoo!, 197, 454
Yahoo! Finance, 455
Yahoo!'s Hadoop, 195

Yamaha, 135
Yipit, 360
Yoplait yogurt, 2, 4, 22, 168
YouTube, 4, 15, 114, 180, 189, 197, 261, 263, 359, 402–403, 411, 418, 434, 455, 462, 465, 469–470, 471, 472, 473, 475, 479
   and Body Glove, 484
   compared to other social media, 466
YoYo, 8
Yum! Brands, 424
Yves Saint Laurent, 108, 334

Z

Zante running shoes, 201
Zappos, 58, 290, 388, 389
   market segmentation, 210–211, 212–213
Zara, 77, 434
Zenith Media Services, 444
Zipcar, 8, 356
Zip2, 5
Zulily, 359, 419

SUBJECT INDEX

Boldface entries denote key terms.

A

above-, at-, or below-market pricing, 307
accelerated development in retail life cycle, 367–368
accessory equipment, 239
account executive, 518
account management, 504
achievement-motivated groups, 113
achievers, 113
action item list, 45
action plan, Pizza Hut, 398
adaptive selling, 499
administered vertical marketing systems, 334
adoption, 414
advertisements
    message content, 439–440
    message creation, 440–441
advertising, 406–407, 430
    advantages to firms, 406–407
    to business buyers, 410
    careers in, 518–520
    challenge to effectiveness of, 428
    cooperative, 449
    costs, 407
    costs with multibranding, 285
    direct-to-consumer, 413
    goals, 430
    Google, Inc., 453–455
    jobs in, 518
    new products, 268
    nonpersonal component, 406
    online behavioral, 420
    paid aspect, 406
    scheduling
        and buyer turnover, 441
        continuous schedule, 441
        flighting schedule, 442
        pulse schedule, 442
        and purchase frequency, 441
    of services, 290
    strengths, 407
    weaknesses, 407
Advertising Age, 417, 424, 434, 522
advertising agencies
    Anomaly, 434–435
    careers in, 520
    commission-based, 443
    fee-based, 443
    full-service, 443

imc^2, 399–400
    incentive-based, 443
    in-house, 443
    limited-service, 443
    PHD agency, 417
advertising budget, 432–433
advertising campaigns, teaser, 115
advertising expenditures
    by media, 435
    media comparisons, 436
advertising media
    bases of selecting, 435–436
    cost per thousand, 436
    gross rating points, 436
    Internet, 440
    magazines, 438–439
    newspapers, 439
    outdoor, 440
    place-based, 440–441
    radio, 438
    rich media, 440
    television, 437–438
    transit advertising, 440
    Yellow Pages, 439
advertising program
    assessing
        making needed changes, 444
        posttesting, 443–444
    designing advertisements
        message content, 433–434
        message creation, 434–435
    executing
        carrying out, 443
        pretesting, 442–443
    identify target audience, 432
    media alternatives
        Internet, 440
        magazines, 438–439
        newspapers, 439
        outdoor, 440
        place-based media, 440–441
        radio, 38
        television, 437–438
        transit advertising, 40
        Yellow Pages, 439
    media selection, 435–436
    scheduling, 441–442
    setting budget, 432–433
    specifying objectives, 432
advertising regulations, 166
Advertising Research Foundation, 432
advocacy institutional advertisements, 431
adware, 441

African Americans, buying patterns, 119–120
agents, 326, 330
    type of, 369
aggregators, online retailing, 360
aided recall, 443
Airbnbmag, 438
air fares, 302
algorithms, 477
all-electric automobiles, 252–253
    slow adoption of, 275
allowances
    everyday low pricing and, 319
    promotional allowances, 318
    trade-in allowances, 318
    in trade promotions
        case allowances, 448
        finance allowances, 449
        floor stock protection program, 449
        freight allowances, 449
        merchandise allowances, 448
all-you-can-afford budgeting, 414
All You Need Is Kill, 178
alternative evaluation
    consideration set, 101
    evaluative criteria, 101
    in organizational buying, 137
American Association of Advertising Agencies, 434
American Community Survey, 185
Americanization of fashion, 158
American Marketing Association, 183
    definition of marketing, 5
America's Got Talent, 187
anchor stores, 363
antecedent states, 105
antitrust laws, 82
Apple Product Matrix strategy, 226
applicant tracking software, 524
approach stage in personal selling, 498
apps, 477–478
    messaging, 460–461
Arms and the Dudes, 178
art director, 518
artificial intelligence, 16, 79
Asian Americans
    assimilated, 120
    buying patterns, 120
    composition of, 120
    nonassimilated, 120
Asia-Pacific markets, 174
aspiration groups, 116
assimilated Asians, 120

Association of Magazine Media, 432
Association of National Advertisers, 443
associative groups, 116
assumptive close, 501
Atomic Blonde, 178
attitude change, 111–112
attitudes, 111
attitude tests, 444
augmented reality, 428–430
Australia, direct marketing requirements, 420
automatic vending, 358
automation, 79
automobile industry
    all-electric automobiles, 252–253, 275
    Apple-enabled car, 238
    Google's driverless car, 255–256
    men as car buyers, 99
    supply chain, 339–340
    Toyota, 92–95
    trade-in allowances, 318
    website performance, 386
    women as car buyers, 98–99
Auto Trader, 439
Avatar, 178
awareness, 414

B

baby boomers, 75
baby bust, 75
Bachelorette, The, 187
back translation, 163
backward integration, 332
bad timing, 247
bait and switch pricing, 316
balance of trade, 151
bankruptcy
    RadioShack, 315
    retailers, 368
barter, 300
Baywatch, 448
BCG; *see* Boston Consulting Group
Begin Again, 178
behavioral evaluation, 507
behavioral learning
    stimulus discrimination, 110–111
    stimulus generalization, 110
    terms/variables in, 110
behavioral segmentation
    business markets, 220
    consumer markets, 218
    at Zappos, 210
behavioral targeting, 391
    online, 413–414
beliefs, 111
believers, 113
benchmark items, 362

Benefit Corporation Movement, 27
Best Global Brands survey, 39
Better Business Bureau, 83
Better Call Saul, 186–187
Better Homes and Gardens, 80
Big Bang Theory, 187
Big Brother, 187
big data, 195
billboards, 440
biometric scanning, 350
Black Panther, 178, 179, 448
Blade Runner 2049, 178
blogs, 389, 463
Bloomberg Businessweek, 520, 525
board of directors, 30
Boston Consulting Group, 44
    business portfolio analysis, 37–39
bots, 388, 461
brand
    and associative groups, 116
    buying and selling of, 282
    creation by Gatorade, 266–268
    evaluating, 101
    global, 157
    imagery-related dimension, 281
    performance-related dimension, 281
brand building
    by Gatorade, 267–268
    Mary Kay, Inc. in, 175
brand community, 116
brand development index, 276, 277
brand dilution, 285
brand equity, 280
    creating
        brand awareness, 281
        consumer–brand connection, 280
        elicit proper response, 281–282
        establish brand's meaning, 281
        valuing, 282
brand extension, 246, 284
branding, 280
branding strategies
    mixed branding, 286
    multibranding
        advantages, 285
        based on price–quality segments, 285
    multiproduct branding, 283–286
        and brand dilution, 285
        brand extension, 284
        co-branding, 284–285
        product line extensions, 284
        subbranding, 284
    private branding, 285
brand licensing, 282
brand loyalty, 111
brand management
    by Gatorade, 266–268
    at Hormel, 295
    at Justin's, 293–296

brand managers, 276, 518
    Facebook strategy, 466–467
    LinkedIn strategy, 469
    Twitter strategy, 468
    YouTube strategy, 470
brand names, 280
    criteria for picking
        favorable phonetic associations, 283
        fit company image, 283
        memorably distinctive, 283
        no regulatory restrictions, 283
        simple and emotional, 283
        suggest product benefits, 282
    language problems, 162
    for services, 289
brand personality, 280
brand sustainability map, 400
breadth of product line, 356–357
break-even analysis, 312
    break-even chart, 313–314
    break-even point, 312–313
break-even chart, 313–314
break-even point, 312–313
bribery, 85, 161
Brigham Young University, 253
brokers, 326, 370
build-to-order, 15
bullet graphs, 35
bundle pricing, 304
Bureau of Labor Statistics, on savings rate, 79
burst schedule, 442
business, 32–33
    and augmented/virtual reality, 428
business analysis, 255
    prototype creation, 255
    sales and profit projections, 255
business cards, 498
business culture
    ethics of competition, 85
    ethics of exchange, 85
business-format franchises, 355
business model, 33
business plan, 56–57
    most-asked questions, 57
    writing and style suggestions, 57–58
business portfolio analysis, 37
    at Apple Inc., 37–39
    growth-share matrix, 38–39
    market growth rate, 38
    relative market share, 38–39
business products, 239
    cost-plus pricing for, 306
    Internet marketing channels, 330
    kinds of, 239
    length of product life cycle, 273
    result of derived demand, 239
business publications, 527
business-to-business exchanges, 140

business-to-business marketing, 130
   JCPMedia, Inc., 128–129
   online buying, 140–142
   order getters, 493
business-to-business products, 239
buy classes, 139
buyers, 18
   in buying centers, 138
   careers as, 518
   decision making stages, 414
   grouped into segments, 216–217
   no economical access to, 248
   potential, 133
   requirements in channel selection, 335
buyer–seller relationships, 34–136
buyer turnover, 441
buying center, 138
   buying situations
      modified rebuy, 139
      new buy, 139
      straight rebuy, 139
   composition of, 138
   guidelines to understanding, 138
   role in, 138
   Trek Bicycle Corporation, 145–146
buying committee, 138
buying situations, 139
buzz, 115
   in online shopping, 390

C

Campbell Interest and Skill
      Inventory, 521
campus career services office, 522
Canada, imports of U.S. services, 152
Can a Song Save Your Life?, 178
canned sales presentation, 498–499
CAN-SPAM Act of 2004, 83, 390
capacity management, 291
career planning publications, 527
careers in marketing, 4–5
   advertising and promotion, 517–519
   diversity of opportunities, 516–517
   getting a job, 516
   information sources
      business and marketing
         publications, 527
      career planning publications, 527
      periodicals, 527
      professional and trade associations,
         527–528
   international careers, 518, 520–521
   job interview, 524–526
   job search process
      identifying opportunities, 521–523
      self-assessment, 521
   marketing research, 518, 520
   physical distribution, 517, 518
   product management, 517, 518
   retailing, 518, 519
   sales, 519–520
   starting salaries, 517
   writing résumé, 523–524
case allowances, 448
cash and carry wholesalers, 369
cash cows, 38
cash discounts, 318
catalog retailing, 358
catalogs, 331
   for online retailing, 358
   reduced printing costs, 420
category development index, 276, 277
category killers, 357
category management, 364
cause marketing, 88–89
caveat emptor (buyer beware), 85
Celebrity Family Feud, 187
Census 2010, 185
Census Bureau, 29, 78, 186
   on population trends, 75
central business district, 363
CEO; *see* chief executive officer
chain stores, 355
channel captain
   influences, 338
   types of, 337
channel conflict, 337
   and disintermediation, 337
   horizontal, 337
   vertical, 337
channel cost, 336
channel of communication, 405
channel strategies
   pull strategy, 412–413
   push strategy, 412
chatbots, 385
Chicago Sun-Times, 439
chief executive officer, 30
chief marketing officer, 30
child-proof caps, 289
Child Protection Act of 1965, 83
children, socialization of, 116
China
   IKEA in, 159
   imports of U.S. services, 152
   Mary Kay, Inc. in, 174
   population, 75
   social and economic statistics, 175
choice, online shopping, 388
choiceboard, 382, 388
classified ads, 440
Clayton Act of 1914, 82
   on price discrimination, 316
click fraud, 441
click-through rate, 475
closed-end questions, 192
closing stage in personal selling, 501
cloud computing, 196
   in India, 149
CNN Early Start, 476

co-branding, 284–285
code of ethics, 86
cognitive dissonance, 103
cognitive learning, 111
cola wars, 86
cold calling, 496–497
cold canvassing, 496–497
Coldest City, 178
collaborative filtering, 382
College Board, 77
college students
   digital natives, 411
   job search on LinkedIn, 469
   as target market, 13–14, 411
   tuition, 77
combination compensation plan, 506
commerce
   online customer experience, 385
   Pizza Hut website, 399
commercialization, 257
   Boeing 787 Dreamliner problem, 257
   Burger King French fries problem,
      257–258
commissions, 300
communication, 404–405; *see also*
      integrated marketing
      communications
   in direct marketing, 409
   encoding and decoding messages, 405
   errors in, 405
   feedback, 405–406
   in logistics management, 343
   message, 404–405
   noise, 406
   online customer experience, 385
   in online shopping, 389–390
   in packaging and labeling, 286–287
   Pizza Hut website, 399
   in publicity, 408
   receivers, 405
   source, 404
communication adaptation, 170
communication infrastructures, 164
community
   online customer experience, 385
   Pizza Hut website, 399
companies; *see also* organizations
   advantages of advertising, 406–407
   core product *vs.* supplementary
      services, 242
   delivery of services, 241
   disadvantages of advertising, 407
   government protection of, 82–83
   hashtags, 473
   joint ventures, 168
   legacy, 380
   overcoming consumer resistance, 275
   role of price, 300
   roles of personal selling in, 491
   two marketing environments, 380
company image, and brand names, 283

comparative advantage, Paradise Kitchens, 60
comparative advertising, 431
compensation of salesforce
   combination compensation plan, 506
   nonmonetary rewards, 506
   straight commission plan, 506
   straight salary plan, 506
   at Xerox, 513
competition, 81
   and antitrust laws, 82
   ethics of, 85
   in global market, 11
   in India, 149
   keeping an eye on, 225
competition-oriented pricing approaches
   above,- at-, or below-market pricing, 307–308
   customary pricing, 307
   loss-leader pricing, 309
competitive advantage from packaging and labeling, 286–288
competitive advertisements
   institutional, 431
   product, 430–431
competitive forces
   forms of competition, 81
   influencing Facebook, 72
   small businesses, 81
competitive intelligence researcher, 518
competitive parity budgeting, 414
competitive position, 223
   salesforce, 504
competitive products, ideas from, 252–253
competitors
   asking customers about, 503
   imitation of low-learning products, 273
   ineffective, 18
   reacting to position of, 278–279
   reactions by, 41
competitors' prices
   and Carmex, 322
   as pricing constraint, 315
complete delivery, 343
complex/professional salesperson, 518
components, 239
computer-assisted telephone surveys, 190
Computer Weekly, 439
concepts, 183
concept testing, 179–180, 254
conference selling, 494
connected cars, 460–461
connecting content, 472
connections
   at LinkedIn, 469
   online customer experience, 384–385
   Pizza Hut website, 400
consideration set, 101
consistent lead time, 343

constraints, 182–183
consultative selling, 499
consumer behavior, 99; *see also* online consumer behavior
   men as car buyers, 99
   and product life cycle
      diffusion of innovation, 274
      psychological barriers, 275
      risk barriers, 275
      value barriers, 275
   psychological influences
      learning, 110–111
      lifestyle, 112–113
      motivation and personality, 107–108
      perceived risk, 109–110
      perception, 109
      values, beliefs, and attitudes, 111–112
   purchase decision process
      alternative evaluation, 101
      characteristics, 104
      consumer journey map, 106
      consumer touchpoints, 105–106
      information search, 100–101
      level of involvement, 103–105
      postpurchase behavior, 102–103
      problem recognition, 100
      purchase decision, 102
      situational influences, 105
   sociocultural influences
      culture, 118–120
      family, 116–118
      personal influences, 113–115
      reference groups, 116
      subcultures, 119–120
   women as car buyers, 98–99
Consumer Bill of Rights, 85, 86
consumer–brand connection, 282
Consumer Electronics Show, Las Vegas, 80
consumer ethnocentric ism, 163
consumer-generated content, 462
consumer income
   discretionary income, 78–79
   disposable income, 78
   effect on demand, 310
   in global marketing, 164–165
   gross income, 78
consumer involvement, 103–105
consumerism, 82–83
consumer journey map, 106, 394
consumer learning, 110–111
consumer lifestyle
   achievement-motivated groups, 113
   differing behaviors, 112–113
   high- and low-resource groups, 113
   ideals-motivated groups, 113
   and psychographics, 112
   self-expression motivated groups, 113
consumer market segmentation
   behavioral segmentation, 218
   demographic segmentation, 217

   geographic segmentation, 217
   group buyers into segments, 216–217
   by product features, 218
   psychographic segmentation, 217–218
consumer-oriented sales promotions, 444
   contests, 445–446
   coupons, 445
   deals, 445
   loyalty programs, 446–447
   point-of-purchase displays, 447
   premiums, 445
   product placements, 447–448
   rebates, 447
   samples, 446
   sweepstakes, 446
consumer packaged goods, 246–247
consumer products, 239
   classification of, 240
   Internet marketing channels, 330
   kinds of, 239
   length of product life cycle, 273
   marketing channels for, 328–329
Consumer Product Safety Act of 1972, 83
Consumer Product Safety Commission, 83
consumer promotions, 444
consumer protection, desire for, 9
Consumer Reports, 100, 225–226
consumers
   benefits from intermediaries, 327
   benefits of direct marketing, 419
   benefits of marketing for, 18
   cross-channel, 393–394
   effects of protectionism, 152–153
   global, 158
   government protection of, 82–83
   main types of, 17–18
   motivation, 107–108
   online *vs.* offline shopping, 393
   personality, 108
   types of motivation, 112–113
   utilities from retailing, 352–353
   value perception, 102–103
   values, beliefs, and attitudes, 111–112
consumer socialization, 116
consumer spending
   by ethnic groups, 76, 119–120
   by global teenagers, 158
   monitored by Dept. of Labor, 79
consumer tastes
   changing, 3–4
   effect on demand, 309
consumer-to-consumer chat rooms, 389
consumer-to-marketer requests, 389
consumer touchpoints, 105–106
consumer trends, 279
content
   online customer experience, 384
   Pizza Hut website, 399
content marketing, 263

561

contests, 445–446
context, online customer experience, 384
continuous improvement at Amazon, 348–349
continuous innovation, 245
continuous schedule, 441
contractual vertical marketing systems
　franchise systems, 333–334, 355–356
　retailer-sponsored cooperatives, 333, 355
　wholesaler-sponsored voluntary chains, 333, 355
control, in online shopping, 391
controllable factors, 10
controlled test markets, 256
Controlling the Assault of Non-Solicited Pornography and Marketing Act of 2004, 83, 390
convenience
　in logistics management, 343
　online shopping, 387–388
　for organizational buyers, 335
convenience products, 239
conversational commerce, 461
conversation velocity, 193
cookies, 391
　Pizza Hut website, 399
cooperative advertising, 449
copyright law, 82
copywriters, 434, 518
core values, 31, 111
　at Zappos, 211
corporate branding, 284
corporate chain, 355
corporate culture; *see also* organizational culture
　codes of ethics, 86
　co-workers, 86
　top management, 86
　at Zappos, 211
corporate level, 30
corporate vertical marketing systems
　backward integration, 332
　forward integration, 332
corruption, 86
cost-effective logistics, 338
cost of production as pricing constraint, 315
cost-oriented pricing approaches, 304–306
　cost-plus pricing, 305–306
　standard markup pricing, 305
cost per action on social media, 474
cost per click on social media, 473–474
cost per thousand, 436
　media comparisons, 436
　on social media, 473–474
cost-plus fixed-fee pricing, 306
cost-plus percentage-of-cost pricing, 306

cost-plus pricing, 305–306
　cost-plus fixed-fee pricing, 306
　cost-plus percentage-of-cost pricing, 306
cost reduction in packaging, 289
costs
　and break-even analysis, 312–314
　importance of controlling, 312
　integrated marketing communications program, 417
　of magazine advertising, 439
　of marketing channels, 336
　in online shopping, 390–391
　performance measures tied to, 473–474
　of reaching segments, 223
　of television advertising, 438
　types of, 312
countertrade, 151
coupons, 445
cover letter, 524
co-workers, ethical behavior, 86
Cre@te magazine, 438–439
CROPing, 98
cross-channel consumers, 393
　document journey of, 394
　showrooming, 393
　webrooming, 393
cross-cultural analysis, 77, 160
cross-functional teams, 31
cross-functional team selling, 494
cross-selling, 499
crowdfunding, 56, 253
crowdsourcing, 252
cue, 110
cultural changes, 77
cultural diversity
　back translation, 162
　cross-cultural analysis, 60
　cultural ethnocentricity, 163
　cultural symbols, 161–162
　customs, 160–161
　languages, 162
　values, 60
cultural ethnocentricity, 163
cultural symbols, 161
　advertising misuse of, 161–162
culture, 76–77
　as socializing force, 84
culture training, 176
currency exchange rate, 165
customary pricing, 307
customer dissatisfaction, 102
customer engagement, 471
customer experience, 16
　online, 383–385
　Pizza Hut, 398–400
customer experience management, 188, 254
customerization, 388–389
customer loyalty, 11

customer relationship management, 15–16, 491
　customer experience, 16
　in direct marketing, 418
customer relationship management systems
　customer service and support automation, 509
　marketing automation, 509
　salesforce automation, 507–509
customer relationship philosophy, 488–489
customer relationships
　building, in multichannel marketing, 394–395
　in marketspace, 382–383
　and personalization, 383
customer requirements, 338
customers, 18
　benefits from branding, 280
　changes in, 41
　connecting with, 288
　differences in, 41
　discovering perceptions of, 228
　finding new, 277–278
　newness from perspective of, 244–246
　new product ideas from, 251–252
customer sales organization, 503
customer satisfaction, 102
　value to companies, 103
customer service, 342
　in direct marketing, 419
　and logistics, 338
　in logistics management, 342–343
　at Nordstrom, 11
　at Zappos, 210–211
customer service and support automation, 509
customer service manager, 518
customer specialists, 503
customer support personnel
　conference selling, 494
　missionary salespeople, 493–494
　sales engineers, 494
　seminar selling, 494
　team selling, 494
customer touchpoints, 414
customer value, 11
　by Chobani, 2–4
　created by personal selling, 491–492
　impact of technology, 80
　from marketspace, 380–381i
　from packaging and labeling
　　communication benefits, 286–287
　　functional benefits, 287–288
　　perceptual benefits, 288
　from product differentiation, 215
　and relationship selling, 491
customer value proposition, 10

customization
  online customer experience, 384
  in online shopping, 388–389
  Pizza Hut website, 399
  Seven Cycles, Inc., 378–379
customized interaction, 406
customs, 160

D

data, 184
  importance in direct marketing, 409
  primary, 186–195
  secondary, 184–185
data analysis, 195
  by product managers, 276
data analytics, 12, 195
  elements of, 196
  refinements, 197
  in retailing, 368
databases, 477
  for direct marketing, 419
data collection methods, 183
data deluge, 195
data mining, 196–197
  downside of, 197
data privacy, 479
Data Protection Directive, European Union, 420
data scientist, 518
data storage, 196
data visualization, 35, 195
dealers, 326
  sales goal incentives, 412
deals, 445
Deceptive Mail Prevention and Enforcement Act of 1991, 83
deceptive pricing, 316
deciders, 138
decision, 181
  evaluating, 200
decision making, 181
  in chain stores, 355
  evaluating, 200
decline stage; *see* product life cycle; retail life cycle
decoding, 405
deletion, 272
Delivering Happiness (Hsieh), 210
demand
  elastic, 311
  factors influencing
    consumer income, 310
    consumer tastes, 309
    price and availability of similar products, 310
  inelastic, 311
  in organizational buying, 132
  as pricing constraint, 315

  primary, 268
  selective, 268
demand curve, 309
  movement along *vs.* shift of, 310
demand estimation, 309–310
demand factors, 310
demand-oriented pricing approaches
  bundle pricing, 304
  odd-even pricing, 304
  penetration pricing, 303–304
  prestige pricing, 304
  skimming pricing, 303
demographics, 74
  generational cohorts, 75–76
  population explosion, 74–75
  population statistics, 74–75
  racial and ethnic diversity, 76
demographic segmentation
  business markets, 220
  consumer markets, 217
density, in target market, 334
Department of Commerce, 29, 186
Department of Energy, 134
Department of Justice, 81, 134
Department of Labor
  on marketing careers, 517
  monitoring consumer spending, 79
  Occupational Outlook Handbook, 522
departments, 31
department store locations, 363
dependability in logistics management, 343
depth interview, 189
depth of product line, 356–357
derived demand, 132, 239
design thinking, 252
desk jobbers, 369
Detroit Institute of Arts, 242, 243
developing countries
  income growth, 165
  per capita income, 164–165
development, 255
deviations
  acting on, 46–47
  identifying, 46
  positive or negative, 47
dichotomous questions, 192
differentiation positioning, 228
digital information manager, 518
digital marketing, 15
Digital Millennium Copyright Act of 1998, 82
digital photography, 251
digital résumé, 524
digital technology, 382
direct channel
  for business products, 329
  for consumer products, 328
direct contact, for job search, 523
direct forecast, 201

direct investment, 168–169
direct mail, 437
direct-mail retailing, 358
direct marketing, 406, 409
  benefits to consumers, 419
  costs, 407
  direct orders, 419
  disadvantages, 409
  ethical issues, 420–421
  expenditures, 418
  forms of, 418
  global issues, 420
  growth of, 418–419
  importance of data for, 409
  lead generation, 419
  marketing campaign methods, 418–419
  strengths, 407
  technology issues, 419–421
  traffic generation, 419
  value of, 419
  weaknesses, 407
Direct Marketing Association, UK, 420
direct marketing channels, 330–331
direct orders, 419
Directory of Corporate Affiliations, 525
direct selling
  growing number of companies, 361
  international expansion of, 361
direct-to-consumer advertising, 413
discontinuous innovation, 246
discounts, 362
  cash discounts, 318
  definition, 317
  quantity discounts, 317
  seasonal discounts, 317–318
  trade discounts, 318
  in trade promotions, 448–449
discretionary income, 78–79
disintermediation, 337
disposable income, 78
dissociative groups, 116
distribution; *see also* marketing channels
  exclusive, 334–335
  in growth stage, 270
  intensive, 334
  regular, 246
  selective, 335
  of services, 290
  for Seven Cycles, Inc., 379
distribution channels, 171
  for gray market, 172
  in introduction stage, 268
  promotional allowances, 318–319
  pull strategy, 412–413
  push strategy, 412
  VIZIO, Inc., 298–299
distribution strategy
  Prince Sports, Inc., 233–234
  worldwide marketing program, 171

563

distributors, 326
    salesforce training by, 449
    trade promotions for, 448–449
Divergent, 214
diversification, 39
    product development, 39
diversification analysis, 40
divestments by Ford Motor Company, 215
dogs, 38
do-not-mail registry, 421
Do Not Track Online Act proposal, 420
downsizing
    definition, 278
    economics of, 279
DRD_2 gene, 492
drivers, 193–194
drives, 110
drop shippers, 369
dual adaptation strategy, 170
dual distribution, 331
dues, 300
dumping, 171–172
Dun & Bradstreet, 522
durable goods, 238
dynamically continuous innovation, 245
dynamic price policy, 317
dynamic pricing, 390–391

E

early adopters, 275
early growth in retail life cycle, 367
echo-boom, 75
economic espionage, 159
    and cola wars, 86
    definition, 85
Economic Espionage Act of 1996, 59
economic forces
    consumer income, 78–79
    influencing Facebook, 72
    macroeconomic conditions, 77–78
    recessions, 78
economic indicators, 77
economic infrastructures, 163–164
economies of scale, 215
economy, 77; *see also* global economy
Edge of Tomorrow, 178
educational content, 472
efficient customer response, 342
e-hubs, 140
eight-second rule, 388
80/20 rule, 218
elastic demand, 311
electronic commerce, 59, 80
electronic intermediaries, 330
Elle, 439, 483
e-marketplaces, 140
emotional intelligence, 505
employee welfare, 33

employment agencies, 522–523
encoding, 405
endorsement, 109
entertaining content, 473
entrepreneurship
    personal selling in, 491
    VIZIO, Inc., 298–299
environmental forces, 10–11
    influencing Facebook, 72–73
    in marketing, 5
    types of, 6
environmental issues
    green marketing, 344
    in packaging, 288
    sustainability, 77
    at Toyota, 93–95
Environmental Protection Agency, 88
environmental scanning, 74
    competitive forces
        forms of competition, 81
        small businesses, 81
    economic forces
        consumer income, 78–79
        macroeconomic conditions, 77–78
    for global marketing
        consumer income, 164
        consumer purchasing power, 164–165
        cultural diversity, 160–163
        currency exchange rates, 165
        economic infrastructures, 163–164
        political stability, 165
        trade regulations, 166
    regulatory forces, 82–84
    social forces
        culture, 76–77
        demographics, 74–76
    technological forces
        data analytics, 80–81
        impact on consumers, 80
        technology of tomorrow, 79–80
environmental sustainability initiatives, 133
equipment-based services, 241
E.T. the Extra Terrestrial, 448
ethical duties, 87
ethical marketing behavior
    business culture, 85
    corporate culture and expectations, 85–86
    industry practices, 85
    personal moral philosophy, 86–87
    societal culture and norms, 84
ethics, 84
    of asking about competitors, 503
    business culture, 85
    corporate culture and expectations, 85–86
    in direct marketing, 420–421
    industry practices, 85

    in marketing, 16
    personal moral philosophy, 86–87
    and protectionism, 153
    societal and cultural norms, 84
ethics of competition, 85
ethics of exchange, 85
ethnic diversity, 76
ethnographic research, 188
European Union
    and antitrust, 81
    Data Protection Directive, 420
    description, 154
    direct marketing requirements, 420
    elimination of trade barriers, 154
    E-Privacy Directive, 420
    General Data Protection Regulation, 479
    marketing opportunities, 154
    membership map, 155
    per capita income, 164
    tariffs on bananas, 152
    tariffs on cars, 152
    withdrawal of United Kingdom from, 154
evaluation, 414
evaluative criteria, 101
everyday fair pricing, 362
everyday low pricing, 319, 362
exchange, 5
    by barter, 300
    in marketing, 7
exchange rate fluctuations, 165
exclusive distribution, 334–335
experiencers, 113
experiments, for primary data, 193–194
expertise influence, 338
exporting, 166, 166–167
    dumping, 171–172
    indirect, 167
exports
    effect on imports, 151
    of United States, 151
extended problem solving, 104
external data, 184, 185
external screening and evaluation, 254
external search, 100
extranets, 80

F

Facebook, 466
    brand manager strategy, 466–467
    capabilities, 465
    dating feature, 467
    e-mail marketing, 467
    live streaming, 467
    mobile marketing at, 467
    overview, 466
    privacy protection, 467

facilitating function, 327
fad products, 274
Fair Packaging and Labeling
        Act of 1966, 83
family branding, 284
family influence
    consumer socialization, 116
    decision making, 118
    family lifestyle, 117
family life cycle, 117
fan service, 475
fares, 300
fashion
    Americanization of, 158
    products, 273–274
Fast and the Furious, The, 180
Fast Company, 435
fast-food restaurants, 218–219
Fate of the Furious, The, 448
fax machines, product life cycle,
        266–272
fear appeals, 433–434
feature bloat, 245
feature fatigue, 245
Federal Communications Commission on
        product placements, 448
Federal Trade Commission, 81
    deceptive pricing, 316
    on Internet fraud, 392
    National Do Not Call Registry,
        360, 420
    on newness, 246
    powers of, 83
    on privacy, 421
    on sweepstakes and contests, 446
Federal Trade Commission
        Act of 1914, 83
Federation of European Direct
        Marketing, 420
FedStats, 186
feedback
    definition, 406
    delayed or distorted, 405
feedback loop, 406
fees, 300
field of experience, 405
fighting brands, 285
final price
    calculating, 301
    factors in setting, 300
    setting
        adjustments to list price, 317
        allowances, 318–319
        approximate level, 316–317
        discounts, 317–318
        set list/quoted price, 317
finance allowances, 449
financial system, in global marketing, 164
financing by crowdfunding, 253
Finding Dory, 174

firms; *see* companies; organizations
fixed alternative questions, 192
fixed cost, 312
fixed pricing, 317
flighting schedule, 442
floor stock protection program, 449
flow of products, 338
focus groups, 189
follow-up stage in personal
        selling, 501
Food and Drug Administration,
        8, 279, 283
food brokers, 370
Forbes, 29, 33, 92, 471
Foreign Corrupt Practices Act, 161
Forest Stewardship Council, 128
form of ownership, 353
    contractual systems, 355–356
    corporate chain, 355
    independent retailers, 354–355
formula selling presentation, 498
form utility, 352–353
    definition, 18, 328
    in marketspace, 381
for-profit organizations, 28
Fortune, 16, 72, 522
Fortune 500 companies, 495
Fortune 1000 companies, 454
47 Ronin, 178
forward integration, 332
four I's of services, 241
four Ps of marketing, 10
franchising, 168
    administered vertical marketing
        systems, 334
    business-format franchises, 355
    definition, 333
    franchise fees, 355–356
    manufacturer-sponsored retail franchise
        systems, 333
    manufacturer-sponsored wholesale
        franchise systems, 333
    product distribution franchises, 355
    service-sponsored franchise
        systems, 334
    service-sponsored retail franchise
        systems, 333–334
free trials, 110
freight allowances, 449
frequency, 436
frequency marketing, 218
full-line wholesalers, 369
full service, 356
full-service ad agencies, 443
functional discounts, 318
functional element in retail
        communication, 364
functional role of packaging,
        287–288
fuzzy front end research methods, 189

G

Game of Thrones, 429
Gantt chart, 45–46
gap analysis, 242
Garden Design, 439
gatekeepers, 138
General Data Protection Regulation,
        United Kingdom, 420
generalized life cycle, 273
general merchandise stores, 357
general merchandise wholesalers, 369
generational cohorts
    baby boomers, 75
    Generation X, 75
    Generation Y, 75–76
    Generation Z, 76
Generation X, 75
Generation Y, 75
Generation Z, 76, 471
    student loan market, 29
geographical sales organization,
        502–503
    Xerox, 513
geographic segmentation
    business markets, 219
    consumer markets, 217
Germany, failure of Walmart, 171
global brand, 157
global companies
    global brands, 157–158
    international firms, 156
    multinational firms, 156–157
    transnational companies, 157–158
global competition, 155–156
global consumers, 158
global economy
    and economic espionage, 59
    impact of retailing, 353
global marketing, 518
    Amazon India, 148–150
    competition, 155–156
    and consumer purchasing power,
        164–165
    and cultural diversity, 160–163
    and direct marketing, 420–421
    economic considerations
        consumer income, 164–165
        infrastructures, 163–164
    economic espionage, 159
    and economic integration, 154–155
    effect of trade regulations, 166
    and exchange rates, 165
    global brands, 157
    global companies, 156–158
    global consumers, 58
    and global economy, 152–154
    market entry strategies
        direct investment, 168–169
        exporting, 166–167

global marketing—Cont.
    franchising, 168
    joint ventures, 168
    licensing, 167–168
    marketing program for, 169–172
    Mary Kay India, 174–176
    multidomestic marketing strategy, 156
    networked global marketspace, 158–159
    and political stability, 165
    and protectionism, 152–154
    strategic marketing alliances, 331–332
global marketing manager, 518
global marketing strategy, 157
global teenagers, 158
goals, 33
    of advertising, 430
goal setting, 43
Good Housekeeping, 439
Good Morning America, 476
goods; *see also* products
    durable, 238
    marketing of, 17
    nondurable, 238
government agencies, 29
    delivery of services, 241
gray market, 172
green marketing, 88, 344
gross domestic product, 77
    small business percentage, 81
    of United States, 151
gross income, 78
gross margin, 362
gross rating points, 436
groupthink, 248–249
growth, expected, 223
growth-share matrix, 38
growth stage; *see* product life cycle
guarantees, 110

H

habit formation, 111
handling costs, 241–242
Harley Owners Group, 116, 385
Harry Potter, 214
harvesting strategy, 272
hashtags, 473
head-to-head positioning, 228
health issues in packaging, 288–289
help-wanted ads, 522
hierarchy of effects, 414
hierarchy of needs, 108
high- and low-resource groups, 113
high-involvement purchase, 103, 105
high-learning products, 273
Hispanics
    buying patterns, 119
    diversity of, 119

horizontal conflict, 337
horizontal price fixing, 316
households
    types of, 116–117
    typical income, 78
hoverboards, 248
humorous appeals, 434
Hunger Games, 214

I

idea generation, 251
    for new products
        competitive products, 252–253
        crowdsourcing, 252
        customers and suppliers, 251–252
        employees and friends, 251
        research and development laboratories, 252
        smaller firms, 253
        universities and inventors, 253
    for questionnaire data, 189
ideals-motivated groups, 113
ideas
    definition, 238
    marketing of, 17
identification influence, 338
idle production capacity, 241–242
image
    and brand name, 286
    of products, 253
    in retail communication, 364
imports, effect of exports on, 151
inbound telemarketing, 493
Inc. magazine, 294
inconsistency of services, 241
independent retailers, 354–355
India
    Amazon in, 148–150
    cloud technology, 149
    competition in, 149
    Mary Kay, Inc. in, 175
    payment systems, 149
    population, 75
    social and economic statistics, 175
    statistics on, 148
    trade regulations, 149
indirect channel
    for business products, 329–330
    for consumer products, 328–329
individual interviews, 189
individuality in marketspace, 382
industrial distributors, 329–330, 369
    exclusive distribution, 335
industrial products, 239
industrial salesperson, 518
industrial services, 239
industry, 29–30
    in marketing plan, 56

industry practices
    ethics of competition, 85
    ethics of exchange, 85
inelastic demand, 311
inflation-adjusted income, 78
influencer marketing, 114, 464–465
influencers, 138
infomercials, 428
information
    for marketing research
        primary data, 186–195
        secondary data, 184–185
    for organizational buyers, 335
    privacy issues, 420
informational interview, 523
information content, 433
information search, 100–101
    external search, 100
    internal search, 100
    marketer-dominated sources, 100
    in organizational buying, 137
    and perceived risk, 109
    personal sources, 100
    public sources, 100
information technology, 195
    for direct marketing, 419
    and relationship marketing, 12
infrastructures
    communication, 164
    economic, 163–164
in-house ad agencies, 443
in-house research staff, 520
innovation
    at Apple Inc., 236
    by Chobani, 22
    continuous, 245
    discontinuous, 246
    dynamically continuous, 245
    open, 249
innovators, 113, 275
input-related measures, 507
inquiry tests, 444
inseparability of services, 241
Inside Edition, 476
inside order takers, 493
inspirational content, 472
installations, 239
institutional advertisements, 431
    advocacy, 431
    competitive, 431
    pioneering, 431
    reminder, 431
intangibility of services, 241
integrated marketing communications, 404
    and advertising agencies, 443
    channel strategies, 410
    and product life cycle, 410–412
    sales promotion managers, 519
    spending on, 415

integrated marketing communications—Cont.
  at Taco Bell, 424
  target audience, 410
integrated marketing communications program
  design promotion, 416
  executing and assessing
    expensive and time-consuming, 417
    facilitate design and uses, 417–418
    testing procedures, 417
  identify target audience, 413–414
  scheduling, 416
  select promotional tools, 415–416
  setting budget, 414–415
  specify objectives, 414
integrated marketing databases, 419
intelligent enterprise, 195
intensive distribution, 334
interaction rate, 475
interactive content, 472
interactive marketing, 382
  choiceboards, 382
  collaborative filtering, 382
  permission marketing, 383
  personalization, 382–383
  Seven Cycles, Inc., 379
interactivity, 382–383
interest, 300, 414
intermediaries, 171
  conflict between, 337
  consumer benefits, 327
  electronic, 330
  focus of promotions, 410
  functions
    facilitating function, 327
    logistical function, 327
    transactional function, 326–327
  merchant wholesalers, 369
  online retailing, 360
  terminology for, 326
  trade promotions for, 448–449
intermittent schedule, 442
internal data, 184–185
internal screening and evaluation, 252–254
internal search, 100
International Anti-Dumping and Fair Competition Act of 1998, 161
international careers in marketing, 520–521
international firms, 156
international trade; see world trade
Internet advertising, 440, 460
  advantages and disadvantages, 437
  and click fraud, 441
Internet marketing channels, 330
Internet of Everything, 12
Internet of Things, 79, **80,** 195, 350, 355
Internet privacy and security, 392

Internet surveys, 190
intranets, 80
introduction stage; see product life cycle
inventors, for new product ideas, 253
inventory control manager, 518
inventory of services, 241–242
involvement, 103
  and problem solving, 103–105
Italy guide book, 408

J

Japan
  direct marketing requirements, 420
  Fran Wilson Creative Cosmetics in, 167
  imports of U.S. services, 152
  tariffs on rice, 152
job analysis, 505
job description, 505
job interview
  follow-up on, 526
  frequently asked questions, 525
  handling rejection, 526
  preparing for, 524–525
  succeeding in, 525–526
job opportunities, identifying, 522–523
job search, at LinkedIn, 468–469
joint family decision making, 118
joint venture, 168
Journal of Marketing, 183
Journal of Marketing Research, 183
judgment of decision makers, 201
jury tests, 442

K

Keeping Up with the Kardashians, 280
key account management, 503
key success factors at Justin's, 294
key traits, 108
kickbacks, 85, 161

L

label, 286
labeling
  challenges and responses
    connecting with customers, 288
    cost reduction, 289
    environmental concerns, 288
    health, safety, and security issues, 288–289
  cost to companies, 286
  creating customer value
    communication benefits, 286–287
    functional benefits, 287–288
    perceptual benefits, 288
laboratory test markets, 256–257

laggards, 275
La La Land, 448
languages
  back translation, 163
  number of, 161–162
Lanham Act of 1946, 83, 280
late majority, 275
lead, 496
Leadership in Energy and Environmental Design, 76, 354
lead generation, 419
learning, 110
  behavioral, 110–111
  and brand loyalty, 111
  cognitive, 111
LEED; see Leadership in Energy and Environmental Design
legacy companies, 380
legal fees, 306
legal forces; see regulatory forces
legal systems in global marketing, 164
legitimate right, 338
Lego Batman Movie, The, 448
length of product life cycle, 273
level of service, 354
  full service, 356
  limited service, 356
  self-service, 356
library reference materials, 522
licensing, 167–168
  of brands, 282
life-cycle curve
  fad products, 274
  fashion products, 273–274
  generalized life cycle, 273
  high-learning products, 273
  low-learning products, 273
lifestyle
  of consumers, 112–113
  family, 117
lifestyle segmentation, 217–218
Likert scale, 192
likes, Facebook, 2–7, 193
limited-line wholesalers, types of, 369
limited problem solving, 104
limited service, 356
limited-service ad agencies, 443
linear trend extrapolation, 201–202
LinkedIn, 469
  brand manager strategy, 469
  college senior's job search, 469
  main purpose, 468
  overview, 469
list/quoted price
  adjustments to, 317–319
  setting, 317
location-based promotions, 478
logistical function, 327
logistics, 338
  and electronic marketing channels, 330
  reverse, 343–344

logistics management, 338
  at Amazon, 348
  automobile industry, 339–340
  functions, 339
  in supply chain
    customer service concept, 342–343
    total cost concept, 342
loss-leader pricing, 309
lost-horse forecast, 201
Louvre, Paris, 17
low-involvement purchase, 103, 104
low-learning products, 273
loyalty card apps, 350
loyalty programs, 446–447, 478

M

MacGyver, 438
macroeconomic conditions, 78–79
magazine advertising
  advantages and disadvantages, 437
  costs, 439
  specialized medium, 438–439
mail surveys, 189–190
maintained markup, 361–362
makers, 113
Malcolm Baldrige National Quality Award, 507
mall intercept interview, 192
Mall of America
  idea for, 372–373
  management of, 373
  as market, 373–374
  marketing, 374
  and social media, 374
  stores and features, 373
management of Mall of America, 373
managing for long-run profits, 314
manufacturers
  cooperative advertising, 449
  pull strategy, 412–413
  push strategy, 412
  salesforce training by, 449
manufacturers' agents, 369
Manufacturers' Agents National Association, 369
manufacturer's branch office, 370
manufacturer-sponsored retail franchise systems, 333
manufacturer-sponsored wholesale franchise systems, 333
manufacturers' representatives, 369
manufacturer's sales office, 370
markdown, 362
market, 9
  reaching new, 279
market attractiveness, too little, 248
market development, 39
market environments, 380

marketer-dominated information sources, 100
marketer-to-consumer e-mail, 389
market growth rate, 38
marketing, 5; *see also* global marketing; interactive marketing
  benefits of, 18
  at Body Glove, 483
  breadth and depth of, 17–18
  and careers, 4
  challenges of two environments, 380
  concepts in, 183
  at Coppertone, 174
  customer relationship management, 15–16
  discovering and meeting needs, 8–9
  ethics in, 16
  factors required for
    ability to satisfy needs, 6
    communication, 6–7
    exchange, 7
    unmet needs, 6
  of Gatorade, 268
  at GoPro, 262–263
  impact of, 4–5
  at Justin's, 295–296
  Mall of America, 374
  marketing concept, 15
  market orientation, 15
  in maturity stage, 271
  mobile, 440
  objectives, 5
  objectives in product life cycle, 269
  personal selling in, 491
  social responsibility, 16–17
  success at Seven Cycles, Inc., 378
  trends in social media
    convergence, 477–478
    mobile marketing, 478–479
marketing actions
  evaluating results, 200
  identify data needed for, 183
  identifying, 182
  implementing, 200
  influences on, 5
  in mobile marketing, 478–479
  objectives and rationale, 14
  product differentiation, 212
  to reach market segments, 224–225
  recommendations, 199–200
  responsibility for, 198
  Taco Bell, 402–404
marketing analytics, 34–36
marketing automation, 509
marketing channel, 326
  for business products, 329–330
  Cereal Partners Worldwide, 332
  consumer benefits, 327
  for consumer products, 328–329
  direct, 330–331

  dual distribution, 331
  Eddie Bauer, 324
  factors affecting choice/management
    buyer requirements, 335
    profitability, 336
    target market coverage, 334–335
  functions, 326–327
  Internet, 330
  multichannel marketing, 331
  securing cooperation in
    channel captains, 337–338
    legitimate right, 338
  strategic channel alliances, 331–332
  types of intermediaries, 326
  vertical marketing systems
    administered, 334
    contractual, 333–334
    corporate, 330–333
marketing channel relationships
  channel conflict, 337
  and logistics, 338–339
  securing cooperation in, 337–338
  and supply chains, 339–340
marketing concept, 15
marketing dashboards, 34
  Tony's Pizza, 199
marketing database manager, 518
marketing department, 5
  activities, 9
  in organizational structure, 6
marketing drivers, 193–194
marketing input data, 184
marketing managers, 43, 518
  setting final price, 303–309
marketing metrics, 35
  above-, at-, or below-market pricing, 308
  advertising media selection, 436
  Apple Stores, 365
  Ben & Jerry's, 36
  brand development index, 277
  Carmex and social media, 194
  category development index, 277
  channel sales and profit, 336
  integrated marketing communications budgeting, 415
  for new product performance, 249–250
  salesperson performance, 508
  site stickiness, 386
marketing mix, 10
  actions in product life cycle, 269
  controllable factors, 10
  four Ps of, 10
  and marketing program, 43
  poor execution of, 248
  price in, 302
  product differentiation, 212
  promotion in, 404
  for services, 289–291
  uncontrollable factors, 10–11

568

Marketing News, 522
marketing organization, 44–45
marketing outcome data, 184–185
marketing plan, 34, 56
   compared to business plan, 56–57
   industry, 56
   kind of organization and
      complexity, 56
   most-asked questions, 57
   for Paradise Kitchens, Inc., 58–69
   target audience, 56
   writing and style suggestions, 57–58
marketing program, 12
   executing, 46
   and four Ps of marketing mix, 43
   and market segments, 12
   relationship marketing, 11–12
   strategy at 3M Corporation, 13–14
   worldwide
      distribution strategy, 170
      price strategy, 170–171
      product strategy, 169–170
      promotion strategy, 170
marketing publications, 527
marketing research, 101
   careers in, 518, 520
   by Carmex, 205–207
   challenge of, 181
   collect relevant information
      data types, 188
      primary data, 186–195
      secondary data, 184–185
   decision and decision making in, 181
   develop findings
      data analytics, 195
      data mining, 196
      information technology, 195–196
      predictive modeling, 197–198
   as five-step approach, 181
   job in, 518
   measures of success, 182
   by movie industry
      concept testing, 179–180
      fixing bad titles, 178
      test screenings, 180
      tracking studies, 180
   plan development
      determine data collection
         methods, 183
      identify needed data, 183
      specify constraints, 182–183
   precise questions, 192
   present findings, 198–199
   problem definition
      identify marketing actions, 182
      at LEGO Group, 181–182
      set objectives, 182
   and sales forecasting, 200–202
   take marketing actions, 199–200
marketing research analyst, 518

marketing research companies, 185
marketing research consulting firms, 520
marketing strategy, 46
   Ben & Jerry's, 26–28
   consumer involvement, 104–105
   in diversification analysis, 40
   product differentiation, 212
   to reduce perceived risk, 109–110
   and supply chain management
      alignment steps, 340–341
      at Dell, 341
      at Walmart, 341–342
   Tiffany/Walmart strategy, 215
   Walmart/Dollar Store strategy, 216
marketing synergies, 226–227
marketing tactics, 46
market modification, 277
   creating new use situation, 278
   finding new customers, 277–278
   increasing product use, 278
market orientation, 15
market penetration, 39
marketplace
   definition, 380
   legacy companies, 380
   online retailing, 360
market price, 307–308
market-product focus, 43
market-product grid, 213
   for market size estimation,
      222–223
market-product synergies, 226–227
market segmentation, 43, 212
   Apple's strategy, 226–227
   business markets, 219–220
   customer value from, 215
   grouping buyers into segments
      criteria, 217
      fast-food restaurants, 218
      means of, 217–218
      variables to use, 219
   group products into categories,
      220–222
   marketing actions, 223–225
   market-product grid, 213, 222–223
   market-product synergies, 225–226
   market size estimation, 222–223
   Prince Sports, Inc., 232–234
   and product differentiation, 212
   reasons for, 212
   target market selection, 223
   timing and means of, 213–216
      build to order, 215
      mass customization, 215
      multiple products, multiple
         segments, 214–215
      one product, multiple segments, 214
      synergies *vs.* cannibalization,
         215–216
   at Zappos, 210–211, 212–213

market segments, 12
   criteria for forming
      differences in needs, 217
      marketing action, 217
      potential for profit, 217
      similarity of needs, 217
      simplicity and cost
         effectiveness, 217
   definition, 212
   at 3M Corporation, 14
market share, 33
   Chobani, 4
   in maturity stage, 271
   organizational goal, 33
   pricing objective, 314
   relative, 38
   VIZIO, Inc., 299
market size estimation, 222–223
marketspace, 80, 380
   achieving success in, 380–383
      creating customer value, 380–381
      customer relationships, 382–383
      interactivity, 382
   Internet companies, 380
   online customer experience
      commerce, 385
      communication, 385
      community, 385
      connection, 384–385
      content, 384
      context, 384
      customization, 384–385
market testing, 256
   controlled test markets, 256
   simulated test markets, 256–257
   standard test markets, 256
markup, 361
   in supermarkets, 305
Maslow's hierarchy of needs, 108
mass customization, 15
mass selling, 406
mass-tige pricing, 175
maturity stage; *see* product life cycle;
      retail life cycle
maximizing current profit, 314
measures of success, 182
media; *see* advertising media;
      social media
media buyer, 518
media richness, 462–463
merchandise allowances, 448
merchandise line, 354
   breadth of product line, 356–357
   depth of product line, 356–357
   scrambled merchandising, 357
merchandise management
   category management, 364
   sales per square foot, 365
   same-store sales growth, 365
merchant wholesalers, 369

message, 404–405
　in advertising, 407
　encoding and decoding, 405
　field of experience, 405
message content
　fear appeals, 433–434
　humorous appeals, 434
　informational, 433
　persuasive, 433
　sex appeals, 434
message creation, 434–435
methods of data collection, 183
Metro, 439
Mexico, imports of U.S. services, 152
middle-aged married couples, 117
middleman, 326
Milk Street, 439
millennials, 75; *see also* Generation Y
mission, 32
　Ben & Jerry's, 26
missionary salespeople, 493–494
mission statement, 32
mixed branding, 286
mobile apps, 477–478
mobile direct marketing, 418–419
mobile marketing, 440
　buyer control, 479
　on Facebook, 467
　and marketing actions
　　location-based promotions, 478
　　loyalty programs, 478
　　price comparison searches, 478–479
　privacy in, 479
　sensor control, 479
mobile marketing communications, 460
Modern Family, 438
modified rebuy, 139
　and order getters, 493
　Trek Bicycle Corporation, 146
money income, 78
monopolistic competition, 81
monopoly, 81
Moody's manuals, 524
moral idealism, 86–87
moral philosophy
　learning of, 86
　moral idealism, 86–87
　utilitarianism, 87
motivation, 108
　of salesforce, 506
　types of, 112
　at Xerox, 513
Motor Trend, 238
movement along a demand curve, 310
movie industry
　marketing research, 178–180
　market segments, 214
　product placements, 447–448
multibranding, 284, 285
multichannel marketing, 331

Eddie Bauer, 325
implementing, 393–395
　document cross-channel consumer journey, 394
　mutually reinforcing channels, 94–395
　performance measurement, 395
Pizza Hut, 397–401
Seven Cycles, Inc., 378–379
multichannel retailers, 364
multicultural marketing, 76
multidomestic marketing strategy, 156
multinational firms, 156–157
multiproduct branding, 284
Mummy, The, 178
Myers-Briggs Type Indicator, 521
mystery shoppers, 188

N

National Aeronautics and Space Administration, 131, 306
National Association of Colleges and Employers, 522
National Do Not Call Registry, 360, 420, 497
near field communication, 350–351
needs
　compared to wants, 9
　discovering, 7–8
　hierarchy of, 108
　and marketing, 6
　met with new products, 8–9
　not satisfying, 247
　perceiving, 100
　satisfying, 1011
need-satisfaction presentation, 499
　adaptive selling, 499
　consultative selling, 499
networked global marketspace, 158–159
networking, 523
neuromarketing methods, 188
neuroscience tools, 188
New Breed documentary, 29
new buy, 139
　and order getters, 493
　Trek Bicycle Corporation, 146
new markets, reaching, 279
newness
　degrees of, 244–246
　as pricing constraint, 315
new-product concept, 183
new-product development process, 250
　business analysis, 255
　commercialization, 257–258
　development stage, 255–256
　feature bloat, 245
　feature fatigue, 245
　financing by crowdfunding, 253

at GoPro, 261–262
idea generation
　competitive products, 252–253
　crowdsourcing, 252
　customers or suppliers, 251–252
　employees or friends, 251
　research and development laboratories, 252
　smaller firms, 253
　universities and inventors, 253
market testing, 256–257
screening and evaluation, 253–254
Stage Gate process, 250
from technology, 80
new-product failures, 8
　at Apple Inc., 237–238
　at commercialization stage, 257–258
　reasons for
　　bad timing, 247
　　incomplete protocol, 247
　　insignificant points of difference, 247
　　marketing failures, 247–248
　　no access to buyers, 248
　　not satisfying needs, 247
　　organizational inertia, 248–249
　　poor execution of marketing mix, 248
　　poor quality, 248
　　too little attractiveness, 248
new products
　Apple's successes, 236
　degrees of newness, 244–246
　examples of failure, 8
　feature bloat, 245
　feature fatigue, 245
　marketing metrics for performance of, 249–250
　meeting needs with, 8–9
　need for protocol, 246
　number of, introduced monthly, 8
　penetration pricing, 303–304
　reasons for success, 246–247
　regional rollout, 256
　skimming pricing, 303
new-product strategy development, 251
　disruptive innovation, 251
　SWOT analysis, 250–251
news conference, 450
newspaper advertising, 439
　advantages and disadvantages, 437
news release, 449–450
newsworthy content, 473
New York Times, The, 385, 439, 464
NFL Football, 187
noise, 406
nonassimilated Asians, 120
nondurable goods, 238
nonmonetary rewards, 506
nonpersonal component of advertising, 406

nonprofit marketing, 518
nonprofit organizations, 28–29
   delivery of services, 241
   goals, 34
   promotion by, 290
nonselling duties, 519–520
nonstore retailing, 357–361
   automatic vending, 358
   catalogs, 358–359
   direct mail, 358–359
   direct selling, 361
   online retailing, 359–360
   telemarketing, 360
   television home shopping, 359
norms, 84
North American Free Trade Agreement, 131
   description, 154–155
North American Industry Classification System, 131
   and demographic segmentation, 220
not-invented-here problem, 249

O

Oak Ridge National Laboratory, 134
objections, handling, 499–501
objective and task budgeting, 415
objectives, 33
   of advertising program, 432
   of marketing, 5
   of marketing research, 182
   in organizational buying, 133
   of pricing, 314–315
   of product advertisements, 430–431
   of promotion, 414
   of sales plan, 502
observational data, 184, 186
   from ethnographic research, 188
   mechanical methods, 186–187
   from mystery shoppers, 188
   neuromarketing methods, 188
   personal methods, 188
Occupational Outlook Handbook, 522
odd-even pricing, 304
offerings, 28
off-peak pricing, 289
off-price retailing, 362–363
older married/unmarried people, 117
oligopoly, 81
Olympic Games, 415–416
omnichannel marketing, 331
one-price policy, 317
online advertising, 440, 471
   Google, Inc., 453–455
online auctions
   reverse, 141–142
   traditional, 141

online behavioral advertising, 420
online behavioral targeting, 413–414
online buying
   auctions, 141–142
   e-marketplaces, 140–141
   prominence in organizational markets, 140
   target market coverage, 335
online career employment services, 522
online consumer behavior
   behavioral targeting, 391
   characteristics of consumers, 386–387
   customerization, 388–389
   eight-second rule, 388
   kinds of purchases, 387
   means of shopping and buying, 392
   privacy and security issues, 392
   reasons for shopping
      choice, 388
      communication, 389–390
      control, 391
      convenience, 387–388
      cost, 390–391
      customization/customerization, 388–389
   and social commerce, 392
   times and marketspaces, 391
   web communities, 389
online consumers, 386–387
online customer experience, 383–385
   commerce, 385
   communication, 385
   community, 385
   connection, 384–385
   content, 384
   context, 384
   customization, 384
   definition, 384
online retailing
   aggregators, 360
   catalogs, 358
   discount service members, 359–360
   failure to purchase, 360
   intermediaries, 360
   marketplaces, 360
online sales, 331
   percentage of world sales, 381
online shopping
   value of products, 380
   website design, 384–385
online surveys, 190
on-the-job training, 506
open-ended questions, 192
open innovation, 249
operations manager, 518
opinion leaders, 114
opportunities; *see also* SWOT analysis
   for Amazon in India, 148
   in Asia-Pacific markets, 174

Oprah Winfrey Show, The, 322
opt-in, 383, 420
opt-out, 383
order clerks, 493
order cycle, 342
order getter, 493
   qualifications, 505
order size in organizational buying, 132–133
order taker, 491
   and inbound telemarketing, 493
   inside, 493
   outside, 493
   problem solving by, 493
organizational buyers, 17, 130
   advertising to, 410
organizational buying
   buyer–seller relationships, 134–136
   buying centers, 137–139
   and channel selection, 335
   characteristics, 132
   criteria, 133–134
   demand characteristics, 132
   dimensions, 132
   function maps, 136–137
   functions in, 136–137
   Harley-Davidson, 135
   JCPMedia, Inc., 128–129
   number of potential buyers, 133
   objectives, 133
   online buying
      auctions, 141–142
      e-marketplaces, 140–141
      prominence of, 140
   reciprocal arrangements, 134–135
   size of order or purchase, 132–133
   stages in process, 137
   supplier development, 134
   supply partnerships, 134–136
   Trek Bicycle Corporation, 145–146
organizational buying behavior, 136
organizational culture, 32
organizational direction
   goals/objectives, 33
   nature of business, 32–33
organizational goals
   customer satisfaction, 33
   profit, 33
   quality, 33
   sales, 33
organizational inertia and product failure
   groupthink, 248–249
   not-invented-here problem, 249
organizational markets
   government markets, 131
   industrial firms, 130
   measuring, 131
   online buying, 140–142
   reseller markets, 130
organizational resources, 41

organizational strategies, 34
organizational synergy, 215
organizations
   corporate level, 30
   departments of, 6
   and environmental forces, 6
   foundations
      core values, 31
      mission, 32
      organizational culture, 32
   functional level, 31
   and industries, 29–30
   marketing concept, 15
   marketing mission, 5
   in marketing plan, 56
   market orientation, 15
   market plan, 34
   newness from perspective of, 246
   strategic business units level, 31
   strategic directions, 36–40
   target market compatibility with objectives, 223
   variation by level, 34
   variation by product, 34
   visionary, 31–36
original markup, 361
Orion Multi-Purpose Crew Vehicle, 131
outbound telemarketing, 493
outdoor advertising, 440
   advantages and disadvantages, 437
output of supply chain, 342
output-related measures, 507
Outside magazine, 263, 483
outside order takers, 493

P

Pacific Rim: Uprising, 447
packaging, 286
   challenge and responses
      connecting with customers, 288
      cost reduction, 289
      environmental concerns, 288
      health, safety, and security issues, 288–289
   cost to companies, 286
   creating customer value
      communication benefits, 286–287
      functional benefits, 287–288
      perceptual benefits, 288
   and shelf life, 289
paid aspect of adverting, 406
paid-to-read websites, 441
Pampers Village, 385
panels for primary data, 193–194
parallel importing, 172
partnership selling, 491

payment systems
   in direct marketing, 420
   in India, 149
payoffs, 161
PC Magazine, 80
Peace Corps, 17, 18
penetration pricing, 303
   conditions favoring, 304
   following skimming pricing, 304
   in introduction stage, 268
people-based services, 240–241, 290
People en Español, 119
per capita income, 164
perceived risk, 109
percentage of sales budgeting, 414
perception, 109
   and perceived risk, 109–110
   selective, 109
perceptual map, 228–229
   for repositioning, 229
performance measures
   in multichannel marketing, 395
   Pizza Hut, 400
   social media programs
      linked to inputs or costs, 473–474
      linked to outputs or revenues, 474–475
periodicals, 527
permission marketing, 383
   rules for, 383
personal contact, in job search, 523
personal influence
   opinion leadership, 113–115
   word of mouth, 114–115
personal information sources, 100
personal interview surveys, 189
personality, 108
personality tests, 521
personalization, 382–383, 388
personal needs, 108
personal selling, 406, 407, 490
   costs, 407
   creating customer solutions, 491
   creating customer value, 492
   and emotional intelligence, 505
   in entrepreneurship, 491
   flexibility, 408
   forms of
      order getters, 493
      order takers, 492–493
      sales support personnel, 493–494
   in marketing, 491
   scope of, 490
   strengths, 407
   wasted coverage, 407
   weaknesses, 407
   at Xerox, 512–513
personal selling process, 495–496, 495–501
   approach stage, 498
   close, 501

   follow-up, 501
   handling objections, 499–501
   preapproach stage, 497–498
   presentation stage, 498–499
   prospecting, 496–497
persuasive content, 433
Pew Internet and American Life Project, 392
Pharmacy Times, 321
physical distribution, careers in, 517, 518
physical distribution specialist, 518
physical environment, of service delivery, 290–291
physical surroundings, 105
physiological needs, 108
pioneering advertisements
   institutional, 431
   product, 430
Pirates of the Caribbean, 180
place, 10; *see also* distribution
place-based media, 440–441
place strategy by Chobani, 22
place utility, 352–353
   definition, 18, 328
   in marketspace, 381
planning gap, 46
point-of-purchase displays, 447
points of difference, 43
   insignificant, 247
   Paradise Kitchens, 65
political stability, 165
Popular Mechanics, 114
population explosion, 74–75
population statistics, 74–75
pop-up blocker, 190
portfolio tests, 442
positioning statement, 228
possession utility, 352–353
   definition, 18, 328
   in marketspace, 381
postpurchase behavior
   consumers, 102–103
   in organizational buying, 137
posttests, 443
   aided recall, 443
   attitude tests, 444
   inquiry tests, 444
   sales tests, 444
   Starch test, 443
   unaided recall, 443
potential buyers, 133
power centers, 363
pre- and postsale services for organizational buyers, 335
preapproach stage in personal selling, 497–498
predatory pricing, 316
predictive modeling, 197
premium, 300
premiums, 445

presentation stage in personal selling
   formula selling format, 498–499
   need-satisfaction format, 499
   stimulus-response format, 498
prestige pricing, 304
preteens as consumers, 118
pretesting, 406
pretests, 442
   jury tests, 442
   portfolio tests, 442
   theater tests, 443
price, 300
   and demand estimation, 309–310
   effect on demand, 310
   and elasticity of demand, 311
   final price, 301
   indicator of value, 301–302
   in marketing mix, 302
   and perception of value, 304
   of services, 289
   setting final price, 316–319
   at Target, 11
   terms for, 300
price comparison searches, 478
price discrimination, 316
price elasticity of demand, 311
price equation, 300, 302
price fixing, 316
price level, approximate, 316–317
price premium, 308
price–quality segments, 285
price strategy
   by Chobani, 21
   worldwide marketing program, 171–172
pricing
   at Carmex, 322
   competition-oriented approaches, 307–309
   cost-oriented approaches, 304–306
   demand-oriented approaches, 303–304
   illegal practices, 316
   in introduction stage, 268
   Mary Kay India, 175
   off-peak, 289
   profit-oriented approaches, 306–307
   value pricing, 302
   VIZIO, Inc., 299
pricing constraints, 315
   competitors' prices, 315
   cost of production, 315
   demand, 315
   legal and ethical considerations, 316
   newness of product, 315
pricing objectives, 314
   market share, 314
   profit, 314
   sales, 314
   social responsibility, 315
   survival, 315
   unit volume, 315

pricing tactics, 300
primary data, 184
   advantages and disadvantages, 195
   observational data, 186–188
   panels and experiments, 193
   questionnaire data, 188–192
   from social media, 192–193
   types, 184
primary demand, 268
prime-time pricing, 318
privacy
   European Union law, 420
   and Federal Trade Commission, 421
   in mobile marketing, 479
   and National Do Not Call Registry, 420
   in online shopping, 392
   United Kingdom law, 420
private branding, 285
private exchanges, 140–141
private labeling, 285
problem identification
   in marketing research
      identify marketing actions, 182
      LEGO Group, 181–182
      set objectives, 182
   in organizational buying, 137
problem recognition, 100
problem solving, 103–105
   extended, 104
   limited, 104
   routine, 104
process of creating and delivering services, 291
product, 10, 17, 238–239
   availability of similar, and demand, 310
   benchmark items, 362
   bought online, 387
   business products, 239
   discretionary items, 305
   flow of, 338
   grouped into categories, 220–222
   in growth-share matrix, 38
   increase use of, 278
      new use situation, 278
   at Starbucks, 11
product adaptation, 169–170
product adopters, categories of, 274–275
product advertisements, 430, 431
   comparative, 431
   competitive, 430–431
   pioneering, 430
   reinforcement, 431
   reminder, 431
product classes, 242, 274
   bought online, 387
product component of services, 289
product deletion, 272
product development
   by Chobani, 21
   by Gatorade, 268

product development manager, 518
product differentiation, 212
   customer value from, 215
   in growth stage, 270
product extension, 169, 246
product failures; *see* new product failures
product features and behavioral segmentation, 218
product form, 242, 274
product image and brand names, 283
product invention, 170
production
   build-to-order, 15
   mass customization, 15
product item, 242–243
product life cycle, 268
   and consumer behavior
      diffusion of innovation, 274–275
      risk barriers, 275
      usage barriers, 275
   decline stage
      drop in sales, 271
      harvesting strategy, 271
      product deletion, 271
   demand and stages of product in, 315
   of fax machines, 266–272
   growth stage
      broadened distribution, 270
      changes during, 270
      profit peak, 270
      repeat purchasers, 270
      sales increase, 270
   introduction stage
      penetration pricing, 268
      primary demand, 268
      selective demand, 268
      skimming pricing, 268
      trial, 268
   length of, 273
   managing
      market modification, 277–278
      product modification, 276
      repositioning, 278–279
      role of product manager, 276
   marketing mix actions, 269
   marketing objectives, 269
   maturity stage
      holding market share, 271
      slowing sales, 271
   multiple cycles, 274
   pioneering ads, 430
   product level, 274
   promotional mix changes
      decline stage, 412
      growth stage, 412
      introduction stage, 410
      maturity stage, 412
   shape of life-cycle curve, 273–274
   video games, 478

product line, 243
   at Amazon, 347
   Carmex, 205
product line extension, 14
   and multiproduct branding, 284
product management
   careers in, 517, 518
   at Hormel, 295
   at Justin's, 293–296
product management team, 517
product manager
   career as, 518
   role in product life cycle, 276
product mix, 243
product modification, 276
product placement, 447–448
product positioning, 228
   differentiation, 228
   head-to-head, 228
   positioning statement, 228
   using perceptual maps, 228229
product repositioning, 228
   catch rising trend, 279
   changing value
      downsizing, 278–279
      trading up or down, 278
   reaching new markets, 279
   reacting to competitors' position, 278–279
product sales organization, 503
product strategy
   by Chobani, 21
   worldwide marketing program, 169–170
product synergies, 226–227
professional organizations, 527–528
profit, 28
   effect of exchange rate fluctuations, 165
   effect of pricing on, 302
   organizational goal, 33
   pricing objective, 314
profitability in channel selection, 336
profit-oriented pricing approaches
   target profit pricing, 306–307
   target return on investment pricing, 307
   target return on sales pricing, 307
profit projections, 255
profit responsibility, 87–88
Programme for the Endorsement of Forest Certification, 128
project manager, 518
promotion, 10
   careers in, 518–520
   communication tools, 404–405
   costs with multibranding, 285
   decision process, 413
   design of, 416
   jobs in, 518
   in marketing mix, 404

   new products, 268
   scheduling, 416
   selection of tools, 415–416
   of services, 290
   use by Taco Bell, 402–404
promotional allowances, 318–319
promotional content, 473
promotional elements
   advertising, 406–407
   direct marketing, 409
   personal selling, 407–408
   public relations, 408–409
   sales promotion, 409
promotional mix, 404
   and product life cycle, 410–412
   target audience, 410
promotion budgeting
   all-you-can-afford budgeting, 414
   competitive parity budgeting, 414
   objective and task budgeting, 415
   percentage of sales budgeting, 414
promotion strategy
   by Chobani, 22
   loss-leader pricing, 309
   Prince Sports, Inc., 233–234
   worldwide marketing program, 170
prospect, 496
prospecting stage of personal selling, 496–497
protectionism, 152
   ethics of, 153
   quotas, 153
   tariffs, 152
protocol, 246
   incomplete, 247
prototype, 255
psychographics, 112
psychographic segmentation, 220–221
psychological attributes in retail communication, 364
psychological influences; *see* consumer behavior
public information sources, 100
publicity, 408
   credibility of, 408
   disadvantages, 408
   lack of control, 408–409
   for services, 290
publicity tools, 449–450
public relations, 406, 408
   costs, 407
   strengths, 407
   weaknesses, 407
public relations manager, 518
public service announcements, 290, 450
pull strategy, 412–413
pulse schedule, 442
purchase
   buyer control, 479
   sensor control, 479

   size of, in organizational buying, 132–133
purchase decision, 102
   in buying cars, 98–99
   in families, 118
   and problem solving, 103–104
purchase decision process, 100
   alternative evaluation, 101
   characteristics, 104
   consumer journey map, 106
   consumer touchpoints, 105–106
   information search, 100–101
   level of involvement, 103–105
   in organizational buying, 137
   postpurchase behavior, 102–103
   problem recognition, 100
   purchase decision, 102
   situational influences, 105
   sun care products, 123–124
purchase frequency, 441
purchase task, 105
purchasing power, 164–165
pure competition, 81
pure monopoly, 81
push strategy, 412

Q

qualified prospect, 496
quality
   organizational goal, 33
   poor, 248
   prestige pricing, 304
quantitative assessments, 507
quantity demanded, and price, 311
quantity discounts, 317
question marks, 38
questionnaire data, 184, 189
   developing precise questions, 190–192
   idea evaluation methods
      mail surveys, 189–190
      online surveys, 190
      personal interviews, 189
      telephone interviews, 190
   idea generation methods, 188–189
      depth interviews, 189
      focus groups, 189
      fuzzy front end methods, 189
      individual interviews, 189
   mall intercept interviews, 192
   types of questions, 192
   Wendy's survey, 190–191
questions in questionnaire data, 190–192
quick response, 342
quotas, 153
quoted price; *see* list/quoted price

R

racial diversity, 76
rack jobbers, 369
radical invention, 246
radio advertising
    advantages and disadvantages, 437
    limited use, 438
    number of stations, 438
radio frequency identification tags, 355
railroads, 32
reach, 435–436
Real Yellow Pages, 439
rebates, 447
receivers, 405
recessions, 78
recycling, 344
reference groups, 116
reference value, 302
Regional Planning Association, Ohio, 363
regional rollout, 256
regional shopping centers, 363
regional trade agreements, 153
regular distribution, 246
regulation, 82
regulatory forces
    and brand names, 283
    influencing Facebook, 72
    and monopoly, 81
    protecting competition, 82
    protecting producers and consumers, 82–83
    self-regulation, 83–84
reinforcement, 110
reinforcement advertising, 431
relationship marketing, 11–12
relationship selling, 491
relative market share, 38
reminder advertising
    institutional, 431
    for products, 431
rent, 300
repeat purchasers, 270
replenishment time, 342
research and development laboratories, 252
research plan
    determine data collection methods, 183
    identify needed data, 183
    specify constraints, 182–183
reseller branding, 285
resources, obtaining, 44
response, 110, 405–406
Restaurant Business, 410
résumé
    cover letter, 524
    preparing, 524
    sections, 523
    video, 524

retail communication
    functional element, 364
    image element, 364
    psychological attributes, 364
    shopper marketing concept, 364
    shopping experience, 364
    store atmosphere, 364
retailers, 326
    supple partnerships, 136
    trade promotions for, 448–449
retailer-sponsored cooperatives, 355
retailing, 352
    careers in, 518, 519
    changing nature of
        data analytics, 368
        retail life cycle, 367–368
        wheel of retailing, 366–367
    consumer utilities from, 352–353
    global impact, 353
    jobs in, 518
    multichannel retailers, 364
    pizza business, 397–398
retailing mix, 361
retail life cycle, 367
    accelerated development, 367–368
    decline stage, 368
    early growth, 367
    maturity stage, 368
retail outlets
    category killers, 357
    exclusive distribution, 335
    forms of ownership, 353–356
    general merchandise stores, 357
    level of service, 356
    locations, 363–364
    of Mall of America, 373
    number of, in U.S., 354
    for Seven Cycles, Inc., 379
    smart stores, 350–351
    specialty outlets, 357
    supply chains, 325
    by type of merchandise line, 356–357
    wheel of retailing, 366–367
retail pricing
    for benchmark items, 362
    everyday low pricing, 362
    maintained markup, 361–362
    markdown, 362
    off-price retailing, 362–363
    original markup, 361
retail salesperson, 518
retail-sponsored cooperatives, 333
retail strategy
    communication, 364
    merchandise management, 364–365
    pricing, 361–363
    store location, 363–364
return on assets, 314
return on investment, 33, 307, 314
revenue estimation, 311

revenues, performance measures tied to, 474
reverse auction, 141
reverse logistics, 343–344
    and green marketing, 344
reward influence, 338
rich media, 440
rich site summary, 418
risk
    in direct exporting, 167
    perceived, 109–110
Risky Business, 448
Robinson-Patman Act of 1936, 82, 83
    on price discrimination, 316
Rock and Roll Hall of Fame, 306
Rolling Stone, 439
routine problem solving, 104
Runner's World, 439

S

safe delivery, 343
safety issues in packaging, 288–289
safety needs, 108
salary, 300
sales
    careers in, 518, 519–520
    in decline stage, 271–272
    effect of exchange rate fluctuations, 165
    in growth stage, 270
    in introduction stage, 268
    in maturity stage, 271
    organizational goal, 33
    pricing objective, 314
    by strategic business units, 35
sales analysis, 198–199
sales clerks, 493
sales engineers, 494
salesforce
    manufacturer training of, 449
    Mary Kay India, 175–176
    motivation and compensation, 506
    organizing
        customer organization, 503
        geographical organization, 502–503
        key account management, 503
        product organization, 503
    recruitment and selection, 504–505
    training of, 505–506
salesforce automation, 508
salesforce evaluation, 506–507
    behavioral evaluation, 507
    quantitative assessments, 507
salesforce management process
    customer relationship management systems, 507–509
    salesforce evaluation, 506–507
    sales plan formulation, 502–504
    sales plan implementation, 504–506

sales force survey forecast, 201
sales forecast, 200–201
sales forecasting techniques, 200–202
    judgment of decision makers, 201
    statistical methods, 201–202
    survey of knowledgeable groups, 201
sales management, 490
    at Xerox, 513
sales organization, competitive position, 504
salespeople, creating customer value, 491–492
sales per square foot, 365
sales plan, 502
sales plan formulation
    account management policies, 504
    organizing salesforce, 502–503
    setting objectives, 502
sales plan implementation
    salesforce compensation and motivation, 506
    salesforce recruitment, 504–505
    salesforce training, 505–506
sales professional, 488–489
sales projections, 255
sales promotion, 406, 409
    advantages, 409
    annual expenditures, 444
    consumer-oriented, 444–448
    costs, 407
    strengths, 407
    temporary gains, 409
    trade-oriented, 448–449
    weaknesses, 407
sales promotion manager, 518
sales quota, 507
sales-support duties, 519
sales tests, 444
same-store sales growth, 365
samples, 446
sampling, 183
San Francisco Chronicle, 439
savings rate, 79
scrambled merchandising, 357
screening and evaluation, 253
    external approach, 254
    internal approach, 253–254
seals of approval, 109
seasonal discounts, 317–318
secondary data, 184
    external sources
        advantages and disadvantages, 185
        Census Bureau, 185
        marketing research companies, 185
        syndicated panel data, 185
    internal sources
        marketing input data, 184
        marketing outcome data, 184–185
        online databases, 186
Secret Sales Pitch (Bullock), 110

security issues
    in online shopping, 392
    in packaging, 288–289
selective comprehension, 109
selective demand, 268
selective distribution, 335
selective exposure, 109
selective perception, 109
selective retention, 109
self-actualization needs, 108
self-concept, 108
self-expression motivated groups, 113
self-regulation, 83
self-service, 356
selling, career benefits, 519
selling agents, 369
selling duties, 519
semantic differential scale, 192
seminar selling, 494
semiotics, 161
semitechnical salesperson, 518
sentiment, 193
services, 238–239
    assessing and improving quality, 242
    classification of
        delivery by business firms, 241
        delivery by government agencies, 241
        delivery by nonprofits, 241
        equipment-based, 241
        people-based, 240–241
    electronic marketing channels, 330
    limited capacity, 291
    marketing channels for, 328–329
    marketing mix
        capacity management, 290–291
        distribution, 290
        people-based delivery, 290
        physical environment, 290–291
        price, 289
        process, 290–291
        product component, 289
        promotion, 290
    marketing of, 17
    need for protocol, 246
    new-product development for, 251
    reasons for failure
        marketing reasons, 247–248
        organizational inertia, 248–249
    supplementary, 242
    uniqueness of
        inconsistency, 241
        inseparability, 241
        intangibility, 241
service-sponsored franchise systems, 334
service-sponsored retail franchise systems, 333–334
seven Ps of services, 289
sex appeals, 434

share of voice, 193
shelf life, 289
Sherman Antitrust Act of 1890, 82
    on price fixing, 316
shift of demand curve, 310
shopper marketing, 364
shopping experience, 364
shopping products, 239
showrooming, 393
signpost items, 362
simulated test markets, 256–257
single parents, 117
site stickiness, 386
situational influences, 105
situation analysis, 42
60 Minutes, 187
Skateboarder, 439
skimming pricing, 303
    in introduction stage, 268
    penetration pricing following, 304
small businesses
    as competitors, 81
    marketing careers, 4
    for new product ideas, 253
smart glasses, 351
smartphones
    mobile marketing communications, 460
    and store experience, 350
smart stores, 350–351
smart systems
    definition, 477
    and privacy, 479
smartwatches, 350
social commerce, 392
social commerce technologies, 477
social entrepreneurs, 29
social forces, 74
    culture, 76–77
    demographics, 74–76
    influencing Facebook, 72
social media, 15, 462
    audience data available for, 471
    and Body Glove, 483–484
    classifying, 463
        blogs, 463
        media richness, 462–463
        self-disclosure, 463
        social networking, 463
        virtual social worlds, 463
    company comparisons, 466
    compared to traditional media
        credibility, 464
        expense and access, 464
        permanence, 464
        reach, 464
        social authority, 464
        time to delivery, 464
        training, 464

social media—Cont.
  convergence of real and digital worlds
    apps, 477–478
    databases and algorithms, 477
    social commerce technologies, 477
  Facebook, 465–467
  hashtags, 473
  influencer marketing, 114, 464–465
  LinkedIn, 468–469
  and Mall of America, 374
  and mobile marketing
    buyer control, 479
    links to marketing actions, 478–479
    sensor control, 479
  for primary data, 192–193
  publicity in, 408
  recent activity, 472
  smart systems, 477
  transforming marketing
      communications, 463–465
  Twitter, 467–468
  types of content, 472–473
  use by Carmex, 205–207
  use by Chobani, 2–3
  use by Taco Bell, 402–404, 424
  user-generated content, 462
  and Web 2.0, 462
  and Web 3.0, 462
  YouTube, 469–470
social media channels, 460
social media marketing manager, 518
social media marketing program, 471
  and Carmex, 475–476
  content selection
    development, execution, and
        delivery, 473
    types of content, 472–473
  customer engagement, 471
  media selection
    audience data availability, 471
    recent activity, 472
  performance measures
    linked to inputs or costs, 473–474
    linked to outputs or revenues,
        474–475
  specialized focus, 475
social media metrics, 193
social needs, 108
social networking sites, 463
social responsibility, 87
  in marketing, 16–17
  organizational goal, 34
  pricing objective, 315
  profit responsibility, 87
  societal responsibility, 88–89
  stakeholder responsibility, 87–88
  sustainable development, 89
  at Toyota, 93–95
social surroundings, 105
societal culture, 84

societal marketing concept, 16–17
societal responsibility
  cause marketing, 88–89
  definition, 88
  green marketing, 88
sociocultural influences; *see*
    consumer behavior
source, 404
spam, 190, **389–390**
spark lines, 35
specialty merchandise wholesalers, 369
specialty outlets, 357
specialty products, 239
Sports Illustrated Kids, 116, 439
spot ads, 438
spouse-dominant decision making, 118
Stage Gate process, 250
stakeholder responsibility, 86
stakeholders, 31
Standard & Poor's *Register of
    Corporations, Directors, and
    Executives,* 524–525
standard markup pricing, 305
standard test markets, 256
Starch test, 443
stars, 38
Star Wars, 180
Star Wars: The Last Jedi, 178, 416
Star Wars Show, 416
state employment office, 523
State Hermitage Museum, Russia, 17
statistical inference, 183
statistical sales forecasts
  linear trend extrapolation, 201–202
  trend extrapolation, 201–202
status reports, 343
steady schedule, 441
stimulus discrimination, 110–111
stimulus generalization, 110
stimulus-response presentation, 498
stock keeping units, 243
  number of, in supermarkets, 248
store locations, 363
store manager, 518
straight commission compensation
    plan, 506
straight rebuy, 139
  Trek Bicycle Corporation, 146
straight salary compensation plan, 506
Strategic Business Insights, 112
strategic business units
  at Apple Inc., 39
  in business portfolio analysis, 37–39
  definition, 31
  in growth-share matrix, 38
  sales performance, 35
strategic directions
  growth strategies
    business portfolio analysis, 37–39
    diversification analysis, 40

    present status, 36–37
      competencies, 37
      competitors, 37
      customers, 37
  strategic marketing alliances,
      331–332
strategic marketing process, 41
  evaluation phase
    act on deviations, 46–47
    identify deviations, 46
  implementation phase
    defining tasks and responsibilities,
        45–46
    designing marketing organization,
        44–45
    executing program, 46
    obtaining resources, 44
  planning phase
    goal setting, 43
    marketing program, 43
    market-product focus, 43
    situation/SWOT analysis, 42–43
  principles underlying, 41
strategy, 30
  based on values, 51
  at IBM, 50–52
Street & Smith's Baseball, 214
StrengthFinder 2.0 (Rath), 521
strengths; *see also* SWOT analysis
  job candidates, 521
strip malls, 363
strivers, 113
Strong Interest Inventory, 521
subbranding, 284
subcultures, 119
  African American buying patterns,
      119–120
  Asian American buying
      patterns, 120
  Hispanic buying patterns, 119
subliminal perception, 109, 110
sugar import quotas, 153
suggestive selling, 489
Summer Olympics, Japan 2020, 416
sun care industry, 123–125
Sunday Night Football, 438
Super Bowl, 115
  Apple's ad of 1984, 226
  costs of ads, 432, 436
  effectiveness of ads, 433
  Taco Bell ad, 424
supermarkets
  differing markups, 305
  number of stock keeping units, 248
  virtual shopping, 479
supplier development, 134
suppliers
  to Amazon, 348
  new product ideas from, 251–252
supplies, 239

577

supply chain, 339
    automobile industry, 339–340
    Eddie Bauer, 325
    Mary Kay India, 176
    output, 342
supply chain management, 339
    at Amazon, 348
    at IBM, 341
    and marketing strategy
        alignment steps, 340–341
            at Dell, 341
            at Walmart, 341–342
supply chain manager, 518
supply partnerships, 34–36
support products, 239
surge pricing, 317, 318
survey of buyers' intentions, 201
surveys of knowledgeable groups
    buyers' intentions, 201
    sales force survey, 201
survival, pricing objective, 315
survivors, 113
sustainability, 77
sustainable development, 89
Sustainable Forestry Initiative, 128
sustainable marketing, 881
sustainable procurement, at
    Starbucks, 136
sweepstakes, 446
SWOT analysis, 42
    by Ben & Jerry's, 42–43
syndicated panel data, 185
synergies *vs.* cannibalization, 215–216

T

target audience
    of advertising program, 432
    of integrated marketing
        communications program, 413–414
    in marketing plan, 56
    of promotions, 410
target market, 10
    for competitive advertising, 430–431
    positioning statement, 228
    selection criteria
        compatibility with objectives, 223
        competitive position, 223
        cost of reaching segments, 223
        expected growth, 223
        market size, 223
target market coverage
    density factor, 334
    exclusive distribution, 334–335
    intensive distribution, 334
    selective distribution, 335
target profit pricing, 306–307
target return, 314

target return-on-investment pricing, 307
target return-on-sales pricing, 307
tariffs, 152
tasks, defining, 45
team selling, 494
teaser advertising campaigns, 115
technological change
    current, 79–80
    and length of product life cycle, 273
technological forces
    and data analytics, 80–81
    impact on consumer value, 80
    influencing Facebook, 72
    technology of tomorrow, 79–80
technology, 79
    augmented reality, 428–430
    customer service and support
        automation, 509
    effect on direct marketing, 419–420
    effect on retailing, 350
    marketing automation, 509
    Prince Sports, Inc., 232
    salesforce automation, 507–509
    virtual reality, 428–430
    wearable, 79
teenagers
    as consumers, 118
    global, 158
telemarketing, 360
    inbound, 493
    and National Do Not Call Registry,
        360, 420, 497
    outbound, 493
Telephone Consumer Protection Act of
    1991, 83, 497
television advertising
    advantages and disadvantages, 437
    change in viewing habits, 437–438
    costs, 438
    infomercials, 438
    product placements, 447–448
    spot ads, 438
television home shopping, 359
television ratings, 186–187
temporal effects, 105
tennis market segments, 232–234
testing procedures, integrated marketing
    communications program, 417
test marketing, 256–257
test markets, 194
    controlled, 256
    simulated, 256–257
    standard, 256
test screenings, 180
theater tests, 443
thinkers, 113
threats; *see* SWOT analysis
3D modeling tools, 350
Tiffany/Walmart strategy, 215

Time, 436, 478
    number of editions, 439
time, in logistics management,
    342–343
time utility, 352–353
    definition, 18, 328
    in marketspace, 381
Titanic, 180
Today's Shopping Choice, 359
Top Gun, 448
top management, 30
    ethical behavior, 86
total cost, 312
total logistics cost, 342
total revenue, 311
Toy Story, 448
tracking studies, 180
trade associations, 527–528
trade discounts, 318
trade feedback effect, 151
trade-in allowances, 318
trademark, 280
trademark law, 83
trade-oriented sales promotions, 448
    allowances, 448–449
    cooperative advertising, 449
    salesforce training, 449
trade promotions, 448
trade regulations, 166
    in India, 149
trade salesperson, 518
trade war, 154
trading down, 278
trading up, 278
traditional auction, 141
traditional family, 116
traffic generation, 419
training
    by manufacturers, 449
    on-the-job training, 506
    in retailing, 519
    of salesforce, 505–506
transactional function, 326–327
transit advertising, 440
transnational firms, 157–158
trend extrapolation, 201–202
trend spotting, 205–206
trial, 414
    of new products, 268
trial close, 501
trial size samples, 446
triple bottom line, 88
truck jobbers, 369
tuition, 300
Twilight Saga, 214
Twitter, 468
    brand manager strategy, 468
    number of users, 467
    overview, 468

U

ultimate consumers, 17
unaided recall, 443
uncontrollable factors, 10–11
unethical behavior
    corruption, 85
    economic espionage, 85
United Kingdom
    Direct Marketing Association, 420
    General Data Protection
        Regulation, 420
    on product placements, 448
    withdrawal from European Union, 154
United States
    costs of economic espionage, 59
    ethnic groups, 76
    exports of services, 152
    gross domestic product, 151
    impact of retailing, 353
    number of franchises, 168
    number of retail outlets, 354
    perspective on world trade, 151–152
    population trends, 75
    quotas imposed by, 153
    recent recessions, 78
United States Patent and Trademark
    Office, 280
United States Secret Service, 144
unit variable cost, 312
unit volume, pricing objective, 315
universities, for new product ideas, 253
University of Florida, 266
unsought products, **239**
upselling, 499
urgency close, 501
U.S. Green Retail Association, 354
U.S. News & World Report, 520
usage instructions, 110
usage rate, 218
    and behavioral segmentation, 220
    80/20 rule, 218
USA.gov, 186
USA Today, 436, 439
user-generated content, 462
users, 138
utilitarianism, 87
utility, 18

V

VALS framework of consumer segments,
    112–113
value, 301
    assessing, 101
    buying, 102
    changing, offered, 278
    as consumer's judgment, 302
    of direct marketing, 419
    perception of, 11, 102–103
    price and perception of, 304
    price as indicator of, 301–302
    realizing, 102–103
    seeking, 100–101
value-based pricing strategy, 299
value pricing, 302
values, 111, **160**
    strategy based on, 51
variable cost, 312
variety, for organizational buyers, 335
V-commerce, 358
vending machines, 479
vendor-managed inventory, 343
vendors, 136
venture capitalists, 56
vertical conflict, 337
vertical marketing systems, 332
    administered, 334
    contractual, 333–334
    corporate, 332–333
vertical price fixing, 316
video games
    and apps, 478
    companies, 428–429
video résumés, 524
viral marketing, 390
virtual reality, 350, 428–430
virtual reality campaigns, 429
virtual social worlds, 463
virtual supermarket shopping, 479
vocational interest tests, 521
Vogue, 483
Voice, The, 446

W

wages, 300
Wall Street Journal, The, 257, 439, 524
Walmart/Dollar Store strategy, 216
wants compared to needs, 9
War Dogs, 178
warranties, 110
wasted coverage, 407
weaknesses; *see also* SWOT analysis
    advertising, 407
    job candidates, 521
wearable technology, 79, 350
web communities, 389
webrooming, 393
websites
    customization at Pizza Hut, 399
    design, 384–385
    paid-to-read, 441
    site stickiness, 386
    traffic sources, 35
    visits by state, 36

West Edmonton Mall, 363, 372
what-if questions, 196
wheel of retailing, 366
whistle-blowers, 86
wholesalers, 326
    manufacturer's branch office, 370
    manufacturer's sales office, 370
    merchant wholesalers, 369
    trade promotions for, 448–449
wholesaler-sponsored voluntary
    chains, 355
Wikipedia, 251
Wired magazine, 405
women as car buyers, 98–99
word of mouth, 114, 242
    buzz, 115, 390
    on Internet, 115
    negative information, 115
World Bank, on corruption, 85
world trade
    countertrade, 151
    dollar value, 150
    dumping, 171–172
    and economic integration, 154–155
    effect of exchange rates, 165
    exporting, 166–167
    global brands, 157
    global companies, 156–158
    global competition, 155–156
    global consumers, 158
    global marketing strategy, 157
    global perspective, 150–151
    gray market, 172
    leaders in merchandise trade, 150
    networked global marketspace,
        158–159
    and political stability, 166
    and protectionism, 152, 153
    trade feedback effect, 151
    and trade regulations, 166
    trade wars, 154
    U.S. perspective, 151–152
World Trade Organization, 154

Y

Yachting, 439
year-to-date targets, 35
Yellowbook, 439
Yellow Pages, 439
    advantages and disadvantages, 437
young married couples, 117
Young Sheldon, 187
young singles, 117
YouTube, 470
    brand manager strategy, 470
    overview, 469
    reach, 469